Handbook of
Coastal and Ocean
Engineering

Volume 1

Wave Phenomena and
Coastal Structures

Handbook of Coastal and Ocean Engineering

Volume 1: Wave Phenomena and Coastal Structures

Volume 2: Offshore Structures, Marine Foundations, Sediment Processes, and Modeling

Volume 3: Harbors, Navigational Channels, Estuaries, and Environmental Effects

Gulf Publishing Company
Houston, London, Paris, Zurich, Tokyo

Handbook of
Coastal and Ocean
Engineering

Volume 1

Wave Phenomena and
Coastal Structures

John B. Herbich, Editor

in collaboration with—

C. L. Bretschneider	R. A. Holman	R. O. Reid
P. Bruun	J. R. C. Hsu	D. T. Resio
F. E. Camfield	Y. C. Li	R. Silvester
R. G. Dean	M. A. Losada	J. G. Titus
Y. Goda	J. L. Machemehl	J. W. van der Meer
E. H. Harlow	C. C. Mei	C. L. Vincent

To my wife Margaret Pauline and children, Ann, Barbara, Gregory, and Patricia, who have been a source of encouragement and inspiration during the preparation of this handbook.

Handbook of Coastal and Ocean Engineering

Volume: 1 Wave Phenomena and Coastal Structures

Copyright © 1990 by Gulf Publishing Company, Houston, Texas. All rights reserved. Printed in the United States of America. This book, or parts thereof, may not be reproduced in any form without permission of the publisher.

Printed on Acid-Free Paper (∞)

Library of Congress Cataloging-in-Publication Data
Handbook of coastal & ocean engineering/John B.
  Herbich, editor, in collaboration with C.
  Bretschneider. . . [et al.].
    p. cm.
  Includes bibliographical references.
  Contents: v. 1. Wave phenomena, coastal structures.
  ISBN 0-87201-461-4 (v. 1)
  1. Coastal engineering—Handbooks, manuals, etc. 2.
Ocean engineering—Handbooks, manuals, etc. I. Herbich,
John B. II. Bretschneider, Charles L., 1920–. III. Title:
Handbook of coastal and ocean engineering.
  TC330.H36 1990
  620′.4146—dc20

Series ISBN 0-87

CONTENTS

Wave Phenomena

Wave Climate and Design Waves

Water-Level Changes

Coastal Structures

Breakwaters

PREFACE

There has been an obvious need for a *Handbook of Coastal and Ocean Engineering* providing the latest state-of-the-art as well as research results in this field. Tremendous strides have been made in these specialized fields in recent decades as evidenced by journal publications and proceedings from specialty conferences of many societies and associations.

To develop this Handbook, many internationally-known experts were invited to contribute and agreed to prepare chapters in their respective fields. They were asked to provide background information on critical environmental factors and design criteria for coastal and ocean engineering structures, marine foundations, ports, harbors and navigational channels, beach protection, and environmental effects of coastal projects and oil spills. Beach protection has become a matter of national concern in the United States, Japan, and Europe. Since the population has been increasing in the coastal zone and since there are many conflicting demands for near-ocean space between recreational interests, industry, and preservation of coastal wetlands, the field of coastal engineering has gained importance in recent decades. Oil exploration and exploitation have also affected the coastal zone.

This volume of the Handbook covers wave phenomena and coastal structures. The first part of Volume 1 provides insight into various complex linear and nonlinear wave theories, forcasting, hindcasting, wave statistics, wave probability, and design applications. It thoroughly discusses wave-current interaction and changes in water levels due to many physical phenomena.

The second part of Volume 1 provides methods to compute wave forces on shore structures, covers design of breakwaters and seawalls, and examines forces due to waves and ice on artificial islands.

This volume represents the effort of 19 experts from around the world. In addition, it reflects the opinions of many engineers and scientists who provided valuable assistance in developing this Handbook. All chapters were peer-reviewed, corrected, and finally reviewed by me. This effort took many months and many evenings, weekends, and vacations. I hope all mistakes were found and corrections made. My deepest gratitude is extended to all the contributors to the Handbook. Great appreciation is also extended to the reviewers: Dr. Charles Bretschneider, University of Hawaii; Robert D. Carver, Dr. Yen-Hsi Chu, Dr. Peter L. Crawford, Dr. Nicholas C. Kraus, Dr. Abhimanyu Swain, Dr. Edward F. Thompson, Dr. Todd L. Walton, the Coastal Engineering Research Center, U.S. Army Engineer Waterways Experiment Station, Vicksburg, Mississippi; Jack Fowler, Geotechnical Laboratory, U.S. Army Engineer Waterways Experiment Station, Vicksburg, Mississippi; Dr. C. H. Kim, Dr. Jack Y. K. Lou, Dr. Robert E. Randall, Dr. Joannes Westerink, the Ocean Engineering Program, Civil Engineering Department, Texas A&M University, College Station, Texas; Professor Robert O. Reid, Department of Oceanography, Texas A&M University, College Station, Texas; Devinder S. Sodhi, U.S. Corps of Engineers Cold Regions Research and Engineering Laboratory, Hanover, New Hampshire; Dr. Charles Adams, Coastal Studies Institute, Louisiana State University, Baton Rouge, Louisiana and Dr. Jack Colonell, School of Engineering, University of Alaska.

The manuscript was assembled for publication by Ms. Joyce Hyden, who also typed several chapters, and to whom I am most grateful. Without her expert help this Handbook would have taken much longer to produce.

I am especially grateful to my wife, Polly, for her encouragement and patience during the preparation of this Handbook.

I am indebted to Marcel Dekker, Inc. for permission to incorporate large portions from my books on *Offshore Pipeline Design Elements* and *Seafloor Scour, Design Guidelines for Ocean-founded Structures,* and to other publishers or individuals who have kindly granted permission to reprint copyrighted materials.

John B. Herbich, Ph.D., PE.
W. H. Bauer Professor
Civil and Ocean Engineering
Texas A&M University
College Station, Texas

Publisher's Note

The *Handbook of Coastal and Ocean Engineering* is a collective effort involving many technical specialists. It brings together a wealth of information from worldwide sources to help scientists, engineers, and technicians solve current and long-range problems.

Great care has been taken in the compilation and production of this volume, but it should be made clear that no warranties, express or implied, are given in connection with the accuracy or completeness of this publication, and no responsibility can be taken for any claims that may arise.

The statements and opinions expressed herein are those of the individual authors and are not necessarily those of the editor or the publisher. Furthermore, citation of trade names and other proprietary marks does not constitute an endorsement or approval of the use of such commercial products or services, or of the companies that provide them.

CONTRIBUTORS TO THIS VOLUME

C. L. Bretschneider, Professor Emeritus, University of Hawaii at Manoa, Department of Ocean Engineering, 811 Olomehani Street, Honolulu, HI 96813, U.S.A.

P. Bruun, 34 Baynard Cove Road, Hilton Head Island, SC 29928, U.S.A.

F. E. Camfield, USAE Waterways Experiment Station, 3909 Halls Ferry Road, Vicksburg, MS 39180, U.S.A.

R. G. Dean, Coastal and Oceanographic Engineering, 336 Weil Hall, University of Florida, Gainesville, FL 32611, U.S.A.

Y. Goda, Department of Civil Engineering, Yokohama National University, 156 Tokiwadai Hodogaya-ku, Yokohama, 240, Japan

E. H. Harlow, SOROS Associates, P.O. Box 441734, Houston, Texas 77244, U.S.A.

J. B. Herbich, Ocean and Civil Engineering, Texas A&M University, College Station, Texas 77843-3136, U.S.A.

R. A. Holman, College of Oceanography, Oregon State University, Oceanography Admin. Bldg. 104, Corvallis, OR 97331-5503, U.S.A.

J. R. C. Hsu, Department of Civil Engineering, University of Western Australia, Nedlands, Western Australia 6009

Y. C. Li, Hydraulic Engineering Department, Dalian University of Technology, Dalian, China 116024, China

M. A. Losada, Dept. de Ciencias y Tecnicas de Agua y del Medio Ambiente, ETS Ingenieros de Caminos, C.yP., Universidad de Cantabria, Santander, Spain

J. L. Machemehl, Ocean and Civil Engineering, Texas A&M University, College Station, Texas 77843-3136, U.S.A.

C. C. Mei, Ralph M. Parsons Laboratory, Massachusetts Institute of Technology, Department of Civil Engineering, Rm 48-413, Cambridge, MA 02139, U.S.A.

R. O. Reid, Department of Oceanography, Texas A&M University, College Station, Texas 77843, U.S.A.

D. T. Resio, Offshore and Coastal Technologies, Inc., 911 Clay Street, Vicksburg, MS 39180, U.S.A.

R. Silvester, Department of Civil Engineering, The University of Western Australia, Nedlands, Western Australia 6009

J. G. Titus, Project Manager for Sea-Level Rise, USEPA, Code PM 221, Waterside Mall, Room M3009E, Washington, DC 20460, U.S.A.

J. W. van der Meer, Delft Hydraulics Laboratory, P.O. Box 152, 8300 AD Emmeloord, The Netherlands

C. L. Vincent, Coastal Engineering Research Center, U.S. Army Corps of Engineers, Waterways Experiment Station, 3909 Halls Ferry Road, Vicksburg, MS 39180, U.S.A.

ABOUT THE EDITOR

Dr. John B. Herbich is professor of civil and ocean engineering and W. H. Bauer Professor of Dredging Engineering at Texas A & M University in College Station, Texas. Dr. Herbich is an expert in coastal and ocean engineering with a specialty in coastal and dredging engineering and technology development. He has consulted extensively for U.S. and international industries and governments on coastal developments and uses, and has served on several committees of the National Research Council, including being a vice-chairman of Technical Panel of the Committee on National Dredging Issues. A Fellow of the American Society of Civil Engineers, Dr. Herbich received his B.Sc. degree in civil engineering from the University of Edinburgh, his M.S. in hydromechanics from the University of Minnesota, and his Ph.D. in civil engineering from Pennsylvania State University.

CHAPTER 1

BASIC GRAVITY WAVE THEORY

Chiang C. Mei

Department of Civil Engineering
Massachusetts Institute of Technology
Cambridge, Massachusetts, U.S.A.

CONTENTS

Formulation

Assumptions and Governing Equations

One of the facts of life in the ocean that affects engineering activities is the omnipresence of waves. Water motion in the sea can be initiated by a variety of natural or man-made causes, such as wind in the atmosphere, the attraction between earth and moon, the eruption of submarine volcanos, the passing of a ship, etc. Owing to myriad factors such as gravity, capillarity, compressibility or the rotation of earth, this motion leads to the presence of waves. The wave periods can cover an extremely broad range. They can be several months for planetary waves, half a day for tides, several hours for storm surges, dozens of minutes for tsunamis, a few seconds for swells, and fractions of a second for capillary waves. This chapter focuses on the gravity waves due initially to the action of wind. With the exception of the very short capillary waves, the small viscosity in water plays a minor role in many situations of practical interest. Underwater sound that has a very high speed of propagation and is associated with fluid compressibility is excluded. We shall therefore assume the fluid to be incompressible and inviscid. For many problems in ocean engineering, the effects of density stratification are not important. Therefore, we take the fluid density ρ to be uniform.

At a point $\vec{x}$ in space and time t, the velocity of the passing fluid will be denoted by $\vec{u}$. The assumption of incompressibility implies that the rate of volume dilation is zero, hence

$$\nabla \cdot \vec{u} = 0 \tag{1}$$

Let the fluid pressure at $\vec{x}$ and t be denoted by P. Conservation of fluid momentum leads to

$$\frac{\partial \vec{u}}{\partial t} + \vec{u} \cdot \nabla\vec{u} = -\nabla \left(\frac{P}{\rho} + gz \right) \tag{2}$$

On the right side the effect of gravity is represented by the last term, the effect of viscous stress being omitted.

In this set of equations, the unknowns are $\vec{u}$ and P. A quantity basic in fluid mechanics is the vorticity that is the rate of rotation of a fluid element, $\frac{1}{2} \nabla \times \vec{u}$. By taking the curl of the momentum equation and using the continuity equation, it can be shown that the vorticity around a fluid element never changes for an inviscid and incompressible fluid of uniform density. The simplest situation is one where there is no vorticity anywhere at the initial instant. The flow is then without vorticity all the time. Such a flow is called *irrotational* and its velocity $\vec{u}$ can be expressed as the gradient of a scalar Φ

$$\vec{u} = \nabla \Phi \tag{3}$$

Use of mass conservation then leads to the simple Laplace equation

$$\nabla^2 \Phi = 0 \tag{4}$$

that must govern all of the fluid. The scalar function $\Phi(\overline{x},t)$ is called the velocity potential.

In terms of Φ the momentum equation can be integrated with respect to the space coordinate to give

$$-\frac{P}{\rho} = gz + \Phi_t + \frac{1}{2} |\nabla\Phi|^2 \tag{5}$$

This is the Bernoulli equation, which gives the pressure P once the velocity potential is found. An arbitrary integration constant that can at most be a function of time has been omitted, because it does not affect the velocity field. We may also define the dynamic pressure p by excluding the static pressure, ρgz:

$$p = P + \rho gz = -\rho \left(\Phi_t + \frac{1}{2} |\nabla\Phi|^2 \right) \tag{6}$$

One of the boundary conditions on any material surface is that the flow must be tangential to the surface. If the surface is fixed, say, the sea bottom at $z = -h(x,y)$, the normal velocity must vanish; this implies

$$\Phi_z = -h_x \Phi_x - h_y \Phi_y, \qquad\qquad z = -h \tag{7}$$

If, however, the surface is the moving free surface of the ocean. $z = \zeta(x,y,t)$, then the normal velocity of the fluid on the free surface must equal that of the surface itself; this implies

$$\zeta_t + \zeta_x \Phi_x + \zeta_y \Phi_y = \Phi_z, \qquad\qquad z = \zeta \tag{8}$$

We call these conditions *kinematic* because they are only concerned with the motion of the fluid.

Now, on the free surface, the pressure below must be related to the pressure in the atmosphere. In this survey we shall ignore surface tension and assume the atmospheric pressure to be P_a. As a result, Bernoulli's equation gives

$$g\zeta + \Phi_t + \frac{1}{2} |\nabla\Phi|^2 = -\frac{P_a}{\rho}, \qquad\qquad z = \zeta \tag{9}$$

Since this is a condition relating to forces, it is called the *dynamic* boundary condition.

Note that on the water surface the velocity potential Φ and the free surface displacement ζ are unknown. This makes the problem highly nonlinear and results in the greatest source of mathematical difficulty in the theory of water waves.

Linearization for Infinitesimal Waves

To analyze a physical problem theoretically, one must first decide the pertinent scales of the problem. For wave problems, the characteristic wavelength λ and wave period T are the natural space and time scales used to gauge all other quantities involving length and time. In particular, let the typical amplitude of the free surface be A. Then the fluid velocity on the free surface should be of the order $O(A/T)$. Because the gradient of Φ is the velocity, we infer that the scale of Φ must be $A \lambda/T$. If we compare typical linear and nonlinear terms, we find the ratios to be on the order:

$$(\zeta_x \Phi_x)\big/\zeta_t \sim \left(\frac{A}{\lambda}\frac{A}{T}\right)\bigg/\frac{A}{T} \sim \frac{A}{\lambda}$$

$$|\nabla\Phi|^2\big/ \Phi_t \sim \frac{1}{\lambda^2}\left(\frac{A\lambda}{T}\right)^2\bigg/\frac{1}{T}\frac{A\lambda}{T} \sim \frac{A}{\lambda} \tag{10}$$

Both are of the order of A/λ. This ratio signifies the free surface slope or the wave steepness. When $A/\lambda \ll 1$, the nonlinear terms are negligible to the leading order of approximation; only the linear terms need be kept in the two conditions on the free surface. We have thus *linearized* the boundary conditions for *waves of small slope*.

The location of the free boundary is still unknown. If we perform Taylor expansion of the velocity potential about the still water surface at $z = 0$, we get

$$\Phi_t(x,y,\zeta,t) = \Phi_t(x,y,0,t) + \zeta_{zt}(x,y,0,t) + \dots \tag{11}$$

Every term on the right is evaluated at the still water surface $z = 0$. The ratio of the quadratic term in Equation 10 to the linear term is again of the order A/λ. Thus, for small steepness we can omit the quadratic terms in the expansion, to the leading order accuracy. To summarize, the two conditions on the free surface become

$$\zeta_t = \Phi_z, \qquad\qquad z = 0 \tag{12}$$

and

$$g\zeta + \Phi_t = -\frac{P_a}{\rho}, \qquad\qquad z = 0 \tag{13}$$

With this linearization, we have eliminated the nonlinear terms, and know the location for applying the boundary conditions before the solution. Therefore, a great simplification has been achieved.

Finally, the kinematic and dynamic conditions can be combined to give

$$g\,\Phi_z + \Phi_{tt} = -\frac{1}{\rho}P_{a_t}, \qquad\qquad z=0 \tag{14}$$

Monochromatic Waves Propagating in Water of Constant Depth

Velocity and Pressure Fields

For constant h, the boundary condition on the sea bottom is simply

$$\Phi_z = 0, \qquad\qquad\qquad z = -h \qquad\qquad (15)$$

Now all governing conditions are linear and have constant coefficients. When atmospheric forcing is absent: $P_a = 0$, there is an elementary solution that represents free progressive waves along the positive x axis:

$$\Phi(x,z,t) = \text{Re}\left\{-\frac{igA}{\omega}\frac{\cosh k(z+h)}{\cosh kh} e^{ikx-i\omega t}\right\} \qquad (16)$$

with

$$\omega = \omega(k) \equiv \sqrt{gk \tanh kh} \qquad\qquad (17)$$

The corresponding free surface height is

$$\zeta(x,t) = \text{Re}\left\{A\, e^{ikx-i\omega t}\right\} \qquad\qquad (18)$$

where A represents the wave amplitude. The symbol Re (real part of) can be omitted for brevity. k is the wave number and ω the frequency, and they are proportional to the reciprocals of the wavelength and period according to

$$k = 2\pi/\lambda, \qquad\qquad\qquad \omega = 2\pi/T \qquad\qquad (19)$$

Equation 17 states that for each ω there can only be one very special k. From elementary physics, the phase velocity C of waves is the ratio

$$C = \frac{\omega}{k} = \sqrt{\left(\frac{g}{k}\tanh kh\right)} \qquad\qquad (20)$$

For long waves or shallow water, $kh = 2\pi h/ \ll 1$. We can approximate Equation 20 by

$$C = \sqrt{gh} \qquad\qquad\qquad\qquad (21)$$

Thus, the phase velocity is the same for all wavelengths. For short waves or deep water, $kh \gg 1$, then from Equation 20 we have

$$C = \sqrt{g/k} = \sqrt{g\lambda/2\pi} \tag{22}$$

Thus, the shorter waves are slower. For intermediate values of kh, C grows monotonically with kh. In the linearized context, any two-dimensional disturbance can be regarded as the superposition of a broad spectrum of sinusoidal waves, each of which propagates according to the laws just described. Thus, after the initial instant, long waves will run away to the front, leaving the short waves behind. This natural process of sorting according to wavelength is called *dispersion*. Equation 17 is therefore called the *dispersion relation*. In view of Equation 17, long waves in very shallow water are non-dispersive.

By taking the spatial gradient of Equation 16 we get the velocity components

$$u = \frac{gkA}{\omega} \frac{\cosh k(z+h)}{\cosh kh} e^{ikx - i\omega t}$$

$$v = 0 \tag{23}$$

$$w = - \frac{igkA}{\omega} \frac{\sinh k(z+h)}{\cosh kh} e^{ikx - i\omega t}$$

The symbol Re { } has been omitted for brevity. From the linearized Bernoulli equation, the total pressure is

$$P = \rho(gz + \Phi_t) \tag{24}$$

We easily find from Equation 16

$$p = P + \rho gz = \rho g \zeta \frac{\cosh k(z+h)}{\cosh kh} \tag{25}$$

For very shallow water kh ≪ 1, we obtain the following limits

$$u = \frac{gkA}{\omega} e^{ikx - i\omega t} \tag{26}$$

$$w = 0$$

Thus, the fluid motion is essentially horizontal. Furthermore, the horizontal velocity is essentially uniform in depth. The total fluid pressure can be written in the form:

$$P = \rho g(\zeta - z) \tag{27}$$

Thus, the pressure is essentially hydrostatic.

In very deep water kh $\gg$ 1, Equations 23 and 25 can be approximated by

$$
\left.\begin{array}{l}
u = \dfrac{gk}{\omega}\, A \\[2ex]
w = -\dfrac{igkA}{\omega} \\[2ex]
p = \rho gA
\end{array}\right\} e^{kz}\, e^{ikx - i\omega t}
\tag{28}
$$

Thus, the vertical and horizontal velocities have the same amplitude. From this, one can deduce that the fluid particles have circular orbits. Also, the velocity and pressure attenuate in z exponentially. Only in a layer of thickness comparable to a wavelength is there significant motion. For this feature of attenuation with depth, gravity waves are *surface waves*.

Group Velocity and Energy Propagation

If there are two trains of sinusoidal waves with slightly different frequencies, $\omega_1 = \omega + \Delta\omega$ and $\omega_2 = \omega - \Delta\omega$, the corresponding wave numbers must also be slightly different: $k_1 = k + \Delta k$ and $k_2 = k - \Delta k$. Since both wave trains must satisfy the same dispersion relation, we have upon Taylor expansion,

$$
\Delta\omega = \left(\frac{d\omega}{dk}\right) \Delta k
\tag{29}
$$

when $\Delta\omega$ or Δk is small enough. The derivative $d\omega/dk$ is evaluated at the central wave number k. Using these results, we can express the sum of the two wave trains as

$$
\begin{aligned}
\zeta &= A\, [e^{i(k_1 x - \omega_1 t)} + e^{i(k_2 x - \omega_2 t)}] \\[2ex]
&= A\, e^{ikx - i\omega t} \left[\exp\left(i\Delta k \left(x - \left(\frac{d\omega}{dk}\right) t \right) \right) + \exp\left(-i\Delta k \left(x - \left(\frac{d\omega}{dk}\right) t \right) \right) \right] \\[2ex]
&= \left\{ 2A \cos\left(\Delta k \left(x - \left(\frac{d\omega}{dk}\right) t \right) \right) \right\} e^{ikx - i\omega t}
\end{aligned}
\tag{30}
$$

This can be viewed as a nearly sinusoidal wave train with the carrier wave frequency ω and wave number k. The envelope has the maximum amplitude 2A and is modulated slowly and sinusoidally in x and t according to

$$
2A \cos\left[\Delta k \left(x - \left(\frac{d\omega}{dk}\right) t \right) \right]
\tag{31}
$$

The envelope can be viewed as sinusoidal groups with the group length $2\pi/\Delta k$ and the speed of propagation equal to

$$C_g = \frac{d\omega}{dk} = \frac{1}{2}\left(1 + \frac{2kh}{\sinh\ kh}\right) \qquad (32)$$

which is called the *group velocity.*

In very shallow water, $kh \ll 1$, we find from Equation 32 that

$$C_g = C = \sqrt{gh} \qquad (33)$$

Thus, for long waves, the phase velocity and the group velocity are equal to and independent of the wavelength. In deep water, $kh \gg 1$, we have

$$C_g = \frac{1}{2}\sqrt{\frac{g}{k}} = \frac{C}{2} \qquad (34)$$

Thus the group velocity is only one-half of the phase velocity. At the speed C the carrier wave must move twice as fast as the envelope, hence the crests move through the envelope from the rear to the front.

Aside from the kinematic significance, the group velocity is also the speed of energy transport. To see this, we first calculate the energy density in gravity waves and then the rate of energy flux through a given station. Within a wavelength, the kinetic energy below the free surface is

$$KE = \frac{k}{2\pi} \int_0^{2\pi/k} dx \int_{-h}^0 dz \frac{\rho}{2}(u^2 + w^2) = \frac{1}{4}\rho g\ |A|^2 \qquad (35)$$

while the potential energy is

$$PE = \frac{k}{2\pi} \int_0^{2\pi/k} dx \int_0^\zeta dz\ \rho gz = \frac{1}{4}\rho g\ |A|^2 \qquad (36)$$

Thus, the total energy density per wavelength is

$$E = KE + PE = \frac{1}{2}\rho g\ |A|^2 \qquad (37)$$

Now the rate of energy flux through any section x averaged over a wave period is equal to the rate of work done by the dynamic pressure:

$$W = \frac{k}{2\pi} \int_0^{2\pi/k} dt \int_{-h}^0 dz\ pu = E\ C_g \qquad (38)$$

In view of this, the rate of energy flux is C_g.

With these preliminaries, we are ready to examine situations that are more common in nature.

Refraction in a Slowly-Varying Environment

When a train of plane monochromatic waves of fixed frequency ω enters a zone of slowly varying depth, the wave number can be expected to change with depth in accordance with Equation 17, resulting in a gradual change in the phase velocity. In general, the spacing between, and the amplitude of, crests and troughs will vary from place to place. Similar changes can also occur for waves riding on a current whose intensity varies in horizontal directions. These phenomena, which are related mainly to the variation in phase velocity, are well known in optics and acoustics and are called *refraction*. In this chapter, we sketch an approximate ray theory (or geometrical optics theory) for the effects of varying depth on the propagation of infinitesimal waves. The evolution equations will be deduced by the so-called WKB method, which is a special version of the multiple-scales method. While these equations are normally solved numerically for practical problems, we shall extract from them physical insights through some analytical examples. A brief discussion is also included, for varying depth only, on the local remedy needed when the ray approximation fails. Modifications for slowly-varying currents will also be introduced at the end.

The Ray Approximation for Slowly-Varying Depth

An important assumption is that the bottom variation is so mild that the change of depth within a wavelength is very small. It is convenient to define an ordering parameter μ that measures the fractional change of depth within a wavelength,

$$\mu = \frac{\nabla h}{kh} \tag{39}$$

When this parameter is small, reflection is weak, and both the direction and amplitude of waves will change slowly in the course of propagation. It is reasonable to expect that certain laws in optics, governing the analogous refraction of light, should apply to water waves. The first is Snell's law, which governs the direction of wave rays. The second is that energy flux in a channel formed by adjacent rays will be conserved; this gives a rule for the variation of the amplitude. While they have been the intuitive basis for engineering predictions for many years, these two laws have sometimes been used beyond their realm of validity. In order to see the restrictions, it is helpful to derive the laws by a systematic procedure, known as the WKB method in physics, which can be applied to many problems involving propagation in slowly-varying media. For simplicity, the algebra will be demonstrated for the two-dimensional case of normal incidence on a bottom with contours parallel to the y axis.

We first express the slow variation of depth by renormalizing the horizontal coordinate x

$$\bar{x} = \mu x \tag{40}$$

and write $h = h(\bar{x})$. The bottom slope is then $h_x = \mu h_{\bar{x}}$; in this way the bottom slope smallness is explicitly displayed. In order to describe long wave groups associated with a narrow-banded spectrum, we anticipate slow variation in time as well. Therefore, we also introduce a slow time:

$$\bar{t} = \mu t \tag{41}$$

With these replacements, the linearized governing equations become

$$\mu^2 \Phi_{\bar{x}\bar{x}} + \Phi_{zz} = 0 \qquad\qquad -h(\bar{x}) < z < 0 \tag{42}$$

$$\mu^2 \Phi_{\bar{t}\bar{t}} + g\Phi_z = 0 \qquad\qquad z = 0 \tag{43}$$

$$\Phi_z = \mu^2 h_{\bar{x}} \Phi_{\bar{x}} \qquad\qquad z = -h \tag{44}$$

The wave potential is expected to have fast variations in phase, while being modulated slowly by the varying depth and narrow spread of frequencies. Therefore, we expand the propagating wave in the perturbation series:

$$\Phi = [\phi_0 + (-i\mu)\phi_1 + (-i\mu)^2\phi_2 + \ldots]e^{iS/\mu} \tag{45}$$

where

$$\phi_j = \phi_j(\bar{x},z,\bar{t}) \qquad\qquad \text{for } j = 0,1,2,\ldots \tag{46}$$

and

$$S = S(\bar{x},\bar{t}) \tag{47}$$

is the phase function. By straightforward differentiation we get

$$\Phi_x = \mu \Phi_{\bar{x}} = \{iS_{\bar{x}} [\phi_0 + (-i\mu)\phi_1 + \ldots] + \mu [\phi_{0_{\bar{x}}} + (-i\mu)\phi_{1_{\bar{x}}} + \ldots]\} \, e^{iS/\mu} \tag{48}$$

$$\Phi_{xx} = \mu^2 \Phi_{\bar{x}\bar{x}} = S_{\bar{x}}^2 [\phi_0 + (-i\mu)\phi_1 + \ldots] + \mu \, \}iS_{\bar{x}} [\phi_{0_{\bar{x}}} + (-i\mu)\phi_{1_{\bar{x}}} + \ldots]$$
$$+ i [(S_{\bar{x}} \phi_0)_{\bar{x}} + (-i\mu)(S_{\bar{x}} \phi_1)_{\bar{x}} + \ldots]\} \, e^{iS/\mu} \tag{49}$$

The t-derivatives can be obtained similarly. Let's define

$$S_{\bar{x}} = k(\bar{x},\bar{t}) \text{ and } S_{\bar{t}} = -\omega(\bar{x},\bar{t}) \tag{50}$$

as the local wave number and frequency, respectively. Separating the various orders, we find from the order $O(\mu)^0 = O(1)$,

$$\phi_{0_{zz}} - k^2\phi_0 = 0, \qquad\qquad -h < z < 0 \tag{51a}$$

$$\phi_{0_z} - \frac{\omega^2}{g} = 0 \qquad\qquad z = 0 \tag{51b}$$

$$\phi_{0_z} = 0, \qquad\qquad z = -h \tag{51c}$$

and from order $O(-i\mu)$:

$$\phi_{1_{zz}} - k^2\phi_1 = k\phi_{0_{\bar{x}}} + (k\phi_0)_{\bar{x}}, \qquad\qquad -h < z < 0 \tag{52a}$$

$$\phi_{1_z} - \frac{\omega^2}{g}\phi_1 = -\frac{1}{g}[\omega\phi_{0_{\bar{t}}} + (\omega\phi_0)_{\bar{t}}], \qquad\qquad z = 0 \tag{52b}$$

$$\phi_{1_z} = -h_{\bar{x}}\,\phi_{0_{\bar{x}}} \qquad\qquad z = -h \tag{52c}$$

Higher order equations are of similar structure, but will be omitted here. The leading order problem is homogeneous and has the following solution

$$\phi_0 = -\frac{igA}{\omega}\frac{\cosh k(z+h)}{\cosh kh} \tag{53}$$

with

$$\omega^2 = gk \tanh kh \tag{54}$$

Thus, to the leading order, the waves behave as if they were propagating over a horizontal bottom; k and ω are related to the *local* depth $h(\bar{x})$ by the dispersion relation. The amplitude $A(\bar{x},\bar{t})$ is, however, not yet determined. At the next order, the form of the boundary value problem is inhomogeneous but of the same type. Consider the Green identity between two functions f and F:

$$\int_{-h}^{0} [f(F_{zz} - k^2F) - F(f_{zz} - k^2f)]\ dz = [fF_z - Ff_z]_{-h}^{0} \tag{55}$$

Now we choose $f = \phi_0^*$, which is the complex conjugate of ϕ_0, $F = \phi_1$ and make use of all the conditions governing them to get

$$\int_{-h}^{0} dz\ \phi_0^*[k\phi_{0_{\bar{x}}} + (k\phi_0)_{\bar{x}}] = -\frac{1}{g}\{\phi_0[\omega\phi_{0_{\bar{t}}} + (\omega\phi_0)_{\bar{t}}]\}_{z=0} - kh_{\bar{x}}\,[|\phi_0|^2]_{z=-h} \tag{56}$$

By Leibnitz's rule the preceding equation can be regrouped

$$\frac{\partial}{\partial\bar{x}}\int_{-h}^{0} k|\phi_0|^2\ dz + \frac{\partial}{\partial\bar{t}}[\omega\,|\phi_0|^2]_{z=0} = 0 \tag{57}$$

Substituting the known expression of ϕ_0 and making use of the dispersion relation, we finally obtain a conservation law:

$$\frac{\partial}{\partial \bar{x}}\left(\frac{E}{\omega}C_g\right) + \frac{\partial}{\partial \bar{t}}\left(\frac{E}{\omega}\right) = 0 \tag{58}$$

The quantity E/ω is known as the *wave action*, and the result above is called the *conservation law of wave action.*

If the topography is slowing varying in both x and y directions, we must add the slow variable $\bar{y} = \mu y$, and change $\partial/\partial \bar{x}$ to $\bar{\nabla} = (\partial/\partial \bar{x}, \partial/\partial \bar{y})$, k to $\vec{k}$, and C_g to $\vec{C}_g$. The wave number vector is in the direction θ so that the components are

$$\alpha = k \cos \theta, \; \beta = k \sin \theta \tag{59}$$

The group velocity vector is parallel to $\vec{k}$. Equation 58 is then generalized to

$$\bar{\nabla} \cdot \left(\frac{E}{\omega}\vec{C}_g\right) + \frac{\partial}{\partial \bar{t}}\left(\frac{E}{\omega}\right) = 0 \tag{60}$$

with

$$\bar{\nabla}S = \vec{k}, \qquad\qquad\qquad S_{\bar{t}} = -\omega \tag{61a,b}$$

instead of Equation 50. As a consequence of the preceding definitions, we also have the following consistency relations:

$$\bar{\nabla} \times \vec{k} = 0, \qquad\qquad\qquad \vec{k}_{\bar{t}} + \bar{\nabla}\omega = 0 \tag{62a,b}$$

In general, there are four unknowns: the two components of $\vec{k}$, ω and A. They are governed by Equations 60 and 62a,b and the dispersion relation, Equation 54. Given $h(\bar{x},\bar{y})$, initial and boundary conditions must be specified to complete the problem.

For a more physical insight, consider in particular the one-dimensional version of the equation

$$k_{\bar{t}} + \omega_{\bar{x}} = 0 \tag{63}$$

Being the number of wave crests per unit horizontal distance, k is the density of crests. Now ω is the number of crests passing a fixed station, hence it is the rate of flux of crests. Equation 62b is therefore the conservation law of wave crests.

While we have derived laws valid for wave trains that vary slowly in both space and time, we shall deal with a simple case where there is no dependence on the slow time. This amounts to restricting ourselves to monochromatic waves with constant ω. The governing equations are then reduced to

$$\bar{\nabla} \times \vec{k} = 0 \tag{64}$$

$$\bar{\nabla} \cdot (E\vec{C_g}) = 0 \tag{65}$$

Given the depth $h(\bar{x},\bar{y})$, the magnitude of $\vec{k}$ is obtained from the dispersion relation, and the two components of $\vec{k}$ can be integrated from the differential Equation 64. As for the wave amplitude, we define a *ray* to be a curve in the $\bar{x},\bar{y}$ plane tangent to the local wave-number vectors. Two adjacent rays form a *ray tube*. Consider the area formed by two cross sections and two walls of a ray tube. Integrating over this area, using the Gaussian theorem and the fact that $\vec{k}$ is tangent to the walls of the ray tube, we get

$$E\ C_g\ d\sigma = (E\ C_g\ d\sigma)_0 = \text{constant} \tag{66}$$

where $d\sigma_0$ and $d\sigma$ are the widths of the tube at the entry and exit cross sections, respectively. Thus the rate of energy flux is constant along the ray tube. Because $E = \frac{1}{2}\,\rho g\,|A|^2$, we have

$$\frac{|A|}{A_0} = \left[\frac{(C_g d\sigma)_0}{C_g d\sigma}\right]^{1/2} \tag{67}$$

which gives the amplitude after the ray geometry is known.

This kind of analysis is called the *ray* or *geometrical optics approximation*. Let us now examine the physical implications for cases where h can be described by one coordinate.

Depth With Straight and Parallel Contours h = h(x̄)

We now consider a train of long-crested monochromatic incident waves from a region of constant depth toward a region of variable depth. From the irrotationality of wave-number vector we get

$$\frac{\partial \beta}{\partial \bar{x}} = 0 \tag{68}$$

which can be integrated to give

$$\beta = k \sin \theta = k_o \sin \theta_o = \text{constant } K \tag{69}$$

where the subscript ( )$_o$ refers to a station where all parameters of the wave are known. Thus, the y component of the wave-number vector remains constant. The phase velocity is defined by $C = \omega/k$, and Equation 69 may be written

$$\frac{\sin \theta}{C} = \frac{\sin \theta_o}{C_o} \tag{70}$$

which is the famous Snell's law in optics. Conservation of energy flux, Equation 65, then gives

$$\frac{\partial}{\partial \bar{x}}\,(E\,C_g\,\cos\theta) = 0,\;\text{ or }\; \frac{|A|}{A_0} = \left[\frac{(C_g\,\cos\theta)_0}{C_g\,\cos\theta}\right]^{1/2} \tag{71}$$

Let us study the ray geometry first. In the zone of constant depth all rays are straight and parallel. Suppose $\bar{y} = y(\bar{x})$ is the equation for a ray in general. Since $\bar{y}' = d\bar{y}/d\bar{x} = \tan\alpha$ we can write Equation 70 as

$$\frac{k\bar{y}'}{\sqrt{1+\bar{y}'^2}} = k\,\sin\theta = K \tag{72}$$

which can be solved for $\bar{y}'$,

$$\bar{y}' = \pm\,\frac{K}{\sqrt{h^2 - K^2}} \tag{73}$$

The sign can be chosen later. The ray equation is clearly

$$\bar{y} - \bar{y}_0 \pm \int_{\bar{x}_0}^{\bar{x}} \frac{K\,d\bar{x}}{\sqrt{k^2 - K^2}} \tag{74}$$

Note that

$$\sqrt{k^2 - K^2} = \alpha = k\,\cos\theta \tag{75}$$

Consider first a submarine canyon flanked on both sides by a horizontal bed of constant and equal depth. A train of plane waves of frequency ω approaches from the left with $0 < \theta_0 < \pi/2$. The wave number k is a constant, say k_{max}, to the left of the canyon, drops to the lowest value k_{min} along the trough, and then increases to k_{max} again to the right of the canyon, see Figure 1a. Since the square root is real only when K is less than k, rays can exist, i.e., propagation is possible, only when the initial incidence is not too far from being normal or when the initial wavelength is sufficiently long. Consider first the case when $K = K_2 < k_{min}$. Propagation is possible for all $\bar{x}$. To the left of the canyon all rays are straight and parallel. When a ray first enters the canyon, the wave-number component α decreases with k. Since β remains constant the ray turns away from the $\bar{x}$ axis, i.e., away from the normal to the depth contours. After crossing the deepest contour of the canyon the tendency is reversed, the ray then leans toward the $\bar{x}$ axis instead. After leaving the canyon the ray returns to the incident direction again, see Figure 1b. A positive sign must be chosen in Equations 73 and 74.

Now consider the case where $k_{min} < K = K_1 < k_{max}$ (see Figure 1a,b). This is possible when the incident ray is rather oblique. The ray can exist only to the left of the line $\bar{x} = \bar{x}_1$, along which $k = K$. Before reaching this line we must take the positive sign in Equations 73 and 74. At this line $\bar{y} \uparrow \infty$, so that the ray becomes tangent to the contour at the point $\bar{y}(\bar{x}_1)$. Afterwards the ray is reflected to the left of

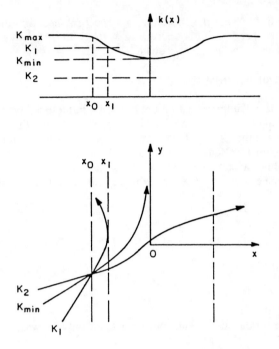

Figure 1. (a) Variation of k across a submarine trough; (b) Wave rays over a submarine trough.

$\bar{x} = \bar{x}_1$. Obviously, all entering rays that are parallel outside the canyon are reflected in the same way. The line $\bar{x} = \bar{x}_1$ is the envelope of all rays and is called a *caustic*. Since two neighboring rays must intersect near the caustic, the width of the ray tube must vanish, hence the amplitude must become unbounded. Our approximate theory then breaks down and a better theory is needed. A *boundary layer* approximation treating the details of the neighborhood of the caustic is possible within the framework of the linearized approximation and will be described later.

In the case of a submarine ridge, the incident ray first enters a region where h first decreases, then increases until the region of constant depth is again reached. The wave number must first increase from k_{min} to k_{max} then decrease. Thus, the incident ray first bends toward then away from the $\bar{x}$ axis. If $k_{min} < K < k_{max}$, there must be two lines, say, $\bar{x} = a$ and b along which k = K. Then rays can only exist inside the strip $a < \bar{x} < b$. This phenomenon is called *trapping*. Both lines $\bar{x} = a$ and b are caustics.

Let us now examine the variation of amplitude. In very shallow water, $kh \ll 1$. The dispersion relation requires that $k \cong \omega/\sqrt{gh}$, which implies $\alpha \cong k$, and all waves must be parallel to the depth contours. It follows from Equation 71 that

$$\frac{A}{A_0} \cong (C_g \cos \theta_0)_0^{1/2}/(gh)^{1/4} \tag{76}$$

Thus, A increases as $h^{-1/4}$. Near the shoreline of a beach, A becomes unbounded and the local wave slope becomes unbounded also as $h^{-3/4}$. In reality, waves break and the linearized theory is no longer adequate.

The Neighborhood of a Caustic

As noted already, the ray approximation breaks down in the neighborhood of a caustic. Let us first diagnose the nature of the breakdown by taking the ray theory to this neighborhood, and then seek a local remedy. The idea is very similar to the boundary layer approximation familiar in fluid mechanics.

Consider a straight line caustic coinciding with $\bar{x} = 0$ and a ray approaching from the left and touching the caustic at $\bar{y} = \bar{y}_*$. Near this caustic we let $|\bar{x}|$ be small and assume

$$k^2 \cong K^2 - \gamma\bar{x} \tag{77}$$

so that

$$\alpha = \sqrt{k^2 - K^2} \cong (-\gamma\bar{x})^{1/2} \tag{78}$$

Because $\sin \alpha \cong 1$ near the caustic we can approximate the incident wave amplitude as

$$\frac{A}{A_0} = \left[\frac{(C_g \cos \theta)_0}{C_g \cos \theta}\right]^{1/2} = \left[\frac{C_g \alpha}{k}\right]_0^{1/2} \left[\frac{K}{C}\right]_{\bar{x}=0}^{1/2} (-\gamma\bar{x})^{-1/4} \equiv \tau(-\gamma\bar{x})^{-1/4} \tag{79}$$

where τ is a constant, and $(\ )_0$ corresponds to a reference line $\bar{x} = \bar{x}_0$ different from $\bar{x} = 0$. Obviously, Equation 79 cannot hold too close to the caustic. Outside a thin layer of certain width the reflected wave must follow a ray that is symmetric with respect to the line $\bar{y} = \bar{y}_*$ and can still be described by the ray approximation. Hence, we can write the total free surface displacement as

$$\eta = e^{i\beta\bar{y}/\mu} A \left[\exp\left(i \int \alpha \, d\bar{x}/\mu\right) + R \exp\left(-i \int \alpha \, d\bar{x}/\mu\right)\right] \tag{80}$$

where R is the unknown reflection coefficient. The approximation of η for small $|\bar{x}|$, but outside the boundary layer, is

$$\eta \cong \tau(-\gamma\bar{x})^{1/4} e^{i\beta\bar{y}/\mu} \left\{\exp\left[-i \frac{\gamma^{1/2}}{\mu} \frac{2}{3} (-\bar{x})^{3/2}\right] + R \exp\left[i \frac{\gamma^{1/2}}{\mu} \frac{2}{3} (-\bar{x})^{3/2}\right]\right\} \tag{81}$$

This may be called the *inner limit* of the *outer solution*, in the language of matched asymptotics.

Now let us take a closer look at the boundary layer itself. Because the ray approximation blows up very near $\bar{x} = 0$, we must expect the $\bar{x}$ derivative to be very important. Assuming the following solution

$$\Phi = \frac{-igX(\bar{x})}{\omega} \frac{\cosh k(z+h)}{\cos kh} e^{iK\bar{y}/\mu - i\omega\bar{t}/\mu} \tag{82}$$

we rewrite the Laplace equation

$$\mu^2 X_{\bar{x}\bar{x}} + (k^2 - K^2)X = \mu^2 X_{\bar{x}\bar{x}} - \gamma\bar{x}X = O(\mu) \tag{83}$$

This implies immediately that the boundary layer thickness is of the order

$$\Delta = O(\mu^{2/3}) \tag{84}$$

Introducing the boundary layer coordinate

$$\sigma = \gamma^{1/3} \, \bar{x}/\mu^{2/3} \tag{85}$$

Equation 83 can be written in the form

$$X_{\sigma\sigma} - \sigma X \cong 0 \tag{86}$$

which is called the Airy equation; it has the general solution

$$X = a \, Ai(\sigma) + bBi(\sigma) \tag{87}$$

It is well known that both $Ai(\sigma)$ and $Bi(\sigma)$ are oscillatory in σ for $\sigma < 0$, for σ large and positive, Ai decays while Bi grows exponentially as follows

$$Ai(\sigma) \sim \frac{1}{2\sqrt{\pi}} \frac{1}{\sigma^{1/4}} \exp\left(-\frac{2}{3} \sigma^{3/2}\right)$$

$$\text{(88a,b)}$$

$$Bi(\sigma) \sim \frac{1}{\sqrt{\pi}} \frac{1}{\sigma^{1/4}} \exp\left(\frac{2}{3} \sigma^{3/2}\right)$$

For boundedness at $\sigma \sim \infty$ we discard Bi and take only

$$\eta = DAi(\sigma)e^{iK\bar{y}/\mu} \tag{89}$$

This is the inner solution good for the boundary layer. To determine the constants D and R, we try to match the inner limit of the outer (ray) solution to the outer limit of the inner solution. The latter is obtained by taking $-\sigma \gg 1$ in

$$\eta \sim \frac{D}{\sqrt{\pi}} \frac{1}{\sigma^{1/4}} \frac{1}{2i} \left\{ \exp\left(i\frac{2}{3}(-\sigma)^{3/2} + \frac{\pi}{4}\right) - \exp\left(-i\frac{2}{3}(-\sigma)^{3/2} - \frac{i\pi}{4}\right) \right\}$$

$$\text{(90)}$$

Rewriting Equation 90 in terms of the outer coordinate $\bar{x}$ through Equation 85 we have

$$\eta \sim -\frac{D}{2i} \frac{e^{-i\pi/4} \mu^{1/6}}{\sqrt{\pi} (-\gamma^{1/3}\bar{x})^{1/4}} \left\{ \exp\left[-i \frac{2}{3} \frac{\gamma^{1/2}}{\mu} (-\bar{x})^{3/2} \right] \right.$$
$$\left. - e^{i\pi/2} \exp\left[i \frac{2}{3} \frac{\gamma^{1/2}}{\mu} (-\bar{x})^{3/2} \right] \right\}$$

$$(91)$$

Comparison of the coefficients of the two exponentials in Equations 91 and 81 gives two conditions for D and R, which in turn yield the results

$$D = -2i \sqrt{\pi} \, \tau \, e^{i\pi/4} \, (\gamma\mu)^{-1/6} \qquad\qquad (92)$$

and

$$R = -e^{i\pi/2}$$

Thus, the reflection is complete and the amplitude is finite, though as large as $O(\mu^{-1/6})$. Using the ray approximation away from the caustic and the Airy function to account for the details of reflection near it, we now have a solution that is finite everywhere.

Besides the straight caustic discussed here, there are many other varieties. For a survey of the rich literature on the subject of caustics one should consult Stamnes [52].

Refraction of Narrow-Banded Waves

So far, only monochromatic waves have been studied. To show how transient waves are refracted, we consider a train of waves with a narrow frequency band, incident from a zone of constant depth. As is shown earlier, the incident waves then have a slowly varying envelope that travels at the group velocity of the carrier waves. What happens when the waves enter a zone of slowly varying depth?

The envelope must be governed by the law of wave action conservation. Because the waves have a fixed central frequency, ω, the envelope equation may be written,

$$\frac{\partial A}{\partial t} + \vec{C}_g \cdot \overline{\nabla} A + A/2 + \overline{\nabla} \cdot \vec{C}_g = 0 \qquad\qquad (93)$$

Let us consider a one-dimensional bathymetry with h(x). In the zone of incidence where h is constant we take the envelope to be

$$A = A_0 \cos \mu(\alpha_0 x + \beta_0 y - \Omega t) = A_0 \, \text{Re} \, \exp i\mu(\alpha_0 x + \beta_0 y - \Omega t) \qquad\qquad (94)$$

This corresponds to a wave train whose frequency spectrum consists of two lines shifted from the central frequency ω by $\pm \mu\Omega$. Substituting Equation 94 into Equation 93 we find

$$\Omega = C_{g0}k_0 \quad \text{where} \quad k_0^2 = \alpha_0^2 + \beta_0^2 \tag{95}$$

Over the zone of variable depth Equation 93 has coefficients that depend on $\bar{x}$ only, so we try a solution of the type

$$A = \text{Re } \hat{A}(\bar{x}) \exp i\mu(\beta_0 \, y - \Omega t) \tag{96}$$

The equation for $\hat{A}$ is then

$$\frac{d\hat{A}}{d\bar{x}} + \hat{A}\left[i\mu \, \beta_0 \left(\frac{C_{g2}}{C_{g1}} - \frac{\Omega}{C_{g1}}\right) - \frac{1}{2C_{g1}}\frac{dC_{g1}}{d\bar{x}}\right] = 0 \tag{97}$$

where C_{g1} and C_{g2} are the x, y components of $\vec{C}g$. Since $C_{g2}/C_{g1} = \beta_0/\alpha$, we may rewrite Equation 97 as

$$\frac{d\hat{A}}{d\bar{x}} + \hat{A}\left[i\mu \, \beta_0 \left(\frac{\beta_0^2}{\alpha_2} - \frac{\Omega}{C_{g1}}\right) - \frac{1}{2C_{g1}}\frac{dC_{g1}}{dx}\right] = 0 \tag{98}$$

Let $\bar{x} = 0$ be the line where h starts to deviate from the constant h_o. The initial condition must be

$$\hat{A}\,(0) = A_0 \tag{99}$$

The solution is easily found to be

$$\hat{A} = A_0 \sqrt{\frac{(C_{g1})_0}{C_g}} \exp \int_0^{\bar{x}} d\bar{x}' \, K_1(\bar{x}') \tag{100}$$

where $K_1 = \dfrac{\Omega}{C_{g1}} - \dfrac{\beta_0^2}{\alpha} = \dfrac{C_{g0}k_0}{C_{g1}} - \dfrac{k^2 - \alpha^2}{\alpha}$

$$= \alpha + \frac{k^2}{\alpha}\left(\frac{C_{g0}}{C_g}\frac{k_0}{k} - 1\right)$$

$$= \alpha + \frac{k^2}{\alpha}\left(\frac{C_{g0}}{C_g}\frac{C_0}{C_0} - 1\right) \tag{101}$$

Along the starting line $h = h_o$ so that $K_1 = \alpha = \alpha_0$. Now

$$\frac{C_{g0}}{C_0}\frac{C}{C_g} = \frac{\omega}{k_0}\left(1 + \frac{2k_0h_0}{\sinh 2k_0h_0}\right) / \frac{\omega}{k}\left(1 + \frac{2kh}{\sinh 2kh}\right) \tag{102}$$

As kh decreases from k_0h_0, C_g/C increases toward unity. Hence, the parenthesis in the last of Equation 101 increases toward zero from negative values, i.e., $K_1 < \alpha$. Thus, the envelope wave-number vector $\vec{K}$ tends to have a greater inclination away from the x axis than $\vec{k}$. But as h decreases monotonically to 0, both these two rays become parallel again and normal to the depth contours. If on the other hand, h increases from h_0, the parenthesis in Equation 102 is greater than 1. When a straight caustic is approached, $\alpha \to 0$ and $K_1 \to \infty$; we find $\vec{k}$ to be parallel but $\vec{K}$ normal to the caustic. The rays of a sinusoidally-modulated incident and reflected envelopes form a cusp at the caustic. In this neighborhood the ray approximation of course breaks down; a uniformly valid theory is still wanting.

Comments on Seabed with Curved Contours

For more general variations of the bottom depth, we appeal to the eikonal equation

$$(\overline{\nabla}S)^2 = S_{\bar{x}}^2 + S_{\bar{y}}^2 = k^2 \tag{103}$$

Let $\bar{y} = \bar{y}(\bar{x})$ be the equation of a ray. Since the ray must be in the direction of $\overline{\nabla}S$ we have

$$\bar{y}' = \frac{d\bar{y}}{d\bar{x}} = S_{\bar{y}}/S_{\bar{x}} \tag{104}$$

Using the eikonal equation we can show that

$$\frac{d}{d\bar{x}}\left(\frac{k\bar{y}'}{\sqrt{1+\bar{y}'^2}}\right) = \frac{\partial k}{\partial \bar{y}}\sqrt{1+\bar{y}'^2} \tag{105}$$

Because $k = k(\bar{x},\bar{y}(\bar{x}))$ on the ray, this is a nonlinear second order differential equation for $\bar{y}(\bar{x})$, which can be solved numerically once two initial conditions at a point on the ray are known. Alternately, one can say that a ray which passes two known points must extremize the following functional,

$$L = \int_{P_1}^{P_2} F(\bar{x},\bar{y}(\bar{x}),\bar{y}'(\bar{x}))d\bar{x} = \int_{P_1}^{P_2} k\sqrt{1+\bar{y}'^2}\ d\bar{x} \tag{106}$$

By the calculus of variations, the extremization of L implies and is implied by Equation 105, which is called the Euler-Lagrange equation. This alternative is known as Fermat's principle.

The special case of circular depth contours, h = h(r), can be worked out easily. Many physically revealing examples can be found in Mei [36].

Refraction by Slowly-Varying Currents

When ebb tides retreat from a river entrance, swift currents run against the wind-induced waves. This can create a choppy sea surface and makes the maneuvering of small fishing vessels hazardous. Because variations of the current are often associated with variations in bathymetry, the horizontal scales are usually large compared to the typical wind wavelength. Hence, reflection is again weak and refraction is the main feature.

A recent impetus for studying current-induced refraction is the revelation of bottom features by satellite images. As a tool of remote-sensing, satellite radar imagery is advantageous in being able to survey a very large area at a time. There are now strong evidences that bathymetrical variations can be read from radar images of the sea surface. However, radar images are due primarily to Bragg reflection of electromagnetic waves of O(30 cm) length or less from the the sea surface. Because these short waves are quickly attenuated within a depth comparable to their wavelength from the sea surface, bottom features cannot be sensed directly by radar. One possibility is that depth variations can affect the large-scale current that in turn affects the short surface waves responsible for Bragg scattering.

Because of the sharp contrast in length scales, it is possible to employ the WKB method again to get the asymptotic equations governing the evolution of waves. Detailed development of the theory and various examples can be found in Mei [36]. We only summarize some essentials here. The assumptions are:

1. Waves: small slope, $kA \ll 1$ and intermediate length, $kh = O(1)$.
2. Current: long period and wavelength, $Kh \ll 1$, but the current velocity U_i, $i = 1,2$, can be comparable to the phase velocity of the short waves.

Under these assumptions, the current is described by the long-wave equations

$$\frac{\partial Z}{\partial \bar{t}} + \frac{\partial Z}{\partial \bar{x}_i} \left[U_i(Z + h) \right] = 0 \tag{107}$$

$$\frac{\partial U_i}{\partial \bar{t}} + U_j \frac{\partial U_i}{\partial \bar{x}_i} = -g \frac{\partial Z}{\partial \bar{x}_i} \tag{108}$$

where U_i represents the current velocity and Z the free surface displacement induced by the current. In these equations the current velocity can be of the order $\sqrt{gh}$. Because of its greater strength, the current is not affected by the waves and can be found first.

We note that the Equation 107 is an exact statement of mass conservation when U_i refers to the depth averaged horizontal velocity. It can be derived from the continuity equation by integrating with respect to ζ and by using the kinematic boundary conditions on the bottom $z = -h$ and on the free surface $z = Z$. The momentum equation can be heuristically justified by the observations made after Equations 6 and 7 that for long waves (a) the vertical velocity is much less important than the horizontal velocity, (b) the horizontal velocity is essentially independent of depth, and (c) the total pressure is hydrostatic $P = \rho g(Z - \zeta)$. Because of (b) there is little distinction between the horizontal velocity and its depth average.

Let the short wave properties be represented by lower case symbols. Assume that the waves are progressive and narrow-banded, then the following results can be derived.

The free surface is given by

$$\zeta = Z + \text{Re A exp } iS(\bar{x},\bar{y},\bar{t})/\mu \qquad (109)$$

where A and S are the amplitude and phase of the short waves. The phase function is related to the local wave number k_i and absolute frequency ω by

$$k_i = \frac{\partial S}{\partial \bar{x}_i} \quad i = 1,2,\ldots \quad \omega = \frac{\partial S}{\partial \bar{t}} \qquad (110)$$

The intrinsic frequency σ is related to the absolute frequency by

$$\sigma = \omega - U_i k_i \qquad (111)$$

and satisfies the following dispersion relation,

$$\sigma^2 = gk \tanh kH \qquad (112)$$

where $H = h + Z = $ total mean depth $\qquad (113)$

If we define the group velocity by

$$C_g = \frac{\partial \sigma}{\partial k}\bigg|_H = \frac{\sigma}{2k}\left(1 + \frac{2kH}{\sinh 2kH}\right) \qquad (114)$$

and the energy density by

$$E = \frac{2}{3}\rho g \,|\, A \,|^2 \qquad (115)$$

then the amplitude variation is governed by

$$\frac{\partial}{\partial \bar{t}}\left(\frac{E}{\sigma}\right) + \frac{\partial}{\partial \bar{x}_i}\left[(U_i + C_{gi})\frac{E}{\sigma}\right] = 0 \qquad (116)$$

The ratio E/σ is the *wave action* for waves on a slowly-varying depth and current.

The corresponding pressure and velocity fields of the short waves are

$$p = \rho g A \,\frac{\cosh k(z + h)}{\cosh kH} \qquad (117)$$

and

$$u_i = \frac{k_i p_o}{\rho \sigma} \quad i = 1,2 \tag{118}$$

Simple quantitative deductions of these equations can be made for monochromatic waves and a steady current. For monochromatic waves ω = constant and the wave action is independent of t, i.e.,

$$\frac{\partial}{\partial \bar{x}_i} \left[(U_i + C_{gi}) \frac{E}{\sigma} \right] = 0 \tag{119}$$

In principle, we first compute the current velocity $\vec{U}(x,y)$ and then find $\vec{k}$ according to

$$\beta_{\bar{x}} - \alpha_{\bar{y}} = 0 \tag{120}$$

and the dispersion relation Equation 112. Let us define in the $\bar{x}, \bar{y}$ plane a family of curves such that each point along the curve is tangent to the local vector of $\vec{U} + \vec{C}g$. Equation 119 then states that the flux of wave action between two adjacent curves of this kind is conserved, and can be used to find the local wave amplitude.

Let us examine an example where analytical considerations are possible.

Waves in a Jet Stream

Consider a jet stream in the y direction with its strength varying in the $\bar{x}$ direction, i.e., U = 0, and V = V($\bar{x}$) > 0. Waves, originally plane away from the jet stream, are propagating at the angle θ with respect to the $\bar{x}$ axis. From Equation 120, $\beta = k \sin \theta$ = constant. Hence

$$\alpha = \sqrt{k(\bar{x}) - \beta^2} , \quad \omega - V(\bar{x})\beta = \sqrt{gk \tanh kH}$$

From these we get the equation for a ray

$$\frac{d\bar{y}}{d\bar{x}} = \pm \frac{\beta}{\alpha} \text{ or } \bar{y} - \bar{y}_0 = \pm \int_{\bar{x}_0}^{\bar{x}} \frac{\beta}{\alpha} d\bar{x} = \pm \int_{\bar{x}_0}^{\bar{x}} \frac{\beta d\bar{x}}{\sqrt{k^2(\bar{x}) - \beta^2}} \tag{121}$$

As V increases (decreases), k decreases (increases). Hence, the effects of a jet stream are similar to that of a submarine trough. If $\beta > 0$, an obliquely incident ray is bent away from the $\bar{x}$ axis. After crossing the axis of the current, the ray bends back toward the $\bar{x}$ axis. If the angle of incidence is large enough, a ray is reflected by a caustic along which $\alpha = 0$.

The wave amplitude is derived from the law of wave action conservation:

$$\frac{\alpha E C_g}{k(\omega - V\beta)} = \text{constant} \tag{122}$$

which gives

$$\left[\frac{A}{A_0}\right] = \frac{C_g \cos \theta_0}{C_g \cos \theta} \frac{\omega - V\beta}{\omega - V_0\beta} \tag{123}$$

In particular for deep water, $kH \gg 1$, we have from

$$\omega - V\beta = \sqrt{gH} \quad \text{and} \quad C_g = \frac{\omega - V\beta}{2k} \tag{124}$$

If we assume $V_0 = 0$, then

$$C_g \equiv \frac{\sigma}{2k} = \frac{\omega - U k \cos \theta}{2k} \tag{125}$$

and

$$\frac{A}{A_0} = \frac{\cos \alpha_0 \left[1 - \dfrac{V}{C_0} \sin \theta_0\right]^2}{1 - \dfrac{\sin^2\theta_0}{\left(1 - \dfrac{V}{C_0} \sin \theta_0\right)^4}} \quad \text{with } C_0 = \frac{\omega}{k_0} \tag{126}$$

Some sample results for this special case are plotted in Figure 2. Other examples may be found in Mei [36].

Diffraction of Infinitesimal Waves

One of the primary concerns in ocean engineering is the mutual effects of waves on structures such as ships, drilling platforms, breakwaters, harbors, etc. The size of these structures is often comparable to, or greater than, a wavelength, so that their presence drastically changes the direction of the incoming waves. The wave forces on the structure also depend strongly on this change. If the structure is further allowed to move, the induced body motion also radiates waves which produce hydrodynamic reaction on the body. The interaction between an incident wave and stationary scatterers is called *diffraction*, while the generation of waves by bodies forced to move in a quiescent water is called *radiation*. Since an unconstrained-, or partially-constrained body can move in incident waves, an engineering problem involves both diffraction and radiation in general. In this chapter some aspects of diffraction will be discussed for long-crested incident waves of a single frequency

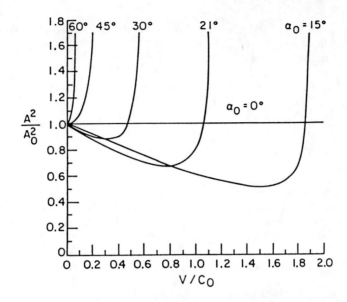

Figure 2. Wave amplitude vs. jet stream velocity for various incidence angles α_0; C_0 is the phase velocity outside the jet stream.

only. To bring out the essential physical features without lengthy mathematics, we shall devote much of our discussions to long waves in shallow water. The mathematics of radiation is very similar to that of diffraction [36].

Formulation of a Diffraction Problem

Long Waves in Shallow Water. For long waves of infinitesimal amplitudes, we can linearize Equations 107 and 108 to get

$$\zeta_t + \nabla \cdot (\vec{u} \, h) = 0 \tag{127}$$

and

$$\vec{u_t} = -g \nabla \zeta \tag{128}$$

Because only long waves are considered here, we shall not use the upper case symbols and omit the overhead bars from the coordinates. By eliminating $\vec{u}$ from these equations, we get the equation governing the free surface displacement

$$\nabla \cdot (h \nabla \zeta) = \frac{1}{g} \zeta_{tt} \tag{129}$$

Note that in Equations 127 and 128, the horizontal scales of $h, \overline{u}$ and ζ are assumed to be comparable.

For simple harmonic waves of frequency ω we write

$$\zeta = \text{Re } \eta(x,y) \, e^{-i\omega t} \tag{130}$$

so that

$$\nabla \cdot (h\nabla\eta) + \frac{\omega^2}{g} \, \eta = 0 \tag{131}$$

Let us consider an incident wave train approaching a finite region of variable depth. The ocean depth far away is taken to be constant $h = h_0$. In this finite region there can also be structures with irregular boundaries. Let the incident wave train be long-crested so that

$$\eta_I = A_0 \, e^{i(\alpha x + \beta y)}, \quad \alpha^2 + \beta^2 = k^2 = \omega^2/gh_0 \tag{132}$$

Because of linearity we split the total η into two parts

$$\eta = \eta_I + \eta_S \tag{133}$$

where η_S denotes the scattered waves. From Equation 131 we have

$$\nabla \cdot h\nabla\eta_S + \frac{\omega^2}{g} \, \eta_S + \nabla \cdot h\nabla\eta_I + \frac{\omega^2}{8} \, \eta_I = 0 \tag{134}$$

In the zone of constant depth, we have

$$\nabla^2\eta_I + k^2\eta_I = 0, \; \nabla^2\eta_S + k^2\eta_S = 0 \tag{135}$$

On the boundary of a surface-piercing structure, or a coastline with a steep shore, where breaking is unimportant, we require that

$$h \frac{\partial\eta}{\partial n} = h \left(\frac{\partial\eta_I}{\partial n} + \frac{\partial\eta_S}{\partial n} \right) = 0 \tag{136}$$

At infinity we must require the *radiation condition* that the scattered waves be outgoing. The precise statement of this last condition depends on the problem. For example, if the ocean depth depends only on x and is the same constant at both infinities, then η_S takes the form:

$$\eta_S = \xi(x)e^{i\beta y} \tag{137}$$

where ξ depends only on x. The reduced problem is now one-dimensional and the radiation condition reads

$$\xi \sim e^{\pm i\alpha x} \quad \alpha x \to \pm \infty \tag{138a}$$

or, equivalently,

$$\left(\frac{\partial}{\partial x} \mp i\alpha\right) \xi \to 0, \quad \alpha x \to \pm \infty \tag{138b}$$

where $\alpha^2 + \beta^2 = k^2$. If, on the other hand, the scatterer lies within a circle of finite radius, the outgoing waves must be radially outgoing so that

$$\eta_S \sim A_0 \, A(\theta) \, \frac{1}{\sqrt{\pi k r}} \, e^{ikr - i\pi/4}, \quad kr \gg 1 \tag{139a}$$

or, equivalently,

$$\sqrt{kr} \left(\frac{\partial}{\partial r} - ik\right) \eta_S \to 0, \quad kr \to \infty \tag{139b}$$

This completes the formulation of the diffraction problem for long waves of infinitesimal amplitudes.

Arbitrary Depth. When $kh = O(1)$ we need to consider variations in all three directions. The velocity potential is then governed by

$$\Phi(x,y,t) = \text{Re} \, \phi(x,y,z) \, e^{-i\omega t} \tag{140}$$

$$\phi_{xx} + \phi_{yy} + \phi_{zz} = 0 \tag{141}$$

in the fluid,

$$\phi_z + \frac{\omega^2}{g} \phi = 0 \tag{142}$$

on the free surface, and

$$\frac{\partial \phi}{\partial n} = 0 \tag{143}$$

on the sea bottom and the rest position of a structure. In terms of the free surface displacement, the radiation condition is still expressed by Equation 138 or 139 if we consider full dispersion relation for ω and k.

We now discuss a few examples.

One-Dimensional Diffraction

Scattering of Shallow Water Waves by a Depth Discontinuity. Consider the simplest problem of a scattering by an abrupt change of depth from h to h' along the line x = 0. The solution on two sides of the step is

$$\eta = A(e^{i\alpha x} + Re^{-i\alpha x})\, e^{i\beta y}, \quad k = \omega/\sqrt{gh}, \quad x < 0$$

$$= A\, T\, e^{i\alpha' x}\, e^{i\beta y}, \quad k' = \omega/\sqrt{gh'}, \quad x > 0 \tag{144a,b}$$

which satisfies the radiation condition. T and R are the transmission and reflection coefficients, respectively. Along the line x = 0 we require continuity of pressure

$$\eta = \eta', \quad x = 0 \tag{145}$$

and of normal flux

$$h\,\frac{\partial \eta}{\partial x} = h'\,\frac{\partial \eta'}{\partial x}, \quad x = 0 \tag{146}$$

It is then easily found that

$$T = \frac{2\alpha h}{\alpha h + \alpha' h'}, \quad R = \frac{\alpha - \alpha' h'}{\alpha h + \alpha' h'} \tag{147}$$

The directions of the incident and transmitted waves measured from the positive x axis are

$$\theta = \tan^{-1} \frac{\beta}{\sqrt{k^2 - \beta^2}}, \qquad \theta' = \tan^{-1} \frac{\beta}{\sqrt{k'^2 - \beta^2}} \tag{148}$$

If the water depth is greater on the transmission side, h < h', then $\theta < \theta'$ and the transmitted wave inclines further away from the x axis. This is qualitatively the same as that of refraction by slowly changing depth. For sufficiently oblique incidence it is possible that

$$k'^2 < \beta^2 < k^2 \tag{149}$$

so that α' and θ' are imaginary. Propagation into deeper water is then impossible and waves are *trapped* on the shallow side. If the analysis is extended to a submarine shelf of width comparable or greater than the typical wavelength, we can show that the shelf can trap waves and acts as a wave guide (see Mei [36]).

We remark that in the neighborhood of the step defined by x = O(h), the vertical velocity is as important as the horizontal velocity, hence the long-wave approximation is no longer valid. Nevertheless, it is possible to show for the special case of normal incidence that Equation 147 is valid with an error of $O(kh)^2$ in the outgoing energy $|T|^2$ or $|R|^2$. This justifies the use of Equations 145 and 146.

Long Waves Scattered by a Gradual Transition of Finite Length. To see the effect of a gradual transition we consider a simple case [21] where the depth is $h_1 = ax_1^2$ for $x < x_1$, ax^2 for $x_1 < x < x_2$, and $h_2 = ax_2^2$ for $x > x_2$. The incident waves propagate from the shallower water on the left toward the deeper water on the right. The governing equation in the transition zone is

$$(x^2\eta')' + \frac{\omega^2}{ga}\eta = 0, \; x_1 < x < x_2 \tag{150}$$

which admits the general solution

$$\eta = ax^\alpha = bx^\beta \tag{151}$$

with

$$\begin{bmatrix} \alpha \\ \beta \end{bmatrix} = -\frac{1}{4} \pm \mu^{1/2}, \text{ where } \mu = \frac{1}{4} - \frac{\omega^2}{ga} \tag{152}$$

The solutions on two sides of the transition are

$$\begin{aligned} \eta &= (A\, e^{ik_1x} + R e^{-ik_1x}), \; x < x_1 \\ &= A\, Te^{ik_2x}, \; x > x_2 \end{aligned} \tag{153}$$

where $k_n = \omega/\sqrt{gh_n}$, $n = 1,2$. By matching at x_1 and x_2 we obtain all the coefficients a, b, R and T. If $\mu > 0$, the reflection intensity is

$$|R|^2 = \frac{\sinh^2\left(\mu^{1/2}\ln\frac{x_2}{x_1}\right)}{4\mu + \sinh^2\left(\mu^{1/2}\ln\frac{x_2}{x_1}\right)} \tag{154}$$

If $\mu < 0$, one simply changes the sign of μ and replaces sinh by sin everywhere. Let $L = x_2 - x_1$ be the length of transition. We may write

$$\frac{x_2}{x_1} = \sqrt{\frac{h_2}{h_1}} \text{ and } \frac{L}{\lambda_2} = \frac{\omega}{2\pi\sqrt{ga}}\left(1 - \sqrt{\frac{h_1}{h_2}}\right) \tag{155}$$

Figure 3 gives a sample plot of R vs. L/λ_2 for various $\sqrt{h_2/h_1}$. Note that $\omega/\sqrt{ga}$ increases with L/λ_2. As the former exceeds 1/4, $|R|$ becomes oscillatory. Physically this is because reflected waves from different parts of the transition interfere with one another.

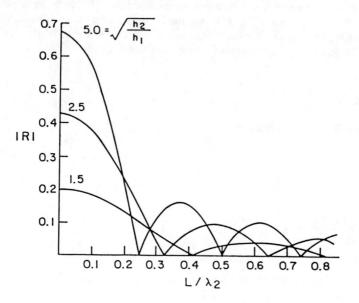

Figure 3. Reflection coefficient for a depth transition from depth h_2 to depth h_1 [21].

Identities on Long Waves over Continuously-Varying Depth. For $h = h(x)$ and oblique incidence, the solution may be written

$$\zeta = \xi(x)\, e^{i(\beta y - \omega t)} \tag{156}$$

Equation 150 then requires

$$L\xi \equiv (h\xi')' + \left(\frac{\omega^2}{g} - \beta^2 h\right)\xi = 0 \tag{157}$$

For generality, we assume $h \to h_\pm$ as $x \to \pm\infty$ where h_+ and h_- are not necessarily the same.

Only a few special forms of $h(x)$ can be solved analytically. However, the mathematical problem here involves only a linear ordinary differential equation and can be solved numerically by a variety of methods. To help check the correctness of a numerical solution let us discuss some identities that are dictated by the boundary value problem. Let ξ_1 and ξ_2 be two solutions of Equation 157, i.e.,

$$L\xi_1 = 0 \text{ and } L\xi_2 = 0 \tag{158}$$

By putting these into Green's formula

$$\int_{-\infty}^{\infty} (\xi_1 L\xi_2 - \xi_2 L\xi_1)dx = [h(\xi_1\xi_2' - \xi_2\xi_1')]_{-\infty}^{\infty} \tag{159}$$

we obtain

$$h_-(\xi_1\xi_2' - \xi_2\xi_1')_{-\infty} = h_+ (\xi_1\xi_2' - \xi_2\xi_1')_{\infty} \tag{160}$$

We now specify ξ_1 and ξ_2 further by adding boundary conditions at infinities. As a first example we choose $\xi_1 = \xi$ to be the solution of a scattering problem with the incident wave arriving from the left $(x - \infty)$ and $\xi_2 = \xi^*$ the complex conjugate of ξ. The asymptotic behaviors are

$$\begin{aligned}\xi &= A (e^{ik_-x} + R e^{ik_-x}) \quad x \simeq \infty \\ &= A T e^{ik_+x} \quad x \sim \infty\end{aligned} \tag{161}$$

With these Equation 160 gives

$$k_-h_- (1 - |R|^2) = k_+h_+ |T|^2 \tag{162}$$

or

$$\sqrt{gh_-} (1 - |R|^2) = \sqrt{gh_+} |T|^2 \tag{163}$$

Since $\sqrt{gh}$ is the group velocity of shallow water waves, Equation 163 implies the conservation of energy flux, i.e., the outward flux of energy by reflected and transmitted waves must equal that of the incident wave.

As a second example, we let ξ_1 and ξ_2 correspond to two scattering problems with incident waves from the left and right, respectively. Their asymptotic behaviors are

$$\begin{aligned}\xi_1 &= A(e^{ik_-x} + R_1 e^{-ik_-x}) \qquad && x \sim - \infty \\ &= A T_1 e^{ik_+x} \qquad && x \sim + \infty\end{aligned} \tag{164}$$

$$\begin{aligned}\xi_2 &= A T_2 e^{-ik_-x} \qquad && x \sim - \infty \\ &= A (e^{-ik_+x} + R_2 e^{ik_+x}) \qquad && x \sim + \infty\end{aligned} \tag{165}$$

Equation 160 then gives

$$k_-h_- T_2 = k_+h_+ T_1 \tag{166}$$

This is a *reciprocity relation*. When one scattering problem is solved, the transmission coefficient for the other can be obtained without repeating the full procedure of calculation.

Similar relations for kh = O(1) can be derived and found in Mei [36].

Two-Dimensional Scattering

Diffraction by small islands, headlands, breakwaters near a coast and submersibles falls under this category. We shall illustrate the physics for a few simple examples of long waves in shallow water, and then sketch a numerical method for harbors and islands of general geometries.

It is useful to point out that, if the ocean depth is constant everywhere and the scatterer is a vertical cylinder extending the full depth of water, the theory is the same whether kh is small or O(1). This is so because the normal at any point on the cylinder is not only horizontal, but the same, along the vertical line passing through that point. As a consequence the velocity potential for any kh can be expressed as

$$\Phi = \frac{id}{\omega} \frac{\cosh k(z+h)}{\cos kh} \eta(x,y)e^{-i\omega t} \tag{167}$$

where η satisfies the two-dimensional Helmoltz equation:

$$\eta_{xx} + \eta_{yy} + k^2\eta = 0 \tag{168}$$

with the boundary condition

$$\frac{\partial \eta}{\partial n} = 0 \text{ on B} \tag{169}$$

where B is the projection of the cylinder in the x,y plane and $\overrightarrow{n}$ is a unit normal to B. With the plane incident wave, the diffraction problem for η is virtually the same as that of two-dimensional scattering of shallow water waves in constant depth, except for the dispersion relations between ω and k.

We now turn to some examples.

A Vertical Cylinder of Circular Section. Let the radius of the cylinder be a. We use polar coordinates (r,θ,z) with the z axis coinciding with the axis of the cylinder. The free surface displacement can be easily found by the method of separation of variables:

$$\eta(r,\theta) = A \sum_{m=0}^{\infty} \epsilon_m \, i^m \left\{ J_m(kr) - H_m(kr) \frac{J'_m(ka)}{H'_m(ka)} \right\} \cos m\theta \tag{170}$$

where J_m is the Bessel function, H_m is the Hankel function of the first kind with the superscript $(\ )^{(1)}$ omitted for brevity. Primes indicate differentiation with respect to the argument, and ϵ_m is the Jacobi symbol defined by $\epsilon_0 = 1$, $\epsilon_m = 2$, m = 1,2,3,.... The value of η along the cylinder is the run-up:

$$\eta(a,\theta) = A \sum_{m=0}^{\infty} \frac{2\epsilon_m i^{m+1} \cos m\theta}{\pi ka \, H_m'(ka)} \tag{171}$$

where a Wronskian identity between two Bessel functions has been used. Figure 4 shows the normalized run-up for several values of ka. When ka is small, the run-up is nearly uniform all around the cylinder. As ka increases, the run-up increases toward 2 at $\theta = \pi$ where the situation is close to that of a total reflection from a plane wall. On the shadow side $\theta = 0$ the angular variation becomes more complicated but the value is small.

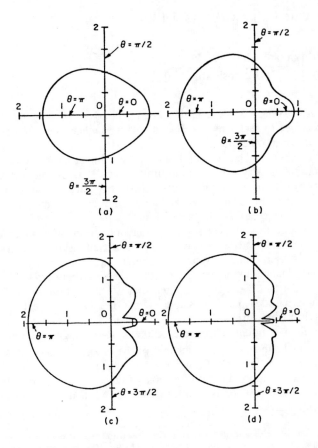

Figure 4. Maximum free surface displacement (run-up) around a circular cylinder with incident plane wave in the direction $\theta = 0$: (a) ka = 0.5; (b) ka = 1; (c) ka = 3; (d) ka = 5.

Aside from the difference in the dispersion relation, this result applies for any constant water depth kh = O(1). We now use Equation 171 to calculate the dynamic pressure on the cylinder for any kh = O(1).

$$p(a,\theta,z) = \rho g \eta(a,\theta) \frac{\cosh k(z+h)}{\cosh kh} \tag{172}$$

$$F_x = -a \int_{-h}^{0} dz \int_{0}^{2\pi} p(a,\theta,z) \cos\theta \, d\theta = \frac{4\,\rho g\,Aah}{kaH_1{}'(ka)} \frac{\tanh kh}{kh} \tag{173}$$

The torque about the axis x = 0, z = − h is

$$M_y = a \int_{-h}^{0} (z+h)\, dz \int_{0}^{2\pi} p(a,\theta,z) \cos\theta \, d\theta$$

$$= \frac{-4\,\rho g\,Aah^2}{ka\,H_1{}'(ka)} \left[\frac{kh \tanh kh - \cosh kh + 1}{(kh)^2 \cosh kh} \right] \tag{174}$$

In the limit of shallow water, kh < < 1, the factor [.] above becomes 3/2. These force formulas were due to McCamy and Fuchs [34] who made use of the diffraction theory well known in other fields.

We caution that these formulas are useful only if the cylinder ka is not too small and the wave amplitude is very small. In the limit of small radius, the diffraction wave force is very small and is usually overwhelmed by a drag force associated with flow separation and eddy production. For a thorough discussion of small cylinders, the reader is referred to Sarpkaya and Issacson [47].

Let us discuss an application of these results to a laboratory phenomenon.* When a bottom-seated structure is tested in a wave tank, significant discrepancy in vertical force and torque is often found between measurement and theory. In most cases the discrepancy is attributable to the existence of a narrow gap between the bottom of the structure and the tank floor, necessitated by instrumentation setup [7]. To have a quick quantitative idea on the possible effects of a gap, we treat the case where the gap width d is uniform.

When space is needed to mount instruments on the bottom, the gap is often much wider than the viscous boundary layer thickness of the order $\sqrt{2\nu/\omega}$. In this case, the direct effect of viscosity is weak. Flow near the edges may be turbulent if the gap is wide enough. As an approximation for most of the gap, we take the flow in the gap to be potential and essentially two dimensional in x and y. The hydrodynamic pressure then satisfies

---

* Pressure beneath the foundation of a platform is also of practical interest for designing protection against wave induced scour. See G. F. Clauss & R. Schmitz (1989), "Deformation and Associated Flow Phenomena of Flat Foundations in the Sea Way," Proc. 8th Int'l. Conf. Offshore Mech. Arctic Eng.

$$p_{zz} + p_{yy} = 0, \quad x,y \text{ in } S \tag{175}$$

where S is the horizontal projection (the foot print) of the gap. At the outer edge C of the gap p must be essentially equal to that given by the diffraction theory calculated by ignoring the gap:

$$p(x,y) = -i\omega\rho\phi(x,y,-h), \quad x,y \text{ on } C \tag{176}$$

Thus, once the diffraction problem is solved for a bottom seated structure, the boundary condition for the gap pressure is known and the Dirichlet problem for the gap pressure can be solved.

If, on the other hand, the gap is so narrow that viscosity dominates, arguments of the lubrication theory can be used to show that Equations 175 and 176 still apply [39]. In both cases, p is independent of the gap width d.

For explicit results, consider the effect of a gap beneath a vertical circular cylinder. When Equation 172 is used at $z = -h$ for the boundary condition, the gap pressure is easily found to be

$$p(r,\theta) = \frac{\rho p A}{\cosh kh} \sum_{n=0}^{\infty} \frac{2\epsilon_n i^n \cos n\theta}{\pi ka\, H_n'(ka)} \left[\frac{r}{a}\right]^n; \tag{177}$$

this gives rise to a vertical force acting on the base of the cylinder

$$F_z = \int_0^a r\,dr \int_0^{2\pi} p(r,\theta)\, d\theta = \frac{\rho g A}{\cosh kh} \frac{2a^2}{ka\, H_1'(ka)} \tag{178}$$

In normalized form we have

$$\bar{F}_z = \frac{F_z \cosh kh}{\rho g A\, \pi a^2} = \frac{2}{\pi\, ka\, H_1'(ka)} \tag{179}$$

For small ka, $\bar{F}_z \rightarrow -i$; for large ka, $\bar{F}_z$ decays monotonically as $\sqrt{2/\pi ka}$. The gap pressure also gives rise to a torque about the axis $x = 0$, $z = -h$,

$$M_y = \int_0^a r^2 dr \int_0^{2\pi} P \cos\theta\, d\theta = \frac{\rho g A}{\cosh kh} \frac{i\, a^3}{ka\, H_1'(ka)} \tag{180}$$

This torque can indeed be quite comparable with that due to the pressure on the vertical side of the cylinder (Equation 174), if a is comparable to h.

A Long and Thin Breakwater. As a second example we consider a long and thin breakwater in waves. Let the breakwater coincide with the x,z plane for $x < 0$, and the incident wave arrive normally from $y \sim -\infty$. This mathematical problem can be solved exactly in many ways, but a simple analysis suffices to give most of the essential results. As a crude description, the x, y plane can be divided according to the ray picture. In the third and fourth quadrant waves propagate from left to right without interruption. In the second quadrant there are both the incident wave propagating toward the right and the perfectly reflected wave toward the left. The first quadrant is a shadow where there is no wave. Thus,

$$n \sim A_0 \, e^{iky} \, |y| < \infty, \; x > 0$$
$$\sim A_0 \, (e^{iky} + e^{-iky}) \; y < 0, \; x < 0 \qquad\qquad (181)$$
$$\sim 0 \; y > 0, \; x < 0$$

This crude description is essentially the ray approximation, according to which η is discontinuous across the y axis, which coincides with the rays separating these regions. A correction is therefore needed to provide a smooth transition.

Let us concentrate on the neighborhood of the shadow boundary, i.e., the positive y-axis. Along the positive x axis we expect the form of η to be

$$\eta = A(x,y) \, e^{iky} \qquad\qquad (182)$$

where the amplitude must be modulated in both x and y. From the Helmholtz equation it follows that

$$(2ik \, A_y + A_{yy} + A_{xx}) \, e^{iky} = 0 \qquad\qquad (183)$$

Anticipating the spatial modulation of A to be slow across, and still slower along, the ray of discontinuity (the x axis), we assume $\partial/\partial y \ll \partial/\partial x$ and obtain the Schrödinger equation

$$2ik \, A_y + A_{xx} = 0 \qquad\qquad (184)$$

at the leading order. Since this equation is of the parabolic type, with y playing the role of time, this type of approximation is known as the *parabolic approximation*. In the region where Equation 184 is valid, the scales of x and y must be related by

$$kx = O\left(\sqrt{ky}\right) \qquad\qquad (185)$$

which implies a boundary layer of parabolic shape. The boundary conditions are

$$A \rightarrow \begin{bmatrix} A_0 \\ 0 \end{bmatrix} \qquad x \rightarrow \pm \infty \qquad y > 0 \qquad\qquad (186)$$

while the "initial" condition is that

$$A = \begin{Bmatrix} A_0 \\ 0 \end{Bmatrix} \qquad x \gtrless 0 \qquad y = 0 \qquad\qquad (187)$$

$$\frac{A}{A_0} = \sqrt{\frac{k}{2\pi}} \, e^{-\frac{i\pi}{4}} \int_{-\infty}^{x/\sqrt{y}} e^{ikz^2/2} \, dz \qquad\qquad (188)$$

Introducing the dimensionless similarity variable

$$\beta = kx / \sqrt{\pi ky} \tag{189}$$

we have

$$\frac{A}{A_0} = \frac{1}{\sqrt{2}} \, e^{i\pi/4} \left\{ \left[\frac{1}{2} + C(\beta) \right] + i \left[\frac{1}{2} + S(\beta) \right] \right\} \tag{190}$$

where

$$C(\beta) = \int_0^{\beta} \cos \frac{\pi v^2}{2} \, dv, \; S(\beta) = \int_0^{\beta} \sin \frac{\pi v^2}{2} \, dv \tag{191}$$

are the cosine and sine integrals. This result is good as long as kx and ky are large compared to unity (in practice no smaller than 2). The variation of the normalized energy $|A|/A_0$ is plotted in Figure 5. Starting from deep inside the shadow ($x \sim -\infty$) and moving across the dividing ray, $|A|$ first increases monotonically. After crossing the dividing ray (y axis), $|A|$ overshoots, then settles to the ultimate value of A_0 in an oscillatory manner. This oscillation gives rise to bands of large and small amplitudes. In optics these bands are called the diffraction fringes.

On the left of the breakwater there is a similar boundary layer providing smooth transition across the dividing ray (here the negative y axis) for the reflected wave. If the incidence is oblique, the dividing rays and hence the axis of the two boundary layers are inclined. Modification of the theory is straightforward.

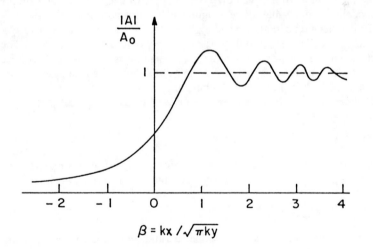

Figure 5. Diffraction factor across the shadow boundary of a thin breakwater.

Resonant Scattering by a Harbor. We now discuss the combined effect of diffraction and resonance. Consider first shallow water in a close basin. For simplicity we assume constant depth and a rectangular basin of horizontal dimensions a and b. For sinusoidal oscillations, the free surface height η satisfies Equation 135 inside the basin $0 < x < a$, $0 < y < b$ and the condition of Equation 136 on the sides. Clearly we may have the following solution

$$\eta = A_{mn} \cos \frac{m\pi x}{a} \cos \frac{n\pi y}{b} \tag{192}$$

where m and n can be any integer but cannot be zero at the same time, and

$$\frac{\omega}{\sqrt{gh}} = \frac{\omega_{mn}}{\sqrt{gh}} = \sqrt{\left[\frac{m\pi}{a}\right]^2 + \left[\frac{m\pi}{b}\right]^2} \tag{193}$$

Equation 192 describes a *natural mode* of oscillation and Equation 193 gives the *natural frequency*. For increasing m and/or n, i.e., higher mode, the frequency increases, and the free surface assumes more complicated forms. These modes can be excited by wind or by landslides.

If the basin opens to the sea, it becomes a harbor. Incident waves of distant origin may excite the natural modes through the harbor entrance. The scattered waves are contributed not only by the coastal line but by fluid motion across the harbor entrance which is affected by and responsible for oscillation inside the harbor. While the subject of harbor oscillation will be more extensively discussed in Volume 3 we give a short example here to illustrate how resonance and diffraction affect each other.

To illustrate the main features, we now give an approximate analysis of a simple theoretical model. A narrow bay of rectangular plan form with length L and uniform width 2a is indented normally to a straight coast. We choose a coordinate system such that the x axis is normal to the coast and the y axis is along the coast. The origin coincides with the bay entrance. The ocean depth h is constant everywhere and the incident waves arrive normally from the right $x \sim \infty$. The basic assumption is that $ka \ll 1$ and $kL = 0(1)$. In the narrow bay, long waves are expected to be one-dimensional, except very near the entrance. The free surface displacement is

$$\eta_B = B \cos k(x + L) \tag{194}$$

almost everywhere. In the ocean there are incident waves and waves reflected by the straight coast. For normal incidence, this combination is simply

$$\eta_I = 2A \cos kx \qquad x > 0 \tag{195}$$

In addition, there are the scattered waves due to fluid motion across the bay entrance, i.e.,

$$\eta = \eta_I + \eta_S \qquad x > 0 \tag{196}$$

in the ocean. The corresponding displacement η_S may be represented formally by distributing oscillatory sources along the line segment $-a < y < a$, $x = 0$.

$$\eta = \eta_I + \eta_S \quad \eta_S = \frac{\omega}{2g} \int_{-a}^{a} U(y') \, H_0 \, (kR) \, dy' \tag{197}$$

where $U(y')dy'$ is the flux from the source stretched over the width y' to $y' + dy'$ and $R^2 = x^2 + (y - y')^2$. As an heuristic approximation we replace U by its average $Q/2a$ where Q is the strength of the oscillatory discharge through the entrance; thus

$$\eta_S \cong \frac{\omega Q}{2g} \frac{1}{2a} \int_{-a}^{a} H_0 \, (kR) \, dy' \tag{198}$$

Since the entrance is narrow, we can approximate Equation 198 by expanding the Hankel function for small ka if $kR = O(ka)$:

$$H_0 \, (kR) = 1 + \frac{2i}{\pi} \ln \frac{\gamma kR}{2} + O \, (k^2R^2) \tag{199}$$

Now as another crude step we match the pressure by equating η_S and η_B,

$$B \cos kL \cong 2A + \frac{\omega Q}{2\,g} \left(1 + \frac{2i}{\pi} \ln \frac{\gamma ka}{2} \right) \tag{200}$$

and also the flux:

$$-kB \sin kL \cong \frac{i\omega}{g} \frac{Q}{2a} \tag{201}$$

only at the center of the entrance $x = y = 0$. These two equations can be solved for two constants Q and B. In particular the latter is

$$\frac{B}{2A} = \left\{ \cos kL + \frac{2}{\pi} ka \sin kL \ln \frac{\gamma ka}{2} - ik \sin kL \right\}^{-1} \tag{202}$$

By a more elaborate analysis of matched asymptotics, a slightly different result can be obtained in which the term $\ln \gamma ka/2$ is replaced by $\ln 2\gamma ka/\pi e \cong \ln \gamma ka/4$. Since $\ln 2 = 0.69$ the error of Equation 202 is only of the order $O(ka)$. With the simple formula (Equation 202) we can examine the dependence of the magnification factor $|B/2A|^2$ on the parameters kL and ka. The plot of $|B/2A|^2$ vs. kL may be called the response curve, as shown in Figure 6.

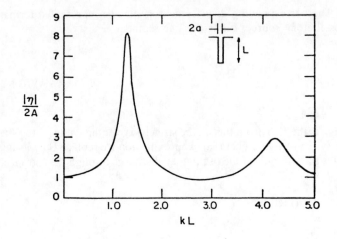

Figure 6. Magnification factor vs. kL for a narrow bay.

First of all, resonance happens when kL is near the a zero of cos kL, i.e., near

$$k_nL = \left(n + \frac{1}{2}\right)\pi \tag{203}$$

More accurately the resonance peak is found by equating to zero the real part of the denominator in Equation 202. Let $\tilde{k}_n$ be the nth peak of resonance, then

$$k_n - k_n = \frac{2k_na}{\pi L} \ln \frac{\gamma ka}{2} < 0 \tag{204}$$

Thus there is a small shift to the left of the crude estimate k_n. The shift is smaller for smaller ka. At the peak we have

$$\left|\frac{B}{2A}\right|^2 \cong (k_na)^{-2} = \left[\left(n + \frac{1}{2}\right)\frac{\pi a}{2}\right]^{-2} \tag{205}$$

which is larger for lower modes (smaller n) and increases with decreasing ka. The lowest mode corresponds to $n = 0$ or $k_0L = \pi/2$ or $L = \frac{1}{4}$ wavelength; this is called the *quarter wavelength* mode. For any n, the value of kL at which $|B/2A|^2$ equals half of its peak value can be estimated as $(n + \frac{1}{2})\,\pi a/L$, which decreases with increasing n and decreasing ka. Thus, the area of the resonance peak is of the order $O[(n + \frac{1}{2})\,\pi a/L]^{-1}$. As the entrance width is reduced, the peak area increases. This is caused by the increasing difficulty for energy to be radiated out of the entrance. In reality, however, additional effects ignored by the present theory may become important near these peaks. The first may be friction due to vortices generated near the harbor entrance. This leads to dissipation, which becomes larger for smaller entrance, hence is opposite in trend to the radiation damping [57]. The second is nonlinearity, whereby energy can be transferred to higher harmonics [27, 46].

A Numerical Method. For large harbors potentially affected by tsunamis, or for small harbors affected by long swells, it is necessary to have a numerical model to aid either the initial planning or later modifications. An effective numerical scheme must be versatile enough to handle irregular plan forms and nonuniform depth. The following section describes the basis of such a method that employs finite elements [8].

Consider an area of scatterers surrounded on all sides by an ocean of constant depth $\bar{h}$. Let a circle C be drawn to enclose this area of complex geometry or bathymetry. The regions in and outside the circle C are called Ω and $\bar{\Omega}$, respectively. The mathematical problem can be restated as follows

$$\nabla \cdot h \nabla \eta + \frac{\omega^2}{g} \eta = 0, \quad (x,y) \text{ in } \Omega \tag{206}$$

and

$$\nabla^2 \bar{\eta} + k^2 \bar{\eta} = 0, \quad (x,y) \text{ in } \bar{\Omega} \tag{207}$$

where $k = \omega/\sqrt{gh}$. The radiation condition is

$$\bar{\eta}_S = \bar{\eta} - \eta_I \sim A_0 \, \mathcal{A}(\theta) \, \frac{1}{\sqrt{\pi kr}} \, e^{ikr - i\pi/4}, \qquad kr \gg 1 \tag{208}$$

where $\mathcal{A}(\theta)/$depends on θ only.
Along the circle C we require that

$$\eta = \bar{\eta} \tag{209}$$

and

$$h \frac{\partial \eta}{\partial r} = \bar{\eta} \frac{\partial \bar{\eta}}{\partial r} \tag{210}$$

If there is any vertical wall C_o within Ω, we also insist that

$$h \frac{\partial \eta}{\partial n} = 0 \qquad \text{on } C_0 \tag{211}$$

In $\bar{\Omega}$, the solution can be formally written as

$$\bar{\eta} = \eta_I + \bar{\eta}_S \tag{212}$$

It is convenient to express the incident plane wave as a Fourier-Bessel series:

$$\eta_I = A_0 \, e^{ikx} = A_0 \sum_n \epsilon_n \, i^n \cos n \, \theta \, J_n(kr) \tag{213}$$

Similarly, the scattered wave is formally

$$\eta_S = A_0 \sum_n \epsilon_n \, i^n \, (A_n \cos n \, \theta + B_n \sin n\theta) \, H_n(kr) \tag{214}$$

where the coefficients A_n and B_n are yet to be found.

It can be shown that the boundary value problem defined above for η and $\bar{\eta}$ is equivalent to the stationarity of the functional

$$J(\eta,\bar{\eta}) = \int\!\!\int_\Omega \frac{1}{2}\left[h \, (\nabla\eta)^2 - \frac{\omega^2}{g} \, \eta^2\right] dA + \oint_C \bar{\eta} \left[\left(\frac{1}{2} \, \bar{\eta}_S - \eta_S \right) \frac{\partial\bar{\eta}}{\partial n} - \frac{\bar{\eta}_S}{2} \frac{\partial\eta_I}{\partial_n}\right] ds \tag{215}$$

when errors in η and $\bar{\eta}$ are small. The proof can be found in Mei [36].

With this variational principle, we can apply a finite element approximation in Ω. This involves the discretization of Ω into small polygons within which η is represented by polynomials with unknown coefficients, say a_i, $i = 1,\dots$ N. Extremizing J with respect to each of a_i, A_n and B_n, we obtain a linear matrix equation for all these coefficients, which can be solved numerically. The computational advantages of this variational formulation are that the resulting matrix is symmetric and the band width of the matrix is governed by the number of modes along C, which has a finite circumference, irrespective of the number of Fourier-Bessel coefficients. Practical applications have been made to islands [18] and harbors on a straight coast [81, 18].

We remind the reader that the variational principle (Equation 215) is exact. For a practical application, approximations stem from the discretization in Ω and truncation of series in Ω. To illustrate the point, we consider the problem of scattering by a circular seamount. The seamount is simply a shelf of radius a and constant depth h, surrounded by an ocean of larger depth $\bar{h}$. The following matching conditions must be required:

$$h \frac{\partial\eta}{\partial r} = \bar{h} \frac{\partial\bar{\eta}}{\partial r}, \; r = a \tag{216}$$

The circle C is chosen to coincide with r = a. The variational principle (Equation 215) still holds. (If the depth is continuous along C, $\bar{h}$ in the line integral along C can be replaced by h, but not otherwise.) Now in both Ω and $\bar{\Omega}$, we can use exact representations,

$$\eta = \Sigma \, \epsilon_n i^n C_n \cos n\theta \, J_n(kr) \qquad r < a$$
$$\bar{\eta} = \Sigma \, \epsilon_n i^n \cos n\theta \, [J_n(\bar{k}r) + B_n H_n(\bar{k}r)] \qquad r > a \tag{217}$$

We now substitute these in J, and then require

$$\frac{\partial J}{\partial B_n} = \frac{\partial J}{\partial C_n} = 0, \qquad \text{for all n} \tag{218}$$

Thanks to the orthogonality of the trigonometric functions, we can solve for the coefficients explicitly,

$$B_n = [J_n(v) \, J_n'(sv) - sJ_n'(sv)]/\Delta_n \tag{219}$$

$$C_n = -2i/\pi s v \Delta_n \tag{220}$$

where

$$v = ka, \quad s = hk/\overline{kh}$$
$$\Delta_n = -J_n(v) \, H_n'(sv) + sJ_n'(v) \, H_n(sv) \tag{221}$$

Longuet-Higgins [31] obtains the same solution directly by solving the boundary value problem. He has given detailed discussions of the physical implications. An interesting property of this geometry is that there are modes that are almost trapped on the seamount. Therefore, incident waves tuned to certain frequencies can excite resonance on the seamount.

General Identities

As in one-dimensional scattering, a number of reciprocity relations can be derived for two dimensions. Consider two different long-wave scattering problems η_1 and η_2 for the same bathymetry and frequency. Let S_B denote the structure walls or island shores and S_∞ be a large circle containing the region of variable depth $h(x,y)$, breakwaters and islands, and all other scatterers. Applying the Green theorem to η_1 and η_2 over the fluid within S_∞ we get

$$\iint_A [\eta_1 \, \nabla \, (h\nabla\eta_2 - \eta_2 \, \nabla \, (h\nabla\eta_1)dA = \oint_{S_B} h \left(\eta_1 \frac{\partial \eta_2}{\partial n} - \eta_2 \frac{\partial \eta_1}{\partial n}\right) ds$$

$$+ \oint_{S_\infty} h \left(\eta_1 \frac{\partial \eta_2}{\partial n} - \eta_2 \frac{\partial \eta_1}{\partial n}\right) ds \tag{222}$$

Because of the governing conditions in the fluid and along S_B we get

$$\oint_{S_\infty} h \left(\eta_1 \frac{\partial \eta_2}{\partial n} - \eta_2 \frac{\partial \eta_1}{\partial n}\right) ds = 0 \tag{223}$$

More explicit results can be obtained by specifying the conditions at infinity for both η_1 and η_2.

As the first example, we let $\eta_1 = \eta$ be the response to certain incident wave and $\eta_2 = \eta^*$, i.e., its complex conjugate. Equation 223 then gives

$$\text{Im} \oint_{S_\infty} \eta \, \frac{\partial \eta^*}{\partial n} \, ds = 0$$

Since the complex amplitude of the pressure is proportional to η and the complex amplitude of the radial velocity is proportional to i $\partial n/\partial n$, the preceding result implies that the net energy flux across the circle S_∞ is zero. In other words, the influx of energy must equal the outflux. By using the asymptotic expression

$$\eta \cong A\left(e^{ikx} + \frac{\mathcal{Q}_1(\theta)}{\sqrt{\pi kr}} \, e^{ikr - i\pi/4}\right) \tag{224}$$

(where $\mathcal{Q}_1(\theta)$ is the scattered wave amplitude) and the method of stationary phase, one may further show that

$$\frac{1}{2\pi} \int_0^{2\pi} |\mathcal{Q}_1(\theta)|^2 \, d\theta = -\text{Re} \, \mathcal{Q}_1(\theta_1) \tag{225}$$

see Mei [36]. Note that the left side is a measure of the total scattered energy in all directions, while the right side refers to the scattered wave amplitude in the direction of the incident waves. This relation is called the *optical theorem* in theoretical physics.

For the second example we let η_1 and η_2 correspond to responses to two different incident waves: one along θ_1 and the other along θ_2. We can then obtain the following reciprocity relation:

$$\mathcal{Q}_1 (\theta_2 + \pi) = \mathcal{Q}_2 (\theta_1 + \pi) \tag{226}$$

Note that $\mathcal{Q}_1 (\theta_2 + \pi)$ is the wave amplitude scattered in the direction opposite to the second incident wave, due to the first incident wave. There are other similiar relations derived by choosing different pairs of η_1 and η_2. Again they can be used to check the correctness of a numerical scheme, besides giving theoretical insight.

Comments on Arbitrary Depth/Wavelength Ratio

When kh = O(1), vertical variation of the flow field becomes important and cannot be adequately described by the propagating wave, which alone depends on z in the special way of cosh k(z + h). More general variations must be allowed to represent the effect of body geometry. Consider, for example, the two-dimensional diffraction with normally incident waves. In the zone just outside the scatterers, $|x| < L$, say, the general solution can be written as a series:

$$\phi = a_0 f_0(z) \, e^{\pm ikx} + \sum_{n=1}^{\infty} b_n f_n(z) \, e^{\mp k_n x} \qquad \begin{matrix} x > L \\ x < -L \end{matrix} \qquad (227)$$

where

$$f_0 = \frac{\sqrt{2} \cosh k(z+h)}{(h + \sigma^{-1} \sinh^2 kh)^{1/2}}, \quad f_n = \frac{\sqrt{2} \cos k_n(z+h)}{(h - \sigma^{-1} \sin^2 k_n h)^{1/2}} \qquad (228)$$

and k_n is the nth real root of the transcendental equation

$$\sigma = \frac{\omega^2}{g} = -k_n \tan k_n h \qquad n = 1,2,3\dots \qquad (229)$$

The set of functions $\{f_n\}$ $n = 0,1,2,3\dots$ are orthonormal, i.e.,

$$\int_{-h}^{0} dz \, f_n f_m = \delta_{nm} \qquad (230)$$

and complete in the range $[-h,0]$, hence can be used to construct the flow field induced by any scatterer. Except for the first term, $n = 0$, all terms in the set are exponentially attenuating for large $|x|$. Therefore they are called the *evanescent modes*.

For three-dimensional scatterers located within a finite radius $r < L$, the scattered wave can be written as

$$\phi = \sum_{m=0}^{\infty} H_m(kr)(\alpha_{0_m} \cos m\theta + \beta_{0_m} \sin m\theta) \, f_0(z)$$

$$+ \sum_{m=0}^{\infty} \sum_{n=1}^{\infty} K_m(k_n \gamma)(\alpha_{nm} \cos m\theta + \beta_{nm} \sin m\theta) \, f_m(z) \qquad (231)$$

where $K_m(k_n r)$ are the modified Bessel functions, which correspond to the evanescent modes and decay to zero as $r \to \infty$.

A variety of numerical methods now exist for general geometries. They can be broadly classified as the integral equation method (also called the boundary element method), and the finite element method. Interested readers may wish to consult Mei [35] and Yeung [60].

Combined Refraction and Diffraction

The Mild Slope Equation

If an ocean structure is to be built at site A in an area of changing depth, and wave data are known only at a distant site B, one must first trace the refraction and diffraction of waves from B to A. Although fully three-dimensional numerical schemes are available in principle, it is often impractical to implement the numerical task of wave estimation. The reason is that the task can be large due to two contrasting requirements. Sufficient resolution demands that any discretization must be fine enough within a wavelength, but the computational domain must be large enough to include the area of variable depth. On the other hand, in pure refraction problems, the ray approximation is very economical because it reduces the mathematical problem from three to one. This approximation nevertheless becomes cumbersome if the scatterer has a complex geometry, and breaks down either near a caustic or the boundary of a shadow unless remedies are made. Can there be intermediate methods that are more economical than the fully three-dimensional treatment and more accurate than the ray approximation?

Heuristically, over a slowly varying bottom, the evanescent modes must be unimportant except in the immediate neighborhood of a three-dimensional structure. It is therefore reasonable to try the following representation

$$\Phi = -\frac{ig\zeta}{\omega} \, f_0(z) \tag{232}$$

where f_0 is chosen to be formally given by Equation 228 with h and k being slowly varying in x and y and connected by the usual dispersion relation. Substituting Equation 232 into the three-dimensional equations for infinitesimal waves, Equations 141 to 143, we can show that η must satisfy

$$\nabla \cdot (C \, C_g \, \nabla \, \eta) + (\omega^2 \, C_g/C) \, \eta = 0 \tag{233}$$

where C and C_g are the local phase and group velocities of a plane progressive wave. This equation is now known as the *mild slope equation* [5]. Let μ represent the order of magnitude of the bottom slope $\mu = O(|\nabla h|/kh)$, then this equation can deal with diffraction at order and $O(\mu^0)$ and refraction at order $O(\mu)$; the omitted terms are of order μ^2 or smaller. Systematic derivations can be found in Smith & Sprinks [50], Lozano & Meyer [33], and Mei, [36]. To see its broad range of applicability, we examine two extremes. In the limit of constant depth h, i.e., $\mu = 0$ and kh = O(1), k, C and C_g are all constants. The resulting Helmholtz equation is known to be exact. On the other hand, if kh ≪ 1 but varying in x and y, Equation 233 reduces to

$$\nabla \cdot (h\nabla\eta) + (\omega^2/g)\eta = 0 \tag{234}$$

which is also known to describe long waves over variable depth.

Since Equation 234 involves only two dimensions, its computational task lies between the ray approximation and the fully three-dimensional calculation. If the wetted sides of a structure have only vertical walls, the variational principle and finite element method described earlier can be directly applied. Such examples have been given by Houston [20]. If the structure is fully three-dimensional, then one may use the idea of matched asymptotics. In the near field of the structure we ignore the depth variation but account for the three-dimensional geometry of the structure with all the evanescent modes. In the far field we need only consider the propagating mode with the mild slope equation.

The Parabolic Approximation

The mild slope equation can still be demanding computationally for practical problems, as it involves two dimensions, and the steps in the numerical discretization must be much smaller than a wavelength. In recent years considerable efforts have been devoted to the modification of the ray approximation, which involves one-dimensional calculations with large steps of discretization. Such modifications are useful if the ray approximation is valid almost everywhere except in a limited neighborhood where diffraction is important. As examples, one may list the following types of structures on a gently sloping bottom: a thin breakwater, where narrow zones of diffraction exist near the boundaries of the shadow and the reflection zones; a slender structure of finite thickness heading into the incident waves; and an elongated region of caustics. In all these cases, the region of diffraction is relatively narrow and nearly parallel to a ray. The parabolic approximation illustrated earlier for the case of pure diffraction can be extended. As will be shown, the mathematical task is reduced to solving an initial value problem of diffusion in two space dimensions, with one space coordinate behaving like time. Also, the unknown is the wave envelope, which varies slowly within a wavelength. Therefore, coarse discretization is sufficient for high accuracy.

The idea can be easily explained for the example of a long breakwater extending normally from the shore into the sea [28]. The axis of the breakwater is parallel to the x axis and perpendicular to the bottom contours (x = constant), as depicted in Figure 7. An incident wave train arrives obliquely. According to the geometric ray approximation, the wave field near the breakwater is divided by the incident and reflected rays into three zones: the (I) incidence, (II) reflection, and (III) shadow zones. We expect diffraction to be important in a narrow region around the incident ray O1 and the reflected ray O2. It is sufficient to examine the former.

In the absence of the breakwater, the direction of the incident rays is given by

$$\frac{dy}{dx} = -\tan \theta(x) = -\frac{\beta}{\sqrt{k^2 - \beta^2}} \tag{235}$$

The equation of a ray passing through a point x_0 and y_0 is

$$y - y_0 = -\int_{x_0}^{x} \tan \theta \, dx \tag{236}$$

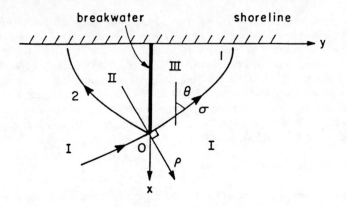

Figure 7. A thin breakwater intersecting the shore line normally. Incident ray $\overline{01}$ and reflected ray $\overline{02}$ from the tip divide the zones of incidence (I), reflection (II) and shadow (III).

The equation of a constant phase (wave crest) is

$$y - y_0 = \int_{x_0}^{x} \cot \theta \; dx \tag{237}$$

We may choose these two sets of curves as coordinate curves. In particular let the origin coincide with the tip of the breakwater ($x_0 = L$, $y_0 = 0$), then the new curvilinear coordinates are

$$\rho = y + \int_{L}^{x} \tan \theta \; dx, \quad \sigma = y - \int_{L}^{x} \cot \theta \; dx \tag{238}$$

In the absence of the breakwater, the velocity potential can be expressed as

$$\Phi_I = \mathrm{Re} \left\{ -\frac{igA}{\omega} \frac{\cosh k(z+h)}{\cosh kh} \; e^{i(\beta\sigma - \omega t)} \right\} \tag{239}$$

where $\dfrac{A(x)}{A_0} = \left[\dfrac{C_{g0}k_0 \cos \theta_0}{C_g k \cos \theta} \right]^{1/2}$ \tag{240}

We now introduce the diffraction factor D which is expected to vary slowly in σ and ρ such that

$$\Phi_I = \mathrm{Re} \left\{ -\frac{ig}{\omega} A \; D(\sigma,\rho) \frac{\cosh k(z+h)}{\cosh kh} \; e^{i(\beta\sigma - \omega t)} \right\} \tag{241}$$

Substituting $\eta = AD$ into the mild-slope equation, it can be shown that the leading order approximation is

$$2i\beta \cot^2 \theta \frac{\partial D}{\partial \sigma} + \frac{\partial^2 D}{\partial \rho^2} \cong 0 \qquad (242)$$

This is the extended Schrödinger equation for slowly-varying depth. Being parabolic, it requires an initial condition along curve $\sigma = 0$:

$$D = 1 \qquad \sigma = 0 \qquad (243)$$

The boundary conditions are

$$D \rightarrow 1 \qquad \rho \rightarrow \infty \qquad (244)$$

and

$$D \rightarrow 0 \qquad \rho \rightarrow -\infty \qquad (245)$$

By the change of variable:

$$Y = \int_0^\sigma \tan^2 \theta \, d\sigma \qquad (246)$$

Equation 242 reduces to

$$2i\beta \frac{\partial D}{\partial Y} + \frac{\partial^2 D}{\partial \rho^2} = 0 \qquad (247)$$

The solution is obtained explicitly,

$$D = \frac{1}{\sqrt{2}} \left\{ \left[\frac{1}{2} + C(q) \right] + i \left[\frac{1}{2} + S(q) \right] \right\} e^{-i\pi/4} \qquad (248)$$

where

$$q = \beta\sigma/\sqrt{\pi\beta Y} \qquad (249)$$

The diffraction factor has been plotted in Figure 5.

Within the linearized framework, the idea of parabolic approximation has been extended for a circular shoal by Radder [45], and for general two-dimensional topography by Lozano and Liu [32]. Assuming that the rays are found and the ray and crest coordinates are defined, Lozano and Liu showed that the diffraction factor satisfies the following Schrödinger equation:

$$2ik \frac{1}{h_1} \frac{\partial D}{\partial \sigma} + \frac{1}{h_2^2} \frac{\partial^2 D}{\partial \rho^2} + \frac{1}{h_1 h_2} \left[\frac{\partial}{\partial \rho} \left(\frac{h_1}{h_2} \right) \right] \frac{\partial D}{\partial \rho} = 0 \qquad (250)$$

where h_1 and h_2 are related to the arc length ds along the ray

$$(ds)^2 = h_1^2 \, d\sigma^2 + h_2^2 \, d\rho^2 \tag{251}$$

The equation is again of the diffusion type with σ behaving as time. Therefore, existing methods of finite difference can be applied to march forward in the direction of the ray.

Note that in Equation 250, the last term represents the effect of the curvature of the rays. The coefficient of $\partial D/\partial \rho$ is of the order $O\,(|\nabla h|/kh)$, which becomes important in very small depth. However, the original ray approximation outside the diffraction zone fails if the above ratio is no longer small. Therefore, curvature correction is not a major factor whenever the parabolic approximation can be legitimately applied.

Lozano and Liu [32] and Liu and Tsay [29] also applied this equation to bathymetries over which a caustic can occur. Their approach is to introduce first another slowly-varying depth $\bar{h}$, which differs slightly from the original h and does not lead to caustics. Based on the ray approximation associated with $\bar{h}$, the parabolic approximation for the diffraction factor needs an additional term $(k^2 - \bar{k}^2)D$ on the left. The numerical solution presents no new difficulty.

Because the wave amplitude is expected to be large near the caustic, it is natural to include both nonlinearity and diffraction. For this purpose, the parabolic approximation is particularly advantageous. This has been demonstrated by Yue and Mei [62] for the case of pure diffraction by a thin and straight breakwater in head seas in glancing incidence, and for the focusing of waves by Stamnes et al. [52]. Nonlinear extension to include both refraction and diffraction has been made by Kirby and Dalrymple [24], and Liu and Tsay [30]. In Holland these new calculation techniques have found their way to practical application of large scales [12].

Strong Reflection by Longshore Bars

Submerged bars that are parallel to the shorelines of lake and ocean beaches have been studied by geologists for a long time. Extensive reports include those by Evans [14], Saylor and Hands [48] for Lake Michigan, Short [49] for Alaskan Arctic, and Kindle [23] and Dolan [13] for Chesapeake Bay. Along most of these shores the beach slope is gentle and lies between 0.001 and 0.01. The number of parallel bars ranges from a few to more than a dozen. Their spacing can range from 10 m to several hundred meters. At least two scientific questions may be raised: Why do longshore bars exist and how do they affect the nearshore waves?

Laboratory studies by Bagnold [4] show that near a seawall where the incident waves are totally reflected, bars grow from an initially flat sandy bottom at the interval equal to half of the incident wavelength. Prior to the landing of Allied Forces on the shores of Normandy, Keulegan [22] studied a sandy beach of gentle slope in the laboratory, and showed that the plunging crest of a breaking wave can dislodge sand particles and then deposit them a short distance seaward, thus creating a *break-point bar*, even without strong reflection at first. More recently, Boczar-Karakiewicz et al. [6] performed experiments on a sandy slope ended by a steep inshore. They found that parallel bars can form at the intervals equaling half the incident wavelength, but for steep waves in shallow depth these bars can deform as the waves evolve nonlinearly by generating higher harmonics and breaking.

On the other hand, Heathershaw [17] examined the effects of periodic bars of wooden construction on waves, and demonstrated that many small bars can cause strong reflection if the bar spacing is close to one-half of the length of the incident waves. This condition is that of *Bragg resonance*, well known in crystallography. Together the experiments by Bagnold, Boczar-Karakiewicz et al. and Heathershaw, indicate that strong reflection and periodic bars may enhance each other. The full details of sand-bar formation must involve the difficult subject of sediment transport, and are beyond the scope of this survey. We shall only examine how longshore bars on a beach alter the reflection of waves.

The mechanism of Bragg resonance is simply a matter of constructive interference and is particularly simple in the case of normal incidence and constant mean depth. If the bars are parallel to the depth contours $x =$ constant and spaced at half of the incident wavelength, then all reflected crests originated from different periods arrive at a given station with the phase difference of $2n\pi$ where n is an integer, no matter how many bars they may have passed previously during transmission and reflection. Because these bars normally occur on a beach, both reflection and refraction are important features. For simplicity, let us consider a sloping beach with all contours given by $x =$ constant and normal incidence. The mean depth is given by $h(x)$, which varies with x slowly. Restricting our discussion to infinitesimal waves, the linearized governing equations are:

$$\Phi_{xx} + \Phi_{zz} = 0, \quad -h + \mu\delta < z < 0 \tag{252}$$

in the fluid where $h(x)$ denotes the mean depth and $\mu\delta(x)$ the height of bars above the mean bottom, and μ is a small parameter comparable to the mean bottom slope. On the free surface we have

$$g\Phi_z + \Phi_{tt} = 0 \tag{253}$$

The boundary condition on the bars is

$$\Phi_z = -h_x\Phi_x + \mu(\delta\Phi_x)_x + O(\mu)^2 \tag{254}$$

Let the bars have the wave number $2k(x)$ where $k(x)$ is the wave number of an incident wave train that would be perfectly tuned to the bars according to Bragg's condition, the corresponding frequency being ω, which is related to k and h by the well known dispersion relation. For generality let there be a slight detuning so that the incident wave has the wave number $k + \mu K$ and frequency $\omega + \mu\Omega$ where

$$\Omega = C_g K \tag{255}$$

The free surface of the incident wave is then given by

$$\zeta = A_0 \exp \{i[\int(k + \mu K)dx - (\omega + \mu\Omega)t]\} = A(x,t)e^{iS^+} \tag{256}$$

where S^+ is its phase of the perfectly tuned "right-going" wave:

$$S^+ = \int kdx - \omega t \qquad (257)$$

In Equation 256 the incident wave amplitude A is slowly modulated in x and t. This suggests the use of slow coordinates

$$\bar{x} = \mu x \quad \bar{t} = \mu t \qquad (258)$$

and the WKB method. Thus we assume the perturbation expansion

$$\Phi = \mu\phi^{(1)} + \mu^2\phi^{(2)} + \ldots \qquad (259)$$

with

$$\phi^{(1)} = \phi^{(1)} (x,z,t; \bar{x}, \bar{t}) \qquad (260)$$

etc., and find at the first order:

$$\begin{aligned}
&\phi^{(1)}_{xx} + \phi^{(1)}_{zz} = 0 \qquad -h < z < 0 \\
&g\phi^{(1)}_z + \phi^{(1)}_{tt} = 0 \qquad z = 0 \\
&\phi^{(1)}_z = 0 \qquad z = -h(\bar{x})
\end{aligned} \qquad (261a,b,c)$$

At $O(\mu^2)$ we have

$$\phi^{(2)}_{xx} + \phi^{(2)}_{zz} = -\left(\frac{\partial^2}{\partial x \partial \bar{x}} + \frac{\partial^2}{\partial \bar{x} \partial x} \right) \phi^{(1)} \qquad (-h < z < 0)$$

$$\phi^{(2)}_{tt} + g\phi^{(2)}_z = -\frac{\partial^2 \phi^{(1)}}{\partial t \partial \bar{t}} \qquad z = 0 \qquad (262a,b,c)$$

$$\phi^{(2)}_z = -h_{\bar{x}} \phi^{(1)}_x + (\delta\phi^{(1)}_x)_x \qquad z = -h(\bar{x})$$

Anticipating that the reflected waves can be as strong as the incident waves, we allow wave trains propagating in opposite directions, hence

$$\phi^{(1)} = \psi^+ e^{iS^+} + * + \psi^- e^{iS^-} + * \qquad (263)$$

with * denoting the complex conjugate of the immediately preceding term, and S^- being the phase of the "left-going" wave:

$$S^- = -\int kdx - \omega t \qquad (264)$$

Substituting Equation 263 into Equation 261a,b,c, we find after some algebra similar to that in an earlier section that at the leading order, ψ^+ is governed by the homogeneous boundary value problem defined by Equation 51a–c. The solutions are therefore

$$\psi^+ = -\frac{ig}{\omega}\frac{\cosh k(z+h)}{\cosh kh} A^\pm \tag{265}$$

with

$$\omega^2 = gk \tanh kh \tag{266}$$

Substituting the first order results into the right side of the second order equations we get

$$\phi_{xx}^{(2)} + \phi_{zz}^{(2)} = -i \, [k \, \psi_x^+ + (k\psi^+)_{\bar{x}}] \, e^{iS^+} + i \, [k\psi_{\bar{x}}^- + (k\psi^-)_{\bar{x}}] \, e^{iS^-} + *.$$
$$-h < z < 0 \tag{267}$$

$$g\phi_z^{(2)} + \phi_{tt}^{(2)} = 2i\omega\left(\frac{\partial\psi^+}{\partial\bar{t}} \, e^{iS^+} + \frac{\partial\psi^-}{\partial\bar{t}} \, e^{iS^-}\right) + *, \qquad z=0 \tag{268}$$

and

$$\phi_z^{(2)} = -i \, h_{\bar{x}} \, [k\psi^+e^{iS^+} - k\psi^-e^{iS^-}) + * + \frac{1}{2} \, Dk^2(\psi^-e^{iS^+} + \psi^+e^{iS^-}) + * + \ldots$$
$$z = -h \tag{269}$$

Here only the terms with the phases S^+ and S^- are kept as other terms do not force resonance. Now we specify the profile of the sandbars by

$$\delta = \frac{1}{2} \, D[\exp{(2i \int k \, dx)} + \exp{(-2i \int k \, dx)}] \tag{270}$$

where the bar amplitude D can vary slowly in x. If the second order potential $\phi^{(2)}$ is expressed as

$$\phi^{(2)} = i\gamma^+e^{iS^+} + * + i\gamma^-e^{-iS^-} + * + \ldots \tag{271}$$

we obtain from Equations 268 to 270 that

$$\gamma_{zz}^+ - k^2\gamma^+ = k\psi_x^+ + (k\psi^+)_{\bar{x}} \qquad -h < z < 0$$

$$\gamma_z^+ - \frac{\omega^2}{g} \, \gamma^+ = -\frac{2\omega}{g} \, \psi_t^+ \qquad z = 0 \tag{272a,b,c}$$

$$\gamma_z^+ = h_{\bar{x}} \, k\psi^+ + \frac{i}{2} \, D \, k^2 \, \psi^- \qquad z = -h$$

γ^- satisfies a similar set of equations if the superscripts $^+$ and $^-$ are interchanged. Solvability of the inhomogeneous problem then gives

$$\frac{\partial A^+}{\partial \bar{t}} + C_g \frac{\partial A^+}{\partial \bar{x}} + \frac{1}{2} \frac{dC_g}{d\bar{x}} A^+ = -i\Omega_0 A^-$$

$$\frac{\partial A^-}{\partial \bar{t}} - C_g \frac{\partial A^-}{\partial \bar{x}} + \frac{1}{2} \frac{dC_g}{d\bar{x}} A^- = -i\Omega_0 A^+ \qquad (273a,b)$$

where Ω_0 is proportional to the local amplitude of the bars,

$$\Omega_0 = \frac{\omega k D}{2 \sinh 2kh} \qquad (274)$$

These equations show that the amplitudes of the incident and reflected waves A^+ and A^- are coupled through the bars.

Some ideas of the effect of these bars may be gained from the special case of constant mean depth. Then h, k, and C_g are constants. Let the bars be confined in a finite strip of width $-L < x < 0$ where $kL = O(\mu^{-1})$. Continuity of pressure $\phi^{(1)}$ and normal velocity $\phi_x^{(1)}$ dictate that A^+ and A^- must be continuous separately. The result depends on the ratio Ω/Ω_0. If $\Omega/\Omega_0 < 1$, i.e., subcritical detuning, the reflection coefficient varies monotonically with respect to x according to

$$|R(\bar{x})|^2 = \frac{\sinh^2\left\{\frac{\Omega_0 L}{C_g}\left[1 - \left(\frac{\Omega}{\Omega_0}\right)^2\right]^{1/2}\frac{\bar{x}}{L}\right\}}{\cosh^2\left\{\frac{\Omega_0 L}{C_g}\left[1 - \left(\frac{\Omega}{\Omega_0}\right)^2\right]^{1/2}\right\} - \left(\frac{\Omega}{\Omega_0}\right)^2} \qquad (275)$$

where $R(\bar{x}) = A^-(\bar{x})/A^+(-L)$. If on the other hand $\Omega/\Omega_0 > 1$, i.e., supercritical detuning, the reflection coefficient is oscillatory.

$$|R(\bar{x})|^2 = \frac{\sin^2\left\{\frac{\Omega_0 L}{C_g}\left[\left(\frac{\Omega}{\Omega_0}\right)^2 - 1\right]^{1/2}\frac{\bar{x}}{L}\right\}}{\left(\frac{\Omega}{\Omega_0}\right)^2 - \cos^2\left\{\frac{\Omega_0 L}{C_g}\left[\left(\frac{\Omega}{\Omega_0}\right)^2 - 1\right]^{1/2}\right\}} \qquad (276)$$

The quantity Ω_0 is therefore a *cutoff* frequency. Only if the detuning frequency is within a frequency band of width Ω_0 is Bragg resonance effective. The important parameters are Ω/Ω_0 and $\Omega_0 L/C_g$.

For bars on a sloping beach the evolution equations depend on x but can be solved numerically. Mei, Hara, and Naciri [39] have obtained results for a plane beach with bars occupying a stretch of the shoreline as depicted in Figure 8 and used the seaward edge of the bar strip as the reference station subscript $(.)_0$. Then both the parameters Ω/Ω_0 and $\Omega_0 L/C_g$ increase with decreasing depth as shown in Figures 9a

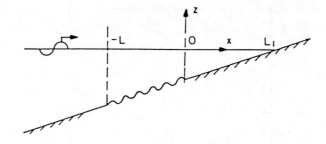

Figure 8. Longshore bars on a plane beach.

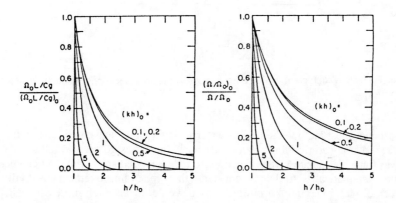

Figure 9. (a) Variations of local bar parameter $\Omega_0 L/C_g$ as a function of local depth and incident wave parameter $(kh)_0$; (b) Variation of local detuning ratio vs. local depth and $(kh)_0$.

and b. Figure 10 shows the typical dependence of the reflection coefficient at the seaward edge of the strip on the strip width $\Omega_0 L/C_g$ and detuning parameter Ω/Ω_0. Because Ω_0 changes with the mean depth, incident waves that are subcritical offshore may become supercritical inshore. The increasingly oscillatory behavior of R is caused by the increase of Ω_0 when h decreases.

Related studies of scattering by periodic bottoms can be found in Davies and Heathershaw [11], Yoon and Liu [56], Kirby [25], Dalrymple and Kirby [9], Hara and Mei [16], and Naciri and Mei [42].

Literature of Nonlinear Theories

Because of mathematical simplicity, linearized theories for infinitesimal waves of very small wave slope have been most extensively developed. In nature the wave slope is often so large that the linearized approximation is inadequate. A better the-

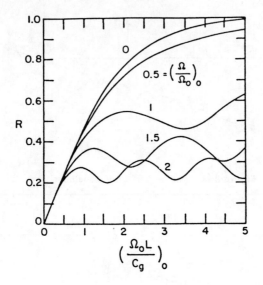

Figure 10. Reflection coefficient at the seaward edge of the field of longshore bars on a sloping beach.

oretical account must include the nonlinear terms in the boundary conditions on the free surface. Among all possibilities it is obviously the easiest to study small amplitude waves for which successive corrections to the linearized approximation can be carried out systematically. At the present stage, this type of improvement has dominated much of water wave research in the past two decades. Much more difficult, but potentially more important to both oceanography and engineering, are the steep and breaking waves.

The development of nonlinear wave theories has been most dramatic as a branch of geophysical science. Since surface waves serve as small-scale roughness that affects the large-scale interaction of air and sea, it is important to understand the generation of waves by wind and the evolution of waves in the course of propagation. This roughness is a dynamic one, in that its size and kinematics depend on the interaction with the wind itself. In particular, surface waves absorb momentum and energy of, and provide drag force to, the air flow above, which therefore affects the wind stress on the sea surface. The wind stress in turn is most responsible for driving the ocean circulation on the global scale. This kind of global interaction between air and sea ultimately influences our weather system. Because of these incentives, oceanographers and fluid dynamicists have pursued vigorously the generation of waves by wind and propagation of waves in the open ocean. In these searches the ocean depth is usually regarded as infinite compared to the wavelengths of interest. On the subject of wind generation of waves in deep water, comprehensive reviews of theories and ideas can be found in Phillips [44] and LeBlond and Mysak [26]. During the course of propagation, waves from different parts of the frequency spectrum exchange energy through nonlinear processes. For small amplitude waves these nonlinear exchanges may be insignificant over a short fetch but their effects can accumulate to cause dramatic changes over a long fetch. For reviews of these weakly nonlinear processes, references may again be made to Phillips [44] and LeBlond and Mysak [26]. Special mention should be made of waves with a narrow frequency band; their nonlinear evolution has been a focal point of research in the recent past. Introductory accounts of this subject can be found in Mei [36], while more advanced surveys can be found in Yuen and Lake [63] and Craik [9].

The propagation of steep waves in deep water is a formidable challenge in fluid mechanics, and the pioneering efforts of M. S. Longuet-Higgins in this area have been outstanding. His contributions span the whole gamut of exact identities, efficient numerical solutions, instability of steep waves, and the evolution of spilling breakers. Perhaps the best sources are his original papers in the past decade.

The theory of nonlinear long waves in shallow water dates back to the classical works of Airy and Korteweg and DeVries. Airy theory is for highly nonlinear waves of large amplitude but small slope so that dispersion is negligible. It is mathematically related to the dynamics of compressible gases and leads to discontinuous solution (shocks) under certain conditions. However, when shocks develop from the mathematics, the basic assumption of the long wave is violated, so that the prediction of shock formation is not reliable. For weakly nonlinear waves of not too great length, the theory of Korteweg, de Vries and of Boussinesq accounts for both nonlinearity and dispersion to the leading order. This makes it possible for waves of permanent form to exist while the opposing effects of nonlinearity and dispersion are in perfect dynamical balance. Of special importance is a permanent wave called the solitary wave or the soliton, for it shows up as basic elements in many transient processes. For example, over a horizontal bed, any localized disturbance on the free surface leads to a train of solitons that would eventually line up in the order of their amplitudes. Their speeds increase with the amplitude so that the larger soliton will outrun the smaller ones. A soliton climbing a shelf will first deform and then enter the region of the smaller depth in a state of imbalance. Solitons may then be emitted and dispersed according to their sizes. For a general survey of this subject, including the waves of other physical origin, one should read the mathematical treatises such as Whitham [59] and Ablowitz and Segur [1]. For water waves an introductory account is contained in Mei [36]. Shoaling of steep and breaking waves on beaches have been surveyed by Peregrine [43] who also discusses works similar to those of Longuet-Higgins for deep water. Applications of these numerical theories have been discussed by Sobey et al. [51] and Swift and Dixon [56].

In ocean engineering, one is more interested in the effects of waves on solid boundaries, whether man-made or natural, and less on the propagation process without the interruption by boundaries. This difference in emphasis is similar to that between the disciplines of physics and electrical engineering on the subject of electromagnetic waves. The interactions between waves and a shoreline, topographical irregularity, a breakwater, a ship, a semi-submersible, or a harbor, etc. . . are the main motivations for engineering interest in ocean waves. In this regard we may distinguish the cases of intermediate depth or deep water ($kh \lesssim O(1)$) and shallow water, ($kh \ll 1$). Most of the published theories are for weakly nonlinear waves so that systematic correction by perturbations can be applied.

For intermediate depth kh = O(1) and broad-banded incident waves, small perturbation theories allow us to treat the first-order problem frequency by frequency. In the second order one must treat diffraction problems involving the sum and difference frequencies. The free-surface boundary conditions are now very complicated and affect the radiation condition at large distances. On this point, which has been a point of contention for many years, Molin [41] has made an important contribution by deducing the radiation condition within the framework of quasi-steady formulation. His result has been recently confirmed by Wang [58] by starting from an initial-value problem.

For narrow-banded waves, the difference frequency is much smaller than the typical frequency of the first-order waves. This implies that there are second-order waves of very long period. For kh = O(1) these second-order long waves are in shallow water. If there are no structures interrupting the propagation, these long waves are locked to the short-wave groups and move at the group velocity of the short waves. However, when there is a scatterer, additional long waves moving at the speed $(gh)^{1/2}$ will appear. For a floating body, these long waves enhance the radiation damping of the so-called slow-drift oscillations. On a submarine ridge, incident groups of short waves may generate long waves that are then trapped on the ridge. A number of these problems have been studied by Agnon, Choi, and Mei [3] and Agnon and Mei [2].

In shallow water, the literature of nonlinear diffraction is limited. One of the cases studied is the nonlinear modification of harbor resonance. It has been found that nonlinearity generally helps the transfer of energy from low to high harmonics, therefore reducing the amplitude of the resonating mode [27, 46]. There are also interesting works on Mach diffraction [15, 40], and on the scattering of solitary waves by a step, where Sugimoto et al. [53–55] used the idea of the inner and outer expansions. The technique can be extended to study the scattering of small bodies in shallow water and long waves.

Much more work on finite amplitude waves needs to be done in ocean engineering.

Acknowledgment

This chapter was prepared while the author was supported by the U.S. National Science Foundation (Fluid Mechanics and Hydraulics Program, Grant MSM 8514919) and by the U.S. Office of Naval Research (Ship Hydrodynamics Program, Contract N00014-86-K-0121, and Ocean Engineering Program, Contract N00014-83-K-0550).

Notation
(frequently used symbols only)

A   wave amplitude
C   phase velocity

C_g group velocity
g   gravitational acceleration
h   still water depth
$H_n(z)$ Hankel function of the first kind, order function
k   wave number
$O(\ )$ order of ( )
p   dynamic pressure
P   total pressure
R   reflection coefficient
S   phase function
t   time
$\bar{t}$ slow time
T   wave period or transmission coefficient
$\bar{u}$ velocity vector
$\bar{x}$ spatial coordinate
$\bar{x}, \bar{y}$ slow coordinates

Greek Symbols

δ sand bar height
ζ free-surface displacement
η spatial amplitude of time harmonic free surface
θ angle of incidence
λ wavelength
μ small parameter
ρ water density
ϕ_0, ϕ_1, etc.   perturbation potentials
ω wave frequency
Ω detuning frequency
Ω_0 cut-off frequency
$(\ )_I$ incident wave
$(\ )_s$ scattered wave
$(\ )^+$ incident wave
$(\ )^-$ reflected wave

References

1. Ablowitz, M. J. and Segur, H., 1981. *Solitons and the Inverse Scattering Transform,* Society of Industrial and Applied Mathematics, Philadelphia.
2. Agnon, Y. and Mei, C.C., 1988, "Excitation of Long Internal Waves by Groups of Short Surface Waves Incident on a Barrier," Vol. 192, pp. 17–31, *J. Fluid Mech.*
3. Agnon, Y., Choi, H. S., and Mei, C. C., 1988, "Slow Drift of a Floating Cylinder in Narrow-Banded Beam Seas," Vol. 190, pp. 141–163, *J. Fluid Mech.*
4. Bagnold, R. A., 1947, "Sand Movement by Waves: Some Small-Scale Experiments with Sand of Very Low Density," *J. Inst. Civil Eng.* 27:447–469.
5. Berkhoff, J. C. W., 1972, "Computation of Combined Refraction-Diffraction," *Proc. 13th Cong. Coastal Eng.* ASCE 1:471–490.

6. Boczar-Karakiewicz, B., Pablinska, B. and Winiecki, J., 1981, "Formation of Sandbars by Surface Waves: Laboratory Experiments," *Rozprawy Hydrotechniczne* 43:111–125.

7. Chakrabarti, S. K., 1987, "Wave Forces on an Open-Bottom Submersible Drilling Structure," 9:2–6. *Appl. Ocean Res.*

8. Chen, H. S. and Mei, C. C., 1974, "Oscillations and Wave Forces in a Man-Made Harbor in the Open Sea," *Proc. 10th Symp. Naval Hydrology*, 573–594.

9. Craik, A. D. D., 1985, *Wave Interactions and Fluid Flows*, Cambridge University Press.

10. Dalrymple, R. A. and Kirby, J. T., 1986, "Water waves over ripples," *J. Waterways Port. Coastal & Ocean Eng*, 112.

11. Davies, A. G. and Heathershaw, A. D., 1984, "Surface wave propagation over sinusoidally varying topography," *J. Fluid Mech.* 144:419–433.

12. Dingemans, M. W., 1985, "Surface Wave Propagation Over an Uneven Bottom: Evaluation of 2-D Horizontal Wave Propagation Models," Delft Hydraulics Laboratory Report W301, Part 5.

13. Dolan, T. J., 1983, "Wave Mechanics for the Formation of Multiple Longshore Bars with Emphasis on the Chesapeake Bay," M.S. thesis, Civil Engineering, University of Delaware.

14. Evans, O. F., 1940, "The Low and Ball of the Eastern Shore of Lake Michigan," *J. Geol.* 48:476–511.

15. Funakoshi, M., 1980, "Reflection of Obliquely Incident Solitary Waves," *J. Phys. Soc. Japan* 109:2371–2379.

16. Hara, T. and Mei, C.C., 1987, "Bragg Scattering of Surface Waves by Periodic Bars: Theory and Experiment," *J. Fluid Mech.* 178:221–241.

17. Heathershaw, A. D., 1982, "Seabed-Wave Resonance and Sandbar Growth." *Nature* 296:343–345.

18. Houston, J. R., 1976, "Long Beach Harbor: Numerical Analysis of Harbor Oscillations," U.S. Army Engineering Waterways Experiment Station, Vicksburg, MS, Report 1, Misc. Paper H-76-20.

19. Houston, J. R., 1978, "Interaction of Tsunamis with the Hawaiian Islands Calculated by a Finite Element Numerical Model," *J. Phys. Ocean.* 8:93–102.

20. Houston, J. R., 1981, "Combined Refraction and Diffraction of Short Waves Using the Finite Element Method," *Appl. Ocean Res.* 3:163–170.

21. Kajiura, K., 1961, "On the Partial Reflection of Water Waves Passing over a Bottom of Variable Depth," *Proc. Tsunami Meeting 10th Pacific Science Congress*, IUGG Monograph 24, 206–234.

22. Keulegan, G. H., 1944, "An Experimental Study of Submarine Sand Bars," Tech. Report No. 3, Beach Erosion Board.

23. Kindle, E. M., 1936, "Notes on Shallow Water Sand Structures," *J. Geol.* 44:861–869.

24. Kirby, J. T. and Dalrymple, R. A., 1983, "A Parabolic Equation for the Combined Refraction-Diffraction of Stokes Waves by Mildly Varying Topography," *J. Fluid Mech.* 136:446–453.

25. Kirby, J. F., 1986, "A General Wave Equation for Waves Over Rippled Beds," *J. Fluid Mech.* 162:171–186.

26. LeBlond, P. H. and Mysak, L. A., 1978, "Waves in the Ocean," Elsevier, Amsterdam.

27. Lepelletier, T. G., 1980, "Tsunamis-Harbor Oscillations Induced by Nonlinear Transient Long Waves," Report No. KH-R-41. Keck Laboratory, California Institute of Technology.

28. Liu, P. L. F. and Mei, C. C., 1976a,b, "Water Motion on a Beach in the Presence of a Breakwater: 1. Waves 2. Mean Currents," *J. Geophys. Res.-Oceans Atmos.* 81:3079–3084; 3085–3094.

29. Liu, P. L. F., and Tsay, T. K., 1982, "Numerical Solution of Water-Wave Refraction and Diffraction Problems in the Parabolic Approximation," *J. Geophy. Res.* 87:C10, 7932–7940.

30. Liu, P. L. F., and Tsay, T. K., 1984, "Refraction-Diffraction Model for Weakly Nonlinear Water Waves," *J. Fluid Mech.* 141:265–274.

31. Longuet-Higgins, M. S., 1967, "On the Trapping of Wave Energy Around Islands," *J. Fluid Mech.* 29:781–821.

32. Lozano, C. J. and Liu, P. L. F., 1980, "Refraction-Diffraction Model for Linear Surface Water Waves," *J. Fluid Mech.* 101:705–720.

33. Lozano, C. J. and Meyer, R. E., 1976, "Leakage and Response of Waves Trapped Around Islands," *Phys. Fluids* 19:1075–1088.

34. McCamy, R. C. and Fuchs, R. A., 1954, "Wave Forces on a Pile: A Diffraction Theory," Tech Memo 63, *Beach Erosion Board*, U.S. Army Corps of Engrs.

35. Mei, C. C., 1978, "Numerical Methods in Water Wave Diffraction and Radiation," *Annual Rev. Fluid Mech.*, 10:393–416.

36. Mei, C. C., 1983, "The Applied Dynamics of Ocean Surface Waves," Wiley-Interscience, New York.

37. Mei, C. C., 1985, "Resonant Reflection of Surface Water Waves by Periodic Sandbars," *J. Fluid Mech.* 152:315–335.

38. Mei, C. C., 1987, "Effects of a Narrow Gap Between a Bottom-Seated Structure and the Sea Floor," (Tech Note) 9:51–52 *Appl. Ocean Res.*

39. Mei, C.C., Hara, T., Naciri, M., 1988, "Note on Bragg Scattering of Water Waves by Parallel Bars on a Seabed," *J. Fluid Mech.* 186:147–162.

40. Miles, J. W., 1977, "Diffraction of Solitary Waves," *ZAMP* 28:889–902.

41. Molin, B., 1979, "Second Order Diffraction Loads Upon Three-Dimensional Bodies," *Appl. Ocean Res.* 1:197–202.

42. Naciri, M., and Mei, C. C., 1988, "Bragg Scattering of Water Waves by a Doubly Periodic Bed," *J. Fluid Mech* 192, 51–74.

43. Peregrine, D. H., 1983, "Breaking Waves on Beaches," *Ann. Rev. Fluid Mech.* 15:149–178.

44. Phillips, O. M., 1977, "Dynamics of the Upper Ocean," 2nd ed. Cambridge University Press, London.

45. Radder, A. C., 1979, "On the Parabolic Equation Method for Water Wave Propagation," *J. Fluid Mech.* 95:159–176.

46. Rogers, S. R. and Mei, C. C., 1978, "Nonlinear Resonant Excitation of a Long and Narrow Bay," *J. Fluid Mech.* 88:161–180.

47. Sarpkaya, T. and Issacson, M. St. Q., 1981, *Mechanics of Wave Forces on Offshore Structures*, Van Nostrand Reinold, New York.

48. Saylor, J. H. and Hands, E. B., 1970, "Properties of Longshore Bars in the Great Lakes," *Proc. 12th Cong. Coastal Engineering*, 2:839–853.

49. Short, A. D., 1975, "Multiple Offshore Bars Along the Alaskan Arctic Coast," *J. Geol.* 83:209–211.

50. Smith, R., and Sprinks, T., 1975, "Scattering of Surface Waves By a Conical Island," *J. Fluid Mech.* 72:373–384.

51. Sobey, R. J., Goodwin, P., Thicke, R. J., and Westberg, Jr., R. J., 1987, "Application of Stokes, Cnoidal and Fourier Wave Theories," *J. Waterways Port. Coastal and Ocean Eng.* 113:569–587.

52. Stamnes, J. J., Louhaugen, O., Spjelkavik, B., Mei, C. C., Lo, E., Yue, D. K. P, 1983, "Nonlinear Focusing of Surface Waves by a Lens-Theory and Experiment," *J. Fluid Mech.* 135:71–94.

53. Sugimoto, N. and Kakutani, T., 1984, "Reflection of a Shallow Water Soliton Part I: Edge Layer Theory for Shallow Water Waves," *J. Fluid Mech.* 146:369–382.

54. Sugimoto, N., Kusaka, Y., and Kakutani, T., 1987a, "Reflection of a Shallow-Water Soliton Part II Numerical Evaluation," *J. Fluid Mech.* 178:99–117.

55. Sugimoto, N., Nakajima, N., and Kakutani, T., 1987b, "Edge Layer Theory for Shallow Water Waves Over a Step—Reflection and Transmission of a Soliton," *J. Phys. Soc. Japan* 56:1717–1730.

56. Swift, R. H. and Dixon, J. C., 1987, "Transformation of Regular Waves," *Proc. Inst. Civil Engrs.* 83:359–380.

57. Ünlüata, Ü. and Mei, C. C., 1975, "Effects of Entrance Loss on Harbor Oscillations," 101: 161–180 *J. Waterways, Harbors and Coastal Eng. Div. ASCE.*

58. Wang, P. F., 1988, "The Radiation Condition and Numerical Aspects of Second-Order Surface Wave Radiation and Diffraction," Ph.D. thesis, Dept. of Ocean Eng., Mass. Inst. Tech.

59. Whitham, G. B., 1974, *Linear and Nonlinear Waves*, Wiley-Interscience, New York.

60. Yeung, R. W. (1982). "Numerical methods in free-surface flows," Ann. Rev. Fluid Mech. 14:395-442.

61. Yoon, S. B. and P. L. F. Liu (1987). "Resonant Reflection of Shallow Water Waves Due to Corrugated Boundaries," *J. Fluid Mech.* 180: 451–469.

62. Yue, D. D. P., and C. C. Mei (1980). "Forward Diffraction of Stokes Waves by a Thin Wedge," *J. Fluid Mech.* 99: 33–52.

63. Yuen, H. C. and B. Lake (1982). "Nonlinear Dynamics of Deep Water Waves," *Adv. Appl. Mech.* 22: 67–229.

CHAPTER 2

STREAM FUNCTION WAVE THEORY AND APPLICATIONS

Robert G. Dean

Coastal and Oceanographic Engineering Department
University of Florida
Gainesville, Florida, U.S.A.

CONTENTS

Introduction

The stream function (SF) wave theory [1–4] is of analytical form with the wavelength, L, coefficients, X(n), and value of stream function on the free surface, ψ_η, determined numerically. The expression for the stream function, ψ for a wave system rendered stationary by a reference frame moving with the speed of the wave, C, is

$$\psi = \left(\frac{L}{T} - U\right) z + \sum_{n=1}^{NN} X(n) \sinh\left[\frac{2\pi n}{L}(h+z)\right] \cos\left(\frac{2\pi nx}{L}\right) \qquad (1)$$

with the coordinate z referenced to the mean water level and U is a uniform current. Figure 1 presents a definition sketch of the system under consideration. Equation 1 satisfies exactly the governing differential equation (Laplace equation) for irrotational flow, and the kinematic bottom and free surface boundary conditions. For a specified wave height, water depth, and wave period, the wavelength, L, coefficients X(n), and stream function evaluated on the free surface, ψ_η, are determined to best satisfy the dynamic free surface boundary condition in the least squares

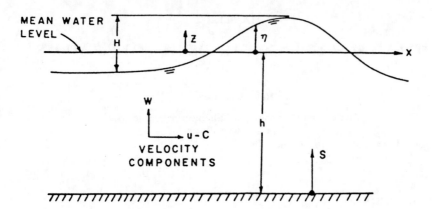

Figure 1. Definition sketch of "arrested" wave system [13].

sense. Advantages of the stream function wave theory include one theory of variable order that spans the full range from shallow to deep water and from small to breaking wave heights, and the availability of fairly comprehensive tables [5] that are usually suitable for preliminary design or in some cases final design. The order, NN, of the water theory is variable and can be extended as appropriate to provide a good fit to the governing boundary conditions. In the tables, the order of the theory has been selected to provide approximately 1% accuracy in water particle kinematics. The SF wave theory has been demonstrated to provide good "analytical validity" [1, 6], which is a measure of the fit to the nonlinear free surface boundary conditions and good "experimental validity" [7].

It is noted that Equation 1 is applicable for the case of irrotational flows; Dalrymple [3, 4] has developed a procedure for extending the stream function wave theory to rotational flows characterized by linear or bilinear shear currents. Numerous extensions and improvements have been made on the original stream function wave theory [3, 4, 8–10], and other representations in terms of the stream function or velocity potential, extendable to very high order, have been developed [11, 12]. Also it should be noted that versions of the stream function wave theory now exist for microcomputers.

This chapter introduces the reader, through application, to the stream function tables. The results in the stream function tables [5] are presented in non-dimensional form for ten values of relative water depth, h/L_o, and for each relative water depth, four values of relative wave height, H/L_o, at relative breaking heights of 0.25, 0.50, 0.75, and 1.0 (see Figure 2). At each of these pairs, $(h/L_o, H/L_o)$, fairly complete geometric, kinematic, and dynamic information is presented in non-dimensional form. Table 1 presents a summary of the information available in the various tables for each pair $(h/L_o, H/L_o)$ of wave conditions considered. Table 2 presents numerical values of selected dimensionless stream function quantities that may be of interest. In addition to the variables tabulated directly, it is possible to use the stream function tabulations to develop other results of interest. To illustrate the stream function wave theory application, the remainder of this chapter is organized in three sections. The first develops geometric and kinematic information for one

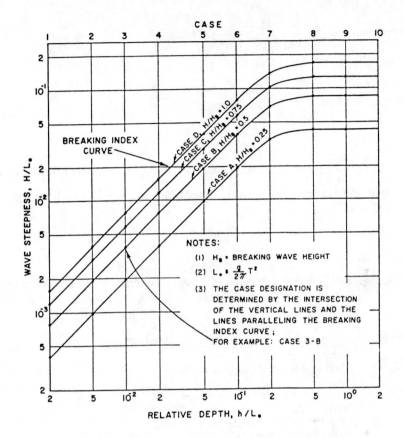

Figure 2. Wave characteristics selected for tabulation [13].

particular wave, the second applies the tables to the case of wave force and moment calculations on an offshore platform for the same wave conditions, and the third summarizes information from the tables and/or develops additional information from the tables. Most of the early examples are from Dean [13].

In the following two sections, numerical results will be calculated using the tables for the following specific breaking wave conditions

Wave height, H = 31.78 ft

Wave period, T = 20.0 sec

Water depth, h = 41.0 ft

The relative water depth and wave height are

Relative water depth: $\dfrac{h}{L_o} = \dfrac{41}{\dfrac{gT^2}{2\pi}} = \dfrac{41}{2,048} = 0.020$

Relative wave height: $\dfrac{H}{L_o} = \dfrac{31.78}{\dfrac{gT^2}{2\pi}} = \dfrac{31.78}{2,048} = 0.0155$

where $L_o \left(= \dfrac{gT^2}{2\pi} \right)$ is the linear deep water wave length. It is noted that these are quite shallow water wave conditions corresponding to case 4-D, i.e., breaking conditions (Figure 2).

Table 1
Dimensionless Variables Presented in Stream Function Theory Tabulations [13]

Table of Dean [5]	Variable Tabulated
—	Stream Function Coefficients
I	Horizontal Velocity Component Field
II	Vertical Velocity Component Field
III	Horizontal Acceleration Component Field
IV	Vertical Acceleration Component Field
V	Drag Force Component Field
VI	Inertia Force Component Field
VII	Drag Moment Component Field
VIII	Inertia Moment Component Field
IX	Dynamic Pressure Component Field
X	Kinematic and Dynamic Free Surface Boundary Condition Errors (Depend on θ)
XI-1	Wave Length
XI-2	Average Potential Energy
XI-3	Average Kinetic Energy
XI-4	Total Average Energy
XI-5	Total Average Energy Flux
XI-6	Group Velocity
XI-7	Total Average Momentum
XI-8	Total Average Momentum Flux
XI-9	Root-Mean-Square Kinematic Free Surface Boundary Condition Error
XI-10	Root-Mean-Square Dynamic Free Surface Boundary Condition Error
XI-11	Maximum Kinematic Free Surface Boundary Condition Error
XI-12	Maximum Dynamic Free Surface Boundary Condition Error
XI-13	Kinematic Free Surface Breaking Parameter
XI-14	Dynamic Free Surface Breaking Parameter

Calculation of Wave Properties

Examples are presented of the wavelength and variation with phase angle of a number of wave properties of interest. Denoting below the dimensionless quantities as primed, the dimensional quantities are defined in terms of the dimensionless tabulated wave parameters as

$$L = L' L_o$$

$$\eta(\theta) = H \eta' \tag{2}$$

$$\begin{Bmatrix} u(\theta,S) \\ w(\theta,S) \end{Bmatrix} = \frac{H}{T} \begin{Bmatrix} u'\ (\theta,S') \\ w'\ (\theta,S') \end{Bmatrix} \tag{3}$$

$$\begin{Bmatrix} \dfrac{Du(\theta,S)}{Dt} \\ \dfrac{Dw(\theta,S)}{Dt} \end{Bmatrix} = \frac{H}{T^2} \begin{Bmatrix} \dfrac{Du'(\theta,S')}{Dt} \\ \dfrac{Dw'(\theta,S')}{Dt} \end{Bmatrix} \tag{4}$$

$$p_D\ (\theta,S) = \frac{\gamma H}{2}\ p_D'\ (\theta,S') \tag{5}$$

in which θ is the phase angle and S is the distance above the bottom. The dynamic pressure represents the departure from hydrostatic pressure (or barometric pressure above the mean water line) due to the presence of the waves.

The non-dimensional wavelength, L', is presented in Table XI-1 of Dean [5] as $L' = 0.422$. The wavelength is then

$$L = L' L_o = (0.422)\ \frac{gT^2}{2\pi} = (0.422)(2{,}048) = 864.3 \text{ ft}$$

Table 3 presents the table for the non-dimensional horizontal velocity field for case 4-D. The calculations are summarized in Table 4 and the dimensional variables are presented in Figure 3, where mid-depth (S = h/2) position has been selected for those variables that depend on elevation within the water column (i.e., all but η). The extreme nonlinearity of this wave is evident by the departure of the variables plotted in Figure 3 from sine and cosine forms as would be predicted by linear wave theory.

Forces and Moments on Individual Platform Members

Consider the platform shown in Figure 4 and suppose that it is desired to calculate the forces and moments on Members "a," "b," and "c." The dimensionless drag and inertia components of force and moment are each presented in a separate

(text continued on page 74)

Table 2
Selected Summary of Tabulated Dimensionless Stream Function Quantities [5]

Case	h/L_o	H/L_o	L'	η'_c	η'_t	u'_c	w'_m**	$\theta(w'_m)$**	$(F'_I)_m$	$(F'_I)_m$**	$\theta(F'_I)_m$**	p'_{bc} (Bottom)	p'_{bx} (Bottom)
1-A	0.002	0.00039	0.120	0.910	−0.090	49.68	13.31	10°	2574.0	815.6	10°	1.57	−0.18
1-B	0.002	0.00078	0.128	0.938	−0.062	47.32	15.57	10°	2774.6	1027.0	10°	1.45	−0.12
1-C	0.002	0.00117	0.137	0.951	−0.049	43.64	14.98	10°	2861.0	1043.5	10°	1.35	−0.10
1-D	0.002	0.00156	0.146	0.959	−0.041	40.02	13.63	10°	2985.6	1001.7	10°	1.29	−0.09
2-A	0.005	0.00097	0.187	0.857	−0.143	29.82	8.70	20°	907.0	327.1	20°	1.46	−0.29
2-B	0.005	0.00195	0.199	0.904	−0.096	29.08	9.29	10°	1007.9	407.1	10°	1.36	−0.19
2-C	0.005	0.00293	0.211	0.927	−0.073	26.71	9.85	10°	1060.7	465.7	10°	1.23	−0.15
2-D	0.005	0.00388	0.223	0.944	−0.056	23.98	9.47	10°	1128.4	465.2	10°	1.11	−0.11
3-A	0.01	0.00195	0.260	0.799	−0.201	19.83	6.22	30°	390.3	162.1	30°	1.34	−0.40
3-B	0.01	0.00389	0.276	0.865	−0.135	19.87	7.34	20°	457.3	209.0	20°	1.28	−0.27
3-C	0.01	0.00582	0.292	0.898	−0.102	18.47	6.98	20°	494.7	225.6	10°	1.16	−0.20
3-D	0.01	0.00775	0.308	0.922	−0.078	16.46	6.22	10°	535.4	242.4	10°	1.04	−0.16
4-A	0.02	0.00390	0.359	0.722	−0.278	12.82	4.50	30°	156.3	82.2	30°	1.18	−0.55
4-B	0.02	0.00777	0.380	0.810	−0.190	13.35	5.38	30°	197.6	103.4	20°	1.16	−0.38
4-C	0.02	0.01168	0.401	0.858	−0.142	12.58	5.29	20°	222.9	116.1	20°	1.06	−0.28
4-D	0.02	0.01555	0.422	0.889	−0.111	11.29	4.99	20°	242.4	113.5	20°	0.97	−0.23
5-A	0.05	0.00975	0.541	0.623	−0.377	7.20	3.44	50°	44.3	37.6	50°	0.93	−0.70
5-B	0.05	0.01951	0.566	0.716	−0.284	7.66	3.69	50°	59.1	38.5	50°	0.94	−0.55
5-C	0.05	0.02916	0.597	0.784	−0.216	7.41	3.63	30°	72.0	47.1	30°	0.88	−0.42
5-D	0.05	0.03900	0.627	0.839	−0.161	6.47	3.16	30°	85.5	45.1	20°	0.76	−0.33

Dimensionless Quantities*

Case													
6-A	0.10	0.0183	0.718	0.571	−0.429	4.88	3.16	75°	17.12	22.62	75°	0.73	−0.67
6-B	0.10	0.0366	0.744	0.642	−0.358	5.09	3.07	50°	22.37	23.67	50°	0.73	−0.61
6-C	0.10	0.0549	0.783	0.713	−0.287	5.00	2.98	50°	28.79	23.64	30°	0.70	−0.51
6-D	0.10	0.0730	0.824	0.782	−0.218	4.43	2.44	50°	36.48	22.43	30°	0.62	−0.41
7-A	0.20	0.0313	0.899	0.544	−0.456	3.63	3.05	75°	6.69	13.86	75°	0.46	−0.46
7-B	0.20	0.0625	0.931	0.593	−0.407	3.64	2.93	75°	8.60	13.61	75°	0.47	−0.47
7-C	0.20	0.0938	0.981	0.653	−0.347	3.54	2.49	50°	11.31	13.31	50°	0.47	−0.45
7-D	0.20	0.1245	1.035	0.724	−0.276	3.16	2.14	50°	15.16	11.68	50°	0.44	−0.39
8-A	0.50	0.0420	1.013	0.534	−0.466	3.11	2.99	75°	2.09	6.20	75°	0.090	−0.090
8-B	0.50	0.0840	1.059	0.570	−0.430	3.01	2.85	75°	2.71	6.21	75°	0.101	−0.102
8-C	0.50	0.1260	1.125	0.611	−0.389	2.86	2.62	75°	3.53	5.96	75°	0.116	−0.118
8-D	0.50	0.1681	1.194	0.677	−0.323	2.57	1.94	50°	4.96	5.36	50°	0.120	−0.120
9-A	1.00	0.0427	1.017	0.534	−0.466	3.09	2.99	75°	1.025	3.116	75°	0.004	−0.004
9-B	1.00	0.0852	1.065	0.569	−0.431	2.98	2.85	75°	1.329	3.126	75°	0.005	−0.006
9-C	1.00	0.1280	1.133	0.609	−0.391	2.83	2.62	75°	1.720	3.011	75°	0.008	−0.007
9-D	1.00	0.1697	1.211	0.661	−0.339	2.60	1.99	75°	2.303	2.836	50°	0.009	−0.011
10-A	2.00	0.0426	1.018	0.533	−0.467	3.09	2.99	75°	0.513	1.558	75°	−0.001	−0.001
10-B	2.00	0.0852	1.065	0.569	−0.431	2.98	2.85	75°	0.664	1.563	75°	0.000	0.000
10-C	2.00	0.1275	1.134	0.608	−0.392	2.83	2.63	75°	0.860	1.510	75°	−0.001	−0.001
10-D	2.00	0.1704	1.222	0.657	−0.343	2.62	2.04	75°	1.137	1.479	50°	0.000	0.000

* See Equations 2–5, Tables 4 and 6, and Reference 5 for definition of dimensionless quantities.

** These values are taken from the tabulations of Reference 5, which are presented at θ values as shown in Table 3. Additional Notes: (1) Except where obvious or noted otherwise, dimensionless quantities are presented for mean water elevation, (2) The maximum dimensionless drag and inertial forces apply for a piling extending through the entire water column, (3) subscripts "m," "c" and "t" denote "maximum," "crest," and "trough," respectively.

Table 3
Dimensionless Horizontal Velocity Component Field Defined in Equation 3, Case 4-D [5]

θ = η/Height =	.0	10.0	20.0	30.0	50.0	75.0	100.0	130.0	180.0
	.889	.583	.284	.101	-.055	-.101	-.110	-.112	-.111
	43.7%	15.5%	-65.4%	-326.7%	681.4%	227.7%	21.4%	-242.4%	-348.7%
Surface**	19.899	12.419	5.621	1.840	-.953	-1.636	-1.789	-1.799	-1.780
	51.9%	24.1%	-59.5%	-347.1%	******%	245.1%	12.9%	-273.2%	-388.6%
S*/Depth = 1.6	18.167								
	100.0%								
S/Depth = 1.5	16.533								
	100.0%								
S/Depth = 1.4	15.137	11.986							
	36.7%	21.4%							
S/Depth = 1.3	13.942	11.246							
	32.3%	17.3%							
S/Depth = 1.2	12.919	10.598	5.627						
	28.0%	13.6%	-55.3%						
S/Depth = 1.1	12.043	10.030	5.637						
	23.9%	10.0%	-52.8%						
S/Depth = 1.0	11.294	9.535	5.627	2.046					
	19.9%	6.6%	-51.1%	-283.0%					
S/Depth = .9	10.655	9.106	5.603	2.266	-.869	-1.630	-1.788	-1.799	-1.780
	16.1%	3.3%	-49.9%	-241.7%	******%	242.0%	13.2%	100.0%	100.0%
S/Depth = .8	10.113	8.736	5.570	2.445	-.733	-1.603	-1.780	-1.798	-1.783
	12.5%	.3%	-49.2%	-213.2%	******%	242.8%	13.7%	-273.2%	100.0%
S/Depth = .7	9.657	8.420	5.534	2.592	-.614	-1.579	-1.773	-1.798	-1.785
	9.3%	-2.5%	-48.7%	-192.7%	******%	243.6%	14.2%	-273.1%	-387.1%
S/Depth = .6	9.278	8.155	5.497	2.709	-.510	-1.556	-1.768	-1.798	-1.787

S/Depth = .5 6.4%	-4.9%	-48.5%	-177.7%	******%	244.5%	14.7%	-270.1%	-386.1%
8.968	7.935	5.462	2.803	-.423	-1.537	-1.762	-1.798	-1.788
S/Depth = .4 3.8%	-7.0%	-48.4%	-166.5%	******%	245.2%	15.0%	-267.5%	-382.3%
8.722	7.760	5.431	2.875	-.351	-1.521	-1.758	-1.798	-1.789
S/Depth = .3 1.7%	-8.8%	-48.4%	-158.3%	******%	245.9%	15.3%	-265.4%	-379.2%
8.535	7.626	5.406	2.928	-.296	-1.508	-1.755	-1.798	-1.790
S/Depth = .2 -.0%	-10.2%	-48.4%	-152.5%	******%	246.5%	15.5%	-263.8%	-376.8%
8.404	7.531	5.387	2.965	-.256	-1.498	-1.753	-1.798	-1.791
S/Depth = .1 -1.2%	-11.3%	-48.4%	-148.5%	******%	247.0%	15.7%	-262.6%	-375.1%
8.326	7.475	5.375	2.987	-.233	-1.493	-1.751	-1.797	-1.791
S/Depth = .0 -2.0%	-11.9%	-48.4%	-146.2%	******%	247.2%	15.8%	-261.9%	-374.1%
8.300	7.456	5.372	2.994	-.225	-1.491	-1.751	-1.797	-1.791
-2.2%	-12.1%	-48.5%	-145.5%	******%	247.3%	15.8%	-261.7%	-373.8%

* S = distance above bottom

** Note: The row labeled "surface" represents the dimensionless velocities evaluated at the free surface; the percentage differences for velocities are calculated as defined below. The percentage below each of the entries represents the difference between stream function and Airy theory, defined as

$$\% = \frac{\psi - \text{Airy}}{\psi} \, (100\%)$$

The remaining part of the table represents the dimensionless velocities and percentage differences evaluated on a grid of $(\theta, S/h)$. The lack of entries for the higher S/h and higher theta values (right side of page) results from the wave profile in the trough region being lower than in the crest region (left side of page). Two additional comments pertaining to the percentage values will complete the description of the sample table. A percentage difference value of exactly 100% implies that the stream-function profile occurred at a $(\theta, S/h)$ value, however, the Airy profile was lower than the particular S/h at the phase angle, θ, i.e., this grid point was not "covered" by the Airy profile. For example, this is the case at $\theta = 0°$, S/h = 1.5 and 1.6 and $\theta = 180°$, S/h = 0.8 and 0.9. Finally, the asterisks indicate that the percentage differences were not calculated because the stream-function value was less than 5% of the maximum stream-function value. This avoided the tabulation of very large percentages that would have been the result of division by a small number.

Table 4

Calculated Wave Profile, Kinematics and Dynamic Pressure (Kinematics and Pressure Calculated at Mid-Depth) [13]

Variable	Dimensionalizing Constant	$\theta(°)$								
		0	10	20	30	50	75	100	130	180
η'	H = 31.78 ft	0.89	0.58	0.28	0.10	-0.06	-0.10	-0.11	-0.11	-0.11
η(ft)		28.28	18.43	8.90	3.18	-1.90	-3.18	-3.50	-3.50	-3.50
u'	H/T = 31.78/20	8.97	7.94	5.46	2.80	-0.42	-1.54	-1.76	-1.80	-1.79
u(ft/sec)	= 1.589 ft/sec	14.25	12.62	8.68	4.45	-0.67	-2.45	-2.80	-2.86	-2.84
w'	Same as for u	0.00	1.46	2.14	1.95	0.81	0.17	0.03	0.01	0.00
w(ft/sec)	= 1.589 ft/sec	0.00	2.32	3.40	3.10	1.29	0.27	0.05	0.02	0.00
$\frac{Du'}{Dt}$	$H/T^2 = 31.78/(20)^2$	0.00	51.89	80.18	76.41	32.40	6.73	1.16	0.28	0.00
$\frac{Du}{Dt}$ (ft/sec^2)	= 0.0795 ft/sec^2	0.00	4.12	6.37	6.07	2.58	0.53	0.09	0.02	0.00
$\frac{Dw'}{Dt}$	Same as for $\frac{Du}{Dt}$	-39.21	-25.66	2.27	21.80	18.01	4.04	1.04	0.04	-0.28
$\frac{Dw}{Dt}$ (ft/sec^2)	= 0.0795 ft/sec^2	-3.12	-2.04	0.18	1.73	1.43	0.32	0.08	0.00	-0.02
p_D'	$\frac{\gamma H}{2} = \frac{(64)(31.78)}{2}$	1.03	0.93	0.67	0.37	-0.04	-0.19	-0.22	-0.23	-0.23
p_D(lb/ft^2)	= 1,017 lb/ft^2	1047.5	945.8	681.4	376.3	-40.7	-193.2	-223.7	-233.9	-228.8

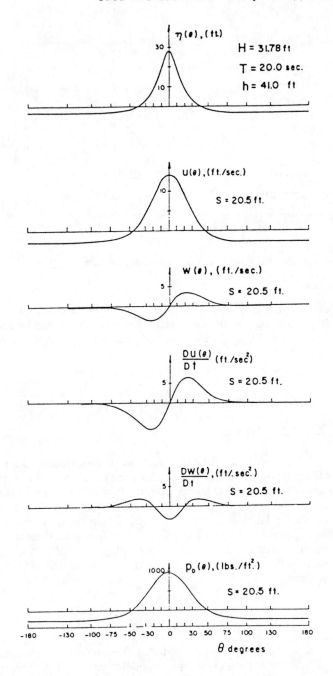

Figure 3. Example of calculations of wave profile, kinematics, and dynamic pressure [13].

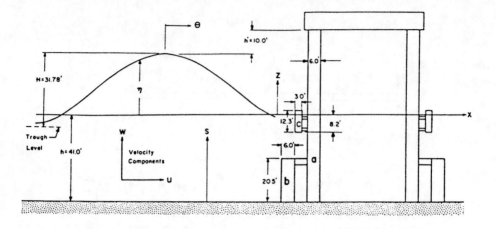

Figure 4. Definition sketch of wave interaction with platform [13].

(text continued from page 67)

table (four tables in all for each wave case). Table 5 presents a tabulation for the dimensionless drag force component as an illustration. Note the format is identical to that discussed previously for u′. The dimensionless drag force component is presented as

$$F_D' \, (\theta, S') = \int_0^{S'} u' |u'| dS' \tag{6}$$

so that in order to recover the dimensional drag forces,

$$F_D(\theta, S) = \frac{C_D \rho D(H/T)^2 h}{2} \cdot F_D'(\theta, S') \tag{7}$$

Member "a"—Calculation of the total drag and inertia components of force on Member "a" is straightforward. Equation 6 shows that the values tabulated represent the integration of the force distribution from the bottom up to the level tabulated. Since the forces and moments are desired for a piling that extends through the water surface, the values labeled "Surface" in Table 5 apply. The results of the calculations are summarized in Table 6 and are presented in graphical form in Figures 5 and 6. In this and other examples requiring drag, C_D, and inertia, C_M, coefficients, the following values were used for illustration purposes only, but are not recommended for design.

$$C_D = 1.05$$

$$C_M = 1.5$$

Member "b"—For Member "b," the desired forces and moments are the result of force distributions from the bottom (S′ = 0) up to mid-depth S′ = 0.5. Therefore, the pertinent tabulated values are those listed for S′ = 0.5. The results of these computations are presented in graphical form in Figures 7 and 8.

Member "c"—The forces and moments (about the bottom) on Member "c" would be determined in a similar way as described previously for Members "a" and "b," except that (1) in order to determine the force (or moment) on this member, it is necessary to subtract a tabulated value at the bottom of the member from one at the upper end; and (2) because the upper end may be either submerged or surface-piercing, at certain phase angles the "Surface" value would be employed, corresponding to phase angles where the water level is less than the elevation of the upper end of the member; at phase angles for which $\eta' + 1 > 1.1$, the values tabulated for $S' = 1.1$ would be employed.

Forces and Moments on a Multi-Legged Platform Due to a Wave of Oblique Incidence

Suppose that it is desired to calculate the wave forces and moments on the platform support piling shown in Figure 9a. All of the piling are of different diameters, and it is desired to investigate waves approaching from various directions. For this example, an efficient graphical procedure can be employed which only requires a small desk calculator. First the dimensionless "Surface" forces and moments are plotted as a function of distance to the same distance scale as the drawing of the platform. Distance, x, is related to the phase angle, θ, by

$$x = \frac{L}{360°} \theta \tag{8}$$

Figures 9b, c, d, e represent plots of F_D', F_I', M_D', and M_I', for Case 4-D. Next, a wave direction is selected and an overlay constructed to represent the proper piling spacing for the relative direction selection. For this example, a wave propagation direction of 30° south of east is considered. The platform orientation relative to the plot of dimensionless drag force properly sequences all piling for encountering the various phases of the wave, see Figure 10. Denoting x' as the distance between piling Number 1 and the approaching wave crest, the total wave forces and moments on the platform piling are given by

$$F(x') = \left\{ \begin{array}{c} \displaystyle\sum_{i=1}^{6} \alpha_{D_i} F_{D_i}'(x' + \delta_i) \\[2em] + \displaystyle\sum_{i=1}^{6} \alpha_{I_i} F_{I_i}'(x' + \delta_i) \end{array} \right\} \tag{9}$$

$$M(x') = \left\{ \begin{array}{c} \displaystyle\sum_{i=1}^{6} \alpha_{D_i} M_{D_i}'(x' + \delta_i) \\[2em] + \displaystyle\sum_{i=1}^{6} \alpha_{I_i} M_{I_i}'(x' + \delta_i) \end{array} \right\} h \tag{10}$$

Table 5
Dimensionless Drag Force Component Field Defined in Equation 6 Case 4-D [5]

θ =	.0	10.0	20.0	30.0	50.0	75.0	100.0	130.0	180.0
η/Height =	.889	.583	.284	.101	-.055	-.101	-.110	-.112	-.111
	43.7%	15.5%	-65.4%	-326.7%	681.4%	227.7%	21.4%	-242.4%	-348.7%
Surface**	242.396	119.800	37.004	7.722	-.254	-2.190	-2.844	-2.951	-2.919
	55.0%	12.1%	-155.2%	******%	******%	******%	******%	******%	******%
S*/Depth = 1.6	209.482								
	100.0%								
S/Depth = 1.5	179.432								
	100.0%								
S/Depth = 1.4	154.400	111.892							
	29.4%	5.9%							
S/Depth = 1.3	133.295	98.412							
	24.2%	.4%							
S/Depth = 1.2	115.284	86.495	36.344						
	20.0%	-3.4%	-124.1%						
S/Depth = 1.1	99.730	75.868	33.170						
	16.1%	-7.0%	-122.8%						
S/Depth = 1.0	86.134	66.307	29.996	7.423					
	12.5%	-10.3%	-121.9%	******%					
S/Depth = .9	74.106	57.628	26.843	6.957	-.207	-2.134	-2.799	-2.909	-2.877
	9.2%	-13.2%	-121.3%	******%	******%	******%	******%	******%	******%
S/Depth = .8	63.337	49.677	23.721	6.400	-.143	1.873	-2.480	-2.586	-2.559
	6.3%	-15.9%	-121.0%	******%	******%	******%	******%	******%	******%
S/Depth = .7	53.577	42.326	20.639	5.764	-.097	-1.620	-2.165	-2.262	-2.241
	3.7%	-18.2%	-120.8%	******%	******%	******%	******%	******%	******%
S/Depth = .6	44.624	35.464	17.597	5.060	-.066	-1.374	-1.851	-1.939	-1.922

S/Depth = .5	1.5%	-20.3%	-120.7%	******%	******%	******%	******%	******%
	36.310	28.997	14.595	4.300	-1.135	-1.540	-1.616	-1.603
	-.4%	-22.0%	-120.7%	******%	******%	******%	******%	******%
S/Depth = .4	28.495	22.844	11.629	3.493	-.901	-1.230	-1.293	-1.283
	-2.0%	-23.4%	******%	******%	******%	******%	******%	******%
S/Depth = .3	21.058	16.931	8.693	2.650	-.672	-.921	-.969	-.962
	-3.2%	-24.5%	******%	******%	******%	******%	******%	******%
S/Depth = .2	13.893	11.193	5.782	1.781	-.446	-.614	-.646	-.642
	-4.0%	******%	******%	******%	******%	******%	******%	******%
S/Depth = .1	6.903	5.568	2.887	.895	-.222	-.307	-.323	-.321
	******%	******%	******%	******%	******%	******%	******%	******%
S/Depth = .0	.000	.000	.000	.000	.000	.000	.000	.000
	******%	******%	******%	******%	******%	******%	******%	******%

* S = distance above bottom

** Note: The row labeled "surface" represents the dimensionless velocities evaluated at the free surface; the percentage differences for drag forces are calculated as defined below. The percentage below each of the entries represents the difference between stream function and Airy theory, defined as

$$\% = \frac{\psi - \text{Airy}}{\psi} \, (100\%)$$

The remaining part of the table represents the dimensionless drag forces and percentage differences evaluated on a grid of (θ, S/h). The lack of entries for the higher S/h and higher theta values (right side of page) results from the wave profile in the trough region being lower than in the crest region (left side of page). Two additional comments pertaining to the percentage values will complete the description of the sample table. A percentage difference value of exactly 100% implies that the stream-function profile occurred at a (θ, S/h) value, however, the Airy profile was lower than the particular S/h at the phase angle, θ, i.e., this grid point was not "covered" by the Airy profile. For example, this is the case at $\theta = 0°$, S/h = 1.5 and 1.6, and $\theta = 180°$, S/h = 0.8 and 0.9. Finally, the asterisks indicate that the percentage differences were not calculated because the stream-function value was less than 5% of the maximum stream-function value. This avoided the tabulation of very large percentages that would have been the result of division by a small number.

Table 6
Example 2—Wave Forces and Moments on Member "a" [13]

Variable	Dimensionalizing Constant	$\theta(°)$								
		0	10	20	30	50	75	100	130	180
F_D'	$\alpha_D = \dfrac{C_D\rho D(H/T)^2h}{2} \times 10^{-3}$ $= 0.6526$ kips	242.4	119.8	37.0	7.7	-0.3	-2.2	-2.8	-3.0	-2.9
F_D(kips)		158.2	78.2	24.1	5.0	-0.2	-1.4	-1.8	-2.0	-1.9
F_I'	$\alpha_I = \dfrac{C_M\rho\pi D^2(H/T^2)h}{4} \times 10^{-3}$ $= 0.2757$ kips	0.0	112.1	113.5	84.6	30.1	6.1	1.0	0.3	0.0
F_I(kips)		0.0	30.9	31.3	23.3	8.3	1.7	0.3	0.1	0.0
F(kips) $= F_D + F_I$		158.2	109.0	55.4	28.3	8.1	0.3	-1.5	-1.9	-1.9
M_D'	$\alpha_D \cdot h$ $= 27.76$ ft-kips	268.1	102.6	23.0	3.6	-0.2	-1.0	-1.3	-1.3	-1.3
M_D(ft-kips)		7,442.0	2,849.0	641.0	100.0	-6.0	-28.0	-36.0	-36.0	-36.0
M_I'	$\alpha_I \cdot h$ $= 11.30$ ft-kips	0.0	101.7	78.5	47.5	13.5	2.5	0.4	0.1	0.0
M_I(ft-kips)		0.0	1,149.0	887.0	537.0	153.0	28.0	4.0	1.0	0.0
M(ft-kips) $= M_D + M_I$		7,442.0	3,998.0	1,528.0	637.0	147.0	0.	-32.0	-35.0	-36.0

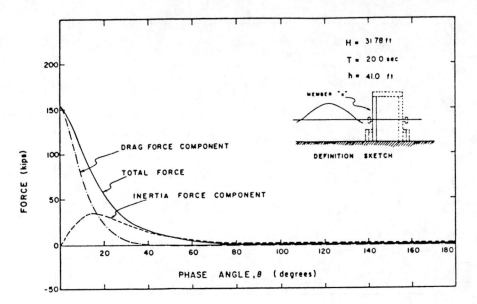

Figure 5. Horizontal wave forces on member a [13].

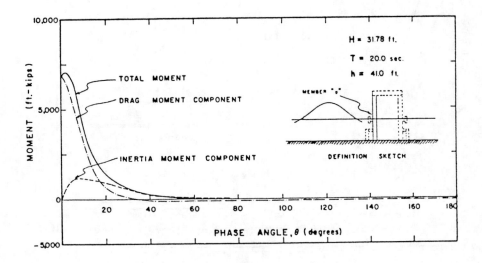

Figure 6. Wave moments on member a [13].

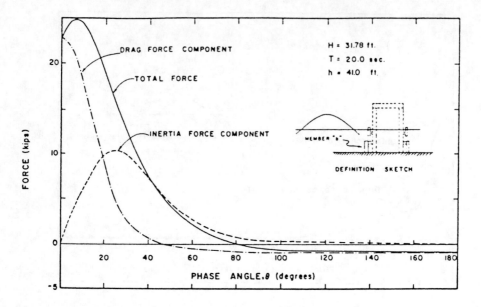

Figure 7. Horizontal wave forces on member b [13].

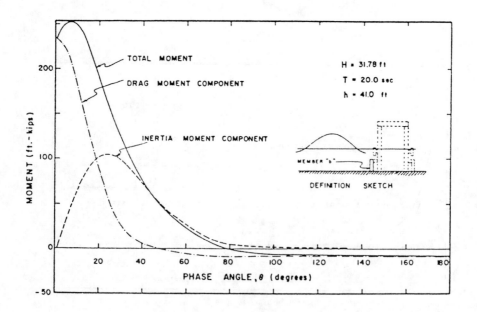

Figure 8. Wave moments on member b [13].

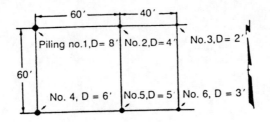

Figure 9a. Plan view of platform support piling [13].

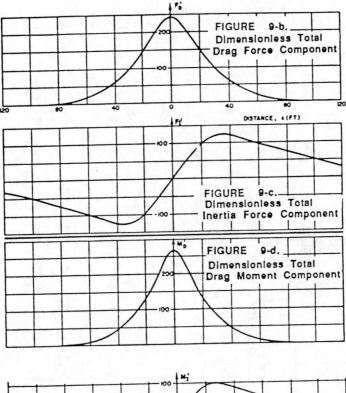

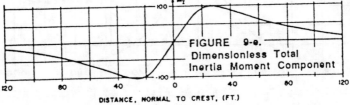

Figure 9. Example platform and dimensionless force and moment components [13].

in which

$$\alpha_{D_i} \equiv \frac{C_D \rho D_i (H/T)^2 h}{2} \tag{11}$$

$$\alpha_{I_i} \equiv \frac{C_M \rho \pi D_i^2 H/T^2 h}{4} \tag{12}$$

and δ_i represents spatial separations along the direction of wave propagation between the various other piling. The values $F'_{D_i}(x' + \delta_i)$, $F'_{I_i}(x' + \delta_i)$, etc., are determined by the overlay, which accounts for the spacing of the platform piling in relation to the wavelength and relative propagation direction. The drag and inertia components and total forces and moments are presented in Figures 11a and b.

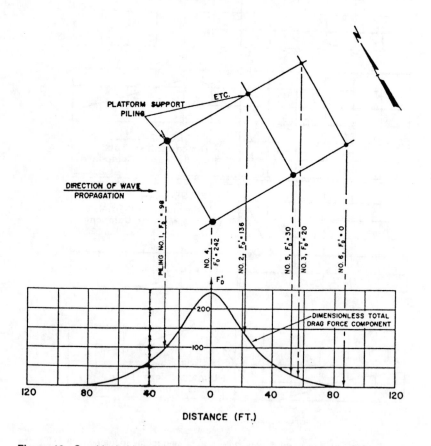

Figure 10. Graphical aid to the determination of wave forces on vertical piling [13].

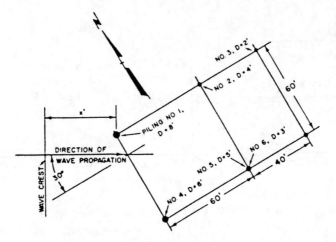

Figure 11a. Plan of platform support piling and wave orientation [13].

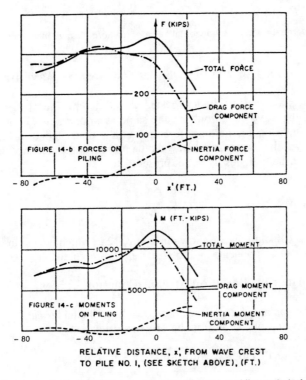

Figure 11b. Determination of total forces and moments on a multilegged platform for oblique wave incidence [13].

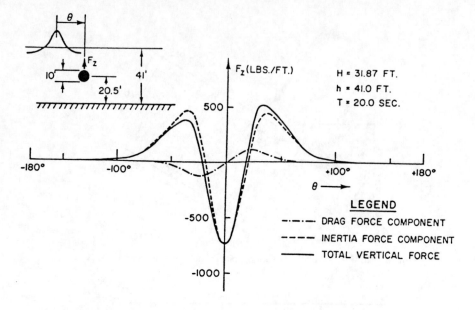

Figure 12. Vertical force on a horizontal cylinder for normal wave incidence [13].

Vertical Forces on a Horizontal Cylinder for Normal Wave Incidence

Figure 12 depicts a circular cylinder located at mid-depth. The diameter of the cylinder is 10 ft; the wave conditions are the same as in previous examples. The usual assumption is made that the total force per unit cylinder length, F_z/ℓ, can be expressed in terms of the kinematics that would be present at the center of the cylinder cross-section if the cylinder were not present:

$$F_z/\ell = C_D \rho \, \frac{D}{2} \left(\frac{H}{T}\right)^2 \, w' \, |\, w'\, | + C_M \, \frac{\rho \pi D^2}{4} \, \frac{H}{T^2} \, \frac{Dw'}{Dt} \tag{13}$$

The results of these calculations are shown in Figure 12 in which the per unit length drag and inertia force components and total force are presented.

Additional Information Based on Stream Function Tables

In addition to the applications presented, the results in the tables can be summarized or used to develop other information of general interest.

Wave Energy, Group Velocity, Shoaling, and Refraction

The definitions of potential energy, PE, and kinetic energy, KE, each averaged over a wavelength, are

$$PE = \frac{\rho g}{L} \int_o^L \frac{\eta^2}{2} \, dx \tag{14}$$

$$KE = \frac{1}{L} \int_o^L \int_{-h}^{\eta} \frac{\rho}{2} (u^2 + w^2) \, dz \, dx \tag{15}$$

The resulting expression for total wave energy density, E, based on linear wave theory is

$$E = PE + KE = \rho g \frac{H^2}{8} \tag{16}$$

and the average potential and kinetic energy are each equal to one-half of the above. Due to nonlinearities, the total energy can be substantially less than given by Equation 16, and it is convenient to define a coefficient, F,

$$E = F \rho g \frac{H^2}{8} \tag{17}$$

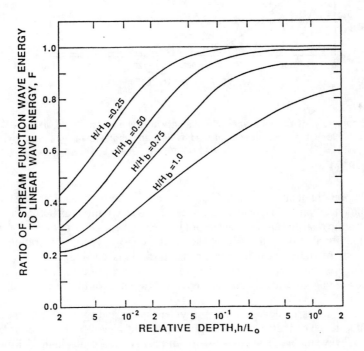

Figure 13. Relative wave energy, stream function to linear waves, for relative breaking wave heights, H/H_b = 0.25, 0.50, 0.75, and 1.0.

where $F \leqslant 1$. Figure 13 presents the value of F as a function of $(h/L_o, H/L_o)$, and it is seen that for the very shallow water, near-breaking waves, linear wave theory overestimates the actual energy in excess of a factor of 4!

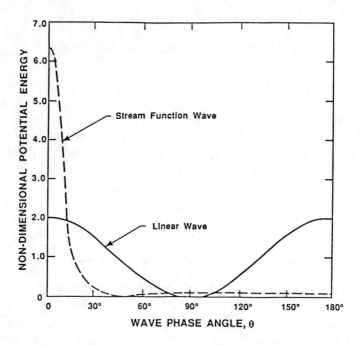

Figure 14. Comparison of potential energy variation with wave phase angle, θ, linear vs. stream function wave. Values non-dimensionalized to yield an integrated value of unity for linear wave threory; H = 31.78 ft, T = 12 s, h = 41.0 ft. (Note: This is a breaking wave.)

The distribution of potential and kinetic energy are of interest and differ substantially from the linear values. Considering the same wave conditions as before, Figure 14 presents the distribution with phase angle of the potential energy and Figure 15 presents the distribution with (θ, S) of the kinetic energy. The concentration of both components of energy near the crest phase position is striking.

Although not presented here in detail, the group velocities based on linear and SF wave theories are in good accord with the greatest difference for the 40 cases being 7%.

The previously discussed deviation in energy density, E, and agreement in group velocity results in waves increasing in height significantly more rapidly than predicted by linear wave theory. The conservation of energy flux results in the following for the combined effects of shoaling and refraction over straight and parallel bottom contours.

$$H = H_o \sqrt{\frac{F_o}{F}} \sqrt{\frac{C_{Go}}{C_G}} \sqrt{\frac{\cos \alpha_o}{\cos \alpha}} \qquad (18)$$

where the subscript "o" denotes deep water conditions, α is the angle between the wave crests and the bottom contours, F is defined in Equation 17, and the last radi-

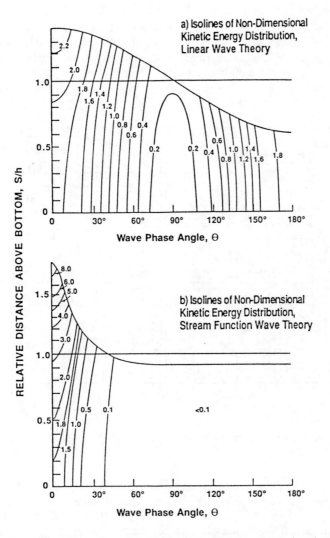

Figure 15. Comparison of kinetic energy distributions, linear vs. stream function wave theories. Values are non-dimensionalized to yield an integrated value of unity for linear wave theory; H = 31.78 ft, T = 12 s, h = 41.0 ft. (Note: This is a breaking wave.)

cal represents the effects of refraction and Snell's law of refraction applies for the case of straight and parallel bottom contours in the form

$$\frac{\sin \alpha}{C} = \frac{\sin \alpha_o}{C_o} \tag{19}$$

Figures 16–20 present results of nonlinear shoaling and refraction as determined from the SF theory for deep water directions of $0°$, $10°$, $20°$, $40°$, and $60°$, respectively. The dotted lines delineate the limits of linear wave theory applicability as defined by failing in wave direction by one degree or in wave height by one percent.

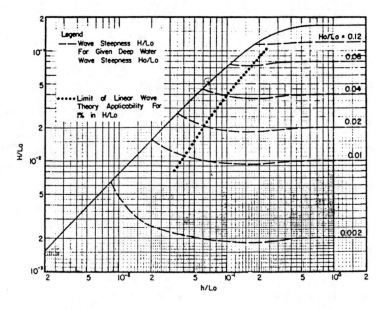

Figure 16. Shoaling for a deepwater wave direction $\alpha_o = 0°$ [5].

Swift and Dixon [10] have developed an improved method for stream function solution and applied the results to shoaling of normally incident waves. Their results are presented in Figure 21 in terms of H/H_o versus h/L_o for isolines of H_o/L_o. Comparison of results from Figures 16 and 21 demonstrate good agreement for $H_o/L_o > 0.01$; however, for lower deep water deepness values, Figure 16 predicts greater shoaling in shallow water than the results of Swift and Dixon ($H/H_o = 2.3$ versus 1.65 for $h/L_o = 0.01$, $H_o/L_o = 0.002$).

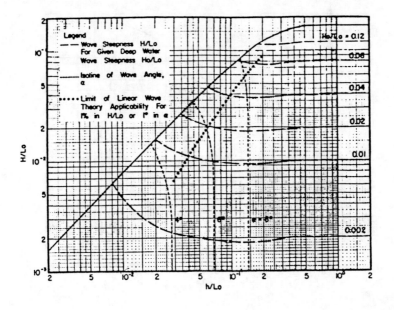

Figure 17. Combined shoaling-refraction for a deepwater wave direction $\alpha_o = 10°$ [5].

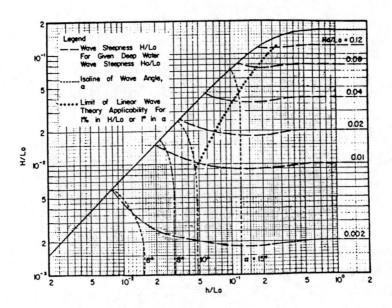

Figure 18. Combined shoaling-refraction for a deepwater wave direction $\alpha_o = 20°$ [5].

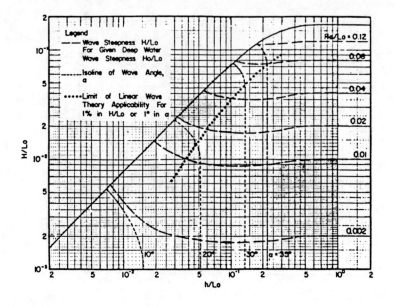

Figure 19. Combined shoaling-refraction for a deepwater wave direction $\alpha_o = 40°$ [5].

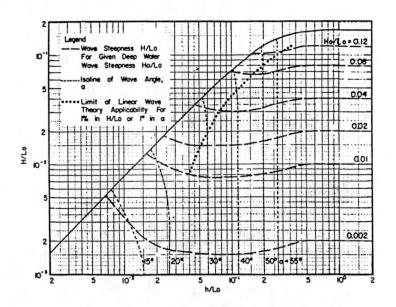

Figure 20. Combined shoaling-refraction for a deepwater wave direction $\alpha_o = 60°$ [5].

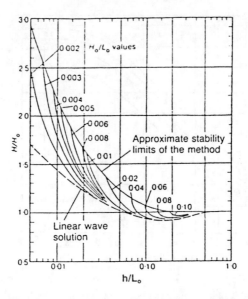

Figure 21. Wave shoaling for a wave of normal incidence, based on stream function wave theory as determined by Swift and Dixon [10].

Bottom Water Particle Velocities and Shear Stresses

Figure 22 presents the ratio $(u_b)_c/(u_b)_t$, where the subscripts "c" and "t" denote crest and trough, respectively. This ratio is very large for shallow water near breaking waves. Recalling the threshold velocities for sediment motion, this has considerable implications for sediment transport. Even though the bottom water particle velocity averaged over a wave period is zero (this must be the case as the bottom velocity, u_b, is represented as a sum of cosines, and the average of each is zero), the average bottom shear stress, τ_b, is not. The bottom shear stress, τ_b, is given in terms of the Darcy Weisbach coefficient, f, as

$$\tau_b = \frac{\rho f}{8} \mid u_b \mid u_b \tag{20}$$

Figure 23 presents the non-dimensional average bottom shear stress, $\overline{\tau_b'}$, where

$$\overline{\tau_b'} = \frac{\overline{\tau_b}}{\rho \frac{f}{8} (H/T)^2} = \frac{\overline{|u_b| u_b}}{(H/T)^2} = \overline{|u_b'| u_b'} \tag{21}$$

Finally, Figure 24 presents one example of the bottom shear stress variation over a representative one-half period of a wave cycle. Included in this figure is the critical bottom stress τ_{bc}. It is seen that accounting for the critical bottom stress would fur-

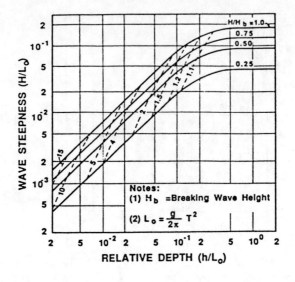

Figure 22. Isolines of ratios of peak crest to trough bottom velocities, $(u_b)_c/|(u_b)_t|$, vs. relative depth h/L_o and wave steepness, H/L_o.

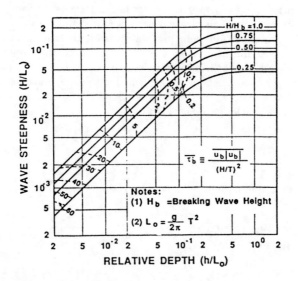

Figure 23. Isolines of non-dimensional average bottom shear stress $\overline{\tau_b}'$ vs. relative depth h/L_o, and wave steepness, H/L_o [14].

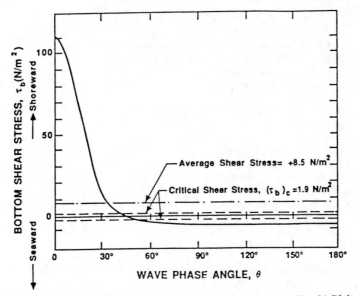

Figure 24. Example of bottom shear stress under a nonlinear wave; H = 31.78 ft, T = 12 s, h = 41 ft, D = 0.2 mm [14].

ther accentuate any onshore sediment transport. On the basis of the net onshore shear stress, cross-shelf profiles, and shoreline change data in some locations [14], there is undoubtedly significant onshore sediment across the continental shelf, thus providing substantial additional sediment input to the nearshore system.

Summary

Previous comparisons have demonstrated that the "analytical validity" of the stream function wave theory is relatively good over wide ranges of wave height, wave period and water depth. In addition, the "experimental validity" based on the agreement between theory and laboratory data appears to be generally better for the stream function theory than other theories tested.

The stream function wave theory tables can be readily applied to preliminary design for several offshore problems. This chapter has illustrated the application of these tables to a number of examples including: (1) wave profiles, velocity and acceleration components and dynamic pressures, (2) wave forces and moments on individual vertical members of an offshore platform, (3) total wave forces and moments on a multi-legged platform for oblique wave incidence, (4) wave forces on a horizontal cylinder for normal wave incidence, (5) comparisons of energy distribution in linear and nonlinear waves, and (6) bottom water particle velocities and shear stresses which are relevant to sediment transport.

For problems that are more complex or require more detail than those examined in this chapter, stream function coefficients are tabulated or may be generated using programmed microcomputers.

References

1. Dean, R. G., 1965, "Stream Function Representation of Nonlinear Ocean Waves," *Journal of Geophysical Research*, Vol. 70, Sept. pp. 4561–4572.
2. Dean, R. G., 1965, "Stream Function Wave Theory; Validity and Application," *Proceedings, ASCE Specialty Conference on Coastal Engineering*, Chapter 12, pp. 269–300.
3. Dalrymple, R. A., 1974, "A Finite Amplitude Wave on a Linear Shear Current," *Journal of Geophysical Research*, Vol. 79, No. 30, Oct., pp. 4498–4504.
4. Dalrymple, R. A., 1974, "A Finite Amplitude Wave on a Bilinear Current," *Proceedings, Fourteenth Conference on Coastal Engineering*, Chapter 36, pp. 626–641.
5. Dean, R. G., 1974, "Evaluation and Development of Water Wave Theories for Engineering Application," Vols. I and II, Special Report No. 1, *U.S. Army Coastal Engineering Research Center*, Fort Belvoir, Virginia.
6. Dean, R. G., 1970, "Relative Validities of Water Wave Theories," *ASCE, Journal of Waterways, Harbors and Coastal Engineering*, Feb. pp. 105–119.
7. Dean, R. G. and LeMehaute, B., 1970, "Experimental Validity of Water Wave Theories," Paper Presented at the *1970 ASCE Structural Engineering Conference*, Portland, Oregon, April 8.
8. Chaplin, J. R., 1980, "Developments of Stream Function Wave Theory," *Coastal Engineering*, Vol. 3, pp. 179–205.
9. Rienecker, M. M. and Fenton, J. D., 1981, "A Fourier Approximation Method for Steady Water Waves," *Journal of Fluid Mechanics*, V. 104, pp. 119–137.
10. Swift, R. H. and Dixon, J. C., 1987, "Transformation of Regular Waves," *Proceedings of the Institution of Civil Engineers*, Part 2, Vol. 83, pp. 359–380.
11. Cokelet, E. D., 1977, "Steep Gravity Waves in Water of Uniform Arbitrary Depth," *Philosophical Transactions of the Royal Society of London*, A286, pp. 182–230.
12. Schwartz, L. W., 1974, "Computer Extension and Analytical Continuation of Stokes' Expansion For Gravity Waves," *Journal of Fluid Mechanics*, Vol. 62, pp. 555–578.
13. Dean, R. G., 1972, "Application of Stream Function Wave Theory to Offshore Design Problems," *Proceedings, Offshore Technology Conference*, Paper No. OTC 1613, pp. I-925 to I-940.
14. Dean, R. G., 1987, "Additional Sediment Input to the Nearshore Region," Special Edition *Shore and Beach*, Symposium to Honor Dean Morrough O'Brien, Vol. 55, Nos. 3–4, July–October, pp. 76–81.

CHAPTER 3

SHORT-CRESTED WAVES

John R. C. Hsu

Department of Civil Engineering
The University of Western Australia
Nedlands, Western Australia

CONTENTS

Introduction

A short-crested wave, being a typical three-dimensional wave phenomenon, is a propagating surface wave with a free surface elevation which is doubly periodic in two perpendicular directions, these being along and normal to the direction of propagation. As shown in Figure 1, a short-crested wave system can be produced either by the interaction of two progressive waves angled to each other, or by oblique reflection from a maritime structure. The double periodicity is characterized by the pattern of island crests that are formed at intersections of the component waves as seen in Figure 2, hence the surface undulations of such a wave system are more complex than its wave components. These isolated crests propagate in a combined

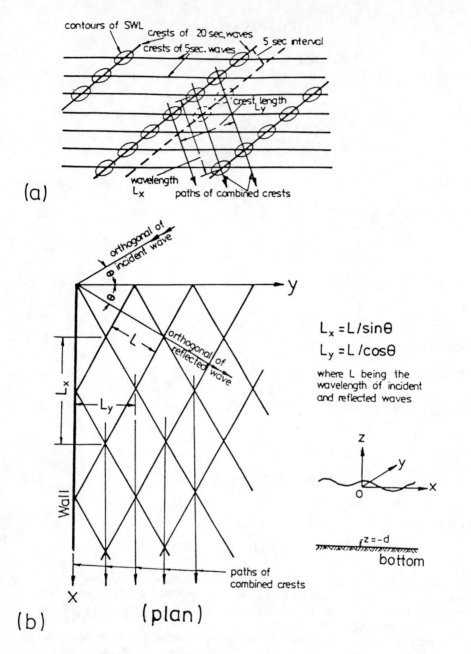

$$L_x = L/\sin\theta$$
$$L_y = L/\cos\theta$$

where L being the wavelength of incident and reflected waves

Figure 1. Formation of short-crested waves, (a) by two progressive waves angled to each other [58], (b) by oblique reflection from a vertical wall.

direction, providing not only a wavelength but also a definite crest length that is the distance between successive crests normal to the former at the same time. Unlike the two-dimensional wave motions, or the long-crested waves, in which the crest length may be considered as infinite, the transverse distance between adjacent crests in a short-crested system is finite, thus introduction of the term "short-crested."

Short-crested waves have wider occurrence in nature than their two-dimensional counterparts and are extremely important in engineering applications on a sedimentary bed, especially in their great propensity for scouring the bed in front of a reflecting structure. The advancement of studying this wave phenomenon, from the two to the three-dimensional case, is not a simple mathematical matter of introducing one additional dimension to the governing equations, nor adding extra terms to the final expressions for its pertinent wave quantities, but rather of including a very complicated field of wave motions in a physical sense. This section discusses the engineering significance of such a wave system and provides a detailed literature review of the development of short-crested wave theories.

Engineering Significance

Jeffreys [1, 2] investigated short-crested waves near the shore, and pointed out that water waves generated by weak and relatively strong winds blowing over the ocean surface are short-crested; whereas those influenced by strong winds are more long-crested. Because most gravity waves are generated by winds, short-crested

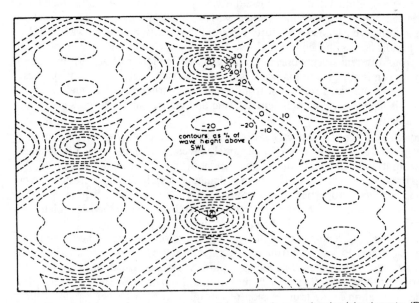

Figure 2. Sketch of the surface contours of a short-crested wave, showing island crests. (Reproduced with permission of R. Silvester, University of Western Australia.)

waves can be developed right from the beginning of this generation process. With frequent cyclonic activity associated with some specific areas of the world, the generation of a short-crested wave system may be considered paramount; whereas the long-crested waves appear to be predominant in shallow water.

Consider a simple interaction of two trains of long-crested waves at an angle to each other, of which the amplitudes and wavelengths of these two primary interacting waves may or may not differ from each other. As mentioned earlier, island mounds are created at the intersections of the crests, and at the intersections of troughs cumulative depressions occur. The combined crests travel along the diagonal direction formed by successive crests of the longer waves and the crest alignments of the shorter ones, if they differ in wave period, as illustrated in Figure 1. The wavelength (L_x) is the distance between the successive combined crests in the direction of propagation, while the crest length (L_y) is gauged in the traverse direction between adjacent crests. The ratio of wavelength to crest length is dependent upon the angle between the two interacting wave trains.

The symmetrical crest patterns produced by oblique interaction may be accepted as diamond shaped, which is an ideal case for linear wave superposition; whereas it may be hexagonal in shape with stems of finite dimension at the island crest due to nonlinear wave interaction between the two component trains [3]. For such a wave system induced by winds, irregular hexagons have been observed [4]. These crest patterns have flat troughs and steep crests. Apart from being doubly periodic in two perpendicular directions in surface elevations, the resulting wave height is more than double of its component waves, and the combined crest also travels faster than its long-crested components.

It has been submitted that short-crested wave systems occur more often than their long-crested counterparts. Short-crested waves can be found through diffraction behind an offshore island or structure, differential refraction of swell waves of differing period across the continental shelf or shoal, concurrent arrival of swell waves from different storm zones, oblique wave reflection from a maritime structure, and even in the generation process itself as already mentioned. Among these examples, oblique wave reflection from a maritime structure, be it land-based or offshore, is the most unfavorable engineering application, and is discussed later in this handbook.

Although short-crested waves have wide occurrence in nature, they have long been neglected compared to two-dimensional waves. This omission is understandable owing to the complexity of the phenomenon, the non-recognition of its engineering importance, and the difficulty in adequately describing short-crested waves and their pertinent properties. Short-crested waves are only now beginning to be appreciated, as evidenced by the theoretical research into wave theories related to this wave system [5–12], and in practical engineering applications [13–25].

Silvester [13] has reported tests of ripple patterns on a movable bed model involving short-crested waves in front of a wall (see Figure 3). Bands of swirling and snake-like ripples have been found among parallel ripples, which are both normal and parallel to the reflecting wall in an alternating manner. He has also noted a possible application in the transmission of littoral drift across river mouth or harbor entrance without bar formation [14]. Gjertveit [15] mentioned the effect of short-crestedness in sea waves when designing large floating pontoons or structures. Wave loading on large cylinders in short-crested seas using a spectral approach has been examined [16], short-crested breaking waves and the practical consideration of this wave system in the loss of ships in the North Sea has been discussed [18, 19].

The water-particle motions within this wave system have been shown to vary spatially, both in the horizontal plane and in the vertical direction as depicted in Figure 4, for a short-crested wave with wave obliquity $\theta = 45°$ defined in Figure 1 [13, 17, 24]. Kinematics of the water-particle motions exhibit strong shearing of the sediment close to the bed at certain alignments parallel to a reflecting structure. Due to this complexity of water-particle motions, it has an extremely important effect on a sedimentary bed.

It may be concluded that a short-crested wave system is more complicated in free surface profiles and steeper than its primary component waves. It creates higher

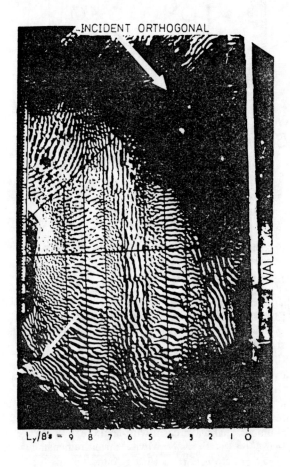

Figure 3. Patterns of sand ripple resulting from wave reflecting at 45° on a wall, showing bands of swirling and parallel ripples [13].

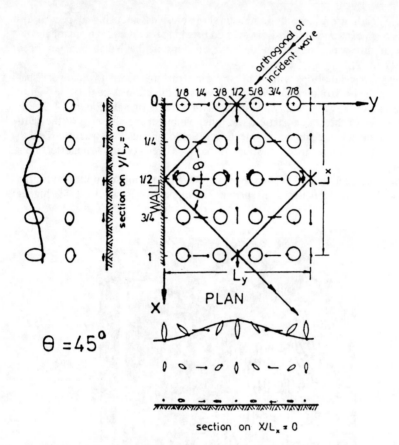

$\theta = 45°$

Figure 4. Sketches of orbital motions of water particles within a short-crested wave system, showing spatial variations in vertical and horizontal directions; $\theta = 45°$.

breaking waves than the usual standing waves [18], has very complicated water-particle motions [13, 24], produces higher wave pressures on a vertical wall than the normal standing waves [25], and has a great propensity for scouring the bed in front of maritime structures [23].

Literature Review

Two-dimensional surface gravity waves, such as progressive and usual standing waves, have been extensively studied over the past 140 years since Stokes [26]. However, the three-dimensional wave case, with lateral extent, has received rather little attention. Research on short-crested waves started rather late as compared to that on long-crested waves. No report had been found on this topic before 1924, when wind-generated short-crested waves near the shore were examined by Jeffreys. It was not until the early 1950s that limited observations of this phenomenon had been made by Keulegan [27] and Van Dorn [28]. The generation of short-crested waves was later carried out in the laboratory using wind tunnels [4].

Although the linear theory of short-crested waves was first sought [1] in 1924, it was only extended in 1952 to a second-order solution by Fuchs, based upon the work of Stokes [26]. In 1957, a rather complicated solution for the diffraction of short-crested waves around an obstacle using Green function was developed [6]. Chappelear [7] systematically extended Fuchs' solution further to a third-order approximation using a classical power expansion. Both solutions were in dimensional form, derived from an assumption of steady motion when viewed from a coordinate system moving parallel to the direction of propagation of the combined crests. Later, a second-order solution for wave interaction was derived [8], also using a perturbation method. Despite these pioneer works, short-crested waves have received very little attention and have generally been ignored in engineering design, until the early 1970s, when mass transport due to interacting waves was investigated by several researchers [29–32], in which only linear wave theory was used.

Linear wave theory by superposition of two velocity potentials and water surface elevations is the simplest form of short-crested waves. For such a wave of finite amplitude, wave theories have been systematically derived using a perturbation method, which is a successive process similar to that for two-dimensional waves. Such a method can be employed to solve the nonlinear governing equations for three-dimensional irrotational wave motion in water of finite depth. The set of linear equations to each order of approximation so deduced then yields the desirable solution to the original problem.

In applying this method to the motion of short-crested waves, the primary wave quantities, such as velocity potential ϕ, water surface elevation η, and wave angular frequency ω, are expanded as a power series. Certain final forms in a trigonometrical function are presumed for these wave quantities in the process of deriving them, which provides a solution to each order of approximation. Because the short-crested wave is the result of two long-crested wave trains interacting at an angle to each other, its solution should yield a standing wave at one end and a progressive wave at the other, which are limiting cases. This physical interpretation is a desirable criterion for checking the validity of the wave theory.

The second-order solution obtained by Fuchs [5] for the velocity potential and water surface elevation was not tested to the limit of a standing wave. The expression of velocity potential to the second order did not include a necessary term in the time t, which is now accepted as a characteristic feature of standing waves. His equation for mass-transport velocity within the fluid domain was independent of the vertical coordinate y, which was later identified as the condition at the free surface [32]. However, Fuchs was first to consider the energy flux and the transformation of short-crested waves in shoaling water over gently sloping beaches.

Chappelear [7] found a third-order approximation to short-crested waves, using a classical power expansion in terms of a parameter that was proportional to the ratio of wave height to wavelength of the short-crested wave itself. This is similar to the derivation of a progressive wave of finite amplitude in that direction, implying the possible preclusion of yielding a standing wave in that limit. However, Chappelear's solution could not yield even the well known forms of Stokes nor the standing waves in the limiting angles of approach. This difficulty was acknowledged by

Chappelear himself. He further suggested that the problem of the limiting two-dimensional case can easily be solved by direct calculation from the original governing equations, rather than be reduced from the general three-dimensional case derived [7]. The solutions developed by Chappelear were complicated by interrelated coefficients and were very lengthy mathematically, making them rather difficult for engineers. It is interesting to note that Mollo-Christensen [33] reported that Chappelear's solution was stable for short-crested but modulationally unstable for long-crested wavelengths.

To overcome these difficulties, a different perturbation parameter was employed, in which the expansion parameter was related to the wavelength of the component waves [9, 10]. Consequently a third-order approximation was derived. This permitted the final solution for the general three-dimensional case to be directly reduced to the two-dimensional limiting cases of standing and Stokes waves.

Another innovation made by Hsu et al. [9] was to apply a dimensionless wave angular frequency, ω_o, which had been previously employed in deriving standing wave theory to finite amplitude [34] to simplify this complex analysis. This variable, ω_o, makes the complicated higher-order solution in power expansions simpler to express. Thus, the resultant solutions for velocity potential and water surface elevation up to third-order were more systematic [9]. These solutions were later critically examined [25] and were found to be correct to that order in wave height, but the original expressions for wave pressure required minor correction.

Because the complex manipulations in using a perturbation method makes manual higher-order derivations very laborious, especially to a three-dimensional wave, wave theory higher than a third-order has not been developed analytically for the present short-crested waves. Instead, a numerical scheme employing Fourier series has been reported [11, 12]. Roberts [11] and Roberts and Schwartz [12] presented a numerical method involving truncated Fourier series up to a 27th order for a short-crested wave in an infinitely deep ocean.

Short-crested waves can also be derived from wave interactions directly. Based upon works on wave interactions in the early 1960s, Hamada [8] studied the characteristics of the secondary wave interaction in two dimensions to a second-order. The problem of partial oblique reflection from a rigid vertical wall was investigated, and it was found that it can be reduced to the solution for a simple short-crested wave system [9]. The calculation of energy flux associated with short-crested waves has been reported [5, 12], as well as the radiation stresses within this wave system [35].

All the short-crested wave theories previously mentioned, whether being derived by a perturbation or numerical method or even from wave interaction, are only applicable for the cases of a reflecting structure with infinite extent and for full oblique reflection without attenuation. In reality, because the reflecting structure is finite lengthwise, and the resultant wave profiles of the short-crested waves attenuate in amplitude in the direction away from the structure, Goda [36] proposed to treat the dispersion of the reflected wave using a linear approach that was similar to wave diffraction.

The quantities derived directly from a wave theory, either being velocity potential, surface elevation, or wave angular frequency, are beyond the immediate reach of an engineer. It is therefore beneficial to derive other physical quantities associated with this wave system, which can be of direct engineering applications. These quantities include the crest height above the still water level, maximum wave height in a higher-order solution, wave speed, the displacements of water particles, the Eulerian water-particle velocities in the interior, and pressure variations throughout the whole region. Among these quantities, the breaking height of a short-crested wave system has recently been proposed [10, 18, 19, 38, 39, 40]. The complex water-particle motions close to the bed have been studied for the laminar case [10, 13, 24, 37], and considered for a rough turbulent condition [41].

Wave Theory by Perturbation

Velocity potential ϕ (or stream function φ) and water surface elevation η, as primary wave variables, have traditionally been employed to formulate wave theories for surface gravity waves. Secondary quantities, such as kinematics of water particles (velocity field and displacement of particles) and pressure distribution, are then obtained from relevant governing equations using these primary variables. To derive these quantities, first, a coordinate system is assigned in relation to the proposed direction of wave propagation. The relationship between the potential function and velocity components is then set, assuming either $u = \partial\phi/\partial x$ or $u = -\partial\phi/\partial x$, implying that the velocity potential is either increasing or decreasing in the positive direction of the x-axis, the direction of wave propagation; likewise to velocities in other directions in a three-dimensional case.

From wave theories available for short-crested waves, it was revealed that many different expressions of velocity potential and water surface elevation exist. A brief discussion of the factors affecting the magnitude of a velocity potential is necessary in order to address these discrepancies. Velocity potential ϕ is normally the product of four independent factors: the overall sign (positive or negative), dimension (or magnitude), depth and phase factors. The phase factor employs a trigonometric function (either sine or cosine), while the depth factor is often in hyperbolic form. The dimension factor includes wave amplitude, wave frequency, and wave number or acceleration of gravity. Several basic forms of velocity potential can be found in progressive wave theory, often with different orientations of coordinate systems and symbols.

In the two-dimensional wave case, the expression for velocity potential is relatively simple compared to three-dimensional waves. However, for short-crested waves, as produced by oblique reflection from a long maritime structure, the expression is further complicated by the relationship between the assumed direction of propagation for the incident and reflected waves to the orientation of the x-y axes in plan. Either sine or cosine functions can be selected to express the phase factor for the propagating direction (presently in the positive x-direction, see Figures 1 and 5) and the direction perpendicular to the wall (now the positive y-direction). There is no fixed rule to this selection, nor the orientation of the coordinate system. As a result of these free choices, there is a variety of forms to velocity potential, and hence to water surface elevation [5, 7, 8, 9, 11]. Such a difference can also be detected in the linear theory [29–32]. As a matter of fact, different symbols so used make a uniform comparison unattainable.

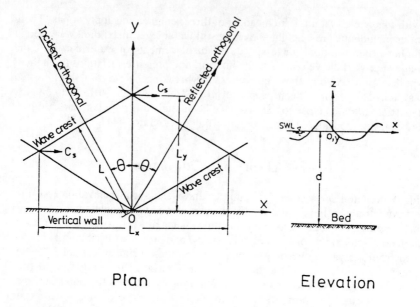

Plan   Elevation

Figure 5. Definition sketch of short-crested waves produced by oblique reflection, showing a diamond-shaped crest pattern and Cartesian coordinate system.

An attempt should be made to compare short-crested wave theories available on the same common grounds, using the same coordinate system, the same direction in which the incident and reflected waves travel, and identical mathematical symbols (see "Notation" at the end of the chapter for a list of symbols and Figure 5 for a common Cartesian coordinate system).

To meet these requirements, a typical velocity component in the x-direction is defined as $u = \partial\phi/\partial x$ from the velocity potential, implying increasing potential in the positive x-direction. Consequently, surface elevation is derived from $\eta = -(\partial\phi/\partial t)/g$, which is evaluated at the still water level $z = 0$. It is further assumed that an observer stands on the crest of a vertical wall at the origin of a Cartesian coordinate system, as shown in Figure 5, hence having the incident wave approaching the wall from his left. The angle of approach θ for the incident wave is measured between its orthogonal and the normal to the wall, or alternatively, between the wave crest and the reflecting wall [the x-axis]. Simple reflection from the vertical wall ensures the same angle θ can conveniently be assumed to be the reflecting orthogonals.

A "simple short-crested wave system," as will be implied from time to time within this chapter, is defined as a wave system formed by two progressive waves of equal amplitudes and periods propagating at an oblique angle to each other. In the case of oblique reflection from a maritime structure, full reflection will be assumed, accepting the same amplitudes and wavelengths for both component waves. Although, fully reflected waves may only be applicable over a short length and width of water area adjacent to a reflecting wall. Where component waves of different amplitude are applicable, a reminding note will be made.

Governing Equations

Consider a three-dimensional irrotational wave motion bounded above by a free surface, below by an impermeable horizontal bed and to one side by a rigid vertical wall [9] , as in Figure 5. Suppose the fluid to be inviscid, incompressible, and of uniform depth, with wave damping neglected. The simplest form of short-crested wave results from oblique reflection from a vertical wall, implying equal periods at least, and similar amplitudes for incident and reflected waves. The angle (θ) of waves approaching and leaving the reflecting wall are measured between the orthogonals and the normal to the wall, as also depicted in Figure 5. Island wave crests appear at the intersection of wave crests. The resulting diamond-shaped crest patterns due to oblique reflection are assumed. The Mach-stem effect, which occurs at large angles of θ, will be ignored.

The irrotationality of the fluid motion leads to the existence of a velocity potential ϕ which gives rise to the Eulerian water-particle velocity components as

$$u = \phi_x, \ v = \phi_y, \ w = \phi_z \tag{1}$$

in the x, y, and z-directions, respectively, where the velocity potential $\phi(x,y,z,t)$ satisfies Laplace's equation

$$\nabla^2\phi = \phi_{xx} + \phi_{yy} + \phi_{zz} = 0 \tag{2}$$

The dynamic boundary condition at the free surface (DFSBC) is

$$\phi_t + g\eta + \frac{1}{2} (\phi_x^2 + \phi_y^2 + \phi_z^2) = 0, \text{ at } z = \eta \tag{3}$$

and the kinematic boundary condition at the free surface (KFSBC) is

$$\eta_t - \phi_z + \phi_x \ \eta_x + \phi_y\eta_y = 0 \text{ at } z = \eta \tag{4}$$

while the bottom and wall boundary conditions are

$$\phi_z = 0 \text{ at } z = -d, \ \phi_y = 0 \text{ at } y = 0 \tag{5}$$

where $\eta = \eta(x,y,t)$ is the water surface elevation of the short-crested waves

g = acceleration due to gravity

subscripts (x,y,z,t) = differentiations with respect to the Cartesian coordinates (see Figure 5) and the time t.

The problem set is to determine solutions for the physical quantities ϕ, η, and velocity components [u, v, and w] that satisfy Equations 2 to 5 and other additional conditions to be specified. The required solutions can be cast in dimensional or dimensionless form. As mentioned earlier, a dimensional approach was employed [5, 7, 8]. On the other hand, Hsu et al. [9] worked on a dimensionless form that made high-order solutions simpler to present.

The velocity potential ϕ at the free surface η is then expressed in terms of the Taylor expansion at $z = 0$ instead of $z = \eta$. Substituting the resultant expansion of ϕ, which now contains the perturbed components, into Equations 3 and 4 and collecting terms of each order in ϵ yields the necessary dynamic and kinematic boundary conditions to each order of approximation for condition at $z = 0$. Appropriate solutions at each order of approximation can then be obtained. Only third-order solutions derived by a perturbation method are discussed in the following section.

Third-Order Solution

Chappelear [7] and Hsu et al. [9] have presented analytical solutions to third-order for a short-crested wave, employing a perturbation method. Both solutions give expressions of velocity potential and water surface elevation using amplitude of the resultant short-crested wave itself. Therefore, the relationship between the resultant wave system and its component waves cannot directly be correlated.

However, there are three major differences in these two solutions. First, Chappelear's solutions were in dimensional form, while the solution of Hsu et al. was cast in dimensionless form. Second, different expansion parameters ϵ were used to derive the primary wave quantities in a perturbation method, in which Chappelear related wave steepness to the wavelength of the short-crested wave itself, but Hsu et al. used that of the component waves. Third, Chappelear's solution was complicated by interrelated coefficients, while the coefficients of Hsu et al. were very simple. Finally, Chappelear's solution could not yield the well-known forms of Stokes and standing waves in the limiting angles of approach; on the other hand, the solution of Hsu et al. can produce both limiting conditions.

To overcome the difficulty experienced by Chappelear [7] in yielding the desired expressions for the limiting two-dimensional cases directly from the final equations of the general three-dimensional case, Hsu et al. [9] have recalculated a third-order solution, also using a perturbation method. They used an expansion parameter in wave steepness, which related wave amplitude of the short-crested wave to the wavelength of the incident or reflected waves. This encompassed all angles of incidence and thus the solution could be extended to both standing and Stokes waves. Another innovation, previously employed [34], was to introduce a dimensionless angular wave frequency ω_0 (see Equation 17), which makes the complicated series involved in this higher order solution simpler to express.

The third-order approximation so derived is in a dimensionless form, reducible to standing and Stokes waves at the limiting angles of approach to the same order [9]. The pertinent physical quantities associated with this short-crested wave system, i.e., the velocity potential, water surface elevation, wave angular frequency, wave celerity, Eulerian water-particle velocities plus the wave pressure, are also available to third-order. All solutions are presented without interrelating coefficients, as required by Chappelear [7]. Only a condensed version of the third-order approximation [9] will be included here.

A set of non-dimensional quantities was introduced to transform the nonlinear governing equations that describe the three-dimensional irrotational water waves in finite depth of water, as given by Equations 1 to 5. Let ϵ represent the small parameter ka, where a is the amplitude of the short-crested wave to the first order, and k is the wave number $2\pi/L_A$, L_A being the wavelength of the incident or reflected wave also to first order. The following dimensionless quantities may be introduced:

$$
\left.
\begin{aligned}
&\hat{x} = k\,x,\ \hat{y} = k\,y,\ \hat{z} = k\,z,\ \hat{t} = \sigma\,t,\ \hat{d} = k\,d \\
&\hat{\phi}\,(\hat{x},\ \hat{y},\ \hat{z},\ \hat{t}) = k^2\epsilon^{-1}\,(gk)^{-0.5}\,\phi(x,\ y,\ z,\ t) \\
&\hat{\eta}\,(\hat{x},\ \hat{y},\ \hat{t}) = k\,\epsilon^{-1}\,\eta\,(x,\ y,\ t) \\
&\hat{\omega} = \sigma/(gk)^{0.5}
\end{aligned}
\right\}
\tag{6}
$$

where σ = angular frequency of the incident (or reflected) wave (i.e., $2\pi/T$, where T is the wave period in seconds)

z, y, z = Cartesian co-ordinates

t = time

Had the relationships $\hat{x} = k_x x$ and $\hat{y} = k_y y$ been used, instead of the present $\hat{x} = kx$ and $\hat{y} = ky$, it would not be possible to separate completely the x from the y components in the final equations for the two-dimensional case.

The carets (ˆ) denoting dimensionless quantities will now be omitted for the sake of simplicity, and unless otherwise specified. The dimensional governing equations (Equations 1 to 5) may now be transformed in terms of these dimensionless quantities to

$$
\nabla^2\phi = 0
\tag{7}
$$

$$
\eta + \omega\phi_t + \frac{1}{2}\,\epsilon\,(\phi_x^2 + \phi_y^2 + \phi_z^2) = 0 \quad \text{at } z = \epsilon\eta
\tag{8}
$$

$$
\phi_z - \omega\eta_t - \epsilon\eta_x\phi_x - \epsilon\eta_y\phi_y = 0 \quad \text{at } z = \epsilon\eta
\tag{9}
$$

$$
\phi_z = 0 \text{ at } z = -d,\ \phi_y = 0 \quad \text{at } y = 0
\tag{10}
$$

To solve for the current unknowns (ϕ, η, and ω), additional conditions are further required to specify the short-crested wave, which include conditions mainly in periodicity and relationships between wave number components. First, as shown in Figure 5, let L be the wavelength of the incident and reflected waves, and L_x and L_y the distances between crests in the x and y directions, then the components of the wave number k may be defined, respectively, as

$$
\left.
\begin{aligned}
k_x &= \frac{2\pi}{L_x} = \frac{2\pi}{(L/\sin\theta)} = \sin\theta\; k = mk \\[2mm]
k_y &= \frac{2\pi}{L_y} = \frac{2\pi}{(L/\cos\theta)} = \cos\theta\; k = nk
\end{aligned}
\right\}
\tag{11}
$$

where θ is defined as in Figure 5; thus

$$
k_x^2 + k_y^2 = k^2, \text{ or } m^2 + n^2 = 1
\tag{12}
$$

When θ becomes zero, a normal standing wave occurs ($m = 0$, $n = 1$); while a progressive wave equal to the incident component results, if θ is $\pi/2$ ($m = 1$, $n = 0$).

Second, additional boundary conditions from the limiting cases of $\theta = 0°$ and $\pi/2$ are required. For the complete standing wave, conditions for conservation of water mass, the periodicity of the wave motion, the phase and amplitude of wave motion are specified. Similar conditions are also required for the progressive wave, which preserves the water mass and the periodicity in time and space [9]. Third, a further condition to provide a unique solution, which was introduced firstly by Tadjbakhsh and Keller [34], is also imposed.

Solutions for the dimensionless quantities ϕ, η and ω are required to satisfy Equations 7 to 10 and the additional conditions previously mentioned. It is assumed that these quantities can be expanded as power series in the small parameter ϵ as

$$
\left.
\begin{aligned}
\phi(x,y,z,t) &= \phi_1 + \epsilon\phi_2 + \frac{1}{2}\epsilon^2\,\phi_3 + \ldots \\[4mm]
\eta(x,y,t) &= \eta_1 + \epsilon\eta_2 + \frac{1}{2}\epsilon^2\,\eta_3 + \ldots \\[4mm]
\omega &= \omega_1 + \epsilon\omega_2 + \frac{1}{2}\epsilon^2\,\omega_3 + \ldots
\end{aligned}
\right\}
\tag{13}
$$

where ϕ_1 and η_1 are first-order components, ϕ_2 and η_2 second-order, and ϕ_3 and η_3 third-order, and so on. The dimensionless velocity potential at the free surface may be expressed in terms of the Taylor expansion at $z = 0$ instead of $z = \epsilon\eta$, so that

$$
\phi(x,y,\epsilon\eta,t) = \phi_1 + \epsilon\,(\eta_1\phi_{1z} + \phi_2) + \epsilon^2\left(\eta_2\phi_{1z} + \frac{1}{2}\eta_1^2\phi_{1zz} + \eta_1\phi_{2z} + \frac{1}{2}\phi_3\right)
$$

$$
+ \epsilon^3\left(\frac{1}{2}\eta_3\phi_{1z} + \eta_1\phi_2\phi_{1zz} + \frac{1}{6}\eta_1^3\phi_{1zzz} + \eta_2\phi_{2z}\right.
\tag{14}
$$

$$
\left. + \frac{1}{2}\eta_1^2\phi_{2zz} + \frac{1}{2}\eta_1\phi_{3z} + \frac{1}{6}\phi_4\right) + O(\epsilon^4)
$$

Substituting Equation 14 into Equations 8 and 9, i.e., the DFSBC and KFSBC, and collecting terms of each order in ϵ yields the necessary equations for each order of approximation for conditions at $z = 0$. The solutions in dimensionless form that satisfy the boundary conditions can then be derived to each order of approximation. Solutions for the lower orders will be used to obtain solutions for the higher orders.

The resulting expressions for the velocity potential, water surface elevation and angular frequency to each order of approximation have been reported [9, 10] and summarized as follows: To the first-order approximation in dimensionless form,

$$\phi_1 = \omega_o \frac{\cosh (z + d)}{\sinh (d)} \cos (ny) \sin (mx - t) \tag{15}$$

$$\eta_1 = \cos (ny) \cos (mx - t) \tag{16}$$

$$\omega_1 = [\tanh (d)]^{0.5} = \omega_o \tag{17}$$

in which $m = \sin \theta$ and $n = \cos \theta$ are defined in Equation 11.

The complete solutions in dimensionless form for the second-order approximation are given by

$$\phi_2 = \beta_1 t + \beta_2 \cosh 2(z + d) \cos 2ny \sin 2(mx - t) \\ + \beta_3 \cosh 2m(z + d) \sin 2(mx - t) \tag{18}$$

$$\eta_2 = b_1 \cos 2ny \cos 2(mx - t) + b_2 \cos 2(mx - t) + b_3 \cos 2ny \tag{19}$$

$$\omega_2 = 0 \tag{20}$$

in which

$$\beta_1 = \frac{1}{8} (-\omega_o^{-3} + \omega_o), \quad \beta_2 = \frac{3(\omega_o^{-7} - \omega_o)}{16 \cosh (2d)} \\ \\ \beta_3 = \frac{K_2}{16 \cosh (2md)} = \frac{(1 + \omega_m^4)K_1}{16 \cosh (2md)} \tag{21}$$

and

$$b_1 = \frac{1}{8} (3\omega_o^{-6} - \omega_o^{-2}), \quad b_2 = \frac{1}{8} [3\omega_o^2 - \omega_o^{-2} (m^2 - n^2) + \omega_o K_2] \\ \\ b_3 = \frac{1}{8} [\omega_o^2 - \omega_o^{-2} (m^2 - n^2)] \tag{22}$$

where

$$K_2 = \frac{(1 + \omega_m^4)\ [(2m^2 - 2n^2 + 1)\omega_o^{-3} - 3\omega_o]}{[(1 + \omega_m^4) - m(\omega_m/\omega_o)^2]}$$

$$K_1 = K_2/(1 + \omega_m^4), \quad \omega_m^2 = \tanh\ (md) \tag{23}$$

It is worth noting that the second-order velocity potential ϕ_2 contains one time-dependent term and one progressive form propagating in the x-direction (along the wall), in addition to the primary term showing double periodicity in both x and y-directions. This is similar to the result of Hamada [8] for the case of a simple short-crested wave, in which his $B_{24} = 0$. However, as reported [8], a fourth term in "sin(2ny)" may be included in the second-order ϕ_2 if the reflected wave has different wave height and period. Also, the water surface elevation to the second-order η_2 has a non-constant term that is dependent upon distance from the wall (in the y direction), which is equivalent to η_{24} of Hamada [8]. At the limiting angles of approaches, Equations 18 and 19 can readily be reduced to the forms of two-dimensional waves. There is no change of wavelength to the second-order approximation, according to Equation 20.

Solutions obtained for the third-order approximation are given as follows:

$$\begin{aligned}
\phi_3 = &\ \beta_{13} \cosh \gamma_{13}(z + d) \cos 3ny \sin (mx - t) \\
&+ \beta_{31} \cosh \gamma_{31}(z + d) \cos ny \sin 3(mx - t) \\
&+ \beta_{33} \cosh 3(z + d) \cos 3ny \sin 3(mx - t)
\end{aligned} \tag{24}$$

$$\begin{aligned}
\eta_3 = &\ [b_{11} \cos ny + b_{13} \cos 3ny] \cos (mx - t) \\
&+ [b_{31} \cos ny + b_{33} \cos 3ny] \cos 3(mx - t)
\end{aligned} \tag{25}$$

$$\omega_3 = \frac{1}{32}\ (6\omega_o^{-7} - 8\omega_o^{-3} - 6\omega_o - 8\omega_o^5) - \frac{1}{8}\ m\omega_o^2\omega_m^2\ K_1 - \frac{1}{16}\ (\omega_o^4 - 4m^2 + 1)K_2$$

$$+ m^2 \left[\frac{1}{32}\ (3\omega_o^{-7} - 2\omega_o^{-3} + 43\omega_o) - \frac{1}{8}\ (m^2 - n^2)\omega_o^{-3}\right]$$

$$+ n^2 \left[\frac{1}{32}\ (3\omega_o^{-7} - 2\omega_o^{-3} + 5\omega_o) + \frac{1}{8}\ (m^2 - n^2)\omega_o^{-3}\right] \tag{26}$$

in which β and b constants are given by

$$\begin{aligned}
\beta_{13} = &\ [16 \cosh \gamma_{13}d\ (\gamma_{13} \tanh \gamma_{13}d - \omega_o^{-2})]^{-1}\ [(-3\omega_o^{-7} + 8\omega_o^{-3} - 3\omega_o + 2\omega_o^5) \\
&+ m^2(-6\omega_o^{-7} + 4\omega_o^{-3} - 10\omega_o) + n^2(6\omega_o^{-7} - 4\omega_o^{-3} - 2\omega_o) \\
&+ 4\ n^2(m^2 - n^2)\omega_o^{-3}]
\end{aligned} \tag{27a}$$

$$\beta_{31} = [16 \cosh \gamma_{31}d \ (\gamma_{31} \tanh \gamma_{31}d - 9\omega_o^2)]^{-1} \ [(- 9\omega_o^{-7} + 64\omega_o^{-3} - 33\omega_o + 18\omega_o^5)$$
$$+ 36m \ \omega_o^2\omega_m^2 K_1 + 2(3\omega_o^4 - 8m^2 - 1)K_2 + m^2 \ (- 18\omega_o^{-7} + 4\omega_o^{-3} - 30\omega_o)$$
$$+ 4m^2 \ (m^2 - n^2) \ \omega_o^{-3} + n^2 \ (18\omega_o^{-7} - 4\omega_o^{-3} + 2\omega_o)] \tag{27b}$$

$$\beta_{33} = [(1 + 3\omega_o^4) \ (9\omega_o^{-13} - 22\omega_o^{-9} + 13\omega_o^{-5})]/[128 \cosh (3d)] \tag{27c}$$

and

$$b_{11} = \frac{1}{16} \ (5\omega_o^{-4} - 4 + 4\omega_o^4) + \frac{1}{8} \ m\omega_o\omega_m^2 K_1 + \frac{1}{16} \ (\omega_o^3 + 2m^2\omega_o^{-1} - \omega_o^{-1})K_2$$

$$+ \frac{1}{32} \ (m^2 + n^2) \ (3\omega_o^{-8} - 2\omega_o^{-4} - 1) - \frac{1}{8} \ (m^2 - n^2)^2 \ \omega_o^{-4} \tag{28a}$$

$$b_{13} = \frac{1}{16} \ (9\omega_o^{-4} - 6 + 2\omega_o^4) - \frac{1}{16} \ m^2(3\omega_o^{-8} + 5) + \frac{1}{16} \ n^2(3\omega_o^{-8} + 1)$$

$$+ [16(\gamma_{13} \tanh \gamma_{13}d - \omega_o^2)]^{-1} \ [(- 3\omega_o^{-6} + 8\omega_o^{-2} - 3\omega_o^2 + 2\omega_o^6)$$
$$+ m^2(- 6\omega_o^{-6} + 4\omega_o^{-2} - 10\omega_o^2) + n^2(6\omega_o^{-6} - 4\omega_o^{-2} - 2\omega_o^2)$$
$$+ 4n^2(m^2 - n^2)\omega_o^{-2}] \tag{28b}$$

$$b_{31} = \frac{1}{16} \ (21\omega_o^{-4} - 10 + 6\omega_o^4) - \frac{3}{4} \ m\omega_o\omega_m^2 K_1 - \frac{1}{16} \ m^2(3\omega_o^{-8} + 5)$$

$$+ \frac{1}{16} \ n^2(3\omega_o^{-8} + 1) + \frac{1}{8} \ (\omega_o^3 - m^2\omega_o^{-1})K_2$$

$$+ 3 \ [16(\gamma_{31} \tanh \gamma_{31}d - 9\omega_o^2)]^{-1} \ [(- 9\omega_o^{-6} + 64\omega_o^{-2} - 33\omega_o^2 + 18\omega_o^6)$$
$$+ 36m\omega_o^3\omega_m^2 K_1 + 2K_2(3\omega_o^5 - 8m^2\omega_o - \omega_o) + n^2(18\omega_o^{-6} + 4\omega_o^{-2} + 2\omega_o^2)$$
$$+ m^2(- 18\omega_o^{-6} + 4\omega_o^{-2} - 30\omega_o^2) + 4m^2(m^2 - n^2)\omega_o^{-2}] \tag{28c}$$

$$b_{33} = \frac{1}{16} \ (-3\omega_o^{-8} + 21\omega_o^{-4} - 15)$$

$$+ (- 27\omega_o^{-6} + 66\omega_o^{-2} - 39\omega_o^2)/[16(\tanh (3d) - 3\omega_o^2)] \tag{28d}$$

in which $\gamma_{13} = (m^2 + 9n^2)^{0.5}$, $\gamma_{31} = (9m^2 + n^2)^{0.5}$ \qquad (28e)

Based upon Equation 26, it is required to modify the wavelength and wave celerity given initially by the first-order solution, when the short-crested wave theory is considered to this third-order. It has been confirmed [9] that this short-crested wave theory to third-order can be reduced to the normal standing and Stokes wave, respectively, at the limiting angles of approaches. The reduced form for standing waves is identical to that derived elsewhere [34, 42] for finite depth of water. Also at $\theta = \pi/2$, the general three-dimensional solutions render the Stokes wave [43, 44]. After deriving the water surface elevation η, the total wave height for the short-crested wave, considered to the third-order, can then be obtained. Other pertinent wave quantities associated with this wave system are developed in the following sections.

Wave Kinematics

Although velocity potential has been employed to describe a wave phenomenon, the realization of wave motion using this quantity is rather abstract. Instead of using velocity potential, some other physical variables may be accepted as explicit means of describing wave action. These pertinent quantities include water surface elevation, crest height, wave steepness, wave speed, water-particle velocities, and wave pressure. Mathematical expressions for these quantities can be obtained from the description of a short-crested wave theory. Preliminary attempts in determining the breaking criteria for this three-dimensional wave case are also discussed.

In this section, the discussion of wave kinematics is based upon the third-order solution [9]. Substituting the results of each order of approximation up to the third, for primary wave variables (ϕ, η and ω), from Equations 15 to 17, 18 to 20, and 24 to 26, into the perturbed series given by Equation 13, the third-order solutions in dimensionless form can be completely formulated. The dimensional form of these quantities can then be obtained by putting the dimensionless variables into Equation 6.

Surface Elevations

The water surface elevation $\eta(x,y,t)$ up to the third-order derived [9] can be summarized as

$$k\eta(x,y,t) = \epsilon\hat{\eta}(\hat{x},\hat{y},\hat{t})$$
$$= \epsilon \cos Y \cos X + \epsilon^2 (b_1 \cos 2Y + b_2) \cos 2X + \epsilon^2 b_3 \cos 2Y$$

$$+ \frac{1}{2} \epsilon^3 (b_{11} \cos Y + b_{13} \cos 3Y) \cos X$$

$$+ \frac{1}{2} \epsilon^3 (b_{31} \cos Y + b_{33} \cos 3Y) \cos 3X \qquad (29)$$

in which $X = (m\hat{x} - \hat{t})$, $Y = n\hat{y}$; and all b_i constants are given by Equation 22 and b_{ij} is specified in Equations 28a to 28d. These constants are a function of "kd" only, i.e., ω_0 of Equation 17. It is implicit in Equation 29 that water surface along the centerlines of the combined crests (i.e., at $y/L_y = 0$, $1/2$, 1 . . .) are similar to a progressive wave, with wave profiles more like a cnoidal wave. Along the crest length direction, it will have minimal fluctuations at the alignments half-way between (i.e., at $y/L_y = 1/4, 3/4 \ldots$). Normal to the wall at the crests and troughs, the profile resembles a standing wave.

Examples of surface profiles are plotted in Figures 6 and 7. The former figure shows the variation of the surface elevation $k\eta$ according to Equation 29 as a function of distance from a reflecting wall for various dimensionless amplitudes in $\epsilon = ka$ for the case of $\theta = 45°$, $d/L_A = 0.1$ at time $t = 0$, with $L_A =$ the wavelength of the incident waves to first-order. A comparison of surface profiles for different orders of wave theory is depicted in Figure 7. The property of a flat trough and steep crest is more pronounced in the third-order solution.

For the crest along the wall at $x = 0$ and $t = q\pi$ (where q is an even integer), the greatest surface elevation η_{max} in dimensionless form given by Equation 29 becomes

$$k\eta_{max} = \epsilon + \epsilon^2 (b_1 + b_2 + b_3) + \frac{1}{2} \epsilon^3 (b_{11} + b_{13} + b_{31} + b_{33}) \tag{30}$$

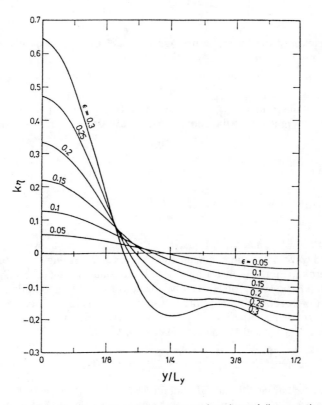

Figure 6. Surface profiles for short-crested waves as functions of distance along crest length and dimensionless amplitude ϵ; $\theta = 45°$, $d/L_A = 0.1$, $t = 0$.

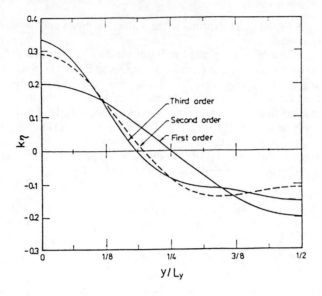

Figure 7. Surface profiles of short-crested waves as functions of distance along crest length and the order of the wave theory; $\theta = 45°$, $d/L_A = 0.1$, $t = 0$, $\epsilon = 0.2$.

The lowest section of the trough, η_{min}, occurs at $t = q\pi$ (for q being an odd integer). Thus the total wave height H_{sc} of the short-crested wave at the wall to the third-order is given by

$$k\,H_{sc} = k(\eta_{max} - \eta_{min})\,|\,x,y = 0$$

$$= 2\epsilon \left[1 + \frac{1}{2}\,\epsilon^2\,(b_{11} + b_{13} + b_{31} + b_{33})\right] \tag{31}$$

The presence of b_{11}, b_{13}, b_{31}, and b_{33} in Equation 31 influences the total wave height of the short-crested wave in the same manner as in Stokes and standing waves to the third-order of approximation. By inserting all the b_{ij} constants in Equations 28a to 28d into 31, the full expression for H_{sc} can be formulated. Based upon this equation, the effect of third-order solution to the first-order wave height H_A can be calculated. Figure 8 shows the ratios of wave heights of H_A to H_{sc} for short-crested waves, as functions of d/L_A and H_A/d, for the case of $\theta = 45°$.

Crest Height

It is implicit that Equations 29 and 30 contain a sinusoidal term of first-order, plus terms that represent an elevation (ΔH) of the mean water level (MWL) above that of the still-water level (SWL). The MWL is an imaginary elevation midway

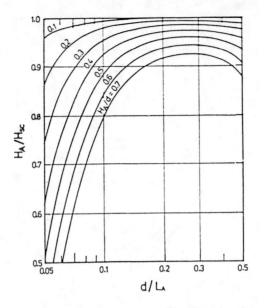

Figure 8. Ratio of first-order wave height to the third-order as functions of d/L$_A$ and H$_A$/d; $\theta = 45°$.

between the crest and the trough of the wave when considered to the third-order. However, the engineer is more interested in the crest height (a$_c$) above the SWL as this is the datum normally used.

The ratio of the maximum crest height η_{max}, or a$_c$, above the SWL to the total wave height H$_{sc}$ for the short-crested wave system can be expressed as

$$\frac{\eta_{max}}{H_{sc}} = \frac{1 + \epsilon\,(b_1 + b_2 + b_3) + \dfrac{1}{2}\,\epsilon^2\,(b_{11} + b_{13} + b_{31} + b_{33})}{2 + \epsilon^2\,(b_{11} + b_{13} + b_{31} + b_{33})} \tag{32}$$

An example of Equation 32 is illustrated in Figure 9, for a$_c$/H$_{sc}$ as functions of d/L$_A$ and H$_A$/d, for the case $\theta = 45°$, where H$_A$ is the height of the short-crested wave to the first-order as also L$_A$ the incident wavelength to that order. In following along any particular H$_A$/d curve, the variation in a$_c$/H$_{sc}$ with respect to the increase of d/L$_A$ should be observed. The increase of a$_c$/H$_{sc}$ in the shallower water depths results from the shoaling effect of wave height; on the other hand, it may be attributed to the fact that a relatively larger wave is used for the same value of H$_A$/d in the deeper waters. The breaking limit, taken temporarily from the case of the usual progressive wave, is proposed as an upper limit to a$_c$/H$_{sc}$. (The breaking criterion is discussed later.)

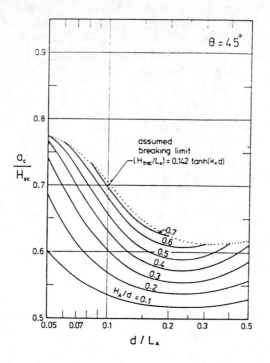

Figure 9. The ratio of crest height a_c to the total wave height of the short-crested wave H_{sc} to third-order, as functions of d/L_A and H_A/d; $\theta = 45°$.

Wave Steepness

The wave steepness of a short-crested wave must account for the change in wavelength of the third-order solution. The perturbed quantity ω from Equation 13 and ω_3 from Equation 26 gives

$$\omega = \omega_1 + \frac{1}{2}\,\epsilon^2\omega_3 = \omega_o\left(1 + \frac{1}{2}\,\epsilon^2\omega_o^{-1}\omega_3\right) \tag{33}$$

or

$$L = \frac{gT^2}{2\pi}\,\omega^2 \approx \frac{gT^2}{2\pi}\,\omega_o^2\,[1 + \epsilon^2\omega_o^{-1}\omega_3 + O(\epsilon^3)] = mL_x \tag{34}$$

This is a similar expression as obtained by Skjelbreia [43] for a Stokes wave and by Goda and Kakizaki [42] for a standing wave. The values of ω_3 from Equation 26 are depicted in Figure 10. As seen from this figure, the change of sign to ω_3, for the cases of $\theta = 0°$ to 22.5° approximately, implies that there is a decrease or increase of the wavelength either side of a critical value of d/L_A for $\omega_3 = 0$. Taking a standing wave for example ($\theta = 0°$), the wavelength is shortened as compared with its progressive component wave, for $d/L_A > 0.17$, as ω_3 has the negative sign. This phenomenon was predicted [34, 45]. For θ greater than 22.5° approximately, the increase in wavelength can be as expected where a wave travels into shallower depths of water, while the rate of increase depends upon the values of d/L_A and wave height.

In terms of the distance between the island crests (L_x) in the direction of wave propagation, the wave provides a steepness of

$$\frac{H_{sc}}{L_x} = \frac{m\epsilon \, [2 + \epsilon^2(b_{11} + b_{13} + b_{31} + b_{33})]}{2\pi \, (1 + \epsilon^2 \omega_o^{-1}\omega_3)} \tag{35}$$

Figure 11 shows the wave steepness H_{sc}/L_x of the short-crested wave to the third-order, for the case of $\theta = 45°$, showing also the tentative breaking limit as used in Figure 9.

Wave Celerity

To the first-order, the phase speed of the combined crests in the short-crested wave system can be easily obtained by any linear wave theory, for example, from

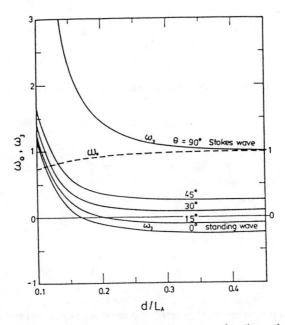

Figure 10. Dimensionless angular frequencies of waves as functions of d/L_A and angle of wave incidence θ.

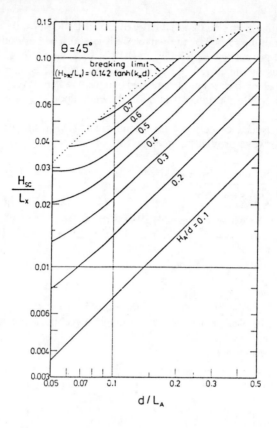

Figure 11. Wave steepness H_{sc}/L_x of the short-crested wave to the third order, as functions of d/L_A and H_A/d; $\theta = 45°$.

Equations 15 and 17 of the present third-order solution. Given the relationship that $\cos(m\hat{x} - \hat{t}) = \cos(k_x x - \sigma t) = \cos k_x(x - C_s t)$, the dimensional phase speed of the wave to this order is thus defined as

$$C_s = \frac{\sigma}{k_x} = \frac{\omega_o(gk)^{0.5}}{m\,k} = \frac{1}{m}\left[\frac{g}{k}\tanh(kd)\right]^{0.5} \tag{36}$$

where ω_o is given by Equation 6. The dimensionless parameter $C_s/\sqrt{(gd)}$ of the short-crested waves is graphed in Figure 12 as functions of d/L_A and θ. Equation 36 is found to be the same as Fuchs [5], in which the compound expression of $[1 + (L_x/L_y)^2]^{0.5}$ is equivalent to $(1/m)$ or $(1/\sin\theta)$ in the present notation.

It is also implicit from Equation 36 that, to the first-order, the ratio of the phase speed of a short-crested system (C_s) to its progressive wave component (C), which makes up the system, can be given by

$$C_s = \frac{1}{m} C, \text{ or } \frac{C_s}{C} = \frac{1}{m} \tag{37}$$

This is graphed in Figure 13. For the limiting angles of incidence, i.e., $\theta = 0°$ and 90° for a standing and progressive wave, respectively, the ratios are also included in the same figure. However, Equation 37 precludes the condition for a short-crested wave produced by an incident wave nearly normal to the reflecting wall, or with a very small angle of θ as in Figure 5. It is obvious that C_s is greater than C for waves of all obliquity $\theta > 0°$, because in the the same wave period T it must traverse the diagonal of the diamond shaped crest pattern, where $L_x > L$ (see also Figure 5).

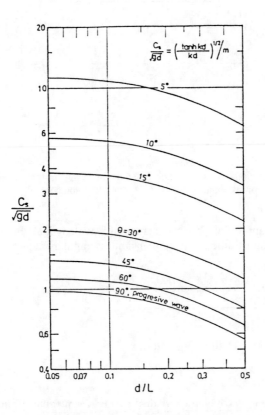

Figure 12. Dimensionless phase speed of short-crested waves as functions of d/L_A and angle of incidence θ, first-order solution.

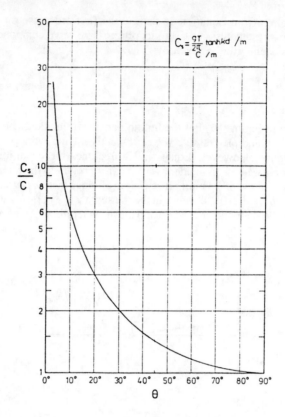

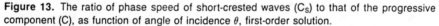

Figure 13. The ratio of phase speed of short-crested waves (C_S) to that of the progressive component (C), as function of angle of incidence θ, first-order solution.

To the third-order approximation, the change of wavelength as influenced by ω_3 must be considered. Substitution of the dimensionless angular frequency ω given by Equation 33 yields

$$C_s = \frac{\sigma}{k_x} = \frac{\omega(gk)^{0.5}}{m\,k} = \frac{\omega_o\left(1 + \frac{1}{2}\,\epsilon^2\omega_o^{-1}\omega_3\right)(gk)^{0.5}}{m\,k} \tag{38}$$

in which ω_3 is given by Equation 26, and m = sinθ.

Breaking Criteria

Determining breaking wave characteristics, in a uniform finite depth and over a sloping bottom, is of great engineering importance and theoretical interest. This subject has been extensively studied both mathematically and experimentally for two-dimensional wave cases. It has been submitted that short-crested breaking waves can produce larger waves on offshore or coastal structures and has wider occurrence than that of long-crested waves. Therefore, for practical engineering applications, it is important to estimate a suitable limiting height for this wave system. Several reports on the limiting conditions are available for short-crested waves [10, 11, 18, 19, 38, 39, 40].

To investigate the breaking height of a short-crested wave for practical uses, it seems logical to start from the criterion that governs the two-dimensional wave case, thereby extending it further for the three-dimensional case. For long-crested waves over a uniform finite depth, two kinds of stability parameters have been employed as possible mechanisms in limiting the height. These are called by Dean [46] as Kinematic Stability Parameter (KSP) and Dynamic Stability Parameter (DSP), respectively.

The KSP relates the maximum water-particle velocity at the crest to the phase velocity of the wave, i.e. u_{max}/C_s at the crest, commonly referred to as the Rankine-Stokes condition in the literature [44, 47, 48]. The wave form becomes asymmetric and finally curves over when u_{max} exceeds C_s and breaking occurs. This criterion has been accepted for progressive waves. On the other hand, the DSP proposes that the limit of the vertical acceleration at the wave crest to the magnitude of the acceleration of gravity, i.e., $(Dw/Dt)/g$, is applicable to the case of normal standing waves [42, 49, 50]. When this parameter exceeds unity, it has been shown that the pressure gradient at the crest is zero [46] and the wave form becomes unstable.

It may serve as a practical purpose in using wave theory at relatively low order to generate a crude but useful estimation of breaking height. A recent study of Le Méhauté [40] suggests that the Stokes criterion (i.e., the KSP condition) for limiting waves is also valid for short-crested waves, providing that corresponding variables in short-crested waves are used to replace equivalent quantities in the formulas developed for the two-dimensional long-crested waves. Some modified equations can be rewritten in the current notations as

$$\frac{H_{bsc}}{L_x} = 0.140 \tanh\left(\frac{2\pi d}{L_x}\right), \text{ or } \frac{H_{bsc}}{(L/\sin\theta)} = 0.14 \tanh\left(\frac{2\pi d}{L/\sin\theta}\right) \tag{39}$$

where L is the wavelength of the progressive wave component that makes up the short-crested system. Under this relationship, the ratio of the maximum height (H_{bsc}) of a short-crested wave to that of a long-crested component wave (H_b) is then given by

$$\frac{H_{bsc}}{H_b} = \frac{1}{\sin\theta} \frac{\tanh(kd\sin\theta)}{\tanh(kd)} \tag{40}$$

Equations 39 and 40 are graphed in Figure 14, as functions of d/L_A and H_A/d. Employing only the similarity of the breaking condition for a two-dimensional wave case [40], the limiting short-crested wave height is approximately twice the height of its component progressive waves, i.e., $H_{bsc} = 2 H_b$. The maximum possible height will be $H_{bsc} = 0.78d$, which is identical to that of a two-dimensional wave. However, with resonant interactions between the fundamental and its har-

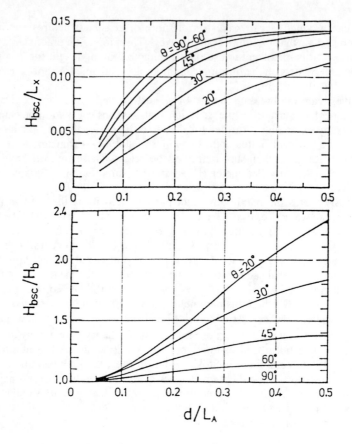

Figure 14. Tentative limiting wave steepness H_{bsc}/L_x, and ratio of breaking height of short-crested waves H_{bsc} to that of the progressive waves H_b, as function of d/L_A and angle of incidence θ.

monics within a short-crested wave system, and upon considering higher order effects, ratios higher than two are possible.

The breaking criteria of KSP and DSP are two extremes of the limiting conditions of a short-crested wave, when $\theta = 90°$ and $0°$, respectively, in the case of oblique reflection to a vertical wall. Because a short-crested wave can be viewed as one kind of progressive wave propagating in the x-direction (along the wall, see Figure 5), it also has the characteristics of a standing wave in the other direction normal to the former, a rational criterion should therefore be attempted. But before this can be achieved, the domain of application of these two breaking criteria (KSP and DSP) as functions of wave obliquity θ and relative water depth d/L_A should be investigated [38, 40].

For deep-water waves, Longuet-Higgins [51] has indicated that many characteristics of gravity wave, such as wave speed, energy, and momentum, are not monotonic functions of the wave amplitude, as has always been assumed, but in fact increase up to a certain value of wave amplitude and then diminish before the wave of greatest amplitude (for a given wavelength) is reached. Thus, the highest waves are not necessarily the fastest or the most energetic.

Because, when near breaking, the kinematics of wave motion are highly nonlinear, theories of the first-order in amplitude are of questionable value, hence wave theories of higher order approximation should be used for this purpose. In considering an accurate limiting height to short-crested waves, it should be borne in mind that a wave theory with a much higher than a third-order approximation should be used.

The range of applicability has been tested [10, 38] in which these two breaking criteria may be satisfied. To verify the domain of applicability of the DSP for small θ values, the dimensionless momentum equation Dw/Dt that governs the vertical acceleration of a water-particle was used. The numerical calculations were made using the third-order theory [9], for θ from 2° to 20° at increments of 2° in a short-crested system. First-order variables (H_A, L_A) were used as input quantities in all numerical calculations, such as d/L_A and expansion parameter $\epsilon = k\,a = \pi H_A/L_A$. The results showed that the DSP condition was satisfied for all d/L_A from 0.05 to 0.5, for $\theta \leq 20°$, and applicable for some limited values of d/L_A for θ between 20° and 34°, but become totally inapplicable for $\theta \geq 35°$. This domain of applicability of DSP is depicted in Figure 15, in which the cross sign, (+), denotes the said breaking condition is satisfied at that combination of d/L_A and θ.

For the range of $35° \leq \theta \leq \theta_m$, the well-known Rankine-Stokes condition of $u_{max} = C_s$ was applied, in which θ_m is the critical angle to prevent the Mach-stem effect. KSP condition for short-crested waves using the third-order solution [9] was also carried out numerically, using first-order quantities such as d/L_A and H_A/d as inputs [10, 38]. For a specific θ and with ϵ values increasing, the ratio of u_{max}/C_s equal to unity or a maximum for each given d/L_A from 0.1 to 0.5 was determined. A sample result for short-crested wave calculation with $\theta = 45°$ is shown in Figure 16, in which the ϵ values that produce the maximum u_{max}/C_s ratio are also recorded.

As seen in Figure 16, although the curves for u_{max}/C_s versus ϵ for d/L_A greater than 0.17 showed decreasing trend after reaching a maximum, their corresponding values of a_c/H_{sc} increased uniformly throughout the range of ϵ proposed in the calculations. This implies that for a given wave height and depth the greatest possible wave is not necessarily the fastest, or has the greatest u_{max}. This agrees with Longuet-Higgins [51] and Cokelet [52]. The limiting condition for KSP may therefore be assumed as $u_{max}/C_s = 1$ or from the maximum ratio of it for a specific ratio of depth to wavelength.

The calculated values of H_{bsc}/L and H_{bsc}/L_x for short-crested wave with $\theta = 45°$ are graphed as function of d/L in Figure 17, showing also the well-known limiting steepness of the usual progressive and standing waves, with all quantities to the third-order. It is seen from this figure that the limiting H_{bsc}/L values suggested for the short-crested wave follow the "0.218 tanh kd" curve [49] for the standing waves, except unexpected peaking of the steepness curve occurs in the d/L range from 0.1 to 0.2. The similarity of wave steepness to the standing waves is to be

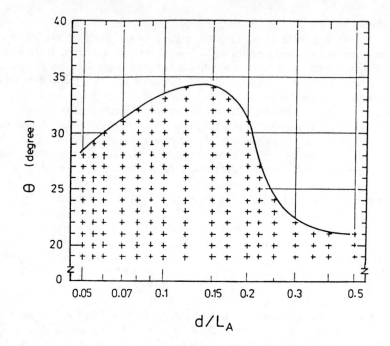

Figure 15. Domain of applicability calculated from the dynamic stability parameter in testing the limiting wave conditions to short-crested waves, as functions of d/L$_A$ and angle of incidence θ.

expected, since the total wave height of the short-crested wave system (H$_{sc}$) is about double that of its incident component, and the steepness is related to the wavelength of the component wave (L). On the other hand, the actual wave steepness of the short-crested wave H$_{bsc}$/L$_x$ itself, being a factor of m (= sin θ) difference than that of H$_{bsc}$/L, is also greater than the limiting condition of the usual progressive wave, i.e., "0.142 tanh kd," when d/L is used as abscissa. The exact solution of Cokelet [52] is shown to be lower than the traditional relationship, while the limiting case of $\theta = 90°$ derived from the present third-order theory is the lowest.

Refined calculations of the maximum height based on KSP, using small increments of d/L$_A$ over the range of 0.1 and 0.2, showed the details of the artificial peaking of the steepness curves to short-crested waves, for the cases of $\theta = 30°$, 45° and 60°, but not that of $\theta = 20°$ and 90°. These are depicted in Figure 18. This phenomenon cannot be explained satisfactorily, although it was thought that over this d/L range that incidentally the wave angular frequency ω_3 changes almost exponentially (see Figure 10). The current calculation of breaker height implies an important but as-yet unjustified assumption that the results for long-crested waves can be applied directly to the unsteady short-crested wave, and only a third-order wave theory used. It is also worth noting that the region in which this peaking applies is the shallow water region where such Stokes' type theories do not strictly apply.

Although only a crude approximation has been presented, the limiting steepness of a short-crested wave with $\theta = 45°$ can be higher than that of a long-crested wave at any given d/L. Moreover, the wave obliquity θ of the component wave has a significant effect on the magnitude of the resultant short-crested wave. It had also been found [10, 38] that H_{bsc}/L for $\theta = 30°$ is higher than that of $\theta = 45°$, as given in Figure 18, with that of $\theta = 60°$ the lowest. Based upon Equation 39, the limiting wave steepness H_{bsc}/L suggested by Le Méhauté [40] is also drawn for the case of $\theta = 45°$, showing much lower values compared to that from the present third-order theory. The previous discussion gives some insight into the limiting wave steepness, as given by the third-order wave theory presented [9] for a simple short-

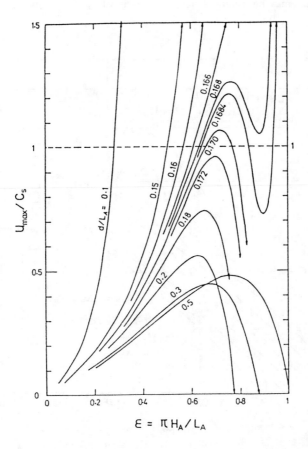

Figure 16. Ratio of the maximum horizontal water-particle velocity u_{max} at the surface of wave crest to phase speed C_s, for short-crested waves, as functions of d/L_A and the expansion parameter ϵ.

crested wave system. However, it is doubtful that a third-order solution can yield extremely accurate estimates of the maximum steepness.

No quantitative measurements have been available on the short-crested breaking waves until Halliwell and Machen [18] reported some preliminary experiments. Only a part of their research program was available at the time of publication. Four short series of runs were made and the data summarized. The height of short-crested breaking waves was found experimentally to be higher than that of long-crested breaking waves. Resonance was also mentioned.

To compare these experimental results of limiting steepness with the current theoretical prediction (Figure 18, for example), the given data of H_{bsc} and d_b (the breaking height and depth at breaking) are transformed into H_{bsc}/L using the given wave period T, where L is the wavelength of the component wave to third-order at the depth d_b. Obliquity to the equivalent reflecting wall was not specified [18]. The value of $\theta = 45°$ may be assumed from their plan of the test basin.

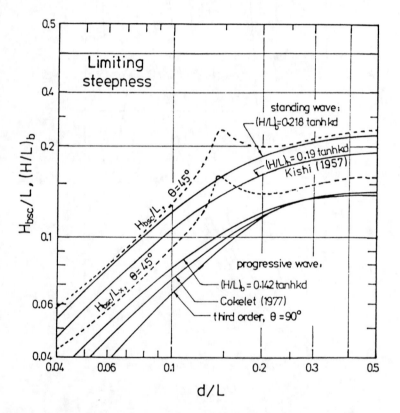

Figure 17. Comparison of the tentative limiting values of H_{bsc}/L and $H_{bsc}L_x$ for the short-crested wave with $\theta = 45°$, third-order solution, with others for progressive and standing waves, L being the wavelength to third-order.

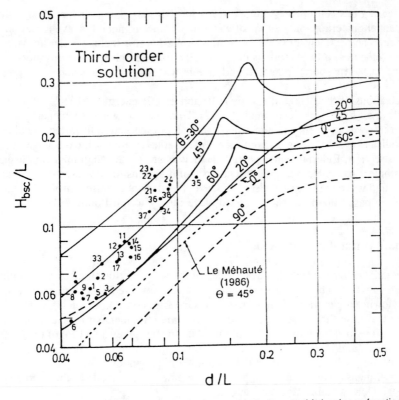

Figure 18. Limiting wave steepness H_{bsc}/L of short-crested waves to third-order as functions of angle of incidence θ and d/L, showing experimental data of Halliwell and Machen [18].

All data available are used and placed in Figure 18, each being labeled with its original run number in the series for direct reference [18]. It is apparent that they follow the theoretical curve of $\theta = 45°$ generally, except for those in series 2 (dots numbered 21 to 24), which were noted as having strong interaction only at breaking. Nevertheless, the agreement seems encouraging, confirming that the height of short-crested breaking waves can be significantly higher than that of the long-crested waves at a given d/L.

The Interior

The interior of a prescribed wave motion constitutes nearly all of the water column over which a wave propagates, because the boundary layers at the free surface and at the bottom are generally very much smaller, particularly the latter being in the order of a few centimeters at most. It is within this large domain that most of the important engineering applications of water motion occur, notably wave forces on a structure. The pertinent physical quantities in the interior include Eulerian water-particle velocities, orbital motions in Lagrangian form (displacements of water-particle and mass transport), potential and kinetic wave energy flux, and wave pressure.

Calculations of the potential energy (PE) and kinetic energy flux (KE) of short-crested waves have been performed [11, 12]. Diagrams showing mean energy densities of this wave system as a function of the steepness squared for selected values of θ, indicate about the same magnitudes of PE and KE for each case presented.

In this section, Eulerian water-particle velocities are presented graphically, using dimensionless parameters to ease the number of diagrams to be presented. Orbital motions and wave pressure are also discussed. The derivations used throughout this section are based upon the short-crested wave theory to third order [9].

Eulerian Water-Particle Velocities

Kinematics of a flow field is a description of the wave motion. It takes no account of how the motion is brought about, nor of the forces involved. There are two methods of viewing the motion of fluid particles. One is to concentrate on a fixed point in space and note the changes that occur with time. Another is to travel with the particle and record the temporal variations. The former gives a picture of the flow of streamlines and is termed the Eulerian description, while the latter provides the trajectory viewpoint and is called the Lagrangian description.

To non-dimensionalize the water-particle velocities, use is made of the following conditions from variable transformations:

$$\hat{u} = \epsilon \, (\partial\hat{\phi}/\partial\hat{x}), \ \hat{v} = \epsilon \, (\partial\hat{\phi}/\partial\hat{y}), \ \hat{w} = \epsilon \, (\partial\hat{\phi}/\partial\hat{z}) \tag{41}$$

in which $\hat{\phi}$ is the perturbed value of Equation 13, obtained by inserting the solutions of $\hat{\phi}_1$, $\hat{\phi}_2$, and $\hat{\phi}_3$ from Equations 15, 18, and 24, respectively. This leads to the velocity potential in dimensionless form to third order as

$$\hat{\phi} = \hat{\phi}_1 + \epsilon\hat{\phi}_2 + \frac{1}{2} \, \epsilon^2\hat{\phi}_3 + O(\epsilon^4)$$

$$= \left[\omega_o \, (\cosh Z/\sinh \hat{d}) \cos Y + \frac{1}{2} \, \epsilon^2\beta_{13} \cosh \gamma_{13}Z \cos 3Y \right] \sin X$$

$$+ \, [\epsilon\beta_2 \cosh 2Z \cos 2Y + \epsilon \, \beta_3 \cosh 2mZ] \sin 2X$$

$$+ \frac{1}{2} \, \epsilon^2 \, [\beta_{31} \cosh \gamma_{31}Z \cos Y + \beta_{33} \cosh 3Z \cos 3Y] \sin 3X + \epsilon \, \beta_1 \, \hat{t} \tag{42}$$

in which $X = (m\hat{x} - \hat{t})$, $Y = n\hat{y}$, and $Z = (\hat{z} + \hat{d})$.

The full expressions of the water-particle velocity components in dimensionless form in the x, y and z-directions, respectively, can thus be obtained as

$$\frac{\hat{u}}{m} = \epsilon\beta_o \cosh Z \cos Y \cos X + \epsilon^2 (2\beta_2 \cosh 2Z \cos 2Y + 2\beta_3 \cosh 2mZ) \cos 2X$$

$$+ \frac{1}{2} \epsilon^3 (\beta_{13} \cosh \gamma_{13} Z \cos 3Y) \cos X$$

$$+ \frac{1}{2} \epsilon^3 (3\beta_{31} \cosh \gamma_{31} Z \cos Y + 3\beta_{33} \cosh 3Z \cos 3Y) \cos 3X \qquad (43)$$

$$\frac{\hat{v}}{n} = -\epsilon\beta_o \cosh Z \sin Y \sin X - \epsilon^2 (2\beta_2 \cosh 2Z \sin 2Y) \sin 2X$$

$$- \frac{1}{2} \epsilon^3 (3\beta_{13} \cosh \gamma_{13} Z \sin 3Y) \sin X$$

$$- \frac{1}{2} \epsilon^3 (\beta_{31} \cosh \gamma_{31} Z \sin Y + 3\beta_{33} \cosh 3Z \sin 3Y) \sin 3X \qquad (44)$$

and

$$\hat{w} = \epsilon\beta_o \sinh Z \cos Y \sin X + \epsilon^2 (2\beta_2 \sinh 2Z \cos 2Y + 2m\beta_3 \sinh 2mZ) \sin 2X$$

$$+ \frac{1}{2} \epsilon^3 (\gamma_{13} \beta_{13} \sinh \gamma_{13} Z \cos 3Y) \sin X$$

$$+ \frac{1}{2} \epsilon^3 (\gamma_{13} \beta_{31} \sinh \gamma_{31} Z \cos Y + 3\beta_{33} \sinh 3Z \cos 3Y) \sin 3X \qquad (45)$$

in which $\beta_o = \omega_o/\sinh\hat{d}$, $X = (m\hat{x} - \hat{t})$, $Y = n\hat{y}$, and $Z = (\hat{z} + \hat{d})$.

Similar to the factors that made up the velocity potential that was discussed earlier, there are four common elements in each order of contributions to the velocity expressions as can be noted in Equations 43 to 45. In dimensionless form, these are:

1. Dimensionless factor, ϵ, of velocity directly proportional to wave height and inversely related to wave period.
2. Depth factors, such as "coshZ/sinhd" and "sinhZ/sinhd" etc., which determine the variation of magnitude of particle motion from the water surface to the bottom.
3. Modulation factors, such as sin Y, cos Y and sin 2Y etc., in the y-direction (i.e., in the direction normal to the reflecting wall).
4. Phase factors, such as sin X, cos X, and sin 2X etc., showing the change of velocity with time and position in the x-direction (i.e., the direction of wave propagation).

Equations 43 to 45 can be reverted back to dimensional quantities by the prescribed variable transformations as in Equation 6, i.e., $\dot{\phi} = k^2/(\epsilon\sqrt{gk})\,\phi$. Because the velocities are functions of (kd, x, y, z, t, θ), a set of proper groupings of wave variables should be selected to ease the task of graphical presentation. For engineering applications, suitable parameters such as $u_{max}/\sqrt{(gd)}$, d/L_A, z/d, and H_A/d are used in the following figures. As it is impossible to cover wave conditions ranging from $\theta = 0°$ to $90°$ and with all d/L_A, z/d and H_A/d values, only some typical results of practical importance are presented.

For a third-order solution, maximum Eulerian velocity $u_{max}/\sqrt{(gd)}$ is illustrated in Figure 19, as functions of d/L_A and angle of incidence θ, for $H_A/d = 0.3$, at both the free surface and the bed. Upon viewing this figure, an apparently misleading picture appears for the Stokes waves case ($\theta = 90°$), $u_{max}/\sqrt{(gd)}$ being superior numerically to that of the short-crested wave. This can be attributed to the equal use of

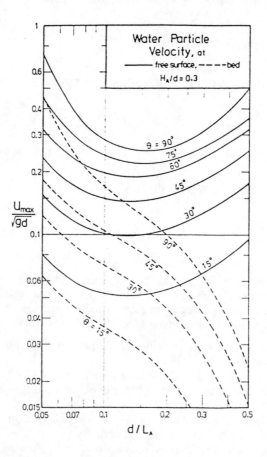

Figure 19. The maximum of Eulerian water-particle velocity u at the free surface and at the bed as functions of θ and d/L_A; $H_A/d = 0.3$.

the same parameters d/L_A and H_A/d for all angles of incidence. In practice, all H_A values for short-crested waves will be about double those of the component progressive waves. This increases $u_{max}/\sqrt{(gd)}$ in this proportion so that, for angle $\theta >$ 45° approximately, u_{max} will exceed that of the Stokes wave, for most d/L_A values.

The maximum forward and backward magnitudes of $u_{max}/\sqrt{(gd)}$, that occur at wave crest and trough, respectively, are demonstrated in Figure 20, as functions of H_A/d through relative depth z/d, for $\theta = 45°$ and $d/L_A = 0.2$. On a semi-log plotting, the parallel curves give an increase of $u_{max}/\sqrt{(gd)}$ generally as H_A/d increases. The ratios of crest height and trough depth divided by water depth are also included in this figure. It is seen that the former is greater than the latter when reasonably large waves are considered.

To exhibit a clearer picture of the maximum water-particle velocity, the case of a short-crested wave with $\theta = 45°$ is now examined more closely. Figure 21 shows the velocity at the free surface and at SWL, and Figure 22 at the bed, as functions of H_A/d and d/L_A, at the position $x = 0$ (i.e., at the reflecting wall) with time $t = 0$. In following along any particular H_A/d curve, the variation in $u_{max}/\sqrt{(gd)}$ with respect to the increase of d/L_A should be observed. Their differences are quite apparent, including the velocity at the bed showing a very steep drop, or swift attenuation, as d/L_A increases. The tentative breaking limit discussed earlier is proposed as an upper limit to $u_{max}/\sqrt{(gd)}$ for engineering purposes.

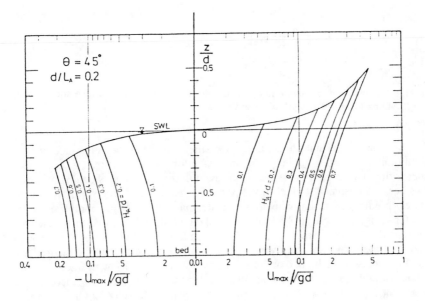

Figure 20. The maximum (at wave crest) and the minimum (at trough) values of Eulerian water-particle velocities of u through the water depth as function of H_A/d; $\theta = 45°$, $d/L_A = 0.2$.

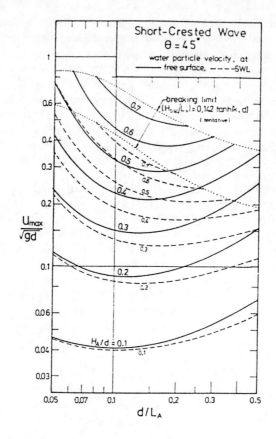

Figure 21. The maximum Eulerian water-particle velocity of u at the free surface and still water level (SWL) as functions of d/L_A and $H_A d$; $\theta = 45°$.

It has been accepted that an accurate assessment of water-particle velocity and acceleration is very important in calculating wave forces on structures, as any error in either is directly proportional. However, even in the two-dimensional wave case that has been extensively studied in the past 150 years, no theory yet derived can adequately predict the orbital velocities of water-particles over the complete range of d/L_A for design purposes [53]. Experimental data [54] indicate that for d/L ratios greater than 0.2 the linear theory gives maximum horizontal velocities at the SWL and bed accurately, but for shallower water conditions these exceed the theoretical values. In other words, higher order solutions are likely to be warranted for the latter conditions because it predicts higher values than does the linear theory.

No attempt is made here on the validity of water-particle velocities as predicted theoretically up to the third order. However, comparison between the first- and third-order solutions are demonstrated in Figures 23 to 25, as function of d/L_A and H_A/d at various depths, for $\theta = 45°$. Figure 23 reveals that the values of $u_{max}/\sqrt{(gd)}$

obtained from the first order are slightly higher than those from the third order at $d/L_A = 0.2$, while this effect is reversed dramatically at $d/L_A = 0.1$ as depicted in Figure 24.

To highlight the comparison for u_{max} obtained from different orders of wave theory, the ratios of $u_1/\sqrt{(gd)}$ to $u_3/\sqrt{(gd)}$ over the full range of H_A/d for velocities at SWL and $\theta = 45°$ are illustrated in Figure 25 (where u_1 and u_3 are u_{max} to the first and third order, respectively). It is seen that the relationship can be well represented by a series of straight lines for d/L_A when H_A/d is used as abscissa on a semi-log scale. The termination of some d/L_A lines refers to the tentative breaking limit as previously used.

Based on Equation 43, a similar diagram for Stokes waves ($\theta = 90°$) is depicted in Figure 26 to facilitate due comparison of maximum horizontal velocities with the case of short-crested wave with $\theta = 45°$, as given by Figure 21. In Figures 21 and

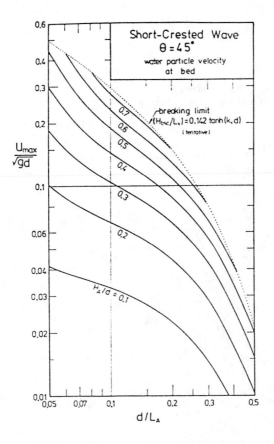

Figure 22. The maximum Eulerian water-particle velocity of u at the bed as functions of d/L_A and H_A/d; $\theta = 45°$.

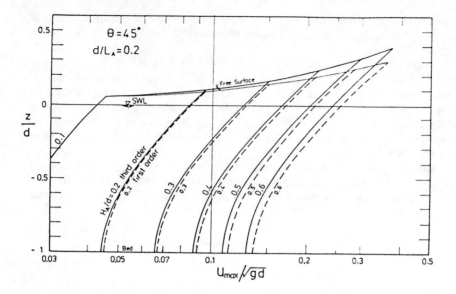

Figure 23. Comparison of the maximum Eulerian water-particle velocity through the water depth as functions of the order of the wave theory and H_A/d; $\theta = 45°$, $d/L_A = 0.2$.

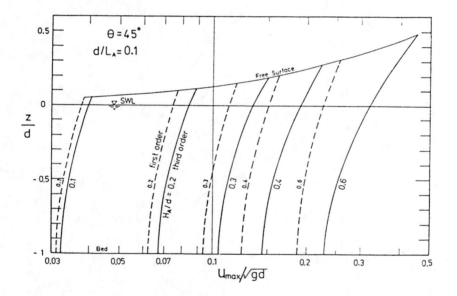

Figure 24. Comparison of the maximum Eulerian water-particle velocity through the water depth as functions of the order of the wave theory and H_A/d; $\theta = 45°$, $d/L_A = 0.1$.

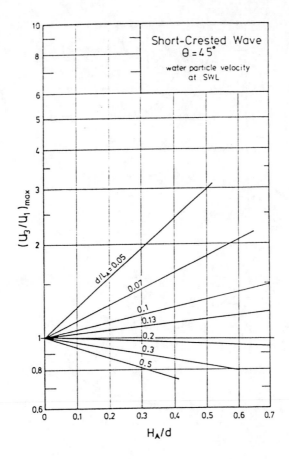

Figure 25. The ratio of the Eulerian water-particle velocity to third-order u_3 to that of the first-order u_1 at the still water level, as functions of d/L_A and $H_A d$; $\theta = 45°$.

26, $u_{max}/\sqrt{(gd)}$ are plotted in terms of L_A of the component waves. To compare the motions of waves traveling in a short-crested wave with $\theta = 45°$ to that of its component progressive wave, the H_A/d value of the former should be at least doubled, due to wave interactions. It is then obvious that $u_{max}/\sqrt{(gd)}$ of $\theta = 45°$ is higher that of $\theta = 90°$, for conditions at the same d/L_A.

Orbital Motions

In Lagrangian description of water-particle motions, it is necessary to follow an individual fluid particle and to refer its movements to a mean position (x_o, y_o, z_o). Therefore, the expression of fluid velocities (u, v, w) depend upon these mean positions.

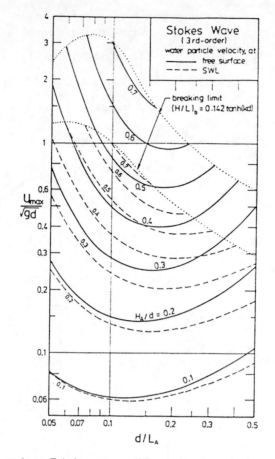

Figure 26. The maximum Eulerian water-particle velocity of u at the free surface and still water level as functions of d/L_A and H_A/d, for Stokes waves ($\theta = 90°$).

In considering a small-amplitude motion in the general three-dimensional wave case, the displacements (ξ_1, ξ_2, ξ_3) in the (x, y, z) directions, respectively, can be formulated by a Taylor series, listing to third-order,

$$f(x_o + \xi_1, y_o + \xi_2, z_o + \xi_3) = f(x_o, y_o, z_o) + [\xi_1\, f_x + \xi_2\, f_y + \xi_3\, f_z] \Big|_{(x_o,\, y_o,\, z_o)}$$

$$+ \frac{1}{2!} [\xi_1^2\, f_{xx} + \xi_2^2\, f_{yy} + \xi_3^2\, f_{zz} + 2\xi_1\xi_2\, f_{xy} + 2\xi_2\xi_3\, f_{yz} + 2\xi_3\xi_1\, f_{zx}] \Big|_{(x_o,\, y_o,\, z_o)}$$

$$+ \frac{1}{3!} [\xi_1^3\, f_{xxx} + \xi_2^3\, f_{yyy} + \xi_3^3\, f_{zzz} + 3\xi_1^2\, (\xi_2\, f_{xxy} + \xi_3\, f_{xxz}) + 3\xi_2^2\, (\xi_3\, f_{yyz}$$

$$+ \xi_1\, f_{yyx}) + 3\xi_3^2\, (\xi_1\, f_{zzx} + \xi_2\, f_{zzy}) + 6\xi_1\xi_2\xi_3\, f_{xyz}] \Big|_{(x_o,\, y_o,\, z_o)} \tag{46}$$

Therefore, in putting $f = d\xi_1/dt = \partial\phi/\partial x$, $f = d\xi_2/dt = \partial\phi/\partial y$, and $f = d\xi_3/dt = \partial\phi/\partial z$, respectively, into Equation 46, a set of equations for $(d\xi_1/dt, d\xi_2/dt, d\xi_3/dt)$ in dimensional form can be formulated.

Introducing the dimensionless quantities for (x, y, z, t, ω) as of Equation 6, velocity potential ϕ and displacement $\hat{\xi} = k\xi$ in a perturbed series, Equation 46 yields the necessary equations for deriving the water-particle displacements in the order of expansion parameter ϵ. The water-particle velocities in Lagrangian form can be obtained for each order of wave theory. The governing equations in each order of approximation have been presented elsewhere [10], only their solutions are presented here for the sake of simplicity.

To the first-order, the displacements of a water-particle $(\hat{\xi}_{11}, \hat{\xi}_{21}, \hat{\xi}_{31})$ from its mean position $(\hat{x}_o, \hat{y}_o, \hat{z}_o)$ are given in dimensionless form as

$$\xi_{11} = -m \frac{\cosh (z_o + d)}{\sinh d} \cos (ny_o) \sin (mx_o - t) \tag{47}$$

$$\xi_{21} = -n \frac{\cosh (z_o + d)}{\sinh d} \sin (ny_o) \cos (mx_o - t) \tag{48}$$

$$\xi_{31} = \frac{\sinh (z_o + d)}{\sinh d} \cos (ny_o) \cos (mx_o - t) \tag{49}$$

where the double subscripts associated with ξ_{ij}, for $i = 1...3$ and $j = 1...3$, denote the direction in (x,y,z) co-ordinate system and to the order of approximation of wave theory, respectively. Taking an initial time $t = 0$, then $\xi_{11} = x(t) - x_o$, $\xi_{21} = y(t) - y_o$ and $\xi_{31} = z(t) - z_o$ at time t, for $t > 0$.

Thus on each projection plane the orbital motions are:

elliptical for the x-y plane,

$$\frac{(\hat{x} - \hat{x}_o)^2}{\left(m \dfrac{\cosh Z}{\sinh d} \cos Y\right)^2} + \frac{(\hat{y} - \hat{y}_o)^2}{\left(n \dfrac{\cosh Z}{\sinh d} \sin Y\right)^2} = 1 \tag{50}$$

also as elliptical for x-z plane,

$$\frac{(\hat{x} - \hat{x}_o)^2}{\left(m \dfrac{\cosh Z}{\sinh d} \cos Y\right)^2} + \frac{(\hat{z} - \hat{z}_o)^2}{\left(\dfrac{\sinh Z}{\sinh d} \cos Y\right)^2} = 1 \tag{51}$$

and for y-z plane as

$$\frac{(\hat{y}-\hat{y}_o)^2}{\left(n\dfrac{\cosh Z}{\sinh d}\sin Y\right)^2}+\frac{(\hat{z}-\hat{z}_o)^2}{\left(\dfrac{\sinh Z}{\sinh d}\cos Y\right)^2}=0 \tag{52}$$

in which the dimensionless variables $\hat{d}=kd$, $\hat{x}=kx$, $\hat{y}=ky$, $\hat{z}=kz$, $Y=n\hat{y}_o$, and $Z=(\hat{z}+\hat{d})$, with carets denoting dimensionless quantities omitted in Equations 50 to 52.

From the elliptical paths the lengths of the semi-major and semi-minor axes are readily obtainable from Equations 50 and 52. The focal distance is twice the square root of the difference between the squares of the semi-axes.

A further investigation of the particle paths in the x-z plane shows that it has one axis in the direction of propagation of the combined crests, and makes an angle β with the vertical plane. This angle of inclination is given by

$$\tan \beta = \xi_{21}/\xi_{31} = -n \coth k(z_o + d) \tan (nky_o) \tag{53}$$

which is equivalent to that of Fuchs [5].

The physical interpretation of the negative sign in Equation 53 can be determined from the coordinate system used. As the z-axis is given positive upwards from the still water level, it implies that β is greater than $90°$ measuring anti-clockwise from the positive z-direction, being in the second quadrant. The greatest inclination occurs at the crest, where $z_o = \epsilon\eta$, while it becomes $90°$ (i.e, horizontal motion only) at the bed where $z_o = -d$ as the value of $\coth(0) \to \infty$. A sketch of orbital motions as derived from Equation 53 is given in Figure 27, after Wiegel [55].

It can be said that the water-particle motions in short-crested waves vary spatially both in the vertical and horizontal directions. For the simplest case of two wave trains of equal height and period, the ideal orbital motions are sketched in Figure 4. It is seen that rectilinear and elliptical orbits exist along certain alignments. Along that of the combined crest propagation (i.e., $y/L_y = 1/2$, $1,\dots$) water-particle orbits are in a vertical plane. Half-way between, rectilinear horizontal oscillations occur (i.e., at $y/L_y = 1/4$, $3/4,\dots$); and where at $y/L_y = 1/8$, $3/8$, $5/8,\dots$, the orbits are ellipses at an angle to the vertical, which depends upon their depth, being in a horizontal place at the bed. The maximum orbital velocities, resulting from the combined wave height, are nearly double those of the progressive waves making up the system.

To the second-order, the components of displacements in dimensionless form are given as

$$\hat{\xi}_{12} = -m\,\omega_o^{-1}\,[\beta_2 \cosh Z \cos 2Y + \beta_3 \cosh 2mZ \sin 2X]$$

$$+\frac{1}{8}\frac{m}{\sinh^2 d}\,[(n^2 \cosh 2Z - \cos 2Y - m^2)\sin 2X$$

$$+2\,(m^2 \cosh 2Z - n^2)\,t \cos 2Y + 2\,t \cosh 2Z] \tag{54}$$

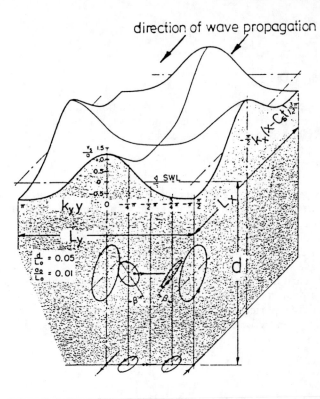

Figure 27. Spatial variations of the orbital motions of water-particles in a short-crested wave. (From R.A. Fuchs, "On the Theory of Short-Crested Oscillatory Waves," in *Gravity Waves*, U.S. National Bureau of Standards, Circ. 521, pp. 187–200, 1952.)

$$\hat{\xi}_{22} = -n \, \omega_o^{-1} \, [\beta_2 \cosh 2Z \sin 2Y \cos 2X]$$

$$+\frac{1}{8} \frac{n}{\sinh^2 d} \sin 2Y \cos 2X \tag{55}$$

$$\hat{\xi}_{32} = \omega_o^{-1} \, [\beta_2 \sinh 2Z \cos 2Y + m \, \beta_3 \sinh 2mZ] \cos 2X$$

$$+\frac{1}{8} \frac{n^2}{\sinh^2 d} \sinh 2Z \cos 2X \tag{56}$$

in which constants β_2 and β_3 are given by Equation 21, and again $X = (m\hat{x} - \hat{t}) = (k_x x - \sigma t)$, $Y = n\hat{y}_o = nky_o$ and $Z = (\hat{z}_o + \hat{d}) = k(z_o + d)$.

Therefore, to correct water-particle displacements up to the second-order, the overall expressions will read

$$\hat{\xi}_1 = \epsilon\ \hat{\xi}_{11} + \epsilon^2\ \hat{\xi}_{12} + O(\epsilon^3),$$
$$\hat{\xi}_2 = \epsilon\ \hat{\xi}_{21} + \epsilon^2\ \hat{\xi}_{22} + O(\epsilon^3),$$
$$\hat{\xi}_3 = \epsilon\ \hat{\xi}_{31} + \epsilon^2\ \hat{\xi}_{32} + O(\epsilon^3),$$

(57)

for the displacement components in x, y, and z-directions, respectively. To the orbital motions in Lagrangian form for the limiting two-dimensional cases, expressions can readily be reduced from these equations [10].

Wave Pressure

Since various pressure-sensing instruments have been placed beneath the water surface as wave recorders in the field, it is important that wave pressure can be correctly calculated. While it is rather easy to determine the locations of wave crests in a two-dimensional wave case, the desirable locations within a short-crested wave system are difficult, because it has been submitted that the wave profile of such a wave system is periodical in two directions, being in the direction of wave propagation and normal to it. As a consequence of these spatial and temporal changes to wave properties, so does the wave pressure vary.

Hsu et al. [9] have reported that the wave pressure of a wave motion in an incompressible fluid is given by Bernoulli theorem

$$\frac{p}{\rho} = -gz - \frac{\partial\phi}{\partial t} - \frac{1}{2}\ (\phi_x^2 + \phi_y^2 + \phi_z^2)$$

(58)

in which ρ is the density of the fluid. After substituting the non-dimensional variables $(\hat{x},\ \hat{y},\ \hat{z},\ \hat{t},\ \hat{\phi})$ as in Equation 6 into Equation 58, a wave pressure equation in dimensionless form is given as

$$\hat{p} = -z - \epsilon\omega\phi_t - \frac{1}{2}\ \epsilon^2(\phi_x^2 + \phi_y^2 + \phi_z^2)$$

(59)

where $\hat{p} = (k/\rho g)p$ is the departure of wave pressure from that of the atmosphere. It is seen from Equation 59 that the total wave pressure at a given elevation z from the still water level in water of depth d is the sum of the hydrostatic pressure plus two additional terms—one arising from the passage of the wave form and the other due to the local kinetic energy of the wave.

Omitting the carets as before, assume the perturbed solution of pressure p in dimensionless form as

$$\hat{p} = -\hat{z} + \epsilon\left(\hat{p}_1 + \epsilon\hat{p}_2 + \frac{1}{2}\ \epsilon^2\ \hat{p}_2\right) + O(\epsilon^4)$$

(60)

to the third-order approximation.

The substitution of ϕ and ω from Equation 6 into Equation 60 gives the following equations for each order of approximation, in dimensionless form,

$$p_1 = -\omega_o \, \phi_{1t} \tag{61}$$

$$p_2 = -\omega_o \, \phi_{2t} - \frac{1}{2} \left(\phi_{1x}^2 + \phi_{1y}^2 + \phi_{1z}^2 \right) \tag{62}$$

$$p_3 = -\omega_3 \, \phi_{1t} - \omega_o \phi_{2t} - 2(\phi_{1x}\phi_{2x} + \phi_{1y}\phi_{2y} + \phi_{1z}\phi_{2z}) \tag{63}$$

Further by inserting the solutions of ϕ_1, ϕ_2, and ϕ_3 from Equations 15, 18, and 24 into Equations 61 to 63, the dimensionless pressure components are given as

$$p_1 = \frac{\cosh(Z)}{\cosh(d)} \cos Y \cos X \tag{64}$$

$$
\begin{aligned}
p_2 = & \left[-\omega_o\beta_1 - \frac{\omega_o^2}{8 \sinh^2 d} \cos 2Z \right] \\
& + 2\omega_o \left(\beta_2 \cosh 2Z \cos 2Y + \beta_3 \cosh 2mZ \right) \cos 2X \\
& + \frac{\omega_o^2}{8 \sinh^2 d} \left(n^2 \cosh 2Z - m^2 - \cos 2Y \right) \cos 2X \\
& + \frac{\omega_o^2}{8 \sinh^2 d} \left(n^2 - m^2 \cosh 2Z \right) \cos 2Y
\end{aligned}
\tag{65}
$$

$$
\begin{aligned}
p_3 = \frac{\omega_o}{\sinh d} \Bigg\{ & \left[\omega_3 \cosh Z + \frac{1}{2} \beta_2 (m - n + 1) \cosh Z + \frac{1}{2} \beta_2 (m - n - 1) \cosh 3Z \right. \\
& \left. + 2m\beta_3 \cosh (2m - 1) Z \right] \cos Y \cos X \\
& + \left[\frac{1}{2} \beta_2 (m + n + 1) \cos Z + \frac{1}{2} \beta_2 (m + n - 1) \cosh 3Z \right. \\
& \left. + \beta_{13} \sinh d \cosh \gamma_{13} Z \right] \cos 3Y \cos X \\
& + \left[\frac{1}{2} \beta_2 (m + n - 1) \cosh Z + \frac{1}{2} \beta_2 (m + n + 1) \cosh 3Z + \frac{1}{2} m\beta_3 \right. \\
& \left. \cosh (2m + 1) Z + 3\beta_{31} \sinh d \cosh \gamma_{31} Z \right] \cos Y \cos 3X \\
& + \left[\frac{1}{2} \beta_2 (m - n - 1) \cosh Z + \frac{1}{2} \beta_2 (m - n + 1) \cosh 3Z \right. \\
& \left. + 3\beta_{33} \sinh d \cosh 3Z \right] \cos 3Y \cos 3X \Bigg\}
\end{aligned}
\tag{66}
$$

in which $X = (m\hat{x} - \hat{t})$, $Y = n\hat{y}$, $Z = (\hat{z} + \hat{d})$, and $d = \hat{d}$.

The pressure to the first-order, being in the simplest form, has been examined extensively in the literature for the two-dimensional cases [55–58]. The pressure to this order in the short-crested system is converted back from Equations 60 and 64 into dimensional form as

$$\frac{p}{\rho g} = -z + \frac{\cosh k(z+d)}{\cosh(kd)} \cos (k_y y) \cos k_x (x - C_s t) \tag{67}$$

Equation 67 is identical to that of Fuchs [5]. The quantity in depth factor "$\cosh k(z + d)/\cosh kd$," being referred as the "pressure response factor Kp," has a value less than unity for all depths below the SWL, with its rate of decreasing dependent upon d/L_A, as shown in Figure 28. It is implicit from this equation that the pressure recorded at the bed at $y/L_y = 1/4, 3/4$, etc. (half-way between the combined crests) is a constant value of hydrostatic pressure as $\cos k_y y = 0$ due to this being the nodal position of wave action.

Furthermore, Figure 29 shows the effect of d/L_A in influencing the variation of wave pressure distribution to the third-order through the whole depth. This is based on the familiar combination of the dimensional quantities (except that p_1, p_2, and p_3 being still in dimensionless form as given by Equations 64 to 66) and is given as

$$\frac{p}{\rho g H_A} = -\left(\frac{z}{d}\right)\left(\frac{d}{H_A}\right) + \frac{1}{2}\left(p_1 + \epsilon p_2 + \frac{1}{2}\epsilon^2 p_3\right) \tag{68}$$

Only the contribution arising from the wave alone (not the hydrostatic part) is graphed in Figure 29, for $\theta = 45°$ and $H_A/d = 0.3$. It is seen that for very shallow water the pressure is transmitted downwards virtually unattenuated from the surface to the bottom, while it decreases exponentially with depth for deep water (i.e., $d/L_A = 0.5$). Wave pressure above the still water level is not included in this figure.

Fenton [25] has verified the correctness of the third-order theory of Hsu et al. [9], stating that it is correct to the third order. But in a subsequent numerical checking on the proposed expressions of pressure components (p_1, p_2, p_3) given in Equations 64 to 66, at the free surface $z = \eta$, he found that the accuracy was wrong at the second order. An alternative solution was then proposed as a part of a third-order expansion in wave height in his paper. Explicit formulations to the third order for the force and moment on a vertical wall are developed, and numerical results are also provided. His formulae contain some new features, such as the second-order contribution to force may dominate the solution to third-order. He also concludes that the maximum force per unit length of structure is caused by obliquely-incident waves (i.e., short-crested waves) rather than the normal standing waves.

For a position just under the wave crest but above the SWL, the traditional calculations of wave pressure have been physically inconsistent. This is because at the real free surface p has been set as zero; but in determining ϕ, the free surface

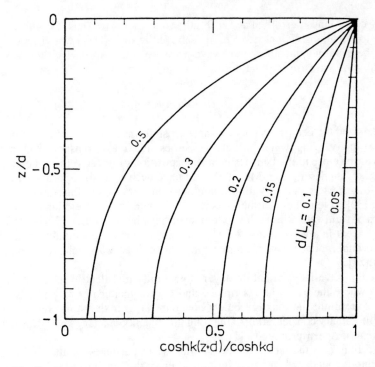

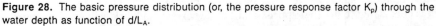

Figure 28. The basic pressure distribution (or, the pressure response factor K_p) through the water depth as function of d/L_A.

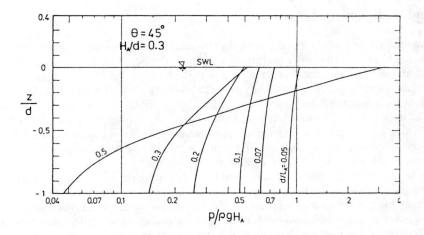

Figure 29. Variations of dimensionless pressure $p/\rho g H_A$ from the wave through the water depth below SWL, as function of d/L_A; $\theta = 45°$, $H_A/d = 0.3$.

boundary condition is perturbed at $z = 0$ rather than at $z = \eta$. Thus, Equation 60 is not valid for locations with positive z, i.e., above the still water level. This simple fact may be equally applicable to all wave pressure equations derived for two-dimensional wave cases in the literature.

The Bottom Layer

To understand the bed forms under a short-crested wave, it is necessary to investigate the time-varying water-particle velocities and mass transport within the boundary layer close to the bed. Using a superposition of linear velocity potentials and a Lagrangian description, Mei et al. [29] have derived a first approximation to the mass-transport velocities within a laminar boundary layer. Tanaka et al. [30] and Dore [32] have calculated the velocity at the outer edge of the laminar layer. Directions of fluid velocities in the bottom layer have been reported [30] using coal and sand tracers in a wave flume 2.5 m wide. However, no quantitative measurements of orbital motions have been made in short-crested waves closed to the bed until Hsu [24].

Because the wave-induced bottom layer is generally turbulent in relatively shallow water where the ocean bed is rippled and hydrodynamically rough, it is also necessary to examine the rough turbulent boundary layer in the short-crested wave system. Preliminary consideration to the rough turbulent boundary layer within this wave system has been proposed [41].

In this section, only the second-order Eulerian water-particle velocities within the laminar bottom boundary layer are considered. From this, the resulting mass transport is considered to the first approximation. Experimental work [10, 17, 37] using a unique experimental wave basin is also reported.

Laminar Boundary Layer

An approximate solution to the three-dimensional unsteady boundary layer equations has been derived using a perturbation method, for incompressible flow over a rigid and smooth horizontal bed within a simple short-crested wave system. The wave theory to third-order derived by Hsu et al. [9] is used to specify the Eulerian fluid velocities at the outer edge of the viscous boundary layer. The Eulerian fluid velocities within this bottom layer are then obtained by solving the dimensionless governing equations that satisfy the various boundary conditions specified. Effects of wave damping due to viscosity and heat transfer are neglected. The work on laminar boundary layer [10, 17] will be reported here.

There are minor differences in the procedure used for deriving fluid velocities in the viscous bottom layer, as compared to that for deriving the wave theory. First, to facilitate the development of velocity field within the bottom layer, it is necessary to use a new Cartesian coordinate system that has the z-axis vertically upwards from the bed where the origin is located, the x and y-axes are horizontal (x along the reflecting wall and y normal to it, as used previously). This is different from the one used in deriving the wave theory as discussed previously, where the origin is at the still water level with its z-axis vertically upwards. Second, after examining the orders of magnitude of various terms in the governing Navier-Stokes equations in dimensional form, which is applicable to the bottom layer, a new set of dimensionless quantities differing from Equation 6 is used. All physical quantities associated with vertical dimension will have different scale effects from those in the horizontal dimensions.

Upon introducing the new set of dimensionless quantities as

$$\left.\begin{aligned}
&\hat{x} = kx, \; \hat{y} = ky, \; \hat{z} = [(gk)^{0.5}/\nu]^{0.5} \, z, \; \hat{d} = kd, \; \hat{t} = \sigma t, \\
&\hat{\phi}(\hat{x}, \hat{y}, \hat{z}, \hat{t}) = k^2 \epsilon^{-1} \, (gk)^{-0.5} \, \phi(x, y, z, t), \\
&\hat{u} = (k/g)^{0.5} \, u, \; \hat{v} = (k/g)^{0.5} \, v, \; \hat{w} = [\nu \, (gk)^{0.5}]^{-0.5} \, w, \\
&\hat{\omega} = \sigma/(gk)^{0.5}, \; \hat{p} = (k/\rho g) \, p.
\end{aligned}\right\} \tag{69}$$

the usual three-dimensional Navier-Stokes equations are transformed into dimensionless form (omitting the carets):

$$\omega u_t + u u_x + v u_y + w u_z = \omega U_t + U U_x + V U_y + u_{zz} \tag{70}$$

$$\omega v_t + u v_x + v v_y + w v_z = \omega V_t + U V_x + V V_y + v_{zz} \tag{71}$$

$$u_x + v_y + w_z = 0 \tag{72}$$

where the subscripts x, y, z, and t are partial derivatives to the fluid velocities u, v, and w within the boundary layer, and to that at the edge of the layer, i.e., U, V, and W; ω is the dimensionless wave angular frequency as defined by Equation 13.

An additional change of variable for z within the boundary layer is also introduced [59, 60],

$$\zeta = \left(\frac{1}{2} \, \omega_0\right)^{0.5} z \tag{73}$$

or physically $\zeta = z/(\nu T/\pi)^{0.5}$ in dimensional form, as a measure of distance from the bed within the boundary layer. Theoretically, the value of $\zeta \to \infty$ has been taken as the distance to the edge of the boundary layer. However, it is worth noting that $\zeta = 2\pi$ corresponds to the outer edge of the boundary layer, since the boundary-layer thickness is usually calculated by $\delta = 2(\pi\nu T)^{0.5}$, i.e., from replacing z in the dimensional form of Equation 73 by the value of δ.

The dimensionless velocity components (U, V, W) assume the expansion series in a small parameter ϵ as:

$$f = \sum_{i=1}^{\infty} \epsilon^i f_i \quad \text{for (U, V, W)} \tag{74}$$

and fluid velocities (u, v, w) in the form of

$$f = \sum_{i=1}^{\infty} \epsilon^i f_i = \sum_{i=1}^{\infty} \epsilon^i (f_{ip} + f_{is}) \quad \text{for } (u, v, w) \tag{75}$$

in the latter, f_{ip} are time-dependent and f_{is} are time-independent terms. For velocities in dimensionless form, the following relationships exist

$$\hat{u} = \epsilon\phi_x, \; \hat{v} = \epsilon\phi_y, \; \hat{w} = \epsilon\phi_z \tag{76}$$

in which ϕ is the perturbed value using the first and second-order solutions previously derived.

The boundary conditions at the real bottom of the layer are all velocity components equal to zero; while at the outer edge, the Eulerian water-particle velocities are represented by the velocities on the bed from the inviscid wave theory for $z = -d$. The dimensionless quantities of these free-stream velocities U, V, and W are,

$$U = \epsilon\phi_x|_{z=-d}$$
$$= \epsilon \, (m\omega_o/\sinh \hat{d}) \cos Y \cos X + \epsilon^2 \, (2m\beta_2 \cos 2Y \cos 2X + 2m\beta_3 \cos 2X)$$
$$= \epsilon \, U_1 + \epsilon^2 U_2 + O(\epsilon^3) \tag{77}$$

$$V = \epsilon\phi_y|_{y=-d}$$
$$= -\epsilon \, (n\omega_o/\sinh \hat{d}) \sin Y \sin X - \epsilon^2 \, (2n\beta_2 \sin 2Y \sin 2X)$$
$$= \epsilon \, V_1 + \epsilon^2 V_2 + O(\epsilon^3) \tag{78}$$

and

$$W = \epsilon\phi_z|_{z=-d} = 0, \text{ more particularly at the bed,} \tag{79}$$

in which $X = (m\hat{x} - t)$, $Y = n\hat{y}$.

Inserting the perturbed quantities of velocities from Equations 75 and 77 to 79 into Equations 70 to 72, and collecting terms of each order in ϵ yields the necessary equations to each order of approximation. The governing equations in dimensionless form [17] are not reproduced here. Only the resultant Eulerian water-particle velocities to the first order are given here in dimensionless form as

$$u_1 = \frac{m \, \omega_o}{\sinh \hat{d}} \cos(n\hat{y}) \, [\cos(m\hat{x} - \hat{t}) - e^{-\zeta} \cos(m\hat{x} - \hat{t} + \zeta)] \tag{80}$$

$$v_1 = -\frac{n \, \omega_o}{\sinh \hat{d}} \sin(n\hat{y}) \, [\sin(m\hat{x} - \hat{t}) - e^{-\zeta} \sin(m\hat{x} - \hat{t} + \zeta)] \tag{81}$$

$$w_1 = \frac{\omega_0^{0.5}}{\sinh \hat{d}} \cos(n\hat{y}) \left[\sqrt{2}\, \varsigma \, \sin(m\hat{x} - \hat{t}) - \sin\left(m\hat{x} - \hat{t} + \frac{1}{4}\,\pi\right) \right.$$

$$\left. + e^{-\varsigma} \sin\left(m\hat{x} - \hat{t} + \varsigma + \frac{1}{4}\,\pi\right) \right] \tag{82}$$

Complete solutions for these velocities to the second-order are

$$u_2 = Q_1 \cos 2X + (6Q_3 - 4Q_2)\, e^{-\varsigma} \cos(2X + \varsigma) + (Q_3 - Q_2)\, e^{-2\varsigma} \cos(2X + 2\varsigma)$$

$$- 2\sqrt{2}\, Q_3 \, \varsigma \, e^{-\varsigma} \cos\left(2X + \varsigma - \frac{1}{4}\,\pi\right)$$

$$- (Q_1 - 5Q_2 + 7Q_3)\, e^{-\sqrt{2}\,\varsigma} \cos(2X + \sqrt{2}\,\varsigma)$$

$$+ Q_3 \left[2e^{-\varsigma} (\sin \varsigma - 2 \cos \varsigma) - 2\sqrt{2}\varsigma\, e^{-\varsigma} \cos\left(\varsigma - \frac{1}{4}\,\pi\right) + e^{-2\varsigma} + 3 \right] \tag{83}$$

and

$$v_2 = \left[-Q_4 \sin 2X - 2Q_5 e^{-\varsigma} \sin(2X + \varsigma) + 2\sqrt{2}\, Q_5 \, \varsigma \, e^{-\varsigma} \sin\left(2X + \varsigma - \frac{1}{4}\,\pi\right) \right.$$

$$\left. + (Q_4 + 2Q_5)\, e^{-\sqrt{2}\,\varsigma} \sin(2X + \sqrt{2}\,\varsigma) \right] \sin(2n\hat{y})$$

$$+ Q_5 \left[2n^2 (4e^{-\varsigma} \sin \varsigma + e^{-2\varsigma} - 1) + 2\sqrt{2}\, \varsigma \, \epsilon^{-\varsigma} \sin\left(\varsigma - \frac{1}{4}\,\pi\right) \right.$$

$$\left. + 2e^{-\varsigma} \cos \varsigma - e^{-2\varsigma} - 1 \right] \sin(2n\hat{y}) \tag{84}$$

in which $X = (m\hat{x} - \hat{t})$ and the Q constants are given by

$$Q_1 = 2m\beta_2 \cos(2n\hat{y}) + 2\,m\,\beta_3$$

$$Q_2 = \frac{m\omega_0}{8 \sinh^2 \hat{d}} [\cos(2n\hat{y}) + 2\,m^2 - 1] \tag{85}$$

$$Q_3 = \frac{m\omega_0}{8 \sinh^2 \hat{d}} [\cos(2n\hat{y}) + 1]$$

$$Q_4 = 2\,n\,\beta_2$$

$$Q_5 = \frac{n\omega_0}{8 \sinh^2 \hat{d}} \tag{86}$$

The vertical velocity component w_2 is then obtained from the continuity equation, i.e., Equation 72, and is given as

$$w_2 = \sqrt{(2/\omega_o)} \left[Q_6 \, \zeta \sin 2X - Q_7 \sin\left(2X + \frac{1}{4}\pi\right) - 8Q_8 e^{-\zeta} \sin\left(2X + \zeta + \frac{1}{4}\pi\right) \right.$$

$$- Q_8 e^{-2\zeta} \sin\left(2X + 2\zeta + \frac{1}{4}\pi\right) + Q_9 \zeta e^{-\zeta} \sin(2X + \zeta)$$

$$\left. + Q_{10} e^{-\sqrt{2}\,\zeta} \sin\left(2X + \zeta + \frac{1}{4}\pi\right) \right]$$

$$+ \sqrt{(2/\omega_o)} \left\{ 2n^3 Q_5 \left[4\sqrt{2}\, e^{-\zeta} \sin\left(\zeta + \frac{1}{4}\pi\right) + e^{-2\zeta} + 2\zeta - 5 \right] \cos(2n\hat{y}) \right.$$

$$\left. + 2nQ_5 \left[2\zeta e^{-\zeta} \sin\zeta - 2e^{-\zeta} \cos\zeta - \frac{1}{2} e^{-2\zeta} + 2\zeta - \frac{3}{2} \right] \cos(2n\hat{y}) \right\} \qquad (87)$$

in which the Q constants are specified as

$$Q_6 = 2\, mQ_1 + 2\, nQ_4 \cos(2n\hat{y})$$

$$Q_7 = m\, [Q_1 - 5Q_2 + 7Q_3 + 9(Q_2 - Q_3)/\sqrt{2}] + n\,(Q_4 + 2Q_5)\cos(2n\hat{y})$$

$$Q_8 = m\,(Q_3 - Q_2)/\sqrt{2} \qquad\qquad (88)$$

$$Q_9 = 4\, mQ_3 + 4\, nQ_5 \cos(2n\hat{y})$$

$$Q_{10} = m\,(Q_1 - 5Q_2 + 7Q_3) + n\,(Q_4 + 2Q_5)\cos(2n\hat{y})$$

The physical meaning of the solutions presented are explained as follows. All Eulerian velocities consist of boundary layer independent and dependent terms (the latter being in $e^{-\zeta}$, $e^{-2\zeta}$, $\zeta e^{-\zeta}$, etc.). Equation 82 indicates that outside the bottom boundary layer the third term tends to zero, while the first term represents continuity of the mean flow and the second the displacement effect of the boundary layer on the external flow, or in other words, the diffusion of periodic vorticity. More precisely, the so-called "secular-term," i.e., the first term in the bracket of Equation 82, fulfills the need for the continuity condition within the layer. Therefore, its presence is entirely consistent with the unsteady boundary layer theory where an external mean flow exists.

The limiting two-dimensional expressions for progressive wave with $m = 1$ and $n = 0$, and for the normal standing wave with $m = 0$ and $n = 1$, can be readily obtained. The results so reduced are similar to those [59–64], for these two-dimensional cases, in which a "secular term" of ζ also appears within w_1 in these solutions.

It is worth stating, from a theoretical point of view, that because the boundary layer has been considered to be of infinite extent in the vertical z-direction, it is necessary that the transition of (u, v) into (U, V) is asymptotic in nature. However, in practice, it has been shown by many researchers that these free-stream velocities (i.e., U and V) are reached very rapidly, and the assumption of a finite thickness to boundary layer is therefore justified and meaningful. The "secular term" of ζ in Equation 82 for w_1 becomes infinite theoretically at the edge of the boundary layer, due to the bottom layer being considered of infinite thickness. Because in practice this layer is of finite size, as just mentioned, some millimeters in magnitude in models and on the order of centimeters in prototype condition, it appears efficacious to use the maximum value of ζ, which has been shown from numerical evaluation to approximate 2π. This is the dimensional meaning of Equation 73, and therefore represents the condition at the outer edge of the laminar bottom layer.

It is also clear, from Equations 83, 84, and 87, that u_2, v_2, and w_2 consist of some periodic parts, with and without boundary layer variables, plus the time-independent terms, which are varying across the direction normal to the reflecting wall. The secular term in w_2 of Equation 87 serves the need of satisfying the continuity equation, similar to that for the first-order. It may also be assumed that the vorticity is diffused away from the bottom boundary layer by molecular action and convected by the flow, particularly the vertical velocity components relative to the main flow in the interior.

It is desirable to show a test case of short-crested wave produced by an incident wave 76 mm in height and period T = 1 second in 300 mm of water, with approaching angle $\theta = 45°$ to a reflecting wall. A maximum value of u = 190 mm/s occurs at the alignments of the combined crests. Figure 30 depicts the vectorial sums of Eulerian fluid velocities (u_1, v_1, u_2, v_2) up to the second-order, for specific y/L_y at various time intervals t/T. It is seen that the maximum values of u and v occur at different y/L_y and t/T, for example, the maximum u appears at $y/L_y = 0$, $1/2$, 1,... at t/T = 0, $1/2$, 1,...; while v becomes maximum along alignments $y/L_y = 1/4$, $3/4$,... From this figure, it can also be observed, among various t/T, that along alignments of combined crests the water-particle motions are predominantly in the x-direction, and that half-way between they are mainly transverse but with some forward motions. Half-way between again, i.e., in the vicinity of $y/L_y = 1/8$ water-particle orbits rotate in ellipses, being anti-clockwise at $y/L_y = 1/8$ and $5/8$, and clockwise at $y/L_y = 3/8$ and $7/8$.

Knowing that u and v reach their maxima at different y/L_y and t/T as noted, it is beneficial to display the vertical distribution of velocity profiles within the laminar layer as a function of time t/T for the alignments where the velocity is at its maximum as already illustrated in Figure 30. This is depicted in Figure 31. From this figure, it can be seen that flow reversal exists in the lower portion of the bottom layer at certain combinations of y/L_y and t/T, even when fluid velocities to the first-order are considered. From Figures 31 and 32, the relative ordering of velocity components can be realized from the dimensional values presented. The maximum ratio of u_1 and u_2 (first to second-order velocity), as given in these two figures, is $u_1 \approx 10u_2$. It also shows that the maximum magnitudes of the second-order velocities $u_2 \approx 4v_2$ and $u_2 \approx 4 w_1$, for the same wave conditions as used for deriving Figure 30. In other words, $u_1 \approx 40 v_2$ and $u_1 \approx 40w_1$. Further calculations show that the maximum ratio of $w_1/w_2 \approx 10$, and therefore $u_1 \approx 400 w_2$ for this particular case.

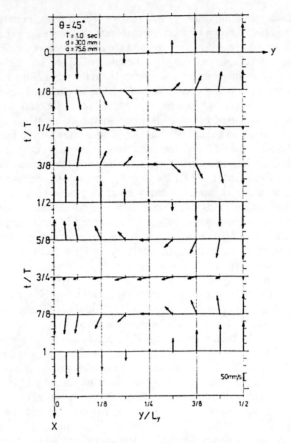

Figure 30. Variations of vectorial sum of Eulerian fluid velocities to second-order, in magnitude and direction, as functions of y/L$_y$ and t/T, in a laminar bottom layer. For the short-crested wave produced by incident wave height = 75.6 mm, period = 1.0 sec in 300 mm water depth, $\theta = 45°$.

From the previous example, it is clear that the vertical velocity components, w_1 and w_2, are negligibly small, particularly w_2. However, the vertical velocity components, although relatively small in value, might help initiate or maintain suspension of sedimentary particles, besides the turbulent effect in a real situation.

The effect of wave obliquity on the magnitude of fluid velocities is given in Figure 33, using the same wave conditions as for deriving Figure 30, except for varying obliquities. It is found that $u_1 \approx 10u_2$ for the case of $\theta = 60°$, and u_2 remains seemingly unchanged for all the three angles presented. The value of u_1 decreases as the approaching angle decreases, which is as expected.

The Lagrangian mean velocity of a water-particle with continuous path in the fluid is defined as the time-averaged value over one complete wave cycle. This is the convective derivative of particle position when moving with the particle. This velocity is termed as "mass transport velocity" in the literature [65]. Defining the mass transport velocity in dimensionless form as

$$U_M = \epsilon \ U_{M1} + \epsilon^2 U_{M2} + \frac{1}{2} \ \epsilon^3 \ U_{M3} + O(\epsilon^4) \qquad (89)$$

with similar expressions for V_M and W_M, (and with carets omitted hereafter for the sake of simplicity). There is no first-order motion for mass transport, because the time-averaged value of any periodic function over a complete wave cycle will vanish, or $U_{M1} = 0$, similarly $V_{M1} = 0$ and $W_{M1} = 0$. Therefore, the first approximation to mass transport is defined only by using U_{M2}, V_{M2}, and W_{M2}.

Using the Eulerian water-particle velocities derived up to the second-order for the bottom boundary layer [17], the mass-transport velocity components U_{M2}, V_{M2}, and W_{M2} have been derived in dimensionless form, within a laminar bottom boundary layer in the simple short-crested wave, as

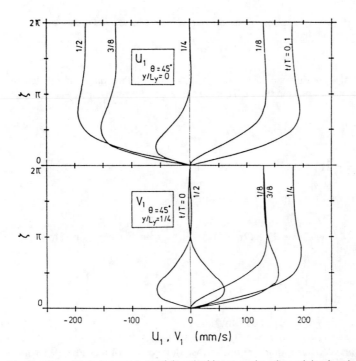

Figure 31. Profiles of Eulerian water-particle velocities u_1 and v_1, through laminar bottom layer at various time steps at locations where the velocities u and v are maximal according to Figure 30. For the same incident wave conditions as in Figure 30.

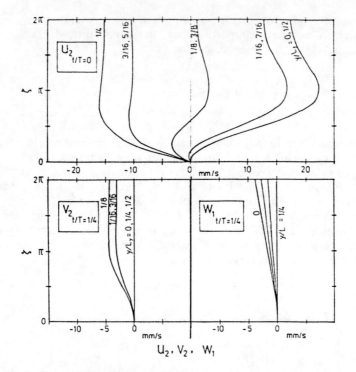

Figure 32. Profiles of Eulerian fluid velocities u_2, v_2 and w_1, through laminar bottom layer at various y/L_y locations and time steps t/T. For the same incident wave conditions as in Figure 30.

$$U_{M2} = \frac{m\,\omega_o}{8\,\sinh^2 d}\,\{[5 + 3e^{-2\varsigma} - 8e^{-\varsigma}\cos\varsigma]$$

$$+ [(4m^2 + 1) + (2m^2 + 1)\,e^{-2\varsigma} - 8m^2\,e^{-\varsigma}\cos\varsigma]\}\,\cos(2ny) \qquad (90)$$

$$V_{M2} = \frac{n\,\omega_o}{8\,\sinh^2 d}\,[-(2n^2 + 1) + (2n^2 + 1)\,e^{-2\varsigma} + 8n^2\,e^{-\varsigma}\sin\varsigma]\,\sin(2ny) \qquad (91)$$

$$W_{M2} = \frac{\sqrt{(2\omega_o)}}{8\,\sinh^2 d}\,\left\{n^4\left[8\,\sqrt{2}\,e^{-\varsigma}\sin\left(\varsigma + \frac{1}{4}\pi\right) + 2e^{-2\varsigma} + 4\varsigma - 10\right]\right.$$

$$\left. + n^2\,[e^{-2\varsigma} + 2\varsigma - 1]\right\}\,\cos(2ny) \qquad (92)$$

Both U_{M2} and V_{M2} are identical with those derived by Mei et al. [29] from using the Lagrangian form and linear superposition of two first-order velocity potentials. The described alternative approach to the second-order directly (with Eulerian description and the short-crested wave theory) has produced similar results. This is because the present boundary layer analysis is the first approximation. Also, the time averaged values of u_2 and v_2 retain only those time-independent terms originating from the first-order velocity components. The common result is therefore to be as expected. However, the equation for U_{M2} cannot be reduced to the well-known expression for the two-dimensional progressive waves given by Longuet-Higgins [65], as discussed elsewhere [17].

As water surface profiles in short-crested waves vary spatially in two directions, so do velocity components. Figure 34 depicts values of all mass-transport velocity components at the outer edge as functions of the specific distance across the crest length direction (y/L_y) and the angles of incidence (θ), for the case of $d/L_A = 0.1$. It is clear that U_{M2} is unidirectional with one sign throughout, while V_{M2} and W_{M2} are sinusoidal with changes in direction at various locations.

For the short-crested wave generally, it can be seen from Figure 34 that the water-particle moves forward as well as upward along the combined crests alignments (at $y/L_y = 0$, $1/2$, 1,... etc.). Half-way between, a rather slow forward but setting-down movement occurs at $y/L_y = 1/4$, $3/4$,... etc. Half-way between again, where $y/L_y = 1/8$, $3/8$, $5/8$,... etc., the water-particle is shifting towards its neighboring alignment of the combined crest thus ready for moving forward from this latter position.

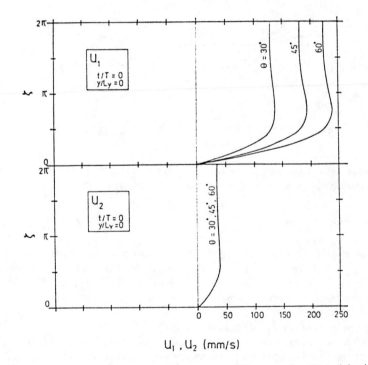

U_1, U_2 (mm/s)

Figure 33. Profiles of the maximum Eulerian fluid velocities u_1 and u_2, through laminar bottom layer at $y/L_y = 0$ and $t/T = 0$. For the same incident wave conditions as in Figure 30.

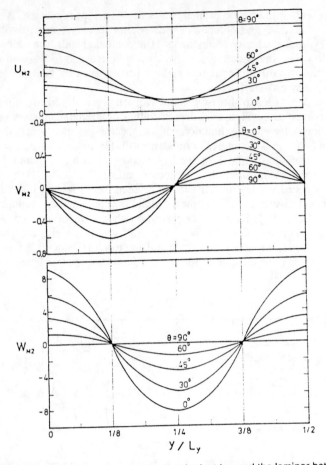

Figure 34. Variations of mass-transport velocities for just beyond the laminar bottom layer as functions of specific distance from the reflecting wall and the angles of incidence; $d/L_A = 0.1$.

The order of magnitude of W_{M2} in Figure 34 is not directly comparable with that of U_{M2} and V_{M2} within the same figure, as it originates from different variable transformation as in Equations 69 and 73, and hence is rather distorted. But, it is sufficient for the purpose of explaining the combined effect of mass-transport velocities.

The maximum mass-transport velocities for various locations are illustrated in Figures 35 to 37, as functions of the relative vertical distance ζ and angle of incidence θ, where the value of ordinate at 32 represents $\zeta = 2\pi$, which is the realistic distance at the outer edge of the laminar layer. It is worth noting that both V_{M2} and W_{M2} show a flow reversal near the lower part of the bottom layer for $\theta < 45°$, as given in Figures 36 and 37. Mei et al. [29] have indicated this flow reversal in V_{M2}, but the same phenomenon for W_{M2} has not been reported.

For the case of $\theta = 45°$ and $d/L_A = 0.1$, each of the prescribed mass-transport velocities at various y/L_y alignments are graphed in Figures 38 to 40. Again, it is clear that not only the magnitudes of the velocity profiles are varied across the crest length direction, but also U_{M2}, V_{M2}, and W_{M2} possess different kinds of velocity profiles generally. The graphical examples mentioned are derived from Equations 90 to 92 in dimensionless form. A comparison of these mass-transport velocities in real magnitudes is beneficial. For the wave conditions specified for Figure 30, the mass-transport velocities U_{M2} and V_{M2} in dimensional form are shown in Figure 41. The forward velocity U_{M2} reaches its maximum along the combined crests and is minimal along ¼ of y/L_y, where at this latter alignment V_{M2} is zero. Therefore, all

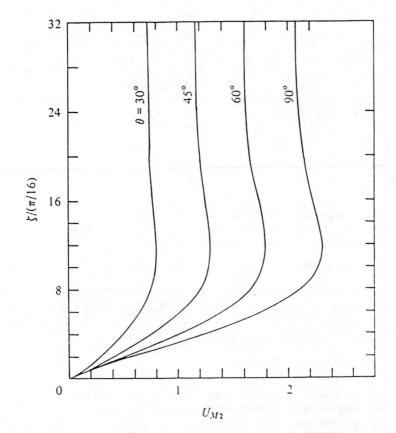

Figure 35. Mass-transport velocity profiles of U_{M2} through the laminar bottom layer for various angles of incidence. The curve for $\theta = 90°$ (progressive wave) agreeing with that of the Longuet-Higgins [65]; $d/L_A = 0.1, y/L_y = 0,1/2$ and 1.

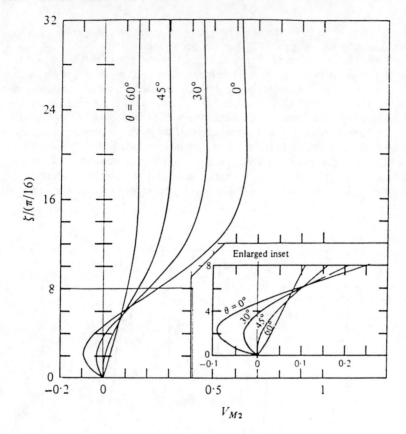

Figure 36. Mass-transport velocity profiles of V_{M2} through the laminar bottom layer for various angles of incidence. The curve for $\theta = 0°$ (standing wave) agreeing with that of Longuet-Higgins [65]; $d/L_A = 0.1$, $y/L_y = 1/8$, 3/8, 5/8, and 7/8.

water-particles within the short-crested wave system have a net movement forward irrespective of their positions across the crest length direction. This also confirms that in the vicinity of $1/8$ of y/L_y, the resultant mass-transport velocity vector is inclined towards its neighboring alignment of the combined crest.

Observation of Orbital Motions

Observations of water-particle motions close to the bed have been reported [10, 17, 24, 41] using polystyrene beads with diameters between 1 and 1.5 mm and specific gravity of about 1.03. These tracer beads were carefully placed on the perspex zone of the bed in an outdoor wave basin, as shown in Figure 42. The wave basin, located at the Shenton Park Research Station of the University of Western Australia, had a unique T-shaped tunnel of 1.8×2.1 m cross-section constructed beneath it.

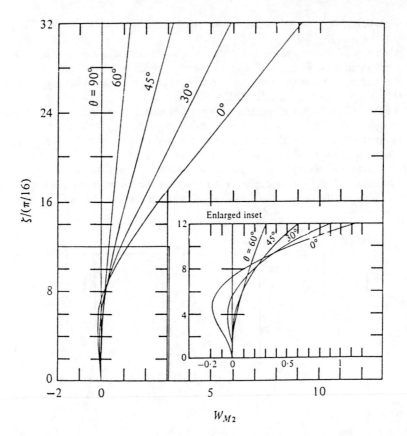

Figure 37. Mass-transport velocity profiles of W_{M2} through the laminar bottom layer for various angles of incidence; $d/L_A = 0.1, y/L_y = 0, 1/2$ and 1.

The tracers used were about one-third of the laminar boundary-layer thickness, which would have made comparison with theory difficult. But as a first attempt at verification of orbital motions and mass transport close to the bed in a three-dimensional wave case, the procedure was believed to be both novel and realistic. The introduction of a slight negative buoyancy to the tracer beads helped to retain the beads in the bottom layer during motion.

Tests were first conducted on pure progressive waves as this case is well established. A comparison was made with the particle velocity and mass transport in progressive waves in order to assess a scale factor, if any, which could then be applied to the case of short-crested waves. With the size of tracers about one-third of the boundary layer thickness, it was found that the recorded velocities corresponded consistently to the theoretical values at about one-eighth of the layer thickness from the bed. Therefore, it was possible to compare the measured Eulerian water-particle velocities and mass-transport obtained from various test runs, upon neglecting the scale factor.

The effects of varying wave incidence and wave period are important to engineering applications. Figures 43 and 44 present orbital paths of beads recorded at specific distances from the reflecting wall (y/L_y), for wave conditions $\theta = 45°$, T = 0.974 seconds, $d/L = 0.221$, $H/L = 0.060$; and $\theta = 30°$, T = 1.00 seconds, $d/L = 0.220$, $H/L = 0.063$ respectively, where H and L are the wave height and wavelength of the incident waves. Circular dots indicate positions at $1/12$ time intervals of the wave period, with squared points for positions after each wave cycle, the latter being a measure of mass transport velocities.

The variations in inclination of the mass-transport vectors (in plan) with respect to the positive x-direction are depicted in Figure 45. The fluctuating but very small inclination within the range of $y/L_y = 0$ to $1/8$ indicates a wider band of y/L_y near the

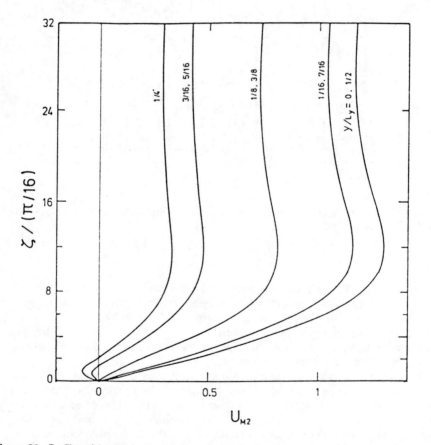

Figure 38. Profiles of the maximum mass-transport velocity of U_{M2} through the laminar bottom layer, at various distances from the wall; $\theta = 45°$, $d/L_A = 0.1$.

wall having forward motion for the case of $\theta = 45°$, while they are mainly moved laterally towards the reflecting wall for the case of $\theta = 30°$. Over the range of $y/L_y = 1/4$ to $1/2$, strong inclinations towards the combined crest alignment at $y/L_y = 1/2$ are seen for both cases. However, the case of 30° had greater transverse motions towards the combined crest at $y/L_y = 1/2$ than that of $\theta = 45°$.

A careful comparison of the horizontal particle velocities and mass transport at various alignments across the crest length direction thus shows that a change of incident wave direction would produce different bed forms. It also enhances different speeds of scouring at various alignments within the resultant short-crested wave system. This suggests that the capacity of scouring or removal of particles from within certain alignments parallel to the wall would be more uniform with a particular approach angle, while the wave conditions of d/L and H/L remain relatively constant.

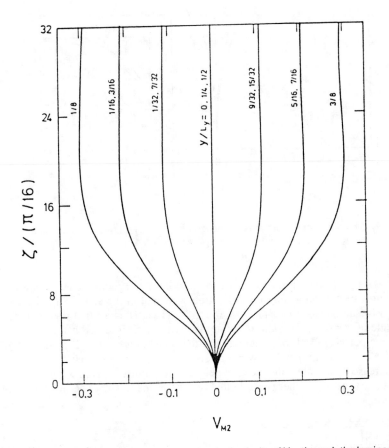

Figure 39. Profiles of the maximum mass-transport velocity of V_{M2} through the laminar bottom layer, at various distances from the wall; $\theta = 45°, d/L_A = 0.1$.

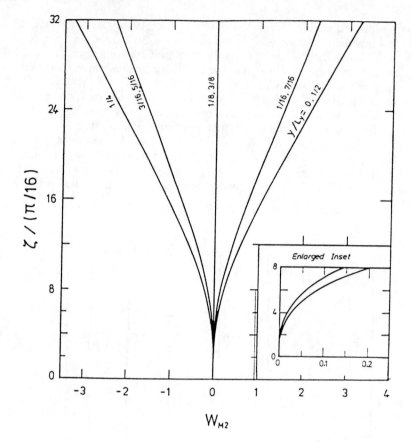

Figure 40. Profiles of the maximum mass-transport velocity of W_{M2} through the laminar bottom layer, at various distances from the wall; $\theta = 45°$, $d/L_A = 0.1$.

Another group of test runs was aimed to examine the effect of changing wave period, with waves approaching the reflecting wall within the same obliquity and the same wave height over constant water depth. These runs all had the same approach angle of $\theta = 45°$. Only the results of two runs are discussed here, one with shorter wave period (T = 0.833 second) and the other longer (T = 1.25 seconds). Because the wave energy per unit width of crest is proportional to H^2L, it was decided to increase deliberately the incident height of the shorter period wave, so as to equalize at least the wave energy for both cases mentioned. The experimental conditions were:

Case 3   T = 0.833 second
         H = 81 mm
         d = 310 mm
         $\theta = 45°$

Case 4 T = 1.25 seconds
       H = 74 mm
       d = 304 mm
       θ = 45°

The only differences were the resulting values of H/L and d/L as a result of changing wave period. These represented H/L = 0.076 and d/L = 0.289 for the case of
shorter wave period, and H/L = 0.039 and d/L = 0.162, respectively, to the case of
longer period.

   Samples of the measured orbital paths across the crest length direction for these
two runs are shown in Figures 46 and 47. It is obvious that the longer period wave

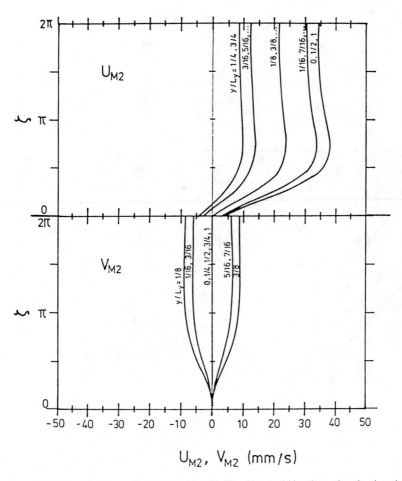

Figure 41. Dimensionless mass-transport velocities U_{M2} and V_{M2} through a laminar bottom
layer within a short-crested wave system. Incident wave conditions same as in Figure 30.

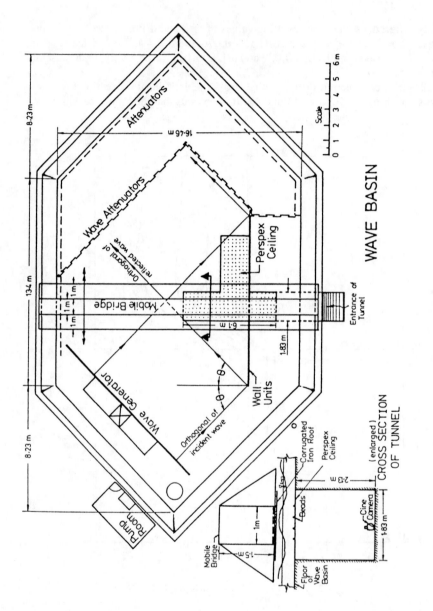

Figure 42. Plan view of an outdoor wave basin with details of the tunnel constructed beneath it.

RUN 1 [1] (45°-0.975-290), $d/L_A = 0.221$, $H/L_A = 0.060$

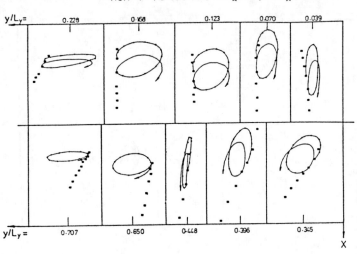

RUN 1 [2] (4.5°-0.975-290), $d/L_A = 0.221$, $H/L_A = 0.060$

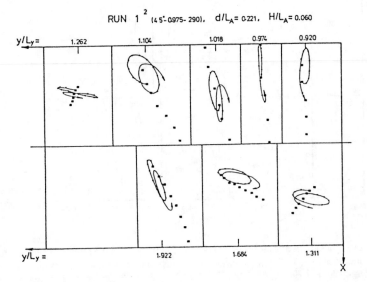

Figure 43. Orbital paths of beads recorded at specific distances from the reflecting wall. Circular dots indicating position at 1/12 time intervals of the wave period, squared points for position after each wave cycle. For Run 1, $\theta = 45°$, T = 0.975 sec, d = 290 mm, incident wave height H = 79 mm, resulting steepness $H/L_A = 0.060$, and $d/L_A = 0.221$.

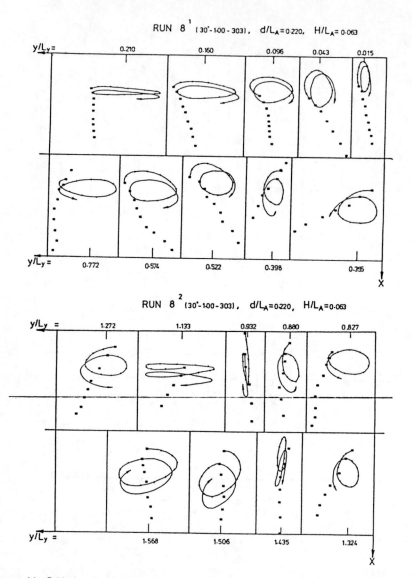

Figure 44. Orbital paths of beads recorded at specific distances from the reflecting wall. Circular dots indicating positon at 1/12 time intervals of the wave period, squared points for position after each wave cycle. For Run 8, $\theta = 30°$, T = 1.00 sec, d = 303 mm, incident wave height H = 86 mm, resulting steepness H/L_A = 0.063, and d/L_A = 0.220.

still had about twice the orbital amplitude of the shorter period, and hence the mass transport, even though the latter was given a higher wave energy, about 10% more than the former. Apparently, the concept of total wave energy is incapable of explaining this seemingly contradicting result obtained for the mass transport in the

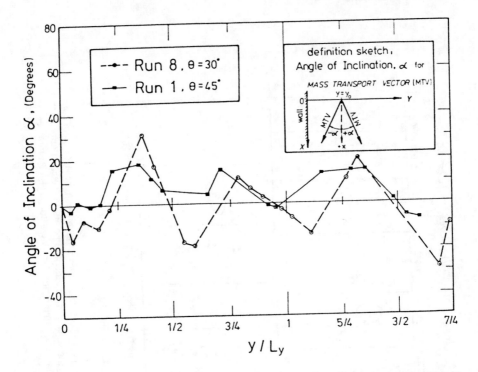

Figure 45. Variations of the inclination of the measured horizontal mass-transport vectors to the reflecting wall, for angles of incidence $\theta = 30°$ and $45°$.

bottom layer. However, according to a dimensional expression of mass-transport velocity,

$$U_{M2} = \frac{5 \; k \; \sigma \; a^2}{4 \; \sinh^2 \; kd} \tag{93}$$

for the progressive wave, it was realized that the existence of "$\sinh^2 \; kd$" in the denominator of Equation 93 is of vital importance in reducing the magnitude of the theoretical values of U_{M2}. In spite of the magnitude of wave energy available in this equation, i.e., $H_{sc}^2/L_x T$, where H_{sc} and L_x is the wave height and wavelength of the resulting short-crested waves, the shorter period wave was far superior to that of the longer period (about 2.59 times greater). The measured U_{M2} at $y/L_y = \frac{1}{2}$ were 21 and 9 mm/sec for the longer and shorter period wave, respectively, presenting a ratio about 2.44 against the theoretical value of 2.39 from the given equation. This agreement is thus reasonable between the theory and experimental results. This may imply that the wave energy, which is normally applicable to the interior of the fluid, cannot be used directly in the viscous bottom boundary layer. This example demonstrates that the effect of wave period is influential in the bottom layer, rather than the traditional concept of wave energy.

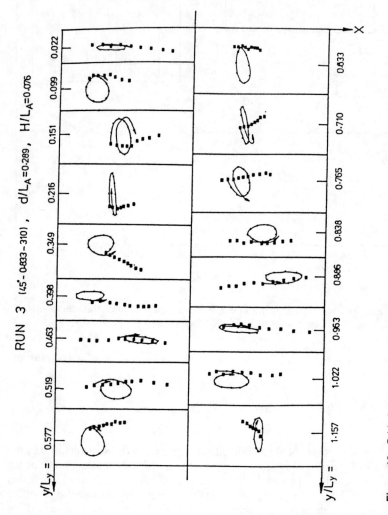

Figure 46. Orbital paths of beads recorded at specific distances from the reflecting wall. Circular dots indicating position at 1/12 time intervals of the wave period, squared points for position after each wave cycle. For Run 3, $\theta = 45°$, T = 0.833 sec, d = 310 mm, incident wave height H = 81 mm, resulting steepness $H/L_A = 0.076$, and $d/L_A = 0.289$.

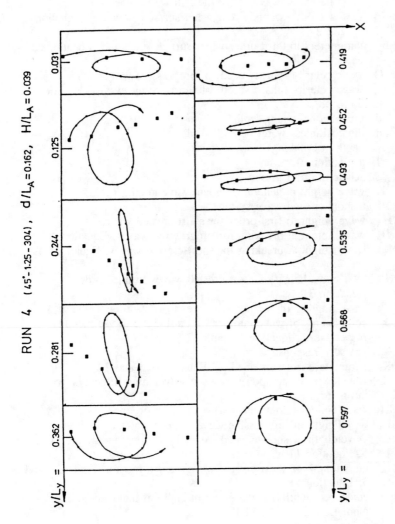

Figure 47. Orbital paths of beads recorded at specific distances from the reflecting wall. Circular dots indicating position at 1/12 time intervals of the wave period, squared points for position after each wave cycle. For Run 4, $\theta = 45°$, $T = 1.250$ sec, $d = 304$ mm, incident wave height $H = 74$ mm, resulting steepness $H/L_A = 0.039$, and $d/L_A = 0.162$.

Notation

a wave amplitude of short-crested wave to first-order

a_c crest height of wave above the still water level

b_1, b_2, b_3 parameters to second-order water surface elevation, Equations 19 and 22

$b_{11}, b_{13}, b_{31}, b_{33}$ parameters to third-order water surface elevation, Equations 25 and 28a–d

C wave celerity (phase speed) of progressive waves

C_s wave celerity (phase speed) of short-crested waves, Equations 36 to 38

d dimensional water depth

$\hat{d}$ dimensionless water depth ($= kd$)

d_b depth at breaking

f a function of

g acceleration of gravity

H wave height in general; incident wave height in a short-crested wave system

H_A wave height to first-order for short-crested waves

H_b wave height at breaking for progressive waves, Equation 40

H_{bsc} wave height at breaking for short-crested waves, Equations 39 and 40

H_{sc} total wave height of short-crested waves to third-order, Equation 31

k wave number of component waves to first-order ($= 2\pi/L_A$)

k_x, k_y components of wave number "k" in the x and y-directions, respectively, Equations 11 and 12

K_p pressure response factor

K_1, K_2 parameters in terms of "kd," Equations 21 and 23

L wavelength of component waves; wavelength in general to third-order

L_A wavelength of component waves to first-order

L_o wavelength of progressive wave in deep water

L_x wavelength of short-crested waves in x-direction, Figures 1 and 5, Equation 11

L_y crest length of short-crested waves in y-direction, Figures 1 and 5, Equation 11

m, n constants identifying the effect of angle of incidence in the plan, Equations 11 and 12

$O(\ )$ order of a parameter or variable

p dimensional wave pressure

$\hat{p}$ dimensionless wave pressure ($= (p/\rho g)p$), Equations 59 and 60

$\hat{p}_1, \hat{p}_2, \hat{p}_3$ components of wave pressure in each order of wave theory, Equations 61 to 66

Q_i a parameter relating to second-order Eulerian water-particle velocities u_2, v_2, and w_2, Equations 85, 86, and 88

T wave period in seconds

t time

$\hat{t}$ dimensionless time $(= \sigma t)$

t_o initial time used in the displacement of water particles

u,v,w Eulerian water-particle velocities in the x, y, and z-directions, respectively

$\hat{u}$ dimensionless velocity in x-direction $(= (k/g)^{0.5}u)$, Equation 69

u_1,u_2 components of velocity u in each order of wave theory, Equations 80 and 83

u_{max} maximum value of Eulerian water-particle velocity u, Figures 16 and 19 to 26

$\hat{v}$ dimensionless velocity in y-direction $(= (k/g)^{0.5}v)$, Equation 69

v_1,v_2 components of velocity v in each order of wave theory Equations 81 and 84

$\hat{w}$ dimensionless velocity in z-direction $= (\nu \sqrt{(kg)})^{-0.5}w$ Equation 69

w_1,w_2 components of velocity w in each order of wave theory, Equations 82 and 87

U,V,W Eulerian water-particle velocities at the outer edge of the bottom boundary layer, in the x, y, and z-directions, respectively, Equations 77 to 79

U_M,V_M,W_M mass-transport velocities in the x, y, and z-directions, respectively, Equation 89

U_{M1},U_{M2} components of mass-transport velocity U_M to the first and second order of the wave theory, Equations 89 and 90

V_{M1},V_{M2} components of mass-transport velocity V_M to the first and second order of the wave theory, Equation 91

W_{M1},W_{M2} components of mass-transport velocity W_M to the first and second order of the wave theory, Equation 92

x,y,z Rectangular Cartesian coordinates, Figures 1 and 5

$\hat{x}$ dimensionless parameter $(= kx)$

X dimensionless parameter $(= (m\hat{x} - \hat{t}))$

$\hat{y}$ dimensionless parameter $(= ky)$

Y dimensionless parameter $(= n\hat{y})$

$\hat{z}$ dimensionless parameter $= kz$, in Equation 6; $= ((\sqrt{gk}/\nu)^{0.5}z,$ in Equation 69)

Z dimensionless parameter $(= (\hat{z} + \hat{d}))$

x_o,y_o,z_o averaged initial position of a water-particle at time $t = t_o$, in three-dimensional case, Equation 46

Greek Symbols

β_o parameters related to relative water depth "kd," Equations 43 to 45

β_1,β_2,β_3 parameters to second-order velocity potential β_1,β_2,β_3, Equations 18 and 21

$\beta_{13},\beta_{31},\beta_{33}$ parameters to third-order velocity potential, Equations 24, and 27a–c

γ_{13}, γ_{31} parameters associated with the angle of incidence, Equation 28e

δ thickness of a laminar boundary layer

ϵ an expansion parameter in a perturbed series ($= ka$)

ζ a parameter associated with the vertical dimension of the bottom boundary layer, Equation 73

η water surface elevation

$\hat{\eta}$ dimensionless water surface elevation ($= k\eta/\epsilon$)

η_1, η_3, η_3 components of water surface elevation in each order of wave theory

η_{max}, η_{min} the maximum and minimum of wave profiles, respectively, Equations 30 and 31

θ angle of incidence measured between the wave orthogonal and the normal to a reflecting wall, Figures 1 and 5

θ_m the critical angle at which the Mach-stem effect occurred when waves reflected obliquely from a maritime structure

ν kinematic viscosity of water

ξ displacement of water-particles

ξ_1, ξ_2, ξ_3 components of water-particle displacement in x, y, and z-directions, respectively, Equation 57

$\xi_{11}, \xi_{21}, \xi_{31}$ components of displacement of water-particles to first-order in x, y, and z-directions, respectively, Equations 47 to 49

$\xi_{12}, \xi_{22}, \xi_{32}$ components of displacement of water-particles to second-order in x, y and z-directions, respectively, Equations 54 to 56

ρ density of water

Σ summation sign

σ angular frequency of wave ($= 2\pi/T$)

σ_o angular frequency of wave to first-order, Equation 36

ϕ velocity potential of waves

$\hat{\phi}$ dimensionless velocity potential of ϕ, [$= k^2 \epsilon^{-1} (gk)^{-0.5} \phi$], Equations 6 and 69

ϕ_1, ϕ_2, ϕ_3 components of velocity potential in each order of wave theory, Equations 13, 15, 18, and 24

$\hat{\omega}$ dimensionless angular frequency of wave [$(= \sigma/(gk)^{0.5}]$

ω_m a dimensionless angular frequency, Equation 23

ω_o dimensionless parameter as function of "kd," ($= \omega_1$ in Equation 17)

$\omega_1, \omega_2, \omega_3$ components of dimensionless angular frequency in each order of wave theory, Equations 13, 17, 20, and 26

∞ at infinity

π a constant ($= 3.141596$)

Subscripts

i,j general parameters for superscripts and subscripts

p periodic or time-dependent parts

s steady state solution; time-independent parts

t partial derivative with respect to time

x,y,z   partial derivatives of a function with respect to x, y, and z
         coordinates, respectively
ʆ   partial derivative with respect to dimension related to the
         thickness of bottom boundary layer

Mathematical Functions

cos, sin, tan   trigonometric functions
cosh, sinh,
tanh, coth   hyperbolic functions
dx, dy, dz, dt   ordinary derivatives with respect to x, y, z, and t, respectively
∂x, ∂y, ∂z   partial derivatives with respect to x, y, and z, respectively

References

1. Jeffreys, H., 1924, "On Water Waves Near the Coast," *Philosophical Magazine*, Series 6, Vol. 48, pp. 44–48.
2. Jeffreys, H., 1925, "On the Formation of Water Waves by Wind," *Proceedings Royal Society London*, Series A, Vol. 107, pp. 189–206.
3. Scheffner, N. W., 1986, "Bi-Periodic Waves in Shallow Water," *Proceedings, 20th International Conference on Coastal Engineering*, Vol. 1, pp. 724–736.
4. Ralls, G. C. and Wiegel, R. L., 1956, "A Laboratory Study of Short-Crested Wind Waves," *Beach Erosion Board*, U.S. Army, Corps of Engineers, *Technical Memorandum*, No. 81.
5. Fuchs, R. A., 1952, "On the Theory of Short-Crested Oscillatory Waves," *Gravity Waves*, U.S. National Bureau Standards, Circular 521, pp. 187–200.
6. MacCamy, R. C., 1957, "A Source Solution for Short-Crested Waves," *La Houille Blanche*, Vol. 3, pp. 379–389.
7. Chappelear, J. E., 1961, "On the Description of Short-Crested Waves," *Beach Erosion Board*, U.S. Army Corps of Engineers, *Technical Memorandum*, No. 125.
8. Hamada, T., 1965, *The Secondary Interactions of Surface Waves*, Port & Harbour Technical Research Institute, Japan, Report No. 10.
9. Hsu, J.R.C., Tsuchiya, Y. and Silvester, R., 1979, "Third-Order Approximation to Short-Crested Waves," *Journal Fluid Mechanics*, Vol. 90, pp. 179–196.
10. Hsu, J.R.C., 1979, *Short-Crested Water Waves*, Ph.D. Thesis, Department of Civil Engineering, University of Western Australia.
11. Roberts, A. J., 1983, "Highly Nonlinear Short-Crested Water Waves," *Journal Fluid Mechanics*, Vol. 135, pp. 301–321.
12. Roberts, A. J. and Schwartz, L. M., 1983, "The Calculation of Nonlinear Short-Crested Gravity Waves," *Physics of Fluids*, Vol. 26, No. 9, pp. 2388–2392.
13. Silvester, R., 1972, "Wave Reflection at Seawalls and Breakwaters," *Proceedings, Institution Civil Engineers*, Vol. 54, pp. 123–131.
14. Silvester, R., 1975, "Sediment Transmission Across Entrances by Natural Means," *Proceedings, 16th Congress International Association of Hydraulic Research*, Vol. 1, pp. 145–156.
15. Gjertveit, B., 1974, *An Investigation about the Crest Length Distribution for Short-Crested Waves*, Report, Division of Port & Ocean Eng., Norwegian Institute of Technology Trondheim.

16. Huntington, S.W., 1978, "Wave Loading on Large Cylinders in Short-Crested Seas," *Proceedings, International Association of Hydraulic Research, Symposium on Mechanics of Wave-Induced Forces on Cylinders*, Bristol, pp. 636–649.

17. Hsu, J.R.C., Silvester, R. and Tsuchiya, Y., 1980, "Boundary-Layer Velocities and Mass Transport in Short-Crested Waves," *Journal Fluid Mechanics*, Vol. 99, pp. 321–342.

18. Halliwell, A. R. and Machen, P. C., 1981, "Short-Crested Breaking Waves in Water of Limited Depth," *Proceedings, Institution of Civil Engineers*, Part 2, Vol. 71, pp. 663–674.

19. Machen, P. C., 1984, "Short-Crested Breaking Waves," *Proceedings, 19th International Conference on Coastal Engineering*, American Society Civil Engineers, Vol. 1, pp. 912–928.

20. Irie, I. and Nadaoka, K., 1984, "Laboratory Reproduction of Seabed Scour in Front of Breakwaters," *Proceedings, 19th International Conference on Coastal Engineering*, American Society Civil Engineers, Vol. 2, pp. 1715–1731.

21. Silvester, R., 1986, "The Influence of Oblique Reflection on Breakwaters," *Proceedings, 20th International Conference on Coastal Engineering*, American Society Civil Engineers, Vol. 3, pp. 2253–2267.

22. Irie, I., Kuriyama, Y. and Asakura, H., 1986, "Study on Scour in Front of Breakwaters by Standing Waves and Protection Methods," Report, *Port and Harbour Research Institute*, Japan, Vol. 25, No. 1, pp. 4–86.

23. Silvester, R. and Hsu, J.R.C., 1987, "Scouring due to Reflection of Oblique Waves on Breakwaters," *Proceedings, 8th Australian Conference Coastal & Ocean Engineering*, pp. 145–149.

24. Hsu, J.R.C., 1977, "Kinematics of Short-Crested Waves," *Proceedings, 6th Australasian Conference Hydraulics & Fluid Mechanics*, pp. 56–59.

25. Fenton, J. D., 1985, "Wave Forces on Vertical Walls," *Journal of Waterway, Port, Coastal and Ocean Engineering*, American Society Civil Engineers, Vol. 111, No. 4, pp. 693–718.

26. Stokes, G. G., 1847, "On the Theory of Oscillatory Waves," *Transactions, Cambridge Philosophical Society*, Vol. 8, pp. 441–455.

27. Keulegan, G. H., 1951, "Wind Tides in Small Closed Channels," *Journal of Research*, National Bureau of Standards, Vol. 46, No. 5, pp. 358–381.

28. Van Dorn, W. G., 1952, *Wind Stress Over Water*, Scripps Institute of Oceanography, SIO Reference No. 52–60.

29. Mei, C. C., Liu, P.L-F. and Carter, T. G., 1972, *Mass Transport in Water Waves*. Ralph M. Parsons Laboratory, Massachusetts Institute of Technology, Report No. 146.

30. Tanaka, N., Irie, I. and Ozasa, H., 1972, "A Study on the Velocity Distribution of Mass Transport Caused by Diagonal, Partial Standing Waves," *Report Port & Harbour Research Institute*, Japan, Vol. 11, No. 3, pp. 112–140 (in Japanese).

31. Carter, T. G., Liu, P. L-F., and Mei, C. C., 1973, "Mass Transport by Waves and Offshore Sand Bedforms," *Journal of Waterway, Harbours & Coastal Engineering Division*, American Society Civil Engineers, Vol. 99, pp. 165–184.

32. Dore, B. D., 1974, "The Mass Transport Velocity Due to Interacting Wave Trains," *Meccanica*, Vol. 9, pp. 172–178.

33. Mollo-Christensen, E., 1981, "Modulational Stability of Short-Crested Free Surface Waves," *Physics of Fluids*, Vol. 24(4), pp. 775–776.

34. Tadjbakhsh, I. and Keller, J. B., 1960, "Standing Surface Waves of Finite Amplitude," *Journal Fluid Mechanics*, Vol. 8, pp. 442–451.

35. Battjes, J. A., 1972, "Radiation Stresses in Short-Crested Waves," *Journal Marine Research*, Vol. 30, pp. 56–64.

36. Goda, Y., 1985, *Random Seas and Design of Maritime Structures*. Toyko: University of Tokyo Press.
37. Hsu, J.R.C., 1981, "Particle Kinematics in the Bottom Layer of Short-Crested Waves," *Proceedings, 5th Australian Conference on Coastal and Ocean Engineering*, pp. 121–124.
38. Hsu, J.R.C., 1983, "On the Limiting Conditions for Short-Crested Waves," *Proceedings, 6th Australian Conference on Coastal and Ocean Engineering*, pp. 42–46.
39. Hsu, J.R.C. and Silvester, R., 1982, Discussion of paper "Short-Crested Breaking Waves in Water of Limited Depth," by A. R. Halliwell and P. C. Machen, *Proceedings, Institution of Civil Engineers*, Part 2, Vol. 73, pp. 489–491.
40. Le Méhauté, B., 1986, "On the Highest Periodic Short-Crested Wave," *Journal of Waterway, Port, Coastal and Ocean Engineering*, American Society Civil Engineers, Vol. 112, No. 2, pp. 320–330.
41. Hsu, J.R.C., 1986, "Rough Turbulent Boundary Layer in Short-Crested Waves," *Proceedings, 20th International Conference on Coastal Engineering*, pp. 271–285.
42. Goda, Y. and Kakizaki, S., 1966, "Study on Finite Amplitude Standing Gravity Waves and Their Pressure on a Vertical Wall," Report, *Port & Harbour Research Institute*, Japan, Vol. 5, No. 10, (in Japanese).
43. Skjelbreia, L., 1959, *Gravity Waves, Stokes' Third-Order Approximation: Tables of Functions*, Berkeley, California: Engineering Foundation Council on Wave Research.
44. Laitone, E. V., 1962, "Limiting Conditions for Cnoidal and Stokes' Waves," *Journal Geophysical Research*, Vol. 67, pp. 1555–1564.
45. Goda, Y. and Abe, Y., 1968, "Apparent Coefficient of Partial Reflection of Finite Amplitude Waves," Report, *Port & Harbour Research Institute*, Japan, Vol. 7, No. 3.
46. Dean, R. G., 1968, "Breaking Wave Criteria: A Study Employing a Numerical Wave Theory," *Proceedings, 11th International Conference on Coastal Engineering*, Vol. 1, pp. 108–123.
47. Stokes, G. G., 1880, "On the Theory of Oscillatory Waves. Appendix B: Considerations Relative to the Greatest Height of Oscillatory Waves which can be Propagated without Change of Form," *Mathematical Physics Papers*, Cambridge University Press, Vol. 1, pp. 225–228.
48. Lenau, C. W., 1966, "The Solitary Waves of Maximum Amplitudes," *Journal Fluid Mechanics*, Vol. 25, pp. 309–320.
49. Penney, W. G. and Price, A. T., 1952, "Finite Periodic Stationary Gravity Waves in a Perfect Liquid; Part II, Some Gravity Wave Problems in the Motion of Perfect Fluid," *Philosophical Transactions Royal Society London*, Series A, Vol. 244, pp. 254–284.
50. Kishi, T., 1957, "Clapotis in Shallow Water," *Journal of Research, Public Works Research Institute*, Japan, Vol. 2, Paper 5, pp. 99–108.
51. Longuet-Higgins, M. S., 1975, "Integral Properties of Gravity Waves of Finite Amplitude," *Proceedings Royal Society London*, Series A, Vol. 342, pp. 157–174.
52. Cokelet, E. D., 1977, "Steep Gravity Waves in Water of Arbitrary Uniform Depth," *Philosophical Transactions Royal Society London*, Series A, Vol. 286, pp. 183–230.
53. Silvester, R., 1974, "Water Particle Orbits in Deep-to-Shallow Water Waves," *Proceedings, 5th Australasian Conference Hydraulics & Fluid Mechanics*, pp. 310–316.
54. Goda, Y., 1964, "Wave Forces on a Vertical Circular Cylinder: Experiments and a Proposed Method of Wave Force Computation," Report, *Port & Harbour Research Institute*, Japan, No. 8.
55. Wiegel, R. L., 1964, *Oceanographical Engineering*, Englewood, N.J.: Prentice-Hall, Inc.
56. Ippen, A. T. (ed.), 1966, *Estuary and Coastal Hydrodynamics*, New York: McGraw-Hill, Inc.

57. Kinsman, B., 1965, *Wind Waves*, Englewood, N.J.: Prentice-Hall, Inc.
58. Silvester, R., 1974, *Coastal Engineering, 1*, Amsterdam: Elsevier Scientific Publishing Company.
59. Noda, H., 1968, "A Study on Mass Transport in Boundary Layers of Standing Waves," *Proceedings, 11th International Conference on Coastal Engineering*, Vol. 1, pp. 227–247.
60. Noda, H., 1970, *The Basic Study on Coastal Littoral Drift*, Ph.D. Thesis, Kyoto University, Japan, (in Japanese).
61. Stuart, J. T., 1963, "Unsteady Boundary Layer," in *Laminar Boundary Layers*, L. Rosenhead, ed. Oxford University Press, pp. 349–408.
62. Schlichting, H., 1979, *Boundary-Layer Theory*, translated from German by J. Kestin, 6th ed. New York: McGraw-Hill Book Company, pp. 428–431.
63. Issacson, M. De St Q., 1976, "The Second Approximation to Mass Transport in Cnoidal Waves," *Journal Fluid Mechanics*, Vol. 78, pp. 445–457.
64. Liu, A-K. and Davis, S. H., 1977, "Viscous Attenuation of Mean Drift in Water Waves," *Journal Fluid Mechanics*, Vol. 81, pp. 63–84.
65. Longuet-Higgins, M.S., 1953, "Mass Transport in Water Waves," *Philosophical Transactions Royal Society London*, Series A, Vol. 245, pp. 535–581.

CHAPTER 4

RANDOM WAVES AND SPECTRA

Yoshimi Goda

Yokohama National University
Yokohama, Japan

CONTENTS

Introduction

   The sea surface is ever changing, sometimes undulating under swell, sometimes choppy under gale, and on rare occasions being heavily tossed up and down amid storms. The instantaneous configuration of the sea surface is quite complex with humps and hollows scattered in random manner. A beautiful pattern of long wave crestlines in quasi-regular manner is observable only in a shallow water area, when swell generated far away is approaching the shore.

   Randomness is the important feature of ocean waves. Application of the wave theory to the design of offshore and coastal structures requires incorporation of the stochastic approach to ocean waves into engineering practice. This chapter introduces the concept of random waves, provides the readers with workable formulas of frequency and directional wave spectra, and describes the statistical properties of individual wave heights and periods. The stochastic approach discussed here is essentially a linear one in the sense that many wave systems can be superimposed without causing interference. In reality, however, there is evidence of nonlinear interaction among wave systems, though its intensity is weak at least in deep water. The last part of this chapter discusses the nonlinear properties of random water waves.

Description of Random Ocean Waves

Gaussian Distribution of Surface Elevation

Since the late 1940s, many instrumental observations of ocean and coastal waves have been made around the world. Most wave recordings were made with a single stationary sensor, which yields the time history of surface elevation or its equivalent (underwater pressure variation). Because the record of surface elevation never duplicates itself in the sea, the only available method of analysis is the statistical one.

The first step in the analysis of a wave record at a single point is the examination of the distribution of instantaneous surface elevation sampled at a certain time interval. Such examinations by many investigators have led to the conclusion that the distribution of the surface elevation of ocean waves is closely approximated by the Gaussian distribution, i.e.,

$$p(\eta)d\eta = \frac{1}{(2\pi)^{1/2}\,\eta_{rms}}\exp\left[-\frac{\eta^2}{2\eta_{rms}^2}\right] \tag{1}$$

where $p(\eta)$ = the probability density function of the surface elevation η
η_{rms} = root-mean-square value of η

It is an established rule that the mean water level (arithmetic mean, straight regression line, or parabolic regression curve) is deducted from the record of surface elevation before any meaningful analysis of a wave record will be made. Thus, the mean water level $\bar{\eta}$ is zero, and Equation 1 is presented without $\bar{\eta}$.

As will be discussed later in this chapter, actual wave records exhibit certain deviations from Equation 1. However, the degree of deviation is small at least in deep water, and the equation is used as the basis of the stochastic analysis of ocean waves.

The Gaussian distribution is also applicable to the time derivative of the surface elevation and the surface slope to the same degree of approximation as the surface elevation itself.

Description of Random Ocean Waves by Means of Variance Spectrum

The present understanding of random ocean waves is such that they are composed of an infinite number of regular wave trains with various frequencies, wave numbers, and directions, which are superimposed on each other. Each wave train is of sinusoidal form, long-crested, and has an infinitesimally small amplitude. The Gaussian distribution of the surface elevation is a logical conclusion of this interpretation by virtue of the central limit theorem.

The interpretation remains as a hypothesis. No direct proof to support or deny the hypothesis has yet been obtained. However, many ocean wave phenomena have successfully been analyzed and explained by using this hypothesis. Many useful applications of ocean wave theories have been made to various engineering problems with this hypothesis. In this sense, the previous interpretation is regarded as an assumption sufficiently accurate for scientists and engineers.

Under this assumption, the surface elevation η at the coordinate x and y at the time t may be expressed after Longuet-Higgins [1] as

$$\eta(x,y,t) = \sum_{n=1}^{\infty} a_n \cos(k_n x \cos \theta_n + k_n y \sin \theta_n - 2\pi f_n t + \epsilon_n) \tag{2}$$

where a_n = amplitudes
k_n = wave numbers
θ_n = directions of propagation
f_n = frequencies
ϵ_n = phase angles of the n-th component waves

Each component wave obeys the hydrodynamical laws, and there exists the dispersion relation of

$$(2\pi f_n)^2 = gk_n \tanh k_n h \tag{3}$$

where h represents the water depth.

The important conditions in Equation 2 are that the frequencies f_n must be densely distributed between 0 and ∞ and so do the directions θ_n between 0 and 2π, and that the phase angles, ϵ_n, must be randomly but uniformly distributed between 0 and 2π. Though the amplitudes a_n are infinitesimal, the summation of their squares over the infinitesimal intervals in f and θ should have a finite and unique value. By denoting this value as S(f, θ), it is expressed as

$$\sum_{f}^{f+\delta f} \sum_{\theta}^{\theta+\delta \theta} \frac{1}{2} a_n^2 = S(f, \theta)\delta f \delta \theta \tag{4}$$

The function defined by Equation 4 is a variance spectrum, and is called the directional wave spectral density function, or the directional wave spectrum, in ocean wave studies.

When the surface elevation is expressed as the function of time t only, such as in the case of wave observation at a fixed point, it is written as

$$\eta(t) = \sum_{n=1}^{\infty} a_n \cos (2\pi f_n - \epsilon_n) \tag{5}$$

The summation of the squares of the amplitudes a_n should have a finite and unique value $S(f)$ in the sense that

$$\sum_{f}^{f+\delta f} \frac{1}{2} a_n^2 = S(f)\delta f \tag{6}$$

The function $S(f)$ is called the frequency spectral density function, or the frequency spectrum.

Equation 2 is a simple way of representing random wave profiles. There are several other methods of mathematical representations of random wave profiles including one using complex vectors. They differ in the degree of statistical rigor and in the convenience for the mathematical manipulations of particular interest. However, the underlying concept is the same and the difference will be of little interest for practicing engineers.

Simulation Formulas. In many problems related to random ocean waves, simulation of random wave profiles often helps to solve the problems. For the purpose of wave simulation, the following form of representation is often used:

$$\eta(x,y,t) = \sum_{m=1}^{M} \sum_{n=1}^{N} a_{m,n} \cos (k_m x \cos \theta_n + k_m y \sin \theta_n - 2\pi f_m t + \epsilon_{m,n}) \tag{7}$$

where $a_{m,n}^2 = 2 S(f_m, \theta_n) \Delta f_m \Delta \theta_n$ \hfill (8)

In this expression, the frequency range is divided into M segments and the directional range into N segments. The numbers M and N are required as large as practicable. One simulation study [2] employs $M = 200$ and $N = 36$ ($-\pi/2 < \theta \leq \pi/2$). The directional bandwidths $\Delta \theta_n$ may be taken as equal, but the frequency bandwidths Δf_m should vary in order to avoid the recurrence of wave profiles with the period 2M due to the properties of the finite Fourier series [3].

When simulation is required of the wave profile at a fixed point, the computational efficiency is increased by employing the following formulas [4], which are revised forms of Equation 7:

$$\eta(t|x,y) = \sum_{m=1}^{M} A_m \cos (2\pi f_m t - \phi_m) \tag{9}$$

where $A_m = [C_m^2 + S_m^2]^{1/2}$
$\phi_m = \tan^{-1} (S_m/C_m)$

$$C_m = \sum_{n=1}^{N} a_{m,n} \cos (k_m \ x \cos \theta_m + k_m \ y \sin \theta_m + \epsilon_{m,n})$$

$$S_m = \sum_{n=1}^{N} a_{m,n} \sin (k_m \ x \cos \theta_m + k_m \ y \sin \theta_m + \epsilon_{m,n})$$

If no consideration for the directional spectrum but only for the frequency spectrum is necessary, then the inverse fast Fourier transform technique (FFT) is the most economical way of wave profile simulation. The number of frequency components M is set as 2^r, where the integer r is so determined that the number of data points 2^{r+1} should be large enough to cover the length of wave profiles to be studied.

Wave Spectra

Frequency Spectra

Spectral Model of Wind Waves in Terms of Generating Conditions. With accumulation of a large volume of measured wave records, the structure of the spectrum of wind waves has become quite known, and several formulations of the standard frequency spectra have been presented. The spectral models often referred to and used in wave hindcasting and forecasting projects are the Pierson-Moskowitz and the JONSWAP spectra.

The Pierson-Moskowitz spectrum [5] is expressed as

$$S(f) = 8.10 \times 10^{-3}(2\pi)^{-4} \ g^2 \ f^{-5} \exp[-0.24(2\pi U_{19.5} f/g)^{-4}] \tag{10}$$

where $U_{19.5}$ = wind speed at the elevation 19.5 m above the sea surface
   g = acceleration of gravity

Equation 10 is based on early measurements of wave spectra in the ocean and is considered to represent the spectrum of fully-developed seas or the equilibrium form of wave spectrum.

The JONSWAP spectrum [6] is expressed as

$$S(f) = \alpha(2\pi)^{-4} \ g^2 \ f^{-5} \exp\left[-\frac{5}{4}\left(\frac{f}{f_p}\right)^{-4}\right]$$

$$\times \gamma \exp[-(f/f_p - 1)^2/2\sigma^2] \tag{11}$$

where $f_p = 3.5 \ (g/U_{10})(gF/U_{10}^2)^{-0.33}$
   $\alpha = 0.076 \ (gF/U_{10}^2)^{-0.22}$
   $\gamma = 1 \sim 7$ (mean of 3.3)
   $\sigma = \begin{cases} 0.07 : f \le f_p \\ 0.09 : f > f_p \end{cases}$

where   F = fetch length
   U_{10} = wind speed at the elevation 10 m above the sea surface
   f_p = frequency at the spectral peak

Equation 11 is based on the Joint North Sea Wave Project (JONSWAP) in the late 1960s and is considered to represent the spectrum of fetch-limited wind waves. Modified forms for the scaling parameter α and the peak enhancement factor γ have been proposed by Mitsuyasu [7] on the basis of additional wave data at various locations. These are

$$\alpha = 0.0817 \ (gF/U_{10}^2)^{-2/7}$$

$$\gamma = 7.0 \ (gF/U_{10}^2)^{-1/7} \tag{12}$$

Equation 12 suggests that wind waves generated by very strong wind in relatively short fetch has a high value of γ, while those generated by relatively mild wind over sufficiently long fetch have the γ-value close to 1.

Spectral Model of Wind Waves in Shallow Water. In the open water where the depth is relatively shallow and waves can "feel" the bottom, the wave spectrum exhibits some deviation from Equations 10 and 11. A noticeable change is that the slope of the high frequency part of spectrum becomes milder than f^{-5}. Kitaigorodoskii et al. [8] showed that the equilibrium range of wind waves in arbitrary depth is proportional to the -3 power of wave number and gave a universal dimensionless function Φ to represent the effect of water depth on wave spectrum. The function Φ is graphically presented with a dimensionless variable $2\pi f(h/g)^{1/2}$. According to them, frequency spectra of wind waves in very shallow water will have the form of f^{-3} in the high frequency range. Bouws et al. [9] proposed a spectral model of wind waves in finite water depth that is the product of the JONSWAP spectrum and the function Φ of Kitaigorodoskii et al. They called it the TMA spectrum after the names of the three sources of spectral data used in calibration.

The TMA spectral model is intended for use in wave hindcasting and forecasting in water of finite depth. Various mechanisms of wave attenuations by bottom friction, percolation, breaking, and others are supposed to be included in the function Φ implicitly. Use of the TMA model in general wave transformation problems in shallow water should be made with caution, because the model is essentially for wind waves at a growing stage.

Spectral Model of Swell. As wind waves propagate away from their generating area, low-frequency components travel faster than high-frequency components, and the process of velocity dispersion develops. A spectrum of swell observed at a fixed location shows concentration of wave energy in a narrow frequency range compared with spectra of wind waves owing to the velocity dispersion effect. However, observational data of swell spectra are rather limited so that no spectral model has yet been proposed for swell spectra. In one of a few available reports, Goda [10] suggests that the spectral shape of the JONSWAP model with $\gamma = 7$ to 10 can be a good approximation to the spectrum of swell that has traveled over several thousands of kilometers, on the basis of his analysis of such swell records [11].

Spectral Model in Terms of Sea State Parameters. Applications of the spectral concepts to various engineering problems are often made without specific information on wave spectral densities. The input data are mostly a few sea state parameters such as the significant wave height and period, or the mean wave period. Thus arises the need for allocating some spectral model with the given sea state parameters. Several formulas are given below to fill such need.

The commonest formula is of the following two-parameter model, which has the same functional shape with Equation 10:

$$S(f) = A f^{-5} \exp [- Bf^{-4}] \tag{13}$$

The constants A and B are dimensional quantities. According to the statistical theory of wave heights discussed later in this chapter, the significant wave heights $H_{1/3}$ is related to the zeroth moment of the spectrum as

$$H_{1/3} = 4.004 \ (m_0)^{1/2} \tag{14}$$

$$\text{where } m_n = \int_0^\infty f^n \ S(f) \ df \tag{15}$$

With the condition of Equation 14, the constants A and B are given the following values according to the two formulas:

Bretschneider-Mitsuyasu Spectra [12–14]:

$$\left. \begin{array}{l} A = 0.257 \ H_{1/3}{}^2 \ T_{H1/3}{}^{-4} \\[2mm] B = 1.03 \ T_{H1/3}{}^{-4} \end{array} \right\} \tag{16}$$

where $T_{H1/3}$ denotes the period of significant wave defined by either the zero-upcrossing or the zero-downcrossing method. It is assumed to have the relation of $T_{H1/3} = T_p/1.05$, where T_p denotes the period corresponding to the spectral peak $(= 1/f_p)$.

ISSC Spectrum [15]:

$$\left. \begin{array}{l} A = 0.11 \ H_{1/3}{}^2 \ T_{0.1}{}^{-4} \\[2mm] B = 0.44 \ T_{0.1}{}^{-4} \end{array} \right\} \tag{17}$$

where $T_{0.1}$ is the mean wave period defined as $T_{0.1} = m_0/m_1$ and is related to T_p as $T_{0.1} = 0.772 \ T_p$. The difference between the Bretschneider-Mitsuyasu and the ISSC spectra is the selection of period parameter and its relation to the spectral peak period.

The formula of Equation 13 alone cannot cover the variety of wave spectra in the field. Also the relation of Equation 14 does not hold true among field waves when the significant wave height is calculated by the zero-crossing method. The constant 4.004 in Equation 14 should be replaced by the value 3.8 to yield a better fit to most field data. The amount of the deviation in the constant value depends on the spectral shape; the sharper the spectral peak is, the less the deviation becomes.

Among several multi-parameter spectral formulas, the following two formulas by Goda [10] are suggested for engineering applications:

Modified Wallops-type Spectrum [10]:

$$S(f) = \beta_w \, H_{1/3}{}^2 \, T_p{}^{1-m} \, f^{-m} \, \exp\left[-\frac{m}{4}\,(T_p \, f)^{-4}\right] \tag{18}$$

where $\beta_w = \dfrac{0.06238 \, m^{(m-1)/4}}{4^{(m-5)/4} \, \Gamma\,[(m-1)]}\,[1 + 0.7458(m+2)^{-1.057}]$

$$T_p = \begin{cases} T_{H1/3}/[1 - 0.238(m - 1.5)^{-0.684}] \\ \bar{T}/[1 - 1.295(m - 0.5)^{-1.072}] \end{cases}$$

and $\bar{T}$ is the mean wave period defined by the zero-crossing method.

Modified JONSWAP-type Spectrum [10]:

$$S(f) = \beta_J \, H_{1/3}{}^2 \, T_p{}^{-4} \, f^{-5} \, \exp\left[-\frac{5}{4}\,(T_p \, f)^{-4}\right]$$

$$\times \gamma \exp\left[-(f/f_p - 1)^2/2\sigma^2\right] \tag{19}$$

where $\beta_J = \dfrac{0.06238}{0.230 + 0.0336\gamma - 0.185(1.9 + \gamma)^{-1}}\,[1.094 - 0.01915 \ln \gamma]$

$$T_p = \begin{cases} T_{H1/3}/[1 - 0.132(\gamma + 0.2)^{-0.559}] \\ \bar{T}/[1 - 0.532(\gamma + 2.5)^{-0.569}] \end{cases}$$

The Wallops spectrum was originally proposed by Huang et al. [16] as the spectral model that can cover the general sea state including decaying seas. The formulations of Equations 18 and 19 are based on the result of statistical analysis of individual wave heights and periods of linearly simulated wave profiles for a wide range of spectral shapes (Table 1).

To illustrate the differences between various spectral formulas, a calculation is made for the wave condition $H_{1/3} = 10.0$ m and $T_{H1/3} = 14$ s. Figure 1 shows the frequency spectra of the Bretschneider-Mitsuyasu spectrum, the modified Wallops-type spectrum, and the modified JONSWAP-type spectrum. The Bretschneider-Mitsuyasu spectrum and the modified Wallops-type spectrum with m = 5 have the same functional form with respect to the frequency f. However, the peak of the latter spectrum is shifted toward the upper left, because the peak period is estimated larger than that by the former. The total area under the latter spectrum is about 10%

Table 1

Mean Values of Statistical Parameters of the Wallops-type and the
JONSWAP-type Spectra ($f_{max} = 6\ f_p$)

Parameter	Wallops-type				JONSWAP-type				Rayleigh
	m = 3	m = 5	m = 10	m = 20	$\gamma = 1.5$	$\gamma = 3.3$	$\gamma = 7$	$\gamma = 14$	
$[\eta_{max}/\eta_{rms}]^*$	0.992*	1.000*	0.998*	0.981*	1.000*	0.996*	0.983*	0.969*	1.000*
$[H_{max}/\eta_{rms}]^*$	0.893*	0.925*	0.956*	0.961*	0.929*	0.935*	0.934*	0.931*	1.000*
$[H_{max}/H_{1/3}]^*$	0.958*	0.967*	0.984*	0.976*	0.968*	0.969*	0.962*	0.954*	1.000*
$H_{1/10}/\eta_{rms}$	4.658	4.781	4.912	5.007	4.801	4.849	4.894	4.938	5.090
$H_{1/3}/\eta_{rms}$	3.736	3.830	3.895	3.948	3.842	3.866	3.895	3.920	4.004
$\bar{H}/\eta_{rms}$	2.359	2.448	2.495	2.504	2.452	2.461	2.476	2.490	2.507
σ_H/η_{rms}	1.201	1.218	1.230	1.261	1.226	1.242	1.253	1.261	1.309
$T_{max}/T_{1/3}$	1.066	0.987	0.985	0.994	0.989	0.987	0.987	0.988	1.000
$T_{H1/10}/T_p$	0.824	0.889	0.927	0.959	0.891	0.933	0.954	0.968	1.000
$T_{H1/3}/T_p$	0.782	0.883	0.934	0.960	0.901	0.934	0.957	0.970	1.000
$\bar{T}/T_p$	0.579	0.740	0.885	0.946	0.760	0.804	0.851	0.892	1.000
σ_T/T_p	0.252	0.246	0.198	0.155	0.247	0.244	0.238	0.208	0.000
r_{HT}	0.711	0.595	0.336	0.173	0.596	0.587	0.553	0.497	0.000
r_{HH}	0.172	0.293	0.445	0.611	0.334	0.446	0.561	0.671	1.000

Remarks: The asterisk * refers to the ratio of the observed value to the theoretical prediction by the
Rayleigh distribution.
Source: Goda [10]

larger than that under the former. This is due to the difference in the estimate of
significant wave height with respect to the zeroth spectral moment.

The selection of the shape parameters m and γ rests upon the experience and
judgment of engineers. As indicated by Equation 12, a small value of the dimensionless fetch gF/U^2 is associated with a high value of γ or m, and a large value of
the dimensionless fetch leads to the value $\gamma = 1$ or m = 5. In shallow water, however, the modified Wallops-type spectrum with m = 3 to 4 will be appropriate. The
selection of m = 5 in Equation 18 or $\gamma = 1$ in Equation 19 yields the spectral shape
same as Equation 13, but the constants A and B differ from Equation 16 or 17 and
become:

$$\left. \begin{array}{l} A = 0.205\ H_{1/3}^2\ T_{H1/3}^{-4} \\ B = 0.75\ T_{H1/3}^{-4} \end{array} \right\} \tag{20}$$

or

$$\left. \begin{array}{l} A = 0.103\ H_{1/3}^2\ \bar{T}^{-4} \\ B = 0.38\ \bar{T}^{-4} \end{array} \right\} \tag{21}$$

A complex sea state of coexisting seas and swell can be represented by adding the
spectrum of wind waves and that of swell together with the respective parameters of
wave heights, periods, and shape parameters. Observed spectra of complicated sea

state exhibiting double peaks can also be fitted to such a combined spectral formula. Ochi and Hubble [17] proposed six-parameter spectra for ocean waves with a data base of 800 spectra. The parameters are expressed in terms of the significant wave height and thus the change of spectral shape with respect to the sea state conditions can be estimated. The proposed spectral model is composed of a mean spectrum and its ten variations corresponding to 95% confidence level.

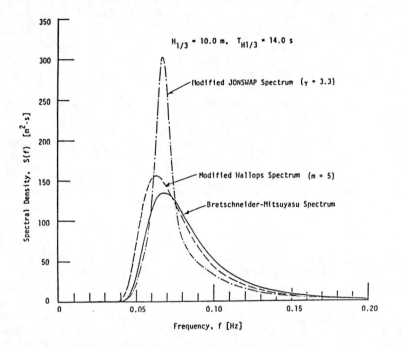

Figure 1. Comparison of three spectral models for the wave condition $H_{1/3} = 10$ m and $T_{H1/3} = 14$ s.

Directional Spectrum

As defined in Equation 4, the directional spectrum $S(f, \theta)$ is a function of the frequency f and the direction θ. It is usually expressed as the product of the frequency spectrum $S(f)$ and a function $G(f, \theta)$, which describes the angular distribution of wave energy at respective frequencies. Thus,

$$S(f, \theta) = S(f) \, G(f, \theta) \tag{22}$$

The function $G(f, \theta)$ is called the directional spreading function. It is also called the spreading function, the angular distribution function, or the directional distribution.

Because the dimension of $S(f, \theta)$ is same as that of $S(f)$, the directional spreading function carries no dimension and is normalized as

$$\int_{-\pi}^{\pi} G(f, \theta) \, d\theta = 1 \tag{23}$$

Equation 23 is the condition imposed upon the directional spreading function estimated from the field data of directional wave measurements.

Directional Spreading Function of the Mitsuyasu-type. The first formula of the directional spreading function was of $\cos^2 \theta$ type. It has been used in several occasions concerned with directional wave spectra, but it was not verified by field data. Measurements of directional spectra in the field require much effort compared with measurements of frequency spectra, because a minimum of three wave sensors (three wave gauges, heave-pitch-roll of buoy, underwater pressure-velocity meters, etc.) must be operated simultaneously. Thus, reliable data of directional wave spectra are much more limited than the data of frequency spectra. There are still arguments regarding the shape of the directional spreading function and the values of the parameters that define the function. Nonetheless, available field data indicate the following functional form to be most appropriate:

$$G(f, \theta) = G_0 \cos^{2s} (\theta/2) \tag{24}$$

where θ = azimuth measured counterclockwise from the principal wave direction
G_0 = a constant introduced to satisfy the normalization condition of Equation 23
s = a parameter that controls the angular distribution

The parameter s is known to vary with respect to the frequency. Mitsuyasu et al. [18] gave the following formula for s:

$$s = \begin{cases} s_{max} \, (f/f_p)^5: & f \leq f_p \\ s_{max} \, (f/f_p)^{-2.5}: & f \geq f_p \end{cases} \tag{25}$$

This functional form has been supported by Holthuijsen [19] with his directional measurements using stereophotography.

According to Mitsuyasu et al. [18], the maximum value of the parameter s is related to the stage of wave development as

$$s_{max} = 11.5 \, (2\pi f_p \, U/g)^{-2.5} \tag{26}$$

This formula is for wind waves only. Goda and Suzuki [20] proposed to use the following value of s_{max} for wind waves and swell in deep water for engineering applications (see Goda [21], pp. 30–32).

Wind waves: $s_{max} = 10$
Swell with short decay distance: $s_{max} = 25$
  (with relatively large wave steepness)   (27)
Swell with long decay distance: $s_{max} = 75$
  (with relatively small wave steepness)

As waves propagate from deep water to shallow water, they are subjected to the process of shoaling, refraction, and other transformations. Among them, the refraction process causes concentration of the directional spreading function in a narrower range. This effect can be addressed by increasing the s_{max} value. Figure 2 provides an estimate of the increase of the spreading parameter s_{max}, which was obtained for the coast with parallel straight depth contours [20, 21]. The notation $(\alpha_p)_0$ in Figure 2 represents the angle of incidence of the deepwater waves, and L_0 appearing in the abscissa is the length of the deepwater waves corresponding to the significant wave period.

Cumulative Distribution Curve of Wave Energy. The characteristics of the directional wave spectrum can also be expressed from the viewpoint of the directional distribution of total wave energy. For this purpose the cumulative relative energy $P_E(\theta)$ is defined:

$$P_E(\theta) = \frac{1}{m_0} \int_{-\pi/2}^{\theta} \int_0^{\infty} S(f, \theta) df\, d\theta \qquad (28)$$

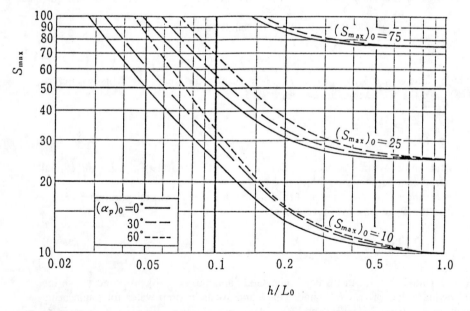

Figure 2. Estimated variation of the spreading parameter s_{max} in shallow water area [20].

Calculation of $P_E(\theta)$ was done by Goda and Suzuki [19] for the directional spectrum, which is the combination of the Bretschneider-Mitsuyasu frequency spectrum and the Mitsuyasu-type directional spreading function. Figure 3 shows the result of the calculation for the spreading parameter $s_{max} = 5$, 10, 25, and 75. The curve denoted with SWOP represents the cumulative distribution for the directional spreading function obtained by the Stereo Wave Observation Project [22].

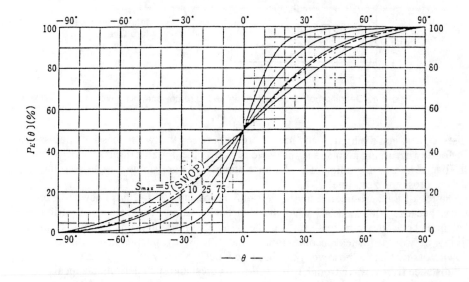

Figure 3. Cumulative distribution of relative wave energy with respect to azimuth from principal wave direction [20].

Statistical Properties of Individual Waves

Definition of Individual Waves by the Zero-Crossing Method

In this section, discussion is focused on the statistics of one-dimensional wave profiles such as those recorded at a fixed location. A time-history record of sea surface elevation usually exhibits a random form with many small maxima and minima superposed on irregular undulations. It is difficult to define individual waves from such a wave record without some criterion to distinguish a single wave from local humps and hollows. The present standard is the adoption of the zero-crossing definition. As shown in Figure 4, a wave sets in when the surface elevation crosses the zero-line (or the mean water level) upward and is set down at the next zero-upcrossing. This is called the zero-upcrossing method. A wave can also be defined with the downward crossing of the zero-line by the surface elevation. This is called the zero-downcrossing method. The wave height is defined as the vertical

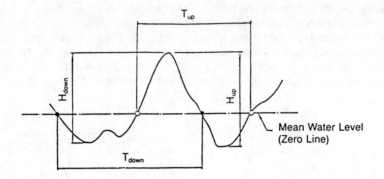

Figure 4. Definition of zero-upcrossing and zero-downcrossing waves.

distance between the highest and lowest points between the two successive upcrossing or downcrossing points, and the wave period as the horizontal distance between the two zero-crossing points. Local humps and hollows are simply discarded if they do not cross the zero-line.

Choice of the zero-upcrossing or zero-downcrossing method is somewhat arbitrary, because both methods yield the statistically same mean values of various height and period parameters except in the area near to the surf zone where forward tilting of wave profiles becomes noticeable [2]. Many people favor the zero-downcrossing method however [23], because it defines the wave height as the vertical distance from a wave trough to the following crest and such definition appeals to visual images of extreme waves.

After a wave record is dissected by either the zero-upcrossing method or the zero-downcrossing method into a series of individual wave heights and periods, several height and period parameters are calculated. They are listed below with the notations recommended by the International Association of Hydraulic Research (IAHR) [23].

H_{max} and $T_{H,max}$: Height of the maximum wave in a wave record and its period.
$H_{1/10}$ and $T_{H1/10}$: Mean height of the highest one-tenth waves and mean period of these waves.
$H_{1/3}$ and $T_{H1/3}$: Mean height of the highest one-third waves and mean period of these waves.
$\bar{H}$ and $\bar{T}$: Mean height and period of all waves.

Among these height and period parameters, $H_{1/3}$ and $T_{H1/3}$ are called the significant wave height and period, respectively, after the definition by Sverdrup and Munk in 1942 when they first introduced the scientific method of wave forecasting [24]. Although the recommendation by IAHR requires the use of the subscript u or d, depending on the use of the zero-upcrossing or the zero-downcrossing method, the subscripts are not used in this chapter, because of little difference between the mean values of the above height and period parameters for most wave conditions.

Distribution of Wave Heights

Rayleigh Distribution of Wave Heights. The heights of individual waves are regarded as a stochastic variable for which a certain distribution function can be fitted. We can examine such a function by collecting many wave records and by taking a histogram of wave heights normalized with some reference value such as the mean heights of respective wave records. If the wave spectrum has a narrow band (the wave energy is concentrated in a very narrow frequency range), most of the maxima of a wave profile coincide with the wave crests and most of the minima become the wave troughs. Under such condition, the distribution of wave heights is expressed by the following Rayleigh distribution:

$$p(x) \, dx = 2 \, a^2 \, x \, \exp[-a^2 \, x^2] \, dx \tag{29}$$

where $p(x)$ = probability density function
x = wave height normalized with an arbitrary reference height H_* with the constant a taking the following value depending on the selection of H_*:

$$x = H/H_*$$

$$a = \begin{cases} 1/8^{1/2} & : \; H_* = m_0^{1/2} = \eta_{rms} \\ \pi^{1/2}/2 & : \; H_* = \overline{H} \\ 1 & : \; H_* = H_{rms} \\ 1.416 & : \; H_* = H_{1/3} \end{cases}$$

The distribution function of wave heights, or the non-exceedance probability, is given as

$$P(x) = 1 - \exp[-a^2 \, x^2] \tag{30}$$

Longuet-Higgins [25] verified the applicability of the Rayleigh distribution to the heights of sea waves and calculated the expected values of various wave height parameters. The results are summarized:

$$\left. \begin{aligned} H_{1/10} &= 5.090 \; \eta_{rms} = 2.031 \; \overline{H} = 1.800 \; H_{rms} \\ H_{1/3} &= 4.004 \; \eta_{rms} = 1.597 \; \overline{H} = 1.416 \; H_{rms} \\ \overline{H} &= (2\pi)^{1/2} \; \eta_{rms} = (\pi^{1/2}/2) \; H_{rms} \end{aligned} \right\} \tag{31}$$

where H_{rms} = root-mean-square value of wave heights

Details of the derivation of the Rayleigh distribution and the calculation of wave height parameters are found in textbooks (e.g., Goda [21] pp. 221–226).

The maximum wave height H_{max} cannot be expressed in a form similar with Equation 31, because its value gradually increases as the number of waves increases. It has its own probability density function which is given:

$$p^* (x_{max}) \, dx_{max} = 2 \, a^2 \, x_{max} \, \xi \, e^{-\xi} \, dx_{max} \qquad (32)$$

where $\xi = N_0 \exp[- a^2 \, x_{max}^2]$

The notation N_0 refers to the number of zero-crossing waves under consideration, and the constant a is given by Equation 30. The expected value of H_{max} is obtained from Equation 32 as

$$(x_{max})_{mean} \doteqdot \frac{1}{a} \, (\ln N_0)^{1/2} + \frac{C}{2a(\ln N_0)^{1/2}} - \frac{\pi^2 + 6C^2}{48a(\ln N_0)^{3/2}} \qquad (33)$$

where C is Euler's constant (0.5772...). Furthermore, the largest wave height $(x_{max})_\mu$ such that the probability of being exceeded is μ is obtained as (see Goda [21], p. 229)

$$(x_{max})_\mu \doteqdot \frac{1}{a} \left\{ \ln \left[\frac{N_0}{\ln 1/(1 - \mu)} \right] \right\}^{1/2} \qquad (34)$$

If storm waves with the mean period of 12 seconds continue for 3 hours, there will be 3 hours × 3,600 s/12 s = 900 waves. By setting $N_0 = 900$ and a = 1.416 in Equation 33, we obtain the estimate $(H_{max})_{mean} = 1.91 \, H_{1/3}$. Also by setting $\mu = 0.05$ in Equation 34 for the same condition, we get $(H_{max})_{0.05} = 2.21 \, H_{1/3}$.

Effect of Spectral Bandwidth on the Distribution of Wave Heights. The frequency spectra of ocean waves are not of narrow-band as assumed in the theory of Rayleigh distribution. The narrowness of spectral bandwidth is measured with the following parameters [1, 26]:

$$\nu = [m_0 \, m_2/m_1^2 - 1]^{1/2} \qquad (35)$$

$$\epsilon = [1 - m_2^2/(m_0 \, m_4)]^{1/2} \qquad (36)$$

where m_n are the spectral moments defined by Equation 15. Both parameters take values between 0 and 1, and waves are said to have narrow-band spectra when ν and ϵ are quite close to 0. The Pierson-Moskowitz and the JONSWAP spectra yield $\nu = 0.425$ and 0.389, respectively, and both spectra yield $\epsilon = 1$. Therefore, ocean waves should be regarded as having broad-band spectra. Nevertheless, the Rayleigh distribution serves as a good engineering formula for the distribution of zero-crossing wave heights as demonstrated in various field data, though actual data show a slight deviation from the theory.

As mentioned earlier, the ratio $H_{1/3}/\eta_{rms}$ takes the value 3.8 on the average instead of the theoretical value 4.004. Details of the distribution function of wave heights themselves have been examined by several investigators. They have proposed the Weibull distribution of the following form:

$$P[x] = 1 - \exp[-(x/\rho)^{\beta}] \tag{37}$$

The parameters ρ and β are given the following values by the best fitting to the field data:

Forristall [27]: $x = H/\eta_{rms}$, $\rho = 2.724$, $\beta = 2.126$

Nolte and Hsu [28]: $x = H/4\,\eta_{rms}$, $\rho = 1/1.467$, $\beta = 2.138$

Myrhaug and Kjeldsen [29]: $x = H/H_{rms}$, $\rho = 1.05$, $\beta = 2.39$

Equation 37 with the value of β greater than 2 results in the smaller probability for large wave heights than that predicted by the Rayleigh distribution, and the difference increases with the increase in the wave height level. Figure 5 illustrates a difference between the Rayleigh distribution and the empirical distribution function by Forristall [27]. The result by Nolte and Hsu [28] gives almost the same value as that of Forristall, because the data base is common. Furthermore, Forristall [27] calculated various wave height parameters such as $H_{1/3}$ based on Equation 37. He derived the following formula for the expected value of the maximum wave height in a normalized form:

$$(x_{max})_{mean} \fallingdotseq \rho(\ln N_0)^{1/\beta} \left[1 + \frac{C}{\beta \ln N_0}\right] \tag{38}$$

Myrhaug and Kjeldsen [29] also presented a similar expression. Equation 38 corresponds to Equation 33 with the omission of the third term in its right side.

The deviation of the observed wave height distribution from the Rayleighan is caused by the tendency for there to be some difference between a crest height and the following trough depth as the spectrum becomes of broad-band, while the theory assumes the equality of the successive crest height and trough depth or the wave height being twice the crest height. A theory of the wave height distribution that addresses the effect of spectral bandwidth was presented by Tayfun [30], and its applicability to the field data was verified by Forristall [31]. The theory is based on the calculation of the amplitudes of wave envelope at the two points being separated by the half wave period. Another theory to account for the effect of spectral bandwidth on the wave height distribution was derived by Naess [32], who introduced the normalized autocorrelation coefficient of the surface elevation with the time lag of one-half the characteristic wave period.

The effects of wave spectral shapes on the wave height parameters are shown in Table 1, which lists the mean values of various height and period parameters for the Wallops-type and the JONSWAP-type spectra of Equations 18 and 19. The data were obtained by Goda [10] through the numerical simulations of 2,000 wave profiles for each spectrum. The simulation was done in the frequency range f = (0.6 ~

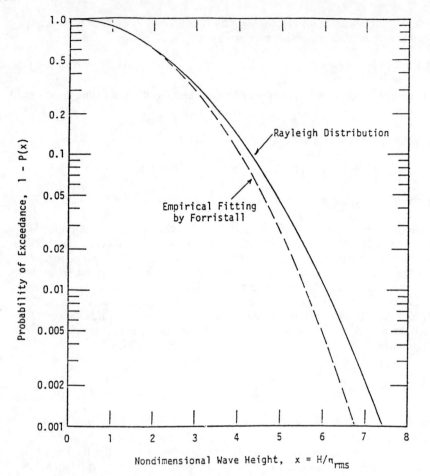

Figure 5. Probability of exceedance of wave heights according to the Rayleigh distribution and the empirical one by Forristall [27].

$6.0)f_p$ with 4,096 data points per wave record, the length of which is equal to 341.4 T_p. Table 1 indicates several interesting points.

First, the simulated data of H_{max} is smaller than the prediction by the Rayleigh distribution by several percent. When H_{max} is expressed in terms of $H_{1/3}$, the difference between the observation and the theoretical prediction decreases but does not disappear. On the other hand, the simulated data of the highest surface elevation in a wave record η_{max} exhibit the value quite close to the theoretical prediction. These data suggest that the highest surface elevation is followed with a trough of lesser magnitude and the largest wave height in a wave record is less than twice the largest crest height, as analyzed by Tayfun [30]. Thus, the highest crest elevation becomes greater than 50% of the largest wave height on the average even with no consideration for wave nonlinearity effects.

Second, other wave height parameters such as $H_{1/3}$ also exhibit the mean values less than the prediction by the Rayleigh distribution. The deviation increases as the level of wave heights increases. This is in support of the Weibull distribution with the value of β greater than 2. As expected, the deviation of the wave height parameters from those of the Rayleigh distribution decreases as the wave spectrum becomes sharply peaked (increase in the value of m or γ). The exception in this tendency is the case of η_{max}, which shows an increase of the deviation with sharpening of spectral peaks. It is due to the presence of strong correlation between successive wave heights. (The assumption in theoretical derivation that individual wave heights are independent does not hold for wave data with sharply peaked spectra.) The effect of the correlation between wave heights on the estimation of largest wave height was theoretically examined by Naess [33].

Distribution of the Maxima of Surface Elevation

When waves are not of narrow-band spectra, wave profiles have a number of local ups and downs that do not cross the zero-line or the line of the mean water level, and thus do not contribute to the counting of zero-crossing waves. The distribution of such local maxima and minima was studied by Cartwright and Longuet-Higgins [26]. The probability density function of the local maxima of the surface elevation normalized with η_{rms}, which is denoted by $x_* = \eta_{max}/\eta_{rms}$, is given by

$$p(x_*)\,dx_* = \frac{1}{(2\pi)^{1/2}} \left\{ \epsilon \, \exp\left[-\frac{x_*^2}{2\epsilon^2}\right] + (1-\epsilon^2)^{1/2} \, x_* \right.$$

$$\left. \times \exp\left[-\frac{x_*^2}{2}\right] \int_{-\infty}^{x_*\,(1-\epsilon^2)^{1/2}/\epsilon} \exp\left[-\frac{x_*^2}{2}\right] dx_* \right\} dx_* \tag{39}$$

The parameter ϵ is the spectral width parameter defined by Equation 36.

The number of the maxima N_1 in a wave record is related to the number of zero-crossing waves N_0 as

$$N_1 = N_0/(1 - \epsilon^2)^{1/2}$$

As the value of the spectral width parameter ϵ approaches 1, the number of the maxima of the surface elevation increases rapidly as predicted by the above formula.

The expected value of the highest maximum in a wave record is calculated as

$$\left[\frac{\eta_{max}}{\eta_{rms}}\right]_{mean} \fallingdotseq (2 \ln N_0)^{1/2} + \frac{C}{(2 \ln N_0)^{1/2}} \tag{40}$$

This becomes the same as Equation 33 by the change of $H_{max} = 2\,\eta_{max}$ with the omission of the third term in the right side of the latter.

It should be mentioned here that the highest surface elevations of real ocean waves are higher than the prediction by Equation 40 because of the wave nonlinearity effects, which are discussed later in this chapter.

Statistics of the Length of Wave Group

Wave Grouping. Although a first look at the sea surface gives the impression of a very random condition, detailed inspection of wave records indicates a tendency of grouping of high waves. The degree of wave grouping is rather weak in wind waves, but it is quite strong among swell from a remote source. The phenomenon of wave grouping is related with several engineering problems such as the long-period oscillations of moored vessels, surf beats and irregular wave runups, resonant interaction between structures and irregular waves, and others.

The length of wave grouping can be quantitatively described by measuring the fluctuation of wave envelopes or by counting the number of waves exceeding some threshold value of the wave height H_c without falling below that height. A practical way of the former measurement was proposed by Funke and Mansard [34] by means of the smoothing of the instantaneous energy level of wave profile (square of surface elevation). The result is called the smoothed instantaneous wave energy history, which is abbreviated as SIWEH. Funke and Mansard have proposed a parameter called the groupiness factor to describe the degree of wave grouping in a wave record. A sophistication of the concept of SIWEH has been elaborated by Bitner-Gregersen and Gran [35].

Probability Distribution of Run Length. The latter method of counting the number of consecutive high waves is based on the concept of the run of wave heights, which is illustrated in Figure 6. If successive wave heights are uncorrela-

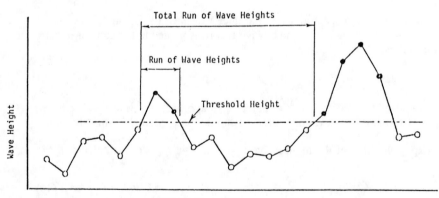

Figure 6. Definition sketch of the run of wave heights and the total run.

ted, the probability distribution of the run length is derived by a simple calculation of the probability as presented by Goda [36, 37]. Let the occurrence probability H $>$ H_c be denoted by p_0 and its non-exceedance probability by $q_0 = 1 - p_0$. Then, the probability that the j_1 consecutive wave heights exceeds H_c is expressed as

$$P(j_1) = p_0^{j_1-1} q_0 \tag{41}$$

The mean length of the run of the wave heights and its standard deviation are calculated using the above probability as

$$\bar{j}_1 = \sum_{j_1=1}^{\infty} j_1 P(j_1) = \frac{1}{q_0} \tag{42}$$

$$\sigma(j_1) = \frac{(p_0)^{1/2}}{q_0}$$

In real ocean waves, successive wave heights are mutually correlated to a certain degree. The degree of correlation is governed by the sharpness of a spectral peak. The parameter that best describes the spectral peakedness seems to be the correlation coefficient of wave envelope of the following form:

$$\varkappa(\overline{T}) = \frac{1}{m_0} \left\{ \left[\int_0^{\infty} S(f) \cos 2\pi f \overline{T} \, df \right]^2 \right.$$

$$\left. + \left[\int_0^{\infty} S(f) \sin 2\pi f \overline{T} \, df \right]^2 \right\}^{1/2} \tag{43}$$

This parameter has been derived by the theory of wave envelopes (see Middleton [74], for instance) and proposed by Battjes [38] and Longuet-Higgins [39]. The same wave envelope theory was used by Tayfun [30] in his analysis of the spectral bandwidth effect on wave height distribution. The correlation coefficient r_{HH} between successive wave heights is calculated as

$$r_{HH} = \frac{E(\varkappa) - (1 - \varkappa^2) K(\varkappa)/2 - \pi/4}{1 - \pi/4} \tag{44}$$

in which K and E denote the complete elliptic integrals of the first and second kind.

A probability theory of run length for waves with mutually correlated heights was given by Kimura [40]. By assuming the Rayleigh distribution for the wave heights, the joint probability density function $p(H_1, H_2)$ for two successive wave heights H_1 and H_2 is obtained as

$$p(H_1, H_2) = \frac{4 H_1 H_2}{(1 - x^2) H_{rms}{}^4} \exp\left[-\frac{H_1{}^2 + H_2{}^2}{(1 - x^2) H_{rms}{}^2}\right]$$

$$\times I_0\left[\frac{2 H_1 H_2 x}{(1 - x^2) H_{rms}{}^2}\right] \tag{45}$$

where I_0 is the modified Bessel function of zero-th order.

Let the probability that both H_1 and H_2 exceeds a threshold height H_c be denoted as p_{22}. This probability is defined as

$$p_{22} = \int_{H_c}^{\infty} \int_{H_c}^{\infty} p(H_1, H_2)\, dH_1\, dH_2 / [1 - P(H_c)] \tag{46}$$

Then the probability of a run of length j_1 is given by

$$P(j_1) = p_{22}{}^{j_1 - 1} (1 - p_{22}) \tag{47}$$

The mean and the standard deviation of the run length is calculated as

$$\bar{j}_1 = 1/(1 - p_{22})$$

$$\sigma(j_1) = (p_{22})^{1/2}/(1 - p_{22}) \tag{48}$$

Run Length of Ocean Waves. The calculation of run length by Kimura's theory can be made by estimating the parameter x with Equation 43 based on spectral information. The result yields a slight underestimation of the mean run length, however, as demonstrated by Battjes and van Vledder [38]. The difference seems to originate from the assumption that a wave height is equal to twice the envelope amplitude, which is used in the derivation of Equation 44, as suspected by Goda [41]. It is advisable to estimate the parameter x by solving Equation 44 with the input of r_{HH} as was done by Kimura [40], if the correlation coefficient r_{HH} is known.

For wind waves the correlation coefficient r_{HH} takes a value around 0.2, while the coefficient may exceed the value 0.6 in case of swell from a remote source, though individual wave records exhibit quite large variations in the value of r_{HH}. The simulation data listed in Table 1 indicate the mean value of r_{HH} for several spectral shapes. With a small value of r_{HH}, wind waves do not develop significant grouping of high waves. The mean length of the run of wave heights exceeding the median height rarely exceeds four waves, and that exceeding the significant height usually remains below two waves. The wave group containing the highest wave in a record is naturally longer than ordinary groups of high waves. Su [42] demonstrated that on the average such an extreme wave group consists of three high waves with the heights greater than the significant height.

Analysis of wave grouping is further made for the interval between the successive wave groups. It is defined as the sum of the run with the height exceeding a threshold value and the succeeding run with the height underlying below the threshold value (see Figure 6 for the definition). Goda [36] called it the total run. The probability distribution of the length of a total run for mutually correlated wave heights has been given by Kimura [40]. In case of wind waves with low correlation between successive heights, the mean length of the total run with the threshold value being the median height is about five waves on the average and that with the significant height is about ten waves.

Marginal Distribution of Wave Periods and Joint Distribution of Wave Heights and Periods

Mean Period of Zero-Crossing Waves. According to Rice's theory [43], the mean period of zero-crossing waves is given as

$$\overline{T} = T_{0,2} = (m_0/m_2)^{1/2} \tag{49}$$

where m_0 and m_2 are the spectral moments calculated by Equation 15. Because Equation 49 contains the second spectral moment, the mean wave period is influenced by the high-frequency tail of the frequency spectrum. As the frequency resolution of the wave recorder becomes finer or the sampling interval of surface elevations becomes shorter, the mean wave period becomes shorter even though the spectral peak period remains unchanged.

The mean wave period $T_{0,2}$ estimated by Equation 49 usually agrees with the mean period $\overline{T}$ calculated from individual zero-crossing wave periods counted on a wave registration. When the wave spectrum carries an appreciable amount of nonlinear components, however, $T_{0,2}$ becomes smaller than $\overline{T}$.

Marginal Distribution of Wave Periods. The marginal distribution of wave periods or the distribution of wave periods without consideration of wave heights is theoretically derived for narrow-band spectra as done by Longuet-Higgins [1, 44]. The probability density function for the nondimensional wave period is expressed as

$$p(\tau)\, d\tau = \frac{\nu^2}{2[\nu^2 + (\tau - 1)^2]^{3/2}}\, d\tau, \quad \tau = T/\overline{T} \tag{50}$$

where ν is the spectral bandwidth parameter defined by Equation 35.

For waves with ν less than about 0.1, Equation 50 describes the distribution of wave periods quite well [45]. For waves with broad-band spectra, adjustment of the ν value based on the observed period distribution makes Equation 50 still applicable. Longuet-Higgins [44] recommends the use of the following formula for ν using the interquartile range (IQR) of the observed distribution:

$$\nu = (\sqrt{3}/2)\, IQR(\tau)$$

Joint Distribution of Wave Heights and Periods. The period parameters of zero-crossing waves such as the significant wave period are dependent on the functional shape of the joint distribution of wave heights and periods. Figure 7 is an example of the joint distribution of the nondimensional wave heights and periods, which was prepared by Goda [45] by analyzing 23 sea wave records having the correlation coefficient r_{HT} between individual wave heights and periods within the range from 0.40 to 0.59. Among waves of small heights, strong correlation is observed between wave heights and periods, but the correlation is almost non-existent among waves of large heights. This tendency is consistent throughout the observable range of r_{HT}.

Because of such tendency of the joint distribution of wave heights and periods, there exist the following mean relations between the zero-crossing wave period pa-

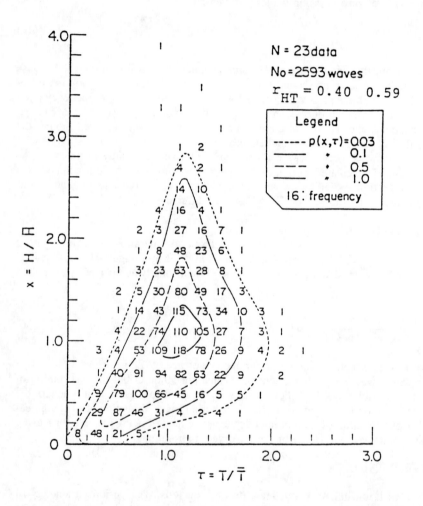

Figure 7. Example of the observed joint distribution of wave heights and periods [45].

rameters almost regardless of the shape of wave spectrum:

$$T_{H.max} \doteqdot T_{H1/10} \doteqdot T_{H1/3} \doteqdot (1.1 \sim 1.3)\, \overline{T}$$

The existence of such relations is confirmed by the simulation data listed in Table 1, in which the mean values of period parameters relative to the spectral peak period are shown for various wave spectra. Individual wave records exhibit a certain deviation from the above relation, as will be discussed in the next section. Among several period parameters, the calculated value of mean wave period is most sensitive to various wave conditions and data processing techniques. It is mostly influenced by the spectral shape: the narrower the spectral peak is, the less the difference between the mean period and the spectral peak period becomes. The mean wave period is also affected by the sampling interval of surface elevations and frequency resolution of wave recorders as discussed in connection with Equation 49. Thus, the mean wave period is not considered as a stable statistical parameter of ocean waves.

Theoretical efforts to describe the joint distribution of the heights and periods of sea waves were made by Cavanié et al. [46] and Longuet-Higgins [47] with partial success. If one is interested in the upper portion of the joint distribution (waves of large heights) only, an earlier theory by Longuet-Higgins [44] can describe several features of the joint distribution (see Goda [21], pp. 243–246, for example). According to this theory, the joint distribution density function for the nondimensional wave heights and periods is given by

$$p(x,\tau) = \frac{ax}{\pi^{1/2}\, \nu} \exp\left\{ -a^2\, x^2 \left[1 + \frac{(\tau-1)^2}{\nu^2} \right] \right\} \qquad (51)$$

where $x = H/H_*$ with a given by Equation 30
$\qquad \tau = T/\overline{T}$

The marginal distribution of wave periods given by Equation 50 is easily obtained from Equation 51 by integrating it for the full range of $x = 0$ to ∞. The Rayleigh distribution for the wave heights is also obtained by integrating Equation 51 for the full range of τ.

Statistical Variability of Sea State Parameters

A record of wave registration is a statistical sample taken from the population of wave records for that particular sea state condition. Any sea state parameter analyzed from a wave record is accompanied by a certain amount of sampling error. A wave spectrum obtained from a wave record is also subject to the sampling error, the amount of which depends on the degree of freedom in spectral analysis. A case study of the sampling variability of spectral estimates is found in Donelan and Pierson [48].

In case of the highest wave height H_{max}, its probability density function is given by Equation 32 and its standard deviation is calculated as

$$\sigma(x_{max}) \doteq \frac{\pi}{2\sqrt{6}\ a\ (\ln N_0)^{1/2}} \tag{52}$$

where x = nondimensional wave height
       a = a constant given by Equation 30

Actual sea waves exhibit the distribution of wave heights slightly narrower than the Rayleighan as discussed earlier. Because of this deviation, the standard deviation of H_{max} tends to become smaller than the prediction by Equation 52 as the bandwidth of wave spectrum becomes broad. This tendency is indicated in the entry of the coefficient of variation of H_{max} in Table 2, which was obtained by the analysis of numerically simulated wave profiles for various wave spectra [10]. The data source is same as that of Table 1.

Theoretical estimate of sampling variability is also available for the correlation coefficient between two statistical variables such as r_{HT} and r_{HH}. The correlation coefficient has the following variance (e.g., Kendall and Stuart [49], p. 236):

$$\text{Var}[r] = (1 - r^2)^2/n \tag{53}$$

in which n is the number of samples and r denotes the correlation coefficient in the ensemble.

Table 2
Proportionality Coefficient α of the Standard Deviation (S.D.) and the
Coefficient of Variation (C.D.) of Various Statistical Parameters of the
Wallops-type and the JONSWAP-type Spectra

Parameter	(Type)	Wallops-type				JONSWAP-type			
		m = 3	m = 5	m = 10	m = 20	$\gamma = 1.5$	$\gamma = 3.3$	$\gamma = 7$	$\gamma = 14$
$\sqrt{\beta_1}$	(S.D.)	0.93	0.72	0.32	0.08	0.69	0.62	0.52	0.42
β_2	(S.D.)	2.29	2.57	3.05	3.49	2.62	2.77	2.96	3.36
[C.V.(H_{max})]*	(C.V.)	0.85*	0.90*	0.95*	1.01*	0.91*	0.94*	0.98*	1.04*
η_{rms}	(C.V.)	0.49	0.55	0.65	0.77	0.58	0.68	0.80	0.94
$H_{1/10}$	(C.V.)	0.64	0.70	0.81	0.94	0.73	0.83	0.95	1.09
$H_{1/3}$	(C.V.)	0.57	0.60	0.69	0.80	0.62	0.72	0.84	0.97
H	(C.V.)	0.61	0.64	0.70	0.81	0.67	0.77	0.89	1.03
σ_H	(C.V.)	0.74	0.79	0.93	1.09	0.82	0.92	1.04	1.21
$H_{1/10}/\eta_{rms}$	(C.V.)	0.37	0.40	0.45	0.53	0.40	0.42	0.46	0.53
$H_{1/3}/\eta_{rms}$	(C.V.)	0.22	0.17	0.17	0.20	0.17	0.16	0.17	0.18
H/η_{rms}	(C.V.)	0.33	0.30	0.25	0.24	0.31	0.32	0.33	0.36
$T_{H1/10}$	(C.V.)	0.64	0.48	0.31	0.22	0.44	0.35	0.26	0.20
$T_{H1/3}$	(C.V.)	0.49	0.35	0.24	0.17	0.32	0.26	0.20	0.15
T	(C.V.)	0.51	0.40	0.28	0.22	0.40	0.40	0.39	0.35
σ_T	(C.V.)	0.66	0.66	0.74	0.88	0.64	0.66	0.82	1.14

Remarks: The asterisk * refers to the ratio of the observed value to the theoretical prediction by the
         Rayleigh distribution.
Source: Goda [10]

Furthermore, the coefficient of variation of the mean length of the run of wave heights is derived by the general statistical theory as [40]

$$C.V.[\bar{j}_1] = \sigma(\bar{j}_1)/E(\bar{j}_1) = p_{22}^{1/2}/N_R^{1/2} \tag{54}$$

where E expresses the expected value and N_R denotes the number of the run of wave heights within a wave record. Because an ordinary wave record of 20 minutes length contains only 10–20 runs of wave heights, the statistics of wave groups are hampered by large amounts of sampling variability. Reliable analysis of wave group statistics requires the wave data of quite long duration under the stationary sea state condition, which is not easily obtained.

For other sea state parameters, their standard deviations are known to vary in proportion to $N_0^{-1/2}$. Thus by denoting the sea state parameter with x in general, its standard deviation or its coefficient of variation is expressed as

$$\sigma(x) = \alpha \ N_0^{-1/2}, \text{ or } C.V.(x) = \alpha \ N_0^{-1/2} \tag{55}$$

The proportionality constant α for η_{rms} is estimated by Tucker's theory [50] as

$$\alpha(\eta_{rms}) = \frac{1}{2m_0} \left[\int_0^\infty \bar{f} \ S^2(f) \ df \right]^{1/2} \tag{56}$$

where $\bar{f}$ is the mean frequency of $\bar{f} = 1/\bar{T}$. The proportionality coefficient can also be evaluated for $T_{0,2}$ with the theory by Cavanié [51] as

$$\alpha(T_{0,2}) = \frac{1}{2} \left\{ \bar{f} \int_0^\infty S^2(f) \left[\frac{f^4}{m_2^2} - \frac{2f^2}{m_0 \ m_2} + \frac{1}{m_0^2} \right] df \right\}^{1/2} \tag{57}$$

As no theory is available for the proportionality constant α for other sea state parameters, it has been estimated by means of a numerical simulation technique by Goda [10]. Table 2 lists the result of analysis. The parameters $\sqrt{\beta_1}$ and β_2 are the skewness and kurtosis of the surface elevation to be discussed later in this chapter. According to the result of Table 2 with Equation 55, the significant wave height and period calculated from a wave record that contains 100 waves have the sampling error of 6.0% and 3.5%, respectively, when the wave spectrum is of the Pierson-Moskowitz type. As the wave spectrum becomes narrow-banded, the sampling error of wave height parameters increases while that of period parameters decreases.

Nonlinear Characteristics of Random Sea Waves

Wave Nonlinearity Effects on Surface Elevation

Distribution of Surface Elevation. Though the surface elevation of waves in the sea is regarded as Gaussian as the first approximation, detailed examination reveals some deviation from the Gaussian distribution. The degree of deviation is measured with the skewness $\sqrt{\beta_1}$ and the kurtosis β_2 defined:

$$\sqrt{\beta_1} = \frac{1}{\eta_{rms}{}^3} \cdot \frac{1}{N} \sum_{n=1}^{N} (\eta_n - \bar{\eta})^3 \tag{58}$$

$$\beta_2 = \frac{1}{\eta_{rms}{}^4} \cdot \frac{1}{N} \sum_{n=1}^{N} (\eta_n - \bar{\eta})^4 \tag{59}$$

where N is the number of surface elevation observations.

For the Gaussian distribution, $\sqrt{\beta_1}$ is 0 and β_2 takes the value 3.0. Ocean waves usually have a positive value of the skewness, reflecting the tendency that wave crests are sharp and peaked, while wave troughs are flat and shallow. This is due to the finite amplitude effect, similar with the case of regular waves. Theoretical treatment of nonlinear random waves requires calculation of wave interactions between linear component waves as will be discussed later in this chapter. The skewness of the surface elevation of wind waves seems to be governed by the wave steepness. Huang and Long [52] found the following relation for wind waves in deep water:

$$\sqrt{\beta_1} \approx 8\pi \, \eta_{rms}/L_P \tag{60}$$

where L_P denotes the wavelength corresponding to the spectral peak period. According to Challenor and Srokosz [53], however, the proportionality constant is not unique but dependent on the functional shape of wave spectrum.

In shallow water, nonlinear characteristics of sea waves become more pronounced. Figure 8 shows examples of the statistical distribution of surface elevation recorded by Kadono et al. [54] at a fixed tower in the 7-m-deep water. As the significant wave height increases, the deviation of surface elevation from the Gaussian distribution (thin solid lines) becomes quite noticeable. Goda [55] proposed the following parameter to describe nonlinear characteristics of water waves from deep water to very shallow water:

$$\Pi = (H/L_A) \, \coth^3 k_A h \tag{61}$$

where   h = water depth
L_A = wavelength given by Airy's theory (small amplitude wave theory)
k_A = wave number $2\pi/L_A$

This parameter becomes the same as the wave steepness in deep water, while it approaches the Ursell parameter in very shallow water. For random sea waves, the significant wave height $H_{1/3}$ is employed as the representative wave height for the above wave nonlinearity parameter. Goda [55] showed for example that the skewness of the surface elevation of sea waves is related with the nonlinearity parameter as

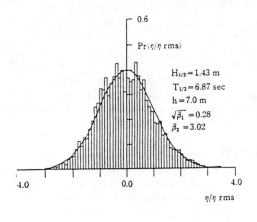

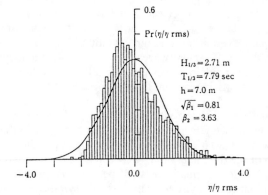

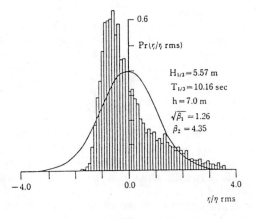

Figure 8. Example of the observed distribution of surface elevation in shallow water area [54].

$$\sqrt{\beta_1} \approx 4.2\Pi_{1/3}$$

Kadono et al. [54] have confirmed the above relation with the field data.

As for the kurtosis, many wave records exhibit the value slightly greater than 3.0, indicating that the distribution of surface elevation has its mode more peaked and its tails more extended than the Gaussian distribution. The factors that affect the value of the kurtosis are not known yet, but Kadono et al. [54] presented data of strong correlation between the kurtosis and the skewness.

Asymmetry of Wave Profiles. Waves at sea are not symmetric in their profiles. In the vertical direction, the heights of wave crests are greater than the depths of wave troughs. In the horizontal direction, breaking waves and those near to breaking have their front faces steeper than the rear faces. The skewness discussed previously serves as the overall measure of the former asymmetry.

The former asymmetry also governs the height of the highest surface elevation, and thus affects the design of many coastal and ocean facilities. There are not sufficient field data of η_{max} relative to η_{rms}, $H_{1/3}$, or H_{max}, and the estimation of the height of the highest surface elevation for a design condition is usually made by applying the finite amplitude theory of regular waves. However, it should be recalled that the highest elevation among random waves exceeds 50% of the largest wave height even in a linear system, as implied in Table 1, because of the effect of spectral bandwidth.

The latter asymmetry in the horizontal direction is evaluated by two parameters. One is the vertical asymmetry factor (asymmetry with respect to the vertical axis passing through a wave crest) proposed by Kjeldsen and Myrhaug [28, 55, 56]. It is defined as the ratio of the time interval T'' between a wave crest and the following downcrossing point and to the time interval T' between that wave crest to the preceding upcrossing point (see Figure 9). The vertical asymmetry factor $\lambda = T''/T'$ characterizes the asymmetry of individual wave profiles. Kjeldsen and Myrhaug showed that extreme waves generally have the λ value greater than 1, indicating steeper front faces than rear faces.

Another parameter for the asymmetry of wave profiles in the horizontal direction is the wave atiltness proposed by Goda [2, 41]. It is defined as the skewness of the time derivative of surface elevation as

$$\beta_3 = \frac{1}{N-1} \sum_{n=1}^{N-1} (\dot{\eta}_n - \bar{\dot{\eta}})^3 / \left[\frac{1}{N-1} \sum_{n=1}^{N-1} (\dot{\eta}_n - \bar{\dot{\eta}})^2 \right]^{3/2} \tag{62}$$

A positive value of β_3 means the front slope of wave profiles are steeper than the rear slope on the average, and wave profiles look tilted forward. Wind waves in developing or equilibrium stage seem to have some positive value of the wave atiltness parameter, but swell shows the null value for β_3 on the average. As waves enter into shoaling water and approach toward the shore, wave profiles are gradually deformed and exhibit forward tilting. Around the outer edge of the surf zone, the wave atiltness attains the value greater than 1. For waves with a large value of β_3, the zero-upcrossing method yields larger values of wave period parameters and

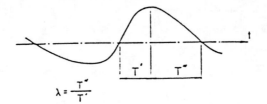

Figure 9. Definition of vertical asymmetry factor by Kjeldsen and Myrhaug [56].

the correlation coefficient between wave heights and periods compared with the zero-downcrossing method, but wave height parameters do not seem to be affected by the degree of wave atiltness [2].

Wave Nonlinearity Effects on Wave Heights and Periods

The effect of wave nonlinearity upon the distribution of wave heights has been investigated by Longuet-Higgins [58] and Tayfun [59] theoretically. Tayfun verified that to the second order of approximation the wave height distribution is not influenced by the wave nonlinearity, although the wave crest elevation is affected at that order. Longuet-Higgins calculated the potential energy of irregular, finite amplitude waves, the heights of which are assumed to follow the Rayleigh distribution. By using the third order approximation to deepwater waves, he demonstrated that the ratio H_{rms}/η_{rms} increases a few percent with the increase in wave steepness.

In shallow water, the effect of wave nonlinearity is much pronounced. The deviation of wave heights from the Rayleigh distribution due to the spectral bandwidth effect is gradually canceled by the nonlinearity effect. As waves propagate into shallower water, the latter effect surpasses the former and the distribution of wave heights may become broader than the Rayleighan, until wave breaking occurs in very shallow water. Figure 10 shows an example of the variation of the ratio $H_{1/3}/\eta_{rms}$ with respect to the wave nonlinearity parameter $\Pi_{1/3}$ defined with the significant wave height and period [55]. The solid curve is the result of a calculation under the assumption that the wave heights follow the Rayleigh distribution and each wave can be replaced by the third-order Stokes wave or the cnoidal wave. An almost identical relation between $H_{1/3}/\eta_{rms}$ and $\Pi_{1/3}$ has been obtained by Kadono et al. [54].

Wave periods counted on a record of wave profiles are not affected by the wave nonlinearity. The mean wave period $T_{0,2}$ evaluated from the wave spectrum, however, becomes shorter than the arithmetic mean of zero-crossing wave periods $\overline{T}$. It is due to the growth of the second harmonics of spectral components by the nonlinear interaction to be discussed in the following section. The nonlinear second harmonics increases the second spectral moment superficially at the rate faster than the zeroth moment, and thus the mean period $T_{0,2}$ is underestimated. Goda [55] and Kadono et al. [54] report examples that the mean periods estimated from spectra are less than 70% of the mean period actually counted on wave records, when the wave nonlinearity parameter $\Pi_{1/3}$ exceeds about 0.3.

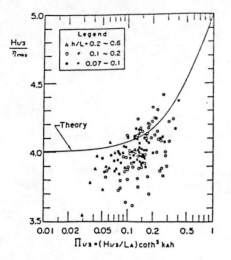

Figure 10. Coastal wave data of the ratio of significant wave height to root-mean-square surface elevation versus wave nonlinearity parameter defined with significant wave [55].

Nonlinear Wave Spectrum and Bound Waves

Nonlinear characteristics of random sea waves are understood at present as the result of the nonlinear interaction between linear wave components. The terminology of "nonlinear interaction" refers to the fact that wave components of higher orders must be present to satisfy the nonlinear boundary conditions on the undulating water surface. Such wave components are not freely propagating waves but waves bounded within the wave group. In regular waves with a single frequency, the bound waves have the harmonic frequencies and are phase-locked to the fundamental waves, as seen in the theory of Stokes waves and the stream function theory of finite amplitude waves. In a random wave system, two groups of bound waves exist. The first group has the frequencies equal to the sum of the frequencies of interacting linear components at the second order of approximation. Bound waves within this group include the harmonics of the linear components, which are the result of the interaction with themselves. The second group has the frequencies equal to the difference of the frequencies of interacting linear components.

Figure 11 shows an example of the resolution of recorded spectrum into the first-order and second-order spectra [11]. The calculation was made using an iterative technique based on the theory of Tick [60] corrected by Hamada [61]. The secondary spectral peak at the frequency about twice the main peak frequency is almost entirely composed of the secondary nonlinear components, which belong to the first group of bound waves. The low frequency part of the recorded spectrum, on the other hand, is explained as the bound waves of the second group. An overestimation of bound waves by theory is probably due to the inadequacy of the presently-available theory, which does not consider the higher order interaction terms beyond the second order.

The bound waves of the first group with same frequencies artificially raise the spectral density level at the high frequency part, and increase the values of spectral moments. This causes errors in the estimate of several statistical parameters including the mean wave period previously discussed. Several researchers [28, 39] rec-

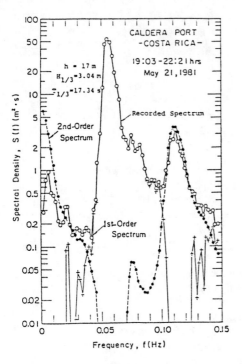

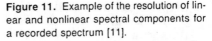

Figure 11. Example of the resolution of linear and nonlinear spectral components for a recorded spectrum [11].

ommend an application of a band-pass filter to a recorded spectrum before calculating spectral moments in order to eliminate the effect of bound waves, when statistical wave parameters are estimated by the theory.

The bound waves of the second group with difference frequencies appear as the long-period oscillation of the mean water level or the group-bounded long waves, which are out-of-phase from the envelope of surface waves. Local depression of the mean water level beneath groups of high waves was predicted by Longuet-Higgins and Stewart [62] with the concept of radiation stress. The phenomenon has attracted the attention of many investigators from the viewpoints of surf beat by Gallagher [63], ship-mooring problems and harbor resonance by Bowers [64, 65], and control of long waves in laboratory flumes by Ottesen-Hansen [66, 67], Sand [68], Barthel et al. [69], and others.

Mathematical expressions of the velocity potential and wave profiles of nonlinear secondary waves are presented by Hudspeth [70], Bowers [64], Sharma [70], Sand [72], and Kimura [73]. These expressions look different, but they are essentially the same.

Notation

a constant in Rayleigh distribution (Equation 30)
a_n amplitude of the n-th component wave
A constant in spectral model of ocean waves
B constant in spectral model of ocean waves

C	Euler's constant (0.5772. . .)
C.V.[]	coefficient of variation
E[]	expected value
f	frequency in general
f_p	frequency at spectral peak
F	fetch length
g	acceleration of gravity
$G(f,\theta)$	directional spreading function
h	water depth
H	wave height in general
H_{max}	largest wave height in a wave record or in a group of waves
H_{rms}	root-mean-square value of wave heights
$H_{1/3}$	average height of the highest one-third waves
$H_{1/10}$	average height of the highest one-tenth waves
$\bar{H}$	mean wave height
H_*	reference wave height
i	order number
j_l	length of the run of wave height exceeding a threshold height
k_A	wave number calculated by Airy theory
k_n	wave number of the n-th component wave
L_A	wavelength calculated by Airy theory
L_p	wavelength corresponding to spectral peak frequency
m	order number, or spectral shape parameter of Wallops spectra
m_0	zero-th moment of wave spectrum
m_n	n-th moment of wave spectrum
M	number of frequency components
n	order number
N	number of data
N_0	number of zero-crossing waves
N_1	number of maxima of surface elevation
p()	probability density function
p_0	occurrence probability of wave height exceeding a threshold value
p_{22}	probability that two waves in succession exceeds a threshold height
P()	probability in general
q_0	non-exceedance probability of wave height over a threshold value
r_{HH}	correlation coefficient between two wave heights in succession
r_{HT}	correlation coefficient between individual wave heights and periods
s	directional spreading parameter
s_{max}	maximum value of directional spreading parameter for a given spectrum
S(f)	frequency wave spectrum
$S(f,\theta)$	directional wave spectrum
t	time
T	wave period in general
$T_{H,max}$	period of the highest wave in a wave record
$T_{H1/3}$	mean period of the highest one-third waves
$T_{H1/10}$	mean period of the highest one-tenth waves
T_p	wave period corresponding to spectral peak

$\overline{T}$ mean wave period

U   wind speed

Var[]   variance

x   horizontal coordinate, or nondimensional wave height ($= H/H_*$)

y   horizontal coordinate

α proportionality constant in JONSWAP spectrum or in sample variability

β shape parameter in wave height distribution (Equation 37)

β_J nondimensional constant in modified JONSWAP spectrum (Equation 19)

β_w nondimensional constant in modified Wallops spectrum (Equation 18)

$\sqrt{\beta_1}$ skewness (Equation 58)

β_2 kurtosis (Equation 59)

β_3 wave atiltness (Equation 63)

γ shape parameter of JONSWAP spectrum

ϵ spectral bandwidth parameter (Equation 36)

ϵ_n phase angle of the n-th component wave

η surface elevation

η_{max} highest value of surface elevation in a wave record

η_{rms} root-mean-square value of surface elevation

$\overline{\eta}$ mean water level

θ azimuth measured counter-clockwise from the principal wave direction

θ_n direction of propagation of the n-th wave component

$\varkappa$ correlation coefficient of wave envelope

λ wave asymmetry factor in horizontal direction (vertical asymmetry factor)

ν spectral width parameter (Equation 35)

Π wave nonlinearity parameter (Equation 61)

$\Pi_{1/3}$ wave nonlinearity parameter defined with $H_{1/3}$

ρ shape parameter in wave height distribution (Equation 37)

σ shape parameter in JONSWAP spectrum (Equation 11)

$\sigma()$ standard deviation

τ nondimensional wave period ($= T/\overline{T}$)

References

1. Longuet-Higgins, M. S., 1957, "The Statistical Analysis of a Random, Moving Surface," *Phil. Trans. Roy. Soc. London,* Ser. A(966), pp. 321–387.
2. Goda, Y., 1986, "Effect of Wave Tilting on Zero-Crossing Wave Heights and Periods," *Coastal Engng. in Japan,* Vol. 29, pp. 79–90.
3. Borgman, L. E., 1969, "Ocean Wave Simulation for Engineering Design," *J. Waterways and Harbors Div., Proc. ASCE,* Vol. 95, No. WW4, pp. 557–583.
4. Goda, Y., 1977, "Numerical Experiments on Statistical Variability of Ocean Waves," *Rept. Port and Harbour Res. Inst.,* Vol. 16, No. 2, pp. 3–26.
5. Pierson, W. J., Jr. and Moskowitz, L., 1964, "A Proposed Spectral Form for Fully Developed Wind Seas Based on the Similarity Law of S. A. Kitaigorodoskii," *J. Geophys. Res.,* Vol. 69, No. 24, pp. 5181–5190.
6. Hasselmann, K. et al., 1973, "Measurements of Wind-Wave Growth and Swell Decay during the Joint North Sea Wave Project (JONSWAP)," *Deutsche Hydr. Zeit,* Reihe A(8°), No. 12.

7. Mitsuyasu, H. et al., 1980, "Observation of the Power Spectrum of Ocean Waves using a Cloverleaf Buoy," *J. Physical Oceanogr.*, Vol. 10, No. 2, pp. 286–296.

8. Kitaigorodoskii, S. A. et al., 1975, "On Phillips' Theory of Equilibrium Range in the Spectra of Wind-Generated Gravity Waves," *J. Physical Oceanogr.*, Vol. 5, No. 3, pp. 410–420.

9. Bouws, E. et al., 1984, "Similarity of the Wind Wave Spectrum in Finite Depth Water. Part I—Spectral Form," *J. Geophys. Res.*, Vol. 89, No. Cl, pp. 975–986.

10. Goda, Y., 1987, "Statistical Variability of Sea State Parameters as a Function of Wave Spectrum," *Proc. IAHR Seminar on Wave Analysis and Generation in Laboratory Basins*, Lausanne, Sept.

11. Goda, Y., 1983, "Analysis of Wave Grouping and Spectra of Long-Travelled Swell," *Rept. Port and Harbour Res. Inst.*, Vol. 22, No. 1, pp. 3–41.

12. Bretschneider, C. L.,1968, "Significant Waves and Wave Spectrum," *Ocean Industry*, Feb., pp. 40–46.

13. Mitsuyasu, H., 1970, "On the Growth of Spectrum of Wind-Generated Waves (2)— Spectral Shape of Wind Waves at Finite Fetch," *Proc. 17th Conf. Coastal Engng.*, pp. 1–7 (in Japanese).

14. Goda, Y., 1979, "A Review on Statistical Interpretation of Wave Data," *Rept. Port and Harbour Res. Inst.*, Vol. 18, No. 1, pp. 5–32.

15. ISSC, 1967, *"Rept. Committee 1 on Environmental Conditions,"* 3rd Int. Ship Structures Congr., Oslo.

16. Huang, N. E. et al., 1981, "A Unified Two-Parameter Wave Spectral Model for a General Sea State," *J. Fluid Mech.*, Vol. 112, pp. 203–224.

17. Ochi, M. K. and Hubble, E. N., 1976, "On Six-Parameter Wave Spectra," *Proc. 15th Int. Conf. Coastal Engng.*, Hawaii, pp. 301–328.

18. Mitsuyasu, H. et al., 1975, "Observation of the Directional Spectrum of Ocean Waves Using a Cloverleaf Buoy," *J. Physical Oceanogr.*, Vol. 5, No. 4, pp. 750–760.

19. Holthuijsen, L. H., 1983, "Observation of the Directional Distribution of Ocean-Wave Energy in Fetch-Limited Conditions," *J. Physical Oceanogr.*, Vol. 13, No. 2, pp. 191–207.

20. Goda, Y. and Suzuki, Y., 1975, "Computation of Refraction and Diffraction of Sea Waves with Mitsuyasu's Directional Spectrum," *Tech. Note, Port and Harbour Res. Inst.*, No. 230, 45 pp. (in Japanese).

21. Goda, Y., 1985, *Random Seas and Design of Maritime Structures*. Tokyo: Univ. Tokyo Press.

22. Kinsman, B., 1965, *Wind Waves*. Englewood Cliffs, N.J.: Prentice-Hall, Inc., p. 401 and pp. 460–471.

23. IAHR Working Group on Wave Generation and Analysis, 1986, "IAHR List of Sea State Parameters," *Supplement to Permanent Int. Assoc. Navigation Congr. Bulletin*, No. 52, Jan.

24. Sverdrup, H. U. and Munk, W. H., 1947, "Wind, Sea and Swell. Theory of Relations for Forecasting," *U.S. Hydrogr. Office, Wash., Publ.* No. 601.

25. Longuet-Higgins, M. S., 1952, "On the Statistical Distributions of the Heights of Sea Waves," *J. Marine Res.*, Vol. IX, No. 3, pp. 245–266.

26. Cartwright, D. E. and Longuet-Higgins, M. S., 1956, "The Statistical Distribution of the Maxima of Random Function," *Proc. Roy. Soc. London*, Ser. A., Vol. 237, pp. 212–232.

24. Forristall, G. Z., 1978, "On the Statistical Distributions of Wave Heights in a Storm," *J. Geophys. Res.*, Vol. 83, No. C5, pp. 2353–2358.

28. Nolte, K. G. and Hsu, F. H., 1979, "Statistics of Larger Waves in a Sea State," *J. Waterway, Port, Coastal & Ocean Div., Proc. ASCE*, Vol. 105, No. WW4, pp. 389–404.

29. Myrhaug, D. and Kjeldsen, S. P., 1986, "Steepness and Asymmetry of Extreme Waves and the Highest Waves in Deep Water," *Ocean Engng.*, Vol. 13, No. 6, pp. 549–568.

30. Tayfun, M. A., 1983, "Effects of Spectrum Band Width on the Distribution of Wave Heights and Periods," *Ocean Engng.*, Vol. 10, No. 2, pp. 107–118.

31. Forristall, G. Z., 1984, "The Distribution of Measured and Simulated Wave Heights as a Function of Spectral Shape," *J. Geophys. Res.*, Vol. 89, No. C6, pp. 10,547–10,552.

32. Naess, A., 1985, "On the Distribution of Crest to Trough Wave Heights," *Ocean Engng.*, Vol. 12, No. 3, pp. 221–234.

33. Naess, A., 1985, "The Joint Crossing Frequency of Stochastic Processes and Its Application to Wave Theory," *Applied Ocean Res.*, Vol. 7, No. 1, pp. 35–50.

34. Funke, E. R. and Mansard, E. P. D., 1980, "On the Synthesis of Realistic Sea State," *Proc. 17th Int. Conf. Coastal Engng.*, Sydney, pp. 2974–2991.

35. Bitner-Gregersen, E. M. and Gran S., 1983, "Local Properties of Sea Waves Derived from a Wave Record," *Applied Ocean Res.*, Vol. 5, No. 4, pp. 210–214.

36. Goda, Y., 1970, "Numerical Experiments on Wave Statistics with Spectral Simulation," *Rept. Port and Harbour Res. Inst.*, Vol. 9, No. 3, pp. 3–57.

37. Goda, Y., 1976, "On Wave Groups," *Proc. BOSS '76*, Vol. I, Trondheim, pp. 115–128.

38. Battjes, J. A. and van Vledder, G. Ph., 1984, "Verification of Kimura's Theory for Wave-Group Statistics," *Proc. 19th Int. Conf. Coastal Engng.*, Houston, pp. 642–648.

39. Longuet-Higgins, M. S., 1984, "Statistical Properties of Wave Groups in a Random Sea State," *Phil. Trans. Rov. Soc. London, Ser. A*, Vol. 312, pp. 219–250.

40. Kimura, A., 1980, "Statistical Properties of Random Wave Groups," *Proc. 17th Int. Conf. Coastal Engng.*, Sydney, pp. 2955–2973.

41. Goda, Y., 1985, "Numerical Examination of Several Statistical Parameters of Sea Waves," *Rept. Port and Harbour Res. Inst.*, Vol. 24, No. 4, pp. 65–102 (in Japanese).

42. Su, M.-Y., 1984, "Characteristics of Extreme Wave Groups," *Proc. Oceans '84*, Washington, D.C., Sept.

43. Rice, S. O., 1944, "The Mathematical Analysis of Random Noise," *Bell Syst. Tech. J.*, Vol. 23, pp. 282–332, and Vol. 24, 1945, pp. 46–156, also reprinted in *Selected Papers on Noise and Stochastic Processes*, Dover Pub., Inc., 1954, pp. 133–294.

44. Longuet-Higgins, M. S., 1975, "On the Joint Distribution of the Periods and Amplitudes of Sea Waves," *J. Geophys. Res.*, Vol. 80, No. 18, pp. 2688–2694.

45. Goda, Y., 1978, "The Observed Joint Distribution of Periods and Heights of Sea Waves," *Proc. 16th Int. Conf. Coastal Engng.*, Hamburg, pp. 227–246.

46. Cavanié, A. et al., 1978, "A Statistical Relationship between Individual Heights and Periods of Storm Waves," *Proc. Boss '76*, Vol. II, Trondheim, pp. 354–360.

47. Longuet-Higgins, M. S., 1983, "On the Joint Distribution of Wave Periods and Amplitudes in a Random Wave Field," *Proc. Trans. Roy. Soc. London, Ser. A*, Vol. 389, pp. 241–258.

48. Donelan, M. and Pierson, W. J., Jr., 1983, "The Sampling Variability of Estimates of Spectra of Wind-Generated Gravity Waves," *J. Geophys. Res.*, Vol. 88, No. C8, pp. 4381–4392.

49. Kendall, M. G. and Stuart, A. S., 1969, *The Advanced Theory of Statistics, Vol. 1*, 3rd ed. London: Griffin.

50. Tucker, M. J., 1957, "The Analysis of Finite-Length Records of Fluctuating Signals," *Brit. J. Applied Phys.*, Vol. 8, Apr., pp. 137–142.

51. Cavanié, A. G., 1979, "Evaluation of the Standard Error in the Estimation of Mean and Significant Wave Heights as Well as Mean Period from Records of Finite Length," *Proc. Int. Conf. Sea Climatology*, Édition Technip, Paris, pp. 73–88.

52. Huang, N. E. and Long, S. R., 1980, "An Experimental Study of the Surface Elevation Probability Distribution and Statistics of Wind-Generated Waves," *J. Fluid Mech.*, Vol. 101, pp. 179–200.

53. Challenor, P. G. and Srokosz, M. A., 1984, "Extraction of Wave Period from Altimeter Data," *Proc. Workshop on EPS-1 Radar Altimeter Data Products*, pp. 121–124.

54. Kadono, T. et al., 1986, "An Observation of Non-linear Coastal Waves," *Proc. 33rd Japanese Conf. Coastal Engng.*, pp. 149–153 (in Japanese).

55. Goda, Y., 1983, "A Unified Nonlinearity Parameter of Water Waves," *Rept. Port and Harbour Res. Inst.*, Vol. 22, No. 3, pp. 3–30.

56. Kjeldsen, S. P. and Myrhaug, D., 1979, "Formation of Wave Groups and Distribution Parameters for Wave Asymmetry," *Norwegian Hydrodynamics Laboratories, Report* No. STF60, A79044, Trondheim, Norway.

57. Myrhaug, D. and Kjeldsen, S. P., 1984, "Parametric Modeling of Joint Probability Density Distributions for Steepness and Asymmetry in Deep Water Waves," *Applied Ocean Res.*, Vol. 6, No. 4, pp. 207–220.

58. Longuet-Higgins, M. S., 1980, "On the Distribution of the Heights of Sea Waves: Some Effects of Nonlinearity and Finite Band Width," *J. Geophys. Res.*, Vol. 85, No. C3, pp. 1519–1523.

59. Tayfun, M. A., 1983, "Nonlinear Effects on the Distribution of Crest-to-Trough Wave Heights," *Ocean Engng.*, Vol. 10, No. 2, pp. 97–106.

60. Tick, L. J., 1963, "Nonlinear Probability Models of Ocean Waves," *Ocean Wave Spectra*, Englewood Cliffs, N.J.: Prentice-Hall, Inc., pp. 163–169.

61. Hamada, T., 1965, "The Secondary Interaction of Surface Waves," *Rept. Port and Harbour Res. Inst.*, No. 10, 28 p.

62. Longuet-Higgins, M. S. and Stewart, R. W., 1964, "Radiation Stresses in Water Waves; a Physical Discussion, with Applications," *Deep-Sea Res.*, Vol. 11, pp. 529–564.

63. Gallagher, B., 1971, "Generation of Surf Beat by Nonlinear Wave Interaction," *J. Fluid Mech.*, Vol. 49, pp. 1–20.

64. Bowers, E. C., 1976, "Long Period Oscillations of Moored Ships Subject to Short Wave Seas," *Trans. Roy. Inst. Naval Arch.*, Vol. 118, Supplm. Paper, pp. 1–8.

65. Bowers, E. C., 1977, "Harbour Resonance Due to Wave Groups," *J. Fluid Mech.*, Vol. 79, pp. 71–92.

66. Ottesen-Hansen, N.-E., 1978, "Long Period Waves in Natural Wave Trains," *Inst. Hydrodyn. and Hydraulic Engng., Tech. Univ. Denmark. Prog. Rept.* 46, pp. 13–48.

67. Ottesen-Hansen, N.-E. et al., 1980, "Correct Reproduction of Group-Induced Long Waves," *Proc. 17th Int. Conf. Coastal Engng.*, Sydney, pp. 784–800.

68. Sand, S. S., 1982, "Long Wave Problems in Laboratory Models," *J. Waterway, Port, Coastal & Ocean Div., Proc. ASCE*, Vol. 108, No. WW4, pp. 492–503.

69. Barthel, V. et al., 1983, "Group Bounded Long Waves in Physical Models," *Ocean Engng.*, Vol. 10, No. 4, pp. 261–294.

70. Hudspeth, R. T., 1974, "Prediction of Wave Forces from Nonlinear Random Sea Simulation," *Ph.D. Disst., Univ. Florida*, 168 p.

71. Sharma, J. N., 1979, "Development and Evaluation of a Procedure for Simulation of a Random Directional Second Order Sea Surface and Associated Wave Forces," *Ph.D. Disst., Univ. Delaware*, 136 p.

72. Sand, S. S., 1982, "Long Waves in Directional Seas," *Coastal Engng.*, Vol. 6, No. 3, pp. 195–208.

73. Kimura, A., 1984, "Averaged Two-Dimensional Low-Frequency of Wind Waves," *Comm. Hydraulics, Dept. Civil Engng., Delft Univ. Tech., Rept.* No. 84-3, 54 p.

74. Middleton, D., 1960, *An Introduction to Statistical Communication Theory*, McGraw-Hill, New York.

CHAPTER 5

WAVE FORECASTING AND HINDCASTING IN DEEP AND SHALLOW WATER

Charles L. Vincent

Coastal Engineering Research Center (CERC)
U.S. Army Engineer Waterways Experiment Station
Vicksburg, Mississippi, U.S.A.

and

Donald T. Resio

Offshore & Coastal Technologies, Inc. (OCTI)
Vicksburg, Mississippi, U.S.A.

CONTENTS

Introduction

Because many economic activities requiring coastal or ocean engineering studies occur in relatively shallow water rather than deep ocean basins, estimating wave conditions often requires including the effects of water depth on wave generation, propagation, and decay. For the purpose of this chapter, three idealized wave growth cases are differentiated. First is wave growth in deep water. Second is the situation in which the entire wave generation area lies in relatively shallow water. Third is the case in which waves are generated in deep water and then propagate into shallow water. The first case is classic deep-water wave growth. The second case is important in semi-enclosed bays, shallow lakes, or regions where ice cover can restrict fetch to shallow areas along a coast. The third case is important in most coastal areas where large storm-generated waves propagate shoreward from deeper water. These idealized cases can be recognized as asymptotic limits in which deep-water wave growth dominates, or shallow-water generation or shallow-water transformation is the dominant process governing the wave characteristics at a site. At a given time wave conditions at a site can be a mixture of all three limiting cases.

Wave Generation

Deep Water

The database on which present-day wave prediction methods rely developed subsequent to World War II and was summarized in Sverdrup and Munk [20]. Key to the development of wave forecast curves was the use of several dimensionless quantities:

$$
\begin{aligned}
\text{Height} &= gH_s/u^2 = \bar{H} \\
\text{Period} &= gT_s/u = \bar{T} \\
\text{Fetch} &= gF/u^2 = \bar{F} \\
\text{Duration} &= gt/u = \bar{t}
\end{aligned}
$$

to form empirical prediction relationships. Further refinements were made over the next decade and are encompassed in the widely used curves of Bretschneider [5]. Laboratory and field studies [9, 14, 15] provide further significant modifications to the overall pattern of wave growth particularly with respect to spectral characteristics of the sea surface. Three simplified examples of wave growth are provided to illustrate the basic aspects of the problem: fetch-limited wind sea, duration-limited wind sea, and a fully-developed wind sea.

Fetch-limited conditions are easily envisioned if a large and deep lake is considered. When a steady, uniform wind blows over the lake, assumed to have no waves initially, waves very near the upwind coast will be observed to be small with short wavelengths. Progressing farther away from the shore the wave height and length become progressively larger reflecting the longer distance, or fetch, that the wind has along which to add energy to the water surface. If the rate of wave growth is measured at some fixed point, the wave height and period will cease to grow even if the wind continues to blow. This condition is termed fetch-limited because the wave growth has come into equilibrium for the fetch length and wind speed with the primary limiting influence being the distance (fetch) over which the wind has blown.

If a wind is considered to start blowing at a specific time and waves are measured at a great distance from shore, wave height and period will be observed to increase with time. As long as the waves continue to grow and no limitations arise due to upwind fetch, the waves are termed *duration-limited*.

In the preceding case two possible endpoints can occur. In one case the presence of an upwind fetch eventually dominates the wave growth and the waves become fetch-limited. However, if the water body is very large, the waves may be seen to stop growing although no effect of fetch is apparent. This appears to result from the constraint that the wind does not transfer energy to waves moving faster than the wind. Hence there appears to be a wave period beyond which, for a given wind speed, waves are not generated. This case is termed a *fully developed wind sea*.

If the wind speed drops or the wind direction shifts, the waves that were actively growing become decoupled from the wind and are termed *swell*. Swell can travel for thousands of miles across the ocean and hence become a feature of the sea surface totally unrelated to local winds in the area at the present or past.

The simple wave growth cases have been used to illustrate the significant aspects of wave growth. Waves at a site, however, may reflect combinations of sea and swell, and the wind sea may not be a result of one of the three classic cases but may represent waves resulting from variable winds. The early wave prediction methods, such as those in Bretschneider [5] and *Shore Protection Manual* [25], were based on applications of the three simple wave growth cases along with rules to attempt to handle the effect of variable winds. These methods can produce reasonable answers if applied carefully by someone of considerable skill; however, numerical models have been developed to allow a more rigorous treatment of spatially-complex and temporally-variable wind fields.

To a large degree deep-water wave growth can be considered as an asymptotic limit for intermediate and shallow-water wave growth curves. As will be discussed next, the shallow-water wave growth curves are a depth-dependent modification to the deep-water curves. The deep-water wave growth formulas will be presented as part of the shallow-water curves to reduce duplication.

Shallow Water

The shallow-water wave generation problem occurs when wave growth is confined to fetches that are predominantly over shallow water and where no outside wave energy in the form of swell is present. As an example, wave growth over a circular lake with constant, very shallow-water depth is discussed. First, some definition of the term "shallow water" must be made. If the water depth is greater than one half the wavelength, the water may be considered deep. Otherwise, the bottom may influence the wave motion and the water depth is termed shallow.

As a wind that is constant in time and uniform in space blows over the lake, waves begin to form. Those waves at the upwind side of the lake remain small because they are limited by the shortness of fetch and typically have very short periods and, therefore, small wave lengths. Consequently, if the waves are very close to the upwind shore, the waves may be deep-water waves, even though compared to the oceanic conditions the depths may be considered shallow. As these waves propagate downwind further from shore and grow, the wavelengths will typically increase due to the evolution of the wave field. If the fetch is long enough and the winds strong enough, the wave motion will become influenced by depth once the water-depth-to-wavelength ratio is less than one half.

The foregoing discussion illustrates two points. First, shallow-water wave growth comes as a limit to waves that initially began as deep-water waves. Second, whether or not wave conditions can be classified as shallow water depends upon fetch, water depth, and wind speed. A significant problem in the study of wave mechanics is the absence of a large number of observations in shallow water that are not influenced by presence of swell or that are not more nearly deep-water waves; that is, depth has had only a minor effect. Adequate data to address the effects of bottom material on the rate of wave growth are also unavailable. The methods available to estimate waves in shallow water have been developed through asymptotic relationships and limited empirical data.

Parametric Relationships

Historical Perspective. The fundamental basis for the parametric wave-growth curves in general use today are the deep-water wave growth relationships that were developed during World War II [20] modified by application of a bottom friction and percolation theory [6] and asymptotic limits on wave height and period derived from field studies performed by the U.S. Army Corps of Engineers [27]. Deepwater wave growth relationships between dimensionless fetch, $\bar{F}$, and dimensionless significant wave height, $\bar{H}_s$, and dimensionless significant wave period, $\bar{T}$, were based on field data. Until the JONSWAP experiment [8] the Sverdrup-Munk-Bretschneider curves [6] were the most widely used wave growth expressions and remain in wide use today. Expressions for the rate of wave growth with duration were derived from the fetch curves, and a joint nomogram for predicting significant wave height and significant period as a function of wind speed, fetch, and duration was developed.

Field data, assembled by the U.S. Army Corps of Engineers [27] allowed development of relationships between $\bar{H}$ and dimensionless depth, $\bar{d}$, and between $\bar{T}$ and $\bar{d}$. These data, largely based on observations of hurricane waves in a shallow-water lake, provide an asymptotic limit. Bretschneider and Reid [6] developed a bottom friction theory and Bretschneider [5] applied it to the deep-water fetch curves to estimate the decay due to bottom friction. This method combined with the depth-limited conditions provided a method for producing shallow-water wave growth curves as a smoothly varying departure from the deep-water growth curves which asymptotically approach the depth limits observed. These curves are given by:

$$g\ H_s/u^2 = 0.283\ \tanh\ [0.530(gd/u^2)^{3/4}] \times \tanh\ \left\{\frac{0.0125\ (gF/u^2)^{0.42}}{\tanh\ 0.530(gd/u^2)^{3/4}}\right\} \tag{1}$$

$$\frac{gT_s}{2\pi u} = 1.2\ \tanh\ [0.833\ (gd/u^2)^{3/8}] \times \tanh\ \left\{\frac{0.77\ (gF/u^2)^{1/4}}{\tanh\ 0.833\ (gd/u^2)^{3/8}}\right\} \tag{2}$$

where T_s is the significant wave period. Bretschneider assumed a bottom friction coefficient of .01. It should be noted that no method was provided to estimate wave height or period as a function of duration for the shallow-water case. For deep water the duration curves are provided graphically in Bretschneider [5] and *Shore Protection Manual* [25].

The wave growth relationships produced by Bretschneider [5] remain in wide-spread use today. However, it is important to recognize that the basis for the shallow-water aspects of the growth curves are a theoretical calculation of wave energy loss due to bottom friction as the only mechanism for wave decay (no account is made for steepness induced breaking as an example). Few observations of the wave growth are available along a fetch where waves make a clear transition from deep- to intermediate- to fully shallow-water conditions. Although the basis for the wave growth curves might be considered primitive, it must be stressed that they have been widely and successfully used, which reflects the skill and judgment incorporated into their development. Given the complexities of many shallow-water sites, the absence of information about bottom materials, and uncertainties in wind estimates, it is apparent that some errors in the wave growth curves will tend to be masked. Likewise in deep water, uncertainties in the wind field specification and spatial and temporal gradients in the wind field often add more uncertainty than the uncertainties in the wave growth curves. However, it should always be noted that any biases existing in these curves can create comparable biases in one's results.

The latest edition of the *Shore Protection Manual* [26] provides an alternate set of wave growth curves. These curves are based on identical application of the Bretschneider [5] depth functions to the JONSWAP [8] deep-water growth curves rather than the Sverdrup-Munk-Bretschneider deep-water curves. A variation on these curves is presented here:

$$\frac{gH_s}{u_*^2} = 200 \tanh 0.003877 \, (gd/u_*^2)^{3/4} \times \tanh \left\{ \frac{0.0002129 \, (gF/u_*^2)^{1/2}}{\tanh 0.003877 \, (gd/u_*^2)^{3/4}} \right\} \tag{3}$$

$$\frac{gT_m}{u_*} = 200 \tanh 0.07125 \, (gd/u_*^2)^{3/8} \times \tanh \left\{ \frac{0.00426 \, (gF/u_*^2)^{1/3}}{\tanh 0.07125 \, (gd/u_*^2)^{3/8}} \right\} \tag{4}$$

The equations for duration-limited growth of deep-water waves [28] were derived from an analytic integration of the parametric wave model of Hasselmann et al. [8] because no well accepted empirical growth curve exists:

$$\frac{gH_s}{u_*^2} = 5.767 \times 10^{-3} \left(\frac{gt}{u_*} \right)^{5/7} \tag{5}$$

and

$$\frac{gT_m}{u_*} = 4.86 \times 10^{-1} \left(\frac{gt}{u_*} \right)^{0.411} \tag{6}$$

The basis for the shallow water adjustments to these curves is no different than that of Bretschneider. The curves presented here differ from those in the *Shore Protection Manual* [26] in that the velocity scaling uses a friction velocity, u_*, explicitly. The conversion of the JONSWAP curves used a $c_d = 0.001$ in the *Shore Protection Manual*, here $c_d = .00142$ was used. Since these curves are not explicitly those of the *Shore Protection Manual*, they will be called JONSWAP-based curves. The

Shore Protection Manual provides nomograms in which an estimate of duration on shallow-water wave growth is provided. It is not included here.

Because neither set of curves can be considered extensively verified, calculations by each of the methods may be expected to provide some concept of the range in estimates that might be expected. The Bretschneider curves have a longer history of use. The JONSWAP-based curves include results from more recent deep-water wave growth observations and appear to be more accepted in the scientific community. However, neither should be considered definitive. Intercomparison of empirical fetch-limited wave growth curves from independent field experiments show differences of up to one decade on log-log graph paper. The reasons for the differences can in part be explained, but the lack of agreement is of significance and deserves additional research in the future.

The two curves presented in this chapter reflect the trend of most of the data. Comparisons of the two growth curves over a range of fetches (10 to 100 km), depths (2 to 20 m), and wind speeds (10 to 30 m/s) indicated that the estimated wave heights and periods were normally well within 15%, with the sign of the deviations varying with fetch, wind speed, and depth. Table 1 provides examples of the values. Certainly the back-up data for either curve is no better than this difference.

Two approaches have been given for the simple parametric wave estimation method. The comparisons suggest that they can produce similar results. Both have been given because the Bretschneider curves have a wide history of use and the 1984 *Shore Protection Manual* curves are relatively new. An advantage of the JONSWAP-based curves is that the effects of atmospheric stability may be included in the calculations. Furthermore, in the deep-water asymptotic limit of the new curves, the growth of energy with fetch appears to be linear, which is in agreement with recent detailed measurements of waves growing along a fetch. The deep-water Bretschneider curves have a 0.84 slope that can produce a significant deviation from the linear relationship at long fetches.

Application. The wave height and period will be estimated for a wind speed of 30 m/sec, a depth of 10 m, and a fetch of 100 km for both curves. The wind speed is measured at 10 m above the surface. A general method for making wind estimates for both curves is provided in Appendix A at the end of this chapter.

Bretschneider: The dimensionless fetch is calculated as

$$gF/u^2 = (9.8)(100,000)/(30)^2 = 1.089 \times 10^3$$

and the dimensionless depth as

$$gd/u^2 = (9.8)(10)/(30)^2 = 1.089 \times 10^{-1}$$

Equation 1 is entered with these values and a height of 2.56 m is obtained. Equation 2 is entered and a period of 6.9 sec is obtained.

JONSWAP-based: These curves use friction velocity as a scaling parameter rather than wind velocity at 10 m. From Appendix A the method of estimating friction velocity is given by calculating the coefficient of drag

Table 1
Comparison of Wave Estimation Techniques

Fetch (km)	Wind Speed (m/s)	Depth (m)	Significant Height		Significant Period	
			Bretschneider (m)	JONSWAP-based (m)	Bretschneider (sec)	JONSWAP-based (sec)
10	10	4	0.52	0.44	2.7	2.5
10	10	10	0.61	0.49	2.9	2.6
10	10	20	0.63	0.50	3.0	2.7
10	30	4	1.23	1.36	4.4	4.0
10	30	10	1.86	1.85	4.9	4.3
10	30	20	2.13	2.02	5.2	4.4
100	10	4	0.73	0.72	3.6	3.7
100	10	10	1.17	1.14	4.2	4.3
100	10	20	1.40	1.34	4.6	4.7
100	30	4	1.31	1.55	5.5	5.8
100	30	10	2.56	3.00	6.9	7.2
100	30	20	3.86	4.46	7.7	8.0

$$c_d = 10^{-3} (0.75 + 0.067 \, u_{10}) = 0.00276$$

and then the friction velocity

$$u_* = \sqrt{c_d} \, u_{10} = (0.05254)(30) = 1.58 \text{ m/sec}$$

assuming that the air-sea temperature difference is zero. From the friction velocity, the dimensionless fetch and depth for the JONSWAP-based curves are obtained

$$gF/u_*^2 = (9.8)(100,000)/(1.58)^2 = 3.9257 \times 10^5$$

$$gd/u_*^2 = (9.8)(10)/(1.58)^2 = 3.9257 \times 10^1$$

It should be noted that the difference between these values and that in the Bretschneider approach is due to normalization by a different speed scale and that the two cannot be intermixed. These values are substituted in Equations 3 and 4 to obtain a height value of 3.0 m and a period value of 7.2 sec.

Definition of Fetch. In the foregoing discussion, the fetch length was assumed and the calculations made. In practice, definition of the fetch value is often one of the most difficult parts of the wave estimation problem. Very often the upwind shoreline can be highly irregular, the water body may have a bifurcation, islands or peninsulas can partially block the fetch, and so forth. On the open ocean delineation of a fetch from a curved wind field can be difficult and requires experience and judgment. The Bretschneider curves illustrate the concept of an effective fetch (see

Shore Protection Manual [25]), that attempts to incorporate the width of the fetch into the fetch-averaging process. The *Shore Protection Manual* [26] approach now suggests a simple arithmetic averaging over a 22° upwind sector centered on the wind direction. This method was suggested because the physics behind the effective fetch method today can be questioned. In the effective fetch method, it was assumed that wind input to the waves was primarily within 45° of the wind direction with a cosine distribution. High-resolution measurements of the directional spectrum indicate that the spreading function in wave energy is

$$\cos^{2s} (\theta - \theta_w) \tag{7}$$

where s is very large (5–10) in the region of the peak frequency. Hence, a simple averaging function was suggested.

Little information is available on the possible effect of fetch width on wave generation. For very narrow fetches, such as in river valleys or fjords, width may possibly be a significant factor. On narrow fetches, slight deviations in wind direction can significantly alter the apparent fetch. However, no guidance is available to provide a definitive treatment of this effect. The engineer should consider that either approach can give misleading answers as the fetch geometry becomes complicated, and that a simple estimate of fetch may be impossible to guess. One of the advantages of a numerical model for wave growth is the ability to handle complicated fetches. The engineer should consider alternative estimates of the fetch and the relative influence this introduces into the wave estimates. If the range in values is too large to accept, more detailed analysis with a more sophisticated model or collection of field data might be considered.

Advantages and Disadvantages. The principal advantages of the parametric approach is the ability to rapidly and simply obtain an estimate of the height and period. The disadvantages of the parametric approach are that no estimate of the effect of duration, based on shallow-water observations, is available and, hence, all calculations are fetch limited. Inclusions of the effects of irregular fetch geometries are difficult and judgmental. Effects of refraction are not considered (a uniform depth assumption is required). Also, spatial variations in the wind field are presently not considered.

Numerical Models for Shallow-Water Wave Growth

Historical Perspective. Consideration of the limitation of parametric relationships provided much of the motivation for beginning research into more sophisticated wave models. The primary limitation in applying parametric wave models is the necessity of having to describe meteorological and bathymetric conditions in terms of constant values over a broad area. Wind fields can be rapidly varying in both time and space, and only rarely are the depths constant across a basin.

In order to extrapolate from concepts of constant conditions over a large area to non-constant conditions, methods had to be developed that could discretize a study area into small regions of nearly constant conditions. Early wave models first attempted to model significant wave parameters. In this context, wave conditions are considered to be representable by a small number of parameters, typically wave height, wave period, and wave direction. The evolution of these wave parameters at a point can be solved by evaluating the energy being advected into the site (wave propagation), the energy transformations accompanying the propagation (refraction and shoaling), the energy being added to the wave system (wind input), and the energy being lost from the wave system (mechanisms related to interactions between wave motions and bottom materials in finite-depth water). Similarly, cumulative effects of these mechanisms on wave periods and wave directions must also be considered. Thus, in a shallow-water parametric model, there are three equations to be solved.

Efforts to model incoming waves on a parametric basis usually focused on only one or two mechanisms at a time and assumed that others could be neglected. However, even under such simplifying assumptions, no widely accepted numerical models based on wave parameters were ever developed. There are probably two primary reasons for this. First, in many coastal applications an *ad hoc* separation was made between two regions. In the first region, the basin bottom was considered either flat or sufficiently deep relative to the wavelength to be treated under the simple framework of constant conditions. In the second region, the effects of wind inputs were neglected and only wave transformations were considered. Under these assumptions available tools provide a reasonable approximation to more generalized techniques. The second reason for the lack of development of generalized parametric models was the development of spectral models for this same purpose. The remainder of this section shall concentrate on models such as these.

To obtain a clear picture of the development of general depth spectral models, it is helpful to examine first the asymptotic deep-water form. In such a model, wave conditions at a point are considered as part of a wave field consisting of continuous directional spectra. Thus, wave energy at a point is considered to be made up by (hypothetically) an infinite number of linearly superimposed components each traveling with its own characteristic speed and direction.

The evolution of a surface wave field in space and time is governed by a balance equation for each spectral component, i.e.

$$\frac{\partial E(f,\theta)}{\partial t} = \underset{\text{advection}}{\vec{V} \cdot \nabla E(f,\theta)} + \underset{\substack{\text{source/sink} \\ \text{terms}}}{\sum S_k(f,\theta)} \tag{8}$$

where $E(f,\theta)$ = energy density at frequency f and propagation direction θ
$\quad\quad\quad$ V = group velocity of this component
$\quad\quad\quad$ $S_k(f,\theta)$ = k^{th} source/sink mechanism acting to add energy to or remove energy from that spectral component

In deep water the principal source/sink terms are wind input, nonlinear transfer of wave energy among wave components and dissipation.

Much of our understanding of deep-water wave generation comes from studies of fetch-limited waves, where the two terms on the right side of Equation 8 exactly balance. The largest experiment of this kind has been the Joint North Sea Wave Project (JONSWAP) as reported in Hasselmann et al. [8]. Following this experiment, it has been generally accepted that the wave spectrum can be conceptually partitioned into three regions as shown in Figure 1. The forward face region shown there represents the actively growing portion of the spectrum. The middle region is in a dynamic-equilibrium state, where wind inputs are balanced by fluxes due to nonlinear wave-wave interactions and/or wave breaking. The high-frequency tail of the spectrum is the major dissipative region of the spectrum, where energy losses are due to white-capping, turbulence, and viscous effects.

Numerous deep-water wave models have been developed for predicting the directional spectrum of the sea surface on global, ocean basin, and regional scales. A detailed summary of many of them is provided in the *SWAMP* study [21], which provides intercomparisons for several idealized wave growth cases. Review of these and other models not covered indicated a diversity of approaches and in some instances substantial differences in results in the idealized test cases. The models contain differing combinations of source terms and different formulations of individual source terms, reflecting divergent technical opinions on the mechanics of wave growth. Most of the models have been used extensively in practical wave prediction problems and displayed reasonably adequate skill. The reason for the paradox lies in calibrating or tuning the model for specific ranges of events typical to the areas in which they are applied. Thus, a critical concern to the use of a particular model for a wave prediction problem is demonstration that the model can function adequately for the situation required. These differences represent a lack of a definitive understanding of the physics of wave growth and decay.

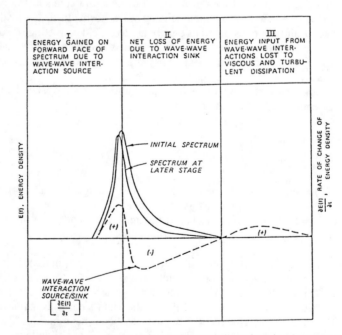

Figure 1. Conceptual diagram showing three dynamic regions in a wave spectrum.

In terms of shallow-water spectral models, a major question that arises concerns what differences exist between the picture of spectral development previously shown and spectral development in shallow water. Rewriting Equation 8 into a more general form for arbitrary depth yields

$$\frac{\partial E(f,\theta)}{\partial t} = V_x \frac{\partial E(f,\theta)}{\partial x} + V_y \frac{\partial E}{\partial y} \ (f,\theta) \tag{9}$$

advection

$$+ V_x \frac{\partial E(f,\theta)}{\partial k_x} \frac{\partial k_x}{\partial x} + V_y \frac{\partial E(f,\theta)}{\partial k_y} \frac{\partial k_y}{\partial y}$$

refraction and shoaling

$$+ \sum S_k(f,\theta)$$

source terms

where   x, y = two spatial coordinates

V_x, V_y = group velocities in the x, y directions, respectively

k_x, k_y = x, y components of the wavenumber vector associated with frequency f and direction θ

As expected, refraction and shoaling now must be addressed. Also, the possibility of additional source terms in shallow water must be examined. Hence, there are two ways in which shallow-water spectral models generally differ from deep-water models: the manner in which they treat wave propagation (including refraction and shoaling) and the presence of additional source terms (relating to finite depth effects). It is beyond the scope of this chapter to go into details of the numerics of calculating wave refraction and shoaling for wave spectra. The reader is directed to Longuet-Higgins [13], Karlsson [12], and Shiau and Wang [19] to obtain additional information on this subject.

Probably one of the most controversial areas in shallow-water wave prediction is the understanding and treatment of various finite-depth source terms. It is highly unlikely that all of the many mechanisms described in the literature have been properly quantified. In fact, in many calibration attempts, all source terms except the single term being investigated are neglected and all energy losses are ascribed to that one mechanism. If all the source terms calibrated in this manner were inserted into a single wave model, energy dissipation rates would be greatly exaggerated.

For the sake of simplicity, let us divide the source terms proposed to date into four broad categories as follows

1. Percolation source terms
2. Bottom friction source terms
3. Wave breaking source terms
4. Miscellaneous other source terms

Percolation was considered as a potential dissipator of wave energy in 1949 by Putnam. The basic mechanism of energy loss is the viscous drag of wave-induced water motions through a porous bottom material. The general form for this source term can be written as [18]

$$S_p(f,\theta) = -E(f,\theta)\,k\alpha_o\,\cosh kd \tag{10}$$

where d = water depth
  α_o = decay constant

Bottom friction was investigated in an early work by Bagnold [1]. This mechanism represents the energy loss due to drag on the wave motions at the water-bottom interface. Bretschneider and Reid [6] presented a classic treatment of the hypothetical effects of bottom friction on wave height decay.

Hasselmann and Collins [9] extended parametric energy loss equations into a spectral source term of the form

$$S_B(\vec{k}) = c_f \nu_{xy} k_x k_y \rho g F(\vec{k}) \tag{11}$$

where c_f is the drag coefficient and ν_{xy} is given by

$$\nu_{xy} = \frac{g}{\omega^2 \cosh^2 kd}\left\{\delta_{xy} <W> + \left\langle\frac{W_x W_y}{W}\right\rangle\right\} \tag{12}$$

where W is the bottom velocity.

Jonsson [31] observed that wave boundary layers were affected by coexisting currents and hypothesized that this could lead to increased drag on the bottom and increased rates of decay. Grant and Madsen [30] also contributed to the estimation of variations of the mean boundary layer in combined wave-current systems. In this context, the value of c in Equation 11 becomes dependent on a wide range of factors such as grain size, ripple formation, and mean current velocities. Little has been done as yet to verify that actual wave energy losses are in quantitative agreement with these theories.

Wave breaking is always observed as a by-product of wave generation in any depth. Recently, Resio [17] proposed a mechanism by which fluxes of energy due to nonlinear wave-wave interactions would depend strongly on the depth of water. Because these fluxes govern the rate of transport of energy into the high-frequency region of the spectrum where it is presumed lost, the rate of wave generation along a fetch is expected to be altered by water depth. Resio [31] suggests that such an alteration would lead to an asymptotic situation in which the wave energy growth with fetch is only one-half of its equivalent deep-water value. Resio [17] has also suggested that due to shallow-water effects, wave spectra with peak periods greater than about $8\sqrt{(h/g)}$ cannot be generated. Vincent [28] has shown that wave data collected during high wind conditions over Lake Okeechobee support the existence of such a limit.

Because source terms related to wave breaking are nonlinearly coupled among various spectral components, the source term is usually represented in an integrated parametric fashion. Typically, this is accomplished by either estimating the complete fluxes as described in Resio [17] or by including a Jacobian term in the representation of the equilibrium form of the spectrum, i.e.

$$E(f,\theta)_h = E(f,\theta)_o J^{-1} \tag{13}$$

where the subscripts o and h refer to deep-water and shallow-water spectra and J^{-1} is given by

$$J^{-1} = \left(\frac{k_o}{k_h}\right)^3 \tag{14}$$

Application Example. The application of a shallow-water spectral model usually requires that a grid of the type shown in Figure 2 be laid out. For each point in the grid a depth must be input into the model; and, in models with source terms sensitive to bottom material, information on the bottom material at each grid point must also be input.

Wind fields must be input into the model at time intervals sufficiently small to resolve any significant temporal variations in the winds over an area of interest. Typically, hourly winds derived by methods described earlier will suffice to drive the model.

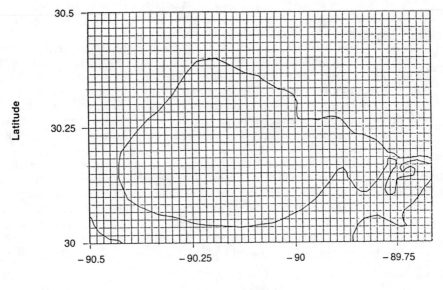

Figure 2. Wave model grid for sample application to Lake Pontchartrain.

Advantages and Disadvantages. The main problems associated with using a deep- or shallow-water spectral model are that the initial set-up for a basin can be tedious and the computer resources in terms of memory and run-time can be large. Advantages in using these models are that they are sufficiently general to treat most practical problems, they do not have to represent winds and bathymetries as constants over a large area, and they can provide a wealth of additional data to a user.

Wave Transformations Near a Coast

The prediction techniques discussed have been largely directed at estimating the significant wave height and associated wave period. In the parametric approach these are the only parameters that can be predicted. In the spectral model approach, the spectrum of the sea surface may be predicted from which the height and period can be determined. Most observations of the active wind sea spectrum indicate a wide band of energy with a well defined peak. On open-ocean coasts observations of the spectra frequently indicate presence of multiple wave trains. Thompson [23], for example, found that only about one third of the observations he analyzed on U.S. Atlantic Ocean, Gulf of Mexico, and Pacific Ocean coasts could be considered as having a single peak, i.e., single wave train system. Thus, in two thirds of the cases the spectrum was more complicated than the simple cases discussed so far.

Given the possible mixtures of sea and swell in shallow water, the general shallow water wave prediction problem becomes quite complicated. The transformation of wind sea from deep to shallow water on a sloping bottom is a different theoretical problem from the case of an assumed flat bottom for which the parametric curves discussed earlier were devised. In the general case of a sloping bottom with irregular depth contours, no simple approximation is possible. For the case in which the bottom is gently sloping, a parametric estimate of the wind sea is possible based on some assumptions about spectral shape in shallow water.

In the next section an empirical-based shape for the wind sea spectrum is introduced. In addition to its possible use in parametric transformation of wind sea, it may be used in conjunction with estimates of the wind sea period from the parametric curves to give an approximation of the energy distribution about the peak frequency. Next, a parametric method for estimating the wind sea transformation with depth is provided. It must be emphasized that as in any parametric transformation method the accuracy is limited to idealized cases. However, the results may serve as a useful first estimate.

Brief discussions follow on the use of numerical models to estimate wave transformation and on the relationship between different estimates of significant wave height in shallow water. These discussions are abbreviated because other chapters treat wave propagation models and wave height distributions in more detail.

In most wave record analyses and in most wave prediction methods, the predicted parameter is an estimate of significant wave height, H_s, obtained from an estimate of the variance of the water surface σ^2. This estimate is called H_{m_0} and is defined

$$H_{m_0} = 4\sigma \qquad (15)$$

In deep water, H_{m_0} and H_s essentially yield the same value when applied to a time history of the water surface. Thompson and Vincent [24] showed that in shallow water, H_{m_0} and H_s do not always yield the same value when applied to a water surface history and that the difference was large if the wave steepness was low. In some laboratory cases H_s was 30 to 50% larger than H_{m_0}. The difference results from the nonsinusoidal shape of many shallow-water waves. After the waves begin to break the ratio decreases and H_s may actually become slightly less than H_{m_0}.

Spectral Shape

Background. Observations of the water surface in deep- and shallow-water depths indicate that under steady winds the spectrum of the sea surface has considerable content in a range of frequencies about a single peak frequency. As the fetch or wind field becomes more complicated, the spectrum likewise becomes more complicated. Shallow-water data collected outside the surf zone for quasi-steady conditions indicate that the spectrum has a self-similar shape not unlike that of the JONSWAP spectrum but scaled by slightly different relationships [3]. The spectrum may be written as

$$E(f) = J(f) \; \Phi(\omega_d) \tag{16}$$

$$J(f) = \alpha g^2 (2\pi)^{-4} f^{-5} \exp(-1.25(f/f_m)^{-4}) \; \gamma^{\exp\{-(f-f_m)^2/2\mu \, f_m\}} \tag{17}$$

$$\Phi(\omega_d) = \frac{k^{-3}(\omega,d)\partial k(\omega,d)/\partial\omega}{k^{-3}(\omega,\infty)\partial k(\omega,\infty)/\partial\omega} \tag{18}$$

$$\mu = 0.07 \text{ for } f < f_m \qquad\qquad \mu = 0.09 \; f \geq f_m$$

$$\alpha = 0.194 \; K_*^{0.49} \qquad\qquad \gamma = 31.9 \; K_*^{0.39}$$

$$K_* = u_*^2 \, k_m/g \qquad\qquad \omega_d = 2\pi f(d/g)^{1/2}$$

The function $\Phi(\omega_d)$ may be approximated (error less than $\pm 10\%$) by

$$\Phi(\omega_d) = \tfrac{1}{2} \; \omega_d^2 \qquad\qquad \omega_d < 1 \tag{19}$$

$$\Phi(\omega_d) = 1 - \tfrac{1}{2}(2 - \omega_d)^2 \qquad 1 \leq \omega_d < 2 \tag{20}$$

$$\Phi(\omega_d) = 1 \qquad\qquad \omega_d \geq 2 \tag{21}$$

The function $J(f)$ is the JONSWAP spectrum [8] for deep water, and the shallow-water spectral form is seen to converge to the deep-water spectrum in the deep-water limit. Thus, under simple conditions, an estimate of the spectrum may be obtained under the conditions of quasi-steady state local wind sea and no swell. Vincent [28] suggested an approximation for the surf zone. It should be noted that the method only considers free wave energy and no harmonic content is predicted.

Parametric Transformations

Given a wave height, period, and wind speed in a given depth of water, the problem of estimating the wave conditions in a nearby, but shallower-water depth requires a wave model that can handle all the many complexities possible for the general case. If the wind is steady and equal at both sites and wave convergence/divergence is not strong, Hughes [10] and Resio [17] suggest that the ratio of wave heights is given by the following relation

$$\left(\frac{H_1}{H_2}\right) = \left(\frac{L_{m_1}}{L_{m_2}}\right)^{3/4} \tag{22}$$

and indicated it may also be a reasonable estimate for steeper swell. Hughes and Miller [11] in further examination of the field data indicate that an approximation including both a shoaling factor n and Equation 22 given as a simple average

$$\frac{H_1}{H_2} = \frac{1}{2} \left\{ \left(\frac{L_{m_1}}{L_{m_2}}\right)^{3/4} + \frac{n_1}{n_2} \right\} \tag{23}$$

is an even better approximation. Such approaches have a partial basis in wave mechanics [17] but should be considered useful only as an approximation. The underlying assumption is that the wave field is in local equilibrium with the same wind speed and direction, that no swell is present, and that no other mechanism significantly modifies the wave field.

Modeling Nearshore Transformations in a Spectral Model

In recent years substantial evidence has been accumulated to demonstrate that wave transformations in wave spectra can be dramatically different from transformations of monochromatic waves [3, 17, 24]. Due to this there has been a change-over from monochromatic-based concepts to spectral concepts in both numerical models and physical models. In particular, essentially all modern shallow-water spectral models have now adopted a depth-dependent form for their equilibrium range. In the TMA spectral shape [3] the energy densities in this region represent a transformation of the JONSWAP deep-water spectrum that is based on an f^{-5} equilibrium range. In the work of Resio [17] energy densities in the equilibrium range represent a transformation of an f^{-4}-based deep-water spectrum. Both approaches appear to provide a good representation of spectral transformations in shallow water.

The question of source terms to be treated in shallow-water spectral models is still somewhat of an open issue. As discussed earlier, various source terms have been introduced as possible energy dissipators in shallow water. To that list, in very shallow water irregular wave breaking and turbulent dissipation in bores must be added. It should be pointed out that, even though a complete understanding of all of the physics of shallow-water transformations may not exist, the performance of several nearshore spectral models has been shown to have good skill [22]. One reason for this ability to predict comparable wave conditions in tests probably relates to the dominance of the equilibrium range constraints in all of these models. Thus, even though additional percolation, bottom friction, and other such source terms are present in many of these models, their net effect relative to energy losses due to spectral-shape adjustments tends to be quite small.

Advantages and Disadvantages of Parametric and Spectral Models for Nearshore Wave Transformations

Figure 3 shows two conceptual diagrams of waves propagating toward a coast. In the upper diagram the classic case of monochromatic, unidirectional waves propagating toward a coast is described. In the context of this figure, nonlinear phenomena such as wave-wave interactions become essentially non-existent. As the wavelength becomes less than one-half the water depth, shoaling and refraction become dominant mechanisms affecting wave conditions (Zone II) with possibly some bottom-related dissipative mechanisms also contributing. Finally, wave breaking becomes important (Zone III) as the wave height approaches the water depth. At one

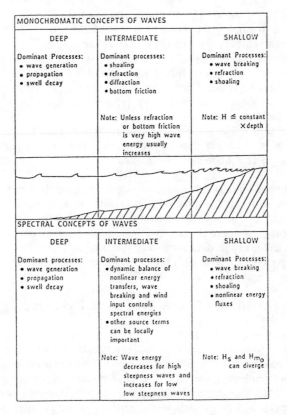

Figure 3. Conceptual diagrams of monochromatic and spectral waves propagating toward a coast.

time, this concept of wave transformations was regarded as almost universally valid. Now it appears that only for the case of very low-steepness, long-period swell do incoming wave spectra become sufficiently peaked and directionally narrow-banded to permit this approximation to be valid.

In most cases in open coastal areas, locally-generated waves constitute an important portion of the overall wave climate. For these waves, concepts of significant wave height transformations based on monochromatic theories do not provide an adequate representation of wave transformations [24]. Instead, complete spectral theories are found to provide a better representation of the overall pattern of change [17]. As seen in the lower diagram in Figure 3, wave spectra in moderate depths (say, L/20 < h < L/2) tend to equilibrate to a depth-dependent balance (Zone II) between wind inputs and certain nonlinear factors (possibly wave-wave interaction fluxes) as shown by Bouws et al. [2]. As the depth becomes still shallower, additional factors such as shoaling, refraction, diffraction, etc. become increasingly important relative to the wind-balance terms; consequently, in this zone (Zone IV), wave breaking becomes the controlling factor for local wave conditions.

In nature, waves at any given location might be classified as belonging to any of the zones in either of the diagrams shown in Figure 3. This presents a potential pitfall to attempts to employ simple parametric models in coastal applications. Parametric transformation techniques that cover the entire range of conditions expected, including complex mixed-sea-swell conditions, presently do not exist. Therefore, it is usually advisable to consider a full spectral model if applying the results to plans or designs can have significant economic consequences. In Zone III it is particularly important to recognize the potential effects of shoaling and refraction for the complete directional spectrum, not an "equivalent" monochromatic wave. Because these effects require a knowledge of the three-dimensional bathymetry near the coast and cannot be truly simulated by simple parallel-contour assumptions, it is unlikely that parametric models will ever be capable of producing accurate answers in this zone.

It appears that the primary advantage of parametric models is the simplicity with which one can obtain quick estimates of nearshore wave conditions. Under most storm conditions the results from spectrally-based parametric models should provide a reasonable first approximation to the expected wave conditions. However, with computer technology continuing to advance rapidly, the availability of well-calibrated complete spectral models for microcomputers should soon replace these simpler models.

Accuracy of Wave Prediction Techniques

A definitive statement of the accuracy of the wave prediction techniques summarized is impossible to provide. Scientific quality evaluations require "blind" experiments in which parties collecting the data and providing the wave estimates perform their studies independently. Few such experiments have been performed. Rarely have they included a sufficiently wide range of wind speeds, depths, fetches, and durations to provide a clear exposition of the quality of the prediction methods over the entire range of applicability. Many studies have been made for selected sites and limited ranges of conditions, but these are often made with data in hand. For most studies, the desire is to obtain a prediction method that reproduces known wave conditions in an area as well as possible before the predictions are extended to unknown cases. This invariably has led to site specific adjustments or tuning of the prediction model to the site. Some methods require less of this than others. This process recognizes that none of the wave (or wind) prediction techniques is perfect and represents an honest attempt to calibrate for these possible errors.

In our experience, if high quality wind field measurements are available, the wave prediction techniques approach error bands of $\pm 10\%$. As the wind generation scenario becomes more complex or less well known, the error can become substantial. Often the knowledge of the wind field is sufficiently poor that it is difficult to ascertain whether the error source is the wind or wave prediction model.

Efforts to obtain high-quality wind and wave measurements at the site of interest are justified if the cost of the project is large. Although current wave prediction methods represent a significant capability, the methods still embody uncertainties and unknowns. Checking with site specific information is a wise and prudent precaution wherever possible.

Summary

This chapter has introduced several techniques for making estimates of deep- and shallow-water wave conditions. Parametric methods are useful when the conditions can be simplified and should be considered most useful for initial estimates. As the fetch and wind field become more complicated, the parametric methods are generally not adequate and a numerical wave model should be used. The numerical models are substantially more complicated technically and on the basis of their input requirements. Historically, they have required very large computers and were not widely available. The development of powerful microcomputers should make it possible for these types of models for most of the parametric approaches and should increase the overall accuracy of wave computations.

Historically, many coastal wave studies have been made by making a deep-water estimate (or shallow-water estimate up to the point of complicated bathymetry). These data might be input to a physical model using monochromatic waves to obtain wave estimates in shallow water. More recently, sophisticated numerical models for monochromatic waves have been developed to replace the physical model for some types of studies. If the propagation distance is short, bathymetry is the controlling influence, there is no substantial wind input and the incident wave energy is narrowly focused, the monochromatic approach (numerical or physical) is adequate. These conditions are somewhat restrictive.

The descriptions of the parametric and numerical model approaches represent an overview of the current state-of-the-art in shallow-water wave estimation. In both cases the physical basis of the techniques, the empirical data on which the techniques are based, and the quality of the confirmation/validation must be considered weak. The lack of a definitive theoretical basis for wave prediction methods represents the extreme complexity of the problem. Both approaches depend upon theoretical assumptions and asymptotic limits to transform deep-water methods into shallow-water methods. The amount of independent confirmatory data is low. However, the methods have been used successfully in many areas, which must be indicative that approximate scaling of wave growth rates is adequate, although the details of the processes are not well understood.

Appendix A—Estimating Winds for Wave Prediction Curves

The wave height prediction curves presented are highly dependent upon the wind speed. For example, in deep water the fetch-limited wave height is directly proportional to wind speed. Errors in wind speed can quickly create large errors in wave estimates. Although the discussions of the wave growth curves were kept at a generalized level, it is not recommended that the parametric methods be applied for situations beyond which relatively simple assumptions about the uniformity of the wind field in space and steadiness in time are assured. If the wind field changes significantly in time or space, a numerical wave model is appropriate and an equally sophisticated wind interpolation or prediction model is warranted.

For the situation where the parametric models will be useful, a simple set of wind transformation formulas are suggested. These methods are somewhat approximate and it should be noted that a realistic solution for the boundary layer problem such as that of Brown and Levy [4] can be programmed for a microcomputer with very quick run times for a simple conversion. The methods presented here are a simplification, with modification, of those given in the *Shore Protection Manual* [26], which provides a more detailed description with examples.

Correction for Observation Elevation. The formulas presented in the chapter are all for winds at 10 m above the water surface. A simple power law relation can be used to move the observation up or down

$$u_{10} = u_z \left(\frac{10}{z}\right)^{1/7} \tag{24}$$

It is recommended that this be used for modest adjustments in elevation (5–20 m, not 100 m).

Wind Speed Observed Over Land. If the wind is observed over land near the water body of interest, but with the wind passing primarily over land, the *Shore Protection Manual* suggests a velocity dependent relationship given in Figure 4. This function was based on a summary of data from the Great Lakes and should be considered highly site dependent. It is preferable to derive a relation such as this based on local data correlations. Use of local ships' observations or mounting an anemometer over water at the site of interest is highly desirable, and use of the general curve should be considered as an approximate approach. If the wind is observed on land adjacent to the water and such that winds from some directions pass primarily overwater with no significant intervening dune, vegetation, or other obstruction, the wind from those directions may be assumed to be an overwater observation. The primary assumption that must be used in performing transformations of winds over land to winds over water is that both the water body and observation site are located in the same principal airstream and that the only difference is due to the

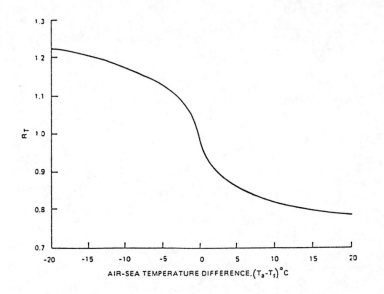

Figure 4. Amplification ratio, accounting for effects of air-sea temperature difference [31].

frictional differences of the sites. If there is a gradient in the wind field due to large-scale or small-scale meteorological structures, presence/absence of thunderstorms, or convergence/divergence due to topography, the method can be in significant error.

Adjustments to Friction Velocity. All the wave growth relationships but that of Bretschneider presented are based on the assumption that friction velocity is the proper wave growth scale factor, not wind velocity. For neutral stratification (difference between air and water temperature of 0°) this may be estimated by the coefficient of drag relation given by Garratt [7] as an example,

$$c_d = 10^{-3}(0.75 + 0.067 \ u_{10})$$ (25)

$$u_* = \sqrt{c_d} \ u_{10}$$ (26)

The wind speed at 10 m may be estimated by the methods discussed previously and then converted to a friction velocity.

Adjustment of the Friction Velocity for Air-Sea Temperature Differences. For winds observed over water and less than 20 m/sec, some adjustment for air-sea temperature is required. Figure 5 (U.S. Army Corps of Engineers, 1984) provides an estimate of the ratio of the stability factor versus temperature difference. This is

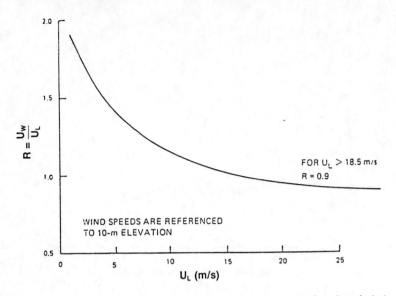

Figure 5. Ratio of windspeed over water to windspeed over land, as a function of windspeed over land [31].

an overestimate for the conditions near 20 m/sec. For winds estimated from over-land (site surrounded by trees, no overwater assumption is possible), the correction should be applied at all velocities. This correction is best handled by use of a boundary layer model and the corrections noted here are approximate.

Summary. The wind field transformations given here illustrate some of the adjustments necessary to estimate the wind stress over the water surface. The problem at a real site can be very complicated. The simple procedures given here may not be highly accurate at a site. It is always preferable to have measurements or a calibrated set of transformations for the specific site.

Appendix B—Wave Growth Curves

Figures 6 through 16 reproduce the *Shore Protection Manual* [26] deep- and shallow-water curves. The wave growth formulas given in Equations 3–6 may be approximated in these curves by using the adjusted wind factor u_A defined as

$$u_A = (0.53 + 0.047\ u_{10})^{1/2}\ u_{10} \tag{27}$$

for u_{10} in m/sec. (It should be noted that the *Shore Protection Manual* uses $u_A = 0.71 u_{10}^{1.23}$ for u_{10} in m/sec.) These curves may be used to obtain a quick estimate, but the use of the wave equations is the preferred approach.

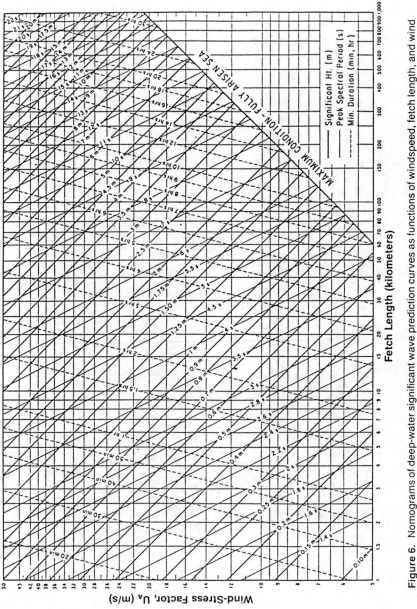

Figure 6. Nomograms of deep-water significant wave prediction curves as functions of windspeed, fetch length, and wind duration (metric units) [26].

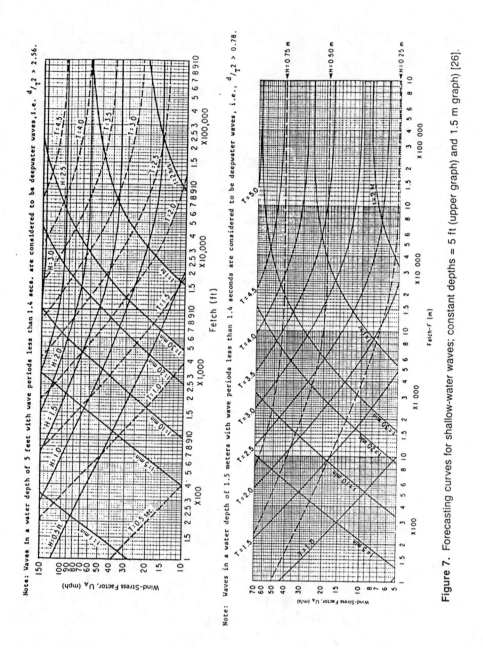

Figure 7. Forecasting curves for shallow-water waves; constant depths = 5 ft (upper graph) and 1.5 m graph) [26].

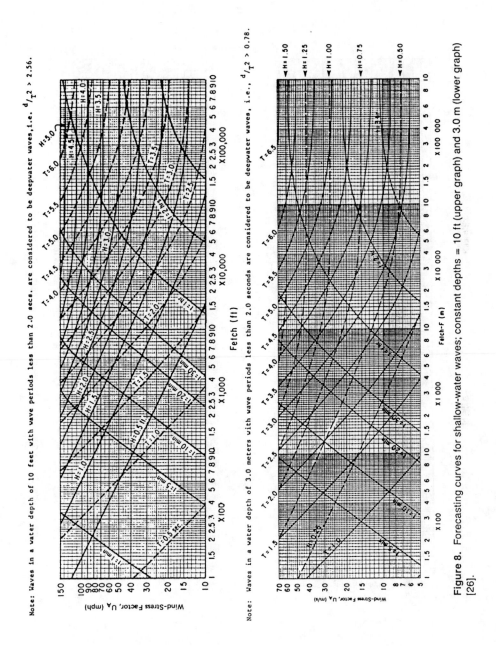

Note: Waves in a water depth of 10 feet with wave periods less than 2.0 secs. are considered to be deepwater waves, i.e., $d/_T{}^2 > 2.56$.

Note: Waves in a water depth of 3.0 meters with wave periods less than 2.0 seconds are considered to be deepwater waves, i.e., $d/_T{}^2 > 0.78$.

Figure 8. Forecasting curves for shallow-water waves; constant depths = 10 ft (upper graph) and 3.0 m (lower graph) [26].

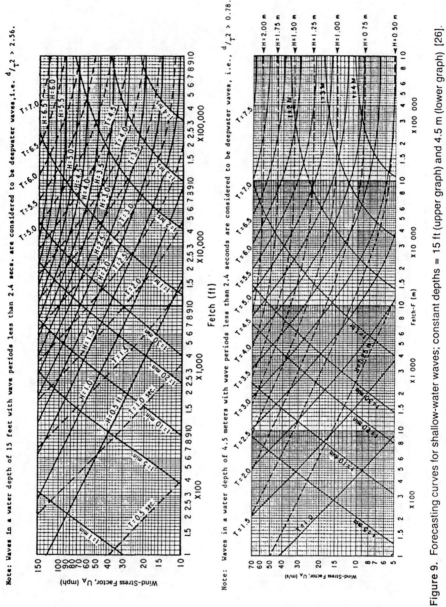

Figure 9. Forecasting curves for shallow-water waves; constant depths = 15 ft (upper graph) and 4.5 m (lower graph) [26].

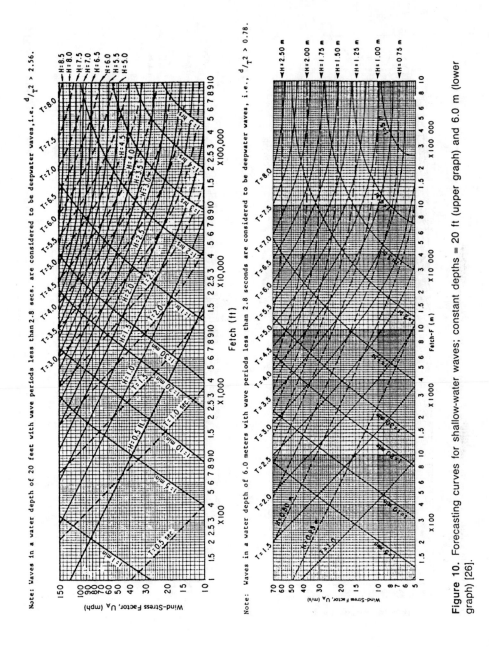

Figure 10. Forecasting curves for shallow-water waves; constant depths = 20 ft (upper graph) and 6.0 m (lower graph) [26].

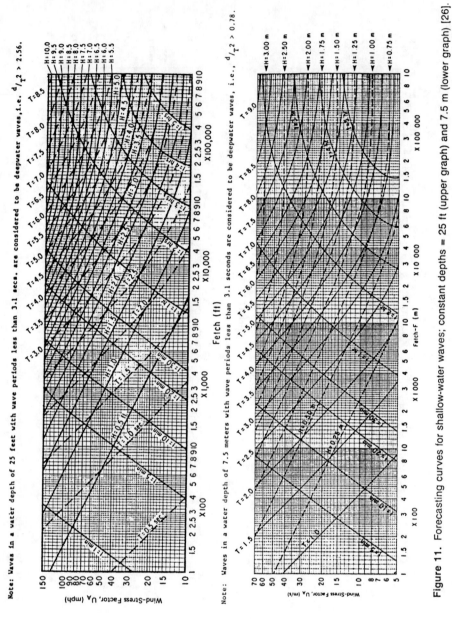

Figure 11. Forecasting curves for shallow-water waves; constant depths = 25 ft (upper graph) and 7.5 m (lower graph) [26].

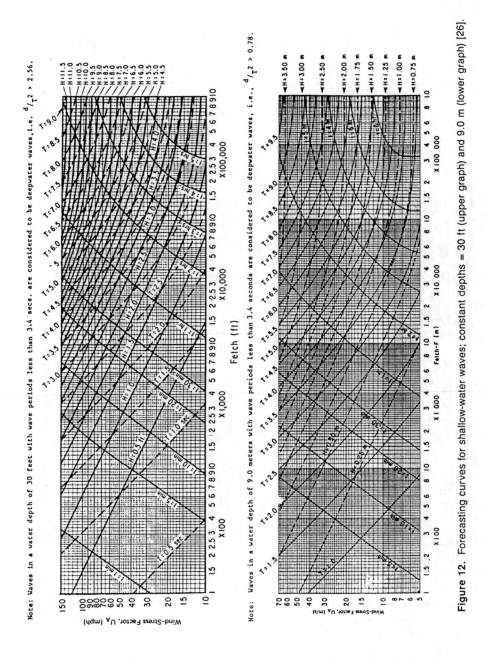

Figure 12. Forecasting curves for shallow-water waves; constant depths = 30 ft (upper graph) and 9.0 m (lower graph) [26].

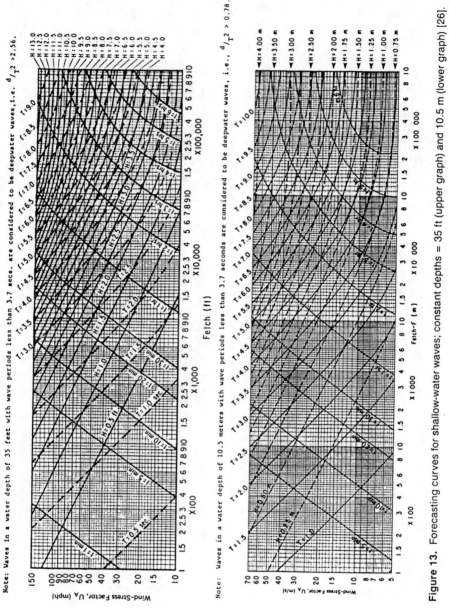

Figure 13. Forecasting curves for shallow-water waves; constant depths = 35 ft (upper graph) and 10.5 m (lower graph) [26].

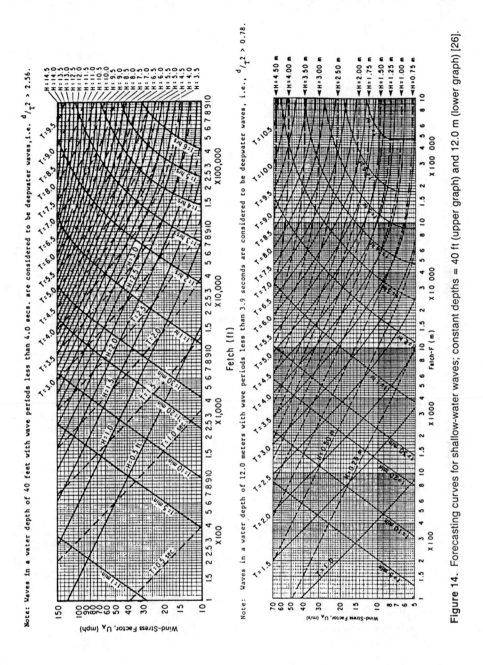

Figure 14. Forecasting curves for shallow-water waves; constant depths = 40 ft (upper graph) and 12.0 m (lower graph) [26].

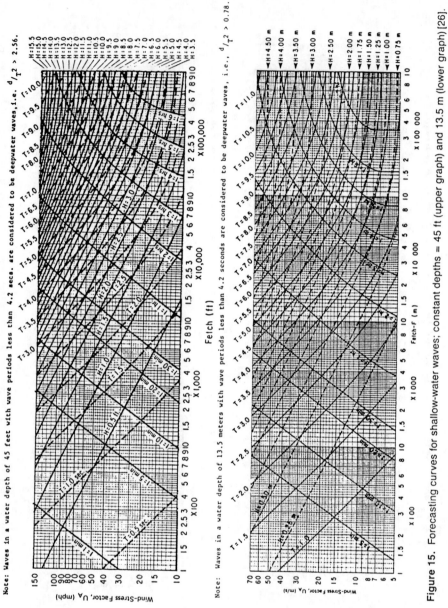

Figure 15. Forecasting curves for shallow-water waves; constant depths = 45 ft (upper graph) and 13.5 m (lower graph) [26].

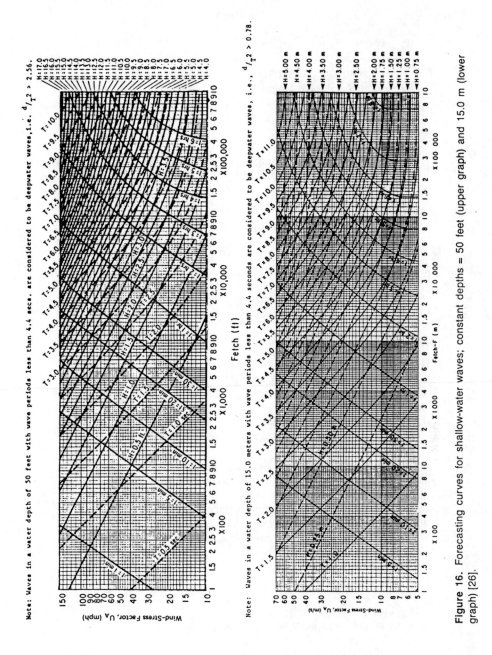

Figure 16. Forecasting curves for shallow-water waves; constant depths = 50 feet (upper graph) and 15.0 m (lower graph) [26].

Notation

c_f	bottom friction coefficient
f	frequency
g	gravitational acceleration
H_s	significant wave height
T_s	significant wave period
F	fetch
t	duration
$\underline{u}$	wind speed
$\underline{H}$	dimensionless wave height
$\underline{T}$	dimensionless wave period
$\underline{F}$	dimensionless fetch
$\underline{t}$	dimensionless duration
d	depth
$\underline{d}$	dimensionless depth
π	3.14592 . . .
u_*	friction velocity
T_m	peak period
c_d	coefficient of drag
S	angular spreading coefficient
θ	angle
θ_w	mean wave angle
$E(f,\theta)$	directional spectrum
$S_k(f,\theta)$	directional spectral source/sink term
Vx, Vy	group velocity components
kx, ky	wave number components
x, y	Cartesian coordinates
$S_p(f,\theta)$	percolation sink function
α_o	percolation decay constant
μ	spectral width
j	depth transformation, Jacobian
H_{m_o}	significant wave height based on surface variance
σ	standard deviation of surface
$E(f)$	one dimensional frequency spectrum
$J(f)$	JONSWAP spectrum
Φ	Kitaigorodskii depth transformation function
ω_d	relative depth
f_m	peak frequency
γ	spectral peakedness
ω	angular frequency, $2\pi f$
α	Phillips' coefficient
K_*	dimensionless peak wave number
H_1, H_2	wave height in different depths
L_{m_1}, L_{m_2}	wavelengths of the peak frequency in different depths of water
n_1, n_2	shoaling coefficient in different depths of water
L	wavelength

u_z	wind speed at elevation z
u_{10}	wind speed at elevation 10 m
u_A	wind factor
z	elevation of wind observation
T_a	air temperature
T_s	sea temperature
ΔT_{a-s}	air-sea temperature difference
$F(k)$	directional spectrum, wave-number space
W,Wx,Wy	bottom velocity and its components
ν_{xy}	anisotropic viscosity term
δ_{xy}	dirac delta function
$S_B(\overline{k})$	bottom friction sink term

References

1. Bagnold, R. A., 1946, "Motion of Waves in Shallow Water—Interaction Between Waves and Sand Bottoms," *Royal Society of London*, Vol. 187, pp. 1–18.

2. Bouws, E. et al., 1983, "A Similarity Based Spectral Form for Finite Depth Water: Wave Growth Relationships for the Entire Depth TMA Spectral Form," International Association for Hydraulic Research, Conference, Moscow.

3. Bouws, E., Gunther, H., and Vincent, C., 1985, "Similarity of the Wind Wave Spectrum in Finite Depth Water, Part I—Spectral Form," *Journal of Geophysical Research*, Vol. 85, No. C3, pp. 1524–1530.

4. Brown, R. A., and Levy, G., 1986, "Ocean Surface Pressure Fields, from Satellite-Sensed Winds," *Monthly Weather Review*, Vol. 114, pp. 2197–2206.

5. Bretschneider, C. L., 1958, "Revisions in Wave Forecasting; Deep and Shallow Water," Proceedings of the Sixth Conference on Coastal Engineering, ASCE, Council on Wave Research.

6. Bretschneider, C. L., and Reid, R. O., 1953, "Change in Wave Height Due to Bottom Friction, Percolation and Refraction," 34th Annual Meeting of American Geophysical Union.

7. Garratt, J. R., Jr., 1977, "Review of Drag Coefficients over Oceans and Continents," *Monthly Weather Review*, Vol. 105, pp. 915–929.

8. Hasselmann, K., et al., 1973, "Measurements of Wind-Wave Growth and Swell Decay During the Joint North Sea Wave Project (JONSWAP)," Deutsches Hydrographisches Institut, Hamburg, 95 pp.

9. Hasselmann, K., and Collins, J. I., 1968, "Spectral Dissipation of Finite-Depth Gravity Waves Due to Turbulent Bottom Friction," *Journal of Marine Research*, Vol. 26, No. 1, pp. 1–12.

10. Hughes, S. A., 1984, *The TMA Shallow-Water Spectrum Description and Application*, Technical Report CERC-84-7. Vicksburg, MS: U.S. Army Engineer Waterways Experiment Station, Coastal Engineering Research Center.

11. Hughes, S. A., and Miller, H. C., 1987, "Transformation of Significant Wave Heights," American Society of Civil Engineers, *Journal of Ports, Waterways, Coasts, and Oceans*.

12. Karlsson, T., 1969, "Refraction of Continuous Ocean Wave Spectra," American Society of Civil Engineers, *Journal of the Waterways and Harbors Division*, Vol. 95, No. WW4, pp. 437–448.

13. Longuet-Higgins, M. S., 1957, "On the Transformation of a Continuous Spectrum by Refraction," *Proceedings, Cambridge Philosophical Society*, Vol. 53, pp. 226–229.

14. Mitsuyasu, H. et al., 1975, "Observations of the Directional Spectrum of Ocean Waves Using a Cloverleaf Buoy," *Journal of Physical Oceanography*, Vol. 5, pp. 750–760.

15. Pierson, W. J., and Moskowitz, L., "A Proposed Spectral Form for Wind Seas Based on the Similarity Theory of S. A. Kitaigorodskii," *Journal of Geophysical Research*, Vol. 69, pp. 5181–5190.

16. Resio, D. T., and Vincent, C. L., 1977, "Estimation of the Winds Over the Great Lakes," *Journal of Waterways, Ports, Coastal and Ocean Engineering*, Vol. 103, pp. 265–283.

17. Resio, D. T., 1987, "Shallow-Water Waves, I: Theory," *Journal of Waterways, Ports, Coastal and Ocean Engineering*, Vol. 113, No. 3, pp. 266–283.

18. Shemdin, O. H., et al., "Mechanisms of Wave Transformation in Finite Depth Water," *Journal of Geophysical Research*, Vol. 85, pp. 5012–5018.

19. Shiau, J. C., and Wang, H., 1977, "Wave Energy Transformation over Irregular Bottom," *Journal of the Waterway, Port, Coastal and Ocean Division*, Vol. 103, No. WW1, pp. 57–68.

20. Sverdrup, H. U., and Munk, W. H., 1947, *Wind, Sea, and Swell: Theory of Relations for Forecasting*, Publication No. 601. Washington, D.C.: U.S. Navy Hydrographic Office, Mar.

21. The SWAMP Group, 1985, *Ocean Wave Modeling*, Plenum Press, 256 pp.

22. The SWIM Group, 1985, "A Shallow Water Intercomparison of Three Numerical Wave Prediction Models (SWIM)," *Quarterly Journal of the Royal Meteorological Society*, Vol. 111, pp. 1087–1112.

23. Thompson, E. F., 1977, *Wave Climate at Selected Locations Along U.S. Coasts*, Technical Report 77-1. Vicksburg, MS: U.S. Army Engineer Waterways Experiment Station, Coastal Engineering Research Center.

24. Thompson, E. F., and Vincent, C. L., 1985, "Significant Wave Height for Shallow Water Design," *Journal of the Waterway, Port, Coastal and Ocean Division*, American Society of Civil Engineers, Vol. 111, No. 5, pp. 828–842.

25. U.S. Army Corps of Engineers, 1977, *Shore Protection Manual*, Ft. Belvoir, VA: Coastal Engineering Research Center.

26. U.S. Army Corps of Engineers, 1984, *Shore Protection Manual*, Vicksburg, MS: Coastal Engineering Research Center.

27. U.S. Army Engineer District, Jacksonville, 1955, "Waves and Wind Tides in Shallow Lakes and Reservoirs, Summary Report, Project CW-167," South Atlantic-Gulf Region, Jacksonville, FL.

28. Vincent, C. L., 1984, "Shallow Water Waves: A Spectral Approach," Proceedings of the Nineteenth International Conference on Coastal Engineering, American Society of Civil Engineers, pp. 370–382.

29. Grant, W. D., and Madsen, O. S., 1979, "Combined Wave and Current Interaction with a Rough Bottom," *Journal of Geophysical Research*, Vol. 84, pp. 1797–1808.

30. Resio, D. T., 1982, "Wave Prediction in Shallow Water," paper presented at 14th Annual Offshore Technology Conference, Houston, TX, Paper 4242.

31. Jonsson, I. G., 1966, "Wave Boundary Layers and Friction Factors," *Proceedings of Coastal Engineering Conference 10th,* Vol. 1, pp. 127–148.

CHAPTER 6

TROPICAL CYCLONES

Charles L. Bretschneider

Professor Emeritus
Department of Ocean Engineering
University of Hawaii at Manoa
Honolulu, HI U.S.A.

CONTENTS

Introduction

Wave forecasting was born in 1943. There was a war-time feverish activity in 1943–1944 to develop wave forecasting methods. The sequence of development appears to be as follows:

1. Sverdrup and Munk prepared a draft report "Wind Waves and Swell: Principles in Forecasting." This was an excellent draft, but it contained no work on the dimensionless fetch graphs. Also, there was no mention of dimensionless fetch in H.O. Misc. 11, 275, under the same title.

2. O'Brien prepared a memo concerning "Wind Waves and Swell, A Basic Theory of Forecasting," dated December 31, 1943. In this memo, O'Brien presented the relationship, H/U^2, F_0/U^2.

3. In a letter to O'Brien on January 18, 1944, Water Munk referred to O'Brien memorandum.

4. O'Brien prepared a more detailed memorandum on F/U^2, H/U^2, t/U, L_D/L_F, H_D/H_F, and T_D/T_F; this memo was dated September 5, 1944. This is HEL-116-7, and a handwritten note showed one copy to Lt. Stump and two copies to Sverdrup.

5. The short report "Non-Dimensional Presentation of Generation and Decay of Waves" was issued by Scripps Institution of Oceanography as S.I.O. Report No. 30 on December 7, 1944.

6. The dimensionless method appeared as Equation 72, page 19 of "Wind, Sea, and Swell: Theory of Relation for Forecasting," by H. U. Sverdrup and W. H. Munk, U.S. Navy Hydrographic Office Pub. No. 601, March 1947. In this publication they referred to their Equation 52, just as O'Brien referred to it in his memo of December 31, 1943, in which he gave the dimensionless method of presentation.

Wave Forecasting Philosophies

Of the various methods of wave forecasting, there are primarily only two concepts: the significant wave [4–7] and the wave spectrum [18, 36].

1. The *significant wave concept* is a very simple method that forecasts the principal parameters, i.e., the significant wave height, H_s, and the significant wave period, T_s. The normal unit form of the theoretical spectrum can be used to estimate the wave spectrum; and the normal form of the directional spectrum, frequency dependent, can be used to estimate the complete directional spectrum.

2. The *wave spectrum* concept is in reverse to the significant wave method, i.e., the wave spectrum method predicts the directional spectrum, from which the one-dimensional spectrum and the significant waves are determined.

3. Both methods use the Rayleigh distribution to determine the most probable maximum wave height.

4. Both methods are based upon use of measured wave data for calibration. If the same or similar wave data are used for calibration, then both methods should give essentially the same results in regard to directional spectrum, the significant wave height and period, and the period (f_0^{-1}) of maximum energy density.

5. The significant wave method is easier to use and certainly less costly, whereas the wave spectrum method requires a highly sophisticated and expensive computer program.

6. Both methods are needed to complement each other, and also serve as calibration techniques for each other.

7. The methods concern only the extreme wave conditions associated with design criteria and not associated necessarily with the day by day or operational wind and wave criteria.

8. Presently, there are about seven methods used in wave forecasting and some methods are not necessarily better than others. Wave forecasting, or wave hindcasting, as the case may be, is an art as well as a science. The accuracy of any method depends upon practice, experience, verification, and correlation.

9. This chapter includes (a) forecasting in two directions and two-parameter wave spectrum; and (b) introduction of the three-parameter Significant Wave forecasting and the use of the three parameter wave spectrum. It is pointed out in this chapter that additional wave generated wave spectra are required to establish the third parameter, which is

$$\frac{g^3 S_{max}}{U^2} = \Psi_1 \left[\frac{gF}{U^2}, \frac{gt}{U} \right]$$

where S_{max} = maximum energy density of the wave spectrum

The Two-Parameter Wave Forecasting Relationships and the Two Parameter Wave Spectrum

In this method we are interested in a characteristic wave height and a characteristic wave period. Generally, the term significant height and period are used. However, because we are also interested in the two-parameter wave spectrum, we will use the modal wave period of the wave spectrum. The significant wave height H_s and the modal wave period f_0^{-1} (sometimes given as T_{max}) are functions of wind speed, U, fetch length, F, and wind duration, t.

It can be shown by use of the Buckingham [16] π theory and dimensional analysis that:

$$\frac{gH}{U^2} = \psi_1 \left[\frac{gF}{U^2}, \frac{gt}{U} \right] = \phi_1 \left[\frac{gF_e}{U^2} \right] \tag{1}$$

$$\frac{gf_0^{-1}}{2\pi U} = \psi_2 \left[\frac{gF}{U^2}, \frac{gt}{U} \right] = \phi_1 \left[\frac{gF_e}{U^2} \right] \tag{2}$$

In these expressions $F_e = F_{min}$ at $t = t_{min}$. In other words this defines minimum fetch corresponding to minimum wind duration, which can be obtained from

$$\frac{gt}{U} = 2 \int_0^{gF_e/U^2} \left[\frac{gf_0^{-1}}{2\pi U} \right]^{-1} \delta \left[\frac{gx}{U^2} \right] \tag{3}$$

In Equations 1–3

g = acceleration of gravity
U = wind speed
F = fetch length
t = wind duration
F_e = effective or minimum fetch
H_s = significant wave height
f_0^{-1} = modal wave period (corresponding to maximum energy density)

ψ_1, ψ_2, ϕ_1, and ϕ_2 are functional notations, and the corresponding functional forms are to be determined in part by theory and assumptions and in part by use of wind and wave data.

The two-parameter wave spectra corresponding to H and f_0^{-1} are given as follows:

$$S(f) = 5\left(\frac{1}{4}H_s\right)^2 f_0^{-1}\left(\frac{f_0}{f}\right)^5 e^{-\frac{5}{4}\left(\frac{f_0}{f}\right)^4} \tag{4}$$

Multiplying both sides of Equation 4 by g^3/U^5 one obtains a dimensionless form of the two-parameter spectrum as follows:

$$\frac{g^3 S(f)}{U^5} = \frac{5\pi}{8}\left(\frac{gH_s}{U^2}\right)^2\left(\frac{gf_0^{-1}}{2\pi U}\right)\left(\frac{f_0}{f}\right)^5 e^{-\frac{5}{4}\left(\frac{f_0}{f}\right)^4} \tag{5}$$

the term $g^3 S(f)/U^5 = \psi_3[gF/U^2, gt/U]$ could also have been determined by use of the Buckingham π theory and dimensional analysis.

Equations 1–5 are the basis of the two-parameter wave forecasting scheme. Assumed analytical expressions for the forecasting equation are:

$$\frac{gH_s}{U^2} = A_1 \tanh\left[B_1\left(\frac{gF}{U^2}\right)^{m_1}\right] \tag{6}$$

$$\frac{gf_0^{-1}}{2\pi U} = A_2 \tanh\left[B_2\left(\frac{gF}{U^2}\right)^{m_2}\right] \tag{7}$$

$$\frac{gt}{U} = 2\int_0^{gF/U^2}\left[\frac{gf_0^{-1}}{2\pi U}\right]^{-1}\delta\left(\frac{gx}{U^2}\right) \tag{8}$$

$$S(f) = 5\left(\frac{1}{4}H_s\right)^2 f_0^{-1}\left(\frac{f_0}{f}\right)^5 e^{-\frac{5}{4}\left(\frac{f}{f_0}\right)^4} \tag{9}$$

$$\frac{g^3 S(f)}{U^5} = \frac{5\pi}{8}\left(\frac{gH_s}{U^2}\right)^2\left(\frac{gf_0^{-1}}{2\pi U}\right)\left(\frac{f_0}{f}\right)^5 e^{-\frac{5}{4}\left(\frac{f}{f_0}\right)^4} \tag{10}$$

$$\frac{g^3 S(f_0)}{U^5} = \frac{5\pi}{8} e^{-5/4}\left(\frac{gH_s}{U^2}\right)^2\left(\frac{gf_0^{-1}}{2\pi U}\right) \tag{11}$$

$$\frac{2\pi H_s}{gf_0^{-2}} = \frac{1}{2\pi}\left[\frac{gH_s}{U^2}\right]\left[\frac{gf_0^{-1}}{2\pi U}\right]^{-2} \tag{12}$$

$$\frac{g^3 S(f_0)}{U^5} = A_1^2 A_2 \frac{5\pi}{8} e^{-5/4}\left\{\tanh\left[B_1\left(\frac{gF}{U^2}\right)^{m_1}\right]\right\}^2\left\{\tanh\left[B_2\left(\frac{gF}{U^2}\right)^{m_2}\right]\right\} \tag{13}$$

$$\frac{2\pi H_s}{gf_0^{-2}} = \frac{A_1}{2\pi A_2^2}\left\{\tanh\left[B_1\left(\frac{gF}{U^2}\right)^{m_1}\right]\right\}\left\{\tanh\left[B_2\left(\frac{gF}{U^2}\right)^{m_2}\right]\right\}^{-2} \tag{14}$$

The upper limits ($gF/U^2 \to \infty$) to the wave forecasting relationships are:

$$\frac{gH_s}{U^2} = A_1 \tag{15}$$

$$\frac{gf_0^{-1}}{2\pi U} = A_2 \tag{16}$$

$$\frac{gt}{U} \to \infty \tag{17}$$

$$S(f) = 5\left(\frac{1}{4} H_s\right)^2 f_0^{-1} \left(\frac{f_0}{f}\right)^5 e^{-\frac{5}{4}\left(\frac{f}{f_0}\right)^4} \quad \text{(same as Equation 9)} \tag{18}$$

$$\frac{g^3 S(f)}{U^5} = \frac{5\pi}{8} A_1^2 A_2 \left(\frac{f_0}{f}\right)^5 e^{-\frac{5}{4}\left(\frac{f}{f_0}\right)^4} \tag{19}$$

$$\frac{g^3 S(f_0)}{U^5} = \frac{5\pi}{8} e^{-5/4} A_1^2 A_2 \tag{20}$$

$$\frac{2\pi H_s}{gf_0^{-2}} = \frac{1}{2\pi} \frac{A_1}{A_2^2} \tag{21}$$

$$\frac{g^3 S(f_0)}{U^5} = \frac{5\pi}{8} e^{-5/4} A_1^2 A_2 \quad \text{(same as Equation 20)} \tag{22}$$

$$\frac{2\pi H_s}{gf_0^{-2}} = \frac{1}{2\pi} \frac{A_1}{A_2^2} \quad \text{(same as Equation 21)} \tag{23}$$

$$\frac{A_1}{A_2^2} = \frac{1.6}{2} \frac{\Gamma(\frac{3}{2})}{[\Gamma(\frac{5}{4})]^2} \alpha^{1/2} = 0.07423 \ (\alpha = 7.4 \times 10^{-3}) \tag{24}$$

The lower limits ($gF_e/U^2 \to 0$) to the wave forecasting relationships are:

$$\frac{gH_s}{U^2} = A_1 B_1 \left(\frac{gF}{U^2}\right)^{m_1} \tag{25}$$

$$\frac{gf_0^{-1}}{2\pi U} = A_2 B_2 \left(\frac{gF}{U^2}\right)^{m_2} \tag{26}$$

$$\frac{gt}{U} = \frac{2}{A_2 B_2} \frac{1}{1 - m_2} \left(\frac{gF}{U^2}\right)^{1 - m_2} \tag{27}$$

$$S(f) = 5\left(\frac{1}{4} H_s\right)^2 f_0^{-1} \left(\frac{f_0}{f}\right)^5 e^{-\frac{5}{4}\left(\frac{f}{f_0}\right)^4} \quad \text{(same as Equations 9 and 18)} \tag{28}$$

$$\frac{g^3 S(f)}{U^5} = \frac{5\pi}{8} (A_1 B_1)^2 (A_2 B_2) \left(\frac{gF}{U^2}\right)^{2m_1 + m_2} \left(\frac{f}{f_0}\right)^5 e^{-\frac{5}{4}\left(\frac{f}{f_0}\right)^4} \tag{29}$$

$$\frac{g^3 S(f_0)}{U^5} = \frac{5\pi}{8} e^{-5/4} (A_1 B_1)^2 (A_2 B_2) \left(\frac{gF}{U^2}\right)^{2m_1 + m_2} \tag{30}$$

$$\frac{2\pi H_s}{g f_0^{-2}} = \frac{1}{2\pi} \frac{A_1 B_1}{(A_2 B_2)^2} \left(\frac{gF}{U^2}\right)^{m_1 - 2m_2} \tag{31}$$

$$\frac{g^3 S(f_0)}{U^5} = \frac{5\pi}{8} e^{-5/4} (A_1 B_1)^2 (A_2 B_2) \left(\frac{gF}{U^2}\right)^{2m_1 + m_2} \quad \text{(same as Equation 30)} \tag{32}$$

$$\frac{2\pi H_s}{g f_0^{-2}} = \frac{1}{2\pi} \frac{A_1 B_1}{(A_2 B_2)^2} \left(\frac{gF}{U^2}\right)^{m_1 - 2m_2} \quad \text{(Same as Equation 31)} \tag{33}$$

The coefficients A_1, A_2, B_1, B_2, m_1, and m_2 are generally obtained by use of data. However, A_1 and A_2 can be obtained by theory. For the special case of unlimited fetch and wind duration we have Equation 24, which can be obtained from theoretical relationships given by Bretschneider [2]. The factor (1.6) is the ratio of the significant wave height to the average or mean wave height. The coefficient $\alpha = 7.4 \times 10^{-3}$ is a universal constant for fully developed seas based on wave data as reported by Burling [17]. Thus, $A_1/A_2^2 = 7.423 \times 10^{-2}$.

If we assume that the very upper limit of wave generation is reached when the group velocity of f_0^{-1} is equal to the wind speed, then

$$C_g = \frac{1}{2} \frac{g f_0^{-1}}{2\pi} = U \tag{34}$$

and we find that $A_2 = 2.0$ and it then follows that $A_1 = 0.297 \approx 0.30$, which is very close to 0.282 previously used by Bretschneider [2] where $A_2 = 1.95$ for the group velocity associated with the significant wave period T_s. According to Rossby and Montgomery [40] $A_1 = 0.30$, and Sverdrup and Munk [44] give $A_1 = 0.26$. The remaining coefficients B_1, B_2 and m_1 and m_2 are obtained by use of data. The lower limits of wave generation equations are given in Equations 25–33.

It is important to note that the overall best relations for the coefficients should be obtained from data such that one obtains the best correlation between equations and data, i.e., Equations 6, 7, 13, and 14.

Based on literature search, we find $A_1 B_1 = .283(.0125)$ from Bretschneider [4, 5], which results in $B_1 = 0.283(.0125) \div 0.3 = .012$ and $m_1 = 0.42 = \frac{5}{12}$.

From Hasselmann et al. [25] we find $m_2 = 0.33 \cong \frac{1}{3}$ and $A_2 B_2 = 1/7\pi$, hence $B_2 = (1/7\pi) \div 2 = 0.0227 = 0.023$. The hyperbolic tangent idea of Wilson [46], although it is not theoretical, seems an excellent means for the transition, and seems to fit the data quite adequately.

Thus, we have the two equations approximately correct.

$$\frac{g H_s}{U^2} = 0.3 \tanh\left[.012\left(\frac{gF_e}{U^2}\right)^{5/12}\right] \tag{35}$$

$$\frac{gf_0^{-1}}{2\pi U} = 2\tanh\left[0.023\left(\frac{gF_e}{U^2}\right)^{1/3}\right] \tag{36}$$

The coefficients $B_1 = 0.012$ and $B_2 = 0.023$ should be further established when more good data become available. One might expect that B_2 could be slightly larger (say, somewhere between 0.023 and 0.024) because of the introduction of the hyperbolic tangent in Equation 7.

The Three-Parameter Wave Forecasting Relationships and the Three-Parameter Wave Spectrum

In the previous section we introduced a new term in wave forecasting:

$$\frac{g^3 S(f_0)}{U^5} \quad \text{(See Equations 5–33.)}$$

In case of the three-parameter wave forecasting system, we can introduce

$$\frac{g^3 S_{max}}{U^5} = \psi_3\left[\frac{gF}{U^2}, \frac{gt}{U}\right] = \phi_3\left[\frac{gF_e}{U^2}\right] \tag{37}$$

in a similar manner that we did for gH_s/U^2 and $(gf_0^{-1}/2\pi U)$ (Equations 1 and 2). Equation 37 can be determined either by use of the Buckingham π theory and dimensional analysis or by substitution into the three-parameter wave spectrum. The three-parameter spectrum from Bretschneider [2] can be written as follows:

$$S(f) = f(\tfrac{1}{4}H_s)^2(af_0)^{-1}\frac{\left[(1 - R) + \sqrt{4/\pi}\,R\left(\frac{af_0}{f}\right)^2\right]^2}{[1 - (4/\pi - 1)R^2]}\left(\frac{af_0}{f}\right)^5 e^{-(af_0/f)^4} \tag{38}$$

where $(af_0)^{-1} = T_s$ the significant wave period and $R = r(\eta, \lambda)$ in the original expression given by Bretschneider [2]. Figure 1 shows the nondimensional spectra based on Equation 38.

We now prefer to call R a correlating parameter as distinguished from the correlation coefficient $r(\eta, \lambda)$, which was never determined by theory for two correlated Rayleigh distributions.

In the original development of Equation 38, $r(\eta, \lambda)$ was by-passed by an algebraic manner.

Thus, R must be determined by statistical curve fitting of Equation 38 using measured wave spectra, and $r(\eta, \lambda)$ must be determined by statistical analysis of wave traces for H_s and T^2. By this method one should be able to establish a relationship between R in the wave spectrum Equation 38 and $r(\eta, \lambda)$ of the joint distribution of wave heights and periods squared.

Returning to Equation 38 and multiplying through by g^3/U^5 to make the expression dimensionless, one obtains:

$$\frac{g^3 S(f)}{U^5} = \frac{\pi}{2}\left[\frac{gH_s}{U^2}\right]^2\left[\frac{gf_0^{-1}}{2\pi U}\right]\frac{\left[(1 - R) + \sqrt{4/\pi}\,R\left(\frac{af_0}{f}\right)^2\right]^2}{[1 - (4/\pi - 1)R^2]}\left(\frac{af_0}{f}\right)^5 e^{-(af_0/f)^4} \tag{39}$$

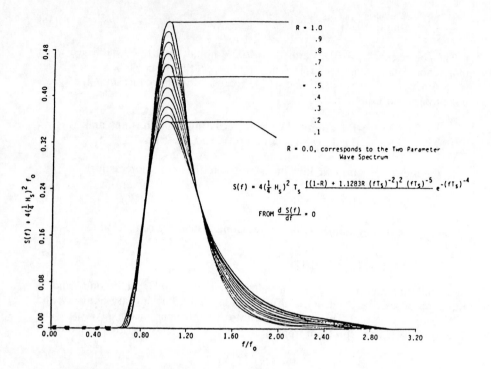

Figure 1. The three-parameter wave spectrum in non-dimensional form.

Differentiating Equation 38 or Equation 39 and setting dS(f)/df = 0, one finds a relationship for S_{max} and a^4 as functions of R. The equations are summarized in the following:

$$\frac{gH_s}{U^2} = A_1 \tanh\left[B_1\left(\frac{gF}{U^2}\right)^{m_1}\right] \tag{40}$$

$$\frac{gf_0^{-1}}{2\pi U} = A_2 \tanh\left[B_2\left(\frac{gF}{U^2}\right)^{m_2}\right] \tag{41}$$

$$\frac{gt}{U} = 2 \int_0^{gF/U^2} \left[\frac{gf_0^{-1}}{2\pi U}\right]^{-1} \delta\left(\frac{gx}{U^2}\right) \tag{42}$$

$$\frac{g^3 S_{max}}{U^5} = G \frac{g^3 S(f_0)}{U^5} = \psi_3\left(\frac{gF}{U^2}\right) \quad \text{(this is the third parameter)} \tag{43}$$

$$S(f) = 4(\tfrac{1}{4}H_s)^2(af_0)^{-1} \frac{\left[(1-R) + \sqrt{4/\pi}\, R\left(\frac{af_0}{f}\right)^2\right]^2}{[1 + (4/\pi - 1)R^2]} \left(\frac{af_0}{f}\right)^5 e^{-(af_0/f)^4} \tag{44}$$

from $dS(f)/df = 0$, $S(f) = S_{max}$

$$R = \frac{-B \pm \sqrt{B^2 - AC}}{A} \tag{45}$$

where $A = \left[(4a^4 - 5) - 2\sqrt{4/\pi}\,a^2(4a^4 - 7) + \frac{4}{\pi}\,a^4(4a^4 - 9)\right]$
$B = \left[-(4a^4 - 5) + \sqrt{4/\pi}\,a^2(4a^4 - 7)\right]$
$C = (4a^4 - 5)$

$$G = \frac{S_{max}}{S(f_0)} = \frac{4}{5}\,a^4 e^{[(5/4) - a^4]}\frac{[(1 - R) + \sqrt{4/\pi}\,Ra^2]^2}{\left[1 + \left(\frac{4}{\pi} - 1\right)R\right]} \quad \text{(See Figure 2.)} \tag{46}$$

where we define an amplification factor G for the peak energy density, which is the ratio of S_{max} of the three-parameter spectrum to $S(f_0)$ of the two-parameter spectrum as follows:

$$\frac{g^3 S_{max}}{U^5} = G\left[\frac{g^3 S(f_0)}{U^5}\right] = \psi_3\left[\frac{gF_e}{U^2}\right] \tag{47}$$

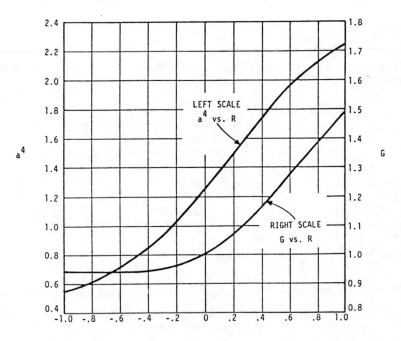

Figure 2. a^4 and G vs. R in the three-parameter wave spectrum.

The family of three-parameter spectra in non-dimensional form is shown in Figures 1 and 2.

What we do not have because of lack of data is the function $\psi_3[gF_e/U^2]$.

However, we do know that when R = 0, G = 1.0, and the terminal limit of Equation 47 becomes

$$\frac{g^3 S_{max}}{U^5} = \frac{g^3 S(f_0)}{U^5} = \frac{5\pi}{8} e^{-5/4} A_1^2 A_2 \tag{48}$$

and for $A_1 = 0.3$ and $A_2 = 2.0$ one obtains

$$\frac{g^3 S_{max}}{U^5} = \frac{g^3 S(f_0)}{U^5} = 0.10 \tag{49}$$

Figure 3 shows a comparison between a measured wave spectrum from Long [32] and theoretical spectra based on Equation 38.

It should be pointed out that G given by Equation 47 is different from the JONSWAP amplification factor used for the Pierson-Moskowitz [36] spectrum first because their U = U (19.5-meter elevation) and second A_1 and A_2 are different.

There are a lot of wave spectra in the literature for which no wind data are given, but one could hindcast the wind data. Where only S_{max}, H_s and f_0 are given, one can determine the amplification factor from

$$G = \frac{S_{max}}{S(f_0)} = \frac{16 e^{5/4} f_0 \cdot S_{max}}{5 H_s^2} \tag{50}$$

A summary of the presently available coefficients from previous studies is as follows:

Coefficient	Value
A_1	(0.26, 0.282, and 0.30, theory and data)
A_2	(2.0 theory)
$A_1 B_1$	(0.0125)(0.282) = 0.012 (data)
$A_2 B_2$	$1/7\pi \cong 0.023$ (data)
m_1	$\frac{1}{2}, \frac{5}{12}$ (data)
m_2	$0.33 \cong \frac{1}{3}$ (data)
A_3	(to be determined)
m_3	(to be determined)

$$A_1/A_2^2 = \frac{1.6}{2} \frac{\Gamma(3/2)}{[\Gamma(5/4)]^2} \alpha^{1/2} \qquad \text{(theory)} \ (\alpha = 7.4 \times 10^{-3}, \text{ data})$$

$$A_1/A_2^2 = 0.07423$$

$$A_3 = \left[\frac{5\pi}{8} e^{-5/4} A_1^2 A_2 \right]^{1-m_3} \qquad \text{(to be determined)} \tag{51}$$

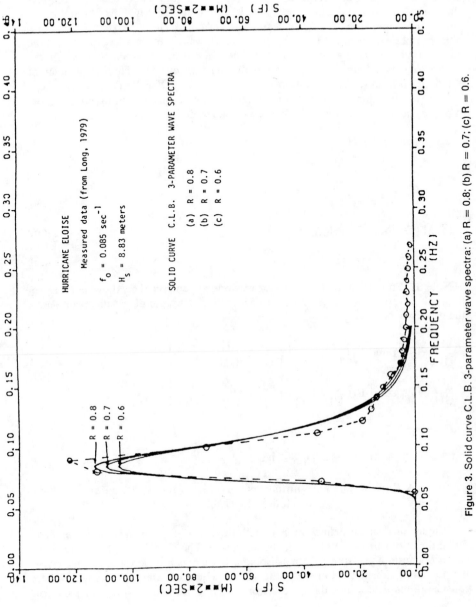

Figure 3. Solid curve C.L.B. 3-parameter wave spectra: (a) R = 0.8; (b) R = 0.7; (c) R = 0.6.

These coefficients should be reevaluated in such a manner that all the equations give overall best correlations between the corresponding values obtained from the prediction equations and the measurements. It should also be noted that A_3 and m_3 or some other expression for S_{max} must still be determined. Once a forecasting relationship has been determined for g^3S_{max}/U^5, we will have information to predict the three-parameter wave spectrum. In fact, the same relations could be used for the JONSWAP type wave spectrum, remembering that our G = factor is a different relationship from the amplification factor used in the JONSWAP spectrum.

The two-direction significant wave forecasting relationships, using an x-y coordinate system and Equations 6–46 are summarized as follows:

$$H^2 = H_x^2 + H_y^2 \tag{52}$$

$$T^4 = T_x^4 + T_y^4 \tag{53}$$

$$t^4 = t_x^4 + T_y^4 \tag{54}$$

$$(S_{max})^{4/5} = (S_{x_{max}})^{4/5} + (S_{y_{max}})^{4/5} \tag{55}$$

$$f_0^{-4} = f_{0x}^{-4} + f_{0y}^{-4} \tag{56}$$

Note: It is not obvious that these expressions are correct. The above axioms, so to speak, can be proven by elementary geometry, or by use of specific example as the case may be, example

$$\left.\begin{aligned} \frac{gH_x}{UU_x} &= A_1 \tanh\left[B_1\left(\frac{gx}{UU_x}\right)^{m_1}\right] \\ \frac{gH_y}{UU_y} &= A_1 \tanh\left[B_1\left(\frac{gY}{UU_y}\right)^{m_1}\right] \end{aligned}\right\} \left\{\begin{aligned} \frac{gH_s}{U^2} &= \frac{gH_x}{UU_x} = \frac{gH_y}{UU_y} \\ \frac{gF}{U^2} &= \frac{gX}{UU_x} = \frac{gY}{UU_y} \end{aligned}\right\} \tag{57}$$

$$F^2 = F_x^2 + F_y^2$$

$$U^4 = U^2U_x^2 + U^2U_y^2 = U^4[\cos^2\theta + \sin^2\sigma] \tag{58}$$

A Rankin Vortex Number as a Guide to the Selection of a Model Hurricane*

A model hurricane is defined by a model pressure profile, which is the same in all radial directions from the center of the hurricane. The model describes concentric circles of constant pressure known as isobars. The slope of the pressure profile gives the pressure gradient used in the gradient wind equation, and together with other considerations determines the time history moving hurricane wind and pressure

---

* Taken from the paper presented by C. L. Bretschneider and J-M. Lo at the 19th Coastal Engineering Conference Proceedings, ASCE, Houston, TX.

fields. The appropriate model hurricane can then be coupled with various other models for the determination of design criteria such as wind, waves, currents, wave forces, storm surge, wave run-up, coastal flooding, and inundation limits. Because of the many requirements for accurate output data, there have always been concerns of the proper use and selection of the appropriate hurricane model for a particular task and location.

Hurricane wind and wave fields are easy to forecast or hindcast by use of the appropriate model applicable to the particular case. The wind field models have had many years of experience. The two-direction significant wave model (applied to the wind model) is a geometrical model and should not be confused with directional spectral models.

The hurricane wind model is first considered as a stationary model, which is a reasonable assumption, and as such can be made into two directional wind stress models, which are coupled with the two directional significant wave forecasting mode. Then one obtains by simple geometric means both the stationary hurricane wind model and the corresponding stationary hurricane wave model. This procedure assumes that steady state is achieved for the stationary wind and wave conditions, which is true for the stationary hurricane wind and wave models.

The hurricane wind and wave models are then coupled with the forward speed of translation, with an increase in wind speed and wave heights to the right of the hurricane path and a decrease in wind speed and wave heights to the left of the hurricane path. The procedure assumes again that steady state is reached and is independent of time. This procedure seems to work very well for hurricanes with forward speeds less than about 15 knots or so, but probably fails for forward speeds greater than about 20 to 25 knots depending on the size of the hurricane, in which case the hurricane begins to move faster than the group velocity of the waves that the wind generates, resulting in reduced wave heights.

Past experience has shown for the more ideal hurricanes that can be represented by the appropriate mode quite accurate wave spectra can be calculated. Thus, wind and wave forecasting or hindcasting for hurricanes (or typhoons) are more easily and more accurately determined than for many extra tropical cyclones, which also depend on wind duration.

The primary purpose of this section is to begin to build a guide for determining the appropriate model to be used for a particular situation and criteria. When the data pressure profile is available, there is no need for a model, because the slope of the data pressure profile gives the pressure gradient, which can be used directly in the gradient wind equation. The data pressure profile can also be fitted to the most appropriate model by various techniques of correlation.

After a sufficient number of data pressure profiles have been determined and correlated with various models to determine the most appropriate model, one should be able to extend the guide for better selection of model. One can then make better use of the standard project, maximum probable and actual tabulated hurricane data (R_G, P_0, P_w, ϕ, V_F, etc.) given in the NOAA Report by Schwerdt, Ho and Watkins [42].

The present guide for selection of a particular model has to do with the hurricane parameters R_G, P_0, P_N, and ϕ as related to the cyclostrophic and gradient wind equations. For the convenience, in this Chapter R is the radius of maximum cyclostrophic wind as distinguished from R_G, the radius of maximum wind in the report by Schwerdt, et al. [42]. The parameters determined by data pressure profile analysis are:

where
$$R = \text{radius of maximum cyclostrophic wind}$$
$$R_R = \text{pressure from the data pressure profile at R}$$
$$\max[r\, dP/dr] = \text{related to the maximum cyclostrophic wind and determine the location of R}$$

Data Pressure Profile

The data pressure profile is determined from the cyclone weather chart and is an average of eight traverses from the center of the cyclone crossing identical isobars to the last closed or nearly closed isobar. The average distance r is plotted versus the corresponding isobar pressure. This method of analysis eliminates or at least minimizes the distortions in the isobar pattern due to personal judgment in construction of the isobars, possible effects due to forward motion to the cyclone, and blocking effects due to adjacent pressure systems or land effects. The net result is a cyclone having concentric circular isobars, the definition of a model cyclone.

The step-by-step procedure is simple and straightforward in this method of analysis. A smooth S-curve is constructed through the data points, defining the data pressure profile. It is not necessary to have a complete data pressure profile, including P_0 and P_N, which can be calculated by theory depending on choice of the model. The pressure gradient is a smooth profile through points calculated from the slope of the data pressure profile. The cyclostrophic profile is calculated from the smooth pressure gradient profile by multiplying corresponding points of the slope of the pressure profile by the radial distance r. Some fine tuning may be required to increase the accuracy in the range of radius of maximum wind, which can easily be estimated at a distance equal to about twice that of the maximum or peak of the pressure gradient profile, which occurs at the inflection point of the data pressure profile. Three important parameters are then determined as follows:

$$R = \text{radius of maximum cyclostrophic wind at } \max[r\, dp/dr]$$
$$\max[r\, dp/dr] \text{ at R}$$
$$P_R = \text{the pressure from that data pressure profile at R}$$

It then follows by theory that P_0 and P_N can be calculated from the following relations:

$$\Delta P_0 = P_N - P_0 = 1/C_1 \max[r\, dp/dr] \tag{59}$$

$$P_0 = P_R - C_2 \Delta P_0 \tag{60}$$

$$P_N = P_0 + \Delta P_0 \tag{61}$$

where C_1 and C_2 are theoretical constants depending on the choice of the model.

The theoretical maximum cyclostrophic wind speed can be determined from:

$$V_c = \sqrt{1/\rho_a \max[r\, dP/dr]} = K\sqrt{\max r\, dp/dr} \qquad (62)$$

where ρ_a = air density of P_R at $r = R$, radius of maximum wind. Equation 62 is independent of choice of model, and $K = 18.7$ to 19.3 for all pressure profiles.

All theoretical pressure profiles will be in agreement with the data pressure profile at P_R, R, and $\max[r\, dp/dr]$ by the very nature of the analysis of the cyclone weather charts. Furthermore all model pressure profiles will be in very close agreement with the data pressure profile over the range of $0.5R < R < 1.5R$ approximately, but there will be deviations outside this range. A high correlation will always be achieved between data pressure profile and model pressure profile because of the above range in agreement, but the choice of the model will be that model that has the overall best correlation with the data pressure profile, excluding P_0 and P_N, except when available by measurements. A spot check of data points such as P_0, P_N, and V_{max} should also be considered, if measured values are available.

Six Indian Seas cyclones have been analyzed by the above method. Regression analysis between the original data of the data pressure profile and the corresponding theoretical pressure points for Bret Model-X was made, and the following regression coefficients were obtained: $\rho = 0.9890, 0.9995, 0.9993, 0.9824,$ and 0.9996. Figure 4 presents the example theoretical hurricane relations for BRET MODEL-X, and Figures 5–10 are the Indian Seas cyclones data pressure profile analysis. Because of the very nature of the method of determining R, P_R, and $\max[r\, dp/dr]$, high regression correlations are expected, and therefore one might reject those cyclones for which $\rho < 0.98$ or 0.99.

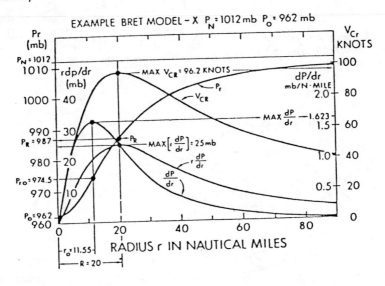

Figure 4. Example theoretical hurricane relations for Bret Model X.

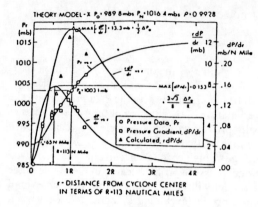

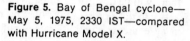

Figure 5. Bay of Bengal cyclone—May 5, 1975, 2330 IST—compared with Hurricane Model X.

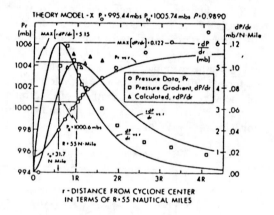

Figure 6. Bay of Bengal cyclone—Dec. 8, 1965, 0830 IST—compared with Hurricane Model X.

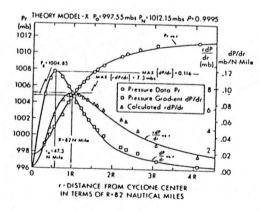

Figure 7. Bay of Bengal cyclone—Oct. 28, 1977, 1800 GMT—compared with Hurricane Model X.

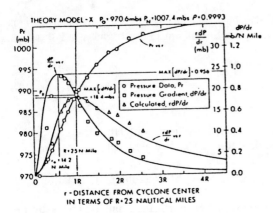

Figure 8. Arabian Sea Porbandar cyclone—Oct. 21, 1975, 0200-1500 GMT—compared with Hurricane Model X.

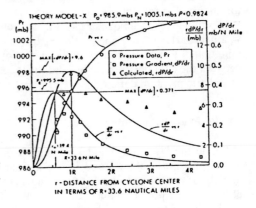

Figure 9. Bay of Bengal cyclone—May 6, 1975, 0530 IST—compared with Hurricane Model X.

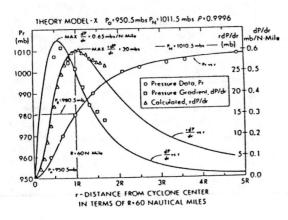

Figure 10. Bay of Bengal Andhra cyclone—Nov. 17, 1977, 0830 IST—compared with Hurricane Model X.

The choice of the model can also be based in part on previous investigations reported in the literature. By theory the maximum cyclostrophic wind speed for model hurricanes is given by:

$$V_c = K_1 \sqrt{P_N - P_0} \tag{63}$$

where $K_1 = (C_1/\rho_a)^{1/2}$
ρ_a = air density and generally increases slightly with latitude
C_1 = theoretical constant, depending on choice of model

Obviously the choice of model depends on V_c of Equation 63 is equal to V_c of Equation 62.

It would seem prudent to analyze cyclones, hurricanes, and typhoons by the simple straightforward method introduced in this section, and determine a large number of values for R, P_R, and max[r dp/dr]. P_0 and P_N can then be determined for choice of model for correlation purposes.

In summary, the uniqueness of this section is the method of analyzing cyclone weather charts to determine the three parameters R, P_R, and max[r dp/dr], the determination of P_0 and P_N by theory depending on choice of model, and the correlation between the data pressure profile and the theoretical pressure profile over the range of isobaric pressure data.

Model Pressure Profiles

Beside the Hydromet model pressure profile, there are several other available model pressure profiles found in the literature. A modification of the Hydromet model was made by Holland [26] giving a family of pressure profiles, of which one of the pressure profiles reduces to the Rankin Vortex model. This family of pressure profiles has been in use with some success by Rosendal and Shaw [38].

Several other pressure profile models from various sources are given in the NOAA Report by Schwerdt, Ho and Watkins [42]. Fujita [21] proposed a different model, which Uji (1975) fitted quite well to Typhoon Vera, September 22–27, 1959, a very large western north Pacific typhoon. Bretschneider [12] proposed a new general form of hurricane models, of which Fujita [21] model is a special case. Jelesnianski [29] used a non-dimensional surface profile corresponding to the Bret Model-X non-dimensional cyclostrophic wind profile.

In summary there are two general types of hurricane models: (1) the modified Rankin Vortex model by Holland [26], of which the Hydromet model is a special case; and, (2) the Bret-General model of which the Bret Model-X, the Fujita model and Jelesnianski model are all special cases. The mathematical form of the pressure profiles for the two families of models are:

$$\frac{P_r - P_0}{P_\infty - P_0} = Ae^{-B[R/r]} \tag{64}$$

and

$$\frac{P_r - P_0}{P_\infty - P_0} = 1 - \left[1 + a\left(\frac{r}{R}\right)^2\right]^{-b} \tag{65}$$

where P_0 = central pressure of hurricanes
P_r = pressure at radial distance r
P_∞ = pressure at infinite distance r
R = radius of maximum cyclostrophic wind

The constants $A = B^{-1}$ and $a = b^{-1}$ must always hold true to satisfy the mathematics of the cyclostrophic wind equation.

Equation 64, proposed by Holland [26], when $A = B = 1$, becomes the original Rankin Vortex model after Schloemer [41]. Equation 65 was proposed by Bretschneider [12] after pressure profile data analysis. When $a = b - 1$, Equation 57 is called Bret Model-X. When $a = b^{-1} = 2$, Equation 65 becomes the same as Fujita model [21].

Equations 64 and 65 represent families of models that overlap. The deviations between models have to do with (1) the size of the hurricane as governed by the radius of maximum cyclostrophic wind, (2) the wind intensity of the hurricane as governed by the central pressure reduction, and (3) an assumption that there is a latitude affect as governed by the Coriolis parameter. These assumptions lead to the introduction of a non-dimensional Coriolis or Rankin Vortex number for hurricane classification. Table 1 presents the theoretical constants K_1 for four hurricane models—Hydromet Model, NOAA Model-I, Fujita Model-J, and Bret Model-X. Table 2 presents the parameters for the six Indian Seas cyclones data pressure profile analysis.

Table 1
Theoretical Constants for Four Hurricane Models

$K_1 = \left(\dfrac{C_1}{\rho_a}\right)^{1/2}$	Hydromet Model-HM $\left(\dfrac{1}{e\rho_a}\right)^{1/2}$	NOAA Model-I $\left(\dfrac{1}{\pi\rho_a}\right)^{1/2}$	Fujita Model-J $\left(\dfrac{2}{3\sqrt{3}\rho_a}\right)^{1/2}$	Bret Model-X $\left(\dfrac{1}{2\rho_a}\right)^{1/2}$
For V = knots and P = in. Hg				
	66.0	61.39	67.51	76.74
K_1	68.0	63.25	69.56	79.28
For V = knots and P = millibars				
	11.34	10.55	11.60	13.22
K_1	11.68	10.87	11.95	13.62

Table 2
Summary Parameters from Six Indian Seas Cyclones

Cyclone Area and Latitude ϕ Date and Time of Weather Chart	I Bay of Bengal 14.8° May 5, 1975 2330 IST	II Bay of Bengal 10° Dec. 8, 1965 0830 IST	III Bay of Bengal 14° Oct. 28, 1977 1800 GMT	IV Arabian Sea* −23° Oct. 22, 1975 0200–1500 GMT	V Bay of Bengal 14.3° May 6, 1975 0530 IST	VI Bay of Bengal 10° Nov. 17, 1977 0830 IST
From Data Pressure Profile and Derivative						
R, radius of maximum cyclone wind, nautical miles	113	55	82	25	33.6	60
P_R, pressure at R (mbs)	1,003.1	1,000.6	1,000.85	989.0	995.5	980.5
Max r dP/dr at R (mbs)	13.3	5.15	7.3	18.4	9.6	30
V_{cR} (max) knots	70.24	43.71	52.04	82.62	59.67	105.5
From Theory, Each Model						
Hydromet Model—HM $K_1 = 11.68; c_1 = 1/e, c_2 = 1/e$						
ΔP_0 (mbs)	36.15	14.00	19.84	50.02	26.10	81.60
P_0 (mbs)	989.8	995.44	997.55	970.60	985.90	950.50
P_N (mbs)	1,026.0	1,009.44	1,017.40	1,020.60	1,012.00	1,032.10
NOAA Model—I $K_1 = 10.87; c_1 = 1/\pi, c_2 = 1/2$						
$\Delta P_0 =$ (mbs)	41.78	16.17	22.92	57.77	30.13	94.20
$P_0 =$ (mbs)	982.2	992.52	993.40	960.10	980.40	933.40
$P_N =$ (mbs)	1,024.0	1,008.69	1,016.30	1,017.90	1,010.60	1,027.60

Fujita Model—J
$K_1 = 11.95$; $c_1 = 2/3\sqrt{3}$
$c_2 = 1 - \sqrt{3}/3$

Bret Model—X
$K_1 = 13.62$; $c_1 = 1/2$, $c_2 = 1/2$

ρ = correlation coefficient

Fujita Model—J						
ΔP_0 (mbs)	34.55	13.38	18.90	47.80	24.94	77.94
P_0 (mbs)	988.50	994.94	996.90	968.80	985.00	947.56
P_N (mbs)	1,023.60	1,008.32	1,015.80	1,016.60	1,009.90	1,025.50
Bret Model—X						
ΔP_0 (mbs)	26.60	10.30	14.60	36.80	19.20	60
P_0 (mbs)	989.80	995.44	997.55	970.60	985.90	950.50
P_N (mbs)	1,016.40	1,005.74	1,012.15	1,007.4	1,005.1	1,010.50
ρ = correlation coefficient	.9928	.9890	.9995	.9993	.9824	.9990
fR_c (knots)	15.1	4.99	10.4	5.10	4.33	5.44
fR_c/V_{R_c}	0.215	0.114	0.199	0.062	0.072	0.052

*Note: Time History Pressure Profile Used

The Gradient Wind Equation

The radius of maximum gradient wind and the maximum gradient wind, respectively, are not identical to the corresponding radius of maximum cyclostrophic wind and the gradient wind at the radius of maximum cyclostrophic wind. This was shown to be the case by Bretschneider [3] using the Hydromet-Rankin Vortex model after Schloemer [41] and Myers [33]. This will be true for any wind field developed from the pressure gradient by the very nature of the gradient wind equation.

The gradient wind equation for a stationary cyclone can be given as follows:

$$V_g^2 + frV_g = \frac{r}{\rho_a}\frac{dp}{dr} \qquad (66)$$

where V_g = gradient wind speed at radial distance r from the center of the cyclone
  f = Coriolis parameter
  ρ_a = air density
  dp/dr = pressure gradient

In the absence of the Coriolis term fr, Equation 66 becomes the cyclostrophic wind equation as follows:

$$V_r^2 = \frac{r}{\rho_a}\frac{dp}{dr} \qquad (67)$$

where V_r is the cyclostrophic wind speed, resulting from the balance between the centripetal force directed toward the center of the cyclone and the force due to the pressure gradient.

Thus Equation 66 can be written as follows:

$$V_g^2 + frV_g = V_r^2 \qquad (68)$$

The maximum cyclostrophic wind velocity can be obtained from

$$V_c^2 = \frac{1}{\rho_a}\max\left[\frac{r}{dr}\frac{dp}{}\right] \qquad (69)$$

where V_c occurs at R radius of maximum cyclostrophic wind. R_G is the radius of maximum gradient wind, and is somewhat smaller than R, depending on the value of fR/V_c or fR_G/V_c.

The most accurate evaluation of Equation 69 would be by using an accurately determined pressure profile from data, but this is seldom possible because of lack of sufficient data. The procedure is to best fit a pressure profile to the data pressure. Then, an analytical pressure profile or model pressure profile can be selected that best fits all the data including the central pressure, if available. Ideally, it would be excellent to have available the pressure at the radius of maximum cyclostrophic wind.

Once the maximum cyclostrophic wind V_c is obtained, one can obtain the gradient wind at R as follows:

$$V_{gR}^2 + fRV_{gR} = V_c^2 \tag{70}$$

or

$$V_{gR} = -(\tfrac{1}{2}fR) + \sqrt{(\tfrac{1}{2}fR)^2 + V_c^2} \tag{71}$$

As can be seen from the works of Bretschneider [3] Equation 70 or Equation 71 does not give the maximum gradient wind V_G and, consequently, the maximum 10-meter level wind speed V_s at the radius of maximum wind. The radius of maximum gradient wind, R_G for V_G is not the same as the radius of maximum cyclostrophic wind $R = R_c$ for V_c.

Actually $R_G = R_c$ and $V_G = V_c$ for the Rankin Vortex model only, which implies that $R_c = R_G$ as $R \to 0$, $V_G = V_c$ as $V \to \infty$. Otherwise everything can only be approximate, the approximation depends upon the Rankin or the Coriolis non-dimensional number, which can be defined as follows:

$$N_c = fR/V_c \tag{72}$$

where f = the well known Coriolis parameter
R = radius of maximum cyclostrophic wind
V_c = maximum cyclostrophic wind

When N_c is very small (0.01 to 0.05) the Rankin Vortex model applies. When $N_c > 0.1$ the Rankin vortex cannot apply. The problem is when does some other model or modification of the Rankin Vortex model become important?

What is required is to establish certain relationships between cyclostrophic wind, gradient wind, and surface wind, usually defined as the 1-minute or the 10-minute average at the 10-meter standard anemometer level.

In sequence of maximum cyclostrophic wind V_c, maximum gradient wind V_G, and maximum surface wind V_s, we have

$$V_G > V_c \quad \text{and} \quad V_{sR_G} = C_f V_G \tag{73}$$

where C_f is the friction reduction factor.

What has not been recognized for hurricanes is that the radii of maximum of the above types of winds are not the same. It is very easy to state that

$$R_s = R_G < R_c \tag{74}$$

In fact, one can prove always for a stationary model hurricane that:

$$R_G < R_c \tag{75}$$

However it is not apparent that R_G is not the same as R_s because of different relationships for reduction friction factors. Unlike R_c and R_G which are quite apparent, it is quite probable that $R_G = R_s$.

An Investigation of a Model Hurricane

To begin with, all model hurricane pressure and wind fields are assumed to be stationary models, after which forward speeds of translation are applied to change only the winds but not the pressures.

What is required here is to establish relationships for the stationary hurricane between R_G, radius of maximum gradient wind, V_{gR} and R, the radius of maximum cyclostrophic wind, V_c.

It is important to note here that R_G and not R, the appropriate parameters to establish the radial distance at which V_G applies.

Three cases will be worked out here: (1) the Hydromet-Rankin Vortex model, (2) the Bret Model-X and (3) the Fujita model. Similar approaches can be worked out for the other models.

Hydromet-Rankin Vortex Model, A = B = 1. The pressure profile is given by:

$$\frac{P_r - P_0}{P_N - P_0} = e^{-R/r} \tag{76}$$

The pressure gradient is obtained as follows:

$$\frac{dp}{dr} = \frac{P_N - P_0}{R} \left(\frac{R}{r}\right)^2 e^{-(R/r)} \tag{77}$$

and the cyclostrophic wind equation by:

$$V_r^2 = \frac{1}{\rho_a} \frac{r \, dp}{dr} = \frac{1}{\rho_a} (P_N - P_0)\left(\frac{R}{r}\right) e^{-R/r} \tag{78}$$

The maximum cyclostrophic wind velocity occurs at r = R. Whence

$$V_c^2 = \frac{1}{\rho_a} \max\left(\frac{r \, dp}{dr}\right) = \frac{1}{\rho_a} (P_N - P_0) e^{-1} \tag{79}$$

Dividing Equation 78 by Equation 79 we obtain

$$V_r^2 = V_c^2 \left(\frac{R}{r}\right) e^{(1 - R/r)} \tag{80}$$

Substituting Equation 80 into Equation 68 we obtain

$$V_g^2 + frV_g = V_c^2 \frac{R}{r} e^{(1 - R/r)} \tag{81}$$

To find the maximum gradient wind V_G at radius of maximum wind R_G, we differentiate Equation 81 and set the results equal to zero and let $r = R_G$.

$$\frac{V_G}{fR_G} = \left(\frac{V_c}{fR}\right)^2 \left(\frac{R}{R_G}\right)^3 \left(\frac{R}{R_G} - 1\right) e^{(1-R/R_G)} \tag{82}$$

For any particular set of conditions

$$\frac{fR}{V_c} = \text{const} = \text{cyclostrophic Coriolis number}$$

when $\dfrac{R}{R_G} = 1$

  $fR_G = fR = 0$

  $\dfrac{V_G}{V_c} = 1$

The simultaneous solution of Equation 82 and Equation 71 gives the proper relationships between R/R and V_G/V_c as functions of the Coriolis number $N_c = fR/V_c$.

Fujita Model, A = B^{-1} = 2. The cyclostrophic wind relationship for the Fujita model is given by

$$V_r^2 = V_c^2 \frac{3\sqrt{3}\left(\frac{r}{R}\right)^2}{\left[1 + 2\left(\frac{r}{R}\right)^2\right]^{3/2}} \tag{83}$$

Substituting Equation 83 into Equation 68, the gradient wind equation becomes

$$V_g^2 + frV_g = V_c^2 \frac{3\sqrt{3}\left(\frac{r}{R}\right)^2}{\left[1 + 2\left(\frac{r}{R}\right)^2\right]^{3/2}} \tag{84}$$

In a similar manner as was done for the Hydromet Rankin Vortex model, differentiate Equation 84 and set dV_g/dr 0 to find the radius, R_G of maximum gradient wind V_G

$$\frac{V_G}{fR_G} = 6\sqrt{3}\left(\frac{V_c}{fr}\right)^2 \frac{1 - \left(\frac{R_G}{R}\right)^2}{\left[1 + 2\left(\frac{R_G}{R}\right)^2\right]^{5/2}} \tag{85}$$

and from Equation 84, let $r = R_g$ it becomes

$$V_G{}^2 + fR_GV_G = \frac{3\sqrt{3}\, V_c{}^2 \left(\dfrac{R_G}{R}\right)^2}{\left[1 + 2\left(\dfrac{R_G}{R}\right)^2\right]^{3/2}} \tag{86}$$

The simultaneous solution of Equations 85 and 86 gives relationships between fR/V_c and R_G/R.

Bret Model-X, $A = B = 1$. The cyclostrophic wind relationship for the Bret Model-X is given by

$$V_r{}^2 = V_c{}^2 \frac{4(rR)^2}{(R^2 + r^2)^2} \tag{87}$$

and the gradient wind equation becomes

$$V_g{}^2 + frV_g = \frac{4(rR)^2}{(R^2 + r^2)^2}\, V_c{}^2 \tag{88}$$

In a similar manner as was done for the Hydromet Rankin Vortex model differentiate Equation 88 and set $dV_g/dr = 0$ to find the radius, R_G of maximum gradient wind V_G.

$$\frac{V_G}{fR_G} = 8\left(\frac{V_c}{fR}\right)^2 \left(\frac{R}{R_G}\right)^4 \frac{\left(\dfrac{R}{R_G}\right)^2 - 1}{\left[\left(\dfrac{R}{R_G}\right)^2 + 1\right]^3} \tag{89}$$

and from Equation 88 let $r = R_G$, we have

$$V_G + fR_GV_G = \frac{4V_c{}^2 \left(\dfrac{R}{R_G}\right)^2}{\left[1 + \left(\dfrac{R}{R_G}\right)^2\right]^2} \tag{90}$$

The simultaneous solution of Equations 89 and 90 gives relationships between fR/V_c and R_G/R_c.

Table 3 presents the relationships between the ratio of radius of maximum gradient wind versus radius of maximum cyclostrophic wind and the Rankin Vortex

Table 3
Radius of Maximum Gradient Wind Versus Radius of Maximum
Cyclostrophic Wind Relationships for Hydromet Rankin
Vortex Model, Fujita Model, and Bret-X Model

$\dfrac{fR}{V_c}$	Hydromet $\dfrac{R_g}{R}$	Fujita $\dfrac{R_g}{R}$	Bret-X $\dfrac{R_g}{R}$
0.0	1.0	1.0	1.0
0.01	0.9903	0.9926	0.9951
0.02	0.9809	0.9856	0.9902
0.03	0.9721	0.9787	0.9855
0.04	0.9636	0.9720	0.9809
0.05	0.9554	0.9656	0.9765
0.06	0.9476	0.9594	0.9721
0.07	0.9401	0.9534	0.9678
0.08	0.9329	0.9476	0.9635
0.09	0.9259	0.9419	0.9594
0.1	0.9192	0.9363	0.9554
0.11	0.9127	0.9310	0.9514
0.12	0.9064	0.9258	0.9476
0.13	0.9003	0.9207	0.9438
0.14	0.8945	0.9158	0.9401
0.15	0.8888	0.9109	0.9364
0.16	0.8832	0.9062	0.9328
0.17	0.8779	0.9016	0.9293
0.18	0.8727	0.8971	0.9259
0.19	0.8676	0.8928	0.9225
0.2	0.8625	0.8884	0.9191

number for Hydromet Rankin Vortex model, Fujita model, and Bret-X model. Table 3 can be used in two ways:

1. Where R_G is given such as for the conditions of previous studies for the Gulf of Mexico, one can calculate the approximate R for the maximum cyclostrophic wind, V_c.
2. Where R is obtained by analysis by pressure profiles, then R_G can be used for the maximum gradient wind V_G.

Non-Dimensional Rankin Vortex Number

The non-dimensional Rankin Vortex number, N_c has been defined in Equation 72. It presents the ratio between the Coriolis velocity (a fictitious velocity) and the cyclostrophic wind velocity (a theoretical velocity) at the radius of the maximum cyclostrophic wind velocity. When $\Delta P_0 = P_N - P_0$ (Equation 59) is given in millibars,

Table 4

Suggested Guide for Selecting a Model [13]

Hydromet Rankin Vortex Model (Equation 64)	
A = B = 1	$0.0 < N_c < 0.05$
A = B = 5/4 (approx. est.)	$0.03 < N_{cR} < 0.08$
Bret Models (Equation 65)	
Fujita (b = 1/2)	$0.03 < N_{cR} < 0.08$
Bret-X (b = 1)	$0.06 < N_{cR} < 0.15$

Note: This table is only suggested. Revisions will be in order after sufficient hurricane analyses.

R in nautical miles, and V_c in knots, Equation 72 becomes

$$N_c = \frac{0.522R \sin \phi}{K \sqrt{\Delta P_0}} \tag{91}$$

where ϕ is the latitude, K = 11.3 to 11.7 depending on the air density at P_R.

Tabulated data from Schwerdt, et al. [42] for 51 U.S. East Coast and 71 Gulf of Mexico hurricanes were used to calculate values of N_{cR} from Equation 91 using K = 11.7. There was found a wide scatter of the data with respect to latitude. The average values of N_{cR} increased from 0.05 at lat $\phi = 24°$, to 0.07 at 30° to 0.165 at 41°, where existing models probably do not apply any way. Two lowest values for N_{cR} were 0.01 for Key West (1909) and 0.018 for Camille (1969), both of which can be considered as classical examples of the Rankin Vortex model. Maximum values for the Gulf were between 0.12 and 0.15, and for the East Coast 0.15 to 0.30. $N_{cR} = 0.15$ for Western Pacific Typhoon Vera (1959), and for Hawaii Hurricane Iwa, $N_{cR} = 0.15$ to 0.22. $N_{cR} = 0.052$ to 0.22 for the Indian Seas cyclones. Data pressure profiles for Vera (1959), Iwa (1982), and Indian Seas cyclones, and also mean, minimum and maximum values of N_{cR} for the U.S. East and Gulf Coast hurricanes were used to suggest a guide for selection of model pressure profiles, given in Table 4.

Summary

The radius of maximum gradient wind and the maximum gradient wind to the corresponding radius of maximum cyclostrophic wind and the maximum cyclostrophic wind have been carefully studied with various theoretical hurricane models. The accuracy of the predicted hurricane wind field heavily depends on the choice of the hurricane model. In the current study, it found that the selection of the hurricane model are determined by the range of the non-dimensional Rankin Vortex number. This number presents the ratio between the Coriolis velocity and the cyclostrophic wind velocity at the radius of the maximum cyclostrophic wind velocity.

Table 4 gives a suggested guidance for the selection of the hurricane model. But it is only a general guide. Additional data pressure profiles need to be analyzed for various P_R, hurricane intensive V_{cR}, and for different latitude ϕ, as well as regional locations.

List of Symbols

$R = R_c$ = radius of maximum cyclostrophic wind

$\quad R_G$ = radius of maximum gradient wind (corresponding to radius of maximum wind of published data on $R = R_G$)

$\quad r$ = distance from center of hurricane

$\quad V_c$ = maximum cyclostrophic wind at R

$\quad V_r$ = cyclostrophic wind at radial distance r

$\quad V_G$ = maximum gradient wind at R_G

$\quad V_g$ = gradient wind at radial distance r

$\quad P_R$ = atmospheric pressure at radius of maximum cyclostrophic wind

$\quad P_r$ = atmospheric pressure at radial distance r

Acknowledgments

The original work on the data pressure profiles Figures 5–9 was done by various members of Engineers India Limited under the support of UNIDO (United Nations Industrial Organization) and Figure 10 at the Coastal Engineering Research Center-Poona under the support of UNDP (United Nations Development Program). The drafting of the figures was done by HIG (Hawaii Institute of Geophysics) and typing of the final manuscript by the Department of Ocean Engineering.

Hurricane Models

Various hurricane model pressure profiles P_r have been proposed in the past. The pressure gradient is the slope, dP_r/dr of the pressure profile. The radial distance from the center of the model hurricane times the pressure gradient, divided by the air density ρ_a at the radial distance is equal to the square of the cyclostrophic wind velocity, $V_{cr}^2 = r\, dP_r/\rho_a\, dr$. The data pressure profile is a smooth S-shaped type of curve constructed through the measured pressure data, including accurately constructed isobars. Generally cross-sections through the isobars are constructed and averaged to give the best fit or best estimate of the data pressure profile. For any particular time and location of any single hurricane, all model pressure profiles including the data pressure profile have a common set of three parameters. These three parameters are: (1) the radius of maximum cyclostrophic wind R_c, (2) the maximum cyclostrophic wind V_{cRc}, and (3) the pressure P_{Rc}, at the radius of maximum cyclostrophic wind. Because all model pressure profiles are identified by some type of analytical or theoretical function, one can determine the above three parameters from the derivatives of (1) the pressure profile (the pressure gradient), (2) the second derivative of the pressure profile, and (3) the derivative of the cyclostrophic wind or the derivative of the product of the radial distance times the pressure gradient. This procedure results in three equations with one constant each. The constants for each model are different depending only on the choice of model pressure profile. The constants for the data pressure profile are determined by graphical or numerical differentiation.

Because of the very nature of this procedure, all model pressure profiles including the data pressure profile will have exactly the same values for the radius of maximum cyclostrophic wind, maximum cyclostrophic wind, and pressure at radius of maximum cyclostrophic wind, and this is true for all acceptable as well for unacceptable model pressure profiles.

The model pressure profile will pass through the common point (R_c, R_{R_c}, V_{cR}) but will depart from each other to the center of the hurricane as well as to the infinite or terminal distance from the radius of maximum wind. That is both the central pressure P_0 and the normal pressure, P_N (as well as the entire pressure profile) except for the common point will be different for each model.

Bretschneider and Jen Men Lo [49] discussed the development of various hurricane models and how to select a particular model based upon certain hurricane parameters. These parameters, quite different from those used in the past, include the following: (1) R_c, the radius of maximum cyclostrophic wind, V_{cR}, (2) P_{Rc}, the pressure; and (3) the maximum value of $(r \, dP/dr)$. These three parameters, R_c, P_{Rc}, and max$(r \, dP/dr)$ are all that are required of any hurricane model, except for ρ_a, the air density at radius of maximum cyclostrophic wind. The selection of the appropriate or best model to use is based upon a non-dimensional Rankin vortex number,

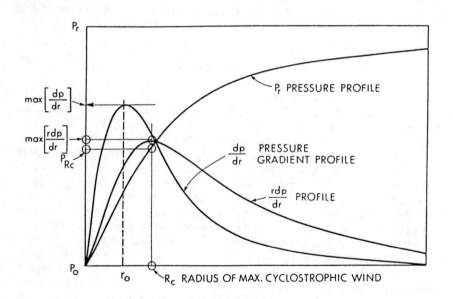

Figure 11. Schematic diagram for determination of R_c, P_{R_c}, and max r (dp/dr).

N_{R_c}. For low values of N_{R_c}, the original Hydromet model is acceptable, but for larger values of N_{R_c} some other model may be more applicable. It was found [12], based on the determinations of R_c, P_R, and max r dP/dr (see Figure 11), that some models gave maximum values of the pressure gradient dP/dr at the center of the hurricane, which is contrary to known pressure profiles. It would then appear that there are several previously proposed model pressure profiles that may not be acceptable even though such models may result in reasonable determinations!

The interesting things about this section concern (1) the determinations of R_c, P_{R_c}, and max r dP/dr; and (2) all model pressure profiles and the corresponding data pressure profiles satisfying R_c, P_{R_c}, and max r dP/dr give surprisingly good agreement for the cyclostrophic wind speed. A typical example is given in regard to the suggested best procedure and comparisons between two types of model pressure profile.

Discussion and Summary of Equations

Figure 12(a–d) shows four models in a non-dimensional form from the report by Bretschneider [12]. An example comparison is made between the models of Figure 12, the Hydromet Model-HM, and a model found in the NOAA Report by Schwerdt, Ho and Watkins [42], which was also used by Garcia and Flor [22] for calculating storm surge and waves for Hurricane Alicia.

For all model pressure profiles, including the data pressure profile, the maximum cyclostrophic wind is given by:

$$V_{cR} = k_0 \sqrt{\max(r\, dP/dr)} \tag{92}$$

where $k_0 = \sqrt{1/\rho_a}$

ρ_a = air density and is a function of temperature and air pressure at radius of maximum cyclostrophic wind.

For V_{cR} = knots, r = nautical miles, and P = mbs, k_0 = 19.26 to 18.70 for all hurricane pressure profiles (see Table 5).

For individual models, one obtains:

$$V_{cR} = k_1 \sqrt{P_N - P_0} \tag{93}$$

where $k_1 = k_0/\sqrt{C_1}$, and C_1 is different for each model. Hence for Equations 92 and 93 to be equal, $P_N - P_0$ must be different for each model, and the following two equations are used:

$$P_0 = P_R - C_2(P_N - P_0) \tag{94}$$

where $P_N - P_0$ is obtained from Equation 93, and

$$P_N = P_0 + (P_N - P_0) \tag{95}$$

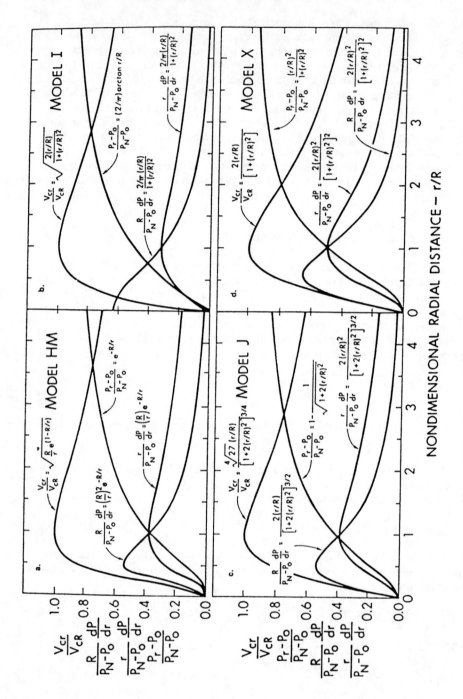

Figure 12. Four hurricane models in non-dimensional form.

Table 5
Theoretical Constants for Four Models

Model	k_0	$k_1 = k_0/\sqrt{C_1}$	k_1	C_2
Hydromet Model—HM	19.26	$k_0/\sqrt{e}$	11.68	$1/e$
	18.70		11.34	
NOAA (Report)	19.26	$k_0/\sqrt{\pi}$	10.87	$1/2$
Model-I	18.70		10.55	
Fujita	19.26	$k_0/\sqrt{2/3\sqrt{3}}$	11.95	$(3-\sqrt{3})/3$
Model-J	18.70		11.60	
Bret	19.26	$k_0/\sqrt{2}$	13.26	$1/2$
Model-X	18.70		13.22	

Example (same for all models). Given: lat $\phi = 20°$, $R_c = 10$ nautical miles, $P_{R_c} = 962$ mbs, and max r dP/dr = 30 mbs

Step 1: Calculate max $V_{cR} = K_0\sqrt{\max(r\,dP/dr)} = 19.26\sqrt{30} = 105.491$ knots.
Step 2: Calculate Rankin Vortex No., $N_{cR} = 0.525R_c \sin \phi/V_{cR} = 0.01702$
Step 3: Select model for $N_{cR} = 0.01702$ (see Table 3 of Ref. 49).
       Hydromet Model applies and $Rg/R_c = 0.9834$
       Radius of maximum gradient wind = $10 \times 0.9834 = 9.8$ nautical miles
Step 4: Calculations for Hydromet Model
       $\max(V_{cR}) = 11.68\sqrt{P_N - P_0}$
       Thus $P_N - P_0 = (105.491/11.68)^2 = 81.57$ mbs
Step 5: $P_0 = P_R - 1/e(P_N - P_0) = 962 - 30 = 932$ mbs
       $P_N = 932 + (P_N - P_0) = 932 + 81.57 = 1{,}013.57$ mbs

Following the same procedure for the NOAA Model-I, using $R_c = 10$ nautical miles, $P_R = 962$ mbs, and max(r dP/dr) = 30 mbs, we find

$$P_N - P_0 = (105.491/10.87)^2 = 94.18 \text{ mbs}$$

$$P_0 = P_R - \tfrac{1}{2}(P_N - P_0) = 962 - 47.1 = 914.91 \text{ mbs}$$

$$P_N = 914.91 + 94.18 = 1{,}009 \text{ mbs}$$

Table 6, based on the above two models gives a summary for the pressure profiles, P_r, pressure gradient, R_c dP/dr, r dP/dr, and V_{cr}. It is interesting to note that the pressure gradient and cyclostrophic wind are both zero at the center of the hurricane for the Hydromet Model, which is as expected, but for the NOAA Model-I, the pressure gradient is maximum at the center of the hurricane and r dP/dr = 0 because r = 0 and so is the cyclostrophic wind $V_{cr} = 0$. One of the above two models must be an unacceptable model! However, as can be seen from Table 6, there is very little

Table 6
Comparison Between Two Hurricane Models With Same
$R_c = 10$ nautical miles, $P_R = 962$ mbs, and max $(r\,dP/dr) = 30$ mbs

	Hydromet Model				NOAA Model-I			
r/R_c	P_r mbs	$\dfrac{R_c\,dP}{dr}$ mbs	$\dfrac{r\,dP}{dr}$ mbs	V_{cr} knots	P_r mbs	$\dfrac{R_c\,dP}{dr}$ mbs	$\dfrac{r\,dP}{dt}$ mbs	V_{cr} knots
0	932.0	0	0	0	914.9	60.0	0	0
.2	932.5	13.74	2.75	31.9	926.7	57.7	11.54	65.4
.4	938.7	41.85	16.74	78.8	937.7	51.7	20.69	87.6
.6	947.4	42.80	25.69	97.6	947.3	44.1	26.47	99.1
.8	955.4	36.52	29.21	104.1	955.4	36.59	29.27	104.2
1.0	962.0	30.00	30.00	105.5	962.0	30.00	30.00	105.5
1.2	967.5	24.62	29.54	104.7	967.4	24.59	29.51	104.6
1.4	971.9	20.37	28.52	102.9	971.9	20.27	28.38	102.6
1.6	975.7	17.06	27.29	100.6	975.6	16.85	26.97	100.0
1.8	978.8	14.45	26.00	98.2	978.7	14.15	25.47	97.2
2.0	981.5	12.37	24.74	95.8	981.3	12.00	24.00	94.4
2.2	983.8	10.70	23.54	93.4	983.5	10.27	22.60	91.6
2.4	985.8	9.34	22.41	91.2	985.4	8.88	21.30	88.9
2.6	987.5	8.21	21.36	89.0	987.1	7.73	20.10	86.4
2.8	989.1	7.28	20.38	87.0	988.5	6.79	19.00	84.0
3.0	990.4	6.49	19.48	85.0	989.8	6.00	18.00	81.7
3.5	993.3	5.00	17.51	80.6	992.4	4.53	15.85	76.7
4.0	995.5	3.97	15.88	76.8	994.4	3.53	14.12	72.4
4.5	997.3	3.23	14.52	73.4	996.0	2.82	12.71	68.7
5.0	998.8	2.67	13.36	70.4	997.3	2.31	11.54	65.4
5.5	1000.0	2.25	12.37	67.7	998.3	1.92	10.56	62.6
6.0	1001.0	1.92	11.51	65.3	999.2	1.62	9.73	60.1
6.5	1001.9	1.66	10.76	63.2	1000.0	1.39	9.02	57.8
7.0	1002.7	1.44	10.10	61.2	1000.6	1.20	8.40	55.8
7.5	1003.4	1.27	9.52	59.4	1001.2	1.05	7.86	54.0
8.0	1004.0	1.12	9.00	57.8	1001.7	.92	7.38	52.3
9.0	1005.0	.90	8.11	54.9	1002.5	.73	6.59	49.4
10.0	1005.8	.74	7.38	52.3	1003.1	.59	5.94	46.9
20.0	1009.6	.19	3.88	37.9	1006.1	.15	2.99	33.3
30.0	1010.9	.09	2.63	31.2	1007.1	.07	2.00	27.7
40.0	1011.6	.05	1.99	27.2	1007.6	.04	1.50	23.6

difference between the two models for the cyclostrophic wind speed except for quite some distance inward and outward from the radius of maximum cyclostrophic wind.

Graphical presentations for the previous example for the range $r = 0$ to $r = 100$ nautical miles and shown in Figures 13, 14, 15, and 16, respectively, for P_r, dP/dr $r\,dP/dr$, and V_{cr}. The differences for the two models can be observed.

Interesting is the fact that the gradient wind speeds and surface wind speeds by the two methods—right model and wrong model—will be much closer together.

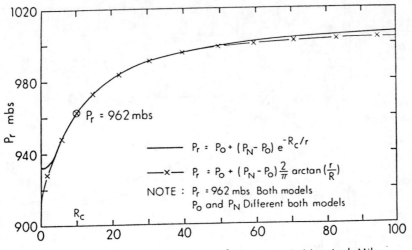

$$P_r = P_o + (P_N - P_o)\, e^{-R_c/r}$$

$$-\times-\quad P_r = P_o + (P_N - P_o)\frac{2}{\pi}\arctan\left(\frac{r}{R}\right)$$

NOTE : P_r = 962 mbs Both models
P_o and P_N Different both models

$\otimes$ P_r = 962 mbs

R_c

Radial Distance from Center of Hurricane in Nautical Miles

Figure 13. Comparison of two hurricane model pressure profiles.

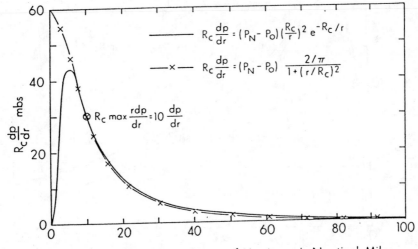

$$R_c\frac{dp}{dr} = (P_N - P_o)\left(\frac{R_c}{r}\right)^2 e^{-R_c/r}$$

$$-\times-\quad R_c\frac{dp}{dr} = (P_N - P_o)\;\frac{2/\pi}{1+(r/R_c)^2}$$

$\otimes$ R_c max $\dfrac{r\,dp}{dr} = 10\,\dfrac{dp}{dr}$

Radial Distance from Center of Hurricane in Nautical Miles

Figure 14. Comparison of two hurricane model pressure gradients (for Figure 13).

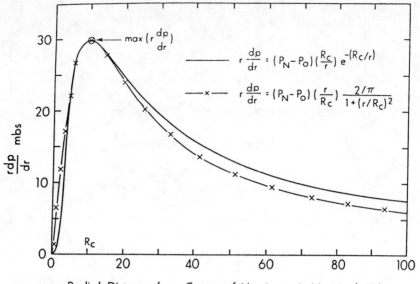

Figure 15. Comparison of two hurricane model r (dp/dr) (for Figure 14).

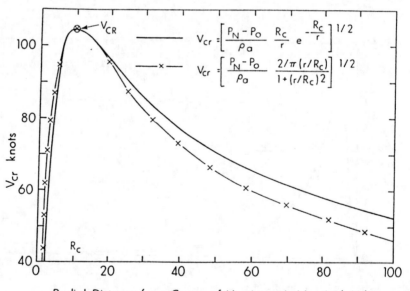

Figure 16. Comparison of two hurricane model cyclostrophic wind speeds.

Summary

There appears to be several acceptable hurricane models for which the pressure gradient is zero at the center of the hurricane, and several unacceptable models for which the pressure gradient is a maximum at the center of the hurricane. An example is given in this section that illustrates these two conditions. For the same data pressure profile all hurricane models will have the same (1) radius of maximum cyclostrophic wind, (2) pressure at radius of maximum cyclostrophic wind, and (3) maximum cyclostrophic wind.

Quick Method for Obtaining Maximum Significant Waves for Hydromet Model Hurricane Wind Fields

A method was given by Bretschneider [6] for obtaining significant wave height and period for Hydromet model Hurricane wind field. Fifty-one hurricanes for various values of a parameter fR/U_R, covering most of all ranges of the stationary hurricane parameters were considered (where R = radius of maximum wind, ΔP_0 = central pressure reduction from normal, $f = 2\omega \sin \phi$, and ϕ = the latitude of the hurricane) (see Figure 17 and Tables 7 and 8). Calculations from the mean curve of K' versus fR/U_R are within less than two percent. In the previous symbols, R = the radius of maximum wind as given in the literature, for example Schwerdt, Ho, and Watkins [42]. It is not known whether R is the radius of maximum gradient wind or R_c, the radius of maximum cyclostrophic wind (see [13]). Because all data

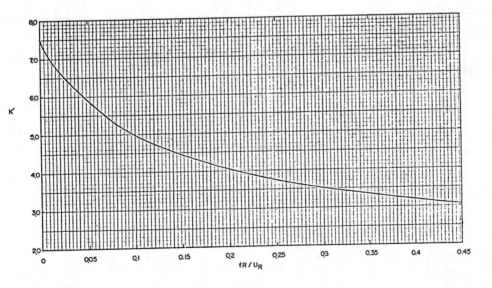

Figure 17. K' vs. fR/U_R for $\beta = 25°$. Note: $H_R = K' \sqrt{R\,\Delta P}$.

Table 7
Significant Wave Calculations for Maximum Significant Waves
(Incurvature Angle $\beta = 25°$)

No.	$\dfrac{fR}{U_R}$	K′	R	ΔP	R ΔP	$H_R = K'\sqrt{R\,\Delta P}$	H_R Comp.
1	0.0	7.50	5	2.0	10	23.7	24.3
2			10	2.5	25	37.5	36.5
3			25	2.0	50	53.0	45.8
4			33.3	3.0	100	75.0	65.5
5	0.025	6.55	6	1.67	10	20.7	20.9
6			10	2.55	25.5	33.1	34.2
7			14	2.88	40.3	41.6	42.9
8			25	2.29	57.3	49.6	46.9
9	0.05	5.80	10	1.19	11.9	20.0	19.8
10			15	1.30	19.5	25.6	25.0
11			20	1.50	30.0	31.8	31.8
12			25	2.34	58.5	44.4	45.2
13	0.10	5.00	20	1.44	28.8	26.8	26.5
14			30	1.79	53.7	36.6	37.5
15			40	1.57	62.8	39.6	39.1
16			45	1.99	89.6	47.3	47.3
17	0.15	4.50	22	1.07	23.5	21.8	20.7
18			25	1.05	26.2	23.0	22.2
19			30	1.51	45.3	30.3	30.1
20			35	1.30	45.5	30.4	30.7
21			40	1.70	67.8	37.1	38.0
22			50	1.15	57.3	34.1	33.0
23	0.20	4.10	30	1.02	30.6	22.7	21.9
24			40	1.00	40.0	25.9	25.9
25			35	1.20	42.0	26.6	26.3
26			40	1.36	54.4	30.2	30.5
27			50	1.52	76.0	35.7	37.1
28			45	2.00	90.0	38.9	39.6
29	0.25	3.80	35	1.07	37.4	23.2	22.5
30			40	1.06	42.4	24.7	24.4
31			42	1.17	49.1	26.6	26.5
32			50	1.04	52.0	27.4	27.8
33			45	1.34	60.4	29.5	29.5
34			50	1.65	82.6	34.5	35.2
35	0.30	3.55	40	1.11	44.4	23.7	21.8
36			45	1.12	50.5	25.2	24.8
37			50	1.20	60.0	27.5	27.5
38			55	1.44	79.3	31.6	32.1
39			65	1.28	83.2	32.4	32.8
40			60	1.73	103.8	36.2	37.1

Table 7   (Continued)

No.	$\dfrac{fR}{U_R}$	K'	R	ΔP	$R\,\Delta P$	$H_R = K'\sqrt{R\,\Delta P}$	H_R Comp.
41	0.35	3.30	45	0.98	44.3	22.0	21.2
42			50	1.06	53.0	24.0	23.4
43			55	1.11	61.1	25.8	25.5
44			60	1.32	79.2	29.4	29.5
45			70	1.14	79.8	29.5	30.0
46			65	1.52	98.9	32.8	33.6
47	0.40	3.15	50	0.97	48.3	21.9	21.0
48			60	1.06	63.6	25.1	24.6
49			65	1.24	80.6	28.3	28.0
50			75	1.15	86.2	29.2	28.0
51			70	1.24	86.8	29.3	29.5

Table 8
K' vs. fR/U_R

fR/U_R	K'	fR/U_R	K'
0	7.50	0.15	4.50
.005	7.25	0.16	4.42
.010	7.05	0.17	4.34
.015	6.85	0.18	4.28
.020	6.70	0.19	4.18
.025	6.55	0.20	4.10
.030	6.40	0.21	4.03
.035	6.25	0.22	3.97
.040	6.10	0.23	3.91
.045	5.95	0.24	3.85
.050	5.80	0.25	3.80
.055	5.70	0.26	3.75
.060	5.60	0.27	3.70
.065	5.49	0.28	3.65
.070	5.42	0.29	3.60
.075	5.34	0.30	3.55
.080	5.27	0.31	3.50
.085	5.20	0.32	3.45
.090	5.13	0.33	3.40
.095	5.06	0.34	3.35
.100	5.00	0.35	3.30
.110	4.88	0.36	3.26
.120	4.76	0.37	3.23
.130	4.66	0.38	3.20
.140	4.57	0.39	3.17
.150	4.50	0.40	3.15

From Bretschneider [6].

on R are given to the closest nautical mile, then truly R = R ± 0.5 nautical miles. This method can be used for the stationary hurricane, and then a correction to both the wind speed and the significant waves can be made for a constant forward speed, not to exceed approximately 20 knots, depending on the size or radius of maximum wind for the particular hurricane.

This method is used here to calculate the significant wave height for Hurricane Camille (August 17, 1969) (see Figure 18); Hurricane Eloise (September 22, 1200 noon), when Eloise was passing over Buoy EB-10, where and wind, wave, wave spectra, and other data were recorded (November 7, 1975) [48]; and Hurricane Eloise (September 23, 0600 a.m.) when Eloise reached near maximum wind and wave intensity (see Figure 19 for path of hurricane Eloise).

Additional figures have been determined by Bretschneider and Tamaye [14] and Bretschneider [9] for the stationary Hydromet model hurricane (Figure 20) and the calculated stationary model hurricane wave field (Figure 21).

For the moving hurricane at constant forward speed, formulas are given for correction, which seem to give very reasonable results as compared with the measurement of both wind and wave data.

Symbols and Definitions Used for the Hurricane Wind and Wave Models

The maximum cyclostrophic wind speed representing the balance between the centrifugal force and the pressure gradient force is given by

$$U_{Rc} = K\sqrt{\Delta P_0} \tag{96}$$

where $\Delta P_0 = P_N - P_0$, the reduction in central pressure p_0 from the normal pressure P_N. The standard $P_N = 29.92$ in. Hg $= 1,013.3$ mbs, but P_N may be as high as 1,014 mbs or as low as 1,008 mbs, depending on surrounding weather pressure conditions.

In Equation 96, $K = \sqrt{\text{constant}/\rho_a}$, where ρ_a is the air density, and the constant depends on the model. K depends on the units of U_{Rc} (knots) (m/s) and ΔP_0 (in. Hg or mbs) [13]. The maximum gradient wind U_{Rg} is approximated by

$$R = U_{Rg} = K\sqrt{\Delta P_0} - \tfrac{1}{2}fR_c \tag{97}$$

where $f = 2\omega \sin \phi$, the Coriolis force parameter
 ω = angular velocity of the earth
 ϕ = the latitude for the moving hurricane the maximum wind at gradient wind level is approximated by

$$U_{Rv} = K\sqrt{\Delta P_0} - \tfrac{1}{2}fR_g + \tfrac{1}{2}V_F \tag{98}$$

where V_F = the forward speed of translations

For other positions in the hurricane see Bretschneider [9]. The 10-meter level sustained wind speed (sometimes called the 10-minute average surface wind speed)

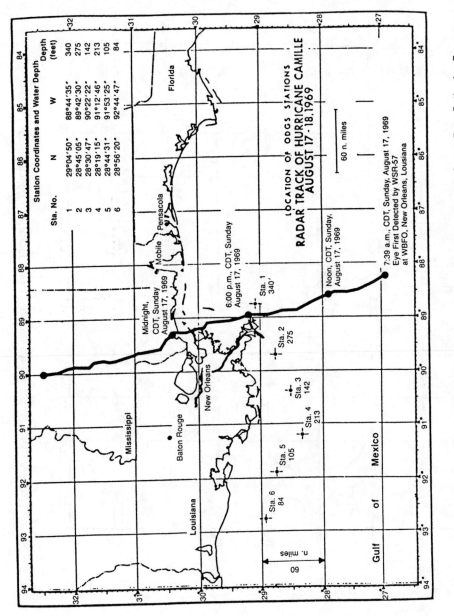

Figure 18. Path of Hurricane Camille (1969) through six measuring stations—of Shell's Ocean Data Gathering Program— in the Gulf of Mexico.

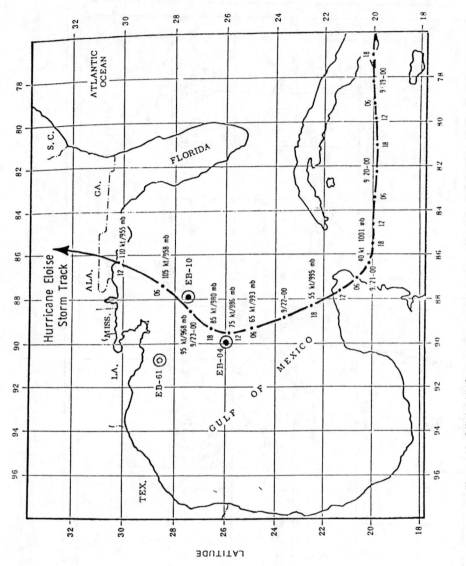

Figure 19. Official NHC storm track of Hurricane Eloise with significant wave heights.

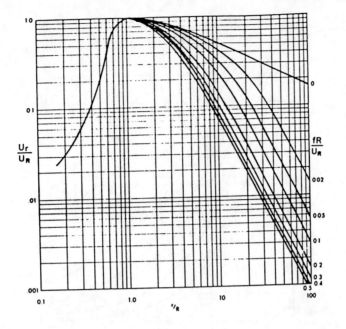

Figure 20. Ratio of wind speed, U_r, at radial distance, r, from center of hurricane to speed, U_R, at radial distance, R, of maximum wind versus r/R with the coriolis (f) function, fR/U_R, as a parameter. For r/R $\geq$ 1 use Equation (15) and for r/R $\leq$ 1 use Graham and Nunn (1972).

is reduced by friction from the gradient wind level. The following equations for the V_{10} are given as follows:

$V_{10} = 0.865 U_{Rv}$, Gulf of Mexico, U.S. East Coast, Bay of Bengal
$V_{10} = 0.82 U_{Rv}$, Western Pacific Ocean
$V_{10} = 0.785 U_{Rv} + 4.5$ (knots), for Hawaiian waters

For the maximum probable hurricane, Gulf of Mexico and U.S. East Coast, the following equation has been used

$V_{10} = 0.886\ V_{10}$

The Rankin Vortex number is given by $N_c = fR_c/U_{Rc}$,

where $f = 2\omega \sin \phi$
R_c = radius of maximum cyclostrophic wind, U_{Rc}
ω = angular velocity of the earth
ϕ = latitude

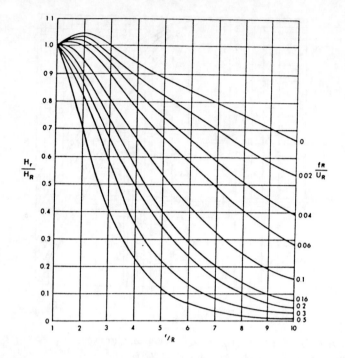

Figure 21. Ratio of significant wave height, H_r, at radial distance, r, from center of a stationary hurricane to that, H_R, at radial distance, R, of maximum wind speed with coriolis (f) function, $fR\,U_R$, as a parameter.

It then follows that

$$\frac{fR_c}{U_{Rc}} = \frac{0.525R_c \sin \phi}{K\sqrt{\Delta P_0}}$$

(99)

where R_c = nautical miles
ΔP_0 = mbs
$K = 11.3$ to 11.7 for the Hydromet model, depending on air density.

The radius of maximum cyclostrophic wind R_c is related to the radius of maximum gradient wind R_g depending on fR_c/U_{Rc} and the choice of model. See Tables 4 and 9 [13].

It is important to note that when R_c is used in the gradient wind equation for hurricanes that the radius of maximum gradient wind (and also the surface wind) for the stationary hurricane will then actually occur at radius of maximum wind, gradient or surface wind. If, however, as has previously been used in the past by most users (including the present author), that when the published radius R is used then Rg is smaller than R, except at very low latitudes. This fact was first noticed in the very early publication "On Hurricane Design Wave Practices," by Bret-

Table 9
Radius of Maximum Gradient Wind Versus Radius of Maximum
Cyclostrophic Wind Relationships for Hydromet Rankin
Vortex Model, Fujita Model, and Bret-X Model [13]

fR_c/U_c	Hydromet R_g/R_c	Fujita R_g/R_c	Bret-X R_g/R_c
0.0	1.0 ,	1.0	1.0
0.01	0.9903	0.9926	0.9951
0.02	0.9809	0.9856	0.9902
0.03	0.9721	0.9787	0.9855
0.04	0.9636	0.9720	0.9809
0.05	0.9554	0.9656	0.9765
0.06	0.9476	0.9594	0.9721
0.07	0.9401	0.9534	0.9678
0.08	0.9329	0.9476	0.9635
0.09	0.9259	0.9419	0.9594
0.1	0.9192	0.9363	0.9554
0.11	0.9127	0.9310	0.9514
0.12	0.9064	0.9258	0.9476
0.13	0.9003	0.9207	0.9438
0.14	0.8945	0.9158	0.9401
0.15	0.8888	0.9109	0.9364
0.16	0.8832	0.9062	0.9328
0.17	0.8779	0.9016	0.9293
0.18	0.8727	0.8971	0.9259
0.19	0.8676	0.8928	0.9225
0.2	0.8625	0.8884	0.9191

schneider [2]. The Rankin Vortex number Equation 99 is used in the later part of this section, whereas the parameter fR/U_R (see Tables 7 and 8 and Figure 17).

$$\frac{fR}{U_R} = \frac{0.525R \sin \phi}{K\sqrt{\Delta P_0} - \frac{1}{2}fR} \tag{100}$$

The reason for the difference for fR/U_R and fR_c/U_{Rc} is that Equation 100 is based on the Hydromet model, gradient wind equation, which is required for determining the corresponding hurricane wind and wave fields, whereas fR_c/U_{Rc} is the Rankin Vortex number, used as a guide to determine the appropriate hurricane model [13].

Determining the Radius of Maximum Cyclostrophic Wind

• Hurricane Camille (August 17, 1969)

$R_c \cong R_g = 10$
$\Delta P_0 = 105 \text{ mbs} = 3.1 \text{ in. Hg}$
$\phi = 29° \text{ lat}$
$V_F = 10 \text{ knots}$

- Hurricane Eloise (September 22, 1975, 1200 noon) Buoy EB-10, 1200 noon September 22, 1975

    $\Delta P_0 = 39$ mbs $= 1.15$ in. Hg (see [39])
    $\phi = 27.5°$ lat
    $V_F = 12.5$ knots (As Eloise approached and R passed over Buoy B-10)
    $R = 15$ nautical miles ($R_g = R$)

    (All values are same as given by Ross [39], except $V_F = 15$ knots.)

- Hurricane Eloise (September 23, 0600 a.m.)

    $\Delta P_0 = 39 + (968 - 958) = 49$ mbs $= 1.45$ in. Hg
    $\phi = 28.5°$ lat
    $V_F = 15$ knots

- Calculating R_c for Hurricane Camille
  Assume $R_c \cong R_g = 10$ nautical miles.
  Calculate Rankin vortex number.

    $$\frac{fR_c}{U_{R_c}} = \frac{0.525R_c \sin \phi}{U_{R_c}}$$
    $$U_{R_c} = 11.68\sqrt{\Delta P_0} = 11.68\sqrt{105} = 119.7 \text{ knots}$$
    $$\frac{fR_c}{U_{R_c}} = \frac{0.525 \times 10 \sin 29°}{119.7} = .0213$$
    $$\frac{R_c}{R_g} \cong 1.0 \text{ (See Bretschneider [13])}$$

    Thus $R_c = R_g = 10$ nautical miles

- Calculating R_c for Hurricane Eloise September 22, 1975, noon
  Given $R = 15$ nautical miles $\Delta P_0 = 39$ mbs $= 1.45$ in. Hg
      $\phi = 27.5°$ lat $V_F = 12.5$ knots
  Assume $R_c \cong R_g = 15 \pm 0.5$ nautical miles.
  Calculate Rankin Vortex number.

    $$\frac{fR_c}{U_{R_c}} = \frac{0.525 \sin \phi R_c}{U_{R_c}}$$
    $$U_{R_c} = 11.68\sqrt{\Delta P_0} = 11.68\sqrt{39} = 72.94 \text{ knots}$$
    $$\frac{fR_c}{U_{R_c}} = \frac{0.525 \sin 27.5° \times 15}{72.94} = 0.05$$

    From Table 9 $R_g/R_c = 0.9554$

    $R_g = 15 \times 0.9554 = 14.35$ (less than $R_g = 15$)

Assume $R_c = 15.5$

$$\frac{fR_c}{U_{R_c}} = 0.05 \frac{15.5}{15} = 0.0517$$

$R_g/R_c = 0.9541$
  $R_g = 0.9541 \times 15.5 = 14.8$

Thus $R_c = 15.5 \pm 0.5$ nautical miles

- Calculating R_c for Hurricane Eloise (September 23, 1975, 0600 a.m.)
  Assume $R = R_g = 15 \pm 0.5$ nautical miles

$$\Delta P_0 = 49 \text{ mbs} = 1.45 \text{ in. Hg}$$
$$\phi = 28.5° \text{ lat}$$
$$V_F = 15 \text{ knots}$$

Calculate Rankin Vortex number
Assume $R = R_g = R_c = 15$ nautical miles

$$\frac{fR_c}{U_{R_c}} = \frac{0.525 \sin \phi \times 15}{11.68 \sqrt{49}} = 0.0460$$

From Table 9

$R_g/R_c = 0.9587$
  $R_g = 15 \times 0.9587 = 14.4$

Assume $R_c = 15.5$

$$\frac{fR_c}{U_{R_c}} = 0.046 \frac{15.5}{14.5} = 0.0495$$

$R_g/R_c = 0.9558$
  $R_g = 14.8$

Thus $R_c = 15.5 \pm 0.5$ nautical miles

All values of R_g and R_c must be considered to be within ± 0.5 nautical miles as reported in the literature. The error in significant wave height will be governed by

$$H_R = K' \sqrt{(R_g \pm 0.5) \Delta P_0}$$

Calculating Significant Waves, Period and Wave Spectra

Once the hurricane parameters lat ϕ, radius of maximum wind cyclostrophic R_c, and central pressure reduction from normal ΔP_0 are given, one can determine the stationary hurricane wind and wave fields, both of which will be symmetric through 360° of the circular model hurricane, thus eliminating the need for defining steady state and time dependency. A correction term is given to take into account both the changes in wind field and the corresponding wave field due to the forward speed of translation. This works very well for slowly moving hurricanes along a straight path. The limit of such conditions is reached when the forward speed of the hurricane becomes equal to the group velocity of the waves being generated, after which the hurricane moves faster than the group velocity of the waves, with lower waves and more confused seas being generated. The limit of forward speed is $V_F \cong 20$ to 22 knots depending on the diameter of the hurricanes. Good results should be expected for $V_F \leq 15$ knots.

Once the significant wave height and corresponding surface wind $(V_{10}) = U_r$ has been calculated, one can make the remaining calculations by calculating the corresponding effective fetch parameter from

$$\frac{gH_s}{U^2} = A_1 \tanh\left[B_1 \left(\frac{gF_e}{U^2}\right)^{m_1} \right]$$

hence

$$\frac{gF_e}{U^2} = \operatorname{arctanh}\left[\left[\left(\frac{1}{A_1}\frac{gH}{U^2}\right)\right]\frac{1}{B_1}\right]\frac{1}{m_1}$$

and then gF_e/U^2 is used in all the other equations.

For the quick method $A_1 = 0.283$ and $B_1 = 0.0125$ and $m_1 = \frac{5}{12}$. For the method given in the next section $A_1 = 0.3$ and $B_1 = 0.0118$. In both methods $A_1 B_1 = 0.00354$, corresponding to high wind speeds and short fetches, such as for hurricanes.

Calculating Significant Wave Height, Period and Wave Spectra for Hurricane Camille and Eloise

- Camille (August 17, 1969) (see Figure 18)
  Given $R = 10$ nautical miles $\Delta P_0 = 105$ mbs $= 3.1$ in. Hg

  $V_F = 10$ knots, $\phi = 29°$, Hydromet model:
  $K = 66$ (ΔP_0 in in. Hg)   11.68 ($\Delta P_0 =$ mbs)
  $U_R = K\sqrt{\Delta P_0} - 0.5fR = 114.9$ knots (stationary)
  $U_{Rs} = 0.865 U_R = 0.865 \times 114.9 = 99$ knots
  $\dfrac{fR}{U_R} = \dfrac{0.525 \sin 29° \times 10}{114.9} = 0.0222.$

From Figure 17 or Table 8

$K' = 6.64$

Stationary $H_{Rs} = K'\sqrt{R \, \Delta P_0} = 6.64\sqrt{10 \times 3.1} = 36.97 \text{ ft} = 11.38 \text{ m}$

Moving $H_{RV} = H_{Rs}\left[1 + \dfrac{0.5V_F}{U_R}\right]^2 = 36.97\left[1 + \dfrac{5}{114.9}\right]^2$

$$= 40.3 \text{ ft} = 12.4 \text{ m}$$

$$U_{Rs} \text{ (moving)} = 0.865(U_{Rs} + \tfrac{1}{2}V_F)$$

$$U = U_{Rs} \text{ (moving)} = 99 + \tfrac{1}{2}(0.865)10 = 103.3 \text{ knots}$$

These results are in excellent agreement with the measured data.

Remaining Calculations to be Made

From $\dfrac{gH_s}{U^2} = 0.3 \tanh\left[0.0118\left(\dfrac{gF_e}{U^2}\right)^{5/12}\right]$

Calculate $\dfrac{gF_e}{U^2} = \left[\dfrac{1}{0.0118} \text{ arctanh}\left(\dfrac{1}{0.3}\dfrac{gH_s}{u^2}\right)\right]^{12/5}$

Then use gF_e/U^2 in the equations for T_s, f_0^{-1}, and other equations for the 3-parameter wave spectrum.

Significant wave calculations for r = 0.5R, 1.5R, 2R, etc. (Use Figures 18 and 19 for obtaining wind speeds and significant wave and spectra, and then for the moving hurricane

$$H_r = H_{rs}\left[1 + \dfrac{0.5V_F[\cos(\theta + \beta)]}{U_{rg}}\right]^2$$

where $(\theta + \beta)$ represents the total angle between V_F and U_r and is positive on the right side $(\theta + \beta) = (+)$ and negative on the left side $(\theta + \beta) = (-)$ the moving hurricane. This is a simple matter of correct geometry. The maximum value of $\cos(\theta + \beta) = 1.0$. Note in the above equation that V_F/U_{rg} should be the same as $0.865V_F \div 0.865U_{rg}$ as used in the past.

- Eloise (September 22, 1200 noon, 1975) (Buoy EB-10) (see Figure 19)
  Given R = R_g = 15 nautical miles,
  ΔP_0 = 39 mbs = 1.15 in. Hg, V_F = 12.5 nautical miles
  lat ϕ = 27.5°

$$U_{Rg} = K\sqrt{\Delta P_0} - \tfrac{1}{2}fR = 72.94 - 3.94 = 69 \text{ knots (gradient)}$$
$$U_{Rs} = 0.865 \times 72.94 = 63.1 \text{ knots (surface)}$$
$$\frac{fR}{U_R} = \frac{0.525(\sin 27.5°)15}{69} = 0.0527 \quad \text{(Note: } U_R = 69 \text{ knots)}$$

From Table 8 $K' = 5.75$

Stationary $H_{Rs} = K'\sqrt{R\ \Delta P_0} = 5.75\sqrt{15 \times 1.15} = 23.88$ ft $= 7.35$ m

Moving $H_{RV} = H_{Rs}\left[1 + \dfrac{1}{2}\dfrac{V_F}{U_R}\right]^2 = 23.88\left[1 + \dfrac{6.25}{69}\right]^2 = 28.40$ ft $= 8.74$ m

Maximum H_s measured given by Ross [39]
$H = 8.7$ m and Huang [28] $H \cong 9.0$ m

The maximum significant wave height is somewhat higher between R and 2R to the right of the center of the hurricane and somewhat within the upper part of the right rear quadrant. The previous calculations are in very good agreement with the measurements of $V_F = 12.5$ knots, then for the moving hurricane

$$H_{RV} = 23.88\left[1 + \frac{6.25}{69}\right]^2 = 28.40 \text{ ft} = 8.7 \text{ m}$$

It must be pointed out that the radius of maximum waves did not pass over the measuring station EB-10, so that the actual maximum conditions will be a little larger than as shown, and which is considered later.

- Eloise (September 23, 0600, 1975)

    Eloise intensified after it passed over Buoy B-10, with a slight increase in forward speed and also with further reduction in central pressure. Calculations are given for the above time and the following conditions:

    lat $\phi = 28.5°$, $R = R_g = 15$ nautical miles (for these calculations)
    $\Delta P_0 = 39 + (968 - 958) = 49$ mbs $= 1.45$ in. Hg (see Figure 19)
    $V_F = 15$ knots
    $U_R = K\sqrt{\Delta P_0} - \frac{1}{2}fR = 78.35 - 3.58 = 74.77$ knots (gradient)
    $\dfrac{fR}{U_R} = \dfrac{0.525 \sin 28.5 \times 15}{74.77} = 0.050$
    $K' = 5.80$

    Stationary $H_{Rs} = 5.80\sqrt{15 \times 1.45} = 27.05$ ft $= 8.32$ m

    Moving $H_{RV} = 27.05\left[1 + \left(\dfrac{1}{2}\right)\dfrac{7.5}{74.77}\right]^2 = 32.75$ ft $= 10.1$ m

All in all, these simplified calculations give very good results when compared with the measured data for both Hurricanes Camille and Eloise. The figures and graphs given with simple calculations with the given formulas are for Hydromet model hurricanes.

Maximum Significant Waves for r > R

The maximum significant waves do not necessarily occur at the radius of maximum wind, but will be somewhere between r = R to 2R as determined from Figures 20 and 21. For example, Hurricane Camille (I) $fR/U_R = 0.0213$, one finds that maximum values for stationary hurricane that occur at $r/R \cong 2$, with a value of 1.03 and that the wind speed $U_r/U_R = 0.9$ approximately.

Thus for a moving hurricane

$$H(2R) = 1.03 \times H_R \left[1 + \frac{0.5V_F}{0.9 \times U_R} \right]^2$$

Hence, for the moving hurricane

$$\frac{H(2R)}{H_{R(Stationary)}} = 1.03 \left[1 + \frac{0.5(10)}{0.9(114.9)} \right]^2 = 1.132$$

Thus, the maximum significant wave (not measured) will be 13.2% greater than that given for the stationary hurricane

$$H_s = 36.97 \times 1.132 = 41.85 \text{ ft} = 12.88 \text{ m}$$

Similar conditions are made for Hurricane Eloise (September 22 and 23) for 1.5R

September 22: $\quad \dfrac{H(1.5R)}{H(R)} = 1.02 \left[1 + \dfrac{6.25}{0.92(69)} \right]^2 = 1.231$

Thus, $H_s = 23.88 \times 1.231 = 29.39 \text{ ft} = 9.04 \text{ m}$
Similar corrections for September 23 are the same as for September 22, i.e.

September 23: $\quad \dfrac{H(1.5R)}{H(R)} = 1.02 \left[1 + \dfrac{7.5}{0.92 \times 74.77} \right]^2 = 1.25$

Thus, $H_s = 27.05 \times 1.25 = 33.94 \text{ ft} = 10.44 \text{ m}$
Thus, the maximum significant wave at 1.5R to 2R is

$$1.26 \times 27.05 = 34.15 \text{ ft} = 10.5 \text{ m}$$

Actually the entire stationary wind and wave fields could be calculated by use of Figures 20 and 21, taking into account the 360° angle in $\cos(\theta + \beta)$. In such case, $\cos(\theta + \beta)$ goes for +1.0 to 0 to (−1). For a stationary hurricane, wind speeds of constant value and significant wave height of constant value are both represented by concentric circles of U_r and H_r. However, the corrections for the moving hurricane are far more tedious by hand calculations, and are best performed on the computer as given in the next section.

The Bretschneider Three-Parameter Wave Spectrum and Two-Direction Wave Forecasting Method

The Bretschneider [3] three-parameter wave spectrum is given by the following equations:

$$S(f) = 4(\tfrac{1}{4}H_s)^2(Af_0)^{-1} \frac{\left[(1 - R) + R\sqrt{4/\pi}\left|\frac{Af_0}{f}\right|^2\right]^2}{[1 + (4/\pi - 1)R^2]} \left(\frac{Af_0}{f}\right)^5 e^{-(Af_0/f)^4} \tag{101}$$

where H_s = significant wave height
    f = wave frequency (hertz)
    f_0 = frequency as $S(f_0) = S(\max)$
    $S(f)$ = energy density (ft^2 sec)
    R = linear regression coefficient between Rayleigh distribution of wave height and Rayleigh distribution of wave length (i.e., T^2)
    A^4 = function of R
    π = 3.1416
    e = 2.7183

Relations between R, A, and $S(f_0)$ max can be obtained by mathematical operations [15, 28].

Procedure for Obtaining the Three-Parameter Wave Spectrum

The Bretschneider three-parameter wave spectrum has been correlated with wind, wave, and wave spectrum from Hurricane Eloise (1975).

The original two-direction wave forecasting model, which has been verified for maximum significant wave heights for Hurricane Camille (1969) was used to predict the significant wave height $H_s = H_{1/3}$ at any location in the hurricane and the corresponding wind speed $V_s = V_{10}$, where V_{10} is the 10-meter, 10-minute average wind speed. The directions of $H_{1/3}$ and V_{10} were also given.

The correlation technique made use of the effective fetch length F_e, which corresponds to the proper dimensionless ratio gH_s/U^2, calculated by the computer program. The nondimensional fetch parameter of gF_e/U^2 was obtained from the inverse significant wave height prediction equation.

The procedure used in these computing techniques has been changed. That is, instead of computing H_s first to obtain F_e and all the other parameters, T_s is computed first to obtain F_e and all the other parameters remain the same. This procedure gives the same wave directions or essentially the same as the previous procedure, except that smooth contours of wave period are obtained. The wave direction is calculated from the significant wave period direction or the propagational direction of the waves. The resolution has also been doubled to increase accuracy, but the accuracy is still essentially the same as before.

The non-dimensional fetch parameter is now obtained from the inverse of the significant wave period prediction equation

$$\frac{gT_s}{2\pi U} = 1.2 \tanh\left[0.077\left(\frac{gF_e}{U^2}\right)^{1/4}\right] \tag{102}$$

where $T_s = T_{1/3}$, significant wave period
$\quad\quad U = V_{10}$, sustained 10-meter level wind speed

The procedure used in the computer calculations now uses the two-direction wave forecasting procedures.

$$2 - x\,\frac{gH_x}{UV_x} = 0.3 \tanh\left[0.012\left(\frac{gF_x}{UU_x}\right)^{5/12}\right]$$

$$2 - y\,\frac{gH_y}{UU_y} = 0.3 \tanh\left[0.012\left(\frac{gF_y}{UU_y}\right)^{5/12}\right]$$

where $H_s^2 = H_x^2 + H_y^2$
$\quad\quad U_x = U \cos\theta$
$\quad\quad U_y = U \sin\theta \tag{103}$
$\quad\quad UU_x = U^2 \cos\theta$
$\quad\quad UU_y = U^2 \sin\theta$

The inverse of Equation 102 becomes:

$$\frac{gF_e}{U^2} = \left[\frac{1}{0.012}\,\text{arctanh}\,\frac{gH}{0.3U^2}\right]^{12/5} \tag{104}$$

Having determined the proper value of gF_e/U^2, then the following equations are solved:

$$\frac{gT_s}{2\pi U} = 1.2 \tanh\left[0.077\left(\frac{gF_e}{U^2}\right)^{1/4}\right] \tag{105}$$

$$\frac{gf_0^{-1}}{2\pi U} = \tanh\left[0.0236\left(\frac{gF_e}{U^2}\right)^{1/3}\right] \tag{106}$$

where $f_0^{-1} = T(f_0) =$ the modal period of the frequency (hertz) spectrum,

$$\omega_0 = 2\pi f_0 = 2\pi/T(f_0) \quad (rad/sec)$$

$$\frac{g^3 S(f_0)}{U^5} = \frac{5\pi}{8} e^{-5/4} \left(\frac{gH}{U^2}\right) \times \left(\frac{gf_0^{-1}}{2\pi U}\right) \tag{107}$$

where $S(f_0)$ is the peak of the Bretschneider two-parameter wave spectrum and corresponds to frequency f_0. The peak of the three-parameter wave spectrum is given by:

$$\frac{g^3 S_{max}}{U^2} = G \cdot \frac{g^3 S(f_0)}{U^5} \tag{108}$$

where G is the amplification factor and is a function of the effective fetch parameter gF_e/U^2. Based on Hurricane Eloise (1975) wave spectra data, the following empirical relationship has been established.

$$G = 1.49 \left\{ -0.45 \, sech[0.6269^{13/12}] \, \ln \frac{1}{10} \frac{U^5}{g^3 S(f_0)} \right\} \tag{109}$$

The amplification G-factor is related to two other parameters in the three-parameter spectrum as follows:

$$G = \frac{4}{5} A^4 e^{(5/4 - A^4)} \frac{[(1 - R) + \sqrt{4/\pi} \, R A^2]}{[1 + (4/\pi - 1)R^2]} \tag{110}$$

where $\left[(1 - R)^2 (4A^4 - 5) + 2\sqrt{4/\pi} \, R(1 - R)A^2(4A^4 - 7) + \frac{4}{\pi} R^2 A^4 (4A^4 - 9) \right] = 0$

$$\tag{111}$$

G is obtained from the forecasting relationships and by use of Equation 109. Then R and A^4 are determined from the simultaneous solution of Equations 110 and 111.

The lower limits for hurricane wind wave generation correspond to $R = 1$ and $A^4 = \frac{9}{4}$, and the upper limits for fully developed sea is $R = 0$ and $A^4 = \frac{5}{4}$, corresponding to the two-parameter wave spectrum. The two-parameter spectrum is a non-dimensional form of the two-parameter wave spectrum, which is identical to that of the Pierson and Moskowitz [36] and the JONSWAP spectra.

In summary the limits of the Bretschreider three-parameter spectrum are as follows:

$0 \le R \le 1$

$\tfrac{5}{4} = A^4 \le \tfrac{9}{4}$

$1 \le G \le 1.49$

and

$$\frac{g\tilde{\tilde{T}}}{2\pi U} = 1.42 \tanh\left[0.043\left(\frac{gF_e}{U^2}\right)^{1/4}\right] \tag{112}$$

In the spectrum analysis the mean apparent wave period is generally called the mean apparent wave period (the zero crossing wave period) and is given the symbol $\tilde{\tilde{T}}$.

Based on the analysis of Eloise (1975) hurricane wave spectra data Bretschneider, et al., [15] determined the following relationship:

$$\frac{g\tilde{\tilde{T}}}{2\pi U} = 1.42 \tanh\left[0.043\left(\frac{gF_e}{U^2}\right)^{1/4}\right] \tag{113}$$

Sample Calculations

Calculations have been made for three hurricane conditions, as follows:

1. Hurricane Camille (Aug. 17, 1969) $\phi = 29°$ lat, $\Delta P_0 = 105$ mbs $= 3.1$ in. Hg, $R_c \cong R_g = 10$ nautical miles, $V_F = 10$ knots, AZM $= 0°$ or $360°$.
2. Hurricane Eloise (Sept. 22, 1975, 12 noon) as it passed over Buoy B-10) $\phi = 27.5°$ lat, $\Delta P_0 = 39$ mbs $= 1.15$ in. Hg, $R_g = 15$ nautical miles, $R_c = 15.5$ nautical miles, $V_F = 12.5$ knots, AZM $= 45°$.
3. Hurricane Eloise (Sept. 23, 1975 0600 a.m.), time and location of greater intensity than for 2 above. No measurement at the location. $\phi = 28.5°$ lat, $\Delta P_0 = 49$ mbs $= 1.45$ in. Hg, $R_g = 15$ nautical miles, $R_c = 15.5$ nautical miles, $V_F = 15$ knots, AZM $= 30°$.

It should be noted that the results of the calculations are in very good agreement with the reported measurements for Hurricane Camille (1) and Hurricane Eloise (2). The radius of maximum waves is to the right of the radius of maximum wind; neither the radius of maximum wind nor the radius of maximum waves passed over Buoy B-10. Hurricane Eloise (3) for a later time and stronger intensity is given to show what one can expect if the hurricane intensity suddenly increases.

In all cases where applicable the computer printouts (see the following pages) are in very good agreement with the measurements, and also for the maximum significant waves given in the previous section on the Quick Method.

It should also be noted for the computed wave spectra that along any traverse passing by a structure that the envelope of wave spectra should apply [8].

1. Hurricane Camille—August 17, 1969

DATE: 5/10/88

HURRICANE : CAMILLE
Lat.= 29 deg.; Rc= 10 n.mi.;ΔPo= 105 mbs; Vf= 10 knts; Dir.= 0 deg.

r N.M.	A0 DEG	Urs KNOTS	Bu DEG	Hs FEET	Bh DEG	Ts SEC.	Tf0 SEC.	Tm SEC.
5.0	115	83.2	180.0	39.7	200.6	13.6	13.0	9.4
10.0	115	95.4	180.0	43.2	211.3	14.1	12.8	9.6
15.0	115	91.8	180.0	44.3	216.6	14.3	13.4	9.8
20.0	115	86.3	180.0	44.7	221.3	14.5	14.0	10.0
25.0	115	81.0	180.0	44.6	222.2	14.5	14.5	10.1
30.0	115	76.2	180.0	43.9	219.3	14.5	14.8	10.1
35.0	115	72.1	180.0	43.4	219.8	14.4	15.2	10.2
40.0	115	68.4	180.0	42.1	216.4	14.2	15.3	10.1
45.0	115	65.1	180.0	42.2	220.5	14.3	15.8	10.3
50.0	115	62.1	180.0	41.7	220.7	14.2	16.1	10.3
55.0	115	59.4	180.0	40.0	217.1	14.0	16.0	10.1
60.0	115	57.0	180.0	39.4	217.3	13.8	16.2	10.1
65.0	115	54.7	180.0	38.7	217.5	13.7	16.4	10.1
70.0	115	52.7	180.0	36.9	213.7	13.4	16.1	9.9
75.0	115	50.8	180.0	36.2	213.8	13.3	16.3	9.9
80.0	115	49.0	180.0	35.5	213.9	13.2	16.4	9.9
85.0	115	47.3	180.0	34.8	214.0	13.0	16.5	9.9
90.0	115	45.7	180.0	32.9	210.2	12.7	16.1	9.6
95.0	115	44.3	180.0	32.2	210.2	12.5	16.2	9.6
100.0	115	42.9	180.0	31.5	210.3	12.4	16.3	9.6
105.0	115	41.6	180.0	30.8	210.3	12.3	16.4	9.6
110.0	115	40.3	180.0	30.2	210.3	12.2	16.4	9.6
115.0	115	39.1	180.0	28.6	209.5	11.8	16.0	9.3
120.0	115	38.0	180.0	27.8	209.5	11.7	16.0	9.3
125.0	115	36.9	180.0	27.0	209.3	11.5	16.0	9.3
130.0	115	35.9	180.0	26.2	206.4	11.4	15.9	9.2
135.0	115	34.9	180.0	25.5	206.4	11.2	16.0	9.2
140.0	115	34.0	180.0	24.9	206.4	11.1	16.0	9.2
145.0	115	33.1	180.0	23.2	205.3	10.7	15.3	8.8

1. Hurricane Camille—August 17, 1969   (Continued)

```
HURRICANE : CAMILLE
Lat.= 29 deg.; Rc= 10 n.mi.;ΔPo= 105 mbs; Vf= 10 knts; Dir.= 0 deg.
```

r N.M.	A0 DEG	Urs KNOTS	Bu DEG	Hs FEET	Bh DEG	Ts SEC.	Tf0 SEC.	Tm SEC.
150.0	115	32.3	180.0	22.5	202.4	10.6	15.2	8.7
155.0	115	31.5	180.0	21.9	202.4	10.4	15.2	8.7
160.0	115	30.7	180.0	21.3	202.3	10.3	15.2	8.7
165.0	115	29.9	180.0	20.6	202.3	10.2	15.2	8.7
170.0	115	29.2	180.0	20.0	202.1	10.0	15.1	8.6
175.0	115	28.5	180.0	19.2	201.8	9.9	14.9	8.5
180.0	115	27.8	180.0	18.5	201.6	9.7	14.7	8.4
185.0	115	27.2	180.0	17.5	198.3	9.4	14.2	8.1
190.0	115	26.6	180.0	16.9	198.2	9.3	14.1	8.1
195.0	115	26.0	180.0	16.4	198.1	9.2	14.1	8.1
200.0	115	25.4	180.0	15.9	198.1	9.0	14.0	8.0
205.0	115	24.8	180.0	15.4	198.0	8.9	13.9	8.0
210.0	115	24.3	180.0	14.8	197.7	8.8	13.7	7.9
215.0	115	23.8	180.0	14.3	197.4	8.6	13.5	7.8
220.0	115	23.3	180.0	13.4	194.2	8.3	12.9	7.4
225.0	115	22.8	180.0	13.0	194.1	8.2	12.8	7.4
230.0	115	22.4	180.0	12.6	194.0	8.1	12.7	7.3
235.0	115	21.9	180.0	12.2	193.9	8.0	12.6	7.3
240.0	115	21.5	180.0	11.8	193.8	7.9	12.5	7.2
245.0	115	21.1	180.0	11.4	193.7	7.7	12.3	7.1
250.0	115	20.7	180.0	11.0	193.4	7.6	12.1	7.0
255.0	115	20.3	180.0	10.6	193.2	7.5	11.9	6.9
260.0	115	20.0	180.0	10.2	193.0	7.3	11.7	6.8
265.0	115	19.6	180.0	9.9	192.7	7.2	11.5	6.7
270.0	115	19.3	180.0	9.4	190.2	7.0	11.1	6.4
275.0	115	18.9	180.0	9.1	190.2	6.9	10.9	6.4
280.0	115	18.6	180.0	8.9	190.1	6.8	10.8	6.3
285.0	115	18.3	180.0	8.6	190.0	6.7	10.7	6.2

1. Hurricane Camille—August 17, 1969   (Continued)

DATE: 5/10/88

HURRICANE : CAMILLE
Lat.= 29 deg.; Rc= 10 n.mi.;ΔPo= 105 mbs; Vf= 10 knts; Dir.= 0 deg.

WIND FIELD , Urs (knots)

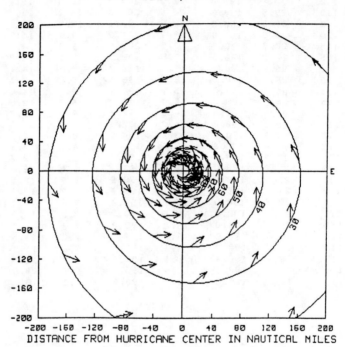

DISTANCE FROM HURRICANE CENTER IN NAUTICAL MILES

1. Hurricane Camille—August 17, 1969   (Continued)

DATE: 5/10/88

HURRICANE : CAMILLE
Lat.= 29 deg.; Rc= 10 n.mi.; ΔPo= 105 mbs; Vf= 10 knts; Dir.= 0 deg.

WAVE FIELD , Hs (feet)

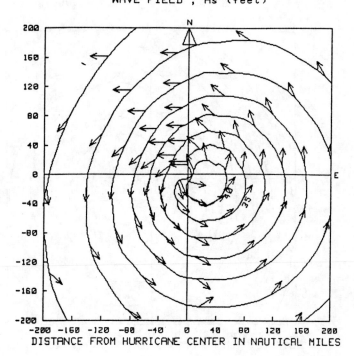

DISTANCE FROM HURRICANE CENTER IN NAUTICAL MILES

1. Hurricane Camille—August 17, 1969 (Continued)

DATE: 5/10/88

HURRICANE : CAMILLE
Lat.= 29 deg.; Rc= 10 n.mi.;ΔPo= 105 mbs; Vf= 10 knts; Dir.= 0 deg.

PERIOD FIELD , Ts (sec.)

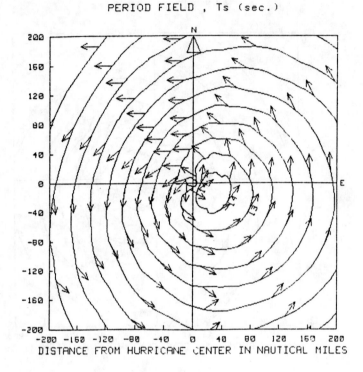

DISTANCE FROM HURRICANE CENTER IN NAUTICAL MILES

1. Hurricane Camille—August 17, 1969   (Continued)

HURRICANE : CAMILLE

Lat.= 29 deg.; Rc= 10 n.mi.;ΔPo= 105 mbs; Vf= 10 knts; Dir.= 0 deg.

X N.M.	t´ HOURS	Urs KNOTS	Bu DEG.	Hs FEET	Bh DEG.	Ts SEC.	Tfθ SEC.	Tm SEC.
-110.0	-11.000	39.7	235.1	26.7	298.8	11.4	14.9	8.8
-105.0	-10.500	41.0	235.1	27.5	300.6	11.6	15.0	8.9
-100.0	-10.000	42.3	235.0	28.4	302.1	11.8	15.0	9.0
-95.0	-9.500	43.7	234.8	29.3	303.4	11.9	15.1	9.1
-90.0	-9.000	45.1	234.7	30.1	304.3	12.1	15.1	9.1
-85.0	-8.500	46.7	234.5	31.0	304.7	12.3	15.1	9.2
-80.0	-8.000	48.3	234.2	31.9	304.6	12.5	15.2	9.3
-75.0	-7.500	50.1	233.9	32.9	303.8	12.7	15.2	9.4
-70.0	-7.000	52.0	233.5	33.8	302.3	12.8	15.2	9.4
-65.0	-6.500	54.1	233.0	34.8	299.9	13.0	15.1	9.5
-60.0	-6.000	56.3	232.4	35.8	296.6	13.2	15.1	9.6
-55.0	-5.500	58.8	231.7	36.9	292.3	13.4	15.1	9.7
-50.0	-5.000	61.5	230.9	38.0	287.8	13.6	15.0	9.7
-45.0	-4.500	64.7	229.9	39.1	285.6	13.7	14.9	9.8
-40.0	-4.000	68.4	228.5	40.1	287.9	13.9	14.7	9.8
-35.0	-3.500	73.0	226.8	41.2	296.8	14.0	14.5	9.9
-30.0	-3.000	77.8	224.6	42.1	300.2	14.1	14.2	9.9
-25.0	-2.500	81.8	221.4	42.8	272.8	14.2	13.9	9.9
-20.0	-2.000	87.7	216.9	43.2	245.4	14.2	13.5	9.8
-15.0	-1.500	91.6	210.1	43.4	242.1	14.2	13.2	9.7
-10.0	-1.000	95.2	199.2	42.9	228.9	14.0	12.7	9.6
-5.0	-.500	95.4	181.5	43.2	212.7	14.1	12.8	9.6
0.0	0.000	95.1	155.9	42.7	188.6	14.0	12.7	9.6
5.0	.500	94.1	130.2	41.1	163.5	13.7	12.4	9.4
10.0	1.000	93.0	112.2	39.5	145.4	13.4	12.1	9.2
15.0	1.500	89.0	101.1	39.1	139.4	13.4	12.3	9.2
20.0	2.000	84.9	94.1	38.4	135.9	13.3	12.5	9.2
25.0	2.500	78.9	89.5	37.5	134.5	13.3	12.8	9.2
30.0	3.000	74.9	86.3	36.5	129.8	13.1	12.9	9.1
35.0	3.500	70.0	84.0	35.2	125.7	12.9	13.1	9.0
40.0	4.000	65.4	82.2	33.9	122.5	12.7	13.2	9.0
45.0	4.500	61.6	80.9	32.6	119.9	12.5	13.2	8.8
50.0	5.000	58.4	79.8	31.3	117.8	12.3	13.2	8.7
55.0	5.500	55.7	79.0	30.1	115.8	12.1	13.2	8.6
60.0	6.000	53.3	78.3	28.9	113.9	11.8	13.2	8.5
65.0	6.500	51.0	77.8	27.8	112.0	11.6	13.1	8.4
70.0	7.000	48.9	77.3	26.8	109.9	11.4	13.0	8.3
75.0	7.500	47.0	76.9	25.8	107.8	11.2	12.9	8.1
80.0	8.000	45.2	76.6	24.8	105.7	11.0	12.8	8.0
85.0	8.500	43.6	76.3	23.9	103.5	10.8	12.7	7.9
90.0	9.000	42.1	76.1	23.0	101.2	10.6	12.6	7.8
95.0	9.500	40.6	76.0	22.1	99.0	10.4	12.5	7.7
100.0	10.000	39.2	75.9	21.2	96.7	10.2	12.4	7.6
105.0	10.500	37.9	75.8	20.4	94.3	10.0	12.2	7.5
110.0	11.000	36.6	75.7	19.6	92.0	9.8	12.1	7.3

1. Hurricane Camille—August 17, 1969   (Continued)

HURRICANE : CAMILLE

Lat.= 29 deg.; Rc= 10 n.mi.;ΔPo= 105 mbs; Vf= 10 knts; Dir.= 0 deg.

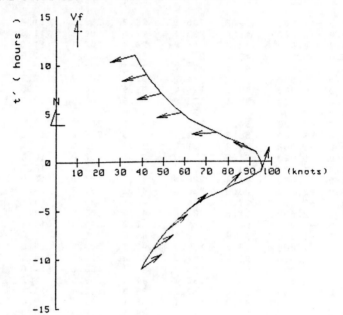

TIME CROSS SECTION THROUGH WIND FIELD (+10.0 N.MILES)

1. Hurricane Camille—August 17, 1969   (Continued)

HURRICANE : CAMILLE

Lat.= 29 deg.; Rc= 10 n.mi.;ΔPo= 105 mbs; Vf= 10 knts; Dir.= 0 deg.

TIME CROSS SECTION THROUGH WAVE FIELD (+10.0 N.MILES)

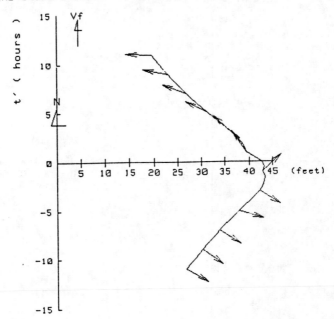

1. Hurricane Camille—August 17, 1969 (Continued)

HURRICANE : CAMILLE

Lat.= 29 deg.; Rc= 10 n.mi.;ΔPo= 105 mbs; Vf= 10 knts; Dir.= 0 deg.

TIME CROSS SECTION THROUGH PERIOD FIELD (+10.0 N.MILES)

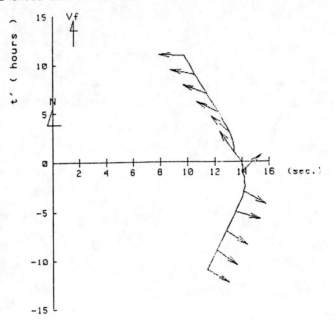

1. Hurricane Camille—August 17, 1969   (Continued)

```
HURRICANE : CAMILLE
Lat.= 29 deg.; Rc= 10 n.mi.;ΔPo= 105 mbs; Vf= 10 knts; Dir.= 0 deg.
```

r	Us	Hs	Tfo	S(fo)	S(max)	G	RHO	A4
n.m.	ft/sec	ft	sec					
5.0	140.4	39.66	12.97	1804	2591	1.44	.8931	2.18

ω rad/s	S(ω) ft^2.s/rad	ω rad/s	S(ω) ft^2.s/rad
.05	0.000	2.05	.038
.10	0.000	2.10	.033
.15	.000	2.15	.028
.20	.000	2.20	.024
.25	.000	2.25	.021
.30	.092	2.30	.018
.35	21.536	2.35	.016
.40	181.897	2.40	.014
.45	376.700	2.45	.012
.50	410.792	2.50	.010
.55	330.077	2.55	.009
.60	229.094	2.60	.008
.65	148.698	2.65	.007
.70	94.054	2.70	.006
.75	59.254	2.75	.006
.80	37.616	2.80	.005
.85	24.210	2.85	.005
.90	15.843	2.90	.004
.95	10.555	2.95	.004
1.00	7.160	3.00	.003
1.05	4.944	3.05	.003
1.10	3.473	3.10	.003
1.15	2.479	3.15	.003
1.20	1.797	3.20	.002
1.25	1.322	3.25	.002
1.30	.985	3.30	.002
1.35	.744	3.35	.002
1.40	.568	3.40	.002
1.45	.439	3.45	.001
1.50	.343	3.50	.001
1.55	.270	3.55	.001
1.60	.215	3.60	.001
1.65	.173	3.65	.001
1.70	.140	3.70	.001
1.75	.114	3.75	.001
1.80	.094	3.80	.001
1.85	.077	3.85	.001
1.90	.064	3.90	.001
1.95	.054	3.95	.001
2.00	.045	4.00	.001

1. Hurricane Camille—August 17, 1969   (Continued)

HURRICANE : CAMILLE
Lat.= 29 deg.; Rc= 10 n.mi.;ΔPo= 105 mbs; Vf= 10 knts; Dir.= 0 deg.

r	Us	Hs	Tfo	S(fo)	S(max)	G	RHO	A4
n.m.	ft/sec	ft	sec					
10.0	161.1	43.24	12.81	2118	3080	1.45	.9275	2.21

w rad/s	S(w) ft^2.s/rad	w rad/s	S(w) ft^2.s/rad
.05	0.000	2.05	.034
.10	0.000	2.10	.029
.15	0.000	2.15	.025
.20	.000	2.20	.021
.25	.000	2.25	.018
.30	.052	2.30	.015
.35	18.318	2.35	.013
.40	187.842	2.40	.011
.45	429.366	2.45	.010
.50	493.141	2.50	.009
.55	407.019	2.55	.008
.60	286.056	2.60	.007
.65	186.386	2.65	.006
.70	117.695	2.70	.005
.75	73.753	2.75	.005
.80	46.454	2.80	.004
.85	29.610	2.85	.004
.90	19.166	2.90	.003
.95	12.618	2.95	.003
1.00	8.452	3.00	.003
1.05	5.760	3.05	.002
1.10	3.991	3.10	.002
1.15	2.810	3.15	.002
1.20	2.009	3.20	.002
1.25	1.457	3.25	.002
1.30	1.071	3.30	.001
1.35	.797	3.35	.001
1.40	.601	3.40	.001
1.45	.458	3.45	.001
1.50	.352	3.50	.001
1.55	.274	3.55	.001
1.60	.215	3.60	.001
1.65	.171	3.65	.001
1.70	.136	3.70	.001
1.75	.110	3.75	.001
1.80	.089	3.80	.001
1.85	.073	3.85	.001
1.90	.060	3.90	.001
1.95	.049	3.95	.000
2.00	.041	4.00	.000

1. Hurricane Camille—August 17, 1969   (Continued)

```
HURRICANE : CAMILLE
Lat.= 29 deg.; Rc= 10 n.mi.;ΔPo= 105 mbs; Vf= 10 knts; Dir.= 0 deg.
```

r	Us	Hs	Tfo	S(fo)	S(max)	G	RHO	A4
n.m.	ft/sec	ft	sec					
15.0	154.9	44.34	13.38	2326	3361	1.45	.9104	2.19

w	S(w)	w	S(w)
rad/s	ft^2.s/rad	rad/s	ft^2.s/rad
.05	0.000	2.05	.034
.10	0.000	2.10	.029
.15	.000	2.15	.024
.20	.000	2.20	.021
.25	.000	2.25	.018
.30	.483	2.30	.016
.35	52.944	2.35	.013
.40	308.601	2.40	.012
.45	523.803	2.45	.010
.50	509.030	2.50	.009
.55	380.887	2.55	.008
.60	252.313	2.60	.007
.65	158.582	2.65	.006
.70	97.994	2.70	.005
.75	60.653	2.75	.005
.80	37.969	2.80	.004
.85	24.156	2.85	.004
.90	15.654	2.90	.003
.95	10.339	2.95	.003
1.00	6.960	3.00	.003
1.05	4.772	3.05	.003
1.10	3.329	3.10	.002
1.15	2.362	3.15	.002
1.20	1.702	3.20	.002
1.25	1.245	3.25	.002
1.30	.923	3.30	.002
1.35	.693	3.35	.001
1.40	.527	3.40	.001
1.45	.405	3.45	.001
1.50	.315	3.50	.001
1.55	.247	3.55	.001
1.60	.196	3.60	.001
1.65	.156	3.65	.001
1.70	.126	3.70	.001
1.75	.102	3.75	.001
1.80	.084	3.80	.001
1.85	.069	3.85	.001
1.90	.057	3.90	.001
1.95	.048	3.95	.001
2.00	.040	4.00	.001

1. Hurricane Camille—August 17, 1969   (Continued)

```
HURRICANE : CAMILLE
Lat.= 29 deg.; Rc= 10 n.mi.;ΔPo= 105 mbs; Vf= 10 knts; Dir.= 0 deg.
```

r	Us	Hs	Tfo	S(fo)	S(max)	G	RHO	A4
n.m.	ft/sec	ft	sec					
20.0	145.6	44.65	13.95	2459	3519	1.43	.8829	2.13

w rad/s	S(w) ft^2.s/rad	w rad/s	S(w) ft^2.s/rad
.05	0.000	2.05	.036
.10	0.000	2.10	.031
.15	.000	2.15	.026
.20	.000	2.20	.023
.25	.000	2.25	.020
.30	2.822	2.30	.017
.35	116.874	2.35	.015
.40	426.632	2.40	.013
.45	567.292	2.45	.012
.50	481.877	2.50	.010
.55	334.004	2.55	.009
.60	211.790	2.60	.008
.65	129.935	2.65	.007
.70	79.337	2.70	.006
.75	48.906	2.75	.006
.80	30.652	2.80	.005
.85	19.595	2.85	.005
.90	12.791	2.90	.004
.95	8.526	2.95	.004
1.00	5.799	3.00	.003
1.05	4.020	3.05	.003
1.10	2.839	3.10	.003
1.15	2.039	3.15	.003
1.20	1.487	3.20	.002
1.25	1.102	3.25	.002
1.30	.827	3.30	.002
1.35	.629	3.35	.002
1.40	.484	3.40	.002
1.45	.377	3.45	.002
1.50	.297	3.50	.001
1.55	.236	3.55	.001
1.60	.189	3.60	.001
1.65	.153	3.65	.001
1.70	.124	3.70	.001
1.75	.102	3.75	.001
1.80	.084	3.80	.001
1.85	.070	3.85	.001
1.90	.059	3.90	.001
1.95	.050	3.95	.001
2.00	.042	4.00	.001

1. Hurricane Camille—August 17, 1969   (Continued)

HURRICANE : CAMILLE
Lat.= 29 deg.; Rc= 10 n.mi.;ΔPo= 105 mbs; Vf= 10 knts; Dir.= 0 deg.

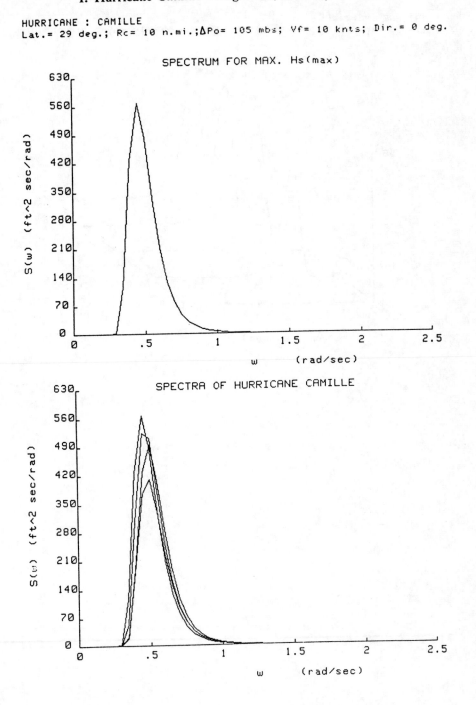

1. Hurricane Camille—August 17, 1969   (Continued)

HURRICANE : CAMILLE
Lat.= 29 deg.; Rc= 10 n.mi.;ΔPo= 105 mbs; Vf= 10 knts; Dir.= 0 deg.

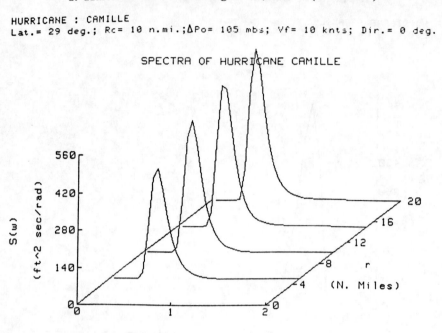

SPECTRA OF HURRICANE CAMILLE

2. Hurricane Eloise—1200 noon, September 22, 1975

DATE: 5/11/88

HURRICANE : ELOISE
Lat.= 27.5 deg.; Rc= 15.5 n.mi.;ΔPo= 39 mbs; Vf= 12.5 knts; Dir.= 45 deg.

r N.M.	Aθ DEG	Urs KNOTS	Bu DEG	Hs FEET	Bh DEG	Ts SEC.	Tfθ SEC.	Tm SEC.
5.0	160	41.1	225.0	28.6	238.2	11.8	15.5	9.1
10.0	160	58.6	225.0	28.8	245.5	11.8	12.4	8.3
15.0	160	61.1	225.0	30.1	251.0	12.0	12.5	8.5
20.0	160	59.8	225.0	30.9	255.6	12.2	12.9	8.6
25.0	160	57.6	225.0	31.3	259.7	12.3	13.4	8.8
30.0	160	55.2	225.0	31.3	257.3	12.3	13.7	8.9
35.0	160	52.8	225.0	31.6	260.9	12.4	14.2	9.0
40.0	160	50.6	225.0	31.1	258.1	12.3	14.4	9.0
45.0	160	48.5	225.0	30.8	258.4	12.3	14.7	9.1
50.0	160	46.5	225.0	30.5	258.6	12.2	15.0	9.1
55.0	160	44.7	225.0	29.4	255.4	12.0	14.9	9.0
60.0	160	43.0	225.0	29.0	255.5	11.9	15.1	9.1
65.0	160	41.5	225.0	28.6	255.6	11.8	15.3	9.1
70.0	160	40.0	225.0	28.1	255.6	11.7	15.5	9.1
75.0	160	38.6	225.0	26.7	252.2	11.4	15.2	8.9
80.0	160	37.4	225.0	26.1	252.2	11.3	15.4	8.9
85.0	160	36.1	225.0	25.6	252.2	11.2	15.5	9.0
90.0	160	35.0	225.0	24.9	252.2	11.1	15.6	9.0
95.0	160	33.9	225.0	24.2	252.0	10.9	15.6	9.0
100.0	160	32.9	225.0	22.9	248.7	10.6	15.2	8.7
105.0	160	31.9	225.0	22.3	248.6	10.5	15.3	8.7
110.0	160	31.0	225.0	21.1	248.0	10.3	14.9	8.5
115.0	160	30.1	225.0	20.4	247.7	10.1	14.9	8.5
120.0	160	29.3	225.0	19.7	247.5	9.9	14.8	8.5
125.0	160	28.5	225.0	19.0	244.9	9.8	14.7	8.4
130.0	160	27.7	225.0	18.4	244.9	9.7	14.7	8.4
135.0	160	27.0	225.0	17.8	244.8	9.6	14.7	8.5
140.0	160	26.3	225.0	17.2	244.5	9.4	14.6	8.4
145.0	160	25.6	225.0	16.1	241.3	9.1	13.9	8.0

(Continued)

2. Hurricane Eloise—1200 noon, September 22, 1975   (Continued)

DATE: 5/11/88

HURRICANE : ELOISE
Lat.= 27.5 deg.; Rc= 15.5 n.mi.;ΔPo= 39 mbs; Vf= 12.5 knts; Dir.= 45 deg

r N.M.	A0 DEG	Urs KNOTS	Bu DEG	Hs FEET	Bh DEG	Ts SEC.	Tf0 SEC.	Tm SEC.
150.0	160	25.0	225.0	15.5	241.2	8.9	13.9	8.0
155.0	160	24.4	225.0	15.0	241.1	8.8	13.8	8.0
160.0	160	23.8	225.0	14.5	241.0	8.7	13.8	8.0
165.0	160	23.3	225.0	13.9	240.8	8.6	13.7	8.0
170.0	160	22.8	225.0	13.4	240.6	8.5	13.6	8.0
175.0	160	22.2	225.0	12.6	237.5	8.1	12.8	7.4
180.0	160	21.8	225.0	12.1	237.4	8.0	12.7	7.4
185.0	160	21.3	225.0	11.7	237.3	7.9	12.6	7.4
190.0	160	20.8	225.0	11.3	237.2	7.8	12.5	7.4
195.0	160	20.4	225.0	10.9	237.1	7.7	12.4	7.3
200.0	160	20.0	225.0	10.5	236.9	7.5	12.2	7.3
205.0	160	19.6	225.0	10.1	236.6	7.4	12.0	7.1
210.0	160	19.2	225.0	9.7	236.4	7.3	11.8	7.0
215.0	160	18.9	225.0	9.2	233.9	7.0	11.3	6.6
220.0	160	18.5	225.0	8.9	233.8	6.9	11.1	6.5
225.0	160	18.2	225.0	8.6	233.7	6.8	11.0	6.5
230.0	160	17.9	225.0	8.3	233.5	6.7	10.8	6.4
235.0	160	17.6	225.0	8.1	233.4	6.6	10.7	6.3
240.0	160	17.3	225.0	7.8	233.1	6.5	10.4	6.2
245.0	160	17.0	225.0	7.5	232.9	6.3	10.2	6.0
250.0	160	16.7	225.0	7.3	232.7	6.2	10.0	5.9
255.0	160	16.5	225.0	7.0	232.5	6.1	9.8	5.8
260.0	160	16.2	225.0	6.8	232.3	6.0	9.6	5.6
265.0	160	16.0	225.0	6.6	232.1	5.9	9.4	5.5
270.0	160	15.7	225.0	6.4	232.0	5.8	9.3	5.4
275.0	160	15.5	225.0	6.2	231.8	5.7	9.1	5.3
280.0	160	15.3	225.0	6.0	230.4	5.6	8.9	5.2
285.0	160	15.1	225.0	5.8	230.3	5.5	8.7	5.1

2. Hurricane Eloise—1200 noon, September 22, 1975   (Continued)

DATE: 5/11/88

HURRICANE : ELOISE
Lat.= 27.5 deg.; Rc= 15.5 n.mi.;ΔPo= 39 mbs; Vf= 12.5 knts; Dir.= 45 deg.

WIND FIELD , Urs (knots)

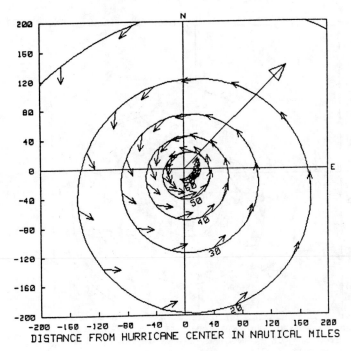

2. Hurricane Eloise—1200 noon, September 22, 1975   (Continued)

DATE: 5/11/88

HURRICANE : ELOISE
Lat.= 27.5 deg.; Rc= 15.5 n.mi.;ΔPo= 39 mbs; Vf= 12.5 knts; Dir.= 45 deg.

WAVE FIELD , Hs (feet)

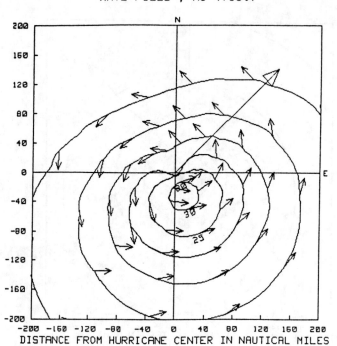

DISTANCE FROM HURRICANE CENTER IN NAUTICAL MILES

2. Hurricane Eloise—1200 noon, September 22, 1975   (Continued)

DATE: 5/11/88

HURRICANE : ELOISE
Lat.= 27.5 deg.; Rc= 15.5 n.mi.;ΔPo= 39 mbs; Vf= 12.5 knts; Dir.= 45 deg.

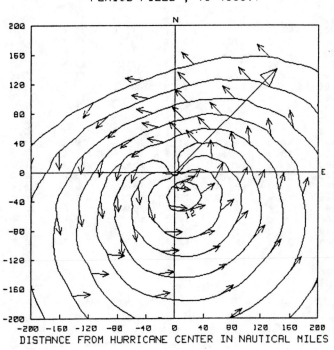

PERIOD FIELD , Ts (sec.)

DISTANCE FROM HURRICANE CENTER IN NAUTICAL MILES

2. Hurricane Eloise—1200 noon, September 22, 1975   (Continued)

HURRICANE : ELOISE

Lat.= 27.5 deg.; Rc= 15.5 n.mi.;ΔPo= 35 mbs; Vf= 12.5 knts; Dir.= 45 deg.

X N.M.	t´ HOURS	Urs KNOTS	Bu DEG.	Hs FEET	Bh DEG.	Ts SEC.	Tfθ SEC.	Tm SEC.
-55.0	-4.400	43.0	279.4	25.2	349.8	11.1	13.4	8.2
-50.0	-4.000	44.0	279.2	25.9	1.4	11.2	13.5	8.3
-45.0	-3.600	45.4	278.8	26.5	9.7	11.4	13.5	8.4
-40.0	-3.200	47.4	278.3	27.0	12.0	11.5	13.3	8.4
-35.0	-2.800	50.3	277.5	27.5	6.2	11.6	13.1	8.4
-30.0	-2.400	54.2	276.5	27.9	349.8	11.6	12.7	8.3
-25.0	-2.000	59.1	275.1	28.1	321.4	11.6	12.0	8.2
-20.0	-1.600	60.6	272.5	27.8	292.7	11.5	11.8	8.1
-15.0	-1.200	56.0	268.1	26.8	281.0	11.3	12.1	8.1
-10.0	-.800	51.4	260.1	27.1	273.1	11.4	13.0	8.3
-5.0	-.400	40.8	242.8	28.1	253.7	11.7	15.3	9.0
0.0	0.000	40.7	202.8	27.8	218.3	11.7	15.2	9.0
5.0	.400	38.3	161.6	22.6	178.9	10.5	13.3	8.0
10.0	.800	48.0	142.3	21.1	161.6	10.1	11.1	7.2
15.0	1.200	52.3	133.6	20.9	152.6	10.0	10.3	7.0
20.0	1.600	56.8	128.6	22.0	154.2	10.2	10.1	7.1
25.0	2.000	55.3	125.9	22.0	157.1	10.2	10.3	7.1
30.0	2.400	50.4	124.6	21.2	158.3	10.1	10.6	7.1
35.0	2.800	46.4	123.6	20.5	157.2	9.9	10.8	7.1
40.0	3.200	43.6	122.9	19.7	154.2	9.8	10.9	7.0
45.0	3.600	41.6	122.3	19.0	149.6	9.6	10.9	7.0
50.0	4.000	40.2	121.9	18.4	144.0	9.4	10.8	6.9
55.0	4.400	39.1	121.6	17.7	137.8	9.3	10.7	6.7

2. Hurricane Eloise—1200 noon, September 22, 1975   (Continued)

HURRICANE : ELOISE

Lat.= 27.5 deg.; Rc= 15.5 n.mi.;ΔPo= 39 mbs; Vf= 12.5 knts; Dir.= 45 deg.

TIME CROSS SECTION THROUGH WIND FIELD (+5.0 N.MILES)

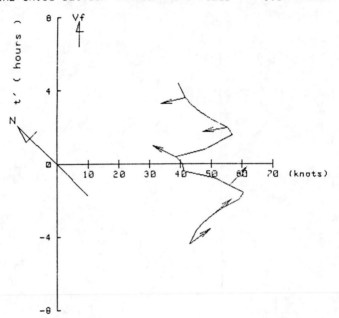

2. Hurricane Eloise—1200 noon, September 22, 1975   (Continued)

HURRICANE : ELOISE

Lat.= 27.5 deg.; Rc= 15.5 n.mi.;ΔPo= 39 mbs; Vf= 12.5 knts; Dir.= 45 deg.

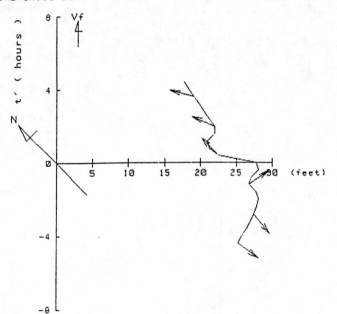

TIME CROSS SECTION THROUGH WAVE FIELD (+5.0 N.MILES)

2. Hurricane Eloise—1200 noon, September 22, 1975   (Continued)

HURRICANE : ELOISE

Lat.= 27.5 deg.; Rc= 15.5 n.mi.;ΔPo= 39 mbs; Vf= 12.5 knts; Dir.= 45 deg.

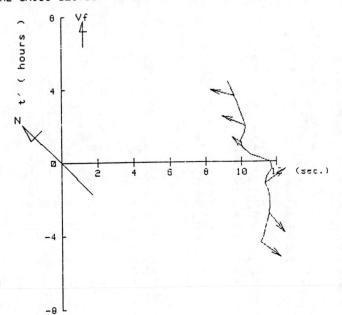

TIME CROSS SECTION THROUGH PERIOD FIELD (+5.0 N.MILES)

2. Hurricane Eloise—1200 noon, September 22, 1975   (Continued)

```
HURRICANE : ELOISE

Lat.= 27.5 deg.; Rc= 15.5 n.mi.;ΔPo= 39 mbs; Vf= 12.5 knts; Dir.= 45 deg.
```

X N.M.	t´ HOURS	Urs KNOTS	Bu DEG.	Hs FEET	Bh DEG.	Ts SEC.	Tf0 SEC.	Tm SEC.
-110.0	-8.800	29.7	277.0	17.8	344.9	9.3	13.0	7.5
-105.0	-8.400	30.7	277.0	18.4	339.5	9.5	13.1	7.6
-100.0	-8.000	31.7	277.0	19.1	334.5	9.7	13.2	7.7
-95.0	-7.600	32.7	277.0	19.7	330.3	9.8	13.3	7.8
-90.0	-7.200	33.7	276.9	20.4	326.9	10.0	13.3	7.8
-85.0	-6.800	34.8	276.8	21.1	324.6	10.2	13.4	7.9
-80.0	-6.400	36.0	276.7	21.8	323.8	10.3	13.5	8.0
-75.0	-6.000	37.3	276.4	22.6	324.5	10.5	13.5	8.0
-70.0	-5.600	38.7	276.1	23.4	327.1	10.7	13.6	8.1
-65.0	-5.200	40.1	275.7	24.2	331.8	10.9	13.6	9.2
-60.0	-4.800	41.8	275.3	25.0	338.8	11.0	13.6	8.3
-55.0	-4.400	43.5	274.7	25.9	348.3	11.2	13.7	8.4
-50.0	-4.000	45.4	274.0	26.8	358.1	11.4	13.6	8.4
-45.0	-3.600	47.5	273.0	27.6	2.2	11.6	13.6	8.5
-40.0	-3.200	49.9	271.8	28.3	354.6	11.7	13.4	8.5
-35.0	-2.800	52.5	270.2	28.7	329.5	11.8	13.2	8.5
-30.0	-2.400	55.2	268.0	28.9	297.3	11.8	12.9	8.4
-25.0	-2.000	57.4	265.0	29.2	284.0	11.9	12.7	8.4
-20.0	-1.600	59.5	260.6	29.0	232.5	11.8	12.3	8.3
-15.0	-1.200	60.3	254.0	29.0	275.2	11.8	12.2	8.3
-10.0	-.800	58.3	243.4	28.4	261.9	11.7	12.3	8.2
-5.0	-.400	58.6	226.4	28.8	246.8	11.8	12.4	8.3
0.0	0.000	58.2	201.9	28.2	224.4	11.6	12.2	8.2
5.0	.400	56.9	177.1	26.1	200.7	11.2	11.7	7.9
10.0	.800	55.7	159.5	24.2	183.1	10.8	11.1	7.6
15.0	1.200	57.2	148.3	24.0	176.5	10.7	10.8	7.5
20.0	1.600	56.1	141.3	23.5	172.3	10.6	10.8	7.4
25.0	2.000	53.8	136.8	23.1	172.6	10.5	10.9	7.4
30.0	2.400	51.5	133.6	22.5	171.3	10.4	11.0	7.4
35.0	2.800	48.8	131.4	21.9	169.4	10.3	11.1	7.3
40.0	3.200	46.2	129.7	21.2	166.6	10.1	11.2	7.3
45.0	3.600	43.8	128.5	20.4	162.9	9.9	11.2	7.2
50.0	4.000	41.7	127.5	19.4	158.9	9.7	11.1	7.0
55.0	4.400	39.7	126.8	18.5	154.8	9.5	11.0	6.9
60.0	4.800	38.0	126.3	17.5	151.1	9.2	10.8	6.8
65.0	5.200	36.3	125.8	16.7	148.0	9.0	10.7	6.6
70.0	5.600	34.8	125.4	15.9	145.3	8.8	10.5	6.5
75.0	6.000	33.5	125.2	15.1	143.1	8.6	10.4	6.4
80.0	6.400	32.2	125.0	14.4	141.2	8.4	10.2	6.3
85.0	6.800	31.0	124.9	13.8	139.7	8.2	10.1	6.1
90.0	7.200	29.9	124.8	13.1	138.5	8.0	9.9	6.0
95.0	7.600	28.8	124.8	12.5	137.5	7.8	9.8	5.9
100.0	8.000	27.8	124.8	11.9	136.7	7.6	9.6	5.8
105.0	8.400	26.9	124.9	11.4	136.0	7.4	9.5	5.7
110.0	8.800	25.9	125.0	10.8	135.5	7.3	9.3	5.6

2. Hurricane Eloise—1200 noon, September 22, 1975   (Continued)

HURRICANE : ELOISE

Lat.= 27.5 deg.; Rc= 15.5 n.mi.;ΔPo= 39 mbs; Vf= 12.5 knts; Dir.= 45 deg.

TIME CROSS SECTION THROUGH WIND FIELD (+10.0 N.MILES)

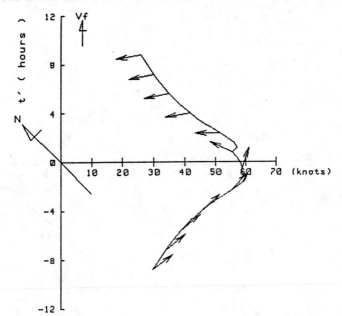

2. Hurricane Eloise—1200 noon, September 22, 1975 (Continued)

HURRICANE : ELOISE

Lat.= 27.5 deg.; Rc= 15.5 n.mi.;ΔPo= 39 mbs; Vf= 12.5 knts; Dir.= 45 deg.

TIME CROSS SECTION THROUGH WAVE FIELD (+10.0 N.MILES)

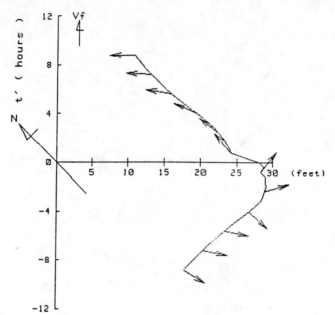

2. Hurricane Eloise—1200 noon, September 22, 1975   (Continued)

HURRICANE : ELOISE

Lat.= 27.5 deg.; Rc= 15.5 n.mi.;ΔPo= 39 mbs; Vf= 12.5 knts; Dir.= 45 deg.

TIME CROSS SECTION THROUGH PERIOD FIELD (+10.0 N.MILES)

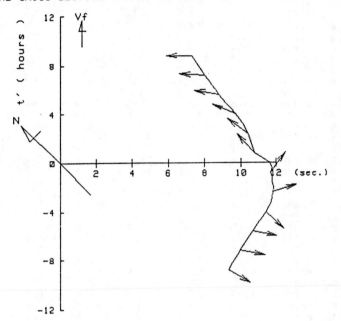

2. Hurricane Eloise—1200 noon, September 22, 1975   (Continued)

```
HURRICANE : ELOISE
Lat.= 27.5 deg.; Rc= 15.5 n.mi.;ΔPo= 39 mbs; Vf= 12.5 knts; Dir.= 45 deg.
```

X N.M.	t' HOURS	Urs KNOTS	Bu DEG.	Hs FEET	Bh DEG.	Ts SEC.	Tfθ SEC.	Tm SEC.
-170.0	-13.600	21.0	273.9	10.9	276.6	7.5	11.6	6.7
-165.0	-13.200	21.7	274.0	11.5	288.5	7.7	11.8	6.8
-160.0	-12.800	22.3	274.1	12.1	300.1	7.8	12.0	6.9
-155.0	-12.400	23.0	274.3	12.7	311.4	8.0	12.1	7.0
-150.0	-12.000	23.7	274.4	13.3	322.2	8.2	12.3	7.1
-145.0	-11.600	24.4	274.5	13.9	332.4	8.3	12.5	7.2
-140.0	-11.200	25.1	274.6	14.5	341.7	8.5	12.6	7.2
-135.0	-10.800	25.8	274.6	15.1	350.1	8.7	12.8	7.3
-130.0	-10.400	26.6	274.7	15.8	357.4	8.8	12.9	7.4
-125.0	-10.000	27.3	274.7	16.4	3.4	9.0	13.1	7.5
-120.0	-9.600	28.1	274.7	17.0	8.0	9.2	13.2	7.6
-115.0	-9.200	28.9	274.7	17.7	11.1	9.3	13.4	7.7
-110.0	-8.800	29.7	274.6	18.3	12.4	9.5	13.5	7.8
-105.0	-8.400	30.6	274.5	19.0	11.9	9.7	13.6	7.8
-100.0	-8.000	31.5	274.3	19.7	9.3	9.8	13.7	7.9
-95.0	-7.600	32.4	274.1	20.4	4.6	10.0	13.8	8.0
-90.0	-7.200	33.4	273.9	21.1	357.6	10.2	13.9	8.1
-85.0	-6.800	34.4	273.6	21.8	348.1	10.3	13.9	8.1
-80.0	-6.400	35.4	273.3	22.5	336.2	10.5	14.0	8.2
-75.0	-6.000	36.6	272.9	23.3	323.0	10.7	14.0	8.3
-70.0	-5.600	37.9	272.3	24.0	309.8	10.8	14.0	8.3
-65.0	-5.200	39.5	271.7	24.8	298.0	11.0	14.0	8.4
-60.0	-4.800	41.4	271.0	25.6	288.8	11.2	13.9	8.4
-55.0	-4.400	43.7	270.1	26.4	283.6	11.3	13.8	8.5
-50.0	-4.000	46.2	269.0	27.2	282.6	11.5	13.7	8.5
-45.0	-3.600	48.3	267.5	27.9	283.9	11.7	13.6	8.5
-40.0	-3.200	49.5	265.7	28.7	285.1	11.8	13.7	8.6
-35.0	-2.800	50.3	263.3	29.4	285.0	12.0	13.8	8.7
-30.0	-2.400	53.8	260.3	29.7	284.0	12.0	13.4	8.6
-25.0	-2.000	56.9	256.4	30.0	282.8	12.0	13.0	8.6
-20.0	-1.600	58.0	251.0	30.2	278.0	12.1	12.9	8.6
-15.0	-1.200	59.6	243.5	30.4	271.0	12.1	12.8	8.6
-10.0	-.800	61.0	233.0	30.1	258.2	12.0	12.5	8.5
-5.0	-.400	61.1	218.9	30.1	245.6	12.0	12.5	8.5
0.0	0.000	60.7	201.9	29.4	230.0	11.9	12.3	8.4
5.0	.400	59.9	184.6	28.2	213.8	11.6	12.0	8.2
10.0	.800	59.0	170.2	26.7	199.8	11.3	11.6	7.9
15.0	1.200	56.9	159.4	26.0	194.0	11.2	11.6	7.9
20.0	1.600	55.0	151.6	25.0	188.6	11.0	11.5	7.7
25.0	2.000	53.7	145.9	24.4	184.9	10.8	11.4	7.6
30.0	2.400	50.4	141.9	23.5	181.3	10.6	11.5	7.6
35.0	2.800	46.8	138.9	22.6	178.4	10.5	11.7	7.5
40.0	3.200	45.9	136.4	21.9	172.7	10.3	11.5	7.4
45.0	3.600	44.7	134.4	21.0	167.9	10.1	11.3	7.3
50.0	4.000	42.5	133.0	20.1	164.7	9.9	11.3	7.2
55.0	4.400	40.0	131.9	19.1	162.5	9.6	11.2	7.0
60.0	4.800	37.7	131.0	18.2	160.5	9.4	11.2	6.9
65.0	5.200	35.8	130.2	17.3	153.4	9.2	11.1	6.8

2. Hurricane Eloise—1200 noon, September 22, 1975   (Continued)

HURRICANE : ELOISE

X N.M.	t' HOURS	Urs KNOTS	Bu DEG.	Hs FEET	Bh DEG.	Ts SEC.	Tf0 SEC.	Tm SEC.
70.0	5.600	34.2	129.6	16.5	156.3	9.0	11.0	6.7
75.0	6.000	32.9	129.2	15.7	154.3	8.8	10.8	6.6
80.0	6.400	31.7	128.8	15.0	152.4	8.6	10.7	6.5
85.0	6.800	30.6	128.5	14.3	150.6	8.4	10.5	6.3
90.0	7.200	29.6	128.2	13.7	148.9	8.2	10.4	6.2
95.0	7.600	28.6	128.0	13.1	147.4	8.0	10.2	6.1
100.0	8.000	27.7	127.9	12.5	146.0	7.8	10.0	6.0
105.0	8.400	26.8	127.8	11.9	144.7	7.6	9.9	5.9
110.0	8.800	26.0	127.8	11.3	143.5	7.4	9.7	5.7
115.0	9.200	25.1	127.8	10.8	142.4	7.2	9.5	5.6
120.0	9.600	24.3	127.9	10.3	141.5	7.1	9.3	5.5
125.0	10.000	23.5	127.9	9.8	140.6	6.9	9.2	5.4
130.0	10.400	22.8	128.1	9.3	139.8	6.7	9.0	5.3
135.0	10.800	22.0	128.2	8.9	139.0	6.5	8.8	5.1
140.0	11.200	21.3	128.4	8.4	138.4	6.4	8.6	5.0
145.0	11.600	20.6	128.6	8.0	137.7	6.2	8.4	4.9
150.0	12.000	19.9	128.8	7.6	137.2	6.0	8.2	4.8
155.0	12.400	19.3	129.0	7.1	136.6	5.9	8.0	4.7
160.0	12.800	18.6	129.3	6.7	136.1	5.7	7.8	4.6
165.0	13.200	17.9	129.5	6.3	135.6	5.5	7.7	4.4
170.0	13.600	17.3	129.8	5.9	135.1	5.4	7.5	4.3

2. Hurricane Eloise—1200 noon, September 22, 1975 (Continued)

HURRICANE : ELOISE

Lat.= 27.5 deg.; Rc= 15.5 n.mi.;ΔPo= 39 mbs; Vf= 12.5 knts; Dir.= 45 deg.

TIME CROSS SECTION THROUGH WIND FIELD (+15.0 N.MILES)

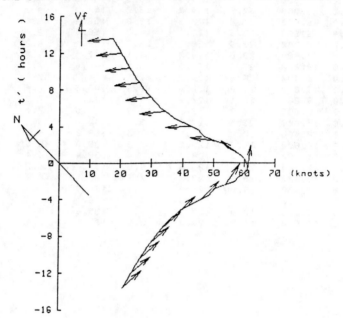

2. Hurricane Eloise—1200 noon, September 22, 1975   (Continued)

HURRICANE : ELOISE

Lat.= 27.5 deg.; Rc= 15.5 n.mi.;ΔPo= 39 mbs; Vf= 12.5 knts; Dir.= 45 deg.

TIME CROSS SECTION THROUGH WAVE FIELD (+15.0 N.MILES)

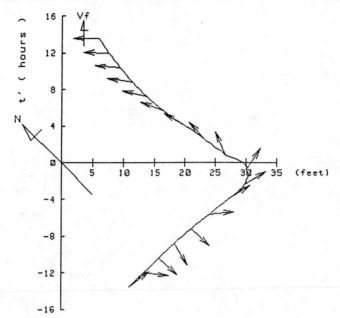

2. Hurricane Eloise—1200 noon, September 22, 1975   (Continued)

HURRICANE : ELOISE

Lat.= 27.5 deg.; Rc= 15.5 n.mi.;ΔPo= 39 mbs; Vf= 12.5 knts; Dir.= 45 deg.

TIME CROSS SECTION THROUGH PERIOD FIELD (+15.0 N.MILES)

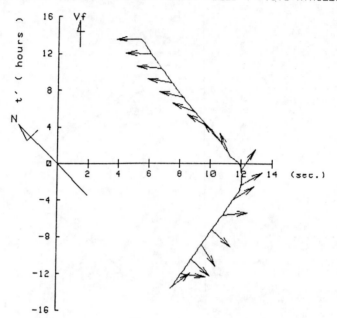

2. Hurricane Eloise—1200 noon, September 22, 1975   (Continued)

HURRICANE : ELOISE

Lat.= 27.5 deg.; Rc= 15.5 n.mi.;ΔPo= 39 mbs; Vf= 12.5 knts; Dir.= 45 deg.

X N.M.	t' HOURS	Urs KNOTS	Bu DEG.	Hs FEET	Bh DEG.	Ts SEC.	Tf0 SEC.	Tm SEC.
-225.0	-18.000	16.6	270.8	7.0	266.4	6.0	9.4	5.4
-220.0	-17.600	17.0	271.0	7.3	267.0	6.1	9.6	5.5
-215.0	-17.200	17.4	271.2	7.6	267.5	6.3	9.8	5.6
-210.0	-16.800	17.7	271.4	7.9	268.1	6.4	10.0	5.7
-205.0	-16.400	18.1	271.5	8.3	268.7	6.5	10.1	5.8
-200.0	-16.000	18.5	271.7	8.6	269.3	6.6	10.3	5.9
-195.0	-15.600	18.9	271.8	9.0	269.8	6.8	10.5	6.0
-190.0	-15.200	19.3	272.0	9.3	270.4	6.9	10.7	6.1
-185.0	-14.800	19.7	272.1	9.7	270.9	7.0	10.9	6.2
-180.0	-14.400	20.2	272.3	10.1	271.5	7.2	11.0	6.3
-175.0	-14.000	20.6	272.4	10.5	272.0	7.3	11.2	6.4
-170.0	-13.600	21.1	272.5	10.9	272.6	7.4	11.4	6.5
-165.0	-13.200	21.6	272.5	11.3	273.1	7.6	11.5	6.6
-160.0	-12.800	22.1	272.6	11.8	273.7	7.7	11.7	6.7
-155.0	-12.400	22.7	272.7	12.2	274.2	7.9	11.9	6.8
-150.0	-12.000	23.2	272.7	12.7	274.7	8.0	12.0	6.9
-145.0	-11.600	23.8	272.7	13.3	275.2	8.2	12.2	7.0
-140.0	-11.200	24.5	272.7	13.8	275.7	8.3	12.4	7.1
-135.0	-10.800	25.1	272.7	14.4	276.2	8.5	12.5	7.2
-130.0	-10.400	25.8	272.6	15.0	276.7	8.6	12.7	7.3
-125.0	-10.000	26.6	272.5	15.6	277.2	8.8	12.8	7.4
-120.0	-9.600	27.3	272.4	16.2	277.6	9.0	13.0	7.4
-115.0	-9.200	28.1	272.3	16.9	278.1	9.2	13.1	7.5
-110.0	-8.800	29.0	272.2	17.7	278.5	9.3	13.3	7.6
-105.0	-8.400	29.9	272.0	18.4	278.9	9.5	13.4	7.7
-100.0	-8.000	30.8	271.7	19.2	279.4	9.7	13.6	7.8
-95.0	-7.600	31.9	271.4	20.0	279.8	9.9	13.7	7.9
-90.0	-7.200	33.0	271.1	20.8	280.2	10.1	13.8	8.0
-85.0	-6.800	34.2	270.6	21.7	280.6	10.3	13.9	8.1
-80.0	-6.400	35.6	270.1	22.5	281.1	10.5	14.0	8.2
-75.0	-6.000	37.0	269.5	23.4	281.5	10.7	14.0	8.3
-70.0	-5.600	38.6	268.8	24.3	282.0	10.9	14.0	8.3
-65.0	-5.200	40.3	268.0	25.1	282.3	11.1	14.0	8.4
-60.0	-4.800	41.9	266.9	26.0	282.6	11.3	14.0	8.5
-55.0	-4.400	43.5	265.7	26.8	282.7	11.4	14.1	8.6
-50.0	-4.000	44.9	264.1	27.6	282.5	11.6	14.1	8.6
-45.0	-3.600	46.6	262.3	28.4	282.5	11.8	14.1	8.7
-40.0	-3.200	48.9	260.0	29.3	283.1	11.9	14.0	8.8
-35.0	-2.800	51.8	257.3	30.0	282.8	12.1	13.8	8.8
-30.0	-2.400	54.4	253.8	30.2	279.6	12.1	13.4	8.7
-25.0	-2.000	54.4	249.2	30.5	275.9	12.1	13.5	8.7
-20.0	-1.600	57.4	243.4	30.9	274.2	12.2	13.2	8.7
-15.0	-1.200	59.0	235.9	30.9	266.0	12.2	13.0	8.7
-10.0	-.800	59.8	226.4	30.9	256.9	12.2	12.9	8.6
-5.0	-.400	59.8	214.9	30.8	246.7	12.2	12.9	8.6
0.0	0.000	59.4	201.9	30.2	235.0	12.0	12.7	8.5
5.0	.400	58.9	188.8	29.2	222.8	11.9	12.5	8.4
10.0	.800	58.2	177.0	28.1	211.6	11.6	12.2	8.2

2. Hurricane Eloise—1200 noon, September 22, 1975   (Continued)

HURRICANE : ELOISE

X N.M.	t' HOURS	Urs KNOTS	Bu DEG.	Hs FEET	Bh DEG.	Ts SEC.	Tfθ SEC.	Tm SEC.
15.0	1.200	56.8	167.3	27.0	203.5	11.4	12.0	8.0
20.0	1.600	54.7	159.6	26.2	199.0	11.2	11.9	8.0
25.0	2.000	51.5	153.7	25.1	189.3	11.0	12.0	7.8
30.0	2.400	51.3	148.9	24.4	186.1	10.9	11.8	7.7
35.0	2.800	48.5	145.2	23.8	186.0	10.7	11.9	7.7
40.0	3.200	45.5	142.4	22.7	181.6	10.5	11.9	7.6
45.0	3.600	43.1	140.2	21.5	176.1	10.2	11.8	7.4
50.0	4.000	41.4	138.3	20.5	172.1	10.0	11.6	7.3
55.0	4.400	39.9	136.7	19.7	169.1	9.8	11.5	7.2
60.0	4.800	38.3	135.4	18.8	166.4	9.6	11.4	7.0
65.0	5.200	36.7	134.3	17.9	163.9	9.3	11.2	6.9
70.0	5.600	35.0	133.5	17.0	161.5	9.1	11.1	6.8
75.0	6.000	33.4	132.8	16.1	159.2	8.9	10.9	6.6
80.0	6.400	31.9	132.3	15.2	157.1	8.6	10.8	6.5
85.0	6.800	30.5	131.8	14.4	155.0	8.4	10.6	6.4
90.0	7.200	29.3	131.4	13.7	153.0	8.2	10.4	6.2
95.0	7.600	28.2	131.1	12.9	151.2	7.9	10.2	6.1
100.0	8.000	27.1	130.9	12.2	149.4	7.7	10.0	5.9
105.0	8.400	26.2	130.7	11.6	147.7	7.5	9.8	5.8
110.0	8.800	25.3	130.6	11.0	146.1	7.3	9.6	5.7
115.0	9.200	24.4	130.5	10.4	144.6	7.1	9.4	5.5
120.0	9.600	23.6	130.5	9.8	143.2	6.9	9.2	5.4
125.0	10.000	22.8	130.4	9.3	141.9	6.8	9.0	5.3
130.0	10.400	22.1	130.5	8.8	140.7	6.6	8.8	5.2
135.0	10.800	21.4	130.5	8.4	139.6	6.4	8.6	5.0
140.0	11.200	20.7	130.6	7.9	138.6	6.3	8.5	4.9
145.0	11.600	20.1	130.7	7.5	137.6	6.1	8.3	4.8
150.0	12.000	19.5	130.8	7.1	136.7	5.9	8.1	4.7
155.0	12.400	18.9	131.0	6.8	135.9	5.8	7.9	4.6
160.0	12.800	18.4	131.2	6.5	135.1	5.7	7.8	4.5
165.0	13.200	17.9	131.4	6.1	134.4	5.5	7.6	4.4
170.0	13.600	17.4	131.6	5.8	133.8	5.4	7.4	4.3
175.0	14.000	16.9	131.8	5.6	133.2	5.3	7.3	4.2
180.0	14.400	16.5	132.1	5.3	132.6	5.1	7.1	4.1
185.0	14.800	16.0	132.4	5.1	132.1	5.0	7.0	4.0
190.0	15.200	15.6	132.7	4.8	131.6	4.9	6.8	3.9
195.0	15.600	15.2	133.0	4.6	131.2	4.8	6.7	3.8
200.0	16.000	14.8	133.3	4.4	130.8	4.7	6.5	3.8
205.0	16.400	14.4	133.6	4.2	130.4	4.6	6.4	3.7
210.0	16.800	14.1	133.9	4.0	130.0	4.4	6.2	3.6
215.0	17.200	13.7	134.2	3.8	129.7	4.3	6.1	3.5
220.0	17.600	13.3	134.6	3.6	129.3	4.2	5.9	3.4
225.0	18.000	13.0	134.9	3.4	129.0	4.1	5.8	3.3

2. Hurricane Eloise—1200 noon, September 22, 1975   (Continued)

HURRICANE : ELOISE

Lat.= 27.5 deg.; Rc= 15.5 n.mi.;ΔPo= 39 mbs; Vf= 12.5 knts; Dir.= 45 deg.

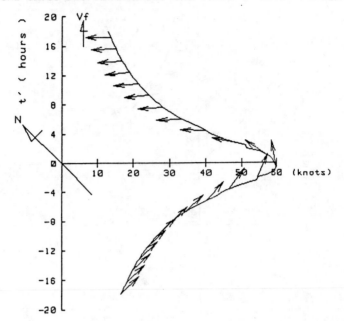

TIME CROSS SECTION THROUGH WIND FIELD (+20.0 N.MILES)

2. Hurricane Eloise—1200 noon, September 22, 1975 (Continued)

HURRICANE : ELOISE

Lat.= 27.5 deg.; Rc= 15.5 n.mi.;ΔPo= 39 mbs; Vf= 12.5 knts; Dir.= 45 deg.

TIME CROSS SECTION THROUGH WAVE FIELD (+20.0 N.MILES)

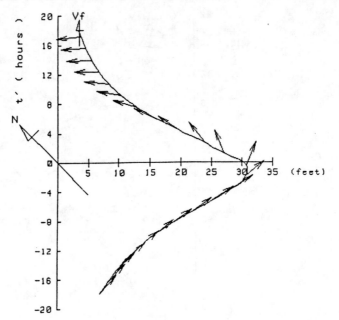

2. Hurricane Eloise—1200 noon, September 22, 1975   (Continued)

HURRICANE : ELOISE

Lat.= 27.5 deg.; Rc= 15.5 n.mi.;ΔPo= 39 mbs; Vf= 12.5 knts; Dir.= 45 deg.

TIME CROSS SECTION THROUGH PERIOD FIELD (+20.0 N.MILES)

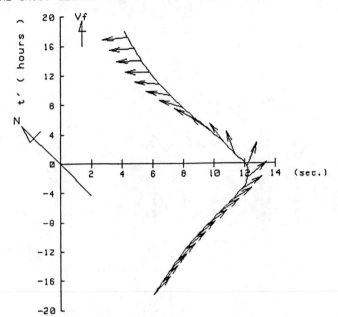

2. Hurricane Eloise—1200 noon, September 22, 1975   (Continued)

```
HURRICANE : ELOISE
Lat.= 27.5 deg.; Rc= 15.5 n.mi.;ΔPo= 39 mbs; Vf= 12.5 knts; Dir.= 45 deg.
```

r n.m.	Us ft/sec	Hs ft	Tfo sec	S(fo)	S(max)	G	RHO	A4
5.0	69.4	28.64	15.47	1122	1233	1.10	.2647	1.59

w rad/s	S(w) ft^2.s/rad	w rad/s	S(w) ft^2.s/rad
.05	0.000	2.05	.135
.10	0.000	2.10	.119
.15	.000	2.15	.106
.20	.000	2.20	.094
.25	.413	2.25	.084
.30	34.883	2.30	.075
.35	143.226	2.35	.068
.40	198.090	2.40	.061
.45	178.424	2.45	.055
.50	134.973	2.50	.049
.55	95.420	2.55	.045
.60	66.103	2.60	.041
.65	45.852	2.65	.037
.70	32.156	2.70	.034
.75	22.893	2.75	.031
.80	16.566	2.80	.028
.85	12.184	2.85	.025
.90	9.103	2.90	.023
.95	6.900	2.95	.021
1.00	5.303	3.00	.020
1.05	4.126	3.05	.018
1.10	3.248	3.10	.017
1.15	2.585	3.15	.015
1.20	2.077	3.20	.014
1.25	1.684	3.25	.013
1.30	1.377	3.30	.012
1.35	1.135	3.35	.011
1.40	.942	3.40	.011
1.45	.787	3.45	.010
1.50	.662	3.50	.009
1.55	.560	3.55	.008
1.60	.476	3.60	.008
1.65	.407	3.65	.007
1.70	.349	3.70	.007
1.75	.301	3.75	.006
1.80	.261	3.80	.006
1.85	.227	3.85	.006
1.90	.198	3.90	.005
1.95	.174	3.95	.005
2.00	.153	4.00	.005

2. Hurricane Eloise—1200 noon, September 22, 1975   (Continued)

```
HURRICANE : ELOISE
Lat.= 27.5 deg.; Rc= 15.5 n.mi.;ΔPo= 39 mbs; Vf= 12.5 knts; Dir.= 45 deg
```

r	Us	Hs	Tfo	S(fo)	S(max)	G	RHO	A4
n.m.	ft/sec	ft	sec					
10.0	98.9	28.83	12.39	910	1249	1.37	.7732	2.10

ω rad/s	S(ω) ft^2.s/rad	ω rad/s	S(ω) ft^2.s/rad
.05	0.000	2.05	.063
.10	0.000	2.10	.054
.15	0.000	2.15	.047
.20	.000	2.20	.041
.25	.000	2.25	.036
.30	.005	2.30	.032
.35	3.739	2.35	.028
.40	54.378	2.40	.025
.45	152.552	2.45	.022
.50	200.668	2.50	.020
.55	183.075	2.55	.018
.60	139.522	2.60	.016
.65	97.517	2.65	.014
.70	65.637	2.70	.013
.75	43.673	2.75	.011
.80	29.136	2.80	.010
.85	19.637	2.85	.009
.90	13.422	2.90	.009
.95	9.321	2.95	.008
1.00	6.580	3.00	.007
1.05	4.721	3.05	.006
1.10	3.441	3.10	.006
1.15	2.546	3.15	.005
1.20	1.911	3.20	.005
1.25	1.453	3.25	.005
1.30	1.119	3.30	.004
1.35	.871	3.35	.004
1.40	.686	3.40	.004
1.45	.546	3.45	.003
1.50	.438	3.50	.003
1.55	.355	3.55	.003
1.60	.290	3.60	.003
1.65	.239	3.65	.002
1.70	.198	3.70	.002
1.75	.165	3.75	.002
1.80	.139	3.80	.002
1.85	.117	3.85	.002
1.90	.100	3.90	.002
1.95	.085	3.95	.002
2.00	.073	4.00	.001

2. Hurricane Eloise—1200 noon, September 22, 1975   (Continued)

```
HURRICANE : ELOISE
Lat.= 27.5 deg.; Rc= 15.5 n.mi.;ΔPo= 39 mbs; Vf= 12.5 knts; Dir.= 45 deg.
```

r	Us	Hs	Tfo	S(fo)	S(max)	G	RHO	A4
n.m.	ft/sec	ft	sec					
15.0	103.1	30.12	12.51	1003	1386	1.38	.7897	2.11

ω rad/s	S(ω) ft^2.s/rad	ω rad/s	S(ω) ft^2.s/rad
.05	0.000	2.05	.059
.10	0.000	2.10	.051
.15	0.000	2.15	.044
.20	.000	2.20	.039
.25	.000	2.25	.034
.30	.010	2.30	.030
.35	5.334	2.35	.026
.40	67.943	2.40	.023
.45	177.307	2.45	.021
.50	223.393	2.50	.018
.55	198.232	2.55	.016
.60	148.208	2.60	.015
.65	102.141	2.65	.013
.70	68.001	2.70	.012
.75	44.844	2.75	.011
.80	29.691	2.80	.010
.85	19.879	2.85	.009
.90	13.508	2.90	.008
.95	9.331	2.95	.007
1.00	6.554	3.00	.006
1.05	4.681	3.05	.006
1.10	3.397	3.10	.005
1.15	2.504	3.15	.005
1.20	1.872	3.20	.005
1.25	1.418	3.25	.004
1.30	1.088	3.30	.004
1.35	.845	3.35	.004
1.40	.663	3.40	.003
1.45	.526	3.45	.003
1.50	.421	3.50	.003
1.55	.340	3.55	.003
1.60	.277	3.60	.002
1.65	.228	3.65	.002
1.70	.188	3.70	.002
1.75	.157	3.75	.002
1.80	.132	3.80	.002
1.85	.111	3.85	.002
1.90	.094	3.90	.002
1.95	.080	3.95	.001
2.00	.069	4.00	.001

2. Hurricane Eloise—1200 noon, September 22, 1975 (Continued)

```
HURRICANE : ELOISE
Lat.= 27.5 deg.; Rc= 15.5 n.mi.;ΔPo= 39 mbs; Vf= 12.5 knts; Dir.= 45 deg.
```

r n.m.	Us ft/sec	Hs ft	Tfo sec	S(fo)	S(max)	G	RHO	A4
20.0	101.0	30.89	12.92	1090	1490	1.37	.7619	2.09

ω rad/s	S(ω) ft^2.s/rad	ω rad/s	S(ω) ft^2.s/rad
.05	0.000	2.05	.063
.10	0.000	2.10	.054
.15	.000	2.15	.047
.20	.000	2.20	.041
.25	.000	2.25	.036
.30	.067	2.30	.032
.35	13.283	2.35	.028
.40	105.563	2.40	.025
.45	215.514	2.45	.022
.50	237.254	2.50	.020
.55	195.021	2.55	.018
.60	139.571	2.60	.016
.65	93.876	2.65	.014
.70	61.726	2.70	.013
.75	40.506	2.75	.012
.80	26.817	2.80	.011
.85	18.011	2.85	.010
.90	12.302	2.90	.009
.95	8.553	2.95	.008
1.00	6.053	3.00	.007
1.05	4.357	3.05	.007
1.10	3.188	3.10	.006
1.15	2.369	3.15	.006
1.20	1.786	3.20	.005
1.25	1.364	3.25	.005
1.30	1.055	3.30	.004
1.35	.825	3.35	.004
1.40	.653	3.40	.004
1.45	.522	3.45	.003
1.50	.421	3.50	.003
1.55	.342	3.55	.003
1.60	.280	3.60	.003
1.65	.232	3.65	.003
1.70	.193	3.70	.002
1.75	.161	3.75	.002
1.80	.136	3.80	.002
1.85	.115	3.85	.002
1.90	.098	3.90	.002
1.95	.084	3.95	.002
2.00	.072	4.00	.002

2. Hurricane Eloise—1200 noon, September 22, 1975   (Continued)

```
HURRICANE : ELOISE
Lat.= 27.5 deg.; Rc= 15.5 n.mi.;ΔPo= 39 mbs; Vf= 12.5 knts; Dir.= 45 d.
```

r n.m.	Us ft/sec	Hs ft	Tfo sec	S(fo)	S(max)	G	RHO	A4
25.0	97.2	31.35	13.37	1162	1560	1.34	.7186	2.06

ω rad/s	S(ω) ft^2.s/rad	ω rad/s	S(ω) ft^2.s/rad
.05	0.000	2.05	.069
.10	0.000	2.10	.061
.15	.000	2.15	.053
.20	.000	2.20	.047
.25	.000	2.25	.041
.30	.374	2.30	.036
.35	29.359	2.35	.032
.40	149.801	2.40	.029
.45	243.722	2.45	.026
.50	237.633	2.50	.023
.55	182.911	2.55	.021
.60	126.464	2.60	.018
.65	83.691	2.65	.017
.70	54.747	2.70	.015
.75	35.988	2.75	.014
.80	23.970	2.80	.012
.85	16.239	2.85	.011
.90	11.206	2.90	.010
.95	7.879	2.95	.009
1.00	5.641	3.00	.009
1.05	4.109	3.05	.008
1.10	3.042	3.10	.007
1.15	2.286	3.15	.007
1.20	1.742	3.20	.006
1.25	1.345	3.25	.006
1.30	1.051	3.30	.005
1.35	.831	3.35	.005
1.40	.663	3.40	.004
1.45	.535	3.45	.004
1.50	.435	3.50	.004
1.55	.357	3.55	.003
1.60	.295	3.60	.003
1.65	.245	3.65	.003
1.70	.205	3.70	.003
1.75	.173	3.75	.003
1.80	.147	3.80	.002
1.85	.125	3.85	.002
1.90	.107	3.90	.002
1.95	.092	3.95	.002
2.00	.080	4.00	.002

2. Hurricane Eloise—1200 noon, September 22, 1975   (Continued)

```
HURRICANE : ELOISE
Lat.= 27.5 deg.; Rc= 15.5 n.mi.;ΔPo= 39 mbs; Vf= 12.5 knts; Dir.= 45 deg.
```

r n.m.	Us ft/sec	Hs ft	Tfo sec	S(fo)	S(max)	G	RHO	A4
30.0	93.1	31.31	13.72	1189	1566	1.32	.6719	2.02

ω rad/s	S(ω) ft^2.s/rad	ω rad/s	S(ω) ft^2.s/rad
.05	0.000	2.05	.078
.10	0.000	2.10	.068
.15	.000	2.15	.060
.20	.000	2.20	.053
.25	.000	2.25	.046
.30	1.118	2.30	.041
.35	46.952	2.35	.037
.40	178.647	2.40	.033
.45	251.074	2.45	.029
.50	227.186	2.50	.026
.55	168.513	2.55	.024
.60	114.643	2.60	.021
.65	75.556	2.65	.019
.70	49.572	2.70	.017
.75	32.820	2.75	.016
.80	22.071	2.80	.014
.85	15.117	2.85	.013
.90	10.553	2.90	.012
.95	7.508	2.95	.011
1.00	5.438	3.00	.010
1.05	4.007	3.05	.009
1.10	2.999	3.10	.008
1.15	2.278	3.15	.008
1.20	1.754	3.20	.007
1.25	1.367	3.25	.007
1.30	1.078	3.30	.006
1.35	.859	3.35	.006
1.40	.692	3.40	.005
1.45	.562	3.45	.005
1.50	.460	3.50	.004
1.55	.380	3.55	.004
1.60	.316	3.60	.004
1.65	.264	3.65	.004
1.70	.223	3.70	.003
1.75	.189	3.75	.003
1.80	.161	3.80	.003
1.85	.138	3.85	.003
1.90	.119	3.90	.003
1.95	.103	3.95	.002
2.00	.089	4.00	.002

2. Hurricane Eloise—1200 noon, September 22, 1975   (Continued)

HURRICANE : ELOISE
Lat.= 27.5 deg.; Rc= 15.5 n.mi.;ΔPo= 39 mbs; Vf= 12.5 knts; Dir.= 45 deg.

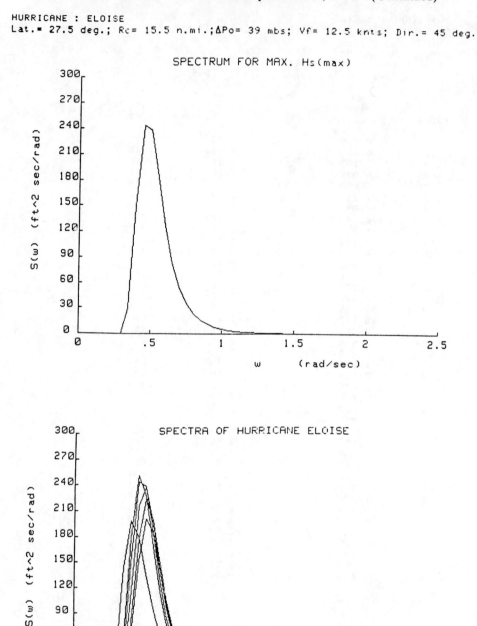

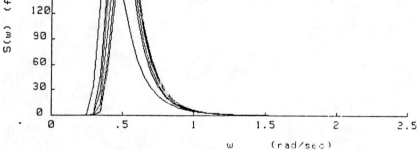

2. Hurricane Eloise—1200 noon, September 22, 1975   (Continued)

HURRICANE : ELOISE
Lat.= 27.5 deg.; Rc= 15.5 n.mi.;ΔPo= 39 mbs; Vf= 12.5 knts; Dir.= 45 deg.

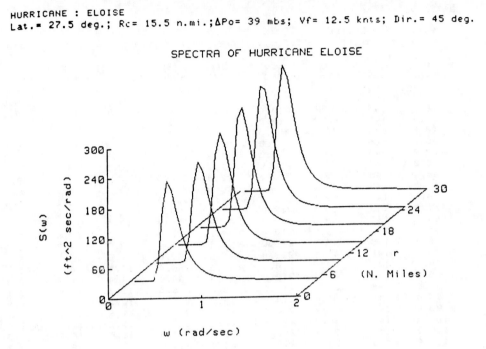

SPECTRA OF HURRICANE ELOISE

3. Hurricane Eloise—0600, September 23, 1975

DATE: 5/10/88

HURRICANE : ELOISE
Lat.= 28.5 deg.; Rc= 15.5 n.mi.;ΔPo= 49 mbs; Vf= 15 knts; Dir.= 30 deg.

r N.M.	A0 DEG	Urs KNOTS	Bu DEG	Hs FEET	Bh DEG	Ts SEC.	Tf0 SEC.	Tm SEC.
5.0	145	46.1	210.0	34.3	223.0	12.9	16.6	9.9
10.0	145	65.7	210.0	34.1	230.2	12.8	13.2	9.0
15.0	145	68.5	210.0	35.6	238.7	13.0	13.4	9.1
20.0	145	67.2	210.0	36.6	240.2	13.2	13.8	9.3
25.0	145	64.7	210.0	37.1	244.1	13.4	14.3	9.5
30.0	145	62.0	210.0	37.4	244.8	13.5	14.7	9.6
35.0	145	59.4	210.0	37.5	245.3	13.5	15.2	9.7
40.0	145	56.9	210.0	37.0	242.5	13.4	15.4	9.8
45.0	145	54.6	210.0	36.8	242.7	13.4	15.7	9.8
50.0	145	52.5	210.0	36.6	242.9	13.3	16.1	9.9
55.0	145	50.5	210.0	35.4	239.8	13.1	16.0	9.8
60.0	145	48.6	210.0	35.0	239.9	13.1	16.3	9.8
65.0	145	46.9	210.0	34.5	239.9	13.0	16.5	9.9
70.0	145	45.3	210.0	34.1	240.0	12.9	16.7	9.9
75.0	145	43.8	210.0	32.5	236.6	12.6	16.5	9.7
80.0	145	42.3	210.0	32.0	236.6	12.5	16.7	9.8
85.0	145	41.0	210.0	31.4	236.6	12.4	16.8	9.8
90.0	145	39.7	210.0	30.8	236.6	12.3	17.0	9.8
95.0	145	38.6	210.0	30.3	236.5	12.2	17.1	9.9
100.0	145	37.4	210.0	28.5	233.1	11.9	16.6	9.6
105.0	145	36.3	210.0	27.9	233.1	11.7	16.7	9.6
110.0	145	35.3	210.0	27.2	233.0	11.6	16.8	9.7
115.0	145	34.4	210.0	26.6	233.0	11.5	16.9	9.7
120.0	145	33.4	210.0	25.9	232.9	11.4	17.0	9.7
125.0	145	32.5	210.0	25.2	232.8	11.3	17.1	9.8
130.0	145	31.7	210.0	23.6	229.4	10.9	16.4	9.4
135.0	145	30.9	210.0	22.9	229.3	10.8	16.4	9.4
140.0	145	30.1	210.0	22.2	229.2	10.7	16.5	9.5

(Continued)

3. Hurricane Eloise—0600, September 23, 1975   (Continued)

```
HURRICANE : ELOISE
Lat.= 28.5 deg.; Rc= 15.5 n.mi.;ΔPo= 49 mbs; Vf= 15 knts; Dir.= 30 deg.
```

r N.M.	A0 DEG	Urs KNOTS	Bu DEG	Hs FEET	Bh DEG	Ts SEC.	Tf0 SEC.	Tm SEC.
145.0	145	29.4	210.0	21.4	228.9	10.5	16.3	9.4
150.0	145	28.7	210.0	20.6	228.6	10.3	16.1	9.3
155.0	145	28.0	210.0	19.8	228.3	10.2	16.0	9.3
160.0	145	27.4	210.0	19.1	228.0	10.0	15.9	9.2
165.0	145	26.7	210.0	18.3	225.5	9.8	15.6	9.1
170.0	145	26.1	210.0	17.7	225.4	9.7	15.6	9.1
175.0	145	25.6	210.0	17.0	225.3	9.6	15.5	9.2
180.0	145	25.0	210.0	16.4	225.0	9.4	15.3	9.1
185.0	145	24.5	210.0	15.8	224.7	9.3	15.1	9.0
190.0	145	24.0	210.0	15.2	224.4	9.1	14.9	9.0
195.0	145	23.5	210.0	14.5	221.9	8.9	14.4	8.6
200.0	145	23.0	210.0	14.0	221.8	8.8	14.3	8.6
205.0	145	22.6	210.0	13.5	221.7	8.7	14.2	8.6
210.0	145	22.2	210.0	13.0	221.5	8.5	14.1	8.7
215.0	145	21.8	210.0	12.5	221.2	8.4	13.8	8.5
220.0	145	21.4	210.0	12.1	221.0	8.2	13.6	8.4
225.0	145	21.0	210.0	11.7	220.7	8.1	13.4	8.3
230.0	145	20.6	210.0	11.3	220.5	8.0	13.2	8.2
235.0	145	20.3	210.0	10.9	220.3	7.8	13.0	8.1
240.0	145	19.9	210.0	10.5	218.3	7.7	12.7	7.8
245.0	145	19.6	210.0	10.2	218.2	7.6	12.5	7.8
250.0	145	19.3	210.0	9.9	218.1	7.5	12.4	7.7
255.0	145	19.0	210.0	9.6	218.0	7.4	12.3	7.7
260.0	145	18.7	210.0	9.3	217.9	7.3	12.1	7.7
265.0	145	18.4	210.0	9.0	217.7	7.2	11.9	7.5
270.0	145	18.1	210.0	8.7	217.5	7.1	11.7	7.4
275.0	145	17.9	210.0	8.5	217.4	6.9	11.5	7.2
280.0	145	17.6	210.0	8.2	216.9	6.8	11.1	6.7
285.0	145	17.4	210.0	8.0	216.7	6.6	10.9	6.6

3. Hurricane Eloise—0600, September 23, 1975 (Continued)

DATE: 5/10/88

HURRICANE : ELOISE
Lat.= 28.5 deg.; Rc= 15.5 n.mi.;ΔPo= 49 mbs; Vf= 15 knts; Dir.= 30 deg.

WIND FIELD , Urs (knots)

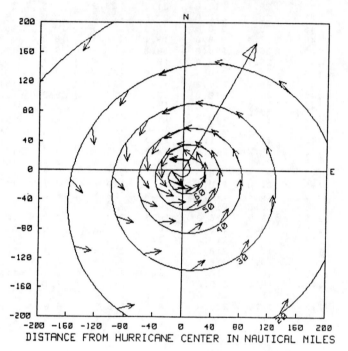

DISTANCE FROM HURRICANE CENTER IN NAUTICAL MILES

3. Hurricane Eloise—0600, September 23, 1975   (Continued)

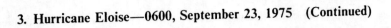

HURRICANE : ELOISE
Lat.= 28.5 deg.; Rc= 15.5 n.mi.;ΔPo= 49 mbs; Vf= 15 knts; Dir.= 30 deg.

WAVE FIELD , Hs (feet)

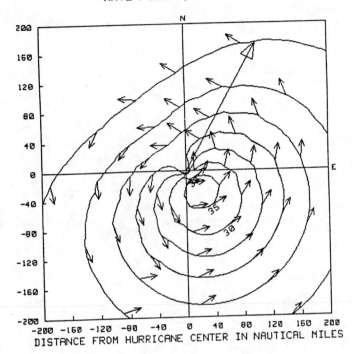

DISTANCE FROM HURRICANE CENTER IN NAUTICAL MILES

3. Hurricane Eloise—0600, September 23, 1975 (Continued)

DATE: 5/10/88

HURRICANE : ELOISE
Lat.= 28.5 deg.; Rc= 15.5 n.mi.;ΔPo= 49 mbs; Vf= 15 knts; Dir.= 30 deg.

PERIOD FIELD , Ts (sec.)

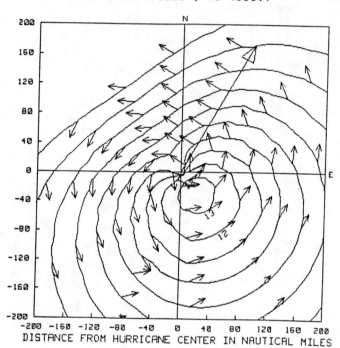

DISTANCE FROM HURRICANE CENTER IN NAUTICAL MILES

3. Hurricane Eloise—0600, September 23, 1975   (Continued)

```
HURRICANE : ELOISE

Lat.= 28.5 deg.; Rc= 15.5 n.mi.;ΔPo= 49 mbs; Vf= 15 knts; Dir.= 30 deg.
```

X N.M.	t´ HOURS	Urs KNOTS	Bu DEG.	Hs FEET	Bh DEG.	Ts SEC.	Tf0 SEC.	Tm SEC.
-170.0	-11.333	24.1	258.3	14.3	260.7	8.6	13.3	7.6
-165.0	-11.000	24.8	258.5	15.0	272.9	8.7	13.4	7.7
-160.0	-10.667	25.5	258.6	15.7	284.9	8.9	13.6	7.8
-155.0	-10.333	26.3	258.7	16.4	296.5	9.1	13.7	7.9
-150.0	-10.000	27.1	258.9	17.0	307.6	9.2	13.8	8.0
-145.0	-9.667	27.8	259.0	17.7	318.1	9.4	14.0	8.0
-140.0	-9.333	28.6	259.1	13.4	327.7	9.6	14.1	8.1
-135.0	-9.000	29.4	259.2	19.1	336.3	9.7	14.2	8.2
-130.0	-8.667	30.2	259.2	19.8	343.8	9.9	14.4	8.3
-125.0	-8.333	31.1	259.2	20.6	350.0	10.1	14.5	8.3
-120.0	-8.000	31.9	259.2	21.3	354.8	10.2	14.6	8.4
-115.0	-7.667	32.8	259.2	22.0	357.9	10.4	14.7	8.5
-110.0	-7.333	33.8	259.2	22.7	359.3	10.6	14.8	8.5
-105.0	-7.000	34.7	259.1	23.5	358.7	10.7	14.9	8.6
-100.0	-6.667	35.7	258.9	24.3	356.1	10.9	14.9	8.7
-95.0	-6.333	36.7	258.7	25.0	351.2	11.1	15.0	8.8
-90.0	-6.000	37.8	258.5	25.8	343.9	11.2	15.1	8.8
-85.0	-5.667	38.9	258.2	26.6	334.1	11.4	15.1	8.9
-80.0	-5.333	40.1	257.9	27.4	321.8	11.6	15.1	8.9
-75.0	-5.000	41.4	257.5	28.2	308.2	11.7	15.1	9.0
-70.0	-4.667	42.8	257.0	29.0	294.6	11.9	15.1	9.0
-65.0	-4.333	44.6	256.4	29.9	282.4	12.1	15.1	9.1
-60.0	-4.000	46.7	255.6	30.7	272.9	12.2	15.0	9.1
-55.0	-3.667	49.2	254.8	31.5	267.5	12.4	14.8	9.2
-50.0	-3.333	52.0	253.7	32.4	266.5	12.5	14.7	9.2
-45.0	-3.000	54.3	252.3	33.2	267.8	12.7	14.5	9.2
-40.0	-2.667	55.6	250.4	34.1	269.1	12.9	14.6	9.3
-35.0	-2.333	56.5	248.0	34.8	269.0	13.0	14.7	9.4
-30.0	-2.000	60.4	245.1	35.2	268.0	13.0	14.3	9.3
-25.0	-1.667	63.9	241.2	35.5	266.8	13.1	13.9	9.3
-20.0	-1.333	65.1	235.8	35.7	262.3	13.1	13.8	9.3
-15.0	-1.000	66.9	228.4	36.0	255.3	13.1	13.7	9.2
-10.0	-.667	68.5	218.0	35.5	245.6	13.0	13.3	9.1
-5.0	-.333	68.5	204.0	35.6	233.4	13.0	13.3	9.1
0.0	0.000	68.1	187.0	34.8	218.1	12.9	13.2	9.0
5.0	.333	67.1	169.9	33.2	202.1	12.6	12.8	8.8
10.0	.667	66.0	155.5	31.4	188.2	12.2	12.3	8.5
15.0	1.000	63.7	144.7	30.4	179.1	12.1	12.3	8.4
20.0	1.333	61.5	137.0	29.3	173.8	11.8	12.2	8.3
25.0	1.667	60.1	131.3	28.4	169.9	11.7	12.1	8.2
30.0	2.000	56.4	127.3	27.4	166.3	11.5	12.2	8.1
35.0	2.333	52.3	124.3	26.5	163.3	11.3	12.4	8.1
40.0	2.667	51.3	121.8	25.6	157.6	11.1	12.2	7.9
45.0	3.000	50.0	119.8	24.6	152.8	10.9	12.0	7.8
50.0	3.333	47.6	118.4	23.5	149.6	10.7	11.9	7.7
55.0	3.667	44.8	117.3	22.4	147.4	10.4	11.9	7.6
60.0	4.000	42.2	116.5	21.4	145.3	10.2	11.9	7.4
65.0	4.333	40.1	115.8	20.4	143.2	10.0	11.8	7.3

(Continued)

3. Hurricane Eloise—0600, September 23, 1975   (Continued)

HURRICANE : ELOISE
Lat.= 28.5 deg.; Rc= 15.5 n.mi.;ΔPo= 49 mbs; Vf= 15 knts; Dir.= 30 deg.

X N.M.	t' HOURS	Urs KNOTS	Bu DEG.	Hs FEET	Bh DEG.	Ts SEC.	Tf0 SEC.	Tm SEC.
70.0	4.667	38.4	115.2	19.5	141.2	9.8	11.7	7.2
75.0	5.000	36.9	114.7	18.6	139.2	9.5	11.6	7.1
80.0	5.333	35.6	114.3	17.8	137.2	9.3	11.4	7.0
85.0	5.667	34.4	114.0	17.1	135.4	9.1	11.3	6.8
90.0	6.000	33.3	113.8	16.3	133.8	8.9	11.1	6.7
95.0	6.333	32.2	113.6	15.6	132.2	8.7	11.0	6.6
100.0	6.667	31.2	113.5	15.0	130.8	8.5	10.8	6.5
105.0	7.000	30.2	113.5	14.3	129.5	8.4	10.7	6.4
110.0	7.333	29.2	113.5	13.7	128.4	8.2	10.5	6.3
115.0	7.667	28.3	113.5	13.1	127.3	8.0	10.3	6.1
120.0	8.000	27.4	113.6	12.5	126.4	7.8	10.2	6.0
125.0	8.333	26.6	113.7	12.0	125.5	7.6	10.0	5.9
130.0	8.667	25.7	113.8	11.4	124.7	7.4	9.8	5.8
135.0	9.000	24.9	114.0	10.9	124.0	7.3	9.7	5.7
140.0	9.333	24.1	114.2	10.4	123.3	7.1	9.5	5.6
145.0	9.667	23.3	114.4	9.9	122.7	6.9	9.3	5.4
150.0	10.000	22.6	114.6	9.4	122.1	6.8	9.1	5.3
155.0	10.333	21.8	114.9	9.0	121.6	6.6	9.0	5.2
160.0	10.667	21.1	115.1	8.5	121.1	6.4	8.8	5.1
165.0	11.000	20.3	115.4	8.0	120.6	6.3	8.6	5.0
170.0	11.333	19.6	115.7	7.6	120.1	6.1	8.4	4.9

3. Hurricane Eloise—0600, September 23, 1975   (Continued)

HURRICANE : ELOISE

Lat.= 28.5 deg.; Rc= 15.5 n.mi.;ΔPo= 49 mbs; Vf= 15 knts; Dir.= 30 deg.

TIME CROSS SECTION THROUGH WIND FIELD (+15.0 N.MILES)

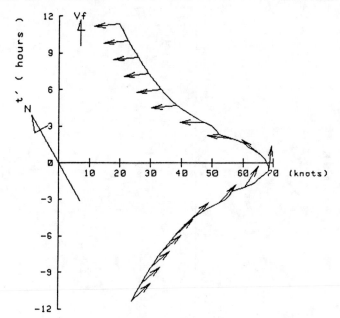

3. Hurricane Eloise—0600, September 23, 1975 (Continued)

HURRICANE : ELOISE

Lat.= 28.5 deg.; Rc= 15.5 n.mi.;ΔPo= 49 mbs; Vf= 15 knts; Dir.= 30 deg.

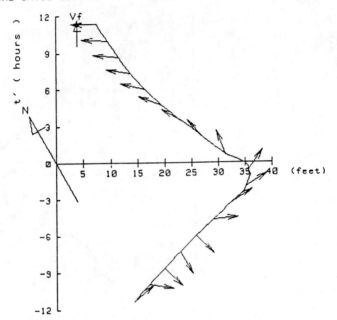

TIME CROSS SECTION THROUGH WAVE FIELD (+15.0 N.MILES)

3. Hurricane Eloise—0600, September 23, 1975   (Continued)

HURRICANE : ELOISE

Lat.= 28.5 deg.; Rc= 15.5 n.mi.;ΔPo= 49 mbs; Vf= 15 knts; Dir.= 30 deg.

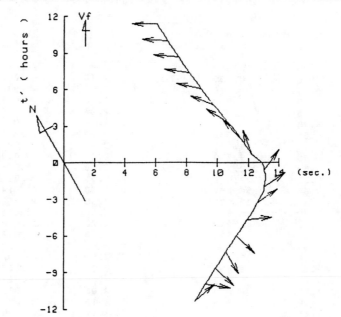

TIME CROSS SECTION THROUGH PERIOD FIELD (+15.0 N.MILES)

3. Hurricane Eloise—0600, September 23, 1975   (Continued)

```
HURRICANE : ELOISE
Lat.= 28.5 deg.; Rc= 15.5 n.mi.;ΔPo= 49 mbs; Vf= 15 knts; Dir.= 30 deg.
```

r n.m.	Us ft/sec	Hs ft	Tfo sec	S(fo)	S(max)	G	RHO	A4
10.0	110.9	34.14	13.24	1364	1891	1.09	.7978	2.12

w rad/s	S(w) ft^2.s/rad	w rad/s	S(w) ft^2.s/rad
.05	0.000	2.05	.054
.10	0.000	2.10	.047
.15	.000	2.15	.041
.20	.000	2.20	.036
.25	.000	2.25	.031
.30	.232	2.30	.027
.35	26.955	2.35	.024
.40	164.191	2.40	.021
.45	289.758	2.45	.019
.50	292.337	2.50	.017
.55	227.090	2.55	.015
.60	156.252	2.60	.014
.65	102.073	2.65	.012
.70	65.598	2.70	.011
.75	42.247	2.75	.010
.80	27.526	2.80	.009
.85	18.230	2.85	.008
.90	12.297	2.90	.007
.95	8.453	2.95	.007
1.00	5.919	3.00	.006
1.05	4.220	3.05	.006
1.10	3.060	3.10	.005
1.15	2.254	3.15	.005
1.20	1.686	3.20	.004
1.25	1.278	3.25	.004
1.30	.981	3.30	.004
1.35	.763	3.35	.003
1.40	.600	3.40	.003
1.45	.476	3.45	.003
1.50	.382	3.50	.003
1.55	.309	3.55	.002
1.60	.252	3.60	.002
1.65	.207	3.65	.002
1.70	.172	3.70	.002
1.75	.143	3.75	.002
1.80	.120	3.80	.002
1.85	.101	3.85	.002
1.90	.086	3.90	.001
1.95	.073	3.95	.001
2.00	.063	4.00	.001

3. Hurricane Eloise—0600, September 23, 1975   (Continued)

```
HURRICANE : ELOISE
Lat.= 28.5 deg.; Rc= 15.5 n.mi.;ΔPo= 49 mbs; Vf= 15 knts; Dir.= 30 deg

    r     Us     Hs    Tfo    S(fo)  S(max)    G     RHO      A4
  n.m.  ft/sec   ft    sec
  15.0  115.7  35.62  13.36   1498   2090    1.39   .8136    2.13
```

ω rad/s	S(ω) ft^2.s/rad	ω rad/s	S(ω) ft^2.s/rad
.05	0.000	2.05	.051
.10	0.000	2.10	.044
.15	.000	2.15	.038
.20	.000	2.20	.033
.25	.000	2.25	.029
.30	.359	2.30	.025
.35	34.830	2.35	.022
.40	193.789	2.40	.020
.45	325.264	2.45	.018
.50	318.290	2.50	.016
.55	242.292	2.55	.014
.60	164.309	2.60	.012
.65	106.147	2.65	.011
.70	67.602	2.70	.010
.75	43.203	2.75	.009
.80	27.960	2.80	.008
.85	18.404	2.85	.007
.90	12.345	2.90	.007
.95	8.441	2.95	.006
1.00	5.883	3.00	.006
1.05	4.174	3.05	.005
1.10	3.014	3.10	.005
1.15	2.211	3.15	.004
1.20	1.647	3.20	.004
1.25	1.244	3.25	.004
1.30	.952	3.30	.003
1.35	.737	3.35	.003
1.40	.578	3.40	.003
1.45	.457	3.45	.003
1.50	.366	3.50	.002
1.55	.295	3.55	.002
1.60	.240	3.60	.002
1.65	.197	3.65	.002
1.70	.163	3.70	.002
1.75	.135	3.75	.002
1.80	.113	3.80	.002
1.85	.095	3.85	.001
1.90	.081	3.90	.001
1.95	.069	3.95	.001
2.00	.059	4.00	.001

3. Hurricane Eloise—0600, September 23, 1975 (Continued)

```
HURRICANE : ELOISE
Lat.= 28.5 deg.; Rc= 15.5 n.mi.;ΔPo= 49 mbs; Vf= 15 knts; Dir.= 30 deg.
```

r n.m.	Us ft/sec	Hs ft	Tfo sec	S(fo)	S(max)	G	RHO	A4
20.0	113.4	36.56	13.79	1630	2251	1.38	.7887	2.11

w rad/s	S(w) ft^2.s/rad	w rad/s	S(w) ft^2.s/rad
.05	0.000	2.05	.054
.10	0.000	2.10	.047
.15	.000	2.15	.041
.20	.000	2.20	.036
.25	.000	2.25	.031
.30	1.469	2.30	.028
.35	66.977	2.35	.024
.40	259.840	2.40	.022
.45	361.912	2.45	.019
.50	319.990	2.50	.017
.55	230.217	2.55	.015
.60	151.332	2.60	.014
.65	96.192	2.65	.012
.70	60.832	2.70	.011
.75	38.828	2.75	.010
.80	25.190	2.80	.009
.85	16.663	2.85	.008
.90	11.249	2.90	.007
.95	7.750	2.95	.007
1.00	5.444	3.00	.006
1.05	3.896	3.05	.006
1.10	2.836	3.10	.005
1.15	2.099	3.15	.005
1.20	1.576	3.20	.004
1.25	1.200	3.25	.004
1.30	.926	3.30	.004
1.35	.723	3.35	.003
1.40	.571	3.40	.003
1.45	.455	3.45	.003
1.50	.366	3.50	.003
1.55	.297	3.55	.002
1.60	.244	3.60	.002
1.65	.201	3.65	.002
1.70	.167	3.70	.002
1.75	.140	3.75	.002
1.80	.118	3.80	.002
1.85	.100	3.85	.002
1.90	.085	3.90	.002
1.95	.073	3.95	.001
2.00	.062	4.00	.001

3. Hurricane Eloise—0600, September 23, 1975   (Continued)

```
HURRICANE : ELOISE
Lat.= 28.5 deg.; Rc= 15.5 n.mi.;ΔPo= 49 mbs; Vf= 15 knts; Dir.= 30 deg.
```

r	Us	Hs	Tfo	S(fo)	S(max)	G	RHO	A4
n.m.	ft/sec	ft	sec					
25.0	109.3	37.13	14.28	1741	2367	1.36	.7496	2.08

w rad/s	S(w) ft^2.s/rad	w rad/s	S(w) ft^2.s/rad
.05	0.000	2.05	.060
.10	0.000	2.10	.052
.15	.000	2.15	.046
.20	.000	2.20	.040
.25	.001	2.25	.036
.30	5.252	2.30	.031
.35	116.830	2.35	.028
.40	322.783	2.40	.025
.45	378.480	2.45	.022
.50	305.728	2.50	.020
.55	209.822	2.55	.018
.60	134.792	2.60	.016
.65	84.927	2.65	.014
.70	53.694	2.70	.013
.75	34.445	2.75	.012
.80	22.532	2.80	.011
.85	15.058	2.85	.010
.90	10.282	2.90	.009
.95	7.169	2.95	.008
1.00	5.098	3.00	.007
1.05	3.693	3.05	.007
1.10	2.721	3.10	.006
1.15	2.037	3.15	.005
1.20	1.547	3.20	.005
1.25	1.191	3.25	.005
1.30	.929	3.30	.004
1.35	.732	3.35	.004
1.40	.583	3.40	.004
1.45	.470	3.45	.003
1.50	.381	3.50	.003
1.55	.312	3.55	.003
1.60	.258	3.60	.003
1.65	.214	3.65	.003
1.70	.179	3.70	.002
1.75	.151	3.75	.002
1.80	.128	3.80	.002
1.85	.109	3.85	.002
1.90	.093	3.90	.002
1.95	.080	3.95	.002
2.00	.069	4.00	.002

3. Hurricane Eloise—0600, September 23, 1975 (Continued)

```
HURRICANE : ELOISE
Lat.= 28.5 deg.; Rc= 15.5 n.mi.;ΔPo= 49 mbs; Vf= 15 knts; Dir.= 30 deg.
```

r	Us	Hs	Tfo	S(fo)	S(max)	G	RHO	A4
n.m.	ft/sec	ft	sec					
30.0	104.7	37.43	14.75	1826	2437	1.33	.7031	2.64

ω rad/s	S(ω) ft^2.s/rad	ω rad/s	S(ω) ft^2.s/rad
.05	0.000	2.05	.068
.10	0.000	2.10	.060
.15	.000	2.15	.053
.20	.000	2.20	.046
.25	.009	2.25	.041
.30	14.016	2.30	.036
.35	174.114	2.35	.032
.40	366.698	2.40	.029
.45	376.089	2.45	.026
.50	284.168	2.50	.023
.55	188.965	2.55	.021
.60	119.939	2.60	.019
.65	75.505	2.65	.017
.70	48.011	2.70	.015
.75	31.095	2.75	.014
.80	20.581	2.80	.013
.85	13.932	2.85	.011
.90	9.641	2.90	.010
.95	6.813	2.95	.010
1.00	4.909	3.00	.009
1.05	3.602	3.05	.008
1.10	2.687	3.10	.007
1.15	2.035	3.15	.007
1.20	1.564	3.20	.006
1.25	1.217	3.25	.006
1.30	.958	3.30	.005
1.35	.763	3.35	.005
1.40	.613	3.40	.005
1.45	.498	3.45	.004
1.50	.407	3.50	.004
1.55	.336	3.55	.004
1.60	.279	3.60	.003
1.65	.234	3.65	.003
1.70	.197	3.70	.003
1.75	.167	3.75	.003
1.80	.142	3.80	.003
1.85	.121	3.85	.002
1.90	.105	3.90	.002
1.95	.090	3.95	.002
2.00	.078	4.00	.002

3. Hurricane Eloise—0600, September 23, 1975   (Continued)

HURRICANE : ELOISE
Lat.= 28.5 deg.; Rc= 15.5 n.mi.;ΔPo= 49 mbs; Vf= 15 knts; Dir.= 30 deg.

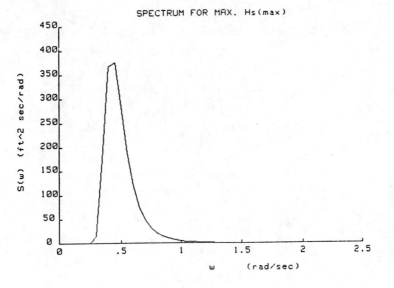

SPECTRUM FOR MAX. Hs(max)

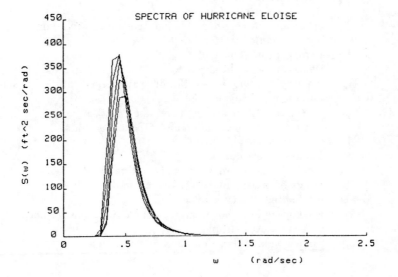

SPECTRA OF HURRICANE ELOISE

3. Hurricane Eloise—0600, September 23, 1975 (Continued)

```
HURRICANE : ELOISE
Lat.= 28.5 deg.; Rc= 15.5 n.mi.;ΔPo= 49 mbs; Vf= 15 knts; Dir.= 30 deg.
```

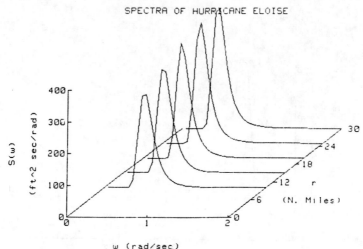

Notation

A_1, B_1, m_1	constants in the wave height prediction equation
U_r	wind speed for stationary hurricane at radial distance r from the center of the hurricane
f	$2\omega \sin \phi$, Coriolis force parameter
F_e	effective fetch length, and is independent of wind duration.
g	acceleration of gravity
H_s	significant wave height
H_R	significant wave height as R
H_{RS}	maximum value of significant wave height at R for stationary hurricane
H_{RV}	maximum H_R for moving hurricane, $V = V_F$
K	constant in wind equation and depends on units
K'	function of fR/U_R
N_C	Rankin vortex number
R	radius of maximum wind as given in the literature
Rg	radius of maximum cyclostrophic wind $R_C > R_g$
U	wind speed (knots or m/s)
U_R	wind speed at radius of maximum wind (probably same as U_{Rg})
U_C	maximum cyclostrophic wind
U_S, V_{10}	surface wind speed, 10-m level and 10-min ave

V_F forward speed of hurricane

ω angular velocity of earth

ϕ degrees in latitude

ΔP_0 $P_N - P_0$, (mbs or in. Hg) reduction in central pressure P_0 from normal pressure P_N

Symbols Used in the Computer Printouts

R_c (n miles)   radius of maximum cyclostrophic wind. R_c (related to R the radius of maximum wind or maximum gradient wind) is required in the model pressure profile, pressure gradient and gradient wind equations

ΔP_0 $P_N - P_0$ (mbs), central pressure reduction from pressure at infinite distance

V_f V_F (knots), forward speed of movement of the hurricane (Typhoon Lex)

r (n miles)   radial distance from center of the hurricane

$A\phi$ Azm direction from center of hurricane to sea location site

U_{rs} V_{10} (knots), sustained 10-m level wind speed at radial distance, r

B_u (deg)   direction from which the wind V_{10} comes

H_s $H_{1/3}$ (ft), significant wave height, average of highest one-third wave

Bh (deg)   direction from which the significant waves come

T_s (sec)   significant wave period, average period of the highest one-third wave

T_{f0} (sec) f_0^{-1}, the spectral peak period of the wave spectrum

T_m $\overline{\overline{T}}$ (sec), the zero crossing wave period from the wave spectrum

N   direction north

X, Y   Cartesian coordinates

r, ϕ polar coordinates

⊛   origin for coordinate system (x, y) (0, 0)

References

1. Atkinson, G. D. and Holliday, C. R., 1977, "Tropical Cyclone Minimum Sea Level Pressure Maximum Sustained Wind Relationship for Western North Pacific," *Monthly Weather Review*, 105, pp. 421–427.
2. Bretschneider, C. L., 1959, "Hurricane Design Wave Practices," Trans. ASCE, Vol. 124, pp. 39–62.
3. Bretschneider, C. L., 1959, "Wave Variability and Wave Spectra for Wind Generated Gravity Waves," U.S. Army Corps of Engineers, Beach Erosion Board, T. M. 118, 192 pp.
4. Bretschneider, C. L., 1970, "Forecasting Relations for Wave Generation," Look Lab of Hawaii, Vol. 1, No. 3, July 1970.
5. Bretschneider, C. L., 1970, "Revisions in Wave Forecasting," Look Lab/Hawaii (a quarterly of the Look Lab University of Hawaii), Vol. 1, No. 3, pp. 31–34.
6. Bretschneider, C. L., 1972, "A Non-Dimensional Stationary Hurricane Wave Model," Proc. 1972 Offshore Technology Conference, Houston, Texas, May, paper no. 1517.

7. Bretschneider, C. L., 1972, "Revisions to Hurricane Design Wave Practices," Proc. 13th Conference on Coastal Engineering, A.S.C.E., Vancouver, July 1972.

8. Bretschneider, C. L., 1975, "The Envelope of Wave Spectrum," Third International Conference on Port and Ocean Engineering Under Arctic Conditions POAC, Fairbanks, Alaska.

9. Bretschneider, C. L., 1978, Significant Wave Hindcasts for Hurricane Camille 1969—(A Verification with Recorded Data—Addendum to Hurricane Wind and Wave Forecasting Techniques), Vol. 8, No. 2, Hawaii: Look Laboratory.

10. Bretschneider, C. L., 1979, "Hurricane Design Wind and Waves and Current Criteria for Potential OTEC Sites," University of Hawaii Department of Ocean Engineering, Look Lab Tech., Report No. 45, April 1979, *Phys. Rev.*, 4.345.

11. Bretschneider Charles L., 1979, "The Two Direction Significant Wave Forecasting Relationships with Special Application to the U.S. Weather Service Hurricane Wind Model," presented at Conference on Marine Science in the Pacific area, Taiwan, January 5–8.

12. Bretschneider, C. L., 1982, "Hurricane Models for Investigating Cyclones of the Indian Seas," Technical Report ANNEX I prepared for Government of India/United Nations Industrial Development Organization (contact Engineer India Ltd., New Delhi).

13. Bretschneider, C. L., 1984, "A Rankin Vortex Number as a Guide to the Selection of a Model Hurricane," 19th Coastal Engineering Conference Proceedings, ASCE, Houston, Texas, September 3–7.

14. Bretschneider, C. L. and Tamaye, E. E., 1976, "Hurricane Wind and Wave Forecasting Techniques," Vol. 6, No. 1, Hawaii: Look Laboratory.

15. Bretschneider, C. L., Huang, T. S. and Endo, H., 1980, "Hurricane Fields and Cross Sections: Surface Winds and Currents, Significant Waves and Wave Spectra for Potential OTEC Sites," Vol. II, University of Hawaii James K. K. Look Laboratory of Oceanographic Engineering Report No. 80-11, July, 95 pp.

16. Buckingham, E., 1914, *On Physically Similar Systems, Phys. Rev.*, Vol. 4, p. 345.

17. Burling, R. W., 1955, "Wind Generated Waves on Water," Ph.D. Dissertation, Imperial College, University of London.

18. Cardone, V. J., et al., 1975, "Hindcasting the Directional Spectra of Hurricane Generated Waves," Proc. of Offshore Technology Conference, Paper No. 2332.

19. Chin, P. C., 1972, "Tropical Cyclone Climatology for the China Seas and Western Pacific from 1884 to 1970," Vol. I *Basic Data*, Royal Observatory, Hong Kong, R.O. T.M. No. 11.

20. Fletcher, R. D., 1955, "Computation of Maximum Surface Winds in Hurricanes," *Bull. Amer. Meteor. Soc.*, 36, 246–250.

21. Fujita, 1962 (see T. Uji, 1975), "Numerical Estimation of Sea Waves in a Typhoon Area," Meteorol. Res. Inst. (JMRI) Tokyo, Papers in *Meteorol. and Geophys.* Vol. 26, No. 4, 199–217.

22. Garcia, W. A. and Flor, T. H., 1984, "Hurricane Alicia Storm Surge and Wave Data." Coastal Engineering Research Center Waterways Experiment Station, U.S. Corps of Engineers, Vicksburg, MS.

23. Gupta, G. R., Mishra, D. K. and Yadav, B. R., 1977, "The Porbandar Cyclone of October (1975)," *Indian J. Met. Hydrol. Geophys.* (1977) Vol. 28, No. 2, 177–188.

24. Hasselmann, K., et al., 1973, "Measurements of Wind-Wave Growth and Swell Decay During Joint Sea Wave Project JONSWAP," Deutsches Hydrographisches Institute, Hamburg, Germany.

25. Hasselmann, K. D., Ross, D. B., Miller, P. and Sell, W., 1976, "A Parametric Wave Prediction Model," *J. Phys. Oceanog.*, Vol. 6, pp. 200–228.

26. Holland, G. J., 1980, An Analytical Model of the Wind and Pressure Profiles in Hurricanes. *Monthly Weather Review*, 108, 1212–1218.

27. Holliday, C. R., 1969: On the Maximum Sustained Winds Occurring in Atlantic Hurricanes. *Tech. Memo.* WBTM-SR-45, 6 pp.
28. Huang, T. S., 1981, "A Three-Parameter Model for Hurricane Waves," Ph.D. Dissertation. Ocean Engineering, University of Hawaii, August, 192 pp.
29. Jelesnianski, C. P., 1966, "Numerical Computations of Storm Surges without Bottom Stress," *Monthly Weather Review*, Vol. 4, No. 6, 379–394.
30. Jelesnianski, C. P., 1973, "A Preliminary View of Storm Surges before and after Storm Modifications," NOAA Tech. Memo ERLWMPO-3.
31. Kraft, R. H., 1961, "The Hurricane's Central Pressure and Highest Wind," *Marines Weather Log*, 5, 157.
32. Long, R. B., 1979, "Forecasting Hurricane Waves," *Mariners Weather Log*, NOAA, Vol. 23, No. 1, pp. 1–10, January 1979.
33. Myers, V., 1954, "Characteristics of United States Hurricanes Pertinent to Levee Design for Lake Okechobee, Florida," *Hydromet Report* 32, 126 pp (GPO No. C30-70:32).
34. Mishra, D. K. and Gupta, G. R., 1976, "Estimating Maximum Wind Speeds in Tropical Cyclones Occurring in Indian Seas," *Indian Jour. Met. Hydrol. Geophys.* (1976) 273, 285–290.
35. Natarajan, R. and Ramamurthy, K. M., 1975, "Estimation of Central Pressures of Cyclonic Storms in the Indian Seas," *Indian J. Met. Hyrol. Geophys.* 26, 60–65.
36. Pierson, W. J., Fr. and Moskowitz, Y., 1964, "A Proposed Spectral Form for Fully Developed Wind Seas Based on the Similarity Theory of S.A. Kitaigorodski," *Journ. Geophys. Res.*, Vol. 69, pp. 5181–5190.
37. Resio, D. T. and Vincent, C. L., 1979, "A Comparison of Various Numerical Wave Prediction Techniques," Offshore Technology Conference, OTC Paper No. 3642, pp. 2471–2478.
38. Rosendal, Hanse and Shaw, Samuel L., 1982, "Relationships of Maximum Sustained Winds to Minimum Sea Level Pressure in Central North Pacific Tropical Cyclones," NOAA Technical Memo NWSTM PR-24.
39. Ross, D., 1979, "Observing and Predicting Hurricane Wind and Wave Conditions," Seminar on Ocean Processing and Service Systems (IDPSS) Morrow, USSR, 2–11 April 1979.
40. Rossby, C. G. and Montgomery, R. B., 1935, "The Layer of Frictional Influence in Wind and Ocean Currents," Papers in *Phys. Oceanog. and Meteorolo.*, Vol. 3, No. 3, 101 pp.
41. Schloemer, R. W., 1954, "Analysis and Synthesis of Hurricane Wind Patterns over Lake Okechobee, Florida," Hydromet Report 31, 49 pp (GPO No. C30. 70:31).
42. Schwerdt, R. W., Ho, F. P. and Watkins, R. R., 1979, Meteorological Criteria for Standard Project and Probable Maximum Hurricane Wind Fields, Gulf and East Coasts of United States, NOAA Technical Report. NWS 25 Dept. of Comm. NOAA NWS.
43. Shell's Ocean Data Gathering Program, Hurricane Camille, 1969.
44. Sverdrup, H. U. and Munk, W. H., 1947, "Wind, Sea, and Swell: Theory of Relations for Forecasting," H.O. Pub. No. 601, U.S. Navy Dept., 44 pp.
45. Takahashi, K., 1939, Distribution of Pressure and Wind in a Typhoon Circulation. J. Meteor. Soc. Japan, Ser. II, 17, 417–421.
46. U.S. Dept. of Commerce, NOAA, Marine Environmental Data and Information Services, *Marine Weather Log*, Vol. 1979–1981.
47. Wilson, Basil W., 1954, "Graphical Approach to the Forecasting of Waves in Moving Fetches," U.S. Army Corps of Engineers, Beach Erosion Board, T. M. No. 73, 31 pp.
48. Withee, G. W. and Johnson, A., Jr., 1975, "Buoy Observations During Hurricane Eloise," Data Buoy Office, National Oceanic and Atmospheric Administration, Bay St. Louis, MS.

49. Bretschneider, C. L. and Jen-Men Lo, 1984, "A Rankin Vortex Number as a Guide to the Selection of a Hurricane Model," Proceedings 1984 Coastal Engineering Conference, Houston, Texas.

50. Garcia, W. Andrews and Flor, Thomas H., 1984, Hurricane Alicia Storm Surge and Wave Data," Coastal Engineering Research Center, Waterways Experiment Station, Corps of Engineers, Vicksburg, Mississippi.

CHAPTER 7

DISTRIBUTION OF SEA STATE PARAMETERS AND DATA FITTING

Yoshimi Goda

Professor of Civil Engineering
Yokohama National University
Yokohama, Japan

CONTENTS

Introduction

Coastal and offshore structures are subject to hostile environmental conditions, and it is critical they maintain their functions properly throughout their design life. Waves are the most dominant and influential environmental factor to be considered in coastal and ocean design. It is important to obtain reliable information on wave conditions at the site of interest before the planning and design of a maritime structure is undertaken. Particularly important is determining the severity of storm waves, which establishes the magnitude of design waves. Underestimation of wave severity leads to the failure of coastal and offshore structures, whereas overestimation results in unnecessary costs. Another vital consideration is the day-to-day conditions of sea state, which governs the construction phase of a structure and controls the operation of the structure after completion.

This chapter deals with the statistics of daily sea states and storm waves. A new concept of "wave climate" is first introduced and then expressed in terms of several wave statistics. Selection of design waves must be based on statistical analysis of extreme wave data, and thus a review of the methodology of extreme wave statistics is presented with an illustrative example of data analysis. However, storm wave statistics still lack reliable data covering sufficiently long periods. Many methods have been proposed for selecting design waves, but no conclusive method has yet been agreed upon. It is left to the experience and sound judgment of coastal and ocean engineers to employ a rational approach to extreme wave analysis and to select the design wave for the project under consideration.

Wave Climate and Data Source

Definition of Wave Climate and Classification of Wave Statistics

Wave climate is a fairly new term created with an analogy of the atmospheric weather climate. It refers to the general condition of sea state at a particular location. The principal elements of wave climate are the wave height and period parameters, and the wave direction. The significant wave height is usually employed as the height parameter. The period parameter is either of the significant wave period determined from time-series analysis or the period corresponding to the spectral peak frequency. The mean wave period either by time-series or spectral analysis is also used as the period parameter. The wave direction in wave climatology is usually expressed with the 16-point bearing system such as NNE, WSW, etc. As in the atmospheric climate, the wave climate is described in terms of months, seasons, and years.

Wave statistics can be classified into several categories according to the time scales concerned. The major classification is short-term and long-term wave statistics. The former deals with the statistical properties of individual waves within a short-time duration, say 20 minutes or so. The topics of short-term wave statistics are fully discussed in Chapter 4 "Random Waves and Spectra." The long-term wave statistics are associated with the wave climate previously defined and with the extreme wave conditions during the lifetime of a structure, and are subdivided accordingly. Long-term wave statistics are formulated for specific time intervals.

The wave climate statistics are sometimes called the medium-term wave statistics, while the extreme wave statistics retain the name of long-term wave statistics [1, 2]. Although the two statistics are occasionally treated as one group without differentiation, the objectives of analyzing these statistics are different and the techniques of data analysis are separate. The wave climate statistics are mostly concerned with operational aspects of maritime structures, while the extreme wave statistics are oriented toward estimating design waves for a certain length of return period. The difference between the two categories of statistics should be kept in mind, and the best use of respective statistics should be made depending on the nature of the problem.

Data Source of Wave Climate and Extreme Wave Statistics

Requirements for the Duration of Data. Analyses of wave climate and extreme wave statistics require a certain amount of wave data covering a sufficiently long period of time. One year is the minimum requirement for the measured wave data, but one year is too short to yield reliable information on wave climate and extreme waves. Goda [3] has demonstrated that the annual mean of significant wave height in a single year may deviate 15% from the average value obtained over long periods. Wave data over several years without significant gaps in data acquisition are the standard requirement for wave climate analysis.

The requirement for long duration of wave data is more severe for the extreme wave statistics. Nolte [4] gives an example showing that estimates of 100-year maximum wave height may vary by a factor of three if it is estimated from different one-year data records. The time duration of several decades is recommended as the requirement for wave data used to determine extreme wave statistics.

Wave data sources currently available are visually observed data, instrument measured data, operational wave forecast data, and wave hindcast data. The nature and limitations of these data sources are discussed in the following subsections.

Visually Observed Wave Data. Visual observations of wave data are routinely made from many ocean weather ships and land-based stations such as lighthouses. Ocean-going vessels and fishing boats also voluntarily comply with the request of meteorological agencies to report the weather and wave conditions regularly. Therefore, visual observation data are the largest in number and cover the large area of the ocean where ships are routinely passing. The most famous compilation of such ship observation data is *Ocean Wave Statistics* by Hogben and Lumb [5] first published in 1967; a revised edition is now available [6]. The U.S. Navy has also published a world-wide marine climatic atlas [7]. Similar efforts have been done in many other countries and some results are available on magnetic tapes [8]. A list of international and national marine data repositories and information, including those of measured wave data, is found in the *Proceedings of the 9th International Ship Structure Congress* [9].

Visually observed data cannot be expected to be of good quality. Accuracy is wholly dependent on the experience and skill of the observer. Even reports from ocean weather ships that are made by trained observers are said to have bias [10]. Synthesis of visual observation data from a large number of ship reports may yield less biased estimation of wave statistics at the site of interest. There have been several efforts to establish the correlation between visually-observed and instrument-measured wave data. The following adjustment is suggested by Guedes Soares [10] for wave heights:

$$H_s = 1.47 + 0.84 \, H_w \quad \text{with s} = 1.19 \, (m) \tag{1}$$

$$H_s = 2.33 + 0.75 \, H_v \quad \text{with s} = 1.59 \, (m) \tag{2}$$

where H_s = significant wave height measured by instruments
        H_w = visually observed height at ocean weather ships
        H_v = wave height reported by voluntary ships
        s = standard deviation

The correlation on wave periods is not well established. A possible reason is the separate reporting of sea and swell periods in visual observations as opposed to a single average (or significant) period provided by instrument measurements. In the North Sea where swells are not influential, a good correlation is reported [11].

Visually observed wave data based on ship reports are used primarily for wave climatic analysis. They are not suitable for extremal analysis because they are random reports, which make it difficult to identify individual storm waves. Also, ships have a tendency to avoid severe storms areas. However, in regions of scarce wave data, ship observations may be the only information available for the estimation of extreme wave conditions.

Measured Wave Data. Many governmental agencies in the world have been conducting long-term wave measurement programs, and many nongovernmental agencies have made project-oriented wave measurements of limited duration at various sites. A comprehensive catalogue of measured wave data in the world has been published by the Marine Information and Advisory Service in U.K. [12]. Most original wave data must be obtained from the source agency.

The quality and duration of measured wave data varies from site to site. Because of the recent development of reliable wave measurement systems, there are few wave stations that have been operating more than 10 years. The Ocean Weather Stations in the North Atlantic, equipped with Tucker wave recorders, are examples of wave stations that have been in operation for an extended period. A drawback of measured wave data is the deficiency of directional information in most cases, because directional wave measurement capability has become commercially available only since the mid-1980s. Some stations employ visual measurements of wave directions or radar image analysis of sea surface scatters to supplement wave measurements by conventional recorders. Another problem in measured wave data is occasional instrument failure, especially during major storms. In analyzing measured wave data, data must be reviewed closely if significant data were lost during storms. If the losses are not trivial, the gaps should be filled in with visual observation or hindcast wave data.

Operational Wave Forecast Data. Since the 1970s, several countries have been conducting daily forecast of wave conditions over the ocean. These forecasts are associated with the global computer forecast of barometric patterns. The U.S. Navy Fleet Numerical Oceanography Center at Monterey, for example, gives the world-wide ocean wave forecast by means of a spectral ocean wave model. Such forecasts are given on a global grid with points spaced at a distance of a few hundred kilometers, and they are mostly used for ship routing to avoid storm areas.

There are several shortcomings in these operational forecast data when used as the wave climate data source. The first is the accuracy of forecast. The second is the scarcity of data points, which results in the lack of information in coastal waters and near some storm centers. The third is the delay in compiling these forecast data into workable wave climatic data bases. However, the operational wave forecast data have the potential of becoming an important data source of wave climate over the ocean in near future.

Hindcast Wave Data. Wave hindcasts are usually done to obtain major storm wave data over 30 to 50 years or longer for extremal wave analysis. A time period covering known storm activity is chosen, and wave hindcasting is performed for that period. Selection of the storms to be analyzed is an important step in the hindcast because failure to pick up all the storm waves above a certain level results in a distortion of extreme wave statistics, leading to an incorrect estimate of design waves. Such hindcasts have been made for many ocean areas by various agencies. Some of the hindcast results have been reported in technical journals and some are deposited in public archives for use by the general public; but other hindcast data are held by private sector sponsoring organizations. Private sector hindcast data, even the more recent data, may often be obtained through negotiations provided it is known where the data were collected.

Another type of wave hindcast involves daily generation of wave data over several years for wave climatic analysis in the area where no wave data are available. Wind data covering the ocean area of interest for the whole time period are constructed from synthetic barometric charts, and wave conditions are hindcast at about six-hour intervals.

Hindcast wave data preferably should be calibrated by instrument measurements before statistical analysis is made. Uncertainty in wave hindcasts originates from the inaccuracy of wind field information and the inadequacy of wave growth models. The former problem is hard to remedy, because old weather maps have been constructed with sparse weather data and there is no way to supplement them. The latter problem is being gradually resolved in recent years with the appearance of several new wave models, which survived various calibration tests. Nevertheless, a factor of 20% is an optimistic estimate of the accuracy of wave hindcasts and a much greater deviation is possible if no calibration with measurement data is performed.

Distribution of Sea State Parameters

Joint Frequency Table of Wave Height and Period Parameters

The general description of wave climate at a certain location is expressed in several ways. The following are typical presentations:

1. Annual, seasonal, and/or monthly averages of significant wave heights and periods (or mean periods), with or without the standard deviations and the maximum values in the corresponding time span.
2. Wave rose or the graphical representation of the histogram of wave heights in several ranks in various directions, which is similar to the wind rose.
3. Join frequency tables of significant wave heights and periods (or mean periods) with or without classification in the wave direction.

The wave height and period parameters employed in these presentations can be either serial data by stationary measurements at regular time intervals or random data such as those by ship reports.

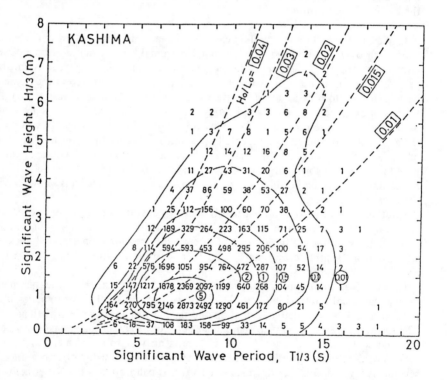

Figure 1. Joint frequency table of significant wave height and period at Kashima Port. [13].

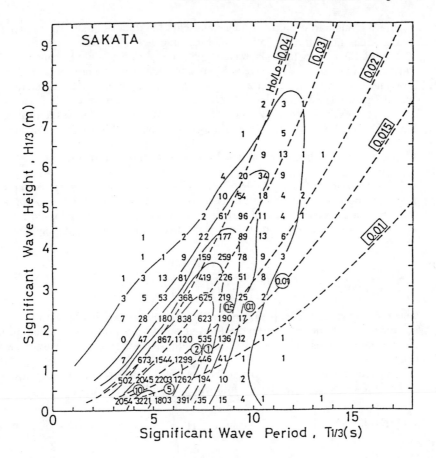

Figure 2. Joint frequency table of significant wave height and period at Sakata Port [13].

Of the above, the joint frequency tables contain the most detailed information on wave climate, and therefore they are employed as the basic form of data representation [5–7]. Figure 1 is an example of the joint frequency table of H_s and T_s representing the results of two-hourly wave measurements over eight years at Kashima Port in Japan, facing the Pacific Ocean at latitude 35° 52′ N and longitude 140° 45′ E [13]. The figures are the number of observations in respective ranks of wave heights and periods, the figures within circles represent their percentile to the whole number of observations (32,346), and the figures within rectangles denote the significant wave steepness.

The example of Figure 1 represents the wave climate under the influence of both wind waves and swell. The correlation between wave heights and periods is insignificant. In the enclosed water areas, the wave climate is governed by local wind waves, and a strong correlation is then observed between wave heights and periods.

Figure 2 is such an example, which represents the data of Sakata Port facing the Sea of Japan at latitude 38° 55′ N and longitude 139° 45′ E [13].

The joint frequency tables of wave heights and periods should be constructed for various wave directions separately. Many engineering problems such as beach erosion and harbor oscillations are quite sensitive to the directional characteristics of wave climate. ("Harbor oscillations" generally mean resonant motions of water body in a harbor excited by long-period incident waves. Here I refer to the problem of maintaining calmness of harbor basin against short-period waves during storms.)

Cumulative Distribution of Wave Height and Period Parameters

From the joint frequency table of wave height and period parameters, the marginal distribution of wave heights or periods is easily obtained. It is expressed in the form of non-exceedance or cumulative probability. The following log-normal distribution has been fitted to many marginal distributions with a varying degree of success:

$$p(Y) = \frac{1}{(2\pi)^{1/2}\sigma_Y} \exp\left\{ -\frac{1}{2}\left(\frac{Y - \mu_Y}{\sigma_Y}\right)^2 \right\} \tag{3}$$

where Y stands for log H, p(Y) denotes the probability density function of Y, and μ_Y and σ_Y are the mean and standard deviation of Y, respectively. The log-normal distribution requires only two easily calculated parameters to describe the wave height distribution.

The good fit of the log-normal distribution to wave data is not universal however. Some data are better fitted by the following Weibull distribution:

$$\left. \begin{aligned} P[H \leq X] &= 1 - \left[-\left(\frac{X - H_c}{H_0}\right)^k \right] : X \geq H_c \\ P[H \leq X] &= 0 \qquad\qquad\qquad : X < H_c \end{aligned} \right\} \tag{4}$$

where $P[H \leq X]$ denotes the probability that the wave height parameter H does not exceed a given level X. The location parameter H_c roughly corresponds to the height of swell persistent at the locality; it is selected by inspection of observed data or by several trials of best fit using different values for H_c. The scale parameter H_0 and the shape parameter k are determined by the best fit to the observed wave data. For the case of wave period distributions, the location and scale parameters H_c and H_0 in Equation 4 are replaced by the corresponding values T_c and T_0 of wave periods.

Battjes [14] applied the Weibull distribution to the data of H_s around the British Isles and reported the range of $H_c = 0 - 0.9$ m, $H_0 = 0.7 - 2.7$ m, and $k = 1.0 - 1.3$. Hirose and Takahashi [13] also applied Equation 4 to the wave data around Japanese Islands. They obtained parameter values similar to Battjes' for H_s, but the shape parameter for T_s ranged from 1.8 to 3.6. Figures 3 and 4 are examples of the Weibull distributions fitted to the data of significant wave heights and periods around Japan by Hirose and Takahashi.

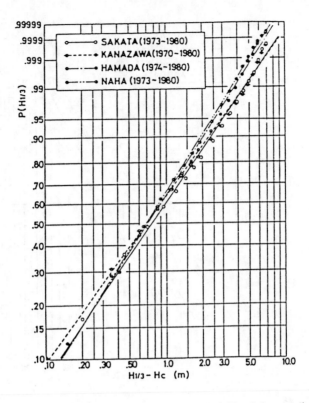

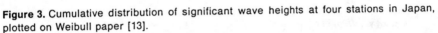

Figure 3. Cumulative distribution of significant wave heights at four stations in Japan, plotted on Weibull paper [13].

Equation 4 fits observed data better than Equation 3, because Equation 4 contains three parameters while the latter has two. However, even Equation 4 cannot represent the full range of the observed distributions of wave heights and periods; the upper tails usually exhibit different behavior than the main parts of the distributions as illustrated in Figures 3 and 4.

Wave Persistency Statistics

Wave Persistence Analysis of Consecutive Wave Data

Wave persistence refers to the tendency of storm waves or calm seas to persist over some time period. Wave persistence is identified and examined by means of the autocorrelation coefficient of time series data of wave height parameter. Goda [15] obtained correlation coefficients of about 0.3 with lags of one day along the coasts

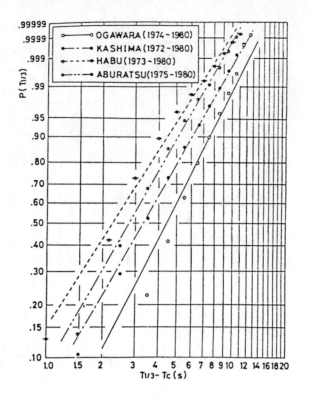

Figure 4. Cumulative distribution of significant wave periods at four stations in Japan, plotted on Weibull paper [13].

of Japan. Lawson and Abernethy [16] found that correlation coefficients remained above 0.5 for data one day apart at the Botany Bay in East Australia. Because many marine operations require a certain duration of calm seas, wave persistence is an important item of wave data analysis.

Wave persistence statistics are quantitatively measured by the number of hours (or days) of the duration of the sea state above or below a certain threshold wave height, which is usually expressed in terms of significant height. Figure 5 is an example of consecutive data of significant wave height with respect to time. The portion of wave height exceeding 2 m is defined as a persistence of storm waves, and that not exceeding 1 m is taken as a persistence of calm seas in this example. There are two occasions of storm waves with durations of 12 and 31 hours, respectively, and two other occasions of calm seas with the durations of 16 and 34 hours, respectively. Time duration of the sea state above or below a predetermined threshold height constitutes a statistical variate, and its cumulative distribution is analyzed by applying various functions including Equations 3 and 4.

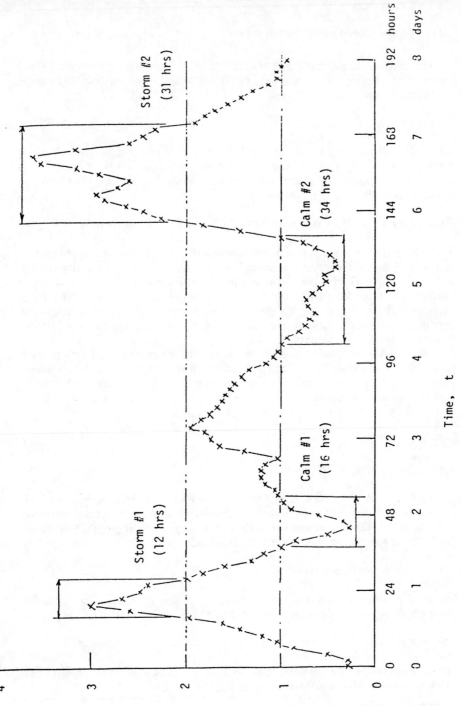

Figure 5. Illustrative sketch of wave history for the definition of wave persistence.

One representative statistic of wave persistence is the mean duration time of the sea state. Lawson and Abernethy [16] employed the following exponential function for the mean duration time of rough seas:

$$D = \alpha(H_s)_c^{\beta} \tag{5}$$

where $(H_s)_c$ denotes the threshold significant height of rough seas. They obtained the values $\alpha = 7$ and $\beta = -2$ when D is expressed in days and H_s is measured in meters. As expected, larger storm wave heights have shorter duration. The values of α and β naturally vary from site to site.

Estimating Wave Persistence from Height and Period Statistics

The basic data of wave persistence is a time series record of wave heights such as shown in Figure 5. On some occasions, however, such data are not available. The joint frequency table of wave height and period parameters or the marginal distribution of wave heights may be the only data available. Because the need for wave persistence statistics is strong, Graham [17] proposed a technique to estimate the persistence statistics from joint frequency tables. Kuwashima and Hogben [18, 19] further refined the technique.

First, the marginal distribution of wave heights is approximated by the two-parameter Weibull distribution (or Equation 4 with H_c being set at 0), and the shape parameter k is estimated. Next, the mean duration (in hours) of the sea state above a predetermined threshold height $(H_s)_c$ which is denoted by $\bar{\tau}$, is related to the exceedance probability Q of the threshold height $(H_s)_c$ by

$$\left.\begin{aligned} Q[H_s > (H_s)_c] &= \exp[-(\bar{\tau}/A)^{-1/\beta}] \\ \bar{\tau} &= A/\{-\ln Q[H_s > (H_s)_c]\}^{\beta} \end{aligned}\right\} \tag{6}$$

The parameters A and β have been determined as functions of the shape parameter k of the Weibull distribution by fitting to various time series data of wave measurements at seven stations around the British Isles, one station in South Africa, and one in Hong Kong. The results are formulated as

$$A = 35/k^{1/2} \quad \text{and} \quad \beta = 0.6k^{0.287} \tag{7}$$

Further the cumulative distribution function of the duration, τ, of the sea state exceeding a threshold height is approximated by the following function:

$$P[\tau] = 1 - \exp[-C(\tau/\bar{\tau})^{\alpha}] \tag{8}$$

The parameters C and α are given the following values as a result of fitting Equation 8 to various wave measurement data:

$$\alpha = 0.267k[(H_s)_c/\bar{H}_s]^{0.24} \quad \text{and} \quad C = [\Gamma(1 + 1/\alpha)]^{\alpha} \tag{9}$$

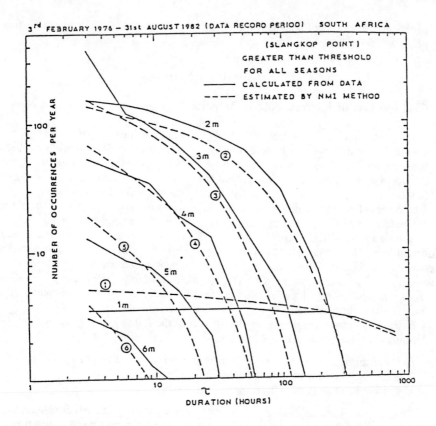

Figure 6. Example of persistence statistics for the duration of sea state above several threshold heights [18].

where $\bar{H}_s$ = mean value of the observed significant wave heights
$\Gamma(\ )$ = Gamma function.

The time duration of the sea state below a predetermined threshold height denoted by τ' is calculated as follows. First, the mean duration $\bar{\tau}'$ is evaluated as $\bar{\tau}' = \bar{\tau}(1 - Q)/Q$. Second, the parameters α and C in Equation 8 are changed to

$$\alpha' = 0.267k[(H_s)_c/\bar{H}_s]^{-0.4} \quad \text{and} \quad C' = [\Gamma(1 + 1/\alpha')]^{\alpha'} \tag{10}$$

Figure 6 is an example of the estimation of persistence statistics for the durations of sea state above several threshold values [18]. The solid lines are the results of direct counting of persistence statistics from the time series data of wave data, while the dashed lines are estimated by the method previously described. For example, rough seas in excess of 4 m with the duration over 10 hours occur about 30 times per year according to Figure 6.

Extreme Wave Statistics

Classification of Extreme Wave Statistics

Extreme wave statistics deal with the heights and periods of storm waves of rare events. The main objective of determining extreme statistics is to provide a reliable basis for selecting design wave conditions. Statistical prediction is often requested for storm wave heights which are probable over a long time span such as 100 years. Similar to other extreme value statistics such as the flood discharge statistics, the return period is used as one of the basic parameters in extreme wave statistics. It is defined as the average waiting time between storm wave heights exceeding a given threshold value. When a return period, say R_p years, is specified, then a storm wave height level, H_R, is predicted such that a storm waves exceeding H_R are expected to occur once on the average during the time span, R_p. The wave height level H_R is called the R_p-years wave height. As general terminology, the "return value" or "return height" is introduced in this chapter to broadly cover the wave height levels for various return periods.

Extreme wave statistics may be classified into the following three categories, depending on wave parameters of interest:

1. Long-term cumulative distribution of individual wave heights.
2. Extreme statistics of significant wave heights.
3. Extreme statistics of highest individual waves.

An example of the application of the first category is fatigue analysis of structural members under cyclic wave loading. The first category can also give information on the return value of the largest individual wave height. The second and third categories are directly concerned with design wave selection, and they are analyzed by the established methods of extreme value analysis.

Although the second category statistics use the significant wave heights of the observed records or the hindcasted waves, the third category statistics employ the largest wave heights from individual records as the basis of the data. Because the method of extreme value analysis is common in both categories of statistics, no further comment is made on the third category statistics.

Long-term Statistics of Individual Wave Heights

The methodology for analyzing long-term statistics of individual wave heights has been given by Battjes [14]. The basic data are the joint frequency table of wave height and period parameters such as shown in Figures 1 and 2. Battjes adopted the significant wave height H_s and the mean zero-crossing wave period T_z as the height and period parameters, but other choices are possible.

Assumptions are made that the sea state remains unchanged between two successive observation hours and the distribution of individual wave heights can be described by the Rayleigh distribution discussed in Chapter 4. Let the joint frequency table be converted into the form of joint probability density function $p(H_s, T_z)$, and let the conditional probability density function of individual wave heights under a given sea state be denoted by $p_0(H|H_s)$. In the case of the Rayleigh distribution, the latter is expressed as

$$p_0(H|H_s) \doteq 4(H/H_s) \exp[-2(H/H_s)^2] \tag{11}$$

and the cumulative distribution is

$$P_0(H|H_s) \doteq 1 - \exp[-2(H/H_s)^2] \tag{12}$$

A slight departure of individual wave height distribution from Rayleigh has been reported in recent years, as discussed in Chapter 4, but it does not affect the method of analysis described in the following.

Because the number of waves per unit time is inversely proportional to the mean wave period T_z, the long-term probability density of individual wave heights is evaluated as a sum of the conditional density $p_0(H|H_s)$ weighted with T_z^{-1} and the probability that H_s and T_z simultaneously fall within certain ranges [14]:

$$p(H) = \frac{\iint p_0(H|H_s)T_z^{-1}p(H_s, T_z)\, dH_s\, dT_z}{\iint T_z^{-1}p(H_s, T_z)\, dH_s\, dT_z} \tag{13}$$

The denominator in Equation 13 represents the long-term average number of waves per unit time and is denoted by $\overline{T_z^{-1}}$.

The cumulative long-term distribution of individual wave heights is obtained by integrating Equation 13 with respect to H:

$$P(H) = \iint P_0(H/H_s)T_z^{-1}p(H_s, T_z)\, dH_s\, dT_z / \overline{T_z^{-1}} \tag{14}$$

Battjes [14] evaluated the long-term distribution of individual wave heights around the British Isles by using the observed joint frequency tables of H_s and T_z. Figure 7 is an example of the results. The probability of the return value for a given return period is given as

$$\text{Prob}[H > H_R] = 1 - P(H_R) = (R_p \overline{T_z^{-1}})^{-1} \tag{15}$$

Caution must be taken to express the return period R_p with the same time unit as T_z. The probability scales indicated in the upper left of Figure 7 are calculated by this method.

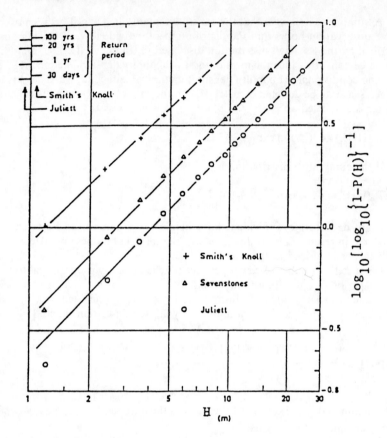

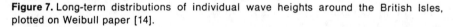

Figure 7. Long-term distributions of individual wave heights around the British Isles, plotted on Weibull paper [14].

The expected number of waves per year exceeding a given height level is easily calculated from the cumulative distribution P(H). Figure 8 presents examples of such estimates at four stations in Japan along the Japan Sea coast and in the East China Sea. In these examples, the total number of waves per year is about 6 million.

Data Set for Extreme Statistics of Storm Wave Heights

Total Sample Analysis versus Peak Value Analysis. In the early days of wave data analysis, the extreme wave height for a certain return period was sometimes estimated by simply extrapolating the marginal distribution of significant wave heights, such as shown in Figure 3. By knowing the time interval between successive wave observation hours Δt, the exceedance probability was estimated as $1/(R_p/\Delta t)$ and

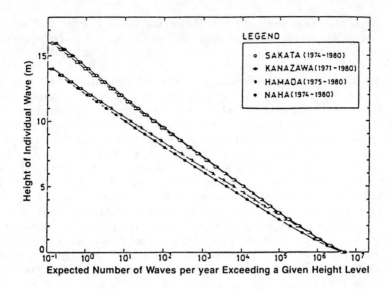

Figure 8. Cumulative distribution of individual wave heights at four stations in Japan [13].

the return value of wave height was read on the extrapolated distribution curve. The method is called the total sample method and is still advocated by some engineers even in the late 1980s. However, the method is statistically unsound for the following reasons and therefore is not recommended for extreme wave analysis:

1. Successive wave data with the time interval of several hours are mutually correlated and do not constitute independent random data. Violation of the assumption of independent random variables excludes the use of most statistical theories.

2. There is no guarantee that data in the upper quartile fit well to the tail of a distribution that governs the whole range of wave heights [20]. Departure of significant wave heights from the log-normal distribution in its upper tail was presented by Battjes [14].

A more statistically sound method is to use only the peak values of storm wave heights. Because individual storms are considered independent, a series of the significant (or maximum) wave heights at the peaks of storms constitute a set of samples from independent random variables. In preparing the data of peak storm wave heights, efforts should be taken to separate storm waves of different nature (waves generated by hurricanes, monsoons, and frontal systems, for example), because they belong to different storm populations and their distribution functions would be different.

Annual Maximum Series and Partial-Duration Series. A series of all peak storm wave heights under the same storm population forms the basis of extreme wave data. The data are called here the peak value series of storm wave heights. In hydrology, such data are called the complete-duration series [21]. When a full record of consecutive wave observations is available for a period of considerable time, a complete-duration series of storm wave heights can be constructed. When storm wave data are constructed by means of wave hindcasting, preparation of the complete-duration series is not practical because of large cost involved in hindcasting all the storm waves over a long period. If one is content with having the data of all storm waves exceeding a certain height level, such data are called the partial-duration series. The process to limit the data only below or above some threshold value is termed "censoring," which commonly appears in the statistical analysis of lifetime data in biomedical sciences and quality control of manufactured goods [22]. The partial-duration series are censored data, and the complete-duration data are uncensored data. A difference between extreme wave statistics and lifetime statistics is the method of censoring. In the extreme wave statistics, data below a threshold height are ignored and are said to be left censored. In the lifetime statistics, data with exceptionally long lifetime are omitted because of test time limitation. Such data are said to be right censored.

An annual maximum series is constructed by drawing the maximum value of significant (or maximum) wave height in every year from the full data of all storm waves. Similarly a monthly maximum series can be constructed and analyzed. When all the annual maxima are known, they form an uncensored data set. If the data of some years with low wave activity are omitted, they become a censored data set. The annual (or monthly) maximum data differs from the peak value data in the sense that the former represents the extreme values among many peak values in the same year (or month). A return value calculated from the former data retains the meaning that it is the lower-threshold of wave height expected to occur as the annual maximum during a given return period. In practice, however, the difference between the return values by the annual maximum data and the peak value data becomes negligible for return periods longer than about 5 years [23].

In the early stage of flood studies, the annual maximum series and the partial-duration series were treated as different data sets. However, the uncensored annual maximum series is a complete-duration series in its own sense, and the censored annual maximum series is regarded as a partial-duration series of annual maximum data. The key factor is the degree of censoring, or the ratio of the number of analyzed data N to the total number of data N_T during the period of analysis. This ratio is called the censoring parameter in this chapter and denoted by $v = N/N_T$; the uncensored data have the parameter $v = 1$, and for the censored data $v < 1$. Another key factor is the mean rate of storm waves, or the mean number of storm waves per year under the same storm population. The mean rate is denoted here with λ. The uncensored annual maximum series can be treated in the extreme value analysis as the case with $\lambda = v = 1$, although the rate λ is absolutely fixed at 1 for the annual maximum series.

In the following, the terminology of "peak value series" is used as inclusive of annual (or monthly) maximum series in order to simplify the description, because the method of data analysis is same for both the peak value series and the annual maximum series.

Fitting of Extreme Wave Data to a Distribution Function

Distribution Function for Extreme Value Analysis. The extreme wave height data inclusive of both annual maximum series and peak value data are fitted to some distribution function. The commonly employed functions in extreme wave analysis are

1. The Fisher-Tippett type I (FT-I), the Gumbel, or the double-exponential type distribution.
2. The Fisher-Tippett type II (FT-II), or the Frechet distribution.
3. The Weibull distribution.
4. The log-normal distribution.

These distribution functions are listed in the forms of the cumulative probability or the non-exceedance probability:

$$
\left.
\begin{array}{l}
\text{FT-I: } F[H < x] = \exp[-\exp\{-(x - B)/A\}] \\
\quad \text{mean:} \quad E[x] = B + \gamma A \quad (\gamma = 0.5772\ldots : \text{Euler's constant}) \\
\quad \text{variance: } E[\{x - E(x))^2] = \pi^2 A^2/6
\end{array}
\right\}
\quad (16)
$$

$$
\left.
\begin{array}{l}
\text{FT-II: } F[H < x] = \exp[-(x/A)^{-k}] \\
\quad \text{mean:} \quad E[x] = \acute{A}\Gamma(1 - 1/k) \\
\quad \text{variance: } E[\{x - E(x)\}^2] = A^2[\Gamma(1 - 2/k) - \Gamma^2(1 - 1/k)]
\end{array}
\right\}
\quad (17)
$$

$$
\left.
\begin{array}{l}
\text{Weibull: } F[H < x] = 1 - \exp[-\{(x - B)/A\}^k] \\
\quad \text{mean:} \quad E[x] = B + A\Gamma(1 + 1/k) \\
\quad \text{variance: } E[\{x - E(x)\}^2] = A^2[\Gamma(1 + 2/k) - \Gamma^2(1 + 1/k)]
\end{array}
\right\}
\quad (18)
$$

$$
\left.
\begin{array}{l}
\text{Log-normal: } F[H < x] = \dfrac{1}{(2\pi)^{1/2}} \displaystyle\int_0^x \dfrac{1}{At} \exp[-\{(\ln t - B)/A\}^2/2]\, dt \\[2mm]
\quad \text{mean:} \quad E[x] = \exp[B + A^2/2] \\
\quad \text{variance: } E[\{x - E(x)\}^2] = \exp[2B + A^2]\{\exp(A^2) - 1\}
\end{array}
\right\}
\quad (19)
$$

where Γ denotes the Gamma function, and E represents the ensemble mean of the expected value.

Other formulas of extreme distribution functions are cited by Isaacson and MacKenzie [24], and Muir and El-Shaarawi [20]. The parameters A, B, and k are usually called the scale, location, and shape parameters, respectively. The FT-I distribution is commonly used by many scientists and engineers.

The FT-II was tried by Thom [25] for annual maximum data of extreme wave heights. The use of the Weibull distribution was advocated by Petruaskas and Aagaard [26], who also presented a procedure to select the best-fitting distribution function among a set of the Weibull and the FT-I distributions. The log-normal distribution is mostly employed in the total sample method discussed earlier. The log-normal distribution has a tendency for the rate of increase of the return wave height to decrease as the return period becomes long, when compared with the FT-I and the Weibull distributions. Use of the log-normal distribution for the peak value series of storm wave heights (inclusive of annual maximum series hereinafter) should not be considered until positive evidence for its support is established.

Method of Data Fitting to a Distribution Function. The data of peak value series must be fitted to some distribution function to enable estimation of the return wave heights for various return periods. There are four methods of data fitting:

1. Graphical method using a specially-devised plotting paper on which the data from a particular distribution are plotted on a straight line.
2. Least squares method.
3. Method of moments.
4. Maximum likelihood method.

The graphical method was used by many engineers for flood analysis in the past when calculation of standard deviations was a tedious job. Presently the least squares method replaces the graphical method, because the calculation is not a burden anymore and the former is a refined version of the latter. In the both methods, the peak value data are first rearranged in descending order of magnitude from the largest to the smallest. The m-th largest datum is denoted as x_m. Then a plotting probability P_m is assigned to x_m, and the reduced variate y_m is calculated from the distribution function in question as

$$y_m = F^{-1}[1 - P_m] \tag{20}$$

The assignment of plotting probability is called the plotting position problem and is discussed in the following section. For the FT-I and Weibull distributions, the formulas for the reduced variate are

FT-I: $y = -\ln[-\ln(1 - P)]$ $\tag{21}$

Weibull: $y = [-\ln(1 - P)]^{-1/k}$ $\tag{22}$

Between the ordered data x_m and the reduced variate y_m, the following linear relation exists and the estimates of the parameters A and B are easily obtained by graphical fitting or by the least squares method:

$$x_m = Ay_m + B \tag{23}$$

The shape parameter k cannot be estimated by this method. Petruaskas and Aagaard [26] proposed to fix k at one of seven values (0.75, 0.85, 1.0, 1.1, 1.25, 1.5, and 2.0), to fit the data to seven alternative Weibull distributions and the FT-I distribution, and to choose an acceptable distribution from the eight alternatives.

The method of moments uses the mean and variance of the peak value series data, and they are equated to the theoretical values listed under Equations 16–19 in order to obtain the estimates of A and B, or A and k for the FT-II distribution. An estimate of the parameter k for the Weibull distribution may be obtained by introducing the skewness, but the approach by Petruaskas and Aagaard previously discussed is perhaps more practical. In the case of the FT-I distribution, Gumbel [27] introduced correction factors for both the mean and the standard deviation for small size data, but Lettenmaier and Burges [28] demonstrated by Monte Carlo simulations that Gumbel's corrections yield poor estimates of the parameters and therefore the ensemble values under Equation 16 should be employed.

The maximum likelihood method makes estimates of parameter values by maximizing the likelihood that the data are from the distribution function under investigation. Likely equations are written down (see Muir and El-Shaarawi [20] for example) and they are numerically solved to get optimum values of parameters. The maximum likelihood method seems to yield more reliable estimates than other methods as exemplified by a Monte Carlo simulation study by Carter and Challenor [29]. Lawless [22] gives full exposure of the maximum likelihood method for life-time data analysis. Its use in extreme wave data analysis is not yet popular, however, probably because of the complexity of numerical analysis involved.

No consensus has yet been established on the best method for data fitting. Furthermore, no one can tell what distribution function is the "right" one to represent the ensemble of extreme storm wave data. One must assume a priori that a certain distribution function should fit the data, or he has to try several distribution functions in search of the most appropriate one. In the former situation, any fitting method will suffice for the purpose, provided a good plotting formula is employed in the case of the least squares method. In the latter situation, the least squares method will provide a easy means of comparing the accuracy of data fit to a distribution function. For the case of censored data, the method of moments has no particular provision and the data are treated the same as uncensored data. The censored data are better analyzed by the least squares method and the maximum likelihood method. In the following, discussion is mainly focused on the least squares method.

Plotting Position Formulas. The problem of assigning a particular plotting probability to each ordered data point has been discussed by many people. Gumbel [27] strongly argued for the use of the Weibull formula $P_i = i/(N + 1)$ by stating five postulates for the selection of plotting position formula. Kimball [30] discussed the problem from the statistical point of view and concluded that the expected value of the i-th reduced variate is most suitable to give the plotting probability, i.e.,

$$P_i = F\{E[y_i]\} \tag{24}$$

where the order i is assigned in the ascending fashion from the smallest to the largest. The ascending order i is related to the descending order m as

$$i = N - m + 1 \tag{25}$$

Cunnane [31] critically reviewed the problem by giving the two criteria for selection of plotting position formulas: unbiasedness and smallest mean square error of plotted results. He supported Kimball's recommendation of Equation 24 and denounced Gumbel's postulates as statistically incorrect. The biased nature of the Weibull formula when applied to the FT-I distribution was demonstrated by a simulation study by Carter and Challenor [29]. Earle and Baer [32] reported on the basis of Monte Carlo simulations that sampling variability causes a positive bias of return values in the case of the log-normal distribution. But it is easily proven that the bias was caused by the use of the Weibull formula and little bias would have been observed if the Blom formula (Equation 30) was used instead.

Equation 24 indicates that the plotting probability differs from one distribution function to another. The following are recommended plotting formulas for the respective distribution functions:

FT-I: Gringorten Formula [33]

$$P_i = (i - 0.44)/(N + 0.12)$$ (26)

Barnett Formula [34]

$$P_i = \exp[-\exp\{\gamma + 3(\ln 2)[2i/(N + 1) - 1]\}]$$ (27)

Weibull: Petruaskas and Aagaard Formula [26]

$$P_i = [i - (0.49 - 0.50/k)]/[N + (0.21 + 0.32/k)]$$ (28)

$$P_m = 1 - [m - (0.30 + 0.18/k)]/[N + (0.21 + 0.32/k)]$$ (29)

Log-normal: Blom Formula [35]

$$P_i = (i - 0.375)/(N + 0.25)$$ (30)

These formulas except for the Petruaskas and Aagaard formula are invariant to the change of the ascending order i to the descending order m. The Blom formula is originally for the normal distribution, but it is also applicable to the log-normal distribution. The Barnett formula was devised to yield the best estimate of the scale and location parameters, but it yields noticeable deviations of plotted data at the upper and lower ends, say about 5% ranges; and thus it is not suitable for competitive comparisons with other distribution functions in the goodness of fit tests. Nevertheless, the mean square errors of the estimates of parameters are smaller than those by the Gringorten Formula.

In the case of censored data, the plotting position should be assigned by using the total number of peak wave data that must have occurred in the time period considered. Let the length of period be K years and the mean rate of storm wave generation be λ, then the total number becomes $N_T = \lambda K$. The descending order number m remains unchanged, but the ascending order number i should be changed to

$$i^* = i + N_T - N \qquad (31)$$

This procedure is due to Muir and El-Shaarawi [20] and is different from the one used by Petruaskas and Aagaard [26] who proposed disregarding the unused data of smaller height and replacing N_T by N. Muir and El-Shaarawi instead adjust the probability of the return value for a given return period. Considering the normal data censored by the rate of 50%, the frequency distribution of the censored data is graphed as the right-hand half of the symmetrical shape distributed from $-\infty$ to $+\infty$. Handling the censored data as if they are uncensored results in distortion of the shape of the frequency distribution, and there will be no chance to recover the original normal distribution from the censored data set. The procedure described at least retains the shape of the frequency distribution at the upper range, and it is recommended here for that reason.

In the case of the annual maximum series, the number N_T is known regardless of censoring. In the case of peak value series in the strict sense, however, the total number N_T is unknown because we are only interested in large storm waves. An appropriate estimate of the mean rate of occurrence of storm waves becomes an important step in the extreme wave data analysis. An accurate estimate is not required according to numerical simulation studies by Goda [36, 37], however, with an allowable magnitude factor of 2. Thus, our meteorological knowledge should make it possible to provide a reasonable estimate of the mean rate, λ, for various storm populations.

Confidence Interval of Parameters. Unless the peak value series of storm wave heights consist of a very large number of data, they cannot escape from the problem of sampling variability, especially when the number of data points is a few dozen or less. This raises the question of the confidence interval of the estimated values of parameters and return values. The standard deviation of the sampled data from the population of the FT-I distribution approximately has the coefficient of variation expressed as $1.0/\sqrt{N}$, and that of the sampled data from the log-normal population about $0.8/\sqrt{N}$ [36]. The Weibull distribution with the shape parameter $k \doteqdot 1.3$ indicates the same order of the coefficient of variation as the FT-I distribution, and the Weibull distribution with a smaller value of shape parameter has a larger coefficient of variation and vice versa.

The sampling variability of the standard deviation directly affects the estimate of the scale parameter A, as indicated by the procedure of the method of moments in which A is linearly estimated by the standard deviation of the sampled data. The confidence intervals of the estimates of the scale and location parameters vary slightly according to the method of data fitting to a distribution function. In the case of the FT-I distribution, the maximum likelihood method seems to provide the narrowest range of confidence intervals. Analytical expression for this case has been given by Lawless [21, 38], and Challenor [39] calculated tables and diagrams of percentage points for the estimates of parameters and return values at several return period levels, according to Lawless's theory. When the scale and location parameters are estimated by the least squares method with the Gringorten plotting formula, the confidence intervals of the parameters are slightly broader than those by the maximum likelihood method. The use of the Barnett plotting formula, however, yields almost the same ranges of the confidence intervals as those by the maximum likelihood method, according to Monte Carlo simulations by Goda [36, 37]. Roughly speaking, an estimate of the scale parameter has the same magnitude of variation as the standard deviation of the sampled data.

Estimating R_p-Years Wave Heights

Return Values and Their Confidence Intervals. Once the extreme wave data are fitted to a distribution function and the parameters are estimated, the return value x_R corresponding to a return period R_p is calculated as

$$x_R = Ay_R + B \tag{32}$$

where $y_R = F^{-1}[1 - 1/(\lambda R_p)]$ $\qquad(33)$

and λ denotes the average number of storm waves per year or N_T/K, where K stands for the time duration (in terms of years) of the period from which the extreme wave data is collected. In the case of the annual maximum series, λ is 1 because $N_T = K$, if the data are not censored. In the case of the peak value series of storm wave data, λ usually takes the value greater than 1.

The return value thus estimated is not a definite one but subject to sampling error in the same way as the parameters of distribution function. The confidence interval of the return value for the data sampled from the population of the FT-I distribution can be evaluated by the following formula, which is due to Gumbel [27]:

$$\text{Var}[x_R] = (\sigma^2/N)[1 + 1.1396(y_R - \gamma)\sqrt{6}/\pi + 1.1000(y_R - \gamma)^2\pi^2/6] \tag{34}$$

where σ denotes the standard deviation of the sampled data or that of storm wave heights under analysis, x_R and y_R are the return value and the reduced variate given by Equations 32 and 33, and γ is Euler's constant. The applicability of Equation 34 to the data sampled from the population of the FT-I distribution has been verified by numerical simulations. Equation 34 only predicts the variance of the return value not the percentile range, but it provides a measure of the variability. Such variability originates from the very nature of the distribution function itself and from a small data sample size. Even if a set of peak value data were fit to the FT-I distribution perfectly, the variance given by Equation 34 still applies to the data, because there is no guarantee that the value of σ of the particular data set is the same as the parent population.

In the case of the Weibull distribution, no analytical expression is available for the confidence intervals of the estimates of parameters and return values. An empirical expression for the standard error of the return value has been derived by Goda

[37, 37] as follows:

$$\sigma[x_R] = (\sigma/\sqrt{N})[1.0 + A_R(y_R - C_R)^2]^{1/2} \tag{35}$$

where $A_R = a_1 \exp[a_2(N)^{-1.3}]$ (36)

and the empirical coefficients $C_R, a_1,$ and a_2 are given the following values depending on the distribution function:

Weibull (k = 0.75): $a_1 = 1.65, a_2 = 11.4, C_R = 0.0$
Weibull (k = 1.0): $a_1 = 1.92, a_2 = 11.4, C_R = 0.3$
Weibull (k = 1.4): $a_1 = 2.05, a_2 = 11.4, C_R = 0.4$ (37)
Weibull (k = 2.0): $a_1 = 2.22, a_2 = 11.4, C_R = 0.5$

Equation 35 has also been applied to simulation data for the FT-I distribution in order to include the effect of sample size N, and the following values of coefficients have been obtained:

$$\text{FT-I} : a_1 = 0.64, a_2 = 9.0, C_R = 0.0 \tag{38}$$

Censoring of extreme data generally increases the range of the confidence interval of the return values in comparison with uncensored data. In the case of the Weibull distribution with k = 0.75, however, censoring yields a decrease in the range of confidence interval. Equation 35 has been extended for censored data (see Goda [36, 37] for details).

Selection of a Distribution Function from Several Alternatives. At present no single distribution function is preferable for extreme wave statistics, even though some favor the FT-I distribution while others argue for the log-normal distribution. Petruaskas and Aagaard [26] proposed selecting one distribution from the FT-I and the Weibull family with k = 0.75, 0.85, 1.0, 1.1, 1.25, 1.5, and 2.0. They employed the mean square deviation of the sample data from the fitted distribution function as a guide for ranking the distributions, but they left the final selection to the design engineers. Simiu and Filliben [40] used the so-called maximum probability plot correlation coefficient criterion to select the closest-fitting distribution function for extreme wind speeds from several alternatives. This correlation coefficient refers to the one between x and y in Equation 23.

Sampling variability of extreme wave data, however, makes it difficult to select the best distribution from a small data sample. Tables 1 and 2 are the results of Monte Carlo simulation tests by Goda [36, 37]. From a given parent distribution, 10,000 samples with the same size were simulated. Each sample was fitted to the FT-I and the Weibull family distributions with k = 0.75, 1.0, 1.4 and 2.0 by the least squares method, and the best-fitting distribution function was selected by the maximum probability plot correlation coefficient criterion. For example, an uncensored data sample with the size N = 10 from the FT-I distribution has a chance of 13.4% of being fitted by the FT-I function, while it has a probability of 48.4% of being

Table 1
Rate of Return of the Best-Fitting Distribution to
the Parent Distribution (per thousand) [36]
(censoring parameter $v = 1.0$)

Best-Fit Distr.	Sample Size N	Parent Distribution				
		Weibull				
		k = 0.75	k = 1.0	k = 1.4	k = 2.0	FT-I
Weibull (k = 0.75)	10	475	287	140	51	113
	20	520	267	68	9	65
	40	588	225	29	1	30
	100	687	173	3	—	5
Weibull (k = 1.0)	10	227	235	174	97	128
	20	304	323	191	59	129
	40	340	443	186	12	117
	100	305	615	124	—	60
Weibull (k = 1.4)	10	172	217	198	138	143
	20	146	279	296	136	163
	40	70	293	419	94	162
	100	8	210	642	41	133
Weibull (k = 2.0)	10	112	223	400	582	484
	20	27	112	346	631	438
	40	2	34	267	708	380
	100	—	22	151	795	280
FT-I	10	14	38	89	132	134
	20	2	19	99	166	206
	40	—	5	99	185	310
	100	—	—	80	164	530

Note: The best fitting distribution is selected as having the largest correlation coefficient between x_m and y_m of Equation 23.

mistaken as belonging to the Weibull distribution with k = 2.0, according to the most right column of Table 1. As the censoring parameter decreases, the chance of hitting the true distribution function is diminished as exhibited in Table 2. Even at the same size N = 100, a sample from either the Weibull with k = 1.4 or the FT-I has a larger chance of being mistaken as that from the Weibull with k = 2.0 than being correctly analyzed as belonging to the parent distribution, if the censoring parameter is $v = 0.25$.

The log-normal distribution exhibits a strong likelihood of overtaking the position of the FT-I and the Weibull distribution with k = 2.0, if it is allowed to compete with them. The shape of log-normal probability density function is quite similar at their tails to that of the Weibull distribution with k = 2.0, and the return values estimated for a sample by both distributions are almost the same. Therefore, dropping

Table 2
**Rate of Return of the Best-Fitting Distribution to
the Parent Distribution (per thousand) [36]**
(censoring parameter $v = 0.25$)

| Best-Fit Distr. | Sample Size N | Parent Distribution | | | | |
| | | Weibull | | | | FT-I |
		k = 0.75	k = 1.0	k = 1.4	k = 2.0	
Weibull (k = 0.75)	10	424	335	274	215	315
	20	446	325	225	159	300
	40	484	316	173	81	272
	100	566	288	93	24	218
Weibull (k = 1.0)	10	83	77	73	67	74
	20	117	112	94	78	96
	40	160	144	115	77	136
	100	212	213	123	50	190
Weibull (k = 1.4)	10	74	75	70	68	71
	20	98	108	105	94	107
	40	119	145	150	136	143
	100	101	190	241	189	202
Weibull (k = 2.0)	10	387	471	539	606	499
	20	286	398	511	605	432
	40	175	306	469	616	356
	100	58	179	401	643	243
FT-I	10	33	43	45	44	42
	20	52	56	65	64	64
	40	63	89	92	91	94
	100	55	130	142	94	147

Note: The best fitting distribution is selected as having the largest correlation coefficient between x_m and y_m of Equation 23.

the log-normal distribution from a list of candidate distributions is recommended, if a family of Weibull and the FT-I distributions are tested for a data sample of extreme waves.

Use of an incorrectly-selected distribution function results in a bias of the estimated return wave heights. When the five distribution functions listed in Tables 1 and 2 are fitted to extreme wave data, the Weibull distribution with k = 0.75 predicts the largest return heights and the Weibull with k = 2.0 the smallest. The FT-I distribution predicts the values between those of the Weibull with k = 1.0 and 1.4. Because the probability of hitting the true distribution function is not large when the sample size is modest as shown in Tables 1 and 2, the estimated values of return heights should be adjusted by considering the previous characteristics. Calculation of return wave heights by all the fitted distribution functions will be useful in judging the extent of adjustment.

Confidence Interval of Return Values for the Case of Unknown Distribution Function. The situation of the true distribution function being unknown for given extreme data generally causes the range of confidence interval of the return values to increase. Goda [36, 37] calculated the weighted mean values of the standard errors of return values for uncensored and censored data ($v = 1.0, 0.5$, and 0.25) for sample sizes between $N = 10$ and 100, based on his simulation data. He assumed that the five distribution functions (FT-I and Weibull $k = 0.75, 1.0, 1.4$, and 2.0) have equal chance as the parent distribution, and he employed the rate of return listed in Table 1 as the weight. The results of the weighted mean errors have been expressed by the following empirical formula:

$$\sigma[x_R] = (\sigma/\sqrt{N})[1.0 + A_s|y_R + \alpha \ln v|^q]$$
(39)

The coefficients A_s and α and the exponent q are given the following values depending on the best-fitting distribution function:

FT-I:

$$A_s = \begin{cases} 0.24 + 0.36 \, (\log_{10} N/80)^2 : v = 1.0 \\ 0.46 + 0.14 \, (\log_{10} N/50)^2 : v = 0.5 \text{ and } 0.25 \end{cases}$$
(40)

$$\alpha = 0.9, \quad q = 1.6$$

Weibull ($k = 0.75$):

$$A_s = \begin{cases} 0.57 + 0.18 \, (\log_{10} N/20)^2 : v = 1.0 \\ 0.41 + 0.22 \, (\log_{10} N/20)^2 : v = 0.5 \text{ and } 0.25 \end{cases}$$
(41)

$$\alpha = 2.7, \quad q = 1.2$$

Weibull ($k = 1.0$):

$$A_s = \begin{cases} 0.55 + 0.15 \, (\log_{10} N/15)^2 : v = 1.0 \\ 0.38 + 0.17 \, (\log_{10} N/20)^2 : v = 0.5 \text{ and } 0.25 \end{cases}$$
(42)

$$\alpha = 1.0, \quad q = 1.7$$

Weibull ($k = 1.4$):

$$A_s = \begin{cases} 0.37 + 0.08 \, (\log_{10} N/1000)^2 : v = 1.0 \\ 0.46 + 0.09 \, (\log_{10} N/20)^2 : v = 0.5 \text{ and } 0.25 \end{cases}$$
(43)

$$\alpha = 0.5, \quad q = 2.3$$

Weibull ($k = 2.0$):

$$A_s = \begin{cases} 0.30 + 0.36 \, (\log_{10} N/80)^2 : v = 1.0 \\ 0.56 + 0.20 \, (\log_{10} N/100)^2 : v = 0.5 \text{ and } 0.25 \end{cases}$$
(44)

$$\alpha = 0.35, \quad q = 3.2$$

Equations 39 to 44 enable estimates of the standard error of a return value, and thus, set its confidence interval according to one-sigma or two-sigma criterion. The distribution of the estimated return values is not the normal one in a strict sense; however, lack of detailed information provides no option but to assume normality for the estimation of confidence interval. The estimates of a return wave height for a given wave height should always be made together with the evaluation of its confidence interval. The design wave height should be selected as a value within a confidence interval with other factors taken into account.

Treatment of Multiple Storm Populations. Extreme wave data from different storm populations such as hurricanes, monsoons, and frontal systems should be analyzed separately. The analysis will yield several best-fitting distributions, one for each storm population. These distributions are combined to yield the overall distribution function for a site of interest. Carter and Challenor [29] introduced the following multiplication probability in order to obtain the distribution of the maxima during the year from the estimated monthly distribution functions $F_j(x)$:

$$\text{Prob}(X < x) = \prod_{j=1}^{12} F_j(x) \tag{45}$$

The same principle is applied for the combination of the estimated distribution functions for multiple storm populations. Thus, the overall distribution function will be calculated as

$$F(x) = \prod_{j=1}^{n} F_j(x) \tag{46}$$

where n denotes the number of storm populations.

Equation 46 is for the data of annual maximum series. For the data of partial-duration series, the estimated distribution functions must be converted to those for the annual maxima. The conversion can be made by assuming a Poisson process. The resulting formula for the overall distribution function for the annual maxima becomes:

$$F(x) = \prod_{j=1}^{n} \exp\{-\lambda_j[1 - F_j(x)]\} \tag{47}$$

Example of Extreme Wave Data Analysis

The procedure of extreme wave data analysis is summarized as follows:

1. Analyze the wave records and pick up the peak storm wave heights above a certain threshold level.
2. Prepare the data of either annual maximum series or partial-duration series.
3. Rearrange the data set in the descending fashion with the largest being assigned the order number $m = 1$.

4. Calculate the plotting probability P_m by Equation 26 for the FT-I distribution function and by Equation 29 for the Weibull distribution. The log-normal distribution is not recommended.

5. In case of censored data, the total number of storms, N_T, which must have occurred during the time period under study, should be used instead of the actual data number N in calculating P_m.

6. Calculate the reduced variate y_m by Equation 21 or 22, and perform regression analysis between x_m and y_m to obtain the estimates of the parameters A and B in Equation 23.

7. Try to fit the extreme wave data to several distribution functions, and select the one having the largest correlation coefficient between x_m and y_m as the best-fitting function.

8. Estimate the return wave height H_R for a given return period R_p by Equations 32 and 33.

9. Make some adjustment for the possible bias arising from not knowing the true distribution function.

10. Estimate the standard error of the return value by Equations 39–44 if the true distribution function is unknown.

11. The true return wave height will be located somewhere in the range of confidence interval, which is evaluated with the estimated return height and its standard error.

Tables 3 and 4 illustrate this procedure. The data represent a set of peak significant heights of typhoon (similar to hurricane) waves taken from measured wave records. The effective duration of wave records excluding the down time is about 10.7 years, and 53 typhoon wave events are thought to have affected the wave station during this period. Among 53 typhoon waves, 21 significant wave heights exceeding 4.0 m were selected for the analysis. Thus, $K = 10.7$, $\lambda = 4.93$, and $v = 0.40$.

Table 3 lists the process of data fitting to the distribution function of the FT-I type and the Weibull family with $k = 0.75$, 1.0, 1.4, and 2.0. The plotting probability for the Weibull distribution is calculated by the following formula derived by Goda [36, 37] as a modification to Equation 29:

$$P_m = 1 - [m - (0.20 + 0.27/\sqrt{k})]/[N_T + (0.20 + 0.23/\sqrt{k})] \qquad (48)$$

The modification was introduced to minimize the bias associated with the original formula by Petruaskas and Aagaard [26], which is noticeable when the shape parameter k is small. The three rows at the bottom of Table 3 list the estimated values of the scale parameter A and the location parameter B as well as the correlation coefficient $r(x_m, y_m)$. In this example, the Weibull distribution with $k = 2.0$ is judged as the best-fitting distribution.

Table 4 lists the estimated values of return wave heights for the return periods from 2 to 100 years. Although the Weibull distribution with $k = 2.0$ was judged as the best-fitting, the return wave heights by the five distribution functions are listed as references. The differences among the return heights by the five distribution functions are rather small compared with the magnitude of their standard errors, which

Table 3
Example of Extreme Wave Data Fitting to Several Distribution Functions (N = 21, N_T = 53, K = 10.7 years) [36]

m	x_m	FT-I P_m	y_m	Weibull (0.75) P_m	y_m	Weibull (1.0) P_m	y_m	Weibull (1.4) P_m	y_m	Weibull (2.0) P_m	y_m
1	8.36	0.9895	4.55	0.9909	7.86	0.9901	4.61	0.9893	2.95	0.9886	2.12
2	7.02	0.9706	3.51	0.9722	5.48	0.9714	3.55	0.9706	2.46	0.9699	1.87
3	6.94	0.9518	3.01	0.9535	4.46	0.9527	3.05	0.9518	2.21	0.9511	1.74
4	6.85	0.9330	2.67	0.9348	3.82	0.9339	2.72	0.9331	2.04	0.9324	1.64
5	6.74	0.9142	2.41	0.9161	3.35	0.9152	2.47	0.9144	1.90	0.9136	1.57
6	6.20	0.8953	2.20	0.8974	3.00	0.8965	2.27	0.8957	1.79	0.8945	1.50
7	5.92	0.8765	2.03	0.8787	2.71	0.8778	2.10	0.8769	1.70	0.8762	1.45
8	5.68	0.8577	1.87	0.8599	2.46	0.8591	1.96	0.8582	1.61	0.8574	1.40
9	5.57	0.8389	1.74	0.8412	2.26	0.8404	1.84	0.8395	1.54	0.8387	1.35
10	5.42	0.8200	1.62	0.8225	2.08	0.8216	1.72	0.8207	1.47	0.8199	1.31
11	5.34	0.8012	1.51	0.8038	1.92	0.8029	1.62	0.8020	1.41	0.8012	1.27
12	5.10	0.7824	1.41	0.7851	1.78	0.7842	1.53	0.7833	1.35	0.7825	1.24
13	5.09	0.7636	1.31	0.7664	1.65	0.7655	1.45	0.7646	1.30	0.7637	1.20
14	4.95	0.7447	1.22	0.7477	1.53	0.7468	1.37	0.7458	1.25	0.7450	1.17
15	4.81	0.7259	1.14	0.7290	1.43	0.7281	1.30	0.7271	1.21	0.7262	1.14
16	4.77	0.7071	1.06	0.7103	1.33	0.7093	1.24	0.7084	1.16	0.7075	1.11
17	4.63	0.6883	0.99	0.6916	1.24	0.6906	1.17	0.6896	1.12	0.6888	1.08
18	4.61	0.6694	0.91	0.6729	1.16	0.6719	1.11	0.6709	1.08	0.6700	1.05
19	4.41	0.6506	0.84	0.6542	1.08	0.6532	1.06	0.6522	1.04	0.6513	1.03
20	4.34	0.6318	0.78	0.6355	1.01	0.6345	1.01	0.6335	1.00	0.6325	1.00
21	4.11	0.6130	0.71	0.6168	0.95	0.6158	0.96	0.6147	0.97	0.6138	0.98
		A = 1.091		A = 0.614		A = 1.147		A = 2.084		A = 3.560	
		B = 3.617		B = 4.029		B = 3.374		B = 2.334		B = 0.786	
		r = 0.9842		r = 0.9621		r = 0.9790		r = 0.9878		r = 0.9910	

Table 4
Example of the Estimation of Return Wave Heights and Their Standard Errors (units in meters) [36]

Return Period	FT-I H_R	σ	Weibull (0.75) H_R	σ	Weibull (1.0) H_R	σ	Weibull (1.4) H_R	σ	Weibull (2.0) H_R	σ
2.0	6.1	0.4	5.9	0.3	6.0	0.4	6.1	0.5	6.2	0.5
5.0	7.1	0.7	6.9	0.5	7.1	0.6	7.1	0.7	7.2	0.8
10.0	7.9	0.9	7.8	0.7	7.8	0.8	7.8	0.9	7.8	1.0
20.0	8.6	1.2	8.7	1.0	8.6	1.1	8.5	1.2	8.4	1.3
50.0	9.6	1.6	10.0	1.4	9.7	1.5	9.4	1.5	9.1	1.7
100.0	10.4	2.3	11.0	2.1	10.5	2.1	10.0	2.2	9.7	2.5

are evaluated by Equations 39–44. As discussed earlier, censored wave data are inclined to show strong affiliation with the Weibull distribution with k = 2.0 even if their true distributions are not. Therefore, it will be safe to assume that the true return wave heights have the values close to or above those by the Weibull distribution with k = 1.4 in this particular example.

The extremal wave analysis can predict the result such as shown in Table 4, but it cannot tell what is the true return wave height. A design engineer must make a decision to select a certain value within the predicted confidence interval. The answer to the question whether the upper or the lower limit of the confidence interval should be employed will depend on the reliability of the wave data, the safety margin of the structure under design, the extent of damages incurred by a possible failure of structure, and other relevant factors.

Design Waves

Selecting Design Wave Height

Return Period and Encounter Probability. The return value of extreme wave heights such as shown in Table 4 provides a basis for selecting the design wave height, but several considerations are required before the selection is made. The major consideration should be the assessment of the risk that a structure under design may fail during its service life by extraordinary waves that exceed the design value. Other factors of considerations include the expected damage (direct and indirect) and the cost of rehabilitation in the event of structural failure. The risk of failure decreases as the design wave height is raised, but the construction cost increases at the same time. The design wave height is determined by the engineer in charge by weighing the cost against the risk.

An useful concept in selecting a design value is the encounter probability presented by Borgman [41]. It is the probability that storm waves with the height exceeding the design value will occur during the service life of a structure. Borgman has given the encounter probability E_p as a function of the return period R_p as

$$E_p = 1 - (1 - 1/R_p)^L \tag{42}$$

where L denotes the service life of the structure. For a very large value of R_p, Equation 42 can be approximated as

$$E_p \doteq 1 - \exp[-L/R_p] \tag{43}$$

If the design wave height is set with the return period equal to the service life of the structure, for example, the structure will have the probability of 0.63 to 0.65 that it will encounter storm waves exceeding the design condition (L = 10 to 100 times units). If the encounter probability is to be set below 0.2 for example, the return period should be greater than about 4.5 times the service life.

Several rules and recommendations for design and construction of offshore structures suggest using a return period of 100 years in selecting the design wave height.

Historic reason for this suggestion is the relatively short service life, say 20 years, of offshore structures for oil exploitation. Because the cost of failure is high, the encounter probability seems to be set low to yield a round figure of 100 years. For coastal structures, there is no particular recommendation for the length of return period to be used in selecting the design wave height. Practices among respective engineer groups are usually followed.

Mean Lifetime Maximum Wave Height and Coefficient of Variation. Another approach to the design wave selection comes from the reliability theory of structural design. In particular, the load and resistance factor design method proposed by Ravindra and Galambos [42] recommends using the mean lifetime maximum load multiplied by a load factor that includes the statistical variation of design load. The mean lifetime maximum load is defined as the expected value of the maximum load during the lifetime of a structure. Let the lifetime maximum wave height during L years be denoted by x_L. Then, its distribution function $\Phi(x_L)$ is derived by definition as

$$\Phi(x_L) = [F(x)]^L \tag{49}$$

In this case, $F(x)$ is the distribution function of the annual maximum wave height. If the distribution function is estimated from the peak-duration series with the mean rate λ greater than 1, the estimated function must be converted into the distribution function of annual maximum with Equation 47 by assuming a Poisson process.

The mean lifetime maximum wave height $E[x_L]$ can be calculated theoretically or numerically from the distribution function of the lifetime maximum wave height $\Phi(x_L)$. For the case when the distribution function of the annual maximum wave height is fitted by the FT-I type, $\Phi(x_L)$ is expanded as

$$\Phi(x_L) = \exp[-\exp\{-[x - (B + A \ln L)]/A\}] \tag{50}$$

Therefore the mean lifetime maximum wave height is immediately obtained from Equation 16 as

$$E[x_L] = B + A(\ln L + \gamma) \tag{51}$$

It is mathematically shown that the return period corresponding to $E[x_L]$ of Equation 51 is equivalent to about 1.8L.

For the cases of the Weibull and the log-normal distributions, the mean lifetime maximum wave height must be evaluated numerically.

The load factor in the load and resistance factor design method uses the coefficient of variation of the lifetime maximum load as the principal parameter. The standard deviation of the lifetime maximum wave height is calculated from the distribution function given by Equation 49. For the case of the FT-I type distribution, the standard deviation of x_L is same as that of the annual maximum derived from Equation 16, i.e.,

$$\sigma_1[x_L] = \pi A/\sqrt{6} \tag{52}$$

For the cases of the Weibull and the log-normal distributions, numerical calculation is required to evaluate the standard deviation of x_L.

The coefficient of variation of the mean lifetime maximum wave height should be calculated by using not only the standard deviation of the lifetime maximum wave height but also the statistical error in estimating the distribution function itself. Equation 35 or 39 for the case when the true distribution function is known or unknown, respectively, can be used to estimate the magnitude of the statistical error. Thus, the coefficient of variation (CV) of the mean lifetime maximum wave height is to be calculated as

$$CV[\bar{x}_L] = [\sigma_1(x_L)^2 + \sigma_2(\bar{x}_L)^2]^{1/2}/\bar{x}_L \tag{53}$$

where σ_1 and σ_2 denote the standard deviation of the lifetime maximum wave height calculated with $\Phi(x_L)$ and the standard error of $\bar{x}_L$ due to uncertainty in estimating the distribution function, respectively.

Selecting Design Wave Period

In contrast to the design wave height, no established procedure exists for the selection of design wave period. The usual practice is the use of a scatter diagram between the peak storm wave heights and associated periods. A regression line is drawn on the scatter diagram, and the wave period corresponding to the design wave height is read from the regression line.

Another practice is to select the period most dangerous for the safety of the structure from the range of period conceivable in nature. This practice is often employed in the design of offshore structures and the period range is specified in terms of the wave height. Examples can be found in various rules and recommendations issued by ship classification institutions.

Notation

a_1, a_2 empirical coefficients for standard error of return value (Equations 37 and 38)

A empirical parameter for wave persistence (Equation 6), or scale parameter of distribution function for extreme statistics (Equations 16 to 19)

A_R empirical coefficient for standard error of return value for the case when the parent distribution is known (Equation 36)

A_s empirical coefficient for standard error of return value for the case when the parent distributions is unknown (Equations 40 to 44)

B location parameter of distribution function for extreme statistics (Equations 16 to 19)

C, C' empirical parameters for wave persistence statistics (Equations 9 and 10).

C_R empirical coefficient for standard error of return value (Equations 37 and 38)

D	mean duration time of rough seas (Equation 5)
E[ ]	expected value of the variable within the brackets
E_p	encounter probability (Equation 42)
F[ ]	distribution function of the variable within the brackets
$F_j(x)$	distribution function for the j-th population
H_c	location parameter for wave height distribution (Equation 4)
H_0	scale parameter for wave height distribution (Equation 4)
H_R	return wave height
$H_s, H_{1/3}$	significant wave height
H_v	visually observed wave height by voluntary ships
H_w	visually observed wave height at ocean weather ships
i	ascending order number $(1, 2, \ldots, N)$
k	shape parameter of Weibull distribution
K	duration of time period from which extreme wave data are drawn
L	lifetime or service life of a structure under design
m	descending order number $(1, 2, \ldots, N)$
n	number of storm wave populations
N	number of data in a sample of extreme statistics
N_T	total number of extreme wave data during the time period under consideration
p( )	probability density function of the variable within the parentheses
$p(H_s, T_z)$	joint probability density function of H_s and T_z
$p_0(H\|H_s)$	conditional probability density function of individual wave heights under a given sea state (Equation 11)
P_i, P_m	plotting probability of the i-th or m-th order statistics
P[ ]	cumulative distribution or non-exceedance probability of the variable within the brackets
$P_0[H\|H_s]$	conditional cumulative distribution of individual wave heights (Equation 12)
q	empirical exponent for standard error of return value (Equations 40 to 44)
Q[ ]	probability of exceedance (Equation 6)
r	correlation coefficient
R_p	return period
s	standard deviation of wave height (Equations 1 and 2)
$T_s, T_{1/3}$	significant wave period
T_z	mean zero-crossing wave period
Var[ ]	variance of the variable within the brackets
x	extremal variate
x_m	m-th variate of ordered statistics
x_L	lifetime maximum wave height during L years
x_R	return value
y	reduced variate of extreme statistics
y_m	m-th reduced variate of ordered statistics
y_R	reduce variate of return value

Y   natural logarithm of wave height ($= \log H$)

α empirical parameter for mean storm wave duration (Equations 5 and 9), or empirical parameter for standard error of return value (Equations 40 to 44)

β empirical parameter for mean storm wave duration (Equation 5)

γ Euler's constant ($0.5772 \ldots$)

λ mean rate of storm waves per year

λ_j mean rate of storm waves of the j-th population

μ_Y mean of $\log H$ (Equation 3)

ν censoring parameter ($= N/N_T$)

σ standard deviation of a sample of extreme statistics

$\sigma(\ )$ standard deviation of the variable within the parentheses

σ_Y standard deviation of $\log H$ (Equation 3)

$\bar{\tau}$ mean duration of sea state above a threshold height

$\Phi(x_L)$ distribution function of lifetime maximum wave height (Equation 49)

References

1. Goda, Y., 1977, "Numerical Experiments on Statistical Variability of Ocean Waves," *Rept. Port and Harbour Res. Inst.*, Vol. 16, No. 2, pp. 3–26.
2. International Ship Structures Congress, 1979, "Report of Committee I.1 on Environmental Conditions," 7th ISSC.
3. Goda, Y., 1984, "Wave Measurements and Utilization of Wave Data," *Civil Engng. Trans., Inst. Engrs., Australia*, pp. 1–9.
4. Nolte, K. G., 1973, "Statistical Methods for Determining Extreme Sea States," *Proc. 2nd Int. Conf. on Port and Ocean Engng. under Arctic Conditions*, Univ. Iceland, pp. 705–742.
5. Hogben, N. and Lumb, F. E., 1967, *Ocean Wave Statistics*, National Phys. Lab., Her Majesty's Stationary Office, 276p.
6. British Maritime Technology Ltd., 1986, *Global Wave Statistics* (Compiled by Hogben, N. et al.), Unwin Brothers Ltd., Surrey, England, 661p.
7. U.S. Navy, 1974–79, *Marine Climatic Atlas of the World*, U.S. Gov. Print. Office, Washington, D.C., Vol. 1–5, 385p. (on the average.)
8. De Graauw, A., 1986, "Wave Statistics Based on Ship's Observations," *Coastal Engng.*, Vol. 10, pp. 105–118.
9. International Ship Structures Congress, 1985, "Report of Committee I.1 on Environmental Conditions," 9th ISSC.
10. Guedes Soares, C., 1986, "Assessment of the Uncertainty in Visual Observations of Wave Height," *Ocean Engng.*, Vol. 13, No. 1, pp. 37–56.
11. Guedes Soares, C., 1986, "Calibration of Visual Observations of Wave Period," *Ocean Engng.*, Vol. 13, No. 6, 1986, pp. 539–547.
12. Marine Information and Advisory Service, Inst. Ocean Sciences, U.K., 1982, "*MIAS Catalogue of Wave Data (2nd Ed.)*," 487p.
13. Hirose, M. and Takahashi, T., 1982, "Statistics of Sea Waves along The Coasts of Japan on The Basis of Nationwide Instrumentally-Measured Data," *Proc. Annual Symp. of Port and Harbour Res. Inst.*, pp. 1–55 (*in Japanese*).
14. Battjes, J. A., 1972, "Long-Term Wave Height Distribution at Seven Stations around The British Isles," *Deutchen Hydr. Zeit, Band 25, Heft 4*, pp. 179–189.

15. Goda, Y., 1967, "Note on The Presentation and Utilization of Wave Observation Data," *Tech. Note of Port and Harbour Res. Inst.*, No. 39, pp. 237–255 (*in Japanese*).
16. Lawson, N. V. and Abernethy, C. L., 1975, "Long Term Wave Statistics off Botany Bay," *Proc. 2nd Australian Conf. on Coastal and Ocean Engng.*, pp. 167–176.
17. Graham C., 1982, "The Parametrization and Prediction of Wave Height and Wind Speed Persistence Statistics for Oil Industry Operational Planning Purposes," *Coastal Engng.*, Vol. 6, No. 4, pp. 303–329.
18. Kuwashima, S. and Hogben, N., 1984, "The Estimation of Persistence Statistics from Cumulative Probabilities of Wave Height," *NMI LTD Report* No. R183, 72p.
19. Kuwashima, S. and Hogben, N., 1986, "The Estimation of Wave Height and Wind Speed Persistence Statistics from Cumulative Probability Distributions," *Coastal Engng.*, Vol. 9, pp. 563–590.
20. Muir, L. R. and El-Shaarawi, A. H., 1986, "On The Calculation of Extreme Wave Heights: A Review," *Ocean Engng.*, Vol. 13, No. 1, pp. 93–118.
21. Chow, V. T. (Ed.), 1964, *Handbook of Applied Hydrology*, McGraw-Hill Book Co., New York.
22. Lawless, J. F., 1982, *Statistical Models and Methods for Lifetime Data*, John Wiley & Sons, New York.
23. Langbein, W. B., 1949, "Annual Floods and The Partial-Duration Flood Series," *Trans. Amer. Geophy. Union*, Vol. 30, No. 6, pp. 879–881.
24. Isaacson, M. de St.Q. and MacKenzie, N. G., 1981 "Long-Term Distributions of Ocean Waves." *J. Wat., Port. Coast., & Ocn. Div.*, *Proc. ASCE*, Vol. 107, No. WW2, pp. 93–109.
25. Thom, H. C. S., 1973, "Extreme Wave Height Distributions over Oceans," *J. Wat., Harb., & Coast. Engng. Div.*, *Proc. ASCE*, Vol. 99, No. WW3, pp. 355–374.
26. Petruaskas, C. and Aagaard, P. M., 1970, "Extrapolation of Historical Storm Data for Estimating Design Wave Heights," *Prepr. 2nd Annual Offshore Tech. Conf.*, OTC 1190.
27. Gumbel E. J., 1958, *Statistics of Extremes*, Columbia Univ. Press, New York.
28. Lettenmaier, D. P. and Burges, S.J., 1982 "Gumbel's Extreme Value I Distribution: A New Look," *J. Hydr. Div.*, *Proc. ASCE*, Vol. 108, No. HY4, pp. 502–514.
29. Carter, D. J. T. and Challenor, P. G., 1983, "Methods of Fitting The Fisher-Tippet Type I Extreme Value Distribution," *Ocean Engng.*, Vol. 10, No. 3, pp. 191–199.
30. Kimball, F., 1960, "On The Choice of Plotting Positions on Probability Paper," *J. Amer. Statist. Assoc.*, Vol. 55, pp. 546–560.
31. Cunnane, C., 1978, "Unbiased Plotting Positions—A Review," *J. Hydrology*, Vol. 37, pp. 205–222.
32. Earle, M. D. and Baer, L., 1982, "Effects of Uncertainties on Extreme Wave Heights," *J. Wat., Port, Coast. & Ocn. Div.*, *Proc. ASCE*, Vol. 108, No. WW4, pp. 456–478.
33. Gringorten, I. I., 1963, "A Plotting Rule for Extreme Probability Paper," *J. Geophys. Res.*, Vol. 68, No. 3, pp. 813–814.
34. Barnett, V., 1975, "Probability Plotting Methods and Orders Statistics," *Applied Statistics*, Vol. 24, No. 1, pp. 95–108.
35. Blom, G., 1958, *Statistical Estimates and Transformed Beta-Variables*, John Wiley & Sons, New York.
36. Goda, Y., 1988, "Numerical Investigations of Plotting Position Formulas and Confidence Interval of Return Values in Extreme Statistics." *Rept. Port and Harbour Res. Inst.*, Vol. 27, No. 1, pp. 31–92 (*in Japanese*).
37. Goda, Y., 1988, "On The Methodology of Selecting Design Wave Height," Proc. 21st Int. Conf. on Coastal Engng., June, pp. 899–913.
38. Lawless, J. F., 1974, "Approximation to Confidence Intervals for Parameters in The Extreme Value and Weibull Distributions," *Biometrika*, Vol. 61, No. 1, pp. 123–129.

39. Challenor, P. G., 1979, "Confidence Limits for Extreme Value Statistics," *Inst. Oceanogr. Sciences, Rept.* No. 82, 27p.

40. Simiu, E. and Filliben, J. J., 1976, "Probability Distributions of Extreme Wind Speeds," *J. Struct. Div., Proc. ASCE*, Vol. 102, No. ST9, pp. 1861–1877.

41. Borgman, L. E., 1963, "Risk Criteria," *J. Waterways & Harbors Div., Proc. ASCE*, Vol. 89, No. WW3, pp. 1–35.

42. Ravindra, M. K. and Galambos, T. V., 1978, "Load and Resistance Factor Design for Steel," *J. Structural Div., Proc. ASCE*, Vol. 104, No. ST9, pp. 1427–1441.

CHAPTER 8

SELECTION OF DESIGN WAVE CHARACTERISTICS*

John B. Herbich

W. H. Bauer Professor
Civil and Ocean Engineering
Texas A&M University
College Station, Texas, U.S.A.

CONTENTS

---

* A large portion of this chapter was performed under an IPA agreement with the U.S. Corps of Engineer Waterways Experiment Station, Vicksburg, Mississippi.

Introduction

Safe design of structures depends to a large extent on the selected wave characteristics. Other design criteria include functional performance, environmental impact,
life-cycle cost, whether in a seismic area (earthquake or tsunami effects), damage
effects on human life and on other structures, whether the structure is to survive a
hurricane (i.e., whether it is designed for non-hurricane or hurricane conditions),
whether it can be damaged by a collision of a large vessel with the structure, etc.

The structural stability criteria are often stated in terms of the extreme environmental conditions (wave heights, wave periods, water levels—tides and storm surges,
winds) that a coastal structure must survive without sustaining significant damage.
The extent to which the survival criteria may be satisfied must, at times, be com-
promised for the sake of reducing project costs. Risk analysis is also employed to
evaluate risks for major structures. Such analysis may prove that the consequences
of occasional damage are more affordable than the additional first capital costs to
provide a structure to survive extremely rare events. A range of survival criteria
should be evaluated prior to selecting the final design.

Waves and currents are the most important environmental phenomena affecting
design of coastal structures and facilities. One of the main difficulties in selecting
design waves is their variability on short-time as well as long-time basis. Wave characteristics such as height and period change from wave to wave and vary from
storm to storm. In addition, waves may be generated from different directions for
any given storm and are affected by refraction, diffraction, reflection and shoaling
in shallow water. Thus, the process of selecting design waves is very complicated,
difficult and site-specific. Ideally, one should make the selection on the basis of
long-term data acquisition at the site, preferably over a period of 15 to 20 years.
However, this is seldom possible and theoretical probability methods have to be
employed to arrive at the design waves.

Statistical Distribution of Waves

Sinusoidal Waves

Longuet-Higgins [89] evaluated the statistical distribution of the wave heights derived on the following assumptions:

1. That the wave spectrum contains a single narrow band of frequencies, and
2. That the wave energy is being received from a large number of different sources whose phases are random.

There are several ways to describe the wave heights, i.e., the mean wave height, the root-mean-square height, the height of significant waves (defined by Sverdrup and Munk [99a] as the mean of the highest one third of all the wave heights), the maximum height over a given interval of time, etc.

The root-mean-square wave height is given by

$$\frac{\pi}{\sigma_1 - \sigma_2} (\bar{a})^2 = \int_0^{\pi/(\sigma_1 - \sigma_2)} 4a_0{}^2 \cos \frac{2^{(\sigma_1 - \sigma_2)}}{2} t \, dt \tag{1}$$

Thus, the various ratios may be computed as follows

$$\frac{a^{(1/10)}}{\bar{a}} = \frac{20\sqrt{2}}{\pi} \sin \frac{\pi}{20} = 1.408 \tag{2}$$

$$\frac{a^{(1/3)}}{\bar{a}} = \frac{6\sqrt{2}}{\pi} \sin \frac{\pi}{6} = 1.350 \tag{3}$$

$$\frac{a^{(1)}}{\bar{a}} = \frac{2\sqrt{2}}{\pi} \sin \frac{\pi}{2} = 0.901 \tag{4}$$

$$\frac{a_{max}}{\bar{a}} = \sqrt{2} \tag{5}$$

The probability that a point in the interval $0 < \theta < \pi/2$ lies in a given region of width $d\theta$ is $2|d\theta|/\pi$. Therefore, the probability $P(r|dr|) = (2/\pi)|d\theta|$, where the statistical distribution of the wave amplitudes is the same as that of the envelope function, or the simple cosine curve

$$r = 2a_0 \cos \theta \tag{6}$$

where $\sigma = \frac{2\pi}{T}$; $\bar{a} = \sqrt{2}a_0$

The successive values of amplitude a in any interval I of the t-axis may be denoted by a, a_2, a_3 ... A_N. If the amplitudes are arranged in descending order of magnitude, the mean value of the first PN of the amplitudes (where P is a fraction between 0 and 1) is denoted by $a^{(P)}$. The significant wave amplitude is thus $a^{(1/3)}$, and the average of 10% of the highest waves is denoted by $a^{(1/10)}$, etc. The root-mean-square amplitude $\bar{a}$ is given by

$$(\bar{a})^2 = \frac{1}{N}(a_1{}^2 + a_2{}^2 + a_3{}^2 + \cdots + a_N{}^2) \tag{7}$$

where N = number of waves

The ratio of amplitudes may be given as

$$\frac{a^{(P)}}{\bar{a}} = \sqrt{2}\frac{2}{P\pi}\sin\frac{P\pi}{2} \tag{8}$$

The probability distribution P(r) of the amplitude a is given by

$$P(r) = \begin{cases} \dfrac{2}{\pi}\dfrac{1}{\sqrt{(2\bar{a}^2 - r^2)}}, & r < \sqrt{2}\bar{a} \\ 0, & r > \sqrt{2}\bar{a} \end{cases} \tag{9}$$

Random Waves—Narrow Spectrum

A case of a narrow spectrum with a disturbance made up of a number of random contributions was considered by Rayleigh [123] in connection with the amplitude of sound. Barber [8] indicated that there is a rough agreement with Rayleigh distribution for waves. Longuet-Higgins pointed out that the wave energy received at any point on the coast originated in many different places over a wide fetch area. If each region of the generating fetch area is large as compared with a wavelength, it may be assumed that the phases of the contribution are independent of each other. Longuet-Higgins assumed that the envelope B is the sum of a very large number of small wave components of random phases (Figure 1). The probability distribution of the sum (known as the "random walk") was developed by Rayleigh. If the component vectors are b_1, b_2, b_m and

$$B = b_1 + b_2 + \cdots + b_m \tag{10}$$

then the mean square value of B is

$$\bar{B}^2 = |b_1|^2 + |b_2|^2 + \cdots + |b_m|^2 \tag{11}$$

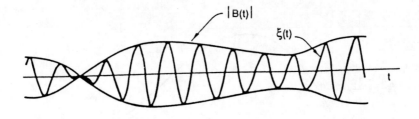

Figure 1. A disturbance $\xi(t)$ with a narrow frequency band and its envelope $|B(t)|$.

The probability that $|B|$ lies between r and (r + dr) is

$$P(r) \, dr = e^{-r^2/\bar{B}^2} \frac{2r}{\bar{B}^2} \, dr \tag{12}$$

Since the probability distribution of $|B|$ is equal to that of the a's, the probability distribution of the a's is

$$P(r) \, dr = e^{-r^2/\bar{a}^2} \frac{2r}{\bar{a}^2} \, dr = -de^{-r^2/\bar{a}^2} \tag{13}$$

The function

$$\bar{a}P(r) = e^{-r^2/\bar{a}^2} \frac{2r}{\bar{a}} \tag{14}$$

and it is presented in Figure 2a. The normalized distribution is presented in Figure 2b. It should be noted that the total area under the curve is equal to 1.0 and that the maximum value occurs when

$$\frac{r}{\bar{a}} = \frac{1}{\sqrt{2}} = 0.717 \tag{15}$$

So that the mode is

$$\frac{\mu(a)}{\bar{a}} = \frac{1}{\sqrt{2}} = 0.717 \tag{16}$$

The chance F(n) that a should exceed a certain value r is

$$F(r) = \int_r^\infty P(r) \, dr = e^{-r^2/\bar{a}^2} \tag{17}$$

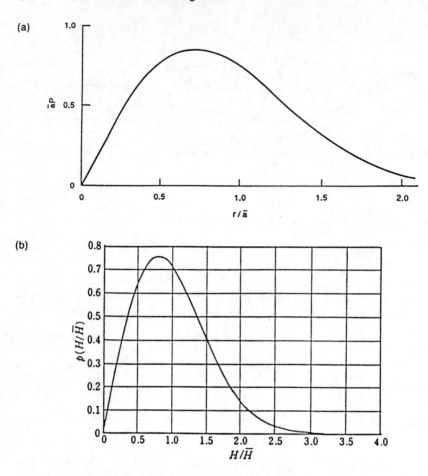

Figure 2. Rayleigh frequency distribution: (a) The "random walk" Raleigh frequency distribution; (b) Normalized Rayleigh distribution.

Numerical values of $a^{(1)}/\bar{a}$ are presented in Table 1 as a function of selected values of P. The mean value of a is

$$\frac{a^{(1)}}{\bar{a}} = \frac{\sqrt{\pi}}{2} = 0.886 \tag{18}$$

The second moment of the distribution about the mean is

$$[d(a)]^2 = \bar{a}^2 - [a^{(1)}]^2 \left(1 - \frac{\pi}{4}\right) \tag{19}$$

Table 1
Representative Values of $a^{(p)}/\bar{a}$ in the Case of a Narrow Wave Spectrum [89]

p	$a^{(p)}/a$	p	$a^{(p)}/a$
0.01	2.359	0.4	1.347
0.05	1.986	0.5	1.256
0.1	1.800	0.6	1.176
0.2	1.591	0.7	1.102
0.25	1.517	0.8	1.031
0.3	1.454	0.9	0.961
0.3333	1.416	1.0	0.886

The standard deviation is

$$\frac{d(a)}{\bar{a}} = \sqrt{1 - \frac{\pi}{4}} = 0.453 \tag{20}$$

The Rayleigh probability density function may also be described in terms of the wave height (trough to crest distance) as follows:

$$R(h) = \frac{d}{dH} \{1 - e^{-(H/H_{rms})^2}\} = \frac{2H}{H_{rms}^2 e^{-(H/H_{rms})^2}} \tag{21}$$

The maximum value for H/H_{rms} occurs at $1/\sqrt{2}$ as in Equation 15 and the most frequent wave is

$$H = 0.707 H_{rms} \tag{22}$$

The mean value, $\bar{H} = 0.886$ (as in Equation 18) $\tag{23}$

The other relationships are

$$H_{1/10} = 1.800 H_{rms} \tag{24}$$

$$H_s = 1.416 H_{rms} \tag{25}$$

The wave height with any given probability η/N of being exceeded may be determined approximately from line a in Figure 3, or from

$$\frac{\hat{H}}{H_{rms}} = -Ln\left(\frac{\eta}{N}\right)^{1/2} \tag{26}$$

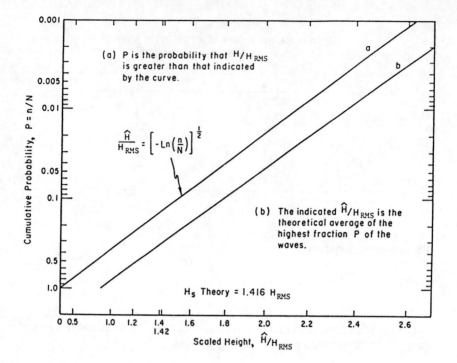

Figure 3. Theoretical wave height distributions [175].

where $\hat{H}$ = arbitrary value (H is greater than an arbitrary value $\hat{H}$)
   η = number of waves larger than $\hat{H}$
   N = total number of waves in the record

The average height of all waves with heights greater than H, denoted $\bar{H}(H)$ can be obtained from

$$\bar{H}(H) = \frac{\displaystyle\int_{H}^{\infty} H^2 \exp -\left(\frac{H}{H_{rms}}\right)^2 dH}{\displaystyle\int_{\hat{H}}^{\infty} H \exp -\left(\frac{H}{H_{rms}}\right)^2 dH} \tag{27}$$

The ratio $\bar{H}(\hat{H})/H_{rms}$ can be estimated from line b in Figure 3. The following example illustrates the use of the theoretical wave height distribution lines in Figure 3.

Given: Based on an analysis of wave records at a coastal location, the significant wave height H_s was estimated to be 3 m (9.84 ft).

Find:

1. H_{10} (average of the highest 10% of all waves).
2. H_1 (average of the highest 1% of all waves).

Solution: $\hat{H} = H_s = 3$ m. Using Equation 25

$$H_s = 1.416H_{rms}$$

or

$$H_{rms} = \frac{H_s}{1.416} = \frac{3}{1.416} = 2.12 \text{ m (6.95 ft)}$$

1. From Figure 3, curve b, it is seen that for $P = 0.1$ (10%)

$$\frac{H_{10}}{H_{rms}} \approx 1.80; \; H_{10} = 1.80H_{rms} = 1.80(2.12) = 3.82 \text{ m (12.53 ft)}$$

2. Similarly, for $P = 0.01$ (1%)

$$\frac{H_1}{H_{rms}} \approx 2.36; \; H_1 = 2.36H_{rms} = 2.36(2.12) = 5.0 \text{ m (16.41 ft)}$$

Note that

$$\frac{H_{10}}{H_s} = \frac{3.82}{3} \quad \text{or} \quad H_{10} = 1.27H_s$$

and

$$\frac{H_1}{H_s} = \frac{5.0}{3} \quad \text{or} \quad H_1 = 1.67H_s$$

Forristall [41] indicated that the Rayleigh distribution overpredicts the heights of the highest waves in the record. He supported this conclusion on the basis of an analysis of 116 hours of hurricane wave data from the Gulf of Mexico. The significant wave height $(H_{1/3})$ was only 94.2% of values predicted by Rayleigh distribution, and the maximum wave in 1,000 waves was 90.7% of the predicted wave height.

The relationship can also be presented in terms of the significant wave height $(H_{1/3})$

$$\bar{H} = 0.626(H_{1/3}) \tag{28}$$

$$H_{1/10} = 2.03\bar{H} = 1.27(H_{1/3}) \tag{29}$$

$$H_{1/3} = 1.597\bar{H} \tag{30}$$

$$H_{rms} = 1.128\bar{H} = 0.706(H_{1/3}) \tag{31}$$

Once H_{rms} is known, the 10% ranges (10% of the waves will have values between a given range) of wave height distribution may be estimated. Table 2 gives the 10% ranges as well as cumulative ascending and descending values.

Table 2
Approximate Wave Height Data*

Ten Percent Ranges (Ten Percent of the Waves Will Have Crest-to-Trough Heights Between the Given Range of Values):

10% between 0.00
10% between $0.64\sqrt{H_{RMS}}$
10% between $0.94\sqrt{H_{RMS}}$
10% between $1.20\sqrt{H_{RMS}}$
10% between $1.42\sqrt{H_{RMS}}$
10% between $1.66\sqrt{H_{RMS}}$
10% between $1.92\sqrt{H_{RMS}}$
10% between $2.20\sqrt{H_{RMS}}$
10% between $2.54\sqrt{H_{RMS}}$
10% greater than $3.04\sqrt{H_{RMS}}$

Cumulative Ascending 10% Values:

10% less than $0.64\sqrt{H_{RMS}}$
20% less than $0.94\sqrt{H_{RMS}}$
30% less than $1.20\sqrt{H_{RMS}}$
40% less than $1.42\sqrt{H_{RMS}}$
50% less than $1.66\sqrt{H_{RMS}}$
60% less than $1.92\sqrt{H_{RMS}}$
70% less than $2.20\sqrt{H_{RMS}}$
80% less than $2.54\sqrt{H_{RMS}}$
90% less than $3.04\sqrt{H_{RMS}}$

Cumulative Descending 10% Values:

10% greater than $3.04\sqrt{H_{RMS}}$
20% greater than $2.54\sqrt{H_{RMS}}$
30% greater than $2.20\sqrt{H_{RMS}}$
40% greater than $1.92\sqrt{H_{RMS}}$
50% greater than $1.66\sqrt{H_{RMS}}$
60% greater than $1.42\sqrt{H_{RMS}}$
70% greater than $1.20\sqrt{H_{RMS}}$
80% greater than $0.94\sqrt{H_{RMS}}$
90% greater than $0.64\sqrt{H_{RMS}}$
100% greater than $0.00\sqrt{H_{RMS}}$

(after S. O. Rice and M. S. Longuet-Higgins)

* From *Practical Methods for Observing and Forecasting Ocean Waves by Means of Wave Spectra and Statistics* by W. J. Pierson, Jr., G. Neumann, and R. W. James, H. O. Pub. No. 603, U.S. Naval Oceanographic Office, 1967.

Wave Period Distribution

Longuet-Higgins [91] proposed the following distribution of wave period:

$$P\left(\frac{T}{\bar{T}}\right) = \frac{n_m{}^2}{2\left[n_m{}^2 + \left(\frac{T}{\bar{T}} - 1\right)^2\right]^{3/2}} \tag{32}$$

where $\bar{T}$ = mean period, usually assumed to be equal to $1/f_{m_2}$ for the zero-crossing method

$$f_{m_2} = \sqrt{\frac{m_2}{m_0}}$$

m_2 = spectral moment of the second order
m_0 = spectral moment of the zero order

$$n_m = \sqrt{\frac{m_0 m_2}{m_1{}^2} - 1}$$

m_1 = spectral moment of the first order

Bretschneider [18] assumed that wavelength variability could be taken as Rayleigh distribution, thus period variability can also be a Rayleigh distribution and a fully developed sea may be given as

$$P(T)\, dT = 2.7\left(\frac{T^3}{\bar{T}^4}\right) \exp\left[-0.675\left(\frac{T}{\bar{T}}\right)^4\right] dT \tag{33}$$

It is assumed that the distribution of T^2 (which is proportional to the wavelength, L) follows the Rayleigh distribution curve. The measurements obtained at Nagoya Harbor [66] showed that

$$\frac{T_{1/10}}{T_{1/3}} = 0.99 \pm 0.06 \quad \text{and} \quad \frac{T_{1/3}}{\bar{T}} = 1.07 \pm 0.08,$$

so that the $T_{1/10}$, $T_{1/3}$, T_{max} are approximately equal to $(1.1 - 1.3)\bar{T}$ [66].

A spectral width parameter was introduced by Cartwright and Longuet-Higgins [24].

$$W_p = \sqrt{1 - \frac{m_0{}^2}{m_0 m_4}} \tag{34}$$

where m_4 = spectral moment of the fourth order

The parameter W_p approaches zero for the narrow-banded spectrum and it approaches one for the broad-banded spectrum. Thus, a determination can be made whether given data represent a narrow- or broad-banded spectrum. Because Rayleigh distribution overpredicts the wave height for broad-banded spectra, this may be taken into account in selecting design waves.

Maximum Waves

The probability distribution of maximum amplitude, a_{max} is

$$N(1 - F)^{N-1}P \tag{35}$$

The probability that a will be less than r is $e^{-e^{-(r^2-r_0^2)/\bar{a}^2}}$ and the probability that a will be greater than r is $1 - e^{-e^{-(r^2-r_0^2)/\bar{a}^2}}$.

The most probable highest individual wave for a given sea state is related to H_s by

$$H_{max} = H_s \sqrt{\frac{\ln(N)}{2}} \tag{36}$$

from Rayleigh extreme density distribution where N = number of waves on record (for which the H_s was calculated).

Example 1:

If N = 1000

$$H_{max} = H_s \frac{\sqrt{\ln(1,000)}}{2} = H_s \frac{\sqrt{6.908}}{2} = 1.858 H_s$$

If N = 400

$$H_{max} = H_s \frac{\sqrt{5.991}}{2} = 1.731 H_s$$

Example 2:

Assume $T_{ave} = 7.5$ sec, N = 10,000

time = 10,000(7.5) = 75,000 sec = 20.83 hr

$$H_{max} = H_s \frac{\sqrt{\ln(10,000)}}{2} = 2.146 H_s$$

{Rule of thumb: $H_{max} = 2(H_s)$}

Table 3
Average Values of H_{max}/H_s and Standard Deviation for
Approximately 150 Waves [64]

Location	H_{max}/H_s	Standard Deviation
Statfjord	1.58	0.11
Halten	1.64	0.20
Utsira	1.65	0.18
Average	1.62	0.16

The extreme Rayleigh distribution is given by

$$R_N(H_N) = \exp\left\{ -N \exp\left[-2\left(\frac{H_N}{H_s}\right)^2 \right] \right\}_0$$

where $R_N(H_N)$ is the probability that the highest among N waves shall not exceed H.

Example 3:

$N = 1000$

$H_N = 15m, H_s = 5m$

$$R_N(H_N) = \exp\left\{ -1,000 \exp\left[-2\left(\frac{15}{5}\right)^2 \right] \right\} = 0.999985$$

i.e., a very low probability that even the highest among 1,000 waves shall exceed $3(H_s)$. For $N = 10,000$, $R_N(H_N) = 0.99848$, still a very low probability. If $T_{ave} = 8.5$ sec, the length of time is 23.6 hr.

Houmb and Overvik [64] reported values of H_{max}/H_s between 1.45 and 1.64 for 115 wave records from the Norwegian Continental shelf (Table 3).

Assuming that there are approximately 150 waves in each record, the theoretical value of H_{max} is equal to $1.58(H_s)$, which correlates well with the experimental data reported by Houmb and Overvik.

The average values and standard deviation for approximately 80 waves are as follows (the theoretical value of $1.48(H_s)$ also agrees well with the measured data):

Location	H_{max}/H_s	Standard Deviation
Famita	1.45	0.13

Long-Term and Extreme Value Statistics

Return Period

The long-term or extreme value statistics deal with wave heights and wave periods of storm, or hurricane events (sometime defined as rare events). The main purpose of employing the extreme statistics is to provide a basis for selection of design wave conditions. In long-term statistics all available data are used to predict the wave distribution of extreme values, and the extreme statistics only employ the extreme data points to predict extreme value distribution. The value of wave height sought is that which may occur on the average once in a 100 yr, or it will have a 100-yr "return period," or a "recurrence interval." The return period T_r is defined as

$$T_r = \frac{N + 1}{m} \tag{37}$$

where m = rank of event
N = number of items

It should also be noted that

$$T_r = \frac{1}{P} \tag{38}$$

Table 4 gives the theoretical distribution of the return period for events having specified average return periods.

It will be noted that the probability of the return period being less than the average value is greater than 0.5. Over a long period of time 25% of the intervals between events equal to, or greater than a 30 year event will be less than 8 years, while an equal number will be greater than 42 years.

Another formula for a return period that can be used is that of Gringorten [50]

$$T_r = \frac{n + 0.12}{m - 0.44} \tag{39}$$

This formula gives longer return periods for the higher values in a series.

Table 4
Theoretical Distribution of the Return Period [88]

Average Return Period T_r	Actual Return Period T_r Exceeded Exceeded Various Percentages of the Time						
	1%	5%	25%	50%	75%	95%	99%
2	8	5	3	1	0	0	0
5	22	14	7	3	1	0	0
10	45	28	14	7	3	0	0
30	137	89	42	21	8	2	0
100	459	300	139	69	29	5	1
1,000	4,620	3,000	1,400	693	288	51	10
10,000	46,200	30,000	14,000	6,932	2,880	513	100

It should be noted that a given wave height will have a given return period *on the average*, and a higher wave height can occur within that period.

The probability j that the actual probability of the mth of N events is less than probability p_0 can be obtained [144] from

$$j = \frac{N!}{m!(N-m)!} \, m \int_1^{1-p_0} p^{m-1}(1-p)^{N-m} \, dp \tag{40}$$

Equation 39 was used to compute Table 5 for rank m values from 1 to 4. It will be noted that there are approximately two chances out of three that the true return period of the largest event in a data series is greater than the period of record.

Extrapolation of wave characteristics for higher return periods is then possible. At least 10 years of data are required, but preferably a longer series of data is required, such as 30 years, to account for meteorological fluctuations. Very few design engineers have the luxury of having long series data, so that predictions of longer return periods must be based on extrapolations. Hindcasted data based on past synoptic weather charts may have to be employed if actual relatively long-term data are not available.

Table 5
Average Return Periods for Various Levels of Probability [88]

Rank From Top m	Number of Years of Record n	Probability				
		0.01	0.25	0.50	0.75	0.99
1	2	1.11	2.00	3.41	7.46	200
	5	1.66	4.13	7.73	17.9	498
	10	2.71	7.73	14.9	35.3	996
	20	4.86	14.9	29.4	70.0	1990
	60	13.5	43.8	87.0	209.0	5970
2	3	1.06	1.48	2.00	3.06	17.0
	6	1.42	2.57	3.78	6.20	37.4
	11	2.13	4.41	6.76	11.4	71.1
	21	3.61	8.12	12.7	21.8	138.0
	61	9.62	23.0	36.6	63.4	408.0
3	4	1.05	1.32	1.63	2.19	7.10
	7	1.31	2.06	2.75	3.95	14.1
	12	1.86	3.32	4.62	6.86	25.6
	22	3.03	5.86	8.35	12.6	48.6
	62	7.76	16.1	23.3	35.8	140.0
4	5	1.03	1.24	1.46	1.83	4.50
	8	1.25	1.80	2.27	3.04	8.26
	13	1.70	2.77	3.63	5.02	14.4
	23	2.67	4.72	6.36	8.98	26.6
	63	6.63	12.5	17.2	24.8	75.2

Extreme wave statistics may be performed from different sets of wave data for a variety of reasons, for example:

1. Extreme statistics of significant wave height (H_s)
2. Extreme statistics of highest individual waves
3. Long-term cumulative distribution of individual wave heights

Normal Distribution. The normal distribution was developed by De Moivre (1733) and later published by Gauss (1809), and is sometimes called the Gaussian distribution. It is usually now referred to as "normal" distribution, as the averages of n observations taken at random from almost any population tend to become normally distributed as n increases.

A variate x is said to be normally distributed if its density function f(x) is

$$f(x) = \frac{1}{\sigma\sqrt{2\pi}} e^{-(x-m)^2/2\sigma^2} \quad (-\infty, \infty) \tag{41}$$

where m can be any real number, and σ any real number > 0. Figure 4 shows normal distributions with m = 0 and selected values of μ.

A normal distribution with m = 0 and $\sigma^2 = 1 = \sigma$ is called the unit normal distribution, or simply normal distribution. Figure 5 shows the normal distribution with fixed m = 0, and selected values of σ. The unit normal distribution is

$$f(x) = \frac{1}{\sqrt{2\pi}} e^{-x^2/2} \quad (-\infty, \infty) \tag{42}$$

Table 6 summarizes the values of f(x) and areas under the bell-shaped curve.

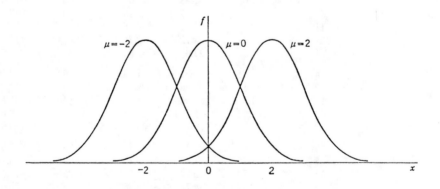

Figure 4. Normal distribution with fixed $\sigma(\sigma = 1)$ and selected values of m.

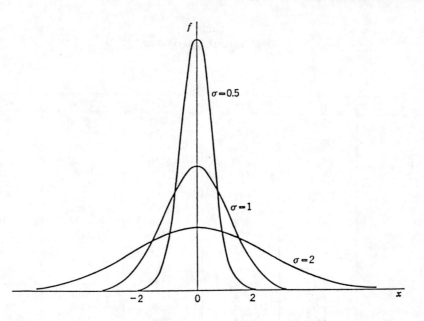

Figure 5. Normal distributions with fixed m(m = 0) and selected values of σ.

Properties of the normal distribution are as follows:

$$\text{Standard deviation} = \sigma = \sqrt{\frac{\Sigma x^2}{N-1}}$$

where x is the difference between the value of individual measurement and the mean of all the measurements in the sample:

$$\text{Mean deviation} = \sigma\frac{2}{\pi} = 0.7979\sigma$$

$$\text{First moment} = m_1 = \text{mean of m}$$

$$\text{Second moment} = m_2 = \text{variance of x}$$

$$\text{Third moment} = m_3$$

$$\text{Fourth moment} = m_4$$

$$\text{Skewness} = \frac{m_3}{(m_2)^{3/2}}$$

$$\text{Kurtosis} = \frac{m_4}{(m_2)^2}$$

Table 6
Unit Normal Distribution*

x	f(x)	F(x)	R(x)	2R(x)	W(x)
.0	.3989	.5000	.5000	1.0000	0
.1	.3970	.5398	.4602	.9203	.0797
.2	.3910	.5793	.4207	.8415	.1585
.3	.3814	.6179	.3821	.7642	.2358
.4	.3683	.6554	.3446	.6892	.3108
.5	.3521	.6915	.3085	.6171	.3829
.6	.3332	.7257	.2743	.5485	.4515
.7	.3123	.7580	.2420	.4839	.5161
.8	.2897	.7881	.2119	.4237	.5763
.9	.2661	.8159	.1841	.3681	.6319
1.0	.2420	.8413	.1587	.3173	.6827
1.1	.2179	.8643	.1357	.2713	.7287
1.2	.1942	.8849	.1151	.2301	.7699
1.3	.1714	.9032	.0968	.1936	.8064
1.4	.1497	.9192	.0808	.1615	.8385
1.5	.1295	.9332	.0668	.1336	.8664
1.6	.1109	.9452	.0548	.1096	.8904
1.7	.0940	.9554	.0446	.0891	.9109
1.8	.0790	.9641	.0359	.0719	.9281
1.9	.0656	.9713	.0287	.0574	.9426
2.0	.0540	.9772	.0228	.0455	.9545
2.1	.0440	.9821	.0179	.0357	.9643
2.2	.0355	.9861	.0139	.0278	.9722
2.3	.0283	.9893	.0107	.0214	.9786
2.4	.0224	.9918	.0082	.0164	.9836
2.5	.0175	.9938	.0062	.0124	.9876
2.6	.0136	.9953	.0047	.0093	.9907
2.7	.0104	.9965	.0035	.0069	.9931
2.8	.0079	.9974	.0026	.0051	.9949
2.9	.0060	.9981	.0019	.0037	.9963
3.0	.0044	.9987	.0013	.0027	.9973
Fractiles					
1.2816	.1755	.9000	.1000	.2010	.8000
1.6449	.1031	.9500	.0500	.1000	.9000
1.9600	.0584	.9750	.0250	.0500	.9500
2.0537	.0484	.9800	.0200	.0400	.9600
2.3263	.0267	.9900	.0100	.0200	.9800
2.5758	.0145	.9950	.0050	.0100	.9900

* From Wadsworth and Bryan, 1960

For the normal distribution $m_1 = m_3 = 0$. Thus the skewness is equal to zero. The Kurtosis is equal to 3.0.

The value of positive skewness is given by different researchers as follows:

Author	Skewness	Remarks
Kinsman [81]	0.168	July Records, 11,786 data points
Kinsman [81]	0.045	November Records, 12,634 data points
Goda and Nagai [45]	(−0.42)–0.168	
Ou and Tang [112]	(−0.0138)–0.0126 ·	

For the purpose of analysis, the bell-shaped curve of a normal distribution can be plotted by accumulating progressively the number of cases equal to, or less than, any particular value.

A cumulative curve is shown in Figure 6 where probable deviations (probable deviation equals 0.6745 times the standard deviation) are used for the vertical scale. Note that in defining a normal distribution 50% of the values are greater than the mean and therefore the value of 50% corresponds to zero on the ordinate scale. The 25% point on the abscissa corresponds to minus-one probable deviation on the ordinate. Plotting the data on the expanded abscissa, in this case a probability scale, produces a cumulative long-normal frequency distribution curve. If data plot as a straight line, it means that the values are normally distributed. The slope of the line is a measure of variability (Figure 7).

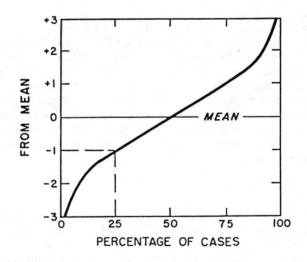

Figure 6. Cumulative normal frequency distribution.

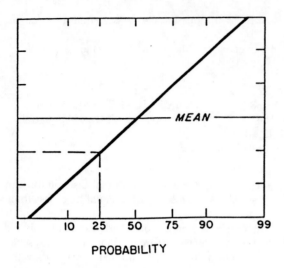

Figure 7. Cumulative log-normal frequency distribution.

Gram-Charlier Distribution

Gram-Charlier distribution considers the effects of non-linearities.

$$p(\eta) = \frac{1}{\sqrt{2\pi m_2}} \exp\left\{-\frac{\eta^2}{2m_2}\left[1 + \frac{1}{6}\sqrt{\beta_1}\left(\frac{\eta^3}{(m_2)^{3/2}} - \frac{3\eta}{(m_2)^{1/2}}\right)\right]\right\} \tag{43}$$

Note that the first term represents the normal distribution.

Two comparisons between the normal and Gram-Charlier distributions were published. Kinsman [81] presented a comparison using July and November wave records (Figure 8). The frequency distribution showed a positive shift from the normal curve at higher values and a negative shift at lower values. The skewing toward high values agrees with observations that the surface waves have relative flatter and longer troughs, and sharper and more peaked crests. Figure 9 displays a comparison between normal and Gram-Charlier distributions for four recorded wave data sets. These comparisons indicate that there is little difference between the two distributions [112].

Gumbel Distribution

The first asymptotic distribution of extreme values has been proposed by Gumbel [51], and is commonly called the Gumbel Type I distribution. The Gumbel distribution has been frequently applied to model natural extremes such as floods or storms. In extreme value statistics the variable is often the annual extreme value, or storm-related extreme values, such as the observed greatest values of wave heights. In most cases the estimates are based on data that are also extremes.

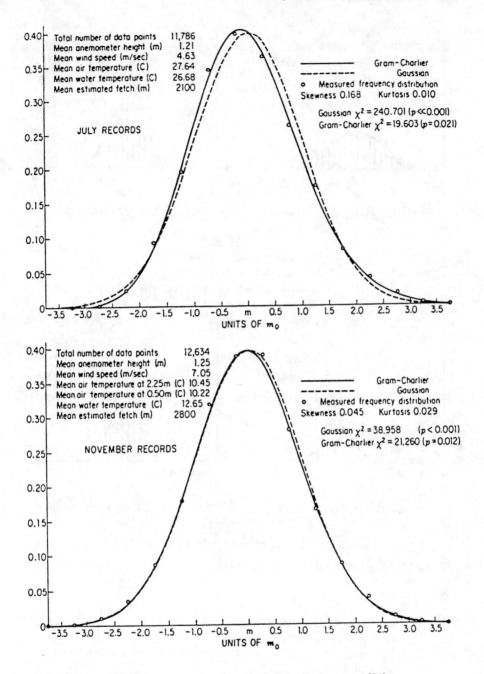

Figure 8. Distributions of water surface displacement [81].

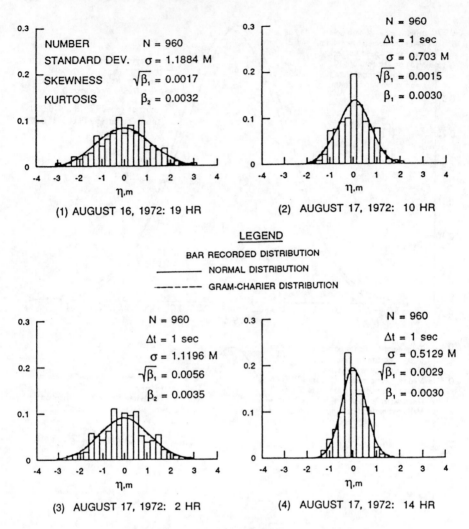

Figure 9. Distributions of water surface a buoy A [112].

Chow [27] has indicated that most frequency function can be generalized to

$$X = \bar{X} + K\sigma_x \qquad (44)$$

where X = an event of specified probability

 $\bar{X}$ = the mean value of the series

 K = frequency factor defined by a selected distribution, and is a function of the return period

 σ_x = standard deviation of the series

Fisher and Tippett [40] discovered that the distribution of maximum (or minimum) data points selected from N samples approached a limiting form as the size of the samples increased. If the initial distributions within the samples are exponential, the distribution is given by

$$P(x) = 1 - e^{-e^{-y}} \tag{45}$$

where   P(x) = probability of a given event being equaled or exceeded
$\qquad$ y = reduced variate
$\qquad$ $= a_n(x - u_n)$
$\quad$ x, a_n, u_n = parameters of the distribution

The distribution function is then

$$F(x) = \exp - e^{(-y)} \tag{46}$$

and Equation 44 may be expressed as

$$X = \bar{X} + (0.7797y + 0.45)\sigma_x \tag{47}$$

where K = (0.7797y + 0.45) for Type I distribution.

Table 7 gives values of K. This distribution is called the Gumbel distribution or Fisher-Tippett Type I distribution.
Equation 46 may be written as

$$y = -\ln\{-\ln[F(H)]\} \tag{48}$$

On the Gumbel probability paper, the abscissa is an arithmetic scale in H, the ordinate is *doubly* logarithmic.

Table 7
Values of K for the Extreme-Value (Type 1) Distribution [88]

Return Period, Years	Reduced Variate Probability	y	K
1.58	0.63	0.000	−0.450
2.00	0.50	0.367	−0.164
2.33	0.43	0.579	0.001
5	0.20	1.500	0.719
10	0.10	2.250	1.30
20	0.05	2.970	1.87
50	0.02	3.902	2.59
100	0.01	4.600	3.14
200	0.005	5.296	3.68
400	0.0025	6.000	4.23

Data *that fit* the distribution then fall on a straight line, and u_n and a_n are given by

$$u_n = \bar{H} - \frac{\bar{Y}_N}{a_n} \tag{49}$$

$$a_n = \frac{\sigma_N}{\bar{H}} \tag{50}$$

where $\bar{H}$ = average of extreme values of H
      y_N = average deviation of y
      σ_N = standard deviation of y

$$\sigma_H{}^2 = \frac{\sum\limits_{i=1}^{N} (H_i - \bar{H})^2}{N - 1} = \text{standard deviation of H} \tag{51}$$

where N = number of extreme wave heights
      σ_H = standard deviation of H

According to Houmb [61] the procedure to calculate the parameters is as follows:

1. Calculate the average of extremes, $\bar{H}$
2. Calculate σ_H from equation 51
3. Knowing N, obtain value of σ_N and y_N from Table 8
4. Calculate u_n (Equation 49)
5. Calculate a_n (Equation 50)

Note: Gumbel [51] introduced the following tests to estimate the goodness of fit between data and distribution.

1. Data between the probability levels 0.15 and 0.85 (or $-0.64 < y < 1.82$) are assumed normally distributed about the theoretical mean. The probability that a data point shall fall within an interval of $\pm\sigma$ is then 0.6827. The standard deviation

$$\sigma_H = \frac{Z}{a_n \sqrt{N}} \tag{52}$$

where

$$Z = \frac{\sqrt{1/F(H) - 1}}{-\ln(F(H))} \tag{53}$$

The control curves are then drawn parallel to the straight line given by Gumbel distribution at $\pm\sigma_H$.

Table 8
Parameters of the Gumbel Distribution [61]

N	Y_N	N	N	Y_N	N
2	0.4043	0.4984	32	0.5380	1.1193
3	0.4286	0.6435	33	0.5388	1.1226
4	0.4458	0.7315	34	0.5396	1.1255
5	0.4588	0.7928	35	0.5403	1.1285
6	0.4690	0.8388	36	0.5410	1.1313
7	0.4774	0.8749	37	0.5418	1.1339
8	0.4843	0.9043	38	0.5424	1.1363
9	0.4902	0.9288	39	0.5430	1.1388
10	0.4952	0.9497	40	0.5436	1.1413
11	0.4996	0.9676	41	0.5442	1.1436
12	0.5035	0.9833	42	0.5448	1.1458
13	0.5070	0.9972	43	0.5453	1.1480
14	0.5100	1.0095	44	0.5458	1.1499
15	0.5128	1.0206	45	0.5463	1.1519
16	0.5157	1.0316	46	0.5468	1.1538
17	0.5181	1.0411	47	0.5473	1.1557
18	0.5202	1.0493	48	0.5477	1.1574
19	0.5220	1.0566	49	0.5481	1.1590
20	0.5236	1.0628	50	0.5485	1.1607
21	0.5252	1.0696	60	0.5521	1.1747
22	0.5268	1.0754	70	0.5548	1.1854
23	0.5283	1.0811	80	0.5569	1.1938
24	0.5296	1.0864	90	0.5586	1.2007
25	0.5309	1.0915	100	0.5600	1.2065
26	0.5320	1.0961	150	0.5646	1.2253
27	0.5332	1.1004	200	0.5672	1.2360
28	0.5343	1.1047	300	0.5699	1.2479
29	0.5353	1.1086	400	0.5714	1.2545
30	0.5362	1.1124	500	0.5724	1.2588
31	0.5371	1.1159	1000	0.5745	1.2685
			∞	0.5772	1.2826

2. Outside the probability level $\langle 0.15, 0.84 \rangle$ asymptotic values are used to determine the distance x from the straight line. At the largest value

$$x = \frac{1.14071}{a_n} \qquad (54)$$

Note: Yearly or monthly data of highest waves may be used for extreme wave analysis. Design conditions are usually given in terms of

$$T_r = \frac{\tau}{1 - e^{-e^{-y}}} \qquad (55)$$

For large values of H, and Gumbel distribution Equation 55 becomes

$$T_r = e^y \tag{56}$$

or the extreme wave height

$$H_R = u_n + \frac{\ln T_r}{a_n} \tag{57}$$

The control curves are usually drawn beyond the largest value at distances $\pm x$, parallel to the straight line. If measured values fall within the control curves, the data may be assumed to follow Gumbel's distribution.

Houmb et al. [65] plotted data obtained from a hindcast project in the North Sea at Utsira. The yearly extreme values were hindcasted for the years 1949–1976 (Figure 10). The significant wave height for a return period of 100 years $H_s(100)$ was taken as 16.0 m. The range of maximum wave height, $H_{max}(100)$ at the 90% confidence level and $N = 1,000$ was 27.2 to 35.6 m.

Weibull Distribution

Another distribution of natural extremes such as floods and storms is the Weibull distribution. During the last decade a number of researchers have tried to apply the Weibull method to describe distributions of wave heights and periods, both within storms and for long-term analysis. The Weibull distribution is given as

$$f(x) = \frac{1}{\beta^\alpha} \alpha x^{\alpha-1} \exp\left[-\left(\frac{x}{\beta}\right)^\alpha\right] \qquad \text{for } x > 0, \alpha > 0, \beta > 0 \tag{58a}$$

$$f(x) = 0 \text{ for other values of } x, \alpha, \beta \tag{58b}$$

where x = random variable
α = shape parameter which determines the basic shape of a given distribution
β = scale parameter which controls the degree of spread along the variate axis (the abscissa).
The mean,

$$m = \beta\Gamma\left(1 - \frac{1}{\alpha}\right) \tag{59}$$

The variance,

$$\sigma^2 = \beta^2\left[\Gamma\left(1 + \frac{2}{\alpha}\right) - \Gamma^2\left(1 + \frac{1}{a}\right)\right] \tag{60}$$

where Γ = gamma function

$$F(z) = \int_0^\infty x^{(z-1)}e^{-x}\,dx = (z - 1)! \tag{61}$$

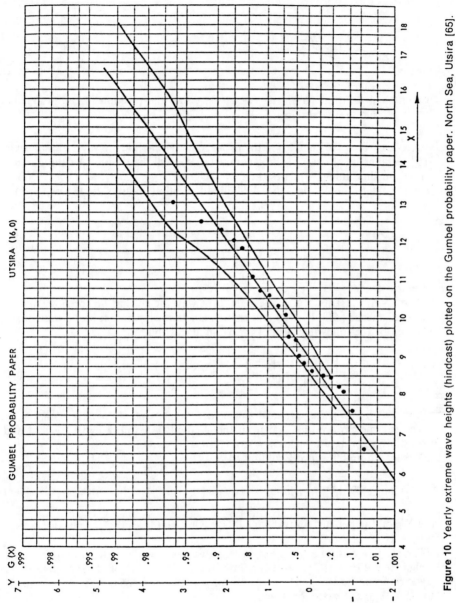

Figure 10. Yearly extreme wave heights (hindcast) plotted on the Gumbel probability paper. North Sea, Utsira [65].

The Weibull distribution can be used with two or three parameters. A three-parameter Weibull distribution is

$$F(x) = 1 - \exp\left[\frac{-(x - \epsilon)}{\beta}\right]^{\alpha} \tag{62}$$

for $\epsilon > 0$

where ϵ = a location parameter, which describes the position of the probability along (the abscissa) [70]

Nordenstrom [107] employed the two-parameter method, however Houmb et al. [65] recommend the use of three-parameter Weibull distribution, as the Nordenstrom's method underestimates the wave heights.

It should be noted that the Weibull distribution reduces to the exponential distribution

$$f(x) = \frac{e^{-x/\beta}}{\beta} \qquad \text{for } x > 0, \beta > 0 \tag{63}$$

when $\alpha = 1$ and $\epsilon = 0$ [107].

A long-term distribution of the significant wave height has not been derived by analytical means [61]. By trial and error it has been shown that best correlation is achieved by the following form of the Weibull distribution

$$F(H_s) = 1 - \exp\left[-\left(\frac{H_s - H_0}{H_c - H_0}\right)\gamma\right] \tag{64}$$

where H_0, H_c and γ are parameters to be determined, based on wave data.

The parameters are obtained from the Weibull probability paper by trial and error plotting of data to achieve a straight line.

The logarithmic form of Equation 64 is

$$\ln\{-\ln[1 - F(H_s)]\} = \gamma[\ln(H_s - H_0) - \ln(H_c - H_0)] \tag{65}$$

The Weibull paper has an ordinate $P(H_s) = \ln\{-\ln[1 - F(H_s)]\}$ and an abscissa $\ln(H_c - H_0)$.

The plotting position of the lowest H_s value has a tendency to deviate from the straight line. For this reason, H_0 is introduced. The value of H_0 is therefore the deviation from the straight line by lowering the plotting position (γ is the slope of the line). H_c is the value for which

$$\ln\{-\ln[1 - F(H_s)]\} = 0 \tag{66}$$

Data must be arranged in frequency tables (normally in classes of 0.5 m or 2 ft). The mid- or the upper-point (more conservative) of each class is used as a plotting position for H. The plotting position for $F(H_s)$ is

$$F(H_{s_i}) = \frac{m}{N + 1} \tag{67}$$

where m is the total number of data less than the upper limit of the class representing H_{s_i}. The *return period* T_r in this case is defined by

$$T_r = \frac{\tau}{1 - F(H_s)} \tag{68}$$

where τ = time between observations (usually = 3 hr)

Taking τ_r = 100 years and τ = 1 units of years, we obtain 100-years significant wave height $H_{s\,100\,yr}$, i.e. the value of H_s that is being exceeded *on the average* once every 100 years.

Note 1: It may be difficult to compare extreme estimates because different values of τ are used (between 12 minutes and 3 hours).

Note 2: Design conditions usually 50- or 100-yr T_r (coastal engineering), 25-yr in other applications. The difference between $(H_s)_{50\,yr}$ and $(H_s)_{100\,yr}$ is only 6%.

Because no analytical expression is available for the confidence intervals of estimates made using Weibull distribution, Goda [44] developed an empirical expression for the standard error of the return period

$$\sigma[T_r] = \left(\frac{\sigma}{\sqrt{N}}\right)[1.0 + A_R(y_R - C_R)^2]^{1/2} \tag{69}$$

where $A_R = a_1 \exp\left[a_2 \left(\frac{N}{10}\right)^{-1.3}\right]$

Empirical coefficients C_R, a_1 and a_2 are given in Table 9 (Weibull) and in Table 10 (Fisher-Tippet Type I, Gumbel).

Table 9
Weibull Empirical Coefficients

K	a_1	a_2	C_R
0.75	1.65	0.57	0.0
1.0	1.92	0.57	0.3
1.4	2.05	0.57	0.4
2.0	2.22	0.57	0.5

Table 10
Fisher-Tippet Gumbel Empirical Coefficient

K	a_1	a_2	C_R
	0.64	0.45	0.0

Houmb examined wave data from a weather ship in the North Sea. The data were analyzed using Weibull distributions with 2- and 3-parameters as shown in Table 11. As shown in Table 11 the three parameter distribution gives the best fit as judged by the coefficient of regression r^2. The Nordenstrom's method uses two-parameter Weibull distribution. Houmb's analysis of the data indicates that the Nordenstrom method underestimates the wave heights as shown in Table 12.

Longuet-Higgins [94] analyzed data on crest-to-trough wave heights and found that the data agreed just as well with the one-parameter Rayleigh distribution as with the two-parameter Weibull distribution, provided that the $\bar{a}_{RMS}$ is taken as $0.925\sqrt{2m_0}$. The $\bar{a}_{RMS}$ amplitude should be evaluated from the original record, and not from the frequency spectrum. He further points out that the two-parameter Weibull distribution offers no obvious advantage, either empirical or theoretical,

Table 11
Parameters from the Long-Term Distribution of Visual Wave Heights from
Weather Ship Station M [65]

Time Period	Number of Parameters	γ	H_c	H_0	$H_v(100)$	$H_s(100)$	Coefficient of Regression r^2
1949	2	1.41	1.95	0	13.5	11.8	0.976
1959	3	0.87	1.98	1.20	19.1	15.4	0.996
1960	2	1.71	2.80	0	13.8	12.0	0.983
1974	3	1.12	2.62	1.15	17.9	14.6	0.998
1949	2	1.63	2.46	0	13.1	11.6	0.984
1974	3	1.00	2.34	1.15	19.3	15.5	0.998

Table 12
Estimates of a 100-Year Storm Based on Nordenstrom Method and
Weibull 2- and 3-Parameter Distribution [65]

Time Period	H(100) Nordenstrom	$H_{max}(100)$ 3-Parameter	$H_{max}(100)$ 2-Parameter
1949–59	23.1	25.1	19.3
1960–74	24.2	23.8	19.5
1949–74	23.2	25.3	18.9

over the one-parameter Rayleigh distribution. The Rayleigh distribution fits the higher wave amplitudes better, which is important in selecting design waves.

Examples of Analysis

Selection Based on Experimentally-Measured Wave Data

Graphical Method. Assuming that wave data for a given location is available, it is possible to calculate the return period (recurrence interval), T_r from the available data and plot it on one of the available probability graph papers. The return period T_r is defined as $T_r = (N + 1)/m$

where m = rank of event
     N = number of items

It would also be noted that $T_r = 1/P$

where P = probability of occurrence

Extrapolation of wave characteristics for higher return periods is then possible. Data may be plotted on a semi-logarithmic, or a logarithmic-logarithmic paper (Figure 11). This may not produce a straight line on the graph paper and other graph papers

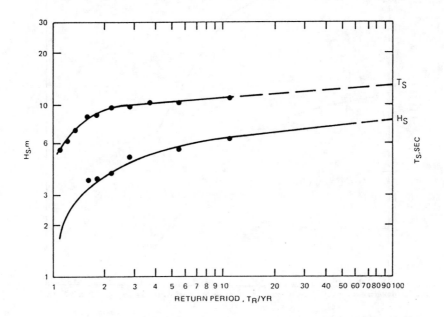

Figure 11. Wave characteristics plotted on a log-log paper.

should be tried. One can select a probability (Figure 12), or a logarithmic probability paper (Figure 13). Other alternatives include the Weibull distribution paper (Figure 14) and the Gumbel extreme value probability paper (Figure 15).

Example 1: Extreme values of the significant wave height (H_s) were observed during a 10-year period (Table 13). Estimate the 25-, 50- and 100-year values of the significant wave height.

The data in Table 13 were plotted on the logarithmic-logarithmic paper (Figure 11), arithmetic-probability paper (Figure 12), logarithmic-probability paper (Figure 13), Weibull distribution paper (Figure 14) and Gumbel extreme probability paper (Figure 15). The dashed portions of the curves indicate extrapolation of the curve beyond measured data.

Tables 14 and 15 present comparisons of wave height and wave period return periods, respectively. Tabulated values of return period correspond to probabilities of 0.10 (10 years), 0.04 (25 years) and 0.01 (100 years).

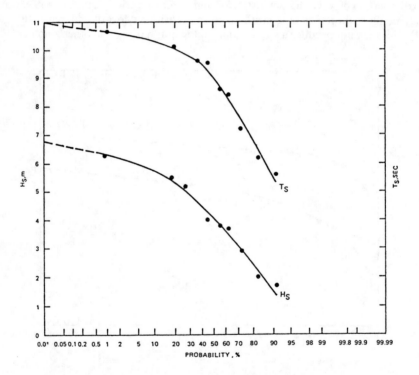

Figure 12. Wave characteristics plotted on an arithmetic-probability paper.

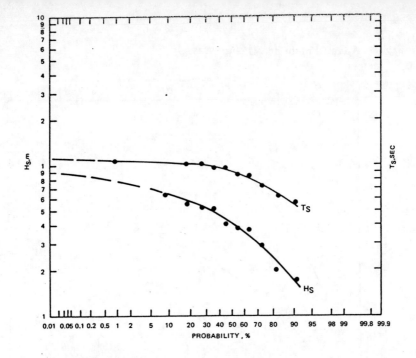

Figure 13. Wave characteristics plotted on a logarithmic probability paper.

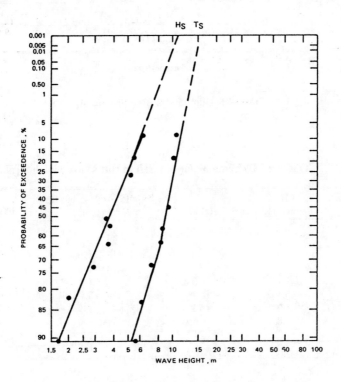

Figure 14. Weibull distribution log(−ln P) as a function of log H.

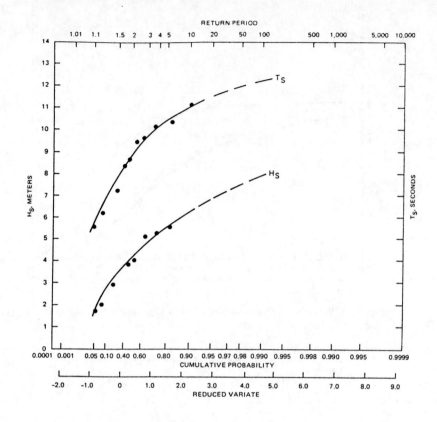

Figure 15. Gumbel extreme probability paper.

Table 13
Observed Extreme Values of Significant Wave Heights [58]

Year	H_s (meters)	Rank, m	Return Period, R_r (years)	Probability, P
1974	4.0	5	2.2	0.45
1975	5.1	4	2.8	0.36
1976	2.9	8	1.4	0.72
1977	3.7	7	1.6	0.63
1978	1.7	10	1.1	0.91
1979	5.5	2	5.5	0.18
1980	5.2	3	3.7	0.27
1981	3.8	6	1.8	0.56
1982	6.3	1	11.0	0.09
1983	2.0	9	1.2	0.83

Table 14
Comparison of Wave Period Return Periods Obtained by Different Methods [58]

	Return Period (T_r) (years)		
Type of Graph Paper	**10**	**25**	**100**
Log-Log (Figure 11)	10.6	11.1	13.0
Arithmetic-Probability (Figure 12)	10.8	10.9	11.0
Logarithmic-Probability (Figure 13)	11.0	11.1	11.3
Weibull (Figure 14)	13.8	14.2	14.7
Gumbel (Figure 15)	11.0	11.6	12.1

Table 15
Comparison of Wave Height Return Periods Obtained by Different Methods [58]

	Return Period (T_r) (years)		
Type of Graph Paper	**10**	**25**	**100**
Log-Log (Figure 11)	6.3	7.0	8.1
Arithmetic-Probability (Figure 12)	6.6	6.7	6.8
Logarithmic-Probability (Figure 13)	8.6	8.8	8.9
Weibull (Figure 14)	8.9	9.4	10.0
Gumbel (Figure 15)	6.2	6.9	7.9

Computation Method. A Microcomputer Applications for Coastal Engineering (MACE) program has been developed by the Coastal Engineering Research Center (1984). The program includes calculation of extremal significant wave height distribution (WAVDIST) and frequency of wave occurrence (FWAVOCUR).

Commercial Firms. There are several commercial firms specializing in wave data hindcasting and prediction for specific locations, principally for the oil industry. Examples of such data presented in graphical form are shown in Figures 16 and 17. Figure 18 shows the significant and maximum wave heights as a function of average interval (return period) in years for a location in the Gulf of Mexico. A similar plot is presented for the storm surge as a function of average interval for the same location (Figure 19).

Duration of Sea State

Duration of sea state is defined as a period during which H_s exceeds a given selected value H_s'. Estimates may be made by the following equation, [63]:

$$\tau_s(H_s') = \frac{\sqrt{2\pi}(H_c - H_0)^\gamma}{\gamma\sigma_h(H_s' - H_0)^{\gamma-1}} \tag{70}$$

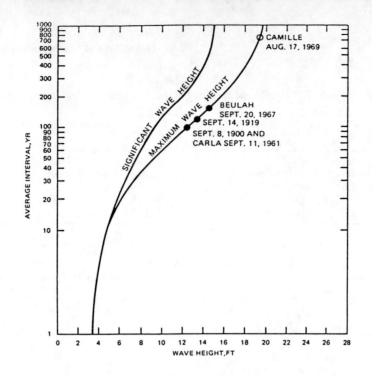

Figure 16. Significant and maximum wave heights as a function of average interval in years for a location in the Gulf of Mexico (Courtesy Glenn and Associates).

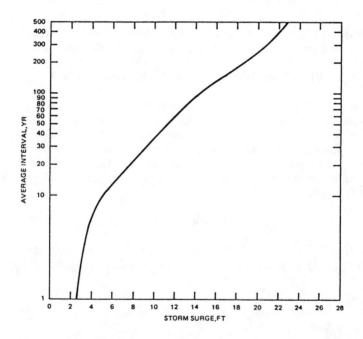

Figure 17. Storm surge as a function of average interval in years for a location in the Gulf of Mexico (Courtesy Glenn and Associates).

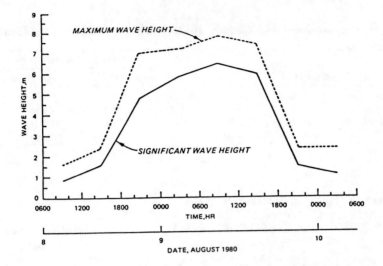

Figure 18. Time history of significant wave height and maximum wave height for Hurricane Allen at a location off Port Mansfield, Texas [58a].

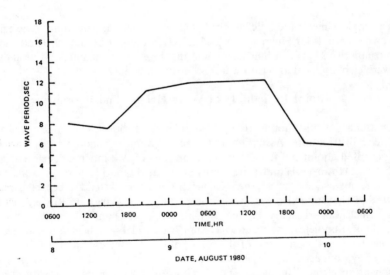

Figure 19. Time history of wave period for Hurricane Allen at a location off Port Mansfield, Texas [58a].

Table 16

Comparison of Recorded and Hindcasted Wave Characteristics [58a]

| Actual Recorded Values | | | Hindcast Values | | | |
| | | | Deep Water | | Water Depth = 18.3 m | |
Maximum Wave Height (m)	Significant Wave Height (m)	Period (secs)	Significant Wave Height (m)	Wave Period (secs)	Significant Wave Height (m)	Wave Period (secs)
7.8	6.50	12.1	7.83	10.8	6.48	10.2

where H_0, H_c, γ = parameters of $F_L(H_s)$ [63]

τ_s = hours

σ_h = standard deviation of H_s (time derivative of H_s) dependent on the wave climate

Note: Selected values may be from 1 to 7 m. The average duration of sea states below level H_s' is:

$$\tau_c(H_s') = \tau_s(H_s')\left(\frac{1}{1 - F_L(H_s')} - 1\right) \tag{71}$$

An example of measured time history of significant wave and maximum wave heights and wave periods for Hurricane Allen is given in Figures 18 and 19. Table 16 shows the comparison between hindcasted and measured wave heights and periods for a waverider buoy located offshore Port Mansfield, Texas.

Joint Probability of Wave Heights and Periods

Bretschneider [18] found that the marginal distributions of H and T followed Rayleigh distributions. Assuming that H and T were independent random variables, he proposed a joint pdf form that was a product of two independent Rayleigh distributions. However, H and T are jointly distributed random variables, and as waves travel a long distance (swell), the wave heights and periods tend to be well correlated. Battjes [10] examined the statistical properties of the bivariate Rayleigh distribution, which was originally derived by Uhlenbeck [152] and Rice [128, 129] in the communication field. The results have not been widely applied in wave studies.

The theoretical derivation of the joint pdf of wave heights and periods was addressed by Longuet-Higgins [93] under the assumption of a linear process and narrow band spectrum. The theoretical distribution of T is symmetrical with respect to $T = \bar{T}$, the mean wave period, $\bar{T}$, and the distribution extends to the negative range. Chakrabarti and Cooley [26] demonstrated that the actual distribution of T exhibited asymmetric behavior. Venezian [159] modified the Longuet-Higgins distribution, to eliminate the negative wave period range. Tayfun [142] examined the effect of the spectrum band width on the Longuet-Higgins distribution. Kimura [80] found that a bivariate Weibull distribution fitted the simulated data well, and the correlation of H and T was related to the spectral band width.

The studies just mentioned are considered as parametric density estimation. Nonparametric density estimation is a major topic in modern statistics that has been extensively studied by mathematical statisticians. Several different techniques have been proposed, but there still remains the question of which technique is superior. Nonparametric density estimation involves smoothing parameters for any type of technique. A major difficulty that arises in various techniques is finding an objective way to choose the smoothing parameters. Spline functions in nonparametric density estimation have been applied and a criterion proposed for objectively choosing the smoothing parameters [171].

The purpose of this section is to introduce available parametric joint pdf and nonparametric density estimation techniques that can be used to describe joint probability of waves and periods.

The Parametric Model of the Joint Probability Density Function

An extensive literature survey was conducted to review available information on joint pdf of wave heights and periods. A limited amount of research has been conducted on this type of problem. This section will introduce several useful joint pdf of wave heights and periods.

Bretschneider [18] proposed a joint pdf of wave heights and periods determined by empirical means, which is a product of marginal distributions, namely

$$f_{XY}(x, y) = 1.35\pi x e^{-(\pi/4)x^2} y^3 e^{-0.675y^4} \tag{72}$$

where $x = \dfrac{H}{\bar{H}}$

$\quad\; y = \dfrac{T}{\bar{T}}$

H, $\bar{H}$, T and $\bar{T}$ are the wave height, the mean wave height, the wave period and the mean wave period, respectively. The marginal distributions are:

$$f_X(x) = \frac{\pi}{2} e^{-(\pi/4)x^2} \tag{73}$$

$$f_Y(y) = 2.7y^3 e^{-0.675y^4} \tag{74}$$

Because $f_{XY}(x, y) = f_X(x)f_Y(y)$, the correlation coefficient is always zero. This is not realistic, because the wave heights and periods appear correlated.

Battjes [10] examined the bivariate Rayleigh distribution, which was originally developed by Uhlenbeck [152]. The bivariate Rayleigh distribution of two random variables U and V, whose means are 1.0, is expressed as

$$f_{UV}(u, v) = \frac{\pi^2}{4} \frac{uv}{1-k^2} \exp\left[-\frac{\pi}{4} \frac{u^2 + v^2}{1-k^2}\right] I_0\left(\frac{\pi}{2} \frac{k}{1-k^2} uv\right) \quad \text{for } u \geq 0, v \geq 0$$

(75)

where k is a shape factor that lies between 0 and 1, and $I_0(.)$ is the modified Bessel function of zeroth order. This distribution has not been successfully applied for the joint variability of wave heights and periods. The examination of this distribution was not pursued. Recently, Kimura [80] examined the applicability of the bivariate Weibull distribution. Because the Rayleigh distribution is a special case of the Weibull distribution, Kimura's work represents a generalized version of the bivariate Rayleigh estimation. In fact, most of the empirical density functions have been proposed for the marginal pdf of wave heights have been forms of the Weibull distribution. The bivariate Weibull pdf of two random variables U and V is written as

$$f_{UV}(u, v) = \frac{mn}{4ab(1-k^2)} u^{m-1}v^{n-1} \exp\left[-\frac{1}{2(1-k^2)}\left(\frac{u^m}{a} + \frac{v^n}{b}\right)\right]$$

$$\times I_0\left(\frac{k^2}{a^{1/2}b^{1/2}(1-k^2)} u^{m/2}v^{n/2}\right) \quad \text{for } u \geq 0, v \geq 0$$

(76)

where m, n, a, b and k are the shape parameters, and $I_0(.)$ is the modified Bessel function of zeroth order. The respective means of U and V are evaluated as

$$E[U] = 2^{1/m}a^{1/m}\Gamma\left(\frac{1+m}{m}\right)$$

(77)

$$E[V] = 2^{1/n}b^{1/n}\Gamma\left(\frac{1+n}{n}\right)$$

(78)

It may be convenient to take the means equal to 1.0, then the random variables are treated as normalized by their respective means. This gives

$$a = \frac{1}{2}\left[\Gamma\left(\frac{1+m}{m}\right)\right]^{-m}$$

(79)

$$b = \frac{1}{2}\left[\Gamma\left(\frac{1+n}{n}\right)\right]^{-n}$$

(80)

Equation 75 is a special case of Equation 76; when m = n = 2, Equation 76 reduces to Equation 75. The marginal distributions of U and V are

$$f_U(u) = \frac{m}{2a} u^{m-1} \exp\left[-\frac{u^m}{2a}\right]$$

(81)

$$f_V(v) = \frac{n}{2b} v^{n-1} \exp\left[-\frac{v^n}{2b}\right] \tag{82}$$

Kimura [80] reproduced a series of random wave trains in a wave tank to obtain the empirical joint pdf of wave heights and periods, taking U as the wave height and V as the wave period. The shape factors were selected to fit the observed data. He found the shape factor m was close to 2.0. Note m = 2.0 corresponds to the Rayleigh distribution. He also stated the shape factor m correlated with the skewness of surface elevation. The shape factor, n, varies depending on the spectral shape, and has a strong association between n and the spectral width parameter. The correlation coefficient has a close connection with the spectral width parameter. Kimura concluded that all the parameters could be estimated from the spectral width parameters. However, this may be possible only if the spectra have a single peak.

Longuet-Higgins [93] extended the Rayleigh law to obtain the theoretical joint pdf of wave heights and periods. The normalized wave height X and period Y, whose means are equal to 1.0, have the following joint pdf:

$$f_{XY}(x, y) = \frac{\pi x^2}{4v} \exp\left[-\frac{\pi}{4} x^2 \left\{1 + \frac{(y-1)^2}{v^2}\right\}\right] \quad \text{for } x \geq 0,\ -\infty < y < \infty \tag{83}$$

where v is a spectral width parameter. The marginal distributions are obtained by integrating $f_{XY}(.,.)$ with respect to x or y.

$$f_X(x) = \frac{\pi}{2} x \exp\left[-\frac{\pi}{4} x^2\right],\ x \geq 0 \tag{84}$$

$$f_Y(y) = \frac{1}{2v\left[1 + \frac{(y-1)^2}{v}\right]^{3/2}},\ -\infty < y < \infty \tag{85}$$

It can be shown that the correlation coefficient is zero; hence, X and Y are linearly uncorrelated random variables. However, the product of marginal distributions is not the joint pdf, therefore X and Y are not independent. Because wave height and period have been observed as correlated random variables, this is not a desirable feature. Another undesirable property of the Longuet-Higgins distribution is that the period has a negative range. Venezian, Bretschneider and Jagannathan [160] describe a modification which removes the negative range from the wave period. The modified Longuet-Higgins distribution is

$$f_{XY}(x, y) = \frac{\pi x^2}{2v} \exp\left[-\frac{\pi}{4} x^2 \left\{1 + \frac{(y-1/y)^2}{v^2}\right\}\right] \quad \text{for } x \geq 0,\ y \geq 0 \tag{86}$$

This density function behaves as the Longuet-Higgins distribution and it does not have a negative range. However, Cov[X, Y] is zero, therefore, the correlation coefficient is always zero.

The shape parameter for the Longuet-Higgins distribution may be evaluated from spectral analysis. Chakrabati and Cooley [26] confirmed the practical applicability of the Longuet-Higgins distribution, provided the spectrum is a narrow band single peak spectrum. However, in many cases, the spectral shape is a broad spectral width and sometimes has multiple peaks. The multiple spectral peaks may suggest the multimodal joint pdf of wave heights and periods. The aforementioned density function never exhibits the multimodal peaks. Thus, nonparametric density estimation should be taken into consideration as an alternative.

Nonparametric Density Estimation

Nonparametric estimation may be categorized into two groups: series estimators and kernel estimators. The series estimator approximates a pdf, which may or may not be known, in terms of an infinite series. The kernel density estimator is a natural extension of the classical histogram estimator. Parzen [114] proposed an alternative method to estimate an unknown density, extending the idea of the autoregressive spectra.

Series Estimators. A mathematical theorem states that an analytic function (such as a pdf) can be expanded into an infinite Maclaurin's series:

$$f(x) = \sum_{j=0}^{\infty} a_j x^j \tag{87}$$

where $a_j = \dfrac{f^{(j)}(\dot{0})}{j!}$

and $f^{(j)}(\dot{0})$ is the j-th derivative of $f(x)$ evaluated at $x = 0$. It is possible to evaluate the coefficients $\{a_j\}$ if the function $f(x)$ is known. In general, if a finite number of samples $\{x_1, x_2, \ldots, x_N\}$ is available, then it is impossible to estimate $\{a_j\}$ from the samples. However, it may be possible to estimate a finite number of coefficients, say $m + 1$, of the following series:

$$f_m(x) = \sum_{j=0}^{m} \hat{a}_j x^j \tag{88}$$

The Gram-Charlier series has the above form. The coefficients $\{\hat{a}_j\}$ are usually estimated from the sample moments. Huang and Long [67] fitted the probability density of surface elevation employing the Gram-Charlier series, and showed the skewed nature of the surface elevation. Unfortunately, the estimated pdf exhibits an undesirable feature of negativity.

A more general expansion of the series estimator is given by

$$f(x) = \sum_{j=-\infty}^{\infty} c_j \phi_j(x) \tag{89}$$

where $\{c_j\}$'s are real valued constants, and $\{\phi_j(x)\}$ are real or complex functions. One would like to estimate the $f(x)$ for $-\infty < x < \infty$, however, the samples have a finite domain, say $[a, b]$. Therefore, the nonparametric density estimators usually have a finite support $[a, b]$. The estimated $f(x)$ is a truncated density of true density, say $g(x)$, such that

$$f(x) = \frac{g(x)}{\int_a^b g(x)\, dx} \tag{90}$$

The support of $f(x)$ in the Equation 89 is $[a, b]$. A general strategy to approach this type of problem is to employ a complete orthonormal set. A complete orthonormal set $\{\phi_j(x)\}$ defined in a finite domain $[a, b]$ with respect to a weighting function $w(x)$ has the property

$$\int_b^a \phi_j(x)\phi_k(x)w(x)\, dx = \delta_{jk} \tag{91}$$

where $\delta_{jk} = \begin{cases} 1.0 & \text{if } j = k \\ 0.0 & \text{otherwise} \end{cases}$

The harmonic function and the orthogonal polynomials, such as the Jacobi, Legendre, Chebyshev, and Laguerre polynomials, are usually applied.

Kronmal and Tarter [83] used the complex harmonic function for $\{\phi_j\}$ to estimate a density function:

$$\phi_j = e^{-2\pi ijx} \tag{92}$$

where $i^2 = -1.0$

Hence, the estimate $\hat{f}_x(x)$ of the pdf $f_x(x)$ for the sample $\{x_1, x_2, \ldots, x_N\}$ can be expressed as

$$\hat{f}_x(x) = \sum_{m=-\infty}^{\infty} \hat{C}_m e^{-2\pi imx} \tag{93}$$

where $\hat{C}_m = \dfrac{1}{N} \sum_{\ell=1}^{N} e^{-2\pi imx_\ell}$

They suggest

$$\hat{C}_m = 0 \qquad \text{if } \hat{C}_m\hat{C}_{-m} < \frac{2}{N+1}$$

where N is the number of samples. Large values of m produce a wiggly form of $\hat{f}(x)$. Kronmal and Tarter suggest the maximum order of $m = 10$. Recently, Woodfield

[168] successfully applied a similar technique to estimate bivariate density functions in the quantile domain. He applied an objective way to choose the optimal order m based on the Akaike Information Criterion, AIC [2a].

Kernel Estimators. Most kernel estimators are based on the idea of a histogram. Rosenblatt [130a] introduced this type of a technique, and Parzen [114a] proposed the detailed theoretical justification. The Rosenblatt estimator of a given sample $\{x_1, x_2, \ldots, x_N\}$ is

$$\hat{f}_N(x) = \frac{\# \text{ of sample points in } (x - h, x + h)}{2Nh} \tag{94}$$

where h is a real constant, which should be a function of sample size and population density. Note that

$$\hat{f}_N(x) = \frac{\tilde{F}_N(x + h) - \tilde{F}_N(x - h)}{2h} \tag{95}$$

where $\tilde{F}_N(x)$ is the empirical distribution function

$$\tilde{F}_N(x) = \frac{\# \text{ of sample points} \leq x}{N} \tag{96}$$

Scott and Thompson [136] proposed an extension of the histogram estimator, which they called the averaged shifted histogram. The estimator is the average of successive adjacent bins of shifted histograms. The extension to the multivariate problem is relatively simple. They successfully applied this technique to represent the multidimensional data in terms of the density function. It should be noted that $\hat{f}_N(x)$ previously mentioned is a discontinuous step function; therefore, it does not have a continuous derivative. To overcome this shortcoming, the smoothing operator, the kernel K(u), may be introduced

$$\hat{f}_N(x) = \int_{-\infty}^{\infty} \frac{1}{h} K\left(\frac{x - y}{h}\right) d\tilde{F}_N(y)$$

$$= \frac{1}{hN} \sum_{j=1}^{N} K\left(\frac{x - x_j}{h}\right) \tag{97}$$

It can be shown when $K(u) = \frac{1}{2}$ for $|u| < 1.0$, and $K(u) = 0$ otherwise, Equation 81 is equivalent to Equation 79. Several useful kernels are shown in Tapia and Thompson [141, p. 60]. The kernel K(u) must satisfy the following properties [168]:

$$\sup_x |K(x)| < \infty$$

$$\int_{-\infty}^{\infty} |K(x)| \, dx < \infty$$

$$\lim_{x \to \infty} |xK(x)| = 0$$

$$\int_{-\infty}^{\infty} K(x)\, dx = 1.0$$

Similar to the difficulty that a series estimator has in choosing the optimal order, the kernel estimator faces the problem of finding objectively a suitable window width, (or bin width), h. Most of the kernel estimators have employed some sort of subjective way to adapt the window width. Depending on the kernel used, negative values may appear in the estimated density function. However, the positivity of density function is constrained by the development of some kernel estimators.

Boneva, Kendall, and Stefanov [15] proposed the "histospline" estimator, which is a smoothed estimator of unknown probability density function f(.) with cdf F(.) having a finite support [a, b]. The histospline estimator $\hat{f}(x)$ is the minimizer of

$$\int_a^b (\hat{f}(x))^2\, dx \tag{98}$$

subject to

$$\int_{x_j}^{x_{j+1}} \hat{f}(t)\, dt = \tilde{F}_N(x_{j+1}) - \tilde{F}_N(x_j) \qquad \text{for } j = 0, 1, \ldots, m \tag{99}$$

where $x_0 = a$ and $x_{m+1} = b$, and $a = x_0, \ldots, x_{m+1} = b$ are an equal partition of [a, b] for the histogram. The base function of the histospline is the deltaspline named by Boneva et al. in their paper, which has the form of a piecewise cubic spline. The histospline estimator is in a class of C^2 function, which is an absolutely continuous function up to the second order derivative. The idea behind the deltaspline is to form a polynomial that acts like the Dirac delta function. It should be noted that the deltaspline has negative tails. Some confusion concerning histospline appears in Tapia and Thompson [141]. They stated that the histospline was a smoothing estimator of the empirical distribution function, but, in fact, it was a smoothing estimator of the histogram.

Because ordinary spline functions do not recover the monotonicity of the empirical distribution function without imposing the side constrains, the density estimator can become negative. Shape preserving spline interpolation has become an important research area in the numerical analysis field. The B-splines have been extensively used in the present study; details concerning the spline functions are discussed in Appendix A.

The B-spline has a high computational efficiency and is easily extended to higher dimensions even though it lacks the shape preserving property. Let the domain of the spline estimator [a, b] be divided into $k - 1$ equal intervals, such as

$$[a, b] = \bigcup_{j=1}^{k-1} [t_j, t_{j+1}] \tag{100}$$

and

$$h = t_{j+1} - t_j = \frac{b - a}{k - 1}$$

The spline estimator is

$$\hat{F}(x) = \sum_{j=1}^{m} C_j B_j(x) \tag{101}$$

where m = the dimension of the B-spline

$$m = k + 2$$

subject to the interpolation conditions

$$\hat{F}(t_j) = \tilde{F}_N(t_j) \tag{102}$$

$$\frac{d\hat{F}(a)}{dx} = \frac{d\hat{F}(b)}{dx} = 0 \tag{103}$$

where $\tilde{F}_N(.)$ is the empirical distribution function. Similar to the other kernel esti-mators, the spline estimator changes the estimated density function in shape de-pending on the bin width h. An objective method to choose h is proposed. The optimal h for the sample $\{x_1, x_2, \ldots, x_N\}$ may be obtained by minimizing the Objective Least square Norm (OLN), which is defined as

$$OLN = \begin{cases} \delta & \text{if } N - m - 1 > 0 \\ \infty & \text{otherwise} \end{cases} \tag{104.1}$$

where $\delta = \dfrac{1}{N - m - 1} \sum_{j=1}^{N} (\tilde{F}_N(x_j) - \hat{F}(x_j))^2$ \hfill (104.2)

The reason for subtracting 1 from the denominator is that the $\{x_j\}$ are normalized by the average value prior to estimates of density for the sake of computational efficiency. If the original sample is $\{y_j\}$, then the normalized sample $\{x_j\}$ is

$$x_j = \frac{y_j}{\bar{y}} \qquad \text{for } j = 1, 2, \ldots, N \tag{105}$$

where $\bar{y} = \dfrac{1}{N} \sum_{j=1}^{N} y_j$

Therefore, the mean of a sample $\{x_j\}$ is 1.0. Having obtained the estimated pdf $f_X(.)$

of X, the pdf $\hat{f}_Y(.)$ of Y can be estimated applying a simple transformation, i.e.

$$\hat{f}_Y(y) = \bar{y}\hat{f}_X(x) \tag{106}$$

The mean $\hat{\mu}_Y$ and variance $\hat{\sigma}_Y{}^2$ are straightforward.

$$\hat{\mu}_Y = \int_{-\infty}^{\infty} y\hat{f}_Y(y)\,dy$$

$$= \bar{y} \int_{-\infty}^{\infty} x\hat{f}_X(x)\,dx$$

$$= \bar{y} \tag{107}$$

$$\hat{\sigma}_Y{}^2 = \int_{-\infty}^{\infty} (\bar{y}x - \hat{\mu}_Y)\hat{f}_X(x)\,dx$$

$$= \bar{y}^2\hat{\sigma}_X{}^2 \tag{108}$$

Knowledge of $\hat{f}_X(.)$ is equivalent to knowledge of $\hat{f}_Y(.)$.

Joint pdf Estimation by Means of Tensor Product Splines

The bivariate extension of nonparametric density estimator by means of B-splines (Spline Density Estimator) is introduced in this section. The technique was independently developed by the authors, therefore much effort was spent on establishing a FORTRAN computer package. A similar technique using the tensor product B-spline was introduced by Bennett [14]; de Boor [35] introduced an extremely efficient algorithm for the tensor product spline. Making use of de Boor's algorihm for the spline density estimator, the technique developed in this study is computationally much faster than Bennett's method.

First, it is necessary to define the empirical bivariate distribution function $\tilde{F}_N(x, y)$ of N pairs of samples $\{x_j, y_j\}_{j=1}^N$ for the random variables X and Y.

$$\tilde{F}_N(x, y) = \frac{\text{\# of sample points} \leq x \text{ and } x \leq y}{N} \tag{109}$$

The function $\tilde{F}_N(...)$ has the same statistical properties as the invariate case and is a consistent and unbiased estimator of the population distribution function $F_{XY}(.,.)$. The bivariate histogram plays a basic role in the spline density estimator. Suppose N pairs of samples $\{x_j, y_j\}_{j=1}^N$ exist in the real domain $[a_X, b_X][a_Y, b_Y]$, (which is a rectangle in the plane). Let the domain be divided into equal rectangular elements, such that

$$[a_X, b_X] = \bigcup_{j=1}^{k_x-1} [t_{j.x} - t_{j+1}, X] \tag{110a}$$

$$[a_Y, b_Y] = \bigcup_{j=1}^{k_Y-1} [t_{j.Y} - t_{j+1}, Y] \tag{110b}$$

and

$$h_X = t_{j+1, X} - t_{j, X} = \frac{b_X - a_X}{k_X - 1} \tag{111a}$$

$$h_Y = t_{j+1, Y} - t_{j, Y} = \frac{b_Y - a_Y}{k_Y - 1} \tag{111b}$$

The bivariate histogram density estimator is

$$\hat{f}_H(x, y; h_X, h_Y) = \frac{\text{\# of samples in } [t_{j, X}, t_{j+1, X}] \times [t_{j, Y}, t_{j+1, Y}]}{h_X h_Y N} \tag{112}$$

where $t_{j, X} \leq x \leq t_{j+1, X}$

and

$$t_{j, Y} \leq y \leq t_{j+1, Y}$$

The corresponding distribution function is

$$\hat{F}_H(x, y; h_X, h_Y) = \int_{a_X}^{x} \int_{a_Y}^{y} \hat{f}_H(u, v; h_X, h_Y) \, du \, dv \tag{113}$$

The population distribution function $F_{XY}(x, y)$ may be estimated by interpolating $\hat{F}_H(x, y; h_X, h_Y)$. The technique used here is the tensor product splines which are a tensor product of one-dimensional B-splines. Let $\hat{F}_S(x, y; h_X, h_Y)$ be the smoothed distribution function of $\hat{F}_H(x, y; h_X, h_Y)$.

$$\hat{F}_S(x, y; h_X, h_Y) = \sum_{i=1}^{m_X} \sum_{j=1}^{m_Y} C_{ij} B_i(x) B_j(y) \tag{114}$$

where
$$m_X = k_X + 2$$
$$m_Y = k_Y + 2$$
$$C_{ij}\text{'s} = \text{constants}$$
$$B_i(.), B_j(.) = \text{the cubic B-spline basis}$$

The number of coefficients to be estimated is $m_X m_Y$; the coefficients are obtained by the following conditions:

$$\hat{F}_S(t_{i, X}, t_{j, Y}; h_X h_Y) = \hat{F}_H(t_{i, X}, t_{j, Y}; h_X, h_Y), \quad \text{for } i = 1, \ldots, k_X \text{ and } j = 1, \ldots, k_Y \tag{115a}$$

$$\frac{d\hat{F}_S(a_X, t_{j, Y}; h_X, h_Y)}{dx} = \frac{d\hat{F}_S(b_X, t_{j, Y}; h_X, h_Y)}{dx} = 0 \quad \text{for } j = 1, \ldots, k_Y \tag{115b}$$

$$\frac{d\hat{F}_s(t_{i,x}, a_Y; h_X, h_Y)}{dy} = \frac{d\hat{F}_s(t_{i,x}b_Y; h_X, h_Y)}{dy} = 0 \qquad \text{for } i = 1, \ldots, k_X \qquad (115c)$$

$$\frac{d^2\hat{F}_s(a_X, a_Y; h_X, h_Y)}{dx\,dy} = \frac{d^2\hat{F}_s(b_X, b_Y; h_X, h_Y)}{dx\,dy} = 0 \qquad (115d)$$

$$\frac{d^2\hat{F}_s(a_X, b_Y; h_X, h_Y)}{dx\,dy} = \frac{d^2\hat{F}_s(b_X, a_Y; h_X, h_Y)}{dx\,dy} = 0 \qquad (115e)$$

The number of conditions provided here is $m_X m_Y = k_X k_Y + 2(k_X + k_Y) + 4$ and the system of equations to obtain $\{C_{ij}\}$ is completed. The matrix to be solved is a $(m_X \times m_Y) \times (m_X \times m_Y)$ matrix. In general, this is a large matrix, so a vast amount of computational effort may be expected. However, the computational load can be reduced by introducing de Boor's algorithm [35], which makes two small tri-diagonal $(m_X \times m_Y)$ and $(m_Y \times m_Y)$ matrices to be solved.

It may be shown that $\hat{F}_s$ is a linear mapping of $\hat{F}_H$ in the spline space. The shape of $\hat{F}_H$ is significantly dependent on the choice of bin widths h_x and h_y, which are called the smoothing parameters. The wider they are, the smoother the estimated density function. The optimal smoothing parameters may be obtained by extending the idea of Objective Least square Norm (OLN) to two dimensions.

$$\text{OLN} = \begin{cases} \delta & \text{if } N - m - 2 > 0 \\ \infty & \text{otherwise} \end{cases} \qquad (116a)$$

$$\text{where} \quad \delta = \frac{1}{N - m - 2} \sum_{i=1}^{N} [\tilde{F}_N(x_i, y_i) - \hat{F}_s(x_i, y_i; h_x, h_y)]^2 \qquad (116b)$$

N = number of samples
m = number of spline coefficients

To make programming easy, the sample variables are normalized by their average values. Suppose the original samples are $\{u_i, v_i\}_{i=1}^{N}$. The normalized samples $\{x_i, y_i\}_{i=1}^{N}$ can be obtained as follows:

$$x_i = \frac{u_i}{\bar{u}} \qquad (117a)$$

$$y_i = \frac{v_i}{\bar{v}} \qquad (117b)$$

$$\text{where} \quad \bar{u} = \frac{1}{N} \sum_{i=1}^{N} u_i \qquad (117c)$$

$$\bar{v} = \frac{1}{N} \sum_{i=1}^{N} v_i \qquad (117d)$$

Because the normalization process reduces two degrees of freedom, an additional number 2 is included in the penalizing factor. In total, one hundred different combinations of h_x and h_y are examined such that

$$h_x = 1/NIX \qquad \text{for NIX} = 1, 2, \ldots, 10 \tag{118a}$$

$$h_y = 1/NIY \qquad \text{for NIY} = 1, 2, \ldots, 10 \tag{118b}$$

It seems reasonable to check the proposed density estimation technique using the data from a known population density function. Figure 20 shows the scatter diagram of 500 samples generated from the independent bivariate normal distribu-

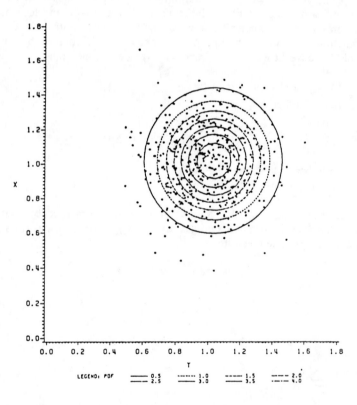

Figure 20. Scatter diagram of 500 samples generated from independent bivariate normal distribution. (Contour lines are the true probability density.)

tion which is

$$f_{xy}(x, y) = \frac{1}{2\pi} \frac{1}{\sigma_x \sigma_y} \exp\left[-\frac{1}{2} \left(\left(\frac{x - \mu_x}{\sigma_x}\right)^2 + \left(\frac{y - \mu_y}{\sigma_y}\right)^2 \right) \right] \tag{119}$$

where $\mu_x = 1.0$
$\quad\quad \mu_y = 1.0$
$\quad\quad \sigma_x = \frac{1}{5}$
$\quad\quad \sigma_y = \frac{1}{5}$

Contour lines in Figure 20 are the probability density of generated samples. The true density function $f_{xy}(x, y)$ is depicted in Figure 21. The contour map of log values of the OLN for this data set is shown in Figure 22. A logarithmic scale is used to

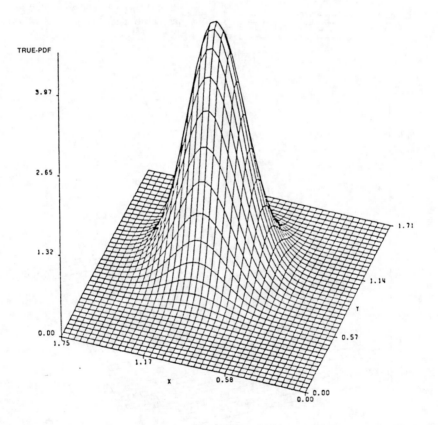

Figure 21. The true independent bivariate normal density function (means = 1.0, variances = 0.04, and correlation coefficient-0) [171].

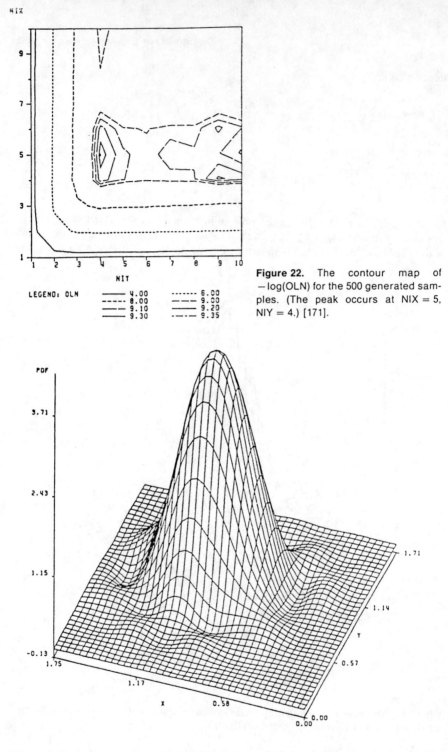

Figure 22. The contour map of $-\log(\text{OLN})$ for the 500 generated samples. (The peak occurs at NIX = 5, NIY = 4.) [171].

Figure 23. The estimated independent bivariate normal density function (means = 1.0, variances = 0.04, and correlation coefficient = 0) [171].

compress deviations of the OLN values. The peak of OLN appears at NIX = 5, NIY = 4. Based on these smoothing parameters, the best estimate of the joint pdf for the proposed criteria is obtained and shown in Figures 23 and 24. The contour plots of the true and estimated densities were visually examined to check whether or not the proposed technique was acceptable. The location of the mode for both densities agrees well, but the peak of the estimated density is slightly less than the true density. Small negative values also appear in the estimated density. Overall, the features of both densities agree well.

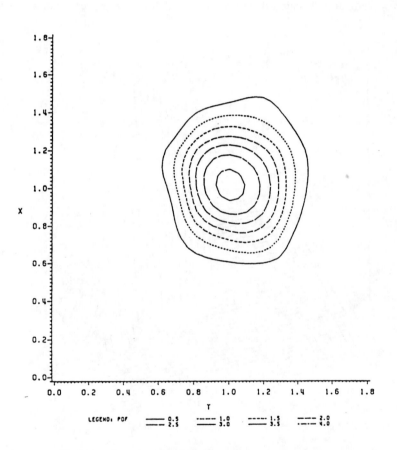

Figure 24. The contour plot of estimated independent bivariate normal density function (means = 1.0, variances = 0.04, and correlation coefficient = 0) [171].

Another numerical evaluation of the density estimation technique was made generating 500 samples from the modified Longuet-Higgins distribution (Equation 86). A series of numerical simulation runs was conducted for different values of the spectral width parameter. The true density function is shown in Figure 25 [171] where the parameter is taken as 0.2. The true density function has a very narrow mode. A realization of 500 samples is depicted in Figure 26. Contour lines in Figure 26 show the true probability density of generated samples. Samples appear around Y = 1.0, which corresponds to the mean of wave period. The estimated joint pdf is shown in Figures 27 and 28. The estimated pdf does not have a density peak as high as the true pdf; however, the basic feature of the true density function is recovered in the estimated pdf. The spline density estimator seems to work well and is acceptable, in a practical sense, even if it shows negative values of estimate.

The joint pdf of wave heights and periods was estimated employing the spline density estimator. A scatter diagram of a typical data set of wave heights and periods

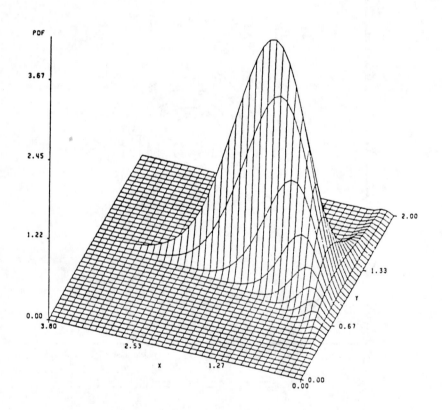

Figure 25. The true modified Longuet-Higgins density function spectral width parameter = 0.2) [171].

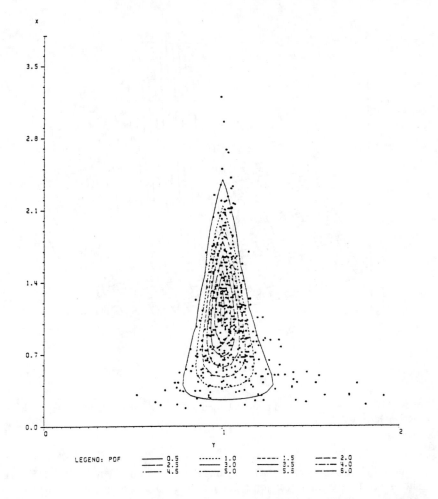

Figure 26. Scatter diagram of 500 samples generated from the modified Longuet-Higgins distribution. (Contour lines are the true probability density.) [171].

is produced from data obtained by a Waverider buoy at 3 p.m. on March 13, 1980, near Port Mansfield, Texas. There are 240 samples shown in Figure 29. The OLN (see Figure 30) chooses the optimal smoothing parameters NIH = 2 and NIT = 4, here NIH, NIT correspond to NIX and NIY, respectively, in the previous notation. The best estimate of joint pdf is shown in Figure 31. The multimodal feature of the pdf can be seen in Figure 31. The contour plot of the estimated pdf clarifies the location of modes and is shown in Figure 32. The negative values may be replaced by zeros without significantly altering the result. For better visualization of the estimated joint pdf, the flat surface appearing in Figure 33 corresponds to the negative

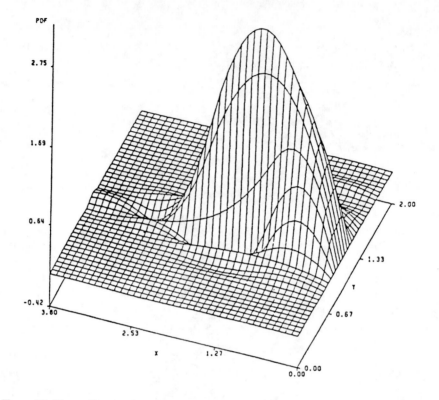

Figure 27. The estimate of modified Longuet-Higgins density function (spectral width parameter = 0.2) [171].

values. Comparing this data set with one obtained in a different season, Figure 34 shows the best estimate of joint pdf based on 319 samples obtained at 3 a.m., August 13, 1981, near Port Mansfield. The corresponding contour map is shown in Figure 35. The multimodal peaks appear in the estimated density. The peaks possibly indicate the different wave generation sourses. The joint pdf estimation for the data obtained in March 1980 and August 1981 was also conducted. The multimodal peaks appeared in all cases, and the location of modes consistently moves with time. Adjacent data sets, six hours apart, do not change the joint pdf dramatically for the March case, but the joint pdf changes significantly in some of the August data sequences. The reason for this may be due to noise from wave sampling. The noise would be more noticeable if the wave heights were not large enough to be measured by the device.

The joint pdf that represents the long-term wave statistics may be obtained using a large sequence of data sets. Figures 36–41 show the estimated joint pdf based on 54 successive data sets, each of which contains approximately 300 waves. The esti-

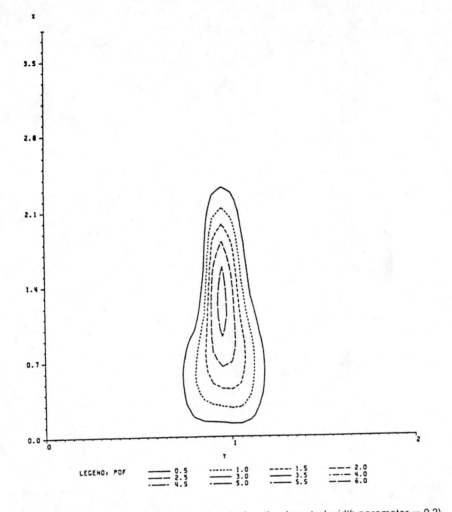

Figure 28. The contour plot of estimated density function (spectral width parameter = 0.2) [171].

mated joint pdf of March 1980 and August 1981 was selected to characterize the wave statistics for each month. Note the single mode that appears in March and the double modes that appear in August. The larger peak in August appears at half the mean period. The second peak in August is located about the mean value of the period. It should be emphasized that the Longuet-Higgins distribution has a single mode located at the mean period; hence, it never shows the multimodal joint pdf features obtained by the proposed nonparametric density estimation technique.

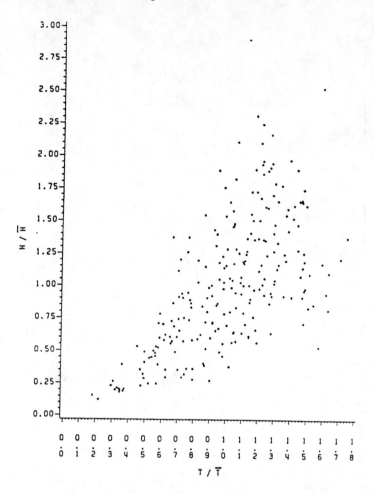

Figure 29. Scatter diagram of wave heights and periods samples. (Data obtained by Wave-rider buoy B at 3 p.m., March 13, 1980, near Port Mansfield, Texas.) [171].

Nonparametric density estimation is an excellent method for representing a large amount of long-term data in a concise form, without masking the statistical charac-teristics of the data set. This was one of the major objectives of the study. The parametric density estimation may significantly alter the estimated density profile from the population density. Nevertheless, the direct practical application of the proposed technique may be difficult in the actual offshore structural design. How-ever, the visual impression of data representation can be achieved by the method presented. A question might be posed on how the joint pdf and spectra are related. Does the spectral information provide the joint pdf estimation? Is it possible to

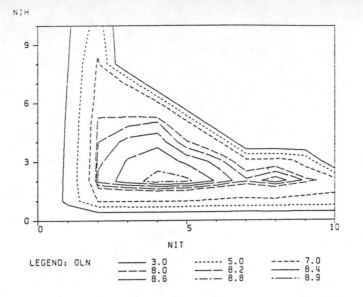

Figure 30. The contour map of −log(OLN) for sample wave heights and periods in Figure 29. (The peak occurs at NIH = 2, NIT = 4.) [171].

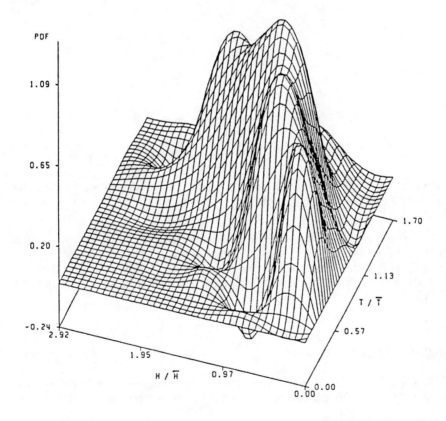

Figure 31. The best estimate of joint pdf for data obtained by Waverider buoy B at 3 p.m., March 13, 1980 near Port Mansfield, Texas [171].

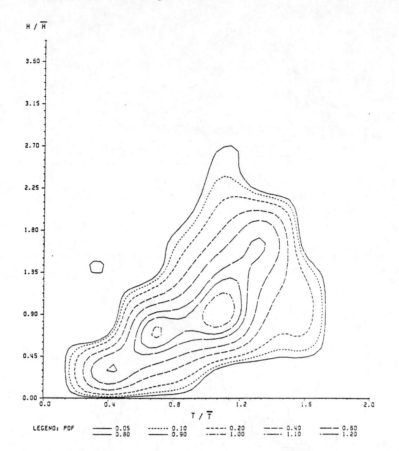

Figure 32. The contour map of best estimate of joint pdf for data obtained by Waverider buoy B at 3 p.m., March 13, 1980, near Port Mansfield, Texas [171].

estimate the spectra from the joint pdf information? The answer to the first question is "NO" unless the parametric density estimation is postulated. Longuet-Higgins [93], Goda [48], and Kimura [80] have examined the correlation between the spectral parameters and the "parametric" joint pdf. The answer to the second question is "YES."

Case Studies

Kodiak, Alaska

An example of application of extremal analysis of hindcasted and measured wave and wind data performed by Andrew et al. [6] is summarized in this section.

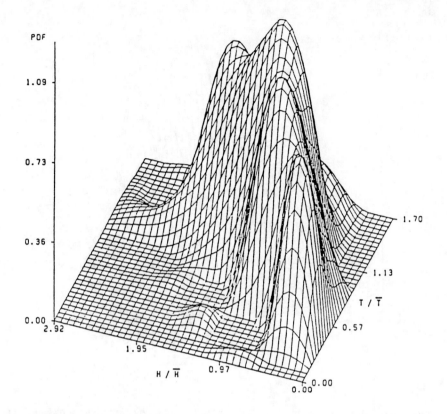

Figure 33. The best estimate of joint pdf. Negative values are replaced by zeros. (Data obtained by Waverider buoy B at 3 p.m., March 13, 1980, near Port Mansfield, Texas.) [171].

The specific area of interest is the deep-draft terminal operated by the Port of Kodiak on St. Paul Harbor. The container dock is fully exposed and its operations are intermittently disrupted by long-period swells which pass during bad weather over reefs.

Probability Distribution

A summary of storms producing significant wave heights (H_s) greater than 6 m (19.4 ft) is given in Table 17 and the frequency of storms per year is listed in Table 18. It will be noted that the frequency of storms observed is quite irregular, and not suitable for simple analysis. One can assume that the Poisson probability distribution could be applied to this case and the probability density

$$p(x) = \frac{u^x e^{-u}}{x!}, \qquad x = 0, 1, \ldots, n \tag{120}$$

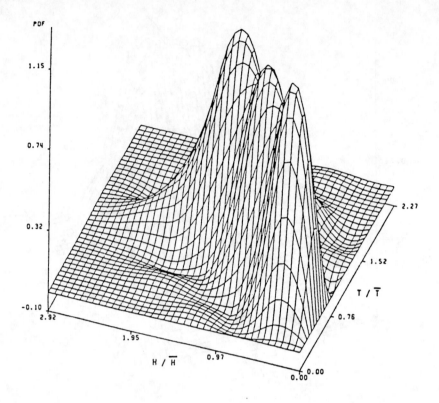

Figure 34. The best estimate of joint pdf for data obtained by Waverider buoy B at 3 a.m., August 13, 1981, near Port Mansfield, Texas [171].

where u is the average number of storms per year, or N/n, where n is the number of years, x is the number of storms per year. For example, for x = 5

$$u = \frac{N}{n} = \frac{78}{29} = 3.89 \approx 3.9$$

$$p(x) = \frac{3.9^5 e^{-3.9}}{5!} = 0.15$$

$$p(x) = \frac{3.9^3 e^{-3}}{3!} = 0.49 \qquad \text{for } x = 3$$

$$p(x) = \frac{3.9^9 e^{-9}}{9!} = 0.71(10)^{-5} \qquad \text{for } x = 9$$

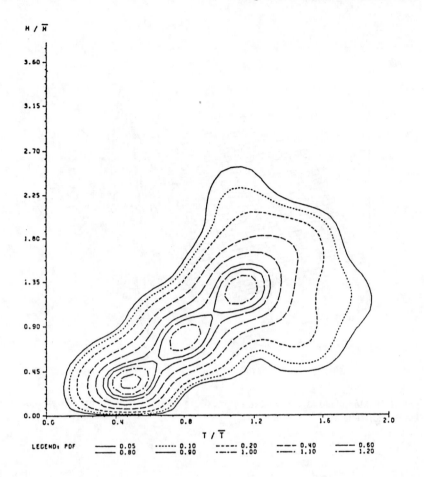

Figure 35. The contour map of best estimate of joint pdf for data obtained by Waverider buoy B at 3 a.m., August 13, 1981, near Port Mansfield, Texas [171].

The "chi square" goodness of fit test may be calculated for the validity for the Poisson assumption

$$X_n^2 = \sum_{i=1}^{n} \frac{(0_i - E_i)^2}{E_i} \tag{121}$$

where 0_1 = observed frequency of years with i = 1 storm
E_i = Poisson expected frequency of years with i = 1 storm

The "chi square" χ_n^2 statistic calculated for the data shown in Table 19 is 0.928.

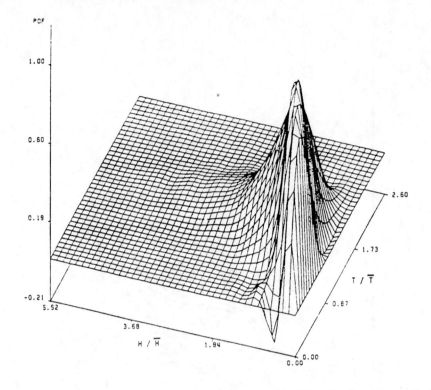

Figure 36. Monthly joint pdf of March 1980. (Data obtained by Waverider buoy B near Port Mansfield, Texas.) [171].

The theoretical "chi square" statistic is 0.92, which indicates that Poisson distribution is correct.

Several theoretical probability distributions have been used in data analysis. These were Extremal Fisher-Tippett Type I distribution, Log-Normal distribution, Log-Extremal distribution and Weibull distribution. The cumulative probability functions are as follows:

Extremal Fisher-Tippett Type I

$$F(x) = \exp\left\{-\exp\left[\frac{-(x-m)}{\sigma}\right]\right\} \qquad -\infty < x < \infty \tag{122}$$

Some of the cells have been combined in the test to minimize the impact of small cell counts on the resulting statistic.

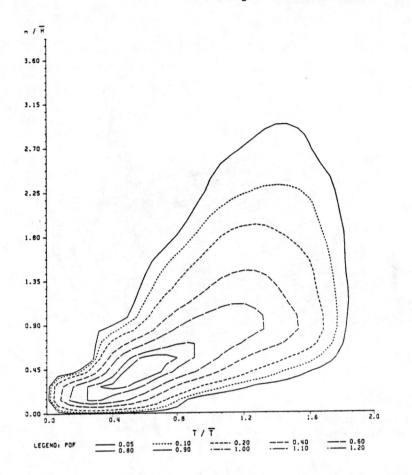

Figure 37. The contour map of monthly joint pdf of March 1980. (Data obtained by Wave-rider buoy B near Port Mansfield, Texas. Mode peak is at H = 0.29 m, T = 2.82 sec.) [171].

Log-Normal:

$$F(x) = \frac{1}{\sqrt{2\pi}} \int_0^x \frac{1}{\sigma h} \exp\left[-\frac{1}{2}\left(\frac{\ln h - m}{\sigma}\right)^2 \right] dh \qquad 0 < x < \infty \tag{123}$$

Log-Extremal:

$$F(x) = \exp\left[-\frac{x^{-m}}{\sigma} \right] \qquad 0 < x < \infty \tag{124}$$

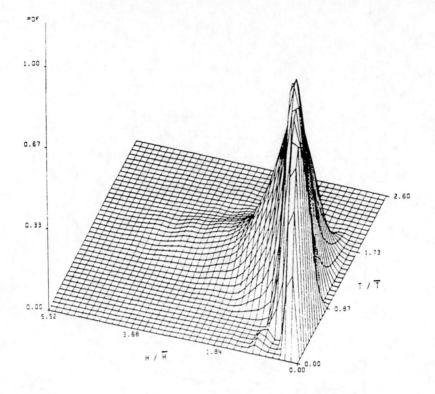

Figure 38. Monthly joint pdf of March 1980. Negative values are replaced by zeros. (Data obtained by Waverider buoy B near Port Mansfield, Texas.) [171].

Weibull:

$$\hat{F}(x) = 1.0 - \exp\left[-\left(\frac{x - m}{\sigma}\right)\right]^{c} \tag{125}$$

The theoretical cumulative probability function is fit to data by means of the plotting position formula. If the data sample given by $x_1, x_2, \ldots n_n$ is ranked in ascending order denoted by $Y_{(1)} < Y_{(2)} < \cdots < Y_{(n)}$ where $Y_{(k)}$ is called the kth order statistic, then the plotting position

$$\hat{F}_k = \frac{k}{n + 1} \tag{126}$$

represents the estimate of the data cumulative probability function. If this is set

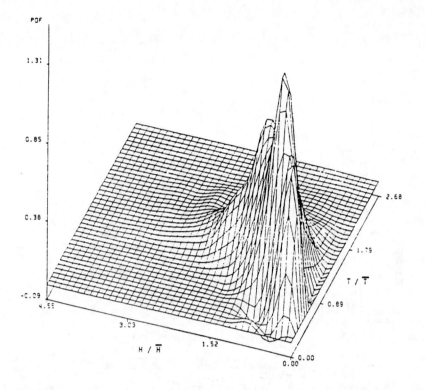

Figure 39. Monthly joint pdf of August 1981. (Data obtained by Waverider buoy B near Port Mansfield, Texas.) [171].

equal to the proposed theoretical cumulative probability function F(x) from Equation 125, then

$$\hat{F}_k = \frac{k}{n+1} = F[AY_{(k)} + B] \tag{127}$$

where A and B are scale and location parameters, respectively. An inverse of the function in Equation 127, is

$$F^{-1}(\hat{F}_k) = (B)Y_{(k)} + A \tag{128}$$

If the plot of $F^{-1}(k/n + 1)$ with $Y_{(k)}$ approximates a straight line with slope A and intercept B then the proposed theoretical distribution is generally accepted. Sometimes more than one of the possible distributions will yield a straight line fit. In this case, the more acceptable of these usually best fits the upper portion of the function

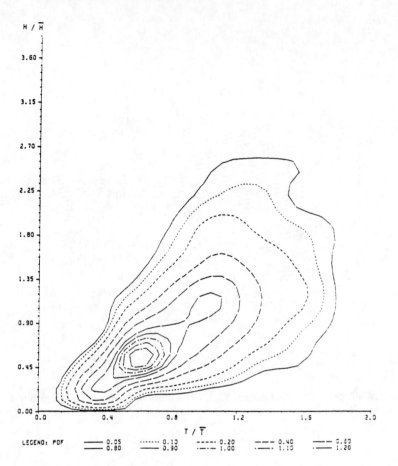

Figure 40. The contour map of monthly joint pdf of August 1981. (Data obtained by Wave-rider buoy B near Port Mansfield, Texas. Higher mode peak is at H = 0.18 m, T = 2.07 sec. Lower mode peak is at H = 0.34 m, T = 3.40 sec.) [171].

F_k. However, some subjective judgment based on experience is required in such cases.

The quantity known as the return period, T_r, is defined to be the mean value of the random number of observations preceding and including the first exceedence of a specified wave threshold x. In terms of the cumulative probability function and the Poisson model parameter u

$$T_r = \frac{1}{u[1 - F(x)]} \tag{129}$$

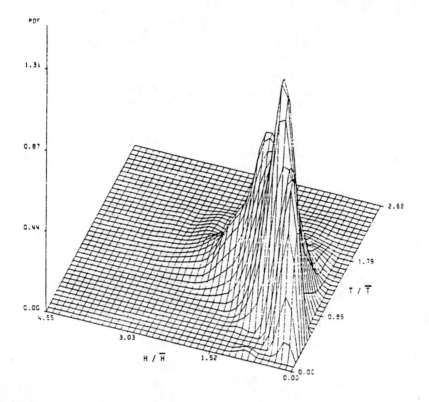

Figure 41. Monthly joint pdf of August 1981. Negative values are replaced by zeros. (Data obtained by Waverider buoy B near Port Mansfield, Texas.) [171].

Andrew et al. [6] computed the constants A and B of Equation 95 for extremal probability functions listed in Equations 122–128. The estimated constants for the hypothesized extremal models are shown in Table 20.

Comparison of Weibull and Extremal-Type Distributions Nagshead, North Carolina and Newport, Oregon

Smith [137] investigated statistical trends of the duration of extreme wave conditions at three specific sites on the Atlantic Coast and two on the Pacific Coast. Only hindcasted waves were employed rather than actual measured wave data.

A comparison was made between the Weibull and Extremal Type I distributions. The Extremal Type I is also known as the Gumbel or Fisher-Tippet type I distribution.

Table 17
Annual Number of Storms Producing Significant
Wave Heights of 6 m or More [6]

Year	Number of Storms
1956	1
1957	0
1958	5
1959	3
1960	5
1961	3
1962	5
1963	7
1964	4
1965	2
1966	3
1967	5
1968	7
1969	7
1970	3
1971	1
1972	5
1973	6
1974	3
1975	3
	$\overline{78 = N}$

Table 18
Frequency Table for the Number of Storms per 1-Year Interval
Producing Significant Wave Heights of 6 m or More [6]

Number of Storms	Frequency
0	1
1	2
2	1
3	6
4	1
5	5
6	1
7	3

Table 19
χ^2 Test for the Poisson Model [6]

Number of Storms	O_i	E_i		$(O_i - E_i)^2 E_i$
0	1	0.40		0.525
	3		1.98	
1	2	1.58		
2	1	3.08		
	7		7.08	0.001
3	6	4.00		
4	1	3.90		1.127
	6		6.94	
5	5	3.04		
6	1	1.98		0.275
	4		3.08	
7	3	1.10		
				$\chi_n^2 = 0.928$

Table 20
Estimated Parameters for the Hypothesized Extremal Models [6]

Model	A	B	μ	σ
Extremal Type I	−6.804	0.981	6.936	1.019
Log Normal	−8.058	1.128	7.144	0.886
Log Extremal	−14.952	7.742	7.742	6.898
Weibull, C = 1.0	−4.615	0.745	6.195	1.342
Weibull, C = 2.0	−1.839	0.363	5.066	2.755

The Weibull distribution employed in these comparisons was:

$$f(x) = \frac{1}{\beta^\alpha} \alpha x^{x-1} \exp\left[-\left(\frac{x}{\beta}\right)^\alpha \right] \qquad \text{for } x > 0, \alpha > 0, \beta > 0 \tag{130}$$

$$= 0 \text{ elsewhere}$$

The corresponding Weibull distribution function is very similar to the exponential distribution:

$$f(x) = 1 - \exp - \left[\left(\frac{x}{\beta}\right)^\alpha\right] \tag{131}$$

The parameter α is the "shape parameter" that defines the basic shape of the function. The β parameter is the "scale parameter" which determines the degree of spread along the abscissa [70]. The mean and variance of the Weibull distribution are:

$$\mu = \beta \Gamma \left(1 - \frac{1}{\alpha} \right) \tag{132}$$

$$\sigma^2 = \beta^2 \left[\Gamma \left(1 + \frac{2}{\alpha} \right) - \Gamma^2 \left(1 + \frac{1}{\alpha} \right) \right] \tag{133}$$

The gamma function is given by:

$$\Gamma(z) = \int_0^\infty x^{z-1} e^{-x} \, dx = (z - 1)! \tag{134}$$

The Weibull distribution has two parameters that make it actually a family of functions. A three-parameter form is sometimes used to provide further flexibility in adapting the distribution to certain phenomena, where

$$F(x) = 1 - \exp \left[-\frac{(x - \epsilon)}{\beta} \right]^\alpha \qquad \text{for } \epsilon > 0 \tag{135}$$

The parameter ϵ is a "location parameter" that locates the position of the probability along the abscissa (x-axis). In the particular case of the Weibull distribution, ϵ is in effect a lower limit to values of x. The ϵ parameter is often taken as zero in practice. The Weibull distribution reduces to the exponential distribution when $\alpha = 1$ and $\epsilon = 0$ [70].

The Extremal Type I distribution is defined as:

$$f(x) = \frac{e^{-e^{-[(x-\epsilon)/\phi]}} e^{-[(x-\epsilon)/\phi]}}{\beta} \qquad \text{for} \begin{cases} -\infty < x < \infty \\ -\infty < \epsilon < \infty \\ \beta > 0 \end{cases} \tag{136}$$

$$F(x) = e^{-e^{-[(x-\epsilon)/\beta]}} \tag{137}$$

The mean and variance are:

$$m = \epsilon - \gamma\beta \tag{138}$$

$$\sigma^2 = \frac{\pi^2 \beta^2}{6} \tag{139}$$

where γ = Euler's constant = 0.5772. The Extremal Type I distribution is also a two-parameter family of functions, in this case with a shape parameter of $\alpha = 1$ in keeping with the usual practice for application to weather-related phenomena [6, 70]. The ϵ parameter is again the location parameter and β the scale parameter. The Extremal Type I distribution is not constrained to positive values of x.

Figure 42 illustrates the relative form of the Exponential, Weibull, Rayleigh, and Extremal Type I distributions. The Exponential and Rayleigh curves shown in Figure 42 have the same mean as the Weibull curve. The Extremal Type I curve of Figure 42 was derived from the same data as the Weibull curve.

Sample comparisons are given for Nagshead, North Carolina (Figure 43), and for Newport, Oregon (Figure 44).

The Weibull distribution in both cases fits the wave data better, but the Extremal Type I comes closer to the most extreme durations.

Figures 45 and 46 are graphs of the sample and distribution standard deviations plotted against percent occurrence and the number of extreme events per year for Nagshead, NC. The Extremal Type I distribution mean and standard deviation are closer to the sample mean and standard deviation.

Smith concludes that the Extremal Type I distribution is superior to the Weibull distribution as a model for both distribution of durations and peak zero moment wave heights of extreme events.

Hurricane Camille

Earle [36] examined ten hours of wave data recorded from a fixed platform during hurricane Camille. The data analysis performed using half-hour records and

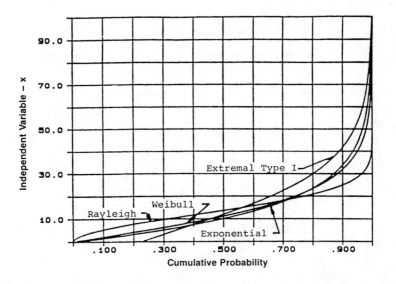

Figure 42. Relative form of four distribution functions [137].

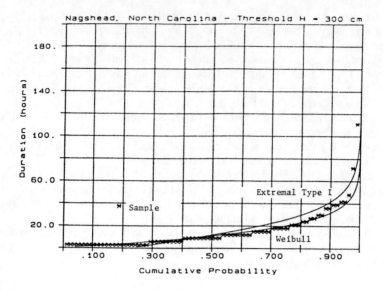

Figure 43. Duration cumulative probability—Nagshead, North Carolina [137].

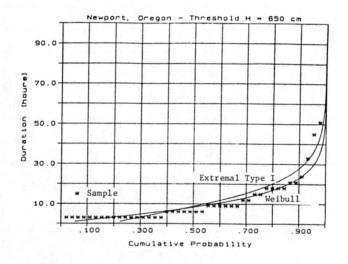

Figure 44. Duration cumulative probability—Newport, Oregon [137].

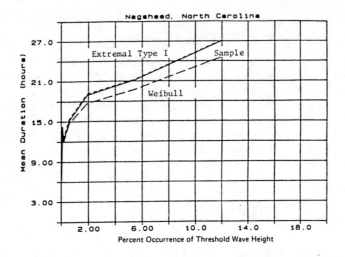

Figure 45. Mean duration vs. percent occurrence of wave height threshold—Nagshead, North Carolina [137].

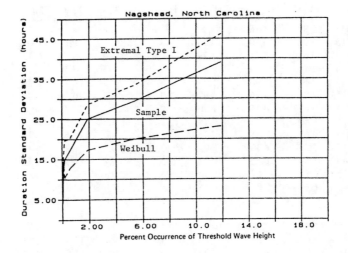

Figure 46. Duration standard deviation vs. percent occurrence of wave height threshold— Nagshead, North Carolina [137].

individual wave heights were computed by the zero up-crossing method. The results of the analysis are shown in Table 21.

Figure 47 shows the time histories of the maximum wave height H_{max}, the significant wave height H_s and the mean wave height $\bar{H}$. Figure 48 is a similar plot for wave periods showing the wave period ($T_{H_{max}}$) associated with the maximum wave height, the significant wave height (T_s), and the mean wave period ($\bar{T}$).

Earle compared the wave height relationships during Hurricane Camille with the Rayleigh distribution, the results are shown in Table 22. It appears that the Rayleigh distribution yielded acceptable wave height relationship for large hurricane-generated waves in deep water.

Borgman [17] proposed a probability equation for non-stationary wave conditions and Rayleigh-distribution wave height in a time interval $(T_s - T_1)$:

$$F_2(H) = \exp \int_{t_1}^{t_2} \ln F_1[H, H_{RMS}(t)] \frac{dt}{\bar{T}(t)} \tag{140}$$

where $F_2(H)$ is the probability that the maximum wave height is less than, or equal to H. The maximum wave height is given by the 50 percentile value of $F_2(H)$. A

Table 21
Wave Parameters During Hurricane Camille, August 17, 1969 [36]

Time	$\bar{H}$, m	H_{rms}, m	H_s, m	H_{max}, m	$\bar{T}$, s	T_s, s	$T_{H_{max}}$, s	Number of Waves
0615–0645	2.82	3.16	4.44	7.02	7.2	8.7	9.8	249
0645–0715	2.90	3.30	4.73	8.39	7.2	9.1	10.6	249
0715–0745	3.05	3.41	4.79	7.67	7.4	9.6	7.7	242
0745–0815	3.10	3.49	4.92	8.50	7.5	9.4	11.0	238
0815–0845	3.50	3.90	5.49	8.54	8.3	10.3	8.6	216
0845–0915	3.85	4.26	5.92	9.49	8.4	10.5	10.4	214
0915–0945	3.87	4.36	6.20	9.58	8.2	10.7	10.9	218
0945–1015	4.60	5.12	7.16	12.12	8.6	10.7	11.4	209
1015–1045	4.65	5.15	7.05	12.02	9.0	11.1	9.7	199
1045–1115	5.37	6.10	8.72	12.15	9.2	11.8	9.3	193
1115–1145	5.84	6.52	9.17	15.12	9.4	11.5	10.5	190
1145–1215	6.23	7.07	9.90	23.60	9.8	12.4	12.5	183
1215–1245	6.38	7.21	10.26	15.18	9.9	12.3	9.1	182
1245–1315	6.32	7.22	10.19	21.37	9.8	12.3	12.1	182
1315–1345	7.58	8.47	11.82	19.26	11.0	12.6	11.1	162
1345–1415	6.97	7.76	10.69	18.99	9.6	11.6	12.9	187
1415–1445	7.00	7.85	11.11	16.02	9.4	12.0	10.1	191
1445–1515	7.75	8.58	12.00	18.82	9.8	11.5	12.4	183
1515–1545	8.35	9.40	13.45	22.90	10.0	11.8	11.9	179
1545–1615	8.12	9.34	13.36	22.22	9.3	11.5	13.7	192

Total number of waves equals 4,058.

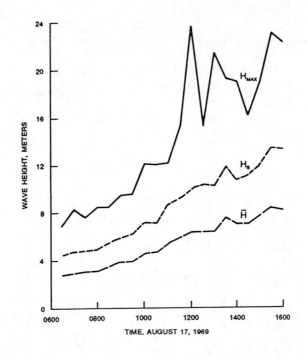

Figure 47. Time variation of wave height parameters during Hurricane Camille [36].

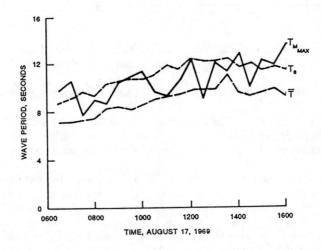

Figure 48. Time variation of wave period parameters during Hurricane Camille [36].

Table 22

Wave Parameter Relationships During Hurricane Camille, August 17, 1969 [36]

Time	$\bar{H}/H_{rms}$	H_s/H_{rms}	H_{max}/H_{rms} Observed	H_{max}/H_{rms} Rayleigh	T/T_s	$T_{H_{max}}/T_s$
0615–0645	0.893	1.41	2.23	2.35	0.826	1.12
0645–0715	0.880	1.43	2.54	2.35	0.785	1.16
0715–0745	0.894	1.41	2.25	2.35	0.765	0.80
0745–0815	0.887	1.41	2.43	2.35	0.802	1.18
0815–0845	0.898	1.41	2.19	2.34	0.804	0.83
0845–0915	0.904	1.39	2.23	2.34	0.797	0.99
0915–0945	0.887	1.42	2.20	2.34	0.769	1.02
0945–1015	0.898	1.40	2.37	2.34	0.799	1.06
1015–1045	0.903	1.37	2.33	2.32	0.816	0.88
1045–1115	0.881	1.43	1.99	2.31	0.780	0.79
1115–1145	0.896	1.41	2.32	2.31	0.819	0.91
1145–1215	0.881	1.40	3.34	2.29	0.788	1.01
1215–1245	0.884	1.42	2.11	2.29	0.801	0.74
1245–1315	0.876	1.41	2.96	2.29	0.795	0.98
1315–1345	0.895	1.40	2.28	2.27	0.877	0.91
1345–1415	0.898	1.38	2.45	2.29	0.814	1.10
1415–1445	0.892	1.42	2.04	2.31	0.782	0.84
1445–1515	0.903	1.40	2.19	2.29	0.853	1.08
1515–1545	0.887	1.43	2.45	2.29	0.843	1.01
1545–1615	0.870	1.43	2.38	2.31	0.811	1.19
Mean	0.890	1.41	2.36	2.32	0.806	0.98
Standard Deviation	0.010	0.02	0.31	0.03	0.028	0.04
Rayleigh	0.886	1.42	2.32	2.32	. . .	. . .

numerical summation over the values listed in Table 22 gives a maximum value of wave height of 24.0 m as compared with measured maximum wave height of 23.6 m.

ARSLOE (Atlantic Remote Sensing Land Ocean Experiment) Study

Ochi et al. [111] conducted an evaluation of wave data obtained at 10 locations in various water depths ranging from 1.35–24.2 m along CERC's Field Research Facility, Duck, North Carolina, and a set of data obtained at Nagshead, North Carolina.

Because waves in coastal waters are non-linear and cannot be considered normal (Gaussian), one way of representing the statistical characteristics of a non-normal random process is to use the probability density function expressed in a series. At present, two probability density functions, both of which are expressed in series form, are available for analysis of non-linear, non-Gaussian random processes. The one was developed by Longuet-Higgins [92] by applying the generating function of a Gaussian random process, while the other expresses the probability density function by the Gram-Charlier series in Edgeworth's form [32, 78]. The probability density function developed by Longuet-Higgins is given as follows:

$$f(z) = \frac{1}{\sqrt{2\pi}} e^{z^2/2} \left\{ 1 + \frac{\lambda_3}{3!} H_3(z) + \frac{\lambda_4}{4!} H_4(z) + \frac{\lambda_3^2}{72} H_6(z) + \frac{\lambda_5}{5!} H_5(z) + \cdots \right\} \quad (141)$$

where $z = \dfrac{x - k_1}{\sqrt{k_2}}$ (standardized random variable)

x = wave deviation from the mean value (wave profile)

$k_1 = m_1$ = mean of x

$k_2 = m_2 - m_1^2$ = variance of x

$k_3 = m_3 - 3m_1 m_2 + 2m_1^3$

$k_4 = m_4 - 4m_1 m_3 - 3m_2^2 + 12m_1^2 m_2 - 6m_1^4$

m_j = the j-th moment of x

$\lambda_3 = k_3/(k_2)^{3/2}$ = skewness

$\lambda_4 = k_4/k_2^2$ = kurtosis

$\lambda_5 = k_5/(k_2)^{5/2}$

$H_n(z)$ = Hermit polynomial of degree n.

On the other hand, the probability density function expressed by the Gram-Charlier series in Edgeworth's form is given by:

$$f(z) = \frac{1}{\sqrt{2\pi}} e^{-z^2/2} \left\{ 1 + \frac{\lambda_3}{3!} H_3(z) + \frac{\lambda_4 - 3}{3!} H_4(z) + \frac{\lambda_5 - 10\lambda_3}{5!} H_5(z) + \cdots \right\} \quad (142)$$

Ochi employed Equation 140 in the wave data analysis. Figures 49 and 50 show comparisons of the probability density functions and histograms obtained during storm conditions.

Several general trends can be observed in Figures 49 and 50. These are:

1. The distributions consisting of the first two terms of Equation 140 taking the skewness, λ_3, into consideration (triangle marks in the figure) differ substantially from the normal distribution, and they agree reasonably well with the histograms over the entire range of wave displacements.

2. The distributions consisting of the first three terms taking the skewness, λ_3, and kurtosis, λ_4, into consideration (cross marks in the figure) agree well with the histograms particularly around the peak value of the distributions. However, some discrepancy between them can be seen for large positive wave displacements.

3. The distributions consisting of the first four or more terms do not necessarily yield a better agreement with the histograms; instead, the agreement is often poor in comparison with that for the distributions consisting of the first two terms.

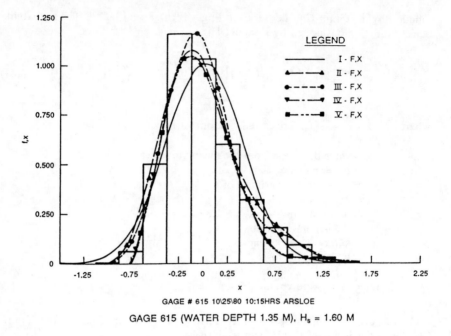

GAGE # 615 10\25\80 10:15HRS ARSLOE

GAGE 615 (WATER DEPTH 1.35 M), H_s = 1.60 M

Figure 49. Comparison between observed histogram, Gaussian distribution, and non-Gaussian distributions with four different terms [111].

It is clear that the skewness, λ_3, is the dominant parameter affecting the non-Gaussian random process at issue. The effect of the kurtosis, λ_4, on non-Gaussian wave characteristics is also significant but not to the same extent as that of the skewness. Hence, skewness alone is considered in the distribution in the following analysis on the effect of sea severity and water depth on non-Gaussian distributions.

It also appears that the non-normal characteristics of shallow water waves are a function of water depth and sea severity. Figure 51 shows the minimum significant wave height above which non-Gaussian characteristics were observed as a function of water depth. Although it is difficult to determine precisely the minimum significant wave height from the limited number of records and the results may be site specific, the figure may provide some insight as to the relationship. For example, at a location of 10 meter-depth, wind-generated waves may be considered to be a Gaussian random process in seas of significant wave height up to 2.75 m. The effect of skewness λ_3 was examined in Figures 52–55 and it can be said that the skewness scatters considerably for a given significant wave height, although in general, the skewness increases with a significant increase in wave height.

The relationship between skewness and significant wave height is represented by the following bi-variate log-normal probability law, because both skewness and sig-

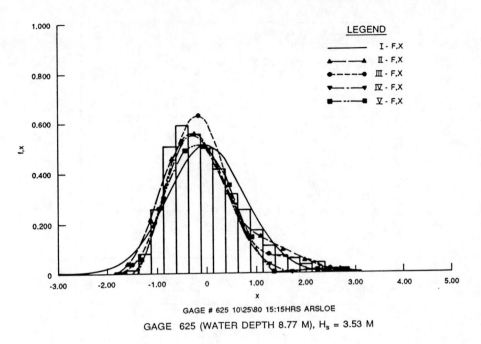

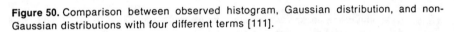

GAGE # 625 10\25\80 15:15HRS ARSLOE

GAGE 625 (WATER DEPTH 8.77 M), H_s = 3.53 M

Figure 50. Comparison between observed histogram, Gaussian distribution, and non-Gaussian distributions with four different terms [111].

nificant wave height approximately follow the log-normal probability distribution:

$$f(H_s, \lambda_3) \sim \Lambda(\mu_{Hs}, \mu_{\lambda3}, \sigma_{Hs}, \sigma_{\lambda3}, \rho) \tag{143}$$

where Λ = bi-variate log-normal distribution

$\mu_{Hs}, \mu_{\lambda3}, \sigma_{Hs}, \sigma_{\lambda3}$ = parameter of the distribution

ρ = correlation coefficient between H_s and λ_3

The expected value of the skewness for a specified significant wave height can be evaluated from the conditional log-normal probability distribution given by:

$$f(\lambda_3 | H_s) \sim \Lambda\left(\mu_{\lambda3} + \rho \frac{\sigma_{\lambda3}}{\sigma_{Hs}} (\ln H_s - \mu_{Hs}), 1 - \rho^2 \sigma_{\lambda3} \right) \tag{144}$$

For this log-normal distribution, the expected value is,

$$E[\lambda_3 | H_s] = \exp\left\{ \mu_{\lambda3} + \rho \frac{\sigma_{\lambda3}}{\sigma_{Hs}} (\ln H_s - \mu_s) + \frac{1}{2} (1 - \rho^2)\sigma_{\lambda3}^2 \right\} \tag{145}$$

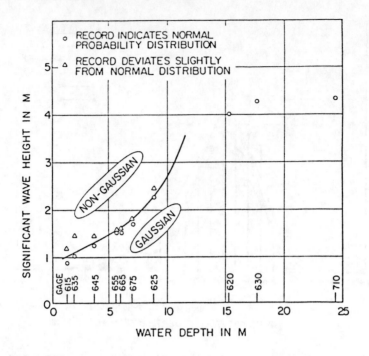

Figure 51. Minimum significant wave height above which non-Gaussian characteristics are observed as a function of water depth [111].

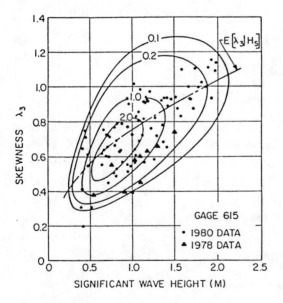

Figure 52. Skewness as a function of significant wave height and the bi-variate log-normal probability density function [111].

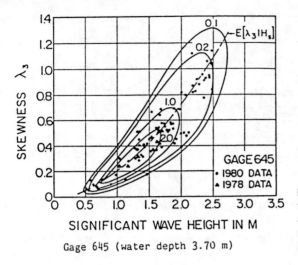

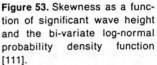

Gage 645 (water depth 3.70 m)

Figure 53. Skewness as a function of significant wave height and the bi-variate log-normal probability density function [111].

The expected skewness for four different water depths is also included in Figures 52–55. It can be seen from the figures that the expected skewness for a given significant wave height increases sharply with increase in significant wave height for waves of shallow water depth on the order of 5 m or less. On the other hand, the expected skewness increases gradually with increase in sea severity for waves of water depth on the order of 7–8 m.

Ochi et al. conclude that the skewness is the dominant parameter affecting the non-normal random characteristics in shallow water. The skewness increases with

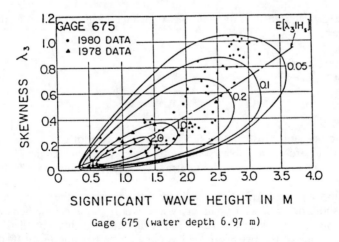

Gage 675 (water depth 6.97 m)

Figure 54. Skewness as a function of significant wave height and the bivariate log-normal probability density function [111].

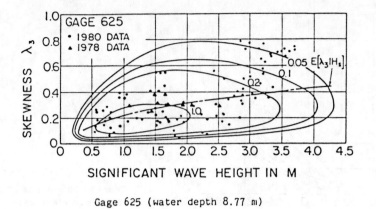

Gage 625 (water depth 8.77 m)

Figure 55. Skewness as a function of significant wave height and the bivariate log-normal probability density function [111].

increase in significant wave height for any water depth. A comparison between histograms and Rayleigh probability distributions of wave heights (peak-to-trough excursions) shows a significant difference. The significant wave heights obtained from the record and those computed based on the generalized gamma probability distribution agree well for all sea states and water depths analyzed.

Summary

There are several statistical distributions that have been applied to analysis of gravity waves:

1. Normal (Gaussian)
2. Gram-Charlier
3. Gumbel
4. Weibull

At present no one single distribution function is preferable for extreme wave analysis. Different researchers and agencies have their own preferences. One of the difficulties is that there are no, or a few, long-term wave measurements to verify different distributions.

The selection of given distribution function results in a bias of the estimated return wave heights and periods. As a preliminary evaluation, graphical methods are recommended, as they provide a quick visual evaluation of different distribution methods. Once one of the two methods is selected, a full evaluation with the aid of a computer should be performed.

The recommended procedure is as follows:

1. Select extreme events above a threshold level from the available data.
2. Employ either an annual maximum, or a partial duration series, depending on the nature of the data.
3. Calculate the return period for all the extreme data.
4. Plot the extreme data on several distribution graphs.
5. In case of Weibull distribution function employ different parameters to achieve a straight line on the Weibull distribution graph.
6. Using computer programs fit the extreme data to one or two distribution functions, and compute correlation coefficients.
7. Summarize the wave height and period data for return periods of interest to a given project.
8. Calculate standard error for the selected return periods.

There are a number of joint probability distributions available; however since research on different methods is continuing, it is too early to recommend any particular method. Several methods look promising but await verification with long-term field data.

Different return periods are considered for coastal and offshore structures. In general, final selection is made on the basis of economics and safety. General guidance is as follows:

1. Coastal structures: 50–100 year return periods. The actual return period depends on the degree of protection and risk analysis.
2. Offshore structures: 30–50 year return period. The actual return period depends on the magnitude of the oil reservoir and risk analysis.

Sources of Wave Data

There are several sources of wave data in the United States and overseas. The earlier published data consisted of ship observations, more recently hindcasted data were published for the coasts of the United States.

Ship observations are obtained from the following centers:

National Climatic Data Center, National Environmental Satellite, Data, and Information Service, N.O.A.A., U.S. Department of Commerce, Ashville, N.C. 2881–2696. These data are collected from the files of ship weather reports:

1. The wave heights are in 0.5 m intervals.
2. Wave periods are logged in 2 sec intervals (0–5 seconds are lumped together).
3. Summaries may be used for the U.S. Coastal waters.

U.S. Naval Weather Service Command Summary of Synoptic Meteorological Observations (SSMO). Information can be obtained from the Federal Clearing-house for Science and Technology Information, Springfield, VA 22151 (1970).

1. This publication is a summary of the 1963–1968 wave data collected from synoptic meteorological observation areas by ships in passage around the world, North American Coastal Summary (Figure 56).

Figure 56. North American coastal summary of synoptic meteorological observation areas.

2. Data for wave heights above 5 meters are questionable, but data above 10 meters are considered good.

Twenty extreme values of temperature, pressure, sea surface temperature, and air-sea temperature difference are tabulated for each month. The parameters were set-up to exclude the obvious errors from the tables. This method is necessarily subjective and frequently there is no concrete evidence to prove or disprove the validity of questionable data. It should also be noted that these data are based on observations made by ships in passage. Such ships tend to avoid bad weather when possible, thus biasing the recorded data toward good weather samples. Of particular interest to the ocean engineer are Tables 23 and 24 (SSMO Publication). Table 23 is a summary of wind speeds (in knots) and corresponding wave heights (in feet); as well as percentage frequency of wind speed (in knots) and direction as a function of wave height (in feet). Table 24 summarized the percent frequency of wave height (in feet) as a function

Table 23

Percent Frequency of Wind Speed (knots) and Direction as a Function of Wave Heights (ft) [155]

PERIOD: (PRIMARY)
(OVER-ALL) 1963-1967

DECEMBER

AREA 009 34-36N
CAPE HATTERAS 73W-COAST

PCT FREQ OF WIND SPEED (KTS) AND DIRECTION VERSUS SEA HEIGHTS (FT)

HGT	**N** 1-3	4-10	11-21	22-33	34-37	48+	TOTAL	**NE** 1-3	4-10	11-21	22-33	34-37	48+	TOTAL
<1	.1	.9	.1	.0	.0	.0	15	.0	.4	.4	.0	.0	.0	6
1-2	.2	2.3	1.1	.1	.0	.0	53	.0	1.2	.6	.0	.0	.0	25
3-4	.0	2.2	4.7	1.2	.0	.0	115	.0	.6	.9	.3	.0	.0	26
5-6	.0	.7	4.2	1.0	.1	.0	85	.0	.4	1.3	.2	.3	.0	28
7	.0	.0	2.7	.9	.0	.0	51	.0	.0	.3	.5	.0	.0	11
8-9	.0	.0	.8	1.0	.1	.0	27	.0	.0	.1	.1	.0	.0	3
10-11	.0	.0	.3	.9	.1	.0	19	.0	.0	.1	.1	.0	.0	1
12	.0	.0	.1	.3	.0	.0	6	.0	.0	.1	.1	.0	.0	3
13-16	.0	.0	.1	.2	.1	.0	5	.0	.0	.0	.0	.1	.0	1
17-19	.0	.0	.0	.0	.0	.0	0	.0	.0	.0	.0	.0	.0	0
20-22	.0	.0	.0	.0	.0	.0	0	.0	.0	.0	.0	.0	.0	0
23-25	.0	.0	.0	.0	.0	.0	0	.0	.0	.0	.0	.0	.0	0
26-32	.0	.0	.0	.0	.0	.0	0	.0	.0	.0	.0	.0	.0	0
33-40	.0	.0	.0	.0	.0	.0	0	.0	.0	.0	.0	.0	.0	0
41-48	.0	.0	.0	.0	.0	.0	0	.0	.0	.0	.0	.0	.0	0
49-60	.0	.0	.0	.0	.0	.0	0	.0	.0	.0	.0	.0	.0	0
61-70	.0	.0	.0	.0	.0	.0	0	.0	.0	.0	.0	.0	.0	0
71-86	.0	.0	.0	.0	.0	.0	0	.0	.0	.0	.0	.0	.0	0
87+	.0	.0	.0	.0	.0	.0	0	.0	.0	.0	.0	.0	.0	0
TOTAL	.4	87	199	80	6	0	376	.0	37	47	19	1	0	104
PCT	.3	6.1	14.0	5.6	.4	.0	26.5	.0	2.6	3.3	1.3	.1	.0	7.3

(Continued)

Table 23 (Continued)

PERIOD: (PRIMARY)
(OVER-ALL) 1963-1967

DECEMBER

AREA 009 CAPE HATTERAS
34-36N 73W-COAST

PCT FREQ OF WIND SPEED (KTS) AND DIRECTION VERSUS SEA HEIGHTS (FT)

E

HGT	1-3	4-10	11-21	22-33	34-37	48+	TOTAL
<1	.0	.0	.0	.0	.0	.0	0
1-2	.0	1.0	.2	.0	.0	.0	17
3-4	.0	.5	.4	.1	.0	.0	12
5-6	.0	.2	.5	.1	.0	.0	12
7	.0	.1	.2	.1	.0	.0	5
8-9	.0	.0	.1	.1	.0	.0	3
10-11	.0	.0	.0	.0	.0	.0	0
12	.0	.0	.0	.1	.0	.0	0
13-16	.0	.0	.0	.1	.0	.0	2
17-19	.0	.0	.0	.0	.0	.0	0
20-22	.0	.0	.0	.0	.0	.0	0
23-25	.0	.0	.0	.0	.0	.0	0
26-32	.0	.0	.0	.0	.0	.0	0
33-40	.0	.0	.0	.0	.0	.0	0
41-48	.0	.0	.0	.0	.0	.0	0
49-60	.0	.0	.0	.0	.0	.0	0
61-70	.0	.0	.0	.0	.0	.0	0
71-86	.0	.0	.0	.0	.0	.0	0
87+	.0	.0	.0	.0	.0	.0	0
TOTAL	.0	26	20	5	.0	.0	51
PCT	.0	1.8	1.4	.4	.0	.0	3.6

SE

HGT	1-3	4-10	11-21	22-33	34-37	48+	TOTAL
<1	.0	.1	.1	.0	.0	.0	3
1-2	.0	.1	.1	.0	.0	.0	10
3-4	.0	.4	.3	.0	.0	.0	19
5-6	.0	.5	.8	.3	.1	.0	14
7	.0	.2	.7	.1	.0	.0	8
8-9	.0	.1	.2	.3	.0	.0	6
10-11	.0	.0	.4	.1	.1	.0	2
12	.0	.0	.0	.1	.0	.0	1
13-16	.0	.0	.1	.1	.1	.0	0
17-19	.0	.0	.0	.0	.0	.0	0
20-22	.0	.0	.0	.0	.0	.0	0
23-25	.0	.0	.0	.0	.0	.0	0
26-32	.0	.0	.0	.0	.0	.0	0
33-40	.0	.0	.0	.0	.0	.0	0
41-48	.0	.0	.0	.0	.0	.0	0
49-60	.0	.0	.0	.0	.0	.0	0
61-70	.0	.0	.0	.0	.0	.0	0
71-86	.0	.0	.0	.0	.0	.0	0
87+	.0	.0	.0	.0	.0	.0	0
TOTAL	.0	19	36	.7	.2	.0	64
PCT	.0	1.3	2.5	.5	.1	.0	4.5

S

HGT	1-3	4-10	11-21	22-33	34-37	48+	TOTAL
<1	.1	.3	.0	.0	.	.	5
1-2	.1	.9	.0	.1	.	.	27
3-4	.	.8	2.1	.1	.1	.	44
5-6	.	.2	1.5	.7	.0	.0	34
7	.	.0	1.1	.8	.1	.	29
8-9	.	.	.4	.4	.1	.1	14
10-11	.	.	.1	.5	.1	.	8
12	.	.	.0	.1	.1	.	4
13-16	.	.	.	.1	.1	.0	2
17-19	.	.	.	.1	.1	.	2
20-22	.	.	.	.0	.0	.	0
23-25	.	.	.	.	.	.	0
26-32	.	.	.	.	.	.	0
33-40	.	.	.	.	.	.	0
41-48	.	.	.	.	.	.	0
49-60	.	.	.	.	.	.	0
61-70	.	.	.	.	.	.	0
71-86	.	.	.	.	.	.	0
87+	.	.	.	.	.	.	0
TOTAL	3	31	84	41	7	1	167
PCT	.2	2.2	5.9	2.9	.5	.1	11.8

SW

HGT	1-3	4-10	11-21	22-33	34-37	48+	TOTAL
<1	.0	.6	.0	.0	.0	.	4
1-2	.1	1.3	1.2	.1	.1	.	38
3-4	.	.6	2.6	.4	.0	.	52
5-6	.	.2	1.5	.6	.1	.	32
7	.	.	.3	.3	.1	.	9
8-9	.	.	.0	.3	.1	.	5
10-11	.	.	.	.1	.1	.	4
12	.	.	.	.0	.0	.	1
13-16	.	.	.	.	.0	.	2
17-19	.	.	.	.	.	.	0
20-22	.	.	.	.	.	.	0
23-25	.	.	.	.	.	.	0
26-32	.	.	.	.	.	.	0
33-40	.	.	.	.	.	.	0
41-48	.	.	.	.	.	.	0
49-60	.	.	.	.	.	.	0
61-70	.	.	.	.	.	.	0
71-86	.	.	.	.	.	.	0
87+	.	.	.	.	.	.	0
TOTAL	1	40	79	28	4	0	152
PCT	.1	2.8	5.6	2.0	.3	.0	10.7

W

HGT	1-3	4-10	11-21	22-33	34-37	48+	TOTAL
<1	.0	.5	.0	.0	.0	.	7
1-2	.1	2.2	2.0	.1	.1	.	63
3-4	.	1.6	2.4	.4	.1	.	62
5-6	.	.0	1.6	1.1	.0	.	39
7	.	.	.4	.9	.1	.	18
8-9	.	.	.2	.6	.1	.	14
10-11	.	.	.0	.2	.1	.	5
12	.	.	.	.1	.1	.	3
13-16	.	.	.	.1	.1	.	3
17-19	.	.	.	.	.	.	0
20-22	.	.	.	.	.	.	0
23-25	.	.	.	.	.	.	0
26-32	.	.	.	.	.	.	0
33-40	.	.	.	.	.	.	0
41-48	.	.	.	.	.	.	0
49-60	.	.	.	.	.	.	0
61-70	.	.	.	.	.	.	0
71-86	.	.	.	.	.	.	0
87+	.	.	.	.	.	.	0
TOTAL	1	60	97	49	7	0	214
PCT	.1	4.2	6.8	3.5	.5	.0	15.1

NW

HGT	1-3	4-10	11-21	22-33	34-37	48+	TOTAL	GRAND TOTAL
<1	.3	.6	.1	.0	.0	.	14	59
1-2	.1	1.5	1.1	.0	.0	.1	37	270
3-4	.	1.8	4.2	.8	.1	.	93	423
5-6	.	.9	3.0	1.5	.2	.	67	311
7	.	.0	.1	.6	.1	.	39	170
8-9	.	.	.2	.4	.1	.	17	89
10-11	.	.	.1	.4	.1	.1	9	47
12	.	.	.1	.1	.2	.	9	28
13-16	.	.	.	.0	.0	.	4	19
17-19	.	.	.	.	.	.	0	1
20-22	.	.	.	.	.	.	0	0
23-25	.	.	.	.	.	.	0	0
26-32	.	.	.	.	.	.	0	0
33-40	.	.	.	.	.	.	0	0
41-48	.	.	.	.	.	.	0	0
49-60	.	.	.	.	.	.	0	0
61-70	.	.	.	.	.0	.	0	0
71-86	.	.	.	.	.	.	0	0
87+	.	.	.	.	.	.	0	0
TOTAL	5	70	142	61	9	2	289	1417
PCT	.4	4.9	10.0	4.3	.6	.1	20.4	100.0

(Continued)

Table 23 (Continued)

DECEMBER

PERIOD: (PRIMARY)
(OVER-ALL) 1963-1967

WIND SPEED (KTS) VS SEA HEIGHT (FT)

HGT	0-3	4-10	11-21	22-33	34-47	48+	TOTAL OBS
<1	1.2	3.4	.3	.0	.0	.0	70
1-2	.3	10.8	7.3	.4	.1	.0	270
3-4	.2	8.5	18.0	2.9	.1	.0	424
5-6	.1	2.9	14.2	4.5	.1	.1	311
7	.0	.2	6.4	5.2	.1	.1	170
8-9	.0	.1	2.2	3.2	.7	.1	89
10-11	.0	.0	.5	2.4	.4	.1	47
12	.0	.0	.5	1.0	.5	.0	28
13-16	.0	.0	.1	.8	.5	.0	19
17-19	.0	.0	.0	.0	.1	.0	1
20-22	.0	.0	.0	.0	.0	.0	0
23-25	.0	.0	.0	.0	.0	.0	0
26-32	.0	.0	.0	.0	.0	.0	0
33-40	.0	.0	.0	.0	.0	.0	0
41-48	.0	.0	.0	.0	.0	.0	0
49-60	.0	.0	.0	.0	.0	.0	0
61-70	.0	.0	.0	.0	.0	.0	0
71-86	.0	.0	.0	.0	.0	.0	0
87+	.0	.0	.0	.0	.0	.0	0
TOTAL	26	370	704	290	36	3	1429
PCT	1.8	25.9	49.3	20.3	2.5	.2	100.0

Table 24

Percent Frequency of Wave Height (ft) as a Function of Wave Period (sec) [155]

PERCENT FREQUENCY OF WAVE HEIGHT (FT) VS WAVE PERIOD (SECONDS)

PERIOD (SEC)	<1	1-2	3-4	5-6	7	8-9	10-11	12	13-16	17-19	20-22	23-25	26-32	33-40	41-48	49-60	61-70	71-86	87+	TOTAL	MEAN HGT
<6	.9	11.7	18.0	9.3	3.4	1.2	.7	.1	.1	.0	.0	.0	.0	.0	.0	.0	.0	.0	.0	670	
6-7	.1	1.6	7.5	10.3	7.2	2.6	1.0	.6	.6	.1	.1	.1	.1	.0	.0	.0	.0	.0	.0	463	
8-9	.0	.7	1.0	2.0	3.7	.7	1.1	.7	.5	.0	.1	.1	.1	.0	.0	.0	.0	.0	.0	169	
10-11	.1	.7	.3	.9	.7	1.2	1.2	.6	.2	.0	.0	.0	.1	.0	.0	.0	.0	.0	.0	86	
12-13	.0	.1	.1	.3	.2	.1	.3	.2	.4	.0	.0	.0	.0	.0	.0	.0	.0	.0	.0	23	
>13	.0	.0	.0	.0	.1	.1	.1	.0	.0	.0	.0	.0	.0	.0	.0	.0	.0	.0	.0	5	
INDET	1.6	.8	.8	.2	.3	.1	.1	.0	.0	.0	.0	.0	.0	.0	.0	.0	.0	.0	.0	58	
TOTAL	40	220	407	338	225	114	65	33	27											1474	
PCT	2.7	14.9	27.6	22.9	15.3	7.7	4.4	2.2	1.8	.1	.1	.1	.1	.0	.0	.0	.0	.0	.0	100.0	

of wave periods (in seconds). In this table when both sea and swell waves are present, the higher of the two is used. If both are of the same height, the longer period is chosen. When only one of the wave types is observed, either sea or swell is used in the tables. Sample data in Tables 23 and 24 are shown for the month of December for Cape Hatteras area.

LEO Program, Corps of Engineers. Observations from shore have been collected in many coastal areas of the United States under the Corps of Engineers' LEO program. General areas for which LEO data are available are shown in Figure 57.

National Oceanographic Data Center, Washington, DC 20235, National Data Buoy Office (NDBO). Spectral wave data are acquired by each operational buoy every three hours at standard synoptic times (hourly data are available from some buoys). Within 30 minutes after the synoptic hour, the data are transmitted via HF (high frequency) to NDBO's Shore Collection Station (SCS) in Miami. At SCS these data are coded and used to compute spectral densities of vertical displacement of the sea surface. These spectral densities are used to calculate significant wave height and average wave period, and sometimes direction. These are sent to the National Meteorological Center (NMC) via teletype along with meteorological data obtained from the buoy in standard ship's weather message format. The displacement spectral densities are then coded into a special format for transmission from SCS to NMC for further dissemination to users involved with: marine forecasting, operational forecasting verification, and development of forecast models.

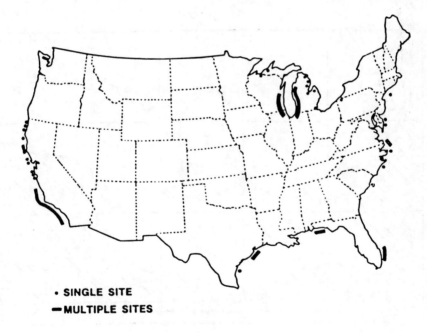

• SINGLE SITE
━MULTIPLE SITES

Figure 57. LEO sites.

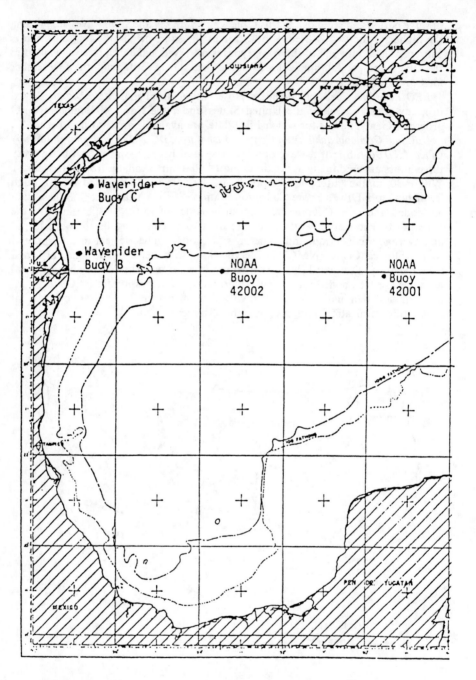

Figure 58. Location of NDBO buoys 42002 and 42001 and Texas A&M buoys B and C.

Once each day SCS sends all raw and processed buoy data to NDBO for evaluation and further processing. All data from the operation buoys are examined for time continuity, internal consistency, and synoptic representativeness. Reports of the status of all operational data are mailed weekly to interested users. When errors are detected in the data, they are flagged on NDBO's data base and deleted from archival tapes, which are prepared monthly and sent to the National Climatic Center and the National Oceanographic Data Center. Two of the Gulf of Mexico buoys, Numbers 42001 and 42002 are located in approximately 6,600 ft water depth (Figure 58). The monthly wave characteristics were summarized for the data from December 1979 to May 1982 by Texas A&M University [172]. The original NDBO data provide the spectral information for each observed wave record.

The following variables are shown in the monthly summaries: significant wave height (m), average wave period (sec), air temperature (degrees °C), sea surface temperature (°C), barometer (mb), wind speed (m/sec) and wind directions (degrees from true North). Sample statistics are shown in Figures 59 and 60. A sample significant wave height rose diagram is shown in Figure 61.

The Coastal Waves Program of the National Ocean Service (NOS), National Oceanic and Administration has been collecting wave data off mid-Atlantic Coast. All data are prepared for submission to NODC for final archival.

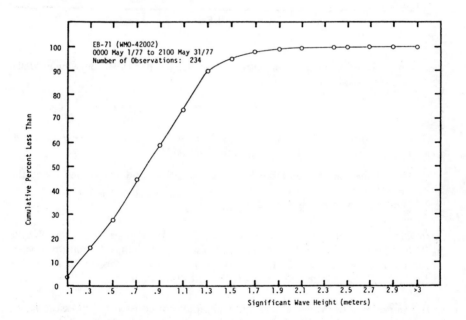

Figure 59. Sample cumulative probability distribution (for NDBO data, buoy WMO-42001, 4/01/79 to 4/30/79) [172].

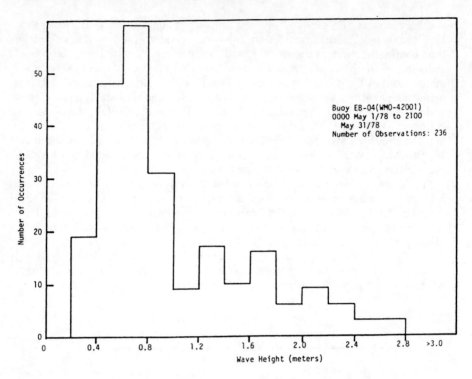

Figure 60. Sample histogram of significant wave heights (for NDBO data, buoy WMO-42001, 4/01/79 to 4/30/79) [172].

Coastal Engineering Research Center, CEWES-CW, Waterways Experiment Station, U.S. Army Engineers. Vicksburg, MS 39181-0631.

1. Wave gauges have been recording since the 1950s and are located along the U.S. Coast.
2. Data are shown in Figures 62–65 [45].

An effort was mounted by the *U.S. Army Engineer Waterways Experiment Station* in 1976 to produce a wave climate for U.S. coastal waters. This information is being produced by numerical simulation of wave growth, propagation, and decay under historical wind fields. The effort was divided into four phases:

1. Examination of available data and techniques for constructing pressure fields.
2. Theoretical estimation of winds at the geostrophic level and the reduction of these wind to surface level. Comparison with wind measurements near the surface.

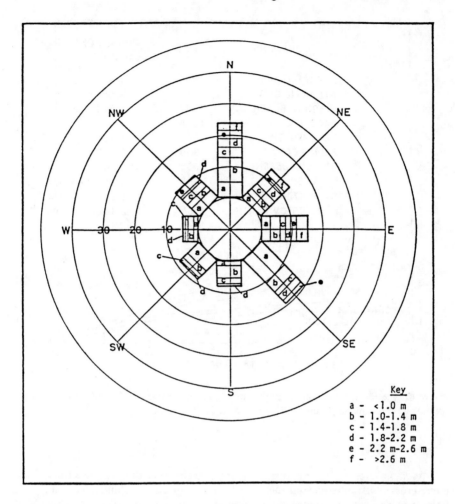

Figure 61. Significant wave height rose diagram (for NDBO Buoy 42001 January 1977) [172].

3. Formulation of a wave hindcast model.
4. Comparison of hindcasted waves using constructed oceanic wind fields with measured wave spectra.

Corson et al. [30] have evaluated pressure fields from two sources for hindcasting purposes and concluded that the sea-level pressure field developed by the National Weather Service should be accepted as a standard compatible with other data. A sample comparison is shown in Figure 66.

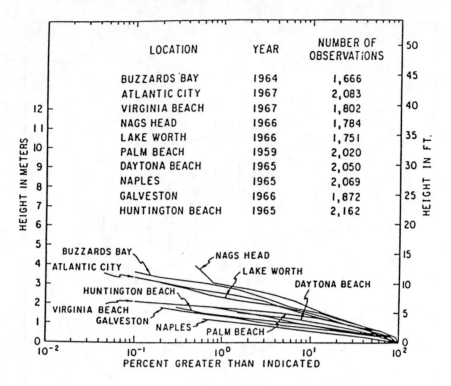

Figure 62. Plotted distribution functions for significant wave heights from wave gauge records as determined by the CERC procedure [145].

Corson and Resio [28] employed descriptive techniques that included time series plots; cross plots; difference of the means and mean absolute difference computations; and percent occurrence computations to compare recorded and computed hindcast wave heights for the Atlantic Ocean. Sample record of measured and computed wave heights is shown in Figure 67. A comparison of time plot of significant wave height, H_s, is shown in Figure 68. The comparisons indicate a random difference of approximately 1.0 m and a bias of approximately 0.04 m. If such is the case in future comparisons at these and other locations, it may be concluded that hindcasting methods should provide sufficient data base at least for feasibility studies. An effort should be made to collect field measurements for as long a time frame possible. It should be pointed out that these hindcasts did not include extreme events.

Another report by Resio et al. [127] presented methodology for estimating surface winds from pressure fields, air and water temperature fields and winds observed from ships.

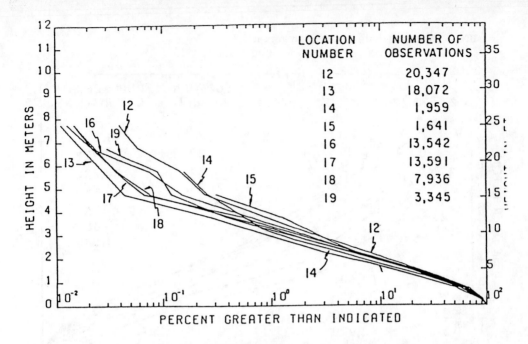

Figure 63. Wave height distribution functions based on shipboard observations from North American coastal SSMO areas along the Atlantic Coast. Wave heights greater than 12 m and height with less than a 0.01% probability of occurrence are not shown [145].

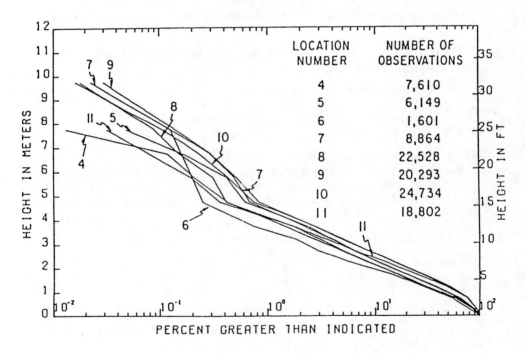

Figure 64. Wave height distribution functions for SSMO areas along the Gulf Coast [145].

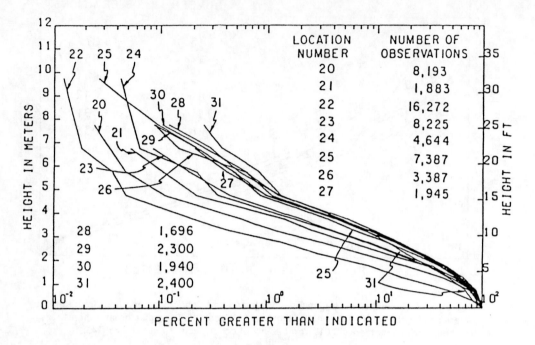

Figure 65. Wave height distribution functions for SSMO areas along the Pacific Coast [145].

The U.S. Atlantic coast water level climate was published by Ebersole [38]. The report includes the following:

1. Trends and variability in mean sea level
2. Magnitudes of the expected water-level climate
3. Duration statistics for both water level and storm surge
4. Extremal storm surge information as a result of extratropical storms

These are presented for 20 locations along the U.S. coast.

The shallow-water hindcast significant wave heights for the Atlantic Coast are presented by Jensen [77]. This report provides computed values for the 20-year period (1956–1975) for 166 stations along the coast. The data are presented in the following form:

1. Geographical variation in the wave climate
2. Twenty-year percent occurrence tables
3. Wave rose diagrams
4. Mean and largest wave-height tables
5. Return period tables
6. Duration tables

A sample output is shown in Tables 25–31 and in Figure 69. This major effort is known as WIS [76, 77].

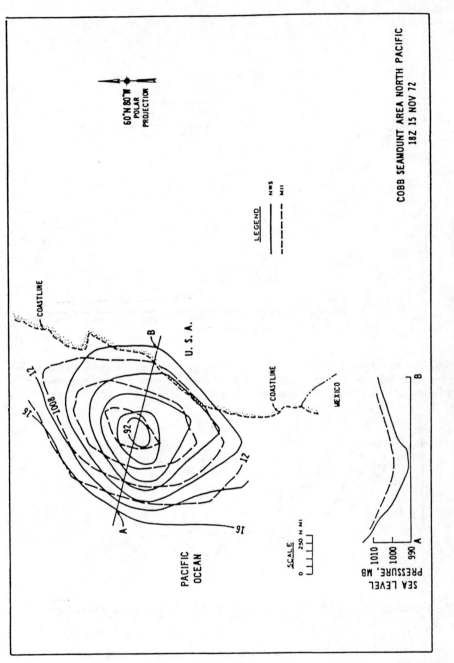

Figure 66. Comparison of sea-level pressure fields [30].

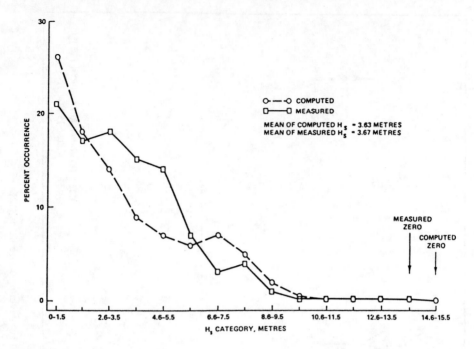

Figure 67. Plot of percent occurrence vs. H_s for time-paired measured and computed data sets. Notice the similiarity of distribution of waves even in extreme categories (measured data set "zeros-out" near computed data set) [28].

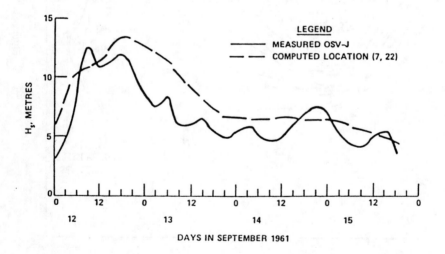

Figure 68. Comparison plot of H_s vs. time for a period in September 1961 at OSV-J [28].

Table 25 [77]

STATION 54 20 YEARS   WAVE APPROACH ANGLE(DEGREES)= 0. - 29.9
SHORELINE ANGLE= 4.0 DEGREES AZIMUTH
WATER DEPTH= 10.00 METRES
PERCENT OCCURRENCE(X1000) OF HEIGHT AND PERIOD BY DIRECTION

HEIGHT(METRES)	0.0-2.9	3.0-3.9	4.0-4.9	5.0-5.9	6.0-6.9	7.0-7.9	8.0-8.9	9.0-9.9	10.0-10.9	11.0-LONGER	TOTAL
0.0 - 0.49	2888	5985	4065	2347	588	869	313	11	6	.	17072
0.50 - 0.99	.	313	1976	1213	388	179	47	5	1	.	4128
1.00 - 1.49	.	.	17	77	100	6	.	.	.	.	201
1.50 - 1.99	.	.	.	.	.	1	.	.	.	.	1
2.00 - 2.49	.	.	.	.	.	.	.	.	.	1	1
2.50 - 2.99	.	.	.	.	.	.	.	.	.	.	0
3.00 - 3.49	.	.	.	.	.	.	.	.	.	.	0
3.50 - 3.99	.	.	.	.	.	.	.	.	.	.	0
4.00 - 4.49	.	.	.	.	.	.	.	.	.	.	0
4.50 - 4.99	.	.	.	.	.	.	.	.	.	.	0
5.00 - GREATER	.	.	.	.	.	.	.	.	.	.	0
TOTAL	2888	6298	6058	3637	1076	1055	360	16	7	1	

PERIOD(SECONDS)

AVERAGE HS(M) = 0.32   LARGEST HS(M) = 1.85   ANGLE CLASS % = 21.4

Table 26 [77]

STATION 54 20 YEARS   WAVE APPROACH ANGLE(DEGREES)= 30.0 - 59.9
SHORELINE ANGLE= 4.0 DEGREES AZIMUTH
WATER DEPTH= 10.00 METRES
PERCENT OCCURRENCE(X1000) OF HEIGHT AND PERIOD BY DIRECTION

HEIGHT(METRES)	0.0-2.9	3.0-3.9	4.0-4.9	5.0-5.9	6.0-6.9	7.0-7.9	8.0-8.9	9.0-9.9	10.0-10.9	11.0-LONGER	TOTAL
0.0 - 0.49	944	1254	1651	340	3237	7493	3879	494	456	465	18059
0.50 - 0.99	.	821	114	665	446	1485	530	205	18	.	5518
1.00 - 1.49	.	.	.	25	154	795	309	37	5	.	1928
1.50 - 1.99	.	.	.	.	27	88	200	10	.	.	678
2.00 - 2.49	.	.	.	.	.	.	113	1	.	.	126
2.50 - 2.99	.	.	.	.	.	.	3	.	.	.	3
3.00 - 3.49	.	.	.	.	.	.	.	.	.	.	0
3.50 - 3.99	.	.	.	.	.	.	.	.	.	.	0
4.00 - 4.49	.	.	.	.	.	.	.	.	.	.	0
4.50 - 4.99	.	.	.	.	.	.	.	.	.	.	0
5.00 - GREATER	.	.	.	.	.	.	.	.	.	.	0
TOTAL	944	2075	1765	1030	3864	9861	5093	747	479	465	

PERIOD(SECONDS)

AVERAGE HS(M) = 0.47   LARGEST HS(M) = 3.05   ANGLE CLASS % = 26.3

Table 27 [77]

STATION 54   20 YEARS   WAVE APPROACH ANGLE(DEGREES)= 60.0 - 89.9
SHORELINE ANGLE= 4.0 DEGREES AZIMUTH
WATER DEPTH=10.00 METRES
PERCENT OCCURRENCE(X1000) OF HEIGHT AND PERIOD BY DIRECTION

PERIOD(SECONDS)

HEIGHT(METRES)	0.0-2.9	3.0-3.9	4.0-4.9	5.0-5.9	6.0-6.9	7.0-7.9	8.0-8.9	9.0-9.9	10.0-10.9	11.0-LONGER	TOTAL
0.0-0.49	634	744			593	2861	2286	992	278	455	8843
0.50-0.99		571	1309	148	137	718	631	277	311	158	4108
1.00-1.49			111	693	147	164	131	64	70	57	1404
1.50-1.99				34	156	159	171		18		560
2.00-2.49					29	285	78				425
2.50-2.99						51					112
3.00-3.49											
3.50-3.99											
4.00-4.49											
4.50-4.99											
5.00-GREATER											
TOTAL	634	1315	1420	875	1062	4238	3297	1333	677	670	

AVERAGE HS(M) = 0.61   LARGEST HS(M) = 3.70   ANGLE CLASS % = 15.5

Table 28 [77]

STATION 54   20 YEARS   WAVE APPROACH ANGLE(DEGREES)= 90.0 - 119.9
SHORELINE ANGLE= 4.0 DEGREES AZIMUTH
WATER DEPTH=10.00 METRES
PERCENT OCCURRENCE(X1000) OF HEIGHT AND PERIOD BY DIRECTION

PERIOD(SECONDS)

HEIGHT(METRES)	0.0-2.9	3.0-3.9	4.0-4.9	5.0-5.9	6.0-6.9	7.0-7.9	8.0-8.9	9.0-9.9	10.0-10.9	11.0-LONGER	TOTAL
0.0-0.49	908	1839	1471	1617	1358	1795	961	123	378	432	10581
0.50-0.99		116	956	1018	316	1651	1245	210	85	1486	
1.00-1.49			17	349	236	586	844	104	55	131	
1.50-1.99				8	123	505	108	46		24	
2.00-2.49					13	45		7		1	
2.50-2.99											
3.00-3.49											
3.50-3.99											
4.00-4.49											
4.50-4.99											
5.00-GREATER											
TOTAL	908	1955	2444	2992	2046	4582	3158	490	518	2074	

AVERAGE HS(M) = 0.61   LARGEST HS(M) = 3.68   ANGLE CLASS % = 21.2

Table 29 [77]

STATION 54 20 YEARS   WAVE APPROACH ANGLE(DEGREES)= 120.0 - 149.9
SHORELINE ANGLE = 4.0 DEGREES AZIMUTH
WATER DEPTH = 10.00 METRES
PERCENT OCCURRENCE(X1000) OF HEIGHT AND PERIOD BY DIRECTION

PERIOD(SECONDS)

HEIGHT(METRES)	0.0-2.9	3.0-3.9	4.0-4.9	5.0-5.9	6.0-6.9	7.0-7.9	8.0-8.9	9.0-9.9	10.0-10.9	11.0-LONGER	TOTAL
0.- 0.49	10	.	.	.	.	.	.	.	.	.	10
0.50- 0.99	.	.	.	.	.	.	.	.	.	.	0
1.0- 1.49	.	.	.	.	.	.	.	.	.	.	0
1.50- 1.99	.	.	.	.	.	.	.	.	.	.	0
2.0- 2.49	.	.	.	.	.	.	.	.	.	.	0
2.50- 2.99	.	.	.	.	.	.	.	.	.	.	0
3.0- 3.49	.	.	.	.	.	.	.	.	.	.	0
3.50- 3.99	.	.	.	.	.	.	.	.	.	.	0
4.0- 4.49	.	.	.	.	.	.	.	.	.	.	0
4.50- 4.99	.	.	.	.	.	.	.	.	.	.	0
5.00-GREATER	.	.	.	.	.	.	.	.	.	.	0
TOTAL	10	0	0	0	0	0	0	0	0	0	10

AVERAGE HS(M) = 0.01   LARGEST HS(M) = 0.01   ANGLE CLASS % = 0.0

Table 30 [77]

STATION 54 20 YEARS   WAVE APPROACH ANGLE(DEGREES)= 150.0 - 179.9
SHORELINE ANGLE = 4.0 DEGREES AZIMUTH
WATER DEPTH = 10.00 METRES
PERCENT OCCURRENCE(X1000) OF HEIGHT AND PERIOD BY DIRECTION

PERIOD(SECONDS)

HEIGHT(METRES)	0.0-2.9	3.0-3.9	4.0-4.9	5.0-5.9	6.0-6.9	7.0-7.9	8.0-8.9	9.0-9.9	10.0-10.9	11.0-LONGER	TOTAL
0.- 0.49	.	.	.	.	.	.	.	.	.	.	0
0.50- 0.99	.	.	.	.	.	.	.	.	.	.	0
1.0- 1.49	.	.	.	.	.	.	.	.	.	.	0
1.50- 1.99	.	.	.	.	.	.	.	.	.	.	0
2.0- 2.49	.	.	.	.	.	.	.	.	.	.	0
2.50- 2.99	.	.	.	.	.	.	.	.	.	.	0
3.0- 3.49	.	.	.	.	.	.	.	.	.	.	0
3.50- 3.99	.	.	.	.	.	.	.	.	.	.	0
4.0- 4.49	.	.	.	.	.	.	.	.	.	.	0
4.50- 4.99	.	.	.	.	.	.	.	.	.	.	0
5.00-GREATER	.	.	.	.	.	.	.	.	.	.	0
TOTAL	0	0	0	0	0	0	0	0	0	0	0

AVERAGE HS(M) = 0.   LARGEST HS(M) = 0.   ANGLE CLASS % = 0.

Table 31 [77]

SHORELINE STATION 54   20 YEARS   FOR ALL DIRECTIONS
ANGLE = 4.0 DEGREES AZIMUTH
WATER DEPTH = 10.00 METRES
PERCENT OCCURRENCE(X100) OF HEIGHT AND PERIOD FOR ALL DIRECTIONS

HEIGHT(METRES)	PERIOD(SECONDS)										TOTAL
	0.0-2.9	3.0-3.9	4.0-4.9	5.0-5.9	6.0-6.9	7.0-7.9	8.0-8.9	9.0-9.9	10.0-10.9	11.0-LONGER	
0.00-0.49	538	.	.	.	.	.	.	.	.	.	538
0.50-0.99	.	982	553	396	577	1301	744	143	85	134	5453
1.00-1.49	.	182	589	272	79	403	272	157	85	127	2066
1.50-1.99	.	.	26	178	88	185	99	107	19	35	2089
2.00-2.49	.	.	.	6	57	57	37	22	3	14	2035
2.50-2.99	.	.	.	.	.	27	15	1	.	1	21
3.00-3.49	.	.	.	.	.	.	.	1	.	.	1
3.50-3.99	.	.	.	.	.	.	.	.	.	.	.
4.00-4.49	.	.	.	.	.	.	.	.	.	.	.
4.50-4.99	.	.	.	.	.	.	.	.	.	.	.
5.00-GREATER	.	.	.	.	.	.	.	.	.	.	0
TOTAL	538	1164	1168	852	805	1973	1189	231	192	318	10000

AVE HS(M) = 0.42   LARGEST HS(M) = 3.70   TOTAL CASES = 58440

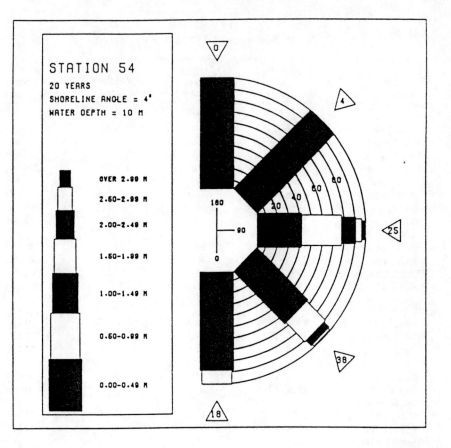

Figure 69. Sample output of shallow-water hindcast significant wave heights for Atlantic Coast [77].

Atlantic and Pacific hindcasts at 3-hour intervals over 20 years are available for deep water summaries (oceanic scale), intermediate summaries (continental shelf scale), and shallow water summaries.

Data for the Atlantic and Pacific Coasts were published and it is expected that wave data for the Gulf of Mexico were published in 1989. The extensive wave data sets for the United States coasts are listed in Table 32.

Texas A&M University Wave Data. Two Waverider buoys were deployed by the Ocean Engineering Program at Texas A&M University offshore, near Port Mansfield, Texas and the Matagorda Peninsula between 1977 and 1981. The buoys were deployed near Mobil Oil Company offshore platforms, and transmitted wave data by radio to receiving stations located on the platforms. Each data set consisted of a 20-minute observation interval at a sampling rate of 0.5 sec. Thus the data set

Table 32
Summary of WIS Data*

Data	Period of Record	Time-Steps GMT	Grid or Stations	Spatial Separation
		Atlantic		
Surface pressure	1956–1975	6-hr	61 × 61	110 km
Phase I wind	1956–1975	3-hr	31 × 31	220 km
Phase II wind	1956–1975	3-hr	41 × 33	55 km
Phase I wave	1956–1975	3-hr	31 × 31	220 km
sea & swell				
parameters	1956–1975	3-hr	13 sites	Variable
2-D spectra	1956–1975	3-hr	96 sites	Variable
Phase II wave	1956–1975	3-hr	41 × 33	55 km
sea & swell				
parameters	1956–1975	3-hr	73 sites	Variable
2-D spectra	1956–1975	3-hr	113 sites	Variable
Phase III wave	1956–1975	3-hr	166 sites	18.5 km
Water level	1927–1981	1-hr	20 sites	Variable
		Pacific		
Surface pressure	1956–1975	6-hr	64 × 123	110 km
Phase I wind	1956–1975	6-hr	32 × 61	220 km
Phase II wind	1956–1975	6-hr	31 × 32	55 km
Phase I wave				
parameters	1956–1975	3-hr	35	Variable
2-D spectra	1956–1975	3-hr	64	Variable
Phase II wave				
parameters	1956–1975	3-hr	53	55 km
2-D spectra	1956–1975	3-hr	53	55 km
Phase III wave				
parameters	1956–1975	3-hr	134	18.5 km
		Gulf of Mexico		
Surface pressure	1956–1975	6-hr	31 × 41	55 km
Wind	1956–1975	6-hr	31 × 41	55 km
Wave				
parameters	1956–1975	3-hr	55	55 km
2-D spectra	1956–1975		55	55 km

* From EM 1110-2-1414 U.S. Army Corps of Engineers (1988).

contained about 2,400 data points. Observations were made four times daily at 6-hour intervals, and data were recorded on magnetic cassettes in the form of a binary code. An analog strip chart recording was also obtained as a visual check on the obtained data.

Sample analyzed data for a Waverider buoy located about 11 miles offshore Padre Island, Texas is shown in Figures 70–71, and Table 33.

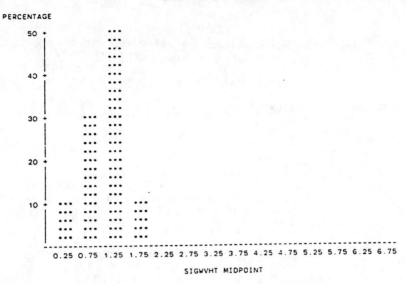

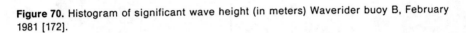

Figure 70. Histogram of significant wave height (in meters) Waverider buoy B, February 1981 [172].

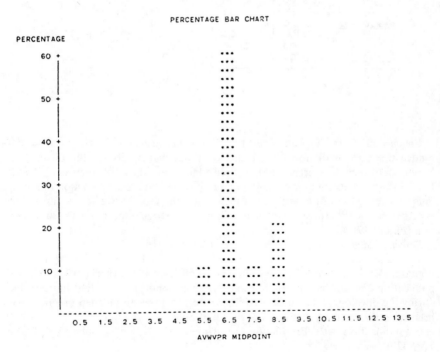

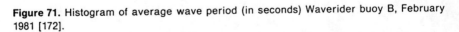

Figure 71. Histogram of average wave period (in seconds) Waverider buoy B, February 1981 [172].

Table 33
Frequency of Significant Height (m) and Average Periods (sec)
Waverider Buoy B, February 1981 [172]

TABLE OF AVWVPR BY SIGWVHT

AVWVPR	SIGWVHT				
FREQUENCY PERCENT ROW PCT COL PCT	<=0.5	<=1.0	<=1.5	<=2.0	TOTAL
<=6.0	0 0.00 0.00 0.00	0 0.00 0.00 0.00	0 0.00 0.00 0.00	1 10.00 100.00 100.00	1 10.00
<=7.0	0 0.00 0.00 0.00	2 20.00 33.33 66.67	4 40.00 66.67 80.00	0 0.00 0.00 0.00	6 60.00
<=8.0	1 10.00 100.00 100.00	0 0.00 0.00 0.00	0 0.00 0.00 0.00	0 0.00 0.00 0.00	1 10.00
<=9.0	0 0.00 0.00 0.00	1 10.00 50.00 33.33	1 10.00 50.00 20.00	0 0.00 0.00 0.00	2 20.00
TOTAL	1 10.00	3 30.00	5 50.00	1 10.00	10 100.00

Commercial Firms. There are several commercial firms specializing in wave data hindcasting and prediction for specific locations, principally for the oil industry. Examples of such data presented in graphical form are shown in Figures 18 and 19. Figure 18 shows the significant and maximum wave heights as a function of average interval (return period) in years for a location in the Gulf of Mexico. A similar plot is presented for the storm surge as a function of average interval for the same location (Figure 19).

Recommended practices–American Petroleum Institute.

The American Petroleum Institute issues the "API Recommended Practice for Planning, Designing, and Constructing Fixed offshore Platforms" (API, 1987). This publication contains engineering design principles and practices that have evolved during the development of offshore oil resources. The recommended practices have been revised over the years and the reader should always obtain the latest edition of the publication (API, Production Department, 211 N. Ervay, Suite 1700, Dallas, TX 75201).

The "Environmental Data" section of the publication covers general meteorological and oceanographic considerations, winds, waves, tides, currents, other environmental information, ice, earthquakes, and marine fouling.

The American Petroleum Institute also issues an "API Bulletin on Planning, Designing and Constructing Fixed offshore Structures in Ice Environments" (1982). This bulletin was developed in connection with oil exploration in the Beaufort Sea, and it is intended to provide guidelines for planning, designing, and constructing of fixed platforms in ice-laden areas.

Another publication is "API Recommended Practice for the Analysis of Spread Mooring Systems for Floating Drilling Units" (API, 1987).

Det Norske Veritas. Det Norske Veritas publishes "Rules for the Design, Construction and Inspection of offshore Structures." The intention of these rules is to lay down minimum requirements regarding structural strength, serviceability, and inspection of offshore structures.

Determination of environmental loads includes those due to wind, wave, current, ice, earthquake, tsunami, and other effects.

The latest edition of the rules may be obtained from:

Det Norske Veritas
Veritasveien 1
P.O. Box 300
N-1322, Høvik, Norway.

Among many other rules are "Rules for the Design, Construction and Inspection of Submarine Pipelines and Pipeline Risers" (DNV 1976, 1980).

Appendix A—Rayleigh Probability Density

The distribution may be written as

$$P\left(\frac{H}{\overline{H}}\right) = \frac{\pi}{\overline{H}}\left(\frac{H}{\overline{H}}\right)\exp\left[-\frac{\pi}{4}\left(\frac{H}{\overline{H}}\right)^2\right] \tag{146}$$

and the probability of exceedance (the probability that a particular wave height exceeds a given value) is

$$P\left(\frac{H}{\overline{H}}\right) = \int_{\overline{H}}^{\infty} p\left(\frac{H}{\eta_{RMS}}\right)^d \left(\frac{H}{\eta_{RMS}}\right) = \exp\left[-\frac{\pi}{4}\left(\frac{H}{\overline{H}}\right)^2\right] \tag{147}$$

where η_{RMS} = root mean square of surface elevation.

The values of probability density and exceedance probability (Rayleigh distribution) are given in Table 34.

Table 34
Probability Density and Exceedance Probability of the Rayleigh Distribution

$H/\bar{H}$	$p(H/\bar{H})$	$P(H/\bar{H})$	$H/\bar{H}$	$p(H/\bar{H})$	$P(H/\bar{H})$
0	0	1.0000	2.0	0.1358	0.0432
0.1	0.1559	0.9922	2.1	0.1033	0.0313
0.2	0.3044	0.9691	2.2	0.0772	0.0223
0.3	0.4391	0.9318	2.3	0.0567	0.0157
0.4	0.5541	0.8819	2.4	0.0409	0.0108
0.5	0.6454	0.8217	2.5	0.0290	0.00738
0.6	0.7104	0.7537	2.6	0.0202	0.00495
0.7	0.7483	0.6806	2.7	0.0138	0.00326
0.8	0.7602	0.6049	2.8	0.0093	0.00212
0.9	0.7483	0.5293	2.9	0.0062	0.00135
1.0	0.7162	0.4559	3.0	0.0040	0.00085
1.1	0.6680	0.3866	3.1	0.0026	0.00053
1.2	0.6083	0.3227	3.2	0.0016	0.00032
1.3	0.5415	0.2652	3.3	0.0010	0.00019
1.4	0.4717	0.2145	3.4	0.0006	0.00011
1.5	0.4025	0.1708	3.5	0.0004	0.000066
1.6	0.3365	0.1339	3.6	0.0002	0.000038
1.7	0.2759	0.1033	3.7	0.0001	0.000021
1.8	0.2219	0.0785	3.8	0.0001	0.000012
1.9	0.1752	0.0587	3.9	0.0000	0.0000065
2.0	0.1358	0.0432	4.0	0.0000	0.0000035

It should be noted that Forristall [41] indicated that Rayleigh Distribution over-predicts the wave heights. Forristall proposed the following equation for the probability of exceedance:

$$P\left(\frac{H}{\eta_{RMS}}\right) = \exp\left[-\frac{1}{8.42}\left(\frac{H}{\eta_{RMS}}\right)^{-2.126}\right] \tag{148}$$

Appendix B—Probability of Exceedance of Wave Crest Elevations

Formula [24]:

$$Q\left(\frac{\eta_{crest}}{\sqrt{m_0}} > \frac{\eta_x}{\sqrt{m_0}}\right)$$

$$= \frac{1}{\sqrt{2\pi}}\left[\int_{\frac{\eta}{\epsilon\sqrt{m_0}}}^{\infty} e^{-x^2/2}\,dx + \sqrt{(1-\epsilon^2)}e^{-\eta_x^2/2m_0}\int_{-\infty}^{\eta_x/\sqrt{m_0}\sqrt{1-\epsilon^2}/\epsilon^2} e^{-x^2/2}\,dx\right]$$

Probability of Exceedance of Wave Crest Elevations

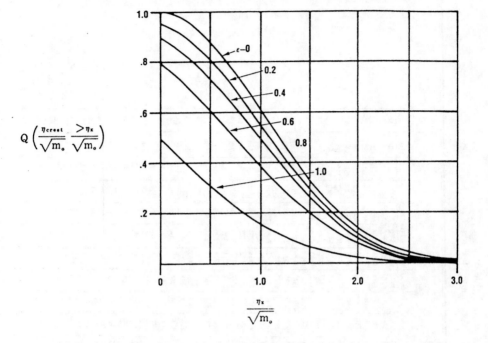

$$Q\left(\frac{\eta_{crest}}{\sqrt{m_o}}, \frac{>\eta_x}{\sqrt{m_o}}\right)$$

Figure 72. Graphs of the cumulative probability Q for different values of the spectral band width ϵ. (Courtesy of *Ocean Resources Engineering*, August 1978.)

where M_0 = zero spectral moment
   ϵ = band width of the spectrum (Figure 72)
   η_x = chosen reference crest elevation above the still water elevation. This includes the elevations of both the primary and secondary crests.
   η_{crest} = Crest elevation above still water level. Note that crest elevations can be negative for secondary crests.

Example:

A form seastate is described by a zero spectral moment of 169 ft/sec. and a band width ϵ of .70. What is the probability of exceedance of a crest elevation of 39 ft?

Table 35

*Probability of Exceedance of Wave Crest Elevations

$$10{,}000\,Q\left(\frac{\eta_{crest}}{\sqrt{m_o}} > \frac{\eta_s}{\sqrt{m_o}}\right)$$

$\dfrac{\eta_s}{\sqrt{m_o}}$	0.0000	0.0500	0.1000	0.1500	0.2000	0.2500	0.3000	0.3500	0.4000	0.4500	0.5000	0.5500	0.6000	0.6500	0.7000	0.7500	0.8000	0.8500	0.9000	0.9500	1.0000	$\dfrac{\eta_s}{\sqrt{m_o}}$
									Band width ε													
0.0	10000	9994	9975	9943	9899	9841	9770	9664	9583	9465	9330	9176	9000	8800	8571	8307	8000	7634	7179	6561	5000	0.0
0.1	9950	9938	9904	9855	9792	9715	9624	9519	9399	9262	9108	8935	8740	8521	8274	7992	7666	7282	6810	6175	4602	0.1
0.2	9802	9789	9753	9695	9619	9528	9422	9301	9164	9011	8840	8651	8440	8205	7941	7644	7304	6906	6422	5777	4207	0.2
0.3	9560	9548	9512	9452	9372	9272	9155	9022	8873	8708	8524	8322	8098	7851	7576	7267	6917	6510	6019	5371	3821	0.3
0.4	9231	9220	9185	9127	9046	8944	8823	8683	8527	8353	8161	7949	7717	7462	7179	6864	6508	6097	5605	4961	3446	0.4
0.5	8825	8814	8781	8725	8647	8547	8426	8285	8126	7948	7752	7537	7301	7041	6755	6438	6081	5672	5184	4551	3085	0.5
0.6	8353	8342	8311	8258	8184	8088	7971	7833	7676	7499	7304	7089	6853	6594	6310	5995	5642	5239	4762	4146	2743	0.6
0.7	7827	7817	7788	7738	7669	7579	7468	7336	7184	7013	6822	6612	6381	6127	5848	5540	5196	4804	4342	3750	2420	0.7
0.8	7261	7252	7225	7179	7114	7031	6927	6804	6660	6498	6315	6113	5890	5646	5377	5080	4749	4372	3930	3367	2119	0.8
0.9	6670	6661	6636	6594	6535	6458	6363	6249	6115	5963	5792	5601	5390	5158	4902	4620	4305	3948	3530	3001	1841	0.9
1.0	6065	6058	6035	5997	5943	5872	5786	5682	5560	5420	5262	5084	4888	4670	4431	4166	3871	3537	3146	2653	1587	1.0
1.1	5461	5454	5433	5399	5350	5287	5209	5115	5005	4878	4734	4572	4391	4191	3970	3725	3451	3142	2781	2328	1357	1.1
1.2	4868	4861	4843	4812	4769	4713	4643	4560	4461	4348	4218	4072	3908	3726	3525	3301	3051	2768	2439	2026	1151	1.2
1.3	4296	4290	4274	4247	4209	4159	4098	4024	3937	3836	3721	3591	3445	3282	3101	2899	2673	2418	2120	1748	966	1.3
1.4	3753	3748	3734	3711	3677	3634	3580	3515	3440	3352	3251	3137	3008	2863	2702	2523	2322	2094	1828	1497	808	1.4
1.5	3247	3242	3230	3210	3181	3143	3097	3041	2975	2899	2812	2712	2600	2474	2333	2175	1998	1797	1562	1270	668	1.5
1.6	2780	2777	2766	2749	2724	2692	2652	2605	2548	2483	2408	2323	2226	2117	1995	1858	1704	1528	1323	1069	548	1.6
1.7	2357	2355	2346	2331	2310	2283	2249	2208	2161	2105	2042	1969	1887	1794	1690	1572	1439	1288	1111	892	446	1.7
1.8	1979	1977	1969	1957	1939	1916	1888	1854	1814	1767	1714	1653	1584	1505	1417	1317	1205	1076	925	737	359	1.8
1.9	1645	1643	1637	1626	1612	1593	1569	1541	1507	1469	1424	1374	1316	1251	1177	1093	999	890	763	604	287	1.9
2.0	1353	1352	1347	1338	1326	1310	1291	1268	1240	1209	1172	1130	1083	1029	968	893	820	729	623	491	228	2.0
2.1	1103	1101	1097	1090	1080	1067	1052	1033	1010	985	955	921	882	838	788	731	667	592	504	395	179	2.1
2.2	889	888	885	879	871	861	848	833	815	794	770	742	711	676	636	590	537	476	405	315	139	2.2
2.3	710	709	706	702	696	688	677	665	651	634	615	593	568	540	507	470	428	379	321	249	107	2.3
2.4	561	561	559	555	550	544	535	526	514	501	486	469	449	427	401	372	338	299	253	195	82	2.4
2.5	439	439	437	434	430	425	419	412	403	392	381	367	351	334	314	291	264	234	197	151	62	2.5
2.6	340	340	339	337	334	330	325	319	312	304	295	284	272	258	243	225	205	181	152	116	47	2.6
2.7	261	261	260	258	256	253	249	245	239	233	226	218	209	198	187	173	157	139	116	89	35	2.7
2.8	198	198	197	196	194	192	189	186	182	177	172	166	159	151	141	131	119	105	88	67	26	2.8
2.9	149	149	148	148	146	144	142	140	137	133	129	125	119	113	106	99	90	79	66	50	19	2.9
3.0	111	111	111	110	109	108	106	104	102	99	96	93	89	84	79	73	67	59	49	37	13	3.0
3.1	82	82	81	81	80	79	78	77	75	73	71	68	66	62	58	54	49	43	36	27	10	3.1
3.2	60	60	59	59	59	58	57	56	55	53	52	50	48	45	43	39	36	32	26	20	7	3.2
3.3	43	43	43	43	42	42	41	40	40	39	37	36	35	33	31	29	25	23	20	14	5	3.3
3.4	31	31	31	31	30	30	29	29	28	28	27	26	25	23	22	20	18	16	14	10	3	3.4
3.5	22	22	22	22	21	21	21	20	20	20	19	18	18	17	16	15	13	11	10	7	2	3.5
3.6	15	15	15	15	15	15	15	14	14	14	13	13	12	12	11	10	9	8	6	5	2	3.6
3.7	11	11	11	11	10	10	10	10	10	10	9	9	9	8	8	7	6	6	4	3	1	3.7
3.8	7	7	7	7	7	7	7	7	7	7	6	6	6	6	5	5	4	4	3	2	—	3.8
3.9	5	5	5	5	5	5	5	5	5	5	4	4	4	4	4	3	3	3	2	1	—	3.9
4.0	3	3	3	3	3	3	3	3	3	3	3	3	3	3	3	2	2	2	1	1	—	4.0
4.1	2	2	2	2	2	2	2	2	2	2	2	2	2	2	2	2	1	1	1	—	—	4.1
4.2	1	1	1	1	1	1	1	1	1	1	1	1	1	1	1	1	1	1	—	—	—	4.2
4.3	—	—	1	1	1	1	1	1	1	1	1	1	1	1	1	1	—	—	—	—	—	4.3
4.4	—	—	—	—	—	—	—	—	—	—	—	—	—	—	—	—	—	—	—	—	—	4.4
4.5	—	—	—	—	—	—	—	—	—	—	—	—	—	—	—	—	—	—	—	—	—	4.5

The cumulative probability Q is giving the probability of exceedance of a certain normalized crest elevation η_s. The crests consists of both the extreme wave elevation as well as the secondary crests.

$$\frac{\eta_x}{\sqrt{m_0}} = \frac{3_g}{\sqrt{16_g}} = 3.0$$

$$Q\left(\frac{\eta_{crest}}{\sqrt{m_0}} > 3.0\right) = .0079 \text{ (see Table 35)}$$

which means that one crest in $1/0.0079 = 127$
Crests will attain an elevation in excess of 39 ft.

Notation

a	amplitude
$\bar{a} = \bar{a}_{RMS}$	root-mean-square amplitude
a_{max}	maximum wave amplitude
a_n	parameter of the distribution
A	scale parameter
B	envelope
.	location parameter
B(t)	envelope
C_R	coefficient (Weibull)
E_i	Poisson expected frequency of years with $i = 1$ storm
$f_U(u)$	marginal distribution of U
$f_{UV}(u, v)$	bivariate Rayleigh distribution function
$f_V(v)$	marginal distribution of V
$f_{XY}(x, y)$	joint probability distribution function
$\hat{F}_K$	data cumulative probability function
F(n)	chance
H	wave height
$\hat{H}$	arbitrary value of wave height
$\bar{H}$	mean value of wave height
H_{max}	highest wave height
H_R	extreme wave height
H_{RMS}	root-mean-square wave height
$H_1 \equiv H_{1/100}$	average of the highest 1% of all waves
$H_{10} \equiv H_{1/10}$	average of the highest 10% of all waves
$H_{1/3} \equiv H_s$	average of the highest 33% of all waves
K	frequency factor
ln	natural logarithm
m	any real number
.	rank of event
.	spectral moment on nth order
.	shape parameter
m_j	the j-th moment of x
m_0	spectral moment of the zero order

m_1 spectral moment of the first order
m_2 spectral moment of the second order
m_3 spectral moment of the third order
m_4 spectral moment of the fourth order
N   number (of items)
NIH   smoothing parameter
NIT   smoothing parameter
O_i observed frequency of years with $i = 1$ storm
$P \equiv P_x$ probability of occurrence
$P(r)$ probability distribution
$P\left(\dfrac{T}{\bar{T}}\right)$ distribution of wave period
$R(h)$ Rayleigh probability density function
r^2 coefficient of regression
T wave period
$T_{1/3} = T_s$ average of the highest 33% periods
$T_{1/10}$ average of the highest 10% periods
$\bar{T} \equiv T_{ave}$ mean wave period
T_{max} maximum period
T_r return period (recurrence interval)
u average number of storms per year
.   variable
u_n parameter of the distribution
v variable
W_p spectral width parameter
X storm of specified probability
$\bar{X}$ mean value of the series
$X_n{}^2$ chi square
y_n average deviation of y

Greek Symbols

α shape parameter (Weibull)
β scale parameter (Weibull)
ϵ location parameter
η number of items larger than an arbitrary value
$\Gamma = \Gamma(2)$ gamma function (Weibull)
γ parameter of $F_L(H_s)$
λ_3 skewness
λ_4 kurtosis
Λ bivariate log-normal distribution
π 3.14
$\phi_j(x)$ orthonormal set
ρ correlation coefficient (log-normal distribution)
σ standard deviation

σ_x standard deviation of the series

σ_H standard deviation of H

σ_{H_s} standard deviation of H_s

θ $2\pi/T$

$\xi(t)$ disturbance

References and Bibliography

1. Agerschou, H., Lundgren, H., Sorensen, T., Ernst, T., Korsgaard, J., Schmidt, L., and Chi, W., 1983, *Planning and Design of Ports and Marine Terminals*, John Wiley and Sons, New York, 320 p.

2. Akaike, H., 1969, "Fitting Autoregressive Models for Prediction," *Ann. Inst. Statist. Math.*, 21, pp. 243–247.

2a. Akaike, H., 1974, "A New Look at the Statistical Model Identification," *IEEE, Trans. Autom. Contr.*, AC-19, pp. 716–723.

3. American Petroleum Institute, 1987, "API Recommended Practice for Planning, Designing and Constructing Fixed Offshore Platforms," API RP 2A, 17th Edition.

4. American Petroleum Institute, 1982, "API Bulletin on Planning, Designing and Constructing Fixed Offshore Structures in Ice Environments," Bul. 2N, 1st Edition.

5. American Petroleum Institute, 1987, "API Recommended Practice for the Analysis of Spread Mooring Systems for Floating Drilling Units," API RP 2P 2nd Edition.

6. Andrew, M., Smith, O., and McKee, J., 1985, "Extremal Analysis of Hindcast and Measured Wind and Wave Data at Kodiak, Alaska," Technical Report CERC-85-4, U.S. Army Engineer Waterways Experiment Station, Vicksburg, MS, 75 pp.

7. Baer, L., Vincent, C. L., 1983, "Atlantic Remote Sensing Land Ocean Experiment (ARSLOE): Overview," *IEEE J. Oceanic Engineering*, Vol. 0E-8, No. 4. (October).

8. Barber, N. F., 1950, "Ocean Waves and Swell," lecture published by Institute of Civil Engineers, London, U.K.

9. Battjes, A., 1970, "Long-Term Wave Height Distribution at Seven Stations Around the British Isles," N.I.O. International Report No. A. 44 (July).

10. Battjes, J. A., 1969, "Fact and Figures Pertaining to the Bivariate Rayleigh Distribution," Department of Civil Engineering, Delft University of Technology, 11 pp.

11. Battjes, J. A., 1971, "Run-up Distributions of Waves on Slopes," Proceedings, American Society of Civil Engineers, 97 WWI, pp. 91–114 (February).

12. Battjes, J., 1977, "Probabilistic Aspects of Ocean Waves," Report No. 77-2, Department of Civil Engineering, Delft University of Technology, Delft, The Netherlands, 52 pp.

13. Bendat, J. and Piersol, D., 1971, *Random Data: Analysis and Measurement Procedures*, Wiley-Interscience, New York, 407 pp.

14. Bennett, J. O., 1974, "Estimation of Multivariate Probability Density Functions Using B-Splines," Ph.D. Dissertation, Rice University, 164 pp.

15. Boneva, L. I., Kendall, D. G., and Stefanov, I., 1971, "Spline Transformations: Three New Diagnostic Aids for the Statistical Data-Analyst," *J. of Royal Stat. Soc.*, Series B33, 1–70.

16. Borgman, L., and Resio, D., 1982, "Extremal Statistics in Wave Climatology," *Topics in Ocean Physics*, Soc. Italiana di Fisica, Corsica, Italy, pp. 439–471.

17. Borgman, L. E., 1973, "Probabilities for Highest Wave in Hurricane," *J. American Society of Civil Engineers*, Vol. 99, WW2, pp. 185–207.

18. Bretschneider, C. L., 1959, "Wave Variability and Wave Spectra for Wind-Generated

Gravity Waves," U.S. Army Corps of Engineers, Beach Erosion Board, Tech Memo. No. 118, 192 pp.

19. Bretschneider, C. L., 1964, "Investigation of the Statistics of Wave Heights Discussion," *J. Waterways and Harbours Division*, No. WWI, pp. 153–166.

20. Bretschneider, C. L., Crutcher, H. L., Darbyshire, J., Neumann, G., Pierson, W. J., Walden, H., and Wilson, B. W., 1962, "Data for High Wave Conditions Observed by the OWS *Weather Reporter* in December 1959," Deutsche Hydrographische Zeitschrift, Band 15, Heft. 6.

21. Brooks, R., 1957, "Statistics on Wave Heights and Periods for the North Atlantic Ocean," David Taylor Model Basin Report 1091, Bethesda, MD, 51 p. (V-024).

22. Brooks, R. M. and Corson, W. D., 1984, "Summary of Archived Atlantic Coast Wave Information Study, Pressure, Wind, Wave, and Water Level Data," WIS Report 13, (September) U.S. Army Engineer Waterways Experiment Station, Vicksburg, MS.

23. Cardone, V. J. and Ross, D. B., 1977, "State-of-the-Art Wave Predictions and Data Requirements," *J. Ocean Wave Climate*, Plenum Press, New York, N.Y., pp. 61–91 (H-025).

24. Cartwright, D. E., Longuet-Higgins, M. S., 1956, "The Statistical Distribution of the Maxima of a Random Function," Proceedings, Royal Society of London, Vol. 237, pp. 212–231.

25. Cavanie, A., Arhan, M. E., 1976, "A Statistical Relationship Between Individual and Periods of Storm Waves, Behavior of Offshore Structures, BOSS '76, Norwegian Institute of Technology, pp. 354–363.

26. Chakrabarti, S. K. and Cooley, R. P., 1977, "Statistical Distribution of Periods and Heights of Ocean Waves," *J. Geophysical Research*, Vol. 82, No. 9, pp. 1363–1368.

27. Chow, V. T., 1959, *Open Channel Hydraulics*, McGraw Hill Co., New York, N.Y.

28. Corson, W. D. and Resio, D. T., 1981, "Comparisons of Hindcast and Measured Deepwater, Significant Wave Heights," WIS Report 3, (May) U.S. Army Engineer Waterways Experiment Station, Vicksburg, MS.

29. Corson, W. D., Resio, D. T., Brooks, R. M., Ebersole, B. A., Jensen, R. E., Ragsdale, D. S., and Tracy, B. A., 1981, "Atlantic Coast Hindcast, Deepwater, Significant Wave Information," WIS Report 2, (January) U.S. Army Engineer Waterways Experiment Station, Vicksburg, MS.

30. Corson, W. D., Resio, D. T., and Vincent, C. L., 1980, "Wave Information Study of U.S. Coastlines; Surfaces Pressure Field Reconstruction for Wave Hindcasting Purposes," TR HL-80-11, Report 1 (July) U.S. Army Engineer Waterways Experiment Station, Vicksburg, MS.

31. Corson, W. D. and Tracy, B. A., 1985, "Atlantic Coast Hindcast, Phase II Wave Information: Additional Extremal Estimates," WIS Report 15, (May) U.S. Army Engineer Waterways Experiment Station, Vicksburg, MS.

32. Cramer, H., 1946, "*Mathematical Methods of Statistics*," Princeton University Press.

33. Darbyshire, J., 1955, "An Investigation of Storm Waves in the North Atlantic Ocean," Proceedings, Royal Society London, Ser, A, Vol. 230, pp. 560–569.

34. Dean, R. and Dalrymple, R., 1984, *Water Wave Mechanics for Engineers and Scientists*, Prentice-Hall, Inc., Englewood Cliffs, N.J., 353 pp.

35. deBoor, C., 1979, "Efficient Computer Manipulation of Tensor Products," *ACM Trns. Math. Software*, Vol. 5, No. 2, pp. 173–182.

36. Earle, M. D., 1975, "Extreme Wave Conditions During Hurricane Camille," *J. Geophysical Research*, Vol. 80, No. 3, pp. 377–379.

37. Earle, M. D. and Baer, L., 1982, "Effects of Uncertainties on Extreme Wave Heights," *J. Coast. Waterways* 108, pp. 456–478.

38. Ebersole, B. A., 1982, "Atlantic Coast Water-Level Climate," WIS Report 7 (April) U.S. Army Engineer Waterways Experiment Station, Vicksburg, MS.

39. Ewing, J. A., 1973, "Mean Length of Runs of High Waves, *J. Geophysical Research*, Vol. 78, No. 12, pp. 1933–1936.
40. Fisher, R. A. and Tippett, L. H. C., 1928, "Limiting Forms of the Frequency Distribution of the Largest or Smallest Member of a Sample," Proc. Cambridge Phil. Society, pp. 24–180.
41. Forristall, G. Z., 1978, "On the Statistical Distribution of Wave Heights in a Storm," *J. Geophysical Research*, Vol. 83, No. C5, pp. 2353–2358.
42. Glenn and Associates., 1982, personal communication.
43. Goda, Y., 1970, "Numerical Experiments on Wave Statistics With Spectral Simulation," Report *Japan, Ministry of Transport, Port & Harbour Research Institute*, Vol. 9, No. 3, pp. 3–57.
44. Goda, Y., 1985, *Random Seas and Design of Maritime Structures*, U. Tokyo Press, 323 pp.
45. Goda, Y. and Nagai, K., 1974, "Investigation of the Statistical Properties of Sea Waves With Field and Simulation Data," Report *Japan Ministry of Transport, Port & Harbour Research Institute*, Vol. 13, No. 1, pp. 3–37 (in Japanese).
46. Goda, Y., 1976, "On Wave Groups," Behavior of Offshore Structures, BOSS '76, The Norwegian Institute of Technology, pp. 1–14.
47. Goda, Y., 1977, "Numerical Experiments on Statistical Variability of Ocean Waves," Report *Japan Ministry of Transport, Port & Harbour Research Institute*, Vol. 16, No. 2, pp. 5–32.
48. Goda, Y., 1978, "The Observed Joint Distribution of Periods and Heights of Sea Waves," Proceedings, 16th Coastal Engineering Conference, Hamburg, pp. 227–245.
49. Goda, Y., 1979, "A Review on Statistical Interpretation of Wave Data, *Japan Ministry of Transport, Port & Harbour Research Institute*, Vol. 18, No. 1, pp. 5–32.
50. Gringorten, I., 1963, "A Plotting Rule for Extreme Probability Paper," *J. Geophysical Research*, Vol. 68, No. 3, (February) pp. 813–814.
51. Gumbel, E., 1958, *Statistics of Extremes*, Columbia University Press, N.Y., 375 pp.
52. Gutman, A. L., 1976, "Delineation of a Wave Climate for Dam Neck, Virginia Beach, Virginia," *Special Report in Applied Marine Science and Ocean Engineering*, No. 125, Virginia Institute of Marine Science, 38 pp.
53. Harris, D. L., 1972, "Wave Estimates for Coastal Regions," Chapter 5, *Shelf Sediment Transport*," edited by Swift, D. and Pilkey, D., Hutchins & Ross, Inc., Stroudsburg, PA.
54. Harris, D. L. and Esteva, D., 1970, "The Analysis of Wave Records," Proceedings, 12th Coastal Engineering Conference, Washington, D.C., pp. 85–100 (M-022).
55. Hasselman, K., et al., 1973, "Measurements of Wind-Wave Growth and Swell Decay During the Joint North Sea Wave Project (JONSWAP)," Deutsche Hydrographische Zeitschrift, Reihe A (8°), No. 12.
56. Hayden, B. P., 1975a, "The Annual Cycle of Wave Climates Along the East Coast of the United States," Proceedings, Coastal Society, Arlington, VA, pp. 225–231 (V-022) (November).
57. Hayden, B. P. and Dolan, R., 1975, "Classification of Coastal Environments of the World," *Coastal Wave Climates of the Americas*, Department of Environmental Sciences, U. of Virginia, Charlottesville, VA, final report prepared under contract number NONr-N00014-69-A-0060-0006, 169 pp. (H-012).
58. Herbich, J. B., 1986, personal communication.
58a. Herbich, J. B. and Watanabe, R. K., 1983, "A Comparison of Actual and Theoretical Values of Waves Generated by Hurricane Allen," 6th Canadian Hydrotechnical Conference, Ottawa, Ontario, pp. 759–775, June.
59. Hotta, S., 1981, "On Wave Height and Wave Period Distributions in the Nearshore

Zone," Proceedings, 28th Japanese Conference on Coastal Engineering, JSCE, pp. 148–152 (in Japanese).

60. Houmb, O. G., 1971, "On the Duration of Storms in the North Sea," Proceedings, Port and Ocean Engineering Under Arctic Conditions, Technical U. of Norway, Trondheim, Norway, pp. 423–439.

61. Houmb, O. G., 1989, "Basic Wave Statistics," Volume 1, *Port Engineering*, 3rd. Ed., P. Bruun, Gulf Publishing Co., Houston, TX.

62. Houmb, O. G. and Vik, I., 1975, "Durations of Storms in Northern Waters," Proceedings, Port and Ocean Engineering Under Artic Conditions, U. of Alaska Fairbanks, AK.

63. Houmb, O. G. and Vik, I., 1977, "On the Duration of Sea State," The Norwegian Institute of Technology, Trondheim, Norway, 33 pp.

64. Houmb, O. G. and Overvik, T., 1977. "On Statistical Properties of 115 Wave Records from the Norwegian Continental Shelf," The Norwegian Institute of Technology, Trondheim, Norway, pp. 183.

65. Houmb, O. G., Mo. K., Overvik, T., 1978, "Reliability Tests of Visual Wave Data and Estimation of Extreme Sea State," The Norwegian Institute of Technology, Tronheim, Norway.

66. Horikawa K., 1978, *Coastal Engineering*, Tokyo University Press.

67. Huang, N. E. and Long, S. R., 1980, "An Experimental Study of the Surface Elevation Probability Distribution and Statistics of Wind-Generated Waves," *J. Fluid Mechanics*, Vol. 101, Part 1, pp. 179–200.

68. Hudspeth, R. T. and Chen, M. C., 1979, "Digital Simulation of Nonlinear Random Waves," Proceedings, American Society of Civil Engineers, Vol. 105, No. WW1, pp. 67–85.

69. Ijima, T. and Tang, F. L. W., 1966, "Numerical Calculation of Wind Waves in Shallow Water," Proceedings, 10th Coastal Engineering Conference, Vol. II, pp. 38–45.

70. Isaacson, M. and MacKenzie, N., 1981, "Long-Term Distributions of Ocean Waves: A Review," Proceedings, American Society of Civil Engineers, Vol. 107, No. WW2, pp. 93–109 (May).

71. Isobe, M., 1982, "Long Period Field Oservation on Horizontal Distribution of Waves and Currents in the Nearshore Zone," NERC Report No. 16, TR-81-2, pp. 26–47 (in Japanese).

72. Isobe, M., 1983a, "Long Period Field Observation on Horizontal Distribution of Waves and Currents in the Nearshore Zone," NERC Report No. 17, TR-82-1, pp. 17–34 (in Japanese).

73. Ito, Y., Tanimoto, K., and Yamamoto, S., 1972, "Wave Height Distribution in the Region of Ray Crossing—Application of the Numerical Analysis Method for Wave Propagation," Report *Japan Ministry of Transport Port and Harbour Research Institute*, Vol. 11, No. 3, pp. 88–109 (in Japanese).

74. Jahns, H. and Wheeler, J., 1973, "Long-Term Wave Probabilities Based on Hindcasting of Severe Storms," *J. Petroleum Tech.*, pp. 473–486.

75. Jensen, A., et al., 1967, "Analyse af Stormflodrisiko," Report on Storm Surges, Technical U. of Denmark, Copenhagen.

76. Jensen, R. E., 1983, "Methodology for the Calculation of a Shallow Water Wave Climate," WIS Report 8 (September) U.S. Army Engineer Waterways Experiment Station, Vicksburg, MS.

77. Jensen, R. E., 1983, "Atlantic Coast Hindcast, Shallow-Water Significant Wave Information," WIS Report 9 (January) U.S. Army Engineer Waterways Experiment Station, Vicksburg, MS.

78. Kendall, M. G. and Stuart, A., 1963, *The Advanced Theory of Statistics*, Hafner, N.Y.

79. Kimura, A., 1980, "Statistical Properties of Random Wave Groups," Proceedings, 17th Coastal Engineering Conference, American Society of Civil Engineers, pp. 2955–2973.

80. Kimura, A., 1981, "Joint Distribution of Wave Heights and Periods of Random Sea Waves," *Coastal Engineering in Japan*, Vol. 24, 77–92.

81. Kinsman, B., 1965, *Wind Waves*, Prentice Hall, Inc., Englewood Cliffs, N.J.

82. Kitaigordskii, S., 1962. "Application of the Theory of Similarity to the Analysis of Wind-Generated Wave Motion as a Stochastic Process," Bull. Acad. of Science, U.S.S.R, Ser. Geophysics, No. 1, Vol. 1, pp. 105–117.

83. Kronmal, R. A. and Tarter, M. E., 1976, "The Estimation of Probability Densities and Cumulatives by Fourier Series Methods," *J. American Stat. Associates*, 63, pp. 925–952.

84. Krusemann, P., 1967, "Two Practical Methods for Forecasting Wave Components with Periods Between 10 and 25 Seconds Near Hook of Holland," Wetenschappelijk Rapport 76-1, Koninklijk Nederlands Meteorologisch Instituut (in Dutch).

85. Le Méhauté, B. and Wang, S., 1984, "Effects of Measurement Error on Long Term Wave Statistics," Proceedings, 19th Coastal Engineering Conference, American Society of Civil Engineers, New York, pp. 345–361.

86. Le Méhauté, B. and Wang, S., 1985, "Wave Statistical Uncertainties and Design of Breakwater," *J. Waterway, Port, Coastal and Ocean Engineering*, American Society of Civil Engineers, New York, Vol. III, No. 5, (September) pp. 921–938.

87. Liang, N. K., 1979, "A Study on Wave Height Comparison Between Penghu and Lukang in Taiwan Strait During Winter Monsoon Season," *Acta Oceanographica Taiwanica*, Science Reports of the National Taiwan University, No. 10, pp. 145–154.

88. Linsley, R. K., Kohler, M. A., and Paulhus, J. L. H., 1982, *Hydrology for Engineers*, McGraw-Hill, New York.

89. Longuet-Higgins, M. S., 1952, "On the Statistical Distribution of the Heights of Sea Waves," *J. Marine Research*, Vol. XI, No. 3, pp. 245–266.

90. Longuet-Higgins, M. S., 1957, "The Statistical Analysis of a Random, Moving Surface," Phil. Trans. Royal Society, Vol. 249 A966, pp. 321–387.

91. Longuet-Higgins, M. S., 1962, "The Distribution of Intervals Between Zeros of a Stationary Random Function, Phil. Trans. Royal Society, London, Serial A, Vol. 254, pp. 557–599.

92. Longuet-Higgins, M. S., 1963, "The Effect of Non-linearities on Statistical Distributions in the Theory of Sea Waves," *J. Fluid Mechanics*, Vol. 17, pp. 459–480.

93. Longuet-Higgins, M. S., 1975, "On the Joint Distribution of the Periods and Amplitudes of Sea Waves, *J. Geophysical Research*, Vol. 80, pp. 2688–2694.

94. Longuet-Higgins, M. S., 1980, "On the Distribution of the Heights of Sea Waves—Some Effects of Non-linearity and Finite Band Width," *J. Geophysical Research*, Vol. 85, pp. 1519–1523.

95. Longuet-Higgins, M. S., 1983, "On the Joint Distribution of Wave Periods and Amplitudes in Random Wave Field," Proceedings, Royal Society London, Ser. A, Vol. 389, pp. 241–258.

96. Longuet-Higgins, M. S., 1984, "Statistical Properties of Wave Groups in a Random Sea State," Phil. Trans. Royal Society London, Ser, A, Vol. 312, pp. 219–250.

97. Longuet-Higgins, M. S. and Stewart, R. W., 1960, "Changes in the Form of Short Gravity Waves on Long Waves and Tidal Currents," *J. Fluid Mechanics*, 8, pt. 4, pp. 565–583.

98. Mase, H. and Iwagaki, Y., 1982, "Wave Height Distribution and Wave Grouping in the Surf Zone," Proceedings, 18th Coastal Engineering Conference, American Society of Civil Engineers, pp. 58–76.

99. Miller, I. and Freund, J., 1985, *Probability and Statistics for Engineers*, 3rd ed., Prentice-Hall, Inc., Englewood Cliffs, N.H., 530 pp.

99a. Sverdrup, H. U. and Munk, W. H., 1947, "Wind, Sea and Swell: Theory of Relations for Forecasting," Publ. No. 601, U.S. Navy Hydrographic Office, Washington, D.C., March.

100. Nagai, K., 1973, "Runs of the Maxima of the Irregular Sea," *Coastal Engineering in Japan*, Vol. 16, Japan Society of Civil Engineers, pp. 13–18.

101. Nagata, Y., 1964, "The Statistical Properties of Orbital Wave Motions and Their Application for the Measurement of Directional Wave Spectra," *J. Oceanogr. Society of Japan*, Vol. 19, pp. 169–181.

102. Nath, J. H. and Ramsey, F. L., 1974, "Probability Distributions of Breaking Wave Heights," Proceedings, International Symposium of Ocean Wave Measurement and Analysis, American Society of Civil Engineers, New Orleans, pp. 379–395 (September 9–11).

103. Neu, H. J. A., 1976, "Wave Climate of the North Atlantic-1970," Bedford Institute of Oceanography, Atlantic Oceanographic Laboratory, Dartmouth, Nova Scotia, Report Series BI-R-76-10, 37 pp. (S-008).

104. Newmann, G. and James, R. W., 1955, "North Atlantic Coast Wave Statistics Hindcast by the Wave Spectrum Method," prepared under contract number DA-49-055-eng-32, U.S. Army Corps of Engineers, Beach Erosion Board, Tech. Memo. No. 57, 22 pp. (H-009).

105. Nolte, K. G., 1973, "Statistical Methods for Determining Extreme Sea States, Proceedings, Second International Conference on Port and Ocean Engineering Under Arctic Conditions (POAC), Iceland (August).

106. Nolte, K. G. and Hsu, F. H., 1973, "Statistics of Ocean Wave Groups," 4th Offshore Technology Conference, No. 1688, also in *J. Society of Petroleum Engineers*, pp. 139–146 (June).

107. Nordenstrom, N., 1969, "Methods for Predicting Long-Term Distributions of Wave Loads and Probability of Failure for Ships, Appendix 1. Long-Term Distributions of Wave Height and Period," Det Norske Veritas, Report No. 69-21-S, Oslo (May).

108. Newmann, G., 1954, "Zur Charakteristik des Seeganges," Arch. fur Meteorol. Geophys. und Biochlimatologie, Serie A7, pp. 352–377 (in German).

109. Ochi, M. K., 1978, "Generalization of Rayleigh Probability Distribution and Its Application," *J. Ship Research*, Vol. 22, No. 4, pp. 259–265.

110. Ochi, M. K. and Hubble, E. N., 1976, "On Six-Parameter Wave Pectra," Proceedings, 15th Coastal Engineering Conference, American Society of Civil Engineers, Honolulu, Hawaii.

111. Ochi, M. K., Malakar, S. B., and Wang, W. C., 1982, "Statistical Analysis of Coastal Waves Observed During the ARSLOE Project, UFL/COEL/TR-045 Coastal and Oceanographic Engineering Department, U. of Florida.

112. Ou, S. H. and Tang, F. L. W., 1974, "Wave Characteristics in the Taiwan Strait," Proceedings, Symposium on Ocean Wave Measurement and Analysis, American Society of Civil Engineers, New Orleans, Vol. II, pp. 139–158.

113. Ou, S. H., 1977, "Parametric Determination of Wave Statistics and Wave Spectrum of Gravity Waves," Dissertation No. 1, Tainan Hydraulics Laboratory, Taiwan.

114. Parzen, E., 1979, "Nonparametric Statistical Data Modeling, *J. American Stat. Assn.*, 74, pp. 105–131.

114a. Parzen, E., 1962, "On Estimation of a Probability Density Function and Mode," *Annals of Mathematical Statistics*, Vol. 33, pp. 1065–1076.

115. Pierson, W. J., 1956, "Visual Wave Observations," Miscellaneous Pub. No. 15921, U.S. Navy Hydrographic Office, Washington, D.C., 50 pp.

116. Pierson, W. J. and Moskowitz, L., 1964, "A Proposed Spectral Form for Fully Devel-

oped Wind Seas Based in the Similarity of S. A. Kitaigorodskii," *J. Geophysical Research*, Vol. 69, No. 24, pp. 5181–5190.

117. Pierson, W. J., 1977, "Wave Conditions, MES New York Bight Atlas," Monograph No. 5, New York Sea Grant Institute, Albany, N.Y.

118. Pierson, W. J., 1982, "Suggested Procedures for Improving Operational Wave Forecasts," Proceedings, 1980 Wave Information Workshop, Bio. Can. Technical Report No. 2.

119. Pierson, W. J., 1982, "The Spectral Ocean Wave Model (SOWM), A Northern Hemisphere Computer Model for Specifying and Forecasting Ocean Wave Spectra," David Taylor Naval Ship Research and Development Center, DTNSRDC-82/0112, Bethesda, MD, 20084.

120. Pierson, W. J., Tick, L. J., and Baer, L., 1966, "Computer Based Procedures for Preparing Global Wave Forecasts and Wind Field Analyses Capable of Using Wave Data Obtained by Spacecraft, Proceedings, 6th Naval Hydrodynamic Symposium, pp. 499–532.

121. Quayle, R. G. and Fulbright, D. C., 1975, "Extreme Wind and Wave Return Periods for the U.S. Coast. Mariners Weather Log, Vol. 19, No. 2, pp. 67–70 (H-019).

122. Ragsdale, D. S., 1983, "Sea-State Engineering Analysis System: Users Manual," WIS Report 10 (August) U.S. Army Engineer Waterways Experiment Station, Vicksburg, MS.

123. Rayleigh, Lord. 1880, "On the Resultant of a Large Number of Vibrations of the Same Pitch and of Arbitrary Phase," Phil. Mag. Series 5, 10 (60). pp. 73–78.

124. Resio, D. T., and Hayden, B., 1973, "An Integrated Model of Storm-Generated Waves," Technical Report 8, Department of Environmental Sciences, U. of Virginia, Charlottesville, VA, 288 pp.

125. Resio, D. T. and Tracy, B. A., 1983, "A Numerical Model for Wind-Wave Prediction in Deep Water, WIS Report 12, U.S. Army Engineer Waterways Experiment Station, Vicksburg, MS.

126. Resio, D. T., 1982, "The Estimation of Wind-Wave Generation in a Discrete Spectral Model," WIS Report 5 (March) U.S. Army Engineer Waterways Experiment Station, Vicksburg, MS.

127. Resio, D. T., Vincent, C. L., and Corson, W. D., 1982, "Objective Specification of Atlantic Ocean Windfields From Historical Data," WIS Report 4 (May) U.S. Army Engineer Waterways Experiment Station, Vicksburg, MS.

128. Rice, S. O., 1945, "The Mathematical Analysis of Random Noise," *Bell Syst. Technical Journal*, 23:282–332, 24:46–156.

129. Rice, S. O., 1954, "Mathematical Analysis of Random Noise," *Noise and Stochastic Processes* (N. Wax, ed.), Dover Publications, Inc. 1954. pp. 133–294.

130. Rijkoort, P. J. and Hemelrijk, J., 1957, "The Occurrence of "Twin" Storms From the North West in the Dutch Coast," *Statistica Neerlandica*, Vol. 11–3.

130a. Rosenblatt, M., 1956, "Remarks on Some Non-parametric Estimates of a Density Function," *Annals of Mathematical Statistics*, Vol. 27, pp. 832–837.

131. Rye, H., 1974, "Wave Group Formation Among Storm Waves," Proceedings 14th Conference Coastal Engineering, Copenhagen, Denmark. pp. 164–183.

132. Sawaragi, T. and Iwata, K., 1984, "A Nonlinear Model of Irregular Wave Run-up Height and Period Distributions on Gentle Beaches," Proceedings, 19th Coastal Engineering Conference, American Society of Civil Engineers, p. 415–434.

133. Sawhney, M. D., 1963, "A Study of Ocean Wave Amplitudes in Terms of the Theory of Runs and a Markov Chain Process," Technical Report, Department of Meterology and Oceanography, New York University, 29 pp.

134. Saville, T., Jr., 1954, "North Atlantic Coast Wave Statistics Hindcast by the Bretschneider-Revised Sverdrup-Munk Method," U.S. Army Corps of Engineers, Beach Erosion Board, Tech. Memo. No. 55, 18 pp + app. (H-003; M-006).

135. Scott, J. R., 1965, "A Sea Spectrum for Model Tests and Long-Term Ship Prediction," *J. Ship Research*, Vol. 9, No. 3.

136. Scott, D. W. and Thompson, J. R., 1983, "Probability Density Estimation in Higher Dimensions," *Computer Science and Statistics*, Netherlands, North-Holland Publishing Company, pp. 173–179.

137. Smith, O. P., 1987, "Duration of Extreme Wave Conditions," Miscellaneous Paper CERC-87-12, U.S. Army Engineer Waterways Experiment Station, Vicksburg, MS, 138 pp.

138. Smith, O, P., 1988, "Duration of Extreme Wave Conditions," *J. Waterway, Port, Coastal and Ocean Engineering*, American Society of Civil Engineers, Vol. 114, No. 1, pp. 1–17.

139. Smith, H. U. and Munk, W. H., 1947. "Wind, Sea, and Swell: Theory of Relationships for Forecasting, U.S. Navy Hydrographic Office, Pub. No. 601, pp. 44.

140. Szabados, M. W., Esteva, D. C., 1983, "Comparison of Offshore Wave Measurements," *IEEE J. Oceanic Engineering*, Vol. OE-8, No. 4 (October) pp. 206–211.

141. Tapia, R. A. and Thompson, J. R., 1978, *Nonparametric Probability Density Estimation*, The Johns Hopkins University Press, Baltimore, MD.

142. Tayfun, M. A., 1983, "Effect of Spectrum Band Width on the Distribution of Wave Heights and Periods, *J. Ocean Engineering*, No. 2, pp. 107–118.

143. Thom, C. S., 1973, "Extreme Wave Height Distributions Over Oceans," Proc. American Society of Civil Engineers, Vol. 99, No. WW3 (August).

144. Thomas, H. A., Jr., 1948, "Frequency of Minor Floods," *J. Boston Society Civil Engineers*, pp. 35:425.

145. Thompson, E. F. and Harris, D. L., 1972, "A Wave Climatology for U.S. Coastal Waters," Proceedings, Offshore Technology Conference, OTC 1693, Houston, TX.

146. Thompson, E. F., 1977, "Wave Climate at Selected Locations Along U.S. Coasts," Technical Report No. 77-1, U.S. Army Corps of Engineers, Coastal Engineering Research Center, Fort Belvoir, VA, 364 pp.

147. Thompson E. F., 1979, "Shallow Water Surface Wave Elevation Distributions," Report NO. CERC-REPRINT-80-1, 6 pp. U.S. Army Corps of Engineers, Coastal Engineering Research Center, Fort Belvoir, VA, also in *J. Waterway, Port, Coastal and Ocean Division*, Proceedings, American Society of Civil Engineers, Vol. 106, No. WW2, pp. 285–289 (May 1980) (M-044).

148. Thompson, E. F., 1980, "Energy Spectra in Shallow U.S. Coastal Waters," U.S. Army Corps of Engineers, Coastal Engineering Research Center, Fort Belvoir, VA, Report No. CERC-TP-80-2, 154 pp. (M-039).

149. Thompson, E. and Vincent, C., 1983, "Prediction of Wave Height in Shallow Water," Proceedings, Coastal Structures 83, American Society of Civil Engineers, New York, pp. 1000–1008.

150. Thompson, W. and Reynolds, F. M., 1977, "Ocean Wave Statistics From Fleet Numerical Weather Central Spectral Analysis," Fleet Numerical Weather Central, T.N. 77-2, Monterey, CA.

151. Tracy, B. A., 1982, "Theory and Calculation of the Nonlinear Energy Transfer Between Sea Waves in Deepwater," WIS Report 11 (May). U.S. Army Engineer Waterways Experiment Station, Vicksburg, MS.

152. Uhlenbeck, G. E., 1943, "Theory of Random Processes," MIT Radiation Lab Report, 454 pp.

153. United States Navy., 1959, "Climatological and Oceanographic Atlas for Mariners," Vol. I, North Atlantic Ocean, U.S. Navy, Division of Oceanography, Washington, D.C., 7 pp. + 182 charts (S-012).

154. United States Navy., 1963, "Oceanographic Atlas of the North Atlantic Ocean, Section

IV, Sea and Swell," Naval Oceanographic Office, Washington, D.C., Publication No. 700 (S-016).

155. United States Navy., 1970, "Summary of Synoptic Meteorological Observations (SSMO) for North American Coastal Marine Areas, Set No. 11: North American Coastal Area," Areas 12–17; 19–21, Vol. 2–3, Naval Weather Service Environmental Detachment, Asheville, NC (S-005).

156. United States Navy., 1974, "U.S. Navy Marine Climatic Atlas of the World, Volume 1, North Atlantic Ocean," NAVAIR Report 50-1C-528, Naval Weather Service Command, National Climatic Center, Asheville, NC (S-017).

157. United States Navy., 1976, "Climatic Study of the Near Coastal Zone: East Coast of the United States," Naval Weather Service Detachment, National Climatic Center, Asheville, NC, 137 pp. (S-011).

158. United States Navy., 1981, "Marine Climatic Atlas of the World, Volume 1, World-Wide Means and Standard Deviations," Naval Air Systems Command, Washington, D.C., Report No. NAVAIR-50-1C-65-VOL-9, 355 pp. (S-018). Van Heteren, J., Bruinsma, J. 1981. "A Method to Calculate the Probability of Exceedance of the Design Wave Height," *J. Coastal Engineering*, 5, pp. 83–91.

159. Venezian, G., 1983, personal communication.

160. Venezian, G., Bretschneider, C. L., and Jagannathan, S., 1980, "Cumulative Distribution of Forces on Structures Subjected to the Combined Action of Currents and Random Waves for Potential OTEC Sites," Vol. III, U. of Hawaii, Look Lab Report 80-1, 244 pp.

161. Wik, I. and Houmb, O. G., 1976, "Wave Statistics at Utsira With Special Reference to Duration and Frequency of Storms," Report by The Ship Research Institute of Norway and The Division of Port and Ocean Eng., The Norway Institute of Technology.

162. Vincent, C. L. and Lichy, D. E., 1981, "Wave Measurements in ARSLOE," Proceedings, Conference on Directional Wave Spectra Applications, pp. 71–86.

163. Walker, R. E., 1976, "Wave Statistics for the North Atlantic—1970," Bedford Institute of Oceanography, Atlantic Oceanographic Laboratory, Dartmouth, Nova Scotia, Report BI-D-76-3, 228 pp. (S-008).

164. Wang, W. C., 1979, "Applications of Beta Distribution Function on the Statistics of Wave Height," Master Thesis, National Cheng Kung University, Tainan City, Taiwan, (in Chinese).

165. Ward, E. G., Evans, D. J., and Pompa, J. A., 1978, "Extreme Wave Heights Along the Atlantic Coast of the United States," *J. Petroleum Technology*, pp. 1697–1705 (H-008).

166. Wiegel, R. L., 1975, "Design of Offshore Structures Using Wave Spectra," Proceedings, Oceanology International, Brighton, United Kingdom (March).

167. Wilson, J. R. and Baird, W. F., 1972, "A Discussion of Some Measured Wave Data, Proceedings, 13th Conference on Coastal Engineering, Vancouver, pp. 113–130.

168. Woodfield, T. J., 1982, "Statistical Modeling of Bivariate Data," Technical Report B-7, Inst. Stat., Texas A&M University, 263 pp.

169. Wooding, R. A., 1955, "An Approximate Joint Probability Distribution for Amplitude and Frequency in Random Noise," N.Z.J. Sci. Tech., Section B, 36, pp. 537–544.

170. Yamada, H. and Shiotani, T., 1968, "On the Highest Water Waves of Permanent Type, Bull. Disaster Prevention Research Institute, Kyoto University, Vol. 18, Part 2, No. 135, pp. 1–22.

171. Yamazaki, H. and Herbich, J. B., 1985a, "Non-Parametric and Parametric Estimation of Wave Statistics and Spectra," Texas A&M University Sea Grant Program, TAMU-SG-86-202.

172. Yamazaki, H. and Herbich, J. B., 1985b, "Monthly Wave Characteristics, National Oceanographic Data Center," Volumes I–III, Texas A&M University Sea Grant Program, TAMU-SG-86-205.

173. Yamazaki, H. and Herbich, J. B., 1985c, "Determination of Wave Height Spectrum by Means of Joint Probability Density Function," *J. Geophysical Research*, Vol. 90, No. C2, pp. 3381–3390.

174. Yang, C. Y., Tayfun, M. A., and Hsiao, G. C., 1974, "Extreme Wave Statistics for Delaware Coastal Waters," paper presented at the American Society of Civil Engineers International Symposium on Ocean Wave Measurement and Analysis, New Orleans, LA, pp. 352–361 (S-009; H-020).

175. U.S. Army Corps of Engineers, 1984, *Shore Protection Manual*, Waterways Experiment Station, Coastal Engineering Research Center, Vicksburg, MS.

CHAPTER 9

TIDES AND STORM SURGES

Robert O. Reid

Distinguished Professor
Department of Oceanography
Texas A&M University
College Station, Texas, U.S.A.

CONTENTS

Introduction

This chapter addresses that portion of the spectrum of water level variations having periods of several hours to several months, with primary focus on those changes caused by astronomically-induced forcing and meteorologically-induced forcing (winds and barometric pressure changes). The term water level (ζ) as employed here is defined as the elevation of the water surface (a) at a given location, (b) for a given time, (c) after removal of variations having periods less than one hour, and (d) referenced to a specified local, continental or global datum. In general, ζ varies with location and time at scales greater than those of surface wind waves, swell, surf beat and tsunamis; moreover it is a relative quantity whose value depends on the adopted datum.

The ideal datum surface to which local water level (ζ) is referenced is one for which the horizontal gradient of ζ times local gravity is a true measure of the gravitationally-induced slope force per unit mass. Such an ideal datum is the geoidal datum surface (or constant geopotential surface). It is a surface everywhere exactly normal to the local value of Earth's effective gravity. Like an inertial reference frame it can be *defined* precisely; but is difficult to implement in terms of physical bench marks for precise measurement. This is particularly true for regions of open water that are not connected by continental land masses and beyond the horizon of any precise line-of-sight geodetic survey technique.

Time variations of water level at given locations can be measured (or inferred from bottom pressure variations) with considerable precision at time scales of hours to months. However, determining absolute water level as referenced to the geoidal datum surface is difficult to achieve with an accuracy required for the evaluation of gravitational slope forces (an exception is for slopes associated with river flow). For large continental shelf and ocean domains, one must rely instead on physically well-founded mathematical models of tides, surges and associated currents to supply an absolute reference by which to relate water levels, and use the measurement of the temporal variations of water level and possibly of currents to supply the means of verification.

The importance of a knowledge of tides and surges is obvious for navigation and berthing of vessels in harbors. The relevance to engineers in the design of protective sea walls and offshore oil platforms is likewise clear, particularly when one bears in mind that during periods of increased water level a higher energy level of short-period surface waves can reach and impact on such structures.

In the sections to follow the primary focus, while confined to tides and surges of long periods, does recognize that there exist some dynamic coupling effects between the long-period and superimposed short-period waves. This is manifested in three ways: (a) short surface waves exert a control on the rate at which momentum is transferred to the water by winds (part of which drives the short waves and part the development of storm surge); (b) the presence of surface waves superimposed on long-period tide or surge can magnify the long-period signal of bottom stress; and (c) short-period waves are associated with the phenomena of radiation stress that can produce an added component of surge near shore (wave set-up) as well as producing littoral currents. These phenomena are at spatial scales that are difficult to resolve in numerical models of tides and storm surges, and their effect is generally incorporated in some parameterized manner, at least with respect to items (a) and (b).

Water Level References and Measurements

The only absolute global datum, which is independent of location and time, is Earth's center of mass, a reference important in describing the orbital path of any Earth-captured satellite (including the moon). In geodesy, the global datum is a hypothetical closed surface (the geoid) whose geocentric radius depends on latitude and longitude. It is a surface of constant geopotential (Φ) the gradient of which is everywhere parallel to the local plumbline and whose magnitude equals the local value of gravity (g). Over the oceanic regions the geoid would correspond to the sea surface *if* the ocean and atmosphere were exactly at rest relative to Earth. The shape of the geoid depends on the distribution of Earth's mass and angular velocity and can be estimated from gravity measurements and/or from satellite altimetry of the ocean surface. The first approximation of the geoid is a spheroid of revolution whose equatorial radius is about 21,500 m greater than its polar radius. Variations of the more precise geoid, relative to the latter spheroid, have elevational variations of order $\pm$ 100 m on horizontal scales of the order of several thousand kilometers to a few meters on horizontal scales of hundreds of kilometers. The geoid can also vary with time due to variations in the configuration of the Earth's mass and its associated effect on the Earth's gravitational field. Of those long-term global processes, climatic warming and the associated melting of glaciers is the most relevant in concerns about increasing trends in the variation of the geoidal datum [47]. However, the most important time variations of the geoid in ocean tidal dynamics are the small amplitude variations occurring on time and space scales comparable to those of the astronomical forcing; these are caused by the elastic distortions of the lithosphere (Earth tide).

The reference datum obviously plays a vital role in the definition of absolute water level. Over the open ocean, there presently exist three ways of estimating water-level variations on time scales of 12 hours to several months: (a) satellite altimetry, (b) benthic pressure gauges, and (c) inverted echo sounders. The first is presently limited to an accuracy of about 10 cm for the measurement of time-varying signals of order 1 m, in a background of geoidal variations that are much larger; the latter can be subtracted out effectively only for exact repeat orbits like GEOSAT. Benthic pressure gauges mounted on the seabed in depths of 5,000 meters measure variations of pressure whose translation into equivalent variation of water level, via the hydrostatic equation, requires a knowledge of atmospheric pressure variations at the sea surface for the same location and a knowledge of the density distribution within the water column. The datum for such gauges is the seabed elevation whose value relative to the local mean sea level is known only to an accuracy of ± 10 m at best. Because of their great depth, pressure gauges filter out the effect of short-period waves (those less than about 1 minute). However they can yield reliable estimates of the diurnal and semidiurnal tidal amplitudes (to within a few cm), because their datum (while unknown) is fixed at least on time scales many times greater than these tidal periods. Inverted echo sounders employ the same acoustic techniques as precision depth sounders, but are upward directed transducers mounted on the seafloor and monitor variations of the sea surface elevation averaged over the spatial beam width of the acoustic pulses.

The vast majority of water-level measurements are made using tide gauges at fixed locations near shorelines of continents and islands. Tide gauges employing stilling wells filter out the short-period waves like their benthic gauge counterparts. Each tide gauge station employs a *local* datum, normally taken as the mean-lower-low-water-elevation (MLLW) for the station. The latter is defined as the arithmetic mean of the lowest water levels occurring during a lunar day, averaged over a specific metonic cycle for that station. A metonic cycle is a period of 235 lunar months (about 19 solar years) which is the period required before the sequence of new and full moon exactly repeats itself on given days of the Gregorian calendar year (CY). This cycle is related to the precession of the plane of the lunar orbit relative to the Earth's orbit. The specific metonic cycle adopted by the National Ocean Survey (NOS) for establishing tide reference levels datums is called the National Tidal Datum Epoch (NTDE); the present NTDE is CY 1960 through 1978 inclusive.

Local MLLW references are useful for pilots of surface vessels in navigating near shore regions, inlet channels and harbors; it should be noted in particular that all navigational charts indicate bathymetry (depths) relative to the local MLLW data (or estimates thereof). A more useful datum for predicting tides and meteorologically-induced surges is the local mean sea level (MSL), which is defined as the arithmetic mean of all hourly water levels observed during an NTDE. Over such a period, virtually all tidally-induced variations and most meteorologically-induced variations are averaged out, leaving only the long-term (secular) trend.

For most mid-latitude and equatorial tide stations the trend from one NTDE/MSL to the next has been upward; while at high latitudes the trend is generally downward. The average rise per century at mid-latitudes varies considerably (10 to 100 cm) due to local or regional factors [47]. A rise in local MSL implies only that the local mean water level is increasing *relative* to local land level, based on gauges that are fixed relative to a nearby land-based benchmark. The melting of glaciers can explain the general global picture of trends (increasing amount of water added to the ocean at all latitudes, but with upward rebound of those continental areas supporting the glaciers). The anomalously high positive trends of MSL (like at Galveston, Texas or Venice, Italy) are no doubt due to land subsidence associated with depletion of ground water. Such local effects can be verified by repeated regional geodetic surveys or satellite altimetry in which local benchmark elevations can be determined relative to some common continental benchmark.

Even in the absence of (or correction for) secular vertical motions of the land relative to the Earth's center of mass, the local MSL values do not necessarily correspond to the same level geoidal reference surface. Indeed, in tidal estuaries like Delaware Bay or Chesapeake Bay the absolute mean water level is several centimeters higher on one side than the other; this is due to the combined effect of the net outward flow due to mean river discharge and the Earth's rotation (D. W. Pritchard, personal communication). This is aside from any longitudinal variation of absolute mean water level as would be required in a riverine system to balance the retarding stress due to the flow.

The difference of sea level between the Pacific coast and the Atlantic coast of the United States is even more dramatic: it averages about 70 cm based on geodetic surveys [69]. Two thirds of this difference can be explained by the fact that the Pacific Ocean is less salty than the Atlantic Ocean and hence stands higher because it's less density. The remaining difference is associated with the effect of the northward moving Gulf Stream off the eastern seaboard, which has lower water on its inshore side due to the rotation of the Earth.

Some Characteristics of Tidal Forcing

Because of the quasi-periodic and global scale character of the forcing, the astronomically-induced tides are the most regular and predictable of the water level variations in the ocean. Later sections will cover the quantitative aspects of tidal prediction. In this section some of the important conceptual aspects of tidal forcing and the response of an idealized ocean are highlighted. It necessarily involves the concepts of celestial mechanics.

The Newtonian attraction exerted by the sun and moon on Earth as a whole produces an acceleration of Earth's center that controls its orbit in the solar system; the orbit lies in a plane containing the sun's center of mass known as the ecliptic plane. The attractive force acting on a unit mass of the ocean facing the sun (or moon) is larger than that acting on a unit mass at the antipode position (diametrically opposite point of the globe), because of the different distances from the attracting body. The effective tide-producing force per unit mass is the difference between the attractive force by the sun (or moon) and the acceleration of Earth's center (the acceleration related to Earth's spin being accounted for in the effective gravitational force of Earth). Because the acceleration of Earth's center is the same as the attractive force per unit mass by the sun (or moon) at that point, and because Earth's radius is small compared with the distance to the sun (or moon), the result is that the same *net outward* effective force occurs at the point facing the sun (or moon) *and* at its antipode. At every point on Earth 90° arclength from these points, the net effective force is inwards; and halfway between these extremes the net force is nearly tangential to the geoid. The overall effect on a deep hypothetical ocean that covers the globe would be to produce a configuration of the fluid surface that resembles a football with the elongated axis directed towards the attracting body. The difference in water level from that of the geoid for this hypothetical ocean is called the *equilibrium tide*; its maximum value is less than one meter for the sun or moon.

Now imagine a solar system in which the centers of Earth, moon, and sun all lie in the same plane *and* where Earth's axis is perpendicular to the ecliptic plane.

For such a system, each new moon represents a total eclipse of the sun by the moon, and each full moon is culminated by its eclipse by Earth. Assume Earth's spin and orbit speeds are the same as the real solar system. In such a hypothetical system, with a hypothetical ocean covering the globe, the solar-induced water-level variation at some fixed point on the globe would have a period of exactly 12 solar hours while the lunar-induced water-level change would have a period of exactly 12 lunar hours (i.e., half the time interval between successive culminations of the sun or moon, respectively, at the chosen point on the globe). The maximum amplitude for this hypothetical tide scenario would occur at the equator and be zero at the poles. There would exist no diurnal tide and virtually no long-period tide. However, because of the changing position of the moon relative to the Earth-sun line, there would exist a fortnightly (14-day) variation of the tidal amplitude at a given location on Earth. Maximum amplitude would occur when Earth, moon, and sun are colinear (new or "full" moon) and minimum amplitude would occur when the moon is at quadrature with the Earth-sun (i.e., when the moon is exactly half illuminated by the sun). These extremes in amplitude occur also for the real world and are called spring and neap tides; note that the time interval between these extremes is about 7 days. It is important to emphasize that the fortnightly variation in amplitude (or amplitude modulation) is phase locked to the lunar orbit relative to the Earth-sun line.

Now consider some of the complications introduced by the real solar system. Most important is the tilt of Earth's spin axis away from perpendicular to the ecliptic plane, the tilt being 23.5°. Because the spin axis is nearly invariant in its orientation during an annual orbit cycle, the apparent declination of the sun (i.e., its latitude relative to Earth's equatorial plane) varies through a range of $\pm 23.5°$, thus producing the different thermal seasons. And while there does in fact exist a slow precession of the spin axis, our adopted Gregorian calendar is phase locked to the time of the vernal equinox (zero declination), rather than the time of perigee (minimum solar distance).

The time-varying declination of the sun (or of moon as well) introduces two additional nominal periods of the tide. With no tilt there are two potential high tides of equal magnitude per lunar or solar day; with tilt the two highs are of different magnitude and the cycle must be represented as the sum of a semidiurnal and a diurnal component. Also the tilt not only produces thermal seasons but also long-period components of the tide: annual and semiannual for solar tides and lunar monthly and fortnightly for lunar tides. The latter should not be confused with the fortnightly modulation produced by successive reinforcement or beating due to the combination of solar and lunar tides. The long-period tides have a period governed by the periodic variation of the solar or lunar declinations and are therefore also called declinational tides. Remember, however, that the declination is also responsible for producing the diurnal component.

Another effect of Earth's tilt (or equivalently solar declination) is that the semidiurnal solar forcing is a maximum at the time of the equinoxes (while the diurnal forcing vanishes at those times). This implies that at the time of a new or full moon closest to that of one of the equinoxes (spring or autumnal), the fortnightly spring tide should be at a maximum.

A third fact that complicates matters is that the lunar orbit does not lie in the ecliptic plane, but is inclined by about 5° from that plane. Thus, while the solar declination has a range of ±23.5°, the lunar declination has a maximum range of about ±28.5°. Moreover, a consequence of the lunar tilt off the ecliptic plane is that the sun exerts a torque on the Earth-moon bodies as a pair and causes a precession of the axis of the lunar orbit having a period of about 19 years (the Metonic cycle). This effect produces a modulation of the maximum declination of the moon with a range of about 10° (18.5° to 28.5°) and a period of 19 years between greatest declination. This in turn causes a modulation of the lunar forcing having the same period.

A fourth complicating factor is the variable Earth-sun distance and Earth-moon distance. The percent variation is greatest for the lunar orbit because of its greater eccentricity. Moreover, the position of lunar perigee, like the line of intersection of the lunar orbit with the ecliptic plane (line of nodes), rotates slowly with time but with a different period from that of the Metonic cycle. All these different factors conspire to make the tidal forcing almost but not exactly periodic, but nevertheless as predictable as the motion of the planets.

The last celestial mechanics type phenomenon mentioned in this overview of tide related factors is Earth's wobble. This is a free or natural precessional perturbation of the angular velocity of Earth relative to its geometrical axis of symmetry. Like a spinning ballistic missile or satellite that has an axis of symmetry (i.e., departing from an exact sphere), it can wobble. Observational evidence for Earth's wobble relies on precise measurements of the apparent oscillation of stars (e.g., the North Star). The magnitude in terms of arc distance is extremely small as one might expect, because of the minimal external impulses that might excite and maintain the wobble (random meteorite impact perhaps). The important observational fact established by Chandler and confirmed by Jeffreys [31] is the wobble period of 14.4 months. Many generations prior to these observations, Euler set forth a theoretical relation for the wobble period of a *rigid* spheroid of revolution having a prescribed spin velocity. Application of Euler's relation to Earth, assuming that it acts like a rigid body, gives a period of 10.0 months. The ratio of Euler's period to observed period of wobble is 0.69, which is a global measure of the effective rigidity of the Earth (unity being absolutely rigid). This factor plays an important role in determining the effective tidal forcing as will be discussed in a subsequent section. In particular Earth tides can exist because Earth is elastic rather than rigid, and the tidal deformations, while small, are enough to significantly alter the field of gravity on time and space scales comparable to those of the external forcing.

Tides of the Real Ocean

The most profound factor governing tidal response, aside from the effective tidal forcing, is the actual morphology of the world oceans, i.e., the continental boundary configuration and the bathymetry within each of the interconnected ocean basins and their marginal seas. Because of the boundary constraints, the actual response of the water level to the tidal forcing differs considerably from that of the equilibrium tide, with possible exception of the very long period declinational tides. The configuration of certain basins can amplify the tidal amplitude if the natural period of oscillation is close to that of the tidal forcing. This occurs notably in marginal regions having relatively shallow depths; examples are the Bay of Fundy, Bristol Bay in England, and Cook Inlet in Alaska. In larger marginal seas like the Mediter-

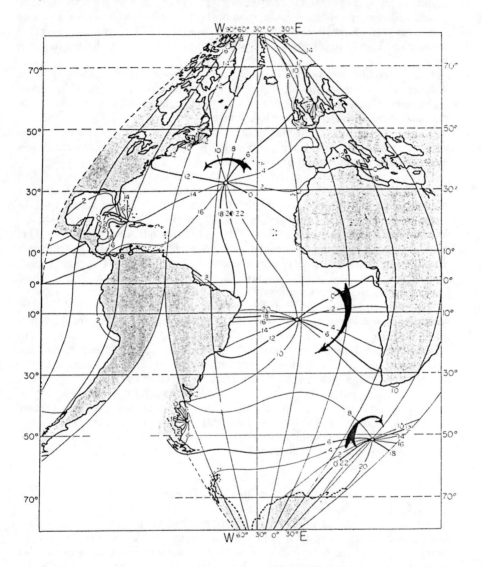

Figure 1. Diurnal luni-solar (K_1) cotidal lines (in solar hours GMT) for the Atlantic Ocean as interpreted by Dietrich [13]; figure adapted from Chart II of Defant [11].

ranean and the Gulf of Mexico the tidal response is small because of their relative isolation.

The general picture of tidal response for the large ocean basins is one in which the largest amplitudes occur generally along the coastlines with small amplitudes in the ocean interior. There exist certain locations (amphidromic points) in the basins where the tidal amplitude is zero and the tide in the region surrounding these points propagates in a rotary manner either clockwise or counterclockwise. Figure 1 shows the cotidal lines for the K_1 tide (one of the diurnal tidal constituents) in the Atlantic Ocean, as analyzed by Dietrich [13]. The cotidal tides are phase lines indicating the relative time at which high tide occurs for that constituent. For the K1 tide one notes three central basin amphidromic points, one in the North Atlantic and two in the South Atlantic. In the northern hemisphere the tide propagates counterclockwise, the high water level occurring first along the coast of Europe and later along the coast of North America. The sense of propagation is reversed for the southern hemisphere amphidromic systems, but both are consistent with the concept of Kelvin wave dynamics, in which Earth rotation plays an important role.

Figures 2 to 4 give example predicted tidal hydrographs for selected one month periods at three selected locations for the coast of North America. The water level

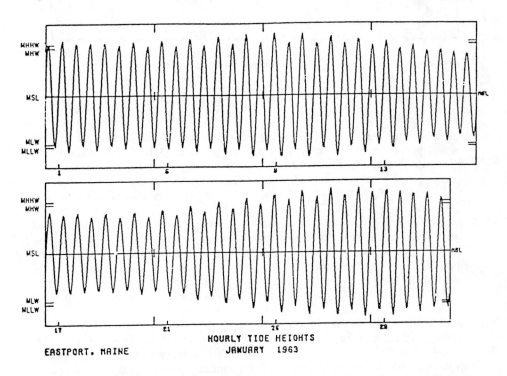

Figure 2. Predicted hourly tidal water level relative to MSL for the month of January 1963 at Eastport, Maine; values of MHHW, MHW, MLW and MLLW can be found in Table 1 [24].

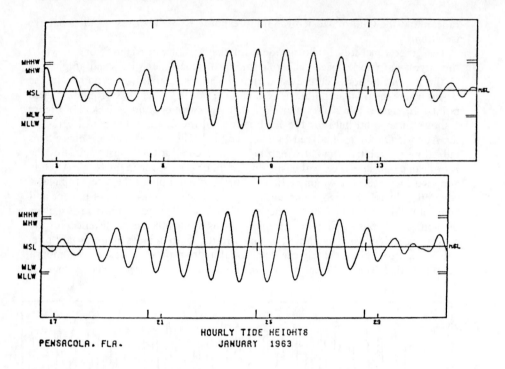

Figure 3. As in Figure 2 for January 1963 at Pensacola, Florida [24].

scale indicates the values of the local references such as MSL, MLLW (defined earlier) plus mean low water (MLW), mean high water (MHW), and mean higher high water (MHHW). The values of these references, along with other statistical quantities are listed in Table 1 for all NOS tide stations in the United States (see Harris [24] for further details). The mean ranges vary from less than 1 ft (0.3 m) at Galveston to about 26 ft (7.9 m) at Anchorage. Each of the figures shows a clear modulation of the water-level range with two maxima of range about fourteen days apart, which occur at times of new and full moon. Figure 2 for Eastport, Maine shows a predominantly semidiurnal signal, while Figure 3 for Pensacola, Florida shows a diurnal signal. Humbolt Bay, California (Figure 4) shows a mixed signal with two unequal highs and two unequal lows per lunar day.

The tides in the Gulf of Mexico, while small in amplitude compared with those on the east and west coasts of North America, are somewhat unique because of the ambivalent character of their forcing. The observations show a sharp change in the character of the tides between the west coast of Florida and the rest of the Gulf, the change occurring at Cape San Blas. The tide is predominantly diurnal (like that at Pensacola) west of Cape San Blas and predominantly semidiurnal east and south of that cape (see Figure 5 for locations of key points in Gulf). Moreover, the greatest semidiurnal amplitude occurs just east of Cape San Blas at Cedar Key in the West

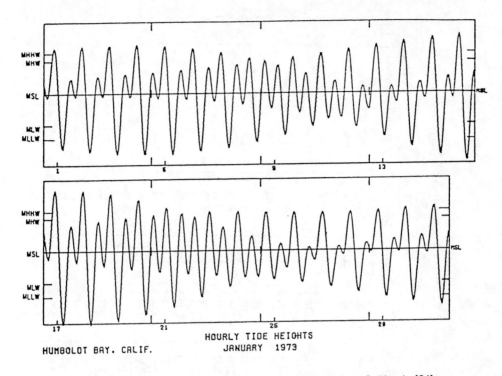

Figure 4. As in Figure 2 for January 1973 at Humbolt Bay, California [24].

Florida Bight. Also in contrast to the spatially varying amplitude and phase of the semidiurnal tide along the west Florida shelf, the diurnal tide is nearly uniform in amplitude and phase throughout the Gulf (with the exception of the region near the Yucatan Channel and Florida Strait).

This unusual character of the Gulf tides can be explained in terms of the nature of the forcing, the bathymetry of the west Florida shelf, and verified via a numerical model. The diurnal tide is forced primarily by in-phase volume transport into (or out of) the Gulf through the two open channels; it is a co-oscillation driven by the diurnal tide in the adjacent Atlantic Ocean and Caribbean Sea. The semidiurnal tide in the Gulf is driven primarily within the Gulf by the direct action of the astronomical forcing. This is made feasible by the circumstance that the west Florida shelf has just the right configuration to allow a natural period close to 12 hours [59, 60].

Non-Tidal Water-Level Variations

The observed water level from tide gauges in general differs from that of the predicted astronomically-induced tide. The differences can be attributed to a variety of natural causes that fall in three categories: (a) those of tectonic origin; (b) those

Table 1
Computed Data, Ranges, and Standard Deviations Referred to MSL [24]

Station	Standard Deviation	MHHW	MHW	MLW	MLLW	Mean Range[1] Observed	Mean Range[1] Computed	Diurnal Range[1] Observed	Diurnal Range[1] Computed
Eastport	6.32	9.32	8.88	−9.01	−9.41	18.20	17.89		18.73
Portland	3.24	4.87	4.45	−4.46	−4.80	9.00	8.91		9.68
Boston	3.40	5.16	4.72	−4.86	−5.19	9.50	9.58		10.35
Newport	1.33	2.18	1.93	−1.69	−1.75	3.50	3.62		3.93
New London	0.94	1.48	1.22	−1.34	−1.45	2.60	2.56		2.93
Bridgeport	2.41	3.61	3.31	−3.36	−3.52	6.70	6.67		7.13
Willets Point	2.68	3.85	3.59	−3.58	−3.78	7.10	7.17		7.65
New York (The Battery)	1.65	2.51	2.19	−2.29	−2.42	4.50	4.48		4.94
Albany	1.70	2.76	2.32	−2.51	−2.65	4.60	4.83		5.40
Sandy Hook	1.70	2.66	2.33	−2.34	−2.47	4.60	4.67		5.13
Atlantic City	1.52	2.41	2.01	−2.07	−2.18	4.10	4.08		4.59
Breakwater Harbor	1.53	2.46	2.04	−2.08	−2.15	4.10	4.20		4.60
Reedy Point	1.96	3.07	2.73	−2.77	−2.85	5.50	5.51		5.92
Philadelphia	2.04	3.15	2.82	−3.09	−3.17	5.90	5.91		6.33
Baltimore	0.51	0.74	0.51	−0.52	−0.64	1.10	1.03		1.38
Washington	1.02	1.54	1.39	−1.37	−1.42	2.90	2.76		2.96
Hampton Roads	0.92	1.41	1.22	−1.22	−1.26	2.50	2.44		2.67
Wilmington	1.51	2.26	2.02	−2.24	−2.33	4.20	4.26		4.59
Charleston	1.88	2.87	2.50	−2.67	−2.81	5.20	5.17		5.69
Savannah River Entrance	2.52	3.77	3.38	−3.56	−3.70	6.90	6.94		7.48
Savannah	2.73	4.07	3.65	−3.96	−4.12	7.40	7.61		8.19
Mayport	1.66	2.49	2.20	−2.27	−2.38	4.50	4.46		4.87
Miami Harbor Entrance	0.95	1.33	1.26	−1.26	−1.40	2.50	2.52		2.74
Key West	0.58	0.92	0.63	−0.64	−0.88	1.30	1.26		1.80
Naples	0.94	1.30	1.03	−1.07	−1.69	2.10	2.10	2.80	2.99
St. Petersburg	0.71	1.04	0.72	−0.70	−1.14		1.42	2.30	2.19
St. Marks River Entrance	1.09	1.51	1.23	−1.18	−1.86	2.40	2.41	3.30	3.37
Pensacola	0.54	0.67	0.61	−0.57	−0.63		1.18	1.30	1.30

Station									
Mobile	0.58	0.73	0.65	−0.62	−0.70		1.27	1.50	1.44
Galveston (ship channel)	0.53	0.57	0.47	−0.44	−0.85		0.91	1.40	1.42
San Juan	0.54	0.87	0.57	−0.58	−0.79	1.10	1.15		1.66
San Diego	1.81	2.90	2.11	−2.09	−3.06	4.10	4.20	5.70	5.96
Los Angeles (Outer Harbor)	1.66	2.63	1.91	−1.87	−2.82	3.80	3.78	5.40	5.45
San Francisco (Golden Gate)	1.75	2.59	2.04	−1.93	−3.14	4.00	3.97	5.70	5.73
Humboldt	1.93	2.97	2.26	−2.24	−3.44	4.50	4.50	6.40	6.40
Crescent City	2.12	3.22	2.56	−2.49	−3.75	5.10	5.04	6.90	6.97
South Beach	2.57	3.88	3.17	−3.09	−4.48	6.30	6.26	8.30	8.36
Astoria	2.53	3.98	3.28	−3.19	−4.38	6.50	6.47	8.20	8.37
Aberdeen	2.99	4.54	3.74	−4.03	−5.35	7.90	7.77	10.10	9.89
Pt Townsend	2.66	3.40	2.74	−2.31	−4.80	5.10	5.04	8.30	8.20
Seattle	3.50	4.83	3.94	−3.75	−6.48	7.60	7.69	11.30	11.31
Friday Harbor	2.55	3.23	2.51	−2.17	−4.55	4.50	4.68	7.70	7.78
Ketchikan	4.91	7.36	6.46	−6.47	−8.02	13.00	12.92	15.40	15.38
Juneau	5.31	7.82	6.93	−7.10	−8.72	13.80	14.03	16.40	16.54
Sitka	3.11	4.69	3.92	−3.86	−5.32	7.70	7.77	9.90	10.01
Cordova	3.85	5.81	4.88	−5.03	−6.51	10.10	9.90	12.40	12.31
Seldovia	5.89	8.48	7.70	−7.81	−9.55	15.40	15.51	17.80	18.04
Anchorage	9.01	12.73	11.99	−13.90	−16.18	26.10	25.88	29.00	28.90
Kodiak	2.71	4.29	3.40	−3.39	−4.54	6.60	6.80	8.50	8.83
Dutch Harbor	1.24	1.52	1.21	−1.07	−2.17	2.20	2.28	3.70	3.69
Sweeper Cove	1.40	1.63	1.29	−1.40	−2.26		2.69	3.70	3.89
Massacre Bay	1.19	1.40	1.10	−1.02	−2.01		2.12	3.30	3.41
Nushagak	5.94	9.42	7.46	−7.78	−10.26	15.30	15.24	19.50	19.68
St. Michael	1.24	1.94	1.39	−1.29	−1.64		2.68	3.90	3.58
Honolulu	0.60	1.08	0.58	−0.65	−0.81	1.20	1.23	1.90	1.89

1 Observed values for both mean and diurnal range are not available for all stations.

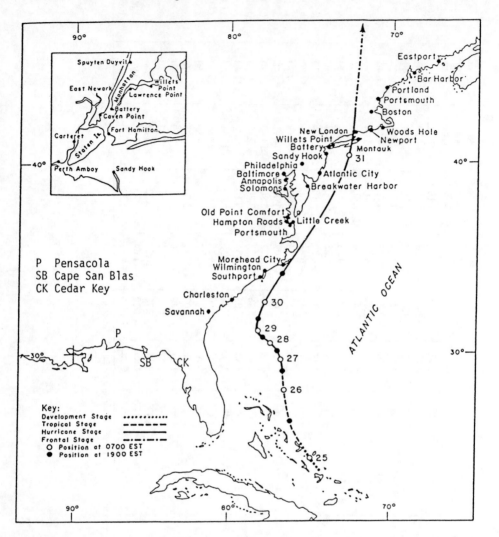

Figure 5. Storm track for hurricane Carol, 27–31 August 1954. Inset map for New York harbor shows locations of additional tide stations supplementing those from Savannah to Eastport [8, 23].

of oceanographic origin; (c) those of meteorological or climatic origin. Category a includes disturbances generated by volcanic eruptions, earthquakes or mudslides that can generate tsunamis having periods from several minutes to about an hour. This subject is treated in Chapter 10. Category b includes water-level variations associated with changes in ocean currents; for example, shifts in the position of a major current like the Gulf Stream or the Loop Current in the Gulf of Mexico, or the migration of cold core or warm core mesoscale eddies towards or away from the continental shelf. The relation to water level is associated with the geostrophic slope of the sea surface, which is governed by the current and the rotation of Earth. These changes can occur without any direct, local meteorological excitation, although the ocean circulation in a global and long-term sense is driven by the climatic wind regime. Category c includes all water-level variations that can be related directly to daily changes in weather conditions, seasonal changes in climate, and long-term climatic changes.

For the Atlantic Ocean and Gulf of Mexico coastal regions the primary non-tidal contribution to water-level variations is due to tropical and extratropical storms (category c), while for the west coast of United States, tsunamis (although rare) have largest impact on water level and potential flooding of lowlands other than tide. Category b has smaller impact on water level than either a or c and, like seasonal thermal effects, are of relatively long time scales (months). The more important impact of oceanographic eddies in engineering design considerations is in respect to currents; such eddies in the North Atlantic or Gulf of Mexico can move onto the continental slope with surface currents > 1 m/s. They are clearly important in deepwater oil platform design and operation. But it is well beyond the scope of this chapter to explore category b further; the reader can find further information on that subject in the proceedings of a recent symposium dealing with the Gulf of Mexico [42]. The remainder of this section focuses on category c.

Figures 6 and 7 shows water-level records over two selected two-month periods for Galveston, Texas; these are based on actual observations in which the semidiurnal

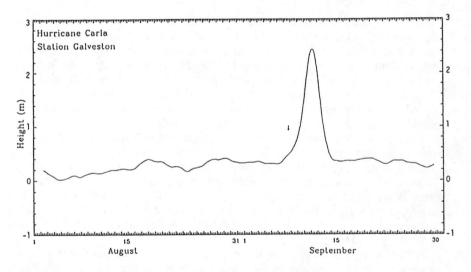

Figure 6. Sample non-tidal water level record at Galveston, Texas, for the two-month period August/September 1961, in which the tide has been removed by a 40-hr low pass filter. The arrow indicates the time at which the center of hurricane Carla entered the Gulf of Mexico. The datum is MSL for the 1941–1959 NTDE [2].

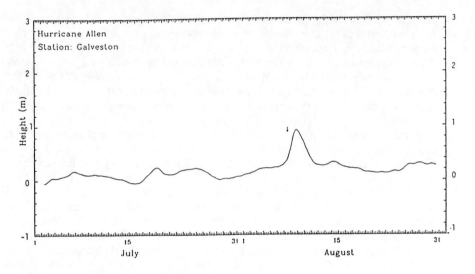

Figure 7. As in Figure 6 for July/August 1980 at Galveston and with MSL datum for the 1960–1978 NTDE [2]. The arrow indicates the time at which the center of hurricane Allen entered the Gulf of Mexico.

and diurnal tides have been removed by a 40-hr low-pass filter (the datum in each case has been taken as the MSL for the NTDE just prior to the year of the record). Each two-month sample was selected to include a major hurricane event: Carla whose center entered the Gulf of Mexico through Yucatan Channel on September 7, 1961; and Allen whose center also entered the Gulf near the same location on August 7, 1980. The landfall for Carla was somewhat west of Galveston, while that for Allen was near Brownsville at the boundary with Mexico. These figures demonstrate several features of the non-tidal water-level signal.

First of all, both records show moderate background variations (aside from the hurricane signal) having a spectral range of period from a few days to a few weeks, which can be attributed to either normal changes in wind patterns or to changes in offshore circulation or both. Secondly, the two-month average level for both periods is about 0.25 m higher than the MSL for the prior NTDE. About 0.15 m is due to the seasonal rise associated with thermal expansion, which is greatest at the end of August. The remainder is probably the secular rise that has occurred from the prior MSL.

A third feature of these example sequences is the expected fact that the greatest water-level response to the hurricane is near (and to the right of landfall); the greatest surge for Allen is somewhat north of Brownsville (not shown here). The last and most intriguing feature is that the apparent hurricane-induced rise in water level seems to start at (or even before!) the time at which the hurricane entered the Gulf; this is the case for both events. This feature tends to be exaggerated due to the 40-hr filtering of the original record; had the predicted tide been subtracted, the initial rise would start somewhat later (about 1 day perhaps). Nevertheless, the observations highlight the possible Gulf-wide response to a hurricane.

Figures 5 and 8 show the effects of a hurricane along the eastern coast of the United States as analyzed by Harris [23]. The first figure shows the track of hurricane Carol in August 1954 and the second figure shows water-level hydrographs at many different stations, after subtracting the predicted tide for the station. Some of the records, notably in the New York Bight, show a continuing but damped oscillation following the initial surge. The greatest surge occurred at Woods Hole on Cape Cod just to the right of landfall. In general the response to the left of the storm during its journey along the coastal region was much less pronounced than that which occurred at its final landfall near Montauk Point, Long Island.

There are four basic mechanisms for surge development at or near the shoreline: (a) inverted barometer effect, (b) set-up due to onshore winds, (c) geostrophic tilt due to alongshore currents driven by alongshore wind, and (d) wave set-up. The inverted barometer effect is the tendency for the water surface to be sucked upwards in regions of low atmospheric pressure; it can account for not more than about 1 m of rise centered at the storm center and depends directly on the central pressure deficit relative to normal sea-level pressure. It is equally effective over deep or shallow water provided that the water domain is large compared with the scale of the storm. Set-up by onshore wind stress is most effective in shallow water and depends directly on the wind stress, the distance over which it acts, and inversely on the depth. Longshore wind stress can generate longshore current, whose upper limit is governed by the wind stress and the opposing bottom stress; if the wind is directed with the land to the right then the tilt of the sea surface caused by the Earth rotation (Coriolis or geostrophic effect) will raise the level along the coast. This is the situation that occurs in the early stages of a hurricane whose path is directed towards the coast in the northern hemisphere. Wave set-up is caused by the radiation stress associated with short surface waves that are also generated by the storm winds. It is a phenomenon confined to the region shoreward of surf zone. Of all these mechanisms the set-up by onshore winds usually has the largest impact for landfalling storms on a coastline with a wide shelf.

In the following section the depth-integrated equations of motion controlling the hourly variations of water level are set forth. Gradients of the tide-generating potential and of the sea-level barometric pressure enter as external body forcing terms; also the wind-induced stress enters as an added external surface forcing term. The effect of mass exchange at the sea surface (precipitation minus evaporation) is neglected. This could be included as an added forcing term in the depth integrated continuity equation, but its *direct* effect on water-level changes at times scales of hours to several weeks is considered negligible. The primary impact of rainfall is in governing the volume of water available to riverine systems from upland watershed areas. This in turn governs the discharge to estuaries and bays. While potential flooding from this source is obviously important, it is beyond the scope of this chapter to pursue the subject of riverine dynamics. Normally, the rainfall-induced effect on water level in bays from a severe storm occurs well after the wind-induced effects.

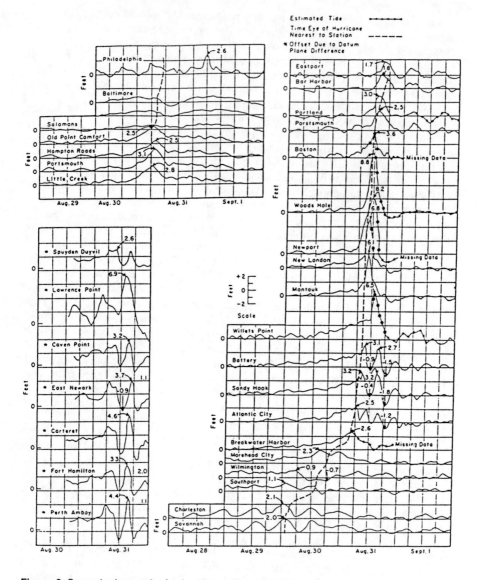

Figure 8. Surge hydrographs for hurricane Carol, 27–31 August 1954, obtained from observed records after removal of predicted tide for those stations shown in Figure 5. Upper inset for stations in Chesapeake Bay; lower left inset for stations in New York harbor [8, 23].

Governing Equations for Tides, Surges, and Circulation

Depth-Integrated Equations of Motion

In the mathematical treatment of tides and surges it is usually adequate to consider only the depth integrated equations of motion if water-level variations are of primary concern. Also, it is usually adequate to ignore the nonlinear convective acceleration terms and that approximation is adopted here; it implies that some of the nonlinear coupling between the transient and steady currents is ignored. For example, if one is concerned with estimating residual circulation associated with tides in shallow water or with distortion of the tidal signal in channels, the nonlinear terms cannot be ignored. The linear approximation also implies that wave radiation stress is ignored in the governing equations; however, its effect can be treated as a nearshore supplement. Otherwise the equations of motion are treated in fairly general form in the sense that they may be applicable to both transient and quasi-steady regimes related to meteorological and tidal forcing.

Because tides are basically global phenomena, as is quasi-steady ocean circulation, the depth integrated equations are represented in spherical geocentric coordinates. Because they contain allowance for meteorological forcing and possible density stratification effects, they constitute generalized Laplace tidal equations (GLTE):

$$\frac{\partial U}{\partial t} - 2\Omega \sin \phi V + \frac{1}{\cos \phi} \int_{r_b}^{r_s} \frac{1}{r} \frac{\partial}{\partial \lambda} (P/\rho_m - \Gamma) \, dr = (\tau_{s\lambda} - \tau_{b\lambda})/\rho_m \tag{1}$$

$$\frac{\partial V}{\partial t} + 2\Omega \sin \phi U + \int_{r_b}^{r_s} \frac{1}{r} \frac{\partial}{\partial \phi} (P/\rho_m - \Gamma) \, dr = (\tau_{s\phi} - \tau_{b\phi})/\rho_m \tag{2}$$

$$\frac{\partial h}{\partial t} + \frac{1}{r_m \cos \phi} \left(\frac{\partial U}{\partial \lambda} + \frac{\partial}{\partial \phi} (V \cos \phi) \right) = 0 \tag{3}$$

and for given λ, ϕ, t

$$dP = \rho g \, dz = \rho \, d\Phi \tag{4}$$

where
- λ = longitude, measured eastward from the Greenwich meridian
- ϕ = latitude, measured northward from the equator
- r = geocentric radial distance
- t = Greenwich mean time reckoned from an appropriate astronomical benchmark
- Ω = angular speed of Earth (7.29212×10^{-5} radians/sec);
- U = zonal volume transport per unit width at λ, ϕ, t and positive northwards
- V = meridional volume transport per unit width at λ, ϕ, t and positive northwards
- P = fluid pressure at λ, ϕ, r, t
- r_s = value of r for sea surface at λ, ϕ, t

r_b = value of r for sea bed at λ, ϕ, t

h = $r_s - r_b$, water depth at λ, ϕ, t

$r_m = (r_s + r_b)/2$ at λ, ϕ, t

ρ = density of the sea water at λ, ϕ, r, t

ρ_m = a typical mean surface value of ρ

Φ = geopotential relative to Earth's center of mass

g = acceleration due to gravity at λ, ϕ, r

Γ = tide generating potential at λ, ϕ, r, t

$\tau_{s\lambda}$, $\tau_{s\phi}$ = λ and ϕ components of surface wind stress at λ, ϕ, t

$\tau_{b\lambda}$, $\tau_{b\phi}$ = λ and ϕ components of resisting bottom stress at λ, ϕ, t

Integration of the hydrostatic Equation 4 yields

$$P = P_s + \rho_m(\Phi_s - \Phi_r) + P' + P_r, \tag{5}$$

where P_s = sea level barometric pressure at λ, ϕ, t

Φ_s = sea surface geopotential at λ, ϕ, t

Φ_r = geopotential of the reference geoid, a constant

P' = baroclinic pressure anomaly defined below

P_r = a function of Φ and Φ_r which is independent of λ, ϕ, t

Let ρ_r be a reference distribution of ρ depending only on Φ and corresponding to an adiabatically leveled state of the ocean, in which P also depends only on Φ for fixed P_s. Then P' has the following meaning:

$$P' = \int_\Phi^{\Phi_r} (\rho - \rho_r)\, d\Phi \tag{6}$$

and

$$P_r = \int_\Phi^{\Phi_r} \rho_r\, d\Phi \tag{7}$$

For a hypothetical ocean that is homogeneous in temperature and salinity, then ρ and ρ_r depend only on total pressure and are essentially the same; hence P' vanishes for such a fluid. The real ocean is stratified in temperature and salinity and the thickness of the upper, less dense water varies considerably with position; for example, the depth of the 10° isothermal surface can change from 200 m to 900 m in a transect across the Gulf Stream [68]. The associated change of P' across the Gulf Stream for $(\Phi_r - \Phi)/g = 1000$ m, is about 1 decibar, which is equivalent to a change in sea surface height of about 1 m. This is due only to the effect of the sloping isopycnals (baroclinic effect); any tidal signal is superimposed on this.

Using Equation 5, the integral terms in Equations 1 and 2 can, with adequate approximation, be replaced by

$$\frac{1}{r_m}\left\{ h\frac{\partial}{\partial\theta}(g_s(\zeta_a - b) - \Gamma_s) + \frac{\partial\chi}{\partial\theta} - \frac{P_b'}{r_m}\frac{\partial h}{\partial\theta} \right\} \tag{8}$$

where θ is either λ or ϕ, g_s is the sea-level gravity, P_b' is P' evaluated at the sea bed, while

$$b = (P_n - P_s)/\rho_m g_s \qquad (9)$$

$$\chi = \frac{1}{\rho_m} \int_{r_b}^{r_s} P' \, dr \qquad (10)$$

and

$$\zeta_a = (\Phi_s - \Phi_r)/g_s \qquad (11)$$

The term b is the barometric pressure deficit expressed as an equivalent height of water, P_n being normal atmospheric pressure (i.e., 1 atm); while χ is the transport potential [16]. The term ζ_a is the elevation of the sea surface above the reference geoid and is therefore the "absolute" water level anomaly at λ, ϕ, t.

One can define another water level anomaly by

$$\zeta_t = h - D \qquad (12)$$

where D is the NTDE time average of h at given λ, ψ. It is the quantity measured by a tide gauge. The difference $(\zeta_a - \zeta_t)$ is a measure of the elevational anomaly of the *seabed* created by Earth tide and/or seabed loading due to the pressure of the water column, or (near shore) to subsidence due to slow compaction of crustal sediments. Even on time scales of tidal periods, the difference is not trivial [26].

The seabed variations $(\zeta_a - \zeta_t)$ and the effective surface tide generating potential Γ_s depend jointly on the pressure variations on the seabed, the time varying distribution of mass of the ocean and the direct Newtonian attraction by the sun and moon. Farrell [14] gives an analysis of these effects for the case where the atmospheric pressure and ocean stratification can be ignored. In order to generalize Farrell's results to include barometric driving, b, and baroclinic effects, it will be assumed that (a) the spatial scales of b are comparable to those of ζ_t and (b) the variation of P at the seabed has no contribution from the baroclinic circulation of the ocean.

The latter assumption implies that

$$P_b' + \rho_m g_s(\zeta_s - b_s) = 0 \qquad (13)$$

where b_s and ζ_s are climatological (NTDE) time average values of b and ζ_t (or ζ_a) at given λ, ϕ. Expression 8 for the gradient terms in Equations 1 and 2 then take the form

$$\frac{1}{r_m} \left\{ g_s h \frac{\partial}{\partial \theta} \left(G(\zeta' - b') - \alpha\eta \right) + \frac{\partial}{\partial \theta} \left(\chi + g_s h(\zeta_s - b_s) \right) \right\} \qquad (14)$$

where η is the Newtonian equilibrium tide potential, while ζ' and b' are the transient parts of ζ and b:

$$\zeta' = \zeta - \zeta_s, \qquad b' = b - b_s \tag{15}$$

and $G(\zeta' - b')$ is an integral convolution of $\zeta' - b'$ over the globe [14]. Schwiderski [65] follows a suggested simplification of Pekeris in using the approximation

$$G(\zeta' - b') = \beta(\zeta' - b') \tag{16}$$

where $\beta = 0.9$. This value of β is appropriate for global tides; for regional disturbances of scales less than 1,000 km it is more common to set $\beta = 1$. The coefficient α modifying η is taken as 0.69 by Schwiderski [65] and Hendershott [27]; this is the effective Earth elasticity factor discussed earlier. Details of η will be given in a subsequent section.

If the previous relations are employed in Equations 1, 2, and 3 then the governing equations take the following form:

$$\frac{\partial U}{\partial t} - 2\Omega \sin\phi V + \frac{g_s h}{r_m \cos\phi} \frac{\partial}{\partial\lambda} (\beta(\zeta' - b') - \alpha\eta) + \frac{1}{r_m \cos\phi} \frac{\partial}{\partial\lambda} (\chi + g_s h(\zeta_s - b_s))$$

$$= (\tau_{s\lambda} - \tau_{b\lambda})/\rho_m \tag{17}$$

$$\frac{\partial V}{\partial t} + 2\Omega \sin\phi U + \frac{g_s h}{r_m} \frac{\partial}{\partial\phi} (\beta(\zeta' - b') - \alpha\eta) + \frac{1}{r_m} \frac{\partial}{\partial\phi} (\chi + g_s h(\zeta_s - b_s))$$

$$= (\tau_{s\phi} - \tau_{b\phi})/\rho_m \tag{18}$$

$$\frac{\partial\zeta}{\partial t} + \frac{1}{r_m \cos\phi} \left(\frac{\partial U}{\partial\lambda} + \frac{\partial}{\partial\phi} (V \cos\phi) \right) = 0 \tag{19}$$

These governing equations involve the dependent variables U, V, ζ', ζ_s, χ, and the components of τ_b (which depend on the fluid velocity); the forcing terms are b', b_s, η, and the components of wind stress $\tau_{s\lambda}$, $\tau_{s\phi}$. The terms g_s and r_m vary by less than 0.5% over the globe and can be taken as their average values 9.81 m/s^2 and 6,371 km, respectively. Likewise, ρ_m can be taken as a constant whose typical value for sea water is about 1.025 gm/cm^3.

Steady Circulation

The NTDE time averages of ζ' and b' are zero by definition. It will also be understood that the NTDE time average of η is essentially zero. The time averages of Equations 17 to 19 over an NTDE then lead to three diagnostic relations involving the steady circulation U_s, V_s and its associated ζ_s and χ_s. The steady counterpart of Equation 19 yields.

$$\frac{\partial U_s}{\partial \lambda} + \frac{\partial}{\partial \phi} (V_s \cos \phi) = 0 \tag{20}$$

which implies that a volume transport stream function ψ_s exists such that

$$U_s = -\frac{1}{r_m} \frac{\partial \psi_s}{\partial \phi} \qquad V_s = \frac{1}{r_m \cos \phi} \frac{\partial \psi_s}{\partial \lambda} \tag{21}$$

The steady counterparts of Equations 17 and 18, after elimination of $(\chi_s + g_s D(\zeta_s - b_s))$ and employing Equation (21), yield the following equation for ψ_s:

$$\frac{\beta_r}{r_m \cos \phi} \frac{\partial \psi_s}{\partial \lambda} = \frac{1}{\rho_m} (\mathrm{curl}(\overline{\tau}_s) - \mathrm{curl}(\overline{\tau}_b)) \tag{22}$$

where $\beta_r = (2\Omega \cos \phi)/r_m$ $\tag{23}$

The overbar implies a temporal average, and curl (τ) is shorthand for the vertical component of the vector curl of the horizontal stress vector. Equation 22 is a generalization of the Sverdrup circulation relation employed by Stommel [68]. The term β_r is the Rossby parameter with units $L^{-1}T^{-1}$. Once ψ_s is determined then $\chi_s + g_s D(\zeta_s - b_s)$ can be recovered from the steady counterparts of Equations 17 and 18 via an appropriate line integral operation. The only boundary condition is that ψ_s vanishes on the coastal boundaries.

If one allows for the slow evolution of the circulation in response to changes in the wind stress curl over the ocean, then Equation 22 is replaced by the relation

$$\frac{\partial}{\partial t} \nabla^2 \psi_s + \frac{\beta_r}{r_m \cos \phi} \frac{\partial \psi_s}{\partial \lambda} = T_s \tag{24}$$

where T_s is the same as the RHS of Equation 22 and ∇^2 is the horizontal Laplacian operator. In fact when $T_s = 0$, Equation 24 admits free wave solutions for ψ_s whose phase propagation is westward for all wave lengths; these are the classical barotropic Rossby waves [27].

The essential feature of the circulation, in contrast to tides and storm surges, is that it is wind stress curl (i.e., wind "torque") which drives it.

Governing Equations for Tides and Surges

If one subtracts the time average counterparts from each of Equations 17 to 19 and ignores time variations of χ and h in the expression $\chi + g_s h(\zeta_s - b_s)$ then the resulting reduced LTE for tides and surges are

$$\frac{\partial U'}{\partial t} - 2\Omega \sin \phi V' + \frac{g_s h \beta}{r_m \cos \phi} \frac{\partial \zeta'}{\partial \lambda} + \tau_{b\lambda}'/\rho_m = \frac{g_s h}{r_m \cos \phi} \frac{\partial}{\partial \lambda} (\alpha \eta + \beta b') + \tau_{s\lambda}'/\rho_m$$

$$(25)$$

$$\frac{\partial V'}{\partial t} + 2\Omega \sin \phi U' + \frac{g_s h \beta}{r_m} \frac{\partial \zeta'}{\partial \phi} + \tau_{b\phi}'/\rho_m = \frac{g_s h}{r_m} \frac{\partial}{\partial \phi} (\alpha \eta + \beta b') + \tau_{s\phi}'/\rho_m \qquad (26)$$

$$\frac{\partial \zeta'}{\partial t} + \frac{1}{r_m \cos \phi} \left(\frac{\partial U'}{\partial \lambda} + \frac{\partial}{\partial \phi} (V' \cos \phi) \right) = 0 \qquad (27)$$

where the primes denote the time variable part of a given term on temporal scales pertinent to tides or surges. All dependent terms are on the left sides and all forcing terms are on the right.

For a hypothetical ocean covering the globe with very great depth h (say, 100 km), then the effect of the stress and inertial terms would be of second order and ζ' would be of order $b' + \alpha\eta/\beta$. Moreover, if b' was negligible and if Earth were rigid, then $\alpha = \beta = 1$ and ζ' would be nearly equal to η, the Newtonian equilibrium tide. For the real world ζ' departs significantly from η, but $\alpha\eta$ still serves as the driving potential for the tides; while $\beta b'$ and the components of τ_s' serve as the driving terms for the storm surges.

Boundary Conditions

From a purely mathematical standpoint, closure of the problem specification for tides and surges requires: (a) that initial conditions on U', V' and ζ' be stipulated for all locations λ, ϕ within the domain of the selected basin; and (b) that a condition on ζ', *or* on the normal component of transport, *or* on a linear combination of these be stipulated at each point of the boundaries of the basin domain. Initial conditions for storm surges are usually taken as U', V', $\zeta' = 0$, i.e., no initial disturbance.

Let Q_n' denote that linear combination of U', V' which represents the *outward* component of transport per unit width at a given boundary point. A possible general open boundary condition is then

$$A\zeta' - BQ_n' = F \qquad (28)$$

where A, B, and F are specified at the boundary point. If the boundary is a rigid impermeable wall, then the physically meaningful condition is that $A = F = 0$ and $B \neq 0$, so $Q_n' = 0$. If the boundary is open and no energy is allowed to enter or leave the basin, then $B = F = 0$ and $A \neq 0$, so $\zeta' = 0$. Both special cases represent adiabatic conditions (i.e., total reflection of energy), $\zeta' = 0$ being a node condition and $Q_n' = 0$ an antinode condition.

If $F = 0$ but neither A nor B is zero, then Equation 28 represents a *radiation* condition provided that A/B is *positive*, the latter quantity having units of velocity.

Positive A/B assures that any net energy flux at the boundary is outwards from the basin (less than total reflection). An optimum value of A/B can assure total transmission (zero reflection) at least for disturbances of particular frequency. This optimum value corresponds to the *group* speed of free gravity waves, which depends on depth, Earth rotation, and frequency. The general condition (Equation 28) with $F \neq 0$ allows some forcing at the boundary; e.g., the ocean tide forcing a co-oscillating tide in a bay (the bay being the domain for which solutions are desired).

A further generalization of Equation 28 is

$$A\zeta' - BQ_n' + C \frac{\partial \zeta'}{\partial t} = F \tag{29}$$

where A, B, and C are positive or zero. A relation similar to Equation 29 was employed by Reid and Whitaker [59] and is nearly equivalent to the complex impedance condition employed by Garrett [20]. Equation 28 is a special case for $C = 0$. When $C \neq 0$ then Equation 29 not only allows some outward radiation of energy, but also introduces some added potential energy to the system. For example Equation 29, when employed as a coastal condition for ocean tide models, can simulate effects of small bays not resolved by the model; both the partial damping effect and the storing of energy by a small bay can be accounted for in this manner.

For limited-area storm surge models where the domain is a reach of the continental shelf, then Equation 28 is recommended for the seaward open condition with A/B taken as $(gD)^{1/2}$ for the open sea and F/A taken as b' along the seaward boundary.

For low-frequency shelf waves excited by winds over the shelf region, the wave energy is trapped on the shelf. In such cases Equation 28 is not appropriate for the seaward boundary. A more appropriate condition is the following *evanescent* condition:

$$\frac{\partial \zeta'}{\partial n} + \mu \zeta' = 0, \tag{30}$$

where n is measured outwards and μ is positive. An example is a Kelvin wave where μ has the value $2\Omega \sin \phi/(gh)^{1/2}$.

Boundary conditions will be discussed further in the section dealing with numerical models, particularly global tide models and regional (or limited area) tide and surge models. The conditions at open lateral boundaries of a reach of continental shelf are the most troublesome in terms of yielding physically satisfying results.

Parameterization of Stress Terms

The wind-induced stress and bottom stress share certain common elements in their parameterization. Let W represent the wind speed at a standard height of 10 m above the sea surface and let θ represent the azimuth measured counterclockwise from east *toward* which the wind is blowing. Then

$$\tau_{s\lambda} = \rho_a C_d W^2 \cos\theta$$

$$\tau_{s\phi} = \rho_a C_d W^2 \sin\theta$$

(31)

where ρ_a is air density at sea level and C_d is a dimensionless drag coefficient whose value depends on W and the air thermal stability (air-sea temperature difference). Values of C_d range from about 1×10^{-3} for low speeds to about 3×10^{-3} for hurricane speeds [e.g., 19, 78]. The gross effect of short surface waves is implicitly included in C_d and its dependence on W; however C_d can also depend on wind duration [30].

In applying Equation(s) 31, it should be noted that the wind stress must be divided by the water density ρ_m in the governing equations. A typical value of ρ_a/ρ_m is about 1.2×10^{-3}.

For extratropical cyclones the information on W and θ can be obtained from surface weather maps. For hurricanes, the data are generally insufficient for giving adequate detail and it is standard practice to adopt a parameterized storm model; this will be considered in a subsequent section.

Relations similar to Equation(s) 31 can be employed for the stress at the seabed. A complication exists, however, in that the appropriate fluid velocity is that just above the benthic boundary layer. The depth-averaged fluid velocity due to tide, surge, and steady currents has components U/h and V/h or magnitude Q/h, where $Q = (U^2 + V^2)^{1/2}$. If one ignores effects of stratification and short surface waves, and employs the above depth-averaged velocity just above the seabed then

$$\tau_{b\lambda} = \rho_m C_b QU/h^2$$

$$\tau_{b\phi} = \rho_m C_b QV/h^2$$

(32)

where C_b is the bottom drag coefficient. It depends on the effective roughness of the seabed. Typical values of C_b fall in about the same range as C_d, but are nearly independent of Q/h.

The presence of superimposed short surface waves will have the effect of increasing Q by an amount depending on their height, period and the depth h [21]. The effect is significant only in shallow water. Earth rotation can produce changes in direction (Ekman veering), such that the near bottom current may differ in direction from the depth-averaged velocity. Stratification of the water column can have more profound effects and is difficult to parameterize in any simple way short of solving the more general three-dimensional spatial problem.

Some investigators [10, 65] employ a linearized version of Equation(s) 32 having the form

$$\tau_{b\lambda} = \rho_m C_b v_r U/h$$

$$\tau_{b\phi} = \rho_m C_b v_r V/h$$

(33)

where v_r is an rms bottom velocity appropriate to a given location and event. If one uses the same coefficient $C_b v_r$ for both the average state and the transient state, then

$$\tau_{b\lambda}' = \rho_m C_b v_r U'/h$$

$$\tau_{b\phi}' = \rho_m C_b v_r V'/h \tag{34}$$

This considerably simplifies the analysis of tides and surges. It is adequately provided that the seabed stress plays only a secondary role, as is the case for non-resonant forcing conditions for the basin.

Tide Potential

The term η in the LTE Equations 25 to 27 is the Newtonian equilibrium tide and the gradient of $\alpha\eta$ yields the effective tide producing force. It can be represented with adequate precision as a function of ϕ, λ for given positions of the Moon and Sun at time t as follows [11]:

$$\eta = (3(\sin \phi)^2 - 1)(F_{mo}(t) + F_{so}(t)) + \sin 2\phi(F_{m1}(\lambda, t) + F_{s1}(\lambda, t))$$
$$+ (\cos \phi)^2(F_{m2}(\lambda, t) + F_{s2}(\lambda, t)) \tag{35}$$

where the F_{ij} terms for $i = m, s$ (moon, sun) have the form

$$F_{i0} = G_i(\sin \delta_i - \tfrac{1}{3})$$

$$F_{i1} = G_i \sin 2\delta_i \cos(\lambda - \lambda_i) \tag{36}$$

$$F_{i2} = G_i(\cos \delta_i)^2 \cos(2\lambda - 2\lambda_i)$$

In these relations

$$G_i = \frac{3}{4} \frac{M_i}{M_e} \frac{r_m^4}{d_i^3} \tag{37}$$

where M_i = mass of the moon or sun
 M_e = mass of Earth
 d_i = time dependent distance between Earth's center and that of the moon or sun

The terms λ_i and δ_i are the time dependent longitude and declination of the moon or sun relative to Earth's reference frame.

While other planets of the solar system can also contribute to η, their effect is negligible compared with the first order effects of the moon and sun. The average ratio of G_m to G_s is about 2.2, the nearness of the moon outweighing its small size compared with the sun. The only other significant supplement to η not included in these relations is the effect of solar radiation pressure, which can modify the solar F_{sj} terms and produce additional ones proportional to $\cos j(\lambda - \lambda_i)$ with $j > 2$ [e.g., 5, 27].

The terms F_{ij} give rise to the declinational ($j = 0$), diurnal ($j = 1$) and semidiurnal ($j = 2$) species of tides. Note in particular that F_{io} does not depend on the longitude of the moon or sun but only on its declination and distance relative to Earth. These relations could be employed directly if one adds further relations for positions of the moon and sun (λ_i, δ_i, d_i) for given time relative to an appropriate astronomical event (e.g., a particular solar eclipse).

The more common procedure in the representation of η, and particularly of its consequences with respect to observed tides, is to decompose its temporal variations for a fixed Earth point λ, ϕ into a sum of many simple harmonic terms having different periods associated with the three general species j. Note, for example, that the mean value of $d\lambda_m/dt$ over a lunar month is approximately $\omega_m - \Omega$ where ω_m is the average angular lunar orbit speed. The practical result, after removal of the steady part of η (whose effect is really incorporated into the geoid), is as follows:

$$\eta(\lambda, \phi, t) = \sum_{n,j} B_{jn} f_{jn}(t_0) L_j(\phi) \cos (2\pi(t - t_0)/T_{jn} + j\lambda + v_{jn}(t_0)) \tag{38}$$

where t_0 is a reference time (e.g., 0000 GMT on 1 January of a given year) and

$$L_0 = 3(\sin \phi)^2 - 1$$

$$L_1 = \sin 2\phi \tag{39}$$

$$L_2 = (\cos \phi)^2$$

The quantities B_{jn} and T_{jn} are constants characterizing the amplitude and period of a given constituent n of species $j(0, 1, 2)$; $v_{jn}(t)$ is the time dependent astronomical argument; and $f_{jn}(t)$ the time-dependent nodal factor for given n, j. Tables for the latter two functions are given by Schureman [63] for the years 1850 to 2000 (see also Schwiderski [65]). The amplitudes and periods of the principal constituents for each tidal species are summarized in Table 2 along with the standard symbols and names for each. More precise values of the angular speeds $360°/T$ are given by Schureman [63].

The spring-neap modulation effect is implicit in Equation 38 by virtue of groups of periods in both the diurnal and semidurnal species, which have only slightly different values. On the other hand, the very long period modulation associated with the motion of lunar and solar perigee and the line of nodes of the lunar orbit is contained explicitly in the nodal factor f, whose mean value for a given constituent is almost unity when averaged over a metonic cycle of 19 years. Its range for the K_1 and M_2 constituents is about 1 ± 0.12 and 1 ± 0.04, respectively. For certain constituents (e.g., S_2) f is unity for all t. The astronomical argument v is also a

Table 2
Constants for the Principal Tidal Constituents

Species		Constituent	B (meter)	T (solar days or hrs[1])
0	M_f	fortnightly lunar	.041742	13.661d
	M_m	monthly lunar	.022026	27.555d
	S_{sa}	semiannual solar	.019446	182.621d
	S_a	annual solar	[2]	365.2425d
1	K_1	luni-solar	.141565	23.93h
	O_1	principal lunar	.100514	25.82h
	P_1	principal solar	.046843	24.07h
	Q_1	elliptical lunar	.019256	26.87h
2	M_2	principle lunar	.242334	12.42h
	S_2	principle solar	.112841	12.00h
	N_2	elliptical lunar	.046398	12.66h
	K_2	luni-solar	.030704	11.97h

[1] One lunar day = 1.035050 solar day or 24.8412 solar hours.
[2] The annual solar tide is heavily dependent on seasonal heating and cooling of the ocean, as well as radiation pressure.

slowly varying function of time and, like the nodal factor, dv/dt is nearly periodic over a metonic cycle. The only principal constituent having constant v is S_2.

Natural Modes of Oscillation

The governing equations 25, 26, and 27 in the absence of any forcing or bottom stress admit free undamped oscillatory solutions. If one adds adiabatic boundary condition constraints for the basin under investigation, there will exist a discrete spectrum of real natural periods of oscillation with associated spatial configurations of ζ' and transports U' and V'. Mathematically this constitutes a two-dimensional eigenvalue problem where the natural periods are the eigenvalues and the associated functions like $\zeta'(\lambda, \phi)$ are the eigenfunctions. A knowledge of these natural modes of oscillation is helpful, if not essential, in understanding and predicting the effects of forcing. In particular any forcing whose period closely matches one of the natural periods will very effectively excite the associated mode of oscillation (quasi-resonant response). If an exact matching of the periods occurs, then the amplitude will grow linearly with time; it will be limited only if some damping mechanism is added (bottom stress or radiation of energy at open boundaries).

The subject of free oscillations of natural bodies of water has a long history; see Wilson [77] for an excellent review of the subject of seiches (oscillations in lakes and harbors), or Defant [11] for a treatment of somewhat larger bodies of water where Earth's rotation becomes important. The possible existence of two distinct classes of free oscillations has been known since the investigations by Laplace in the late 1700s: oscillations of the first class are basically gravity modes; oscillations of the second class are inertial modes whose existence depends on Earth spin and the ocean morphology. Seiches in small bodies of water are basically gravity modes; Rossby waves in the ocean or atmosphere are inertial modes. The primary distinction between these modes lies in their kinematic properties and their energetics. In gravity modes the fluid velocity is divergent, thus accounting for variations of water level; in the inertial modes the flow is almost non-divergent and circulational (i.e., possessing vorticity). Accordingly, the latter are also called vorticity or vortex modes. In the absence of Earth spin the vortex modes are steady (zero frequency or infinite period). In the presence of Earth spin these modes have frequencies usually less than $2\Omega \sin \phi$ except close to the equator. Low-frequency shelf waves are an example of topographically trapped vortex modes [37].

The most comprehensive study of the modes of both classes for the world oceans has been carried out by George Platzman over the last two decades and reported in a series of papers [50–55]. These studies necessarily involve numerical techniques for their solution, some aspects of which will deserve comment in the following section. An important result from the 1981 study [55] is that in the period band from 8 to 80 hours, 56 modes were identified for the world oceans (this includes modes of both classes). The gravity modes and vortex modes overlap in period, but differ in their spatial configuration; the gravity modes have periods generally less than about 30 hours and the vortex modes have periods generally greater than about 20 hours. As a benchmark, it may be remarked that the pendulum rotational period at 30° latitude is 24 hours. The important point is that the natural gravity modes span the range where *tidal forcing* may have nearly matching periods. On the continental shelves both gravity and vortex modes can be excited by *meteorologically-induced forcing*, while it is primarily the vortex modes that can be excited within the ocean basins by such forcing.

Numerical Models of Tides and Surges

Clearly any realistic attempt to solve the LTE for a basin with general configuration and bathymetry requires an appropriate numerical implementation. For the forced tide problem as well as the normal mode problem, both global and limited-domain modeling attempts have been carried out since the early 1960s, and the degree of their reality has in certain respects kept pace with the advancements in computer technology. Storm surge modeling while employing essentially the same equations, but with different forcing and boundary conditions, has generally been confined to limited-domains, with the attendant uncertainties of open boundary conditions (including the most difficult of all—moving boundaries associated with overland flooding).

Tide Modeling

Excellent reviews of global tide modeling are to be found in Hendershott [26, 27] and the reader should consult those reviews for details that are beyond the scope of this brief section (see also [50–55]). An important aspect of global tide models is that there exist basically two quite different types. The first type employs a coastal boundary condition with the constraint of no flow across the boundary; the second employs the specification of the water level ζ' at the coast. Both are mathematically legitimate conditions (they are special cases of Equation 28). The dream of Laplace was to try to explain the observed features of the observed tides from a knowledge of the ocean configuration and the Newtonian tide potential alone. The first type of tidal model is directed towards realizing Laplace's goal. It has almost but not quite been realized in the last decade. The second type model is perhaps the more realistic for satisfying the goal of those who wish to determine the configuration of the tides throughout the ocean interior (where little if any data exist) with optimum precision.

Basically, the first type of tidal model is fully predictive; the second type is diagnostic in the sense that it must employ the observed tides around the boundaries and perhaps at islands to determine the interior tides. In principle, if both employ exactly the same physics and if the numerical rendition is the same and has *adequate resolution* particularly over the continental shelves, then the results ought to be very nearly the same, assuming the common physics is correct; any difference would perhaps be related to insufficient detail for the coastal observations. Figure 9 shows the results of a predictive model of the M_2 global tide by Accad and Pekeris [1]; the figure gives phase (full lines) and amplitude contours (dashed). Figures 10 and 11 show phase and amplitude contours resulting from the diagnostic model of Schwiderski [64, 66]. These figures focus only on the Atlantic portion of the results in order to show the detail clearly; in comparing the two results the different map projections should be borne in mind. The general patterns of the amphidromic systems are remarkably similar, but there exist some differences in location of the amphidromic points. The *major* differences are in the magnitude of the amplitudes, especially near continental boundaries. Both models employ similar physics including allowance for Earth tide, loading, and self-attraction. The Schwiderski model has a resolution of $1°$ in latitude and longitude, while the Accad and Pekeris model employed about $2°$ resolution. This may account for some of the quantitative differences. However, there is reason to believe that, had both models employed $1°$ resolution and *exactly* the same treatment of Earth tide, loading, and self attraction, they probably still would not agree near the continental boundaries. One degree resolution, while adequate over the ocean interior, is *not* adequate over the continental shelf regions.

The evidence to document this statement concerning resolution is a series of studies by different investigators of the normal modes and the M_2 tide in the Gulf of Mexico (GOM), whose observed characteristics were outlined briefly earlier under "Tides of the Real Ocean." Three of the studies employed predictive GOM models with allowance for tidal input at the open straits, the latter tuned to give the best response within the Gulf. The models, identified by reference citation and some crucial features are summarized below:

1. Grijalva [22], 2/3° resolution, tide potential included
2. Mungall, *et al.* [45], 1/2° resolution, no tide potential
3. Reid and Whitaker [59], 1/4° resolution, tide potential included

Of these (1) and (2) could account for at best 70% of the observed variance of the GOM M_2 tide, while (3) accounted for 90% of the M_2 tide variance. The difference

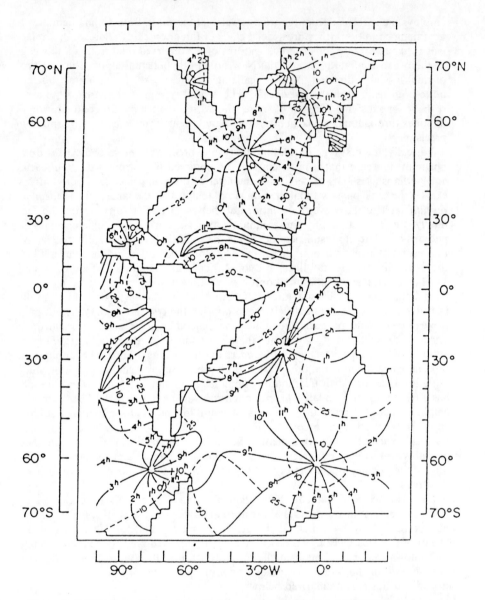

Figure 9. Cotidal lines (full) and amplitude contours (dashed) in hrs GMT and cm, respectively, for the M_2 tide in the Atlantic Ocean as deduced from a global predictive model driven purely by tide potential as modified by Earth tide, loading and self attraction [1].

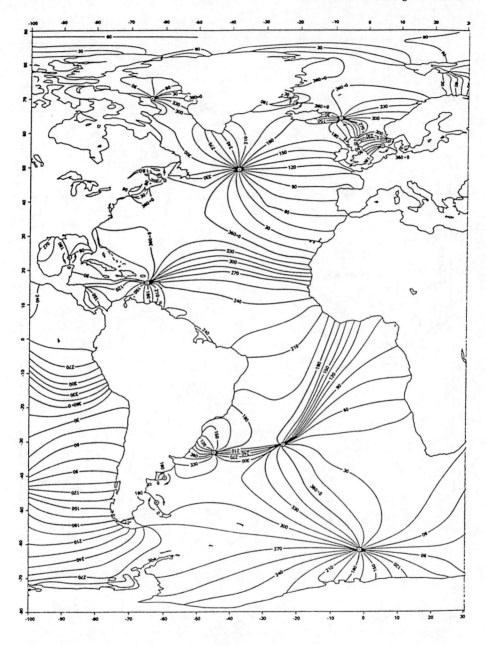

Figure 10. Cotidal lines in degrees GMT for the M₂ tide in the Atlantic Ocean portion of the Schwiderski diagnostic global tide model, which uses observed tidal constants at the coastlines, but otherwise includes interior forcing by tide potential, as modified by Earth tide and approximate effect of loading and self attraction [64].

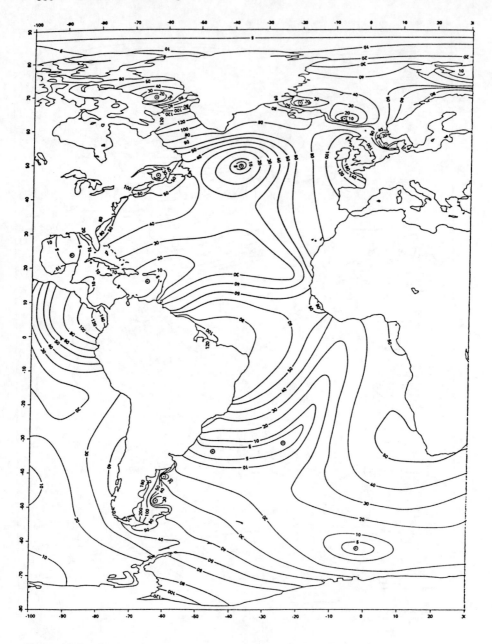

Figure 11. Amplitude contours in cm for the M_2 tide deduced from the diagnostic model as in Figure 10 [64].

between models (1) and (3) is primarily resolution; model (2) while having better resolution than (1) lacked some essential physics: the direct forcing of the GOM M_2 tide by tide potential. Indeed in study (3) it was found that about two-thirds of the explained variance was due to direct forcing within the GOM. This can be possible in such a small basin only if one of the normal modes is close to resonance with the 12.42 hr M_2 period. The poorer resolution of model (1) compared with (3) probably made it unable to achieve such near-resonant conditions. This is supported by the normal mode· study of Platzman [50], which indicates natural periods of about 7 and 21 hours for the GOM but nothing near 12 hours; Platzman's model employed a resolution of 1° similar to that of Grijalva. A recent study by Reid [60] confirms that adequacy of resolution can be critical in the proper simulation of normal mode periods.

Tidal and normal mode models can be formulated either in time marching form or in spectral form where the linearized governing equations are converted to Helmholz form for time periodic solutions. Resonant iteration techniques or variations thereof are usually employed to seek natural periods [50, 51]. Most global tide models employ second-order accurate, centered finite difference forms for spatial and temporal derivatives, although Platzman [52] has used a finite element formulation for one version of the global normal modes. When employing the primitive LTE form, care must be taken in the representation of the Coriolis terms [38, 50]. In the time-marching mode one has a choice of explicit or semi-implicit schemes, the former being accurate but inefficient and the latter efficient but not as accurate in rendition of the correct dispersive properties of free-wave solutions. The common semi-implicit method is the ADI technique of Leendertse [38].

For most studies of concern to engineers the focus is on some limited region (e.g., the North Sea, Bering Sea, or a portion of the continental shelf perhaps adjoining a bay). For such problems one can achieve good resolution with a reasonable number of grid points; the issue here is proper specification of tidal signals at the open boundaries. This is where the global models are of great utility; the costly alternative is to acquire observational data at the open regions. Of the existing global tide models, that of Schwiderski is the most accurate for specifying tide elevation signals at the edge of the continental shelf. If the domain is small and non-resonant to tidal forcing then the tide potential forcing over the domain may be neglected; this is an option the user must decide.

Storm Surge Modeling

Nearly all storm surge models are of limited-domain type with open boundaries; an exception exists for closed lakes. Basically, a good limited-domain tide model can be employed for storm surges with the appropriate addition of the meteorological forcing, and perhaps the capability of inland flooding (which requires a true time dependent h). Indeed one of the common means of partial verification of a model application to a given region is to try to reproduce the tidal regime for the region.

Many different 2-D time marching models exist capable of simulating storm surges over the continental shelf or in bays. Listed in Table 3 is a sample list of

Table 3
Selected Depth-Integrated Storm Surge Models Developed for Use in the Public Domain

Code Name	Originator	Agency User[1]	Characteristics
SPLASH	Jelesnianski [34, 35]	NWS/NOAA	Sheared coordinates, explicit, fixed coast.[2]
SLOSH	Jelesnianski and Chen [36]	NWS/NOAA	Polar coordinates with pole inland, overland flooding allowed.[2]
SURGE II	Reid et al. [58]	CERC/USACE	Bays with sub-grid scale channels, overland flooding and barriers allowed.[2]
SSURGE	Wanstrath [74, 75]	WES/USACE	Coastal boundary—fitted coordinates over shelf, fixed coast.[2]
CFSSM	TetraTech [70]	FEMA/FIA	Rectangular coordinates, overland flooding and barriers allowed.[2]
WIFM	Butler [4]	WES/USACE	Stretched rectangular grid, overland flooding allowed, and ADI.[3]
GOMTS	Bunpapong et al. [2]	CERC/USACE	Gulf of Mexico model for tides and surges, spherical coordinates, two-layers, fixed boundaries, and ADI.[3]

[1] Agency acronyms:
  NWS = National Weather Service
  NOAA = National Oceanic and Atmospheric Administration
  CERC = Coastal Engineering Research Center
  USACE = United States Army, Corps of Engineers
  WES = Waterways Experiment Station
  FEMA = Federal Emergency Management Agency
  FIA = Federal Insurance Administration
  OCE = Office of the Chief of Engineers
[2] Finite difference, explicit code
[3] Finite difference, alternating direction implicit (ADI)

those 2-D model codes developed for use by U.S. government agencies; no attempt is made to include the many models developed and used in the private sector in the United States or abroad. The table lists the adopted code names, the originators, reference citations, the government agency, and some model characteristics. Several of these models have the overland flooding capability (moving coastal boundary) and allowance for sub-grid scale barriers which use the methodology of Reid and Bodine [57]. All but two employ explicit time marching schemes; the two exceptions use the ADI scheme.

An important caveat about the ADI scheme: It can introduce a spurious numerical mode that has no physical counterpart in the continuum equations of motion. Spurious modes commonly occur when one employs more time levels than are consistent with the predictive system being modeled. The ADI scheme has the less obvious feature that there exists four degrees of freedom for the dependent variables U, V, ζ rather than three; the reason is that ζ computed with U at one step is really a different variable than ζ computed with V at alternate steps. The result is that there exist four possible wave speeds for a given wave number rather than three (two gravity speeds of opposite sign and one Rossby speed). This feature is not important for applications in which the primary response involves gravity modes, which is true in most part for tides and storm surges. The caveat is most relevant in applications to slowly evolving circulation where vortex modes play a leading role.

It is well beyond the scope of this review to attempt to discuss any further details of the numerical methodology; the reader should consult the available references for this. The focus here is on the general characteristics and capabilities as summarized in Table 3 and on the performance of these models. Two studies that attempt to assess model performance are pertinent: one of these was by the Committee on Tidal Hydraulics [9] the other by a special *ad hoc* committee of the National Research Council [46]. In the first study several of the models listed in Table 3 were intercompared in simulations of five hurricanes of record (Carla, 1961; Camille, 1969; Gracie, 1950; Hazel, 1954; and Eloise, 1972). The results, after removing some bias due to poor representation of wind forcing, indicated an rms errors of the surge hydrographs of about 2.5 ft (0.76 m); this is to be compared with the average of the observed peak surge of 11.5 ft (3.51 m). The ratio of these (0.22) gives some measure of the collective random error, after removal of bias. Both studies identify the differences employed in storm wind field parameterization as the major source of bias. The National Research Council report of 1983 [46] contains a comparison of three different storm parameterization schemes. Evaluating surge and wind field models and the data requirements for such evaluation is addressed further by Harris [25].

Aside from the paramount role of accurate wind fields for driving storm surge models, there are six important aspects of the surge models that deserve comment:

1. The adequacy of resolution particularly near shore; Harris [24, 25] has emphasized the importance of small-scale features of coastlines and harbors on surge response and this is demonstrated in Figure 8 (note insert hydrographs for New York Harbor).
2. The adequacy of bottom stress parameterization; the model must be calibrated using tidal data and storms of record.
3. The problem of boundary conditions for open *lateral* boundaries along a shelf region; there are currently no truly realistic conditions of this type in any existing models (all produce artificial reflection of energy). The pragmatic solution to the problem is to model a sufficiently wide reach of the shelf such that the effects of such artificial reflection is minimized for the time interval being simulated. This strategy works well for storm surge events but not so well for limited domain tide models.
4. Another potential source of error is the way in which the effect of wave set-up is considered in storm surge models. For nearly all existing models, this source

of added water level signal is either ignored or implicitly allowed for in terms of the choice of wind stress drag coefficient. Clearly, the proper approach is to compute the wave set-up explicitly; it occurs inshore of the breaker point for the conditions prevailing during the storm and depends on the breaker height and period (CERC, 1973, article 3.85). To make such a calculation, one must include the necessary wave predictions concurrently with the surge model. It is presently unclear how much of the discrepancies that exist between surge model predictions and observed data is due to the lack of treating wave set-up in a reasonable way; its potential contribution for hurricane induced waves can be as much as one meter.

5. Wind stress drag coefficient. Clearly the wind stress estimates are only as good as the estimated wind *and* the drag coefficient. All models really ought to employ the same over water drag coefficient; it is not a factor to be tuned to different storms or different regions. The review article by Garratt [19] of over-water drag coefficients suggests the formula

$$C_d = (0.75 + 0.067W) \times 10^{-3} \tag{40}$$

for neutral stability conditions, where W is the 10 m wind speed in m/s. This fits the scatter of estimates in the range $4 < W < 45$ m/s with an rms deviation of about 0.3×10^{-3}. In contrast, some storm surge models employ a constant C_d with a value of order 3×10^{-3}, while others use a relation first suggested by Van Dorn [72].

6. The last factor, which is relevant only in special basins, is the possible excitation of basin wide oscillations in water level by a severe storm. The Gulf of Mexico is an example in which an initial rise in level can occur along the Texas coast long before a hurricane reaches its continental shelf (see Figures 6 and 7). A study by Bunpapong *et al.* [2], which employed a model of the whole Gulf of Mexico, indicates that a volume mode oscillation of the Gulf having a period nearly 30 hrs can be excited as a hurricane enters the Gulf. The simulation of the water-level variation at Galveston due to Carla, 1961, is compared with the observed hourly levels in Figure 12. The observed water level contains the small tide signal, which is not simulated by the model and the rms difference is only slightly greater than the rms tide signal for the seven days shown. A similar comparison between simulated and observed water level caused by Allen, 1980, is shown in Figure 13 for Port Isabel, which is near the landfall location for that hurricane. The shift in phase is probably because the observed gauge is located in a lagoon, while the simulation is for the open coast. Both simulations were carried out via the Gulf wide model, which had a resolution of 1/4° in latitude and longitude. For comparison the simulations were repeated with the same model, but with winds "turned off" everywhere except over a reach of the shelf from south of Brownsville to the Mississippi delta (thus simulating that of a limited area domain having the same resolution). The latter produced responses similar to, but smaller by about 0.5 m during the rising stage.

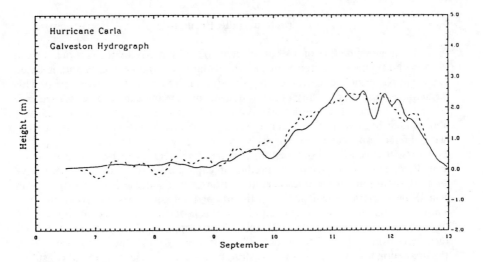

Figure 12. Comparison of computed storm surge and observed water level at Galveston, Texas for hurricane Carla, September 1961. The datum is MSL for the week prior to September 7. The computed surge is from the Gulf-wide model of Bunpapong et al. [2] and does not include the tidal signal.

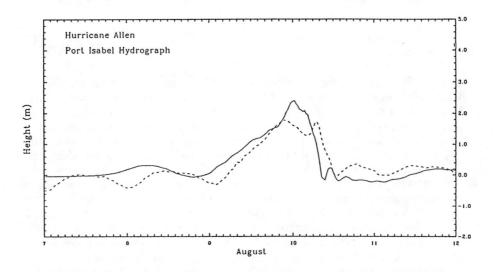

Figure 13. Comparison of computed storm surge and observed water level at Port Isabel, Texas for hurricane Allen, August 1980. The datum is MSL for the week prior to August 7. The computed surge is from the Gulf-wide model of Bunpapong, et al. [2] and does not include the tidal signal. The obvious lag of the observed surge relative to the computed is probably related to the gauge location within Laguna Madre (not resolved by the model).

Practical Tide Prediction

The routine prediction of tides at selected coastal stations, by the National Ocean Survey (NOS) in the United States or the Tidal Observatory in England, is based on a simple principle attributed to Sir William Thompson (Lord Kelvin). This principle asserts that for any linear system whose forcing can be decomposed into a sum of harmonic terms of known frequency (or period), the response can also be represented by a sum of harmonics having the same frequencies (or periods) but with different amplitudes and phases from the forcing. The tides are basically such a system (with exception of some estuaries where nonlinear effects become important). For the open coastal stations the prediction capability requires only that one have prior observations of the tides at that station over a suitable period of time from which the amplitudes and phases of the major tidal constituents (having precisely known periods) can be ascertained. Thus, the problem is reduced to an analysis of the prior observations for the amplitudes and phases of the important periods (generally from about 20 to 40 depending on the station). Once these are known the prediction for subsequent times is straightforward. Normally, the tidal constants are reevaluated for each tide station as more data are acquired in order to assure their validity and/or to allow for real changes that have been produced by natural or manmade changes in local morphology.

Let ζ be the observed water level relative to some selected datum at a given tide station, then its representation for the purpose of tidal decomposition is

$$\zeta = A_0 + \sum_{n=1}^{N} f_n(t_0) A_n \cos(\omega_n(t - t_0) + v_n(t_0) - G_n) + \epsilon \qquad (41)$$

where the A_n are constant amplitudes and the G_n are constant phases (epochs) relative to Greenwich for each of the N tidal constituents. The leading term A_0 is a measure of the gauge MSL relative to the gauge data (which are subject to slow secular change). Term v_n is the astronomical argument as in the representation of η and is a known function of t_0, f_n is the nodal factor also known versus t_0, and $\omega_n = 2\pi/T_n$ are the known constant frequencies of the tidal constituents n. The time t_0 is a reference, e.g. 0000 GMT of January 1 of a given year. The term ϵ contains any residual not explained by all the other terms; it contains any real non-tidal variations plus any measurement error. The analysis problem is to determine the $N + 1$ values of A_n and the N values of G_n such that Equation 41 gives a best fit of the available prior measurements of ζ, in the sense of minimizing the variance of ϵ for the given segment of record. In this way one gets least-squares estimates of $A_n \cos G_n$, and $A_n \sin G_n$ from which A_n and G_n are easily calculated.

Although the procedure is simple in principle, the accuracy of the resulting estimates of the A_n and G_n depends critically on the length of record, the total number of constituents N sought, and the variance of non-tidal signal in the record. The principle of trade-off between accuracy and resolution holds here just as it does in any spectral analysis procedure. The resolution of tides pertains to the ability of distinguishing between two or more constituents having nearly the same frequency or period (e.g., K_1 and P_1 or S_2 and K_2; see Table 2). Good resolution demands a sufficiently long record; namely one long enought to contain at least one modulation produced by closely neighboring periods. The ideal record would be one of length equal to the Metonic cycle. If fact this is required for the long-period solar tides and desirable for the long-period lunar tides. The minimum record length for analysis of the short period tides is a year, but one should select a year of record having minimal variance of ϵ (e.g., not containing the influence of a major hurricane event).

One measure of the ability of the tidal analysis procedure in representing the tide is given by Harris [24] in Table 1 where the observed and computed mean tidal ranges are compared for the NOS tide gauge stations in United States. Precise formulas for the computation of the nodal factors f_n and the astronomical arguments v_n for given t_0 can be found in Schureman [63]. Schwiderski [65] also gives a summary of the relations required to compute v_n (denoted by χ in his Table 1).

The aforementioned summary of tidal prediction and analysis based on observations gives only the basic elements of the most common of several possible methodologies. Another quite different approach is to employ a numerical convolution of the tide potential to represent the tide at a given location [43]. The standard representation, Equation 41, will yield valid predictions over extended time intervals only if the tidal constants are known precisely. Methods of analysis other than simple-least square exist for optimal estimation of the tidal constants; one is the method of cyclic descent, which suppresses aliasing from neighboring major constituents [48]. Moreover for stations where prior records are limited to only a few months, an approximate procedure for estimating the constants for neighboring frequencies is to assume that the ratios of amplitudes (e.g., S_2/M_2, N_2/M_2, K_2/M_2; O_1/K_1, P_1/K_1, Q_1/K_1) are the same as those for a nearby station having adequate records. This reduces the number of variables to be estimated by the least-squares method and improves the accuracy.

For locations where no tide gauges exist (e.g., over the continental shelf or slope), but for which an offshore structure is proposed one has essentially three options:

1. Install a self-contained, retrievable, bottom-mounted pressure gauge for a period of several months from which records can be obtained for analysis.
2. Use the GEOSAT altimeter records for the closest fixed node of the satellite repeat orbit.
3. Use the results of the Schwiderski [65, 66] diagnostic global tide model to estimate the major tidal constants for the location concerned. [Option (3) could be employed for feasibility studies, while (1) or (1) and (2) are desirable for final design considerations (at least with respect to tidal signal).

Practical Guidelines for Storm Surges

One can employ empirical multiple regression techniques for relating the observed peak storm surge elevation (S) for a given storm event to such parameters as:

1. Central pressure deficit (ΔP) for the storm.
2. Storm scale (e.g., the radius R to maximum winds).

3. Storm translational speed v_t.
4. Orientation of the storm track relative to the coast θ_t.
5. Shelf width L at the location where the peak surge is observed.

Conner *et al.* [9a] developed a simple empirical model of this type relating S to ΔP only, the correlation coefficient being 0.68. Harris [23a] found that by adding L along with ΔP the correlation was increased to 0.75 (which still only accounts for 56 percent of the variance of S).

Jelesnianski [34] employed his SPLASH storm surge model to simulate hypothetical hurricanes having different ΔP, R, v_t, θ_t which had landfall positions on many different shoreline points along the east coast and Gulf coast of the United States. From the results of these simulations he was able to construct a series of nomograms giving the dependence of simulated S on ΔP, R, v_t, θ_t, and location of landfall (implying different L). When applied to actual storm surge data, his nomograms for S yield a correlation of 0.85 with the observed S and hence is able to account for 72% of the variance of S among the 52 storms that he employed in the comparison.

The Jelesnianski nomographs emphasize the vital effect of continental shelf width on peak storm surge for given hurricane parameters. The west coast of the United States is not included in the Jelesnianski location nomograph. This is because the shelf width is so narrow that, even when a possible (but rare) hurricane occurs on the west coast, its primary impact is in generating large surface waves rather than increased water level. In contrast, a wide shelf located in "hurricane alley" (e.g., the Texas shelf) is axiomatic of a record surge waiting to happen.

If one needs estimates only of the peak surge S for a hurricane of given characteristics impacting at a given point of the United States' east or Gulf of Mexico coastline, then the Jelesnianski nomographs will provide a very good approximation. These nomograms can be found in the Shore Protection Manual (CERC, 1973 and 1977) as well as in report by Jelesnianski [34] and are not repeated here. They also serve as the benchmark for comparison with other model results.

There is still of course the need for the hydrodynamic storm surge models for giving time histories of water level and details of spatial variations that go well beyond what the nomograms can provide. The latter apply only to the surge at the open coast, with no allowance for overland flooding. No doubt some of the residual variance not explained by the nomograms is produced by such an effect.

Statistical Aspects of Water-Level Extremes

Estimation of extreme water levels for given coastal locations is a subject of vital concern in design of coastal protective structures and in federal insurance studies for coastal communities. In the latter studies the aim is to determine the probability that, in any year, the water level at a selected coastal location will equal or exceed a given value; or alternatively one can ask: What are the expected levels for those combinations of events that have return periods of, say, 50 years, 100 years, 200 years, etc.?

The problem would be very simple if the water level were controlled exclusively by astronomically-induced tides. The tidal water level extremes are in fact deterministic. In contrast, the storm events occur at random times and a peak surge from any given storm is equally likely to occur at any phase of the daily tidal cycle. There does exist of course a seasonal preference for storms of different scales (e.g., extratropical cyclones in winter and hurricanes in summer and early fall for the northern hemisphere).

In high latitude regions of North America and for most regions along its western coast it is feasible to ascertain the statistical properties of extreme water levels directly from the observations at those locations where extensive records are available. In doing this it is usually best to separate the tidal contribution from the nontidal and analyze the latter since its statistical characteristics differ from that of the tidal part. A procedure for carrying out an analysis by this historical method is detailed in a recent U.S. Corps of Engineers Manual published by the Office of the Chief of Engineers [49] (hereafter OCE).

For those regions vulnerable to hurricanes, a synthetic method, employing the concepts of joint probability theory together with a storm surge model, is recommended. The rationale is that the historical records, for any single location, are generally inadequate for yielding meaningful estimates of water level extremes having a return period greater than about 20 years. The synthetic method takes advantage of the fairly well known statistics of hurricane events and the probability distributions of the hurricanes parameters like P, R, etc. If the probability of a given combination of hurricane parameters is known and if the peak surge corresponding to such a hurricane is determined from a surge model, that peak surge has the same probability, given that the hurricane occurs. If the return period of the hurricane is known for a given location, one can establish the statistics of peak surge for given return period. It then remains to combine these statistics with those of the tides, remembering that it is equally likely that the peak surge can occur at any stage of the tide during a daily, fortnightly, or Metonic cycle (subject only to the constraint of the preference of hurricanes during the July to October time window).

The synthetic methodology has been employed extensively by NWS and FEMA in coastal federal insurance studies. Further details of the method and a discussion of some of its limitations will be found in a report of the National Research Council [46], the OCE Manual [49], and the many references contained therein. The report by Harris [24], which contains valuable information on the tidal statistics, is an essential supplement to the OCE Manual [49].

For design of offshore and/or protective structures along the coast, the same concepts of statistics of water level as employed in the FEMA studies could be applied. Engineers often employ the deterministic concept of an adopted "maximum probable hurricane" for design purposes. While this is convenient, it may not be realistic. A hurricane of given intensity, scale, and translational speed has different probability of occurring at different places. Considerations of risk cannot be assessed in terms of a single maximum hurricane, but must be determined from an analysis of the effects of a whole ensemble of possible hurricanes whose probabilities can be determined and which collectively (with known tides) determine the probability of given extreme water levels, as well as wave-induced forces on a structure, at the location under study.

Vertical Structure of Currents

This discourse on tides and storm surges has focused so far primarily on water level and its prediction. This final section addresses the much more difficult problem of predicting currents. The depth-integrated equations of motion governing most models of tides and storm surges are convenient because they involve besides water level, only the volume transport as the dependent variables. While one can estimate the depth-averaged current from the transport by knowing h, the model gives us no information about its depth structure. Such structure depends jointly on internal shear stresses and on any stratification of density in the water column. The former can be important in frictional boundary layers near the sea bed or near the sea surface under the joint effect of stress and Earth rotation (Ekman layers). If the fluid is shallow these boundary layers can merge so as to give structure (velocity shear) throughout the water column. This shear can involve change in direction as well as speed. The stratification effect can produce velocity shear at all levels, even in deep water.

Types of 3-D Models

While vertical structure of currents can affect the way in which the sea bed stress is parameterized, it does not have a first-order effect on water level and volume transport at least for non-resonant forcing. But if one is concerned with current profiles for engineering design considerations, then some supplementary governing equations are needed. These must be provided by the primitive equations of motion in three dimensions (3-D models). Such models are absolutely essential in the study of ocean circulation and many exist, in various degrees of complexity and capability [6, 29, 73]. Versions of such models for engineering application and environmental impact studies also exist in the public and private sector. Mentioned here are two recent versions of models of this type: that of Sheng [67] and that of Liu and Leendertse [39].

Models that allow for vertical structure fall in one of three generic classes: n-levels, n-layers, or spectral (n modes). The n-level models employ n fixed values of the vertical coordinate z (or a stretched version of the latter like z/h). The n-layer models are quasi-Lagrangian in the sense that the thickness of layers having prescribed density are dependent variables (like ζ). The spectral models, while not as common, have certain advantages over the other two classes, in the sense of resolving power. The remainder of this final section focuses on spectral models as the potential future state-of-the-art.

Spectral Models

Spectral models are certainly not new; they are a subset of Galerkin methodology applied with the use of global, rather than local, basis functions. In contrast, finite element models employ local basis functions. Global, in the present context, means over the whole water column. However, modern weather prediction models employ spectral models in the horizontal (spherical harmonic structure functions), but with n-levels. Ocean or coastal problems are better suited to spectral representation vertically with finite grid points or nodes horizontally. The selection of the spectral representation can be ad hoc, or physically motivated, but a desirable property of the chosen global structure functions is that they be *orthogonal* over the domain of the water column. Sets of Legendre or Tschebyscheff polynomials are examples of ad hoc orthogonal functions that can be employed.

Physically motivated (or natural) structure functions are of two types: (a) those based upon internal shear stress as the major mechanism controlling velocity shear; or (b) those in which density stratification dominates in its effect on velocity shear. The first is most meaningful for relatively shallow water that is well mixed vertically; a shallow bay with horizontal rather than vertical stratification of density is an example. The second is the most meaningful for vertically stratified basins with moderate or large depth (typical of the ocean and outer continental shelf). The physical (natural) structure function representation tends to allow realistic structure with a modest number of modes (degrees of freedom).

In the spectral method, one represents the horizontal velocity components u, v in the form:

$$\begin{pmatrix} u \\ v \end{pmatrix} = \sum_{m=0}^{M} \begin{pmatrix} u_m \\ v_m \end{pmatrix} F_m(z, h) \tag{42}$$

where u_m, v_m are functions of horizontal coordinates and t but not of z. The physical structure functions F_m are the eigenfunctions satisfying the following eigenvalue problem:

$$\frac{d}{dz}\left(\xi \frac{dF_m}{dz}\right) + \lambda_m F_m = 0 \tag{43}$$

$$\frac{dF_m}{dz} = -\kappa_s F_m \quad \text{at } z = 0 \tag{44}$$

$$\frac{dF_m}{dz} = \kappa_b F_m \quad \text{at } z = -h \tag{45}$$

where   z = vertical coordinate
      κ_s, κ_b = stipulated parameters
      ξ = function of z dictated by the physics
      λ_m = eigenvalue associated with the eigenmode F_m

For positive κ_s, κ_b, $\xi(z)$ the admissible λ_m are positive real numbers and the F_m are oscillatory functions that possess a simple orthogonality property. They can always be normalized such that

$$\frac{1}{h} \int_{-h}^{0} F_n F_m \, dz = \delta_{nm} \tag{46}$$

where $\delta_{nm} = 1$ for $n = m$ and otherwise zero.

For physical eigenmodes of type (a), ξ is the kinematic eddy viscosity, which may be a function of z as in planetary boundary layer models (e.g., [3, 40, 71]); moreover one chooses $\kappa_s = 0$, $\kappa_b > 0$ such that the surface shear stress is independent of surface water velocity but the bottom stress is proportional to the near bottom velocity. In effect, Equation 45 is neither a free slip nor a zero slip condition; it avoids the necessity of a high resolution bottom boundary layer [18]. In the parameterization of ξ, $(\tau_s/\rho)^{1/2}$ and/or $(\tau_b/\rho)^{1/2}$ serve as natural velocity scales governing the magnitude of ξ/z or $\xi/(z + h)$.

For physical eigenmodes of type (b), ξ is related to the densimetric stability of the stratified water, $\kappa_s \xi^{-1}(0) = g$ and $\kappa_b = 0$. The latter stipulations of κ_s, κ_b allows a free surface motion at the top and a rigid surface at the sea bed. Specifically for stratification eigenmodes one takes

$$\xi = \left(\frac{-g}{\rho_0} \frac{d\rho_0}{dZ} \right)^{-1} \tag{47}$$

where ρ_0 is the rest state potential density (with compressibility effect removed). For a stable state, $\xi > 0$ and $\xi^{-1/2}$ corresponds to a natural buoyant frequency at level z. The stratification eigenmodes are frequently employed in the vertical decomposition of deep ocean currents [15].

The eigenvalues λ_m can be shown to be related in an integral sense to the normalized F_m by the following (Rayleigh type) relation:

$$h\lambda_m = \int_{-h}^{0} \xi \left(\frac{dF_m}{dz} \right)^2 dz + \kappa_s (\xi F_m{}^2)_0 + \kappa_b (\xi F_m{}^2)_{-h} \tag{48}$$

which shows its positive property for all modes m (provided that ξ, κ_s, κ_b are not negative). For the stratification eigenmodes (type b), the *lowest* eigenvalue (λ_0) is associated with a nearly uniform structure ($F_0 = 1$) such that $\lambda_0 = (gh)^{-1}$. Thus, $\lambda_0^{-1/2}$ for this mode corresponds to the barotropic long wave celerity $(gh)^{1/2}$. The values of $\lambda_m^{-1/2}$ for the other modes of type b correspond to the propagational speeds (C_m) associated with internal waves (baroclinic modes). They are of order $0.02 (gh)^{1/2}/m$, $m = 1, 2, \ldots, M$.

In the case of the eddy viscosity eigenmodes (type a), the values of λ_m^{-1} have the physical interpretation of relaxation times for mode m associated with the stress-induced dissipation of kinetic energy. Those modes having the largest λ_m have the greatest contribution to such damping effect; they are the modes with the most detailed structure (large rms value of dF_m/dz).

The strategy of the spectral approach is to convert the 3-D equations of motion into $(M + 1)$ 2-D equation sets, which govern the time evolution of u_m, v_m in addition to ζ (and other variables as needed for the stratified case). The primitive equations involve derivative terms with respect to z and the eigen function analysis allows their elimination. The procedure is facilitated by the orthogonality property of the natural structure functions F_m. The resulting equations differ in important respects for the stratified and non-stratified cases, both of which involve eddy shear stress. The simpler case of a non-stratified fluid is considered first.

Homogeneous Fluid

For the non-stratified case the reduced equations include the depth-integrated equations (LTE) covered earlier under "Governing Equations for Tides, Surges and Circulation" which govern ζ and the depth-averaged current components U/h and V/h. These can be supplemented by predictive equations for the complex quantity $(u_n + iv_n)$, which has the following compact form for given mode n:

$$\left\{\frac{\partial}{\partial t} + (\lambda_n + if)\right\}(u_n + iv_n) = K_n \tag{49}$$

where K_n depends on the gradient of ζ and known forcing; λ_n is the inverse relaxation time for mode n; f is the Coriolis parameter $2\Omega \sin \phi$; and i is the unit imaginary number. The forcing term K_n is specifically as follows:

$$K_n = F_n(0)(\tau_{sx} + i\tau_{sy})/\rho_m h + g\gamma\left(\frac{\partial}{\partial x} + i\frac{\partial}{\partial y}\right)(\alpha\eta + \beta(b - \zeta)) \tag{50}$$

where $dx = r_m \cos \phi \, d\lambda$ and $dy = r_m \, d\phi$; and

$$\gamma = \frac{1}{h}\int_{-h}^{0} F_n \, dz \tag{51}$$

One can employ the LTE to get an update of ζ, then employ Equation 49 to determine an update of the u_n, v_n and also the bottom stress which, in complex form, is given by

$$\tau_{bx} + i\tau_{by} = \rho\kappa_b[\xi F_n(u_n + iv_n)]_{-h} \tag{52}$$

ξ being the eddy viscosity. Relations of this type have been employed in surge/tide models [17, 18, 28, 32, 33].

Equation 49 when applied for steady state conditions yields a generalized Ekman spiral. For the time-evolving case, Equation 49 allows for the possible existence of rotary inertial motion having a frequency close to f and depth dependent amplitude; such inertial motion is commonly found in observed currents, following the sudden onset of winds over a water basin. The presence of the terms λ_n causes such oscillations to be damped in time for a given mode; the lowest eigenmodes (smallest λ_n) being the most persistent. The overall effect on the total velocity, see Equation 42, is that the largest kinetic energy occurs near the sea surface in the initial stages of a storm and then penetrates downward on time scales dictated by the values of λ_n^{-1}.

Stratified Fluid

The simplicity of the homogeneous case is related to the fact that the pressure anomaly at any fixed level z is the same throughout the water column and has the value $\rho_m g\zeta$ (ignoring barometric effect). For the stratified case this is no longer true. One can allow for a z-dependent pressure anomaly in a manner similar to that of u and v, namely

$$P = P_a + P_0(z) + \rho_m \sum_{n=0}^{M} p_n F_n(z, h) \tag{53}$$

where p_n are functions of x, y, t (p_n/g has dimensions of length). The water level ζ is related to the p_n by

$$g\zeta = \sum_{n=0}^{M} p_n F_n(0, h) \tag{54}$$

hence if ζ is known then there exist M extra variables to be determined. The p_n are related to vertical displacement of the isopycnal (density) surfaces whose vertical velocity is controlled by the horizontal divergence associated with u_n and v_n.

The 3-D equations of motion for the stratified fluid can be reduced to (M + 1) sets of equations in the variables u_n, v_n, p_n. The methodology is given for example by Flierl [15], for the case of quasi-geostrophic motion; by McCreary [41], for the primitive equations in constant depth; and by Bunpapong, et al. [2], for the case of two modes in variable depth. For the general case the equations, for a given mode n, resemble the LTE but with some important added coupling terms. When expressed in vector form these are:

$$\left\{ \left(\frac{\partial}{\partial t} + \sigma_n + f\vec{k}x \right) \vec{q}_n + \nabla p_n + F_{nb}\vec{\tau}_b/h\rho_m + \frac{1}{h} \sum_{m=0}^{M} S_{nm} p_m \nabla h \right\}$$

$$= F_{ns}\vec{\tau}_s/h\rho_m + g\nabla(\alpha\eta + \beta b) \delta_{n0} \tag{55}$$

$$\lambda_n \frac{\partial p_n}{\partial t} + \frac{1}{h} \nabla \cdot (h\vec{q}_n) - \frac{1}{h} \sum_{m=0}^{M} S_{mn} \vec{q}_m \cdot \nabla h = 0 \tag{56}$$

where F_{ns}, F_{nb} = F_n at surface and bottom, respectively

$\vec{q}_n$ = 2-D vector with components u_n, v_n

$\vec{k}$ = the unit vertical vector

σ_n = damping coefficients as in McCreary [41]

S_{nm} = coupling parameters

The λ_n are eigenvalues for the stratified case which can be expressed in the form $\lambda_n = c_n^{-2}$ where c_n is the celerity for mode n.

The bottom stress (τ_b) can be parameterized in terms of the bottom velocity as for the LTE, however, the latter depend on the u_n and v_n via Equation 42. This is one of the terms that couples the equations for one mode with those for other modes. The more important coupling terms are those involving the matrix S_{nm}, which appears in Equation 55 and its transpose in Equation 56. These terms arise because of vertical motion of fluid at the seabed caused by horizontal flow across the bathymetric contours. They do not appear in the governing equations given by McCreary [41], because he assumed a horizontal seabed. The bottom slope coupling is included in the two-mode equations used by Bunpapong, et al. [2] and in the quasi-geostrophic vorticity equations of Flierl [15]. It can be shown [61] that for the general case

$$S_{nm} = F_{nb}F_{mb}\lambda_m/(\lambda_n - \lambda_m), \quad n \neq m$$

while

$$S_{nn} = \frac{1}{2}(1 - F_{nb}^2) \tag{57}$$

For the special case of M = 0 (i.e., where all but the barotropic mode are ignored), then $p_0 = g\zeta$, $\sigma_0 = 0$, $S_{00} = 0$, $F_{0s} = F_{0b} = 1$ so Equations 55 and 56 reduce exactly to the LTE for n = 0. In general the barotropic mode (n = 0) and baroclinic modes (n > 0) are coupled and energy can cascade in spectral mode space n in either direction [56].

The general coupled equations for a stratified fluid can be employed to address the problem of baroclinic tides, driven by the barotropic (surface) tide, over a sloping shelf [61]. For such problems horizontal resolution can be a very limiting factor because of the small wavelengths of the baroclinic tides over the shelf.

Equations 55 and 57 also can be employed to study the low frequency baroclinic shelf waves driven by wind stress, which have been studied previously with the 3-D primitive equations [7]. In the case of a homogeneous fluid, momentum and kinetic energy supplied by the wind stress can penetrate downward only by turbulent mixing (parameterized by eddy viscosity or higher order schemes). For a stratified fluid an effective supplement to mixing is the possibility of a downward component of energy propagation by internal waves [44]. In fact this is the major mechanism for transfer across the thermocline, where mixing is suppressed by the high stability. In terms of the spectral mode representation of the velocity structure, the downward propagation is manifested in the form of rapid development of all modes by wind stress in the early stages of a storm, followed by a readjustment of the phasing of these modes with time. In the early stages, the phasing of the modes is such that they reinforce in the upper part of the water column and cancel each other in the lower part. As time goes by the changing phasing of the modes leads to a structure with non-zero abyssal current.

The spectral mode representation for vertical structure of currents in a stratified fluid is particularly advantageous for low (subinertial) frequency phenomena, as in slowly evolving ocean circulation. The reason for this is that the velocity structure in such cases can be very well represented with only a few modes [12, 62]. The alternative of employing a model with n fixed levels requires many levels in order to achieve an equivalent resolution, and can be very demanding in terms of computer resources. The price one must pay for the spectral method is in the solution of the eigenvalue problem, Equations 43 to 45 for the stratification modes $F_n(z)$ and their associated λ_n. However, this need be carried out only once, for given $\rho_0(z)$ and an appropriate array of h; the resulting information is then stored for the routine time marching calculations of u_n, v_n, p_n. The detailed profiles of u and v are readily calculated for those locations of interest as post processing of the results.

Closing Remarks

This single section dealing with the important topic of current structure associated with tide, storm surges, and low-frequency meteorological forcing of the ocean and its marginal shelves is but a brief summary. The intent has been to highlight some of its important aspects in the context of modeling, with particular attention to spectral (or n-mode) models.

This chapter in general has stressed the physics and the continuum representation of the physics of models, rather than the details of its implementation in terms of numerical codes. The most important factor in numerical implementation is proper resolution consistent with those natural scales (like λ_n) dictated by the physics or the basin morphology. The overall credibility of any model that attempts to simulated tides, storm surges, shelf waves, and their associated current structure in time and space rests heavily on careful attention to the following essential elements:

1. The physics of the governing equations.
2. The accuracy of the external forcing.
3. The consistency of boundary constraints with the interior physics.
4. The adequacy of the resolution provided by the numerical methodology.
5. The adequacy of the parameterization of sub-grid scale processes not resolved by the model.
6. The verification of the model via adequate comparison with observations.

An important limitation of the present review is the omission of convective terms. For flow regimes having small Froude number or small Rossby number this approximation may be justified. Convection is vital in studies of flow separation, wakes, wave-wave interaction and small-scale eddy dynamics, which are not addressed here. Many models do in fact include such terms; they are the most difficult to implement in a truly satisfactory manner with the inherent constraints of limited resolution and numerical stability. For a recent treatment of the nonlinear shallow water equation, see Westerink et al. [76].

Modeling of the dynamics of the ocean, like that of the atmosphere has been and remains a learning process, always subject to developments in numerical techniques, new insights provided by new measurement technology, and advances in computer infrastructure capability. The application of some of our yet incomplete and largely unverified models to engineering problems has a definite boldness in it. And while the great German philosopher Goethe tells us that "boldness has genius, power, and magic in it," professional engineering ethics urges us to temper boldness with engineering judgment and insight. There exists no more genius, power, nor magic in a model than that which one builds into it; and its real credibility rests on adequate verification.

Notation

A	boundary condition coefficient, Equations 28, 29
A_n	amplitude of tidal constituent n for given tide station, Equation 41
B	boundary condition coefficient, Equations 28, 29
B_{jn}	amplitude of tide potential constituent n of species j, Equation 38, Table 2
b	barometric pressure deficit expressed an as equivalent height of water, Equation 9
b_s	steady part of b (time average)
b'	$b - b_s$
C	boundary condition coefficient, Equation 29
C_d	wind stress drag coefficient, Equations 31, 42
C_b	seabed drag coefficient, Equation 32
c_n	celerity of given wave mode n
D	time average water depth at given location
d_i	distance between center of mass of body i and Earth's center of mass
e	base of natural logarithm (2.7182818)
F	forcing term in boundary condition, Equations 28, 29
F_{ij}	astronomical function for body i, species j, Equation 36
F_n	vertical structure function for mode n, defined by Equations 43–45
f	Coriolis parameter $2\Omega \sin \phi$
f_{jn}	nodal factor for tide constituent n, species j; a slowly changing function of time.
G	global convolution functional notation, Equation 14
G_i	astronomical coefficient, Equation 37
G_n	phase (or epoch) of tidal constituent n for given tide station, referenced to Greenwich.
g	acceleration due to gravity
g_s	sea-level value of g, about 9.8 m/s^2
h	water depth from seabed to sea surface
i	index; also $\sqrt{-1}$
j	index
K_n	defined by Equation 50
$\vec{k}$	vertical unit vector, positive upward
L	shelf width
L_j	latitude dependence of tide species j, Equation 39
M_i	mass of body i (e = Earth, m = moon, s = sun)
n	index
P	pressure
P_s	steady part of P

P_r reference value of P

P_a atmospheric pressure at sea level

P' pressure anomaly $P - P_r$

p_n see Equation 53

Q_n volume transport component normal to and outward from boundary of fluid domain

$\dot{q}_n$ horizontal velocity vector for spectral mode n

r geocentric radial distance

r_s value of r at sea surface

r_b value of r at seabed

r_m mean radius of Geoid

S_{nm} coupling matrix, Equation 57

T_{jn} period of tidal constituent n, species j

t time

t_0 reference time

U zonal component of volume transport

U_s steady part of U

U' $U - U_s$

u zonal component of velocity

V meridional component of volume transport

V_s steady part of V

V' $V - V_s$

v Meridional component of velocity

v_r RMS fluid speed

v_{jn} Astronomical argument for tide constituent n, species j; a slowly changing function of time

W Wind speed

x Zonal Cartesian coordinate; $dx = r_m \cos \phi \, d\lambda$

y meridional Cartesian coordinate; $dy = r_m \, d\varphi$

z vertical coordinate, $dz = dr$

α coefficient modifying the Newtonian tide potential η caused by Earth tide; accepted value of α is 0.69 (nondimensional)

β coefficient modifying the water level anomaly ζ' in the approximation of the effect of seabed loading and self attraction (change of g associated with water level changes); for global tides the recommended value of β is 0.9; for disturbances of horizontal scale less than 1,000 km one should take $\beta = 1$ (seabed loading and self attraction is negligible)

β_r Rossby parameter, Equation 23

Γ effective tide generating potential; depends on the direct Newtonian potential η but also on changes in g associated with distortion of the Earth (variable r_b) and sea surface (variable r_s); Γ is approximately equal to $g_s(\alpha\eta + (1 - \beta)(\zeta' - b'))$

γ Depth average of F_n, Equation 51

ΔP Central pressure deficit, as for a hurricane

δ_i Declination of body i relative to Earth's equatorial plane

δ_{nm} Identity matrix: 1 for m = n, 0 for m $\neq$ n

ϵ Residual error

ζ Water level realtive to some adopted reference

ζ_a Water level relative to the geoid, Equation 11

ζ_t Water level relative to mean sea level at a given station for given NTDE

ζ_s Steady part of ζ

ζ' $\zeta - \zeta_s$

η Newtonian tide potential or equilibrium tide (units of elevation); $-g\,\nabla\eta$ is the astronomically induced tide producing force acting on a unit mass

θ Wind azimuth; also used to signify 1 or j

θ_t Azimuth of storm track

κ_b Parameter with dimensions of $[L^{-1}]$, Equation 45

κ_s parameter with dimensions of $[L^{-1}]$, Equation 44

λ longitude, positive eastward from Greenwich meridian

λ_i longitude of body i

λ_m eigenvalue for mode m, Equation 43

μ parameter with dimensions of $[L^{-1}]$, Equation 30

ξ a function of z governing the vertical structure functions F_m for physical mode m, Equation 42; for physical modes governed by shear stress ξ is eddy viscosity $[L^2/T]$; for physical modes governed by density stratification ξ is given by Equation 46, with dimension $[T^2]$

π ratio of perimeter to diameter of a circle (3.14159...); 2π radians = 360° of arc or phase

ρ mass density of sea water

ρ_m adopted mean ρ (about 1,030 kg/m³)

ρ_r reference state $\rho(z)$; also denoted $\rho_0(z)$, except that ρ_0 is potential density (adiabatic compression effect removed)

ρ_a density of air at sea level (about 1.2 kg/m³).

σ_n damping coefficient for mode n with dimension $[T^{-1}]$.

τ horizontal shear stress with dimensions of force per unit area; used in vector and component sense; τ_s wind stress; τ_b bottom stress

Φ geopotential with units of energy per unit mass $[L^2T^{-2}]$; $d\Phi = g\,dr = g\,dz$; Φ = constant is a level surface, a particular value of which (Φ_r) corresponds to the reference geoid

Φ_s value of Φ at sea surface

ϕ latitude, positive northward from equator

χ transport potential, Equation 10

Ψ_s volume transport streamfunction for steady circulation, Equation 21

Ω angular speed of Earth (2π radians per sidereal day)

ω_n frequency of tidal constituent, $2\pi/T_n$

∇ gradient operator along a level surface

∇^2 Laplacian operator

Technical Abbreviations

ADI   alternating direction implicit

CY   Gregorian calendar year

GEOSAT	exact repeat orbit satellite for determinating the geoid and sea-level time variations via radio altimetry
GLTE	generalized Laplace tidal equations
GMT	Greenwich mean time
GOM	Gulf of Mexico
LTE	Laplace tidal equations
MLW	mean low-water level
MLLW	mean lower low-water level.
MSL	mean sea level
MHW	mean high water level
MHHW	mean higher high water level
NTDE	national tidal datum epoch, a 19-year time interval used to define a MSL datum
RHS	right hand side
RMS	root mean square

References

1. Accad, Y. and Pekeris, C. L., 1978, "Solution of the Tidal Equations for M_2 and S_2 Tides in the World Oceans from a Knowledge of Tidal Potential Alone," *Phil. Trans., Royal Soc. of London*, A290:235–266.
2. Bunpapong, M., Reid, R. O., and Whitaker, R. E., 1985, "An Investigation of Hurricane-Induced Forerunner Surge in the Gulf of Mexico," Tech. Rep. CERC-85-5, Coastal Engineering Research Center, U.S. Army Engineer Waterways Experiment Station, Vicksburg, Miss.; 201 pp.
3. Businger, J. A. and Arya, S. P. S., 1974, "Height of the Mixed Layer in the Stably Stratified Planetary Boundary Layer," in *Advances in Geophysics*, Vol. 18A, 73–92; Academic Press, New York, N.Y.
4. Butler, H. L., 1978, "Coastal Flood Simulation in Stretched Coordinates," *Proc. 16th Coastal Engineering Conference*, Amer. Soc. Civil Engineers, Vol. 1:1030.
5. Cartwright, D. E., 1977, "Ocean Tides," *Reports on Progress in Physics* 40:665–704.
6. Charney, J. G. and Flierl, G. R., 1981, "Ocean Analogues of Large-Scale Atmospheric Motions," in *Evolution of Physical Oceanography*, Ch. 18:504–549, MIT Press, Cambridge, Mass.
7. Clarke, A. J. and Brink, K. H., 1985, "The Response of Stratified, Frictional Flow of Shelf and Slope Waters to Fluctuating Large-Scale, Low-Frequency Wind Forcing," *J. Phys. Oceanogr.*, 15:439–453.
8. Coastal Engineering Research Center, 1973, *Shore Protection Manual*, Vol. I, U.S. Dept. of the Army, Corps of Engineers.
9. Committee on Tidal Hydraulics, 1980, "Evaluation of Numerical Storm Surge Models," Tech. Bul. No. 21, Office of Chief of Engineers, U.S. Army, Washington, D.C. 26 pp. with 4 appendices.
9a. Conner, W. C., Kraft, R. H., and Harris, D. L., 1957, "Empirical Methods for Forecasting the Maximum Storm Tide Due to Hurricanes and Other Tropical Storms," *Monthly Weather Review*, Vol. 85:113–116.
10. Csanady, G. T., 1981, "Circulation in the Coastal Ocean," in *Advances in Geophysics*, Vol. 23:101–183; Academic Press, New York, N.Y.

11. Defant, Albert, 1961, *Physical Oceanography*, Volume II, Pergamon Press, N.Y., 598 pp.
12. DeMey, P. and Robinson, A. R., 1987, "Assimilation of Altimeter Eddy Fields in a Limited-Area Quasi-Geostrophic Model," *J. Phys. Oceanogr.*, 17:2280–2293.
13. Dietrich, G., 1944, "Die Schwingungssysteme der halb-und eintägigen Tiden in den Ozeanen," *Veröff. Inst. fur Meereskunde*, N.F.A. no. 41, Universitat Berlin.
14. Farrell, W. E., 1972, "Earth Tides, Ocean Tides and Tidal Loading," *Phil. Trans. Roy. Soc. London*, Ser. A, 274:45.
15. Flierl, G. R., 1978, "Models of Vertical Structure and Calibration of Two-Layer Models," *Dynamics of Atmospheres and Oceans*, 2:341–381, Elsevier, Amsterdam.
16. Fofonoff, N. P., 1962, "Dynamics of Ocean Currents," in *The Sea*, Vol. 1, Sec III:323–396. Interscience, John Wiley, N.Y.
17. Forristall,, G. Z., 1974, "Three-Dimensional Structure of Storm Generated Currents," *J. Geophys. Res.*, 79:2721–2729.
18. Forristall, G. Z., Hamilton, R. C., and Cardone, V. J., 1977, "Continental Shelf Currents in Tropical Storm Delia: Observations and Theory," *J. Phys. Oceanogr.*, 7:532–546.
19. Garratt, J. R., 1977, "Review of Drag Coefficients Over Oceans and Continents," *Mon. Wea. Rev.*, 105:915–929.
20. Garrett, Christopher, 1975, "Tides in Gulfs," *Deep-Sea Research*, 22:23–35.
21. Grant, W. D. and Madsen, O. S., 1979, "Combined Wave and Current Interaction with a Rough Bottom," *J. Geophys. Res.*, 84:1797–1808.
22. Grijalva, Nicolas, 1971, "The M_2 Tide in the Gulf of Mexico." *Geofisica Internacional, Mexico*, 11:70–83.
23. Harris, D. L., 1963, "Characteristics of the Hurricane Storm Surge." Technical Paper No. 48, U.S. Dept. of Commerce, Washington, D.C.
23a. Harris, D. L., 1959, "An Interim Hurricane Storm Surge Forecasting Guide," National Hurricane Research Report No. 32, Weather Bureau, U.S. Dept. of Commerce, Washington, D.C., 24 pp.
24. Harris, D. L., 1981, "Tides and Tidal Datums in the United States." Special Report No. 7, Coastal Engineering Research Center, U.S. Army, Corps of Engineers; 382 pp.
25. Harris, D. L., 1982, "Data Requirements for the Evaluation of Storm Surge Models," Coastal and Oceanographic Engineering Dept., Univ. of Florida. Published by the Division of Health, Siting and Waste Management, U.S. Nuclear Regulatory Commission, Washington, D.C. (NUREG/CR-2555). 38 pp.
26. Hendershott, M. C., 1977, "Numerical models of ocean tides," in *The Sea*, Vol. 6, Ch. 2: 47–96. Interscience, John Wiley, N.Y.
27. Hendershott, M. C., 1981, "Long Waves and Ocean Tides," in *Evolution of Physical Oceanography*, Ch. 10:292–341. MIT Press, Cambridge, Mass.
28. Heaps, N. S. and Jones, J. E., 1975, "Storm Surge Computations for the Irish Sea Using a Three-Dimensional Numerical Model." *Mem. Soce.r. Scie. Liege*, Ser. 6, 7:289–333.
29. Holland, W. R., 1977, "Oceanic General Circulation Models," in *The Sea*, Vol. 6, Ch. 1: 3–46. Interscience, John Wiley, N.Y.
30. Huang, N. E., Bliven, L. F., Long, S. R., and DeLeonibus P. S., 1986, "A Study of the Relationship Among Wind Speed, Sea State, and the Drag Coefficient for a Developing Wave Field," *J. Geophys. Res.*, 91, C6:7733–7742.
31. Jeffreys, Sir Harold, 1954, "Dynamics of the Earth-Moon System," in *The Earth as a Planet*, Ch. 2:42–56, Kuiper, G. P., Ed. Univ. of Chicago Press, Chicago, Illinois.
32. Jelesnianski, C. P., 1967, "Numerical Computations of Storm Surges With Bottom Stress," *Mon. Wea. Rev.*, 95:740–756.
33. Jelesnianski, C. P., 1970, "Bottom Stress Time History in Linearized Equations of Motion for Storm Surges," *Mon. Wea. Rev.*, 98:462–478.

34. Jelesnianski, C. P., 1972, "SPLASH (Special Programs to List Amplitudes of Surges from Hurricanes); Part I: Landfall Storms," NOAA Tech. Memo. NWS TDL-46, National Weather Service, Silver Spring, Md.

35. Jelesnianski, C. P., 1974, "SPLASH (Special Programs to List Amplitudes of Surges from Hurricanes); Part II: General Track and Variant Storm Conditions," NOAA Tech. Mem. NWS TDL-52, National Weather Service, Silver Spring, Md.

36. Jelesnianski, C. P. and Chen, J., 1981, "Sea, Lake, and Overland Surges from Hurricanes (SLOSH)," Unpublished report of the Techniques Development Laboratory, National Weather Service, NOAA, Silver Spring, Maryland.

37. LeBlond, P. H. and Mysak, L. A., 1981, "Trapped Coastal Waves and Their Role in Shelf Dynamics," in *The Sea*, Vol. 6, Ch. 10:459–495.

38. Leendertse, J. J., 1967, "Aspects of a Computational Model for long-period water-wave propagation," Memo. RM5294-PR, The Rand Corporation, Santa Monica, CA. 165 pp.

39. Liu, S.-K. and Leendertse, J. J., 1987, "Modeling the Alaskan Continental Shelf Waters," Report R-3567-NOAA/RC, The Rand Corporation, Santa Monica, CA. 136 pp.

40. Madsen, O. S., 1977, "A Realistic Model of the Wind-Induced Ekman Boundary Layer," *J. Phys. Oceanogr.* 7:248–255.

41. McCreary, J. P., 1981, "A Linear Stratified Ocean Model of the Coastal Undercurrent," *Phil. Trans. Roy. Soc.*, London, 302:385–413.

42. Mitchell, T. M. and Brown, M., 1988. Proceedings of Symposium on the Physical Oceanography of the Louisiana/Texas Shelf, Galveston, TX, May 24–26, 1988. To be published by the Minerals Management Service, Gulf of Mexico Region, New Orleans, LA.

43. Munk, W. H. and Cartwright, D. E., 1966, "Tidal Spectroscopy and Prediction," *Phil. Trans. Roy. Soc. London* Ser. A259:533–581.

44. Munk, W. H., 1981, "Internal Waves and Small-Scale Processes," in *Evolution of Physical Oceanography*, Ch. 9:264–291. MIT Press, Cambridge, Mass.

45. Mungall, J. C. H., Able, C. E., and Olling, C. R., 1978, "Hydrodynamic Model Estimates of the M_2 and K_1 Currents of the Gulf of Mexico," Tech. Rep. 78-9-T, Department of Oceanography, Texas A&M University, College Station, TX.

46. National Research Council, 1983, "Evaluation of the FEMA model for Estimating Potential Coastal Flooding from Hurricanes and Its Application to Lee County, Florida," Committee on Coastal Flooding from Hurricanes, Advisory Board on the Built Environment, Commission on Engineering and Technical Systems. National Academy Press, Washington, D.C. 154 pp.

47. National Research Council, 1987, "Responding to Changes in Sea Level, Engineering Implications," Committee on Engineering Implications of Changes in Relative Mean Sea Level. Marine Board. Commission on Engineering and Technical Systems. National Academy Press, Washington, D.C. 148 pp.

48. Nowlin, W. D. Jr., Bottero, J. S., and Pillsbury, R. D., 1982, "Observations of the Principal Tidal Currents at Drake Passage," *J. Geophys. Res.*, C7, 87:5752–5770.

49. Office of the Chief of Engineers, 1986. "Engineering and Design: Storm Surge Analysis and Design Water Level Determinations." Engineer Manual No. 1110-2-1412, Department of the Army, U.S. Corps of Engineers, Washington, D.C. 4 Chapters and 8 Appendices.

50. Platzman, G. W., 1972, "Two-Dimensional Free Oscillations in Natural Basins," *J. Phys. Oceanogr.*, 2:117–138.

51. Platzman, G. W., 1975, "Normal Modes of the Atlantic and Indian Oceans," *J. Phys. Oceanogr.*, 5:201–221.

52. Platzman, G. W., 1978, "Normal Modes of the World Ocean, Part I. Design of a Finite-Element Barotropic model," *J. Phys. Oceanogr.*, 8:323–343.

53. Platzman, G. W., 1984, "Normal Modes of the World Ocean, Part III. A Procedure for Tidal Synthesis," *J. Phys. Oceanogr.*, 14:1521–1531.

54. Platzman, G. W., 1984, "Normal Modes of the World Ocean, Part IV. Synthesis of Diurnal and Semidiurnal Tides." *J. Phys. Oceanogr.*, 14:1532–1550.

55. Platzman, G. W., Curtis, G. A., Hansen, K. S., and Slater, R. D. 1981, "Normal Modes of the World Ocean. Part II. Description of modes in the period range 8 to 80 hours," *J. Phys. Oceanogr.*, 11:579–603.

56. Rhines, P. B., 1977, "The Dynamics of Unsteady Currents," in *The Sea*, Vol. 6, Ch. 7:189–318. Interscience, John Wiley, N.Y.

57. Reid, R. O. and Bodine, B. R., 1968, "Numerical Model for Storm Surges in Galveston Bay," *J. Waterways, Harbors and Coastal Division*, Amer. Soc. of Civil Engineers, 94, WWI, Proc. 5805:33–57.

58. Reid, R. O., Vastano, A. C., and Reid, T. J., 1977, "Development of SURGE II Program with Application to Sabine-Calcasieu Area for Hurricane Carla and Design Hurricanes," Tech. Paper No. 77–13, Coastal Engineering Research Center, U.S. Army Corps of Engineers, 218 pp.

59. Reid, R. O and Whitaker, R. E., 1981, "Numerical Model for Astronomical Tides in the Gulf of Mexico," Tech. Report, Department of Oceanography, Texas A&M University, College Station, TX (prepared for U.S. Army Engineer Waterways Experiment Station, Vicksburg, Miss.).

60. Reid, R. O., 1988, "Sensitivity of Basin Normal Modes to Resolution of Shelf Bathymetry," Abstracts of papers at the International Conference on Tidal Hydrodynamics, Nov. 15–18, 1988, National Bureau of Standards, Gaithersburg, Md. Full papers to be published in 1989 by the National Ocean Service/NOAA and the Marine Technology Society.

61. Reid, R. O. and Dever, E. P., 1988, "Baroclinic Tides in an Axially Symmetric Basin," Abstract in EOS, December 1988 American Geophysical Union. Full paper available as M.S. thesis 1989 by Dever, E. P., Texas A&M University.

62. Rienecker, M. M., Mooers, C. N. K., and Robinson, A. R., 1987, "Dynamical Interpolation and Forecast of the Evolution of Mesoscale Features off Northern California," *J. Phys. Oceanogr.*, 17:1189–1213.

63. Schureman, Paul, 1941, *Manual of Harmonic Analysis and Prediction of Tides*, Special Pub. No. 98, Coast and Geodetic Survey, U.S. Dept. of Commerce. U.S. Government Printing Office, Washington, D.C. 313 pp.

64. Schwiderski, E. W., 1979, "Global Ocean Tides; Part II: The Semidiurnal Principal Lunar Tide (M_2), Atlas of Tidal Charts and Maps," Report NSWC TR 79-414 of the Naval Surface Weapons Center, Dahlgren, VA. 15 pp. plus tables and charts.

65. Schwiderski, E. W., 1980, "On Charting Global Ocean Tides," *Reviews of Geophysics and Space Physics*, 18(1):243–268.

66. Schwiderski, E. W., 1983, "Atlas of Ocean Tidal Charts and Maps, Part I: the Principal Lunar Tide M_2." *Marine Geodesy*, 6:219–265.

67. Sheng, Y. P., 1983, "Mathematical Modeling of Three-Dimensional Coastal Currents and Sediment Dispersion: Model-Development and Application," Tech. Rep. CERC-83-2, Office of Chief of Engineers, U.S. Army Washington, D.C. 288 pp.

68. Stommel, Henry, 1965, "The Gulf Stream, A Physical and Dynamical Description," Univ. of California Press, Berkeley and Cambridge Univ. Press, London. Second Edition. 248 pp.

69. Sturges, W., 1974, "Sea-level Slope Along Continental Boundaries," *J. Geophys. Res.*, 79:825–830.

70. TetraTech, Inc. 1981, "Coastal and Flooding Storm Surge Model. Part I: Methodology; Part 2: Users Guide; Part 3: Codes," Prepared for the Federal Emergency Management Agency, Washington, D.C. by TetraTech, Inc., Pasadena, CA. Approx. 380 pp.

71. Thomas, J. H., 1975, "A Theory of Steady Wind-Driven Currents in Shallow Water with Variable Eddy Viscosity," *J. Phys. Oceanogr.*, 5:136–142.

72. Van Dorn, W. G., 1953, "Wind Stress on an Artificial Pond," *J. Mar. Res.*, 12:249–276.
73. Veronis, George, 1981, "Dynamics of Large-Scale Ocean Circulation," in *Evolution of Physical Oceanography*, Ch. 5:140–183. MIT Press, Cambridge, Mass.
74. Wanstrath, J. J., 1976, "Storm Surge Simulation in Transformed Coordinates," Vols. I and II, Techn Rep. No. 76-3, U.S. Army Coastal Engineering Research Center, Fort Belvoir, VA. Vol I 166 pp.; Vol II 176 pp.
75. Wanstrath, J. J., 1978, "An Open-Coast Mathematical Storm Surge Model with Coastal Flooding for Louisiana," Misc. Paper H-78-5, Reports 1 and 2. U.S. Army Engineer Waterways Experiment Station, Vicksburg, Miss.
76. Westerink, J. J., Connor, J. J., and Stolzenbach, K. D., 1988, "A Frequency-Time Domain Finite Element Model for Tidal Circulation Based on the Least-Squares Harmonic Analysis Method," *Int. J. Num. Methods in Fluids*, 8:813–843.
77. Wilson, B. W., 1972, "Seiches," *Advances in Hydroscience*, Vol 8:1–94. Academic Press, N.Y.
78. Wu, Jin, 1982, "Wind-stress Coefficients Over Sea Surface from Breeze to Hurricane," *J. Geophys. Res.*, 87:9704–9706.

CHAPTER 10

TSUNAMI

Fred E. Camfield

Research Hydraulic Engineer
Coastal Engineering Research Center (CERC)
U.S. Army Engineer Waterways Experiment Station
Vicksburg, Mississippi, U.S.A.

CONTENTS

Introduction

The term "tsunami" is derived from two Japanese words: *tsu*, meaning harbor, and *nami*, meaning wave. Tsunamis, or seismic sea waves, have very long periods and are not easily dissipated. The waves may create large surges or oscillations in bays or harbors that are not responsive to the action of normal sea waves. In the original definition, the term tsunami was applied to all large waves, including storm surges. However, recent definitions have limited its application to waves generated by tectonic or volcanic activity. Western literature previously referred to these waves as tidal waves or seismic sea waves, but those terms have generally been replaced by the term tsunami.

Tsunamis are primarily created by disturbances in the crust of the Earth underlying bodies of water, and the resulting uplifting of the water surface over a large area, which forms a train of very long-period waves. The waves may have periods exceeding 1 hour, in contrast to normally occurring wind-generated sea waves that have periods less than 1 minute. When tsunamis are generated by volcanic activity or landslides, the wave energy tends to spread along the wave crests and the tsunamis affect mainly the areas near their source. Tsunami waves generated by tectonic uplifting may travel across an ocean basin, and can cause great destruction at locations far from their source.

Because of the potential destructive effects of tsunamis, it is necessary to understand the mechanisms of their generation and propagation, and to be able to predict the extent of flooding and the effect of wave forces in coastal areas subject to tsunami attack. Proper control must be exercised over the use of such areas, and in designing structures to be placed in these areas. Also, sufficient warning of a tsunami attack must be given to people located in these areas, and procedures must be established for an orderly evacuation when necessary.

Nature and Origin of Tsunamis

Areas of seismic activity which have a high potential for generating tsunamis occur along the boundaries of the Pacific Ocean, with other regions of strong activity primarily concentrated in the Caribbean and Mediterranean areas. Van Dorn [105] indicated that the Japan Trench radiates detectable tsunamis at the rate of about one per year. Lesser amounts of activity occur elsewhere. Tsunamis can be generated in any coastal area, including inland seas and large lakes. Spaeth [98] provides an extensive bibliography on tsunamis. Additional information is available [2, 24, 36, 86, 96, 97].

Consideration must be given to the fact that records based on visual observations may not include all tsunamis that occurred. The observers probably gave special notice only to those waves that caused substantial flooding or large, rapid variations of the water level in bays and harbors. At a location where the normal tidal range was of the same order as the tsunami height, a tsunami occurring at a low tide stage may have been given only passing notice, if noticed at all, while the same tsunami occurring at a high tide stage would have been recorded as a major tsunami. Likewise, the occurrence of a tsunami in conjunction with high storm waves would have caused more flooding, and therefore, may have been given more significance in the records than a tsunami occurring during a relative calm.

Records of tsunamis in the Mediterranean and Middle East include theories on the eruption of Thira (also known as Santorini) and the tsunami on the coast of Crete that destroyed the Minoan Empire circa 1400 B.C. Factual accounts of tsunamis extend back at least 2,000 years. Accounts of tsunamis in Japan extend back at least 1,300 years. In contrast, records of tsunamis originating in the Chile-Peru coastal areas only cover about 400 years (from 1562 to present), those originating in Alaska about 200 years (from 1788), and those occurring in Hawaii slightly more than 150 years (from 1813). Few records are available of tsunamis occurring on the California-Oregon-Washington coastline. Holden [41] indicates tsunamis occurred at points on the California coastline in 1812, with various occurrences at later dates, mainly recorded or observed at San Francisco. Townley and Allen [103] provide similar information.

Although tsunamis occur frequently in the Caribbean, they are much less frequent in the North Atlantic Ocean. The only major recorded tsunami along the east coast of the United States and Canada was the tsunami generated by the Grand Banks earthquake, which devastated the Burin Peninsula along Placentia Bay, Newfoundland, in November 1929. At least 26 lives were lost [57]. The tsunami was enhanced by an exceptionally high tide and high storm waves; otherwise, it may not have been of major proportions [40]. This tsunami was reported to have had a height of 0.31 m (1 ft) in Atlantic City, New Jersey [79].

The only tsunamis of record that traveled across the North Atlantic were those generated near Lisbon, Portugal, in 1755 and 1761. Both of these were recorded on the south coast of England, as well as in the West Indies [25]. For comparison, the 1755 tsunami had a maximum rise of 2.4 m (8 ft) at Penzance (England) and flowed over the wharves and streets at Barbados (West Indies). In 1761, the sea rose about 1.8 m (6 ft) at Penzance and 1.2 m (4 ft) at Barbados. Other run-up heights in 1755 were estimated at 4.9 m (16 ft) on the coast of Portugal, 18 m (60 ft) at Cadiz (Spain), 1.8 m (5.9 ft) at Gibraltar, 15 m (50 ft) at Tangier (Morocco), 5.6 m (18 ft) at Madeira, 14.6 m (48 ft) at Faial (the Azores), 2.5 m (8.2 ft) at St. Ives (England), 3.7 m (12 ft) at Antigua (West Indies), 6.4 m (21 ft) at Saba (West Indies), and the waves overflowed the lowlands on the coasts of Martinique and other French islands.

Probability of Occurrence

Where sufficient historical data are available on tsunami flood levels, the probability of tsunami flooding at any elevation can be determined by the same methods used for determining the probability of floods on rivers. For a known period of record, the recorded flood levels can be ranked from the largest to the smallest; i.e., the highest flood level is ranked 1, the next highest is ranked 2, and so on. Linsley, Kohler, Paulhus [67] show that the probability of each flood level is then given by

$$P(Z) = \frac{m}{n+1} \tag{1}$$

where P(Z) = the probability of flooding to the evaluation Z in any year
Z = the elevation above a defined datum
m = the rank of the flood level
n = the period of record in years

Houston, Carver, and Markle [45] have determined the probability of tsunami flood levels for the Hawaiian Islands. For recurrence intervals greater than 10 years, i.e., $P(Z) < 0.1$, they give

$$h_{200} = -B - A \log_{10} P(h_{200}) \tag{2}$$

where h_{200} = elevation of the maximum tsunami wave crest above mean sea level (MSL) 200 ft (61 m) shoreward of the coastline

$P(h_{200})$ = the probability of a flood level occurring at elevation h_{200} in any given year

A, B = the empirical coefficients determined for each point on the coastline

Where sufficient historical data were not available, they generated additional data using a mathematical model. The model data were multiplied by correction factors and compared to historical data. This produced additional data at points along the coastline where historical data were not available, and allowed a determination of the empirical coefficients A and B at all coastal points.

It should be noted that there is a probability of some error in the predicted flood elevations based on available historical data. For example, there is a 37% probability that a 100-year flood level (i.e., a flood level with a recurrence interval of 100 years) will not occur in any period of 100 years. Therefore, a 100-year flood level predicted from a 100-year period of record may be too low. Also, there is a 9.5% probability that a 1,000-year flood level will occur at least once in any period of 100 years. Therefore, the predicted 100-year flood level, based on a 100-year period of record, may be too high. Camfield [11] discusses the effects of limited periods of record on tsunami flood level predictions.

Where no historical data are available, data may be constructed entirely from a computer model by assigning magnitudes to various tsunamis in the mathematical model, and by determining the probability of generation for each tsunami magnitude. However, the results will not have the same degree of accuracy.

Iida [51] proposed that tsunamis could be assigned a magnitude based on their energy (the energy of the generated waves), with an increase in magnitude of 0.5 being equal to a doubling of the energy. The probability $n(m)$ of a tsunami with magnitude m being generated in any given year in a specified generating area is given by the empirical equation

$$n(m) = ae^{-bm} \tag{3}$$

where the coefficients a and b are determined by a least-squares analysis of the available data for the generating area. To calculate probabilities tsunamis may be placed in groups; e.g., a group of tsunamis shown with magnitude 3.75 actually includes all tsunamis with magnitudes from 3.5 to 4.0, etc. To analyze the probability of an individual tsunami having a magnitude greater than or equal to 3.5, the probabilities would be summed

$$\sum_{j=0}^{2} n(3.75 + 0.5j) = n(3.75) + n(4.25) + n(4.75) \tag{4}$$

which would include all tsunamis with magnitudes from 3.5 to 5.0. Various definitions have been used for tsunami magnitude, and Abe [1] has related magnitude to seismic moment. It is generally assumed that 5 is the upper limit of magnitude. The 1960 Chilean tsunami had the largest seismic moment ever determined, equal to 2×10^{30} dyne-cm [60].

The method for grouping tsunamis (Equation 4) has been used by Houston and Garcia [46], using statistics for the entire trench along the Chilean coast. Applying revised information for that particular generating area, a major source of tsunamis in the western United States [48], $a = 0.074$ and $b = 0.63$. Taking the value $m = 3.5$ for the magnitude of a design tsunami (to be used for determining potential run-up in coastal areas), the probability for a tsunami with a magnitude of 3.5 or greater being generated in any given year is

$$n(3.5) = 0.074[e^{-0.63(3.75)} + e^{-0.63(4.00)} + e^{-0.63(4.75)}] \tag{5}$$

which gives a value of 0.0166 or a recurrence interval of 60 years. For a 412-year period for the Chilean coast, the prediction would be seven tsunamis of magnitude 3.5 or greater. This agrees with historical records of tsunamis in this area.

Another major source of tsunamis in the western United States is the Aleutian Trench. Only relatively recent records exist for the area. Analysis of these records by Houston and Garcia [46], as revised by Houston, et al. [49] and Houston and Garcia [48], gives

$$n(m) = 0.113^{-0.71m} \tag{6}$$

which is similar to the previous equation for the Peru-Chile Trench. The probability of tsunami occurrence is assumed to be uniform along the trench.

Using Equation 6, the probability of a tsunami with a magnitude of 3.5 or greater is

$$n(3.5) = n(3.75) + n(4.25) + n(4.75) \tag{7}$$

which gives a value of 0.0174 for the Aleutian Trench. This value is based on a relatively short period of data for large tsunamis only. Dividing the trench into 12 segments gives the probability of 0.00145 for a tsunami of the given magnitude of 3.5 or greater to be generated at any particular segment of the trench in any given year, assuming an equal probability for each segment. The general equation for a particular segment of the trench becomes

$$n(i) = 0.0094e^{-0.71i} \tag{8}$$

To determine the probability of run-up of a given height at a given location along the coastline, it is necessary to propagate tsunamis across the ocean by numerical means from each segment of the trench for all tsunami magnitudes (i.e., $i = 2.0, 2.5, 3.0, 3.5, 4.0, 4.5,$ and 5.0). The wave train of each tsunami must be superimposed on segments of the tidal cycle of an interval equal to the duration of the wave train. This superposition must be made for each tidal segment of that interval for a 1-year period, and the probability of the resulting run-up determined. Tidal variations are discussed by Harris [35]. A cumulative probability can then be established for run-up at a particular site.

Determining the probability of tsunami run-up at a particular coastal location for tsunamis generated in the Aleutian Trench area, would require the numerical generation of 84 tsunamis (12 segments of trench and 7 intensities of each segment). As shown by Houston and Garcia [46], each run-up value has an associated probability, and the totality of run-up values at a given shoreline point defines a probability distribution from which the cumulative probability distribution, $P_S(Z)$, can be obtained for run-up greater than or equal to a particular value.

By approximating the probability $f_\beta(Z)$ of the astronomical tide by a Gaussian distribution [46, 89], the probability of run-up to a given elevation is given by

$$P(Z) = \int_{-\infty}^{\infty} f_\beta(\lambda) P_S(Z - \lambda) \, d\lambda \tag{9}$$

Probabilities for a tsunami run-up can then be determined at each coastal point, combining the tsunami with the astronomical tide.

An analysis similar to that used for the Aleutian Trench could be applied to tsunamis generated in other source areas. For the west coast of the United States (excluding Hawaii), only the Aleutian Trench and the Peru-Chile Trench appear to produce a significant tsunami run-up, although Holden [41] indicates some occurrence of tsunamis from sources along the California coastline. Using numerical results obtained for tsunamis generated along the Aleutian and Peru-Chile Trenches, Houston and Garcia [48] have determined probable 100- and 500-year tsunami flood elevations for the west coast of the continental United States.

The Generation and Propagation of Tsunamis

The generation and propagation of tsunamis are discussed by Murty [78] and Camfield [9]. Tsunami-type waves can be generated by several sources, including shallow-focus submarine earthquakes, volcanic eruptions, landslides and submarine slumps, and explosions. Each of these sources has its own generating mechanism, and the characteristics of the generated waves are dependent on the generating mechanism. The tsunami waves that travel long, transoceanic distances are normally generated by the tectonic activity associated with shallow-focus earthquakes. However, large waves can be generated locally by the other generating mechanisms.

Tsunami Generation

As shown by Iida [52], tsunamis are generated by shallow-focus earthquakes of a dip-slip fault type; i.e., vertical motion upward on one side of the fault and downward on the other side (Figure 1). Shepard, MacDonald, and Cox [95] indicate that tsunamis traveling long distances across the ocean are probably caused by unipolar disturbances. (An example of a unipolar disturbance would be the uplift of a large area of the sea floor where there is a net change in volume.) Waves generated from a unipolar source decay much less rapidly with distance than waves generated by a

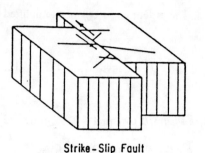 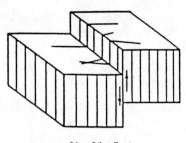

Strike-Slip Fault   Dip-Slip Fault

Figure 1. Movement along faultlines.

bipolar disturbance; i.e., a combination uplifting and subsidence, or other apparent transfer of material on the sea floor, without a net change in volume. Hammack and Segur [34] studied the propagation of waves both experimentally and numerically. They indicate that where there is a positive net change in volume (e.g., a unipolar uplifting of the sea floor), waves of stable form (solitons) evolve, followed by a dispersive train of oscillatory waves. The number of amplitude of the solitons depends on the initial generating mechanism. Van Dorn [105] discusses the generating mechanism of the 1964 Alaskan tsunami. The ground motion was dipolar, having a positive pole (uplifting) under the sea and a negative pole predominantly under the land. As a positive pole was the main tsunami-generating mechanism, this was equivalent to a unipolar source.

Iida [52] shows that major tsunamis (those that cause high water levels at many different coastal locations) do not appear to occur as the result of deep-focus earthquakes or the strike-slip fault type, i.e., horizontal motion along the faultline (Figure 1). A general expression for the lower limit of the earthquake magnitude, M, of tsunamigenic earthquakes is given by Iida [52] as

$$M = 6.3 + 0.005D_f \qquad (10)$$

where D_f is the focal depth in kilometers and M the magnitude on the Richter scale. The Richter scale is given by

$$M = \frac{(\log E - 11.8)}{1.5} \qquad (11)$$

where E is the earthquake energy in ergs.

The generation of large, transoceanic tsunamis results from the displacement of water above the area of uplifted sea bottom associated with a dip-slip fault movement. An uplifting of the sea bottom will produce a vertical uplifting of the overlying water. As a first approximation, it may be assumed that the uplifting of the water surface equals the uplifting of the sea bottom. The potential energy of the uplifted water is then given as

$$E = \sum_{i=1}^{n} \rho g A_i h_i \frac{h_i}{2} \tag{12}$$

where E = the energy in ergs (ft-lb)

ρ = the density of the seawater and is assumed to equal 1.0252 grams/cc (1.989 slugs/ft^3)

g = gravitational acceleration and is equal to 980.7 cm (32.174 ft)/sec^2

A_i = an incremental area of uplifting

h_i = the height of uplifting over the incremental area A_i

or alternatively

$$E = \rho g A \frac{(h^2)_{avg}}{2} \tag{13}$$

where $(h^2)_{avg}$ is the average value of the square of the uplifted heights.

Because of their long periods and corresponding long wavelengths, the train of waves forming a tsunami is taken to be shallow-water waves at their origin, and propagates across the ocean as shallow-water waves. The actual form of the wave train is determined by the initial generating mechanism, i.e., the area of the uplifted sea bottom, the height and variation of the uplift within the area of uplift, and the depth of water and coastal characteristics in the generating area. While ordinary sea waves are assumed to have a cnoidal shape as they approach shore (i.e., high crests and shallow troughs), the waves in a tsunami may have various combinations of forms.

Where the actual sea bottom displacement is known, the initial displacement of the water surface may be taken as equal to the sea bottom displacement. Where an actual sea bottom displacement is not known, an initial displacement may be assumed. Houston, et al. [49] use an assumed elliptical-shaped generating area with an instantaneously displaced water surface, as input data for a standard design tsunami in a numerical solution. They define the surface displacement as a modified elliptic paraboloid, having a parabolic cross section parallel to the major axis of the ellipse, and a triangular cross section parallel to the minor axis of the ellipse. The potential energy of the uplifted water surface for this type of surface displacement is given by

$$E = 4\left(\frac{\rho g}{6}\right) \frac{b}{a} \frac{c^2}{a^4} \int_0^a (a^2 - x^2)^{5/2} \, dx \tag{14}$$

where x = distance measured along the major axis of the ellipse

a = length of the semimajor axis

b = length of the semiminor axis

c = maximum uplifted elevation at coordinates (x = 0, y = 0, z = c)

ρ = the density of the seawater (taken as 1.026 g/cc)

Tsunami Propagation

The initial mound of water described in the previous section will evolve into a wave train. This is discussed in detail by Carrier [13], and by Kajiura [58]. The initial wave train will normally have a broad spectrum, and dispersion effects will result in the longer period waves separating from the shorter period waves, with the longer waves leading the wave group as it propagates away from the source. When waves propagate long distances over the ocean, they will also be subject to lateral spreading.

Tsunamis are long-period waves with long wavelengths in relation to both the water depth and the wave height. Numerical simulation of tsunami propagation may be carried out using either long-wave equations or Boussinesq type equations. Some care must be exercised in applying the numerical methods in order to avoid inaccurate results. Reid [91] points out that for the long-wave equations to be correctly applied, the grid spacing, Δs, should be of the same order as the water depth, d. When Δs is much larger than d, the numerical model may predict too much dispersion and underestimate the amplitude of the leading waves for large propagation distances.

When a tsunami travels a long distance across the ocean, the sphericity of the Earth must be considered to determine the effects of the tsunami on a distant shoreline. Hwang and Divoky [50] give numerical equations in spherical coordinates for computing the propagation of a tsunami. These equations are, at times $t + \Delta t/2$, $t + 3 \Delta t/2$, $t + 5 \Delta t/2$, ...

$$u_{n+1/2} = u_n - \frac{g}{2R_e} \frac{\Delta t}{\Delta \theta} \left(\frac{\partial \eta}{\partial \theta}\right)_{n+1/2} + \frac{1}{2} \Delta t \, f_c \bar{\bar{v}}_n \tag{15}$$

$$\eta_{n+1/2} = \eta_n - \frac{\Delta t}{2R_e \sin \theta} \left\{ \frac{1}{\Delta \theta} \frac{\partial}{\partial \theta} \left[\overline{(d + \eta)}^\phi u \sin \theta \right]_{n+1/2} \right.$$
$$\left. + \frac{1}{\Delta \phi} \frac{\partial}{\partial \phi} \left[\overline{(d + \eta)}^\theta v \right]_n \right\} \tag{16}$$

$$v_{n+1/2} = v_n - \frac{g}{2R_e \sin \theta} \frac{\Delta t}{\Delta \phi} \left(\frac{\partial \eta}{\partial \phi}\right)_n - \frac{1}{2} \Delta t \, f_c \bar{\bar{u}}_{n+1/2} \tag{17}$$

and at times $t + \Delta t$, $t + 2 \Delta t$, $t + 3 \Delta t$, ...

$$v_{n+1} = v_{n+1/2} - \frac{g}{2R_e \sin \theta} \frac{\Delta t}{\Delta \phi} \left(\frac{\partial \eta}{\partial \phi}\right)_{n+1} - \frac{1}{2} \Delta t \, f_c \bar{\bar{u}}_{n+1/2} \tag{18}$$

$$\eta_{n+1} = \eta_{n+1/2} - \frac{\Delta t}{2R_e \sin \theta} \left\{ \frac{1}{\Delta \theta} \frac{\partial}{\partial \theta} \left[\overline{(d + \eta)}^\phi u \sin \theta \right]_{n+1/2} \right.$$
$$\left. + \frac{1}{\Delta \phi} \frac{\partial}{\partial \phi} \left[\overline{(d + \eta)}^\phi v \right]_{n+1} \right\} \tag{19}$$

$$u_{n+1} = u_{n+1/2} - \frac{g}{2R_e} \frac{\Delta t}{\Delta \theta} \left(\frac{\partial \eta}{\partial \theta} \right)_{n+1/2} + \frac{1}{2} \Delta t \, f_c \bar{\bar{v}}_{n+1} \qquad (20)$$

where R_e = radius of Earth

$\quad\quad\; \theta$ = degrees latitude (measured from the pole)

$\quad\quad\; \phi$ = degrees longitude (measured eastward)

$\quad\quad\; u$ = velocity in the θ-direction

$\quad\quad\; v$ = velocity in the ϕ-direction

$\quad\quad\; t$ = time

$\quad\quad\; f_c$ = the coriolis parameter = $2\Omega \cos \theta$

$\quad\quad\; \Omega$ = the rotational speed of the Earth in radians/sec

$$\bar{\bar{u}} = \tfrac{1}{4}(u_{j-1/2,\,k} + u_{j+1/2,\,k} + u_{j-1/2,\,k+1} + u_{j+1/2,\,k+1}) \qquad (21)$$

$$\bar{\bar{v}} = \tfrac{1}{4}(v_{j,\,k-1/2} + v_{j+1,\,k-1/2} + v_{j,\,k+1/2} + v_{j+1,\,k+1/2}) \qquad (22)$$

and terms like $\overline{(d + \eta)}^{\,\theta}$ are computed by averaging in the θ-direction, and $\overline{(d + n)}^{\,\phi}$ in the ϕ-direction. The coordinate system is shown in Figure 2.

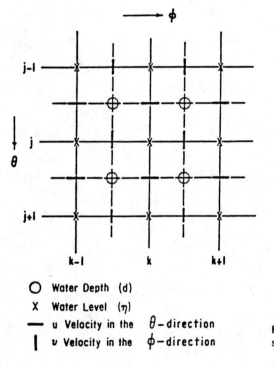

O Water Depth (d)

X Water Level (η)

— u Velocity in the θ – direction

| v Velocity in the ϕ – direction

Figure   2. Coordinate   system, spherical coordinates.

Nearshore Propagation

For refracting waves approaching the shoreline and propagating in two dimensions in the plane of the water surface, Chen, Divoky, and Hwang [21] give the equations below using dimensionless expansions similar to those proposed by Peregrine [87]. A time-staggered scheme is used, with the velocities and wave amplitudes calculated explicitly at alternate time steps of $\Delta t/2$. The amplitudes at $t_0 + \Delta t/2$ will be calculated using amplitude at $t_0 - \Delta t/2$ and velocities at t_0; then, the velocities at $t_0 + \Delta t$ will be calculated using velocities at t_0 and amplitudes at $t_0 + \Delta t/2$. At time $t_0 + \Delta t/2$, the amplitude is

$$\eta_{j,k} = \eta_{j,k} - \frac{\Delta t}{2\,\Delta x}\left[\{(d+\eta)\bar{u}\}_{j+1,\,k} - \{(d+\eta)\bar{u}\}_{j-1,\,k}\right]$$

$$-\frac{\Delta t}{2\,\Delta y}\left[\{(d+\eta)\bar{v}\}_{j,\,k+1} - \{(d+\eta)\bar{v}\}_{j,\,k-1}\right] \tag{23}$$

where the j, k subscripts refer to positions in the plane of the still-water surface, and $\bar{u}$ and $\bar{v}$ the velocities satisfying the linear long-wave equations. Where the initial velocity field is known, $\bar{u}$ and $\bar{v}$ can be computed at time $t_0 + \Delta t$ using values of $\bar{u}$ and $\bar{v}$ at time t_0 and amplitudes at time $t_0 + \Delta t/2$. This gives the equations

$$\bar{u}_{j,k} = \bar{u}_{j,k} - \frac{\Delta t}{2\,\Delta x}\left(\eta_{j+1,\,k} - \eta_{j-1,\,k}\right) \tag{24}$$

$$\bar{v}_{j,k} = \bar{v}_{j,k} - \frac{\Delta t}{2\,\Delta y}\left(\eta_{j,\,k+1} - \eta_{j,\,k-1}\right) \tag{25}$$

At time $t_0 + \Delta t$, the velocities $\bar{u}$ and $\bar{v}$ are given by

$$u_{j,k} = u_{j,\,k} - \frac{\Delta t}{2\,\Delta x}\,\bar{u}_{j,k}(\bar{u}_{j+1,\,k} - \bar{u}_{j-1,\,k}) - \frac{\Delta t}{2\,\Delta y}\,\bar{v}_{j,\,k}(\bar{u}_{j,\,k+1} - \bar{u}_{j,\,k-1})$$

$$-\frac{\Delta t}{2\,\Delta x}\left(\eta_{j+1,\,k} - \eta_{j-1,\,k}\right) \tag{26}$$

$$v_{j,k} = v_{j,\,k} - \frac{\Delta t}{2\,\Delta x}\,\bar{u}_{j,k}(\bar{v}_{j+1,\,k} - \bar{v}_{j-1,\,k}) - \frac{\Delta t}{2\,\Delta y}\,\bar{v}_{j,\,k}(\bar{v}_{j,\,k+1} - \bar{v}_{j,\,k-1})$$

$$-\frac{\Delta t}{2\,\Delta y}\left(\eta_{j,\,k+1} - \eta_{j,\,k-1}\right) \tag{27}$$

where the values on the right side of the equations are previous time steps as indicated.

Chen, Divoky, and Hwang [21], using a stability criterion obtained by Benjamin, Bona, and Mahony [3], used a higher order solution for the amplitude when

$$d < \frac{\Delta x}{(20\,\Delta t)^{1/3}} \tag{28}$$

where the variables are expressed in dimensionless form. The solution then becomes

$$\eta_{j,k} = \eta_{j,k} - \frac{\Delta t}{2\,\Delta x}\left[\{(d+\eta)\bar{u}\}_{j+1,k} - \{(d+\eta)\bar{u}\}_{j-1,k}\right]$$

$$- \frac{\Delta t}{2\,\Delta y}\left[\{(d+\eta)\bar{v}\}_{j,k+1} - \{(d+\eta)\bar{v}\}_{j,k-1}\right]$$

$$- \Delta t \text{ (higher order derivative terms)} \tag{29}$$

The higher order derivatives are approximated by central difference equations as follows

$$\frac{\partial^3 \bar{u}}{\partial x^3} = \frac{1}{2(\Delta x)^3}\left[\bar{u}_{j+2,k} - 2\bar{u}_{j+1,k} + 2\bar{u}_{j-1,k} - \bar{u}_{j-2,k}\right] \tag{30}$$

$$\frac{\partial^3 \bar{v}}{\partial y^3} = \frac{1}{2(\Delta y)^3}\left[\bar{v}_{j,k+2} - 2\bar{v}_{j,k+1} + 2\bar{v}_{j,k-1} - \bar{v}_{j,k-2}\right] \tag{31}$$

$$\frac{\partial^2 d}{\partial x\,\partial y} = \frac{1}{4\,\Delta x\,\Delta y}\left[d_{j+1,k+1} - d_{j-1,k+1} - d_{j+1,k-1} + d_{j-1,k-1}\right] \tag{32}$$

etc. Computed surface elevations were smoothed when one of the following conditions was satisfied:

1. A crest or trough has wave amplitude less than 25% of the maximum wave amplitude at that instant.
2. The local velocity component (u) or (v) has a different sign from the average value of the surrounding four points.
3. At a matching point where equations change from linear to higher order equations.

Smoothing is accomplished by the average

$$\eta_{j,k} = 0.5[\eta_{j,k} + \bar{\eta}_{j,k}] \tag{33}$$

where the values on the right side are before smoothing, and

$$\bar{\eta}_{j,k} = \frac{\tilde{\eta}_{j,k}}{12k+4} \tag{34}$$

where

$$\tilde{\eta}_{j,k} = (1+4k)(\eta_{j-1,k} + \eta_{j+1,k} + \eta_{j,k-1} + \eta_{j,k+1})$$

$$- k(\eta_{j-2,k} + \eta_{j+2,k} + \eta_{j,k-2} + \eta_{j,k+2}) \tag{35}$$

and k represents a weighting spline coefficient that varies from 0 to ∞. The influence from the surrounding points is controlled by the values of (k). For the case $k = 0$, the equation reduces to Laplacian interpolation.

To avoid numerical instability, Chen, Divoky, and Hwang [21] imposed the condition at matching points that

$$\eta_{\text{matching}} = 0.5(\eta_{\text{linear}} + \eta_{\text{higher order}}) \tag{36}$$

Also, the partial derivative with respect to time was approximated by

$$\frac{\partial n}{\partial t} = \frac{\eta_{j,k} - \bar{\eta}_{j,k}}{\Delta t} \tag{37}$$

where η is taken at time $t_0 + \Delta t/2$ and $\bar{\eta}$ at $t_0 - \Delta t/2$, and

$$\bar{\eta}_{j,k} = 0.5\eta_{j,k} + 0.125(\eta_{j-1,k} + \eta_{j+1,k} + \eta_{j,k-1} + \eta_{j,k+1}) \tag{38}$$

Listings of typical computer programs for solutions of long-wave equations can be found in Brandsma, Divoky, and Hwang [6] for linear long-wave equations, and in Chen, Divoky, and Hwang [21] for Boussinesq-type equations.

Tsunamis Approaching the Shoreline

As a tsunami approaches a coastline, the waves are modified by the various off-shore and coastal features. Submerged ridges and reefs, continental shelves, head-lands, various shaped bays, and the steepness of the beach slope may modify the wave period and wave height, cause wave resonance, reflect wave energy, and cause the waves to form bores that surge onto the shoreline.

Ocean ridges provide very little protection for a coastline. While some amount of energy in a tsunami might reflect from the ridge, most of it will be transmitted across the ridge and into the coastline. The 1960 tsunami that originated along the coast of Chile is an example of this. That tsunami had high wave heights along the coast of Japan, including Shikoku and Kyushu, which lie behind the South Honshu Ridge [39].

Abrupt-Depth Transitions

An ocean shelf along a coastline may cause greater modification to a tsunami than an ocean ridge. Waves may become higher and shorter, and dispersion may occur. Lamb [63] gave the equations for a single wave passing over an abrupt change in water depth as shown in Figure 3. He considered only the case of a wave at a zero angle of incidence, i.e., $\theta_1 = \theta_2 = 0$. The equations he derived are

$$\frac{H_r}{H_i} = \frac{d_1^{1/2} - d_2^{1/2}}{d_1^{1/2} + d_2^{1/2}} \tag{39}$$

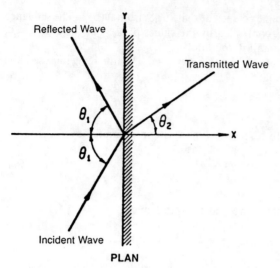

PLAN

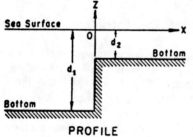

PROFILE

Figure 3. Wave passing onto shelf.

$$\frac{H_t}{H_i} = \frac{2d_1^{1/2}}{d_1^{1/2} + d_2^{1/2}} \tag{40}$$

and

$$\frac{H_t}{H_i} = 1 + \frac{H_r}{H_i} \tag{41}$$

where H_i = incident wave height
  H_r = reflected wave height
  H_t = transmitted wave height
  d_1 = initial water depth
  d_2 = water depth under the transmitted wave

The equations predict that substantial reflection will occur when a wave passes from deep water into shallow water, and also when a wave passes from shallow water to deep water. It is assumed that no energy loss occurs, and that a single incident wave splits into a single reflected wave and a single transmitted wave.

Cochrane and Arthur [23] extended Lamb's work to consider waves approaching a shelf at varying angles of incidence. They give the ratio of reflected wave height to incident wave height as

$$\frac{H_r}{H_i} = \frac{\sqrt{d_1}\cos\theta_1 - \sqrt{d_2}\cos\theta_2}{\sqrt{d_1}\cos\theta_1 + \sqrt{d_2}\cos\theta_2} \tag{42}$$

for an abrupt change in water depth. The water depths d_1 and d_2, and the angles θ_1 and θ_2, are defined in Figure 3. This equation also applies to a single wave with a reflected component and a transmitted component.

The ratio of transmitted wave height H_t to the incident wave height is given by

$$\frac{H_t}{H_i} = 1 + \frac{H_r}{H_i} \tag{43}$$

as before.

Cochrane and Arthur [23] compared a calculated value for a wave from the 1946 tsunami, which reflected from the continental slope off southern Oregon, with an actual recorded wave height at Hanasaki, Japan. Using a rough approximation for the wave height at the top of the continental slope, it was determined that the reflected wave arriving at Hanasaki would have a height of 17 cm (0.56 ft). The observed wave height, for an arrival time equal to the calculated time for the reflected wave, was in good agreement with the calculated wave height. Cochrane and Arthur note that reflected waves are normally of secondary, but not negligible, magnitude according to theory. At given stations, convergence may cause reflected waves to be of primary magnitude, but this occurs only in relatively few cases. Shepard, MacDonald, and Cox [95] note that the highest and most damaging waves at Napoopoo and Hokeena, on the island of Hawaii, from the April 1, 1946 tsunami originating in the Aleutian Islands, Alaska, were reflected waves from the continental slopes of Japan and the Bonin Islands.

Nonlinear Depth Transitions

Kajiura [58] investigated waves passing from deep water to shallow water over the nonlinear slope profile shown in Figure 4. The profile is defined by

$$\frac{1}{d(x)} = \frac{1}{2}\left(\frac{1}{d_1} + \frac{1}{d_2}\right) - \frac{1}{2}\left(\frac{1}{d_2} - \frac{1}{d_1}\right)\tanh\left(\frac{nx}{2}\right) \tag{44}$$

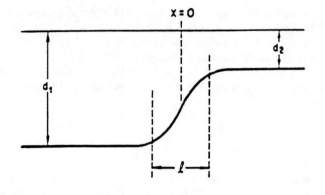

Figure 4. Slope and shelf.

where the effective slope length is given by

$$\ell = \frac{2\pi}{n} \tag{45}$$

L_1 = wavelength at depth d_1
L_2 = wavelength at depth d_2
 n = arbitrary small number in Equation 43 that fits the equation to the actual
       slope and determines the length of the slope in Equation 44

The reflection coefficient obtained by Kajiura is given by

$$\frac{H_r}{H_i} = \left| \frac{\sinh\left[\pi\left(\dfrac{\ell}{L_2} - \dfrac{\ell}{L_1}\right)\right]}{\sinh\left[\pi\left(\dfrac{\ell}{L_2} + \dfrac{\ell}{L_1}\right)\right]} \right| \tag{46}$$

If no energy loss is assumed, then the transmitted wave height can be determined as before for non-dispersive waves. For dispersive waves, a different analysis is required.

Solitons and Shoaling-Induced Dispersion

For certain conditions, a wave will decompose into a train of waves. This train of waves will consist of an initial wave having the highest amplitude, followed by a finite number of waves of decreasing amplitude. Wave dispersion has been investigated by Mason and Keulegan [71], Horikawa and Wiegel [42], Benjamin and Feir [4], Street, Burgess, and Whitford [100], Madsen and Mei [69], Byrne [8],

Street, Chan, and Fromm [102], Galvin [29], Zabusky and Galvin [112], and Hammack and Segur [34].

Benjamin and Feir [4] discuss the stability of waves, and indicate that the waves will only be unstable if kd > 1.363, where k is the wave number $2\pi/L$. Whitham [108] showed that equations governing extremely gradual variations in wave properties are elliptic if kd > 1.363, and hyperbolic if kd < 1.363. For tsunamis, where $d/L \ll 1$, the equations will be hyperbolic and the waves will be stable, at least in a constant water depth.

Galvin [29] investigated waves propagating through water of uniform depth in a laboratory wave tank. He found that the initial generated wave broke down into several waves called solitons. For a water depth of 0.15 m (0.5 ft) and a generator period of 5.2 sec, each of the initial waves broke down into five solitons. Taking these waves as shallow-water waves, the wavelength was approximately 6.4 m, and $kd \simeq 0.15$, which would indicate that the waves were stable. However, it may be assumed that the generated waves were not actually single waves, but rather a combination of several solitons. Galvin noted that if a group of such waves traveled over a sufficiently long distance, the solitons would recombine into a single wave, separate again into solitons, etc. There are commonly two or three solitons, but as many as seven could exist in some instances. If a generated tsunami had the characteristics of a group of solitons, it could appear differently at various coastal points, depending on the distance from the generating area.

Zabusky and Galvin [112] compared numerical and experimental results for solitons, using the Korteweg-deVries equations, for cases where $22 \leq U \leq 777$, where U is defined as $(H/d)(L/d)^2$. They found good comparisons for slightly dissipative waves. Hammack and Segur [34] also studied numerical and experimental results. They found that soliton generation is dependent on the net volume change in the body of water. When the net volume of the initial wave system was positive (e.g., from uplifting of the sea bottom), solitons evolved, followed by a dispersive train of oscillatory waves. If the initial generating mechanism was negative everywhere (sea bottom subsidence), no solitons evolved.

Street, Burgess, and Whitford [100] investigated solitary waves passing from an initial water depth, over a steep slope, and into a shallower water depth. They obtained results similar to those of other investigators, showing that each wave changed from a single wave into a train of several waves. In some instances, there was also a significant increase in wave height.

Madsen and Mei [69] obtained numerical results for the propagation of long waves for a solitary wave passing over a slope and onto a shelf. The numerical results of Street, Chan, and Fromm [102] give results for a solitary wave, and results for a train of waves. Goring [30] has also carried out experiments on solitary waves propagating onto a shelf. His results are similar to those of Street, Chan, and Fromm [102] and Madsen and Mei [69].

In all cases where a single wave produced a series of wave crests, the first wave crest of the series was the highest. It may be presumed that a number of initial wave crests will produce the same number of groups of wave crests, each having a high initial wave followed by smaller waves.

Tsunami-Shoreline Interaction

In addition to the shoaling of waves on the nearshore slope, a tsunami may inter-act with a shoreline in a number of different ways, including standing wave resonance at the shoreline, the generation of edge waves by the impulse of the incident waves, the trapping of reflected incident waves by refraction, and as the reflected wave from the shoreline propagates seaward, the reflection of wave energy from an abrupt change in water depth at the seaward edge of a shelf. Also, a wave arriving at an oblique angle to the shoreline may produce a Mach-stem along the shoreline. All of these interactions depend on wave reflection at the shoreline. Tsunamis entering inlets and harbors may also produce resonant conditions within the inlets and harbors. LeBlond and Mysak [64] provide a general discussion of edge waves and wave trapping.

Wave Reflection

The reflection of an incident wave ray from a shoreline is illustrated in Figure 5. The angle, α_1, between the wave ray and a line normal to a tangent to the shoreline will have the same value for the incident and the reflected wave rays. For a steep nearshore slope, the reflected wave will be in phase with the incident wave.

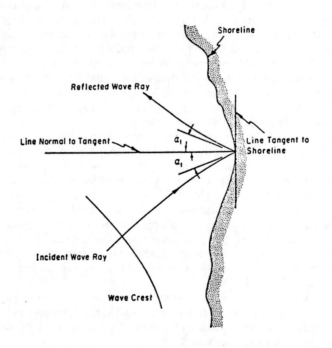

Figure 5. Wave reflection from a shoreline.

Miche [73] defined the wave reflection at a shoreline in terms of a critical wave steepness, $(H/L)_c$, which is given by

$$\left(\frac{H}{L}\right)_c = \left(\frac{2\beta}{\pi}\right)^{1/2} \frac{\sin^2 \beta}{\pi} \tag{47}$$

where β is the angle of the beach slope in radians. Complete reflection will occur if the wave steepness, H/L, in deeper water is less than $(H/L)_c$.

Shelf Response

Investigations of shelf resonance were carried out by Hidaka [38], and Wilson [110]. Their results compare favorably and Wilson's method is easier to apply and will account for refraction affects. The equations given by Wilson [110] for calculating a dimensionless amplitude, U, are

$$N_{j+1} = \frac{(B_j D_j - C)N_j - U_j}{C + B_j D_{j+1}} \tag{48}$$

$$U_{j+1} = U_j + 2C(N_{j+1} + N_j) \tag{49}$$

$$B_j = \frac{2}{[\Delta(b_{j+1} + b_j)]} \tag{50}$$

$$C = \frac{\Delta \omega^2}{(4g)} \tag{51}$$

$$D_j = b_j d_j \tag{52}$$

$$j = 1, 2, 3, \ldots$$

where b_j and b_{j+1} represent the distance between refracted wave rays at stations j and $j + 1$, respectively, N the horizontal displacement of a water particle, and Δ the horizontal distance between stations j and $j + 1$. For an unrefracted wave,

$$B_j D_j = \frac{d_j}{\Delta} \tag{53}$$

$U_0 = 1$ at the shoreline (as in the case of Hidaka) and $N_0 = 0$ at the shoreline. Figure 6 is a dimensionless plot showing an example of Wilson's results. A solution using the earlier method of Hidaka is shown for comparison. The slope of the shelf is S, and the water depth at the nearshore edge of the shelf is d_s.

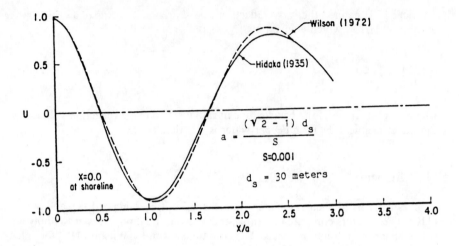

Figure 6. Resonant amplification on a shelf.

Reflection from Seaward Edge of Shelf

When a wave propagates seaward from the shoreline some of the wave energy is reflected shoreward from the transition in water depth at the seaward limit of the shelf. This is illustrated in Figure 7 where d_s is the water depth at the toe of the nearshore slope, d_2 the water depth at the seaward limit of the shelf, d_1 the water depth

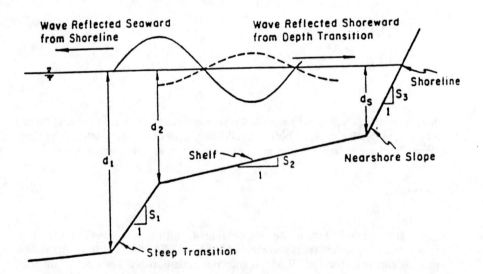

Figure 7. Reflected waves on a shelf.

at the seaward limit of the steep transition in water depth, S_1 the slope of the steep transition, S_2 the slope of the shelf, and S_3 the nearshore slope.

The wave reflected shoreward from the steep transition may be π radians out of phase with the wave transmitted seaward across the transition. However, the actual phase difference will depend on the geometry of the shelf and transition, and the water depth. For perfect reflection, the wave reflected from the shoreline will be in phase with the initial wave incident on the shoreline. The time, t_s, for the wave to travel the distance, l_s, from the steep transition to the nearshore slope will be the same as the time required for the reflected wave from the nearshore slope to travel back to the steep transition in depth. Therefore, where the wave reflected from the transition is π radians out of phase with the incident wave, resonance will occur if

$$2t_s = \frac{nT}{2} \tag{54}$$

where T is the incident wave period, and n = 1, 2, 3, ... As shown by Camfield [9],

$$T = \frac{8}{n} \frac{(d_2^{1/2} - d_s^{1/2})}{S_2 g^{1/2}} \tag{55}$$

where T is a resonant wave period where the reflected wave and incident wave are π radians out of phase, and n = 1, 2, 3, ... Equation 55 provides a first approximation for the resonant wave periods.

Edge Waves

The impulse of incident waves reflecting from the shoreline may generate edge waves in the longshore direction. These edge waves, the trapped mode of longshore wave motion, have longer wave periods than the incident wave periods; standing edge waves will have peaks and nodes at points along the shoreline, although edge waves may be either standing or progressive waves. Guza and Bowen [31] indicate that experimental results confirm the work of Galvin [28] and Bowen and Inman [5], which shows that incident waves that are not strongly reflected will not excite edge waves visible at the shoreline.

Guza and Davis [33] carried out a theoretical investigation of the mechanism of edge wave generation by normally incident, shallow-water waves on a constant beach slope. They define the longshore wavelength of the edge wave by the longshore wave number, k_y, given by

$$k_y = \frac{2\pi}{L_y} = \left(\frac{2\pi}{T_y}\right)^2 \frac{1}{g(2n + 1)\tan \beta} \tag{56}$$

where L_y = wavelength of the edge wave
T_y = period of the edge wave
β = the angle of the nearshore slope in radians

Guza and Davis attribute the generating mechanism to a nonlinear interaction between the incident wave and a pair of progressive edge waves with frequencies defined by ω_1 and ω_2 where $\omega = 2\pi/T$ and

$$\omega = \omega_1 + \omega_2 \tag{57}$$

i.e., the incident wave frequency is equal to the sum of the two edge wave frequencies. The two edge waves have the same wavelength, but propagate in opposite directions along the shoreline. Therefore, the edge wave pair forms a standing wave. This standing wave will always have a frequency equal to one-half the incident wave frequency (a period twice the incident wave period) even though the frequencies of the edge wave pairs may vary. Where the frequencies of the two progressive edge waves forming the pair are different, the nodes and antinodes of the standing wave will move in the direction of the edge wave with the higher frequency (shorter period). The locations of edge wave peaks define locations where wave run-up on the shoreline may be higher.

Guza and Bowen [32] discuss the height of the edge waves occurring along a coastline. They show that the maximum edge wave amplitude at the shoreline is theoretically three times the amplitude of the incident wave for a straight coastline. Gallagher [27] indicates that energy would be lost because of bottom friction and the dispersion caused by irregularities in the coastline. Guza and Bowen [32] indicate that edge wave growth is limited by radiation of energy to deep water and by finite-amplitude demodulation; i.e., as the edge waves increase in height their natural frequency increases and no longer matches the forcing frequency. From Equation 56 and the work of Munk, Snodgrass, and Gilbert [77] relating trapped modes to leaky modes, it can be seen that leaky modes (i.e., edge waves radiating energy to deep water) will only occur on steep nearshore slopes. These nearshore slopes are very short in comparison to the tsunami wavelength, and are not of concern here. The edge waves associated with the tsunami are assumed to occur over the wider and flatter shelf slope shown in Figure 7.

Refracted Waves and Caustics

When very long waves such as tsunamis arrive at a shoreline, a substantial amount of wave energy will be reflected seaward from the shoreline. These reflected waves will interact with the bottom topography, and will refract as they travel seaward. Refraction diagrams of these waves show a tendency for the waves to turn parallel to the shoreline as they move into deeper water. When a shelf slopes away from the shoreline, and extends a sufficient distance seaward, the waves may be turned back shoreward (see Figure 8). The line tangent to the wave rays where they turn shoreward is a caustic. The wave rays will not cross the caustic, and the wave energy tends to be trapped, although some wave energy will leak across the caustic [18, 19, 90].

Chao [18] and Chao and Pierson [19] investigated higher frequency waves trapped by a caustic. They demonstrate that lower frequency (longer period) waves will form caustics closer to the coastline, and that waves with frequencies above some maximum value will propagate seaward into deep water. For tsunamis, only the lower frequency waves are significant.

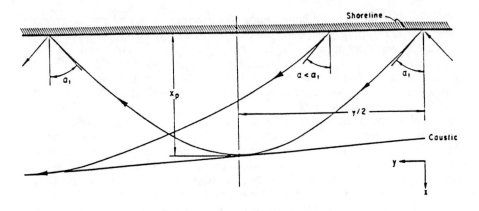

Figure 8. Schematic of caustic (uniform bottom slope).

As the wave rays are not normal to the shoreline, different parts of the wave crest would arrive at the shoreline at different times. Where a coastline is irregular, parts of a wave crest reflected from one section of coastline may be refracted and trapped so that they coincide with an incident wave on another section of coastline. Palmer, Mulvihill, and Funasaki [85] illustrated the effects of wave trapping at Hilo, Hawaii, where the reflected wave rays were turned by refraction so that they arrived simultaneously at a point inside Hilo Harbor.

The case of wave energy being trapped by refraction can be most easily illustrated for a long, shallow-water wave on a straight section of shoreline, with some water depth, d_s, at the toe of the shoreline slope, and with a constant shelf slope extending seaward. It is assumed that the wave reflects from the shoreline slope and refracts on the shelf. Camfield [9] shows that

$$x_p = \frac{d_s}{S \sin^2 \alpha_1} - \frac{d_s}{S} \tag{58}$$

and that

$$\frac{y}{2} = \frac{2d_s}{S \sin^2 \alpha_1} \left[\frac{\pi}{4} - \frac{\alpha_1}{2} + \frac{\sin 2\alpha_1}{4} \right] \tag{59}$$

where α_1 is measured in radians.

These equations are limited to the particular case of a long, straight coastline, but may provide a first approximation for solutions on some sections of continental shelves. Refraction diagrams would be required to obtain exact solutions for irregular coastlines. If the waves travel for long distances over a shelf, it may be desirable to use wave refraction equations in spherical coordinates such as the equations given by Chao [18].

When the tsunami energy becomes trapped between a caustic and a coastline, the energy will tend to propagate along the coastline. This will excite long-shore edge waves along the coastline, and may substantially increase observed wave heights. When the coastline is irregular, the trapped waves may concentrate their energy at particular coastal points. An investigation of the wave rays using the usual wave refraction techniques will define the caustic locations, and the locations of any coastal points where energy concentrates.

Tsunamis generated in coastal areas may have part of their energy trapped along the coastline, as waves radiating away from a source area may become trapped within a caustic in the same manner as reflected waves, as illustrated in Figure 9. For a wave ray originating within the coastal area, d_s is the water depth at the point of origin, x_p the distance seaward from the point of origin, and α_1 the angle between the wave ray and the orthogonal to the bottom contours as before.

Figure 9 shows that wave rays trapped on a shelf may diverge. These wave rays may reconverge at various points along the coastline, producing high waves at the points of convergence. For the straight coastline considered above, Camfield [9] showed that the travel time of a reflected wave from the shoreline to the caustic would be

$$t = \frac{2\sqrt{d_s}}{S \sin \alpha_1 \sqrt{g}} \left[\frac{\pi}{2} - \alpha_1 \right] \tag{60}$$

where α is given in radians.

Camfield [10] extended the work of Shen and Meyer [94] and Shen [93] to obtain solutions for trapped waves on coastlines with curved plan forms. Using the definitions in Figure 7, he showed that a necessary condition for wave trapping to occur is that

$$\frac{d_s}{S_2 R_s} < 0.5 \tag{61}$$

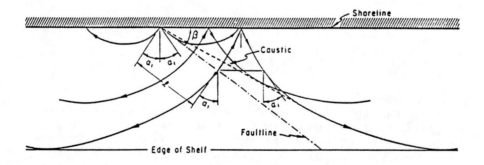

Figure 9. Trapping of generated tsunami.

where R_s is the radius of curvature of the shoreline. The parameter $d_s/(S_2R_s)$ is a shelf parameter that determines wave trapping. A continuous band of solutions exists for values of n_2 between the minimum and maximum values defined as

$$(n_2)_{min}^2 = \frac{R_s}{R_s S_2 - d_s} \tag{62}$$

$$(n_2)_{max}^2 = \frac{\dfrac{(R_s)^2 S_2}{d_s} - R_s}{R_s S_2 - d_s} \tag{63}$$

where integer values of n_2 between the minimum and maximum values define resonant periods for a circular island where the periods T are obtained from values of $2\pi d_s n_2/(gT^2)$, which can be determined numerically. Camfield showed that solutions come from the equations

$$\left(\frac{1 + c^2 \tan^2 \alpha_1}{\tan^2 \alpha_1}\right)^{1/2} \tanh\left[\left(\frac{1 + c^2 \tan^2 \alpha_1}{\tan^2 \alpha_1}\right)^{1/2} \frac{n_2^2 d_s}{c^2 R_s}\right] = \frac{R_s}{r_p} \tag{64}$$

and

$$c \tanh\left[\frac{n_2^2 d}{r_p c}\right] = 1 \tag{65}$$

where r_p is the radius of the caustic, d is the water depth at the caustic, and c is a dimensionless value. Equation 65 can be restated by noting

$$d = d_s + (r_p - R_s)S_2 \tag{66}$$

so that

$$c \tanh \frac{n_2^2 d_s}{R_s} \frac{1}{c} \frac{R_s}{r_p} + \frac{S_2 R_s}{d_s} - \frac{R_s}{r_p} \frac{S_2 R_s}{d_s} = 1 \tag{67}$$

From Equation 64, values of R_s/r_p vs. c can be obtained for a constant value of $n_2^2 d_s/R_s$ for a given value of α, and from Equation 65 for a given shelf parameter $d_s/S_2 R_s$, values of R_s/r_p and c are determined for a given value of n_2. The corresponding wave period, T, for the value of n_2 is determined from

$$\frac{2\pi d_s n_2}{gT^2} = \frac{1}{2\pi c}\left(\frac{R_s}{r_p}\right)\left(\frac{n_2^2 d_s}{R_s}\right) \tag{68}$$

Longuet-Higgins [68] discusses trapping of waves around islands, and Meyer [72] provides a review of the subject. Studies of particular islands have included Wake Island [106, 107] and the Hawaiian Islands [47]. These studies demonstrate tsunami amplification at preferred periods, dependent on island configuration and associated bathymetry. The response will vary, dependent on the direction of incident waves, i.e., the source of the tsunami. It is of interest to note that the maximum response is not necessarily on the incident wave side of the island [91].

Mach-Stem Formation

Perroud [88] showed that $\alpha_1 = 45°$ defines a critical angle for wave reflection. When $\alpha_1 < 45°$ regular reflection occurs, i.e., the wave reflects in a manner previously described. When $\alpha_1 = 45°$ the end of the wave crest at the shoreline turns perpendicular to the shoreline (see Figure 10). Regular reflection no longer occurs when $\alpha_1 > 45°$.

Perroud showed that, for $\alpha_1 > 45°$, the incident wave produces two components. The first is a reflected wave, lower than the incident wave, and with the angle, α_2, between the reflected wave ray and the normal to the shoreline defined by $\alpha_2 < \alpha_1$. The second component is a Mach stem, which moves along the shoreline in the direction of the longshore component of the incident wave, growing in size as it progresses along the shoreline.

Experimental measurements by Perroud [88] show that the Mach stem has a profile at the shoreline similar to the profile of the incident wave, giving the Mach stem the appearance of a large wave moving along the shoreline. The Mach stem remains attached to the shoreline end of the incident wave crest, so its speed of

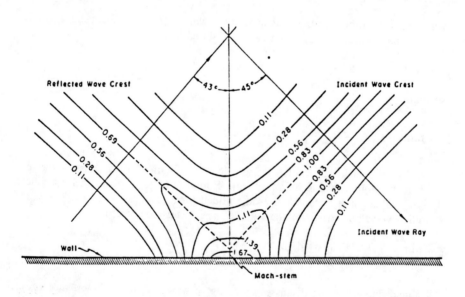

Figure 10. Mach-stem formation, solitary wave. Lines of equal surface elevation above still water normalized to unit incident wave amplitude.

propagation, C, along the shoreline is given as

$$C_\ell = \frac{C}{\sin \alpha_1} \qquad (69)$$

where C is the celerity of the incident wave near the shoreline.

Chen [22] studied Mach-stem development using a range of values for the near-shore slope. He showed that where the angle of the nearshore slope $\beta < 60°$, and $\alpha_1 > 55°$, the Mach stem formed a breaking wave along the shoreline. The relationship between the wavelength and the slope length was not considered in this case, and was not varied during the experiments.

It was generally found by Perroud [88] and Chen [22] that the incident waves neither reflected from the shoreline nor formed Mach stems when $\alpha_1 > 70°$. This would be the case for an incident wave traveling nearly parallel to the section of shoreline; e.g., a wave entering an inlet with a gradually-varying cross section.

Bay and Harbor Resonance

When a bay or harbor is very long in relation to the tsunami wavelength, the tsunami may cause resonance if a natural mode of oscillation of a bay or harbor corresponds to the period of the tsunami. Murty, Wigen, and Chawla [80] have tabulated the approximate periods of inlets on the Pacific coast of North and South America based on the formula

$$T_1 = \frac{4L_b}{\sqrt{gd_a}} \qquad (70)$$

Referring to the work of Nakano [81] that showed secondary undulations to be proportional to the length of an inlet, L_b, and inversely proportional to the width, B, and to $d_a^{3/2}$, Murty, Wigen, and Chawla [80] proposed that the relative intensity, I, of the secondary undulations could be given as

$$I = \frac{L_b}{Bd_a^{3/2}} \qquad (71)$$

As indicated by Murty, Wigen, and Chawla, some bays that have small ratios of L_b/B have large secondary oscillations. They point out that Equations 70 and 71 are based on a one-dimensional theory that is not valid for low ratios of L_b/B, and that transverse motion is important in these cases.

Various investigators have considered harbor resonance for idealized geometries. These have included Ippen, Raichlen, and Sullivan [54], Nishimura, Horikawa, and Shuto [83], and Ippen and Goda [53].

Miles [75] indicated that for waves passing from a continental shelf into a harbor, where the dimensions of the harbor and the entry channel are small compared to the local wavelength of the tsunami, the response of the harbor is essentially restricted to the Helmholtz mode; i.e., the lowest mode of resonance. The harbor undergoes a pumping motion where the water level in the harbor is assumed to rise and fall uniformly across the total area of the harbor [14]. The water passing through the entry channel is assumed to have a high velocity, represented as kinetic energy; the water in the harbor has a much lower velocity, and the rise and fall of the water level in the harbor is represented as potential energy.

For a harbor with an entrance channel, Miles [75] indicates that narrowing the entrance width or increasing the length of the entrance channel will significantly increase the response of the harbor to the Helmholtz mode, which may dominate tsunami response. This narrowing or lengthening also has the effect of decreasing the resonant frequency [14]. Carrier, Shaw, and Miyata point out that lengthening the entrance channel to a harbor also increases the frictional resistance so amplification factors for a very long entrance channel may be significantly reduced (although the resonant frequencies would still be less than for a harbor without an entrance channel).

Seelig, Harris, and Herchenroder [92] present a numerical means for analyzing harbors responding to the Helmholtz mode of resonance. The method uses a Runge-Kutta-Gill technique where

$$\frac{dh_b}{dt} = \frac{Q}{A_b} \tag{72}$$

h_b = surface elevation of the water in the harbor above some arbitrary fixed datum
Q = the flow rate through the entrance channel
A_b = surface area of the harbor ($A_b = L_b B$)

The governing differential equation is

$$\frac{dQ}{dt} = \frac{I_g}{2}\left(\frac{1}{A_{bc}{}^2} - \frac{1}{A_{sc}{}^2}\right)Q^2 - gI_g(h_b - h_s) - I_g F \tag{73}$$

where $\quad I_g = \dfrac{1}{\displaystyle\int_{x_s}^{x_b} \frac{d_x}{A_c}} \tag{74}$

A_c = cross-sectional area of flow through the entrance channel at any point X between the seaward end at X_s and the harbor end X_b (A_c, therefore, being a function of X)
A_{bc} = the cross-sectional area at the bay end
A_{sc} = the cross-sectional area at the sea end
h_s = the height of the sea level above the arbitrary fixed datum
F = total bottom friction in the entrance channel

A sample computation for a tsunami entering a bay is given in Figure 11. It can be seen that the peak water levels in the bay occur slightly after the peak water levels just seaward from the entrance channel. Also, the peak water levels were slightly lower in this case.

Miles [74] found that he could transform his equations for wave-induced oscillations in a harbor to an integral equation equivalent to the equation formulated by Lee [65, 66]. Lee expresses the governing equations for wave oscillations in an arbitrary-shaped harbor as

$$\frac{d^2Z}{dZ^2} = K^2Z \tag{75}$$

and

$$\frac{\partial^2 f(x, y)}{\partial x^2} + \frac{\partial^2 f(x, y)}{\partial y^2} + k^2 f(x, y) = 0 \tag{76}$$

where

$$Z = -\frac{ag \cosh[k(z + d)]}{\cosh(kd)} \tag{77}$$

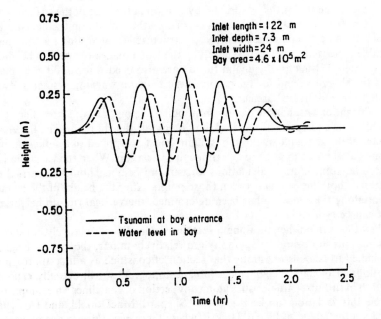

Figure 11. Tsunami water levels in a bay (tide excluded).

and f(x, y) is a wave function to be determined. Equation 76 is the Helmholtz equation. The following boundary conditions are assumed:

1. f(x, y)/∂n = 0 along all fixed boundaries where n is in the normal direction to the boundary.
2. The harbor does not affect the wave system where $(x^2 + y^2)^{1/2} \to \infty$; i.e., at large distances from the harbor entrance.

Lee [65] obtained numerical solutions for a harbor with an arbitrary shape.

Chen and Mei [20] have developed a finite-element numerical model that can be used to study water level oscillations in a harbor. Houston [43, 44] applied Chen and Mei's model to studies of Los Angeles and Long Beach harbors.

Tsunami Run-up on the Shoreline

The arrival of a tsunami at a shoreline may cause an increase in water level as much as 30 m or greater in an extreme case. Increases of 10 m (32.8 ft) are not uncommon. The large increase in water level, combined with the surge of the tsunami, can impose powerful forces on shore protection structures and on structures located near the shoreline. Structures may be seriously damaged or destroyed by the tsunami. Damage may be caused by strong currents produced by waves overtopping the structures, by the direct force of the surge produced by a wave, by the hydrostatic pressure created by flooding behind a structure due to extreme drawdown of the water level when the waves recede, and by erosion at the base of the structure. Major damage may also be caused by debris carried by the tsunami in the nearshore area.

To determine the potential damage to structures located along a shoreline, the probable increase in water level caused by the tsunami, i.e., the run-up height, must be estimated. Estimates of tsunami run-up are also needed for flood zone planning along the shoreline, and for operation of the tsunami warning system to evacuate people from endangered areas.

The height of a tsunami will vary from point to point along a coastline. The numerical models for prediction of tsunami height at the shoreline, i.e., the elevation of water at the shoreline due to the tsunami, must be applied to a sufficient number of points along the shoreline to determine this variation. When the variation is large between adjacent points, calculations for tsunami heights should be carried out at additional shoreline points between those points. After the height of the tsunami at a point along the shoreline has been determined, the vertical run-up height at that point can be estimated.

When the tsunami height along a section of coastline is relatively constant, and the variations in onshore topography are relatively minor, the run-up height may be assumed to be constant along that section of coastline as a first approximation. Variations in tsunami height and shoreline topography will actually cause some variation in run-up characteristics along any section of coastline. An example of how extreme this variation can be is given by Shepard, MacDonald, and Cox [95] for Haena, on the Island of Kauai, Hawaii, where there was a gentle rise of water level on the western side of the bay, but less than 1 mile to the east, waves rushed onshore, flattening groves of trees and destroying houses. An example of the variation in run-up height is given by Wilson and Tørum [111] for Kodiak City, Alaska (Figure 12). The mean run-up height at Kodiak City was a little more than 6 m (20 ft) above mean lower low water (MLLW), with variations from about 5 to 8 m (17 to 27 ft). Because these variations are difficult to predict, the predicted run-up heights may contain substantial errors. Where tsunamis of a known height have produced

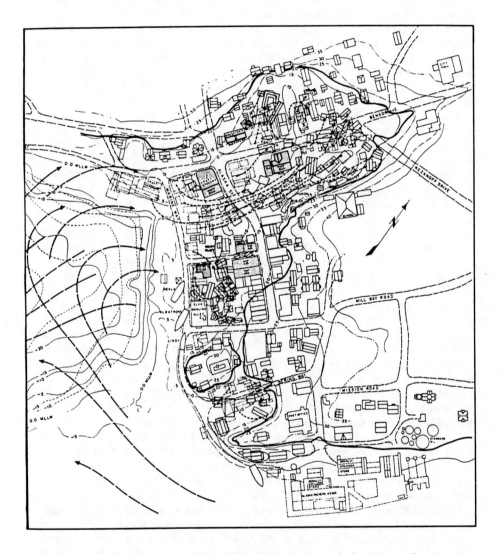

Figure 12. 1964 tsunami runup, Kodiak City, Alaska (contours in feet); heavy line is maximum flood level.

variations in run-up at a particular section of coastline, the higher heights should normally be used for conservative design.

It should be noted that the characteristics of the waves may vary from one wave to another at the same coastal point. Shepard, MacDonald, and Cox [95] cite a case in Hawaii where the first wave came in so gently that a man was able to wade through chest-high water ahead of the rising water. Later waves were so violent that they destroyed houses and left a line of debris against trees 150 m (500 ft) inland.

An added complication, which is an important consideration in computing run-up heights, is the possibility of storm waves occurring simultaneously with the tsunami. The prediction of maximum run-up heights would require the consideration of joint probabilities of tsunamis and storm waves, as well as the probability of a high tidal stage. The probability of a high tide, tsunami, and storm waves occurring simultaneously may appear to be small; however, such an event did occur in Newfoundland in 1929 [40].

Because a tsunami has a very long period relative to storm waves, it causes an apparent variation in water depth over a long distance. Storm waves riding on top the tsunami will have a wave celerity corresponding to the depth (including tsunami height) at any particular point. If two storm waves are otherwise equivalent (e.g., the same period and wave height), and one is at the crest of the tsunami while the other is at the leading edge, the storm wave at the tsunami crest will have a higher celerity [104]. Therefore, the tsunami can cause one storm wave to overtake and superimpose itself on another storm wave, producing higher waves at the shoreline.

Storm waves alone may be more severe than a tsunami at some exposed coastal points. Shepard, MacDonald, and Cox [95] refer to the Kalaupapa Peninsula, on the Island of Molokai, Hawaii, where the 1946 tsunami left driftwood at elevations slightly more than 2 m (7 or 8 ft) above normal sea level, but winter storms had left driftwood 6 m above the same datum plane. A combination of a winter storm and a large tsunami could be very destructive.

Houston and Garcia [46] assume that tsunami run-up on a shoreline will have a run-up height (vertical rise) equal to the wave height at the shoreline. This assumption is based on the idea that a tsunami will act like a rapidly rising tide. The assumption was compared with a few cases where both height and run-up data were available. For those cases, which included the 1960 tsunami at Hilo, Hawaii, that produced a bore-fronted wave, the predicted value of run-up equal to wave height at the shoreline compared well with the maximum run-up measured in the area. Nasu's [82] data for a tsunami occurring in Japan also indicated that the total run-up was about equal to the wave height at the shoreline at many locations. Wiegel [109] reports that maximum run-up elevations above MLLW at Crescent City, California, were equal to or greater than the maximum wave height (crest-to trough) at the Crescent City tide gauge for the 1952, 1960, and 1964 tsunamis. Magoon [70] indicates that the 1964 tsunami at Crescent City had an elevation of about 6 m above MLLW along a substantial length of shoreline, and that the line of maximum tsunami inundation generally followed a contour at that elevation. While the assumption that maximum run-up heights will equal the tsunami height at the shoreline provides an initial estimate, this assumption cannot always be used with accuracy. The effects of ground slope, wave period, and the possible convergence or divergence of the run-up must be considered.

The results of Nasu [82] indicate that the tsunami height at the shoreline and the run-up height are dependent on the configuration of the coastline. At Kamaisi, Japan, on the north side of a bay, the run-up height was actually somewhat less than the wave height at the shoreline, equal to slightly more than 3 m. At Hongo, at the head of a bay, the tsunami flowed directly up a canyon along a streambed, and the maximum run-up height was about 11 m (36 ft). At Ryoisi, the tsunami intruded into a small inlet opening onto the main bay, flowed up a canyon along a streambed and highway, and reached a maximum run-up height equal to about 10.5 m (34 ft). The wave at Kamaisi was probably traveling parallel to the shoreline as it flooded into the bay. The wave at Hongo and Ryoisi was probably traveling in a direction oriented directly along the axis of the canyons as the surge came onshore.

Iwasaki and Horikawa [56] show that the period of the waves will be a major factor in determining maximum inundation levels. The waves from the tsunami that struck the coast of Japan on May 24, 1960 had periods of about 60 minutes, while the 1933 tsunami reported by Nasu [82] had wave periods of about 12 minutes. The 1960 tsunami did not form a bore or a spilling front, and the water level gradually gained height over the entire surface of the bays where it was observed. For the longer period waves of the 1960 tsunami, the orientation of the bays appeared to have no influence on the run-up heights; the height of the run-up was equal to (or sometimes less than) the height of the wave at the shoreline.

Tsunamis at a shoreline could be categorized into three types of waves: nonbreaking waves (i.e., a tsunami that acts as a rapidly rising tide); waves that break far from the shoreline and become fully developed bores before reaching the shoreline; and waves that break near the shoreline and act as partially developed bores that are not uniform in height. In addition, there are some cases where reflected waves become bores after reflecting from a shoreline.

For the nonbreaking wave, the assumption that the run-up height equals the wave height at the shoreline may be reasonable and possibly even conservative. Field observations (e.g., Nasu, [82]) indicate that the run-up height is sometimes less than that value. To analyze the run-up of breaking waves and fully developed bores, where maximum run-up heights have been observed to be much higher than the wave or bore height at the shoreline, it is necessary to consider the actual form of the run-up.

Using solitary waves, Camfield and Street's [12] experimental results for an $8°$ nearshore slope fronted by a slope $S_2 = 0.01$ indicated that the run-up takes the initial form of a horizontal water surface at an elevation equal to the wave height at the shoreline (Figure 13), and (from Camfield [9]) that the higher run-up on the slope washes up the slope at a shallow depth. Results for plunging breakers on $4°$ and $8°$ slopes fronted by a slope $S_2 = 0.01$, and on $4°$, $8°$, and $12°$ slopes fronted by a slope $S_2 = 0.03$, indicated similar run-up characteristics. The higher, shallow run-up may cause some flooding, but would not be expected to otherwise cause damage because of the shallow depth. Also, this higher, shallow run-up may not be representative of prototype run-up. O'Brien [84] points out that a fraction of the uprush

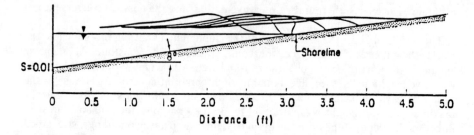

Figure 13. Solitary wave runup.

percolates into a natural, permeable beach. This percolation tends to partially dissipate the shallow part of the run-up observed on the impermeable model beach.

Kononkova and Reihrudel [62] studied the run-up of solitary waves on uniform slopes that were apparently fronted by a horizontal tank bottom. For nearshore slopes less than 8°, their results were comparable to those of Camfield and Street [12]. For nearshore slopes greater than 8°, they found run-up values higher than the wave height at the shoreline.

Miller [76] gives results for borelike waves that act as surge run-up on a shoreline. He shows that the run-up in this case also takes the initial form of a horizontal water surface at an elevation equal to the wave height at the shoreline, and that the higher run-up flows up the slope as a thin sheet. Miller comments that, "In the later stages of run-up, the form of the wave was of a thin, fast-moving greatly elongated wedge."

The experimental work of Camfield and Street [12], Miller [76], and Kononkova and Reihrudel [62] was for flat, uniform slopes with no convergence of the wave crest. In general, the experiments show that for flatter slopes ($<8°$) the run-up height appears equal to or less than the wave height at the shoreline. For steeper slopes, the run-up height increases as the slope increases, and the ratio of run-up height to wave height at the shoreline appears to reach a maximum value for vertical walls. However, the higher run-up on the steeper slopes appears to have a relatively shallow depth.

Bretschneider and Wybro [7] investigated the effect of bottom friction on tsunami inundation by using the Manning n to describe the roughness of the onshore slope. Although this is not entirely correct (the Manning relationship was developed for uniform flow), it provides a simple means of investigating the effects of roughness on the limits of inundation. It was shown that decreasing the Manning roughness coefficient, n, from n = 0.025 (long grass with brush) to n = 0.015 (short, cut grass and pavement) could increase the distance required for dissipation of the surge by 160% (from 670 to 1,770 m or 2,200 to 5,800 ft in the example used, where $h_s = 10$ m or 33 ft). Bretschneider and Wybro also demonstrated that a bore would be dissipated faster than a tsunami acting as a rapidly rising tide.

Chan, Street, and Strelkoff [17] and Chan and Street [15, 16] use a modified Marker and Cell (SUMMAC) numerical finite-difference technique for calculating the wave run-up of solitary waves on a 45° slope and on a vertical wall. Their results compared well with the experimental results of Street and Camfield [101], but their numerical method was not applied to wave run-up on the shoreline for flatter slopes. Heitner [37] developed a numerical method based on finite elements. However, he provides only limited results for simulating waves in laboratory channels, and the results depend on the choice of a bottom-friction factor and an artificial viscosity.

Spielvogel [99] developed a theoretical solution for tsunami run-up based on the wave or surge height at the shoreline, h_s, and the wave height, $\hat{H}$, at the point where the leading edge of the wave is at the shoreline. This related the run-up to the rate of shoaling just before the wave reaches the shoreline, and effectively includes the influence of the bottom slope and the wave period. Replotting Spielvogel's results into a more usable form gives the equation

$$\frac{R}{h_s} = \frac{2.94}{\dfrac{h_s}{\hat{H}} - 0.8} \tag{78}$$

Equation 78 indicates that the higher values of relative run-up, R/h_s, occur when the values of $h_s/\hat{H}$ are the lowest. Spielvogel indicates that Equation 77 is correct for $3.74 > h_s/\hat{H} > 2.12$, has limited application where $2.12 > h_s/\hat{H} > 1.76$, and is invalid where $h_s/\hat{H} < 1.76$. This latter, invalid case would be a nearshore bore or breaking wave.

In addition to considering wave run-up, it is necessary to consider the drawdown of the water when the wave trough arrives at the shoreline. Not as much attention has been given to wave run-down; however, the drawdown of the water level may result in the seaward collapse of seawalls, result in damage to ships in a harbor, or expose seawater-intake pipelines. It should also be noted that a gradual increase in water level, with very low-velocity currents, may be followed by a sudden withdrawal of water producing very strong currents.

During the 1946 tsunami in Hawaii, waves at Hanamaulu Bay rose 2.7 m at a breakwater and wharf, but the water receded to a level 5.6 m below normal sea level between waves [95]. Most of the damage was caused by the violent withdrawal of the water.

The run-down elevations will depend on the wave train generated at the tsunami source. For the 1946 tsunami, the tide gauge record at Honolulu, Hawaii, indicated some very narrow, deep wave troughs with the initial troughs having greater amplitudes than the initial crests.

Consideration must also be given to the current velocities of the run-up. Ishimoto and Hagiwara [55] investigated the large 1933 tsunami at Kamaisi, Japan, and estimated current velocities with a maximum value of 1 m/sec. Houston and Garcia [46] estimated that small tsunamis in southern California acting as rapidly rising tides would have maximum current velocities of about 0.5 m/sec. The current velocity for the 1933 tsunami, which was about double the velocity estimated by Houston and Garcia for small tsunamis, destroyed some buildings when the water depth reached a height of 2 m (6.15 ft).

Water overflowing a coastal barrier will have a current velocity determined by the difference in height between the top of the barrier and the ground level behind the barrier, as well as the quantity of water overtopping the barrier, rather than acting like a rapidly rising tide. The barrier will also limit the height of the run-up; however, large drain openings must be provided to prevent water levels from building up behind the barrier if it is overtopped by successive waves. Magoon [70] cites one example south of Crescent City, California, during the 1964 tsunami where water flowed over narrow coastal dunes. The quantity of water overflowing the dunes was insufficient in some instances to fill the low areas to landward, reducing the resulting run-up height.

Where the slope is very long compared to the wavelength, and friction effects must be considered, it can be seen that for low velocities the retarding effect of the slope roughness (deceleration) may prevent the water from rising to a run-up height equal to the wave height at the shoreline (i.e., drawdown will start at the shoreline, reversing the direction of flow). As previously noted, the currents associated with the run-down might have much higher velocities than the currents associated with the run-up. No estimates are available for the run-down currents.

Surge run-up on a dry bed will have a much higher velocity than the values given by Houston and Garcia [46] for a tsunami that acts like a rapidly rising tide. Keulegan [61] gives

$$u = 2(gh)^{1/2} \tag{79}$$

where h is the surge height at any point and u the water velocity at the same point. Fukui, et al. [26] give a lower value of velocity as

$$u = 1.83(gh)^{1/2} \tag{80}$$

The higher value would be conservative.

Notation

A   coefficient area of uplifting
a   wave amplitude; coefficient; semimajor from the shoreline $= (\sqrt{2} - 1)d_s/S$
B   mean width of a harbor or inlet; coefficient
B_j variable used in determining wave amplitude
b   coefficient; semiminor axis of ellipse
C   wave celerity; a coefficient
c_ℓ longshore propagation speed of a Mach stem
c   maximum uplifted elevation; constant
D_f focal depth of earthquake
D_j variable used in determining wave amplitude
d   water depth; projected dimension transverse to direction of flow
d_a depth of water at toe of nearshore slope
d_1 depth of deeper water
d_2 depth of shallower water
E   energy

F	bottom friction
f	friction factor
f_c	coriolis parameter $= 2\Omega \cos \theta$
$f_{\beta(Z)}$	probability of astronomical tide elevation Z
g	acceleration due to gravity
H	wave height
H_i	incident wave height
H_r	reflected wave height
H_t	transmitted wave height
$\hat{H}$	wave height when the leading edge is at the shoreline
h	surge height; uplifting height
h_s	surge height at the shoreline
I	relative intensity of secondary undulations
j	integer used for increments
k	an integer used for increments; wave number $= 2\pi/L$
L	wavelength
L_b	length of bay, harbor, or inlet
L_y	longshore wavelength
L_1	wavelength in deeper water
L_2	wavelength in shallower water
ℓ	length of slope connecting sea bottom to a shelf
M	Richter magnitude of earthquakes
m	tsunami magnitude
N	normalized horizontal water particle displacement
n	Manning roughness coefficient
n(m)	probability of tsunami with magnitude m being generated in any given year
P(Z)	probability of run-up to elevation Z
Q	flow rate under a wave
R	vertical height of run-up above the stillwater level at the shoreline
R_e	radius of Earth
R_s	radius from the center of curvature to the shoreline
r_p	radius from the center of curvature to where the wave ray turns parallel to the bottom contours
S	slope of sea bottom in direction of wave motion
S_1	slope of steep transition
S_2	slope of shelf
S_3	nearshore slope
T	wave period
T_1	period of bay or inlet
t	time
t_s	time required for a wave to travel across a shelf
U	normalized wave amplitude; $(H/d)(L/d)^2$
u	current or particle velocity in direction of wave motion; velocity in the θ-direction (spherical coordinates)
v	velocity in the ϕ-direction (spherical coordinates)
x	horizontal coordinate in direction of wave motion

x_p distance between the shoreline and the point where a wave ray turns parallel to bottom contours

y horizontal coordinate in direction transverse to x-direction

z vertical coordinate

α_1 angle in wave refraction between the incident wave ray and an orthogonal to the contour of the sea bottom

β angle of the beach slope; angle of nearshore slope given in radians

γ specific weight of water

Δ an incremental distance

δ a small value

ϵ an arbitrary increment

η water surface elevation above still water at an arbitrary point

θ degrees latitude measured from the pole

ρ density

ϕ longitude of a point

Ω rotational speed of Earth in radians per second

ω wave frequency $= 2\pi/T$

References

1. Abe, K., 1979, "Size of Great Earthquakes of 1837-1974 Inferred from Tsunami Data," *Journal of Geophysical Research*, Vol. 84, No. B4, Apr. pp. 1561– 1568.
2. Ambraseys, N. N., 1965, "Data for the Investigation of Seismic Sea-Waves in Europe," Monograph No. 29, European Seismological Commission, International Union of Geodesy and Geophysics, Paris, France, Nov.
3. Benjamin, T. B., Bona, J. L., and Mahony, J. J., 1972, "On Model Equations for Long Waves in Nonlinear Dispersive Systems," *Philosophical Transactions of the Royal Society*, Series A, Vol. 272, pp. 47–78.
4. Benjamin, T. B. and Feir, J. E., 1967, "The Disintegration of Wave Trains on Deep Water," *Journal of Fluid Mechanics*, Vol. 27, Part 3, pp. 417–430.
5. Bowen, A. J. and Inman, D. L., 1971, "Edge Waves and Crescentic Bars," *Journal of Geophysical Research*, Vol. 76, No. 36, Dec. pp. 8662–8671.
6. Brandsma, M., Divoky, D., and Hwang, L-S., 1975, "Seawave—A Revised Model for Tsunami Applications," Final Report, National Science Foundation, Washington, D.C., Apr.
7. Bretschneider, C. L. and Wybro, P. G., 1976, "Tsunami Inundation Prediction," *Proceedings of the 15th Conference on Coastal Engineering*, American Society of Civil Engineers, Ch. 60, pp. 1006–1024.
8. Byrne, R. J., 1969, "Field Occurrences of Induced Multiple Gravity Waves," *Journal of Geophysical Research*, Vol. 74, No. 10, May, pp. 2590–2596.
9. Camfield, F. E., 1980, "Tsunami Engineering", CERC Special Report No. 6, U.S. Army Engineering Waterways Experiment Station, Feb. 222 pages.
10. Camfield, F. E., 1982, "Long Wave Energy Trapping," *Physics of Fluids*, Vol. 25, No. 2, Feb. pp. 233–237.
11. Camfield, F. E., 1987, "Effects of Insufficient Data on Tsunami Flood Level Predictions," XIXth General Assembly, International Union of Geotesy and Geophysics, August.
12. Camfield, F. E. and Street, R. L., 1967, Stanford University, Department of Civil Engineering, Palo Alto, Calif., unpublished data.

13. Carrier, G. F., 1971, "The Dynamics of Tsunamis," in *Mathematical Problems* in *Geophysical Sciences, Part I, Lectures in Applied Mathematics*, Vol. 13, Amer. Math. Soc., Providence, pp. 157–187.

14. Carrier, G. F., Shaw, R. P., and Miyata, M., 1971, "Channel Effects in Harbor Resonance," *Journal of the Engineering Mechanics Division*, Vol. 97, No. EM6, Dec. pp. 1703–1716.

15. Chan, R. K. C. and Street, R. L., 1970a, "A Computer Study of Finite-Amplitude Water Waves," *Journal of Computational Physics*, Vol. 6, Aug. pp. 68–94.

16. Chan, R. K. C. and Street, R. L., 1970b, "Shoaling of Finite-Amplitude Waves on Plane Beaches," *Proceedings of the 12th Coastal Engineering Conference*, American Society of Civil Engineers.

17. Chan, R. K. C., Street, R. L., and Strelkoff, T., 1969, "Computer Studies of Finite-Amplitude Water Waves," Technical Report No. 104, Department of Civil Engineering, Stanford University, Palo Alto, Calif., June.

18. Chao, Y-Y., 1970, "The Theory of Wave Refraction in Shoaling Water, Including the Effects of Caustics and the Spherical Earth," Report No. TR-70-7, New York University, Geophysical Sciences Laboratory, New York, N.Y., June.

19. Chao, Y-Y. and Pierson, W. J., 1970, "An Experiment Study of Gravity Wave Behavior Near a Straight Caustic," Report No. TR-70-17, New York University, Geophysical Sciences Laboratory, New York, N.Y., Dec.

20. Chen, H. S. and Mei, C. C., 1974, "Oscillations and Wave Forces in an Offshore Harbor (Applications of the Hybrid Finite Element Method to Water-Wave Scattering)," Report No. 190, Massachusetts Institute of Technology, Cambridge, Mass.

21. Chen, M., Divoky, D., and Hwang, L-S., 1975, "Nearfield Tsunami Behavior," Final Report, National Science Foundation, Washington, D.C., Apr.

22. Chen, T. C., 1961, "Experimental Study on the Solitary Wave Reflection Along a Straight Sloped Wall at Oblique Angle of Incidence," TM 124, U.S. Army, Corps of Engineers, Beach Erosion Board, Washington, D.C., Mar.

23. Cochrane, J. D. and Arthur, R. S., 1948, "Reflection of Tsunami," *Journal of Marine Research*, Vol. 7, No. 3, pp. 239–251.

24. Cox, D. C., Pararas-Carayannis, G., and Calebaugh, J. P., 1976, "Catalog of Tsunamis in Alaska," Report SE-1, World Data Center A, Solid Earth Geophysics, National Oceanic and Atmospheric Administration, Rockville, Md., Mar.

25. Davison, C., *Great Earthquakes*, 1936, Thomas Murby & Co., London.

26. Fukui, Y., et al., 1963, "Hydraulic Study on Tsunami," *Coastal Engineering in Japan*, Vol. 6, pp. 67–82.

27. Gallagher, B., 1971, "Generation of Surf Beat by Non-Linear Wave Interactions," *Journal of Fluid Mechanics*, Vol. 49, Part 1, pp. 1–20.

28. Galvin, C. J., 1965, "Resonant Edge Waves on Laboratory Beaches," *Transactions of the American Geophysical Union*, Vol. 46, p. 112.

29. Galvin, C. J., 1970, "Finite-Amplitude, Shallow Water-Waves of Periodically Recurring Form," *Proceedings of the Symposium on Long Waves*, University of Delaware, Newark, Del., pp. 1–32.

30. Goring, D. G., 1978, "Tsunamis—The Propagation of Long Waves Onto a Shelf," W. M. Keck Laboratory Report No. KH-R-38, California Institute of Technology, Pasadena, Calif., Nov.

31. Guza, R. T. and Bowen, A. J., 1975, "The Resonant Instabilities of Long Waves Obliquely Incident on a Beach," *Journal of Geophysical Research*, Vol. 80, No. 33, Nov. pp. 4529–4534.

32. Guza, R. T. and Bowen, A. J., 1976, "Finite-Amplitude Edge Waves," *Journal of Marine Research*, Vol. 34, No. 1 pp. 269–293.

33. Guza, R. T. and Davis, R. E., 1974, "Excitation of Edge Waves by Waves Incident on a Beach," *Journal of Geophysical Research*, Vol. 79, No. 9, Mar. pp. 1285–1291.

34. Hammack, J. L. and Segur, H., 1974, "The Korteweg-deVries Equation and Water Waves, Part 2, Comparison with Experiments," *Journal of Fluid Mechanics*, Vol. 65, Part 2, pp. 289–314.

35. Harris, D., 1981, "Tides and Tidal Datums in the United States," Special Report No. 7, CERC, U.S. Army Corps of Engineers, Waterways Experiment Station, Vicksburg, MS.

36. Heck, N. H., 1947, "List of Seismic Sea Waves," *Bulletin of the Seismological Society of America*, Vol. 37, No. 4, Oct.

37. Heitner, K. L., 1969, "A Mathematical Model for Calculation of the Run-up of Tsunamis," Dissertation, Earthquake Engineering Research Laboratory, California Institute of Technology, Pasadena, Calif.

38. Hidaka, K., 1935, "A Theory of Shelf Seiches," *The Memoirs of the Imperial Marine Observatory*, Kobe, Japan, Vol. 6, No. 1, Dec. pp. 9–11.

39. Hirono, T., 1961, "The Chilean Earthquake of 1960," *Journal of Geography*, Tokyo Geographical Society, Tokyo, Japan, Vol. 70, No. 3, pp. 20–31 (in Japanese with English abstract).

40. Hodgson, E. A. and Doxsee, W. W., 1930, "The Grand Banks Earthquake, November 18, 1929," *Earthquake Notes*, Vol. 2, Nos. 1 and 2, pp. 72–81.

41. Holden, E. S., 1898, "A Catalogue of Earthquakes on the Pacific Coast, 1769 to 1897," Smithsonian Miscellaneous Collections 1087, Smithsonian Institution, Washington, D.C.

42. Horikawa, K. and Wiegel, R. L., 1959, "Secondary Wave Crest Formation," Series 89, Issue 4, Wave Research Laboratory, Institute of Engineering Research, University of California, Berkeley, Calif., Feb.

43. Houston, J. R., 1976, "Long Beach Harbor Numerical Analysis of Harbor Oscillations, Report 1, Existing Conditions and Proposed Improvements," Miscellaneous Paper H-76-20, U.S. Army Engineer Waterways Experiment Station, Vicksburg, Miss., Sept.

44. Houston, J. R., 1977, "Los Angeles Harbor Numerical Analysis of Harbor Oscillations," Miscellaneous Paper H-77-2, U.S. Army Engineer Waterways Experiment Station, Vicksburg, Miss., Feb.

45. Houston, J. R., Carver, R. D., and Markle, D. G., 1977, "Tsunami-Wave Elevation Frequency of Occurrence for the Hawaiian Islands," Technical Report H-77-16, U.S. Army Engineer Waterways Experiment Station, Vicksburg, Miss., Aug.

46. Houston, J. R. and Garcia, A. W., 1974, "Type 16 Flood Insurance Study: Tsunami Predictions for Pacific Coastal Communities," Technical Report H-74-3, U.S. Army Engineer Waterways Experiment Station, Vicksburg, Miss., May.

47. Houston, J. R., 1978, "Interaction of Tsunamis with the Hawaiian Islands Calculated by a Finite-Element Numerical Model," *Journal of Physical Oceanography*, Vol. 8(1), p. 93–102.

48. Houston, J. R. and Garcia, A. W., 1978, "Type 16 Flood Insurance Study: Tsunami Predictions for the West Coast of the Continental United States," Technical Report H-78-26, U.S. Army Engineer Waterways Experiment Station, Vicksburg, Miss., Dec.

49. Houston, J. R., et al., 1975b, "Effect of Source Orientation and Location in the Aleutian Trench on Tsunami Amplitude Along the Pacific Coast of the Continental United States," Research Report H-75-4, U.S. Army Engineer Waterways Experiment Station, Vicksburg, Miss., July.

50. Hwang, L-S. and Divoky, D., 1975, "Numerical Investigations of Tsunami Behavior," Final Report, National Science Foundation, Washington, D.C., Mar.

51. Iida, K., 1961, "Magnitude, Energy, and Generation Mechanisms of Tsunamis and a Catalogue of Earthquakes Associated with Tsunamis," *Proceedings of the 10th Pacific*

Science Congress Symposium, International Union of Geodesy and Geophysics, Monograph No. 24, pp. 7–18.

52. Iida, K., 1970, "The Generation of Tsunamis and the Focal Mechanism of Earthquakes," *Tsunamis in the Pacific Ocean*, Ch. 1, East-West Center Press, Honolulu, Hawaii, pp. 3–18.

53. Ippen, A. T. and Goda, Y., 1963, "Wave Induced Oscillations in Harbors: The Solution for a Rectangular Harbor Connected to the Open-Sea," Report No. 59, Massachusetts Institute of Technology, Hydrodynamics Laboratory, Cambridge, Mass., July.

54. Ippen, A. T., Raichlen, F., and Sullivan, R. K., Jr., 1962, "Wave Induced Oscillations in Harbors: Effect of Energy Dissipators in Coupled Basin Systems," Report No. 52, Massachusetts Institute of Technology, Hydrodynamics Laboratory, Cambridge, Mass., July.

55. Ishimoto, M. and Hagiwara, T., 1934, "The Phenomenon of Sea Water Overflowing the Land," *Bulletin of the Earthquake Research Institute*, Tokyo Imperial University, Tokyo, Japan, Supplementary Vol. 1, pp. 17–23.

56. Iwasaki, T. and Horikawa, K., 1960, "Tsunami Caused by Chile Earthquake in May, 1960 and Outline of Disasters in Northeastern Coasts of Japan," *Coastal Engineering in Japan*, Vol. III, pp. 33–48.

57. Jaggar, T. A., 1929, "A Big Atlantic Earthquake," *The Volcano Letter*, Dec.

58. Kajiura, K., 1963, "On the Partial Reflection of Water Waves Passing Over a Bottom of Variable Depth," *Proceedings of the 10th Pacific Science Congress on Tsunami Hydrodynamics*, International Union of Geodesy and Geophysics, Monograph No. 24, pp. 206–230.

59. Kajiura, K., 1963, "The Leading Wave of a Tsunami," Bulletin of the Earthquake Research Institute, Vol. 41, p. 535–571, (Reprinted in Selected Papers of Professor Kinjiro Kajiura, University of Tokyo, 1986).

60. Kanamori, H. and Cipar, J. J., 1974, "Focal Processes of the Great Chilean Earthquake, May 22, 1960," *Physics of the Earth and Planetary Interiors*, Vol. 9, pp. 128–136.

61. Keulegan, G. H., 1950, "Wave Motion," *Engineering Hydraulics*, Ch. 11, John Wiley and Sons, Inc., New York, pp. 711–768.

62. Kononkova, G. E. and Reihrudel, A. E., 1976, "Experimental Study of Solitary Tsunami Waves," *Proceedings of the Tsunami Research Symposium*, Bulletin 15, Royal Society of New Zealand.

63. Lamb, H., 1932, *Hydrodynamics*, 6th ed., Dover Publications, Inc., New York.

64. LeBlond, P. H. and Mysak, L. A., 1977, "Trapped Coastal Waves and Their Role in Shelf Dynamics," *Marine Modeling, The Sea*, Ch. 10, Vol. 6, pp. 459–495.

65. Lee, J. J., 1969, "Wave Induced Oscillations in Harbors of Arbitrary Shape," Report No. KH-R-20, W. N. Keck Laboratory of Hydraulics and Water Resources, California Institute of Technology, Pasadena, Calif., Dec.

66. Lee, J. J., 1971, "Wave Induced Oscillations in Harbors of Arbitrary Geometry," *Journal of Fluid Mechanics*, Vol. 45, pp. 375–393.

67. Linsley, R. K., Jr., Kohler, M.A., and Paulhus, J. L. H., 1958, *Hydrology for Engineers*, McGraw-Hill Book Company, New York.

68. Longuet-Higgins, M. S., 1967, "Trapping of Waves Around Islands," *Journal of Fluid Mechanics*, Vol. 29.

69. Madsen, O. S. and Mei, C. C., 1969, "The Transformation of a Solitary Wave Over an Uneven Bottom," *Journal of Fluid Mechanics*, Vol. 39, Part 4, pp. 781–791.

70. Magoon, O. T., 1965, "Structural Damage by Tsunamis," *Proceedings of the Coastal Engineering Specialty Conference*, American Society of Civil Engineers, Ch. 4, pp. 35–68.

71. Mason, M. A. and Keulegan, G. H., 1944, "A Wave Method for Determining Depths Over Bottom Discontinuities," TM-5, U.S. Army, Corps of Engineers, Beach Erosion Board, Washington, D.C., May.

72. Meyer, R. E., 1971, "Resonance of Unbounded Water Bodies," in Mathematical Problems in Geophysical Sciences, Part I, Lectures in Applied Mathematics, Vol. 13, Amer. Math. Soc., Providence, pp. 189–228.

73. Miche, R., 1944, "Movement Ondulatores de Mers en Profondour Cons," *Ann. Ponts Chaussees*, Vol. 114.

74. Miles, J. W., 1971, "Resonant Response of Harbors: An Equivalent-Circuit Analysis," *Journal of Fluid Mechanics*, Vol. 46, Part 2, pp. 241–265.

75. Miles, J. W., 1972, "Wave Propagation Across the Continental Shelf," *Journal of Fluid Mechanics*, Vol. 54, Part 1, pp. 63–80

76. Miller, R. L., 1968, "Experimental Determination of Run-up of Undular and Fully Developed Bores and an Examination of Transition Modes and Internal Structure," Technical Report No. 8, Department of Geophysical Sciences, University of Chicago, Chicago, Ill., June.

77. Munk, W., Snodgrass, F., and Gilbert, F., 1964, "Long Waves on the Continental Shelf: An Experiment to Separate Trapped and Leaky Modes," *Journal of Fluid Mechanics*, Vol. 20, Part 4, pp. 529–554.

78. Murty, T. S., 1977, "Seismic Sea Waves—Tsunamis," Bulletin 198, Department of Fisheries and the Environment, Fisheries and Marine Service, Ottawa, Canada.

79. Murty, T. S. and Wigen, S. O., 1976, "Tsunami Behavior on the Atlantic Coast of Canada and Some Similarities to the Peru Coast," *Proceedings of the Tsunami Research Symposium*, Royal Society of New Zealand, Bulletin 15, pp. 51–60.

80. Murty, T. S., Wigen, S. O., and Chawla, R., 1975, "Some Features of Tsunamis on the Pacific Coast of South and North America," Series No. 36, Marine Sciences Directorate, Department of the Environment, Ottawa, Canada.

81. Nakano, M., 1932, "Preliminary Note on the Accumulation and Dissipation of Energy of the Secondary Undulations in a Bay," *Proceedings of the Physico-Mathematical Society of Japan*, Vol. 14, pp. 44–56.

82. Nasu, N., 1934, "Heights of Tsunamis and Damage to Structures," *Bulletin of the Earthquake Research Institute*, Tokyo Imperial University, Tokyo, Japan, Vo. 1, Mar. pp. 218–226.

83. Nishimura, H., Horikawa, K., and Shuto, N., 1971, "On the Function of Tsunami Breakwaters," *Coastal Engineering in Japan*, Tokyo, Japan, Vol. 14, pp. 63–72.

84. O'Brien, M. P., 1977, Discussion of "Similitude in Coastal Engineering" by B. Le Mehaute, *Journal of the Waterway, Port, Coastal, and Ocean Division*, Vol. 103, No. WW3, Aug. pp. 393–400.

85. Palmer, R. Q., Mulvihill, M. E., and Funasaki, G. T., 1965, "Hilo Harbor Tsunami Model—Reflected Waves Superimposed," *Proceedings of the Coastal Engineering Santa Barbara Specialty Conference*, American Society of Civil Engineers, Ch. 2, pp. 21–31.

86. Pararas-Carayannis, G., 1969, "Catalog of Tsunamis in the Hawaiian Islands," Report WDCA-T 69-2, ESSA—Coast and Geodetic Survey, Boulder, Colo., May.

87. Peregrine, D. H., 1967, "Long Waves on a Beach," *Journal of Fluid Mechanics*, Vol. 27, No. 4, pp. 815–827.

88. Perroud, P. H., 1957, "The Solitary Wave Reflection Along a Straight Vertical Wall at Oblique Incidence," University of California, Institute of Engineering Research, Berkeley, Calif., Series 99, Issue 3, Sept.

89. Petrauskas, C. and Borgman, L.E., 1971, "Frequencies of Crest Heights for Random Combinations of Astronomical Tides and Tsunamis Recorded at Crescent City, Califor-

nia," Technical Report HEL 16-8, Hydraulic Engineering Laboratory, University of California, Berkeley, Calif., Mar.

90. Pierson, W. J., 1972, "Wave Behavior Near Caustics in Models and in Nature," *Waves on Beaches*, Academic Press, New York, pp. 163–180.

91. Reid, R. O., 1988, private communication.

92. Seelig, W. N., Harris, D. L., and Herchenroder, B. E., 1977, "A Spatially Intergrated Numerical Model of Inlet Hydraulics," GITI Report 14, U.S. Army Engineer Waterways Experiment Station, Vicksburg, Miss., Nov.

93. Shen, M. C., 1972, "Wave Resonance Near Shores," *Waves on Beaches*, Academic Press, New York, pp. 123–161.

94. Shen, M. C. and Meyer, R. E., 1967, "Surface Wave Resonance on Continental and Island Slopes," Technical Summary Report No. 781, Army Mathematics Research Center, University of Wisconsin, Madison, Wisc., Sept.

95. Shepard, F. P., MacDonald, G. A., and Cox, D. C., 1950, "The Tsunami of April 1, 1946," *Bulletin of the Scripps Institution of Oceanography*, Vol. 5, No. 6, pp. 391–528.

96. Soloviev, S. L. and Go, C. N., 1974, "A Catalog of Tsunamis on the Western Shore of the Pacific Ocean," Navka Publishing House, Moscow, USSR, 310 pages.

97. Soloviev, S. L. and Go, C. N., 1975, "A Catalog of Tsunamis on the Eastern Shore of the Pacific Ocean," Navka Publishing House, Moscow, USSR, 204 pages.

98. Spaeth, M. G., 1964, *Annotated Bibliography on Tsunamis*, Monograph No. 27, International Union of Geodesy and Geophysics, Paris, France, July.

99. Spielvogel, L. Q., 1975, "Single-Wave Run-up on Sloping Beaches," *Journal of Fluid Mechanics*, Vol. 74, Part 4, pp. 685–694.

100. Street, R. L., Burgess, S. J., and Whitford, P. W., 1968, "The Behavior of Solitary Waves on a Stepped Slope," Technical Report No. 93, Department of Civil Engineering, Stanford University, Palo Alto, Calif., Aug.

101. Street, R. L. and Camfield, F. E., 1966, "Observations and Experiments on Solitary Wave Deformation," *Proceedings of the 10th Conference on Coastal Engineering*, American Society of Civil Engineers, Ch. 19, pp. 284–301.

102. Street, R. L., Chan, R. K. C., and Fromm, J. E., 1970, "The Numerical Simulation of Long Water Waves: Progress on Two Fronts," *Tsunamis in the Pacific Ocean*, Ch. 30, W. M. Adams, ed., East-West Center Press, University of Hawaii, Honolulu, Hawaii, pp. 453–473.

103. Townley, S. D. and Allen, M.W., 1939, "Descriptive Catalog of Earthquakes of the Pacific Coast of the United States 1769 to 1928," *Bulletin of the Seismological Society of America*, Vol. 29, No. 1, Jan. pp. 1–297.

104. U.S. Army Engineer District, Honolulu, "Hilo Harbor, Hawaii, Report on Survey for Tidal Wave Protection and Navigation," Nov. 1960.

105. Van Dorn, W. G., 1965, "Tsunamis," *Advances in Hydroscience*, Vol. 2, Academic Press, New York, (also published as Scripps Institution of Oceanography Report, Federal Clearinghouse No. AD457729, Jan. 1965).

106. Van Dorn, W. G., 1970, "Tsunami Response at Wake Island: A Model Study," *Journal of Marine Research*, Vol. 28(3), p. 336–344.

107. Vastano, A. C. and Reid, R. O., 1970, "Tsunami Response at Wake Island: Comparison of the Hydraulic and Numerical Approaches," *Journal of Marine Research*, Vol. 28(3), p. 345–356.

108. Whitham, G. B., 1967, "Non-Linear Dispersion of Water Waves," *Journal of Fluid Mechanics*, Vol. 27, Part 2, pp. 339–412.

109. Wiegel, R. L., 1965, "Protection of Crescent City, California from Tsunami Waves," Report for the Redevelopment Agency of the City of Crescent City, Crescent City, Calif., Mar.

110. Wilson, B. W., 1972, "Estimate of Tsunami Effect at San Onofre Nuclear Generating Station Units 2 and 3, California," Southern California Edison Co., Los Angeles, Calif., Dec.

111. Wilson, B. W. and Tørum, A., 1968, "The Tsunami of the Alaskan Earthquake, 1964; Engineering Evaluation," TM-25, U.S. Army Coastal Engineering Research Center, Washington, D.C., May.

112. Zabusky, N. J. and Galvin, C. J., 1971, "Shallow-Water Waves, the KortewegdeVries Equation and Solitons," *Journal of Fluid Mechanics*, Vol. 47, Part 4, pp. 811–824.

CHAPTER 11

WAVE SET-UP

R. A. Holman

College of Oceanography
Oregon State University
Corvallis, Oregon, U.S.A.

CONTENTS

Introduction

Any process that raises water level in the nearshore can be an important agent in beach erosion. One such phenomenon that is local to the surf zone and immediate beach vicinity is the phenomenon of wave set-up. In very rough terms, wave breaking causes a stress (a landward push) on the water, causing it to pile up against the shore until the seaward slope of this set-up is sufficient to oppose the wave stresses. The term wave set-up is used to distinguish this phenomenon from storm set-up (surge) or wind set-up, both of which occur over a larger scale. While wave set-up is limited to a much smaller area (the surf zone) the magnitudes of this superelevation can still be appreciable. Set-up on natural beaches will be from 17–50% of the incident wave height, so that values of 1 m are possible during large storms. On a ambient beach slope of 1:50, this results in an inundation of 50 m, making this a first-order problem for coastal engineers.

This chapter summarizes the present knowledge on wave set-up. The topic is introduced historically with the first interest resulting from the impact of the 1938 hurricane in Narragansett, Rhode Island. The laboratory work that established wave set-up as a process is described, followed by the evolution of a theoretical understanding mainly through the introduction of the concept of radiation stress. Finally, there is a summary of results from field data and a discussion of future research.

Early Interest

The first indications that breaking waves could force a rise in sea level against the shore came from an analysis of the damage from a 1938 hurricane that hit the east coast of the United States. Careful assessment of storm surge during the height of the hurricane showed that surge levels at Narragansett Pier, fully exposed to the storm, were 1 m higher than those at the relatively protected Newport shoreline. Models of surge in the area failed to explain the difference, and it was suggested that the sea-level rise may have been a result of wave breaking.

The Beach Erosion Board then began model wave tank tests to validate this hypothesis. Fairchild [5] built a 1-to-75 scale model of the beach profile at Narragansett Pier, and exposed it to equivalent prototype wave heights of up to 10 m. Measurements of wave height and local sea level were made with dual-wire resistance gauges placed in stilling wells. Fairchild found clear indication of landward sloping sea level in the surf zone, with a maximum measured set-up of 1 m, matching the field observations. Saville [13] extended the wave tank work to examine the effect of beach slope and wave conditions. He observed that there was actually a mild depression of sea level in the vicinity of the break point (called set-down) but a clear set-up through the surf zone. On gently sloping beaches the maximum set-up (at his landward-most gauge) was 15% of the incident wave height. Surprisingly in retrospect, on beaches with slopes steeper than 1 to 6 no set-up was observed. Nevertheless, the phenomenon had been demonstrated and now awaited a theoretical foundation.

Theory

The general mechanism whereby waves can exert a stress on the fluid in which they propagate was introduced by Longuet-Higgins and Stewart [9–11]. They defined a stress tensor called the radiation stress, S, as the excess flux of momentum due to the presence of waves. Gradients in the radiation stress then correspond to a net addition or loss of momentum to a water column, in other words a net force. As shown in the following, these gradients can arise from wave shoaling and breaking, and explain the wave set-down at the breakpoint and set-up at the shoreline.

If we assume longshore uniformity, then the analysis of set-up involves only cross-shore quantities. Taking x to be the cross-shore coordinate, positive seaward from the still water shoreline, then the x-directed flux of x-directed momentum is given (correct to second order) by

$$S_{xx} = E\left(\frac{2kh}{\sinh 2kh} + \frac{1}{2}\right) \tag{1}$$

where k = $2\pi/L$, the wave number
      L = wavelength
      h = depth below still water
      E = the wave energy density

$$E = \frac{1}{8}\rho g H^2 \tag{2}$$

where ρ = density of the fluid
      g = acceleration due to gravity
      H = wave height

Any net stress on the fluid will force a response. If the force is steady and acts long enough, equilibrium will be reached (time dependencies will vanish), and the momentum balance will be

$$\frac{dS_{xx}}{dx} + \rho g(\bar{\eta} + h)\frac{d\bar{\eta}}{dx} = 0 \tag{3}$$

where $\bar{\eta}(x)$ is the adjustment of mean sea level away from still water level (the set-up or set-down). Thus, sea level simply adjusts until radiation stress gradients are balanced by sloping sea level. Specification of the gradients of radiation stress will then allow us to find sea level everywhere (assuming a constant of integration, usually $\eta = 0$ well out to sea). We follow the analysis of Longuet-Higgins and Stewart [9] and Bowen et al. [3].

The problem is usually approached by separately considering two regions; the surf zone where radiation stress gradients are related to breaking, and seaward of the breakpoint where shoaling is the dominant process. In the shoaling region, wave height varies to conserve wave energy flux,

$$E \cdot C_g = \text{constant} \tag{4}$$

where C_g is the group velocity. Using Equation 4, Longuet-Higgins and Stewart [9] found an explicit expression for the depression of sea level (the set-down) in the shoaling region,

$$\bar{\eta} = -\frac{1}{8}\frac{H^2 k}{\sinh 2kh} \tag{5}$$

Bowen et al. [3] showed that Equation 5, written in terms of local wave height and wave number, could be re-expressed in terms of deep water wave characteristics in a form

$$\bar{\eta} = -\frac{1}{4}H_0^2 k_0 f(k_0 h) \tag{6}$$

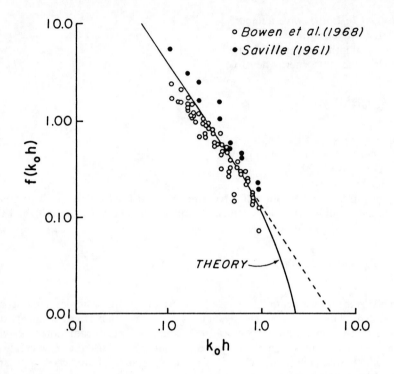

Figure 1. Behavior of set-down outside the surf zone. Solid line corresponds to theory (Equation 6). Data points are obtained experimentally [3, 13].

The function, f, is shown in Figure 1, along with data from Saville [13] and Bowen et al. [3]. The theory clearly provides a good description of set-down for at least these laboratory experiments.

Inside the surf zone the analysis becomes more difficult, a result of our lack of knowledge about wave kinematics in this highly non-linear region. Nevertheless, Bowen et al. [3] pursued the analysis using rough approximations to produce a result that is very consistent with available laboratory and field data. The decay of wave height was modeled as a simple depth-limited process,

$$H = \gamma(\bar{\eta} + h) \tag{7}$$

where γ is approximately constant and of order 1. Assuming Equation 1 to still be valid (despite the fact that processes at higher than second order should not be negligible), the cross-shore dependence of radiation stress is found to be

$$S_{xx} = \frac{3}{16} \rho g \gamma^2 (\bar{\eta} + h)^2 \tag{8}$$

This is then combined with the momentum Equation 3 to yield an explicit form for the set-up gradient

$$\frac{d\bar{\eta}}{dx} = -K\frac{dh}{dx} \tag{9}$$

$$K = \frac{1}{1 + \dfrac{8}{3\gamma^2}}$$

Thus, the set-up slope is just a constant fraction of the local beach slope, the constant being determined solely from the value of γ, the ratio of breaker height to local depth. Equations 6 and 9 can be integrated to yield a predicted cross-shore profile of mean sea level on a beach under monochromatic waves.

The value of γ, the only free parameter in the theory, shows some dependency on wave and beach conditions. Bowen et al. [3] present data that shows γ to be a function of a surf similarity parameter, the Iribarren number, ξ_0, given by

$$\xi_0 = \frac{\beta}{(H_0/L_0)^{1/2}} \tag{10}$$

Bowen et al. continued to carry out a careful laboratory study of the above predictions. An example of their results is shown in Figure 2. Several conclusions were made. First, the theory was shown to provide a very good description of the observations. In the set-down area, the agreement was excellent up to the immediate vicinity of the breakpoint, where the observed set-down profile became flat. The set-up region was linear as predicted, with a slope in agreement with Equation 9. Only in very close proximity to the actual beach face did the set-up profile begin to diverge from prediction, showing an increase in slope to approach the beach face asymptotically. They argue that this is the result of a reflected component in the incident wave field, such that wave height does not go exactly to zero at the shoreline, but tends to a small residual value. Figure 3 shows two examples of this behavior. The presence of this asymptotic region becomes important when examining the field data, since wave run-up is one of the simplest variables to monitor from which set-up can be estimated.

The principle addition to the theory since the work of Bowen et al. has been the extension from monochromatic to random wave forcing by Battjes [1] and Battjes and Janssen [2]. Specification of the gradient of radiation stress for a spectrum of incident waves requires knowledge of the energy dissipation rates (Equation 1), the focus of their work. Starting with an assumed frequency distribution of wave heights, Battjes and Janssen invoke a breaking criteria (based on a critical wave steepness) to determine the portion of the distribution that will break. They then calculate dissipation by assuming those waves that break will show bore-like behavior. Laboratory data provide support for their model on both simple

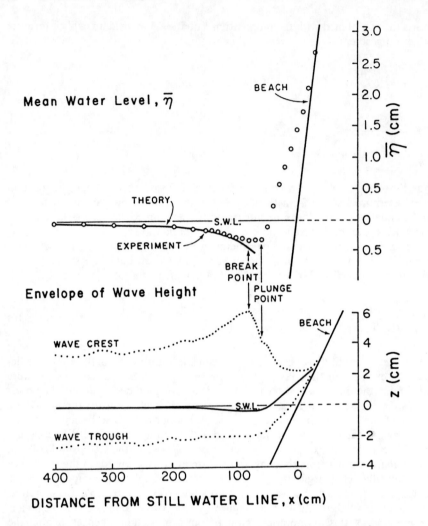

Figure 2. Results of example laboratory experiment. The upper figure shows the data for set-down and set-up, while the lower figure also shows the wave height envelope [3].

and barred beach profiles. The magnitude of the maximum set-up (at the shoreline) was found to be from 14 to 21% of the deep-water significant wave height.

Field Data

In contrast to the elegance of the theory and success of the laboratory data, field data on set-up are remarkable sparse and uncertain, with only three useful data sets presently in the literature. Dorrenstein [4] collected set-up data from a fishing

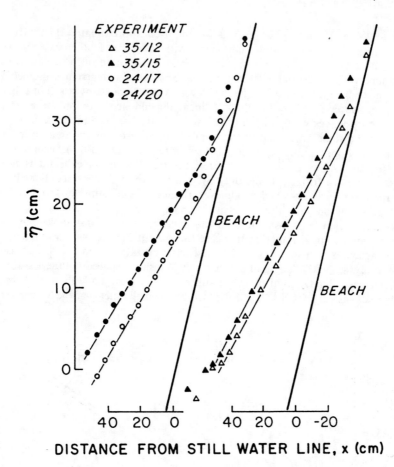

Figure 3. Set-up data from laboratory experiments showing sharp increase in set-up in the vicinity of beach face. Linearity of set-up through the surf zone is obvious [3].

pier on the Atlantic Coast of Florida. Given the primitive equipment available for data acquisition and analysis, the experiment was remarkable and the results apparently useful (Battjes [1] showed the results to be consistent with theory and lab data). However, the set-up estimates were based on very short records (64 second averages) for which infragravity band contamination could be a serious problem. Also, Miller et al. [12] has shown that scour around piers may have a major influence on local processes.

It took 20 years for the next good field data set, results from the large Nearshore Sediment Transport Study (NSTS), to reach publication. Using elevation differences between mean run-up (measured using a dual resistance-wire run-up sensor) and mean offshore elevation (deduced from offshore pressure sensors), Guza and Thronton [6] published set-up estimates from 11 days during which wave height varied from 0.6 to 1.6 m (Figure 4). Set-up was found to be approximately 17% of the deep water significant wave height, consistent with theory and other data. However, the data set was not without problems. First, run-up and offshore elevation were not surveyed to the same reference, so that absolute difference measurements were not made. The difference in reference levels was estimated by assuming that the set-up measurements should follow a linear dependence with zero intercept. Thus, the set-up values were uniformly adjusted to give the zero intercept in Figure 4 (it should also be noted that the amount of this adjustment was in agreement with the known approximate position of the offshore pressure sensors). Second, the data in Figure 4 show considerable scatter; the trend with wave height is not particularly obvious. In fact, it was only by omitting the value labeled 17 that a sensible regression was obtained at all. Nevertheless, these estimates formed the best data on set-up on natural beaches at the time.

A more recent data set is from Holman and Sallenger [8]. Their data were again based on wave run-up, although in this case the run-up time series were digitized from time lapse movies using a computer assisted digitization system [7]. Because the camera view showed a length of beach, many longshore-spaced time series were available for each film. A total of 154 set-up estimates were made from 61 films. Each estimate was calculated as the difference between the mean of the 35 minute

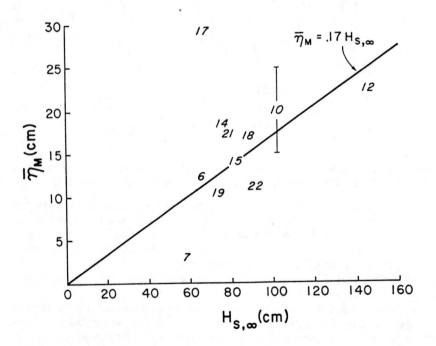

Figure 4. Compilation of set-up data from NSTS Torrey Pines experiment. Solid line is best linear fit with intercept subtracted from all data to force line through origin [6].

run-up time series and the tidal elevation measured offshore in 6-m depth (the depth immediately surrounding the gauge was actually 8 m due to local scour around the pier on which the gauge was mounted).

Holman and Sallenger found that when the set-up data were plotted in dimensional terms (set-up as a function of significant wave height), the data were extremely scattered. Instead, the data were better behaved when non-dimensionalized by incident wave height and plotted against the Iribarren number, ξ_0. Figure 5 shows these set-up data separated according to tide. Several points are apparent. First,

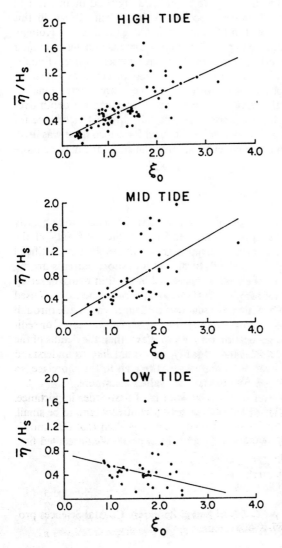

Figure 5. Set-up data from Holman and Sallenger [8] showing 154 points, separated by tidal elevation. The data of Guza and Thornton [6] lie within the scatter of the data set.

some of the values plotted are quite large, much larger than expected by the theory. This is largely due to the nature of the sampling system. Tests show that the depth of water "defined" as the waters edge in the photographic technique is approximately 0.5 cm, much shallower than the 3 cm "definition" of the dual resistance wire run-up meter of Guza and Thornton. Because this is in the asymptotic region discussed by Bowen et al. [3], the observation of larger-set values is not surprising. Second, the scatter of the data is quite large at high Iribarren number (when the beach was reflective and, typically, three-dimensional). This may in part be due to an accidental bias in sampling; on days where longshore variability was observed, time series at many longshore locations (up to nine) were digitized in an effort to understand longshore structure of swash processes. Third, when plotted in this format, the data of Guza and Thornton [6] are consistent with those of Holman and Sallenger [8]. That they were able to plot their data in dimensional terms in their original paper is due to the very narrow range of Iribarren number sampled. Finally, the separation by tidal stage was forced by the unusual behavior of the low tide data. These data are from a barred beach, often with pronounced three-dimensionality. Not only do processes apparently become quite complicated when the depth over the bar becomes quite shallow, but the appropriate definition of a beach slope for calculation of the Iribarren number is unclear. While local foreshore slope was used, the variation by tide suggests that the mean value over the surf zone may be more appropriate.

Discussion

The presence of the asymptotic region of set-up against the beach slope greatly complicates field studies. Results appear quite sensitive to the proximity of the "instrument" to the beach face. It may be argued that this result is an artificial complication. If the primary interest is the dynamics of longshore currents arising from longshore gradients of set-up, then values measured in the thin wedge of set-up at the shoreface are clearly not appropriate. Instead, an approach such as was used by Dorrenstein [4] should be used, with mean sea-level measurements made through the surf zone. However, if interest centers on overtopping, swash processes, or sediment transport and morphology generation on the shoreface, then the details of the asymptotic region are of extreme relevance. Ideally, we would like to understand the entire transect of mean sea level, from deep water through to the shoreface, so that measurements at one point can be used to infer values elsewhere.

The description of mean sea level in the nearshore is of first-order importance. While the dynamics arise at higher order and the set-up gradients tend to be small, the integrated magnitudes are not. It would seem surprising then that our knowledge of mean sea-level behavior on natural beaches is so poor. Well-executed field experiments are clearly needed.

Acknowledgment

This work was supported by the Office of Naval Research, Coastal Sciences program, under contract N00014-87-K-0009.

Notation

C_g   group velocity
C_g group velocity
E   wave energy density
g   acceleration of gravity
h   water depth
H   wave height
k   wave number
K   a constant
L   wavelength
S   radiation stress tensor
x   cross-shore coordinate
0   (as a subscript) referring to deep water
β beach slope
γ a constant of order 1
$\bar{\eta}$ wave set-up
ρ density of water
ξ_0 surf similarity parameter

REFERENCES

1. Battjes, J. A., 1974, "Computations of Set-up, Longshore Currents, Run-up Overtopping Due to Wind-generated waves," Rep. 74-2, Delft Univ. Technol. Delft, The Netherlands.

2. Battjes, J. A. and Janssen, J. P. F. M., 1978, "Energy Loss and Set-Up Due to Breaking of Random Waves," Proc. 16th Conf. Coastal Eng., 569–587.

3. Bowen, A. J., Inman, D. L. and Simmons, V. P., 1968, "Waves 'Set-Down' and Wave Set-Up," *J. Geophys. Res.* 73, 2569–2577.

4. Dorrenstein, R., 1961, "Wave Set-Up on a Beach," 2nd Technical Conference on Hurricanes, Beach Erosion Board, 230–241.

5. Fairchild, J. C., 1958, "Model Study of Wave Set-Up Induced by Hurricane Waves at Narragansett Pier," Rhode Island, bulletin, Beach Erosion Board, U.S. Corps Eng., Washington, D.C.

6. Guza, R. T. and Thornton, E. B., 1981 "Wave Set-Up on a Natural Beach," *J. Geophys. Res.*, 86(C5), 4133–4137.

7. Holman, R. A. and Guza, R. T., 1984, "Measuring Run-up on a Natural Beach," *Coastal Eng.*, 8, 129–140.

8. Holman, R. A. and Sallenger, Jr., A. H., 1985, "Set-Up and Swash on a Natural Beach," *J. Geophys. Res.*, 90(C1), 945–953.

9. Longuet-Higgins, M. S. and Stewart, R. W., 1962, "Radiation Stress and Mass Transport in Gravity Waves with Application to Surf Beats, *J. Fluid Mech.* 13, 481–504.

10. Longuet-Higgins, M. S. and Stewart, R. W., 1963, "A Note on Wave Set-Up," *J. Mar. Res.*, 21, 4.

11. Longuet-Higgins, M.S. and Stewart, R. W., 1964, "Radiation Stress in Water Waves, a Physical Discussion with Applications, *Deep Sea Res.*, 11, 529–562.

12. Miller, H. C., Birkemeier, W. A. and DeWall, A. E., 1983, "Effects of CERC Research Pier on Nearshore Processes," editor J. R. Weggel, Proc. Coastal Structures 83, ASCE, New York, N.Y., 769–784.

13. Saville, T., 1961, "Experimental Determination of Wave Set-Up," Proc. 2nd Tech. Conf. Hurricanes, 242–252.

CHAPTER 12

WORLDWIDE IMPACT OF SEA-LEVEL RISE ON SHORELINES

Per Bruun

Chairman (Retired)
Port and Ocean Engineering
Norwegian Institute of Technology
Trondheim, Norway

CONTENTS

Introduction

Sea level is rising around the world. Anthropogenic emissions may result in a climatic warming through the next few centuries, which could overcompensate the natural cooling that might otherwise be expected. The warming might be a threat to the continued existence of the Greenland and the West Antarctic ice sheets.

This chapter discusses evidence from tidal gauges and archeology that sea level has been rising in the past centuries. Next, it describes methods for assessing erosion caused by sea-level rise. It then describes how people have held back the sea in the past, focusing on the low countries of Europe. Finally, it describes the options available to society for responding to shoreline changes resulting from projected sea-level rise.

Historic Evidence of Sea-Level Rise

Tide-level recordings tell us of sea-level movements over the 200 years. For longer-term developments, we must seek the evidence of such rises in, for example, increased flooding of low coastal areas, drowning of valleys and shore features, including some ancient man-made features, and density currents penetrating further upstream. The findings are not always easy to interpret. Tectonic movements, glacial rebounds, subsidence, consolidation of softer materials in the ground and rebalancing of land masses due to offshore sedimentation have interfered with the relative movement of land and sea. The many authors who have written about above-mentioned phenomena come from a variety of disciplines, including geology, geography, engineering, and archeology, to name a few. Other evidence of sea-level rise comes from historic records of past construction activities.

Recordings of the events were solely descriptive rather than by instruments, although surveys have been made to state the actual situation. An impressive geophysical review was given by Fairbridge [26] who referred to works by Marmar [42], Stommel [54], and Guilcher [29]. Others include Milliman and Emery [43] and Emery [25].

Important reviews of tide-level fluctuation are given by U.S. Department of Commerce [57] for the United States' shores. The recent contribution by Barth and Titus [4] was the first to examine future conditions.

The following text presents a few examples of these reviews [12].

Early Harbor Works

The Port of Alexandria in Egypt was founded by Alexander the Great, who destroyed the ports at Tyre and Sidon. Alexander built the port by connecting through reclamation the island of Pharos (the scene, centuries earlier, of the great harbor works, which had by then mostly disappeared) with the mainland. This formed two harbors protected by the island, in which basins were formed by the construction of walls in the form (on plan) of semicircles, the northeastern basin having an outer mole protecting the single central entrance channel. This was a form of layout that was later adopted by both Greeks and Romans.

The first mention of a lighthouse for the benefit of shipping is that built upon a rock off the northeast of the island of Pharos. This lighthouse appears to have been of considerable height and was circular in plan, tapering to the top.

Of the Greek ports, perhaps the most interesting are those of Piraeus, Zea and Munychia, Rhodes, and Cnidus. All these were natural bays protected on the seaward sides by jetties or breakwaters. In the Mediterranean, where there is practically no rise or fall in water level—and the earlier Greeks had apparently not evolved any means of drying out the sites by cofferdams—these structures were all founded upon beds of tipped impervious material, which were built up until they reached the surface or thereabouts. They were then leveled to receive the masonry that formed the superstructures.

The period of the Roman Empire provides considerably more information about harbors construction along the coast of Italy and Sicily from the accounts written by historians and from remains of the actual works. These works were much more substantial than anything previously existing, both in design and in the means and methods of construction employed. For example, in Italy, as opposed to Greece, natural bays that could readily be formed into harbors were scarce, and the character of the works was therefore somewhat different. Moreover, Roman cement was in general use, which contributed to stability and lasting qualities; again, methods of constructing underwater works were evolved, many of which were founded on piles driven into the seabead; for all Roman jetties and breakwaters were constructed of masonry founded at sea-bed level. Many jetties were of arched formation, probably to avoid the siltation that in some places would be induced by solid walls. To reduce foundation work and masonry in exposed situations, double arcades were formed some distance apart, with the arches staggered to break the force of waves but still allow the passage of water. Cellae-covered recesses for ships of war, which protected the vessels from the sun and inclement weather, were a feature of many Roman ports, but vessels used for purely commercial purposes were berthed at marginal quays or jetties.

In all these ancient ports the piers and wharves today are covered by 2 to 3 meters of water. However, because the structures have deteriorated, this does not provide quantitatively firm figures for the amount of sea-level rise occurring in the last 1,500 to 3,000 years.

Viking Ports

We know little about port development during the centuries following the downfall of the Roman Empire. Sea voyages and trade undoubtedly continued. Ports were river-based; quays or piers hardly existed or were uncommon. The big seafarers for several centuries were the Vikings, whose large fleets enabled them to invade England, France, Ireland, Spain, and the Baltic countries all the way down to Constantinopole (Istanbul). Next they crossed the Atlantic Ocean to Iceland, Greenland, and Vineland (North America). We know about their prowess from historic accounts of what they accomplished. But navies require naval bases for operation; they were found during recent decades of excavations in Denmark (Fyrkat).

From archeological discoveries in Denmark and in the southern part of Sweden we know that the Vikings built large forts at rivers and in fjords. Their vessels were probably moored, or they may have been beached, but we have also found large pile walls, for example, at Hedeby, South Jutland, demonstrating that their vessels, whether built for commerce or for war, used piers for loading or unloading. Sometimes they also built large submerged walls or dams from sunken ships, or from piles across a navigation channel to stop enemies from penetrating into their harbors. A magnificent example of the latter is found in Roskilde Fjord on the Island of Zeeland in Denmark.

The remains of these 1,000- to 1,500-year-old Viking structures do not provide direct data on elevations, but some of them were built in a way that indicates that the water table must have been lower than it is today. The conclusion of the Danish National Museum regarding water tables is that sea level about 1,000 years ago must have been 1 to 1.5 m below present sea level.

Sedimentological Evidence

Coastal geomorphologists observe the elevation of beach ridges and strandlines. In emerged condition they provide evidence of a higher sea level (i.e., as many be seen in Denmark where strandlines are found in up to about 60 to 70 m elevation) generated by the postglacial arctic waters. After melting of the ice cap, the ground experienced a rebound effect, which was much faster than the sea-level rise. That this situation still continues was revealed by Svante Arhenius' famous drilling of holes in vertical rock walls on the Swedish west coast outside Gothenburg. The holes were drilled in 1890 and are now found about 0.6 m above present mean sea level (MSL). (Svante Arhenius is also known for coining the term "greenhouse effect.")

On the Skagen Spit, the northernmost tip of Jutland, the elevation of old beach ridges elevated by the glacial rebound decreases to the north as deposits get younger. One of these changes in elevation occurs rather abruptly, revealing a slowdown in the relative movement of land and sea about 2,500 years ago, demonstrating a rise in sea level elsewhere.

Two examples of sedimentation provide indirect confirmation of the mechanics of the sea/land interaction process. At Penang, West Malaysia, rivers discharge known quantities of sediments on the estuary bottom. If the area of the estuary bottom (500 km^2) is multipled by a sea-level rise of 0.002 m/yr one arrives at 1 million m^3, which corresponds to the annual river discharge of sediments. This is consistent with the observation that water depths have not changed in the last 200 years.

The situation on the 140-km pocket shore on the South Coast of Iceland between Porlakshöfn and Dyrholaey is described by Bruun [15, 16]. The discharge of river sediments of sand size is about 4.5 million m^3/year. This quantity is balanced by deposits of 0.0035 m/yr (which corresponds to the recorded sea-level rise in the Port of Reykjavik) on the 140-km long, 9,000-m wide platform, of which 2,000 m is beach area, extending to 50-m to 60-m depth where there is a steepening of the offshore bottom leaving the impression of a deposit boundary slope. Grain size distributions confirm the existence of an equilibrium condition. A horizontal rock platform is found at 100-m depth, possibly an abrasion platform from a lower sea level during an extending glacial period.

Tidal Gauges

As described by Hicks [35]:

"Tidal data are the fundamental base from which most coastal and marine boundaries are determined. They are also the fundamental references for sounding and depiction of the shoreline on all nautical charts. As such, they are intrinsic to the activities of coastal engineering, surveying, hydrography, and photogrammetry. The most important tidal data are defined, amplified, and their specific uses listed in abbreviated outline form. The definitions are in terms of the procedures used in their computation.

"As 'tide authority' (in the international and legal sense) of the United States of America, the National Ocean Service (NOS) of the National Oceanic and Atmospheric Administration (NOAA), U.S. Department of Commerce, has statutory responsibility for tidal measurements, analyses, predictions, and data determinations. Responsibility for tidal data included the development and any subsequent modifications of the methods of computation.

"The method used for the computation of a tidal datum is specified in the official definition of that datum. The purposes of these 'method definitions' are to:

- Ensure uniformity of computation among oceanographers.
- Ensure uniformity of computation among the various tidal regimes of the U.S.
- Provide for comparisons with foreign data.
- Enable outside scientific verification of results through duplication.
- Provide precise terminology for judicial and legislative acceptance in cases involving coastal and marine boundaries."

Hicks [35] gives twelve references of recordings of sea levels. Tidal-level recordings, however, have been undertaken on a larger scale only in recent decades. Exceptions are the Dutch and British recordings, which date back a few centuries; however, the accuracy of those tidal observations is questionable. In Holland, the influence of sea-level rise is reinforced by subsidence due to the soft underground caused by the large Rhine, Maas, and Scheldt Rivers.

In the United States the trend of relative sea-level rise is fairly well documented by surveys on all shores (Hicks [34], Lisle [40], U.S. Department of Commerce [57], Nummedal [47] for the Louisiana Coast, are among the most important contributions). Sea-level rise during the latest decades ranges from 1 to 4 mm/yr depending upon the location. The subsidence in Louisiana is about 10 mm/yr. On the U.S. east coast the rise is 2–3.5 mm/yr, on the Gulf, 2–3 mm/yr, and on the Pacific, about 2 mm/yr. Rises for east and west coasts of Canada are similar. Germany has kept good records of the rises on the North Sea Coast [53], as may be seen from Table 1. The conclusion of the Siefert paper reads as follows:

"The knowledge of the probable development of the water level of the German North Sea coast—in general on all flat coasts—is of greatest importance for coastal engineering. In Germany an increase of MThw (mean high water) of 25 cm per century has been taken as a basis for dimensioning of coastal protection construction (i.e., dikes or storm surge barrages). If instead one had to reckon with a rise of MThw of 2 m or more in the next 100 years and with at least the same increase of the storm surge levels, all coastal protection works would be ineffective. It is doubtful that an elevation of the dikes for such a water-level rise would be possible everywhere. As one can conclude from the development of MThw at all locations on the German North Sea coast for the last 400 years in connection with the development of temperature in central

Table 1
Trends in Sea Level Along the German North Sea Coast [53]

		Mean High Water			Mean Low Water
		Until 1955	1873–1955	1956–1983	1956–1983
		1	2	2	4
Emden	(1857)	0.25	0.23	0.54	−0.33
Wilhelmshaven	(1873)	0.23	0.23	0.37	−0.15
Cuxhaven	(1843)	0.25	0.24	0.51	−0.21
Busum	(1871)	0.22	0.21	0.62	−0.25
Husum	(1870)	0.30	0.28	0.63	−0.09
Dagebull	(1873)	0.28	0.28	0.65	−0.32

Slope "b" of the regression lines $y = a + bx$ of mean high water in three different periods and of mean low water in the last period.

England, an increase of 2 m or more would be thinkable in the case of an increase of the temperature of about 4 C. The increase of temperature is assumed to be 1 C since the culminating-point of the "little Ice Age." In the same period MThw rose about 1 m.

Therefore it is necessary to intensify investigations in order to predict the probable development of the global sea level as well as that of certain coastal sections for the next 100 years as exactly as possible. Three routes of research are deemed necessary:

1. One has to analyze all the factors responsible for the development of water level in the ocean and on the coasts as exactly as possible. This demands an extensive and close cooperation of the different scientific disciplines of climatology, meteorology, oceanology, glaciology, geodesy and coastal engineering. This cooperation has to be international. Coastal engineers should contact such projects as the International Climate Research Program and the Project No. 200 of the International Geological Correlation Program (Sea-Level Correlation and Applications). The results of these projects are of greatest practical importance for coastal engineering."

From these figures it appears that high tides (Germany) apparently have risen from 2 to 6 mm/yr, m while low tides have dropped 1–3 mm/yr; therefore, tidal ranges have increased. The large differences occur during the 1956–1983 period when the means of high and low tide levels have increased 2–5 mm/yr.

In Denmark the rebound from the glacial period was believed to dominate until recently. The latest decades however, show that relative sea level is rising in the entire country, being highest (1–2 mm/yr) in the southwest part, but close to zero at the northernmost part of Jutland. At the tip of Jutland, the Skagen Spit, the apparent 3-mm rise may be related to the consolidation of thick layers of silt upon which the spit grew out by littoral drift deposits in water depths of about 200 m in "The Norwegian trench."

In Norway it appears that the Oslo fjord area of granite and old lavas may still be rising in comparison with sea level. The rest of the Norwegian coast up to North Cape seems to be in a neutral situation, but at some places sea level is slightly rising compared to land despite the fact that glaciers were roaming only about 10,000 years ago. Movements range from a 1–2 mm/yr sea-level rise in the northern part to a 3–4 mm/yr land level rise (compared to sea level) in the Oslo fjord areas.

In Sweden, glacial rebound is still very predominant, as shown in Figure 1. The southern shore of Sweden, however, now experiences a sea-level rise. The situation in Iceland is described by the already-mentioned recordings in Reykjavik, which show a rise of 3.5 mm/yr.

In Holland and Belgium, sea level is rising 2–3 mm/yr (Table 2). The general situation in northwest Europe is seen in Figure 1. The glacial rebound in Fenno-Scandinavia is still active, up to 10 mm per year in northern Finland and Sweden.

It has not been possible to secure data from the U.S.S.R. In Japan sea level has been observed (i.e., in the Osaka Bay) and is of the order of magnitude of 2 mm/yr. On Hokaido, Japan settling occurs to a considerable extent due to the extraction of gas and water. In China the rise in sea level has been noticed mainly because of the increasing problems of saltwater intrusions in the rivers.

In summary, sea level is rising worldwide at a rate of from 2 to 4 mm annually in the areas discussed. However, it appears to be stable in several places, such as in the vicinity of coral reefs in the Pacific and Australia. As a result, most authors estimate the eustatic rate of rise at 1 to 1.5 mm/yr. There is some indication of an increase in the rise, but the evidence is not too clear at this point.

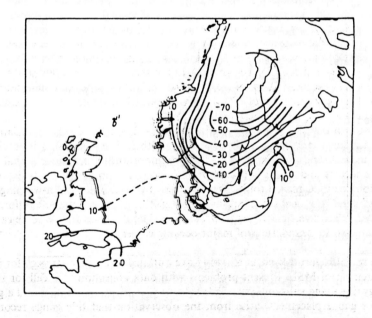

Figure 1. Changes in relation to sea level (cm/year) in NW Europe.

Table 2
Average Rate of Rise of Relative Mean Sea Level (MSL), Mean High-Water
Level (HW), Mean Low-Water Level (LW) and Mean Tidal Difference (TD)
in cm/century in Holland and Belgium (Rijkswaterstaat, Den Haag)

Station	MSL	HW	LW	TD	Period Used
Oostende		17	5	12	1925–1980
Flushing	22	33	19	13	1900–1980
Terneuzen		40	18	22	1900–1980
Hansweert		40	10	30	1900–1980
Bath		44	16	28	1900–1980
Zierikzee	17	26	5	21	1900–1980
Hook of Holland	19	22	16	6	1900–1980
Ijmuiden	21	24	18	6	1900–1980
Den Helder	16	15	7	8	1933–1980
Harlingen	16	27	10	17	1933–1980
Delfzijl	16	21	7	14	1900–1900

The most comprehensive study on the relative movements of land and sea undoubtedly is described by Pirazzolli [48]:

"This paper gives the preliminary results of a new investigation based on the records of 1,178 stations provided by the Permanent Service for Mean Sea Level or found in the literature. The longest series available show that oscillations in Relative Sea Level (RSL) can be averaged satisfactorily by linear trends of secular variation when long enough periods of observation are considered. The calculation has been limited to those stations providing at least 50 year-long records and to some stations where the records are only 30 to 50 years long, if the 5-yr fluctuations of the RSL are weak during the period of observation. This makes a total of 229 stations for which updated trends of secular variation are now available."

"Most of the stations indicate positive upwards trends of secular variation, but at rates changing from one place to another. The conclusion is reached that tectonic and oceanic factors are more important than average global eustatic factors and that the average of all the trends indicated by tide-gauge stations may be biased towards a RSL rise by systematic down-warping of coastlines. On a local scale, secular trends of RSL provide very useful information on relative vertical movements of regional land masses and, in some cases, on large-scale meanderings of major oceanic currents."

In a recent report, Munk, et al. [45] have outlined a scientific strategy for future measurement of MSL. Present problems with data collection that call for such a strategy (involving substantially improved tide gauge instrumentation and a global plan for gauge placement) arise from the observation that tide gauge records of long duration, on the order of a century, appear to be dominated by two processes namely, (1) noisy fluctuations with time scales on the order of a decade and a

RMS (root mean square) amplitude of 50 mm associated with El Nino-like oceano-graphical events; and (2) a long-term, secular trend on the order of 1 mm/yr. See Figure 2 for instance. In spite of careful mathematical analyses of time-series gauge records, the noise-to-"signal" ratio is typically too large to be amenable to accurate interpretation of quantitative trends.

Tide gauges are more commonly placed inside protected water bodies including coastal bays and estuarial mouths than along the open coast for obvious reasons. Dominant tidal frequencies range from 1.1×10^{-5} to $2.2 \times 10^{-5} \text{ sec}^{-1}$ and the tidal range on the order from near-zero to as much as 10 m in some area. Although bay dimensions in general vary widely, information useful to an interpretation of coastal sea level is typically derived from gauges placed in the vicinity of the connection (tidal inlet) to open waters. Furthermore, bays that are either too shallow or small in horizontal dimensions are sometimes unsuitable for tide gauge placement. The reasons are not always "hydraulic." Tide gauges are more commonly placed in rela-tively large bays of commercial/navigational importance than in small, inaccessible locations. Likewise, gauges placed well upland of the inlet tend to be influenced by too many factors that are not sea-related. Accordingly, and in a very approximate manner, we may specify relevant characteristic bay dimensions as follows: horizontal dimension (order of magnitude range) 10^3 to 10^4 m and depth, 10^0 to 10^2 m. The point to be made here is that these dimensions are highly restrictive compared to sea dimensions, and it immediately poses the question: What do we know about bay water-level fluctuations and, particularly, how do they relate to what occurs outside?

This question is by no means new; it has been posed by scientists previously, but it clearly takes on a new meaning in light of the present and future needs for an accurate evaluation of MSL from measurement in bays. One of the early, well-documented and comprehensive studies in the United States was by Johnson and Winter [37] and Johnson [36] whose effort was directed towards disspelling the

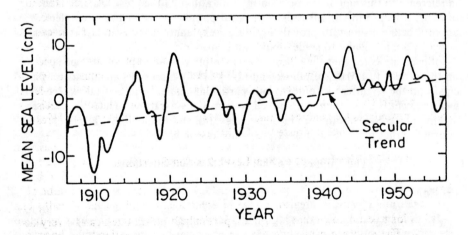

Figure 2. Mean sea-level record from Honolulu, Hawaii with frequencies above 2 cycles/year attenuated [44].

then prevalent view among some that MSL derived from tide gauge records in bays is a reliable indicator of a "geodetic" datum. Johnson noted:

> "A consideration of certain simple facts of shoreline physiography supports the theory that along an irregular coast the mean sea-level surface is an irregularly warped plane which is extremely sensitive to alterations of the form of the shore, depths of tidal channels and other shore features. Changes in these features must accordingly cause local fluctuations of the position of mean sea level, which local and often rapid vertical oscillations of our most important datum plane range from fractions of an inch to a few inches in ordinary cases, but reach values of one or two feet or even more under extreme conditions."

After examining several factors causing superelevation in several bays and waterways, Johnson concluded that "harbors and bays are unfavorable locations for tide gauges intended to give accurate and constant values for mean sea level as a datum plane on which to base geodetic surveys of high precision."

The "theory" that Johnson referred to essentially consisted of a series of qualitative, well thought out explanations of causes for the generation of bay superelevation, i.e. elevation difference between mean bay level (MBL) and MSL. Johnson's basic argument was that because many of the causative factors are influenced by shoreline alterations including the inlet and bay morphology, superelevation in turn changes as a result of these alterations and therefore, in general, MBL bears no unique relationship to MSL.

Superelevation response to shoreline change is by now well recognized by scientists, and the fact of its occurrence does not require overemphasis. However, because considerable information on coastal sea level is presently derived and is likely to be obtained in the future from tide gauges placed in bays, there are associated scientific and engineering implications for which we should restate as well as reevaluate Johnson's argument in a broader and somewhat different context than he intended in reference to this aim. It is worth noting that although the present understanding of MBL response to various coastal physical parameters is far from complete, we are in a better position to provide a physical explanation to several of the causes noted by Johnson, and to some he did not consider.

Johnson indicated that the objective is (1) to provide an appropriate perspective on the problem of MBL response; and (2) to briefly discuss its significance, principally in the engineering context, with particular reference to coastal water-level measurement. In so doing, it is hoped to introduce a rational factor in decision making procedures for analysis of tide gauge data, and to highlight gaps in present knowledge that must be addressed by further research.

The Impact of Sea-Level Rise on Shorelines

Erosion

It has long been known that high tides, particularly storm tides, can be very destructive. The influence of the eustatic rise of sea level on shore stability was "rediscovered" in the early 1960s.

The Bruun Rule of erosion [7], so named by American coastal geomorphologists [50–52], concerns a long-term budget of onshore/offshore movement of material. The rule is based on the assumption of a closed material balance system between (1) the beach and nearshore and (2) the offshore bottom profile. This topic is dealt with extensively in theory [1, 10, 31] and through observations in the field [5–7, 10, 22, 28, 30]. The "rule" has sometimes been used rather indiscriminately without realizing its limitations. One should always remember that it is basically two-dimensional, but it is almost always applied three-dimensionally.

The theory has now been tested extensively in the field [22, 28, 30, 50]. Its overall validity seems unquestionable when boundary conditions are well defined, but this is not always the case. Its mathematics has been proven for two-dimensional conditions [1, 2]. The difficulty lies in clear definitions of boundaries in relation to the composition of materials of which the shores are built up, usually sand particles decreasing in size as distance offshore increases, until silt- and perhaps clay-sized particles finally prevail. Such fine materials may originate from erosion of the shore, but may also originate from rivers or from deserts and volcanoes as windblown dust [10, 30].

As previously explained, the theory of the influence of sea-level rise on erosion is proposed as being two-dimensional, but nature is three-dimensional. This in turn means that in practice one must consider a certain uninterrupted length offshore, when the material transport is contained in a "box," xyz where x is the distance offshore from a defined point on the shoreline; y is the length of the box along the shore; and z is the depth from a defined water table. The numerical material balance in and out of two x-z sections y meters apart is initially assumed to be zero. If there is no balance between the two quantities, this must be considered in the total material balance equations. There are two boundary y-z sections, one located on the beach or in the dunes, the other at a certain water depth, which separates the "nearshore drift" from the "offshore drift" in the x-direction. On the beach, the effect of wind-drift may then have to be added. It is usually negligible, but it may in some cases present a non-negligible quantity. The outer y-z boundary is more difficult to define, because there is no clear distinction between the limit of exchange between beach and offshore drifts of material. In practice these limits are "fading-out."

Often the term "wave base" is used for material agitation on the bottom. Recent research [30, 31] attempts to present rational methods for calculating the limits of active agitation of sand bottom and the long-term erosion rates based on long-term rises of sea level. The short-term "seasonal" limit may be approximately equal to depth $2H_b$, where H_b is the height of the highest breaking waves. The "wave base" is thereby related to the capacity or limit of the wave action in agitating the bottom material "actively," which in a statistical sense depends upon the time interval considered [31]. A "five-year wave base" obviously may not be the same as a "fifty-year based."

In addition to this, there is the problem of diffusion of material along the bottom and other boundary layer phenomena [10]. The original theory [7], however, is based on a quantitative two-dimensional balance between the beach and the nearshore and offshore bottom and there will be a certain transition area between "nearshore" and "offshore" adjustments to a change in sea level. If the physical forces do not change in the nearshore area, the equilibrium-balance condition apparently will be maintained. But the situation may be different in the offshore area, where forces and supplies of materials are very different from those governing the nearshore area. No equilibrium balance situation needs to exist in the offshore area, where currents are offshore-originated. Bottom sediments in movement are clay and silt, occasionally fine sand where currents are strong enough to carry the material. Current-generated ripple marks have been found at very great depths (i.e., at 5,000 ft (1,500 m) on the Blake Plateau), which include indications of scour due to current movement over shells.

Depending upon the grain size, the "base" may extend to shallower or deeper water. This refers to open sea coasts, where sediments of silt and clay size may be carried long distances in suspension before being deposited. In defining the area of exchange between nearshore and offshore drifts, one therefore must consider the grain sizes and materials of certain characteristics available on the shore. The finest parts of this material, which may stay in suspension for long periods, therefore have to be included in the materials balance equations. This refers to a certain depth beyond which fines may still be transported to much deeper water for deposition [10, 30].

The ultimate limit for movement characterized by threshold velocities is discussed by Bruun [15, 16] based on research by Losada and Desire [41]. Results from Iceland [15] point in the direction of ultimate depth

$$d_1 \sim 3.5 \, Hs$$

where Hs then refers to wave heights occurring once, or over a certain number of hours, every 1, 10, 20, 50, 100, and 500 years.

Bruun's two-dimensional theory [7, 11] depends upon a "closing depth" for exchange of material between the offshore bottom and the shore. It must also be adjusted for grain sizes that will eventually wind up far offshore due to their small size and consequent slow settling velocities (i.e., silts and clays). For three-dimensional applications, major adjustments may become necessary, particularly when features like tidal inlets, canyons, and other "sinks" of materials enter the balance picture. The report by Titus, et al. [56] on the erosion at Ocean City, Maryland, is remarkable because it emphasizes the great importance of sea-level rise on a long unobstructed shore.

A quantification of erosion caused by the rise in sea level was attempted by Bruun and Schwartz [13]. Sea-level rise may contribute from 10% to 100% to the total erosion or from 1 to 6 m³/m yr. If erosion is not caused by natural or artificial inlets, breakwaters, groins, or sea walls, the sea-level rise is the only explanation for the occurring erosion [56]. A normal shoreline recession by sea-level rise is 0.3 m/yr. If sea level rises 1.5 m by the year 2100, shoreline recession will be about 200 meters. For the lower bay lagoon, estuary, and other tidelands this may approach catastrophic proportions. Huge areas in Bangladesh, Brazil, China, Egypt, Iraq, Iran, India, Lagos, Nigeria, and areas on the U.S. east and Gulf coasts will be flooded.

Erosion of shores is a worldwide phenomenon. Shores always attempt to adjust their condition to the impact of the acting forces, thereby establishing an "equilibrium condition." But why do they then continue to erode? There is no other explanation than that sea level is rising if erosion is not caused by man-made structures.

The author has observed erosion in many countries all over the world. Table 3 gives a record of his experiences, listing six different reasons for erosion, three "natural" and three "man-induced." Sea-level rise is listed as a reason in all cases, either because no other reason could be given for the erosion of uninterrupted shorelines of extended length or that sea level was known to be rising and consequently erosion must result.

Another "natural" reason is subsidence caused by the consolidation of soft materials, such as that which occurs in Holland; the Po estuary in Italy; Bay of Bengal, India; Louisiana, U.S.A; and elsewhere. Subsidence could, however, also be caused by the extraction of oil and/or gas as it occurs in Japan (Hokaido) and California (Long Beach). Some areas may experience large- or small-scale tectonic movements related to fault lines. The following are other causes of erosion:

- *Tidal entrances* interrupt the normal littoral longshore drift causing erosion because they discharge shore material in the bay and/or in the ocean. Tidal entrances accounted for 28 out of 40 cases in the 40 countries where erosion was observed by the author; some of these cases were very severe [9].
- *Navigation channels*, like the tidal entrances upon which they were often based, constitute littoral barriers to the normal drift by accumulating materials that otherwise could drift to downdrift shores thereby contributing to their stability.
- *Manmade structures* such as breakwaters, jetties, groins, and other shore-perpendicular structures are also barriers to the longshore drift and have also caused severe damages to downdrift shores. It can safely be said that the coastal protective groins have caused *more* erosion than accretion. According to the author's experience, man-made structures (listed in Table 3) are second only to sea-level rise and head of natural tidal inlets as causes of erosion.
- *Mining* for heavy minerals has caused damage in several countries until the adverse effects were observed. Mining also includes extraction of sand, gravel, and stones. Such operations are now largely prohibited, but they still occur in countries where the problems they cause have not yet been realized.

Short-term erosion events of a severe or extreme nature usually catch the eye of the public. To evaluate occurrences of rapid dune erosion due to storm tides, like hurricanes and typhoons, the large-scale experiments by Vellinga [60], Vellinga and Bruun [61], Vellinga, et al. [62], and van de Graaf [58] are important for assessing events of an extreme nature for which preparedness is warranted.

In summary, erosion due to sea-level rise is obvious. Compared to other reasons, particularly the man-made, it is less severe, but as it occurs almost everywhere, it undoubtedly counts for the largest part of erosion worldwide. It is therefore very unfortunate that we, due to "greenhouse effects," may expect (during the next several decades) an accelerated rise in sea level [4].

Table 3
Overview of Causes of Erosion Worldwide [16]

Country	Natural			Man-Induced		
	Sea Level Rise	Subsidence	Tidal Inlets	Navig. Channels	Man-made Structures	Mining
Algeria	X			X	X	
Argentina	X		X	X	X	
Australia	X		X	X		
Belgia	X		X	X	X	
Brazil	X		X	X	X	
Canada	X			X	X	
China	X	X		X	X	
Columbia	X		X	X		
Denmark	X		X	X	X	
Ecuador	X		X	X	X	
Egypt	X	X	X	X	X	
France	X		X	X	X	
Holland	X	X	X	X	X	
Iceland	X		X			
Ireland	X			X	X	
India	X	X	X	X	X	X
Iran	X		X	X		
Israel	X			X	X	
Italy	X	X	X	X	X	
Japan	X	X	X	X	X	
Lebanon	X			X	X	
Malaysia	X			X	X	X
Mexico	X		X	X	X	
Nigeria	X		X	X	X	
New Zealand	X		X		X	
Nicaragua	X		X	X		
Norway	X					
Pakistan	X		X	X		
Portugal	X		X	X	X	
Saudi Arabia	X			X	X	
Spain	X		X	X	X	
Sweden	X	Rise		X	X	
Sri Lanka	X		X	X	X	
Tripoli	X			X	X	
Turkey	X			X	X	
UK	X		X	X	X	
USA	X	(X)	X	X	X	
USSR	X		X	X	X	
Venezuela	X		X	X	X	
West Germany	X	X	X	X	X	
Σ 40	40	7	28	37	33	2

Shoreline Recession

Shoreline recession can be expected on the ocean shore as a result of sea-level rise. The actual shoreline recession depends upon the exposure, the offshore profile-steepness, and the character of the material that builds up the shore and the offshore bottom.

One may get a general impression of the rate of shoreline recession by examining the following data, which are representative of recession rates for exposed shores like those of the Atlantic, the Pacific, and the Indian Oceans:

Rise per year	Shoreline Recession per year
1 cm (1/30 ft)	1–1.5 m (4–5 ft)
2 cm (1/15 ft)	2–3.0 m (7–10 ft)
3 cm (1/10 ft)	3–4.5 m (10–15 ft)
10 cm (1/3 ft)	10–15.0 m (33–50 ft)

These numbers represent large volumes of material lost to the sea or the amount needed to maintain a status quo with respect to erosion. The figures speak for themselves, giving an impression of the severity of the problem we are now facing.

Coastal Protection in the Low Countries in Europe and in England

Erosion is a deficit in the material balance: We lose more than we gain. How old is the art of coastal protection? We do not know; probably very old.

Coastal protective works of major order probably first came into existence when man was forced to protect the land on which he lived to avoid the waters digging away the ground under his feet.

Although a great many training and irrigation walls, dams, or dikes were built in the Far and Middle East, coastal protection *per se* probably first developed in the low countries in Europe where rivers poured soft materials, mainly clay and silt, out in the ocean for settling. Consolidation was a slow process that made the land settle. In addition sea level was rising. To avoid loss of land by flooding and to protect themselves from drowning, the Frisians and the Dutch first built earth mounds. Diking started about the year A.D. 1000. In the 13th century, the Dutch had accomplished major coastal protection and reclamation works, particularly in the Dordrecht area.

van Veen [59] writes:

"The earliest written records about the Frisians (or Coastal Dutch) describe them as water-men and mud-workers. The Romans found in the north of the country the artificial hillocks upon which the inhabitants, already called Frisii, made a living. We shall follow their history, because written records are available about the early reclamation works they made. One and the same race, now called the Dutch, took, held, and made the low country."

"Pliny, who saw these mound-dwelling tribes in the year A.D. 47 described them as a poor people. He apparently exaggerated when he wrote that they had no cattle at all. Or did he see some much-exposed mounds near the outer shores where the sea had swallowed every bit of marshland? At storm tide, Pliny said, the Frisians resembled groups of miserable shipwrecked sailors, marooned on the top of their self-made mounds in the midst of a waste of water. It was impossible to say whether the country belonged to the land or to the sea. 'They try to warm their frozen bowels by burning mud, dug with their hands of the earth and dried to some extent in the wind more than in the sun, which one hardly ever sees.'"

"No doubt the mud Pliny refers to was the peat found in the 'wolds,' or swamps, some distance south of the clay marshes, where the artificial mounds had been made. In all they built 1,260 of these mounds in the northeastern part of the Netherlands, an area of a mere 60 × 12 miles. Further east there are more of them in East Friesland. The areas of the mounds themselves vary from 5 to 40 acres; they rise sometimes to a height of 30 feet above normal sea level. The contents of a single mound may be up to a million cubic yards."

"They built their mounds on the shores of the creeks in which the tide ebbed and flowed. In their scows they went (in their language in which the roots of so many English words can be found): 'uth mitha ebbe, up mitha flood,' out with the ebb, up with the flood. The tide bore them towards the peat regions, or perhaps to the woods still farther inland and then brought them back. Or they went out with the ebb in the morning towards the sea, where they gathered their food, and returned in the evening with the incoming tide."

"The Coastal Dutch have now lived 24 centuries in their marshes and of these the first 20 or 21 were spent in peril. It was not until 1600 or 1700 that some reasonable security from flooding was achieved. During these long treacherous centuries the artificial mounds made their survival possible."

"It was a work which might be compared with the building of the pyramids. The pyramid of Cheops has a content of 3,500,000 cubic yards, that of Cephren 3,000,000 and that of Mycenium 400,000 cubic yards. The amount of clay carried into the mounds of the northeastern part of the Netherlands can be estimated at 100,000,000 cubic yards."

"In Egypt it was a great and very powerful nation which built the pyramids throughout a series of dynasties. The aim was to glorify the Pharaohs. With us it was a struggling people, very small in number and often decimated, patiently lifting their race above the dangers of the sea, creating large monuments, not in stone, but in native clay."

"In this Lex Frisionum of 802 there is not yet any mention of seawalls, but the first attempts at dike building must have been made shortly afterwards. Frisian manuscripts still extant, dating from the early Middle Ages, deal chiefly with the following three points: First, the right of the people to freedom, all of them, 'the bern and the unbern.' Secondly, the 'wild Norsemen' whose invasions took place roughly from 800 to 1000, and thirdly: the Zeeburgh or Seawall."

"This novel means of defense against the sea by means of a continuous clay wall was called a Burgh, or stronghold. The people were apparently very proud of seaburgh, because they described it in poetical language as 'the Golden Hop,' the Golden Hoop."

"This is also the Right of the Land to make and maintain a Golden Hoop that lies all around our country where the salt sea swells both by day and by night."

The spade, the hand barrow, and the fork were the instruments used for diking, the fork presumably for the grass turfs that were used to heighten the dikes and make them stronger. Despite these tremendous efforts, the sea was the strongest.

"This was due partly to our insufficient technical skill and partly to lack of cooperation. For a single night, Dec. 14th 1287, the officials and priests estimated that 50,000 people had been drowned in the coastal district between Stavoren and the Ems. This is a large number considering that this was the area where so many dwelling mounds could be used as places of refuge."

The advances and successes have been tied to a few names. Says van Veen:

"We often wondered who was the master engineer who created marvelous Great Holland Polder, south of Dordrecht, the work which had included the damming off of the tidal mouth of the river Maas, and the leading of that river into the Rhine. This proved to be William I. He had already finished that gigantic undertaking by 1213. The polder was destroyed in 1421 by the St. Elisabeth's flood, described in a former chapter. William was a man of great conceptions. He surrounded the entire area of Holland-Proper with strong dikes and made several canals intended to drain the vast moors. They also served as a splendid network of shipping canals. It is likely that he made the dikes around the Zeeland islands Walcheren and Schouwen too, and that he established the still-existing administrations for the upkeep of these islands. The other part of his clever and amazing reclamation and construction programme cannot be described here, but it is very clear that he knew the geography of his country by heart. No maps as yet existed!"

The earliest reference to the art of accelerating the natural rate of accretion is the manuscript *Tractaet van Dijckagie* (Treatise on Dikebuilding), written by the Dutch dikemaster Andries Vierlingh between 1576 and 1579. Vierlingh discusses the contruction of "cross-dams" on mudflats that are not yet dry at low water. In this connection he also advises that old ships should be sunk and earth dumped on the top of them so as to make artificial islands or flats that could hold back the silt and sand suspended in the water. These islands should subsequently be connected with low dams. Although this method has not been used commonly, it is known that shipwrecks have been used at numerous places to close dike breaches. These wrecks formed the basis for the fill material that was secured with mats or brushwood. Vierlingh, however, was much against closing of dike breaches with shipwrecks due to the non-homogeneity they created in the dike structure. Nevertheless, this method was widely used over a long period of time, not only in Holland but in the (at that time Danish) Schleswig-Holstein.

Vierlingh was found to be a real master of the dikes and waters, a man of great ability and spirit—one of the greatest of his kind. Luckily, the greater part of his manuscript has survived. Its ancient picturesque style is a joy to every hydraulic engineer. This remarkable book already shows the special vocabulary of the Dutch diking people in all its present-day richness. In some ways it is even richer.

His advice is simple and sound. The leading thought is: *Water will not be compelled by any 'fortse' (force), or it will return that fortse onto you.* This is the principle of streamlines. Sudden changes in curves or cross-sections must be avoided. It is the law of action and reaction. And truly, this fundamental law of hydraulics must be thoroughly absorbed by anyone who wants to be a master of tidal rivers.

Andries Vierlingh was a genius. If we had followed his advice on streamlining, the shores would have been better off today. His protection was the streamlined dike. It offered storm tide protection but not necessarily erosion protection unless the dike was provided with a hard surface. And even so, erosion might continue below or in front of the hard surface due to the combined action of waves and currents. To push the currents away, current breakers or groins were then introduced. The hard surface due on the dike was a revetment with a gentle slope reflecting little wave energy, and so it still is in Holland, where vertical walls have long been banned. The groin worked well in certain areas, where currents and waves carried considerable material as they still do on some parts of the Dutch coast and in Denmark [5, 6]. If not, they were of little importance or only of value as a kind of toe protection for the dike. Experiences elsewhere are, of course, similar.

Planning for Sea-Level Rise on the Ocean Shores

We must accept that sea-level rise in all probability is going to accelerate. Consequently, the beach and bottom profiles must adjust to a new situation. As a result erosion will occur. Barth and Titus [4] characterize the issues:

"Ocean beach resorts in the United States have always faced erosion and storm damage. At first, these risks were accepted as inevitable."

"Development was generally sparse, and people often built relatively inexpensive cottages along the ocean that they could afford to lose. When the occasional severe storm destroyed these houses and eroded the beach, replacement structures were frequently built farther inland to maintain the original distance from the shore."

"After World War II, beaches became more popular and were developed more densely than before. The resulting increases in real estate values enabled greater numbers of communities to justify expensive engineering solutions to maintain their shorelines. Frequently subsidized by the federal government, the practice of stabilizing shorelines replaced the previous custom of accepting erosion as inevitable."

"The projected rise in sea level poses a fundamental question: How long should these communities hold back the sea? In the decades ahead, the costs of shoreline protection will rise dramatically and the relative efficiencies of various measures will change. But without such efforts, a 1-ft rise would erode most shorelines over 100 ft, threatening recreational use of both breaches and adjacent houses. Even under the low scenario, this could happen by 2025."

"Although sea level is not expected to rise rapidly until after 2000, resort communities may have to consider its consequences much sooner. After the next major storm, in particular, homeowners whose properties are destroyed will decide whether and how to rebuild; and local governments will decide whether or not to let all of them rebuild, and which options are appropriate to address the storm-induced erosion. How well a community ultimately adapts to sea-level rise will depend largely on the direction it takes when it reaches this crossroads."

Quantification of erosion due to sea-level rise is of course difficult as the rise-induced erosion is mixed with other agents of erosion. Bruun and Schwartz [13] attempted to show that beach erosion due to sea-level rise may amount to about 15–20% of the total erosion occurring on heavily eroding shores. Titus, et al. [56] (for Ocean City, MD.), however, demonstrate that sea-level rise could become the major part of the erosion on extended shores far from tidal inlets or other "sinks." (See also Everts [24] and Bruun [17].)

Beach Nourishment

Future coastal protection must include beach restoration and maintenance as well as storm tide protection by dunes or revetted dunes [8]. In future coastal protection one must think *large*. It will therefore develop as a function of the combined political, administrative and technical structure. There will be little or no use for "one-man shows." Large groups and large areas will have to be accommodated— by large scale measures. Needs will be concentrated on protective and recreational projects and all combinations thereof. Pressure will increase by the need for recreational beaches. Protection will be achieved simultaneously. The question of which protective measure will be most practical under such circumstances may be answered by artificial nourishment with suitable material that offers the large-scale protection [8]. This, however, does not mean that it always suffices. It may need support from dikes and/or sea walls because of the possibility of storm surges or it may need groins to break scouring currents running close to shore. One main technical advantage associated with artificial nourishment is that it is "smooth" and "streamlined" and therefore not only has no adverse leeside effects, but, on the contrary, benefits adjoining shores by a gradual release of material. Other measures, particularly groins and offshore breakwaters, have definite adverse effects on neighboring shores. The importance of streamlining is obvious.

What then shall we do? We shall improve our artificial nourishment technology. For that we need (1) suitable sand, as coarse as possible or coarser than the beach sand (but sand must not be so coarse that it generates a partly reflecting beach that could become dangerous to bathers); (2) the sand must be placed by equipment that is as efficient and economic as possible, (3) the sand shall be placed with the right profile (which means so that we lose as little of it as possible). Although items (1) and (2) have long been recognized as appropriate, that is not the case with item (3).

Table 4
Profile Nourishment [15, 16]

Tide		A: +1, −1	B: −1, −3	C: −3, −5
			Area	
High	Spring	C	C	—
	Mean	C	M	F
	Neap	C	M	F
Mean	Spring	C	M	F
	Mean	—	M	F
	Neap	—	M	F
Low	Spring	—	M	F
	Mean	—	—	F
	Neap	—	—	F

Bruun [15, 16] discusses in theory, as well as in protective equilibrium, profiles including geometries and grain sizes. Theoretical and practical results favor placement of material, not on the beach, but along the entire cross section, all at one time, with grains of various sizes placed "exactly" where they belong in the profile. It is unquestionable that this will cause higher stability and less material loss alongshore as well as offshore.

Table 4 [15, 16] describes an example of profile nourishment, but which three different grain sizes (distributions) are placed in three different depth ranges (see Figure 3). This, of course, requires meticulous planning and supervision of the actual

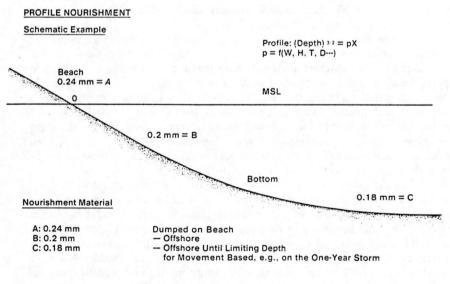

PROFILE NOURISHMENT

Schematic Example

Profile: $(Depth)^{3.2} = pX$
$p = f(W, H, T, D\cdots)$

Beach
0.24 mm = A
0

MSL

0.2 mm = B

Bottom

0.18 mm = C

Nourishment Material

A: 0.24 mm — Dumped on Beach
B: 0.2 mm — Offshore
C: 0.18 mm — Offshore Until Limiting Depth
for Movement Based, e.g., on the One-Year Storm

Figure 3. Profile nourishment [15, 16].

Figure 4. Profile nourishment on the Danish North Sea Coast (Source: Coastal Directorate, Lemvig, 1985).

work in the field under construction. Three different grain sizes—C (0.25 mm), M (0.21 mm), and F (0.18 mm)—are dumped at three tidal elevations (high, mean, and low) on three different bottom areas for the portion of the beach profile extending from 1 m above sea level to 5 m below sea level (A, B, and C).

How shall we accomplish profile nourishment? By using equipment that is able to place on the beach as well as to whatever depth the material shall be placed. This includes pipelines and hopper-dredges as well as split-hull barges and dredges. Figure 4 is a Danish example. Profile nourishment is highly economical compared to conventional beach nourishment due to the lesser costs in offshore dumping bid prices in Queensland [15, 16].

Other Measures

For storm tide protection we neeed dikes of adequate elevation. At some places where the beach has narrowed excessively, dikes must have a hardened surface on the ocean side to resist wave attack and overflows by uprushes. But to keep the dike intact beach stabilization is needed in front of the dike. If we are not able to stabilize the beach, we will have to move the dike back sooner or later and keep moving it back if shore recession continues. We have no other option.

On the large scale we apparently must consider three different possibilities as shown in Figure 5:

1. Stabilization of the shoreline: No further shoreline recession due to the existing land developments.
2. Let nature take its course: Accept the erosion; establish a beach park area instead.
3. Compromise: Establish set-back lines valid for a certain time period before reviewing them for further set-backs.

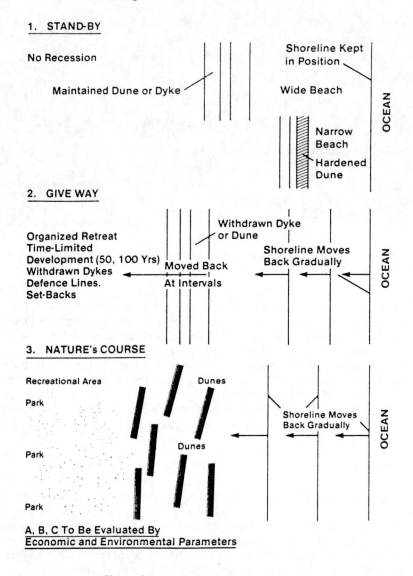

Figure 5. Long-term shore management.

Stabilization. This is a common case, where stabilization is a *must*. Shorelines in Holland, parts of Denmark, the United Kingdom, and Germany must be closely monitored in case stabilization becomes necessary. Shore developments like townships and barriers protecting bays or lagoons do not allow further shoreline recession. Consequently, it is necessary to nourish the beach and to stabilize the dunes.

This will be done for many shores in California and Florida as well as for other shores on the east coast of the United States.

Let nature take its course. This may be done where plenty of undeveloped land is found behind the shoreline, such as in the Outer Banks of North Carolina in the United States. The most practical way of handling such a situation is by constructing withdrawn dikes at considerable distances behind the shoreline and prohibiting any substantial development outside the withdrawn dike. This is already taking place on the Danish North Sea Coast, the Dutch Friesian Islands, and on the Outer Banks in North Carolina. The wisdom of this strategy is obvious—such national and state parks have become very popular and more of these are probably going to be established.

Compromise. Establish a set-back line valid for a certain time period (i.e., 50 or 100 years) and allow a controlled development. Houses can be built in such a way that they can be moved back easily.

While stabilization and letting nature take its course are straightforward, compromise is more complicated because it must be anticipated that the lifetimes of parts of the development are time limited. That would imply, for example, that buildings erected on the property after some time would be moved back to "safer locations." One may imagine the administrative difficulties involved in such an arrangement. One solution, of course would be to lease the coastal properties for limited periods of time (i.e., 20, 30, 50, or 100 years). The buildings eerected on such property should then be designed in such a way that they could be moved landward to another location after a certain time period. Technically, this relocation would not be difficult; the problem would be to make new areas available for the reconstruction of such buildings, which are expendable after so many years.

Financing

Financing possibilities vary from country to country. In the United States the state governments are taking over more and more of the responsibility that earlier rested with the federal government. The Florida task force "Save our Beaches" suggests a 75% financial contribution by the state and a 25% local contribution. In the low countries of Europe, costs will be borne by the national governments either entirely or with some matching funds from the local governments. The contributions by public funds range from 50% to 100%. In some countries, like Spain, the national and state governments will pay all costs of shoreline protection.

Developing countries in general have no provisions or possibilities for public funding. In some of these countries (i.e., large coastal areas in Bangladesh) the situation has become critical. Financing by UN-World Bank is a possibility being explored by Bangladesh.

Conclusion

- Sea level *is* rising. An accelerated rise would cause accelerating erosion of our coastal shorelines. Acceleration of erosion has been noted during recent decades.
- Our ability to quantify the magnitude of the rise is steadily improving.

- It is possible to predict the approximate influence of sea-level rise on shore stability.
- Proper coastal protective measures are available to mitigate the effects of erosion, wherever this is desirable.
- Future coastal protection will involve beach nourishment and storm tide protection by dikes and revetments and offshore (detached) breakwaters (but not groins) where needed, as well as the establishment of practical set-back lines.
- Progress is being made, scientifically and technically, to improve available nourishment procedures and equipment. Future nourishment will be "profile," not "beach," nourishment.

References

1. Allison, H., 1979, "Enigma of the Bruun Formula in Shore Erosion," *Proc. Bruun Symposium*, Newport, RI, International Geographical Union, November.
2. Allison, H., 1981, "Expedious Regimes of Artificial Beach Nourishment or Dredging," *Coastal Eng.*, Vol. 5, pp. 311–330.
3. Birkemeyer, W. A., 1985, "Field Data on Seaward Limit of Profile Change," *Proc. ASCE, Journal Waterway, Port and Coastal Engineering Div.*, Vol. 111, pp. 598–603.
4. Barth, M. C. and Titus, J. G., 1984, *Greenhouse Effect and Sea-Level Rise*, New York: Van Nostrand Reinhold.
5. Bruun, P., 1954a, *Coast Stability*. Danish Engineering Press, Copenhagen, 400 pp.
6. Bruun, P., 1954b, "Coast Erosion and Development of Beach Profile," Tech. Memo No. 44, CERC, USCE, (See also Bruun, P., 1989, *Port Engineering*, 4th Ed., Chap. 7, Houston: Gulf Publishing.)
7. Bruun, P., 1962, "Sea-Level Rise as a Cause of Shore Erosion," *Proc. ASCE. J. Waterways Harbors Divs.*, Vol. 88, pp. 117–130.
8. Bruun, P., 1973, "The History and Philosophy of Coastal Protection," *Proc. 13th Conf. Coastal Engr.*, Vancouver: ASCE, pp. 33–74.
9. Bruun, P., 1978, *Tidal Inlets and Littoral Drift*, Amsterdam: Elsevier.
10. Bruun, P., "The Bruun Rule: Discussion on Boundary Conditions," *Proc. Bruun Symposium*, Newport, RI, International Geographical Union, November 1979.
11. Bruun, P., "Review of Conditions for Uses of the Bruun Rule of Erosion," *Coastal Engineering*, 1983, Vol. 7, pp. 77–89.
12. Bruun, P., "Cost Effective Coastal Protection," *Journal Coastal Research*, 1985, Vol. 1(1), pp. 47–55.
13. Bruun, P. and Schwartz, M., 1985, *Analytical Prediction of Beach Profile Change in Response to a Sea Level Rise*, Stuttgart, W. Germany: Zeitschrift for Geomorphologie, Bd. 36.
14. Bruun, P. et al., 1985, *The Design and Construction of Mounds for Breakwaters and Coastal Protection*, Amsterdam and New York: Elsevier, 1985. (Also see review article by Bruun and Losada, in *Dredging and Port Construction*, November, pp. 25–32.)
15. Bruun, P., 1985, "Sedimentary Balances—Land and Sea With Special Reference to the Icelandic South Coast from Porlakshofn to Dyrholaey," *Proc. Iceland Symposium: Sediment Balances*, Reykjavik, Iceland: The National Energy Authority, September.
16. Bruun, P., 1986, "Sediments Balances—Land and Sea, With Special Reference to the Icelandic South Coast from Porlakshofn to Dyrholey." *Coastal Engineering*, Vol. 10.
17. Bruun, P., 1987, "Discussion of Paper by C. H. Everts titled Sea-Level Rise Effects on Shoreline Position." *ASCE, Journal Waterways, Ports and Coastal Engineering Division*, Vol. 113(3).

18. Dansgaard, W., 1985, "Fast Environmental Changes in the North-Atlantic Region." *Proc. POAC-85*, Greenland: Danish Hydraulic Institute, Horsholm.
19. Dansgaard, W. and Duplessy, J. C. 1981, "The Eemian Interglacial and Its Termination." *The Climate of Europe: Past, Present and Future*, H. Flohn and R. Fantechi (eds.) Dordrecht/Boston/Lancaster: D. Reidel. Chap. 5.3, pp. 208–225.
20. Dansgaard, W., 1984, "The Fugure Degree of Glaciation." *The Climate of Europe*, Chap. 5.4, pp. 225–248
21. Deigaard, R., Fredsoe, J., and Hedegaard, F. B., 1985, "A Mathematical Model for Littoral Drift." Report No. 301, Danish Center for Applied Mathematics and Mechanics, Lyngby.
22. Dubois, R. N., 1976, "Nearshore Evidence in Support in the Bruun Rule on Shore Erosion." *J. Geolo.*, Vol. 83, pp, 485–491.
23. Dubois, R. N., 1982, "Relation Among Wave Conditions, Sediment Texture, and Rising Sea Level: An Opinion." *Shore and Beach*, Vol. 50(2).
24. Everts, C. H., 1985, "Sea Level Rise Effects on Shoreline Position." *Proc. ASCE, Journal Waterways, Ports and Coastal Engineering Division*, Vol. 111, pp. 995–1000.
25. Emery, K. O., 1980, "Relative Sea Levels From Tide-Gauge Records." *Proc. National Academy of Sciences*, Vol. 97, pp. 6968–6972.
26. Fairbridge, R., 1961, "Eustatic Changes in Sea Level." *Physics and Chemistry of the Earth*. Pergamon Press, Vol. 4, p. 99.
27. Fenneman, M. M., 1982, "Development of the Profile of Equilibrium of the Subaquateous Shore Terrace." *J. of Geol.*, Vol. X.
28. Fisher, J. J., 1979, "Shoreline Erosion, Rhode Island and North Carolina Coasts: Tests of the Bruun Rule." In *Proc. Bruun Symposium*, International Geographical Union, Newport, RI, November.
29. Guilcher, A., 1958, *Coastal and Submarine Morphology*. New York: John Wiley and Sons.
30. Hands, E. B., 1979, "Bruun's Concept Applied to the Great Lakes." *Proc. Bruun Symposium*, International Geographical Union, Newport, RI, November.
31. Hallermeier, R. J., 1972, "Calculating a Yearly Limit Depth to the Active Beach Profile." TP77-9, Ft. Belvoir, VA: CERC, USCE.
32. Hallermeier, R. J., 1981a, "Seaward Limit of Significant Sand Transport by Waves." CETA 81-2, Ft. Belvoir, VA: CERC, USCE.
33. Hallermeier, R. J., 1981b, "Critical Wave Conditions for Sand Motion Initiative." CETA 81-10, Ft. Belvoir, VA: CERC, USCE.
34. Hicks, S. D., 1980, "An Average Geopotential Sea Level Series for the United States." *J. Geophys. Res.*, Vol. 83(C3).
35. Hicks, S. D., 1985, *Shore and Beach*, January.
36. Johnson, D., 1929, "Studies of Mean Sea-Level." The National Research Council, The National Academy of Sciences, Washington, D.C., Bulletin No. 70.
37. Johnson, D. and Winter, E., 1927, "Sea-Level Surfaces and the Problem of Coastal Subsidence." *Proc. of the American Philosophical Society*, Philadelphia, PA, April, Vol. 66, pp. 465–496.
38. Kuhn, G. and Sheppard, F., 1983, "Importance of Phreatic Vulcanism in Producing Abnormal Weather Conditions." *Shore and Beach*, October.
39. Leatherman, S. P., 1982, "Barrier Island Evolution in Response to Sea Level Rise: A Discussion." *Journal Sedimentary Petrology*, Vol. 43(3), pp. 1026–1033.
40. Lisle, L. D., 1982, "Annotated Bibliography of Sea Level Changes Along the Atlantic and Gulf Coasts of North America." *Shore and Beach*, Vol. 50(3).
41. Losada, M. and Desire, H., 1985, "Incipient Motion of Horizontal Sand Bottom Under Non-breaking Waves." Report by Dept. Puertos Y Structuras Maritime, Universidad de Santander, Spain, (See also Losada and Desire: *Coastal Engineering*, Vol. 9, pp. 357–370.)

42. Marmar, H. A., 1948, "Is the Atlantic Coast Sinking? The Evidence from the Tides." *Geological Review*, Vol. 38, p. 352.

43. Milliman, J. D. and Emery, K. O., 1968, "Sea Levels During the Past 35,000 Years." *Science*, Vol. 162(3558), pp. 1121–1123.

44. Munk, W. H. and Cartwright, D. E., 1966, "Tidal Spectroscopy and Prediction." *Philosophical Transactions of the Royal Society*, A259, pp. 533–581.

45. Munk, W., Revelle, R., Worcester, P., and Zumberge, M., 1985, "Strategy for Future Measurements of Sea Level." Unpublished Manuscript, Scripps Institution of Oceanography, University of California, LaJolla, CA, June.

46. Neftel, A. M., Oeschager, H., and Stauffer, B., 1985, "Evidence from Polar Ice Cores for the Increase in Atmospheric CO_2 in the Past Two Centuries." Letter, *Nature*, May, Vol. 315, pp. 45–47.

47. Nummedal, D., 1983, "Future Sea Level Changes Along the Louisiana Coast." *Shore and Beach*, April.

48. Pirazzolli, P. A., 1986, "Recent Sea-Level Changes in the North Atlantic," in Pirazzolli, P. A. and Suter, J. R. (eds), "Late Quaternary Sea-Level Changes and Coastal Evolution," *Journal of Coastal Research*, Special Issue, No. 1.

49a. Rosen, P. S., 1978, "A Regional Test of the Bruun Rule on Shoreline Erosion." *Mar, Geol.*, Vol. 26, pp. M7–M16.

49b. Rosen, P. S., 1979, "An Application of the Bruun Rule in the Cheasapeake Bay." In *Proc. Bruun Symposium*, International Geographical Union, Newport, RI, November.

50. Schwartz, M. L., 1967, "The Bruun Theory on Sea Level Rise as a Cause of Shore Erosion." *J. Geol.*, Vol. 75, pp. 79–92.

51. Schwartz, M. L., 1968, "The Scale of Shore Erosion." *J. Geol.*, Vol. 76, pp. 508–517.

52. Schwartz, M. L., 1979, "The Bruun Rule: A Historic Perspective." *Proc. Bruun Symposium*, Newport, RI, International Geographical Union, November.

53. Siefert, W., 1984, "Changes in Tide Levels in the German Bay." *Proc. Coastal Engineering Conf.*, ASCE, Houston, Texas. New York: Am. Soc. Civil Engrs.

54. Stommel, H., 1960, *The Gulf Stream*. Los Angeles: Univ. of California Press.

55. Trask, P., 1955, "Movement of Sand Around Southern California Promontories." Tech. Memo No. 76, Beach Erosion Board, U.S. Army Corps of Engineers.

56. Titus, J. G., Leatherman, S. P., Everts, C. H., Kriebel, D. L., and Dean, R. G., 1985, "Potential Impacts of Sea Level Rise on the Beach at Ocean City, Maryland." EPA 230-1085-013. Washington, D.C.: U.S. Environmental Protection Agency.

57. U.S. Department of Commerce, 1983, *Sea Level Variations for the United States*. Rockville, MD: National Oceanic and Atmosphic Administration.

58. van de Graaf, J., 1986, "Probabilisitic Design of Dunes: An Example from the Netherlands." *Coastal Engineering*, ASCE, Vol. 9, pp. 479–500.

59. Van Veen, J. J., 1962, *Dredge, Drain and Reclaim: The Art of a Nation*. Den Haag, Holland: Martinus Nijhoff.

60. Vellinga, P., 1983, "Predictive Computational Model for Beach and Dune Erosion During Storm Surge." *Proc. Coastal Structures*, ASCE, New York: Vol. 83, pp. 806–820.

61. Vellinga, P. and Bruun, P., 1984, Discussion on "Beach and Dune Erosion During Storm Surges." by P. Vellinga (*Coastal Engineering*, Vol. 6, pp. 361–387). *Coastal Engineering*, Vol. 8, pp. 171–188.

62. Vellinga, P., 1986, "Beach and Dune Erosion During Storm Surges," Delft Hydraulic Communications, No. 372, 170 p.

63. Weggel, R., 1979, "A Method for Estimating Long-Term Erosion Rates From a Long-Term Rise in Water Level." CETA 79-2, Ft. Belvoir, VA: CERC, USCE.

CHAPTER 13

GREENHOUSE EFFECT AND SEA-LEVEL RISE

James G. Titus

U.S. Environmental Protection Agency
Washington, D.C.

CONTENTS

Since people first began to protect land with earthen dikes, sea level has risen (and occasionally fallen) so slowly that for most practical purposes it has been constant. It has thus been reasonable for coastal projects to be designed on the assumption that a given shoreline will be maintained indefinitely, without costs escalating over time. But this fundamental condition of coastal engineering is starting to change.

Increasing atmospheric concentrations of carbon dioxide and numerous other gases are expected to cause the earth to warm several degrees (C) in the next century by a mechanism commonly known as the "greenhouse effect." Such a warming could raise sea level worldwide 50–200 cm by the year 2100, in addition to current trends caused by local factors. Such a rise would inundate coastal wetlands and lowlands, accelerate beach erosion, exacerbate flooding, and increase the salinity of estuaries and aquifers—all of which could threaten the success of coastal projects designed without proper consideration of future sea-level rise.

One must recognize from the outset that we cannot predict future sea-level rise with any more certainty than we can predict the occurence of a 100-year storm in a particular location. A large rise in sea level may be averted if nations throughout the world take steps to curtail emissions of the gases that cause the greenhouse effect, or if currently-unknown natural forces counteract the factors that are known to cause global warming and sea-level rise. But the possibility of a benign outcome does not justify assuming a benign outcome; it is no more reasonable to design projects on the basis of historic trends in sea level than to design projects on the assumption that a 100-year storm will not occur.

This chapter summarizes the basis for expecting an accelerated rise in sea level, the likely impacts, and some possible responses.

Basis for Expecting Accelerated Sea-Level Rise

Past Trends in Sea Level

The worldwide average sea level depends primarily on (1) the shape and size of ocean basins, (2) the amount of water in the oceans, and (3) the average density of seawater. The latter two factors are influenced by climate while the first is not. Subsidence and emergence due to natural factors such as isostatic and tectonic adjustments of the land surface, as well as human-induced factors such as oil and water extraction, can cause trends in "relative sea level" at particular locations to differ from trends in "global sea level."

Hays and Pitman [40] analyzed fossil records and concluded that over the last 100 million years, changes in mid-ocean ridge systems have caused the sea level to rise and fall more than 300 m. However, Clark et al. [14] have pointed out that these changes have accounted for sea-level changes of less than 1 m/century. No published study has indicated that this determinant of sea level is likely to have a significant impact in the next century.

The impact of climate on sea level has been more significant over relatively short periods of time. Geologists generally recognize that during ice ages, the glaciation of substantial portions of the northern hemisphere has removed enough water from the oceans to lower sea level 100 m below present levels during the last (18,000 years ago) and previous ice ages [21, 54, 66].

Although the glaciers that once covered much of the northern hemisphere have retreated, the world's remaining ice cover contains enough water to raise sea level over 75 m [44]. As Table 1 shows, Hollin and Barry [44] and Flint [29] estimate that existing alpine glaciers contain enough water to raise the sea level 30 or 60 cm, respectively. The Greenland and West Antarctic Ice Sheets each contain enough water to raise sea level about seven meters, while East Antarctica has enough ice to raise the sea level over 60 m.

There is no evidence that either the Greenland or East Antarctic Ice Sheets have completely disintegrated in the last two million years. However, it is generally recognized that the sea level was about 7 m higher than today during the last interglacial, which was 1°–2° warmer [44a]. Because the West Antarctic Ice Sheet is marine-based and thought by some to be vulnerable to climatic warming, attention

Table 1
Snow and Ice Components (Modified from [44])

	Area $(10^6$ km$^2)$	Ice Volume $(10^6$ km$^3)$	Sea-Level Equivalent[a] (m)
Land ice: East Antarctica[b]	9.86	25.92	64.8
West Antarctica[c]	2.34	3.40	8.5
Greenland	1.7	3.0	7.6
Small ice caps and mountain glaciers [29, 44]	0.54	0.12	0.3
			0.6
Permafrost (excluding Antarctica):			0.6
Continuous	7.6	0.03	0.08
		to	to
Discontinuous	17.3	0.7	0.17
Sea ice: Arctic[d]			
Late February	14.0	0.05	
Late August	7.0	0.02	
Antarctic[e]			
September	18.4	0.06	
February	3.6	0.01	
Land Snow Cover[f]			
N. Hemisphere			
Early February	46.3	0.002	
Late August	3.7		
S. Hemisphere			
Late July	0.85		
Early May	0.07		

[a] 400,000 km^3 of ice is equivalent to 1 m global sea level.

[b] Grounded ice sheet, excluding peripheral, floating ice shelves (which do not affect sea level). The shelves have a total area of 1.62×10^6 km^2 and a volume of 0.79×10^6 km^3.

[c] Including the Antarctic Peninsula.

[d] Excluding the Sea of Okhotsk, the Baltic Sea, and the Gulf of St. Lawrence (Walsh and Johnson 1979). Maximum ice extents in these areas are 0.7 million, 0.4 million, and 0.2 million km^2, respectively.

[e] Actual ice area excluding open water (Zwally et al. 1983). Ice extent ranges between 4 million and 20 million km^2.

[f] Snow cover includes that on land ice but excludes snow-covered sea ice (Dewey and Heim 1981).

Source: *Glaciers, Ice Sheets, and Sea Level*, National Academy Press, p. 272.

has focused on this source for the higher sea level. Mercer [65] found that lake sediments and other evidence suggested that summer temperatures in Antarctica have been 7°–10°C higher than today at some point in the last two million years, probably the last interglacial 125,000 years ago, and that such temperatures could have caused a disintegration of the West Antarctic Ice Sheet. However, others are not certain that marine-based glaciers are more vulnerable to climate change than land based glaciers (personal communication, Mark Meier, University of Colorado). Robin [71a] suggests that the higher sea level during the last interglacial period may have resulted from changes in the East Antarctic Ice Sheet.

Tidal gauges have been available to measure the change in relative sea level at particular locations over the last century. (The only true measure of absolute sea level would be the rise of sea level relative to the center of the earth. Unfortunately, no such measurements are yet available. Therefore, researchers have had to combine tidal gauge measurements of relative sea-level trends at various locations, filter out known movements of the land surface, and take weighted averages to arrive at estimates of global sea-level trends. Although such estimates are useful, one cannot rule out the possibility that the estimate of 1 to 1.5 mm/yr results from land sinking rather than sea level rising. Although the distinction is academic for purposes of examining the impacts, it could be important for evaluating models of future impacts of a global warming.) Studies combining these measurements to estimate global trends have concluded that sea level has risen 1.0–1.5 mm/yr during the last century [6, 27, 34]. Figure 1 shows the sea level curve estimated by Gornitz et al. [34]. Barnett [6] found that the rate of sea-level rise over the last fifty years had been

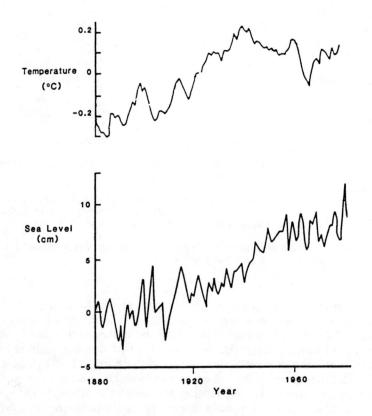

Figure 1. Curve showing temperatures [38] and sea level [34].

about 2.0 mm/yr, while in the previous fifty years there had been little change; however, the acceleration in the rate of sea-level rise was not statistically significant. Emery and Aubrey [23, 24] have accounted for estimated land surface movements in their analyses of tidal gauge records in northern Europe and western North America, and have found an acceleration in the rate of sea-level rise over the last century. (This result was reported in the North America study. The data also shows it to be true in the Northern Europe study, but the result was not reported. David Aubrey, Woods Hole Oceanographic Institute, Woods Hole, Massachusetts, personal communication.) Braatz and Aubrey [11] have found that the rate of relative sea-level rise on the east coasts of North America accelerated after 1934.

Several researchers have sought to explain the source of current trends in sea level. Barnett [6] and Gornitz et al. [34] estimate that thermal expansion of the upper layers of the oceans resulting from the observed global warming of 0.4°C in the last century could be responsible for a rise of 0.4 to 0.5 mm/yr. Roemmich and Wunsch [73] examined temperature and salinity measurements at Bermuda and concluded that the 4°C isotherm had migrated 100 m downward, and concluded that the resulting expansion of ocean water could be responsible for some or all of the observed rise in relative sea level. Roemmich [72] showed that the warming trend 700 m below the surface was statistically significant.

Meier [63] estimates that retreat of alpine glaciers and small ice caps could be currently contributing between 0.2 and 0.72 mm/yr to sea-level rise. The National Academy of Sciences Polar Research Board (Meier et al. [62]) concluded that existing information is insufficient to determine whether the impacts of Greenland and Antarctica are positive or zero. Although the estimated global warming of the last century appears at least partly responsible for the last century's rise in sea level, no study has demonstrated that global warming might be responsible for an *acceleration* in the rate of sea level rise.

The Greenhouse Effect

Although global temperatures and sea level have been fairly stable in recent centuries, the future may be very different. Increasing concentrations of carbon dioxide, methane, chlorofluorocarbons, and other gases released by human activities could heat the earth to temperatures warmer than at any time in the last two million years and thereby accelerate the rate of sea-level rise.

A planet's temperature is determined primarily by the amount of sunlight it receives, the amount of sunlight it reflects, and the extent to which its atmosphere retains heat. When sunlight strikes the earth, it warms the surface, which radiates the heat as infrared radiation. However, water vapor, carbon dioxide, and a few other gases found naturally in the atmosphere absorb some of the energy, rather than allowing it to pass undeterred through the atmosphere to space. Because the atmosphere traps heat and warms the earth in a manner somewhat analogous to the glass panels of a greenhouse, this phenomenon is generally known as the *greenhouse effect*; the relevant gases are known as *greenhouse gases*. Without the greenhouse effect of the gases that occur naturally, the earth would be 33°C (60°F) colder than it is currently [38, 38a].

Since the industrial revolution, the combustion of fossil fuels, deforestation, and cement manufacture have released enough CO_2 into the atmosphere to raise the atmospheric concentration of CO_2 by 20%; the concentration has increased 10% since 1958. Carbon cycle modelers and energy economists generally expect the concentration of CO_2 to increase 50% by 2050 and to double by 2075. Recently, the concentrations of chlorofluorocarbons, methane, nitrous oxide, carbon tetrachloride, ozone, and dozens of other trace gases that also absorb infrared radiation have also been increasing [57]. Ramanathan et al. [66a] estimated that the combined impacts of these other gases are likely to be as great as CO_2, which implies that by 2050, the atmospheric concentration of greenhouse gases will be equivalent to a doubling of carbon dioxide.

All projections of future concentrations have been based on the assumption that current trends continue and that governments do not regulate emissions of greenhouse gases. However, in the fall of 1987, most of the industrial nations agreed to cut emissions of the chlorofluorocarbons by 50% over the following decade. The U.S. Congress has directed the Environmental Protection Agency to examine measures to reduce emissions of the other greenhouse gases. Thus, the Ramanathan et al. projection may prove to be pessimistic (in part because the paper itself helped to motivate political action). Nevertheless, curtailing other gases would be difficult. No one knows how to reduce the methane and nitrous oxide released by agriculture, and reducing CO_2 emissions by shifting away from fossil fuels to alternative energy sources would be costly and controversial.

There is considerable doubt regarding the global warming that would result from a doubling of carbon dioxide. There is general agreement that the average temperature would rise 1.2°C if nothing else changed. However, warmer temperatures would allow the atmosphere to retain more water vapor, which is also a greenhouse gas, increasing the warming. A retreat of ice cover would also amplify the warming, while possible changes in cloud cover could increase or decrease the warming. Two reports by the National Academy of Sciences have developed a consensus estimate that the average warming will be 1.5 to 4.5°C, and that the polar areas will warm two to three times as much.

Impact of Future Global Warming on Sea Level

Concern about a substantial rise in sea level as a result of the projected global warming stemmed originally from Mercer [65], who suggested that the Ross and Filchner-Ronne ice shelves might disintegrate, causing a deglaciation of the West Antarctic Ice Sheet and a resulting 6–7-m rise in sea level, possibly over a period as short as 40 years.

Subsequent investigations have concluded that such a rapid rise is unlikely. Hughes [46] and Bentley [8] estimated that such a disintegration would take at least 200–500 yr, respectively. Other researchers have estimated that this process would take considerably longer [28, 61].

Researchers have turned their attention to the magnitude of sea-level rise that might occur in the next century. The best-understood factors are the thermal expansion of ocean water and the melting of alpine glaciers. In the National Academy of Sciences report *Changing Climate*, Revelle [69] used the model of Cess and Goldenberg [13a] to estimate temperature increases at various depths and latitudes resulting from a 4.2°C warming by 2050–2060, shown in Figure 2. While noting that his assumed time constant of 33 years probably resulted in a conservatively low estimate, he estimated that thermal expansion would result in an expansion of the upper ocean sufficient to raise sea level 30 cm.

Using a model of the oceans developed by Lacis et al. [57], Hoffman et al. [43] examined a variety of possible scenarios of future emissions of greenhouse gases and global warming. They estimated that a warming of between 1 and 2.6°C could result in thermal expansion contribution to sea level between 12 and 26 cm by 2050. They also estimated that a global warming of 2.3 to 7.0°C by 2100 would result in thermal expansion of 28 to 83 cm by that year.

Revelle [69] suggested that while he could not estimate the future contribution of alpine glaciers to sea-level rise, a contribution of 12 cm through 2080 would be reasonable. Meier [63] used glacier balance and volume change data for 25 glaciers where the available record exceeded 50 years to estimate the relationship between historic temperature increases and the resulting negative mass balances of the glaciers. He estimated that a 28-mm rise had resulted from a warming of 0.5°C, and

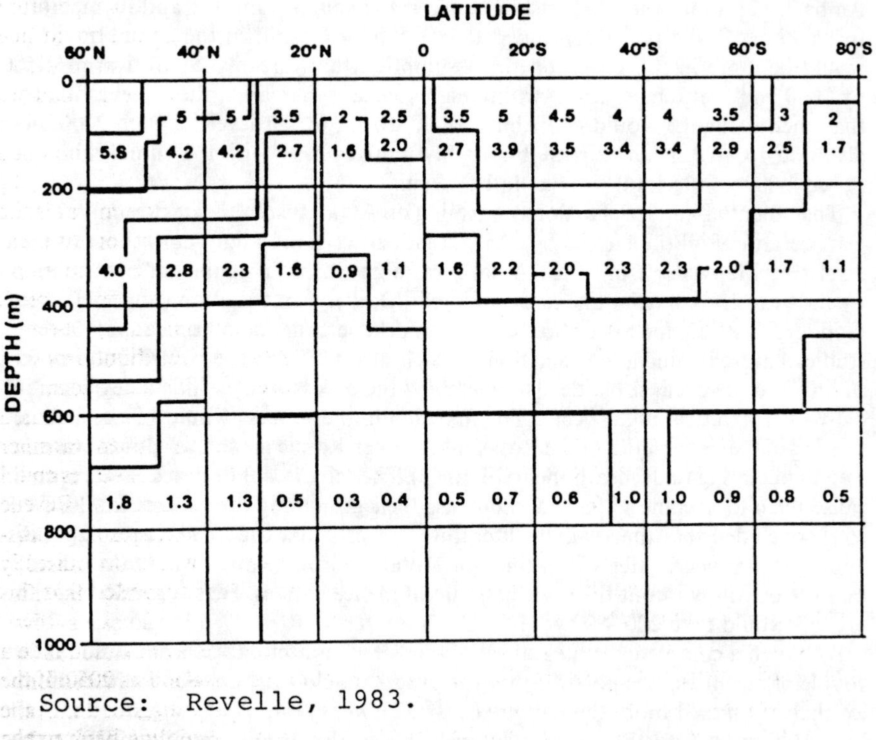

LATITUDE

	60°N	40°N	20°N	0	20°S	40°S	60°S	80°S
		5 — 5	3.5	2 — 2.5	3.5 5	4.5 4	4 3.5	3 2
	5.8	4.2 4.2	2.7	1.6 2.0	2.7 3.9	3.5 3.4	3.4 2.9	2.5 1.7
	4.0	2.8 2.3	1.6	0.9 1.1	1.6 2.2	2.0 2.3	2.3 2.0	1.7 1.1
	1.8	1.3 1.3	0.5	0.3 0.4	0.5 0.7	0.6 1.0	1.0 0.9	0.8 0.5

DEPTH (m): 0, 200, 400, 600, 800, 1000

Source: Revelle, 1983.

Figure 2. Revelle modeled ocean temperature changes [69].

concluded that a 1.5 to 4.5°C warming would result in a rise of 8 to 25 cm in the next century. Using these results, the NAS Polar Board concluded that the contribution of glaciers and small ice caps through 2100 is likely to be 10 to 30 cm [62]. They noted that the gradual depletion of remaining ice cover might reduce the contribution of sea-level rise somewhat. However, the contribution might also be greater, given that the historic rise took place over a 60-yr period, while the forecast period is over 100 years. Using Meier's estimated relationship between global warming and the alpine contribution, Hoffman et al. [43] estimated alpine contributions through 2100 at 12 to 38 cm for a global warming of 2.3 to 7.0°C.

The first published estimate of the contribution of Greenland to future sea-level rise was Revelle's [69] estimate of 12 cm through the year 2080. Using estimates by Ambach [2, 3] that the equilibrium line (between snowfall accumulation and melting) rises 100 m for each 0.6°C rise in air temperatures, he concluded that the projected 6°C warming in Greenland would be likely to raise the equilibrium line 1,000 m. He estimated that such a change in the equilibrium line would result in a 12-cm contribution to sea-level rise for the next century.

The NAS Polar Board (Meier et al. [62]) noted that Greenland is a "significant potential contributor of meltwater." They found that a 1,000-m rise in the equilibrium line would result in a contribution of 30 cm through 2100. However, because Ambach [2] found the relationship between the equilibrium line and temperature to be 77 m/°C, the panel concluded that a 500-meter shift in the equilibrium line would be more likely. Based on the assumption that Greenland will warm 6.5°C by 2050 and that temperatures will remain constant thereafter, the panel estimated that such a change would contribute about 10 cm to sea level through 2100, but also noted that "for an extreme but highly unlikely case, with the equilibrium line raised 1,000 m, the total rise would be 26 cm."

The potential impact of a global warming on Antarctica in the next century is the least certain of all the factors by which a global warming might contribute to sea-level rise. Meltwater from East Antarctica might make a significant contribution by the year 2100, but no one has estimated the likely contribution (James Hansen, Goddard Institute for Space Studies, New York, personal communication). Several studies have examined "deglaciation," which also includes the contribution of ice sliding into the oceans. Bentley [8] examined the processes by which a deglaciation of West Antarctica might occur. The first step in the process would be accelerated melting of the underslides of the Ross and Filchner-Ronne ice shelves due to warmer water circulating underneath them (Figure 3). The thinning of these ice shelves could cause them to become unpinned and cause their grounding lines to retreat. Revelle [69] concluded that the available literature suggests that the ice shelves might disappear in 100 years after which time the Antarctic ice streams would flow directly into the oceans, without the back pressure of the ice shelves. He suggested that this process would take 200–500 yr.

Although a complete disintegration of the West Antarctic Ice Sheet would take a couple of centuries, it is possible that the process could start as soon as 2050. If the ice shelves thinned more than about 1 m/yr, Thomas et al. [81] suggested that the ice would move into the sea at a sufficient speed that even a cooling back to the temperatures of today would not be sufficient to result in a reformation of the ice shelf.

Source: Mercer (1978).

Figure 3. Antarctica.

To estimate the likely Antarctic contribution for the next century, Thomas [80] developed four scenarios of the impact of a 3°C global warming by 2050, estimating that a 28-cm rise would be most likely, but that a rise of 1 to 2.2 m would be possible under certain circumstances.

The NAS Polar Board (Meier et al. [62]) evaluated the Thomas study and papers by Lingle [61] and Fastook [28]. Although Lingle estimated that the contribution of West Antarctica through 2100 would be 3 to 5 cm, he did not evaluate East Antarctica, while Fastook made no estimate for the year 2100. Thus, the panel concluded that "imposing reasonable limits" on the model of Thomas yields a range of 20 to 80 cm by 2100 for the Antarctic contribution. However, they also noted several factors that would reduce the amount of ice discharged into the sea: the removal of the warmest ice from the ice shelves, the retreat of grounding lines, and increased lateral shear stress. They also concluded that increased precipitation over Antarctica might increase the size of the polar ice sheets there. Thus, the panel concluded that Antarctica could cause a rise in sea level up to 1 m, or a drop of 10 cm, with a rise between 0 and 30 cm most likely.

Table 2 summarizes the various estimates of future global sea-level rise for specific years. Using a range of estimates for future concentrations of greenhouse gases, the climate's sensitivity to such increases, oceanic heat uptake, and the behavior of glaciers, Hoffman et al. [42] estimated that the rise would be between 56 and 345 cm, with a rise of 144 to 217 cm most likely; however, they did not examine the impact of deliberate attempts by society to curtail emissions. Revelle [69] estimated that the rise was likely to be 70 cm, ignoring the impact of a global warming on Antarctica; he also noted that the latter contribution was likely to be 1 to 2 m/century after 2050, but declined to add that to his estimate. The NAS Polar Board (Meier et al. [62]) projected that the contribution of glaciers would be sufficient to raise the sea level 20 to 160 cm, with a rise of "several tenths of a meter" most likely.

Table 2
Estimates of Future Sea-Level Rise (cm)
(Year 2100 by Cause (2085 in the case of Revelle [69]))

	Thermal Expansion	Alpine Glaciers	Greenland	Antarctica	Total
Revelle [69]	30	12	12	[a]	70
Hoffman et al. [42]	28–115	[b]	[b]	[b]	56–345
Meier et al. [62]	—	10–30	10–30	−10–+100	50–200[c]
Hoffman et al. [43]	28–83	12–37	6–27	12–220	57–368
Thomas [80]	28–70	14–35	9–45	13–80	64–230

Total Rise in Specific Years:[d]

	2000	2025	2050	2075	2085	2100
Revelle [69]	—	—	—	—	70	—
Hoffman et al. [42]						
low	4.8	13	23	38	—	56.0
mid-range low	8.8	26	53	91	—	144.4
mid-range high	13.2	39	79	137	—	216.6
high	17.1	55	117	212	—	345.0
Hoffman et al. [43]						
low	3.5	10	20	36	44	57
high	5.5	21	55	191	258	368

[a] Revelle attributes 16 cm to other factors.
[b] Hoffman et al. [42] assumed that the glacial construction would be one to two times the contribution of thermal expansion.
[c] This estimate includes extrapolation of thermal expansion from Revelle [69].
[d] Only Hoffman et al. made year-to-year projections for the next century.

Thus, if one extrapolates the earlier NAS estimate of thermal expansion through the year 2100, the 1985 NAS report implies a rise between 50 and 200 cm. The estimates from Hoffman et al. [43] for the year 2100 (57 to 368 cm) were similar to those by Hoffman et al. [42]. However, for the year 2025, they lowered their estimate from 26–39 cm to 10–21 cm.

Future Trends in Local Sea Level

Although most attention has focused on projections of global sea level, impacts on particular areas would depend on local relative sea level. Tidal gauge measurements suggest that relative sea level has risen 10–20 cm more rapidly along much of the U.S. coast than the worldwide average [41]. Important exceptions include Louisiana, which is subsiding close to 1 m/century, and Alaska, which is emerging 10–100 cm/century.

Local subsidence and emergence are caused by a variety of factors. Rebound from the retreat of glaciers after the last ice age has resulted in the uplift of northern Canada, New England, and parts of Scandinavia, while emergence in Alaska is due more to tectonic adjustments. The uplift in polar latitudes has resulted in subsidence in other areas, notably the U.S. Atlantic and Gulf coasts. Groundwater pumping has caused rapid subsidence around Houston, Texas; Taipei, Taiwan; and Bangkok, Thailand, among other areas [53a, 59]. River deltas and other newly created land subsides as the unconsolidated materials compact. Although subsidence and emergence trends may change in the future, particularly where anthropogenic causes are curtailed, no one has linked these causes to future climate change in the next century.

However, the removal of ice from Greenland and Antarctica would immediately alter gravitational fields and eventually deform the ocean floor. For example, the ice on Greenland exerts a gravitational pull on the ocean's water; if the Greenland ice sheet melts and the water is spread throughout the globe, that gravitational attraction will diminish, and could thereby cause sea level to drop along the coast of Greenland and nearby areas such as Iceland and Baffin Island. Eventually, Greenland would also rebound upward, just as northern areas covered by glaciers during the last ice age are currently rebounding. Clark and Lingle [15] have calculated the impact of a uniform 1-m contribution from West Antarctica. They concluded that relative sea level at Hawaii would rise 125 cm, and that along much of the U.S. Atlantic and Gulf Coasts the rise would be 15 cm. On the other hand, sea level would drop at Cape Horn by close to 10 cm, and the rise along the southern half of the Argentine and Chilean coasts would be less than 75 cm.

Other contributors to local sea level that might change as a result of a global warming include currents, winds, and freshwater flow into estuaries. None of these impacts, however, have been estimated.

Effects of Sea-Level Rise

A rise in sea level of 1–2 m would permanently inundate wetlands and lowlands, accelerate coastal erosion, exacerbate coastal flooding, threaten coastal structures, and increase the salinity of estuaries and aquifers.

Submergence of Coastal Wetlands

The most direct impact of a rise in sea level is the inundation of areas that had been just above the water level before the sea rose. Coastal wetlands are generally found at elevations below the highest tide of the year and above mean sea level. Thus, wetlands account for most of the land less than 1 m above sea level.

Because a common means of estimating past sea-level rise has been the analysis of marsh peats, the impacts of sea-level rise on wetlands are fairly well-understood. For the rates of sea-level rise of the last several thousand years, marshes have generally kept pace with sea level through sedimentation and peat formation [16, 25, 67, 68]. As sea level rose, new wetlands formed inland while the seaward boundary was maintained. Because the wetland area has expanded, Titus, Henderson, and Teal [79] hypothesized that one would expect a concave marsh profile, i.e., that there is more marsh area than the area found immediately above the marsh. Thus, if the sea level rose more rapidly than the marsh's ability to keep pace, there would be a net loss of wetlands. Moreover, a complete loss might occur if protection of developed areas prevented the inland formation of new wetlands. (See Figure 4.)

Kana et al. [52, 53] surveyed marsh transects in the areas of Charleston, South Carolina and two sites near Long Beach Island, New Jersey, to evaluate the concavity of wetland profiles and the vulnerability of wetlands to a rise in sea level. Their data showed that in the Charleston area, all of the marsh was between 30 and 110 cm above current sea level, an elevation range of 80 cm. The area with a similar elevation range just above the marsh was only 20% as large. Thus, a rise in sea level exceeding vertical marsh accretion by 80 cm would result in an 80% loss of wetlands. In the New Jersey sites, the marsh was also found within an elevation range of 80 cm; a rise in sea level 80 cm in excess of marsh accretion would result in 67 to 90% losses.

The future ability of marshes to accrete vertically is uncertain. Based on field studies by Ward & Domeracki [87a], Hatton et al. [38b], Meyerson [65a]. Kana et al. [52, 53] concluded that current vertical accretion rates are approximately 4–6 mm/yr in the two case study areas, greater than the current rate of sea-level rise but less than the rates of rise projected for the next century. If current accretion trends continue, then 87- and 160-cm rises by 2075 would imply 50 and 80% losses of wetlands in the Charleston area. Kana et al. also estimated 80% losses in the New Jersey sites for a 160-cm rise through 2075. However, because the high marsh dominates in that area, they concluded that the principal impact of an 87-cm rise by 2075 would be the conversion of high to low marsh.

In both cases, the losses of marsh could be greater if inland areas are developed and protected with bulkheads or levees. Because there is a buffer zone between developed areas and the marsh in South Carolina, protecting development from a 160-cm rise would increase the loss from 80 to 90%. Without the buffer, the loss would be close to 100%.

Louisiana, whose marshes and swamps account for 40% of the coastal wetlands in the United States (excluding Alaska) would be particularly vulnerable to an accelerated rise in sea level. The wetlands there are mostly less than 1 m above sea level, and are generally subsiding approximately 1 m/century as its deltaic sediments compact [10]. Until the last century, the wetlands were able to keep pace with this rate of relative sea-level rise, because of the sediment conveyed to the wetlands by the Mississippi River.

Human activities, however, have largely disabled the natural processes by which coastal Louisiana might keep pace with sea-level rise. Dams, navigation channels, canals, and flood protection levees have interrupted the flow of sediment, freshwater, and nutrients to the wetlands. As a result, over 100 km^2 of wetlands convert to open water every year [31]. A substantial rise in sea level would further accelerate the process of wetland loss in Louisiana, as shown in Figure 5.

Throughout the world, people have dammed, leveed, and channelized major rivers, curtailing the amount of sediment that reaches river deltas. Even at today's rate of sea-level rise, substantial amounts of land are converting to open water in Egypt and Mexico [65b]. Other deltas, such as the Ganges in Bangladesh and India, are currently expanding seaward. These areas would require increased sediment, however, to keep pace with an accelerated rise in sea level. Additional projects to

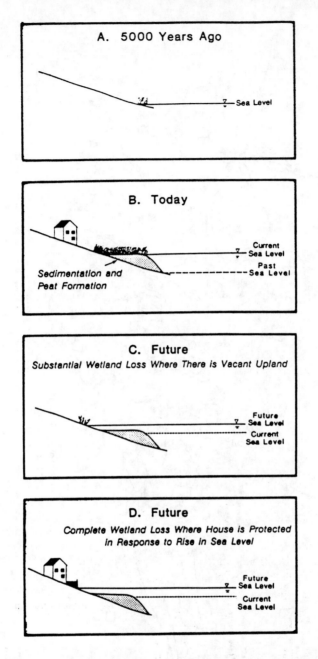

Figure 4. Evolution of marsh as sea level rises. Coastal marshes have kept pace with the slow rate of sea-level rise that has characterized the last several thousand years. Thus, the area of marsh has expanded over time as new lands were inundated, resulting in much more wetland acreage than dry land just above the wetlands (A and B). If in the future, sea level rises faster than the ability of the marsh to keep pace, the marsh area will contract (C). Construction of bulkheads to protect economic development may prevent new marsh from forming and result in a total loss of marsh in some areas (D).

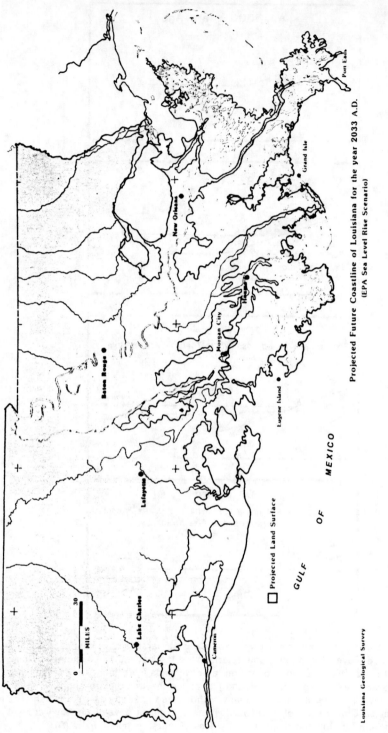

Figure 5. Lousiana land loss (From Louisiana Wetland Protection Panel, 1987, "Saving Louisiana's Coastal Wetlands, EPA, Washington D.C.)

divert the natural flow of river water would increase the vulnerability of these areas to a rise in sea level. Broadus et al. [12] estimated that a 2-m rise in sea level would inundate 20% of Bangladesh and the Nile Delta.

To develop an understanding of the potential nationwide impact of sea-level rise on coastal wetlands in the United States, Armentano et al. [4] used topographic maps to characterize wetland elevations at 52 sites comprising 4,800 km² (1.2 million acres) of wetlands, over 17% of all U.S. coastal wetlands. Using published vertical accretion rates, they estimated the impact of 1.4- and 2.1-m rises in sea level through the year 2100 for each of the sites. Weighting their results according to the coastal wetland inventory by Alexander et al. [1], implied a loss of wetlands between 47 and 82%, which could be reduced to between 31 and 70% if new wetlands are not prevented from forming inland.

Several options have been identified for reducing wetland loss due to sea-level rise. Abandonment of developed areas inland of today's wetlands could permit new wetlands to form inland. In some cases, it might be possible to enhance the ability of wetlands to accrete vertically by spraying sediment on them or, in the case of Louisiana and other deltas, by restoring the natural processes that would provide sediment to the wetlands. Finally, some local governments in Louisiana have proposed the option of artificially controlling water levels through the use of levees and pumping stations [22].

The need for anticipating sea-level rise would vary. Artificial means to accelerate wetland accretion need not be implemented until the rise occurs (although a lead time would be necessary to develop the required technologies). Similarly, there is no reason to build levees and pumping stations today for a rise that is still decades in the future. On the other hand, a planned retreat would require several decades lead time, so that new structures could be designed to be moved and immovable structures had time to be depreciated.

Recognizing this situation, the state of Maine has recently adopted regulations to implement a planned retreat should one be necessary. The state's Dune Rule Number 355 states that houses along the coast are presumed to be movable, and would have to be moved if their presence interferes with the ability of wetlands and beach systems to migrate landward. In the case of large structures that clearly cannot be moved, the regulations state that a structure that would be threatened by a 3-ft rise in sea level can only be built if the owners demonstrate that they have an abandonment plan. A challenge for coastal engineers in Maine and states that follow its lead will be to design buildings so that they can be more easily moved if and when sea-level rise enough for that to be necessary.

Inundation

Although coastal wetlands are found at the lowest elevations, inundation of low land could also be important in some areas, particularly if sea level rises at least 1 m. Unfortunately, the convention of 10-ft contours in the mapping of most coastal areas has prevented a general assessment of land loss. Nevertheless, a few case studies have been conducted.

Kana et al. [51] used data from aerial photographs to assess elevations in the area around Charleston. They concluded that 160- and 230-cm rises would result in 30 and 46% losses of the area's dry land, respectively. Leatherman [59] estimated that such rises would result in 9 and 12% losses of the land in the area of Galveston and Texas City, Texas, assuming that the elaborate network of seawalls and levees was maintained.

The only nationwide assessment of the inundation from a projected sea-level rise was conducted by Schneider and Chen [74]. Unfortunately, the smallest rise in sea level they considered was a 4.5-m (15-ft) rise, in part because smaller contours are not generally available in topographic maps. Nevertheless, their findings suggest which coastal states would be most vulnerable: Louisiana (which would lose 28% of its land and 51% of its wealth), Florida (24 and 52%), Delaware (16 and 18%), Washington, D.C. (15 and 15%), Maryland (12 and 5%), and New Jersey (10 and 9%).

Some nations are far more vulnerable to a rise in sea level than the United States. Broadus et al. [12] estimated that a 2-m rise would inundate 20% of Bangladesh and a similar portion of the Nile Delta, the only part of Egypt that is inhabited. Coral island nations such as the Maldives are even more vulnerable. Close to one-half of the Netherlands is less than 1 m above sea level—most of it being below sea level. However, that nation is not especially vulnerable to sea level rise [33]—it has already spent considerable resources in making most of its coastline invulnerable to a 10,000-year storm; raising the dikes another meter or two and installing additional pumps would be relatively inexpensive. The increased opportunities for Dutch coastal engineers are likely to offset the adverse consequences of sea-level rise for that nation.

As with wetland loss, the responses to inundation broadly fall into the categories of retreat and holding back the sea. Levees in New Orleans already prevent areas that are below sea level from being flooded, and could be similarly constructed around other major cities. In lightly developed areas, however, the cost of a levee might be greater than the value of the property being protected. Moreover, even where levees prove to be cost-effective, the environmental implications of replacing natural shorelines with man-made structures would need to be considered.

The experience of the Dutch is illustrative of the need to consider environmental implications. Considering economics alone, shortening the coastline by closing off estuaries was generally the optimal approach. However, when the Dutch government proposed to close off its only remaining estuary, environmentalists objected. After extensive negotiations, the government agreed to an Eastern Scheldt project that would cost three times as much: a system of flood gates across the mouth of the estuary that are usually left open but can be closed when storm surges occur. As sea level rises, levees along the entire shore of the estuary must be raised and/or the gates closed more frequently.

Coastal Erosion

Sea-level rise can also result in the loss of land above sea level through erosion. Bruun [13] showed that the erosion resulting from a rise in sea level would depend upon the average slope of the entire beach profile extending from the dunes out to the point where the water is too deep for waves to have a significant impact on the bottom (generally a depth of about 10 m), shown in Figure 6. By comparison,

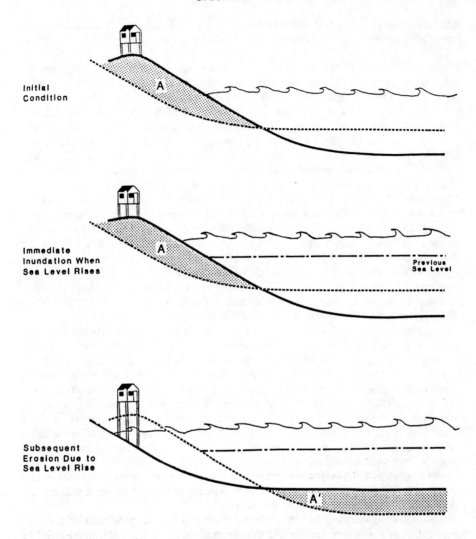

Figure 6. Bruun Rule.

inundation depends only on the slope immediately above the original sea level. Because beach profiles are generally flatter than the portion of the beach just above sea level, the "Bruun Rule" generally implies that the erosion from a rise in sea level is several times greater than the amount of land directly inundated.

Processes other than sea-level rise also contribute to erosion, including storms, structures, currents, and alongshore transport. Because the sea level has risen slowly in recent centuries, verification of the Bruun Rule on the open coast has been difficult. However, water levels along the Great Lakes can fluctuate over 1 m in a decade. Hands [35–37] and Weishar and Wood [89] have demonstrated that the Bruun Rule generally predicts the erosion resulting from rises in water levels there.

The Bruun Rule has been applied to project erosion due to sea-level rise for several areas. Bruun [13] found that a 1-cm rise in sea level would generally result in a 1-m shoreline retreat, but that the retreat could be as great as 10 m along some parts of the Florida coast. Everts [26] and Kyper and Sorensen [56] however, found that along the coasts of Ocean City, Maryland and Sandy Hook, New Jersey, respectively, the shoreline retreat implied by the Bruun Rule would be only about 75 cm. Kana et al. [51] found that along the coast of South Carolina, the retreat could be 2 m. The U.S. Army Corps of Engineers [84] indicated that along the coast of San Francisco, where larger waves are generally found than along the Atlantic Coast, the shore might retreat 2–4 m for a 1-cm rise in sea level.

Dean and Maurmeyer [18] generalized the Bruun Rule approach to consider the "overwash" of barrier islands. Geologists generally believe that coastal barriers can maintain themselves in the face of slowly rising sea level through the landward transport of sand, which washes over the island during storms, building the island upward and landward. Because this formulation of the Bruun Rule extends the beach profile horizontally to include the entire islands as well as the active surf zone, it always predicts greater erosion than the Bruun Rule. However, the formulation may not be applicable to developed barrier islands, where the common practice of public officials is to bulldoze sand back onto the beach after a major storm.

The potential erosion from a rise in sea level could be particularly important to recreational beach resorts, which include some of the nation's most economically valuable and intensely used land. Although nationwide statistics are not available, information on particular locations is instructive. Every weekend in the summer, approximately 250,000 people visit Ocean City, Maryland to sunbathe on its 15 km (9-mile) beach (Sandy Coyman, Department of Planning and Community Development, Town of Ocean City, Maryland, personal communication). Along most of the Ocean City shoreline, the beach is less than 15 m wide during high tide—a width that is typical of the most extensively used beach resorts. Relatively few of the most intensely developed resorts along the Atlantic Coast have beaches wider than about 30 m at high tide. Thus, the rise in relative sea level of 30 cm projected in the next 40–50 years could erode most recreational beaches in developed areas, unless additional erosion response measures are taken.

Responses to coastal erosion have long been a major responsibility of the U.S. Army Corps of Engineers, and have thus been thoroughly studied (Magness in [7]; [85]). The responses fall generally into three categories: walls and other structures, adding sand to the beach, and abandonment. Although seawalls have been used in the past, they are becoming increasingly unpopular among shore communities because erosion can proceed up to the wall, resulting in a complete loss of beach, which has happened, for example, at Sea Bright, New Jersey [45, 56]. A number of other structures have been used to decrease the ability of waves to cause erosion, including groins (jetties) and breakwaters. Bulkheads are often used where waves are small [75].

A more popular form of erosion control has been the placement of sand onto the beach. Although costs can exceed $1 million/mile [56, 83], it is often justified by the economic and recreational value of beaches. A recent study of Ocean City,

Maryland, for example, concluded that the cost of holding back the sea for a 30-cm rise in sea level would be about $0.25/visitor, less than 1% of the cost of a trip to the beach [77]. That community also provides an example of the practical consequences of sea-level rise. Until 1985, the state of Maryland's policy for erosion control was the construction of groins, which curtail erosion causes by sand moving along the shore, but not erosion caused by sea-level rise. Consideration of sea-level rise was cited as motivating the state to abandon the groin plan and use beach replenishment, which can effectively control erosion caused by both types of erosion [5].

Although shore protection is often cost-effective today, the favorable economics might change in the future. A more rapid rise in sea level would increase the costs of shore protection. Several states have adopted erosion policies that assume a retreat from the shore. North Carolina requires homes that can be moved to be set back from the shore equal to 30 years of erosion, while high-rises must be set back 60 years (North Carolina Administrative Code, Chapter 7H, 1983. Raleigh, North Carolina: Office of Coastal Management). As described above, Maine requires abandonment plans for large structures and presumes that small structures will be moved as shorelines retreat. Other jurisdictions discourage the construction of bulkheads and seawalls [45].

Nevertheless, the retreat option will not be a reasonable policy for densely developed barrier island resorts. Studies by the Environmental Protection Agency are currently examining an extended version of beach nourishment: raising entire islands in place. For many narrow islands, the area of the island is about the same as the area of the underwater part of the beach profile that must be raised by conventional beach nourishment. Because grain size is not important for building lots, land sources of material would be acceptable, which in some cases would reduce costs substantially.

The need for anticipating erosion caused by sea-level rise varies. Where communities are likely to adapt to erosion, anticipation can be important. The cost and feasibility of moving a house back depends on design decisions made when the house is built. The willingness of people to abandon properties depends in part on whether they bought land on the assumption that it would eventually erode away or had assumed that the government would protect it indefinitely. Less anticipation is necessary if the shore will be protected; sand can be added to the beach as necessary. Nevertheless, some advanced planning may be necessary for communities to know whether retreat or defending the shore would be least economic.

Flooding and Storm Damage

A rise in sea level could increase flooding and storm damages in coastal areas for three reasons: erosion caused by sea-level rise would increase the vulnerability of communities; higher water levels would provide storm surges with a higher base to build upon; and higher water levels would decrease natural and artificial drainage.

The impact of erosion on vulnerability to storms is generally a major consideration in proposed projects to control erosion, most of which have historically been funded through the U.S. Army Corps of Engineers. The impact of sea-level rise, however, has not generally been considered separately from other causes of erosion.

The impact of higher base water levels on flooding has been investigated for the areas around Charleston, South Carolina and Galveston, Texas [7] Kana et al. [51] found that around Charleston, the area within the 10-year flood plain would increase from 33% in 1980, to 48, 62, and 74% for rises in sea level of 88, 160, and 230 cm, respectively, and that the area within the 100-year flood plain would increase from 63% to 76, 84, and 90% for the three scenarios. Gibbs [32] estimated that even an 88-cm rise would double the average annual flood damages in the Charleston area (but that flood losses would not increase substantially for higher rises in sea level because shoreline retreat would result in a large part of the community being completely abandoned.)

Leatherman [59] conducted a similar analysis of Galveston Island, Texas. He estimated that the area within the 100-year flood plain would increase from 58% to 94% for an 88-cm rise in sea level, and that for a rise greater than 1 m, the Galveston seawall would be overtopped during a 100-year storm. Gibbs estimated that the damage from a 100-year storm would be tripled for a rise of 88 cm.

A wide variety of shore protection measures would be available for communities to protect themselves from increased storm surge and wave damage due to sea level rise [75]. Many of the measures used to address erosion and inundation also provide protection against storms, including seawalls, breakwaters, levees, and rebuilding beaches. In the case of Galveston, which is already protected on the ocean side by the seawall, Gibbs hypothesized that it might be necessary to completely encircle the developed areas with a levee, to prevent flooding from the bay side; upgrading the existing seawall might also be necessary.

Kyper and Sorensen [56] examined the implications of sea level rise for the design of coastal protection works at Sea Bright, New Jersey, a coastal community that currently is protected by a seawall and has no beach. Because the seawall is vulnerable to even a 10-year storm, the Corps of Engineers and the state of New Jersey have been considering a possible upgrade. Kyper and Sorensen estimated that the cost of upgrading the seawall for current conditions would be $3.5 to 6 million/km of shoreline, noting that if designed properly, the seawall would be useful throughout the next century. However, they estimated that a rise in relative sea level of 30–40 cm would be likely to result in serious damage to the seawall during a major storm, due to higher water levels and the increased wave heights resulting from the erosion of submerged sand in front of the seawall. To upgrade the seawall to withstand a 1-m rise in relative sea level would cost $5.7 to 9 million/km (50% more). They concluded that policy makers would have to weigh the tradeoff between the cost of designing the wall to withstand projected sea-level rise and the cost of subsequent repairs and a second overhaul.

In addition to community-wide engineering approaches, measures can also be taken by individual property owners to prevent increased flooding. In 1968, the U.S. Congress created the National Flood Insurance Program to encourage communities to avoid risky construction in flood-prone areas. In return for requiring new construction to be elevated above expected flood levels, the federal government provides flood insurance, which is not available from the private sector. If sea-level rises, flood risks will increase. In response, local ordinances will automatically require new construction to be further elevated and insurance rates on existing properties will rise unless those properties are further elevated. As currently organized, the National Flood Insurance Program would react to sea-level rise as it occured. Various measures to enable the program to anticipate sea level rise have been proposed, including warning policy holders that rates may increase in the future if sea level rises; denying coverage to new construction in areas that are expected to be lost to erosion within the next 30 years; and setting premiums according to the average risk expected over the lifetime of the mortgage [45, 76].

Case studies in Charleston and Fort Walton Beach, Florida have examined the implications of sea-level rise for rainwater flooding and the design of coastal drainage systems. Waddell and Blaylock [88] estimated that a 25-year rainstorm (with no storm surge) would result in no damages for the Gap Creek watershed in Fort Walton Beach. However, a rise in sea level of 30 to 45 cm would result in damages of $1.1–1.3 million in this community of 4,000 residents during a 25-year storm. An upgrade costing $550,000, however, would prevent such damages.

Consulting engineers [79], who had previously developed the master drainage plan for Charleston, South Carolina, evaluated the implications of sea-level rise for the Grove Street watershed in that community. They estimated that the costs of upgrading the system for current conditions would be $4.8 million, while the cost of upgrading the system for a 30-cm rise would be $5.1 million. If the system is designed for current conditions and sea-level rises, the system would be deficient and the city would face retrofit costs of $2.4 million. Titus et al. [78] noted that for the additional $300,000 necessary to upgrade for a 30-cm rise, the city could ensure that it would not have to spend an additional $2.4 million later. Noting that the decision whether to design now for a rise in sea level depends on the probability that sea level would rise, they concluded that the 3% real municipal bond rate that has characterized the last 30 years would imply that designing for sea-level rise is worthwhile if the probability of a 30-cm rise by 2025 is greater than 30%.

Increased Salinity in Estuaries and Aquifers

Although most researchers and the general public have focused on the increased flooding and shoreline retreat associated with a rise in sea-level, the inland penetration of saltwater could be important in some areas.

A rise in sea-level increases the salinity of an estuary by altering the balance between freshwater and saltwater forces. The salinity of an estuary represents the outcome of (1) the tendency for the ocean saltwater to completely mix with the estuarine water and (2) the tendency of freshwater flowing into the estuary to dilute the saline water and push it back toward the ocean. During droughts, the saltwater penetrates upstream, while during the rainy season, low salinity levels prevail. A rise in sea-level has an impact similar to decreasing the freshwater inflow. By widening and deepening the estuary, sea-level rise increases the ability of saltwater to penetrate upstream.

The implications of sea-level rise for increased salinity have only been examined in detail for Louisiana and the Delaware Estuary. In Louisiana, saltwater intrusion is currently resulting in the conversion of cypress swamps—which cannot tolerate saltwater—to open water lakes, as well as the conversion of fresh and intermediate marsh to marsh with greater salinity levels. In response to these trends, numerous projects have been proposed to divert freshwater from the Mississippi River to these wetlands [71, 82, 87]. Although the cause of the saltwater intrusion has been primarily the dredging of canals and the closing of river "distributaries" (streams that flow from the river through the wetlands to the Gulf) that once provided the wetlands with freshwater, relative sea-level rise is gradually increasing the saltwater force in Louisiana's wetlands; a further rise in sea-level would accelerate this process. Haydl [39] also concluded that subsidence may be resulting in increased salinity of drinking and irrigation water supplies in some parts of Louisiana.

The impact of current sea-level trends on salinity has been considered in the long-range plan of the Delaware River Basin Commission since 1981 [19]. The drought of the 1960s resulted in salinity levels that almost contaminated the water supply of Philadelphia and surrounding areas. Hull and Tortoriello [50] found that the 13-cm rise projected between 1965 and 2000 would result in the "salt front" migrating 2–4 km farther upstream during a similar drought. They found that a moderately sized reservoir (57 million m^3) to augment river flows would be needed to offset the resulting salinity increases.

Hull et al. [49] examined the potential impacts of an accelerated rise in sea-level due to the greenhouse warming. They estimated that 73-cm and 250-cm rises would result in the salt front migrating an additional 15 and 40 km, respectively, during a repeat of the 1960s drought. They also found that the health-based 50 ppm sodium standard (equivalent to 73 ppm chloride) adopted by New Jersey would be exceeded 15 and 50% of the time, respectively, and that the EPA drinking water 250-ppm chloride standard would be exceeded over 35% of the time in the latter case. See Figure 7.

Lennon et al. [60] examined the implications of increased estuarine salinity for the Potomac-Raritan-Magothy aquifer system, which is recharged by the (currently fresh) Delaware River and serves the New Jersey suburbs of Philadelphia. During the 1960s drought, river water with chloride concentrations as high as 150 ppm recharged these aquifers. Lennon et al. [60] estimated that a repeat of the 1960s drought with a 73-cm rise in sea-level would result in river water with concentrations as high as 350 ppm, recharging the aquifer, and that during the worst month of the drought, over one-half of the water recharging the aquifer system would have concentrations greater than 250 ppm. With a 250-cm rise, 98% of the recharge during the worst month of the drought would exceed 250 ppm, and 75% of the recharge would be greater than 1,000 ppm.

Hull and Titus [46, 47] examined the options by which various agencies might respond to increased salinity in the Delaware estuary. They concluded that planned but unscheduled reservoirs would be more than enough to offset the salinity increased from a 1-ft rise in sea-level, although those reservoirs had originally been intended to meet increased consumption. They noted that construction of the reservoirs would not be necessary until the rise became more imminent. However, they also suggested that, given the uncertainties, it might be advisable today to identify additional reservoir sites, to ensure that future generations retained the option of building additional reservoirs if necessary.

A rise in sea-level could increase salinities in other areas, although the importance of those impacts has not been investigated. Kana et al. [51] and Leatherman [59]

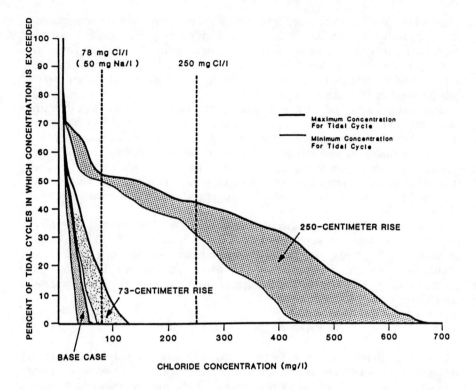

Figure 7. Salinity levels at Torresdale, Pennsylvania, USA [47].

made preliminary inquiries into the potential impacts on coastal aquifers around Charleston and Galveston, respectively. However, they concluded that in-depth assessments were not worthwhile because the aquifers are already salt-contaminated around Charleston due to overpumping, and pumping of groundwater has been prohibited in the Galveston area due to the resulting land subsidence. The potential impacts on Florida's Everglades and the shallow aquifers around Miami are currently being investigated by the U.S. Environmental Protection Agency.

Other Impacts of the Greenhouse Warming

The impacts of sea-level rise on coastal areas, as well as their importance, is likely to depend in part on other impacts of the greenhouse warming. Although future sea-level is uncertain, there is a general consensus that a global warming would cause sea-level to rise; by contrast, the direction of most other changes is unknown.

One of the more certain impacts is that most areas will be warmer. For coastal resorts north of Florida, the beach season would be extended by a number of weeks. For mid-Atlantic resorts with a three-month peak season, such an extension might increase revenues 10 to 25%, far more than the estimated cost of controlling erosion.

Some areas where the ocean is too cold to swim today might find water temperatures more appealing in the future. Warmer temperatures in general might encourage more people to visit beaches in the summer. On the other hand, southern resorts like Miami Beach might lose business because the season during which it is too warm would be extended and because it would no longer be necessary to travel that far south in the winter.

Changing climate could alter the frequency and tracks of storms. Because hurricane formation requires water temperatures of 27°C or higher [90], a global warming might result in an extension of the hurricane season and in hurricanes forming at higher latitudes. Besides increasing the amount of storm damage, increased frequency of severe storms would tend to flatten the typical beach profile, causing substantial shoreline retreat unless additional sand was placed on the beach. A decreased frequency of severe winter storms might have the opposite impact at higher latitudes.

Because warmer temperatures would intensify the hydrologic cycle, it is generally recognized that a global warming would result in increased rainfall in maritime environments. Thus, rainwater flooding could be increased both due to decreased drainage and increased precipitation. The impact of sea-level rise on saltwater intrusion could be offset by decreased drought frequency or exacerbated by increased drought frequency [70].

The Role of the Coastal Engineer

Coastal communities can respond to sea-level rise either by adapting to changes in shorelines by floodproofing and removing structures, or by holding back the sea with structures and fill. In the narrow context of the engineer asked to design a workable system, the major question is whether a significant rise is sufficiently close at hand to warrant designing projects today for an accelerated rise. In many cases, such as the Charleston drainage example previously cited, the cost of designing a structure to accommodate a foot or two of sea-level rise is small compared with the eventual cost of rebuilding a system after the sea has risen.

Whalin and Houston [91], however, argue that coastal engineers do not currently need to consider accelerated sea-level rise for most projects. Even if a major acceleration starts around 2010, it will be at least 50 years before sea-level has risen one-half meter. The extra cost of designing most structures to accommodate accelerated sea-level rise, they suggest, will generally be greater than the present value of the eventual costs of failing to do so, especially if one assumes that the structure would have to be rebuilt in 50 years anyway. Certainly this will be true in many instances. As mentioned previously, a beach nourishment project can always be supplemented in the future with additional sand; so consideration of accelerated sea-level rise can be deferred until another time.

Nevertheless, in the broader context of deciding which type of project to undertake, coastal engineers and their clients must consider accelerated sea-level rise today. Consider this hypothetical example: A state park is rebuilding its road and facilities at a cost of $10 million if rebuilt in the current location, and $15 million if rebuilt 300 feet inland. If beach nourishment through the next 50 years will cost $3 million, the park would decide to rebuild in the current location and nourish the beach. But if sea-level rise would increase beach nourishment costs to a present value of $10 million, the eventual cost of nourishment is greater than the extra cost of rebuilding the facilities inland, and the latter option should be chosen.

Should the coastal engineer be concerned with accelerated sea-level rise? The answer depends in large measure on how one views his or her role. The technician is merely carrying out orders to design the specifications for a project that has already been selected, and in this example can ignore the issue. Consultants and government agencies, however, lose credibility when they ignore the larger question of whether a different type of project is more appropriate. Because future sea-level rise alters the relative merits of retreat, beach nourishment, and structural solutions, most government and consulting engineers need to consider it today.

This perspective was endorsed by a recent panel of the Marine Board of the National Academy of Engineering in a report entitled *Responding to Changes in Sea-Level* [17]. That report concluded that the risk of accelerated sea-level rise is sufficiently established to warrant consideration in the design of coastal facilities. It recommended that the U.S. Army Corps of Engineers consider alternative scenarios of future sea-level rise when evaluating coastal protection projects, and search for options that are likely to be satisfactory for the entire range of uncertainty, rather than picking projects that are optimal if sea-level rise does not accelerate but would fail if it did. The official policy of the Corps of Engineers is to assume current trends in sea level. However, top officials are currently considering whether that policy needs to be changed in light of both the Marine Board report and the recent Congressional finding that sea-level rise will accelerate, expressed in the Water Resources Act of 1986, which authorizes Corps projects.

Coastal engineers also have a role in supporting research. The profession clearly has a need for improved predictions of future sea-level rise, with estimates of the probability distribution. Yet the research necessary to provide better estimates is not taking place. Officials allocating research budgets will only provide funds for that research if the users of the information begin to demonstrate to them the value of this research.

The role of the coastal engineer in addressing sea-level rise can be viewed in an even broader context: the responsibility of an informed citizen. Coastal engineers need not merely react to an accelerated rise in sea level caused by forces outside of their control; they can also participate in the societal process of determining whether to undertake the measures necessary to keep the rate of sea-level rise from exceeding intolerable levels. Already, the efforts of coastal scientists and engineers in Maine, Rhode Island, and Delaware to make the public aware of sea-level rise has encouraged U.S. senators from those states to introduce legislation requiring the U.S. government to seek out ways of reducing emissions of greenhouse gases; and senators from most other coastal states have supported these efforts. In many cases, the fact that constituents were already planning for sea-level rise convinced legislators to take the issue seriously. As a result of public concern over sea-level rise—as well as the depletion of stratospheric ozone—the U.S. Department of State initiated successful international negotiations to limit emissions of chlorofluorocarbons worldwide.

The civic role of the coastal engineering profession leaves us with a paradox: By preparing for an accelerated rise in sea level, coastal engineers may contribute to a state of public awareness that leads to measures that keep the sea from rising. This has already happened to Ramanathan et al., whose article demonstrating the importance of greenhouse gases other than CO_2 helped lead to a treaty that invalidated their projections.

There is no way to escape the fact that expectations of the future can change the future. But if we have to risk being wrong, would we rather prepare for a rise, and in so doing, prevent it from happening, or ignore its possibility, and in so doing, allow it to occur?

References

1. Alexander, C. E., Broutman, M. A., and Field, D. W., 1986, *An Inventory of Coastal Wetlands of the USA*. Rockville, Md.: National Oceanic and Atmospheric Administration, National Ocean Service.
2. Ambach, W., 1985, "Climatic Shift of the Equilibrium Line—Kuhn's Concept Applied to the Greenland Ice Cap," *Annals of Glaciology* 6:76–78.
3. Ambach, W. (translated by Weidhaas G. P.), 1980, "Increased CO_2 Concentration in the Atmosphere and Climate Change: Potential Effects on the Greenland Ice Sheet," *Wetter und Leben* 32:135–142, Vienna. (Available as Lawrence Livermore National Laboratory Report UCRL-TRANS-11767, April 1982.)
4. Armentano, T. et al., 1988, "Nationwide Impact on Coastal Wetlands." In Titus, J. G. *Greenhouse Effect, Sea-Level Rise, and Coastal Wetlands*, Washington, D.C.: Environmental Protection Agency.
5. Associated Press, 1985, "Doubled Erosion Seen for Ocean City," *Washington Post*, November 14th. (Maryland Section).
6. Barnett, T. P., 1984, "The Estimation of "Global" Sea-Level Change: A Problem of Uniqueness," *Journal of Geophysical Research* 89(C5):7980–7988.
7. Barth, M. C. and Titus J. G. (eds.), 1984, *Greenhouse Effect and Sea Level Rise: A Challenge for This Generation*, New York: Van Nostrand Reinhold.
8. Bentley, C. R., 1983, "West Antarctic Ice Sheet: Diagnosis and Prognosis." In *Proceedings: Carbon Dioxide Research Conference: Carbon Dioxide, Science, and Consensus*. Conference 820970. Washington, D.C.: Department of Energy.
9. Bindschadler, R. A., 1985, "Contribution of the Greenland Ice Cap to Changing Sea Level: Present and Future," in Meier, M. F., 1985. *op. cit.*
10. Boesch, D. F. (ed.), 1982, *Proceedings of the Conference of Coastal Erosion and Wetland Modification in Louisiana: Causes, Conseqences, and Options*. FWS-OBS-82/59. Slidell, Louisiana: National Coastal Ecosystems Team, U.S. Fish and Wildlife Service.
11. Braatz, R. V. and Aubrey, D. G., 1987, "Recent Relative Sea-Level Change in Eastern North America, in Nummedal, D., Pilkey, O., and Howard J. (eds.). *Sea Level Fluctuation and Coastal Evolution*. Tulsa, Oklahoma: Society of Economic Paleontologists and Minerologists.
12. Broadus, J. M., Milliman, J. D., Edwards, S. F., Aubrey, D. G., and Gable, F., 1986, "Rising Sea Level and Damming of Rivers: Possible Effects in Egypt and Bangladesh," In Titus, J. G. (ed.), *Effects of Changes in Stratospheric Ozone and Global Climate*. Washington, D.C.: U.S. Environmental Protection Agency and United Nations Environment Programme.
13. Bruun, P., 1962, "Sea-Level Rise as a Cause of Shore Erosion," *Journal of Waterways and Harbors Division* (ASCE) 88:117–130.
13a. Cess, R. D. and Goldenberg, S. D., 1981, "The Effect of Ocean Heat Capacity Upon

Global Warming Due to Increasing Atmospheric Carbon Dioxide," *J. Geophys. Res.*, 86: 498–502.

14. Clark, J. A., Farrell, W. E., and Peltier, W. R., 1978, "Global Changes in Postglacial Sea Level: A Numerical Calculation," Quarternary Research 9:265–87.

15. Clark, J. A. and Lingle, C. S., 1977, "Future Sea-Level Changes Due to West Antarctic Ice Sheet Fluctuations," *Nature* 269:5625:206–209.

16. Davis, R. A., 1985, *Coastal Sedimentary Environments*, New York: Springer Verlag.

17. Dean, R. G. et al., 1987, *Responding to Changes in Sea Level*, Washington, D.C.: National Academy Press.

18. Dean, R. G. and Maurmeyer, E. M., 1983, "Models for Beach Profile Response," CRC *Handbook of Coastal Processes and Erosion*. Boca Raton, Fl.: CRC Press.

19. Delaware River Basin Commission (DRBC), 1981, *The Delaware River Basin Comprehensive (Level B) Study: Final Report and Environmental Impact Statement*, West Trenton, New Jersey: Delaware River Basin Commission.

20. Dewey, K. F. and Heim, R. J., 1981, "Satellite Observations of Variations in North Hemisphere Seasonal Snow Cover," Tech. Report, NESS87, Washington, D.C.

21. Donn. W. L., Farrand, W. R., and Ewing, M., 1962, "Pleistocene Ice Volumes and Sea-Level Lowering," *Journal of geology* 70:206–214.

22. Edmonson, J. and Jones, R., 1985, *Terrebonne Parish Barrier Island and Marsh Management Program*. Houma, La.: Terrebonne Parish Council. (August).

23. Emery, K. O. and Aubrey, D. G., 1986, "Relative Sea-Level Change from Tide-Gauge Records of Western North America," *Journal of Geophysical Research* 91:13941–53.

24. Emery, K. O. and Aubrey, D. G., 1985, "Glacial Rebound and Relative Sea Levels in Europe From Tide-Gauge Records," *Tectonophysics* 120:239–255.

25. Emery, K. O. and Uchupi, E., 1972, "Western North Atlantic Ocean Memoir 17," Tulsa, Oklahoma: American Association of Petroleum Geologists.

26. Everts, C. H., 1985, "Effect of Sea-Level Rise and Net Sand Volume Change on Shoreline Position at Ocean City. Maryland," in *Potential Impacts of Sea Level Rise on the Beach at Ocean City, Maryland*, Washington, D.C.: Environmental Protection Agency.

27. Fairbridge, R. W. and Krebs, W. S., Jr., 1962, "Sea Level and the Southern Oscillation," *Geophysical Journal* 6:532–545.

28. Fastook, J. L., 1985, "Ice Shelves and Ice Streams: Three Modeling Experiments," in Meier et al. [62].

29. Flint, R. F., 1971, *Glacial and Quarternary Geology*, New York: John Wiley and Sons.

30. Flohn, H., 1982, "Climate Change to Ice-free Arctic Ocean," in Clark W. C. (ed.) *Carbon Dioxide Review: 1982*, New York Oxford University Press.

31. Gagliano, S. M., Meyer-Arendt, K. J., and Wicker, K. M., 1981, "Land Loss in the Mississippi Deltaic Plain," in *Transactions of the 31st Annual Meeting of the Gulf Coast Association of Geological Societies*. Corpus Christi, Texas. pp. 293–300.

32. Gibbs, M. "Economic Analysis of Sea-Level Rise: Methods and Results," in: Barth and Titus (eds.). *op. cit.* [7].

33. Geomans, T., 1986, "The Sea Also Rises: The Ongoing Dialogue of the Dutch with the Sea," in Titus, J. G. (ed.). *Effects of Changes in Stratospheric Ozone and Global Climate*, Volume 4. Washington, D.C.: U.S. Environmental Protection Agency and United Nations Environment Programme.

34. Gornitz, V., Lebedeff, S., and Hansen, J., 1982, "Global Sea-Level Trend in the Past Century," *Science* 215:1611–1614.

35. Hands, E. G., 1981, *Predicting Adjustments in Shore and Offshore Sand Profiles on the Great Lakes*, CETA 81-4. Vicksburg, MS: Corps of Engineers. 25 pp.

36. Hands, E. G., 1979, *Changes in Rates of Offshore Retreat: Lake Michigan*. Fort Belvoir: U.S. Army Corps of Engineers Coastal Engineering Research Center publication TP79-4.

37. Hands, E. G., 1976, *Observations of Barred Coastal Profiles Under Influence of Rising Water Levels: Eastern Lake Michigan*, Fort Belvoir: U.S. Army Corps of Engineers CERC publication TR76-1.

38. Hansen, J. E., Johnson, D., Lacis, A., Lebedeff, S., Rind, D., and Russell, G., 1981, "Climate Impact of Increasing Atmospheric Carbon Dioxide," *Science* 213:957–966.

38a. Hansen, J. E., Lacis, A. A., Rind, D. H., and Russell, G. L., 1984, "Climate Sensitivity to Increasing Greenhouse Gases," in Barth and Titus (eds.), see [7].

38b. Hatton, R. S., DeLaune, R. D., and Patrick, W. H., Jr., 1983, "Sedimentation, Accretion and Subsidence in Marshes of Barataria Basin, Louisiana," *Limnology and Oceanography*, 28(3), pp. 494–502, May.

39. Haydl, N. C., 1984, "Louisiana Coastal Area, Louisiana: Water Supply, Initial Evaluation Study," New Orleans: U.S. Army Corps of Engineers."

40. Hays, J. D. and Pitman III, W. C., 1973, "Lithsopheric Plate Motion, Sea-Level Changes, and Climatic and Ecological Consequences," *Nature* 246:18–22.

41. Hicks, S. D., H. A., and Hickman, L. H., 1983, *Sea-Level Variations for the United States 1855-1980*, Rockville, Maryland: U.S. Department of Commerice, NOAA-NOS.

42. Hoffman, J. S., Keyes, D., and Titus, J. G., 1983, *Projecting Future Sea-Level Rise*, Washington, D.C.: Government Printing Office.

43. Hoffman, J. S., Wells, J., and Titus, J. G., 1986, "Future Global Warming and Sea-Level Rise," in G. Sigbjarnarson and Bruun P. (eds.) *Iceland Coastal and River Symposium '85* Reykjavik: National Energy Authority.

44. Hollin, J. T. and Barry, R. G., 1979, "Empirical and Theoretical Evidence Concerning the Response of the Earth's Ice and Snow Cover to a Global Temperature Increase," *Environment International* 2:437–444.

44a. Hollin, J. T., 1972, "Interglacial Climates and Antarctic Ice Surges," *Quaternary Research*, Vol. 2, pp. 401–408.

45. Howard, J. D., Pilkey, O. H., and Kaufman, A., 1985, "Strategy for Beach Preservation Proposed," Geotimes 30:12:15–19.

46. Hughes, T., 1983. "The Stability of the West Antarctic Ice Sheet: What Has Happened and What Will Happen," in Proceedings: Carbon Dioxide Research Conference: Carbon Dioxide, Science, and Consensus. Conference 820970. Washington, D.C.: Department of Energy.

47. Hull, C. H. J. and Titus, J. G. (eds.), 1986, "Greenhouse Effect, Sea-Level Rise, and Salinity in the Delaware Estuary, Washington, D.C.: Environmental Protection Agency and Delaware River Basin Commission.

48. Hull, C. H. J. and Titus, J. G., 1986, "Responses to Salinity Increases," in Hull and Titus (eds.) *op. cit.* [47].

49. Hull, C. H. J., Thatcher, M. L., and Tortoriello, R. C., 1986, "Salinity in the Delaware Estuary," in Hull and Titus (eds.) *op. cit.* [47].

50. Hull, C. H. J. and Tortoriello, R. C., 1979, "Sea-Level Trend and Salinity in the Delaware Estuary," Staff Report. West Trenton, N.J.: Delaware River Basin Commission.

51. Kana, T. W., Michel, J., Hayes, M. O., and Jensen, J. R., 1984, "The Physical Impact of Sea Level Rise in the Area of Charleston, South Carolina," in Barth and Titus (eds.), *op. cit.* [7].

52. Kana, T. W., Baca, B., and Williams, M., 1986, "Charleston Case Study" in *Greenhouse Effect Sea-Level Rise, and Coastal Wetlands*, Titus (ed.), Washington, D.C.: Environmental Protection Agency.

53. Kana, T. W., Baca, B., Eiser, W., and Williams, M., 1988, "New Jersey Case Study" in Titus, J. G. (ed.), *Greenhouse Effect, Sea Level Rise, and Coastal Wetlands*. Washington, D.C.: Environmental Protection Agency.

53a. Kao, C. Y., 1984, "Flooding in Taipei, Taiwan and Coastal Drainage," in *Effects of*

Changes in Stratospheric Ozone and Global Climate, Environmental Protection Agency and United Nations Environment Program, Washington, D. C.

54. Kennett, James, 1982, *Marine Geology*, Prentice-Hall. Englewood Cliffs, New Jersey: Prentice-Hall.

55. Kuo, C. (no date), "Potential Impact of Sea-Level Rise on Coastal Drainage Systems, Washington, D.C.: Environmental Protection Agency. (Draft).

56. Kyper, T. and Sorensen, R., 1985, "Potential Impacts of Selected Sea-Level Rise Scenarios on the Beach and Coastal Works at Sea Bright, New Jersey, in Magoon, O. T., et al. (eds.). *Coastal Zone '85...*, New York: American Society of Civil Engineers.

57. Lacis, A. et al., 1981, "Greenhouse Effect of Trace Gases, 1970–1980," *Geophysical Research Letters.* 81:10:1035–1038.

58. Laroache, T. B. and Webb, M. K., (n.d.), in Kuo, C., *Potential Impacts of Sea-Level Rise on Coastal Drainage Systems.* Washington, D.C.: Environmental Protection Agency (in press).

59. Leatherman, S. P., 1984, "Coastal Geomorphic Responses to Sea-Level Rise: Galveston Bay, Texas," in Barth and Titus (eds.). *op. cit.* [7].

60. Lennon, G. P., Wisniewski, G. M., and Yoshioka, G. A., 1986, "Impact of Increased River Salinity on New Jersey Aquifers," in Hull and Titus (eds.) *op. cit.* [47].

61. Lingle, C. S., 1985, "A Model of a Polar Ice Stream and Future Sea-Level Rise Due to Possible Drastic of the West Antarctic Ice Sheet," in Meier et al. 1985. *op. cit.* [62].

62. Meier, M. F. et al., 1985, *Glaciers, Ice Sheets, and Sea Level.* Washington, D.C.: National Academy Press.

63. Meier, M. F., 1984, "Contribution of Small Glaciers to Global Sea Level," *Science* 226:4681:1418–1421.

64. Mercer, J. H., 1978, "West Antarctic Ice Sheet and CO_2 Greenhouse Effect: A Threat of Disaster?" *Nature* 271:321–325.

65. Mercer, J. H., 1968, "Antarctic Ice and Sangamon Sea Level," *Geological Society of America Bulletin* 79:471.

65a. Meyerson, A. L., 1972, "Pollen and Paleosalinity Analysis from Halocene Tidal Marsh Sequence, Cape May County, New Jersey," *Mar. Geol.* Vol. 12, No. 5, pp. 335–357.

65b. Milliman, J. D. and Meade, R. H., 1983, "Worldwide Delivery of River Sediment to the Ocean," *J. Geol.*, 191:1–21.

66. Oldale, Robert, 1985, "Late Quarternary Sea Level History of New England: A Review of Published Sea-Level Data," *Northeastern Geology* 7:192–200.

66a. Ramanathan, V., Ciceroni, R. J., Singh, H. B., and Kiehl, J. T., 1985, "Trace Gas Trends and Their Potential Role in Climate Change," *J. Geophys. Res.* 90:5547–5566, August.

67. Redfield, A. C., 1972, "Development of a New England Salt Marsh," *Ecological Monograph* 42:201–237."

68. Redfield, A. C., 1967, "Postglacial Change in Sea Level in the Western North Atlantic Ocean," *Science* 157:687–692.

69. Revelle, R., 1983, "Probable Future Changes in Sea Level Resulting from Increased Atmospheric Carbon Dioxide," in *Changing Climate.* Washington, D.C.: National Academy Press.

70. Rind, D. and Lebedeff., S., 1984. Potential Climate Impacts of Increasing Atmospheric CO_2 with Emphasis on Water Availability and Hydrology in the United States. Washington, D.C.: Government Printing Office.

71. Roberts, D., Davis, D., Meyer-Arendt, K. L., and Wicker, K. M., 1983. "Recommendations for Freshwater Diversion to Barataria Basin, Louisiana," Baton Rouge: Coastal Management Section, Louisiana Department of Natural Resources.

71a. Robin, G. de Q., 1985, "Glaciology: Contrasts in Vostok Care, Changes in Climate or Ice Volume?" *Nature* (London) pp. 578–579, August 15.

72. Roemmich, D., 1985, "Sea-Level and Thermal Variability of the Ocean," in *Glaciers, Ice Sheets, and Sea Level,*" Washington, D.C.: National Academy Press.

73. Roemmich, D. and Wunsch, C., 1984, "Apparent Changes in the Climatic State of the Deep North Atlantic Ocean," *Nature* 307:447–450.

74. Schneider, S. H. and Chen, R. S., 1980, "Carbon Dioxide Flooding: Physical Factors and Climatic Impact," *Annual Review of Energy* 5:107–140.

75. Sorensen, R. M., Weisman, R. N., and Lennon., G. P., 1984. "Control of Erosion, Inundation, and Salinity Intrusion," in Barth and Titus (eds.), *op. cit.* [7].

76. Titus, James G., 1984, "Planning for Sea-Level Rise Before and After a Coastal Disaster," in Barth and Titus (eds.), *op. cit.* [7].

77. Titus, James G., 1985, "Sea-Level Rise and the Maryland Coast," in *Potential Impacts of Sea-Level Rise on the Beach at Ocean City, Maryland,*" Washington, D.C.: Environmental Protection Agency.

78. Titus, James G., 1987, "Greenhouse Effect, Sea-Level Rise, and Society's Response," in Devoy, R. J., *Sea Surface Studies.* Beckenham (U.K.): Croom Helm.

79. Titus, J. G., Henderson, T., and Teal, J. M., 1984, "Sea-Level Rise and Wetlands Loss in the United States." *National Wetlands Newsletter.* 6:4.

80. Thomas, R. H., "Responses of the Polar Ice Sheets to Climatic Warming," in Meier et al. 1985, *op. cit.* [62].

81. Thomas, R. H., Sanderson, T. J. O., and Rose, K. E., 1979, "Effect of Climatic Warming on the West Antarctic Ice Sheet." *Nature* 227:355–358.

82. U.S. Army Corps of Engineers, 1982, *Louisiana Coastal Area, Louisiana: Freshwater Diversion to Barataria and Breton Sound Basins.* New Orleans: Army Corps of Engineers.

83. U.S. Army Corps of Engineers, 1980, *Feasibility Report and Final Environmental Impact Statement: Atlantic Coast of Maryland and Assateague Island, Virginia,* Baltimore: Army Corps of Engineers.

84. U.S. Army Corps of Engineers, 1979, *Ocean Beach Study: Feasibility Report.* San Francisco: Army Corps of Engineers.

85. U.S. Army Corps of Engineers, Coastal Engineering Research Center. 1984. *Shore Protection Manual.* Fort Belvoir, Virginia: Coastal Engineering Research Center.

86. U.S. Army Corps of Engineers, 1971, *National Shoreline Study,* Washington, D.C.: Army Corps of Engineers.

87. Van Beek, J. L., Roberts, D., Davis, D., Sabins, D., and Gagliano, S. M., 1982, "Recommendations for Freshwater Diversion to Louisiana Estuaries East of the Mississippi River," Baton Rouge: Coastal Management Section, Louisiana Department of Natural Resources.

87a. Ward, L. G. and Domeracki, D. D., 1978, "The Stratigraphic Significance of Back-Barrier Tidal Channel Migration," *Geol. Soc. Am. Abstr. Programs,* Vol. 10, No. 4. p. 201.

88. Waddell, J. O. Blaylock, R. A., (no date), "Impact of Sea Level Rise on Gap Creek Watershed in the Fort Walton Beach, Florida Area," in Kuo, C. Y. (ed.), *op. cit.* [55].

89. Weishar, L. L. and Wood, W. L., 1983, "An Evaluation of Offshore and Beach Changes on a Tideless Coast. *Journal of Sedimentary Petrology,* 53:3:847–858.

90. Wendland, W. M., 1977, "Tropical Storm Frequencies Related to Sea Surface Temperatures," *Journal of Applied Meteorology* 16:480.

91. Whalin, R. W. and Houston, J. R., 1987 "Implications of Sea-Level Rise to Coastal Structure Design," in *Preparing for Climate Change,* Washington, D.C.: Climate Institute.

92. Zwally, H. J., Parkinson, C. L., Comiso, J. C., 1983, "Variability of Antarctic Sea Ice and Changes in Carbon Dioxide," *Science,* 220:1005–1012.

CHAPTER 14

WAVE-CURRENT INTERACTION

Y. C. Li

Professor, Civil Engineering Department
Dalian Institute of Technology
Dalian, People's Republic of China

CONTENTS

Introduction

Waves generated at sea generally intercept currents. The interacting waves and currents, not only change the characteristics of waves, but at the same time also transform the current flow field. Development in offshore and coastal engineering accelerated research concerning wave-current interaction [1–27] by many scientists and engineers. To evaluate this problem, one may employ

1. The conservation of mass transport, which determines the mean velocity of current profile.

2. The conservation of wave number, or the conservation of wave crest, which determines the transformation of wave celerity, wave number or wave frequency.
3. The conservation of wave energy flux or the conservation of wave action flux, which allows calculations of wave height transformation.

To simplify the practical engineering application, the main results introduced in this chapter are only suitable for steady case and uniform current profile. For shear current profile research by Hughes and Stewart [11] and Dalrymple [17] is introduced, and for nonsteady case, Chen and Wang [28] is recommended.

Principle of Conservation of Wave Energy Flux

Longuet-Higgins and Stewart [7, 10] first dealt with the wave transformation in currents using an analytical approach. In a steady case, for conservative one-dimensional problem the principle of conservation of wave energy flux may be written:

$$\frac{\partial}{\partial x}\left[E(U + Cg)\right] + S_{xx}\frac{\partial U}{\partial x} = 0 \tag{1}$$

The radiation stress term S_{xx} may be determined by the following equation

$$S_{xx} = E\left(\frac{2kd}{\sinh 2kd} + \frac{1}{2}\right) \tag{2}$$

In deep water

$$S_{xx} = \frac{1}{2}E \tag{3}$$

and in very shallow water

$$S_{xx} = \frac{3}{2}E \tag{4}$$

In deep water, Equation 1 may be replaced by

$$E\left(U + \frac{1}{2}C\right)C = E_0\frac{1}{2}C_0^2 \tag{5}$$

If the current is normal to the direction of wave propagation, Equation 1 may be expressed in a two-dimensional case as

$$\frac{\partial}{\partial x}\left[E(U + Cg)\right] + \frac{\partial}{\partial y}(EV) + S_{xx}\frac{\partial U}{\partial x} + S_{yy}\frac{\partial V}{\partial y} = 0 \tag{6}$$

where axis is parallel to the direction of wave propagation.

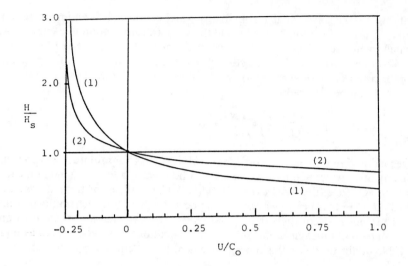

Figure 1. Wave height transformation [8].

Assuming that $\partial E/\partial y = 0$ and in deep water $S_{yy} = 0$, it follows that

$$\frac{E}{C}\left(U + \frac{1}{2}C\right) = E_0 \tag{7}$$

The wave height transformation by Equations 5 and 7 are shown in Figure 1 as curves 1 and 2, respectively.

In very shallow water, from Equation 6,

$$E(U + C) = E_0 C_0 \tag{8}$$

Equation 1 or 6 can be solved analytically only in deep or very shallow water, but in intermediate water depth, which is more important for practical application, these equations can only be solved numerically.

Principle of Conservation of Wave Action Flux

The concept of wave action flux was first developed by Bretherton and Garrett [12]. Wave action A is defined as the ratio of wave energy E to wave frequency ω, i.e. $A = E/\omega$. Jonsson [13, 14] used this principle to solve real problems of wave-current interaction. In a steady case, for conservative one-dimensional case, the principle of conservation of wave action flux may be expressed as follows

$$\frac{d}{dx}\left[\frac{E}{\omega_r}(U + Cg_r)\right] = 0 \tag{9}$$

Equation 8 can be solved analytically in any water depth. This is an important advantage for using Equation 8 to calculate the wave transformation in a current. As indicated by Bretherton, et al. [12] and verified by Christoffersen, et al. [29, 30] the principle of conservation of wave action flux is exactly equivalent to the principle of conservation of wave energy flux. It is indicated by Li and Herbich [31] that Equation 1 can be replaced by

$$\frac{\partial}{\partial x}\left[\frac{E}{\omega_r}(Cg + U)\right] + \left(\frac{C_g}{C} - \frac{1}{2}\right)\frac{E}{\omega_r}\frac{\partial U}{\partial x} = 0 \tag{9a}$$

The second term on the left side of Equation 9 is equal to zero only in deep water, but in any other water depth this term will not be equal to zero. If defining the ratio of term $(C_g/C - 1/2)(E/\omega_r)(\partial U/\partial x)$ to $(E/\omega_r)(U + Cg)$ as the error term, it has been pointed out [31] that before wave breaking occurs this error is generally less than 0.6%. Thus, one may conclude that Equation 9 is exactly equal to Equation 1 only in deep water, but for engineering applications Equation 9 may be treated as Equation 1. No doubt Equation 9 is more convenient for practical applications.

Wave Transformation in Currents (Monochromatic Waves)

One Dimensional Case [32, 33] (for Following or Opposing Currents)

Based on linear wave theory, wave celerity C in current may be determined by

$$C = U + C_r \tag{10}$$

in which

$$C_r = \left(\frac{g}{k}\tanh kd\right)^{0.5} \tag{11}$$

and $k = 2\pi/L$.

The transformation of wavelength or wave celerity can be calculated as follows

$$L/L_s = C/C_s = \left(1 - \frac{U}{C}\right)^{-2}\frac{\tanh kd}{\tanh k_s d} \tag{12}$$

From Equation 9, the transformation of wave height can be obtained by

$$H/H_s = \left(1 - \frac{U}{C}\right)^{0.5}(L_s/L)^{0.5}(N_s/N)^{0.5}\left[1 + \left(\frac{U}{C}\right)\frac{2 - N}{N}\right]^{0.5} \tag{13}$$

where $N = 1 + 2kd/\sinh 2kd$ \hfill (14)

$$N_s = 1 + 2k_s d/\sinh 2k_s d \tag{15}$$

The results given by Equations 12 and 13 are shown in Figures 2 and 3.

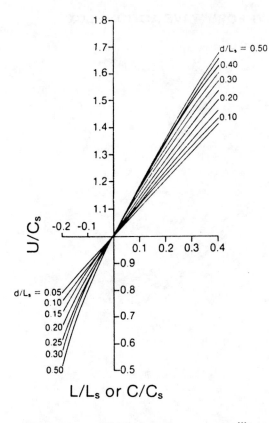

Figure 2. Wave length change computed by linear wave theory [32].

When $U = -0.25C$, the wave energy will stop its propagation and cause wave breaking. This represents the theoretical criterion of wave breaking in opposing current.

Li and Herbich [32] presented the effect of the influence of wave nonlinearity on wave transformation in a current. A comparison was made employing the Stokes third-order theory and Airy theory. Numerical calculations of the wavelength change by nonlinear wave theory are less than 10% within the range $0.15 < d/L_s < 0.40$, $0.01 < H_s/L_s < 0.07$ and $-0.15 < U/C_s < 0.30$; and the error for wave height change by linear wave theory is less than 4%. It is also shown by laboratory experiments that the results using linear wave theory agree well with the laboratory data. Thus, for practical engineering applications, it is recommended one could employ the linear wave theory when evaluating wave-current interaction.

Diagonal Waves

Wave celerity C in a current, as shown in Figure 4, may be determined by

$$C = U \sin \alpha + C_r \qquad (16)$$

H/HS, LINEAR THEORY WAVE ACTION FLUX

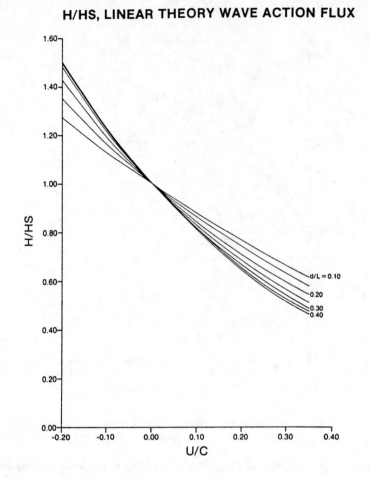

Figure 3. Wave height change computed by linear wave theory [32].

The conservation of wave number is expressed by

$$k \sin \alpha = k_s \sin \alpha_s \tag{17}$$

or

$$L/\sin \alpha = L_s/\sin \alpha_s \tag{18}$$

The concept of wave energy ray in a current is shown in Figure 5. The wavelength transformation can be calculated

$$\frac{L}{L_s} = \frac{C}{C_s} = \left(1 - \frac{U}{C_s} \sin \alpha_s\right)^{-2} \frac{\tanh kd}{\tanh k_s d} \tag{19}$$

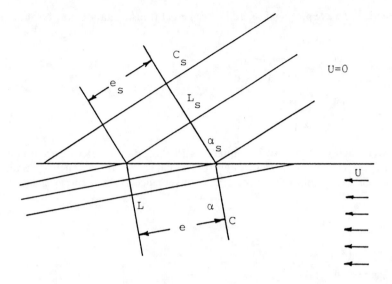

Figure 4. Scheme of refraction of diagonal waves in current.

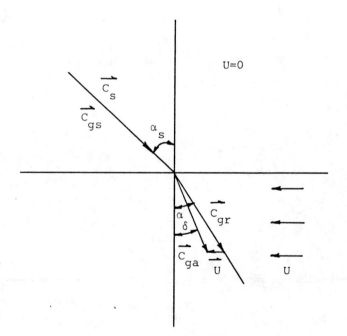

Figure 5. Wave energy ray in currents.

The direction of wave propagation and wave height transformation may be obtained from

$$\sin \alpha = \left(1 - \frac{U}{C_s} \sin \alpha_s\right)^{-2} \frac{\tanh kd}{\tanh k_s d} \sin \alpha_s \tag{20}$$

$$H/H_s = \left[\frac{N_s}{N} \frac{L_s}{L} \frac{\cos \alpha_s}{\cos \alpha}\right]^{0.5} \tag{21}$$

The wave refraction in current by Equations 19 through 21 under different conditions may be given by Figures 6 through 10 where it is shown that when α_s becomes large enough during following current, the convergence of wave energy may occur

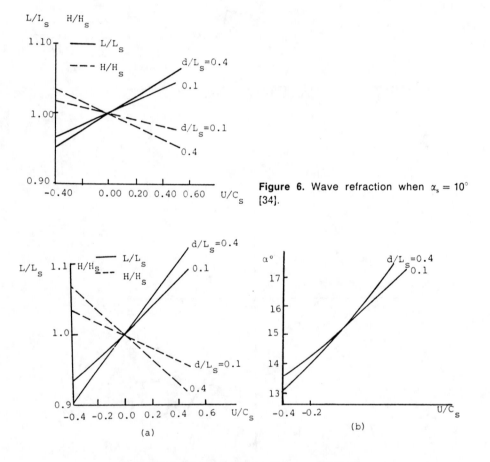

Figure 6. Wave refraction when $\alpha_s = 10°$ [34].

Figure 7a,b. Wave refraction when $\alpha_s = 15°$ [34].

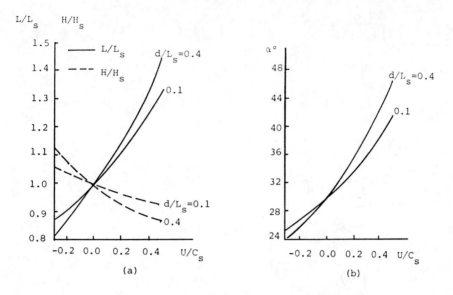

Figure 8a,b. Wave refraction when $\alpha_s = 30°$ [34].

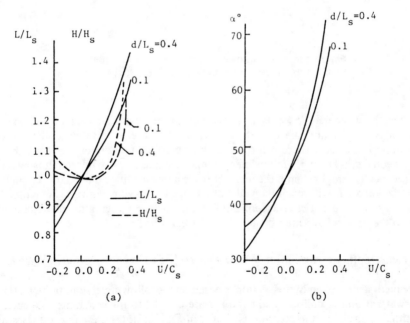

Figure 9a. Wave transformation when $\alpha_s = 45°$ [34].
Figure 9b. Wave refraction when $\alpha_s = 45°$ [34].

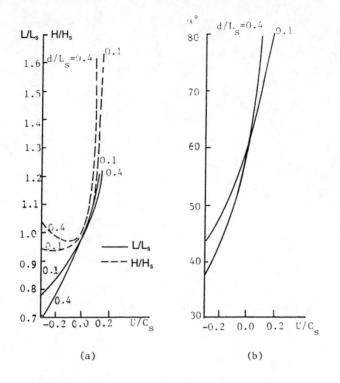

Figure 10a. Wave transformation when $\alpha_s = 60°$ [34].
Figure 10b. Wave refraction when $\alpha_s = 60°$ [34].

and then the wave height would increase. During an opposing current, the wave energy may diverge and the wave height would decrease. It is found that in case of an opposing current there is a discontinuity between one-dimensional problem with diagonal sea. During a following current, the angle of wave refraction is larger than the incident angle; then if the incident wave angle in still water is large enough, the refraction angle will reach the value of 90°, i.e. the wave will propagate parallel to the current. The critical incident angle $[\alpha_s]_{cr}$ for the appearance of refraction angle to the value of 90° may be found in Table 1.

Current-Depth Refraction of Water Waves [35] (Monochromatic Waves)

The method described in this section is based on the following assumptions: (1) the underwater profile is uniform and contours are parallel to the coastline; (2) current direction is parallel to the contour as shown in Figure 11; (3) the current does not vary with depth; (4) only a steady state wave-current combination is considered; and (5) dissipation of wave energy is neglected.

Table 1
Critical Incident Angle for $\alpha \rightarrow 90°$ [34]

U/C_s	d/L_s	$[\alpha_s]_{cr}$ (degree)
0.1	0.4	61
	0.1	64
0.2	0.4	52
	0.1	55
0.3	0.4	46
	0.1	49

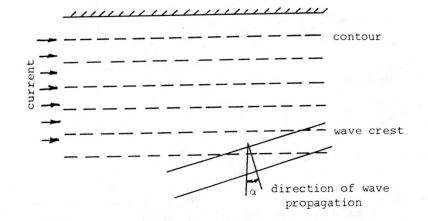

Figure 11. Scheme of current-depth refraction of waves.

Wave celerity at any given point (X_m, Y_n) may be calculated by

$$C_{mn} = U_{mn} \sin \alpha_{mn} + (C_r)_{mn} \tag{22}$$

The wave number alongside the current direction will remain constant in a different current field

$$k_0 \sin \alpha_0 = (k_s)_{mn} \sin(\alpha_s)_{mn} = k_{mn} \sin \alpha_{mn} \tag{23}$$

or

$$L_0/\sin \alpha_0 = (L_s)_{mn}/\sin(\alpha_s)_{mn} = L_{mn}/\sin \alpha_{mn} \tag{24}$$

according to the linear wave theory

$$(C_r)_{mn} = \left[\frac{g}{k_{mn}} \tanh k_{mn}d \right]^{0.5} \tag{25}$$

In a steady case, the absolute wave period will remain constant in a different current field, i.e.,

$$T_0 = (T_s)_{mn} = (T_a)_{mn} \tag{26}$$

The transformation of wavelength or celerity may be obtained from

$$\frac{L_{mn}}{L_0} = \frac{C_{mn}}{C_0} = \left[1 - \frac{U_{mn}}{C_0} \sin \alpha_0 \right]^{-2} \tanh k_{mn} d_{mn} \tag{27}$$

The angle of refraction could be calculated from

$$\sin \alpha_{mn} = \left[1 - \frac{U_{mn}}{C_0} \sin \alpha_0 \right]^{-2} \tanh k_{mn} d_{mn} \sin \alpha_0 \tag{28}$$

The transformation of wave height at any given point with respect to deep still water may be determined by

$$\frac{H_{mn}}{H_0} = \left[\frac{1}{N_{mn}} \frac{L_0}{L_{mn}} \frac{\cos \alpha_0}{\cos \alpha_{mn}} \right]^{0.5} \tag{29}$$

where $N_{mn} = 1 + 2k_{mn}d_{mn}/\sinh 2k_{mn}d_{mn}$ \hfill (30)

Nomograms were calculated from Equations 27 to 29 and are shown in Figures 12 through 16, which may be used for a preliminary evaluation of depth-current refraction of water waves for practical engineering application. As shown by Li [35], if

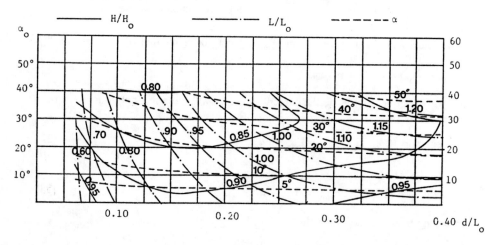

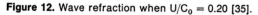

Figure 12. Wave refraction when $U/C_0 = 0.20$ [35].

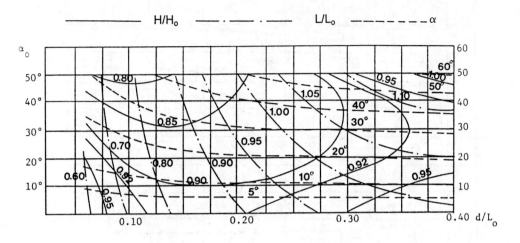

Figure 13. Wave refraction when $U/C_0 = 0.10$ [35].

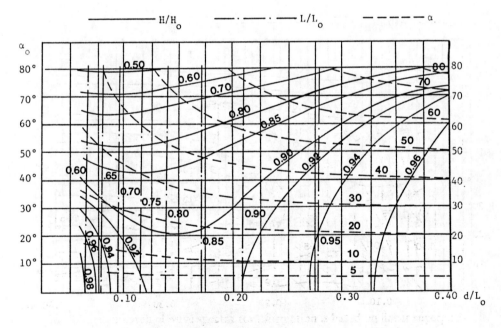

Figure 14. Wave refraction when $U/C_0 = 0.0$ [35].

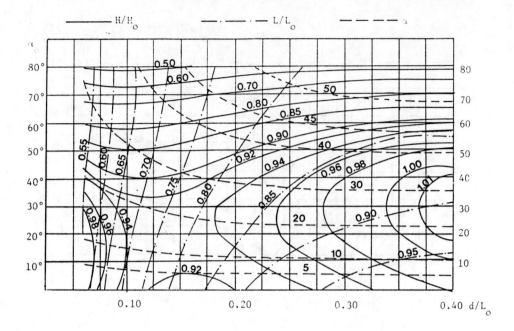

Figure 15. Wave refraction when $U/C_0 = -0.10$ [35].

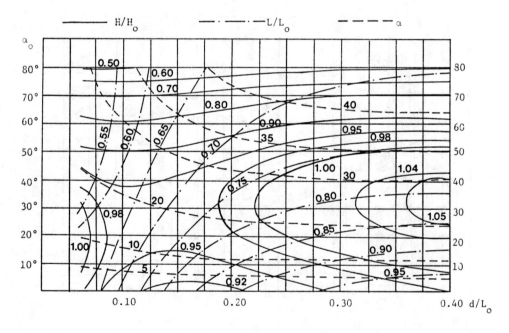

Figure 16. Wave refraction when $U/C_0 = -0.20$ [35].

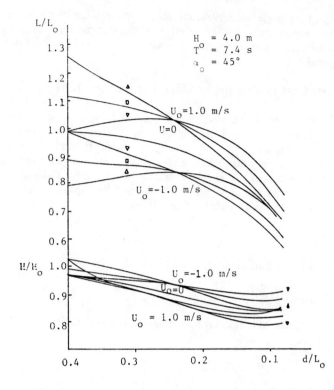

Figure 17. Wave refraction by different current velocity distribution [35].

wave steepness in deep water is less than 0.05, the results of wave transformation by the linear wave theory is very close to that calculated by the Stokes' third-order theory. Comparisons on influence of current velocity distribution on wave refraction are given in Reference 35. Figure 17 [35] shows that the transformation of wave height depends only on the local velocity value of the calculated point and on the wave characteristics in still, deep water. It does not depend on the current magnitude distribution from deep water to the point of calculation. This is only correct when wave energy dissipation is neglected.

However, it should be pointed out that in intermediate water depth, if the distance of wave propagation is sufficiently long, the energy dissipation by bottom friction is significant and should not be neglected.

Wave Frequency Spectra Transformation in a Current

So far most research of wave spectra transformation is based on linear superposition principle. It is also shown previously that linear wave theory will give reasonably good results. Thus, if we neglect the influence of wave-wave interaction, the linear superposition principle will give quite reasonable results. It means that the transformation of wave spectra is the combination of transformation of each spectral component, and for each wave component the method for the calculation of transformation of regular waves can be used.

One Dimensional Case (Following or Opposing Current) [36]

As shown in Figure 18, the calculated frequency range is from ω_1 to ω_2, the omitted energy part in the region of $\omega < \omega_1$ and $\omega > \omega_2$ is less than 0.5% of the total wave spectral energy. Between ω_1 to ω_2, the spectral density curve is divided to n parts with the same frequency range $\Delta\omega$, i.e., $\Delta\omega = \omega_2 - \omega_1/n$. The transformation of spectra (including spectra of surface elevation, particle velocity, and acceleration spectra, etc.) should be calculated in relative frequency domain. The relative frequency of i-th component can be obtained as follows

$$\omega_{ri} = \omega_{si} - k(\omega_i)U \tag{31}$$

For wave spectra transformation,

$$S_{\eta\eta}(\omega_i)\,d\omega_i = |Y_\eta|^2 SS_{\eta\eta}(\omega_{si})\,d\omega_{si} \tag{32}$$

The energy of i-th component in relative frequency domain is the same as in absolute frequency domain, i.e.,

$$S_{\eta\eta}(\omega_i)\,d\omega_i = S_{\eta\eta}(\omega_{si})\,d\omega_{si} \tag{33}$$

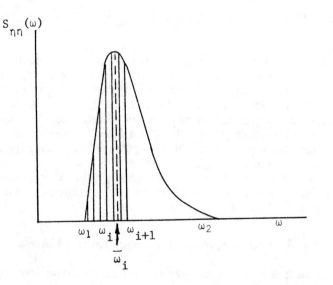

Figure 18. Scheme of wave spectral density curve.

then

$$S_{\eta\eta}(\omega_{si}) = |Y_\eta|^2 SS_{\eta\eta}(\omega_{si}) \tag{34}$$

$$\text{where } |Y_\eta(\omega_i)|^2 = \frac{E(\omega_i)}{E_s(\omega_{si})} \tag{35}$$

Equation 35 is the ratio of wave energy; thus the transformation of wave spectral density can be determined by

$$S_{\eta\eta}(\omega_{si}) = \left[1 - \frac{U}{C(\omega_i)}\right] \frac{C_s(\omega_{si})}{C(\omega_i)} \frac{N_s(\omega_{si})}{N(\omega_i)} \left[1 + \frac{U}{C(\omega_i)} \frac{2 - N(\omega_i)}{N(\omega_i)}\right]^{-1} \times SS_{\eta\eta}(\omega_{si}) \tag{36}$$

and

$$\frac{C_s(\omega_{si})}{C(\omega_i)} = \left[1 - \frac{U}{C_s(\omega_{is})}\right]^2 \frac{\tanh k_s(\omega_{si})d}{\tanh k(\omega_i)d} \tag{37}$$

Similarly, for the transformation of particle velocity and acceleration spectral density, the following formulas are introduced:

$$S_{uu}(\omega_{si}) = |Y_{u\eta}(\omega_i)|^2 S_{\eta\eta}(\omega_{si}) \tag{38}$$

$$\text{where } Y_{u\eta}(\omega_i) = \omega_{ri} \frac{\cosh k(\omega_i)(z + d)}{\sinh k(\omega_i)d} \tag{39}$$

$$S_{aa}(\omega_{si}) = |Y_{a\eta}(\omega_i)|^2 S_{\eta\eta}(\omega_{si}) \tag{40}$$

$$\text{where } Y_{a\eta}(\omega_i) = \omega_{ri}^2 \frac{\cosh k(\omega_i)(z + d)}{\sinh k(\omega_i)d} \tag{41}$$

It should be mentioned that the results by these formulae agree well with the experimental model data. The mean upcrossing wave period in a current is also modified by the effect of currents. [35]

Diagonal Wave Spectra

The main equations used for the transformation of diagonal wave spectra are as follows:

$$\omega_{ri} = \omega_{si} - k(\omega_i) \sin \alpha \tag{42}$$

$$S_{\eta\eta}(\omega_{si}) = |Y_\eta|^2 SS_{\eta\eta}(\omega_{si}) \tag{43}$$

$$\text{where } |Y_\eta|^2 = \frac{N_s(\omega_{si})C_s(\omega_{si}) \cos \alpha_s}{N(\omega_i)C(\omega_i) \cos \alpha(\omega_i)} \tag{44}$$

The refraction angle of i-th component can be evaluated as follows:

$$\sin \alpha(\omega_i) = \left[1 - \frac{U}{C_s(\omega_{si})} \sin \alpha_s \right]^{-2} \frac{\tanh k(\omega_i)d}{\tanh k_s(\omega_{si})d} \sin \alpha_s \tag{45}$$

As a result, the wave component, under the influence of current, will not propagate any more at the same direction. The components in a high-frequency domain are usually refracted more by the current than those in a low-frequency domain. At a certain incident wave angle, during a following current, wave convergence in a high-frequency region will occur and the components higher than this frequency will no longer propagate across the current, but move parallel to the current.

Based on a series of computations [37] it was found that when $\alpha_0 < 30°$, analysis of regular waves will give a sufficiently accurate result; when $\alpha_0 > 30°$, it is more accurate to use spectral analysis. If $d/gT_0^2 \geq 0.06$ and the distance of wave propagation is not too large, the effect of wave energy attenuation by bottom friction can be neglected, otherwise this effect should be considered. [38]

Current-Depth Refraction of Wave Frequency Spectra [39]

It is indicated previously that if the wave steepness in deep water is less or equal to 0.05, then the influence of nonlinearity of waves on wave refraction by currents and depth may be neglected. Generally, the characteristic wave steepness of wave spectra in deep water satisfies this condition. Thus, for calculating current-water depth refraction of wave frequency spectra, the linear superposition principle as described in the previous section can be used.

Assuming that the seabed is uniform and has parallel contours and that steady-state conditions exist, the current flow is parallel to the contour and wave energy dissipation can be neglected. For the calculation of current-depth refraction of wave frequency spectra the following formulation is introduced.

The relative frequency of i-th component at point (X_m, Y_n) may be determined by

$$\omega_{rimn} = \omega_{imn} - k_{imn}(\omega_{imn})U_{mn} \sin \alpha_{imn}(\omega_{imn}) \tag{46}$$

The transformation of spectral density can be calculated as follows

$$S_{\eta\eta mn}(\omega_{simn}) = |Y_{\eta omn}|^2 SS_{\eta\eta o}(\omega_{io}) \tag{47}$$

and

$$|Y_{\eta omn}|^2 = \frac{1}{N_{imn}(\omega_{imn})} \frac{C_{io}(\omega_{io})}{C_{imn}(\omega_{imn})} \frac{\cos \alpha_{io}}{\cos \alpha_{imn}(\omega_{imn})} \tag{48}$$

where $\dfrac{C_{io}(\omega_{io})}{C_{imn}(\omega_{imn})} = \left[1 - \dfrac{U_{mn}}{C_{io}(\omega_{io})} \sin \alpha_{io} \right]^2 \dfrac{1}{\tanh k_{imn}(\omega_{imn})d_{mn}}$ (49)

$$N_{imn}(\omega_{imn}) = 1 + 2k_{imn}(\omega_{imn})d_{mn}/\sinh 2k_{imn}(\omega_{imn})d_{mn} \tag{50}$$

The refraction angle may be obtained by

$$\sin \alpha_{imn}(\omega_{imn}) = \left[1 - \frac{U_{mn}}{C_{io}(\omega_{io})} \sin \alpha_{io} \right]^{-2} \tanh k_{imn}(\omega_{imn})d_{mn} \sin \alpha_{io} \qquad (51)$$

The comparison of the results by this method with the results by the method introduced in the previous section are shown in Figures 19 through 21, which are based on the Pierson-Moskowitz Spectrum in still water. As shown in these figures, in some cases the results obtained by an irregular wave analysis are quite close to that calculated using the regular wave method. Also, it is clear that the type of wave spectra will influence the results of wave transformation. Based on a series of computations, [37] it is concluded that:

1. When $\alpha_0 \leq 30°$ and $d/gT_0^2 \geq 0.05$, in which T_0 is defined as the mean upcrossing wave period of spectra in deep water, the method of regular wave analysis is recommended, which is more convenient to use and gives an accurate result.

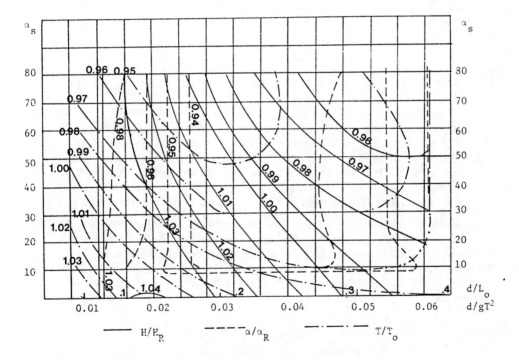

Figure 19. Wave spectra refraction of Pierson-Moskowitz spectrum when $U/C_0 = -0.107$ [39].

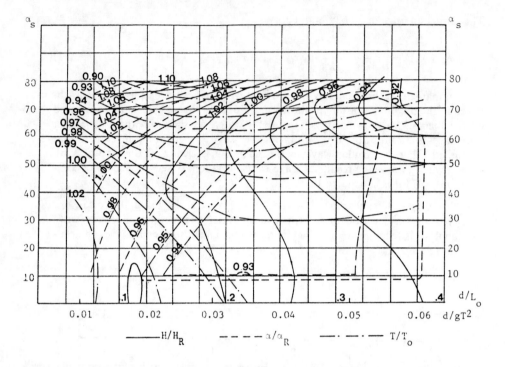

Figure 20. Wave spectra refraction of Pierson-Moskowitz spectrum when $U/C_0 = 0.0$ [39].

2. When $\alpha_0 \leq 30°$ and $d/gT_0{}^2 < 0.05$, the method of spectral analysis must be used, but the type of wave spectra will not significantly affect the results.

3. When $\alpha_0 > 30°$, in any water depth, it is necessary to use the method of spectral analysis. In the following current, the type of wave spectra will significantly influence the result, thus in this case the use of the local spectra based on field observations for the calculation of wave transformation is recommended.

Sakai [40, 41] discussed the influence of wave energy directional spread. He indicated that in the equation of conservation of wave action flux, the "refraction term" should be included, which will cause the directional energy transfer. It is shown by Sakai's calculation that the refraction term significantly influences the result. Then in general, when the wave energy directional spread function is concerned, the simple linear superposition principle for directional spectra analysis will produce some error.

Notation

C   wave celerity
C_g wave group velocity

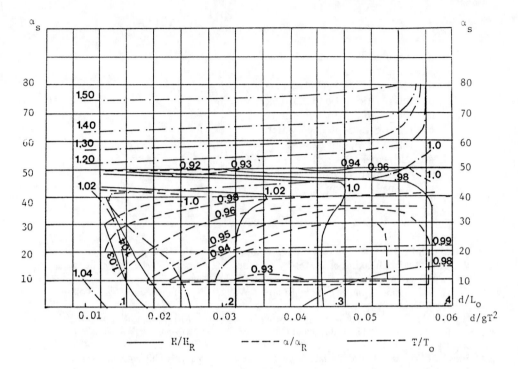

Figure 21. Wave spectra refraction of Pierson-Moskowitz spectrum when $U/C_0 = 0.123$ [39].

d	water depth
E	wave energy per unit column of water
g	gravity acceleration
H	wave height
k	wave number $= 2\pi/L$
L	wavelength
S	spectral density in current
SS	spectral density in still water
S_{xx}, S_{yy}	radiation stress on axis X and Y, respectively
T	wave period
U	current velocity on X axis
V	current velocity on Y axis
Y_η	transfer function of wave surface spectra
$Y_{u\eta}$	transfer function of wave particle velocity
$Y_{a\eta}$	transfer function of wave particle acceleration
α	angle between the current flow and wave crest
ω	wave angular frequency

Subscripts

a   wave particle acceleration
cr   critical value
i   sequence number of wave components
m   the position of points on axis X
n   the position of points on axis Y
o   relative value in deep water
r   relative value in current
s   still water
u   wave particle velocity
η surface elevation

References

1. Unna, P. J. H., 1942, "Waves and Tidal Streams," *Nature.* Vol. 149, p. 219.
2. Yu, Y. Y., 1952, "Breaking of Waves by an Opposing Current," *Tran. Amer. Geophys. Union,* Vol. 33, pp. 39–41.
3. Burns, J. C., 1953, "Long Waves in Running Water," *Proc. Camb. Phil. Soc.,* Vol. 49, pp. 695–703.
4. Hunt, N. J., 1955, "Gravity Waves in Flowing Water," *Proc. Roy. Soc.,* A231, pp. 496–504.
5. Vicefeld, E. A., 1957, "The Influence of Current on Waves," *Symposium of Hydraulic Laboratory,* National Press of Construction, Architecture and Material, USSR, (in Russian).
6. Sun, C., 1959, "Behavior of Surface Waves on a Linearly-Varying Current," *Moskov. Fiz-Tech. Inst., Isstd. Meck, Praki, Mat.,* No. 3, pp. 66–84 (in Russian).
7. Longuet-Higgins, M. S. and Stewart, R. W., 1960, "Changes in the Form of Short Gravity Waves on Long Waves and Tidal Currents," *Jour. of Fluid Mech.,* Vol. 8, pp. 565–583.
8. Longuet-Higgins, M. S. and Stewart, R. W., 1961, "The Changes in Amplitude of Short Gravity Waves on Steady Nonuniform Currents," *Jour. of Fluid Mech.,* Vol. 10, pp. 529–549.
9. Longuet-Higgins, M. S. and Stewart, R. W., 1962, "Radiation Stress and Mass Transport in Gravity Waves with Application to Surf Beat," *Jour. of Fluid Mech.,* Vol. 13, pp. 481–504.
10. Longuet-Higgins, M. S. and Stewart, R. W., 1964, "Radiation Stress in Water Waves: A Physical Discussion with Applications," *Deep Sea Res.,* Vol. II, p. 529.
11. Hughes, B. A. and Stewart, R. W., 1961, "Interaction Between Gravity Waves and a Shear Flow," *Jour. of Fluid Mech.,* Vol. 10, pp. 385–402.
12. Bretherton, F. P. and Garrett, C. J. R., 1969, "Wavetrains in Homogeneous Moving Media," *Proc. Roy. Soc. London,* Series A302, pp. 529–554.
13. Jonsson, I. G., Skougaard, C., and Wang, J. D., 1970, "Interaction Between Waves and Currents," *Proc. 12th Conf. Coastal Eng.,* ASCE, Vol. 1, pp. 489–508.
14. Jonsson, I. G., 1978, "Combinations of Waves and Currents," in *Stability of Tidal Inlets,* Per Bruun, ed. Amsterdam: Elsevier, *Dev. Geotechn. Eng.,* Ch. 23, pp. 162–203.
15. Phillips, C. M., 1966, *The Dynamics of the Upper Ocean,* London and New York: Cambridge Univ. Press.
16. Peregrine, D. H., 1976, "Interaction of Water Waves and Currents," *Adv. Appl. Mech.,* Vol. 16, pp. 9–117.
17. Dalrymple, R. A., 1974, "Models for Nonlinear Water Waves in Shear Currents," *6th Off. Tech. Conf.,* No. 2114.

18. Hales, L. Z. and Herbich, J. B., 1974, "Effects of a Steady Nonuniform Current on the Characteristics of Surface Gravity Waves," Miscellaneous Paper H-74-11, Hydraulic Laboratory, U.S. Army Engineer WES, Vicksburg, MS.

19. Tung, C. C. and Huang, N. E., 1973, "Combined Effects of Current and Waves on Fluid Force," *Ocean Engineering*, Vol. 2, pp. 183–193.

20. Van Hoften, J. D. A. and Karaki, S., 1976, "Interaction of Waves and a Turbulent Current," *Proc. 15th Conf. Coastal Eng.*, ASCE, Vol. 1, pp. 404–412.

21. Horikawa, K., Mizuguchi, M., Kitazawa, O., and Nakai, M., 1977, "Hydrodynamic Forces on a Circular Cylinder," *Annual Report of the Engineering Research Institute*, Faculty of Engineering, Unv. of Tokyo, Vol. 36, pp. 37–48.

22. Iwagaki, Y., Sakai, T., and Asano, Y., 1977, "Wave Refraction and Wave Height Variation Due to Current," *Bull. Dis. Prev. Res. Inst.*, Kyoto Univ., Vol. 27, pp. 73–91.

23. Kamphuis, J. W., 1975, "Friction Under Oscillatory Waves," *Proc. Waterways, Harbors, Coastal and Ocean Division*, ASCE, Vol. 101, WW2, pp. 135–144.

24. Hedges, T. S., 1979, "Measurement and Analysis of Waves on Currents," in *Mechanics of Wave-Induced Forces on Cylinders*. T. L. Shaw, ed. Pitnam Advanced Publishing Program, pp. 249–259.

25. Grant, W. D. and Madsen, O. S., 1979, "Combined Wave and Current Interaction with a Rough Bottom," *Jour. Geophys. Res.*, Vol. 84(C4), pp. 1797–1808.

26. Brevik, I. and Aas, B., 1980, "Flume Experiment on Waves and Currents," *Coastal Engineering*, Elsevier Science Publishers, Vol. 3, pp. 149–177 and Vol. 4, pp. 89–110.

27. Lambrakos, K. F., 1981, "Wave-Current Interaction Effects on Water Velocity and Surface Wave Spectra," *Jour. Geophys. Res.*, Vol. 86(C11), pp. 10955–10960.

28. Chen, Y. H. and Wang, H., 1983, "Numerical Model for Nonstationary Shallow Water Wave Spectral Transformation," *Jour. Geophys. Res.*, Vol. 88(C14), pp. 9851–9863.

29. Christoffersen, J. B. and Jonsson, I. G., 1980, "A Note on Wave Action Conservation in a Dissipative Current Wave Motion," *Applied Ocean Res.*, Vol. 2, M.4, pp. 179–182.

30. Christoffersen, J. B., 1982, "Current Depth Refraction of Dissipative Water Waves," Institute of Hydraulic Engineering, Technical University of Denmark, Series Paper No. 30.

31. Li, Y. C., 1984, "A Discussion on the Equivalence of Conservation of Wave Energy Flux and Conservation of Wave Action Flux in Wave-Current Interaction," Technical Report of RIOE No. 8418, Dalian Institute of Technology, (in Chinese).

32. Li, Y. C. and Herbich, J. B., 1982, "Effect of Wave-Current Interaction on the Wave Parameter." *Proc. 18th Conf. Coastal Eng.*, ASCE, Vol. 1, pp. 413–438.

33. Li, Y. C. and Herbich, J. B., 1984, "Wavelength and Celerity for Interacting Waves and Currents," *Jour. of Energy Res. Tech.*, ASME, Vol. 106, No. 2, pp. 226–227.

34. Li, Y. C., 1984, "Refraction of Diagonal Waves in Currents," *Marine Transportation Engineering*, No. 1, pp. 1–7 (in Chinese).

35. Li, Y. C., 1986, "Current-depth Refraction on Waves," *Proc. of Offshore Mech. and Arctic Eng.*, ASME, Vol. 1, pp. 397–403.

36. Li, Y. C., Wang, F. L., and Teng, B., 1987, "The Transformation of Wave Spectrum in Current," *Proc. 2nd Conf. on Coastal and Port Eng. in Developing Countries*, China.

37. Pan, J. C., 1986, "Nomograms for the Calculation of Current-depth Refraction of Wave Spectra." Tech. Report of RIOE No. 8627, Dalian Institute of Technology, (in Chinese).

38. Li, Y. C. and Teng, B., 1987, "Wave Attenuation by Bottom Friction in Currents," *Proc. Nearshore Hydrodynamics*, ASCE, Delaware.

39. Li, Y. C. and Zhang, C. Y., 1986, "Current-depth Refraction of Wave Spectra," *Acta Oceanologica Sinica*, Vol. 8, No. 4, pp. 510–518 (in Chinese).

40. Sakai, T., Koseki, M., and Iwagaki, Y., 1983, "Irregular Wave Refraction Due to Current," *Jour. Hydraulic Eng.*, ASCE, Vol. 109, No. 9, pp. 1203–1215.

41. Sakai, T., Hirosue, F., and Iwagaki, Y., 1986, "Wave Directional Spectra Change Due to Underwater Topography and Current," *Proc. Offshore Mechanics and Arct. Eng. 5th,* Vol. 1, pp. 59–65.

42. Li, Y. C. and Herbich, J. B., 1982, "Velocity Field for Interacting Waves and Currents," COE Report No. 258, TEES, Texas A&M Univ., College Station, TX.

43. Sakai, S., Ota, K., Oba, H., and Saeki, H., 1985, "Shoaling of Irregular Waves Affected by Opposing Currents," *Proc. of Japanese Conf. on Coastal Eng. 32nd,* pp. 224–228 (in Japanese).

44. Treloar, P. D., 1986, "Spectral Wave Refraction Under the Influence of Depth and Current," *Coastal Engineering,* No. 9, pp. 439–452.

CHAPTER 15

WAVE RUN-UP AND OVERTOPPING

John B. Herbich

Ocean Engineering Program, Civil Engineering Department
Texas A&M University,
College Station, Texas, U.S.A.

CONTENTS

Introduction

The magnitude of wave run-up is of importance in many coastal engineering design projects. The run-up determines the amount of freeboard required to prevent overtopping of dikes, seawalls, breakwaters, etc., and is also used to determine the volume of water that may be transmitted over or through an engineering structure.

The run-up is a function of wave characteristics, water depth, beach slope in front of the structure, slope of the structure, structure's shape, roughness and direction of wave approach with respect to the structure, or

$$R = \underbrace{f[H, L(\text{or } T), C, E,}_{\substack{\text{Wave} \\ \text{characteristics}}} \underbrace{d, \beta, S_b, \alpha, S, r,}_{\substack{\text{Geometric} \\ \text{variables}}} \underbrace{\rho, \mu]}_{\substack{\text{Fluid} \\ \text{properties}}}$$

where H = wave height
       L = wavelength
       T = wave period
       C = wave celerity
       E = wave energy
       d = water depth
       S_b = slope of the beach
       α = slope of the structure
       S = shape of the structure
       r = slope relative roughness
       β = angle of wave approach
       ρ = mass density
       μ = dynamic viscosity

Review of Literature*

Wave Run-up (R)

Before presenting the available wave run-up (R) theories, it is important to describe what physically happens when a wave or wave train propagates from deep water to the shore. As a wave is propagated shoreward on the continental slope its wavelength (L) is shortened, while its wave height (H) first decreases slightly and then increases. As the wave steepness (H/L) reaches a certain limiting value for breaking (which depends on the relative depth d/L), the wave breaks and a substantial amount of energy is dissipated. The wave may continue to break (depending on the wave characteristics and bottom contour) or it may form a nonbreaking wave of smaller height (H) and continue to advance shoreward while growing in steepness. As a wave reaches very shallow water, it falls into the category of a shallow water wave (d/L < 1/25). The shallow water wave may become a bore with its height decreasing as it advances shoreward and finally it runs up the beach. If the wave steepness (H/L) fails to reach the limiting value for breaking (which depends on the relative depth d/L) the wave simply advances to the shore without breaking and runs up the beach or structure.

Theories for Non-breaking Waves

When a long wave (d/L < 1/25) with small amplitude is propagated toward a steep slope, the wave will not break seaward of the slope. This wave is called a non-

* Based in part on Machemehl and Herbich (1970) [55]

breaking wave. If the bottom friction is neglected, the nonbreaking wave will be totally reflected by the steep slope. In the case of a vertical wall the wave run-up (R) for a sinusoidal wave (Airy) will be equal to the wave height (H) of the original wave:

$$\frac{R}{H} = 1.0 \tag{1}$$

For the case of a uniform slope and infinite depth $(d = \infty)$ Miche [34], using linear theory, developed the following equation:

$$R/H = \sqrt{\pi/2\alpha} \tag{2}$$

in which α is the slope angle. For a vertical wall terminating at a finite depth Miche [58] derived the equation:

$$R/H = 1 + \pi \, \frac{H}{L} \, \frac{1}{\tanh \dfrac{2\pi d}{L}} \left(1 + \frac{3}{4 \sinh^2 \dfrac{2\pi d}{L}} - \frac{1}{4 \cosh^2 \dfrac{2\pi d}{L}} \right) \tag{3}$$

by applying correction terms to Equation 1. Equation 3 loses its validity for a small relative depth, because it predicts an infinite relative run-up $R/H \to \infty$. In this case the wave run-up (R) must be approximated by a solitary wave theory. Using a solitary wave theory, Wallace [81] investigated wave reflection from a vertical wall. He found the wave run-up (R) to be two and a half times the solitary wave height (H):

$$R/H = 2.5 \tag{4}$$

For the case of a sloping beach rather than a vertical wall, the superelevation terms found in Equation 3 are added to Equation 2 to obtain

$$R/H = \sqrt{\pi/2\alpha} + \pi \, \frac{H}{L} \, \frac{1}{\tanh \dfrac{2\pi d}{L}} \left(1 + \frac{3}{4 \sinh^2 \dfrac{2\pi d}{L}} - \frac{1}{4 \cosh^2 \dfrac{2\pi d}{L}} \right) \tag{5}$$

which is valid for moderate to steep slopes (S > 1 on 30). Equation 5 also loses its validity for a small relative depth because it predicts an infinite relative run-up $(R/H \to \infty)$.

The propagation of waves in water of nonuniform depth was studied on the basis of linear theory by Lewy [53] and Issacson [36].

For a nonuniformly sloping beach (slowly varying depth) Keller [46] matched the geometrical optics theory in deep water to the linear, standing wave theory, to obtain

$$\frac{R}{H} = \frac{A}{2} = \frac{1}{2} \left(\frac{2\pi}{\alpha} \right)^{1/2} \frac{(K_0 \sinh^2 \gamma K_0 + \gamma K_0)^{1/2}}{\cosh \gamma K_0}, \qquad \text{for } \gamma \gg 1 \tag{6}$$

where α = slope angle of the beach at the shore line
        γ = the dimensionless wave frequency $(2\pi/T\sqrt{g/d})$
        K_0 = root of the equation

$$K_0 \tanh \gamma K_0 = 1.0 \tag{7}$$

For a uniformly sloping beach Keller [45] derived

$$\frac{R}{H} = \frac{A}{2} = \left(J_0{}^2 \frac{2\gamma}{\alpha} + J_1{}^2 \frac{2\gamma}{\alpha} \right)^{-1/2} \tag{8}$$

in which J_0 and J_1 are Bessel functions.

To obtain results for nonlinear shallow water waves on a uniformly sloping beach, Keller and Keller [44] devised a numerical solution to solve the initial boundary value problem and calculate wave run-up (R) numerically. The method enabled an incident wave to be introduced into a one dimensional model bounded by the shoreline. Their results showed fair agreement with the analytical results for waves of low frequency but not for higher frequencies.

To improve the agreement with analytical results at higher frequencies, Keller and Keller [44] used a finite difference scheme of higher order accuracy. The discrepancies between the numerical and analytical results still occurred at the highest frequencies.

Carrier [10] combined nonlinear shallow water theory with the linear dispersive theory for deep water to obtain

$$\frac{R}{H} = \frac{2.1}{\alpha^{1/2} X_0{}^{1/6}} \tag{9}$$

which related run-up to the wave height at the point X_0 for the case of a horizontal bottom for $0 < X < X_0$ and a delta function bottom elevation at $X = 0$.

Theories for Breaking Waves

No generally applicable wave run-up theory exists for breaking waves. Breaking is a nonconservative process and the breaking point is a mathematical singularity.

Bore Run-up Theory. Run-up of a bore on a beach was investigated in a sequence of papers by Ho and Meyer [30], Shen and Meyer [72], Ho, Meyer, and Shen [31]. The bore run-up (R) was found to be independent of slope (S):

$$R = \frac{u_0{}^2}{2g} \tag{10}$$

in which u_0 is the horizontal velocity component at the instant the bore reached the shoreline. (This conclusion was also arrived at separately by Freeman and Le Méhauté [15].) By using an approximation proposed by Whitham [84], the horizontal velocity (u_0) was calculated from bore behavior prior to its intersection with the beach. Keller, Levine, and Whitham [43] compared solutions for bore run-up based on the approximations of horizontal velocity (u_0) by Whitham with numerical solutions obtained by integrating the nonlinear shallow water equations (see Stoker [77]) by finite differences. They found good agreement between the two methods of computing the bore run-up (R).

Nonsaturated Breaker Theory. Le Méhauté [52] first introduced the new concept of saturated and nonsaturated breakers. His theory overcomes a difficulty previously encountered in the long wave theory, which resulted in the premature prediction of bores. Le Méhauté concluded that a solitary wave carries a maximum amount of energy towards the shore and that if excess energy exists in the wave, it will be dissipated in a spilling breaker. Also, if excess energy exists it will be carried along (by a bore instead of a spilling breaker) and will cause wave run-up (R). The following conclusions were drawn from this theory in which S is bottom slope and f_* is a friction coefficient:

1. If $S < 0.01f_*$, the wave does not break due to bottom friction and viscous dissipation and there is no wave run-up (R).
2. When $0.01f_* < S < (0.02 + 0.01f_*)$, the wave breaks as a spilling breaker and the energy dissipated by the breaker increases as the bottom slope increases. All the wave energy is dissipated before reaching the shoreline, and there is no significant wave run-up (R).
3. When $S > (0.02 + 0.01f_*) \approx 0.02$, the breaker becomes saturated and becomes a fully developed bore. In this case, the maximum wave run-up (R) is experienced. Le Méhauté's theory therefore only predicts when appreciable wave run-up (R) will be experienced.

Numerical Methods. Amein [2] investigated the motion of periodic long waves in shoaling water and their run-up on a sloping beach. His theoretical study was confined to waves with periods ranging from 30 seconds to several minutes (waves generally associated with tsunami and explosion waves arriving in coastal waters). The calculations by the linear theory were made by using Friedrich's [16] second asymptotic representation while the calculations by the nonlinear theory were made by using a finite difference scheme based on the method of characteristics. Amein coupled the bore equations to the equations of the nonlinear theory in his numerical procedure to calculate the wave run-up on a dry slope.

Experimental Investigations

Due to the complexity of this phenomenon, theory alone has not always been able to accurately predict wave run-up heights (especially true if the wave breaks seaward of the shore).

Significant Parameters. In formulating the physical laws that govern a natural phenomenon it is normal practice to form dimensionless parameters from the variables involved in the problem.

In determining the height of wave run-up (R) on a rough impermeable continuous slope, the following variables are important:

1. Geometric variables
   Wave run-up, R
   Wave height, H
   Wavelength, L
   Depth of water, d
   Relative roughness, r
   Structure slope, α
   Shape of structure, S
2. Dynamic variables
   Wave celerity, C
   Wave energy, E
   Angle of wave approach, β
3. Fluid properties
   Mass density, ρ
   Dynamic viscosity, μ

The general equation may be written as follows:

$$f_1(R, H, L, d, r, \alpha, C, E, \rho, \mu) = 0 \tag{11}$$

Using the Buckingham π theorem the following dimensionless parameters were obtained:

$$f_2\left(\frac{R}{H}, \frac{H}{L}, \frac{H}{d}, \frac{H^2C^2\rho}{E}, \frac{HC\rho}{\mu}, \alpha, r\right) = 0 \tag{12}$$

where R/H relates the wave run-up (R) to incident wave height (H); H/L and H/d relate the wave run-up (R) to wavelength (L) and water depth (d), respectively; $H^2C^2\rho/E$ is an energy term approximately equal to tanh $2\pi d/L$; $HC\rho/\mu$ is a form of the Reynolds Number, α is (a characteristic of) the slope and r is a term describing the surface roughness.

These parameters must then be investigated to determine their effect upon the wave run-up (R) on a slope or structure.

Investigation by Bruun. A study was conducted by Bruun [8] to determine the effects of structural shape and characteristics on wave run-up (R) and wave reflection. Single slopes, composite slopes, and composite slopes with berms were investigated (Figure 1). For a single impermeable slope Bruun found (1) that the slope should be milder than 1:1.5 to facilitate breaking and (2) that the maximum effect of a roughness element appears on a 1:2 slope. For an impermeable composite slope with berm he found (1) that the berm elevation should be at or near storm water level, (2) that the berm should (for practical reasons) be horizontal or inclined and (3) that a composite section with stilling basin was very effective in reducing wave uprush.

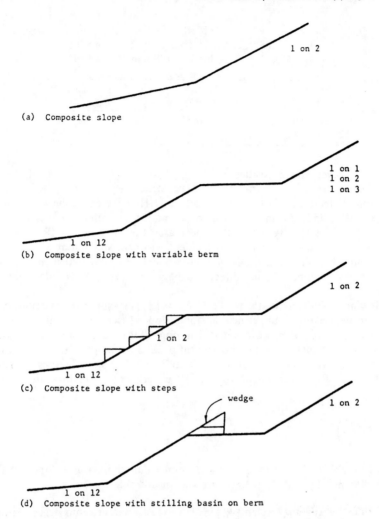

(a) Composite slope

(b) Composite slope with variable berm

1 on 12

1 on 1
1 on 2
1 on 3

(c) Composite slope with steps

1 on 12

1 on 2

1 on 2

(d) Composite slope with stilling basin on berm

1 on 12

wedge

1 on 2

Figure 1. Model structures tested by Bruun [8].

Investigation by Granthem. Granthem [22] investigated constant-slope structures to determine experimentally (1) the effect of slope angle (α) and side slope porosity (n) on wave run-up (R) and (2) to investigate the effect of wave steepness (H/L) and relative depth (d/L) on wave run-up (R). A series of wave uprush tests were run in the 60-ft University of California wave tank for slope angles (α) ranging from 15° to 90°, wave heights (H) from 0.075 ft to 0.307 ft, water depths (d) from 0.98 ft to 1.23 ft, and for wave steepness ratios (H/L) from 0.012 to 0.112. The constant slope models used by Granthem consisted of a smooth flat surface with a porosity n = 0% and two specially constructed model slopes of 1.5 in. maximum angular stone and well

Table 1
Empirical Coefficients and Exponents for Use with
Relative Run-Up Equation by Hall and Watts [26]

Slope (1)	$f_1(S)$ (2)	$f_2(S)$ (3)
$0.09 < S < 0.2$	$11.00S^{0.67}$	$1.90S^{0.35}$
$0.20 < S < 1.0$	$3.05S^{0.13}$	$1.15S^{0.02}$

rounded pea gravel with porosities n = 32.6% and n = 28.9%, respectively. From the investigation Granthem concluded that (1) as structure porosity (n) increases, the wave run-up (R) decreases, (2) as the wave steepness (H/L) increases, the wave run-up (R) increases (this finding is in disagreement with later research conducted by Hunt [35]), and (3) as the relative depth (d/L) decreases, the wave run-up (R) increases. Granthem also found that for a given incident wave the maximum wave run-up (R) will occur when the slope angle is approximately 30° and that if there is any variation from this slope in either direction, the wave run-up (R) will decrease.

Investigation by Hall and Watts. Hall and Watts [26] investigated wave run-up (R) from solitary waves on an impermeable single slope. Tests were conducted in the Beach Erosion Board (BEB) wave tank (85 ft long, 14 ft wide and 4 ft deep) using a wave generator producing a single horizontal push. Slope angles (α) tested ranged from 5° to 45°, water depths (d) from 0.5 ft to 2.25 ft and wave heights (H) from 0.005 ft to 0.5 ft. Results from the run-up (R) experiments were presented in the form:

$$\frac{R}{d} = f_1(S)\left(\frac{H}{d}\right)^{f_2(S)} \tag{13}$$

in which $f_1(S)$ and $f_2(S)$ are empirically-determined functions of the slope (S). The functions obtained by Hall and Watts are shown in Table 1.

Investigation by Kaplan. Kaplan [42] investigated tsunami run-up (R) on smooth continuous slopes. His preliminary tests in the BEB. wave tank (96 ft long, 1.5 ft wide, and 2 ft deep) showed that for a given wave height (H) the initial wave will give the maximum run-up (R) while the wave run-up (R) from the following waves are significantly reduced by backwash. For continuous slopes of 1:30 and 1:60, and for a vertical type reflecting wall, and 1:2 dike type wall installed at the shore line on the 1:60 slope Kaplan obtained the empirical equations in Table 2.

Investigation by Sibul. An experimental investigation was conducted by Sibul [74] to determine the quantity of water pumped over an impermeable uniform slope by wave action. A series of tests were conducted in the University of California wave research laboratory wave tank (60 ft long, 3 ft deep, and 1 ft wide) for smooth and roughened 1:2 and 1:3 slopes. Wave run-up (R) in each test was equal to the elevation of the crest of the structure when the latter was just high enough to prevent

Table 2
Empirical Equations for Relative Wave Run-Up by Kaplan [42]

Slope (1)	Relative Run-Up (2)
1:30 slope	$R/H = 0.381(H/\lambda)^{-0.316}$
1:60 slope	$R/H = 0.206(H/\lambda)^{-0.315}$
1:60 slope with reflecting type wall	$R/H = 0.436(H/\lambda)^{-0.285}$
1:60 slope with 1:2 dike type wall	$R/H = 0.436(H/\lambda)^{-0.283}$

* The wavelength (λ) is defined as twice the distance between the first noticeable rise of the water and the maximum.

overtopping. Sibul found maximum wave run-up (R) occurring at the wave steepness (H/L), which caused breaking at the edge of the structure. When the breaking point moved seaward of the structure, the wave run-up (R) decreased. With the wave breaking seaward of the structure he found a decrease in the wave run-up (R) with decreasing wave steepness (H/L). For a given wave condition the critical wave steepness (H/L) that caused breaking on the structure was higher for the 1:2 slope than for the 1:3 slope.

Wind-generated wave uprush tests were conducted by Sibul on smooth continuous 1:3 and 1:6 slopes rising above a 1:10 bottom slope. Comparing wave run-up (R) from wind-generated waves with wave run-up (R) from mechanically generated waves Sibul found no significant difference in relative run-up (R/H) on the 1:6 slope for low wind velocities (V). On the 1:3 slope, however, he found a 30% increase in the relative run-up (R/H) from the wind-generated waves.

Sibul found the breaker location affecting the wave run-up (R). With the breaking point at the edge of the structure the wave run-up (R) was at a maximum. When the breaking point moved seaward the wave run-up (R) decreased.

Investigation by Saville. Saville [70] analyzed run-up (R) data from a comprehensive test program conducted jointly by Waterways Experiment Station (WES) and Beach Erosion Board (BEB). WES used a large wave flume (120 ft long, 5 ft wide, and 5 ft deep) to collect wave run-up (R) data for a vertical wall, a curved wall (based on the Galveston seawall section), a similar curved wall with a recurvature at the top, smooth slopes of 1:3 and 1:1.5, a step-faced wall of 1:1.5 slope, and a riprap-faced wall of 1:1.5 slope (one layer of riprap on an impermeable base) as shown in Figure 2. All of the structures were fronted by a 1:10 beach slope during testing.

Saville found run-up (R) increasing with depth of structure until a depth-height ratio (d/H_0') of between 1 and 3 was reached.

Evaluating wave run-up (R) for various structures, Saville found the vertical wall more efficient in reducing wave run-up (R) than slopes steeper than 1:4 (for all conditions except that of zero depth at the structure toe). He attributed this decrease in wave run-up (R) to the fact that the waves (horizontal) momentum must be changed instantaneously to vertical momentum to carry the wave up the wall (some momentum may be carried downward if the wave breaks on the wall) whereas on a slope

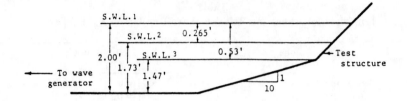

a. Waterways Experiment Station

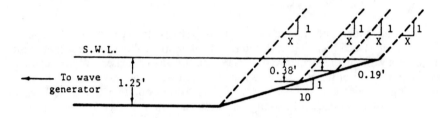

b. Beach Erosion Board

Figure 2. Model structures tested by Waterways Experiment Station and Beach Erosion Board [70].

the waves (horizontal) momentum changes gradually to vertical momentum. Saville found the highest relative run-up (R/H_0') values on the curved walls.

Investigation by WES. An experimental investigation was conducted by the WES [83] to obtain information relative to wave run-up (R) and overtopping of levees. A series of wave uprush (R) tests were conducted on 1:30-scale section models in the WES wave tank (94 ft long, 1.0 ft wide, and 1.5 ft deep). The tests were run to determine the effects of (1) levee slope (α) on wave run-up (R), (2) water depth at toe of beach (d_1) on wave run-up (R), (3) water depth at toe of levee (d_2) on wave run-up (R), (4) various combinations of berms on wave run-up (R) and overtopping, and (5) various combinations of composite slopes on wave run-up (R) and overtopping. A series of single and composite slopes ranging from 1:20 to 1:2 with a beach slope of 1:10 were tested.

WES found the magnitude of wave run-up (R) to be a function of the wave steepness (H/L), slope of levee (α), geometry of levee face, water depth at toe of beach slope (d_1), water depth at toe of levee (d_2), roughness (r) and permeability (n) of levee face, wind speed (V), and time relative to wave period (T) required for water that runs upslope for a given wave to return downslope.

The equation for relative run-up (R) can be expressed as:

$$R/H = f\left(\frac{H}{L}, \alpha, d_1, d_2, \text{berm width, slope geometry, wave backwash}\right) \tag{14}$$

in which d_1 and d_2 are water depth at toe of beach slope and water depth at toe of levee section, respectively. The following conclusions were drawn from the study:

1. Water depth at the beach toe (d_1) had a negligible effect on wave run-up (R).
2. Wave run-up (R) increased as wave steepness (H/L) decreased [for the range $(0.03 < H/L < 0.08)$].
3. Wave run-up (R) decreased as water depth at the levee toe (d_2) decreased.
4. Wave run-up (R) decreased as the berm width increased.
5. An increase in water depth at the break in grade of a composite levee slope resulted in a decrease in run-up (R).
6. Wave run-up (R) decreased as levee slope (α) decreased (this is contrary to Hunt's [35] findings).
7. Wave run-up (R) data was not affected (to a measurable extent) by scale effect.

Investigation by Wassing. Wassing [82] summarized model investigations on wave run-up (R) carried out in the Netherlands over a twenty-year period. His summary included wave run-up (R) on smooth and roughened impermeable slopes (straight, convex, berm dike, and berm dike with stilling basins). As reported by Wassing, the wave run-up (R) was governed by (1) wave characteristics in front of the dike, (2) the direction of wave propagation, (3) the slope of the dike (α), (4) the shape of the dike, (5) the character of the dike facing and (6) the artificial foreshore conditions. Of particular interest herein was the influence of the dike berm and the character of the dike facing. The equation for run-up (R) can be rewritten as:

$$\frac{R}{H} = \phi f\left(\alpha, \frac{H}{L}, \frac{B}{L}, \text{type of facing, and so forth}\right) \tag{15}$$

where the value of ϕ was taken as unity for a revetment of neatly set stones. Values of ϕ for various kinds of artificial roughness are summarized by Wassing.

From various model tests on berm dikes it was found that the berm width should be approximately 1/4L.

Investigation by Savage. Savage [66, 67] investigated wave run-up on smooth, roughened, and permeable structures of constant slope. The objectives of his study were to determine the effects of roughness (r) and permeability (n) on wave run-up (R). A series of wave run-up (R) tests were performed in the Coastal Engineering Research Center (CERC) wave tank (96 ft long, 1.5 ft wide, and 2 ft deep) for slopes ranging from 1:30 to a vertical wall, wave heights (H) from 0.001 ft to largest stable height, and wave periods (T) from 0.5 sec to 5 sec. A constant water depth (d) of 1.25 ft was used in all tests. Savage found the magnitude of wave run-up (R) to be a function of the deep water wave steepness (H_0'/T^2), the structure slope (α), the mean diameter of the roughness material (d') or the permeability of the slope material (n), and the form of wave breaker which, in turn, depends on the behavior and timing of the backwash from the proceeding wave. The equation for relative wave run-up can be expressed as:

$$\frac{R}{H} = f_1\left(\frac{H_0'}{T^2}, \alpha, d' \text{ or } n, \text{ form of the breaker}\right) \tag{16}$$

where H_0' = equivalent deep water wave height
   T = wave period
   d' = particle diameter of the roughness material

Evaluating wave run-up (R) on smooth slopes, Savage found the highest relative run-up (R/H_0') for steep waves occurring on a slope in the order of 1:2 and the highest relative run-up (R/H_0') for waves of low steepness occurring on a slope in the order of 1:4. From his investigation of roughened and permeable slopes he found (1) that the effect of slope roughness (or permeability) increases with an increase in the roughness (or permeability), (2) that the effect of a constant roughness (or permeability) on a given slope increases with decreasing wave steepness (H_0'/T^2) and that (3) the effect of a constant roughness (r) or permeability (n) increases as the slope flattens.

Discussion by Hunt. In 1959, Hunt [35] summarized all the equations (known to him) being used to compute wave run-up (R) on a seawall, he proposed the equations shown in Table 3 be used in seawall design.

Table 3
Empirical Equations for Relative Wave Run-Up by Hunt [35]

Wave and Structure Conditions (1)	Relative Run-up (R/H) (2)	Limitations and Assumptions (3)
Wave run-up on a continuous sloping impermeable structure	$R/H = \dfrac{2.3 \tan \alpha}{(H/T^2)^{1/2}}$	$(\tan \alpha)^2 < H/T^2$ $H \approx H_0'$
Wave run-up (surging wave) on a continuous sloping impermeable structure	$R/H = 3$	$(\tan \alpha)^2 < H/T^2$ $H \approx H_0'$
Wave run-up on a composite slope	$R/H = \dfrac{2.3}{(H/T^2)^{1/2}} \dfrac{\tan \alpha_1 + \tan \alpha_2}{2} S$	SWL at the break in slope $(\tan \alpha_1)^2 < H/T^2$ $H \approx H_0'$ $S \approx 0.8$ to 0.9
Wave run-up on a continuous (roughened) sloping impermeable structure	$R/H = \dfrac{2.3}{(H/T^2)^{1/2}} \tan \alpha \, (r)$	$i^2 < H/T^2$ $H \approx H_0'$ r = roughness factor

Investigation by Hudson. Hudson [34] investigating wave run-up (R) on a model breakwater found the relative run-up (R/H) to be a function of breakwater slope (α), wave steepness (H/L) and, to some extent, the hydraulic roughness (r) of the breakwater surface. A series of wave uprush tests were run for slopes ranging from 1:1.25 to 1:5 with relative depths (d/L) from 0.10 to 0.50. Hudson found the effects of relative depth obscured by a wide range of scatter in the observed values of wave run-up (R). He attributes this scatter to the complexity of defining and observing the phenomenon of wave motion on a roughened slope.

Although his tests were not designed specifically to study the effects of hydraulic roughness (r) on wave run-up (R), he conducted wave uprush (R) tests on breakwater sections composed of 0.10-lb and 0.30-lb stones. For a 1:4 slope Hudson found the effects of hydraulic roughness (r) negligible while on a 1:5 slope the wave run-up (R) was reduced 20%. Hudson states that this phenomenon can probably be explained by the fact that waves tend to break more readily on flatter slopes that provide a greater distance over which energy losses can occur.

Discussion by Saville. Saville [68] discussed the dependency of relative run-up (R/H) on relative depth (d/L). He points out the fact that both wave height (H) and wavelength (L) are dependent on the relative depth (d/L) in which they are measured and that a wave run-up (R) curve independent of relative depth (d/L) will produce an anomaly of wave run-up (R) values for a particular wave train (depending on where the wave characteristics are measured). Saville also suggests that there is a tendency for relative run-up (R) to decrease with decreasing wave steepness (H/L) below a critical steepness value (although this conclusion is largely dependent on the location of a single point).

Investigation by Adam. An experimental investigation was conducted by Adam [1] to determine the height of wave run-up (R) on smooth and roughened structures of constant slope for wave heights in the same dimensional range as the slope riprap material. A series of wave uprush (R) tests were run in the University of Manitoba wave tank (44 ft long, 3 ft wide, and 2.33 ft deep) for slopes ranging from 1:30 to a vertical wall. A constant water depth (d) of 1.50 ft was used in all the tests. The riprap material used in the tests on roughened slopes ranged in size from 0.021 ft ($\frac{1}{4}$ in.) to 0.50 ft (6 in.). From the investigation Adam concluded that (1) as the wave steepness (H_0'/T^2) decreased, the effect of slope roughness on wave run-up (R) increased; (2) as the roughness coefficient ($H_0'T^2/d^2$) (actually the reciprocal of a dimensionless roughness coefficient) decreased, the effect of slope roughness on wave run-up (R) increased; and (3) that for a constant wave steepness (H_0'/T^2) and roughness coefficient ($H_0'T^2/d$), the effect of slope roughness increased as the slope decreased. Adam also found maximum wave run-up (R) occurring on a 1:4 (or 1:6) slope for waves of low steepness ($H_0'/T^2 = 0.005$) and on a 1:1 (or 1:2) slope for waves of high steepness ($H_0'/T^2 = 0.400$).

Investigation by Herbich et al. To determine the limitations of Saville's method for predicting wave run-up on composite beaches Herbich et al. [29] investigated the effect of berm width (B) on wave run-up (R). A composite structure (1:4 slopes) with variable berm) was studied in the Fritz Engineering Laboratory wave tank (67.5 ft long, 2 ft deep, and 2 ft wide).

The theoretical values of wave run-up (R) predicted by Saville's method [69] were compared with experimental values from the study. The theoretical values compared favorably with experimental values for berm to wavelength ratios (X/L) less than 0.15. For berm-to-wave length ratios (X/L) > 0.15 there was little agreement as the experimental run-up (R) remained approximately constant while the predicted values decreased.

Investigation by Hosoi and Mitsui. An experimental investigation was conducted by Hosoi and Mitsui [33] to determine the effect of breaking waves on the run-up (R) on composite slopes. A series of wave uprush tests were run with composite slopes (Figure 3) in the 368-ft Public Works Research Institute wave tank. Results of the tests indicated that the relative run-up (R/H_0') was a function of the characteristics of the breaker within the range of $d/H_0' = 2.3$ to 11.7.

Investigation by Jordaan. Theoretical and experimental studies were conducted by Jordaan [41] to determine maximum wave uprush (R) from an impulsively generated wave train (wave train of continuously decreasing periodicity and varying amplitude). The tests were conducted in the Naval Civil Engineering Laboratory wave basin (94 ft by 92 ft and 3 ft deep). Three rigid beach sections of 1:5, 1:15, and 1:24 provided with smooth, fine-grained and coarse-grained strips were tested to determine the relative effects of surface roughness on wave run-up (R). A plunger in the form of a paraboloid of revolution about the axis of symmetry was used to create the wave train by displacement or impact.

In the impulsively generated wave train Jordaan found maximum run-up (R) produced by the leading wave. The momentum of the subsequent wave was then reduced by the backwash of the leading wave. In the experiments on the 1:15 slope Jordaan found significant wave run-up (R) from every third or fourth wave.

Investigation by Van Dorn. Van Dorn [80] investigated wave run-up (R) on beaches of arbitrary slope. His objectives were to develop a method of predicting wave run-up (R) on a beach, given only the slope of the beach and the characteristics of the offshore incident waves and to determine whether an individual wave in a dispersive system can be treated independently, or whether some cumulative effect of the wave train is of importance in a wave prediction scheme.

Investigations by Le Méhauté et al. Le Méhauté et al. [51] investigated the behavior of gravity waves on gentle slopes to obtain a better understanding of the behavior of explosion-generated waves on a gentle slope. A series of tests were conducted in the National Engineering Science Company weir flume (190 ft long, 4 ft wide, and 4 ft deep) using a 1:107 bottom slope. The waves dissipated their energy completely prior to reaching the shore line, thus verifying the nonsaturated breaker theory proposed by Le Méhauté [52].

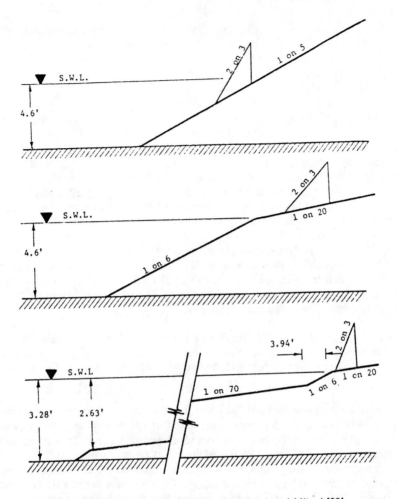

Figure 3. Model structures tested by Hosoi and Mitsui [33].

Investigation by Multer. An experimental investigation was conducted by Multer [60] to determine how the basic laboratory variables (generator stroke, period, and water depth) influenced wave run-up (R). Tests were run in the CERC 72-ft wave tank. Multer found wave run-up (R) varying with test location in the tank. He concluded that this unusual variation of wave run-up (R) with distance from the wave generator was caused by the interaction of primary and secondary waves. He concluded that the relative position of the primary and secondary waves (wave going out of phase, waves coming into phase rapidly, waves coming into phase slowly or waves out of phase) had a major effect on wave run-up (R) and that the run-up (R) could be changed by as much as a factor of 3 because of this effect.

Multer attempted to describe the phase effect by introducing the parameters θ and H_2/H_1. His equation for relative run-up can be expressed as:

$$\frac{R}{H_1} = f_1\left(\frac{H_1}{gT^2}, \frac{H_1}{d}, \frac{H_1}{H_2}, \theta\right) \tag{17}$$

in which θ is the phase angle between the primary and secondary waves and H_1 and H_2 are, respectively, the heights of the primary and secondary waves.

Investigation by Robson. An experimental investigation was conducted by Robson and Jones [65] to determine (1) if an oscillation (seiche) could be induced by an incident train of waves in the water over an offshore submerged shelf, and (2) if so, the effect of the wave system on the wave run-up (R) on an impermeable beach. The tests were conducted in the Navy Civil Engineering Laboratory wave flume (100 ft long and 2 ft wide).

In two of the test runs Robson correlated maximum wave run-up (R) with other than the first wave (probably due to mass oscillation of seiching). He concluded from his investigation that the increase in wave run-up (R) due to seiching could be significant, especially because incident dispersive waves in nature would be higher and would develop greater on-shore mass transport.

Discussion by Haws. Haws [27] discussed wave run-up (R) results obtained for a wind-generated spectrum. He states that no direct relationship has been found to exist between individual wave heights (H) and run-up (R) values in a wind-generated wave train.

Investigation by Jackson. Jackson [38] investigated wave run-up and run down on model rubble-mound breakwaters constructed of rough and smooth quarry-stones, quadripods, tetrapods, hexapods, tribars, modified cubes, and truncated tetrahedrons. Run-up tests were conducted in the WES wave flume (119 ft long, 5 and 12.5 ft wide, and 4 ft deep) for a limited range of wave conditions. For increasing values of wave steepness (H/L) and slope angle (cot α) Jackson found a decrease in relative run-up (R/H). However, for slopes greater than 1:3 he found that the breakwater slope had less effect on wave run-up (R) than wave steepness (H/L). Jackson did not find any appreciable reduction in wave run-up due to slope roughness or method of placement of armor stone.

Investigation by Bowen et al. Wave set-up on a smooth 1:12 slope was measured by Bowen et al. [7] in the Scripps Institution of Oceanography wave flume (130 ft long, 1.65 ft wide, and 2.46 ft deep). Bowen found the maximum set-up on the slope to be of the order of the wave amplitude. He found the wave run-up (R) to be in good agreement with the empirical equations given by Hunt [19].

Summary by Le Méhauté. In 1968, Le Méhauté [50] summarized theories for breaking and nonbreaking waves. From his review of the wave run-up (R) phenomena, he proposed the general equation:

$$\frac{R}{H} = f\left(\alpha, \frac{2\pi d}{L}\right) + g\left(\frac{H}{L}, \frac{2\pi d}{L}\right) - k\left(\alpha, \frac{2\pi d}{L}, \frac{H}{L}\right) \tag{18}$$

where

$$f\left(\alpha, \frac{2\pi d}{L}\right) = \text{run-up contribution by linear approximations}$$

$$g\left(\frac{H}{L}, \frac{2\pi d}{L}\right) = \text{correction due to superelevation by nonlinear effects}$$

$$k\left(\alpha, \frac{2\pi d}{L}, \frac{H}{L}\right) = \text{reduction in relative run-up due to the loss of energy in breaking and bottom dissipation}$$

Investigation by Franzius. Franzius [14b] presented an equation for calculating run-up on smooth slopes. Experimentally-obtained coefficients must be used to obtain wave run-up estimates

$$R = HC_1\left(0.123 \frac{L}{H}\right)^{C_2\sqrt{H/d} + C_3} \tag{19}$$

where
$$\begin{aligned}
H \text{ or } H_i &= \text{incident wave height} \\
L &= \text{wavelength} \\
d &= \text{water depth} \\
C_1, C_2, C_3 &= \text{empirical coefficients}
\end{aligned}$$

Values of empirical coefficients are given in Table 4. A linear interpolation of these values is necessary to obtain coefficients for other slopes.

Investigation by Miller. Miller [59] investigated the run-up (R) of an undular surge (Froude Number, $N_F \leq 1.35$) and a fully developed bore ($N_F \geq 1.55$) on four slopes, each with three different bottom roughnesses in the University of Chicago wave tank (63 ft long, 1.16 ft wide, and 3.0 ft deep). For each combination of slope and

Table 4

Empirical Wave Run-Up Prediction for Smooth Impermeable Slopes [14b]

Front-Face Slope of Breakwater	C_1	C_2	C_3
Vertical	0.958	0.228	0.0578
1:0.5	1.280	0.390	−0.091
1:1.0	1.469	0.346	−0.105
1:1.5	1.991	0.498	−0.185
1:2.25	1.811	0.469	−0.080
1:30	1.366	0.512	0.040

Table 5
Functions for Use With Relative Run-Up Equation by Miller [59]

Condition (1)	$f_1(\sin \alpha_1 f_*)$ (2)	$f_2(\sin \alpha_1 f_*)$ (3)
Undular surge $H_3/d \leq 1.35$ ≤ 1.25	$-3.151 - 15.00 \sin \alpha + 27.88 f_*$	$3.03 + 14.54 \sin \alpha - 22.12 f_*$
Fully developed bore $H_3/d \geq 1.75$ ≥ 1.55	$-0.182 - 9.60 \sin \alpha + 11.82 f_*$	$1.57 + 6.96 \sin \alpha + 9.33 f_*$

bottom roughness he developed a linear equation of the form:

$$\frac{R}{H_3} = f_1(\sin \alpha, f_*) + f_2(\sin \alpha, f_*) \frac{H_3}{d} \tag{20}$$

where H_3 = height of the wave measured from the channel bottom
  d = undisturbed water depth
  α = slope angle
  f_* = dimensionless friction coefficient
 f_1, f_2 = functions

The functions obtained by Miller are shown in Table 5. In all tests Miller found the bore strongly affected by slope (α) and bottom roughness. He also found a general disagreement between theory (based on nonlinear long-wave equations) and his experimental results. In particular, he found that Equation 10 was not valid for the conditions tested (Equation 10 neglects bottom friction).

Investigation by Machemehl and Herbich. Machemehl and Herbich [55] conducted a comprehensive study of the wave run-up phenomena on single and composite slopes and on the effects of slope roughness.

The effects of slope roughness, r, on relative wave run-up, R/H_0', were studied by comparing relative run-up data from two water depths (Figures 4 and 5). The mean wave energy density (E_μ) was obtained from the wave spectrum for both the monochromatic waves and for the wind (irregular) waves. The configuration of parallel strip- and symmetric-block pattern roughnesses is shown in Figure 6.

Relative uprush velocity, V_u/C and a relative downrush velocity, V_d/C values were plotted in Figures 7 and 8. (V_u = uprush velocity, V_d = downrush velocity, and C = wave celerity).

It was concluded that:

1. The water depth, d, affected the relative wave run-up, R/H_0', from the waves in the lower range of mean wave energy densities [i.e., long waves ($L \gg d$) with small wave heights ($H_0' \ll d$)].

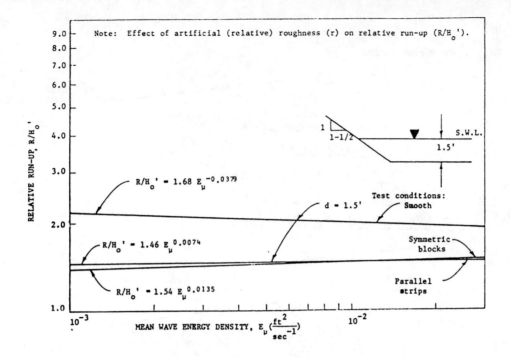

Figure 4. Relative run-up on a smooth and roughened (blocks and strips) 1:1½ slope (d = 1.5 ft) [55].

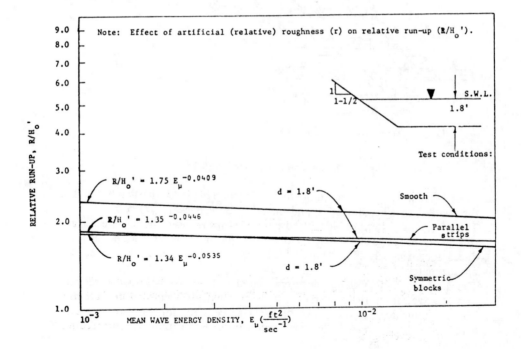

Figure 5. Relative run-up on a smooth and roughened (blocks and strips) 1:1½ slope (d = 1.8 ft) [55].

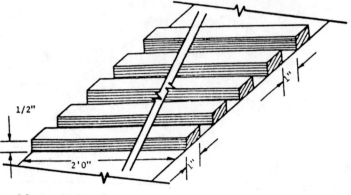

(a) Parallel strips

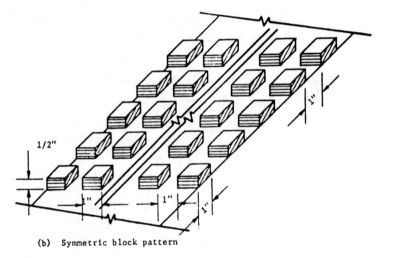

(b) Symmetric block pattern

Figure 6. Model composite section [55].

2. The relative wave run-up was found to be a function of the relative depth (d/L_0), the relative wave height (H_0'/d) and the relative steepness (H_0'/T^2).
3. The symmetric pattern of blocks and parallel strips reduced the relative wave run-up on the single slope. The relative monochromatic wave run-up was reduced approximately 15%, while the relative wind wave run-up was reduced approximately 35%.
4. The wave run-up (R) was significantly reduced by the berm. Maximum reduction of wave run-up (R) occurred with the water depth located at the berm. The maximum reduction of wave run-up also occurred for the short wavelengths $(d < L)$, whereas the least reduction in the wave run-up occurred for the long wavelengths $(d \ll L)$.

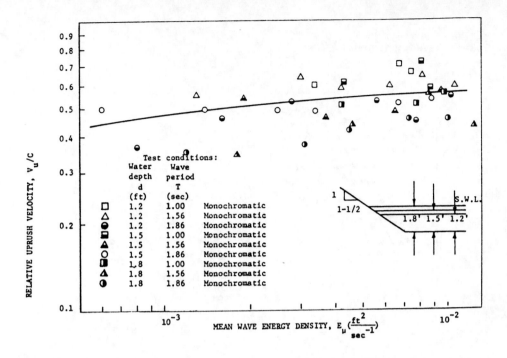

Figure 7. Relative uprush velocity for a roughened (strips) 1:1½ slope (d = 1.2, 1.5, and 1.8 ft) [55].

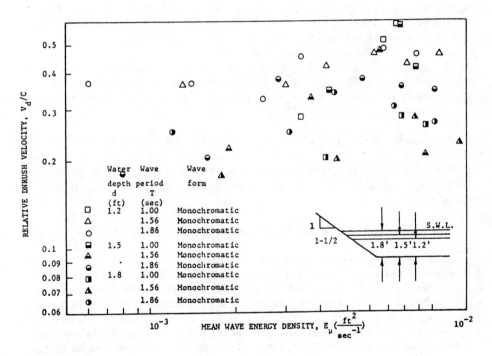

Figure 8. Relative downrush velocity for a roughened (strips) 1 on 1½ slope (d = 1.2, 1.5 and 1.8 ft) [59].

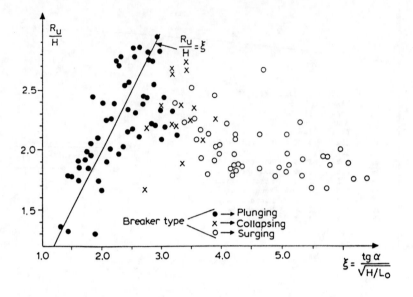

Figure 9. Wave run-up on smooth slopes of 1/1.5, 1/2.0, 1/3.0 (d/H > 3) [22b].

5. The parallel strip roughness element was the most efficient dissipator of the relative wave run-up energy on the composite (1:1.5 slopes with berm) section.
6. The wave uprush velocity, V_u, for the smooth (1:1.5 slope) was approximately seven-tenths of the wave celerity ($V_u = 0.7$ C).
7. The slope roughness, r, reduced the maximum relative uprush velocity, V_u/C, on the 1:1.5 slope. The symmetric pattern of blocks reduced the relative uprush velocity approximately 15%, while the parallel strips reduced the relative uprush velocity approximately 25%.

Investigation by Günbak [22b]. Günbak conducted model tests with monochromatic waves noting the type of wave breaking on smooth slopes of 1:1.5, 1:2 and 1:3. Results are shown in Figure 9 where the dimensionless run-up (R_u/H) is plotted as a function of tan $\alpha/\sqrt{H_0/L_0} = \xi$. The maximum dimensionless run-up is at a ξ value of 3.0.

Methods for Determining Wave Run-up on Composite Slopes

A method for determining wave run-up (R) on composite slopes from laboratory-derived curves for single slopes was first presented by Saville [69]. His method was one of successive approximations that involved replacing the actual composite slope with a hypothetical slope obtained from the breaking depth (d_b) and an estimated wave run-up (R) value. Saville found the wave run-up (R) predicted by his method to be generally within 10% of experimental values except for the longest berms tested. The indications were that, after a horizontal berm had reached a certain width,

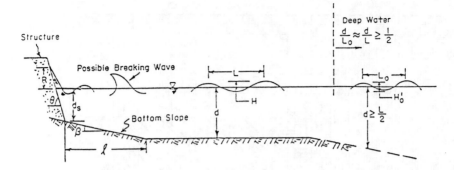

Figure 10. Definition sketch of variables applicable to wave run-up [76].

further widening had no significant effect in reducing wave run-up (R). Saville found the reduction in berm effectiveness (for berm widths greater than $\frac{1}{4}$ L) to be caused by the phenomenon of water "set-up" on the berm. This "set-up" of water (increase in water depth on the berm) was caused by the forward transport of water by waves. Saville found wave run-up (R) affected by reformed waves or surges on the berm.

Modification of Saville's method was first proposed by Hosoi and Mitsui [33]. Due to the characteristics of breakers they proposed that the relationship between cot α and R should be:

$$\cot \alpha = \frac{X_b + X_r}{d_b + R} \tag{21}$$

where X_b = horizontal distance from breaking point to the toe of the structure
X_r = horizontal distance from the toe of the structure to the extent of maximum wave run-up (Figure 3)

Examples of Run-up Calculations

Stoa [76] re-analyzed results of previous tests of monochromatic wave run-up on smooth structures. The definition sketch is shown in Figure 10, the product of acceleration of gravity and wave period squared is used as the principal measure of deepwater wavelength and the undiffracted, unrefracted deep-water wave height is used (H_0').

The run-up results for both breaking and non-breaking waves are reproduced as Figures 11 to 20.

The run-up curves are given for three different cases:

1. Horizontal bottom of structure toe (Figures 11–13).
2. 1:10 sloping bottom at the structure toe, with a zero toe depth ($d_s = 0$) (Figures 14–16).
3. 1:10 sloping bottom at the structure toe, with toe depths greater than zero ($d_s > 0$) (Figures 17–20) [70].

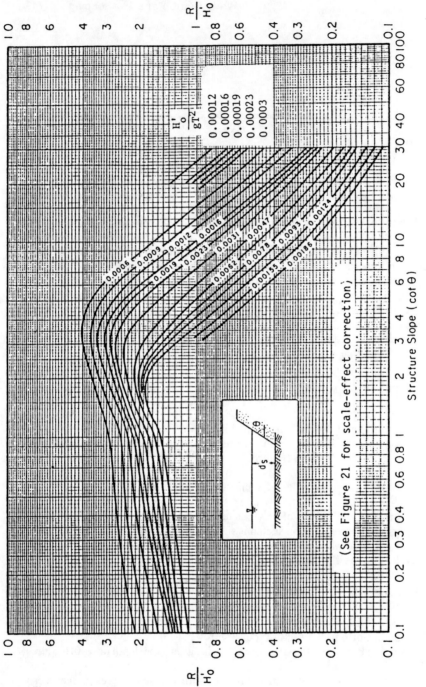

Figure 11. Relative run-up for smooth slope on horizontal bottom; $d_s/H_0' = 3$ [76].

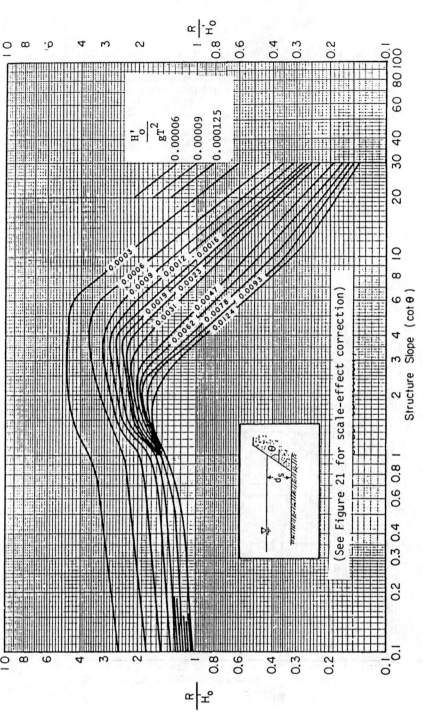

Figure 12. Relative run-up for smooth slope on horizontal bottom; $d_s/H_o' = 5$ [76].

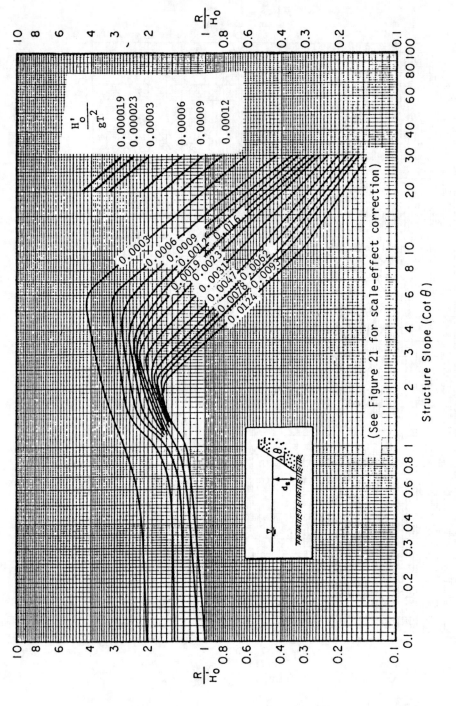

Figure 13. Relative run-up for smooth slope on horizontal bottom; $d_s/H_o' = 8$ [76].

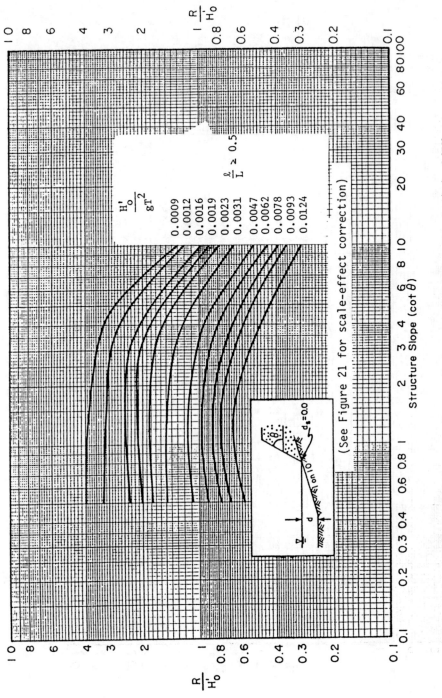

Figure 14. Relative run-up for smooth slopes on 1:10 bottom; $d_s = 0$; $d/H_0' = 3$ [76].

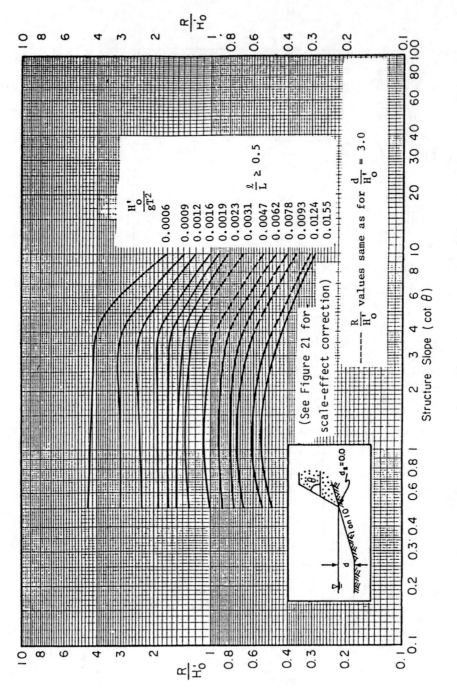

Figure 15. Relative run-up for smooth slopes on 1:10 bottom; $d_s = 0$; $d/H_o' = 5$ [76].

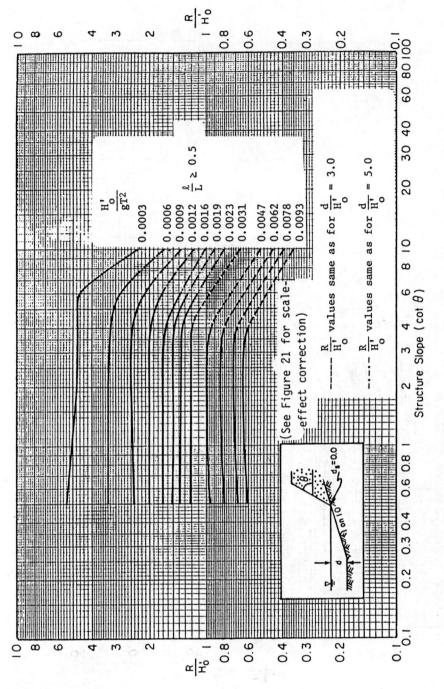

Figure 16. Relative run-up for smooth slopes on 1:10 bottom; $d_s = 0$; $d/H_0' = 8$ [76].

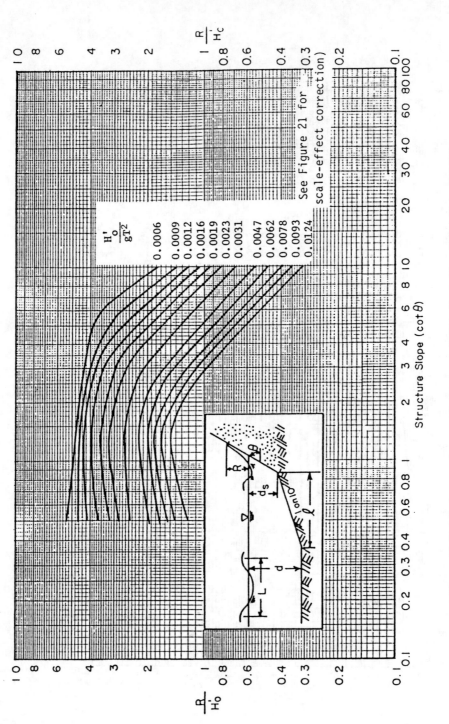

Figure 17. Relative run-up for smooth slopes on 1:10 bottom; $l/L > 0.5$; $d_s/H_o' = 0.6$ [76].

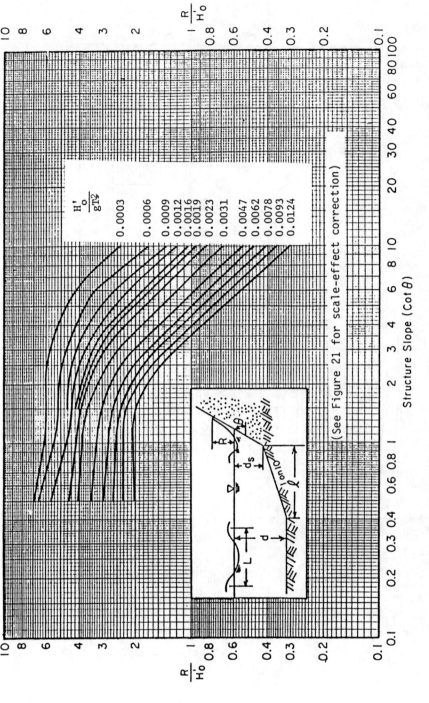

Figure 18. Relative run-up for smooth slopes on 1 on 10 bottom; $\ell/L \geq 0.5$; $d_s/H_0' = 1.0$ [76].

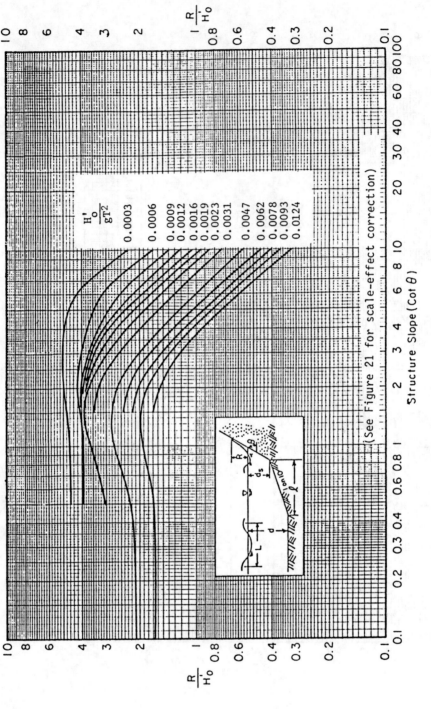

Figure 19. Relative run-up for smooth slopes on 1:10 bottom; $l/L \geq 0.5$; $d_s/H_0' = 1.5$ [76].

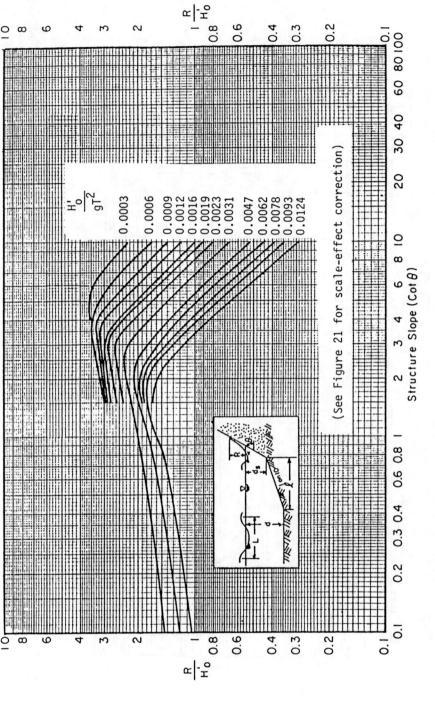

Figure 20. Relative run-up for smooth slopes on 1:10 bottom; $l/L \geq 0.5$; $d_s/H_o' = 3.0$ [76].

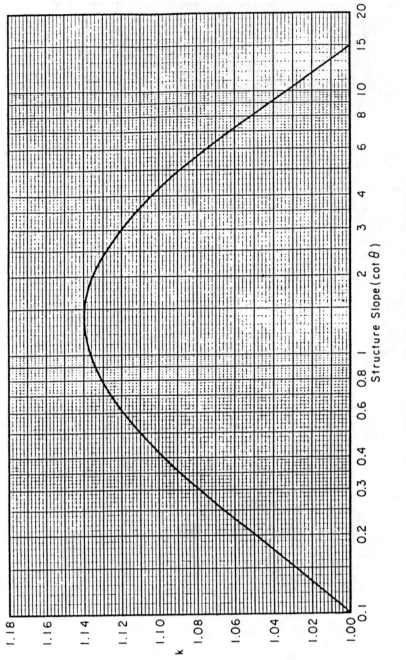

Figure 21. Run-up scale-effect correction factor, k [76].

Because the smooth slope run-up curves (Figures 11–20) are based on small-scale wave-channel tests, a correction factor, k, should be applied to the values obtained from the figures. The scale effect factor, k, is a function of the structure slope as shown in Figure 21.

A comparison of wave run-up on smooth slopes with run-up on permeable rubble slopes is shown in Figure 22.

Examples of run-up calculations follow.

Example 1

Given: An impermeable structure has a smooth slope of 1:3 and is subjected to a design wave, H = 8 ft (2.4 m), measured at a gauge located in a depth, d = 30 ft (9.1 m). Design wave period is T = 8 sec. The structure is fronted by a 1:90 bottom slope extending seaward of the point of wave measurement. Design depth at structure toe is d_s = 25 ft (7.6 m). (Assume no wave refraction between the wave gauge and structure.)

Find: The height above SWL to which the structure must be built to prevent overtopping by the design wave.

Solution: The wave height must be converted to a deep-water value. Using the depth where wave height was measured, calculate

$$\frac{d}{L_0} = \frac{d}{gT^2/2\pi} = \frac{d}{(32.2/2\pi)T^2} = \frac{30}{5.12(8)^2} \tag{22}$$

$$\frac{d}{L_0} = 0.09155$$

To determine the shoaling coefficient, H/H_0',

$$\frac{H}{H_0'} \approx 0.9406 \tag{23}$$

Therefore,

$$H_0' = \frac{H}{0.9406} = \frac{8}{0.9406}$$

$$H_0' = 8.5 \text{ ft (2.6 m)} \tag{24}$$

Calculate, also,

$$\frac{H_0'}{gT^2} = \frac{8.5}{32.2(8)^2} = 0.00412 \tag{25}$$

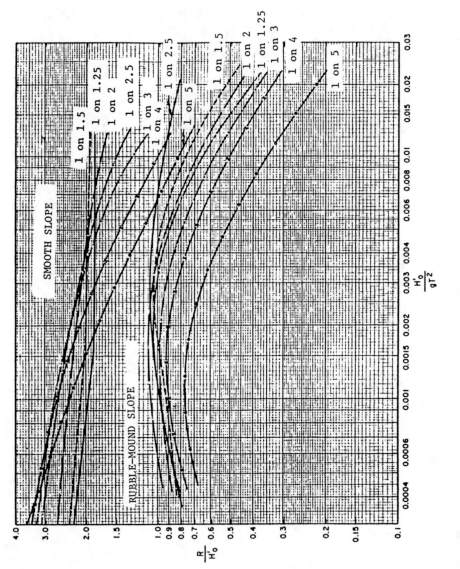

Figure 22. Comparison of wave run-up on smooth slopes with run-up on permeable rubble slopes (data for $d_s/H_0' > 3.0$) [70].

and, for $d_s = 25$ ft

$$\frac{d_s}{H_0'} = \frac{25}{8.5} = 2.94 \tag{26}$$

The bottom slope is very gentle (1:90). Assuming that the slope approximates a horizontal bottom, the appropriate set of curves for $d_s/H_0' = 2.9$ is Figure 11 (for $d_s/H_0' = 3$). For a 1:3 slope and

$$\frac{H_0'}{gT^2} = 0.00412, \frac{R}{H_0'} = 2.1 \tag{27}$$

The run-up, uncorrected for scale effects, is

$$R = (2.1)(H_0')$$

$$= (2.1)(8.5)$$

$$R = 17.9 \text{ ft } (5.5 \text{ m})$$

The scale-correction factor, k, can be determined from Figure 21, and, for cot $\theta = 3$, the correction factor is $k = 1.12$.
   Thus, the corrected run-up is

$$R = (1.12)(17.9) = 20.0 \text{ ft } (6.1 \text{ m}) \tag{28}$$

Example 2

Given: An impermeable, smooth, 1:2 structure is fronted by a 1:10 bottom slope. Toe depth for the structure is $d_s = 10$ ft (3 m), but the bottom slope extends seaward to a depth of 50 ft (15.2 m), beyond which the slope is approximately 1:100. The design wave approaches normal to the structure and has a height of $H = 9$ ft (2.7 m) and period of $T = 9$ sec, measured at a depth of 55 ft (16.8 m).

Find: The height of wave run-up using the appropriate set of curves.

Solution: The wave height given is not the deep-water wave height; it is measured, however, above the gentle 1:100 bottom slope, which approximates a horizontal surface. To determine the shoaling coefficient, K_s, for the location of measurement, calculate

$$\frac{d}{L_0} = \frac{d}{gT^2/2\pi} \tag{29}$$

$$= \frac{55}{(5.12)(9)^2}$$

$$\frac{d}{L_0} = 0.1326 \tag{30}$$

$$K_s = \frac{H}{H_0'} \approx 0.9162 \tag{31}$$

Therefore,

$$H_0' = \frac{H}{K_s} = \frac{9}{0.9162} = 9.82 \text{ ft (3.0 m)} \tag{32}$$

$$\frac{d_s}{H_0'} = \frac{10}{9.82} = 1.018 \approx 1.0 \tag{33}$$

and

$$\frac{H_0'}{gT^2} = \frac{9.82}{(32.2)(9)^2} = 0.00377 \tag{34}$$

Because there is a steeply sloping bottom fronting the structure, the value of ℓ/L must be determined:

$$\ell = (50 - 10)(10) = 400 \text{ ft (122 m)}$$

Next determine the wavelength in water depth of 50 ft (the depth at the toe of the 1:10 slope). For

$$\frac{d}{L_0} = \frac{50}{(32.2/2\pi)(9)^2} = 0.12045 \tag{35}$$

and

$$\frac{d}{L} \approx 0.1585 \tag{36}$$

Therefore,

$$L = \frac{d}{d/L} = \frac{50}{0.1585} = 315.46 \text{ ft (96.1 m)} \tag{37}$$

Then,

$$\frac{\ell}{L} = \frac{400}{315.46} = 1.27 \tag{38}$$

thus,

$$\frac{\ell}{L} > 0.5 \tag{39}$$

From Figure 18, for $H_0'/gT^2 = 0.0038$,

$$\frac{R}{H_0'} \approx 3.0 \tag{40}$$

The run-up is

$$R = \left(\frac{R}{H_0'}\right)(H_0') = (3.0)(9.82)$$

$$R = 29.5 \text{ ft } (9.0 \text{ m})$$

For $\cot \theta = 2$, the scale-correction factor, from Figure 21, is

$$k = 1.136 \tag{41}$$

Thus, the corrected run-up is

$$R = (1.136)(29.5) = 33.5 \text{ ft } (10.2 \text{ m}) \tag{42}$$

Example 3

Given: A design geometrically similar to that in Example 2, where an impermeable, smooth, 1:2 structure is fronted by a 1:10 bottom slope. Toe depth for the structure is $d_s = 10$ ft, but the bottom slope extends seaward to a depth of 50 ft beyond which the slope is approximately 1:100. However, a range of wave periods and deep-water wave heights are known; $H_0' \leq 16$ ft (4.9 m).

Find: Maximum run-up for three different wave conditions: $T_{max} = 7$ sec; $T_{max} = 13$ sec; and constant wave steepness, $H_0'/gT^2 = 0.0101$, with $T_{max} = 7$ sec.

Solution: For any given d_s/H_0' value, the design curves show that relative run-up is highest for the longest wave period (or the lowest wave steepness, H_0'/gT^2). However, for constant toe depth, d_s, and for constant wave steepness, the largest wave height (or lowest d_s/H_0' value) usually results in the largest absolute run-up, R. When a sloping bottom is present, and wave period and toe depth (d_s) are held constant, the maximum run-up may occur at other than the minimum d_s/H_0' value. Thus, run-up for a range of d_s/H_0' values should be investigated.

In the following development, *preliminary* determinations of run-up are not corrected for scale effect. Only the final run-up, as determined for selected wave conditions and structure slope, is corrected.

Table 6

Example Run-Up for T = 7 sec, Constant Depth, and $(H_0')_{max}$ = 16 ft [76]

Figure	d_s/H_0'*	H_0' (ft)	H_0'/gT[†]	R/H_0'	R (ft)
8	≈ 0.6	16.00	0.01014	1.38	22.10
9	1.0	10.00	0.00634	2.35	23.50^2
10	1.5	6.67	0.00423	≈ 2.80	18.70
11	3.0	3.33	0.00211	2.60	8.66

* d_s/H_0' values selected to correspond with values in figures; d_s = 10 ft.
[†] R_{max} = 23.5 feet.

1. The maximum wave height given is H_0' = 16 ft; for this location, the resultant d_s/H_0' value is

$$\frac{d_s}{H_0'} = \frac{10}{16} = 0.63 \tag{43}$$

which is approximately the lowest value used in Figures 17 to 20. The maximum run-up may be determined by constructing a table for varying conditions. Because the maximum wave period is less here than in Example 2, L is also less; thus, $\ell/L > 0.5$ and Figures 17 to 20 may be used.

For d_s = 10 ft, T = 7 sec, and gT^2 = 1,577.8 ft. Table 6 may be constructed with T held constant at 7 sec because the maximum wave period results in the highest relative run-up for each value of d_s/H_0'.

2. For the second condition where T_{max} = 13 sec, the maximum run-up would occur for the lowest d_s/H_0' value. To check ℓ/L, for d = 50 ft:

$$\frac{d}{L_0} = \frac{50}{(32.2/2\pi)(13)^2} = 0.0577 \tag{44}$$

$$\frac{d}{L} = 0.1020$$

$$L = 490.2 \text{ ft};$$

$$\frac{\ell}{L} = \frac{400}{490.2} = 0.82 > 0.5. \tag{45}$$

Table 7 may be constructed for d_s = 10 ft, T = 13 sec, gT^2 = 5,441.8 ft, and by using Figures 17 to 20. Table 7 shows that, in this case, not only is run-up higher for the longer wave period than in Table 6, but the maximum run-up occurs at a lower d_s/H_0' value for the maximum deepwater wave.

Table 7
Example Run-Up for T = 13 sec, Constant Depth, and $(H_0')_{max}$ = 16 ft [76]

Figure	d_s/H_0'*	H_0' (ft)	H_0'/gT^2[†]	R/H_0'	R (ft)
8	≈0.6	16.00	0.002940	2.60	41.6[2]
9	1.0	10.00	0.001840	3.80	38.0
10	1.5	6.67	0.001230	3.90	26.0
11	3.0	3.33	0.000612	3.15	10.5

* d_s = 10 ft
[†] R_{max} = 41.6 ft

3. For the third condition, suppose that wave steepness is expected to be most important, and that the structure is being designed for a constant wave steepness of $H_0'/gT^2 = 0.0101$ and a maximum period of 7 sec.

Table 8 shows the characteristic relationship that the largest run-up, R, occurs for the lowest d_s/H_0' value when H_0'/gT^2 and d_s are constant; the largest *relative* run-up has lower dimensional run-up. However, Table 8 does not indicate the maximum run-up to be expected on this structure for the given conditions; Table 6 shows the maximum (uncorrected for scale effects) to be 23.5 ft when a maximum period of 7 sec is given. Thus, care should be exercised in determining run-up for a particular structure. The results of the three parts of this problem are summarized in Table 9, and the calculated values are corrected for scale effect based on Figure 20.

Example 4

Given: An impermeable structure has a smooth slope of 1:1.5 and is subjected to a design wave, $H_0' = 5$ ft (1.5 m). Design wave period is T = 6 sec. The design water depth at the toe of the structure is $d_s = 0.0$ ft. The bottom has a 1:10 slope from the structure toe to a depth, d = 15 ft (4.6 m), at which point the bottom slope changes to 1:200.

Table 8
Example Run-Up for Constant Wave Steepness, H_0'/gT^2 = 0.0101 [76]

Figure	H_0'/gT^2	d_s/H_0'*	H_0' (ft)	T[†] (s)	R/H_0'**	R[††] (ft)
8	0.0101	≈0.6	16.00	7.0	1.38	22.1
9	0.0101	1.0	10.00	5.5	1.88	18.8
10	0.0101	1.5	6.67	4.5	1.75	11.7
11	0.0101	3.0	3.33	3.2	1.73	5.8

* d_s = 10 ft
[†] T_{max} = 7 sec
** cot θ = 2
[††] R_{max} = 22.1 ft

Table 9
Summary of Maximum Run-Up for Different Conditions [76]

Table	Wave Condition	Maximum R (ft)	Scale-Effect Correction k	Maximum R (ft)
1	Constant period; T = 7 sec	23.5	1.136	26.7
2	Constant period; T = 13 sec	41.6	1.136	47.3
3	Constant steepness; $H_0'/gT^2 = 0.0101$; $T_{max} = 7$ sec	22.1	1.136	25.1

* Uncorrected for scale effect.

Find: Determine run-up on the structure caused by a wave train approaching normally.

Solution: The toe depth is zero, and the bottom slope is 1:10; assuming that the more seaward 1:200 bottom slope approximates a horizontal bottom, Figures 14, 15, and 16 are applicable, subject to the value of d/H_0'.

$$\frac{d}{H_0'} = \frac{15}{5} = 3 \tag{46}$$

Therefore, Figure 14 is applicable;

$$\frac{H_0'}{gT^2} = \frac{5}{(32.2)(6)^2} = 0.0043 \tag{47}$$

The relative run-up for a 1:1.5 structure slope is determined by interpolation to be

$$\frac{R}{H_0'} \approx 1.23 \tag{48}$$

Therefore,

$$R = (1.23)(5)$$

$$R = 6.15 \text{ ft } (1.87 \text{ m})$$

The scale-correction factor, k, from Figure 21, is

$$k = 1.14$$

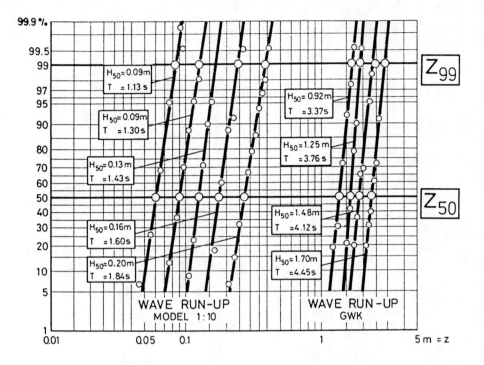

Figure 23. Examples of probability distributions for wave run-up in the model and in the prototype, large wave channel (GWK) [16a].

The corrected run-up is

$$R = (1.14)(6.15) = 7.0 \text{ ft} (2.1 \text{ m}) \tag{49}$$

Investigation by Führböter. Führböter [16a] compared the model and prototype values of run-up (Figure 23) and found the data to agree with a log-normal distribution function. A comparison of experimental data with Wassing's equation indicates the validity of Froude's Law (Figure 24). It should be noted that Wassing's equation neglects the influence of wavelength (or wave period).

$$R = 8 \frac{H_s}{m} = Z_w \tag{50}$$

where H_s = significant wave height

m = slope, i.e., 1 on m

Z_w = run-up calculated from Wassing's equation

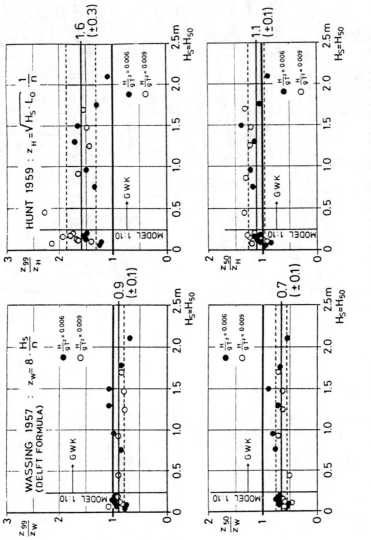

Figure 24. Wave run-up as function of wave height $H_s \sim H_{50}$ [16a].

Hunt's equation includes wave period indirectly as deep-water wavelength (L_0) is part of the equation

$$Z = \frac{1}{n}\sqrt{H_s L_0} = Z_H \tag{51}$$

where Z_H = run-up calculated from Hunt's equation.

Führböter shows that the experimental data indicate higher values than those calculated, the mean value for Z_{w50} is 1.1 and for Z_{w99} is 1.6 (Figure 24). It should be noted that only one smooth slope 1:4 was used in a wave channel equipped with monochromatic waves.

However, even for monochromatic waves, there is scatter due to the stochastic processes in breaking waves. Führböter found that the wave run-up fits the log-normal distribution as shown in Figure 25 and states that Wassing formula shows good agreement with model and prototype results.

Investigation by Goto and Shuto. Goto and Shuto [21] solved the linear and non-linear sets of equations of long waves in the Lagrangian description to obtain run-up heights. The computed values of run-up agreed fairly well with the recorded run-up in Okkirai Bay in Japan. The proposed method may be used to predict run-up caused by tsunamis.

Ogawa and Shuto [62] presented a method for calculation of run-up of periodic waves on gentle and non-uniform slopes.

The relative run-up on a uniform slope may be computed using the Lagrangian description:

$$\frac{R}{H_i} = \left[J_0^2\left(4\pi\frac{\ell}{L_i}\right) + J_1^2\left(4\pi\frac{\ell}{L_i}\right) \right]^{-1/2} \tag{52}$$

where H_i = incident wave height
   L_i = incident wavelength
   J_0 = Bessel function of the zeroth order
   J_1 = Bessel function of the first order
   ℓ = horizontal length between the toe of the slope and the shoreline

As $L \to \infty$, the equation reduces for non-breaking waves to

$$\frac{R}{H_i} = \sqrt{\frac{\pi\sigma}{s}}\left(\frac{d_1}{g}\right)^{1/4} \tag{53}$$

where σ = angular frequency
   s = offshore slope angle
   h_1 = water depth at the change of slope (see Figures 26–28).

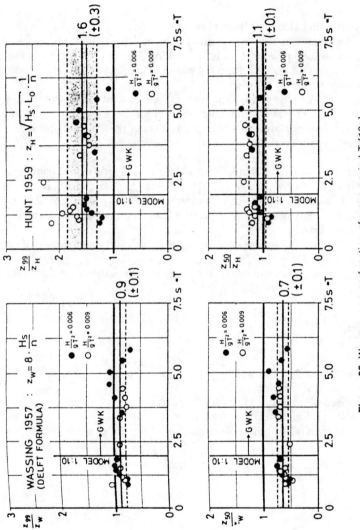

Figure 25. Wave run-up as function of wave period T [16a].

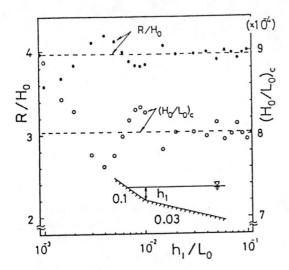

Figure 26. Numerical examples of run-up height and breaking condition of standing waves (bi-linear sloped beach) [62].

If the incident wave height, H_i, is replaced by the deep-water wave height, H_0, Equation 53 is reduced to

$$\frac{R}{H_0} = \sqrt{\frac{\pi}{2s}} \tag{54}$$

which is similar to Miche's [58] equation.

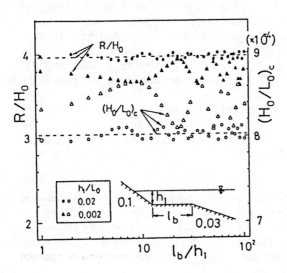

Figure 27. Numerical examples of run-up height and breaking conditions of standing waves (step-type beach) [62].

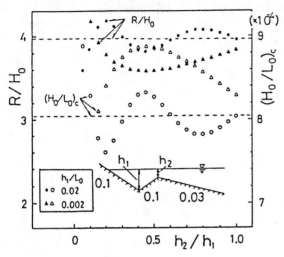

Figure 28. Numerical examples of run-up height and breaking condition of standing waves (bar-type beach) [62].

Similarly, the breaking condition may be derived, which is also analogous to Miche's [57] result.

$$\left(\frac{H_0}{L_0}\right)_{critical} = \sqrt{\frac{2s}{\pi}} \frac{s^2}{\pi} \tag{55}$$

Solutions were obtained by Ogawa and Shuto for different composite beaches as shown in Table 10, and are found to be dependent on foreshore slopes. Regarding breaking waves, the width of the swash zone and run-up height are obtained for relatively gentle slopes ($<1:30$) by dividing the transformation of waves into dissipation and swash processes. The width of the swash zone is mainly determined by the foreshore slope and wave period. For gentle uniform slopes between 1:10 to 1:100, the authors' formula may be used in place of Hunt's formula.

Comparison between the numerical calculations and experimental data for run-up on a uniform slope is shown in Figure 29, and for non-uniform slope in Figure 30.

Run-Up from Irregular Waves

The maximum run-up from irregular waves may be estimated using a method proposed by Ahrens [1a]. The run-up for irregular waves is assumed to follow a Rayleigh distribution.

Investigation by Mase and Iwagaki. Mase and Iwagaki [56] have investigated the run-up of random waves on flat slopes. On such slopes the cycle of run-up and run-down may be longer than the wave period and the waves running down the slope will affect the next wave run-up. The run-up of random waves will also depend on the characteristics of the incoming waves and on the groupiness of incident

Table 10

Solutions of Run-Up Height and Breaking Condition of Standing Waves [62]

$$\frac{R}{H_0} = \frac{1}{Z}\sqrt{\frac{\pi}{2s}} \qquad \left(\frac{H_0}{L_0}\right)_{cr} = z\sqrt{\frac{2s}{\pi}}\,\frac{m^2}{\pi} \qquad J_0, J_1, N_0, N_1;$$

Bessel and Neumann Function of the Zeroth and the First Order

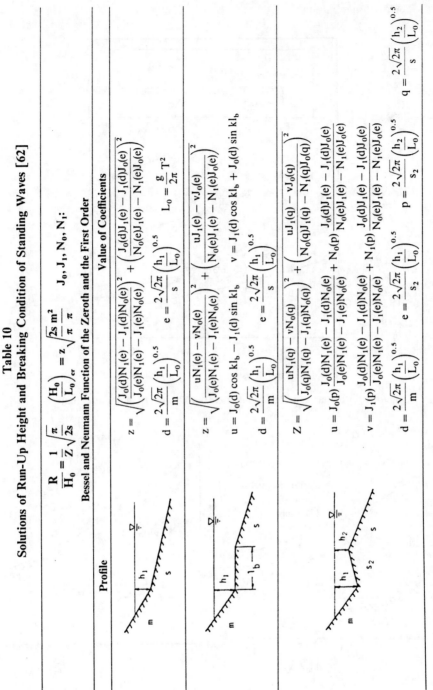

Profile	Value of Coefficients

$$z = \sqrt{\left(\frac{J_0(d)N_1(e) - J_1(d)N_0(e)}{J_0(e)N_1(e) - J_1(e)N_0(e)}\right)^2 + \left(\frac{J_0(d)J_1(e) - J_1(d)J_0(e)}{N_0(e)J_1(e) - N_1(e)J_0(e)}\right)^2}$$

$$d = \frac{2\sqrt{2\pi}}{m}\left(\frac{h_1}{L_0}\right)^{0.5} \qquad e = \frac{2\sqrt{2\pi}}{s}\left(\frac{h_1}{L_0}\right)^{0.5} \qquad L_0 = \frac{g}{2\pi}T^2$$

$$z = \sqrt{\left(\frac{uN_1(e) - vN_0(e)}{J_0(e)N_1(e) - J_1(e)N_0(e)}\right)^2 + \left(\frac{uJ_1(e) - vJ_0(e)}{N_0(e)J_1(e) - N_1(e)J_0(e)}\right)^2}$$

$$u = J_0(d)\cos kl_b - J_1(d)\sin kl_b \qquad v = J_1(d)\cos kl_b + J_0(d)\sin kl_b$$

$$d = \frac{2\sqrt{2\pi}}{m}\left(\frac{h_1}{L_0}\right)^{0.5} \qquad e = \frac{2\sqrt{2\pi}}{s}\left(\frac{h_1}{L_0}\right)^{0.5}$$

$$Z = \sqrt{\left(\frac{uN_1(q) - vN_0(q)}{J_0(q)N_1(q) - J_1(q)N_0(q)}\right)^2 + \left(\frac{uJ_1(q) - vJ_0(q)}{N_0(q)J_1(q) - N_1(q)J_0(q)}\right)^2}$$

$$u = J_0(p)\frac{J_0(d)N_1(e) - J_1(d)N_0(e)}{J_0(e)N_1(e) - J_1(e)N_0(e)} + N_0(p)\frac{J_0(d)J_1(e) - J_1(d)J_0(e)}{N_0(e)J_1(e) - N_1(e)J_0(e)}$$

$$v = J_1(p)\frac{J_0(d)N_1(e) - J_1(d)N_0(e)}{J_0(e)N_1(e) - J_1(e)N_0(e)} + N_1(p)\frac{J_0(d)J_1(e) - J_1(d)J_0(e)}{N_0(e)J_1(e) - N_1(e)J_0(e)}$$

$$d = \frac{2\sqrt{2\pi}}{m}\left(\frac{h_1}{L_0}\right)^{0.5} \qquad e = \frac{2\sqrt{2\pi}}{s_2}\left(\frac{h_1}{L_0}\right)^{0.5} \qquad p = \frac{2\sqrt{2\pi}}{s_2}\left(\frac{h_2}{L_0}\right)^{0.5} \qquad q = \frac{2\sqrt{2\pi}}{s}\left(\frac{h_2}{L_0}\right)^{0.5}$$

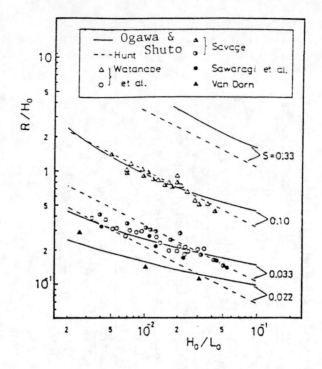

Figure 29. Comparison of calculated R/H_0 with experimental data [62].

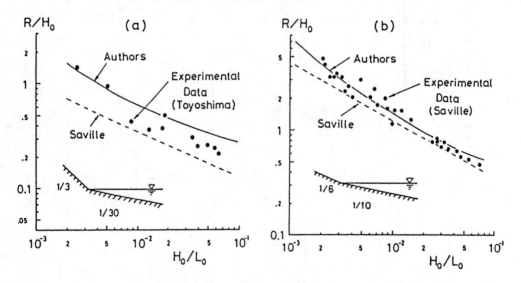

Figure 30. Comparison between Saville's method and Ogawa and Shuto's [62].

Table 11
Experimental Formulas for Run-Up Heights of Random Waves
($R_{1/3}$ = Significant Run-Up, R = Average Run-Up) [56]

(a) $\dfrac{R}{H_0} = \alpha(\tan\theta)^b(H_0/L_0)^c$

	Crest Method				Zero-Up-Cross Method			
	α	b	c	σ	α	b	c	σ
R_{max}	2.565	0.783	-0.367	0.151	2.565	0.783	-0.367	0.151
$R_{1/3}$	1.308	0.696	-0.361	0.095	1.375	0.686	-0.363	0.088
$\bar{R}$	0.946	0.697	-0.330	0.072	0.992	0.668	-0.356	0.079

(b) $\dfrac{R}{H_0} = d\left(\dfrac{\tan\theta}{\sqrt{H_0/L_0}}\right)^e$

	Crest Method			Zero-Up-Cross Method		
R_{max}	2.319	0.771	0.159	2.319	0.771	0.159
$R_{1/3}$	1.378	0.702	0.094	1.497	0.695	0.086
$\bar{R}$	0.878	0.688	0.074	1.085	0.678	0.077

waves in deep water. On flat slopes the number of run-up waves is generally less than the number of incident waves because of the run-down wave interference with the running-up waves.

Mase and Iwagaki proposed two equations for computing wave run-up:

$$\frac{R}{H_0} = a(\tan\theta)^b(H_0/L_0)^c \tag{56}$$

$$\frac{R}{H_0} = d\left(\frac{\tan\theta}{\sqrt{H_0/L_0}}\right)^e \tag{57}$$

where θ = beach slope
a, b, c, d, e = coefficients

The coefficients are based on the experimental data for wave steepness greater than 0.008 for the 1:5 beach slope and larger than 0.005 for the 1:20 and 1:30 beach slopes. Table 11 summarizes the coefficients for the crest method and for the zero up-crossing method defined in Figure 31.

Investigation by Tautenhain. Tautenhain, et al. [78b] investigated the run-up for waves approaching the slope at an angle. Employing the energy conservation concept and assuming that the energy of an incident monochromatic wave $\tilde{E}$ can be equated with the energy E of an equivalent spectrum wave Tautenhain and

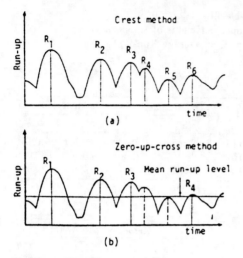

(a)

(b)

Figure 31. Definition method of run-up waves [56].

Kohlhase [78a] proposed that

$$E_{pot_{A_n}} = 2(\psi)\tilde{E}_{pot_{A_n}} - E_{pot_{A_{n-1}}} \tag{58}$$

where A_n = wave run-up of the wave n of a time series
A_{n-1} = run-up of the pertinent previous wave
ψ = form parameter (found experimentally to be between 0.63 and 0.73 with an average value of 0.7).

The run-up A_n is given as:

$$A_n = \tilde{A}_n \sqrt[3]{2(\psi) - \left(\tilde{A}_{n-1} \middle/ \frac{1}{A_n}\right)^3} \tag{59}$$

The wave run-up $\tilde{A}_n$ is

$$\tilde{A}_n = 1.29\sqrt{HL_0}(1 - C_R')/\cos\alpha \tag{60}$$

where C_R' = reflection coefficient.

The run-up for wave approach angle, β, is given as

$$\tilde{A}_\beta = \tilde{A}_n \bar{k}_\beta \tag{61}$$

where $k_\beta = \dfrac{\tilde{A}_\beta}{\tilde{A}_n} = \cos\beta \sqrt[3]{2 - \cos^3 2\beta}$ (62)

It will be noted that k_β includes both the refraction and friction effects, as well as the angle of the running-down wave in relation to the running-up wave. The relative

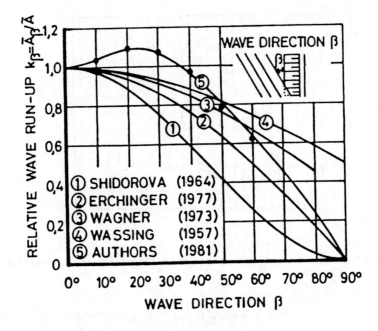

Figure 32. Relative wave run-up. Summation of results for different angles of wave approach, β [78].

run-up, k_β, is plotted as a function of the angle of wave direction, β, from several investigators in Figure 32. The magnitude of run-up is greater for the approach wave angle, β, between the values of 0 and 35°. Because the maximum increase is about 10%, this effect should be considered in design.

Grüne [22a] conducted field measurements of run-up at two locations in the German Bight. A sample comparison of log-normal distributions of waves and wave run-up is shown in Figure 33. The ratios of maximum run-up (R_{max}), 1/100 run-up ($R_{1/100}$), 1/10 run-up ($R_{1/10}$), significant run-up ($R_{1/3}$) and 98% (R_{98}), 95% (R_{95}) and 90% (R_{90}) to average run-up (R_m) are shown in Table 12 for three locations (Wangerooge—beach slope 1:4, Eiderdamm—beach slopes 1:4 and 1:6).

In general, wave run-up measured at these two locations was higher than that predicted by the existing formulas. A comparison of field data with the run-up predicted was based on equation for 98% run-up

$$R_{98} = C(T_m)\sqrt{H_s g}\left(\frac{1}{N}\right) \tag{63}$$

Empirical coefficient C varied from 0.53 to 1.14 at two different locations. Comparisons with studies conducted by Van Oorschot and d'Angremond [80a], Battjes [3a] and Tautenhain are given in Table 13.

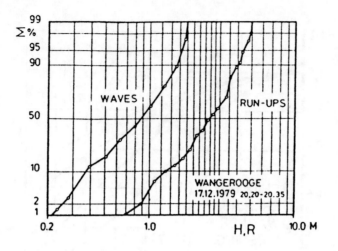

Figure 33. Log-normal distribution of waves and run-ups for one record [22a].

Table 12
Ratios of Statistical Values of Wave Run-Up [22a]

Location	$\dfrac{R_{max}}{RM^*}$	$\dfrac{R_{1/100}}{RM}$	$\dfrac{R_{1/10}}{RM}$	$\dfrac{R_{1/3}}{RM}$	$\dfrac{R_{98}}{RM}$	$\dfrac{R_{95}}{RM}$	$\dfrac{R_{90}}{RM}$
Wangerooge N = 4	2.06	1.90	1.66	1.39	1.75	1.60	1.46
Eiderdamm N = 4	1.97	1.97	1.63	1.38	1.69	1.60	1.43
N = 6	1.90	1.86	1.58	1.34	1.69	1.57	1.40

* RM = mean value of run-up

Table 13
Comparison of Empirical Factors C [22a]

	C	
Van Oorschot/D'Angremond	0.60 to 0.77	$\hat{T}/T_m = 1.05$
Battjes	0.59 to 0.74	analytical model based on Rayleigh-distribution
Tautenhain	0.70 to 0.86	not comparable directly, based on wave distribution
Grüne	0.53 to 1.14	2 different locations

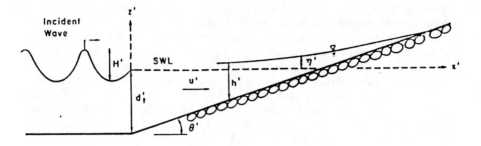

Figure 34. Normally-incident wave train on rough slope [48].

Field Measurements by Holman and Guza. Holman and Guza [32] conducted field experiments to evaluate two methods for measuring run-up on natural beaches, resistance wire sensors and films. Use of the film and resistance sensors showed small differences in the mean set-up elevation (swash elevation), but an 83% difference in swash variance. Both dual resistance wire and time-lapse photography appear to be good methods for measuring wave run-up on natural beaches; each has its advantages and disadvantages.

Numerical Model by Kobayashi and Greenwald. Kobayashi and Greenwald [48] developed a numerical model to predict wave motion on a rough, impermeable slope.

Limiting to the case of a normally-incident wave train on the rough impermeable slope shown in Figure 34, the finite-amplitude, shallow-water equations including the effects of bottom friction may be written as

$$\frac{\partial h'}{\partial t'} + \frac{\partial}{\partial x'}(h'u') = 0 \tag{64}$$

$$\frac{\partial}{\partial t'}(h'u') + \frac{\partial}{\partial x'}(h'u'^2) = -gh'\frac{\partial \eta'}{\partial x'} - \frac{\tau_b'}{\rho} \tag{65}$$

where t' = time
  x' = horizontal coordinate at the still water level (SWL), which is taken to be positive in the landward direction with $x' = 0$ at the toe of the slope
  h' = water depth below the free surface
  u' = depth-averaged horizontal velocity
  g = gravitational acceleration
  η' = vertical displacement of the free surface relative to SWL
  r_b' = bottom shear stress
  ρ = fluid density, which is assumed constant neglecting the effects of air entrainment

The bottom shear stress may be expressed as

$$\tau_b' = \tfrac{1}{2}\rho f'|u'|u' \tag{66}$$

where f' = friction factor associated with the rough impermeable slope, which is simply assumed constant. It should be noted that f' will depend on h' if Manning formula is used to express r_b [63b, 63c]. The empirical formula proposed by Madsen and White [55a] has been found satisfactory in estimating the constant value of f' for riprap slopes although additional calibration may be required [48a].

If the permeability of the underlayer below armor units is not negligible, the flow over the rough permeable bottom and the flow in the permeable underlayer are coupled through the mass and momentum fluxes between these two flow regions. Since Kobayashi assumed an impermeable layer, the numerical model is not applicable to permeable breakwaters.

Denoting the characteristic period and height associated with the normally-incident wave train by T' and H', respectively, the following dimensionless variables are introduced

$$t = \frac{t'}{T'}, \qquad x = \frac{x'}{T'\sqrt{gN'}}, \qquad u = \frac{u'}{\sqrt{gH'}} \tag{67}$$

$$z = \frac{z'}{H'}, \qquad h = \frac{h'}{H'}, \qquad \eta = \frac{\eta'}{H'}, \qquad d_t = \frac{d_t'}{H'} \tag{68}$$

where   z' = vertical coordinate, which is taken to be positive upward in which z' = 0
at SWL as shown in Figure 34
d_t' = water depth below SWL where the incident wave train may be specified
conveniently

Limiting to the case where the incident wave train is well-behaved without any breaking at the toe of the slope, d_t' is taken to be the water depth below SWL at the toe of the slope as shown in Figure 34. Substitution of Equations 66 through 68 into Equations 64 and 65 yields

$$\frac{\partial h}{\partial t} + \frac{\partial}{\partial x}(hu) = 0 \tag{69}$$

$$\frac{\partial}{\partial t}(hu) + \frac{\partial}{\partial x}\left(hu^2 + \frac{h^2}{2}\right) = -\theta h - f|u|u \tag{70}$$

with

$$f = \frac{1}{2}\sigma f', \qquad \sigma = T'\sqrt{\frac{g}{H'}} \tag{71}$$

$$\theta = \sqrt{2\pi}\,\xi, \qquad \xi = \frac{1}{\sqrt{2\pi}}\,\sigma \tan\theta' \tag{72}$$

Equations 69 and 70 are solved numerically in the time domain to compute h and u as a function of t and x for given θ (i.e., ξ), f, initial and boundary conditions. The initial conditions for h and u are taken such that h = normalized depth below SWL (i.e., $\eta = 0$) and u = 0 at t = 0 for the region x ≥ 0 on the rough slope, corresponding to the conditions before the arrival of the incident wave train at the toe of the slope. In general, the computation in the time domain can incorporate nonlinear effects easily relative to the computation in the frequency domain. However, for the incident regular wave train, the time-domain computation starting from the assumed initial conditions at t = 0 needs to be continued until the state of periodicity is reached. For the computation made by Kobayashi et al. [48, 48a] the transient duration has been limited to the relatively short duration 0 ≤ t ≤ 5 where the normalized period of the incident regular wave train is unity. Furthermore, the time-domain computation will become expensive if the number of individual waves in an incident irregular wave train becomes large.

The landward boundary on the rough slope is located at the moving waterline where the water depth h is essentially zero, assuming that no wave overtopping occurs.

Extreme Run-up Statistics on Natural Beaches

Investigation by Holman [32a]. Holman examined wave run-up maxima from experiments conducted on a natural beach. Wave characteristics ranged from 0.4- to 4.0-m wave heights and from 6- to 16-sec wave periods. Beach face slopes ranged from 0.07 to 0.20. Four extreme value statistics of run-up were calculated.:

1. maximum shoreline elevation height, η_{max}
2. 2% exceedance height of run-up, η_2
3. 2% exceedance height for the run-up heights associated with individual run-up peaks, R_2
4. 2% exceedance height for swash range for the individual swashes (defined by the zero up-crossing method), S_2

Holman found that the run-up data best plotted on dimensionless basis as a function of Iribarren number, $\xi = \beta/\sqrt{H/L_0}$, Figure 35. ($\hat{\eta}_{max} = \eta_{max}/H$, $\hat{\eta}_2 = \eta_2/H$, $\hat{R}_2 = R_2/H$, and $\hat{S}_2 = S_2/H$ in Figures 35 and 36).

The extreme swash data were also plotted as a function of Iribarren number in Figure 36. Holman concludes that for Iribarren number greater than 1.5, the run-up was dominated by the incident frequencies, while the longer period motions dominated the swash at lower Iribarren numbers.

Investigation by Resio. Resio [64] presented a method for estimating maximum run-up elevation on a natural sand beach during a storm. Extensive data obtained by Holman [32a] on the Atlantic coast and San Francisco Bay data obtained by Carlson [9] were used in Resio's analysis.

The run-up and incident conditions may be linked by Hunt's equation

$$\frac{R}{H} = \frac{\tan \beta}{\sqrt{H/L}} \tag{73}$$

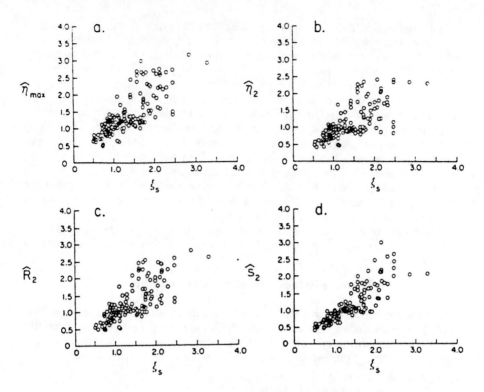

Figure 35. Extreme value run-up statistics normalized by the incident significant wave height, plotted as a function of the Iribarren number, ξ_s [32a].

where R, H, and L are arbitrary run-up parameters, wave height and wave length parameters, respectively, β is a beach slope angle.

Holman used a R_2 parameter defined as

$$\hat{R}_2 = \frac{R_2}{H_{m_0}} \tag{74}$$

where R_2 = run-up exceeded by only 2% of all run-ups
        H_{m_0} = zero-moment wave height

Figure 37 shows a typical relative run-up.

Because each individual run-up is related to incident wave parameters H_{m_0} and T_m in a probabilistic fashion, the relationship between distribution of individual run-ups and incident wave parameters may be written in a condition probability statement.

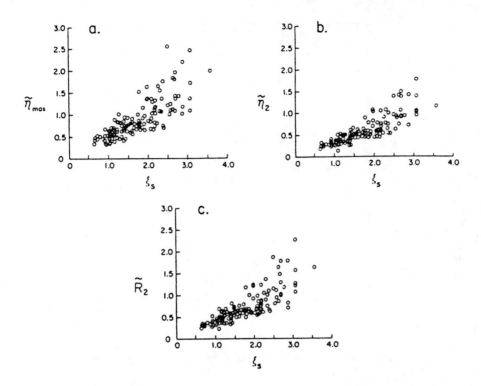

Figure 36. Extreme swash statistics, normalized by incident significant wave height, as a function of the Iribarren number, ξ_s. The swash statistics were calculated by subtracting the set-up from the corresponding run-up statistical measure. There is no plot for S_2 since that measure had already excluded the set-up [32a].

Resio, following the procedure derived by Borgman [6], wrote an integral for the expected largest run-up during the entire storm as

$$F_e(R_i) = 1 - \exp\left\{\int_0^t \ln[P_t(R_i)]\,\frac{dt}{\bar{T}}\right\} \tag{75}$$

where subscript e = the non-exceedance frequency is for an entire event
$\qquad P_t(R_i)$ = non-exceedance probability defined as $P_t(R_i) = 1 - F_t(R_i)$
$\qquad F_t(R_i)$ = cumulative frequency distribution F of individual run-ups in
$\qquad\qquad$ terms of a conditional probability, i.e.
$\qquad F_t(R_i) = f_t(R_i/\epsilon)p(\epsilon)$
$\qquad\qquad \bar{T}$ = mean period of run-ups

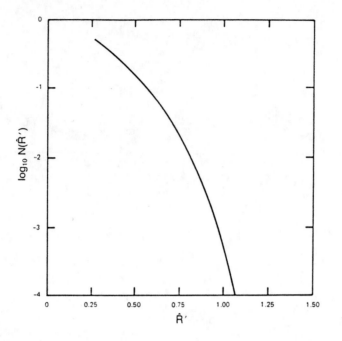

Figure 37. Plot of extremal distribution for expected run-ups [64].

For a complete set of the parameters, a vector $\underline{\epsilon}$ consisting of all parameters influencing the statistical properties of run-up may be expressed as follows:

$$\underline{\epsilon} = (H_{m_0}, T_m, \bar{\theta}, \eta, \beta)$$

where H_{m_0} = zero-moment wave height
T_m = spectral peak period
$\bar{\theta}$ = mean wave direction at the location where H_{m_0} and T_m are obtained
η = mean water level (MWL) (MWT + tide + surge + setup)
β = beach slope angle

Equation 75 can be used in a discretized form in a numerical integration scheme over a storm, i.e.

$$F_e(R_i) = 1 - \exp\left\{\sum_{k=1}^{n} \ln\left[1 - F_{t_k}(R_i)\right]\frac{\Delta t_k}{\bar{T}_k}\right\} \tag{76}$$

where $\dfrac{\Delta t_k}{\bar{T}_k}$ = number of run-ups in the k-th time increment

Accurate estimate of the cumulative distribution function is of importance in determining extreme run-ups. Resio recommends that asymptotic methods should be used rather than theoretical forms such as the Weibull distribution. A generalized extreme value (GEV) may be used to provide good estimate of expected sample extremes. Jenkinson [39a] showed that the three asymptotic limiting forms for extremal distribution may be written as

$$x = x_0 + \alpha\left(\frac{1 - e^{-ky}}{k}\right) \tag{77}$$

where x_0, α, y, and k are parameters in Jenkinson's form of GEV distribution.

For $k = 0$, Equation 66 reduces to asymptote I (called the Gumbel or Fisher-Tippett Type I distribution)

$$x = x_0 + \alpha y \tag{78}$$

For asymptote II, k is negative (Frechet or Fisher-Tippett Type II distribution); for asymptote III, k is positive (Weibull or Fisher-Tippett Type III distribution).

Given values of x_0, α, and k in Jenkinson's equation, a parametric relationship between the value x and return period is

$$x = x_0 + \frac{\alpha}{k} - \frac{\alpha}{k}e^{-ky} \tag{79}$$

where y is a function of return period, or

$$y = -\ln\left[\ln\left(\frac{T}{T-1}\right)\right] \tag{80}$$

Note that $y > 10\ y \approx \ln(T - \frac{1}{2})$.

The equation for the expected extremal values for a given run-up can be given as

$$\hat{R}' = 0.20 + 0.20\left[\frac{1 - \exp(-0.19y)}{0.19}\right] \tag{81}$$

where $y = -\ln\left[\ln\left(\frac{T}{T-1}\right)\right]$ (82)

T = return period given in terms of number of waves

$$= \frac{1}{1 - F(x)} = \frac{1}{N(x)} \tag{83}$$

Using the definition of T, any value of $N(x)$ can be substituted to obtain a corresponding value of $\hat{R}'$. Figure 37 is a plot of extremal distribution for expected run-ups, Figure 38 shows a plot of $\hat{R}$, as a function of $\tan \beta/\sqrt{H_{mo}/L_0}$, and Figures

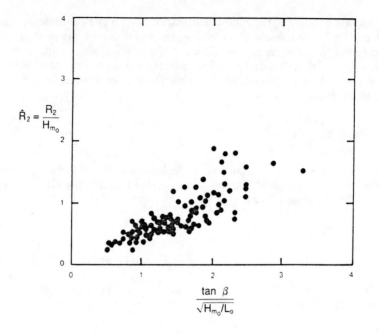

$$\hat{R}_2 = \frac{R_2}{H_{m_0}}$$

$$\frac{\tan \beta}{\sqrt{H_{m_0}/L_0}}$$

Figure 38. Plot of $\hat{R}_2$ versus $\tan \beta/\sqrt{H_{m_0}/L_0}$ [32].

39 and 40 show $\hat{R}_2$ as a function of $\tan \beta/\sqrt{H_{m_0}/L_0}$ obtained by Holman for two locations.

The Alameda Beach Data. Although additional data from other beaches will be needed to verify the proposed method, the indications are that the relationships between wave and run-up parameters based on Holman's data are also valid for other natural beaches.

Run-up on Vertical and Inclined Cylinders

Haney and Herbich [23] studied run-up on model cylinders in the laboratory. A wave that interacts with a vertical cylinder experiences a transformation, resulting in a water-level increase in front of the pile that is generally known as run-up or up-rush. Concurrently, a cavity known as draw-down or down-rush is formed behind the pile.

Haney's and Herbich's study concentrated on wave flow around thin single piles, pile groups, and inclined piles. A thin pile is a cylinder with its diameter, D, much less than a wavelength, L.

The study of wave run-up on vertical cylinders is of interest to basic research, but also has several practical applications. The American Petroleum Institute RP 2A (1) [3] states that wave run-up must be considered when determining the appropriate

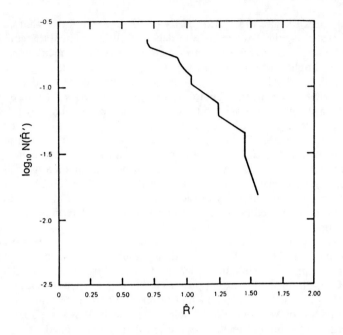

Figure 39. Plot of Alameda Beach data from analysis of the Carlson data [64].

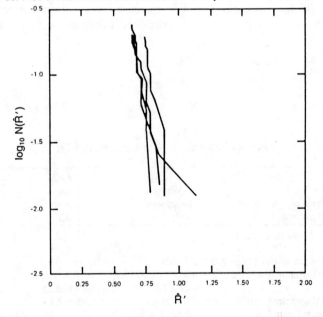

Figure 40. Plot of Coyote Point data from analysis of the Carlson data [64].

deck clearances on offshore platforms to avoid the large forces that could result from waves striking the platform's lower deck and the equipment thereon. However, no recommendations are presented on which to base run-up calculations. As a consequence, a simplification is used in which a small percentage of the water depth, such as 10%, is added to the design crest height and the water depth. To avoid these problems, an accurate calculation of run-up is necessary. Run-up and drawdown can have significant effects on the wave forces encountered by piles.

Another practical application of the results of run-up studies is its use as a device to record wave direction. For single piles, the maximum water level pattern is symmetrical about the direction of wave approach. James and Hallermeier [24] have completed a study in which they considered using this characteristic as a means of recording predominant wave directions in the nearshore zone. Such a device is needed in this zone for the study of sediment transport. This investigation showed that such a device is definitely an accurate method for determining predominant wave direction.

The first study of wave patterns in connection with single cylinders was conducted by Omer and Hall [63] as they studied the result of the tsunami of April 1946 around the periphery of the island of Kauai (Hawaii). Since then, several laboratory studies of run-up on single vertical piles have been conducted as outlined in Table 14. The first five studies of Table 14 had results in good agreement with the linear scattering theory of MacCamy and Fuchs [54], which is an exact solution for the linear scattering of infinitesimal, long-crested water waves incident on a circular vertical pile. Ignoring viscous effects, they found that theoretically the peak water level at the pile depends linearly on the incident wave height for a given scattering parameter, $ka = 2\pi a/L$. They used potential flow theory to derive the expression:

$$W(\alpha) = \frac{H}{2}[1 + (2ka \cos \alpha)^2]^{1/2} \sin(\sigma t - \psi) \tag{84}$$

Table 14
Previous Laboratory Run-Up Studies [23]

Principal Investigator(s)	Wave Steepness H/L	Relative Water Depth D/L	Scattering Parameter $ka = 2\pi a/L$
Hellstrom and Rundgren [28]	0.7	0.12–0.25	0.6–1.3
Laird [49]	0.03	0.1–0.25	0.7–1.7
Bonnefille and Germaine [5]	0.04	0.6–0.9	0.7–1.1
Tsuchiya and Yamaguchi [79]	0.003–0.3	0.3	0.6–4.0
Nagai [61]	0.017–0.055	0.21–0.62	1.05–3.1
Galvin and Hallermeier [18]	0.008–0.4	0.05–0.13	0.09–0.2
Chakrabarti and Tam [11]	0.009–0.06	0.11–0.50	0.34–1.55
Hallermeier [24]	0.006–0.06	0.05–0.13	0.023–0.5

for small values of ka,

where $k = 2\pi/L$
$\quad\quad\quad t = $ time
$\quad\quad\quad H = $ wave height
$\quad\quad\quad a = $ radius
$\quad\quad\quad W(\alpha) = $ water height above still water level for the cylinder for a given orientation angle from the front of the pile α
$\quad\quad\quad \sigma = 2\pi/T$
$\quad\quad\quad \psi = \tan^{-1}(2ka \cos \alpha)$
$\quad\quad\quad T = $ wave period

This expression was derived assuming a sinusoidal wave form (linear wave theory). The run-up ratio at the front of the pile is

$$\frac{W(\alpha)}{P} = [1 + 4(ka)^2]^{1/2} \tag{85}$$

where $P = $ incident crest height

Hellstrom and Rundgren [28] conducted a study on a pile surrounded by a submarine slope. Their results are essentially in agreement with those of Laird [49] for similar waves. Laird based his comparison on the work of Wiener [86] who investigated the diffraction of sound by circular cylinders. Wiener was the first to tabulate the theoretical distribution of pressure around a cylinder for several values of ka between 0.5 and 10.

In the first five studies of Table 14, the scattering parameter, ka, is always greater than 0.6. Of more interest to the present study are the three latest studies, because these tests are more in the scattering parameter range of the present tests. All three of these tests report peak water levels much higher than that predicted by linear scattering theory. They are in the range where viscous effects play an important role in the interaction between piles and waves.

Galvin and Hallermeier [18] used several different pile shapes to investigate run-up. Included in these shapes are circular cylinders, finned cylinders, H-beams, and flat plates. The results obtained were consistent with the hypothesis that run-up on the front of a pile is the velocity head of the water particle in the wave crest. Calculation of the velocity head by linear or solitary wave theory gave run-up values that were within a factor of 2 observed values.

Conservation of mass requires minima somewhere between $\alpha = 0°$ and $\alpha = 180°$ due to the existence of the two maxima. As P increases, the minima shifted more toward 180° and their position seemed to be related to the separation points on the circular cylinder. Galvin and Hallmeier [18] suggested that the symmetry of the maximum water-level distribution be used to determine wave direction and that the results be used in interpreting wave-height statistics from surface-piercing wave gauges. Data obtained from step-resistance wave gauges can overrepresent the high waves, perhaps causing an over-conservative design.

Chakrabarti and Tam [11] employed a cylindrical tank 6.77 ft (2.06 m) in diameter to show that for the lowest values of ka, run-up varies with increasing wave height for the same value of the scattering parameter. This means that for some of the tests nonlinear scattering occurred. In this study, the maximum water level was found to vary largely with the period. They postulated that this contradiction with the work of Galvin and Hallermeier [18] was due to the differences in the scattering parameters, to which the distribution is sensitive. They suggested that as long as ka is less than 0.2, the wave-height distribution is almost independent of period. As the scattering parameter increases beyond 0.2, the distribution changes in shape.

Hallermeier tests with ka = 0.5 resulted in an excellent agreement with the linear scattering theory of MacCamy and Fuchs [54] and the theoretical values of Wiener [86], however, the tests with ka = 0.06 show a significant departure from linear scattering theory. Hallermeier noted that with small values of ka and large wave heights, viscous effects become dominant and linear scattering theory is no longer applicable. In this situation, flow separation occurs [71] along with the generation of a scattered wave by the pile.

Hallermeier concluded that when the Froude number ($F = U^2/2ga$, where U = maximum horizontal water particle velocity and g = acceleration due to gravity) is

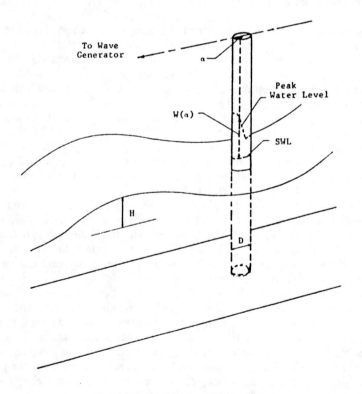

Figure 41. Test setup for Part I [23].

significant compared to unity, nonlinear transformations will occur. These nonlinear processes occurring near peak crest flow result in a momentary stagnation of the flow. The velocity head, as computed by McCowan solitary wave theory, gave a fairly good upper bound for the increase in water level at the pile's front. The waves with the largest d/L gave the lowest run-up compared to calculations, while those with smaller d/L have the best agreement. Hallermeier suggested that this might be due to the uncertainty involved in the velocity calculations and suggested the use of stream function wave theory might give a better correlation.

Test Procedures

The testing was divided into two major parts. Part I included tests using simple piles with two different diameters: 0.062 ft (0.019 m) and 0.100 ft (0.031 m). The test setup for Part I is shown in Figure 41. Part I also included tests on inclined single piles with a diameter of 0.100 ft (0.031 m) as shown in Figure 42. Part II included tests on groups of three piles with varying wave approach angle, θ, and various spacings, s, as shown in Figure 43. All tests were conducted in the Texas A&M University Hydromechanics Laboratories' two-dimensional wave tank, which is 120 ft (36.6 m) long by 2.0 ft (0.61 m) wide by 3.0 ft (0.91 m) deep. The waves were

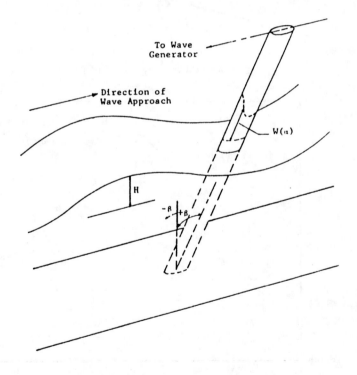

Figure 42. Test setup for inclined piles [23].

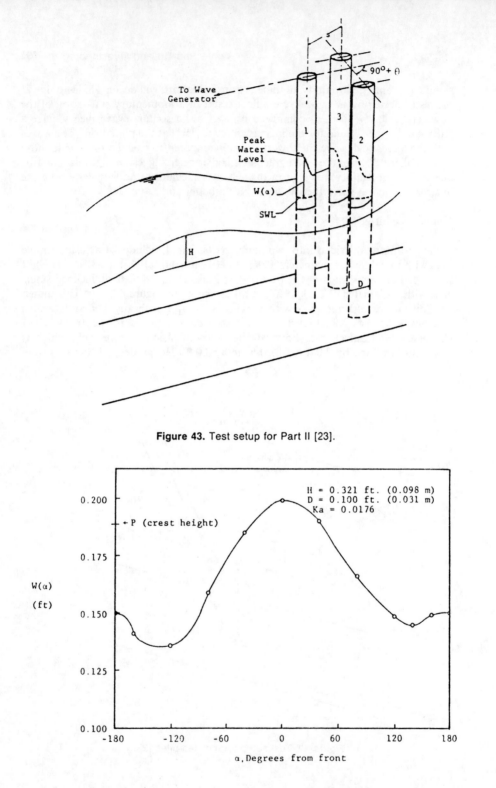

Figure 43. Test setup for Part II [23].

Figure 44. Non-normalized wave profile for a single pile [23].

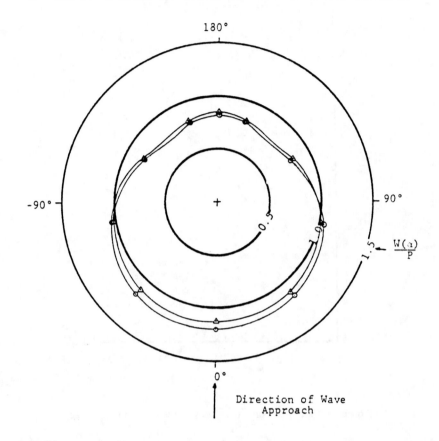

⊙   Run 23   D=0.100 ft. (0.031 m)   H = 0.440 ft. (0.134 m)
△   Run 24   D=0.062 ft. (0.019 m)   H = 0.410 ft. (0.125 m)

Figure 45. Normalized polar plot of the wave profiles for two single piless [23].

generated by a pendulum-type wave generator and a wave height was measured using a parallel-wire (capacitance) wave gauge beside the test pile(s).

The maximum water level around the pile(s) was recorded using a paper sleeve for about ten successive waves, Rhodamine-W dye, which is red in color, was added to the tank water to mark the graph paper sleeve. The dye left a permanent record of the maximum water levels. The water level, $W(\alpha)$, on the paper sleeves was determined by measuring the difference in elevation between the still water level and the dye markings. Figure 44 is the crest height. A normalized plot of two other runs is shown in Figure 45. From both plots it can be seen that the front maximum due to the stagnation of the crest velocity, is much more pronounced than the maximum caused by stagnation of the converging flow.

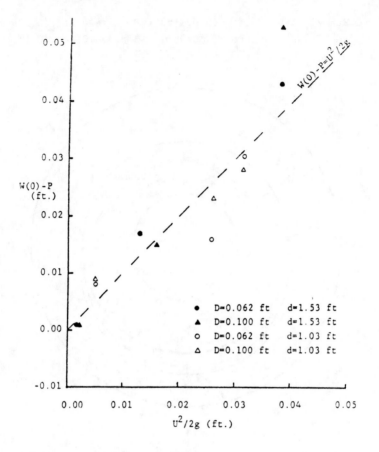

Figure 46. Plot of run-up vs. velocity head for single piles [23].

The fact that the run-up at the front is caused by stagnation of the crest flow is clearly shown in Figure 46, where the maximum run-up, $W(0) - P$, is plotted against the maximum velocity head, $U^2/2g$, at the crest (P is the incident crest height). The velocity U was computed using Dean's fifth-order stream-function wave theory, because this theory best suited the test conditions. Figure 46 shows that for both the diameters investigated, the maximum run-up is equal to the crest stagnation head. These results are consistent with those of previous studies where $ka > 0.6$.

The average slope between $\alpha = 40°$ and $\alpha = 80°$ was found to be proportional to the Froude number up to a maximum slope of about one. Using stream function theory to calculate the Froude number, the average side slope is found to be approximately equal to the Froude number, as opposed to Hallermeier's value of 1.5 times

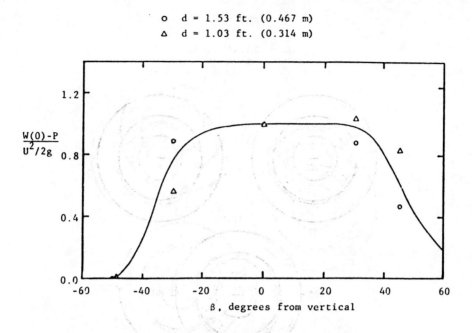

o   d = 1.53 ft. (0.467 m)
Δ   d = 1.03 ft. (0.314 m)

Figure 47. Plot of run-up vs. β for inclined, single piles [23].

the Froude number using solitary wave theory. The relationship between slope and Froude number exists because in these tests the Froude number is actually a slope.

The results of the tests on the inclined piles is shown in Figure 47 where the relative run-up as a portion of the velocity head is plotted against the angle from the vertical, β. As β either increases or decreases from its vertical position, the run-up, which is measured in the vertical direction, decreases for the same velocity head. This decrease is more sudden as β decreases, with the run-up becoming negligible at $\beta = -45°$. As β increases from zero, the significant decrease in run-up does not occur until β is about 35. The decrease for negative β is caused by the water falling away from the pile. For angles greater than about 35 the decrease is due to the water sliding off the thin pile. It should be emphasized that the curve in Figure 47 may vary for different conditions, especially for larger diameters.

The bulk of the testing involved three pile groups with a pile diameter of 0.10 ft (0.031 m). Samples of the collected data are shown in the normalized polar plots in Figures 48, 49, and 50 for the three different wave approach angles. All three figures show the same general results as for single piles. As in the case of the single piles, the run-up was plotted against the velocity head in Figures 51, 52, and 53 for the three piles as numbered in Figures 48, 49, and 50. Again, the general trend is that the maximum run-up is equal to the crest velocity head. There seems to be no consistent

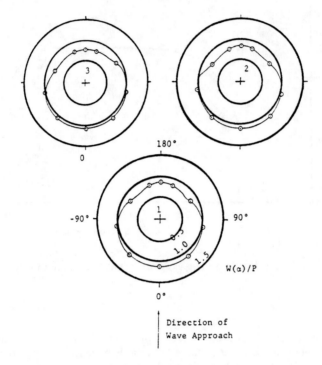

Figure 48. Normalized wave profile for the three pile groups with $\theta = 0°$ [23].

correlation between run-up and spacing, nor run-up and wave approach angle. At the smaller wave heights (smaller velocity head), there is a decrease in run-up on pile #2 (Figure 52) for $\theta = 0°$ and $\theta = 30°$ due to the blockage caused by pile no. 1. A decrease also occurs on pile no. 3 (Figure 53) for the two smallest spacings at all three wave approach angles. However, this trend does not continue into the higher waves. In some cases, the interaction of the three piles caused the rear maximum value to disappear. This occurred mostly for pile no. 1 at the smallest spacing and at $\theta = 30°$ (Figure 52) due to the interruption of the rear converging flow by pile no. 3.

This analysis has shown that even for pile groups the velocity head at the crest is an excellent measure of wave run-up. This is plotted in another form in Figure 54,

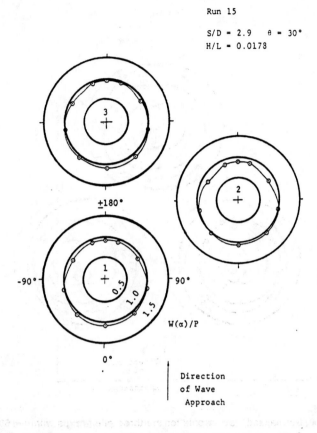

Run 15

S/D = 2.9   θ = 30°
H/L = 0.0178

Figure 49. Normalized wave profile for the three pile groups with $\theta = 30°$ [23].

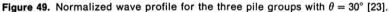

which is a combination of diffraction theory, previous laboratory tests, and this study.

The relationship between run-up and velocity head can be used for piles with scattering parameters as small as 0.0105. However, just below this value, run-up decreases rapidly as a function of the scattering parameter.

These tests have also shown that despite the interaction between cylinders in pile groups, the crest velocity head is a good measure of the amount of run-up. In some cases there is a decrease due to blockage, but this seems to have no practical application as the wave approaches from every direction. The main conclusion for the pile groups is that no significant increase in run-up is caused by the interaction of three piles. The conclusions of this study would hold equally true for pile groups of more than three.

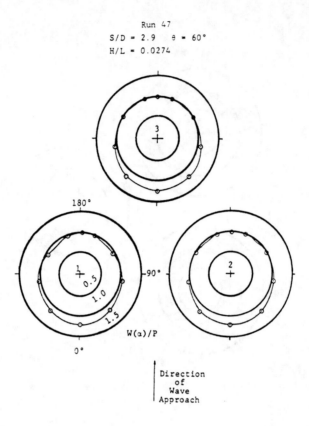

Figure 50. Normalized wave profile for the three pile groups with $\theta = 60°$ [23].

For design purposes the following procedure should be employed for both single piles and pile groups. First, calculate the scattering parameter, $ka = 2\pi a/L$, and the factor $U^2/(2gP)$, using the appropriate wave theory. Using Figure 54, find the correct $W(0)/P$ value. If ka is greater than 0.6, use the diffraction theory portion of Figure 54. The run-up, $W(0) - P$, is found by multiplying $W(0)/P$ by P and then subtracting P. A small percentage, at least 10%, of the calculated run-up should be added to the run-up to account for possible errors in calculating the true velocity as included in the following equation:

$$\text{Design run-up} = 1.10P\left(\frac{W(0)}{P} - 1\right) \tag{86}$$

For piles with scattering parameters smaller than 0.01 the velocity head is an overestimate of the maximum run-up and the total run-up should be calculated

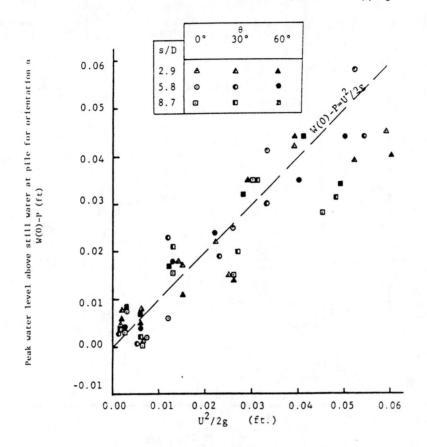

Figure 51. Graph of run-up vs. velocity head for pile #1 [23].

using the velocity head without adding a percentage of error. This will provide a reasonable estimate of run-up for piles with scattering parameters as small as 0.001, which is about the limit of practical application. For inclined piles with β between 0° and 35°, the velocity head provides a good estimate of the run-up. Figure 47 shows how the run-up declines for other values of β for the single pile investigated. More research is needed to determine if this trend holds for piles of larger diameter.

Not only does the velocity head provide a good estimate of the run-up, the opposite is also true: accurate wave run-up measurements can be used as a method to determine maximum wave velocities. However, the scattering parameter must be between 0.5 and 0.01 and the crest height must be known.

Experimental and Analytical Study by Isaacson [36a]. Isaacson conducted a series of experiments to measure wave run-up around conical structures. The results were

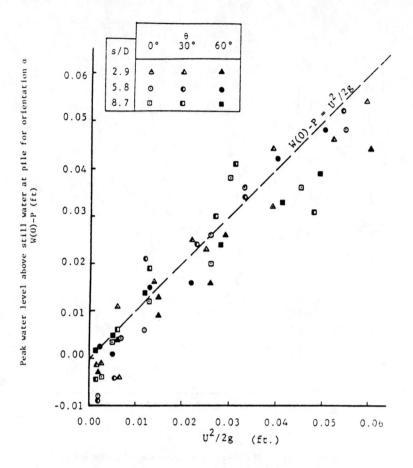

Figure 52. Graph of run-up vs. velocity head for pile #2 [23].

compared with predicted values by linear diffraction theory. Figure 55 shows the dimensionless run-up ($R(\theta)$) measured around the complete circumference of a conical structure. A comparison is made with predicted values by the diffraction theory. Isaacson concludes that the measured maximum run-up values were as much as twice those predicted. Greater values of dimensionless run-up were observed for greater wave steepnesses.

Overtopping

The amount of overtopping depends on location and on the amount of damage that can be caused by overtopping, principally through flooding. It is usually uneconomical to prevent all overtopping.

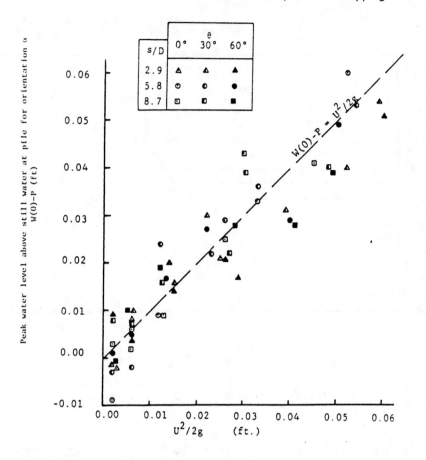

Figure 53. Graph of run-up vs. velocity head for pile #3 [23].

The rate of overtopping during a storm, Q, may be calculated by the addition of the overtopping of individual waves $g(H_1, T_1)$:

$$Q = \frac{1}{t_0} \sum_{i=1}^{i=N} g(H_i, T_i) \tag{87}$$

where $t_0 = \sum_{i=1}^{i=N} T_i$ duration of storm or hurricane

H_i = height of the i-th individual wave
T_i = period of the i-th individual wave

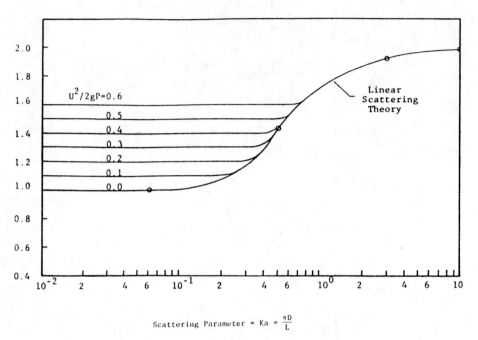

Peak water level above still water at pile for orientation α
W(0)−P (ft)

Scattering Parameter = Ka = $\dfrac{\pi D}{L}$

Figure 54. Run-up curve for design purposes [23].

An approximate value of the mean rate of random wave overtopping is given by Goda [19]:

$$Q = \frac{1}{t_0} \sum_{i=1}^{i=N_o} T_i q_0(H_i, T_i) \tag{88}$$

If a significant wave period, $T_i = T_{1/3}$, is assumed to be representative of the wave periods, then

$$Q = \int_0^\infty q_0\!\left(\frac{H}{T_{1/3}}\right) p(H)\, dH \tag{89}$$

where $q_0\!\left(\dfrac{H}{T_{1/3}}\right)$ = overtopping rate by regular waves with height H, and period
$T_{1/3}$

$p(H)$ = probability density function of wave height

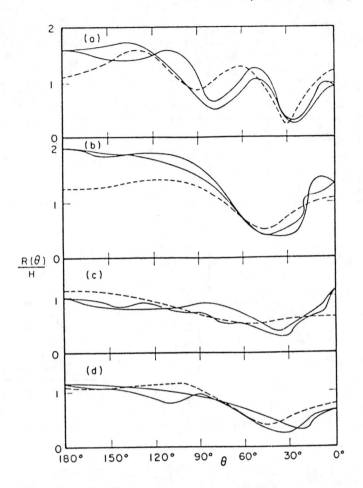

Figure 55. Selected run-up profiles [36a].

Experimental wave overtopping rates for vertical seawalls fronted by 1:10 and 1:30 are shown in Figures 56 and 57, respectively. The overtopping rates for seawalls protected by rubble mound slopes are shown in Figures 58 and 59.

Example: Estimate the overtopping rate for a vertical seawall due to a deep-water wave height, H_0', of 3 m and significant wave period of 7.3 sec. The slope in front of a seawall is 1:30. Crest elevation is 5.0 m above the datum and the seawall toe is at -4.0 m. Tide level is at $+1.0$ m.

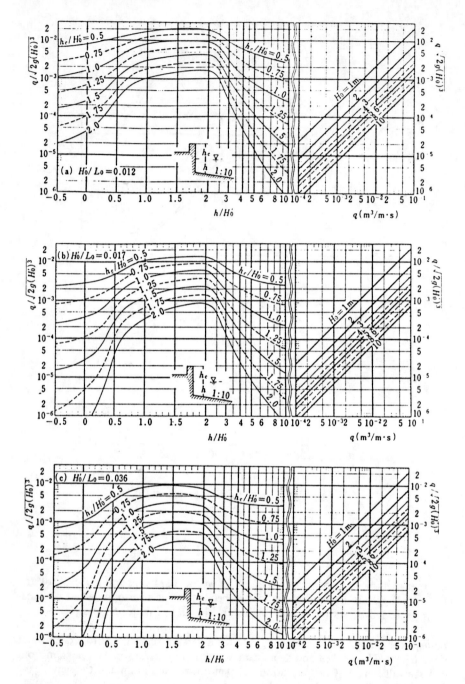

Figure 56. Design diagrams of wave overtopping rate of vertical revetments on sea bottom slope of $\frac{1}{20}$ [19].

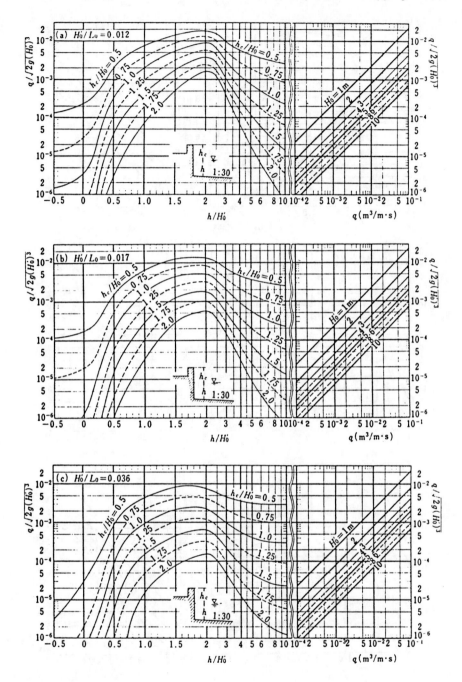

Figure 57. Design diagrams of wave overtopping rate of vertical revetments on a sea bottom slope of $\frac{1}{30}$ [19].

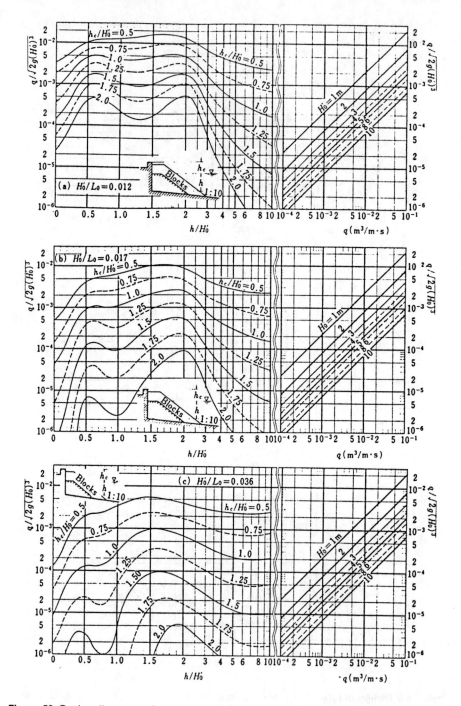

Figure 58. Design diagrams of wave overtopping rate of block mound seawalls on a sea bottom slope of $\frac{1}{10}$ [19].

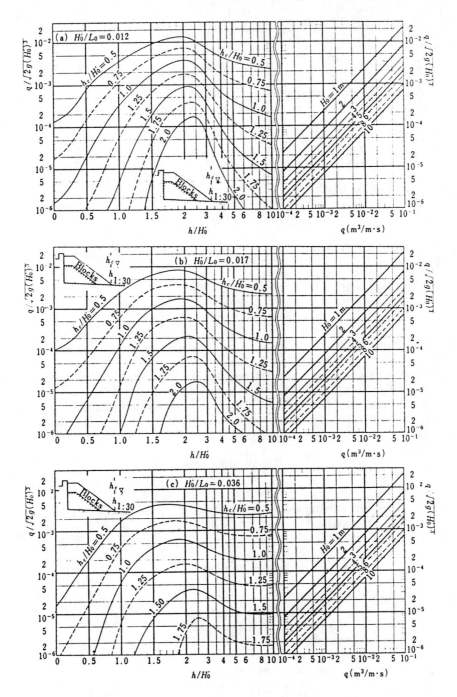

Figure 59. Design diagrams of wave overtopping rate of block mound seawalls on a sea bottom slope of $\frac{1}{30}$ [19].

Deep-water wavelength, $L_0 = 83.3$ m

$$\frac{H_0'}{L_0} = \frac{3}{83.3} = 0.036 \tag{90}$$

$$d/H_0' = (4.0 + 1.0)/3 = 1.67 \tag{91}$$

$$\frac{d_c}{H_0'} - (5 - 1.0)/3 = 1.33 \tag{92}$$

From Figure 57c

$$q/\sqrt{2g(H_0')^3} = 8(10)^{-3}$$

$$q = 8(10)^{-3}\sqrt{2(9.8)(3)^3} = 0.184 \text{ m}^3/\text{m sec} \tag{93}$$

Example: Estimate the overtopping rate for the rubble mound breakwater. From Figure 59c

$$q/\sqrt{2g(H_0)^3} = 5(10)^{-4}$$

$$q = 5(10)^{-4}\sqrt{2(9.8)(3)^3} = 0.0115 \text{ m}^3/\text{m sec} \tag{94}$$

The overtopping rate may be reduced sixteen times by placing a rubble mound in front of the vertical seawall.

Gadd, et al. [16b] conducted large-scale physical model tests with both mono-chromatic and irregular waves of eight types of armor slope designs to protect an offshore island in the Beaufort Sea. The results of these tests indicate that the SPM overtopping equation over-predicts the measured values in the model study.

The form of the wave overtopping for the SPM equation is as follows:

$$Q = [gQ_0^*(H_0')^3]^{1/2} \exp\left[\frac{-0.1085}{\alpha} \ln\left(\frac{R + h - d_s}{R - h + d_s}\right)\right] \tag{95}$$

where Q = unit overtopping rate (volume per unit time per unit crest length)
H = incident wave height
T = wave period
L = incident wave length
H_0' = unrefracted deepwater wave height
g = acceleration due to gravity
R = run-up height
d_s = water depth at the toe of the structure
h = height of structure crest above seabed
θ = structure slope
α = experiment coefficient
Q_0^* = experiment coefficient

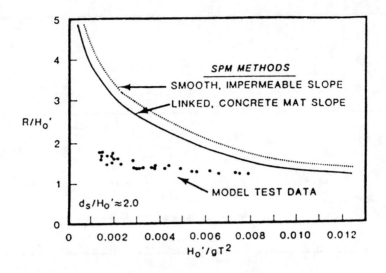

Figure 60. Measured versus predicted wave run-up [16a].

Figure 60 presents the calculated results by the *Shore Protection Manual* method [72a] and the model test data for a constant value of $d_s/H_0' = 2$. The measured data of run-up were only about 58% of the predicted values. Gadd, et al. [166] also reported the concept of employing roughness coefficient, r, to account for slope armor roughness is improper and that the roughness coefficient varies with the wave steepness parameter H_0'/gT^2.

Gadd states that the SPM methods to predict both wave run-up and overtopping greatly overestimate the values measured in these large-scale model tests. The average value of overprediction of the overtopping rate was 165 times greater than the measured value. The SPM method can be improved if large-scale model data are used as input for the overtopping equation. However, this prediction method still overpredicts the measured overtopping by an average factor of ten.

Goda [19] examined the magnitude of structural damage resulting from wave overtopping for levees and breakwaters (Figure 61). Goda [20a] presents the maximum allowable overtopping rate for structural safety for seawalls and rubble mound (Table 15).

Douglass [14a] reviewed four methods for estimating wave overtopping by irregular waves. The methods reviewed were SPM [72a], Goda [19a], Battjes [3a], and Owen [63a].

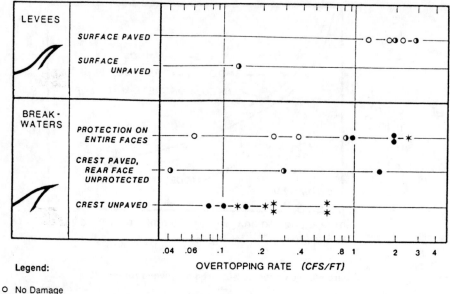

Legend:

o No Damage
ᴑ Minor Damage
● Severe Local Damage
✱ Total Damage

Figure 61. Structural damage resulting from wave overtopping [19].

Weggel [83a] derived the following empirical equation for the monochromatic-wave overtopping rate:

$$Q_{mono} = (gQ_0{}^*H_0{}'^3)^{1/2} \exp\left[-\frac{0.217}{\alpha} \tanh^{-1}\left(\frac{F}{R}\right) \right] \qquad (96)$$

Table 15
Maximum Allowable Overtopping Rate for Structural Safety [20a]

Structure Type	Degree of Protection	Maximum Allowable Overtopping Rate (cfs/ft)
Sea wall	1. No protection on crest surface or rear slope	0.054
	2. Crest surface protected, but no protection on rear slope	0.215
	3. All surfaces protected	0.538
Rubble mound	1. No protection on crest	0.538
	2. Crest protected	2.152

where $\quad Q_{mono}$ = volume rate of overtopping, L^2T
$\qquad\qquad g$ = acceleration due to gravity, L/T^2
$\qquad Q_0^*, a$ = dimensionless empirical coefficients
$\qquad\qquad H_0'$ = monochromatic deepwater wave height, L
$\qquad\qquad F$ = $(h - d_s)$-freeboard above SWL, L
$\qquad\qquad h$ = height of structure, L
$\qquad\qquad d_s$ = depth of water at structure, L
$\qquad\qquad R$ = run-up, L

To apply Weggel's equation to a sea of irregular waves, Ahrens [1a] assumes that the distribution of run-ups (R's) caused by an irregular sea will follow a Rayleigh distribution. Ahrens estimates the overtopping rate by summing the overtopping contributions from the individual run-ups,

$$Q_{SPM} = \frac{1}{199} \sum_{i=1}^{199} Q_i \qquad\qquad (97)$$

where $\quad Q_{SPM}$ = volume rate of overtopping caused by irregular waves, L^2/T
$\qquad\qquad Q_i$ = volume rate of overtopping caused by one run-up in the run-in distribution, L^2/T, or

$$Q_i = [gQ_0^*(H_s)_0^3]^{1/2} \exp\left[-\frac{0.217}{\alpha} \tanh^{-1}\left(\frac{F}{R_p}\right)\right] \qquad\qquad (98)$$

where $\quad (H_s)_0$ = deepwater significant wave height
$\qquad\qquad R_p$ = run-up of probability of exceedance p
$$R_p = \left(\frac{\ln 1/p}{2}\right)^{1/2} R_s$$
$\qquad\qquad p = 0.005 \times i, i = 1, 2, 3, \ldots, 199$
$\qquad\qquad R_s$ = run-up of monochromatic wave with the significant wave height and period

These equations can be considered to "correct" Weggel's monochromatic results for the effect of irregular waves [1a]. Figure 62 shows Ahrens' "correction factors" for freeboards, F, less than the run-up of the significant wave, R_s. When the freeboard is greater than R_s, Weggel's equations yield no overtopping. However, larger run-ups in the run-up distribution may still overtop the structure, and Equations 97 and 98 must be used. For these relatively high freeboards, the run-up distribution should be broken into 999 run-ups, instead of 199, to properly account for the effect of the higher run-ups. Equation 97 becomes

$$Q_{SPM} = \frac{1}{999} \sum_{i=1}^{999} Q_i \qquad\qquad (99)$$

where $p = 0.001 \times i, i = 1, 2, \ldots, 999$

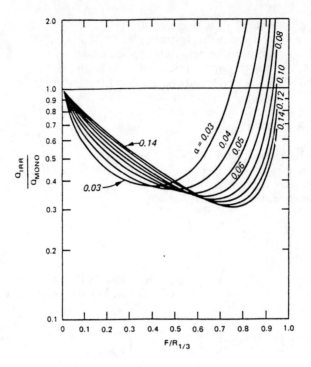

Figure 62. Ahrens' correction factors [1a].

Example: Using the SPM method, an estimation can be made of the overtopping rate for a proposed 15-ft high structure (1:3 smooth slope) (Figure 63) in 10 ft of water caused by waves with a significant wave height H_s of 5 ft and a design wave monochromatic wave of $H_0' = 5$ ft and $T = 8$ sec:

$$\frac{H_0'}{gT^2} = \frac{5}{(32.2)(8)^2} = 0.0024 \qquad \frac{d_s}{H_0'} = \frac{10}{5} = 2 \tag{100}$$

$$R = \frac{R}{H_0'} (H_0')(k) = (2.75)(5 \text{ ft})(1.14) = 15.7 \text{ ft} = R_s \tag{101}$$

(Value of $k = 1.14$ obtained from SPM Figure 7–11).

To calculate Q_{SPM}, and because $F < R_s$, use "correction factor" applied to monochromatic result.

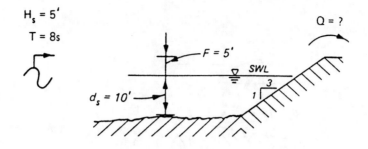

Figure 63. Definition sketch, Example 1.

Equation 96 for Q_{mono} becomes

$$Q_{mono} = [(32.2)(0.033)(5)^3]^{1/2} \exp - \left[\frac{0.217}{0.09} \tanh^{-1}\left(\frac{5}{15.7}\right)\right]$$

$$= 5.2 \text{ ft}^3/\text{sec/ft of seawall} \tag{102}$$

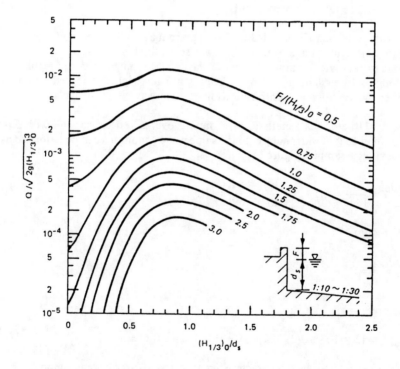

Figure 64. Goda's irregular-wave overtopping rate [19a].

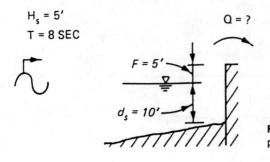

Figure 65. Definition sketch, Example 3.

From Figure 62 with

$$\frac{Q_{irr}}{Q_{mono}} = 0.51 \tag{103}$$

$$Q_{SPM} = Q_{irr} = (0.51)(5.2 \ ft^3/sec/ft)$$
$$= 2.65 \ ft^3/sec/ft \ of \ structure \tag{104}$$

Tsuruta and Goda [79a] and Goda [19a] present a graphical method of estimating the rate of irregular wave overtopping over seawalls (Figure 64).

Goda extrapolates his monochromatic-wave overtopping curves to irregular wave overtopping by assuming that wave heights are Rayleigh distributed and adding together the overtopping contributions from each wave in an irregular sea.

Example: Using Goda's method, overtopping over a vertical seawall with 5 ft of freeboard in 10 ft of water subject to the same wave conditions can be estimated as in the previous Example (Figure 65).

$$\frac{(H_s)_0}{d} = \frac{5 \ ft}{10 \ ft} = 0.5, \qquad \frac{F}{(H_s)_0} = \frac{5 \ ft}{5 \ ft} = 1 \tag{105}$$

From Figure 64,

$$\frac{Q_{Goda}}{\sqrt{2g(H_s)_0^3}} = 2 \times 10^{-3} \tag{106}$$

Therefore,

$$Q_{Goda} = (2 \times 10^{-3})\sqrt{(2)(32.2)(5)^3} = 0.18 \ ft^3/sec/ft \ of \ seawall \tag{107}$$

Battjes [3a] related wave characteristics directly to overtopping smooth, sloped structures. After deriving an expression for overtopping caused by monochromatic waves, he accounts for the irregularity of seas by assuming that deep-water wave height and wavelength are jointly Rayleigh distributed.

In deriving his monochromatic-overtopping equation, Battjes combines a monochromatic run-up formula with laboratory results and then fits the equation to Saville's overtopping data to get

$$b = 0.1 \left(1 - \frac{F}{R} \right)^2 \tag{108}$$

where $b = \dfrac{B}{HL_0 \sqrt{\tan \theta}}$

    b = Battjes' dimensionless overtopping for monochromatic waves
    B = overtopping volume per wave
    θ = structure slope
    F = freeboard
    R = run-up

By assuming that R can be approximated by Hunt's formula ($R = \sqrt{HL_0} \tan \theta$), and by assuming that both H and L_0 are jointly Rayleigh distributed in an irregular sea, Battjes analytically derives an expression for the average overtopping rate created by irregular waves,

$$\beta = \frac{(1 + \kappa)^{3/2}}{\sqrt{\kappa}} \left[\sqrt{\frac{1 + \kappa}{\pi}} \exp\left(-\frac{\pi}{2} \frac{\zeta^2}{1 + \kappa} \right) - \frac{1}{\sqrt{2}} \zeta \operatorname{erfc}\left(\frac{\pi}{2 + 2\kappa} \zeta \right) \right] \tag{109}$$

where $\bar{\beta}$ = Battjes' dimensionless-overtopping volume per average wave period
         = $\bar{B}/(0.1\bar{H}\bar{L}_0 \sqrt{\tan \theta})$
      $\bar{B}$ = average overtopping volume per average wave period
      $\bar{H}$ = average wave height
      $\bar{L}_0$ = average deep-water wavelength
      κ = statistical parameter directly related to $\lambda (0 < \kappa < 1)$
      λ = the coefficient of linear correlation of H and L_0
      ζ = dimensionless freeboard = $F/(\sqrt{HL_0} \tan \theta)$
  erfc = complementary error function [0]

To calculate volumetric overtopping rate, $\bar{B}$ is divided by the average wave period, $\bar{T}$,

$$Q_{\text{Battjes}} = \frac{\bar{B}}{\bar{T}} = \frac{\beta(0.1\bar{H}\bar{L}_0 \sqrt{\tan \theta})}{\bar{T}} \tag{110}$$

Equation 102 is shown graphically in Figure 66.

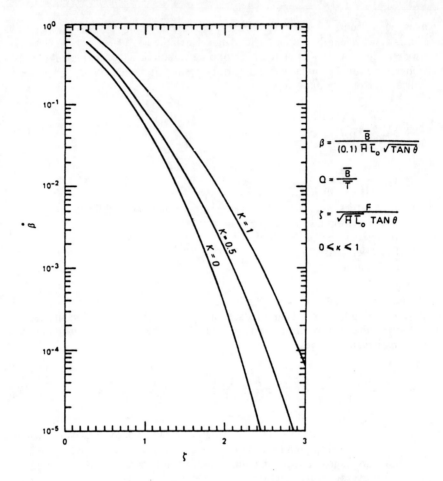

$$\beta = \frac{\overline{B}}{(0.1)\, \overline{H}\, \overline{L}_o\, \sqrt{TAN\, \theta}}$$

$$Q = \frac{\overline{B}}{\overline{T}}$$

$$\zeta = \frac{F}{\sqrt{\overline{H}\, \overline{L}_o\, TAN\, \theta}}$$

$$0 \leqslant \kappa \leqslant 1$$

Figure 66. Battjes' irregular wave overtopping [3a].

Battjes shows that his statistical parameter κ is a function of the linear correlation between H and L, λ. The relationship between λ and κ is shown graphically in Figure 67. When H and L_0 are completely uncorrelated, $\lambda = 0$ and $\kappa = 0$. When H and L_0 are perfectly correlated, $\lambda = 1$ and $\kappa = 1$.

Example: Using Battjes method, an estimation can be made of the volume rate of water which will overtop a smooth 1:6-slope sea dike with a 5-ft freeboard in 10 ft of water caused by waves with an average wave height of $\overline{H} = 3$ ft, and an average wave period of $\overline{T} = 8$ sec (Figure 68).

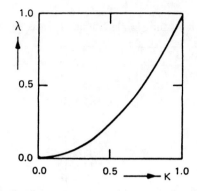

Figure 67. Relationship between Battjes' κ and λ [3a].

To calculate Battjes' dimensionless freeboard, ζ,

$$\zeta = \frac{F}{\sqrt{\bar{H}\bar{L}_0}\,\tan\theta} = \frac{5}{\sqrt{(3)(5.12)(8)^2}\left(\frac{1}{6}\right)} = 0.96 \tag{111}$$

Figure 66 is then entered with ζ to find values of β for $\kappa = 0$, $\kappa = 0.5$, and $\kappa = 1.0$:

$\beta = 0.06, 0.09, 0.2$ as $\kappa = 0, 0.5, 1$, respectively.

Equation (103) is used to calculate overtopping rate,

$$Q_{\text{Battjes}} = \frac{\beta(0.10\bar{H}\bar{L}_0\,\tan\theta)}{\bar{T}} = \frac{\beta(0.1)(3)(5.12 \times 8^2)\frac{1}{6}}{8} \tag{112}$$

Therefore, $Q = 0.30, 0.45.$ $1.0\,\text{ft}^3/\text{sec/ft}$ of dike for $\kappa = 0, 0.5, 1.0$, respectively.

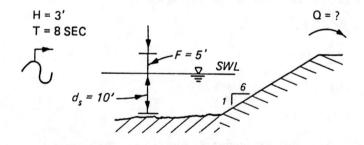

Figure 68. Definition sketch, Example 4.

Table 16
Empirical Coefficients for Simple (Plane in Cross Section) Seawalls [63a]

Seawall Slope	A	B
1:1	7.94×10^{-3}	20.12
1:1.5	1.02×10^{-2}	20.12
1:2	1.25×10^{-2}	22.06
1:2.5	1.45×10^{-2}	26.1
1:3	1.63×10^{-2}	31.9
1:3.5	1.78×10^{-2}	38.9
1:4	1.92×10^{-2}	46.96
1:4.5	2.15×10^{-2}	55.7
1:5	2.5×10^{-2}	65.2

Owen [63a] measured overtopping caused by irregular laboratory waves. Based on the results, an equation is presented for estimating irregular wave overtopping rates:

$$Q_* = Ae^{-BF_*} \tag{113}$$

where Q_* = Owen's dimensionless overtopping
$\quad\quad = Q/(\bar{T}gH_s)$
$\quad Q$ = mean overtopping volume rate, L^2/T
$\quad \bar{T}$ = mean zero upcrossing wave period, T
$\quad F_*$ = Owen's dimensionless freeboard
$\quad\quad = F/(\bar{T}\sqrt{gH_s})$
$\quad F$ = freeboard, L

Values for A and B are presented in Table 16. The values for slopes of 1:1, 1:2, and 1:4 are from the experimental data. The others have been interpolated. Owen cautions against applying his method to situations other than those he tested. His experimental parameter ranges were as follows:

$$0.05 < F_* < 0.30$$

$$10^{-6} < Q_* < 10^{-2}$$

$$1.5 < d_s/H_s < 5.5$$

$$0.035 < H_s/L_0 < 0.055$$

Owen also investigated overtopping of seawalls with large berms (composite slopes). The results are presented in Owen [63a] in the form of different A and B values.

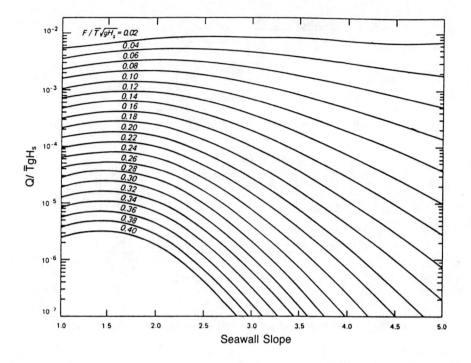

Figure 69. Owen's dimensionless overtopping for smooth, plane-sloped structures [63a].

In order to interpolate between seawall slopes, Owen [63a] plots A and B values for all the situations investigated. Owen goes a step further and generates dimensionless design curves for each berm situation tested. Figure 69 is the design curve for simple seawalls.

Example: Using Owen's method, an estimation can be made of the volume rate of water which will overtop a 15-ft high, 1:3-slope, smooth seawall in 10 ft of water. Wave height and period are $H_s = 5$ ft and $\bar{T} = 8$ sec.

$$F_* = \frac{F}{\bar{T}\sqrt{gH_s}} = \frac{5}{[8\sqrt{32.2(5)}]} = 0.049 \tag{114}$$

From Figure 69,

$$Q_* = 3 \times 10^{-3} \tag{115}$$

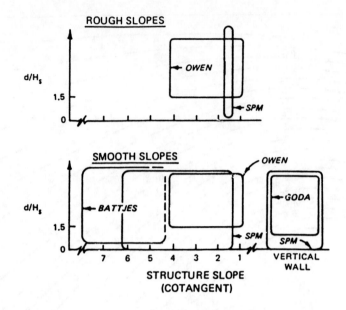

Figure 70. General regions of applicability of overtopping methods [14a].

Therefore,

$$Q_{Owen} = (3.5 \times 10^{-3})\bar{T}gH_s = (3.5 \times 10^{-3})(8)(32.2)(5) \qquad (116)$$

$$= 4.5 \text{ ft}^3/\text{sec/ft of structure}$$

Douglass concludes that for vertical seawalls the SPM method estimates higher rates of overtopping than Goda's method except in shallow water. For sloped structures the SPM method generally estimates lower overtopping rates than Battjes' and Owen's methods. Regions of applicability of overtopping methods are shown in Figure 70 for smooth and rough slopes. Figure 71 presents the comparison of Goda's and SPM's methods for estimating overtopping a vertical wall. Comparison of Battjes' and SPM's methods for estimating overtopping of a 1:6 smooth-slope structure is shown in Figure 72, and Figure 73 presents a comparison of Owen's and SPM's methods for estimating overtopping of a 1:3 smooth-slope structure.

Overtopping rates are also affected by wind velocity. Iwagaki, et al. [37] reported that the overtopping rates increase rapidly for values of

$$\frac{U}{\sqrt{gH_0}} > 5 \qquad (117)$$

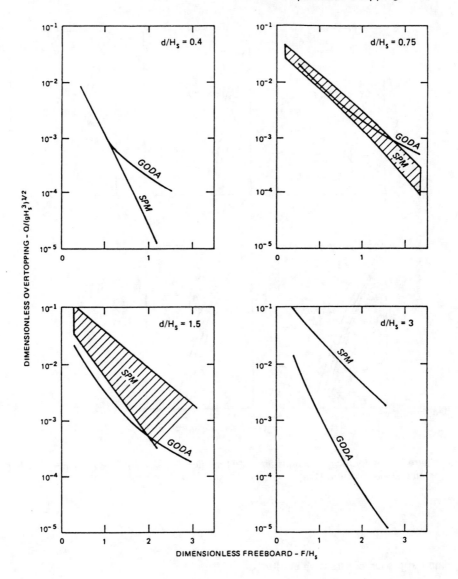

Figure 71. Comparison of Goda and SPM methods for estimating overtopping of a vertical wall [14a].

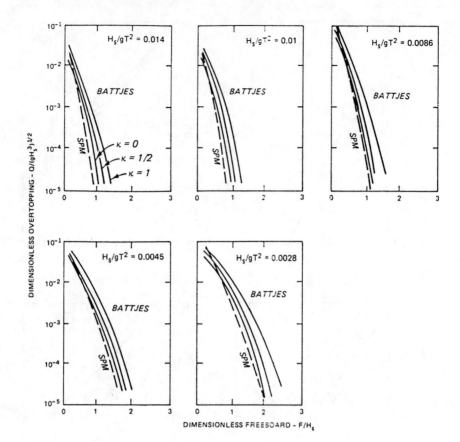

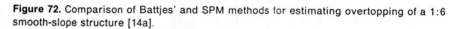

Figure 72. Comparison of Battjes' and SPM methods for estimating overtopping of a 1:6 smooth-slope structure [14a].

and approach constant values for

$$\frac{U}{\sqrt{gH_0}} > 10 \tag{118}$$

where   U = wind velocity
       H_0 = deep-water wave height

Figure 74 shows the effect of wind velocity on overtopping rates for a vertical wall.

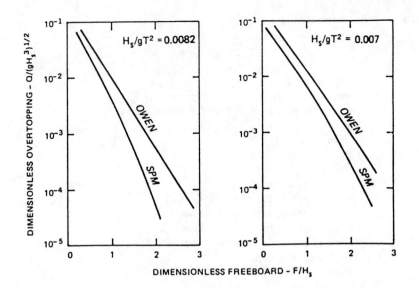

Figure 73. Comparison of Owen and SPM methods for estimating overtopping of a 1:3 smooth-slope structure [14a].

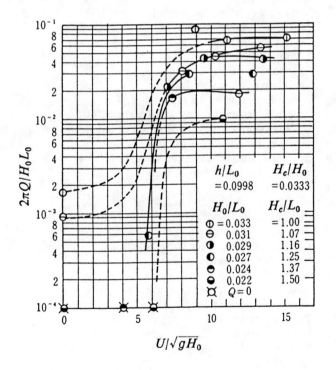

Figure 74. Wind effect on wave overtopping [37].

Notation

a	pile radius, L
A_β	wave runup for wave approach angle β, L
A_n	wave runup of the wave n of a time series, L
A_{n-1}	wave runup of the previous wave, L
C	wave celerity, L/T
C_1, C_2, C_3	empirical coefficients, L/T
C_R	reflection coefficient, L/T
d	still water depth, L
d_1	water depth at toe of beach slope, L
d_1	water depth at the change of slope, L
d_2	water depth at toe of levee station, L
d^1	mean diameter of roughness material, L
d_b	wave breaking depth, L
d_c	wave crest depth, L
d_s	water depth at the structure, L
d_t'	water depth below still water level, L
D	pile diameter, L
E	wave energy, L
$\tilde{E}$	wave energy of monochromatic wave, L
E_μ	mean wave energy density, L
erfc	complementary error function
f_*	friction coefficient, L
F	freeboard, L
F	cumulative frequency, 1/T
F_*	dimensionless freeboard (Owen), L/T
$F_e(R_i)$	expected largest run-up during a storm, L/T
$F_t(R_i)$	cumulative frequency distribution of individual run-ups, 1/T
g	acceleration due to gravity, LT^{-2}
h	height of structure crest above seabed, L
h'	water depth below free surface, L
H	water height, L
H_i	height of the i-th individual wave, L
	incident wave height, L
H_0	deep water wave height, L
H_0'	unmodified deep water wave height, L
H_1	height of the primary wave, L
H_2	height of the secondary wave, L
H_3	wave height measured from the channel bottom, L
H_{mo}	zero-moment wave height, L
J_0	Bessel function of the zeroth order, L
J_1	Bessel function of the first order, L
k	$2\pi/L$ = wave number, L^{-1}
k	scale effect factor, L^{-1}
k_β	$\tilde{A}_\beta/\tilde{A}_n$, L^{-1}

K_0	root of the equation $K_0 \tanh \gamma K_0 = 1$, L^{-1}
K	shoaling factor, L^{-1}
L	wavelength, L
L_0	deep water wavelength, L
L_1	incident wavelength, L
ℓ	length, L
ln	natural logarithm, L
n	porosity, L
	permeability, L
N	number, L
N_F	Froude number, L
p	probability density function, L
P	incident crest height, L
$P_e(R_i)$	non-exceedance probability, L
Q	overtopping rate, L^3/T
Q_0	unit overtopping rate, L^2/T
Q_0^*	dimensionless empirical coefficients, L^2/T
Q_{irr}	volume rate of overtopping (irregular waves), L^2/T
Q_{mono}	volume rate of overtopping (monochromatic waves), L^2/T
Q_{SPM}	volume rate of overtopping caused by irregular waves, L^2/T
r	relative roughness, L^2/T
R	wave run-up, L
R_{max}	maximum wave run-up, L
R_p	run-up of probability of exceedance, p, L
R_s	run-up with the significant monochromatic waves, L
$R_{1/3}$	significant wave run-up, L
$R_{1/10}$	one-tenth wave run-up, L
$R_{1/100}$	one-hundredth wave run-up, L
R_2	run-up exceeded by 2% of all run-ups, L
R_2	dimensionless, 2% run-up, L
s	pile spacing, offshore slope angle, L
S	shape of structure, L
S	slope angle, L
S_b	slope,
t	time, T
t'	time, T
t_0	duration of storm, T
T	wave period, T
T_{max}	maximum wave period, T
$\bar{T}$	mean period of run-ups, T
T_i	period of the i-th individual wave, T
u	depth-averaged horizontal velocity, L/T
U_0	horizontal component of velocity, L/T
U	peak horizontal water particle velocity, L/T
	wind velocity, L/T
V_d	downrush velocity, L/T

V_u uprush velocity, L/T
 x horizontal dimension, L
 x' horizontal coordinate, L
 X distance, L
X_0 distance, L
X_b horizontal distance from breaking point to toe of structure, L
X_r horizontal distance from the toe of the structure to the extent of maximum wave run-up, L
 y vertical dimension, L
$W(\alpha)$ peak water level above still water level at pile for orientation α, L
$W(0)$ water level above still water at pile for orientation 0, L
Z_H run-up calculated from Hunt's equation, L
Z_w run-up calculated from Wassing's equation, L
Z_{w50} 50 median run-up value (Wassing), L
Z_{w99} 99% run-up value (Wassing), L
 Z' vertical coordinate (positive upward), L

Greek Letters

α · orientation angle, L
  slope of structure, L
  beach slope, L
  coefficient (Goda), L
β angle of pile from vertical, T^{-1}
  Battjes coefficient, T^{-1}
  angle of wave approach, T^{-1}
η mean water level, L
  vertical displacement of water level, L
ϵ vector consisting of all parameters influencing the statistical properties of run-up, L
ϕ artificial roughness coefficient (Wassing), L

γ relative roughness of the slope $= \dfrac{2\pi}{T\sqrt{g/d}}$, L

λ coefficient of linear correlation of H and L_0, L
μ dynamic viscosity, M/LT
ρ mass density, M/L^3
κ statistical parameter, M/L^3
σ $2\pi/T$, angular frequency, 1/T
ζ dimensionless freeboard, 1/T
ψ form parameter (Tautenhain), 1/T
  $\tan^{-1}(2ka\cos\alpha)$, 1/T
θ phase angle between primary and secondary waves, 1/T
  slope angle, 1/T

$$\xi \quad \frac{\tan \alpha}{\sqrt{H_0/L_0}} \text{ (Günbak), } 1/T$$

$$\frac{\beta}{\sqrt{H/L_0}} \text{ (Holman), } 1/T$$

τ_b' bottom shear stress, F/L^2

θ beach slope

$\bar{\theta}$ mean wave direction

References

0. Abramowitz, M. and Stegun, I. A., 1965, *Handbook of Mathematical Functions*, Dover Publications, Inc., N.Y.

1. Adam, K. M., 1963, "A Model Study of Wave Run-up on Smooth and Rough Slopes," Unpublished M.S. thesis, University of Manitoba, Winnipeg, Canada, pp. 1–114.

1a. Ahrens, J., 1977, "Prediction of Irregular Wave Overtopping," CETA 77-2, U.S. Army Engineer Waterways Experiment Station, Coastal Engineering Research Center, Vicksburg, MS.

1b. Ahrens, J. P., Heimbaugh, M. S., and Davidson, D. D., 1986, "Irregular Wave Overtopping of Seawall/Revetment Configurations, Roughans Point, Massachusetts," T.R. CERC-86-7, U.S. Army Engineers, Coastal Engineering Research Center, Vicksburg, MS.

2. Amein, M., 1966, "A Method for Determining the Behavior of Long Waves Climbing a Sloping Beach," *Journal of Geophysical Research*, Vol. 71, No. 2, Jan. 15, pp. 401–410.

3. American Petroleum Institute, 1976, "API Recommended Practice for Planning and Constructing Fixed Offshore Platforms." API RP 2A, January, Washington, D.C., p. 13.

3a. Battjes, J. A., 1974, "Computation of Set-up, Longshore Currents, Run-up and Overtopping Due to Wind-Generated Waves," Report No. 74-2, Delft University of Technology, Dept. of Civil Engineering, Delft, the Netherlands.

4. Blackman, R. B. and Tukey, J. W., 1958, *The Measurement of Power Spectra*, Dover, New York.

5. Bonnefille, R. and Germain, R., 1963, "Wave Action on Isolated Vertical Cylinders of Large Dimensions." *Proceedings of the International Association for Hydraulics Research Congress*, London, England, pp. 311–318 (in French, Abstract in English).

6. Borgman, L. E., 1973, "Probabilities for Highest Wave in Hurricane," *Journal of Waterway, Port, Coastal and Ocean Engineering*, ASCE, Vol. 99, No. WW22, pp. 187–207.

7. Bowen, A. J., Inman, D. L., and Simmons, V. P., 1968, "Wave 'Set-down' and Set-up." *Journal of Geophysical Research*, Vol. 73, No. 8, April 15, pp. 2569–2577.

8. Bruun, P., 1953, "Breakwaters for Coastal Protection," *Proceedings, XVIII International Navigation Congress*, Section 2, Question 1, Rome, Italy, pp. 25–35.

9. Carlson, C. T., 1984, "Field Studies of Run-up Generated by Wind Waves on Dissipative Beaches," SRI International, Menlo Park, CA.

10. Carrier, G. F. and Greenspan, H. P., 1958, "Water Waves of Finite Amplitude on a Sloping Beach," *Journal of Fluid Mechanics*, Vol. 4, pp. 97–109.

11. Chakrabarti, S. K. and Tam, W. A., 1975, "Wave Height Distribution Around Vertical Cylinder," *Journal of the Waterways, Harbors and Coastal Engineering Division*, ASCE, Vol. 101, No. WW22, Proc. Paper 11279, May, pp. 225–230.

12. Coastal Engineering Research Center, 1984, *Shore Protection Manual*, U.S. Army Coastal Engineering Research Center.

13. Dean, R. G., 1974, "Evaluation and Development of Water Waves Theories for Engineering Application. Volume I—Presentation of Research Results. Volume II—Tabulation of Dimensionless Stream-Function Theory Variables." Special Report No. 1, U.S. Army Engineers Coastal Engineering Research Center, Fort Belvoir, VA, pp. 133, 534.

14. Douglass, S. L., 1984, "Irregular Wave Overtopping," *Proceedings, Coastal Engineering,* ASCE, pp. 316–326.

14a. Douglass, S. I., 1986, "Review and Comparison of Methods for Estimating Irregular Wave Overtopping Rates," U.S. Army Coastal Engineering Research Center, Vicksburg, MS, T.R. CERC-86-12, December.

14b. Franzius, L., 1965, "Wirkung und Wirtschaftlichkeit von Rauhdeckwerken in Hinblick auf den Wellenauflauf," Mitteilungen des Franzius-Instituts für Grund-und Wasserbau der T.H. Hannover, West Germany, Heft 25, pp. 1949–268, (in German).

15. Freeman, J. C. and LeMéhauté, B., 1964, "Wave Breakers on a Beach and Surges on a Dry Bed," *Journal of the Hydraulics Division,* ASCE, Vol. 90, March, pp. 187–216.

16. Fredrichs, K. O., 1948, "Wave Waves on a Shallow Slopping Beach," *Communication Applied Mathematics,* Vol. 1, pp. 109–134.

16a. Führböter, A., 1986, "Model and Prototype Tests for Wave Impact and Run-up on a Uniform 1:4 Slope," *Coastal Engineering,* Vol. 10, pp. 49–84.

16b. Gadd, P. E., Potter, R. E., Safaie, B., and Resio D., 1984, "Wave Run-up and Overtopping: A Review and Recommendations," Offshore Technology Conference, OTC 4674, pp. 239–245.

16c. Gadd, P. E., Machemehl, J. L., and Manikian, V., 1985, "Comparison of Wave Overtopping Prediction to Measurements from Large-Scale Model Tests," *Proceedings, Civil Engineering in the Arctic Offshore.*

17. Galvin, C. J., Jr., 1968, "Finite-amplitude, Shallow Water Waves of Periodically Recurring Form." Unpublished report, U.S. Army Corps of Engineers Coastal Engineering Research Center.

18. Galvin, C. J. and Hallermeier, R. J., 1972, "Wave Run-up on Vertical Cylinders," *Proceedings, Thirteenth Conference on Coastal Engineering,* ASCE, Vancouver, Canada, pp. 1955–74.

19. Goda, Y., 1970, "Estimation of the Rate of Irregular Wave Overtopping of Seawalls." Port and Harbour Research Institute, Japan, Vol. 9, No. 4, pp. 3–41 (in Japanese with an English Abstract).

19a. Goda, Y., 1971, "Expected Rate of Irregular Wave Overtopping of Seawalls," Coastal Engineering in Japan, Vol. 14.

20. Goda, Y., Kishira Y., and Kamiyama, Y., 1975, "Laboratory Investigation on the Overtopping Rate of Seawalls by Irregular Waves," Port and Harbour Research Institute Report, Japan, Vol. 14, No. 4, (in Japanese).

20a. Goda, Y., 1977, *Wave Analysis for the Design of Coastal Facilities,* Kajima Publishing Co., Tokyo, Japan, 237 p. (in Japanese).

21. Goto, C. and Shuto, N., 1982, "Run-up of Tsunamis by Linear and Nonlinear Theories," Chapter 43, *Proceedings, International Conference on Coastal Engineering,* ASCE.

22. Granthem, K. N., 1953, "Wave Run-up on Sloping Structures." *Transactions, American Geophysical Union,* Vol. 34, No. 5, October, pp. 720–724.

22a. Grüne, J., 1982, "Wave Run-up Caused by Natural Storm Surge Waves," *Proceedings, International Conference on Coastal Engineering,* ASCE, pp. 785–803.

22b. Gunbak, A. R., 1978, "Rubble Mound Breakwaters," unpublished D. Eng. Thesis, Norwegian Institute of Technology, Trondheim, Norway.

23. Haney, J. P. and Herbich, J. B., 1982, "Wave Flow Around Thin Piles and Pile Groups," *Journal Hydraulic Research,* Vol. 20, No. 1.

24. Hallermeier, R. J., 1976, "Nonlinear Flow of Wave Crests Past a Thin Pile." *Journal of the Waterways, Harbors and Coastal Engineering Division*, ASCE, Vol. 102, No. WW24, Proc. Paper 12551, Nov. pp. 365–377.

25. Havelock, T. H., 1940, "The Pressure of Water Waves Upon a Fixed Obstacle," *Proc. Royal Society*, London, U.K. Vol. 175A, July 18, pp. 409–415.

26. Hall, J. V. and Watts, G. M., 1953, "Laboratory Investigation of the Vertical Rise of Solitary Waves on Impermeable Slopes," BEB Technical Memorandum No. 33, U.S. Army Corps of Engineers Beach Erosion Board, March, pp. 1–14.

27. Haws, E. T., 1968, "Discussion of Mangle," *Proceedings of the Institute of Civil Engineers*, Vol. 41, Sept., pp. 145–148.

28. Hellstom, B. and Rundgren, L., 1954, "Model Tests on Olands Sodra Grund Lighthouse," *Bulletin No. 39*, The Institution of Hydraulics, Royal Institute of Technology, Stockholm, Sweden.

29. Herbich, J. B., Sorensen, R. M., and Willenbrock, J. H., 1963, "Effect of Berm on Wave Run-up on Composite Beaches," *Journal of the Waterways and Harbors Division*, ASCE, Vol. 89, No. WW22, May, pp. 55–72.

30. Ho, D. V. and Meyer, R. E., 1962, "Climb of a Bore on a Beach," *Journal of Fluid Mechanics*, Vol. 14, pp. 305–318.

31. Ho, D. V., Meyer, R. E., and Shen, M. C., 1963, "Long Surf," *Journal of Marine Research*, Vol. 21, No. 3, pp. 219–23.

32. Holman, R. A. and Guza, R. T., 1984, "Measuring Run-up on a Natural Beach," *Coastal Engineering*, Vol. 8, pp. 129–140.

32a. Holman, R. A., 1986, "Extreme Value Statistics for Wave Run-up on a Natural Beach," Coastal Engineering, Vol. 9, pp. 527–544.

33. Hosoi, M. and Mitsui, H., 1964, "Wave Run-up on Sea Dikes Located in the Surf Zone or on the Shore," *Coastal Engineering in Japan*, Japan, Vol. 6, pp. 1–6, Vol. 7, pp. 95–99.

34. Hudson, R. Y., 1959, "Laboratory Investigation of Rubble-mound Breakwaters," *Journal of the Waterways and Harbors Division*, ASCE, Vol. 85, No. WW23, Sept., pp. 108–113.

35. Hunt, I. A., 1959, "Design of Seawalls and Breakwaters," *Journal of the Waterways and Harbors Division*, ASCE, Vol. 85, No. WW23, Sept., pp. 123–152.

36. Isaacson, E., 1950, "Water Waves Over a Sloping Bottom," *Comm. Pure and Applied Mathematics*, Vol. 3, pp. 1–32.

36a. Isaacson, M. de St. Q., 1985, "Wave Run-up Around Conical Structures," *Proc. Civil Engineering in the Arctic Offshore*, ASCE, pp. 706–713.

37. Iwagaki, Y., Tsuchiya, Y., and Inoue, M., 1966, "On the Effect of Wind on Wave Overtopping on Vertical Seawalls," Bull. Disaster Prev., Res. Inst., Kyoto Univ., 16(I):11–30.

38. Jackson, R. A., 1968, "Design of Cover Layers for Rubble-mound Breakwaters Subjected to Non-breaking Waves," WES Research Report No. 2–11, U.S. Army Waterways Experiment Station, Vicksburg, MS, June, pp. 20, 30.

39. James, W. R. and Hallermeier, R. J., 1976, "A Nearshore Wave Direction Gage," *Journal of the Waterways, Harbors and Coastal Engineering Division*, ASCE, Vol. 102, No. WW24, Proc. Paper 12552, Nov., pp. 379–393.

39a. Jenkinson, A. F., 1955, "The Frequency Distribution of the Annual Maximum (or Minimum) Values of Meteorological Elements," *Quarterly Journal*, Royal Meteorological Society, Vol. 81, pp. 158–171.

40. Johnson, J. W., 1945, "Rectangular Artificial Roughness in Open Channels," *Transactions of the American Geophysical Union*, Vol. 34, May, pp. 907–914.

41. Jordaan, J. M., Jr., 1965, "Feasibility of Modeling Run-up Effects of Dispersive Water Waves," USNCEL Technical Note N-691, U.S. Naval Civil Engineering Lab., Port Hueneme, May, pp. 1–61.

42. Kaplan, K., 1955, "Generalized Laboratory Study of Tsunami Run-up," BEB Technical Memorandum No. 60, U.S. Army Corps of Engineers Beach Erosion Board, Jan., pp. 1–30.

43. Keller, H. B., Levine, D. A., and Whitham, B. G., 1960, "Motion of a Bore on a Sloping Beach," *Journal of Fluid Mechanics*, Vol. 7, pp. 302–316.

44. Keller, J. B. and Keller, H. B., 1965, *Water Wave Run-up on a Beach*, Service Bureau Corporation Research Report, New York, pp. 1–40.

45. Keller, J. B. and Keller, H. B., *Water Wave Run-up on a Beach*, Service Bureau Corporation Research Report. New York, 1964, pp. 1–A13.

46. Keller, J. B., 1961, "Tsunamis-Water Waves Produced by Earthquakes," *Proceedings Conference on Tsunami Hydrodynamics*.

47. King, L. V., 1914, "On the Convection of Heat from Small Cylinders in a Stream of Fluid: Determination of the Convective Constants of Small Platinum Wires with Application to Hot-Wire Anemometry," *Proceedings Royal Society*, London, U.K. Vol. 214A, No. 14, p. 373.

48. Kobayashi, N., Greenwald, J. H., 1986, "Prediction of Wave Run-up and Riprap Stability," Chapter 144, *Proc. 20th Coastal Engineering Conference*, p. 1958–1971.

48a. Kobayashi, N., Otta, A. K., and Roy, I., 1987, "Wave Relection and Run-up on Rough Slopes," *Journal of Waterways, Port, Coastal and Ocean Engineering*, ASCE, Vol. 113, No. 3, May, pp. 282–298.

48b. Kobayashi, N. and Watson, K. D., 1987, "Wave Reflection and Run-up on Smooth Slopes." *Proceedings Coastal Hydrodynamics*, ASCE.

49. Laird, A. D. K., 1955, "A Model Study of Wave Action on a Cylindrical Island," *Transactions of the American Geophysical Union*, Vol. 36, No. 2, pp. 279–285.

50. Le Méhauté, B., Koh, B. C. Y., and Hwang, L-S., 1968, "A Synthesis on Wave Run-up," *Journal of the Waterways and Harbors Division*, ASCE, No. WW21, Vol. 94, Feb., pp. 77–92.

51. Le Méhauté, B. and Divoky, D., 1966, "Effects of Explosion-Generated Waves on the Hawaiian Islands," NESCO Report No. SN-30, National Engineering Science Co., Pasadena, CA, Dec., pp. 1–74.

52. Le Méhauté, B., 1963 "On Non-Saturated Breakers and the Wave Run-up," *Proceedings Eighth Conference on Coastal Engineering*, Council on Wave Research, Chapter 6, pp. 77–92.

53. Lewy, H., 1946, "Water Waves on a Sloping Beach," *Bulletin American Mathematical Society*, Vol. 52, pp. 737–775.

54. MacCamy, R. C. and Fuchs, R. A., 1954, "Wave Forces on Piles: A Diffraction Theory," Technical Memorandum No. 69, U.S. Army Engineers Beach Erosion Board.

55. Machemehl, J. L. and Herbich, J. B., 1970, "Effects of Slope Roughness on Wave Run-up on Composite Slopes," Texas A&M Sea Grant Program, TAMU-SG-70-222, COE Report No. 129, August.

55a. Madsen, O. S. and White, S. M., 1976, "Energy Dissipation on a Rough Slope," *Journal Waterways, Harbors and Coastal Engineering Division*, ASCE, Vol. 102, No. WW1, pp. 31–48.

56. Mase, H. and Iwagaki, Y., 1984, "Run-up of Random Waves on Gentle Slopes," Chapter 40, International Conference on Coastal Engineering, ASCE, pp. 593–609.

57. Miche, R., 1951, "Le Pouvoir Refléchissant Des Ouvrages Maritimes," *Ann. de Ponts et Chausées*, May to June, pp. 285–319.

58. Miche, R., 1944, "Mouvements Ondulatores de la Mer," *Ann. de Ponts et Chausées*, Jan. to Aug.

59. Miller, R. L., 1968, "Experimental Determination of Run-up of Undular and Fully Developed Bores," *Journal of Geophysical Research*, Vol. 73, No. 14, July 15, pp. 4497–4510.

60. Multer, B., 1967, "Wave Run-up," CERC Memorandum for Record, U.S. Army Corps of Engineers Coastal Engineering Research Center, pp. 1–15.

61. Nagai, S., Tokikawa, K., and Oda, K., 1966, "Report on the Pier of the Suspension Bridge Connecting the Mainland with Shikoku Island in Japan.," Interim Report I, Hydraulic Laboratory, Faculty of Engineering, Osaka City University, Osaka, Japan.

62. Ogawa, Y. and Shuto, N., 1984, "Run-up of Periodic Waves on Beaches of Non-uniform Slope," Chapter 23, *Proceedings, International Conference of Coastal Engineering*, ASCE, pp. 328–344.

63. Omer, G. C. and Hall, H. H., 1949, "The Scattering of a Tsunami by a Cylindrical Island," *Journal of the Seismological Society of America*, Vol. 39, No. 4, pp. 257–260.

63a. Owen, M. W., 1980, "Design of Seawalls Allowing for Wave Overtopping," Report No. Ex 924, Hydraulics Research Station, Wallingford, U.K.

63b. Packwood, A. R., 1980, "Surf and Run-up on Beaches," unpublished Ph.D. Thesis, University of Bristol, U.K.

63c. Packwood, A. R. and Peregrine, D. H., 1981, "Surf and Run-up on Beaches: Models of Viscous Effects," Report No. AM-81-07, School of Mathematics, University of Bristol, U.K.

64. Resio, D. T., 1987, "Extreme Run-up Statistics on Natural Beaches," M.P. CERC-87-11, U.S. Army Corps of Engineers, Washington, D.C.

65. Robson, L. E. and Jones, D. B., 1967, "Laboratory Study of Seiching Induced on an Offshore Shelf," USNCEL Technical Note N-895, U.S. Naval Civil Engineering Lab, Port Hueneme, CA, pp. 1–46.

66. Savage, R. P., 1958, "Wave Run-up on Roughened and Permeable Slopes," *Journal of the Waterways and Harbors Division*, ASCE, Vol. 84, No. WW23, May, pp. 1640-1–1640-38.

67. Savage, R. P., 1959, "Laboratory Data on Wave Run-up on Roughened and Permeable Slopes," BEB Technical Memorandum No. 109, U.S. Army Corps of Engineers Beach Erosion Board, March, pp. 1–28.

68. Saville, T., Jr., 1960, Discussion to "Laboratory Investigation of Rubble-mound Breakwaters," *Journal of the Waterways and Harbor Division*, ASCE, Vol. 86, No. WW23, Sept., pp. 151–156.

69. Saville, T., Jr., 1957, "Wave Run-up on Composite Slopes," *Proceedings Sixth Conference on Coastal Engineering*, Council on Wave Research, Chapter 41, pp. 691–699.

70. Saville, T., Jr., 1956, "Wave Run-up on Shore Structures," *Journal of the Waterways and Harbors Division*, ASCE, Vol. 82, No. WW22, April, pp. 9251–9254.

71. Schlichting, H., 1968, *Boundary Layer Theory*. 6th ed., McGraw-Hill Book Co., Inc., New York, N.Y.

71a. Seyama, A. and Kimura, A., 1986, "Critical Run-up Height on the Sea Wall," Chapter 164, *Proceedings, International Conference on Coastal Engineering*, ASCE.

72. Shen, M. C. and Meyer, R. E., 1963, "Climb of a Bore on a Beach," Part 3, *Journal of Fluid Mechanics*, Vol. 16, pp. 173–175.

72a. *Shore Protection Manual*, 4th ed., 2 Vols., 1984, U.S. Army Corps of Engineers, U.S. Government Printing Office, Washington, D.C.

73. Shrens, J., 1977, "Prediction of Irregular Wave Run-up," CETA 77-4, U.S. Army Corps of Engineers, CERC, Fort Belvoir, VA, July.

74. Sibul, O., 1955, "Flow Over Reefs and Structures by Wave Action," *Transactions of the American Geophysical Union*, Vol. 36, No. 1, Feb., pp. 61–71.

75. Sibul, O. J. and Tickner, E. G., 1955, "A Model Study of the Run-up of Wind-generated Waves on Levees With Slopes of 1:3 and 1:6," BEB Technical Memorandum No. 67, U.S. Army Corps of Engineers Beach Erosion Board, Dec., pp. 1–19.

76. Stoa, P. N., 1978, "Revised Wave Run-up Curves for Smooth Slopes," CETA 78-2, U.S. Army Corps of Engineers, CERC, Fort Belvoir, VA, July.

77. Stoker, J. J., 1957, *Water Waves*. Interscience, New York.

77a. Synolakis, C. E., 1987, "The Run-up and Reflection of Solitary Waves," *Proceedings, Coastal Hydrodynamics*, ASCE, pp. 533–547.

78. Tautenhain, E., 1981, "Der Wellenüberlauf an Seedeichen unter Berücksichtigung des Wellenüberlaufs," Mitteilungen des Franzius-Instituts, Heft 53, Hannover, West Germany, (in German).

78a. Tautenhain, E. and Kohlhase, S., 1980, "Investigations on Wave Run-up and Overtopping at Seadikes, *International Conference on Water Resources Development*, Taipei.

78b. Tautenhain, E., Kohlhase, S., and Partenscky, H. W., 1982, "Wave Run-up at Sea Dikes Under Oblique Wave Approach," *Coastal Engineering*, pp. 804–810.

79. Tsuchiya, Y. and Yamaguchi, M., 1971, "Studies of Waves Forces Exerted on Large Cylindrical Piles (1)—Characteristics of the Distribution of Wave Pressure and the Variation of Water Level," *Annual Report of the Disaster Prevention Research Institute*, Kyoto University, Kyoto, Japan, No. 14B, pp. 373–390 (in Japanese, abstract in English).

79a. Tsurata, S. and Goda, Y., 1968, "Expected Discharge of Irregular Wave Overtopping," 11th Conference on Coastal Engineering, London, U.K., pp. 833–852.

80. Van Dorn, W. G., "Theoretical and Experimental Study of Wave Enhancement and Run-up on Uniformly Sloping Impermeable Beaches," SIO-66-11 Scripps Institute of Oceanography, San Diego, CA, pp. 1–95.

80a. Technical Advisory Committee on Protection Against Inundation, 1974, "Wave Run-up and Overtopping," Government Publishing Office, den Haag, the Netherlands.

81. Wallace, N. R., 1963, "Deformation of Solitary Waves, Part I: Reflection from a Vertical Wall," URS-631-1, United Research Services, Burlingame, CA, pp. 1–56.

82. Wassing, F., 1957, "Model Investigations on Wave Run-up Carried Out in the Netherlands During the Past Twenty Years," *Proceedings, Sixth Conference on Coastal Engineering*, Council on Wave Research, pp. 700–713.

83. Waterways Experiment Station, 1957, "Wave Run-up and Overtopping Levee Sections Lake Okeechobee, Florida," USWES Technical Report No. 2–449, U.S. Waterways Experiment Station, Vicksburg, MS. Jan., pp. 1–26.

83a. Weggel, J. R., 1976, "Wave Overtopping Equation," *Proceedings, 15th Coastal Engineering Conference*, ASCE, Honolulu.

84. Whitham, J. B., 1958, "On the Propagation of Shock Waves Through Regions of Non-uniform Area or Flow," *Journal of Fluid Mechanics*, Vol. 4, pp. 337–360.

85. Whitham, J. B., 1969, "Hot Film and Hot Wire Anemometry Theory and Application," TSI Bulletin TB-5, Thermo-Systems, Inc., St. Paul, MN, pp. 1–13.

86. Wiener, F. M., 1947, "Sound Diffraction by Rigid Spheres and Circular Cylinders," *Journal of the Acoustical Society of America*, Vol. 19, No. 3, pp. 444–451.

CHAPTER 16

RANDOM WAVE INTERACTION WITH STRUCTURES

Yoshimi Goda

Department of Civil Engineering
Yokohama National University
Yokohama, Japan

CONTENTS

Introduction

The fundamental property of sea waves is their randomness. When the first coastal engineering conference was held at Long Beach, California in 1950, the concept of random waves was not familiar to coastal engineers. Thus, various formulas and techniques to evaluate wave transformation and action upon structures were derived only with regular monochromatic waves. At present, however, the randomness of sea waves is well known (as discussed in Chapter 4). As it will be shown in this chapter, wave randomness can yield different results in wave transformation and action on structures compared with the results obtained with regular waves.

Wave refraction, shoaling, diffraction, and breaking are discussed in this chapter. The overtopping rate of seawalls, wave transmission behind breakwaters, and design wave pressure for vertical breakwaters are also discussed.

Wave Transformation and Deformation

Overview of the Transformations and Actions of Sea Waves

Flow Chart for Calculating Wave Transformations and Actions. Sea waves under-go several transformation and deformation processes before they interact with off-shore and coastal structures. Figure 1 presents an overview of such processes in a form of flow chart [1]. As the chart is self-explanatory, only a few comments are made here.

First, the boundary between deep and shallow water is rather vague. It is cus-tomary to take the water depth being one-half the deep-water wavelength as the boundary between deep and shallow waves. However, for random waves with spec-tra spreading over a frequency range, the boundary differs for various frequency components. For convenience, the wavelength corresponding to a representative period such as the spectral peak period, significant wave period, or the mean wave period can be employed to define the boundary between deep water and shallow (or intermediate depth) water.

Second, wave refraction and shoaling occur simultaneously at sea, but they are listed separately in Figure 1. This is done to clarify the concept of equivalent deep-water waves. The equivalent deep-water wave height is defined as

$$H_0' = K_d K_r K_f (H_{1/3})_0 \tag{1}$$

where K_d, K_r, and K_f denote the diffraction coefficient, the refraction coefficient, and the coefficient of wave attenuation due to bottom friction etc, respectively. As indicated, the equivalent deep-water waves are referred to as the significant waves and therefore serve as a representative of random sea waves in shallow water for the convenience of design calculation. The period of equivalent deep-water waves is usually taken as the significant wave period, the spectral peak period, or the mean wave period. In this chapter, the significant wave period is employed to define the equivalent deep-water wave period.

Third, waves may experience appreciable amount of attenuation due to bottom friction, percolation, and other phenomena while propagating in shallow water. The degree of attenuation depends on the expanse of shallow water portion (or the slope of sea bottom), sediment characteristics, etc. Although the phenomenon of wave attenuation is not explicitly shown in Figure 1, it could be inserted between the wave refraction ⑥ and the equivalent deep-water waves ⑧. The calculation method for wave attenuation due to bottom friction was first presented by Bretschneider [2] and is described in Reference 3. A review of various wave attenuations in shallow water was provided by Shemdin et al. [4].

Methods of Analysis for Random Wave Transformations and Actions. Figure 1 describes each phenomenon with the capital letters A to E. These letters symbolize the methods of analysis that are best suited to the phenomena in question according

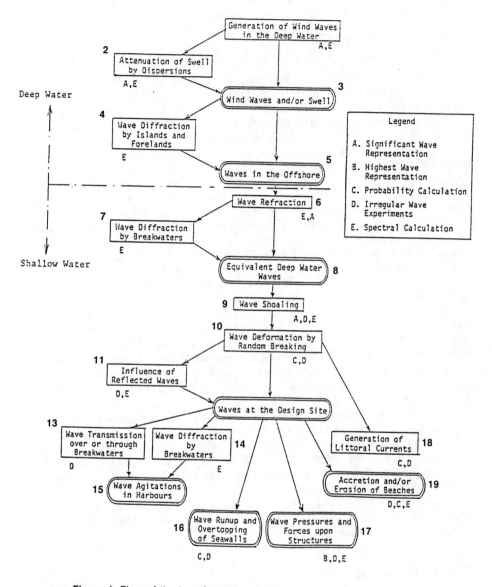

Figure 1. Flow of the transformations and actions of sea waves [1].

to Goda [1, 5]. They are

- A. Significant wave representation method
- B. Highest wave representation method
- C. Probability calculation method
- D. Irregular wave method
- E. Spectral calculation method

The significant or highest wave representation method is based on the assumption that actual wave trains could be represented with a train of regular waves having the height and period equal to those of significant or highest waves. Theory or laboratory data of regular waves are used to calculate transformations and actions of sea waves in these methods. Although both methods are convenient to use, they remain as crude approximations to the actual phenomena of random waves, and their use should be restricted to the phenomena in which the accuracy of approximation is within acceptable limits. Wave generation by wind and wave shoaling can be analyzed by the significant wave representation method, and wave pressures and forces are often estimated by the highest wave representation method.

The probability calculation method makes use of the probability distribution of the height and period of individual waves in random seas. Transformations and actions of individual waves are estimated with knowledge of regular waves, and they are added together with the probability of occurrence of individual waves. Wave deformation by random breaking and wave overtopping rate of seawalls are typical examples of the application of this method.

The irregular wave method is extensively employed in scale model tests of structures and harbors. Monochromatic wave tests for mound breakwaters are becoming obsolete as many hydraulic laboratories are now equipped with irregular wave flumes and basins. New facilities capable of reproducing three-dimensional random waves with given directional spectra are available at a limited number of laboratories around the world, and they expand the applicability of the irregular wave method even further.

The spectral calculation method is based on linear superpositions of spectral wave components, which undergo various transformation processes or exert certain influence on structures. The method is most powerful in evaluating the change in wave height due to diffraction and refraction. It is also employed for calculating wave forces on offshore structures of large diameters, because linear inertia forces dominate over nonlinear drag forces.

Because of the complex nature of sea waves, no single method can deal with all problems of wave transformations and actions on structures. Depending on the nature of a problem in question, a wise selection of the best method is recommended. The procedures regarded most appropriate are described in the following sections.

Wave Refraction and Shoaling

Wave Refraction. The phenomenon of wave refraction is easily recognized as wave crests are gradually bent to the shape of shorelines. Techniques to analyze the change in wave direction and height due to refraction are well established for the case of regular waves, and they are described in many textbooks and engineering manuals.

The techniques can be directly applied for the case of random waves using the significant wave representation method, if the bathymetric topography is relatively simple. In complicated bathymetry, however, simple application of monochromatic refraction analysis often yields mutual crossing of wave rays in certain areas and thus assessment of refraction coefficient becomes impractical. It is then advisable to employ the spectral calculation method. This method yields higher accuracy than the former method even in the case of monotonic geometry.

The basic technique of the spectral calculation method for any linear process inclusive of a refraction phenomenon is to derive the directional wave spectrum after wave transformation by means of the following formula:

$$S_{xx}(f, \theta) = \int_0^\infty \int_{\theta_{min}}^{\theta_{max}} S_{\eta\eta}(f, \theta) K_{xx}^2(f, \theta) \, d\theta \, df \tag{2}$$

where S_{xx} and $S_{\eta\eta}$ denote the directional spectra of transformed and incident waves, respectively, and K_{xx} represents the transfer function or the ratio of the transformed to incident amplitudes of monochromatic waves. In case of wave refraction, the transfer function is given as

$$K_{xx}(f, \theta) = K_{rr}(f, \theta) = K_s(f) K_r(f, \theta) \tag{3}$$

where $K_s(f)$ stands for the shoaling coefficient of regular waves with frequency f, and $K_r(f, \theta)$ represents the refraction coefficient of regular waves with frequency f and direction θ.

The effective refraction coefficient of random waves, denoted by $(K_r)_{eff}$, is then evaluated by

$$(K_r)_{eff} = \left[\frac{1}{m_{s0}} \int_{\theta_{min}}^{\theta_{max}} S_{rr}(f, \theta) \, d\theta \, df \right]^{1/2} \tag{4}$$

in which S_{rr} is the spectrum of refracted waves and m_{s0} is the zeroth moment of wave spectrum after transformation by shoaling only, i.e.,

$$m_{s0} = \int_0^\infty \int_{\theta_{min}}^{\theta_{max}} S_{\eta\eta}(f, \theta) K_s^2(f) \, d\theta \, df \tag{5}$$

The effective refraction coefficient of sea waves along a coast with straight, parallel depth-contours has been calculated with the previous method by Goda and Suzuki [6] for the directional spectrum of the following form:

$$S(f, \theta) = S(f) G(f, \theta) \tag{6}$$

where
$$\begin{aligned}
S(f) &= 0.257 \, H_{1/3}^2 T_{H1/3}^{-4} f^{-5} \exp[-1.03(T_{H1/3}f)^{-4}] \\
G(f, \theta) &= G_0 \cos^{2s}(\theta/2) \\
s &= \begin{cases} s_{max}(f/f_p)^5, & f < f_p \\ s_{max}(f/f_p)^{-2.5}, & f \geq f_p \end{cases} \\
f_p &= 1/(1.05 \, T_{H1/3})
\end{aligned} \tag{7}$$

This is the Bretschneider-Mitsuyasu frequency spectrum combined with the Mitsu-yasu-type directional spreading furnction (see Chapter 4). The results of calculation for $s_{max} = 10$, 25, and 75 have been reproduced in Reference 5b.

Refraction of random waves can also be computed by solving the following energy flux equation for a given directional spectrum of incident waves:

$$\frac{\partial}{\partial x} (Sv_x) + \frac{\partial}{\partial y} (Sv_y) + \frac{\partial}{\partial \theta} (Sv_\theta) = 0 \tag{8}$$

The wave propagation velocity vectors v are given by

$$v_x = c_g \cos \theta$$

$$v_y = c_g \sin \theta$$

$$v_\theta = \frac{c_g}{c} \left(\frac{\partial S}{\partial x} \sin \theta - \frac{\partial S}{\partial y} \cos \theta \right) \tag{9}$$

in which c_g and c denote the group and phase velocities, respectively. The above energy flux equation was first given by Karlsson [7] in 1969 for wave refraction problems and has been employed in many engineering problems since then. A numerical scheme for solving Equation 8 requires that all frequency components should propagate in the positive x-direction and no wave diffraction phenomenon should occur in the area of simultaneous computation. It should be mentioned here that Equations 8 and 9 conform with the basic equation for wave refraction.

Wave Shoaling. Shoaling of random waves can be treated with the technique of linear spectral transformation in Equation 2. The transfer function is taken as the shoaling coefficient K_s. Difference between regular and random wave shoaling co-efficients is found to be on the order of 2 to 3%.

Much larger deviation from linear wave shoaling is observed by introduction of wave nonlinearity. Such deviation becomes quite noticeable as waves approach the surf zone. Shuto [8] obtained a closed-form expression for nonlinear wave shoaling coefficient, and Goda [5c, 9] presented a design diagram for estimating nonlinear shoaling coefficient. Figure 2 is a reproduction of the diagram by Goda [9]. The notations h and L_0 represent the water depth and the deep-water wavelength, respectively, and $\tan \theta$ denotes the bottom slope. The portion of curves above dash-dots lines belong to the waves within the surf zone.

Wave Diffraction

Diffraction of random waves is calculated by the linear wave transformation formula of Equation 2. The transfer function in this case is

$$K_{xx}(f, \theta) = K_d(f, \theta) \tag{10}$$

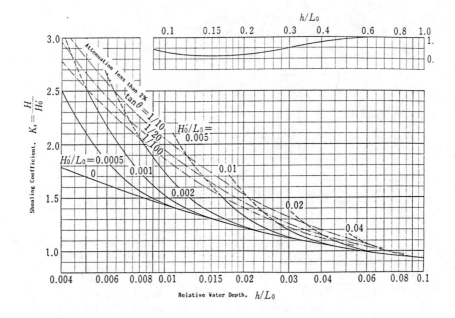

Figure 2. Diagram of nonlinear wave shoaling coefficient [9].

where $K_d(f, \theta)$ denotes the diffraction coefficient of regular waves with frequency f and direction θ. Once the spectrum of diffracted waves is calculated, the significant height and the mean wave period are evaluated by Equations 14 and 49 of Chapter 4, respectively.

The diffraction diagrams of sea waves have been computed by Goda et al. [10] with the directional spectrum defined by Equations 6 and 7. Figures 3 and 4 are examples of diffraction coefficient of random sea waves. A full set of random wave diffraction diagrams with the directional spreading parameter $s_{max} = 10$ and 75 is found in Reference 5d.

It should be noted that diffraction diagrams of random sea waves are quite different from those of regular waves. For example the diffraction coefficient along the x-axis for a semi-infinite breakwater takes the value about 0.7 as seen in Figure 3, while the coefficient is about 0.5 in case of regular waves. Diffraction diagrams of a breakwater opening also exhibit smaller wave height along the central axis and larger height in the shadow zone than those of regular waves, as indicated in Figure 4. Such differences originate from the directional spreading of wave energy, which is expressed by directional wave spectra.

Several field measurements on wave diffraction [10] have verified the reliability of random wave diffraction calculation and proved inapplicability of regular wave diffraction diagrams. Because of a large difference between random and regular wave diffraction, the use of regular diffraction diagrams for actual problems at sea causes

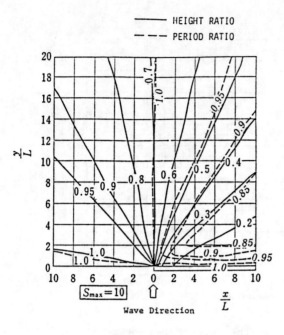

Figure 3. Diffraction diagram for a semi-infinite breakwater for random sea waves of normal incidence (solid lines for wave height ratio and dash lines for wave period ratio) [10].

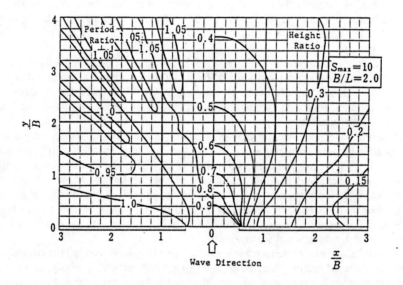
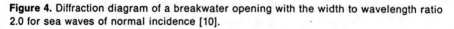

Figure 4. Diffraction diagram of a breakwater opening with the width to wavelength ratio 2.0 for sea waves of normal incidence [10].

large errors in the estimate of diffracted wave height; therefore, diffraction diagrams of random sea waves should be used instead.

An interesting feature of random wave diffraction is the change in wave period. This is shown in Figures 3 and 4 as the ratio of diffracted to incident wave periods. The verification of period change by wave diffraction remains a subject of future research.

Wave Deformation Due to Random Breaking

A regular train of waves generated in a laboratory flume break at a fixed point with an almost constant.height. Then their heights decrease rapidly due to energy dissipation after breaking. Breaking of random waves nearshore, however, is not confined at any fixed location but spread over a broad area, which is called the surf zone. Decrease of wave heights such as the significant wave height within the surf zone is gradual. Direct application of regular wave breaking to sea waves nearshore only yields inaccurate estimate of wave behavior in the surf zone.

Several studies have been carried out to clarify the nature of random wave breaking in the surf zone and to evaluate the change of wave characteristics. It may be some time before we can clearly understand the wave deformation process taking place in the surf zone. From the engineering point-of-view, the changes in the largest and significant wave heights and the mean water level in the surf zone are of most concern. For this purpose, a model developed by Goda [5e, 9] provides a good working tool for engineers. The model includes the breaking of individual waves as a function of wave height relative to water depth, the wave set-down and set-up due to the change in radiation stress, and the presence of surf beats near the shoreline.

Figure 5 shows an example of the diagrams for estimating significant wave height in the surf zone with the bottom slope 1/20 [9]. The equivalent deep-water wave height H_0' is employed as the reference height for the change of wave height. Similar diagrams for the bottom slope of 1:10, 1:30, and 1:100 and those for the largest wave height are listed in reference [5e]. The applicability of the random wave diffraction model has been verified by field observation data. The tendencies of wave height variations compiled in the diagrams such as Figure 5 have been formulated into the following expressions by Goda [9]:

$$H_{1/3} = \begin{cases} K_s H_0', & h/L_0 \geqq 0.2 \\ \min\{(\beta_0 H_0' + \beta_1 h), \beta_{max} H_0', K_s H_0'\}, & h/L_0 < 0.2 \end{cases} \tag{11}$$

$$H_{max} \equiv \begin{cases} H_{1/250} = 1.8\, K_s H_0', & h/L_0 \geqq 0.2 \\ \min\{(\beta_0^* H_0' + \beta_1^* h), \beta_{max}^* H_0', 1.8\, K_s H_0'\} & h/L_0 < 0.2 \end{cases} \tag{12}$$

where
$$\left. \begin{aligned} \beta_0 &= 0.028(H_0'/L_0)^{-0.38} \exp[20 \tan^{1.5} \theta] \\ \beta_1 &= 0.52 \exp[4.2 \tan \theta] \\ \beta_{max} &= \max\{0.92, 0.32(H_0'/L_0)^{-0.29} \exp[2.4 \tan \theta]\} \end{aligned} \right\} \tag{13}$$

$$\left. \begin{aligned} \beta_0^* &= 0.052(H_0'/L_0)^{-0.38} \exp[20 \tan^{1.5} \theta] \\ \beta_1^* &= 0.63 \exp[3.8 \tan \theta] \\ \beta_{max}^* &= \max\{1.65, 0.53(H_0'/L_0)^{-0.29} \exp[2.4 \tan \beta]\} \end{aligned} \right\} \tag{14}$$

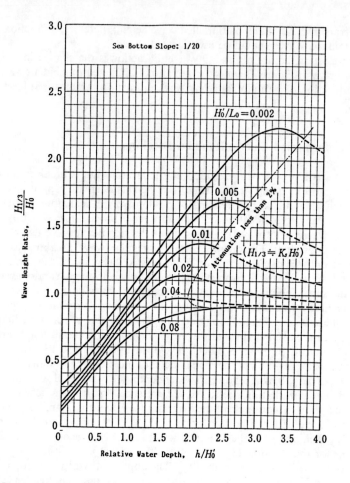

Figure 5. Diagram for the estimation of significant wave height in the surf zone with the sea bottom slope 1 on 20 [9].

and min{a, b, c} stands for the minimum value among a, b, and c, while max{a, b} gives the larger of a or b.

Equations 11 and 12 are approximate representations of smooth curves such as shown in Figure 5 with a set of a straight line proportional to the water depth h, a horizontal line limiting a maximum value, and a curve corresponding to wave shoaling. Therefore, an error of a few percent due to approximation should be expected.

Gradual change in the wave height causes a variation of local mean water level in the surf zone, which is known as the wave set-down and set-up. Figure 6 shows the variation of mean water level calculated by Goda [9]. Calculation has shown

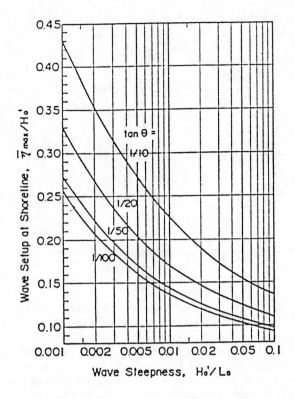

Figure 6. Diagram for the estimation of wave setup at the shoreline [9].

that the variation of mean water level is enhanced as the bottom slope becomes steep.

Wave Overtopping and Transmission over Shore Structures

Overtopping Rate of Seawalls by Random Waves

The quantity of water overtopping a shore structure has been investigated by many researchers, because it is an essential part of seawall design. Most of the studies were based on laboratory tests using regular waves, and some of the results are presented in Reference 3. Such data of regular wave overtopping may often provide inaccurate information, because the irregularity of wave trains can have a major influence on the volume of wave overtopping. For example, if a shore structure is designed to have its crest elevation higher than the run-up height of regular waves equivalent to the design significant wave, engineers may expect no wave overtopping of the structure. In reality, however, the structure will experience considerable overtopping by individual waves higher than the significant wave when the design storm waves attack the shore structure.

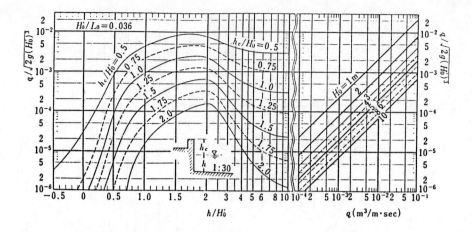

Figure 7. Design diagram of wave overtopping rate of vertical revetments on a sea bottom slope of $\frac{1}{30}$ [11].

At present the only available data of random wave overtopping are those of Goda [5f, 11]. The data are presented in a set of twelve design diagrams of two types of structures (vertical revetments and block-mound seawalls), two values of sea bottom slopes (1/10 and 1/30), and three values of equivalent deep-water wave steepness (0.012, 0.017, and 0.036). Figures 7 and 8 are examples of these diagrams; the former is for vertical revetments and the latter is for seawalls built with concrete block mounds of the energy-dissipating type such as tetrapods.

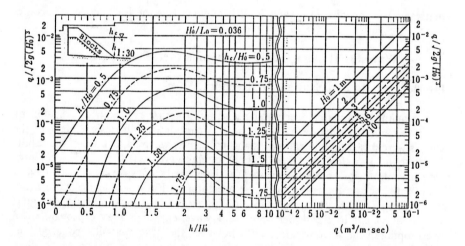

Figure 8. Design diagram of wave overtopping rate of block-mound seawalls on a sea bottom slope of $\frac{1}{30}$ [11].

An illustrative example is given here. Suppose a seawall of vertical wall type is designed at the water depth 6 m with the bottom slope 1/30. The crest elevation is 4 m. Both the depth and elevation is referenced to the design storm tide level. The equivalent deep-water wave for design is $H_0' = 3.0$ m and $T_{1/3} = 7.0$ s. Because the wave steepness is $H_0'/L_0 = 0.039$, Figure 7 is approximately applicable. The relative water depth is $h/H_0' = 2.0$ and the relative crest elevation is $h_c/H_0' = 1.33$. The dimensionless wave overtopping rate is read from Figure 7 as $q/\sqrt{2g(H_0')^3} = 10^{-3}$. Thus $q = 0.035$ m³/m/s. If the seawall is built with a concrete block mound of the energy-dissipating type, the wave overtopping rate is estimated to decrease to 0.004 m³/m/s by using Figure 8.

The amount of allowable wave overtopping rate depends on the state of land use behind a seawall, the strength of pavement against the impact of falling water mass, the capacity of pumps and flumes to dispose the accumulated water, and other factors. Presently in Japan, the overtopping rate $q = 0.01$ m³/m/s is employed for design of seawalls protecting the densely inhabited area.

Wave Transmission Behind Breakwaters

Although the breakwater is built to prevent waves propagating into a harbor, a certain amount of wave energy is usually allowed to penetrate through the breakwater because of economical or design constraints. One source of energy transmission is the regeneration of waves by water overtopping the breakwater. This process occurs when the crest elevation of breakwater is lower than the wave run-up height along the front face of the breakwater. The other source of energy transmission is the wave penetration through the voids of the breakwater core. This latter process may become significant in the case of sloping breakwaters. A system of segmented breakwaters to prevent beach erosion is often designed to permit some wave transmission in order to enhance beach accretion behind the system.

The degree of wave transmission behind a breakwater largely depends on the structural type of the breakwater and the materials employed. Because theoretical analysis of wave transmission by overtopping is almost impossible, many laboratory investigations have been undertaken to provide design data for breakwaters. Some of the results are presented in the following discussion as reference data for breakwater design. It should be cautioned, however, that the laboratory data are usually quite scattered and the design curves or empirical formulas are drawn as the average relation among the scattered data. The estimated height of transmitted waves may deviate more than 10% in terms of the incident wave height from the actual value. As in many other problems of wave and structure interactions, a scale-model test is recommended whenever a reliable information of wave transmission is required.

Upright Impermeable Breakwater. A caisson or masonry type breakwater rested upon a rubble-mound foundation permits little penetration of wave energy through it. Wave transmission is mostly due to overtopping. Figure 9 by Goda [12] enables an approximate estimate of the wave transmission coefficient or the ratio of transmitted to incident wave heights over an upright impermeable breakwater. The governing factor is the crest elevation above the water level h_c relative to the incident

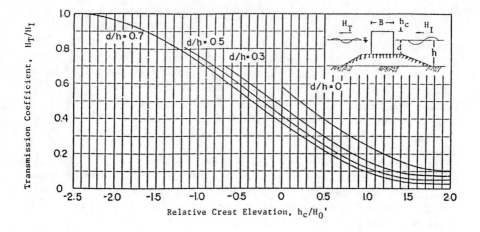

Figure 9. Wave transmission coefficient for a vertical breakwater [12].

wave height H_I. The height of the rubble-mound is a secondary factor affecting the wave transmission coefficient. The diagram was prepared on the basis of laboratory experiments using regular waves, but it has been verified as applicable for random waves through laboratory tests. The width B of the upright section tested, covers a range $B/h = 0.8 \sim 1.1$, which represents standard geometry of upright breakwaters.

A rubble-mound foundation of upright breakwater allows a small amount of wave energy passing through it. The portion of empirical curves in the range $h_c/H_I > 1.5$ represents a crude estimation of wave transmission through the rubble-mound foundation.

Rubble-Mound Breakwater. Wave transmission behind a rubble-mound breakwater is caused by both overtopping and penetration. It is affected by many factors such as the crest elevation, crest width, front and rear face slopes, rubble size, and porosity of the breakwater mound. The wave height, wavelength, and water depth also affect the wave transmission. Several laboratory investigations have been carried out to provide design information on wave transmission behind rubble-mound breakwaters. Seelig [13], for example, has combined his own data and several other studies and proposed the following procedure to estimate the wave transmission coefficient:

$$K_T = H_T/H_I = [(K_T)_0{}^2 + (K_T)_P{}^2]^{1/2} \tag{15}$$

where $(K_T)_0$ and $(K_T)_P$ denote the transmission coefficient due to wave overtopping and penetration, respectively.

For wave transmission through a porous rubble structure, Seelig recommended using the analytical model by Madsen and White [14]. Seelig [13] wrote a computer program to obtain the transmission coefficient. For the wave transmission over a rubble-mound breakwater, Seelig has proposed an empirical formula as

$$(K_T)_0 = C(1 - h_c/R), \quad 0 \leqq (K_T)_0 \leqq 1.0 \tag{16}$$

where C is an empirical coefficient given by

$$C = 0.51 - 0.11 B/(h + h_c) \tag{17}$$

and R is the run-up height. Seelig's recommendation for predicting run-up height on a rough slope was

$$\frac{R}{H} = \frac{0.692\xi}{1 + 0.504\xi} \tag{18}$$

where ξ is the surf parameter defined by

$$\xi = \tan \theta / \sqrt{(H/L_0)} \tag{19}$$

and tan θ represents the slope of front face.

For a quick reference to the overall wave transmission coefficient of rubble-mound breakwaters, Figure 10 can be useful. The diagram was prepared by Tanaka [15] based on his laboratory tests of model breakwaters with the front slope 1:2. The study conducted with regular waves covered a wide range of crest elevation and width for nonbreaking to breaking waves. The diagram indicates that a very broad breakwater can dissipate a considerable amount of wave energy, even if it is submerged. Adams and Sonu [16] applied the diagram for the submerged break-water at Santa Monica to predict the transmission coefficient and compared it with the result of a three-dimensional scale-model test using irregular waves. They reported that Tanaka's diagram yielded predictions in agreement with the model study, although the diagram showed a slight tendency of underestimation.

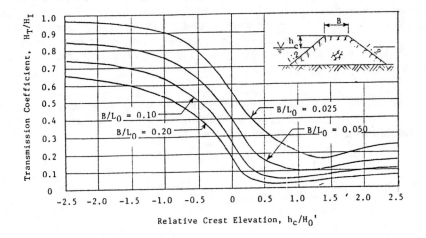

Figure 10. Wave transmission coefficient for a rubble mound breakwater [15].

Wave Pressure on Upright Structures

Wave Pressure Formulas Based on a Monochromatic Wave Concept

The wave pressure exerted upon a vertical wall is the major design load of vertical breakwaters. The wave height, period, and direction are the major parameters of breakwater design. Many analytical studies, laboratory investigations, and field observations have been undertaken to clarify the phenomenon of wave pressure and to derive certain wave pressure formulas since the 19th century. Most of wave pressure formulas, however, are based on the concept of monochromatic waves or regular waves with the constant height and period, despite the fact that actual sea waves are irregular. Also most of existing formulas are designed to deal with either nonbreaking waves or breaking waves.

These wave pressure formulas based on a monochromatic wave concept are generally not recommended for design for two reasons. The first is the ambiguity in the definition of wave height to be employed with the pressure formula. It is not specified whether H_{max} or $H_{1/3}$ should be used, even though the resulting differences in wave pressure are great. The second is the discontinuity in the predicted wave pressure at the threshold condition from nonbreaking waves to breaking waves. A breakwater extending over a long distance from shallow to deep-water areas would be designed with the pressure formulas of breaking waves in the shallow portion and those of nonbreaking waves in the deep portion. At the threshold water depth, two predictions for the shallow and deep portions should meet together, and they usually indicate an abrupt change of more than 30% in the predicted value of wave pressure. A slight modification in the design wave height would shift the location of the threshold condition. Engineers in charge of the breakwater design would face the problem of how to adjust two breakwater designs across the threshold point.

These problems originate from the inadequacy in the pressure formulas with the monochromatic wave concept. In the next subsection a method of wave pressure calculation based on the random wave concept is introduced where such problems do not appear. However, a few standard pressure formulas are discussed in this subsection in order to acquaint the readers with a historical background of wave pressure problems.

Sainflou's Formulas. These formulas are for the pressure caused by standing waves. The rise of the mid-height level δ and the pressure intensities p_1 and p_2 shown in Figure 11 are calculated as follows:

$$\delta = (\pi H^2/L) \coth(2\pi h/L)$$

$$p_1 = (p_2 + wh)(H + \delta)/(h + H + \delta) \tag{20}$$

$$p_2 = wH/\cosh(2\pi h/L)$$

where w denotes the specific weight of sea water.

Sainflou [17] proposed these formulas in 1928 as simplified forms of his trochoidal wave theory of standing waves in finite water depth. Immediately after the publication of his paper, Sainflou's formulas were widely accepted by harbor engineers. However, the use of the significant wave height $H_{1/3}$ in Sainflou's formula results in seriously underestimating maximum wave force during the design sea state, and it might cause a failure of the structure.

There are several other formulas of standing wave pressures, including the Miche-Rundgren method cited in Reference [3]. They can be fitted to laboratory data better than Sainflou's formulas, but the question of the wave height to be used in design calculation still remains.

Hiroi's Formula. This formula is for breaking wave pressures and assumes a uniform distribution of pressure along the vertical wall with the intensity of

$$p_b = 1.5wH \tag{21}$$

Hiroi [18] proposed this formula in 1919, based on his field experiments and experiences in vertical breakwater construction in Japan at that time. When the concept of wave irregularity became known to engineers in Japan, it was decided to incorporate the significant wave height into Hiroi's formula based on the comparison of design wave heights at various harbors. Although it is a very simple formula,

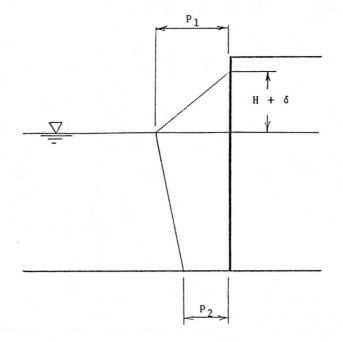

Figure 11. Wave pressure distribution in Sainflou's formulas.

it was accepted by engineers through the design, construction, and performance of many vertical breakwaters. Use of Hiroi's formula, however, became infrequent since 1979, when the new wave pressure formulas based on the random wave concept by Goda [20] were officially adopted in engineering manuals for harbor design in Japan.

Minikin's Formulas. Minikin's formulas are for estimating breaking wave pressures on a vertical breakwater rested upon a rubble mound. Wave pressure is divided into the dynamic and hydrostatic components, which are given as follows (see Figure 12):

Dynamic pressure:

$$\left.\begin{array}{l} p_m = p_{max}(1 - 2|z|/H)^2, \\ p_{max} = 101wd(1 + d/h)H/L \end{array} \quad |z| \leqq H/2\right\} \tag{22}$$

Hydrostatic pressure:

$$p_s = \begin{cases} 0.5wH(1 - 2z/H), & 0 \leqq z < H/2 \\ 0.5wH, & z < 0 \end{cases} \tag{23}$$

The notation z refers to the elevation measured upward from the still water level and d stands for the water depth above the rubble foundation.

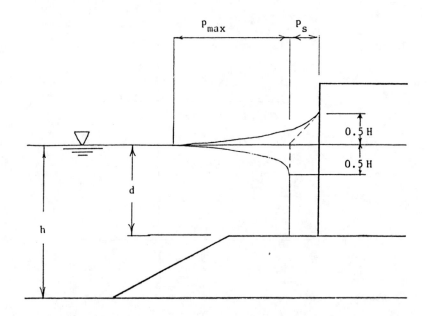

Figure 12. Wave pressure distribution in Minikin's formulas.

Minikin [19] proposed these formulas in 1950 based on speculations on the mechanism of impulsive breaking wave pressures. Although the formulas have been cited in many textbooks and engineering manuals, few breakwaters have been designed with Minikin's formulas. One reason is the tendency that the formulas predict the pressure of excessively large intensity and a vertical breakwater capable of withstanding such large pressure becomes uneconomical. The tendency of overestimation was demonstrated by Goda [20] in a case study of breakwater performance during high waves. Another reason is the fact that vertical breakwaters have not been built in many countries because of the failure of Mustapha Jetty at Port of Algiers in 1932. Exceptions are the countries of Japan, Korea, and Taiwan, where vertical breakwaters have been favored over rubble-mound breakwaters and have been built without serious failures over many years. Hiroi's formula has been used in these countries.

At present, Minikin's formulas can be considered to belong to a group of pressure formulas of historical interest.

Wave Pressure Formulas with a Random Wave Concept

Wave Pressure under a Wave Crest. In 1973, Goda [20] presented a method of predicting wave pressures exerted on an upright section of a vertical breakwater for design purposes. The basic concept was to design the upright section against the largest single wave force expected during the design sea state and to assume that the largest force could be evaluated with the highest wave in a wave group. The method was slightly modified in 1975 to incorporate the model of random wave breaking within the surf zone into the evaluation of H_{max}, and is currently used as the standard design formula in Japan.

The wave pressure formulas are also characterized with a smooth transition from nonbreaking to breaking wave pressures without the necessity for changing the design formula. The following is a brief account of the method by Goda [20]; additional details can be found in Reference 5g.

Design Wave. The highest wave in the design sea state is employed. Its height is evaluated by Equation 12 or read from the design diagrams for H_{max} by the random wave breaking model by Goda [5e, 9]. The wave height H_{max} is estimated not at the breakwater site but at the location at a distance $5H_{1/3}$ seaward of the breakwater. By means of this procedure, the effect of sea bottom slope on breaking wave pressure is considered indirectly. The period of the highest wave $T_{H,max}$ is taken equal to the significant period $T_{H1/3}$.

Wave Pressure Distribution. As shown in Figure 13, a trapezoidal shape of pressure distribution is assumed along the face of the front wall (Figure 13). It should be noted that the water depth above the rubble foundation d is measured from the top of armor layer but the wave pressure is exerted down to the bottom of the upright section; therefore, $h' \geq d$. The uplift pressure is acting along the bottom of the upright section. The distribution of the uplift pressure is assumed to be triangular.

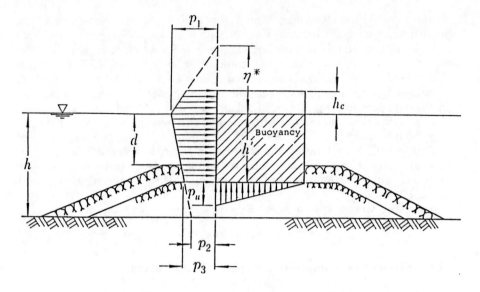

Figure 13. Wave pressure distribution in Goda's method.

Elevation to which the Wave Pressure Is Exerted.

$$\eta^* = 0.75(1 + \cos \beta)H_{max} \tag{23}$$

in which β denotes the angle between the direction of wave approach and a line normal to the breakwater. For incident waves normal to the breakwater, $\beta = 0°$ and $\eta^* = 1.5H_{max}$. The wave direction should be rotated by an amount of up to $15°$ toward the line normal to the breakwater from the principal wave direction in order to offset the uncertainty in estimating the design wave direction to allow for greater design safety.

Wave Pressure on the Front of a Vertical Wall.

$$\left.\begin{array}{l} p_1 = 0.5(1 + \cos \beta)(\alpha_1 + \alpha_2 \cos^2 \beta)wH_{max} \\ p_2 = p_1/\cosh(2\pi h/L) \\ p_3 = \alpha_3 p_1 \end{array}\right\} \tag{24}$$

$$\text{where } \left.\begin{array}{l} \alpha_1 = 0.6 + 0.5\left[\dfrac{4\pi h/L}{\sinh(4\pi h/L)}\right]^2 \\[2mm] \alpha_2 = \min\left\{\left[\dfrac{h_b - d}{3h_b}\left(\dfrac{H_{max}}{d}\right)^2\right], \dfrac{2d}{H_{max}}\right\} \\[2mm] \alpha_3 = 1 - \dfrac{h'}{h}\left[1 - \dfrac{1}{\cosh(2\pi h/L)}\right] \end{array}\right\} \tag{25}$$

where h_b denotes the water depth at the location at a distance $5H_{1/3}$ seaward of the breakwater and $\min\{a, b\}$ represents the smaller of a or b.

Buoyancy and Uplift Pressure. The buoyancy is to be calculated for the displacement volume of the upright section in still water below the design water level regardless of the state of wave overtopping or non-overtopping. The uplift pressure at the toe of the upright section is given by

$$p_u = 0.5(1 + \cos \beta)\alpha_1\alpha_3 wH_{max} \tag{26}$$

Wave Pressure under a Wave Trough. When a wave trough makes contact with a vertical wall, the water pressure on the wall is less than the hydrostatic pressure under the still water level. The decrease in the pressure under a wave trough can be approximately estimated as follows:

$$p = \begin{cases} wz & : -0.5H_{max} \leqq z < 0 \\ -0.5wH_{max} & : z < -0.5H_{max} \end{cases} \tag{27}$$

For the case of standing wave pressures, a more accurate estimation is possible by means of the fourth-order finite amplitude wave theory by Goda [21]. A set of calculation diagrams for standing wave pressure under a wave trough can be found in References 5g and 21. An interesting feature is the fact that the wave force under a wave trough directing seaward exceeds the force under a wave crest directing shoreward when the water depth is greater than about a quarter of the wavelength. This reversal of the absolute magnitudes of wave forces at the crest and the trough is caused by the second and fourth harmonic components of wave pressures inherent to standing waves.

Notation

B	width of breakwater
c	phase celerity of waves
c_g	group celerity of waves
C	empirical coefficient of wave transmission given by Equation 17
d	water depth above the top of rubble-mound foundation
f	frequency
f_p	frequency at the peak of wave spectrum
g	acceleration due to gravity
$G(f, \theta)$	directional spreading function (Equation 7)
h	water depth
h′	height of upright section of vertical breakwater below the mean water level
h_c	crest elevation of breakwater or seawall above the mean water level
H	wave height
H_0'	equivalent deep-water wave height (Equation 1)

$H_{1/3}$ significant wave height
$(H_{1/3})_0$ significant wave height at deepwater
H_{max} largest wave height in an irregular wave train
H_I incident wave height
H_T transmitted wave height behind breakwater
K_d diffraction coefficient
K_f coefficient of wave attenuation due to bottom friction, etc.
K_r refraction coefficient
K_s shoaling coefficient
K_T transmission coefficient
K_{xx} spectral transfer function of the phenomenon X
L_0 deepwater wavelength corresponding to significant wave period
m_{s0} zeroth moment of wave spectrum after transformation by shoaling only (Equation 5)
p wave pressure
p_1, p_2, p_3 intensity of wave pressure at various elevations (Equations 20 and 24)
p_b breaking wave pressure by Hiroi (Equation 21)
p_m dynamic component of wave pressure by Minikin (Equation 22)
p_{max} maximum intensity of the dynamic component of wave pressure
p_s hydrostatic component of wave pressure
p_u uplift pressure at the toe of upright section
q wave overtopping rate of seawall
R height of wave run-up above the mean water level
s directional spreading parameter (Equation 7)
s_{max} maximum value of directional spreading parameter
$S(f)$ frequency spectra of waves
$S(f, \theta)$ directional wave spectra
$S_{xx}(f, \theta)$ directional spectra of waves transformed by the phenomenon X
$S_{\eta\eta}(f, \theta)$ directional spectra of incident waves
$T_{H_{1/3}}$ significant wave period
$T_{H,max}$ period of highest wave
$\mathbf{v}(v_x, v_y, v_\theta)$ wave propagation celerity vector (Equation 9)
w specific weight of sea water
z elevation measured upward from the still water level

Greek Letters

$\alpha_1, \alpha_2, \alpha_3$ coefficients of wave pressure given by Equation 25
β angle between the direction of wave approach and a line normal to the breakwater
$\beta_1, \beta_2, \beta_{max}$ coefficients of significant wave height in the surf zone (Equation 13)
$\beta_1{}^*, \beta_2{}^*, \beta_{max}{}^*$ coefficient of largest wave height in the surf zone (Equation 14)
δ rise of mid-height level above the still water level (Equation 20)
η^* elevation to which the wave pressure is exerted (Equation 23)

θ direction of spectral wave component, or angle of inclination of sea bottom or breakwater face from the horizontal line

ξ surf parameter defined by Equation 19

References

1. Goda, Y., 1976, "Irregular Sea Waves for the Design of Harbour Structures (Integrated Title)," *Trans. Japan Soc. Civil Engrs.*, Vol. 8, pp. 267–271.
2. Bretschneider, C. L. and Reid, R. O., 1954, "Modification of Wave Height Due to Bottom Friction, Percolation, and Refraction," *U.S. Army Corps of Engrs., Beach Erosion Board, Tech. Memo.*, No. 45.
3. U.S. Army Coastal Engng. Res. Center, 1984, *Shore Protection Manual* (4th Ed.), U.S. Gov. Printing Office, Washington, D.C.
4. Shemdin, O.H. et al., 1980, "Mechanisms of Wave Transformation in Finite-Depth Water," *J. Geophys. Res.*, Vol. 85, No. C9, pp. 5012–5018.
5. Goda, Y., 1985, *Random Seas and Design of Maritime Structures*, Tokyo, Univ. Tokyo Press, 323p.: (a) pp. 5–10, (b) pp. 49–50, (c) pp. 68–70, (d) pp. 54–58, (e) pp. 71–87, (f) pp. 145–154, (g) 114–139.
6. Goda, Y. and Suzuki, Y., 1975, "Computation of Refraction and Diffraction of Sea Waves with Mitsuyasu's Directional Spectrum," *Tech. Note of Port and Harbour Res. Inst.*, No. 230, 45p. (*in Japanese*).
7. Karlsson, T., 1969, "Refraction of Continuous Ocean Wave Spectra," *Proc. ASCE*, Vol. 95, No. WW4, pp. 437–448.
8. Shuto, N., 1974, "Nonlinear Long Waves in a Channel of Variable Section," *Coastal Engng. in Japan*, Japan Soc. Civil Engrs., Vol. 17, pp. 1–12.
9. Goda, Y., 1975, "Deformation of Irregular Waves Due to Depth-Controlled Wave Breaking," *Rept. Port and Harbour Res. Inst.*, Vol. 14, No. 3, pp. 59–106 (*in Japanese*), or *Coastal Engng. in Japan*, Vol. 18, pp. 13–26.
10. Goda, Y. et al., 1978, "Diffraction Diagrams for Directional Random Waves," *Proc. 16th Int. Conf. Coastal Engng.*, Hamburg, pp. 628–650.
11. Goda et al., 1975, "Laboratory Investigation on the Overtopping Rate of Seawalls by Irregular Waves," *Rept. Port and Harbour Res. Inst.*, Vol. 14, No. 4, pp. 3–44 (*in Japanese*).
12. Goda, Y., 1969, "Re-analysis of Laboratory Data on Wave Transmission over Breakwaters," *Rept. Port and Harbour Res. Inst.*, Vol. 8, No. 3, pp. 3–18.
13. Seelig, W. N., 1980, "Two-Dimensional Tests of Wave Transmission and Reflection Characteristics of Laboratory Breakwaters," *U.S. Army Coastal Engng. Res. Center, Tech. Rept.*, No. 80-1., 187 pp.
14. Madsen, O. S. and White, S. M., "Reflection and Transmission Characteristics of Porous Rubble-Mound Breakwaters," *U.S. Army Coastal Engng. Res. Center. Misc. Rept.*, No. 76-5.
15. Tanaka, N. 1976, "Effects of Submerged Rubble-Mound Breakwater on Wave Attenuation and Shoreline Stabilization," *Proc. 23rd Japanese Coastal Engng. Conf.*, pp. 152–157 (*in Japanese*).
16. Adams, C. B. and Sonu, C. J., 1986, "Wave Transmission across Submerged Near-Surface Breakwaters," *Proc. 20th Int. Conf. Coastal Engng.*, Taipei, pp. 1729–1738.
17. Sainflou, G., 1928, "Essais sur les Digues Maritimes Verticales," *Annales de Ponts et Chaussées*, Vol. 98, No. 4.
18. Hiroi, I., 1919, "On a Method of Estimating the Force of Waves," *Memoirs of Engng. Faculty, Imperial Univ. Tokyo*, Vol. X, No. 1, p. 19.

19. Minikin, R. R., 1950, *Winds, Waves, and Maritime Structures*, London, Griffin, pp. 38–39.
20. Goda, Y., 1973, "A New Method of Wave Pressure Calculation for the Design of Composite Breakwater," *Rept. Port and Harbour Res. Inst.*, Vol. 12, No. 3, pp. 31–70 (*in Japanese*), or *Proc. 14th Int. Conf. Coastal Engng.* Copenhagen, 1974, pp. 1702–1720.
21. Goda, Y. and Kakizaki, S., 1966, "Study on Finite Amplitude Standing Waves and Their Pressures upon a Vertical Wall," *Rept. Port and Harbour Res. Inst.*, Vol. 5, No. 10, 57 pp. (in Japanese), or *Coastal Engng. in Japan*, Vol. 10, 1967, pp. 1–11.

CHAPTER 17

RUBBLE MOUND AND ARTIFICIAL STONE BREAKWATERS

Eugene H. Harlow

Civil Engineer
Houston, Texas

CONTENTS

Rubble-Mound Breakwaters

Historical Perspective

Rubble mounds are the oldest form of coastal protection because they are the simplest to build and the easiest to maintain. It is apparent that large pieces of stone are not as easily moved by waves and currents as smaller particles of sand or silt. Also, larger pieces are readily available near the coasts in many parts of the world. Even where stone is far away, quarries where rock may be excavated are often within a small distance.

The earliest seafaring people built protection for their harbors and waterfronts with windrows of stone and rock. In Roman times, the methodology became quite sophisticated, and remains of breakwaters built by Romans have been found that resemble the latest in present-day rubble-mound structures.

Furthermore, the cost of construction was found to be generally less than other types of breakwaters, because nothing more is required than manpower and simple skids and levers. Complex mining and processing of mortars is not needed, nor is heavy lifting equipment, as may be the case with synthetic blocks.

Configurations

The shapes of rubble-mound structures vary considerably, depending on the coast being protected, no two of which are exactly alike.

Harbors in general need breakwaters to prevent large waves from entering and causing such turbulence as to interfere with shipping. Yet sufficient opening through the breakwater is needed to allow safe passage of ships. The orientation of the breakwater, sometimes with one arm projecting from the shore, sometimes with two, is chosen as a compromise between stopping all waves or stopping all navigation, in a way that gives maximum use at the least cost—like all engineering objectives.

Frequently, this leads to overlapping arms intended to block the worst waves almost completely, yet allow room for vessel passage. At other locations, where waves may come from several directions, more nearly symmetrical arms are more appropriate, counting on preventing the major energy of any storm waves from entering the harbor. Or, in the case of a river estuary, it may be necessary to allow the river channel to continue to sea in its normal direction (Figure 1).

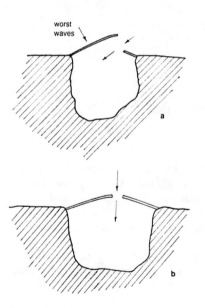
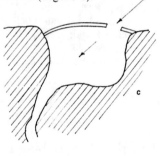
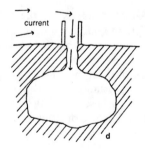

Figure 1.

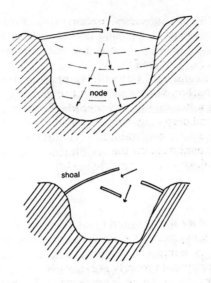

Figure 2.

Attention must be given to reflected waves within the harbor, as, at some harbors, energy entering the opening between breakwaters may be reflected off the interior shore in such a way as to produce nodes where wave heights may equal or surpass the outside waves. In such cases, however, it may be desirable to provide an asymmetrical enclosure, or even secondary breakwater arms to break up the reflected waves (Figure 2).

In all cases, ship navigation should be made as simple and safe as possible, bearing in mind the effect of wind and currents on a vessel as it is piloted through a rough sea into the shelter of a harbor. A typical problem is met where a channel perpendicular to a straight coast is protected by jetties on each side (Figure 1d). If the coastal current is strong, as may be the case where storms come down the coast, there is a sudden shift in forces as the vessel enters between the jetties. As the ship advances crab-wise into the channel, the bow is all at once shielded from the lateral forces of wind and current, while the stern is not. Unless steering is quickly corrected, the ship may plow along in the direction of its keel toward the inside of the windward breakwater.

Ideally, the approach to a harbor should be straight, so that the pilot may judge the direction and rate of side-slip, and correct for it with the rudder. The perception of side-slip on a curved course is much more difficult and likely to lead to error.

Many factors, however may force the breakwater configuration to require vessels to follow a curved course. Not the least of these factors is the natural depth of the water, along the consideration of construction costs.

The worst storms do not often come from prevailing wind or current directions. There is also benefit from placing breakwaters in such an orientation to guide currents in the direction of the channel, so as to minimize the rate of sedimentation and reduce dredging costs (Figure 3).

Another factor to be considered is the effect a breakwater will have on the bathymetry of the coast or harbor. Wave and current action may be radically affected by the presence of a breakwater, causing a change in the coastal processes, shoals where there were no shoals, and deep water where it used to be shallow. This is particularly true of coasts where there is considerable littoral drift. In such cases, an obstruction to the drift causes impoundment on the updrift side and erosion on the downdrift side, sometimes with disastrous results (Figure 4).

Components

Stone components of a rubble-mound breakwater or revetment may come from local sources, stones from glacial debris, or quarries near or far. Consequently, the variation in sizes, shapes, mineral content hardness, abrasion resistance, fracturing, color and every other physical property is extremely wide.

Quarrying for breakwater materials is art as well as science. The method of drilling and blasting, the arrangement and depth of holes, the timing and amount of the charges, the sorting of rocks of different weights and shapes and their handling and transportation to the waterfront site are all devised with a plan for placement. And of course, the placing is an art in itself.

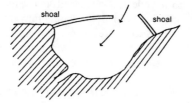

Figure 3.

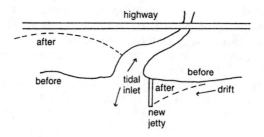

Figure 4.

The sizes of the components vary from many tons to virtual powder. The maximum size that can be counted upon with any regularity depends mostly on the native rock deposit, but also on the method of recovery. The best and largest pieces are set aside for outer armor, and these should be selected for hardness and the absence of fracture planes as well as size. This calls for judicious planning of the shooting of the quarry face so as to take advantage of the laminations, the dip, and type of minerals that appear. Knowledge of the geologic history of the deposit is essential.

Criteria for Component Sizes

Rubble-mound breakwaters and revetments are composed of rock pieces graded, inner core to outer slope, from finer to larger. The outer stones, or "armor," are theoretically large enough to resist being moved about under the onslaught of storm waves. The criteria for the size of the armor relate to the slope (a/b), the wave height (H), the weight and density of the armor pieces (Figure 5). The formula developed by Iribarren et al. [20a] modified by Hudson [11] to determine the weight required for these armor pieces is

$$Q = \frac{\gamma_s H^3}{K_D(\gamma_s/\gamma_f - 1) \cot \alpha}$$

where
Q = weight of armor unit
γ_s = density of material
γ_f = density of water
H = wave height at toe
α = angle between slope and horizontal
K_D = coefficient determined experimentally

The validity of this equation is subject to a number of variables, such as the nature and permeability of underlayers and the core materials, the presence or absence of a capwall, the height and width of the crown above still water and the uniformity of both waves and structure.

Table 1 [42] gives the K_D values used in the formula.

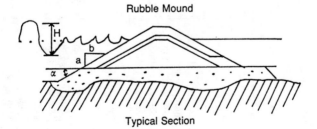

Rubble Mound

Typical Section

Figure 5.

Table 1 [42]
No-Damage Criteria and Minor Overtopping

Armor Units	n^3	Placement	Structure Trunk K_D^2		Structure Head K_D		Slope
			Breaking Wave	Nonbreaking Wave	Breaking Wave	Nonbreaking Wave	Cot θ
Quarrystone							
Smooth rounded	2	Random	*1.2*	*2.4*	*1.1*	*1.9*	1.5 to 3.0
Smooth rounded	>3	Random	*1.6*	*3.2*	*1.4*	*2.3*	[5]
Rough angular	1	Random[4]	*[4]*	*2.9*	*[4]*	*2.3*	[5]
Rough angular	2	Random	2.0	4.0	3.2 / 2.8 / 2.3	1.9 / 1.6 / 1.3	1.5 / 2.0 / 3.0
Rough angular	>3	Random	2.2	4.5	*2.1*	*4.2*	[5]
Rough angular	2	Special[6]	5.8	7.0	*5.3*	*6.4*	[5]
Parallelepiped[7]	2	Special[1]	7.0–20.0	8.5–24.0	—	—	
Tetrapod and Quadripod	2	Random	7.0	8.0	5.0 / 4.5 / 3.5	6.0 / 5.5 / 4.0	1.5 / 2.0 / 3.0
Tribar	2	Random	9.0	10.0	8.3 / 7.8 / 6.0	9.0 / 8.5 / 6.5	1.5 / 2.0 / 3.0
Dolos	2	Random	15.8[8]	31.8[8]	8.0 / 7.0	16.0 / 14.0	2.0[9] / 3.0

	Placement	n[3]					
Modified cube	Random	2	6.5	7.5	—	*5.0*	[5]
Hexapod	Random	2	8.0	9.5	*5.0*	*7.0*	[5]
Toskane	Random	2	*11.0*	22.0	—	—	[5]
Tribar	Uniform	1	12.0	15.0	7.5	9.5	[5]
Quarrystone (K_RR)							
Graded angular	Random	—	2.2	2.5	—	—	—

Caution: Those K_D values shown in *italics* are unsupported by test results and are only provided for preliminary design purposes.

[1] *Caution:* Those K_D values shown in *italics* are unsupported by test results and are only provided for preliminary design purposes.

[2] Applicable to slopes ranging from 1 on 1.5 to 1 on 5.

[3] n is the number of units comprising the thickness of the armor layer.

[4] The use of single layer of quarrystone armor units is not recommended for structures subject to breaking waves, and only under special conditions for structures subject to nonbreaking waves. When it is used, the stone should be carefully placed.

[5] Until more information is available on the variation of K_D value with slope, the use of K_D should be limited to slopes ranging from 1 on 1.5 to 1 on 3. Some armor units tested on a structure head indicate a K_D-slope dependence.

[6] Special placement with long axis of stone placed perpendicular to structure face.

[7] Parallelepiped-shaped stone: long slab-like stone with the long dimension about 3 times the shortest dimension (Markle and Davidson, 1979).

[8] Refers to no-damage criteria (<5% displacement, rocking, etc.); if no rocking (<2%) is desired, reduce K_D 50% (Zwamborn and Van Niekerk, 1982).

[9] Stability of dolosse on slopes steeper than 1 on 2 should be substantiated by site-specific model tests.

Other expressions have been recommended in recent years, taking into account additional variables, such as wave period and permeability of the core material. One of them, advocated by Hedar [41] is summarized for uprush and downrush of waves, and for pervious and impervious core materials in a series of graphs for different angles of repose.

These formulas have often been used to size armor units made of concrete, cast in various shapes, rather than natural rock. Such applications are open to question, and several large breakwaters from these designs have suffered severe damage.

Underlayers beneath the armor may be single or double, and are generally sized to act as filters. Their purpose is to prevent core material from penetrating up through the voids. The criteria for filter material, as given by Terzaghi and Peck [43], for materials with similar gradation (parallel grain size curves) include the following:

Rounded particles:
   Ratio R_{50} = 12 to 58
   Ratio R_{15} = 12 to 40

Angular particles:
   R_{50} = 9 to 30
   R_{15} = 6 to 18

Maximum filter <3-in. for soils, and <5% passing #200
Permeability = K in cm/sec for:
      gravel = 1.0 to 10^2
   clean sand = 10^{-3} to 1.0
      silts, etc = to 10^{-6}

The U.S. Army Corps of Engineers also stipulates that:

$$\frac{D_{15} \text{ filter}}{D_{85} \text{ base}} < 5$$

$$\frac{D_{85} \text{ filter}}{D_{\text{voids}}} < 2$$

The core material, often described as "run-of-bank" quarry, consists of what remains in the quarry after the armor and underlayer stones have been sorted out. Sometimes there is a specification limiting the percentage of "fines," or material passing a certain sieve size. There is almost always a grain-size to produce some desired coefficient of permeability. Yet recent tests [44] and [41] have shown permeability to have a strong effect on the stability of the larger stones at the surface of the rubble mound, which should set a lower limit on permeability. All other things being equal, the greater the permeability the more stable the armor.

This leads to the necessity of establishing limits for the particle size distribution for the core material. The design must have due regard for the sizes of superimposed armor and underlayers, as well as for the particle size of the sea-bottom materials,

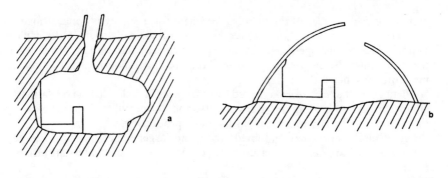

Figure 6.

in keeping with the purpose of the breakwater. For example, a jetty alongside an entrance channel into a deep harbor with natural topographic protection from big waves, as in Figure 6a, will not require the same low transmissibility of waves as an enclosing-arm breakwater that furnishes the sole protection for the harbor, as in Figure 6b.

Behavior vs. Wave Characteristics

Wiegel [45] states: ". . . our direct knowledge of the wave water particle motions is small . . . due to several reasons. The first is the complexity of ocean waves, especially while they and the drift currents are still being generated by winds, and when they are breaking in the surf zone. The second is because of the difficulty of measuring the water motion. Usually, something else is actually measured that must be related to the water motion through theory and/or calibration."

Therefore, direct and sure knowledge of the behavior of a particular breakwater subjected to the innumerable uncertain wave characteristics is not available. For example, non-breaking waves against a vertical wall on a level bottom develop a typical standing wave pattern, where the forces can be calculated with some degree of accuracy if the waves approach at 90°. But on the other hand, breaking waves against a sloping bottom—whether regular or non-regular waves, mono-directional or multi-directional, exhibiting extreme variation, depending on the nature of the slope and what it is composed of, smooth or rough, with changes in slope or not, causing more or less turbulence, trapped air, bubbles or foam currents along shore and transverse—provide so many independent variables that precise analysis is not possible.

Model Studies

Physical models of rubble-mound breakwaters have been relied upon for design information. Two-dimensional (2D) models are built in large tanks, with bathymetry accurately reproduced, to determine slopes and configurations, roundhead design and armor size at areas in the breakwater where wave energy is concentrated. For example, it is often found that waves break at roundheads so that the explosive impact strikes downslope in a much more destructive direction than they do against the main seaward-facing slopes. This may require flatter slopes, larger armor, submerged berms, or all three.

All models suffer from errors caused by differences in scale [26]. The relationships among energy, force, drag, inertia, viscosity, and permeability do not follow both Froude's Law and Reynolds' Law in the same proportion.

Recent model tanks have adopted larger and larger scales in efforts to reduce these errors. More extensive measurements on prototype breakwaters are also being made.

There is a strong emphasis, because of the cost of large models, on numerical models for analyzing breakwater behavior. But a numerical model depends on clear understanding of the physics of the complex phenomena involved in breakwater damage. Such knowledge is far from adequate for reliance on the mathematical formulas we now have. Numerous technical groups are attempting to improve this understanding. One is the Permanent International Association of Navigation Congresses (PIANC), whose Permanent Technical Committee II (PTC II) has organized a second working group to investigate rubble-mound breakwaters. Another is the Marine Board, National Research Council, U.S.A., which established a Committee on Coastal Engineering Measurement Systems, one of whose considerations is how to make detailed prototype measurements of pore pressures.

Construction

Methods and equipment for transporting and depositing quarry stone at a breakwater site depend on the location and nature of the quarry, the distance to the site and the configuration and cross-section of the breakwater.

Some breakwaters are built from the shore out into deeper water. For example, the breakwater at Antifer, the deep-water oil terminal serving the Port of Le Havre, starts at the land next to a rock cliff that provides the quarry material. This, of course, is ideal, because there is good rock adjacent to the port. Quarry material was crushed to provide the aggregate for making the concrete in the cubes comprising the armor. Trucks were used to move the quarry-run core material out onto the breakwater, end-dump it, and then carry underlayer stone and armor to cranes that placed those materials on the outer slopes and under water.

The nature of cross-section developed by this method varies with the nature of stone encountered in the quarry and with the detailed succession of truck loads dumped or set by crane. The variation is in three dimensions, as the roundhead is extended.

Occasional storms are likely to ravel the stone exposed without armor, or even to cause breaches in the incomplete portions. An example of this was the breakwater at Apra Harbor, Guam, which was also built from the land outward. A typhoon in the fall of 1946, when about 800 feet at the outer end had not yet been protected with limestone armor, created two breaches, each about 150 feet long, where the breakwater was leveled to mean sea level. It was then rebuilt with flatter slopes.

Other breakwaters may be built either entirely offshore, necessitating the use of floating equipment, bottom-dump barges and floating cranes, or using floating plant for placing the underwater rock at depths below the keels of barges and tugs and lighters, for the sake of greater economy, where distance from shore makes trucking uneconomical.

In either case, it will be seen that any given cross-section of the breakwater will have a different stratification of materials than at other sections, because complete uniformity is not possible, either with respect to source materials or method of placement. It is not surprising, therefore, that when rubble-mound breakwaters sustain damage from violent storms, the damage is never uniform, but more severe at some sections than at others. This occurs even if wave attack is the same along the entire structure, which is not likely because of the heterogeneous nature of large waves.

Transportation and placing of armor, whether of stone or specially cast concrete shapes, is given much attention, because the pieces are heavy, easily broken or damaged, and need to be placed in a fairly regular pattern. For example, one contractor of considerable experience with a quarry site where basalt rock breaks off in large, flat slabs, developed a system using a ringer crane at the roundhead with a very long reach. Using a computerized grid, the polar coordinates of each piece were established and set on a plan for the crane operator, who could control the orientation and tilt of the slabs, each being longer than its width. Each slab would then be placed with the flat side down, long axis perpendicular to the slope or axis of the breakwater, and at a slight angle from the horizontal, outer end up. Succeeding layers would overlap somewhat, thus keying in each armor piece. The result was a remarkably stable slope.

Often, as in the case of the breakwater at Ashdod, Israel, a large rail-mounted crane is used to set the armor pieces—in this case, tetrapods. The system provided speedy and direct access for rail cars carrying the large units from a distance along the lengthening breakwater, as its curving arm extended from a beach around the synthetic port.

Maintenance

Rubble-mound breakwaters have been characterized as "flexible," meaning not that they behave like rubber, but rather that wave action remolds their shape in a way that can readily be added to and rebuilt. This means that the personnel, materials, and equipment for repair should be promptly mobilized so that storm damage can be quickly noted and repaired.

Access to the damaged portions must also be possible. Accordingly, many breakwaters are constructed with roadways, capwalls or other means of access along the crest. Capwalls, however, have suffered extreme damage in the case of some breakwaters, notably at Sines, Portugal, and Algiers, Morocco, as well at other sites. There is evidence that a large concrete mass at the crest of a rubble-mound is a target for wave impact forces, concentrating energy to an extent that can scarcely be withstood, particularly when perched at the top of a slope of stones with limited stability.

Access from the sea requires an almost prohibitive crane reach unless placement of units is confined to the underwater seaward slopes of a breakwater. And, of course, it is not possible to control position and orientation of pieces accurately under water.

An example of the value of careful maintenance is the breakwater at Plymouth, England. This stone structure, built first in 1806, is quite exposed to view at low tide, because of large tidal fluctuation. After every storm, it is carefully inspected, and the displaced rock is either replaced or a substitution made. The structure appears as good as new.

Research

Many agencies are conducting research into the behavior of rubble-mound break-waters. Among them are:

- Studies by the National Hydraulics Laboratory of Canada into the effect of permeability of underlayers and core upon the stability of armor. This has lead to the "berm" concept of the profile [34] in which the underwater slope is extended seaward and the quarry materials are mixed in only two gradations.
- Field measurements by the U.S. Army Corps of Engineers, Coastal Engineering Research Center (CERC), on the resistance against fracture and breakage of dolos armor units at the Crescent City breakwater, California.
- Installations of "berm" type breakwaters.
- Development of statistical methods applying principles of risk analysis.

Artificial Stone Breakwaters

Blocks

"Blocks" are concrete objects used as armor on the outer slopes of breakwaters. The ideal block is:

- Heavy and tough
- Easily cast and carried
- Strong
- Nests securely with other blocks
- Provides a rough external surface facing the sea
- Economical to build

There are endless varieties of shapes that have been advocated. Some are claimed to resist wave run-up most effectively, others are easier and cheaper to cast, some nest together in almost monolithic solidity. Figure 7 illustrates a few names and shapes:

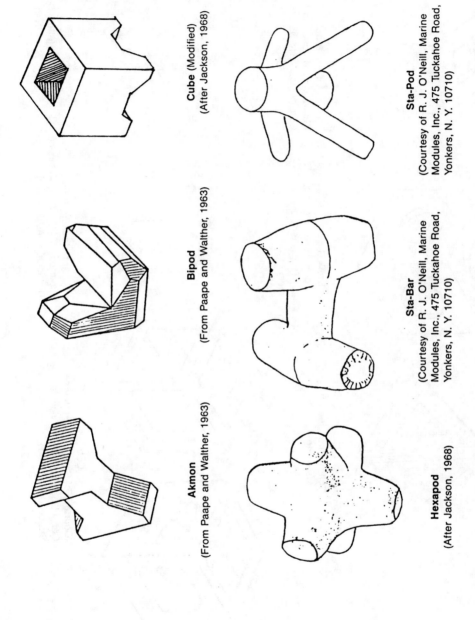

Cube (Modified)
(After Jackson, 1968)

Bipod
(From Paape and Walther, 1963)

Akmon
(From Paape and Walther, 1963)

Sta-Pod
(Courtesy of R. J. O'Neill, Marine Modules, Inc., 475 Tuckahoe Road, Yonkers, N. Y. 10710)

Sta-Bar
(Courtesy of R. J. O'Neill, Marine Modules, Inc., 475 Tuckahoe Road, Yonkers, N. Y. 10710)

Hexapod
(After Jackson, 1968)

Figure 7.

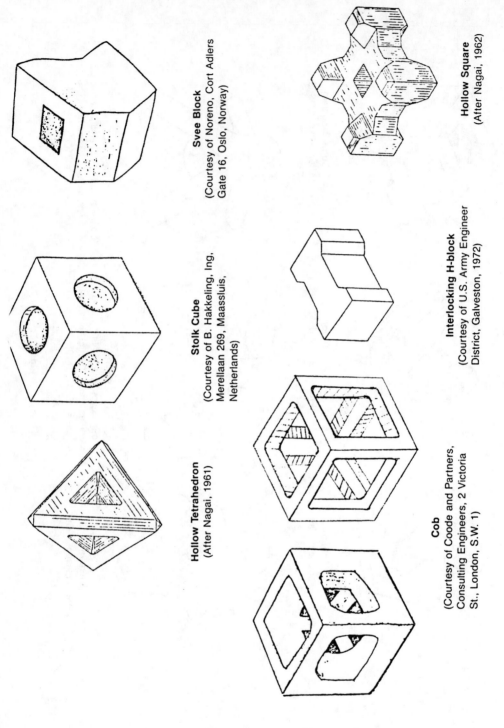

Svee Block
(Courtesy of Noreno, Cort Adlers
Gate 16, Oslo, Norway)

Hollow Square
(After Nagai, 1962)

Stolk Cube
(Courtesy of B. Hakkeling, Ing,
Merellaan 269, Maassluis,
Netherlands)

Interlocking H-block
(Courtesy of U.S. Army Engineer
District, Galveston, 1972)

Hollow Tetrahedron
(After Nagai, 1961)

Cob
(Courtesy of Coode and Partners,
Consulting Engineers, 2 Victoria
St., London, S.W. 1)

Figure 7. (Continued)

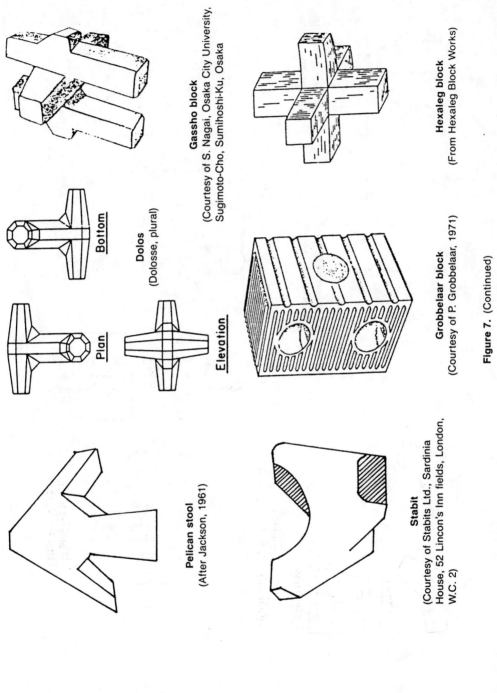

Gassho block
(Courtesy of S. Nagai, Osaka City University,
Sugimoto-Cho, Sumihoshi-Ku, Osaka

Hexaleg block
(From Hexaleg Block Works)

Bottom

Plan

Elevation

Dolos
(Dolosse, plural)

Grobbelaar block
(Courtesy of P. Grobbelaar, 1971)

Figure 7. (Continued)

Pelican stool
(After Jackson, 1961)

Stabit
(Courtesy of Stabits Ltd., Sardinia
House, 52 Lincon's Inn fields, London,
W.C. 2)

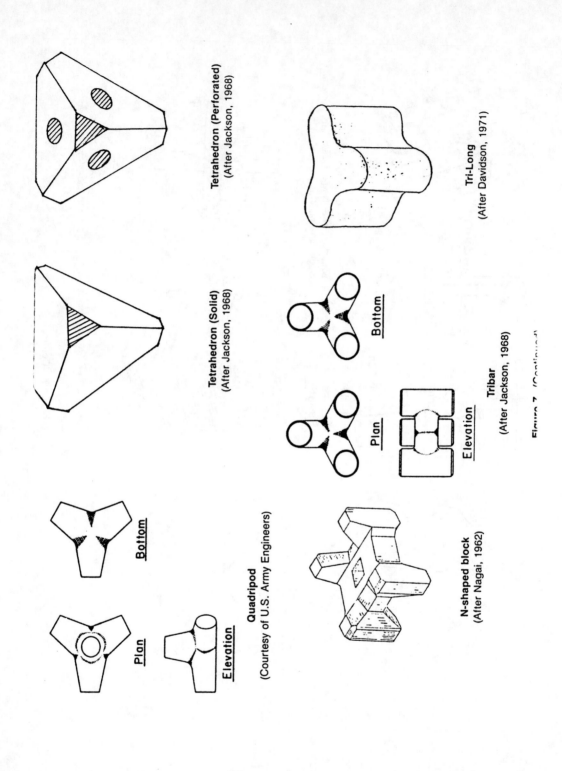

Tetrahedron (Perforated)
(After Jackson, 1968)

Tetrahedron (Solid)
(After Jackson, 1968)

Tri-Long
(After Davidson, 1971)

Bottom

Plan

Bottom

Plan

Elevation

Tribar
(After Jackson, 1968)

Elevation

Quadripod
(Courtesy of U.S. Army Engineers)

N-shaped block
(After Nagai, 1962)

Figure 7. (Continued)

VOLUME OF BLOCK : 0.3h³

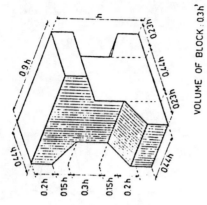

0.9h

h

0.23h

0.47h

0.17h

0.23h

0.17h

0.2h

0.15h

0.3h

0.15h

0.2h

Details of Akmon Armor Unit
(From Paape and Walther, 1963)

Tripod
(From Paape and Walther, 1963)

Quadripod
(After Jackson, 1968)

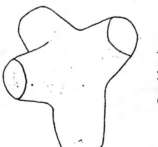

Quadripod

Figure 7 (Continued)

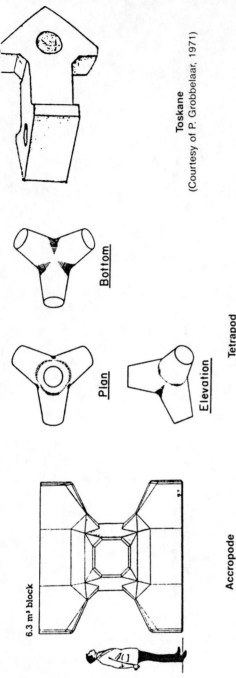

Toskane
(Courtesy of P. Grobbelaar, 1971)

Bottom

Plan

Elevation

Tetrapod
(Courtesy of Sogreah, 1967)

6.3 m³ block

Accropode
(Courtesy of Sogreah, 1988)

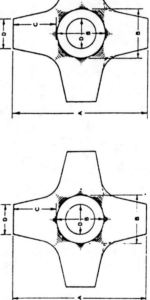

PLAN

ELEVATION

Hexapod

NOTE: DATA BASED ON HEXAPODS USED IN MODEL TESTS
CONDUCTED AT THE WATERWAYS EXPERIMENT STATION.

Figure 7 (Continued)

Caissons

A caisson is a large, generally rectangular concrete box, usually not solid, but composed of walls and internal diaphragms to give it strength, and filled with sand or gravel to give it weight (Figure 8). This differs from caissons as used in, say, bridge foundations. It rests on the sea bottom, or on a layer or mound of stone, relying on its mass to resist wave action. A string of such caissons can make a continuous breakwater, presenting a wall with a vertical face to the sea. Individual caissons are often used as dolphins for breasting or mooring of ships.

A line of caissons forming a breakwater is sometimes topped with a parapet wall of concrete, gaining additional height in order to limit overtopping by storm waves.

One of the characteristics of a vertical wall breakwater is that the kinetic energy of wave advance is stopped suddenly at the wall face, and absorbed by reflection and by translation of water motion upwards and downwards. The upwards component known as clapotis, causes wave crests to rise to double their deepwater height in the case of non-breaking waves. A wave that happens to break at the wall creates a vertical jet of water and air that explodes to a height limited by the quantity of gases, either in dissolved form or in bubbles.

The downward component causes very high water velocities at the base of the wall, and for $\frac{1}{2}$ wavelength horizontally away from it. For this reason, such walls are often set on a layer of stone or other material to prevent erosion. Where this has not been done, large cavities have been found in front of walls, sometimes so large as to cause entire sections to be undermined and to topple forward into the waves.

Caissons are sometimes cylindrical in shape, with curved surfaces to cut down the drag coefficient of waves moving past individual units. Although separate caissons offer less obstruction to wave energy than a continuous wall, the dangers of clapotis and undermining are still very real, and must be guarded against.

An example of this was an installation on the north shore of Lake Ontario, Canada, where circular caissons were built to support a series of trusses carrying pipe lines from an offshore tanker berth to a refinery onshore. The seabed at this

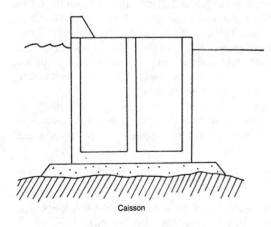

Caisson   **Figure 8.**

site consisted of bare shale rock. To provide a suitable base for the caissons, and avoid rocking, the designers had specified that the smooth shale surface be broken up and covered with a layer of broken stone, screeded level to receive the caisson bases, and that each base be protected from scour by a "necklace" of concrete slabs of trapezoidal shape, covering the annular space of broken stone around the caisson base, the slabs being held together by chains.

However, before the contractor managed to place the necklaces, a storm on the lake caused large waves to undermine a number of caissons, both tilting and sliding them off their planned positions.

Sometimes caissons are designed with irregular or perforated [46] walls toward the sea. The object is to allow some wave energy to pass through the outer wall into the next interior portion of the box, so that energy is absorbed more gradually, and the impact is reduced in intensity. One of the early applications of this type of design was the very large structure for offshore oil drilling at the Ekofisk field in the North Sea. The outer wall was built with circular holes and the inner walls were solids. In the rough sea states, water poured in either direction through the holes, almost continuously.

Other designs in Japan provided slits in the outer concrete wall, so as to break up wave energy in a similar fashion.

A breakwater of "stepped bin" caissons was proposed in 1974 to protect offshore floating nuclear power plants, and tested in a model tank. In this design, two outer walls were to be perforated and built with the tops at increasingly high levels, so that very large waves would overtop each wall in succession, except for the inner one, which was solid. The water cascaded from bin to bin, pouring back out through the perforations in a manner to spread the turbulent absorption of wave energy over a considerable distance, and time. Overtopping was prevented, except for spray and foam in the highest waves.

Composite Breakwaters

Where the depth of water is so large as to require very large caissons, one alternative is to build a submerged mound of rubble and place caissons upon it. Berms of rubble, or armor, or concrete slabs stacked in front of the caissons may help reduce wave impact, and berms behind them may reinforce against sliding. There are many combinations [46]. Study of some 44 breakwaters of composite type and differing degrees of embedment of caissons within a rubble mound seems to indicate that where the percentage of protruding vertical wall exposed to wave breaking becomes large, the damage is likely to be more severe [44].

In all cases, the nature of the foundation soils determines its susceptibility to erosion or overstressing. In some installations, foundations have been prepared by driving piling or sand drains, or by excavation and replacement, or by extended anti-scour layers.

Concrete Requirements

Concrete for use in the salty marine environment must be (a) dense and impervious, (b) strong, and (c) protected from rusting of the steel reinforcing bars.

To accomplish (a), the aggregate must be well graded, the water content must be controlled, mixing must be thorough, and vibratory methods of placing are imperative.

Strength requires chemically resistant, non-fracturing minerals, high-tension cement, adequate cement content, and steel or other reinforcement in the right places. The tension fibers must be adequate to limit cracking, and if made of steel rods or mesh or even fabric, covered with sufficient thickness of concrete to prevent oxidation.

Joints

The spaces between caissons, or other large units in a breakwater, must be sealed against rapid movement of water. Otherwise, particles of material will be carried away, the openings become larger, and just as in the case of dam, progressive piping and failure may occur.

When caissons are set on the sea bottom or on a prepared layer of stone, the adjacent faces are neither exactly plumb nor parallel: and because of small settlements and adjustments, the openings are likely to change dimension slightly with time. Numerous strategies have been applied to seal them in a manner to prevent erosion under the attack of waves. Some of them are:

- Grouting
- Filter layers
- Plastic materials
- Flexible joints
- Overlapping membranes
- Cylindrical plugs
- Sheetpiling
- Shear keys in the caisson faces

None of the strategies can withstand unlimited differential movement of adjacent caissons, and all must be monitored and, if necessary, repaired. The amount of relative motion in a given period of time depends on several factors, such as:

- Compaction of the foundation
- Erosion of the foundation
- Decomposition of sealing materials
- Changes in lateral forces
- Severity of wave impact
- Build-up of water behind the caissons

The selection of a sealing method may vary with the type of foundation materials, the backfill, the type and size of caisson and the exposure.

Pervious Components

Recognizing the potential severity of breaking wave impacts against a caisson wall, numerous designs have been developed for walls with openings that will break up wave energy, providing a pervious face into which much water may move without shock. Among these are:

- Circular or rectangular holes
- Vertical or horizontal slots
- A series of walled bins
- Irregular surfaces
- Steps
- Combinations of these

The double wall, with the outer one perforated, as at Ekofisk, was mentioned. Another design, common in revetments on the Gulf coast, is the stepped slope—frequently built on piles in cases where the foundation is easily eroded.

Still another is the U-shaped wall, in which wave reflection is employed to create turbulence in front of the structure.

Bottom Scour

Breakwaters tend to interrupt normal coastal currents and cause velocities to increase around them. Vertical-wall structures cause the greatest increases, particularly during storms when large waves cause vertical surges of water, backwashing down so as to scour the materials at the base of the wall and move them offshore.

A blanket of stone, or other coarse material not likely to be moved by high-velocity water, is customarily placed on the seabed in these areas. Some designs provide for excavating a trench in front of the breakwater, and filling it with well-graded stone, up to considerable sizes.

A trench was scoured by large waves in front of a vertical-wall breakwater at Genoa in 1898, undermining the toe of the foundation until extensive lengths of the wall toppled forward into the sea, burying parts of it. At Sines, Portugal, in 1978, large percentages of the dolos concrete armor units disappeared, possibly from undermining of the toe of the rubble mound and burial of many units in the moving sand.

Protection against scour requires an understanding of the effect of the breakwater upon the coastal regime during storms—a subject not easily observed and about which much is still to be learned. Model studies are helpful, but not conclusive because of differences in scale and difficulty in reproducing combined wind and sea behavior. Prototype measurements are needed.

References

1. Sainflou, M., 1928, "Essai sur les Digues Maritimes Verticales," *Annales des Ponts et Chaussées*, Vol. 98, Pt. I, Tome II.
2. Caples, W. G., 1932, "Steel Breakwaters," *The Military Engineer*, Mar, Apr. p. 120.
3. Ogden, D. A. D. 1932, "Experience with Breakwaters at Milwaukee," *The Military Engineer*, Mar. Apr. p. 146.
4. Heavey, W. F., 1932, "Breakwaters on the Great Lakes," *Journal, Shore and Beach Protection Assoc.* Nov. Dec. p. 486.

5. Molitor, David A., 1935, "Wave Pressures on Seawalls and Breakwaters," *Trans. ASCE*, Vol. 100, p. 984.

6. Condron, T. L., 1935, "Cellular Steel Breakwater for Calumet Harbor," *Eng. News-Record*, Vol. 115, p. 86.

7. Larras, J., 1937, "Les Déferlement des Lames sur les Jetée Verticales," *Ponts et Chaussées*, France, May.

8. Bagnold, R. A., 1938-9, "Interim Report on Wave Pressure Research," *Journal ICE*, Vol. 2.

9. De Rouville, A., Besson, P., Petry, P., 1938, "Etat Actuel des Études Internationales sur les Efforts Dus aux Lames" *Annales des Ponts et Chaussées, Vol. 108, No. 7, pp.* 5-113.

10. Karl Terzaghi, 1945, "Stability and Stiffness of Cellular Cofferdams", *Trans. ASCE*, Vol. 110, p. 1083.

11. Hudson, Robert Y., 1953, "Wave Forces on Breakwaters," *Trans. ASCE*, Vol. 118, p. 653.

12. Mason, Martin A., 1953, "Surface Water Wave Theories," *Trans. ASCE*, Vol. 118, p. 546.

13. Thorndike Saville, Jr., 1958, "Wave Run-up on Shore Structures," *Trans ASCE*, Vol. 123, p. 139.

14. Nagai, S., 1961, "Shock Pressures Exerted by Breaking Waves on Breakwaters," *Trans. ASCE*, Vol. 126, Part IV, p. 772.

15. Hudson, Robert Y., 1961, "Laboratory Investigation of Rubble-Mound Breakwaters," *Trans. ASCE*, Vol. 126, Part IV, p. 492.

16. Nagai, S., 1963, "Stable Concrete Blocks on Rubble-Mound Breakwaters," *Trans ASCE*, Vol. 128, Part IV, p. 227.

17. Nagai, S., 1964, "Sliding of Composite-Type Breakwaters by Breaking Waves," *Trans. ASCE*, Vol. 129, p. 370.

18. Nagai, S., 1969, "Pressures of Standing Waves on Vertical Wall," *Journal WW&H Div.*, *ASCE*, Vol. 95, p. 53, Feb.

19. Broeders W. P. A., and van Loenen G., 1974, "Wave Conditions and Coastal Structures," *Ocean Wave Measurement Analysis, ASCE*, Proc. of International Symposium on Ocean Wave Measurement and Analysis, *ASCE*/Dept. of Public Works Canada/U.S. Army Corps of Engineers, New Orleans, La, Sept 9-11, pp. 543.

20. Per Bruun and Johannesson, P., 1974, "A Critical Review of the Hydraulics of Rubble-Mound Structures," *Report R-3, Univ. Trondheim*, Norway.

20a. Iribarren, Cavanilles, R. and Nogales y Olano, C., 1950, "Generalization of the Formula for Calculation of Rock Fill Dikes and Verification of its Coefficients," *Revista de Obras Publicas*, Spain.

21. Noble, R. M., and Dornhelm, R. B., 1974, "Deterministic and Probabilistic Design Wave Approach to Engineering Application," *Ocean Wave Measurement Analysis, ASCE*, Proc. of International Symposium on Ocean Wave Measurement and Analysis, *ASCE*/Dept. of Public Works Canada/U.S. Army Corps of Engineers, New Orleans, La, Sept 9-11, pp. 856.

22. Takezawa, M., "Experimental Study of Wave Forces on a Vertical Wall," *Coastal Structures '79, ASCE*, p. 48.

23. Harlow, E. H., 1980 "Large Rubble-Mound Breakwater Failures," *Journal WWPCO Div.*, *ASCE*, Vol. 106, No. WW2, May.

24. Marr W. A., Jr. and Christian, J. T., 1981, "Permanent Displacements Due to Cyclic Wave Loading," *Journal Geotechnical Engng. Div., ASCE*, Vol. 107, No. GT8, p. 1129, Aug.

25. Walton, T. L., Jr. and Weggel, J. R., 1981, "Stability of Rubble-Mound Breadwaters," *Journal WWPCO, Div., ASCE*, Vol. 107, WW3, Aug.

26. Vasco Costa, F., 1981, "Forces Associated to Different Fluid Properties as Affected by Scaling," *Coastal Engng. 5*.

27. Salih Kirkgoz, M., 1982, "Shock Pressure of Breaking Waves of Vertical Walls," *Journal WWPCO, Div. ASCE*, Vol. 108, WW1, Feb.
28. Ching S. Chang, 1982, "Residual Undrained Deformation from Cyclic Loading," *Journal Geotechnical Engng. Div., ASCE*, Vol. 108, 6T4, Apr.
29. Vasco Costa, F., 1982, "Consideration of Critical Flow Velocities in Hydraulic Modeling," *Int'l Conf. on Hydraulic Modeling of Civil Engng. Structures, Univ. Warwick, Coventry, England*, Sep.
30. FBJ Barends, H. van der Kogel et al., 1983, "West Breakwater—Sines, Dynamic—Geotechnical Stability of Breakwaters," *Coastal Structures '83 ASCE*, Arlington VA., Mar.
31. Jensen, O. J., 1983, "Breakwater Structures," *Coastal Structures '83 ASCE*, Arlington, VA., Mar.
32. Smith, A. W. S., and Gordon, A. D., 1983, "Large Breakwater Toe Failures," *Journal WPCO, Engng. Div. ASCE*, May.
33. Hedges, T. S., 1983, "The Core and Underlayers of a Rubble-Mound Structure," *Inst. Civil Engineers, London, U.K.*, May.
34. Baird W. F. and Hall, K. R., 1983, "The Design and Armour Systems for the Protection of Rubble-Mound Breakwaters," *Inst. Civil Engineers*, May.
35. Owen, M. W. and Allsop, N. W. H., 1983, "Hydraulic Modeling of Rubble-Mound Breakwaters," *Inst. Civil Engineers, London, U.K.* May.
36. Timco, G. W., 1983, "An Analysis of the Breakage of Concrete Armour Units on Rubble-Mound Breakwaters," *Nat'l Research Council Canada*, 09.
37. PIANC, 1985, "Report of Working Group on the Stability of Rubble-Mound Breakwaters in Deeper Water," PIANC.
38. Fang, T., 1984, "Dolos Breakwater Design Improvements," *Journal WWPCO, ASCE* Nov. 1982 & discussion Harlow E. H. Feb. Vol. 110, No. 1.
39. Mizumura, K., 1984, "Flow Analyses in Idealized Rubble-Mound Breakwater," *WWPCO Div. ASCE.*, Vol. 110, No. 3, Aug.
40. The Swamp Group, 1985, "Ocean Wave Modeling," (See Wave Modeling Project) published by Plenum, New York.
41. Hedar, P. A., 1986, "Armor Layer Stability of Rubble-Mound Breakwaters," *J. WPC and OE, ASCE*, Vol. 112, No. 3, 1986, pp. 343–350.
42. *Shore Protection Manual*, 1984, CERC, U.S. Army Corps of Engineers, Vicksburg, Mississippi.
43. Terzaghi, K. and Peck, R., 1967, *Soil Mechanics in Engineering Practice*, 2nd Edition, John Wiley & Sons, New York.
44. Harlow, E. H., 1985, "Factors Affecting Behavior of Composite Breakwaters," Bulletin No. 50, PIANC.
45. Wiegel, R. L., 1981, "Recent Developments in Ocean Engineering," Seminar at U. of California, Berkeley.
46. Nakayama, S., 1985, "Present Situation of Caisson Type Breakwaters in Japan," Bulletin No. 50, PIANC.

CHAPTER 18

RUBBLE MOUNDS—RECENT MODIFICATIONS

Jentsje W. van der Meer

Harbors, Coasts, and Offshore Technology Division
Delft Hydraulics,
Emmeloord, The Netherlands

CONTENTS

Introduction

The use of coarse materials, such as gravel and natural stone for slope revetments and breakwaters, is very common in civil engineering. In recent years, there has been an increasing demand for reliable design formulas, because of the ever-growing dimensions of structures and the necessity to move into more hostile environments.

The Hudson formula has been found by many users to have a lot of shortcomings. It does not include, for example, the influence of the wave period and does not consider random waves. The study of Ahrens [1] in a large wave tank showed the importance of the wave period on the stability of riprap. The tests, however, were performed with regular waves. Evaluation of Ahrens' data by Pilarczyk and den Boer [2] produced stability formulas that included the wave period. Losada and Giménez-Curto [3] gave formulas for the stability of rubble-mound slopes under regular wave attack, which also included the wave period. Hedar [4, 5] showed the importance of the permeability of the structure. His tests were also performed with regular waves.

An extensive investigation was performed by Thompson and Shuttler [6] on the stability of rubble-mound revetments under random waves. One of their main conclusions was that, within the scatter of the results, the erosion damage showed no clear dependence on the wave period. By reanalyzing their data, however, it was found, in fact that there was a clear dependence on the wave period. The work of Thompson and Shuttler [6] has been used, therefore, as a starting point for an extensive model research program. More than two hundred and fifty physical model tests have been performed. Analysis of the results from these tests has resulted in two practical design formulas that describe the influence of wave period, storm duration, armor grading, spectrum shape, groupiness of waves, and the permeability of the core.

The development of these formulas has been described by Van der Meer [7]. The following section restates the formulas and describes the relevant parameters. The formulas are then used in a deterministic approach to produce design graphs, showing the influence of the parameters.

Comparison with Hudson Formula

The Hudson formula is well known because of its simplicity. Stone mass, relative mass density, and wave height are directly related to the slope angle, given by cot α.

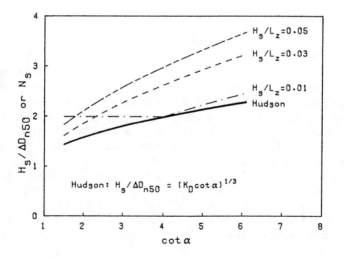

Figure 1. Comparison of Hudson and new formulas for a permeable core and after 1,000 waves (H_s is the wave height at the toe of the structure).

The Hudson formula, written in a simple form, is given by

$$H_{10}/\Delta D_{n50} = (K_D \cot \alpha)^{1/3} \qquad (1)$$

where H_{10} = average of the highest 10% of the waves
Δ = relative mass density
D_{n50} = nominal diameter
K_D = stability coefficient
$\cot \alpha$ = slope angle

Figures 1 and 2 illustrate this relationship, which is independent of wave period, storm duration, and permeability of the structure. Figures 1 and 2 show the Hudson formula ($K_D = 4.0$ and $H_{10} = 1.27H_s$ in *Shore Protection Manual* [8]), and are compared with the new stability formulas, described in the following. Curves have been drawn for several values of the deep water wave steepness. Figure 1 shows the curves for a permeable structure after a storm duration of 1,000 waves (a little more than the number used by Hudson). Figure 2 gives the stability of an impermeable revetment after a wave attack of 5,000 waves (equivalent to 5 to 10 hours in nature).

The conclusion is clear. The Hudson formula can only be used as a very rough estimate for a particular case. It should be borne in mind that a difference of a factor 2 in the N_s-number means a difference in the stone mass of a factor 8. These figures should be sufficiently convincing for the designer to apply the new formulas instead of the simple Hudson formula.

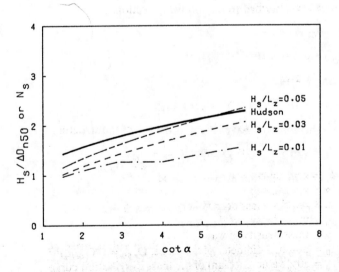

Figure 2. Comparison of Hudson and new formulas for an impermeable core (after 5,000 waves). H_s/L_z = fictitious wave steepness = significant wave height at the toe of the structure/Deep-water wavelength.

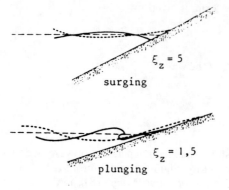

$\xi_z = 5$

surging

$\xi_z = 3$

collapsing

$\xi_z = 1,5$

plunging

Figure 3. Plunging, collapsing, and surging waves.

Stability Formulas

The analysis of all the results of the investigation, which led to the final stability formulas, is given in Van der Meer [7]. Two stability formulas were derived, one for plunging (breaking) waves and one for surging (non-breaking) waves, Figure 3. The main basic assumptions for the formulas are:

1. A rubble-mound structure with an armor layer consisting of rock.
2. There should be little or no overtopping.
3. The slope of the structure should be generally uniform.

The formulas are described in the following sections:

For plunging waves:

$$H_s/\Delta D_{n50} * \sqrt{\xi_z} = 6.2P^{0.18}(S/\sqrt{N})^{0.2} \tag{2}$$

For surging waves:

$$H_s/\Delta D_{n50} = 1.0P^{-0.13}(S/\sqrt{N})^{0.2} \sqrt{\cot \alpha}\, \xi_z{}^P \tag{3}$$

where H_s = significant wave height at the toe of the structure

ξ_z = surf similarity parameter, $\xi_z = \dfrac{\tan \alpha}{\sqrt{2\pi H_s/gT_z{}^2}}$

T_z = zero up-crossing wave period
α = slope angle
Δ = relative mass density of the stone, $\Delta = \rho_a/\rho - 1$
ρ_a = mass density of the stone
ρ = mass density of water
D_{n50} = nominal diameter of the stone, $D_{n50} = (W_{50}/\rho_a)^{1/3}$
W_{50} = 50% value (median) of the mass distribution curve
P = permeability coefficient of the structure
S = damage level, $S = A/D_{n50}{}^2$
A = erosion area in a cross-section, Figure 4
N = number of waves (storm duration)

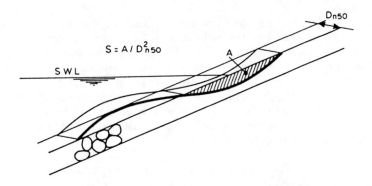

Figure 4. Erosion area and damage level, S.

Governing Variables

Slope. The slope, cot α, should lie between 1.5 and 6.

Wave Height. The significant wave height is used. In the tests performed in order to establish formulas, the significant wave height was defined as the average of the highest one third of the waves. This definition is similar to the significant wave height derived from the spectrum: $H_s = 4\sqrt{m_0}$, where m_0 is the zeroth moment of the energy density spectrum. Both can be used in the formulas.

A small number of tests was performed with a 1:30 uniform foreshore in front of the structure, causing breaking waves on the foreshore. Analysis of these tests indicated that if the structure is located in relatively shallow water and that if the wave height distribution is truncated, the 2% value of the wave height exceedance curve gives the best agreement with results showing a Rayleigh distribution. This means that for shallow-water locations the parameter $(H_{2\%}/1.40)$ must be used in Equations 2 and 3 instead of H_s. The factor 1.40 is the ratio $H_{2\%}/H_s$ for a Rayleigh distribution.

Wave Steepness. The wave steepness, $2\pi H_s/gT_z^2$, should be between 0.005 and 0.06. For a wave steepness greater than 0.06 waves become unstable, and break because of their steepness. This value can, therefore be regarded as an upper boundary. The average wave period is used in the formulas defined by the zero up-crossings in the wave record or by the formula: $T_z = \sqrt{m_0/m_2}$, where m_2 is the second moment of the energy density spectrum. This average period is preferred as it gave the same stability for different spectral shapes, where the peak period for instance, gave different stability curves.

Permeability. The permeability coefficient P was introduced to describe the influence of the permeability of the structure on its stability. Three structures have been investigated. The lower boundary value of P is that given by an impermeable core (clay or sand), see Figure 5a. With this impermeable core a value of $P = 0.1$ was assumed. The upper boundary value of P is that given by a homogeneous structure, consisting only of armor stones, see Figure 5d. For this structure a value of

P = 0.6 was assumed. The third structure consisted of a two-diameter-thick armor layer on a permeable core. The ratio of armor/core stone diameter was 3.2, see Figure 5c. For this structure a value of P = 0.5 was assumed. The first and third structures are close to the structures investigated by Hedar [4, 5], who also found that the permeability had a large influence on stability.

The value of P for other structures with, for example, more than one layer of stones (Figure 5b) or a thicker armor layer must be estimated from the values established for the three specific structures. The design engineers experience is obviously important when selecting the value of P.

Damage Level, S. The damage level S is the "number of cubic stones with a side of D_{n50}, eroded around the water level within a width of one D_{n50}," see Figure 4. For a two-diameter-thick armor layer the lower and upper damage levels have been assumed to be the values shown in Table 1. The definition of start of damage (S = 2 for steep slopes and S = 3 for milder slopes) is the same as that used by Hudson [9] and Ahrens [1]. The definition of "filter layer visible" may be assumed as failure of the armor layer (although not the immediate failure of the structure).

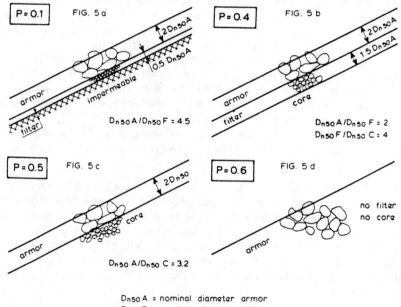

$D_{n50}A$ = nominal diameter armor
$D_{n50}F$ = nominal diameter filter
$D_{n50}C$ = nominal diameter core
Structures on Fig. 5a, 5c and 5d have been tested.
The value of P for Fig. 5b has been assumed.

Figure 5. The permeability coefficient P.

Table 1
Lower and Upper Damage Levels for Two-Diameter-Thick Rock Slopes

	Damage Level $S = A/D_{n50}^2$	
Cot α	Start of Damage	Filter Layer Visible
1.5	2	8
2.0	2	8
3.0	2	12
4.0	3	17
6.0	3	17

Storm Duration. The formulas can be used when the number of waves, or storm duration, is in the range $N = 1{,}000$–$7{,}000$. For $N > 7{,}000$ the damage tends to be overestimated. The maximum damage is, in fact, observed for $N = 8{,}000$–$9{,}000$.

Mass Density. The mass density of the stones used in the tests was between 2,000 and 3,000 kg/m^3 giving relative mass densities, Δ, in the range 1.0 to 3.0.

Other Parameters. Equations 2 and 3 do not include parameters for the grading of the stones (riprap or uniform stones) or for the spectrum width or the groupiness of the wave signal. The investigation showed no difference in stability between riprap and uniform stones, and the spectrum shape and groupiness of waves did not appear to influence the stability, provided that the average wave period was used and not the peak period.

Deterministic Design Graphs

Design graphs can be drawn using Equations 2 and 3. To demonstrate the influence of the different parameters the graphs are given for an assumed structure. The properties of this structure are:

Nominal diameter	$D_{n50} = 1.0$ m
Mass density stone	$\rho_a = 2{,}600$ kg/m^3, that is $W_{50} = 2{,}600$ kg
Mass density water	$\rho = 1{,}000$ kg/m^3, equivalent to a relative mass density, Δ, of 1.6
Slope angle	cot $\alpha = 3.0$
Damage level	$S = 5$ (tolerable damage in 50 years)
Permeability	$P = 0.5$ (permeable core, see Figure 5c)
Storm duration	$N = 3{,}000$ waves

Influence of Wave Height, Period and Damage Level

Most of the design graphs are shown on graphs where the significant wave height (H_s) is plotted as a function of the surf similarity parameter (ξ_z). The wave height is plotted on the vertical axis and the surf similarity or breaker parameter on the horizontal. The breaker parameter considers the influence of the wave period and slope angle. The damage levels $S = 2$ (start of damage), $S = 5$ and 8 (tolerable damage) and $S = 12$ (filter layer visible, failure) have been plotted in Figure 6. Equation 2 is plotted on the left side of the figure (plunging waves) and Equation 3 on the right side (surging waves).

By using the assumed parameters for the structure given above, the plunging wave curve for $S = 5$ can be found from Equation 2:

$$H_s = 5.43\xi_z^{-0.5} \tag{4}$$

and the surging wave curve from Equation 3:

$$H_s = 1.88\xi_z^{0.5} \tag{5}$$

The transition from plunging to surging waves occurs at:

$$\xi_z = (6.2P^{0.31}\sqrt{\tan\alpha})^{1/(P+0.5)} \tag{6}$$

This transition (collapsing waves) gives the minimum stability. In the plunging region wave run-up is decisive for stability and in the surging region wave run-down. In the collapsing region both run-up and run-down forces are high, which causes the minimum of stability.

Influence of Slope Angle

Figure 7 shows the stability formulas for slope angles with $\cot\alpha = 1.5$, 2.0, 3.0, 4.0 and 6.0. The left side (plunging waves) is given by one curve, which means that

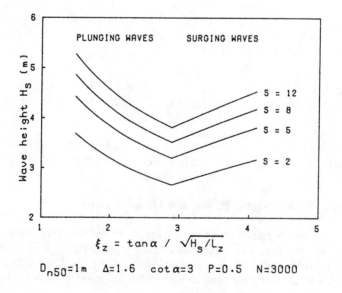

Figure 6. Influence of damage level.

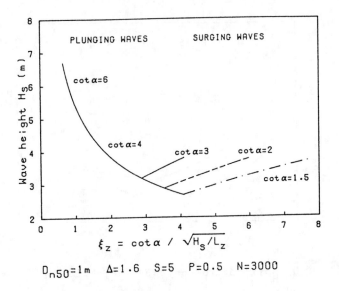

Figure 7. Influence of slope angle.

the breaker parameter is an excellent parameter in the breaking wave region. For slopes gentler than 1:4 surging waves do not occur. For steeper slopes the minimum decreases, i.e., a lower wave height causes instability, and the transition from plunging to surging waves moves to the right.

Influence of Permeability

Figure 8 shows the curves for four values of the permeability coefficient. The value of $P = 0.1$ (impermeable structure) gives the lower boundary and the value of $P = 0.6$ (homogeneous structure) gives the upper boundary. The influence of the wave period for plunging waves (left side of Figure 8) shows the same trend for all four structures, although a more permeable structure is more stable. A more permeable structure is also more stable for surging waves ($\xi_z > 3.5$), but the stability increases with larger wave periods. The curves are steeper for larger permeability.

This phenomenon can be explained in physical terms by the difference in water motion on the slope. For a slope with an impermeable core the flow is concentrated in the armor layer causing large forces on the stones during run-down. For a slope with permeable core the water dissipates into the core and the flow becomes less violent. With longer wave periods (larger ξ_z) more water can percolate and flow down through the core. This reduces the forces and stabilizes the slope.

The stability increases by more than 35% as P shifts from 0.1 to 0.6 in relation to the wave height. This means a difference of a factor 2.5 in mass of stone for the same design wave height. And this is only caused by a difference in permeability. This aspect is included in the berm breakwater concept (Baird and Hall [10]) where a permeable berm is applied.

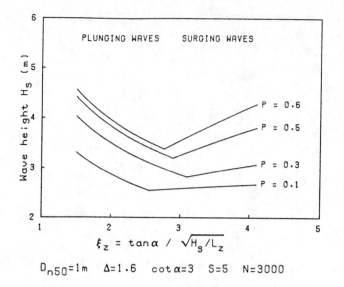

Figure 8. Influence of permeability.

Influence of Storm Duration

Figure 9 shows the damage level of S = 5 for different storm durations, i.e., different numbers of waves. For $\xi_z = 2$ and N = 1,000 this damage level is reached with a wave height of $H_s = 4.3$ m. For a very long storm (N > 7,000) it is reached with $H_s = 3.5$ m. The storm duration is a parameter that only becomes obvious when testing with random waves. For monochromatic waves equilibrium is found within 1,000 waves. This means that it is not so easy to use stability formulas developed with monochromatic waves for prototype conditions where the waves are random. It is not simply a matter of replacing H by the significant wave height H_s or even a higher wave height.

Damage Curves

Another graph that can be calculated from the formulas is the damage curve in which the damage is plotted as a function of the wave height. Figure 10 gives these damage curves for two different values of wave steepness, $H_s/L_z = 0.02$ (S = $0.00907H_s^5$, from Equation 2) and 0.05 (S = $0.00289H_s^5$, also from Equation 2) where $L_z = gT_z^2/2\pi$.

Conclusions

New stability formulas have been derived from the results of extensive model investigations. These formulas have been used to develop design graphs, Figures 6 to 10, and to provide a good representation of the influence of the governing

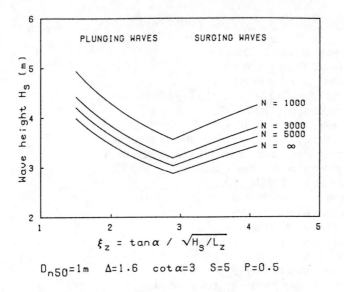

Figure 9. Influence of storm duration.

parameters on stability. Formulas and graph plotting can be programmed on a personal computer. This makes it relatively easy for the engineer to design the armor layer of a rubble mound and to investigate the effects of various changes on the breakwater stability and provides possibilities for improving design.

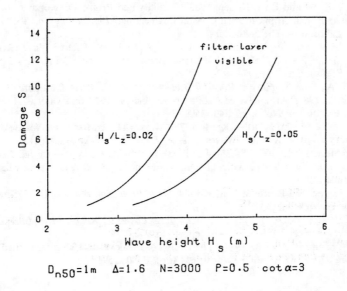

Figure 10. Damage curves. H_s/L_z = fictitious wave steepness = significant wave height at the toe of the structure/Deep-water wavelength.

Notation

A   erosion area in a cross-section
D_{n50} nominal diameter $(W_{50}/\rho_a)^{1/3}$
g   acceleration due to gravity
H_s significant wave height at the top of the structure
H_{10} average of the highest 10% of the waves
L_z deep-water wavelength $(gT_z^2/2\pi)$
m_0 zeroth moment of the energy density spectrum
m_2 second moment of the energy density spectrum
N   number of waves (storm duration)
N_s stability number $(H_s/\Delta D_{n50})$
P   permeability coefficient
S   damage level (A/D_{n50}^2)
T_z average wave period
W_{50} 50% value of mass distribution curve
α slope angle
Δ relative mass density $(\rho_a/\rho - 1)$
ξ_z surf similarity parameter $(\tan\alpha/\sqrt{H_s/L_z})$
ρ_a mass density of stone
ρ mass density of water

References

1. Ahrens, J. P., 1975, *Large Wave Tank Tests of Riprap Stability*, C.E.R.C. Technical Memorandum No. 51, Fort Belvoir, VA.
2. Pilarczyk, K. W. and Boer, K. den, 1983, "Stability and Profile Development of Coarse Material and Their Application in Coastal Engineering," *Publication No. 293*, Delft Hydraulics Laboratory, The Netherlands.
3. Losada, M. A. and Giménez-Curto, L. A., 1979, "The Joint Effect of Wave Height and Period on the Stability of Rubble-Mound Breakwaters Using Iribarren's Number," *Coastal Engineering*, 3, pp. 77–96.
4. Hedar, P. A., 1960, *Stability of Rock-fill Breakwaters*, Ph.D. thesis, Goteborg, Sweden
5. Hedar, P. A., 1986, "Armor Layer Stability of Rubble-Mound Breakwaters," *J. WPC and OE*, ASCE, Vol. 112, No. 3, pp. 343–350.
6. Thompson, D. M. and Shuttler, R. M., 1975, "Riprap Design for Wind Wave Attack. A Laboratory Study in Random Waves," *Report EX 707*, Wallingford, U.K.
7. Van der Meer, J. W., 1987, "Stability of Breakwater Armor Layers—Design Formula," *J. of Coastal Engineering*, Vol. 11, No. 3, Sept., pp. 219–239, Amsterdam, The Netherlands.
8. Coastal Engineering Research Center, 1984, *Shore Protection Manual*, U.S. Army Corps of Engineers, Vicksburg, MS.
9. Hudson, R. Y., 1958, *Design of Quarry Stone Cover Layers for Rubble-Mound Breakwaters*, U.S. Army Engineer WES, Research Report No. 2-2.
10. Baird, W. F. and Hall. K. R., 1984, "The Design of Breakwaters Using Quarried Stones," *Proceedings 19th ICCE*, ASCE, Houston, IX, pp. 2580–2591.

CHAPTER 19

PILE AND OFFSHORE BREAKWATERS

John B. Herbich

W. H. Bauer Professor
Ocean Engineering Program,
Civil Engineering Department
Texas A&M University
College Station, Texas U.S.A.

CONTENTS

Pile Breakwaters

Introduction

Pile breakwaters consist of closely-spaced, rigid, vertical piles (cylindrical or rectangular) [20]. Vertical and horizontal slotted screens have also been used to form a breakwater. Examples of pile breakwaters include:

1. Cylindrical reinforced concrete breakwater consisting of 12.5-m (41-ft) diameter units with a 0.25-m (0.8-ft) wall thickness installed in 12 m (39 ft) of water in Hanstholm, Denmark.
2. Cylindrical shells in caissons that are 53.8 m (177 ft) long and 16 m (52 ft) wide at Marsa el Brega, Libya.

3. A steel pipe breakwater consisting of 2-m (6.6-ft) diameter pipes with an average spacing between pipes of 5-cm (0.16-ft) constructed in Port of Osaka, Japan.
4. A concrete pipe breakwater consisting of 1.4-m (4.6-ft) diameter pipes with average spacing between pipes of 15.2 cm (0.5 ft) at Pass Christian, Mississippi.

Laboratory Studies

Several laboratory investigations have been conducted to evaluate the transmission and reflection of waves from permeable-pile breakwaters. Published data include studies by Wiegel [52], Hayashi, et al. [19], Allsop and Kalmus [2], Truitt and Herbich [49] and Herbich and Douglas [20].

Hayashi, et al. [19] derived an expression for wave transmission based on water jets discharging through the pile gaps:

$$\frac{H_t}{H_i} = 4\left(\frac{d}{H_i}\right)E\left[-E + \sqrt{E^2 + \frac{H_i}{2d}}\right] \qquad (1)$$

where H_t = height of transmitted wave
  H_i = height of incident wave
  d = water depth

$$E = c\left(\frac{b}{D+b}\right)\sqrt{1 - \left(\frac{b}{D+b}\right)^2} \qquad (2)$$

where c = constant
  b = spacing between piles
  D = pile diameter

Wiegel [52] derived an expression for wave transmission based solely on geometry of the piles:

$$\frac{H_t}{H_i} = \frac{b}{D+b} \qquad (3)$$

Model studies performed later showed a greater wave transmission rate (up to 25%) than the rate predicted by Equation 3.

Recent Laboratory Studies

Truitt and Herbich conducted experimental studies on wave transmission through a breakwater consisting of a single row of piles employing both monochromatic and random waves. The results of experiments with random waves indicate that the relationships developed for monochromatic waves may be applicable to random

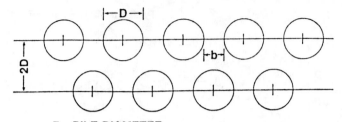

D - PILE DIAMETER

b - PILE SPACING

RATIO (b/D) CHOSEN TO BE 0.10, AND 0.20

Figure 1. Definition sketch for pile geometry [20].

waves. Very good agreement was observed between the values of wave transmission predicted by Hayashi's equation and experimentally-obtained values with random waves, provided the coefficient employed was equal to 0.9. It was also found that two dimensionless ratios affect the transmission coefficient:

1. b/d, a ratio of breakwater spacing to pile diameter
2. d/H_s, a ratio of water depth to wave height

The influence of the second ratio on the transmission coefficient is more pronounced.

Herbich and Douglas [20] conducted additional experimental studies in the same facility as Truitt and Herbich [49], with two staggered rows of piles employing both monochromatic and irregular wave spectra including the Darbyshire, I.T.T.C., Pierson-Moskowitz, and JONSWAP.

The experiments consisted of passing waves through the pile breakwater and measuring both incident and transmitted wave heights. Definition sketch for pile geometry is shown in Figure 1. The models were built using a steel conduit to assure rigid and uniform piles. Two sizes of conduit were used: 3.0-cm diameter (1–3/16-in.) and 2.4-cm diameter (15/16-in.). Four models were employed as shown in Table 1.

Table 1
Dimensions of Pile Breakwaters

Pile Diameter (D) (cm)	b/D	Distance Between Rows (cm)
2.4	0.1	2 (D) = 4.8
3.0	0.2	2 (D) = 6.0
2.4	0.1	2 (D) = 4.8
3.0	0.2	2 (D) = 6.0

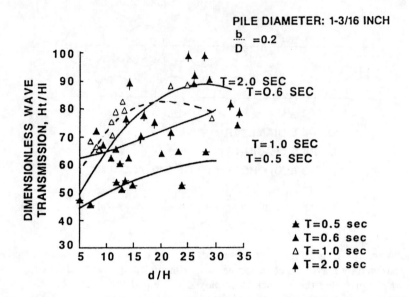

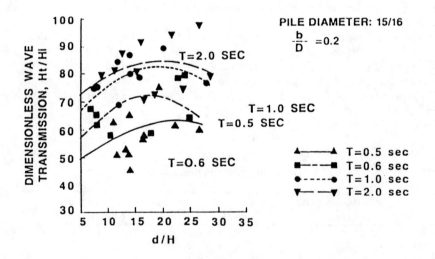

Figure 2. Dimensionless wave transmission as a function of depth-to-wave-height ratio for four wave periods; $D = 3.0$ cm ($1\frac{3}{16}$ in.), $b/D = 0.2$, two rows, monochromatic waves [20].

Figure 3. Wave transmission as a function of depth-to-wave-height ratio for four wave periods. $D = 2.4$ cm ($\frac{15}{16}$ in.), $b/D = 0.2$, two rows, monochromatic waves [20].

Wave Transmission Rates

Sample plots of dimensionless wave transmission (H_t/H_i) as a function of water depth to wave height ratio (d/H) are shown in Figures 2 and 3). The increase of wave transmission with an increase in wave period and d/H ratio (up to 25) can be seen in these figures. As anticipated, the smaller the gap ratio, the lower the wave transmission. Reducing the gap space from 20 to 10% results in transmission for a gap ratio of b/D = 0.1 being reduced to 60 to 80% of the transmission for a gap ratio of b/D = 0.2. The wave transmission was reduced even more at lower wave periods.

Plots of dimensionless wave transmission, (H_t/H_i), as a function of d/H for random waves are shown in Figures 4 and 5. Even though scatter occurred, data for the four wave spectra tended to plot together. The curves for the two sizes of pile were similar for the same gap ratios. The reduction in gap spacing from 20 to 10% reduced the values of wave transmission by approximately 30%.

A comparison between wave transmission for one and two row of piles is shown in Figures 6 and 7. Figure 6 shows a comparison for a b/D ratio of 0.2 and Figure 7 for a b/D ratio of 0.1. For these plots all data points for the same gap ratio have been plotted together regardless of pile diameter. The data for one row of piles covered a very narrow range of d/H values and the resulting curve represents linear regression of the data. For a gap ratio of b/D = 0.2, wave transmission was reduced by about 15%, while for a gap ratio of b/D = 0.1 it was reduced by 5 to 10%.

The monochromatic wave data are plotted using the dimensionless parameter d/gT^2 where d is the water depth, g is the gravitational acceleration and T is the wave period. Figure 8, which is a plot of wave transmission as a function of d/gT^2,

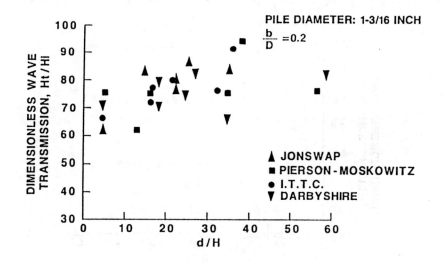

Figure 4. Wave transmission as a function of water-depth-to-wave-height ratio for random waves; D = 3.0 cm ($1\frac{3}{16}$ in.), b/D = 0.2 [20].

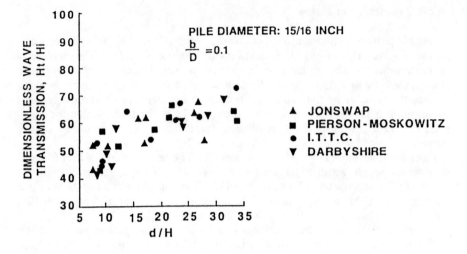

Figure 5. Wave transmission as a function of water depth-to-wave-height ratio for random waves; D = 2.4 cm ($\frac{15}{16}$ in.), b/D = 0.1 [20].

indicates that the wave transmission decreases as d/gT^2 increases. Values of wave steepness H_i/L are also shown next to the individual data points. The general trend is for the wave transmission to decrease as the wave steepness increases.

These data were also compared with a similar breakwater model consisting of one row of piles [24]. This study was performed with slightly different pile diameters:

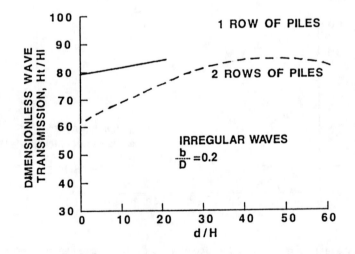

Figure 6. Wave transmission for one and two rows of piles, random waves, b/D = 0.2 [20].

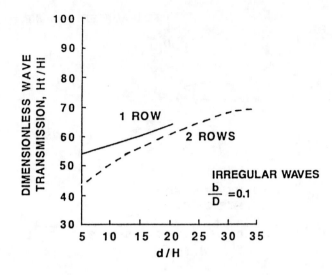

Figure 7. Wave transmission for one and two rows of piles, random waves, b/D = 0.1 [20].

0.63 cm (4/16 in.) and 1.9 cm (12/16 in.) but with the sample gap ratios (0.1 and 0.2). It has already been shown that pile diameter has a minimal effect on transmission and that the b/D (gap ratio) is the more important variable. Several plots of wave transmission as a function of d/gT^2 for the monochromatic waves present a comparison between the single- and double-pile breakwaters (Figures 9–12).

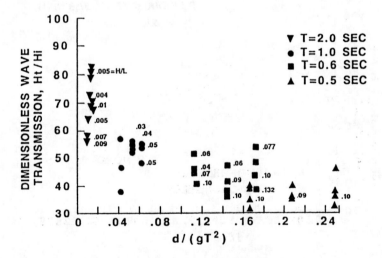

Figure 8. Wave transmission as a function of relative depth ratio for four wave periods, monochromatic waves; D = 3.0 cm ($1\frac{3}{16}$ in.), b/D = 0.1 [20].

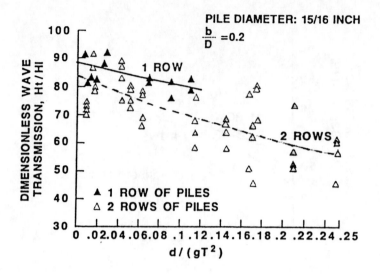

Figure 9. Wave transmission as a function of relative depth ratio for one and two rows of piles; monochromatic waves; D = 2.4 cm ($\frac{15}{16}$ in.), b/D = 0.2 [20].

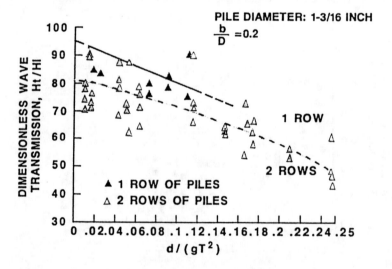

Figure 10. Wave transmission as a function of relative depth ratio for one and two rows of piles; monochromatic waves; D = 3.0 cm ($1\frac{3}{16}$ in.), b/D = 0.2 [20].

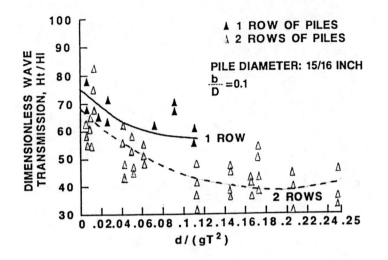

Figure 11. Wave transmission as a function of relative depth ratio for one and two rows of piles; monochromatic waves; D = 2.4 cm ($\frac{15}{16}$ in.), b/D = 0.1 [20].

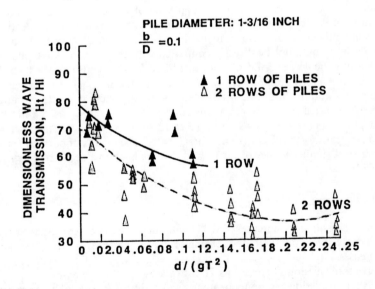

Figure 12. Wave transmission as a function of relative depth ratio for one and two rows of piles; monochromatic waves; D = 3.0 cm ($1\frac{3}{16}$ in.), b/D = 0.1 [20].

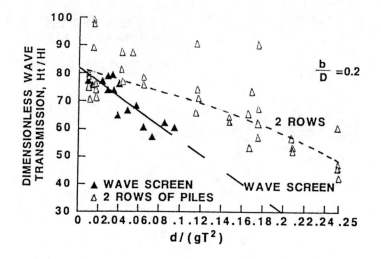

Figure 13. Wave transmission as a function of relative depth ratio; comparison between two rows of piles and a wave screen [20].

The results were also compared with wave transmission data presented by Allsop and Kalmus [2] for wooden wave screens. An arrangement of wooden wave screens was proposed to provide the wave protection for a new marina at Plymouth, United Kingdom. The wave screen breakwater consisted of vertical, rectangular slats with a gap ratio of 0.2. Experiments were performed with irregular wave spectra. The results were published for wave transmission as a function of wave frequency.

These results could not be directly compared with the random wave pile experiments because the wave period was not measured for the random wave tests. However, the wave screen results were compared with the monochromatic wave pile experiments. Caution should be used when comparing these two sets of data. The wave screen experiments were conducted using irregular waves, an 8.6-m (28.2-ft) water depth, 12-m (39.4-ft) long slats and 3 to 12-sec wave periods. The wave screen allowed less transmission than the pile breakwater. The results of both experiments agree better at smaller values of d/gT^2 and diverge as the value of d/gT^2 increases (Figure 13).

Conclusions

1. Wave transmission increases as d/H (water depth/wave height ratio) increases.
2. Wave transmission for monochromatic waves increases as the wave period increases.
3. Wave transmission decreases as H/L (wave steepness) increases.
4. Wave transmission for monochromatic waves decreases as d/gT^2 (water depth/gravitational acceleration (wave period)^2) values increase.
5. For a 10% gap ratio, the addition of a second row of piles reduced the wave transmission by 5 to 10%.

Offshore Breakwaters

Introduction

Offshore breakwaters are built to protect the shoreline from wave action, prevent beach erosion, and replenish beach sand by interrupting longshore and wave-generated currents. When properly designed, an offshore breakwater will either form a tombolo or a sand-spit, as desired. Formation of the sand-spit begins soon after construction of the breakwater. Approximately 50% of the sand volume is deposited in the first year with a steady state usually being reached after 4 to 5 years. After that time it will remain relatively stable undergoing minor or moderate seasonal changes. The process of beach accretion may be accelerated by depositing sand on the shoreline behind the breakwater employing pumping (dredging) or trucking methods.

Offshore breakwaters dissipate incident wave energy through wave reflection and diffraction. They act as a countermeasure against beach erosion and provide a sheltered area for small craft and bathers. The sheltered area serves as a littoral reservoir for materials brought in by waves diffracted by the breakwaters.

In the last 20 years the number of offshore breakwaters in Japan has increased approximately 1,000% while the increase in groin-type structures has increased only 100%. This shows a strong trend in that country toward the use of offshore breakwaters over groins as a means of beach stablization and protection. Offshore breakwaters have been constructed in South Africa, Italy, Spain, and Israel. In this country, offshore breakwaters have been constructed in California, Hawaii, Illinois, Louisiana, Massachusetts, Ohio, Pennsylvania, and Virginia.

Design procedures have been largely empirical and have varied from project to project. This has resulted in highly successful projects in most cases, however, some projects experienced beach erosion on the downstream side of the breakwaters. Additional research both in the laboratory and in the field is needed to develop more comprehensive design criteria.

The theory describing offshore, detached breakwaters (approximately parallel to the shore) is that they serve to diminish incoming wave energy, principally by the diffraction process, which reduces the potential sediment carrying capacity resulting in deposition of sediment in the form of salients (spits) or tombolos. At present there is interest in the design of offshore breakwaters which have the crest height slightly above or below the mean water level, this reduces construction costs. Wave forces acting on the breakwater are also reduced because during major storms the breakwaters are submerged by the generated storm surges.

Model Studies

The performance of a detached breakwater depends on the geometry of breakwater placement, wave properties, and sediment characteristics. Dimensional analysis of relevant parameters yields the following relationship:

$$Q_b/XBD = fn(X/B, X_{br}/B, H_0/L_0, G/B, \alpha, \ldots) \tag{4}$$

where Q_b = volume of sand moved into the sheltered volume of the breakwater defined by (X)(B)(D)

 X = distance from original shoreline to seaward edge of breakwater

 B = length of breakwater

 D = depth of water at seaward edge of breakwater

 X_{br} = distance from shoreline to breaker line

 G = gap distance between successive breakwaters

 α = angle of incident wave crests

The functional expression indicates a dependence on the geometric parameters of the breakwater in determining the amount of sand deposited in the sheltered volume of the breakwater.

The effects of G/B and X/B on Q_b were examined by Harris and Herbich [18]. Generally, sand volume increases as X/B decreases. For all field data and most model data examined, tombolos formed for values of X/B less than one. No tombolos formed for X/B equal to or greater than one. The effect of G/B is significant but not as pronounced as that of X/B. Sand volume trapped in the sheltered area generally increases as G/B decreases.

The effect of the location of the breaker line in relation to the location of the breakwater was reported by Rosen and Vajda [38] who showed the importance of having the breaker line seaward of the breakwater to get a maximum spit length. Shinohara and Tsubaki [41] showed the importance of deep-water wave steepness (H_0/L_0) in determining the amount of sand deposited in the sheltered area of a breakwater. Their data clearly showed that as wave steepness increases the amount of sand deposited in the sheltered area increases.

Figure 14 shows a relationship between Q_b and X/B [18]. Figure 15 shows the effect of gap spacing accreted behind each breakwater and the gap. $Q_{b+g}/XD(G + B)$ is the average sand behind each breakwater plus the sand moved into or out of the gap between the breakwaters divided by the control volume XD(G + B). The figure

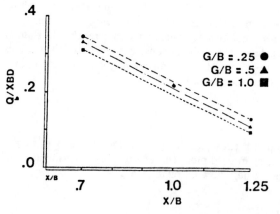

Figure 14. Effect of gap spacing on sand accreted behind each breakwater [18].

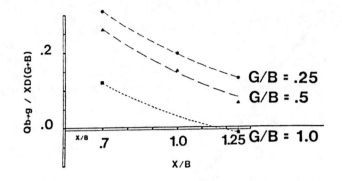

Figure 15. Effect of gap spacing on sand accreted behind each breakwater and gap [18].

indicates that as the gap gets smaller, more sand is accumulated. This plot is dimensionless and may be used to determine expected sand volumes in the sheltered area of one breakwater and one gap. Of particular note is that there can be a net loss of sand in the sheltered area for large gap spacings. Figure 16 is a plot of sand accumulated or lost in the gap versus X/B. As seen in the graph for the range of X/B

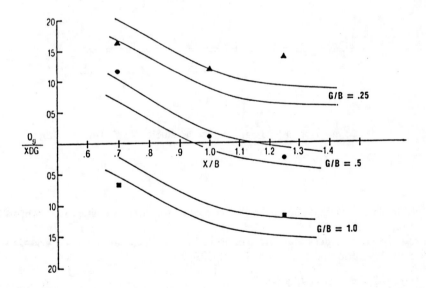

Figure 16. Effect of gap spacing on sand accreted behind each gap [18].

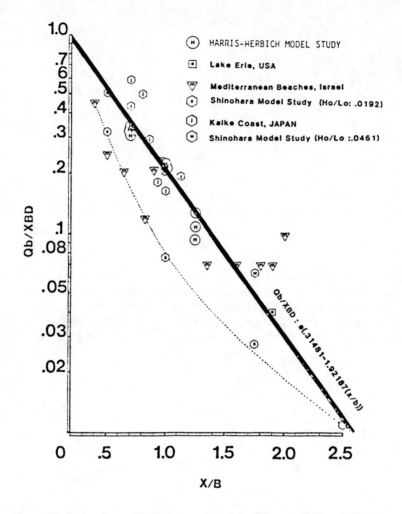

Figure 17. Comparison of field data and model studies, Q_b/SBD vs X/B [18].

shown, for large spacings the sand will erode while for larger spacings there will be accretion of sand.

Prototype and model data were plotted in Figure 17, the agreement appears to be reasonably good and the equation for the line is

$$Q_b/XBD = e^{(0.31481 - 1.92187(X/B))}$$ (5)

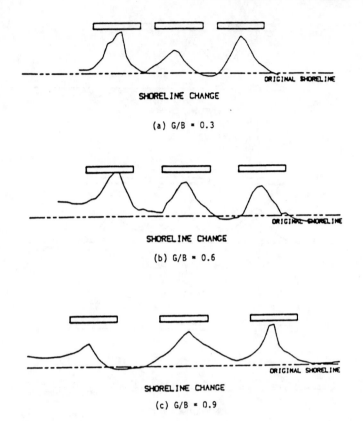

Figure 18. Shoreline response for a series of offshore breakwaters with X/B = 0.9 for three different gap distances (G/B) [8].

This formula is applicable for X/B between 0.5 and 2.5. For X/B less than 0.5 very little information is available but the curve should not go above a theoretical maximum of $0.5 = Q_b/XBD$ for subaqueous volume only and the slope should reverse so that Q_b/XBD would equal zero at X/B = 0. Toyoshima [48] reported that for continuous breakwaters with small X/B values tombolos did not form.

Cords [8] evaluated the shoreline changes for three breakwaters as a function of the breakwater position and the wave steepness. Figures 18–21 show the effect of gap for different distances from shore to breakwater length ratios (X/B) on shoreline changes. As expected the effect of gap on shoreline changes is considerable, the effect of wave steepness (H_0/L_0) should also be noted. Cords also observed that most of the sand transport is caused by steep waves. Thus, only small changes in

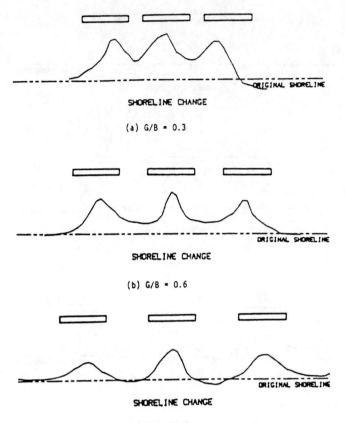

Figure 19. Shoreline response for a series of offshore breakwaters with X/B = 1.2 for three different gap distances (G/B) [8].

the shoreline behind the breakwaters can be expected from low steepness waves. Most of the sand transport and salient formation occur during the short periods when storm waves are present. Figure 22 shows the average volume gain/loss behind a gap between breakwaters.

Tallent [46] studied the effect of submerged breakwaters on seafloor topography. He observed that, similarly to the emergent breakwaters studies, increasing wave steepness increases sand movement to the lee side of the breakwater. However, waves of large steepness increase the scouring potential of gap areas. Tallent's study also indicates that there exists an intermediate relative submergence at which maxi-

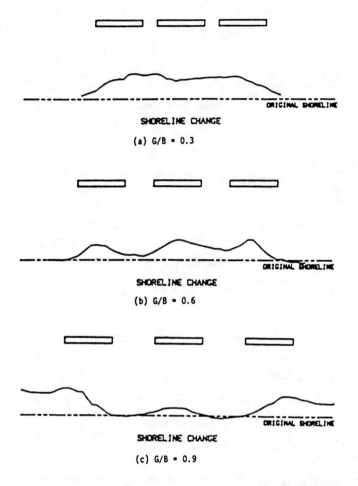

Figure 20. Shoreline response for a series of offshore breakwaters with X/B = 1.5 for three different gap distances (G/B) [8].

mum accretion occurs. Any further decrease in relative submergences beyond this optimum point drastically reduces accretion potential as shown in Figure 23.

Comparison of Model and Field Studies

Krafft and Herbich [26] compared the laboratory and field data for several existing offshore breakwaters. In spite of scatter of data points, the relationship between the volume of sediment deposition (or the volume of sediment accreted since

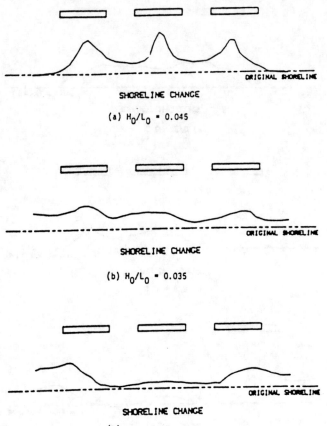

SHORELINE CHANGE

(a) $H_0/L_0 = 0.045$

SHORELINE CHANGE

(b) $H_0/L_0 = 0.035$

SHORELINE CHANGE

(c) $H_0/L_0 = 0.027$

Figure 21. Shoreline response for a series of offshore breakwaters with $X/B = 1.2$ and $G/B = 0.6$ for three different wave steepness (H_0/L_0) [8].

construction) Q has a reasonable relationship with sheltered volume defined as

$$XBD \tag{6}$$

where X = distance from original shoreline to breakwater
      B = breakwater length
      D = water depth at the structure

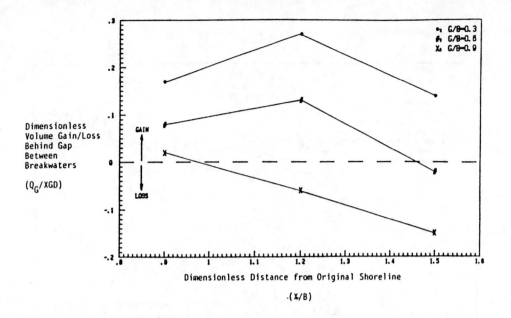

Figure 22. Average volume gain/loss behind a gap between breakwaters [8].

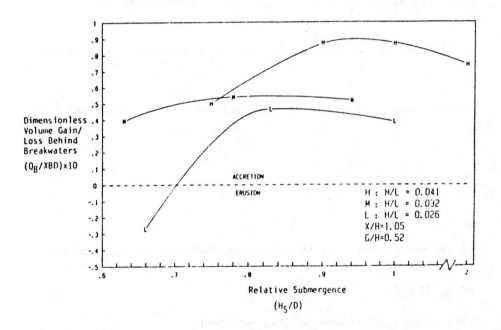

Figure 23. Effect of wave steepness and relative submergence on volume gain/loss behind a breakwater [46].

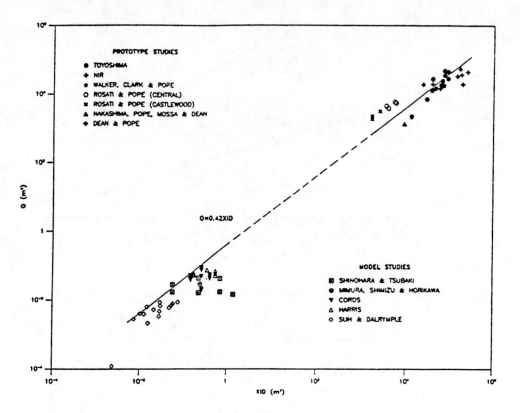

Figure 24. Sheltered volume relative to sediment deposition for all studies [26].

Figure 24 summarizes all data from the model studies and the field measurements. The relationship between the two volumes is

$$Q = 0.42\,XBD \tag{7}$$

This equation reflects a bias toward prototype studies.

A summary of the characteristics of offshore breakwaters constructed in the United States is presented in Table 2 [26].

Table 2
Summary of Characteristics of United States Detached Breakwaters

Project	Type of Breakwater*	When Built	Total Length of Breakwater Project (B)	No. of Segments	Length of Segments (B$_s$)	Gap Width (G)	Distance Offshore (X)
Venice, CA	Si	1905	183 m	N/A	N/A	N/A	366 m $\overline{213\ m}$
Santa Barbara, CA	Si	1929	434 m	N/A	N/A	N/A	305 m
Santa Monica, CA	Si	1934	610 m	N/A	N/A	N/A	610 m
Haleiwa Beach, HI	Si	1965	49 m	N/A	N/A	N/A	91 m original $\overline{49\ m\ w/fill}$
Winthrop Beach, MA	Se	1935	625 m	5	91 m	30 m	305 m
Lakeview Park, OH	Se	1977	403 m	3	62 m	49 m	137 m original $\overline{76\ m\ w/fill}$
Presque Isle, PA	Se	1978	440 m	3	38 m	60, 91 m	46 m
Colonial Beach, VA (Central)	Se	1982	427 m	4	61 m	45 m	64 m
Colonial Beach, VA (Castlewood)	Se	1982	335 m	3	61, 93 m	26, 40 m	46 m
Lakeshore Park, OH	Se	1982	244 m	3	38 m	60 m	120 m original $\overline{75\ m\ w/fill}$
East Harbor, OH	Se	1982	244 m	3	46 m	90, 105, 120 m	180 m
Lincoln Park, IL	Si	1939	457 m	N/A	N/A	N/A	183 m
Channel Islands, CA	Si	1960	700 m	N/A	N/A	N/A	550 m
Waikiki Beach, HI	Si	1938	213 m	N/A	N/A	N/A	76 m
Holly Beach, LA	Se	1985	555 m	6	46, 50 m	93, 89 m	78, 61 m
Redington Shores, FL	Si	1986	112 m	N/A	N/A	N/A	91.5 m
York River Gloucester Pt., VA	Se	1983	62.2 m	3	11 m 11 m 7.3 m	14.6 18.3 m	12.2 m 10.7 m 15.2 m

* Si = single, Se = segmented
** Datum used is local MLW (unless otherwise stated) or Low Water Datum (LWD) for the Great Lakes.

Table 2   (Continued)

Water** Depth (D)	Crest** Elevation	Tombolo (T) or Salient (S)	Comments	Fill Placed	B_x/X	B/X
1.8 m	3.7 m	S / T	Pre 1940s / 1940s–1960s groin installed early 1960s	No	N/A	0.5 / 0.9
7.6 m	3.7 m	T	Project dredged and shoreward connection added to prevent tombolo formation	No	N/A	1.4
7.6 m	3.0 m	S	Periodic dredging prevents tombolo formation	No	N/A	1.0
2.4 m	1.5 m	S / Near T	159 m groin nearby	No / Yes	N/A	0.5 / 1.0
3 m MLW / 5.7 m MHW	5.5 m MLW / 2.8 m MHW	T / S	Two beach planforms as a result of 2.7 m tidal range	No	0.3 / 0.3	2.0
3.0 m	2.4 m	S	Terminal groins at both ends	No / Yes	0.5 / 0.8	2.9 / 5.3
0.3 m	1.8 m	T/S	Tombolos form during low wave energy condition, removed by storms	Yes	0.8	9.6
1.2 m	0.4 m	T/S	Tombolos behind breakwaters, salients behind others	Yes	0.9	6.7
0.61 m	0.4 m	T/S			1.3, 2.0	6.7
1.5 m	2.0 m	S	Still adjusting, fine size fill being lost longshore	Yes	0.3 / 0.5	2.0 / 3.3
1.5 m	2.4 m	S	Still adjusting, low sand supply	No	0.3	3.1
3.7 m / 4.3 m	−1.2 m	F	Fill placed and held satisfactory	Yes	N/A	2.5
9.1 m MLLW	+4.3 m	T	Tombolo is periodically bypassed	No	N/A	1.3
—	0 m	S	Fill placed which eroded slowly over 8-year period	Yes	N/A	2.8
2.5 m	1.2, 2.4 m	S	1 riprap 5 pile w/used tire	No	0.8	9.1
2.4 m	0.46 m	S	Accumulated 24 m of beach in less than 20 days	Yes	N/A	3.8
0.41 m	0.3 m / 0.3 m / 0.5 m	T / S	Estuary unattached groins nearby	No	0.9	4.90

Summary and Conclusions

1. Offshore (detached) breakwaters have been successful in stopping further beach erosion and in forming salients (spits) and tombolos provided there is an adequate sand supply. In case of low sand supply sand artificially placed on beaches in the shadow of the breakwaters will generally remain in place.
2. Geometry of breakwaters including elevation, length, gap length, and distance from shoreline all affect the overall performance. Either salients or tombolos will form in the shadow of the breakwaters.
3. Wave diffraction analysis should be performed as part of the design process. Tombolos will generally form when the distance offshore to breakwater length ratio is less than one, i.e.

$$\frac{X}{B} < 1 \tag{8}$$

Salients will generally form when

$$\frac{X}{B} > 1 \tag{9}$$

Breakwaters are ineffective for beach augmentation when

$$\frac{X}{B} > 2 \tag{10}$$

The relative gap ratio affects the breakwater performance.
4. Preliminary budget estimates may be made on the basis of Figures 14, 16, and 17.

References

1. Adams, C. and Sonu, C., 1986, "Wave Transmission Across Near-Surface Breakwaters," *Proc.* 20th Coastal Engineering Conference, ASCE, pp. 1729–1738.
2. Allsop, N. W. H. and Kalmus, D. C., 1985, "Plymouth Marine Events Base: Performance of Wave Screens," Report No. EX 1327, Hydraulics Research, Wallingford, U.K.
3. Anglin, C. D., MacIntosh, K. J., Baird, W. F., and Werren, D. J., 1987, "Artificial Beach Design, Lake Forest, Illinois," *Proc.* Coastal Zone '87, ASCE, pp. 1121–1129.
4. Beach Erosion Control, Colonial Beach, Virginia, 1980, Detailed Project Report, U.S. Army Corps of Engineers, Baltimore District, May.
5. Brasfield, C. W. and Chatham, C. E., Jr., 1967, "Magic Island Complex Including Kewala Basin and Ala Wai Harbor, Honolulu, Oahu, Hawaii," U.S. Army Corps of Engineers, Waterway Experiment Station, Vicksburg, MS, TR 2-767.
6. Bruno, R. O., Watts, G. M., and Gable, C. G., 1977, "Sediments Impounded by an Offshore Breakwater," *Proc.* Coastal Sediments '77, ASCE, pp. 1006–1025.

7. Clark, G., 1988, *Warzyn Engineering*, personal communication.

8. Cords, D., 1986, "Model Study of Shoreline Changes Due to a Series of Offshore Breakwaters," unpublished Master of Science thesis, Ocean Engineering, Texas A&M University, College Station, TX.

9. Dally, W. R. and Pope, J., 1986, "Detached Breakwaters for Shore Protection," TR CERC-86-1, U.S. Army Engineering Waterways Experiment Station, Coastal Engineering Research Center, U.S. Government Printing Office, Washington, D.C.

10. Dean, J. and Pope, J., 1987, "The Redington Shores Breakwater Project: Initial Response," *Proc.* Coastal Sediments '87, ASCE, pp. 1369–1384.

11. Dean, R. G., 1973, "Heuristic Models of Sand Transport in the Surf Zone," *Proc.* Conf. on Engineering Dynamics in the Surf Zone, Sydney, Australia, pp. 208–214.

12. Dean, R. G. and Dalrymple, R., 1984, *Water Wave Mechanics for Engineers and Scientists*, Prentice-Hall, Inc., Englewood Cliffs, New Jersey, p. 72.

13. Dyer, K., 1986, *Coastal and Estuarine Sediment Dynamics*, Wiley-Interscience, New York, N.Y., p. 191.

14. Fried, I., 1976, "Protection by Means of Offshore Breakwaters," *Proc.* 15th Coastal Engineering Conference, ASCE, pp. 1407–1425.

15. Hardaway, C. S., 1985, "Estuarine Shore Erosion Control: Gapped Breakwaters," Proc. Coastal Zone '85, ASCE.

16. Harris, M. M., 1984, "Offshore Breakwater Placement Criteria," unpublished Master of Engineering Report, Ocean Engineering, Texas A&M University, College Station, TX.

17. Harris, M. M. and Herbich, J. B., 1986a, "Effects of Breakwater Spacing on Sand Entrapment," *Proc.* Symposium on Scale Effects in Modeling Sediment Transport Phenomena, Symposium '86, International Association of Hydraulic Research, Toronto, Canada, August 25–28, 1986.

18. Harris, M. M. and Herbich, J. B., 1986b, "Effects of Breakwater Spacing on Sand Entrapment," *Journal of Hydraulic Research*, Vol. 24, No. 5, International Association of Hydraulic Research.

19. Hayashi, T., et al., 1966, "Hydraulic Research on Closely Spaced Pile Breakwaters," *Proc.* 10th Coastal Engineering Conference, Vol. II, Chapter 50, pp. 873–884.

20. Herbich, J. B. and Douglas, B., 1989, "Wave Transmission Through a Double-Row Pile Breakwater, *Proc.* 21st International Conference on Coastal Engineering, ASCE, Chapter 165, pp. 2229–2241, Torremolinos, Spain.

21. Herbich, J. B., 1988, "The Concept of Offshore Breakwaters for Mitigating Beach Erosion," PIANC.

22. Herron, W. J. and Harris, R. L., 1966, "Littoral Bypassing and Beach Restoration in the Vicinity of Port Hueneme, California," *Proc.* Coastal Engineering Conference, ASCE, pp. 651–675.

23. Inman, L. D. and Frautschy, J. D., 1965, "Littoral Processes and the Development of Shorelines," *Proc.* Coastal Engineering, Santa Barbara, pp. 511–536.

24. Kilpatrick, W. S., 1984, "Wave Transmission Through a Row of Rigid, Vertical Piles," Unpublished report, Ocean Engineering Program, Texas A&M University.

25. Komar, P. D., 1976, *Beach Processes and Sedimentation*, Prentice-Hall, Inc., Englewood Cliffs, New Jersey, p. 207.

26. Krafft, K. and Herbich, J. B., 1988, "Literature Review and Evaluation of Offshore Detached Breakwaters," prepared for CERC, USAE Waterways Experiment Station, Vicksburg, MS, Texas A&M University, Report No. COE-297, September, 98 pp.

27. Kriebel, D., Dally, W., and Dean, R., 1986, "Undistorted Froude Model for Surf Zone Sediment Transport," *Proc.* 20th Coastal Engineering Conference, American Society of Civil Engineers, pp. 1296–1310.

28. Lakeview Park, Lorain, Ohio, "General Design Memorandum," 1975, U.S. Corps of Engineers, Buffalo, New York.
29. Mimura, N., Shimizu, T., and Horikawa, K., 1983, "Laboratory Study on the Influence of Detached Breakwater on Coastal Change," *Proc.* Coastal Structures '83, ASCE, pp. 740–752.
30. Nakashima, L. D., Pope, J., Mossa, J., and Dean, J. L., 1987, "Initial Response of a Segmented Breakwater System, Holly Beach, Louisiana," *Proc.* Coastal Sediments '87, ASCE, pp. 1399–1414.
31. Nance, T. F. and Hirota, P. M., 1974, "Magic Island . . . Ten Years After," *Shore and Beach*, Vol. 42, No. 2, pp. 19–22, Oct.
32. Nir, Y., 1982, "Offshore Artificial Structures and Their Influence on the Israel and Sinai Mediterranean Beaches," *Proc.* 18th Coastal Engineering Conference, ASCE, pp. 1837–1856.
33. Orville, M. T., 1976, "Offshore Breakwaters at Winthrop Beach, Massachusetts," *Shore and Beach*, Vol. 44, No. 3, Oct., pp. 34.
34. Peraino, J., Chase, B. L., Plodowski, T., and Amy, L., 1975, "Features of Various Offshore Structures," Miscellaneous Paper No. 3–75, U.S. Army Corps of Engineers, Coastal Engineering Research Center, Fort Belvoir, VA, April.
35. Pope, J. and Dean, J., 1986, "Development of Design Criteria for Segmented Breakwaters," *Proc.* 20th Coastal Engineering Conference, American Society of Civil Engineers, pp. 2144–2158.
36. Rosati, J. and Pope, J., 1989, "The Colonial Beach, Virginia Breakwater Project," Technical Report CERC-MP-89-2, Department of the Army, Waterways Experiment Station, Corps of Engineers, Vicksburg, MS.
37. Rosati, J., 1988, personal communication.
38. Rosen, D. S. and Vajda, M., 1982, "Sedimentological Influences of Detached Breakwaters," *Proc.* 18th Coastal Engineering Conference, American Society of Civil Engineers, pp. 1930–1949.
39. Seabergh, W. C., 1983, "Design for Beach Erosion at Presque Isle Beaches, Erie, Pennsylvania," CERC Technical Report HL-83-15, U.S. Army Engineers, Waterways Experiment Station, Vicksburg, MS.
40. Shinohara, K. and Tsubaki, T., 1966, "Model Study on the Change of Shoreline of Sandy Beach by the Offshore Breakwater," *Proc.* 10th Coastal Engineering Conference, ASCE, pp. 550–563.
41. *Shore Protection Manual*, 4th ed., 1984. U.S. Army Waterways Experiment Station, CERC, U.S. Government Printing Office, Washington, DC, p. 4–94.
42. Silvester, R. and Ho, S., 1972, "Use of Crenelate Shaped Bays to Stabilize Coasts," *Proc.* 13th Coastal Engineering Conference, ASCE, pp. 1347–1365.
43. Sonu, C. and Warwar, J., 1987, "Evaluation of Sediment Budgets in the Lee of a Detached Breakwater," *Proc.* Coastal Sediments '87, American Society of Civil Engineers, pp. 1361–1368.
44. Suh, K. and Dalrymple, R. A., 1987, "Offshore Breakwaters in Laboratory and Field," *Journal of Waterway, Port, Coastal and Ocean Engineering*, Vol. 113, No. 2. pp. 105–121.
45. Tallent, J., 1986, "The Submerged Offshore Breakwater and Its Effect on Seafloor Topography," unpublished Masters Thesis, Civil Engineering, Texas A&M University, College Station, Texas.
46. Toyoshima, O., 1982, "Variation of Foreshore Due to Detached Breakwaters," *Proc.* 18th Coastal Engineering Conference, ASCE, pp. 1872–1892.

48. Toyoshima, O., 1974, "Design of a Detached Breakwater System," *Proc.* Coastal Engineering Conference, American Society of Civil Engineers, pp. 1419–1431.

49. Truitt, C. L. and Herbich, J. B., 1987, "Transmission of Random Waves Through Pile Breakwaters," *Proc.* 20th International Conference on Coastal Engineering, ASCE, Ch. 169, pp. 2303–2313, Taipei, Taiwan.

50. Walker, J., Clark, D., and Pope, J., 1980, "A Detached Breakwater System for Beach Protection," *Proc.* 17th Coastal Engineering Conference, American Society of Civil Engineers, pp. 1968–1987.

51. Water Resources Development, 1979, U.S. Army Corps of Engineers in Hawaii, Pacific Coast Division, Ft. Shafter, HI.

52. Wiegel, R. L., 1961, "Closely Spaced Piles as a Breakwater," *Dock and Harbour Authority*, Vol. 42, *No.* 491.

CHAPTER 20

FLEXIBLE MEMBRANE UNITS FOR BREAKWATERS

Richard Silvester

Department of Civil Engineering
University of Western Australia
Nedlands, Western Australia

CONTENTS

Introduction

Construction of breakwaters with rubble stone has been in vogue since this type of coastal structure was devised in the last century. In more recent decades, as stone has become more uneconomical in the larger sizes to quarry and transport, it has been replaced by precast concrete units with a plethora of shapes. The fact that so many such armor units have been devised points to the fact that none have provided the stability in the face that was desired. If any particular solution had proved successful beyond all competitors it would have usurped the market.

The fact is that unreinforced concrete monoliths touch each other in spots and are therefore subject to rocking with all the heavy impacts that are involved. Cracking then occurs and the units are halved in weight, making them more mobile by even smaller waves. Being thrown around, they then proceed to break others and so the process continues.

The method of construction by dump truck at the end of the structure and later by crane to place the larger units on the seaward and leeward faces requires a wide surface for vehicular traffic. This access path must be located well above the highest tide level and reach of storm waves in order that the work, lasting many years, can be carried out continuously. Breakwaters thus have mammoth proportions to accommodate these constructional needs, much more than is required to prevent wave overtopping. The face slopes are relatively mild in order to provide stability for units covering them and hence the cross-sectional area of breakwaters is excessive in achieving the task of breaking or reflecting waves.

As these structures have been taken into ever larger depths, the demand for bigger precast concrete units has escalated costs. The quarrying and crushing of stone to suitable sizes for concrete production, its transport to the site, the mixing and subsequent cartage of units to the breakwater require much energy and equipment. This has made the provision of breakwaters the largest cost component in the building of a port.

Many theories have been put forward for the design of units in breakwaters, treated elsewhere in this handbook, but one significant conclusion reached by Sawaragi et al. [1] was: "Design formulas in future must take the hydrodynamic forces produced by resonance into consideration as an external disturbing force." This points to a new approach in breakwater design that permits large-scale voids to exist throughout the structure to obviate the use of small-scale material that may be dislodged in this resonance mechanism.

Another link in the design chain for these large structures is between them and the supporting bed material. Reflections of waves either normally or obliquely can scour material from adjacent to the face and cause slumping, perhaps accompanied by pore pressure build up. This topic is discussed in Volume 2. But the bed in the vicinity of breakwaters must be given attention if further failures are to be avoided.

Flexible Membrane Units

If progress is to be made in breakwater design, and this must encompass economic factors, the following requirements appear paramount:

1. Armor units should be designed that fit snugly together, giving resistance to movement by friction and shape over wide surface areas.
2. Core material should consist of units equally as large as other armor blocks if they can be manufactured from low-grade concrete.
3. Spaces should be provided between elongated units to permit wave absorption, reduce reflection, and attenuate upward pressures.
4. The bed seawards of the breakwater should be protected from scouring over wide widths by an impermeable mat for either traditional rubble-mound structures or other designs.

These various demands can be met by casting in-situ large units whose formwork comprises flexible skins of strong fabric, which is readily available today. Such nylon or other type of material can be sewn into any desired shape before it is filled with a slurried mortar comprising only sand and a cementing mixture. There is no need for stone to constitute a concrete because the strengths required are much less than those for precast concrete monoliths. The reason for this is that these membrane units are not handled after they are formed in place, and they will not rock because of their intimate contact with each other. The only compressive force required is that to support the load from above and that due to the overturning moment produced by horizontal wave forces. This can normally be met with a compressive strength of limestone or about 0.2 of normal concrete.

Engineers in Mexico [2–6] have pioneered the development of flexible membranes as formwork for cement mortar cast in-situ. Their purpose was to use local unskilled labor in developing countries rather than expensive imported technology. Although it has served its purpose in this context, it has application in western economies, where isolated sites with little infrastructure, cause quarrying and transport of rock to be extremely expensive. As good quality material becomes harder to locate, costs rise very quickly. The use of sand, which is generally available at the coast, makes for large reductions in cost.

Fabrics are available today with high strengths that can be readily sewn into bags or sausage proportions of any desired dimensions, resulting in units of very large weight. The greatest benefit is their assuming the shape of monoliths on which they rest, so producing a saw-tooth contact which, together with friction over large surfaces, provides good shear resistance to horizontal forces. Suction from waves is applied only to the ends of these large units, which can extend across the full width of the breakwater.

The mortar used needs to be a slurry that can flow to all parts of the fabric container without the use of vibrators. Once set, the formwork is no longer required and hence deterioration of the membrane is of no concern. The final hard-set mortar must be able to withstand the wear from wave swashing with suspended sand. Mortar of strength equal to that of limestone has sufficient wearability as exemplified by the resistance of limestone in many breakwaters throughout the world.

As in any engineering structure, costs of alternatives must be considered. In such comparisons it is not the unit cost (e.g. cost per m^3) that is relevant, but the overall expense of establishment, relative volumes of material, interruption of construction, and subsequent maintenance that must be considered. Methods of handling the large rock or precast concrete units involve sophisticated mechanical equipment in the form of intricate formwork, trucks, and cranes, that require technical know-how, large quantities of fuel, and good quality roads to the site. The provision of such infrastructure is all part of the overall cost.

It is believed that longer containers, in the form of sausage skins, have great advantages over the shorter alternative, equivalent to large bags. The overall size of each homogeneous mass can be so large that it is inconceivable that any wave could disturb or remove it. The weight of individual units can be such, and their frictional and form resistance so effective, that even the stability coefficient [7] normally used in the design of breakwaters becomes irrelevant. Laboratory tests are required to prove this contention, but if part of the research funds devoted to precast concrete units could be applied to this new concept, its characteristics could quickly be obtained. The high compressive, shear and tensile strengths required by precast monoliths are not required for these cast in-situ units, which do not rock or suffer associated dynamic forces.

The trapezoidal shapes of rubble-mound breakwaters cause a variable compressive force on the bed material, which results in differential slumping. This is accommodated by the rock material moving to new stable shapes prior to the final armor units being positioned. The flexible membrane structures are rectangular in shape and built from the bottom upwards, which therefore apply a more even pressure on the bed. Hence, differential settlement is not envisaged. Even if some of the internal segments are cracked by such slight adjustments the volumes and intimate contact will retain units of large volume or weight.

Design of Units

The specific gravity of these mortar units has been shown by tests [8] to approximate 2.0, which are cast underwater with the outside pressure medium of unit SG. Tests can therefore be conducted to derive shapes by using plastic containers filled with water in air. Such verification of theoretical shapes has been carried out as per Figures 1 and 2, which used the same circumference S = 92.8 cms. [9, 10]. The difference in shape was produced by applying pressure heads b_1 = 17.9 and 39.4 cms. In Figure 1 it is seen that the height of the water column is just above the soffit of the spheroidal shape, while in Figure 2 it is 1.7 times this vertical dimension. It is possible to increase this head to such an extent that the container becomes circular, but the tension in the plastic, or fabric in the case of the prototype, becomes very

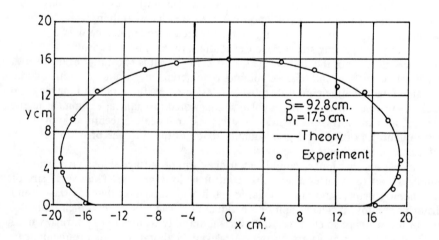

Figure 1. Comparison of measured and theoretical shapes for a water pressure head b_1 = 17.9 cm.

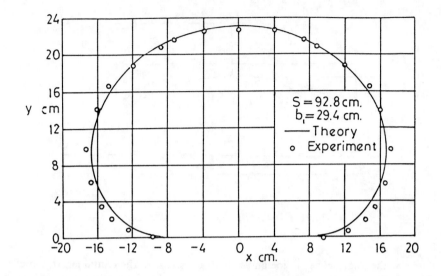

Figure 2. Comparison of measured and theoretical shapes for a water pressure head $b_1 = 39.4$ cm.

high. This may cause tearing in the material or the longitudinal seams. As seen in the two figures, the experimental shapes match the theory reasonably well.

Relationships were derived and measured between the input parameter of pressure head (b_1) divided by circumference S and the following ratios:

Sausage height/width	H/B
Height/circumference	H/S
Width/circumference	B/S
Cross-sectional area	A/BH
Contact width at base	B′/B
Height of greatest width	H′/H
Hoop tension in fabric	$T/\gamma S^2$ where γ is specific weight of water.

The variables are defined in Figure 3 and the parameters are presented in Figure 4. It is seen that A/BH varies very little for $b_1/S > 0.4$, implying that the cross-sectional area, or weight per unit length, is virtually the same for H/B ratios from 0.67 to 0.92. Because tension in the fabric increases some 600% over this range, it appears better to pour a flatter sausage in order to reduce stresses, while the cross-sectional area remains sensibly constant.

As the membrane tends towards a circular section so the contact width at the base (B′) decreases, while the height-to-maximum cross-section (H′) approaches 0.5. This condition is not recommended because it also involves high-pressure heads of

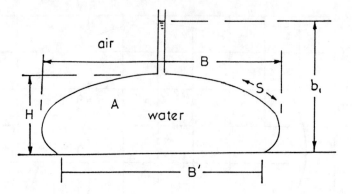

Figure 3. Definition sketch of sand sausage.

slurry on the joint between pipe and cylindrical sleeve of the container. It is preferable to have a pressure head equal to 150% of the height of the sausage, or $b'/H = 1.5$ or $b_1/S = 0.35$. This ordinate is specifically drawn to assist in the evaluation of parameters.

The proportional height at the greatest width (H') has a value of 0.375H for $b_1/S = 0.35$, which permits sausages placed in contact to form below and above units already in place. This provides an excellent interlocking mechanism. It tends

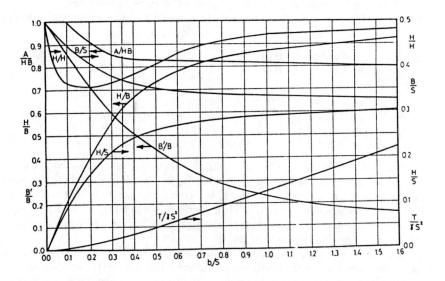

Figure 4. Dimensionless parameters from theory and experiment.

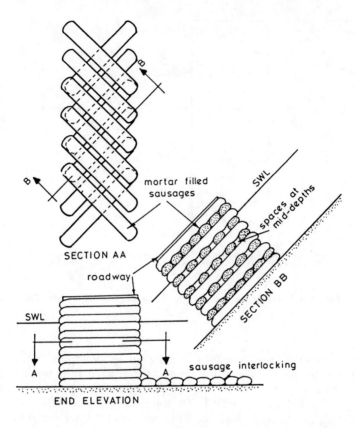

Figure 5. Orientation of sausage units to maximize surface contact.

towards 0.5 for large b_1/S and also for very small values, which might be used where a mattress-like cover is required.

As indicated in Figure 5, the sausage layers could be aligned alternately at 45° to the breakwater axis, to make each unit longer and heavier. This crossing at right angles permits an undulating surface contact that provides good shear resistance against horizontal wave forces. Positioning of units in the same orientation should be directly one above the other in order that they do not sit over spaces between supports. This can be achieved by nailing empty skins to those already cast. These will pull out as filling proceeds.

The exposed face should be essentially vertical to prevent uplift forces breaking the ends of units, which should be loaded with sausages from above. The cross-sectional area of the breakwater thus becomes rectangular, but with smaller height

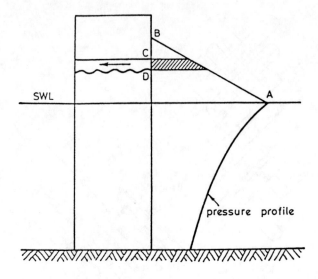

Figure 6. Wave pressures exerted on sausage units above SWL.

than for the equivalent rubble-mound structure. Some overtopping can be countenanced during the more severe storms due to the sausage units withstanding the
forces of sheet flow over them. As seen in Figure 6, the pressure forces from waves
vary in triangular fashion above SWL. The top units must have sufficient weight to
provide the frictional and form resistance to withstand the horizontal forces from
pressure and water friction. The 45° orientation aids in this stability by not having
any single sausage experience the full impact of a wave, which will vary in height
along the breakwater due to the generation process in storm conditions. Oblique
approach also results in wave height variation along the face.

As suggested in Figure 5, spaces could be left between units in the mid-depths to
allow for wave dissipation, with water oscillating through the corrugated channels
both across and along the breakwater. Water could jet through the leeward exit of
these tubes and may transmit some wave motion to this sheltered zone. However,
these jets will be at right angles to each other in alternate layers and hence will
attenuate readily. The exits are rounded nozzle turned inwards and therefore provide
a diffusing effect with reduced velocities. Tests are required to measure transmission
coefficients for various widths of structure and different spacing of sausage units.

The lower three and top three layers should be cast next to each other to prevent
such swashing. This would obviate scouring of the bed beneath the structure and
provide a reasonably smooth surface at the top for access during construction and
later maintenance if required. The spaces so provided should give excellent breeding
grounds for small fish. Barnacle growth will increase friction for flow through these

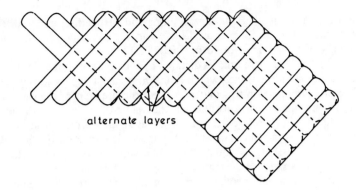

Figure 7. Method of making all units of equal length at the end of a breakwater.

conduits and hence will diminish wave transmission over time. Sand could be lodged in these spaces that could promote the growth of seaweed.

At the end of breakwaters the 45° alignment of units would normally mean that some of the sausages would be short in length and hence not so stable. This can be overcome by making them of equal length to those in the trunk, which implies the construction of a square end comprising units of similar length, as depicted in Figure 7. This shows units placed adjacent to each other, which will make for greater stability at this critical location.

All breakwaters reflect some energy from incident waves, either approaching normally or obliquely. This is especially so for long-period swell, which arrives persistently from one direction. Structures consisting of flexible membranes will have vertical faces and, in spite of the perforations suggested, may reflect waves more readily. This characteristic could be used in by-passing sediment across harbor of river mouths [11–13] by forming short-crested waves that expedite the passage of material across the opening. Even for rubble-mound structures bed protection could prevent scouring. [14, 15].

As noted in Figure 5, this protection could be afforded by similar sausage units to the breakwater construction. These could be laid parallel to the breakwater face out to a width covering the zone where reflected waves have heights equal to about half those of the incident waves. This may extend over a triangular area from the breakwater tip to a width of 200–300 m at the landward margin. The greatest scour will occur up to one *crest* length away from the face in a short-crested system. For waves arriving normal to a structure where standing waves are formed, bed cover should be taken out to one half wavelength, where accretion normally occurs.

When laid, alternate sausages should be cast first, with a space between that is filled later, so these mold around the initial ones to form a tongue and grooved joint. This close contact prevents vortices, formed in short-crested wave systems

[16], from penetrating to the sedimentary floor and suspending material from beneath the sausages. If rock cover is used these vortices will penetrate the voids and cause slumping of material, as found by Irie et al. [17].

The mean thickness of these units is dictated by the uplift produced in the troughs of short-crested or standing waves, which cause the greatest depressions in the water surface. The pressure beneath this mattress-like structure is from the water column of mean sea level, while the pressure above is the weight of water beneath the trough. The greatest uplift will therefore occur at $\frac{1}{4}$, $\frac{3}{4}$, wavelengths from the structure, and hence cover should be provided for at least one wavelength from the face. Because the buoyant force is essentially equal to the differential water column, their thicknesses should equate or exceed the trough-to-mean-sea-level height. The interlocking of sausages, as noted, should provide some safety factor. Here again some research could determine the minimum values to be employed.

Design of Mortar Mix

The largest cost in fabricating these cast in-situ units is the cement employed, therefore mixtures that minimize this content or replace the cement with an admixture should be sought. Extensive tests have been conducted [8, 18, 19] to determine a mix that will provide the necessary strength, which as noted before could be one fifth of the normal strength of concrete, or equivalent to limestone. Besides the compressive strength these sausages must withstand the wear of water, perhaps with suspended sand, from eroding the surfaces. The fabric used as formwork is not required after setting and hence can deteriorate from such wear or from ultraviolet (UV) rays in sunlight.

Other requirements of the mix are:

1. It must have 100% slump or be a slurry, in order to flow to any part of the container without vibration.
2. It must provide a tensile strength equal to that of limestone.
3. It must have a specific gravity equal to or exceeding that of limestone.
4. It must be as cheap as possible for the cementing materials available.

The strength of a cement mortar varies with the proportions of sand to cement, [2, 20, 21] decreasing with increase in the sand component. Due to the fine beach sand used, a ratio of 5:1 was used throughout the experiments [8]. This could be increased if coarser sediment is available. Tests should be carried out for the material available on the site.

For comparison, limestone samples were obtained from seven different sites, which varied greatly in strength. One exceeded the others by far and hence was used as the criterion. Replacements for portions of the portland cement were ground, granulated blast furnace slag, fly ash, and diatomite. Of these only the first improved the characteristics of the test cylinders. Sand was used both from the beach and from terrigenous sources. Also, seawater was used in some specimens in place of

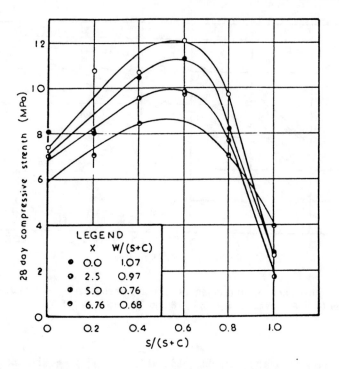

Figure 8. Compressive strength vs. blast-Furnance slag (S) plus cement (C) for variations in freshwater (W) and detergent X (ml/kg of S + C) for terrigenous sand/(S + C) = 5.0.

freshwater. To reduce the water/cement ratio while maintaining a high slump and easy flow through pumping equipment, various percentages of detergent were added. Results from the tests on best limestone were as follows:

Compressive strength:	1,335 psi (9.2 MPa)
Tensile strength:	170 psi (1.17 MPa)
Compressive strength for zero scour*:	1,510 psi (10.4 MPa)
Specific gravity:	1.95

Specimens with sand/cement of 5:1 with fine sand, and water/cement around 1.0, should give a compressive strength of 1,450 psi (10.0 MPa). Cement (C) was replaced with ground granulated blast furnace slag (S) in various proportions with detergent (X) added at rates of 0, 2.5, 5.0, and 6.76 ml/kg of cementing agents (S + C) (equivalent of up to 0.676% by weight approximately). As seen in Figure 8, optimum 28-day

---

* This comparative measure was for a water jet under constant head for 72 hours.

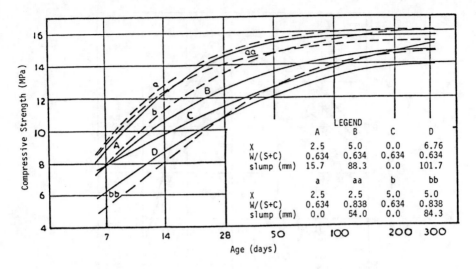

Figure 9. Strength vs. age for (a) terrigenous sand and freshwater (–) and (b) beach sand and seawater (– –). All cases, S/(S + C) = 0.6 and Sand/(S + C) = 5.0.

strength was obtained with S/(S + C) = 0.6 and X = 2.5. This is equivalent to 150% more slag than cement. These proportions were then used to compare beach sand and seawater with tests conducted at 7, 14, and 28 days. Strength with age are graphed in Figure 9 for terrigenous sand with freshwater and beach sand with seawater. As seen, curves were extrapolated to 300 days with increases of 70% over 28-day strength for this long period. This age characteristic has been observed elsewhere [22, 23]. The reasons for beach sand and seawater providing optimum results could be the increased content of calcium carbonate in beach sand (15.5%) compared to 0.1% in terrigenous material. The presence of sodium and magnesium compounds in seawater complements those found in portland cement [25].

The mixes used had limited slump and hence it is necessary to extrapolate strengths for complete slump. This indicated that a compressive strength of 1,720 psi (11.8 MPa) was possible [19]. The W/(S + C) ratio was also extrapolated for 100% slump to give a value of 1.18 with X = 2.5. Tests should be conducted on local sand with the cements, additives, and detergent available to obtain strengths of this order.

Brazil tests for tensile strength indicated again that S/(S + C) = 0.6 and X = 2.5 gave optimum values when reduced for 100% slump of 220 psi (1.52 MPa), which was higher than for the limestone specimens. With the same jet conditions as for the limestone sample, it was found that the mortar specimen required only a compressive strength of 1,020 psi (7 MPa) to prevent scour. This was an improvement on the limestone with the need for 1,510 psi (10.4 MPa) to achieve this capacity to withstand wear. The specific gravity of these mortar mixes was related to compressive strength in the same manner as limestone, giving 2.07 for the accepted strength.

Thus, the following proportions are recommended as a starting point for testing agents on-site and from local suppliers:

Beach sand/(slag + cement) = 5.0
Slag/(slag + cement) = 0.6 by weight
Seawater/(slag + cement) = 1.18 by weight
Detergent/(slag + cement) = 0.25% by weight

These should give the following values:

28-day compressive strength = 1,600 psi (11 MPa)
28-day tensile strength =   205 psi (1.4 MPa)
Specific gravity = 2.07

This mixture should give adequate wear resistance against water scour, certainly better than limestone, which is widely used in marine structures.

Comparative Costs

It is difficult to compare costs of a flexible membrane structure with equivalent rubble-mound construction due to many factors, namely:

1. A specific situation must be analyzed that may not be appropriate at any other site where material supply conditions differ.
2. The methods of costing equipment in different construction situations may vary greatly.
3. The purchase price of cement and additives (the bulk of the cost) is determined by local suppliers and can change swiftly.
4. The wave climate for any area is unique and may determine costs of construction by varying methods.

A comparison has been made between a limestone breakwater enclosing a marina and its membrane alternative [8]. The cost of the former was known and the same wave conditions were used in the design of the latter. The breakwater had been completed in 1978 at a cost of A$1,125,000, whereas the cost of the alternative was derived with 1982 prices. An inflation factor of 2.5 applied to the original estimates causing it to rise to A$2,800,000. This is one of the unknowns in the equation.

For the mortar version the price of three concrete mixers, one for standby, two slurry pumps (again one as standby), water pumps, and a compressor to supply air for divers were obtained. This total was divided by 5 as depreciation for this one job. Labor costs and fuel were assessed for the duration, which had to be estimated. The percentages for each item were as follows:

Nylon fabric	6.3
Cement + slag	73.6
Detergent	2.7
Machinery + running cost	4.2
Labor	13.2
Total	100.0

This total was A$2.5, which was 89% of the limestone version using a protective mat in front of the membrane structure. If this was excluded for a more realistic comparison this percentage became 64%.

Even with some reservations in the manner of estimating, this new approach equals or is more likely to be less expensive than the traditional method of construction. However, a final cost of any complex must account for probable maintenance. During an extreme storm sequence, it is normally accepted that rubble-mound structures will require some rebuilding. Access of heavy equipment on a breakwater with massive armor units placed over its soffit can be very difficult. The massive sausages employed are not likely to rock or be displaced but even if this happens the establishment cost for a concrete mixer plus pump is extremely small. Slurry can be pumped the length of the breakwater and hence access by cranes or trucks is not an issue. Even if an existing rubble-mound structure requires repairs, the use of flexible membranes, which will mold around existing rocks or precast units should be considered as an economical proposition. In the United Kingdom such cast, in-situ replacements were considered in one case with a formwork comprising 10 sides to form an almost spherical block. These would touch others at points and be very subject to movement by waves. A fabric form would provide intimate contact with those beneath and be very much cheaper. Thus, this new approach to overall construction or for repairs should be priced against alternatives using trucks and cranes for breakwaters, groins, and headlands.

Logistics

One of the great advantages of this concept is the simplicity of the operation. Very little equipment is necessary, and it is transportable by trucks of reasonably low capacity. The cement and additives must be delivered in bags or in bulk. If the site is near a city, premixed mortar could be delivered by truck and poured into the pump hopper. But if the structure is in a remote location, perhaps only two concrete mixers, a slurry pump, and a compressor are required. Sand will need to be brought to the mixers by front-end loader and seawater supplied by a modest sized pump.

Filling of mixers could be effected by unskilled labour. Pumping through a 3-in. (75-mm) pipe up to 1,000 ft (305 m) to the point of filling can be carried out. If longer distances are involved an intermediate hopper and pump could be used. Divers can connect the flexible ends of these pipes to containers in turn without stopping the pump. Once the structure reaches above water level, such labor can be unskilled.

The alternative of establishing a ready-mix complex on site will depend upon the site conditions and magnitude of the job. Hoppers for sand, bulk cement, and blast furnace slag would feed mixer trucks that pour continuously into the pump hopper. It is advisable to maintain a continuous flow of slurry because settling in the pipe should be avoided. The volume of any container should be such for it to be filled to a suitable height within, say, 3 hours. This ensures that the mix remains fluid throughout and provides the final shape previously predicted. The output of mixers should match the capacity of the pump used. There is little doubt, from experience in Mexico, that construction by this method can be much faster than for traditional rubble-mound construction. Cessation of operations due to inclement weather, shortage of funds, or labor disputes, does not involve large overheads.

Initial fabric containers placed on the seabed need to be held in place before filling, perhaps with the aid of concrete block anchors with cords attached to strips of fabric sewn at intervals along the sausage skins. These layers could be placed in calm weather with little wave action. Once the first layer is in place, those laid above them can be nailed to the partially set mortar of other units, the nails will pull out as pouring proceeds. To permit any excess water on the surface of the mix to be removed small cuts can be made across the top of the sausage without any ill effects.

There is no doubt that contractors will quickly learn shortcuts and procedures to follow, to minimize costs while providing the structure as designed. Where units are to be placed adjacent to each other, alternate sausages should be cast first with the final ones filled between them. As noted for the bed cover, these will then follow the curved edges of the existing units (See Figure 3) to form an interlocking mechanism. Such intimate contact and interaction is not so readily available even with the best designs of so-called interlocking precast concrete blocks.

Applications

Because of the great variety of sizes possible, these cast in-situ sausages are applicable to all types of marine structure, no matter how massive. Because overtopping will not dislodge units at the crown, it could be accepted during the more severe storms. Many applications for fabric formwork in marine and fluvial situations have been described [25] and even for floor protection around offshore structures. They have been used to protect offshore pipelines and support them over rocky seabed undulations. Scour holes beneath and adjacent to bridge piers have been protected from wave action by large bag or mattress like units. They have application in causeways for pipes, roads, or dikes for reclaimed areas. In fact, they can be used wherever the traditional but expensive rubble-mound alternative has been used in the past.

The major advantage of the system is that bulk material used in the construction is already available on the site, namely the sand. This obviates quarrying in the provision of large rock units, or crushing and screening of smaller stone for use in concrete. The necessity for infrastructure such as roads is overcome plus the consumption of expensive fuel in transport. For developing countries the expense of importing technology is avoided. As breakwaters are taken into deeper water the size of armor units grows, requiring larger trucks and cranes to place them greater distances out from the breakwater centerline.

The low strength requirement of these cast in-situ structures calls for leaner mixes and less strict demands on the sand used. The smaller cross-section required to achieve the hydraulic task of dissipating or reflecting waves, rather than the larger rubble-mound alternative, whose size is dictated by construction requirements, makes for a more economical approach overall. Interruptions for short or even longer terms does not increase costs greatly due to the lower mobilization charges. The use of more unskilled labor can aid all economies, be they of developing or fully developed countries.

References 2–6, 25 have been cited where the flexible membrane approach has been applied to modest structures such as groins and some offshore applications. Pilot studies are now required in natural settings to refine the logistics and exhibit the advantages or otherwise of this developing technology. The various subsidiary problems can be overcome if the same research effort is applied to them as has been available for development of the multitude of precast concrete blocks, which are still being called into disrepute. Work on soil-cement dams and pavements has application in the sea environment, with slight changes in the slurry mix to be employed. The increasing cost of traditional methods of construction for breakwaters and the like calls for a new approach to be experimented and applied.

Summary

The points raised in this chapter can be summarized as follows:

1. The current inquiries into stability of breakwater armor units should be expanded to include new and more economical methods of construction.
2. Such novel approaches should provide permeability within the structures in order to minimize uplift and scouring forces.
3. Bed protection should be afforded to all marine structures, particularly where persistent swell or storm waves arrive obliquely to their seaward faces.
4. Constructional units are required that have extensive surface contact to prevent rocking and provide good shear strength.
5. Conditions as in (4) above are provided by large monolithic units cast in-situ using flexible membranes as formwork, using mortar consisting of beach sand from the site.
6. This mortar, in the form of slurry for easy placement, needs only the strength of limestone to withstand the wave forces and wear due to sloshing of water with suspended sediment.
7. Units of sausage proportions are preferable to those of bag proportions to provide the weight necessary to impede uplift or horizontal displacement.
8. Shapes and other characteristics of such sausage units when cast underwater are available for design purposes.
9. These units laid trellis fashion across the structure distribute forces along each, thereby minimizing the effects of wave action.
10. Spacing of sausages at mid-depths reduces the forces on them, while leeward waves are minimized by the interaction of vortices from jets at each layer.
11. A mortar mix has been suggested that could lead to economical combinations of sand, cement, and additives to be tested for each site.
12. Costs of structures using sausage-type units could be less than for rubble-mound alternatives, taking both short- and long-term charges into account, and construction time is reduced.

13. Logistics of flexible membrane construction require attention, but the reduced costs of transport, equipment with overheads, technical expertise, and overall volume of material, should lead to reduced costs.

14. There have been many applications of flexible membrane units both on the coast and offshore, hence their expansion to larger marine structures is inevitable.

15. Subsidiary problems could readily be overcome if some research funds are diverted from traditional concepts that are not meeting requirements.

References

1. Sawaragi, T. et al., 1983, "Considerations of the Destruction Mechanism of Rubble-mound Breakwaters due to the Resonance Phenomenon," *Proceedings of the 8th International Navigation Congress*, pp. 3/197–208.

2. Alvariz, J. A. M. et al., 1974, "Breakwater, Rockfill and In situ Rocks Construction with Bolsacreto System," *4th International Annual Conference on Materials Technology*, pp. 1–20.

3. Porraz, M. et al., 1977, "Low Cost Structures using Operational Design Systems," *Proceedings Coastal Sediments Conference*, ASCE, pp. 672–685.

4. Porraz, M. and Medina R., 1977, "Low Cost, Labour Intensive Coastal Development Appropriate Technology," *Sea Technology*, pp. 19–24.

5. Porraz, M. and Medina R., 1978, "Exchange of Low-cost Technology between Developing Countries," *ECOR General Assembly*, Washington, D.C.

6. Porraz, M. et al., 1979, "Mortar-filled Containers, Lab. and Ocean Experiences." *Proceedings Conference on Coastal Structures*, ASCE, pp. 270–289.

7. Hudson, R. V., 1959, "Laboratory Investigation of Rubble-mound Breakwaters," *Journal of the Waterway, Port, Coastal and Ocean Division*, ASCE, Vol. 85, No. WW3, pp. 93–121.

8. Goh, P. J. P., 1983, "Use of Mortar-Filled Containers for Marine Structures," Master of Engineering Thesis, University of Western Australia.

9. Liu, G. S., 1974, "Mortar Sausage Units for Coastal Defense," M. Eng. Sc. Thesis, University of Western Australia.

10. Liu, G. S. and Silvester R., 1977, "Sand Sausages for Beach Defense Work," *Proceedings of 6th Australasian Conference on Hydraulics and Fluid Mechanics*, pp. 340–343.

11. Silvester, R., 1975, "Sediment Transmission across Entrances by Natural Means," *Proceedings 16th Congress International Association of Hydraulic Research*, Vol. I, pp. 145–156.

12. Silvester, R., 1977, "The Role of Wave Reflection in Coastal Processes." *Proceedings Coastal Sediments 1977, ASCE*, pp. 639–654.

13. Silvester, R., 1985, "Sediment By-passing Across Coastal Inlets by Natural Means," *Coastal Engineering*, Vol. 9, pp. 327–345.

14. Silvester, R., 1986, "The Influence of Oblique Reflection on Breakwaters," *Proceedings 20th International Conference on Coastal Engineering*, ASCE, Vol. III, pp. 2253–2267.

15. Hsu, J. R. C. and Silvester, R., 1987, "Scouring due to Reflection of Oblique Waves on Breakwaters," *Proceedings 8th Australasian Conference on Coastal and Ocean Engineering*, pp. 145–149.

16. Silvester, R., 1974, *Coastal Engineering*, Vols. I and II Elsevier Publ. Co., Amsterdam.

17. Irie, I. et al., 1986, "Study on Scour in Front of Breakwaters by Standing Waves and

Protection Methods." *Report of Port and Harbour Research Institute, Japan*, Vol. 25, No. 1., pp. 4–86.

18. Silvester, R., 1983, "Design of In situ Cast Mortar-Filled Armour Units of Marine Structures," *Proceedings 6th Australasian Conference Coastal and Ocean Engineering*, pp. 289–292.

19. Silvester, R., 1986, "Use of Grout-filled Sausages in Coastal Structures," *Proceedings, Waterway, Port, Coastal and Ocean Engineering, ASCE*, Vol. 112, No. 1., pp. 95–114.

20. Neville, A. M., 1973, *Properties of Concrete*, Pitman Press, Bath, U.K.

21. Yen, T. et al., 1978, "A Possibility of Increased Mortar Strength for Ferro-cement," International Conference on Materials Construction for Developing Countries, Bangkok, Thailand, pp. 665–683.

22. Bamforth, P. B., 1980, "In-situ Measurements of the Effect of Particle Portland Cement Replacement Using Either Fly Ash or Ground Granulated Blast-Furnace Slag on the Performance of Mass Concrete," *Proceedings of the Institution of Civil Engineers*, Part 2, pp. 777–800.

23. Anonymous, *Production of Cement from Granulated Blast-furnace Slag* (pamphlet), Nippon Steel Company, Japan.

24. Montgomery, D. C. and Dunstan, M. R. H., 1981, "A Particular use of Fly Ash in Concrete Rolled Concrete Dams," *Civil Engineering Transactions, The Institution of Engineers, Australia*, Vol. CE 23, No. 4, pp. 227–233.

25. Koerner, R. M. and Welsh J. P., 1980, "Fabric Forms Conform to any Shape," *Concrete Construction*, pp. 401–405.

CHAPTER 21

RECENT DEVELOPMENTS IN THE DESIGN
OF MOUND BREAKWATERS

M. A. Losada

Departamento de Ciencias y Técnicas del Agua
University of Cantabria, Spain

CONTENTS

Introduction

The function of a breakwater is to "break" the "water" and provide a sheltered area where vessels can berth, moor, load, and unload their cargo. In addition, breakwaters protect against sediment transports in the littoral zone. Most breakwaters are land-connected. They are usually built in pairs perpendicular to shore and extend to the same depth, narrowing the distance between them to form an entrance.

In many cases the breakwaters are provided with a quay on the inside of sufficient width to allow loading and unloading of certain vessels and the necessary traffic and transport on the quay. This may include space for cranes for loading and unloading and for transportation equipment, such as trucks, low-boys, containers, and space for pipelines for oil, gas, cranes, conveyor belts, etc.

The difference between a breakwater serving only as protection against waves and possibly also littoral drift and a breakwater with a quay on its inside is that while in the case of the former a certain amount of overtopping during storms may be permitted. In the latter case, the breakwater should provide full protection against overtopping of water, and allow some spray carried over the breakwater by wind action if it does not happen too often. In most developing countries the combined breakwater and quay has been preferred because it is more economical than a breakwater and a pier built separately. The drawback with the design has been that because only a certain width of quay is available, it may be inadequate for future requirements.

Figure 1 shows a schematic section of a rubble-mound breakwater. There is an outer layer that must be stable under the wave action; it is constructed with armor units that may be either natural or artificial. A core provides the support or base for the main layer. In between, there are several layers, secondary layers, that are the transition between core and main layer, and have the following functions: to support the main layer by roughness, to filter the transmission of wave pressure, and to provide a filter layer for the core material. It is a common practice for economic or functional reasons to construct a screen and a low berm that limit the extension of the main (armor) layer, the most expensive part of the dike.

The main layer is a granular system, thus it is rough and permeable. It can be built with graded quarry stones, known as rip-rap, comprising uniform quarry stones or artificial units of concrete of different shapes such as cubes, dolos, and tetrapods; the artificial units must be of the same size and weight. To define a section of the dike it is necessary to specify the following items (see Figure 1):

- Characteristics of the armor units, shape and size
- Construction and placement procedure
- α, slope angle
- W, W_i, weight of the pieces of the main layer and of the secondary layers and core
- γ_r, γ_{ri}, specific weight of armor units in the main layer and secondary layers respectively.
- e, e_i, width of the main layer and secondary layers, respectively
- h_i, b_i, geometric definition, height and width of layers and berms

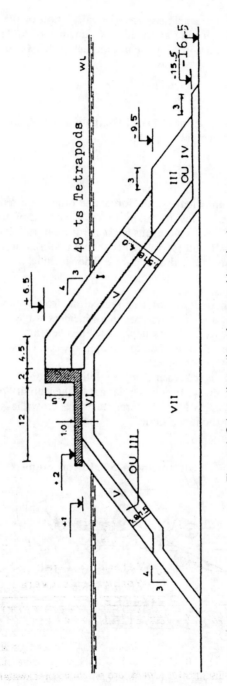

Figure 1. Schematic section of a mound breakwater.

In general all parameters are defined after the calculation of the weight, W, of armor units and most of them are specified as a function of it. The lengths and widths, e_i, are defined in function of a useful parameter, the size of an equivalent cube, defined by

$$1 = (W/\gamma_r)^{1/3} \tag{1}$$

Furthermore, roughness and permeability of the main layer depend on the type of armor units and on the placement procedures.

Possible Damage to Breakwaters

The design requires the knowledge of the forces and other requirements involved. The breakwater is supposed to last for many years. The extent of possible damage also needs to be specified. Common reasons for breakdown of rubble-mound breakwaters are summarized by Bruun [9a] whether the mound is composed of natural or artificial blocks, and are depicted in Figure 2. They include:

1. Knock-outs by waves.
2. Lift-outs (by up-rush, down-rush) usually resulting from combinations of up-rush and down-rush and toe velocities in an incident wave.
3. Sliding of the armor as a whole due to special wave trains.
4. Gradual breakdown or failure due to "fatigue" by special wave trains, wave concentrations or by similar effects.
5. Undermining of the wave screen or upper solid structure.
6. Overwash by water always presents a danger to the stability of the crown as well as to the inner slope. Many failures started as crown failures or failures of the upper part of the inner slope.

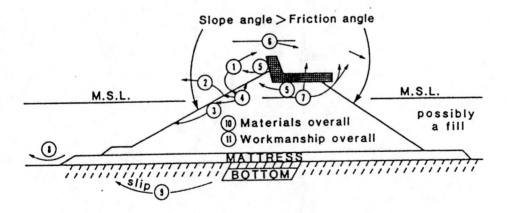

Figure 2. Common reasons for failure of mound breakwaters [9].

7. Lift-ups and through-washes when the core material and/or filter layer are so coarse that they let water pass through the permeable and structural components behind it.

8. Toe erosion is also a common reason for failure at the lower part of the seaward side of a rubble mound that is placed in shallow water or where the depth/wave height ratio is less than 2.0.

9. Soils failures. Sometimes a breakwater must be built on soil that is not very strong. It may include soft silt layers with a high water content and thereby a low bearing capacity, which may cause turnover as well as sliding on or squeezing out of the soft layer.

10. Differences in the soundness of materials used for the construction. Natural materials when carried demonstrate strongly varying characteristics with respect to size, geometry, hardness, wear by rubbing against or knocking to other blocks, resistance to shifting conditions of submergence and emergence, temperature variation, freezing and thawing, etc.

11. Poor workmanship. Although most contractors have no desire whatsoever to produce poor quality work, it occasionally happens.

Stability of Mound Breakwaters: General Principles

Design and construction of mound breakwaters has entered a new area during the last few years. The major reason for that is the realization of problems encountered as it became necessary to erect port structures on more exposed shores and in deeper waters. Progress was achieved by the numerous breakdowns of, or severe damages to, large breakwaters soon after their completion during the period of 1976–1981.

Based on bitter experience, it was realized that damage to mound structures often is a chain process by which failure of one element introduces a chain of failures. To obtain stability, one must therefore consider four different types of stabilities:

1. The overall stability, which is the stability of the breakwater as a whole with special reference to the armor layer.

2. The unit stability, which is the stability of the single unit or its ability to stay in place.

3. The structural unit stability, which is its structural strength.

4. The geotechnical stability including overall soils stability, as well as stability against toe erosion and rock fill stability.

These interdependent stabilities all must be fulfilled. Failure by (2) or (3) or both may cause a failure in (1). Failure in (1) may initially occur without (2) or (3), but it may cause failures in (2) or (3), or both. Overall, soils failures are rare, but toe erosion may occur, causing sliding of the armor layer. This emphasizes the use of a protective mattress on the floor.

The earlier tendency was to define stability solely as "unit stability," as it was expected that such stability would include "everything." Experience, however, demonstrated that stability had to be considered in a much broader sense.

Overall Stability. Overall stability is mainly concerned with:

1. Sliding of the armor layer as a whole, or mass slides penetrating deeper in the mound.
2. Mass departures of blocks from the armor layer by jumps and/or rolling.
3. Toe failures causing breakdown of the lower slope expanding upward, finally causing a mass failure of the armor. Such an occurrence may start as a failure of the mattress below the toe.
4. Mass breakdowns by heavy overwashes of the crown of the mound peeling off layers after washing most of the material down on the inside of the mound. Such failure could start with a turning over of a massive wave screen.

Hydrodynamic Stability of Units in the Mound. Forces on the unit include impact and momentum forces exerting pressures and shear forces on the unit, which will try to push it out of the mound.

The ability of units to stay in place in the mound first of all depends on gravity forces. Gravity forces are exerted directly on a unit and by friction forces on a unit by neighboring units. Units' ability to stay in place depend highly upon their geometry. For the same slope, blocks may show a great variety of reactions caused by hydraulic forces because their ability to "interknit" or "intertangle" varies greatly.

The hydrodynamic "stability," however, should not only be looked upon "statically," because this only provides "static information." A rock-mound structure under wave attack is a "dynamic feature," and may include numerous moving parts. It possesses a certain "brittleness" and is subject to wear and tear. The stability, therefore, cannot be adequately defined without considering the ability of the structure and its units to stand up to certain shocks as well as to wear and tear. The structure must neither be too brittle, nor should it be allowed to wear out too soon, as it should last 100 to 200 years, or more. Port structures should be built to last. They are neither supposed to suffer short-range breakdowns, nor long-range wear and degradation.

Many rock-mound breakwaters built 100–200 years ago are still functioning well. Examples are found at many NW-European countries. Other types of structures have failed during the same period.

Structural Unit Stability. Unit stability includes the ability of the unit to stay in place in the mound and the structural stability of the unit, which must not rupture, crack or break under any load, static or dynamic or both, it may experience. The forces ensuring stability of a unit include gravity and friction forces. In blocks of special geometrical shapes these forces may be assisted by interlocking, making the armor a king-sized "mattress." This, however, may be a very dangerous practice if the single elements (leg or arm) of a block are not strong enough to resist the forces by pressure, momentum, shear, or a combination of these forces. The numerous failures of breakwaters with armor of multilegged blocks have proven the inadequacy of the structural stability of such blocks, which simply was not considered in the design.

Overall Design Criteria. Design is based on a number of "design-criteria" that include:

1. Wave criteria.
2. Geometry criteria (configuration).
3. Materials criteria, including availability of materials.
4. Soils criteria, including a combination of (2) and (3), and bottom soils and geotechnical characteristics.
5. Construction criteria, including availability of equipment and manpower.
6. Maintenance criteria.
7. Economics criteria.
8. Aesthetic criteria.

These criteria are partly independent of each other and partly interrelated. Conditions of waves and soils are given for a particular location. Materials may have alternatives depending upon geometries, construction and maintenance criteria. Choice is usually between rock and concrete, but rock quality and size varies greatly. Construction depends upon geometries, materials, equipment, and labor. Maintenance is a function of materials and of construction procedures. Construction as well as maintenance also have a dependency upon manpower, particularly in developing countries.

Flow Characteristics of Regular Waves

When a regular wave train reaches an undefined slope, the following physical phenomena are produced: breaking, run-up and run-down, reflection, and transmission. Taking Z as a variable to measure these phenomena, Z is a function of the following parameters:

The medium—

1. Depth at the toe of the slope, h
2. Bottom slope, β
3. Specific weight of the water, γ_w
4. Acceleration due to gravity, g
5. Kinematic viscosity, μ

Incident waves, assuming regular waves—

1. Wave height, H
2. Wave period, T
3. Wave approach angle, θ

The structure

1. Geometry, defined by slope angle, α, and a characteristic width, λ.
2. Characteristics of roughness permeability, which will depend on:
   - Type of armor units of the main layer.
   - Physical arrangement of the armor units.

- Size of the armor units, which may be characterized by the length of the side of the equivalent cube, $1 = (W/\gamma_r)^{1/3}$, W being the weight of the armor units and γ_r their specific weight.
- Characteristics of the underlying layers.

Regarding rubble-mound breakwaters designed according to traditional criteria, it is acceptable to say that the mean characteristics of roughness and permeability depend only on the type of the armor units and their size.

From experiments described by the Technical Advisory Committee on Protection Against Inundation [81], it may be concluded that when the incident wave height is considerably greater than the side of the equivalent cube, the magnitudes of the physical phenomena associated with the breaking of the wave on the slope are independent of the height of roughness and, therefore, of the size of the blocks.

On the other hand, when the wave breaks on smooth impermeable slopes, experiments confirm that depth does not influence run-up [5, 35,.72], nor the reflection coefficient [63].

The aforementioned considerations suggest that flow characteristics on a rough, undefined slope under the action of a regular wave train can be approximately governed by an expression of the type:

$$f(Z, \text{type of armor unit}, \alpha, \lambda, \gamma_w, \mu, g, H, T, \theta) = 0 \qquad (2)$$

The following dimensionless numbers may be generated:

Z generic dimensionless variable expressing flow characteristics
α
θ
$H/L_0 = 2\pi H/gT^2$
$H^2/\mu T$
λ/H

Equation 2 in dimensionless form is:

$$Z = f(\alpha, \theta, H/L_0, H^2/\mu T, \lambda/H) \qquad (3)$$

According to Battjes [4] Reynolds' number $H^2/\mu T$ holds for smooth slopes, normally over a minimum threshold above which it has no influence, and assuming perpendicular incidence ($\theta = 0$) and neglecting the variable λ/H (relative width of the breakwater) which only has appreciable influence on the phenomenon of wave transmission. Hence Equation 3 can be further reduced to

$$Z = f(\alpha, H/L_0) \qquad (4)$$

This function can be reduced to a simpler one of a single variable:

$$Z = f(Ir) \qquad (5)$$

Table 1
Breaking on Rip-Rap Slope (Günbak, 1976)

Type of Breaking	Iribarren's Number
Spilling	—
Plunging	Ir < 2.0
Plunging or collapsing	2.0 < Ir < 2.6
Collapsing or surging	2.6 < Ir < 3.1
Surging	3.1 < Ir

$Ir = \tan \alpha / \sqrt{H/L_0}$, which is called the Iribarren's number. This function holds for each type of armor unit and perpendicular incidence.

Breaking. In the classical literature four types of breaking are defined as points of reference [20, 42, 66]: surging, collapsing, plunging, and spilling. Iribarren's number, which originated as an indication of whether or not wave breaking occurred on a flat slope [4], produces not only this information but also *how* the wave breaks [3, 4]. Table 1 shows the results of Günbak [28] on a rough slope, with cot $\alpha = 2.5$.

Run-up and Run-down. In Figure 3 the variables Ru and Rd are defined as the maximum and minimum levels referring to the SWL reached by the water on the slope. With reference to Equation 4 and taking Ru/H and Rd/H as the dimensionless variable, we can express

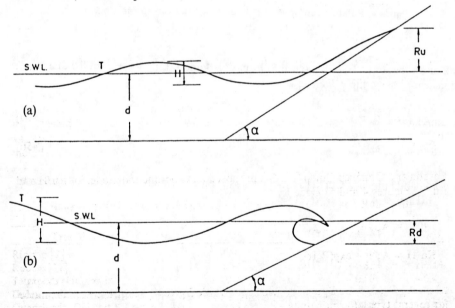

Figure 3. Definition sketch of wave run-up (a) and run-down (b).

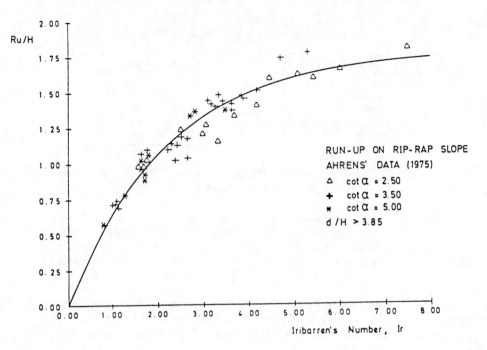

Figure 4. Relative run-up vs. Iribarren's number on rip-rap slope [2].

water on the slope. With reference to Equation 4 and taking Ru/H and Rd/H as the dimensionless variable, we can express

$$Ru/H = f(\alpha, H/L_0) \tag{5a}$$

$$Rd/H = f(\alpha, H/L_0) \tag{5b}$$

Losada and Giménez-Curto [53, 54] proposed an experimental model for Ru/H and Rd/H (Figures 4 and 5) given by

$$Ru/H = A_u(1 - \exp(B_u Ir))$$

$$Rd/H = A_d(1 - \exp(B_d Ir))$$

where A_u, B_u, A_d, and B_d are fit coefficients. Table 2 gives the coefficients of the model for several type of armor units.

Figure 6a,b shows the variation of the coefficients with the porosity, n.

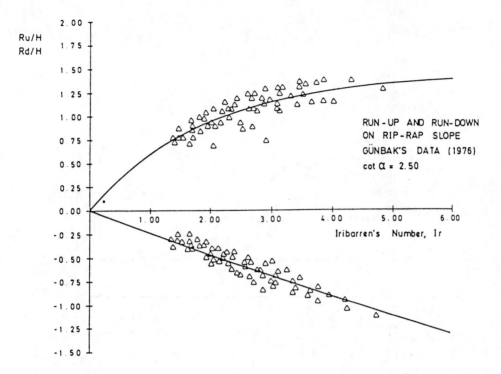

Figure 5. Relative run-up and run-down versus Iribarren's number on rip-rap slope [28].

Structure of the Water Flow on the Slope

It is of interest to know the properties of the mass flow on a specific slope such as water layer thickness, δ; particle velocities, v; uprush-backwash, front velocity, u_c; phase difference, σ; pressure, p; and acceleration, a. These are the dependent variables. If it is desired to know the behavior of these variables, it is necessary to include two new variables, the time, t, and the length, x, in the dimensional analysis.

Table 2
Fitness Coefficient of the Exponential Model for Run-up and Run-down

Type of Armor Unit	A_u	B_u	A_d	B_d
Rip-rap [2]	1.80	−0.46	−1.10	0.30
Rubble [27]	1.37	−0.60	−0.85	−0.43
Tetrapods (Jackson in [26])	0.93	−0.75	−0.80	−0.45
Dolos (Wallingford [26])	0.70	−0.82	−0.75	−0.49
Quadripods (Dai and Kamel in [26])	0.93	−0.75	−0.80	−0.45
Cubes [57]	1.05	−0.67	−0.72	−0.42

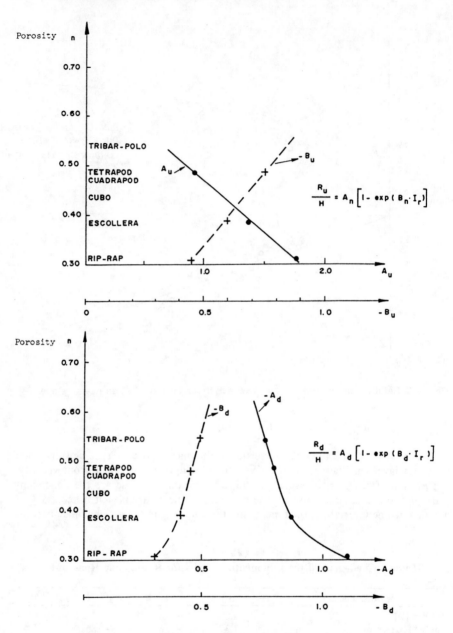

Figure 6a,b. Fit coefficients of the exponential model for run-up and run-down.

Consequently, Equation 2 may be modified as follows, for a specific slope defined by roughness and permeability,

$$Y = f_y(H, T, \mu, \rho, g, \alpha, l, n, x, t) \tag{6}$$

where perpendicular incidence $d/H > 1.5$ and the influence of break-water width is neglected. Equation 6 depends on ten parameters; it is possible to reduce to seven by

$$\pi_Y = \Psi_Y((\nu T/H^2), (gT^2/H), (1/H), nH^2, \alpha, (t/T), (x/T\sqrt{gh})) \tag{7}$$

Making the same assumption as before about Reynolds' number, roughness and permeability, it is possible to reduce Equation 7 to:

$$\pi_Y = \Psi_Y((gT^2/H), \alpha, (t/T), (x/T\sqrt{gH})) \tag{8}$$

The dependent variables, π_Y, are

Water layer thickness, $\delta/T\sqrt{gH}$
Particle velocity, $v/\sqrt{gH}$
Up-rush, backwash front velocity, $u_c/\sqrt{gH}$
Phase difference, t/T
Particle acceleration a/g
Pressure, $p/\sqrt{gH}$

Battjes and Roos [5] reported results of tests on these variables. Unfortunately, they only covered a small range of Iribarren's numbers, $Ir < 2.0$, on smooth plane, mild slopes. With these limitations, the conclusions obtained must be considered with some reservation and the application to engineering practice is still difficult.

Denoting the extreme up-rush and down-rush velocity by V_{max} and V_{min}, respectively, Battjes and Roos concluded that

$$V_{max}/\sqrt{gH} = Irf_1(x/T\sqrt{gH}) \tag{9}$$
$$V_{min}/\sqrt{gH} = Irf_2(x/T\sqrt{gH}) \tag{10}$$
$$u_c/\sqrt{gH} = 0.6\sqrt{Ir}, \quad Ir \le 2.0 \tag{11}$$
$$t/T = 0.7(1/\sqrt{Ir}), \quad Ir \le 2.0 \tag{12}$$

Günbak [26] reported time-dependent mean pressures inside the breakwater with fine and coarse core material and also maximum and minimum pressures in two different types of materials. The general trend of the experimental data confirms a dependence of the pressure with Iribarren's number, and as a crude approximation,

$$p/\rho gH = f(Ir, x/T\sqrt{gH}) \tag{13}$$

where x in this case is taken along the still-water level inside the breakwater.

As before, the formal structure of Equation 13 becomes

$$p/\rho gH = A_p(1 - \exp(B_p Ir)) \tag{14}$$

where A_p and B_p depend on the dimensionless distance and roughness and permeability of core and layer material. More data are needed before practical values for application can be used.

Sawaragi et al. [74] presented distributions of maximum water particle velocity and acceleration (uprush and backwash), along the slope in a permeable slope for a wide range of Iribarren numbers $1.30 < Ir \leq 4.60$. The main conclusions of their study are as follows:

Maximum Water Particle Velocity and Acceleration. Figure 7a gives an example of the effect of the surf-similarity parameter on $V_{max}/\sqrt{gH}$ on a 1:2 slope with various structural characteristics, such as an impermeable smooth surface slope, a rubble-mound slope with an impermeable core, and a permeable rubble-mound slope. $V_{max}/\sqrt{gH}$ has a maximum value in the $2.0 \leq Ir \leq 3.0$ range, with resonance and where the variation of this value with Ir is very large. In other words, it is strongly affected by the incident wave period in the $2.0 \leq Ir \leq 3.0$ range. The maximum value of $V_{max}/\sqrt{gH}$ becomes smaller as the surface roughness and permeability increases.

It is found that the maximum value of $V_{max}/\sqrt{gH}$ is 3.0 on an impermeable smooth slope, 2.0 on an impermeable rough slope and 1.3 on a permeable rough slope.

Furthermore, Figure 7b also shows the effect of $H/h = 0.5$. Thus, we can also see that H/h is strongly affected by the water particle velocity.

Figure 7b shows the effect of the surf-similarity parameter on the water particle acceleration on the permeable rubble-mound slope. In Figure 8 the closed circles and dotted lines show the experimental results, while the full lines show the values calculated by the shallow-water wave theory and the long dash-short dash lines indicate the ratio of the experimental acceleration to the theoretical values. A + symbol indicates where a resonance phenomenon has occurred. In general, the water particle acceleration on the slope tends to increase as Ir decreases. This fact indicates that breaking waves on the slope act by increasing the acceleration. On the other hand, the maximum acceleration in the down-rush appeared in the range $2.0 \leq Ir \leq 3.0$. As stated above, both the water particle velocity and the water particle acceleration reach their maximum values when under resonance conditions. From these facts, we may assume that the resonance phenomenon has a significant effect on the damage or destruction of a breakwater.

Distribution of the Maximum Water Particle Velocity and Acceleration Along the Slope. Figure 8a,b shows the distribution of the maximum water particle velocity and acceleration along the slope. The scattering of the data around the same position is caused by differences in the incident symbol +, which indicates where resonance phenomenon has occurred, and the unbroken lines show the best fit curves. It can

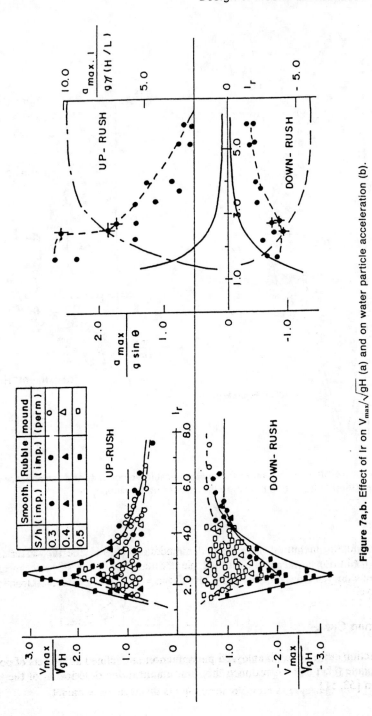

Figure 7a,b. Effect of Ir on $V_{max}/\sqrt{gH}$ (a) and on water particle acceleration (b).

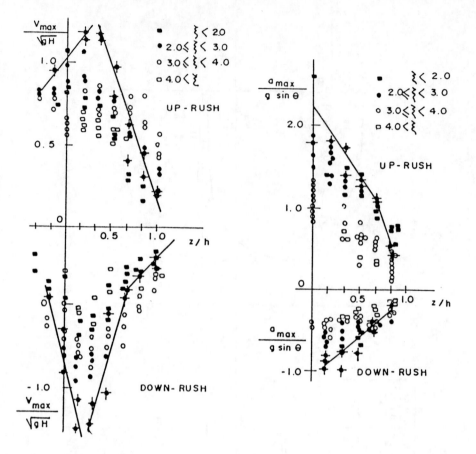

Figure 8a,b. Distribution of the maximum water particle velocity (a) and maximum water particle acceleration (b) along the slope in the permeable slope.

be seen that the maximum value occurs immediately below the still-water level. These distributions confirm that the incipient destruction of the slopes can easily occur immediately below the still-water level: $z/h = 0.1 - 0.2$ (z = depth from still-water level).

Interaction Curves

Interaction curves of each analyzed phenomenon are defined as the sets of points on the plane (H, T) which produce the same quantitative description of the phenomenon [53, 54].

For perpendicular incidence and a specific type of armor unit, the exponential model can be used:

$$Z = A(1 - \exp(B \cdot Ir)) \tag{15}$$

and expressing Iribarren's number as

$$Ir = \sqrt{g/2\pi} \tan \alpha T/\sqrt{H} \tag{16}$$

A function of type:

$$f(Z, H, T, \alpha) = 0 \tag{17}$$

can be obtained by eliminating Ir, thus allowing representation of the curves $Z =$ constant on the plane (H, T) for each slope.

Figures 9 and 10 show some examples of interaction curves of breaking and rundown phenomena. These curves are limited by the curve, which defines the wave stability limit. Maximum value of the wave slope was taken as $(H/L_0)_{max} = 0.142$, which corresponds to $Ir_0 = 2.654 \tan \alpha$.

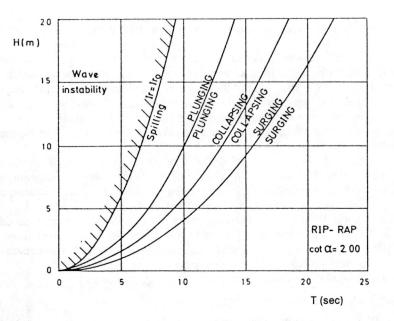

Figure 9. An example of interaction diagram of breaking.

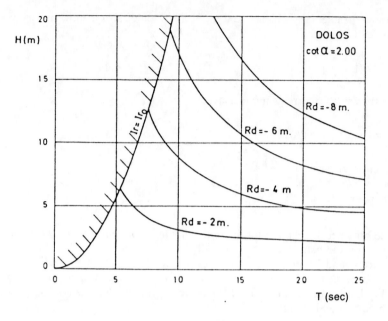

Figure 10. An example of interaction curves of wave run-down.

Flow Characteristics of Irregular Waves

In the case of a sea state, defined by H_s, (significant wave height), T_z, (mean zero-upcrossing wave period) and spectral parameters ε or ν_0, the variables such as type of breaking, Ru, Rd, H_r, H_t, may be considered random variables that acquire a different value for every wave of the sea state. The distribution function of these random variables may be obtained by assigning to each individual irregular wave the same value that would be produced by a periodic wave train of the same height and the same period.

It is important to note the statistical nature of this hypothesis, which does not necessarily imply that each individual wave produces the same phenomenon manifestation as the equivalent regular wave train, but is less restrictive; it refers to averages of many values rather than to individual values.

This hypothesis, known as the hypothesis of equivalence, was introduced by Saville [73] and was empirically proven by Van Oorschot and d'Angremond [86] and Battjes [3] for run-up on smooth slopes, and by Bruun and Johannesson [12] and Bruun and Günbak [10] for run-up on rough, permeable slopes.

Considering that the distribution function of Z is defined by

$$F_Z(x) = \text{Prob}(Z \le x) \tag{18}$$

and that $Z = x$ is an interaction curve, the result is

$$F_Z(x) = \iint_D p^*(H, T) \, dH \, dT \tag{19}$$

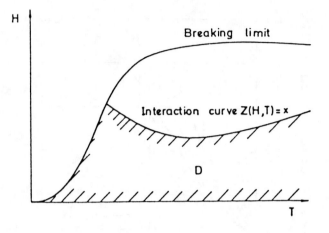

Figure 11. Definition sketch of the integration domain in Eq. 19.

where the integration domain, D, is the shaded area in Figure 11 and p*(H, T) is the joint probability density function of wave heights and periods in the place occupied by the slope.

Thus, knowing the joint probability density function of wave heights and periods and interaction curves, by means of numerical integration, it is possible to obtain the distribution of type of breaking, Ru, Rd, H_r, or H_t in a sea state.

Figures 12 and 13 show examples of distribution functions of type of breaking and H_r.

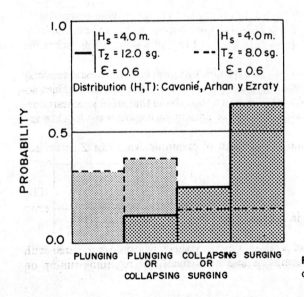

Figure 12. Distribution function of the type of wave breaking.

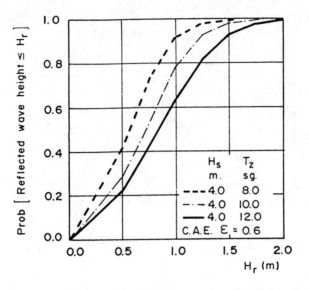

Figure 13. Distribution function of reflected wave, Hr.

It has been assumed that:

$$p^*(H, T) = p(H, T) \Big/ \left[\int_0^\infty dT \int_0^{H_b} p(H, T) \, dH \right] \tag{20}$$

where $p(H, T)$ is a theoretical distribution [18, 52] and H_b is breaking-wave height defined by the breaking limit curve. This curve has been defined in the examples in accordance with Michell [62], Miche [61], Goda [23], and Reid and Bretschneider [69].

Distribution of the maximum value of variables Ru, Rd, H_r, H_t in a sea state may be obtained by accepting statistical independence among the successive values acquired by each of these variables within the sea state. Note that this hypothesis does not necessarily imply statistical independence among successive wave heights and periods.

Taking $F_{MZ}(x)$ as the distribution function of maximum value for Z in the sea state, it follows that

$$F_{MZ}(x) = [F_Z(x)]^N \tag{21}$$

where N = number of waves in the sea state

The probabilistic method of analysis described here has been compared with experiments carried out by Kamphuis and Mohamed [45] regarding run-up on

Table 3
**Data of Experiments from Kamphuis and Mohamed [45] on Smooth,
Impermeable Slopes and h = 0.90 m, T_p Is the Spectral Peak Period**

Case	Spectrum	H_s (m)	T_p (sec)	T_z (sec)	cot α
A	Bretschneider	0.0528	1.59	1.30	1.50
B	Bretschneider	0.0755	1.43	1.20	2.00

smooth, impermeable slopes. Two cases (A and B) have been chosen, details of which are given in Table 3.

The theoretical method has been applied with the following criteria:

- Run-up on smooth, impermeable slopes is represented by the following model:

$$Ru/H = Ir \qquad\qquad \text{for Ir} \leq 2.5 \qquad\qquad (22a)$$

$$Ru/H = 2.5 - (Ir - 2.5)/3 \qquad \text{for } 2.5 < Ir < 4.0 \qquad (22b)$$

$$Ru/H = 2.0 \qquad\qquad \text{for } 4.0 \leq Ir \qquad\qquad (22c)$$

which is based on data from the Technical Advisory Committee on Protection Against Inundation [81], Battjes and Roos [5], and Günbak [28].
- On the basis of this model, interaction curves have been obtained which, together with the breaking limit, are shown in Figures 14 and 15.
- Using Equations 19 and 20 with joint distributions of wave heights and periods of Bretschneider [7], Longuet-Higgins [52], and Cavanié et al. [18], run-up distribution functions have been obtained. Parameters of joint distributions of

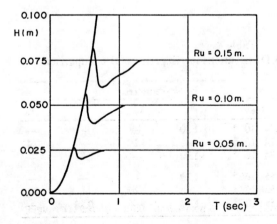

Figure 14. Interaction curves of run-up on smooth impermeable slopes; ctg α = 1.5.

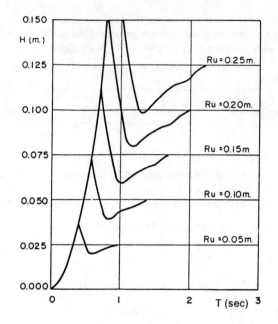

Figure 15. Interaction curves of run-up on smooth, impermeable slopes based on Eq. 22; ctg α = 2.00.

wave heights and period, obtained from spectral moments are given in Table 4.

Figures 16 and 17 represent the values obtained in the experiments and the results obtained by the aforementioned method, together with Rayleigh distribution, for cases A and B, respectively.

Table 4
Values of Parameters Used in Distributions for Experimental Comparison

Case	Distribution	Parameters				
		m_0	T_z	$T_{0,1}$	ϵ	ν_0
A	Bretschneider	$1.74 \cdot 10^{-4}$	1.30	—	—	—
	Longuet-Higgins	$1.74 \cdot 10^{-4}$	—	1.23	—	0.41
	Cavanié et al.	$1.74 \cdot 10^{-4}$	1.30	—	0.80	—
B	Bretschneider	$3.55 \cdot 10^{-4}$	1.20	—	—	—
	Longuet-Higgins	$3.55 \cdot 10^{-4}$	—	1.10	—	0.41
	Cavanié et al.	$3.55 \cdot 10^{-4}$	1.20	—	0.80	—

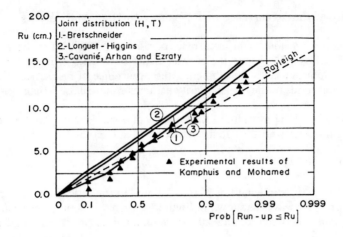

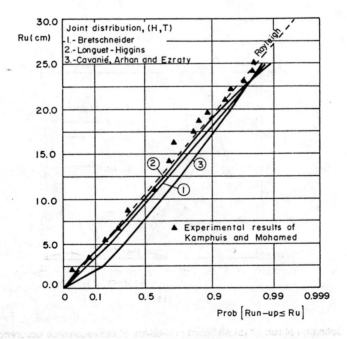

Figure 16. Experimental comparison of the probabilistic method described (Case A).

Figure 17. Experimental comparison of the probabilistic method described (Case B).

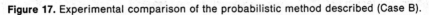

Probability of the Occurrence of Resonance for Irregular Waves

As mentioned previously, the occurrence of resonance is related to the interaction of successive waves. Therefore, the characteristics of a series of irregular waves in time is an important factor in predicting the occurrence of resonance. Notable is that this corresponds to the surf-similarity parameter more closely than wave height alone.

Sawaragi et al., [75] introduced the concept of a run length ξ^*, where the surf-similarity parameter whose value lies between 2.0 and 3.0 is denoted as

$$\xi^* = 2.0 < \xi < 3.0$$

The definition of the run length of ξ^* is as follows. In the series in time of ξ of a sequence of irregular waves as shown in Figure 18 where the solid circles indicate the values of ξ falling between 2.0 and 3.0. The length of the runs ξ^* reading them from

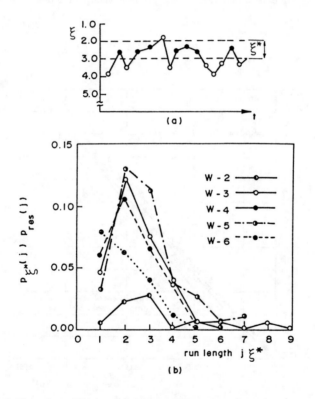

Figure 18. Definition of run ξ^* (a) and joint probability of the resonance occurence $P_{red}(j)$ and the run length j of ξ^*, $P_{\xi^*}(j)$ vs. run length of j_{ξ^*}(b) [73a].

left to right in Figure 18a, are 1, 2, 3, and 1. Using this concept, one can obtain the probability of the occurrence of resonance for ($p_{res}(j)$) for a run length j for $\xi p\xi_*(j)$.

The joint probability given by the product of these two probabilities at every run length was obtained and is shown in Figure 18b, where the joint probability is defined as,

$$P\xi_*(j) \cdot P_{res}(j) = N_j \bigg/ \sum_{j=1}^{\infty} N_j \cdot r_j/N_j = r_j \bigg/ \sum_{j=1}^{\infty} N_j \tag{22}$$

where r_j is the total number of occurrences of resonance for a run length, and N_j is the total number of occurrences for a run length of j.

From Figure 18b, it can be seen that the maximum frequency of the occurrence of resonance for given irregular wave trains appears at the run length of j = 2 for ξ^*.

Functional Design: Reflection, Transmission and Wave Overtopping

Depending on the breakwater's geometry and materials, the arriving wave energy will be partly reflected, partly transmitted, and partly dissipated. The design of the breakwater is highly dependent on the wanted level of reflected, transmitted, and dissipated energy. There are no general rules for these important aspects, however, some researchers have proposed several formulas and design diagrams. Most of these equations have been obtained with regular waves. Their use must be considered as informative and for *preliminary* designs.

Reflection and Transmission Coefficients for Vertical, Permeable and Not Overtopped Dikes

Numata [64], proposed the following formulas for the calculation of the reflection coefficient, K_R, and transmission coefficient, K_T.

$$K_T = 1/(1 + \alpha_T(H/L)^{\beta_T})^2, \qquad h/L < 0.25 \tag{23}$$

$$K_R = \alpha_R(B/D)^{\beta_R}, \qquad\qquad H/L > 0.01 \tag{24}$$

where   B = width of the dike
               D = grain diameter
               h = water depth at the toe of the dike
        H, L = wave height and length at h

α_T, β_T, α_R, and β_R are given in the Tables 5 and 6. The energy dissipation can be calculated directly from the equation

$$K_E^2 = 1 - (K_R^2 + K_T^2) \tag{25}$$

where K_E is the dissipation energy coefficient.

Table 5
Coefficient α_T and β_T [64]

Type of Material	α_T	β_T
Quarry stone	$1.26\,(B/D)^{0.67}$	1/2
Tetrapods	$1.184\,(B/D)^{0.895}$	1/2

Table 6
Coefficient α_R, β_R [64]

Type of Material	B/D	h/L	α_R	β_R
Quarry stone	<8	≤0.15	0.35	$1.7\,(h/L)$
		≥0.15	0.35	$1/0.5\,(2.9(h/L)^{0.2})$
	>8	≤0.15	$1.19\,(h/L)$	0.12
		>0.15	$0.38\,(h/L)^{-0.1}$	0.12
Tetrapods	<5	<0.15	0.35	$0.6\,(h/L)^{-0.49}$
	>5	>0.15	0.35	$0.04\,(h/L)^{-1.1}$

Reflection and Transmission Coefficients for Breakwaters That Are Not Overtopped

Numata [64], proposed the following equation:

$$K_T = 1/(1 + \alpha_T{}^*/Ir)^2 \tag{26a}$$

$$\alpha_T{}^* = 1.48(B_s/D)^{0.66} \tag{26b}$$

where B_s = width of the breakwater at the mean water level
     $Ir = tg\alpha/\sqrt{H/L_0}$
     α = slope angle
     $L_0 = 1.56T^2$
     T = wave period.

The reflection coefficient, K_R is a function of Ir [55]. Some of their results are given in Figure 19.

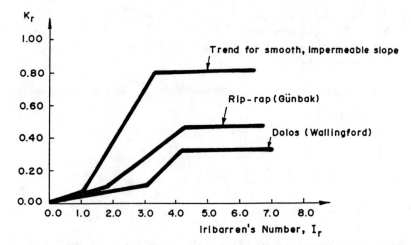

Figure 19. Comparison of reflection coefficient for several types of not overtopped slope vs. Ir.

Overtopped Breakwaters

In that case part of the wave energy can be transmitted over the breakwater. A transmission coefficient is defined by

$$K_{T_0} = H_{T_0}/H_i \tag{27}$$

where H_{T_0} = transmitted wave height over the breakwater
  H_i = incident wave height

Also, some energy is transmitted through the breakwater. This coefficient is defined by

$$K_{T_t} = H_{T_t}/H_i \tag{28}$$

where H_{T_t} = transmitted wave height through the breakwater

The total transmission coefficient is calculated by

$$K_T = (K_{T_0}^2 + K_{T_t}^2)^{1/2} \tag{29}$$

Impermeable Breakwaters. For an impermeable breakwater $K_{T_t} = 0$, but $K_{T_0} \neq 0$. The experimental work by Goda [24], Lamarre [51], and Saville [73a] may be synthesized in the following equations Seelig [76].

$$K_{T_0} = \alpha_{T_0}(1 - (F/R)), \qquad 0 \leq B/h \leq 3.2 \tag{30a}$$

$$\alpha_{T_0} = 0.51 - 0.11(B_c/d^*), \qquad F > 0 \tag{30b}$$

$$K_{T_0} = \alpha_{T_0} - (F/R)(1 - \alpha_{T_0}), \qquad f < 0 \tag{30c}$$

where   F = freeboard of the dike
$\quad\quad$ B_c = width in the upper level
$\quad\quad$ d^* = height of the dike from the mean water level
$\quad\quad$ h = water depth

It is not recommended to use this equation outside the following ranges:

$1.5 \leq \cot \alpha \leq 2.0$
$B/h \leq 3.2$
Bottom slope $\approx 1/15$

The reflection coefficient can be calculated by

$$K_R = (1 - (F/h)^{1/2})/(1 + (F/h)^{1/2}) \tag{31}$$

Reflection and Transmission Coefficient in Permeable Slopes. For this case it is not possible to give a general equation. Only through experimental tests or theoretical calculation it is possible to arrive at the correct value of K_R and K_T. In the case that the breakwater has $F < 0$, $K_{T_0} \gg K_T$, then it is permissible to consider $K_T = K_{T_0}$.

Overtopping by Irregular Waves

After testing several rock-armored, low-crest mound sections in a 2-dimensional wave flume Allsop [1] concluded that for a number of irregular waves, N, overtopping depends chiefly upon wave height and breakwater geometry, but not upon wave steepness. Allsop proposed the following equation to describe N in terms of F/H_s, where F is the freeboard (height of breakwater crest above static-water level), and H_s is the significant wave height at breakwater site in absence of the structure,

$$N = 50\{1 - \sin[C_1(F/H_s) + C_2]\} \tag{32a}$$

$$C_1 = 3.1 - 4.6(F/h) \tag{32b}$$

$$C_2 = \text{coefficient}$$

As Allsop [1] indicated that Equations 32a and 32b do not follow the sharp upwards trend of N at low values of F/H_s. They seriously underpredict K_t at these levels of F/H_s, see Figure 20.

Following Allsop [1], the wave transmission by overtopping can be related to a new parameter R^* defined by

$$R^* = (F/H_s)\left[\left(\frac{1}{2\pi}\right)(H_s/L_0)\right]^{1/2} \tag{33}$$

Figure 21 shows the transmission coefficient versus freeboard R^*.

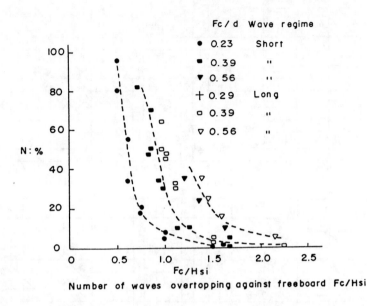

Figure 20. Number of waves overtopping against F/H$_s$ [1].

Wave Overtopping Rate: Goda's Diagrams. Goda [22] gives design diagrams of wave overtopping rate of block mound seawalls and of vertical revetments. These diagrams are given in Figures 22a-d. Figure 23 [22] shows where the effect of crown width of block mound on design crest elevation is included.

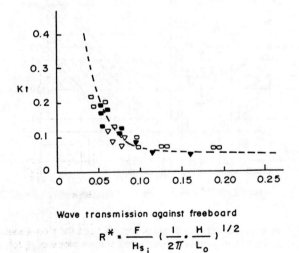

Wave transmission against freeboard

$$R^* = \frac{F}{H_{s_i}} \left(\frac{1}{2\pi} \cdot \frac{H}{L_0} \right)^{1/2}$$

Figure 21. Wave transmission against freeboard R* [1].

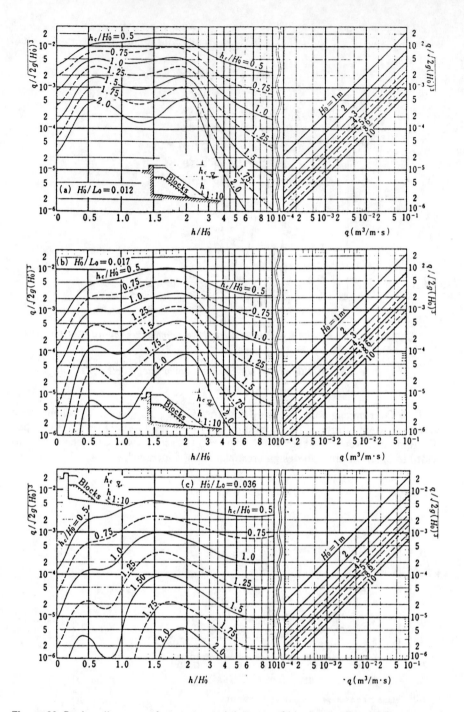

Figure 22. Design diagrams of wave overtopping rate of block mound seawalls on a sea bottom slope of $\frac{1}{10}$ (a), $\frac{1}{30}$ (b) and of vertical revetments on a sea bottom slope of $\frac{1}{10}$ (c), $\frac{1}{30}$ (d) [22].

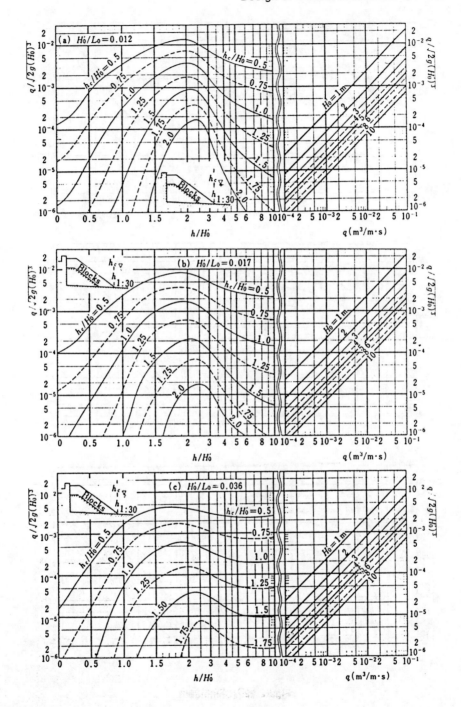

Figure 22. (Continued)

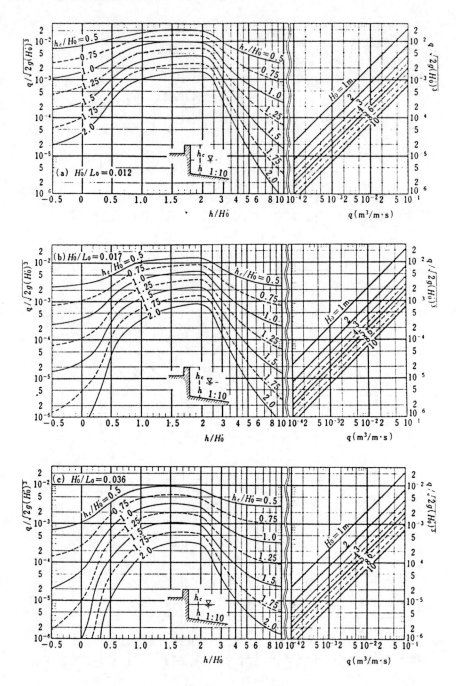

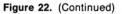

Figure 22. (Continued)

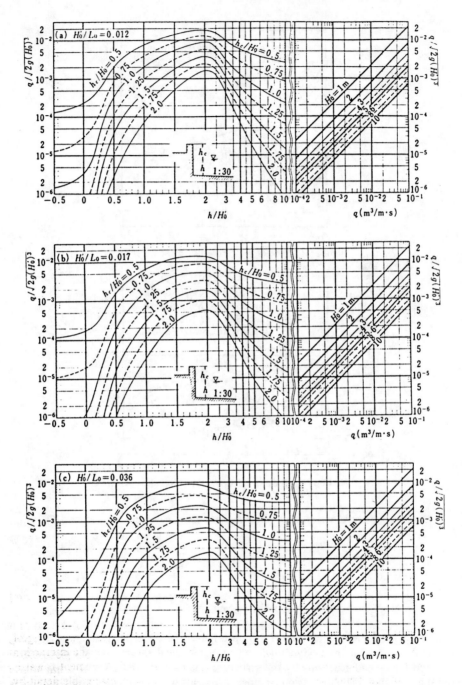

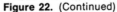

Figure 22. (Continued)

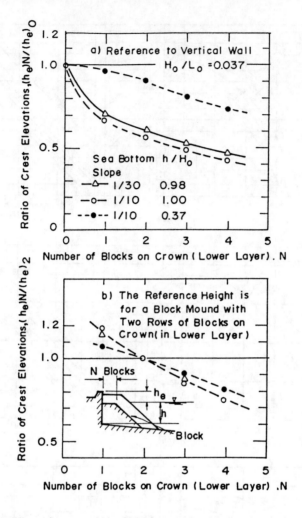

Figure 23. Effect of crown width of block mound on design crest elevation [22].

Stability Analysis

From being a highly empirical "formula-minded" field, deeper understanding of the wave mechanical, hydrodynamic, and geomechanical aspects of the interaction between forces and reactions by the structure has caused a development towards rational design principles. Basic principles are dealt with in considerable detail by Bruun et al. [8].

Hydrodynamic Stability

Stability Criteria. The first problem faced in analyzing stability conditions is the definition of stability or damage criteria. A breakwater under specific wave conditions, may be *stable* or *unstable*. It is said to be *unstable* when incident waves produce a loss of armor units on this main layer. The breakwater is *stable* if the waves are incapable of removing any armor unit from its main layer.

Traditionally, damage was defined as the percentage of armor units displaced with respect to the total number of armor units used in the construction of the main layer (classical definition). This definition is inconsistent, given that damage depends on the size of the main layer. If the dimensions of the latter were to be standardized in relation to the size of the armor unit, then the classical definition of damage would be consistent.

One way of avoiding the existing inconsistency, would be to define "damage" as the percentage of displaced armor units with respect to the number of units initially placed in a band of specific width around the SWL. [27, 65, 84].

The main disadvantage of these definitions is that they do not provide clear information about the possibility of the total destruction of the breakwater.

Iribarren [37] proposed the following definition of *breaking*, which gives a clearer picture of the breakwater's future: "A rubble-mound breakwater has reached its breaking level when the depth of damage on its main layer is equal to the length of the side of the equivalent cube." In Figure 24, the final profile greatly resembles the dynamically stable profile of a rock slope-gravel beach. (See "Dynamic Stability of Rock Slopes and Gravel Beaches" by van der Meer and Pilarczyk [85]).

This indicates that the first layer of armor units of the main layer has been lifted (and displaced) in an area large enough to expose units of the second layer of the main layer to the direct wave action. Once this situation has been reached, the breakwater would be severely damaged and it may be said that its total destruction is merely a question of time. Note that the interlocking of second layer of armor units is usually less effective than that of outer armor units.

Figure 24 shows two examples of damages from experiments carried out by Iribarren, which correspond to this breaking situation (unpublished data). To reach this state, the waves must exceed a certain "threshold value." In order to displace an armor unit integrated in the main layer, the wave must overcome friction and interlocking between existing armor units. Generally, *friction* refers to resistance to displacement of a "microscopic type," due to the roughness of armor units. *Interlocking* refers to resistance of a "macroscopic type" depending upon the shape of the armor units.

Once this threshold value has been exceeded, the only resistance that the armor unit offers against its displacement by waves is its own weight.

Considering this, it is understood that a main layer designed with a type of armor unit that develops a great deal of interlocking possesses a higher threshold, and as a consequence, would require less weight to resist wave action. However, if its level is exceeded, the armor unit is unable to contribute to the stability of the adjacent armor units. If its weight is low, it is easy displaced by wave action. Also, if the armor unit breaks in pieces, each piece will weigh even less and will, as a consequence, be more vulnerable, Magoon and Baird [59a].

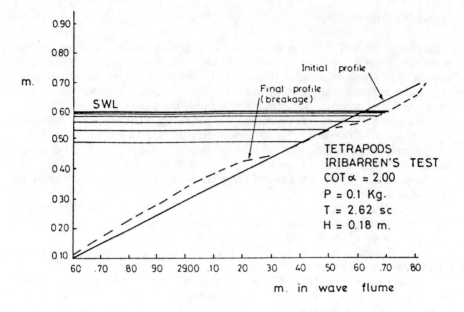

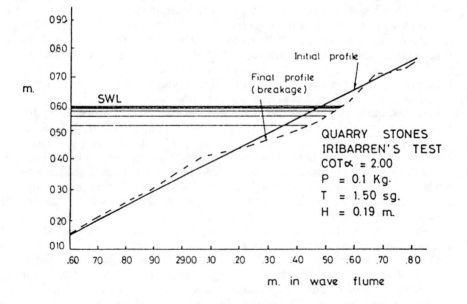

Figure 24. Slope profile in breakage point (Iribarren's criterion).

When waves overcome friction and interlocking among the armor units of the main layer, the only resistance they can offer is their own weight. Under such conditions, they are easily displaced even by lower waves, so damage may occur that is caused by small displacements, including breakdown or failures due to fatigue because of continuous movements of the main layer armor units.

During these movements, some armor units may also hit others and this may cause damage. This means that small initial damages could significantly affect the stability of the structure. Consequently, it seems reasonable to use this threshold criteria in the design, as a level of the beginning of the damage.

The initiation of the damage therefore, is defined as the minimum wave height, for constant period, which is capable of overcoming friction and interlocking among the armor units.

When interpreting experimental results, a problem arises in distinguishing once the first armor units fail, which of these units were part of the main armor layer, and which were not, so that it could be determined whether friction and/or interlocking failed. For this reason, it is necessary to establish a clear criterion.

Bearing in mind these aforementioned points, the criteria for the initiation of severe damage can be defined as the minimum wave height (for constant period) capable of extracting at least 10% of the total number of armor units that are displaced until failure of the breakwater is reached by Iribarren's criterion [37, 41].

Stability Under Regular Waves: General Statement. This considers the problem of the stability of the main layer armor units of an undefined mound under regular wave action and deals almost exclusively with the type of damages considered by Bruun [9a], that is, lift-outs of armor units caused by wave action. The following variables initially play a role in this phenomenon:

Characteristics of the medium: h, β, γ_w, g, μ
Characteristics of incident waves: H, T, θ
Characteristics of the structure:
   Slope angle, α
   Weight of the armor units, W
   Specific weight of the armor units, γ_r
   Interaction forces among armor units (friction and interlocking)
Characteristics of roughness and permeability of the armor layer
Characteristics of the underlying layers.

(See "Flow Characteristics of Regular Waves" for the definition of other variables.)

Regarding mound breakwaters designed in accordance with traditional criteria, it is accepted that the characteristics of the underlying layers depend on those of the main layer (type of armor units, W, e). On the other hand, one may consider that average characteristics of friction and interlocking, as well as roughness and permeability of the armor layer depend on:

Type of armor units
Size of armor units
Method of placement.

The size of armor units may be characterized by means of the length of the side of an equivalent cube:

$$L = (W/\gamma_r)^{1/3} \tag{34}$$

The thickness of the armor layer tends to be a number times the side of the equivalent cube:

$$e = nL \tag{35}$$

Assuming that water depth is deep enough to eliminate the influence of h and β, and that placement of the armor units on the slope is at random, it turns out that *for a given type of armor unit* stable conditions are governed by a function of the type:

$$f(\alpha, W, \gamma_r, H, T, \theta, \gamma_w, \mu, g) = 0 \tag{36}$$

The equality expressed by this equation refers to a *stability limit*. For the wave condition defined by H, T, and θ, and given α, γ_r, γ_w, μ, g, and weight W, is the *minimum* needed for the armor units to remain stable in the mound. Therefore, function "f," carries with it a *stability criterion* (damage or failure criterion).

Using the following six dimensionless parameters:

α
$W/\gamma_w H^3$
$S_r = \gamma_r/\gamma_w$
θ
$H^2/\mu T$
$H/L_0 = 2\pi H/gT^2$

Equation 36 becomes

$$f(\alpha, W/\gamma_w H^3, S_r, \theta, H^2/\mu T, H/L_0) = 0 \tag{37}$$

Accepting, as for flow characteristics, that the Reynolds' number $H^2/\mu T$, is kept above a minimum threshold value so that variation in this value does not significantly affect the resulting phenomenon, and assuming normal incidence of waves ($\theta = 0$), Equation 37 becomes

$$f(\alpha, W/\gamma_r H^3, S_r, H/L_0) = 0 \tag{38}$$

which can also be written as

$$W = \gamma_w H^3 f(\alpha, S_r, H/L_0) \tag{39}$$

On the other hand, existing formulas for calculating the weight of the main armor unit can be written

$$W((S_r - 1)^3/S_r)/H^3\gamma_w = \Psi \tag{40}$$

or

$$W = \gamma_w H^3 [S_r/(S_r - 1)^3] \tag{41}$$

where Ψ is a dimensionless function depending on α in all cases, and on other parameters, such as *the type* of armor unit, H, T, d, L, friction and permeability coefficients and other empirical coefficients.

It can be seen that Equation 39 has the same formal structure as Equation 41. Comparing both expressions one can write

$$f(\alpha, S_r, H/L_0) = R(S_r) \times \Psi(\alpha, H/L_0) \tag{42}$$

where $R = S_r/(S_r - 1)^3$ \hfill (43)

encompasses the effect of S_r (specific relative weight of armor units) in the function f.

Furthermore, it is concluded that for each type of armor unit with an established stability criterion, and for regular waves, that function Ψ depends solely on α and H/L_0 (accepting the aforementioned equivalence hypothesis). This function may be called the *stability function*.

The weight of the armor units required, in order to fulfill the criterion that the stability function implicitly carries with it is then expressed as

$$W = \gamma_w H^3 R \Psi \tag{44}$$

In the following paragraphs, the stability function is studied using experimental results of Iribarren [37], Ahrens and McCartney [2], and Hudson [33].

The Stability Function

The "Fit" Model. It has already been seen that once a stability critierion has been established for each type of armor unit and in the case of normal influence of regular waves, the stability function depends solely upon the slope angle (α) and on the wave steepness (H/L_0)

$$\Psi = (\alpha, H/L_0) \tag{45}$$

Flow characteristics on rough, permeable slopes are well represented by Iribarren's number as the sole parameter:

$$Ir = \tan \alpha / \sqrt{H/L_0} \tag{46}$$

Consequently, it is reasonable to assume that this parameter plays an important role also for the rubble-mound breakwater stability.

Losada and Giménez-Curto [53] proposed an exponential model as a function of Iribarren's number for analysis of stability of a rubble-mound breakwater under regular waves.

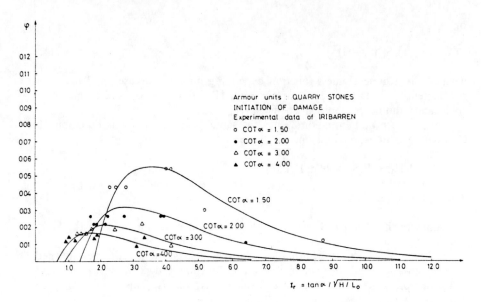

Figure 25. The stability function of quarrystones. Initiation of damage [37, 38].

Using this "fit-model" one may write

$$\Psi = A_w(Ir - Ir_0)\exp(B_w(Ir - Ir_0)), \qquad Ir > Ir_0 \tag{47}$$

where $Ir_0 = 2.654 \tan \alpha$, and A_w and B_w are "fitting-coefficients" (which depend on the type of armor unit and the slope angle).

Figure 25 shows the stability function drawn against Iribarren's number, Ir, for various slope angles and quarry stones. The corresponding values of fitting-coefficients A_w and B_w, and of Ir are given in Table 7 [53] for various types of armor units.

Figure 26 represents the stability function against Iribarren's number for experiments by Ahrens and McCartney [2].

Table 8 gives the values of A_w, B_w, and Ir_0 that are the results of the fit of data from Ahrens and McCartney (Losada and Giménez-Curto [53]).

It should be pointed out that the stability function presents a maximum, which corresponds to a minimum in breakwater stability. The Iribarren's number producing the most unfavorable condition is given by

$$Ir_{crit} = Ir_0 - 1/B_w \tag{49}$$

Table 7
Values of $A_w B_w$ and Ir_0: Initiation of damage

Armor Unit	Cot α	A_w	B_w	Ir_0
Quarry stones	1.50	0.09035	−0.5879	1.77
	2.00	0.05698	−0.6627	1.33
	3.00	0.04697	−0.8084	0.88
	4.00	0.04412	−0.9339	0.66
Parallelopipedic blocks	1.50	0.06819	−0.5148	1.77
	2.00	0.03968	−0.6247	1.33
	3.00	0.03410	−0.7620	0.88
Tetrapods	1.33	0.03380	−0.3141	1.99
	1.50	0.02788	−0.3993	1.77
	2.00	0.02058	−0.5078	1.33

After Iribarren's data.

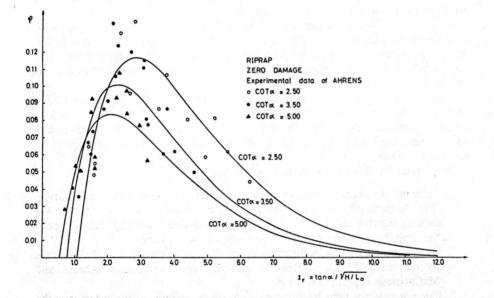

Figure 26. The stability function of rip-rap. Zero damage [2].

Table 8
Values of $A_w B_w$ and Ir_0 for Rip-Rap: Zero damage [2]

Cot α	A_w	B_w	Ir_0
2.50	0.1834	−0.5764	1.06
3.50	0.1819	−0.6592	0.76
5.00	0.1468	−0.6443	0.53

and the maximum value of Ψ is

$$\Psi_{max} = -A_w/Be_w \tag{50}$$

The existence of a stability minimum for a specific wave steepness or combination of wave heights and periods has already been pointed out by Bruun and Johannesson [14] and Günbak [27] and by Ahrens and McCartney [2].

Randomness in the Structural Response—Confidence Bands and Design Curves. Considerable scatter exists in experimental data regarding the stability function. How can this scatter be explained when according to the established general statement, the stability function depends solely upon α and H/L_0?

In the general statement, it is assumed that the characteristic values of friction, roughness, interlocking, and permeability depend solely on the type of the armor unit. Reference was made to *average* values of the characteristics. The situation, however, varies from one armor unit to another, and each type of armor unit was found to have a different stability condition.

What happens is that the behavior of the main layer, as a granular system, introduces a random component into the system [68]. Owing to the fact that in the structural response itself there exists an important random component, it turns out that stability conditions of the main layer armor units vary from one type of armor unit to another and also vary with time.

Losada and Desiré [57] after detailed tests with rectangular blocks concluded that the dispersion in the experimental results depends on the damage criterion, the slope angle, and the shape of the armor unit. Figures 27a-c show the test results and recommended design curves for blocks and three levels of damage as given by Losada and Desiré [57].

The criteria for damage are defined as follows:

1. There are insufficient data for other types of units to propose design curves. Thus, Losada and Giménez-Curto [53, 54] proposed confidence bands for the stability function curve obtained by linear regression, assuming that the deviation may be evaluated through a Gaussian random variable.
2. The control curves can be obtained in (Ir, Ψ) axes by multiplying the fit curves by the factor given in Table 9 obtained from Iribarren's, Ahrens and McCartney's experiments.
3. The upper factor refers to the upper control curve and the lower factor to the lower control curve.
4. This factor can be interpreted as a safety coefficient with respect to the structural response of the mound.
5. From this study, it is concluded that the highest control curve for 95% confidence level, which could be taken as a stability function of design, is $\Psi_v = f(Ir)$, which may be obtained approximately by multiplying coefficient A_w given in Tables 7 and 8 by the following factors:

   Rip-rap   1.5
   Quarry stones   1.5
   Tetrapods   2.0

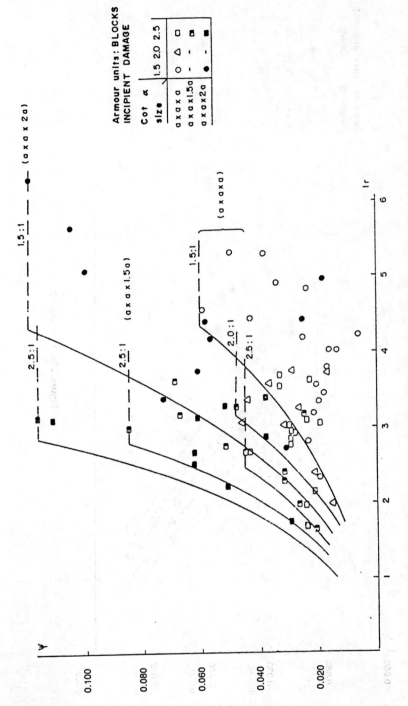

Figure 27a. Stability function for blocks, incipient damage (a), Iribarren's damage (b), destruction (c).

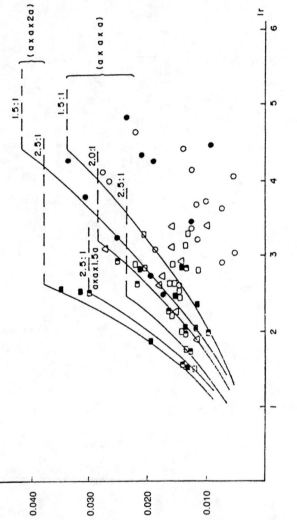

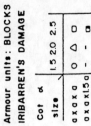

Figure 27b. (Continued)

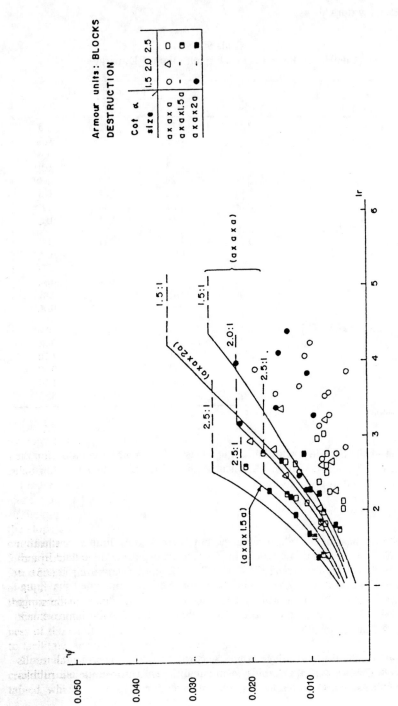

Figure 27c. (Continued)

Table 9
Confidence Band Factors for Initiation of Damage

Armor Units	Cot α	Confidence Level		
		90%	95%	99%
Quarry stones	1.50	1.34	1.41	1.58
		0.75	0.71	0.63
	2.00	1.37	1.46	1.64
		0.73	0.69	0.61
	3.00	1.29	1.35	1.49
		0.77	0.74	0.67
	4.00	1.51	1.64	1.91
		0.66	0.61	0.52
Tetrapods	1.33	1.51	1.64	1.91
		0.66	0.61	0.52
	1.50	1.99	2.27	2.93
		0.50	0.44	0.34
	2.00	1.73	1.93	2.37
		0.58	0.52	0.42
Rip-rap (zero damage) [2]	2.50	1.46	1.57	1.80
		0.69	0.64	0.55
	3.50	1.40	1.50	1.70
		0.71	0.67	0.59
	5.00	1.42	1.52	1.74
		0.70	0.66	0.58

After Iribarren's data.

Variation of the Stability with the Armor Density. The general equation for the stability of armor units, Equation 44, considers the influence of the density through the separated function given by

$$R = S_r/(S_r - 1)^3 \tag{51}$$

This expression has an overall acceptance, but there is only limited verification of its validity. Losada and Giménez-Curto [56a], using experimental data of Brandtzaeg (1.72 < S_r < 4.72), Iribarren [37] (1.54 < S_r < 3.0), and Zwanborn [88] (2.31 < S_r < 2.57), and working with the stability function method, concluded that Equation 51 can be used in engineering practice with some confidence in the range S_r > 2.00 (see Fig. 28). It is important to note that for S_r > 2.5 the improvement in stability is not significant.

Variation of Stability with Slope Angle. According to the experimental results considered, it appears that the stability of the main layer armor units of a rubble-mound breakwater improves as the slope becomes milder.

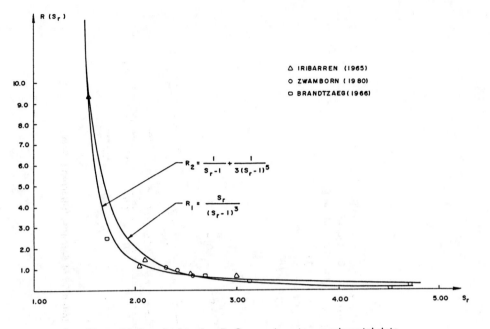

Figure 28. Density function R. Comparison to experimental data.

Starting with a very steep slope and progressively making it milder, the stability condition improves and the slope becomes more stable. But this occurs up to a specific slope angle limit. Stability conditions degrade once the slope angle is exceeded [37].

Figure 29 represents the variation of stability function for tetrapods with a slope angle. Substantial decrease in stability is noted when cot α changes from 2.0 to 2.5.

The question then is: how does the stability level of an armor unit change when the slope angle is varied? Considering a single armor unit placed on a slope, the only force that opposes a wave attack is the block weight. When an armor unit forms part of the main layer, it is clear that it is capable of opposing a far greater force due to the interlocking with the adjacent armor units. Evidently, the stability of an armor unit isolated on a smooth slope depends on the mildness of the slope; the maximum stability being achieved on a horizontal slope.

On the other hand, in order to establish effective armor units, a certain compactness of the main layer is necessary, and contacts among armor units are required to facilitate transmission of forces from one block to another.

If armor units are placed on a horizontal plane that is gradually tilted, an increase in the number of contact points and in the stresses in these points is obtained, which brings about an increase in interaction among the armor units.

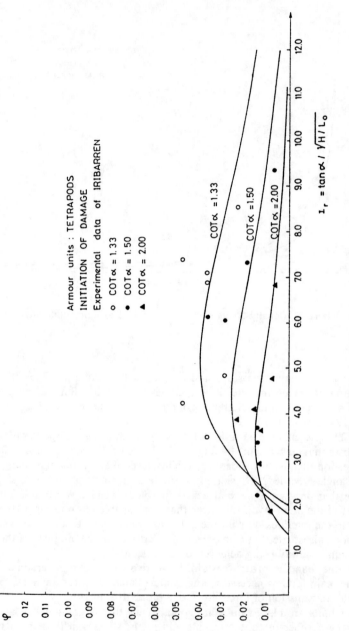

Figure 29. Stability function for tetrapods. Initiation of damage. Iribarren's data.

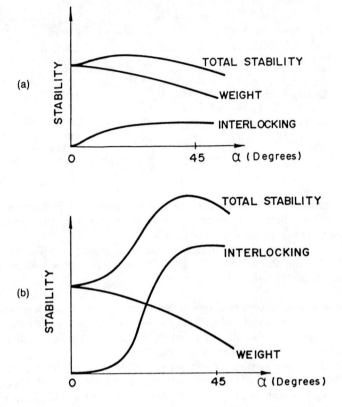

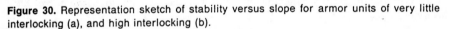

Figure 30. Representation sketch of stability versus slope for armor units of very little interlocking (a), and high interlocking (b).

It seems that interaction between armor units increases as the slope angle increases. Brebner [6] showed that a certain slope angle is required for dolos units to achieve full interlocking. Bearing in mind the above-mentioned reasoning, it is possible to explain the presence of a maximum stability for a specific slope by assuming that stability conditions for each armor unit are determined by two factors: the armor unit's own weight and the interaction between adjacent armor units, producing friction and interlocking. Naturally, this interaction largely depends on the type of armor unit.

Figure 30a shows schematically the variation of stability with the slope angle, when the type of armor unit is such that interaction between armor units is of little importance. Figure 30b demonstrates the variation of stability with slope angle for armor units with high interlocking. Finally, it may be concluded that all types of armor units capable of developing interaction have a maximum stability for a specific slope.

Table 10
Values of A_w, B_w, and Ir_0: Initiation of Damage

Type of Armor Unit	cot α_{opt}
Rip-rap	> 5.00
Quarry stones	4.00 to 6.00
Parallelopipedic blocks	3.00 to 4.00
Stabits	2.00 to 2.50
Tetrapods	2.00 to 2.50
Dolos	1.75 to 2.00

This optimum slope will be steeper and the maximum of stability more effective as the level of interaction that can be developed among armor units becomes more important, depending on the degree of interlocking.

Table 10 summarizes the experimental results of Iribarren [37], Ahrens and McCartney [2], and Price [68]. It shows the maximum stability slope angle of various types of armor units.

Variation of Armor Layer Stability with Sublayers. To arrive at the general equation for the stability of armor units, (Equation 44) it has been assumed that the friction between layers is sufficient to guarantee the stability against sliding. Now is the time to reconsider that important aspect.

To clarify the importance of friction between cover and sublayer on the cover-layer's angle of repose, ϕ, tests were conducted in the air [11, 14]. Based on the studies by Eagleson and Dean [19a] and Miller and Byrne [62a] the following expression for the average angle of repose of a single particle on a rough bed has been developed:

$$\phi = f(C_s, D/\bar{K}, \beta_s) \tag{52}$$

where
ϕ = average angle of repose
C_s = parameter that incorporates the effect of shape and roundness of the particle as well as in the bed
$D/\bar{K}$ = ratio of the diameter of a single grain to the average diameter of the bed grains
β_s = parameter incorporating the effect of the sorting of the bed grains

The following equation was developed (Figure 31):

$$\phi = a(D/\bar{K})^{-0.3} \tag{53}$$

The value of ϕ increases from 50 for spheres to 70 for crushed quartzite. In Figure 31 the popular ratios used for filter layers in rubble mound by U.S. Army Corps of Engineers standards are also shown [42a]. The values refer to weights that were

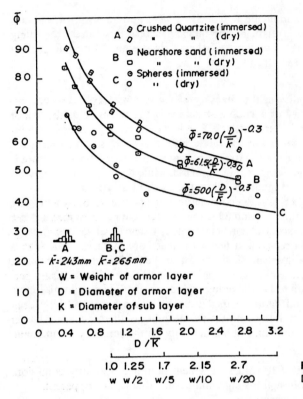

Figure 31. ϕ as function of D/K ratio [14].

converted to grain diameter ratios (Table 11). The ϕ's corresponding to crushed quartzite rubble-mound blocks are also listed in Table 11.

It may be noted that the improvement of slope stability *against sliding* by the use of W/10 instead of W/20 as sublayer is 1.4/1.2 = 1.15. The improvement of the stability by the use of a W/2 layer between the W and the W/10 layer is 1.75/1.4 = 1.25.

Table 11
Popular Weight Ratios in Rubble Mounds and the Corresponding Ratios Between Diameters in Armor and Sublayers' ϕ's and tan ϕ (approximately) for Crushed Quartzite [14]

Weight Ratios	Diameter Ratios	ϕ	tan ϕ
W to W	1	70°	2.75
W to W/2	1.25	65°	2.1
W to W/10	2.15	55°	1.4
W to W/20	2.7	50°	1.2
W/2 to W/10	1.7	60°	1.75
W/2 to W/20	2.15	55°	1.4

Other interesting details should be noted. SPM [79] and Jackson [42a] warn against the use of only one layer of armor blocks because this lowers the safety factor and increases the risk of collapse of the entire design. More information about this aspect is included in Bruun [8].

Influence of the Permeability in the Stability of the Armor Layer. Another important factor in the stability of a rubble structure is the porosity of the armor layers, underlayers, core, and filter material. This is a determining factor in the intensity of in- and out-flow, as well as for the level of the water surface within the breakwater core. For very fine core material the water level within the structure is located almost at the elevation of maximum up-rush, while for very coarse material the water surface oscillates and tends to follow the up- and down-rush.

Hedar [30] and Hudson [32] found a considerable increase in stability for highly permeable core material. Figures 32 and 33 show the damage ratio plotted against the wave height for various sizes of core material. It demonstrated that damage was more pronounced and occurred earlier with finer core material than with a coarser material in the core. This is particularly noticeable for higher damage ratios. Stability, within certain limits, therefore appears to increase with increasing permeability (Figure 34). Similar results have been obtained by Sawaragi et al. [73c].

Detailed tests on cubes and parallelepipedic blocks by Losada et al. [57] confirmed the same trend of the stability with the permeability of the main layer. Other important conclusions of the influence of permeability on the stability of cubes and parallelepipedic blocks are [57]:

1. There is a broad band of Ir values in which minimum stability conditions seems to be present, although a single minimum value is not apparent.
2. Considerable scatter is present.
3. Scattering decreases as the damage criterion becomes more severe, i.e., as the corresponding damage level is higher.

Considering this and Sawaragi's et al. [73b] conclusions, it seems reasonable to attribute the lack of appearance of a maximum value in the stability function for blocks to the superior permeability and roughness of the blocks' armor layer. It should be noted that steep maximum values are observed for rip-rap at Ir values between 1.5 and 3.5 (Figure 26).

Variation of Stability with H/h. In the previous analysis, it has been assumed that the waves break on the slope. To fulfill the criterion it is required that $H/h < 0.5$, where h is the depth on the toe of the dike, and H is the wave height. Two aspects are important if $H/h > 0.5$: (1) Broken waves will arrive at the breakwater; (2) the maximum wave can occur many times during a storm and during the life of the structure. In relation to breaking waves, there is not much information about the stability of the slope under such conditions, but it is generally agreed that broken waves are less dangerous than breaking waves.

The second aspect is more important, it is related to fatigue and to slope response that has a certain random nature. Consequently, it is recommended under such

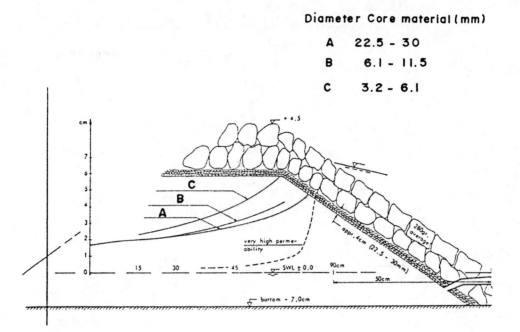

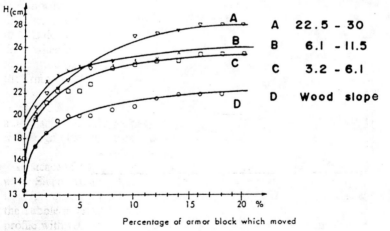

Figure 32. Water elevation in the core at maximum uprush for varying permeability of the core [14].

Figure 33. Damage ratio versus wave height for different core material [14].

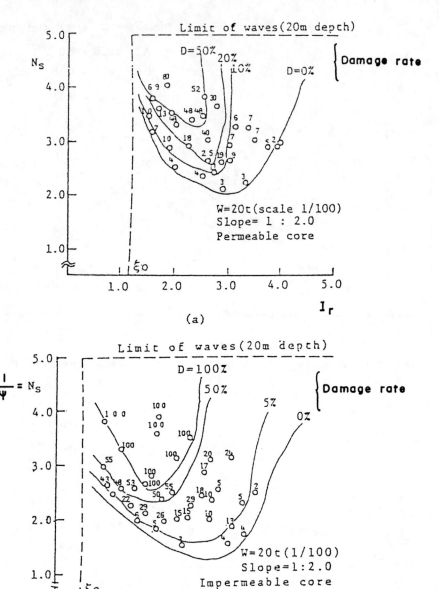

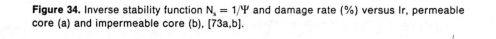

Figure 34. Inverse stability function $N_s = 1/\Psi$ and damage rate (%) versus Ir, permeable core (a) and impermeable core (b), [73a,b].

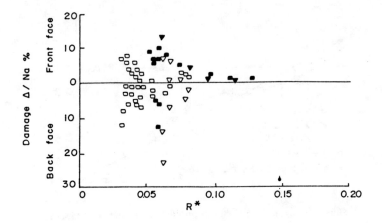

Figure 35. Damage to front and back faces against $R^* = F/H_s$ [1].

conditions that a broader confidence band be employed to increase the confidence level of the stability curve up to 95–99%. It is noted that the design procedure under limited depth conditions can be simplified; however, a careful evaluation of bottom erosion under mean water level fluctuation and sequence of waves must be performed.

Variation of Slope Stability by Overtopping. If the breakwater will be overtopped by highest waves, its stability conditions are different from those considered in the present analysis, because a part of the water volume overtopping the breakwater does not return as down-rush flow. Unfortunately, there is an insufficient number of systematic tests to evaluate the slope stability as the upper level, or crown of the dike, is decreased. It is recommended to use the same weight of armor units at the crest, when the crown or upper berm is higher than 1.2 H measured from the design mean water level. In any case, special attention should be given to the stability of the armor at the crest and the development of damage in the back face. Figure 35 shows damage to both front and back face, obtained by Allsop [1] for the quarry-stone breakwater. Although these data are insufficiently defined to allow further analysis, it is important to note that the overtopping has an important bearing on the design of such beakwaters.

Influence of Slope Geometry on the Slope Stability—Self-Adjusted Stable Breakwater Slope. A general stability equation (44) has been developed on the assumption that the breakwater slope is plane and undefined. After damage has progressed, the rubble-mound breakwater slope tends to adopt or develop the most stable profile with respect to the disturbing force. Typical stable breakwater profiles are shown in Figure 36.

It has been known for a long time that rubble-mound structures, when damaged or when the slopes are readjusted, may develop an S-shape. Figure 37 (*The Dock*

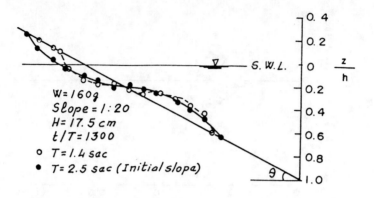

Figure 36. Examples of stable profiles for breakwater slopes.

and Harbour Authority, No. 633, July 1973) shows breakwaters at Plymouth, England and Cherbourg, France, built 150–200 years ago. Similar experiences were observed at many places in Iceland, Norway, and Spain. Due to these and other observations, Bruun [8] proposed to divide the rubble-mound slope for design and construction into three zones, each with its characteristic block properties (Figure 38). The "platform" BC, has a relatively gentle slope, e.g., 1:3. Waves plunge at point C. Run-up is reduced by turbulence and energy absorption due to the phase difference between up-rush and down-rush. The breaking wave usually does not strike the exposed breakwater slopes, but plunges into a "stilling basin" on the gentle part of the breakwater. The steep slope, CD, separates backwash from the retreating velocity field in the down-rush at the toe of the breaking waves, and therefore makes the backwash incipient breaker interaction less violent. This reduces the maximum normal and parallel forces at the lowest level of wave retreat,

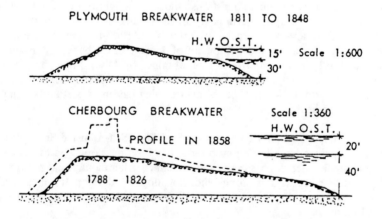

Figure 37. Ancient breakwaters at Plymouth and at Cherbourg.

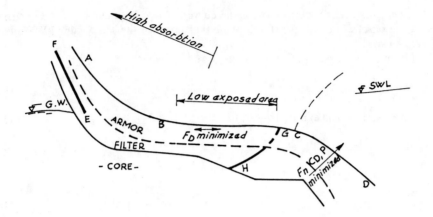

Figure 38. Optimization of breakwater properties [8].

and these forces are usually most critical for the stability of a breakwater. Furthermore, a layer HG with low permeability prevents outflow from being concentrated at the breaking point where the external forces, primarily suction in the toe of the breaking wave, are maximized.

Another layer, FE, with lower permeability, prevents inflow above point E, which reduces the build up of hydrostatic pressure in the mound during wave retreat. In zone BC the drag coefficient of the blocks should be minimized.

In zone CD the drag coefficient of the armor blocks perpendicular to the slope should be minimized due to the high normal forces and the concentrated outflow. The upper slope AB may be relatively rough as it is not exposed to high velocities. Roughness decreases up-rush and lowers down-rush velocities. Both are advantageous.

Other researchers studied the stability of S-shape breakwaters, Sawaragi et al. [73d] and Kobayashi and Jacobs [49, 49a, 50]. Some of their results will be given in another section.

Interaction Curves. The variable that governs the stability of the main layer composed of armor units in a rubble-mound breakwater is the weight W. Given the type of armor unit, slope (α) and the specific weights (γ_r and γ_w), the stability conditions refer to

$$W = \gamma_w H^3 R \Psi \tag{44}$$

However, for each combination of wave height and period, the value of W defined by Equation 44 is different. If this value is less than the actual weight of the armor units, W_0, the breakwater will be stable (according to the criterion established).

Consequently, it is useful to know the curves W = constant on the (H, T) plane, i.e., the set of points on the (H, T) plane that produce the same value of W (*interaction curve*).

Given the type of armor unit, W, α, γ_r, and γ_w, where

$$W = \gamma_w H^3 R \Psi \tag{44}$$

$$\Psi = A_w(Ir - Ir_0) \exp(B_w(Ir - Ir_0)), \qquad Ir > Ir_0 \tag{47}$$

$$Ir = \sqrt{g/2\pi} \tan \alpha \, T/\sqrt{H} \tag{46}$$

$$Ir_0 = 2.654 \tan \alpha \tag{48}$$

$$R = S_r/(S_r - 1)^3 \tag{43}$$

$$S_r = \gamma_r/\gamma_w$$

The function

$$f_0(H, T) = 0 \tag{54}$$

can be obtained defining the corresponding interaction curve.

Figure 39 shows an example of a stability interaction curve for the case of rip-rap, $W_{50} = 3.0$ ts, cot $\alpha = 3.50$, $\gamma_r = 2.6$ ts/m^3 and $\gamma_w = 1.0$ ts/m^3.

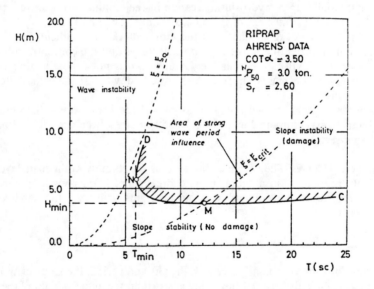

Figure 39. Stability interaction curve for rip-rap. Zero damage criterion.

The concept of stability interaction curves, introduced by Losada and Giménez-Curto [53], clearly reflects the joint influence of period and wave height on stability of the breakwater, separating on plane (H, T) stability and instability zones.

The minimum wave height that can produce damage to the breakwater corresponds to Iribarren's number defined by:

$$Ir_{crit} = Ir_0 - 1/B_w \qquad (55)$$

and the minimum period is defined by Iribarren's number:

$$Ir_1 = (1/28)(5 + B_w \cdot Ir_0 - \sqrt{B_w^2 \cdot Ir_0^2 - 14B_w \cdot Ir_0 + 25}) \qquad (56)$$

It may be noted that the three parabolas that define Iribarren's number Ir_0, Ir_1, Ir_{crit}, depend solely on Ir and B, i.e., the type of armor units and slope angle. Therefore, all resulting interaction curves for the different values of W (or W_{50}), γ_r and γ_w have points corresponding to the minimum wave height on the parabola $Ir = Ir_{crit}$.

Figures 40 and 41 present some examples of how interaction curves vary with the weight of armor units, their specific weight, and the type of armor units.

Stability under Irregular Waves: The Failure Probability and Storm Duration. In the case of regular waves, the weight of armor units required for the stability of the breakwater is given by

$$W = \gamma_w H^3 R \Psi \qquad (44)$$

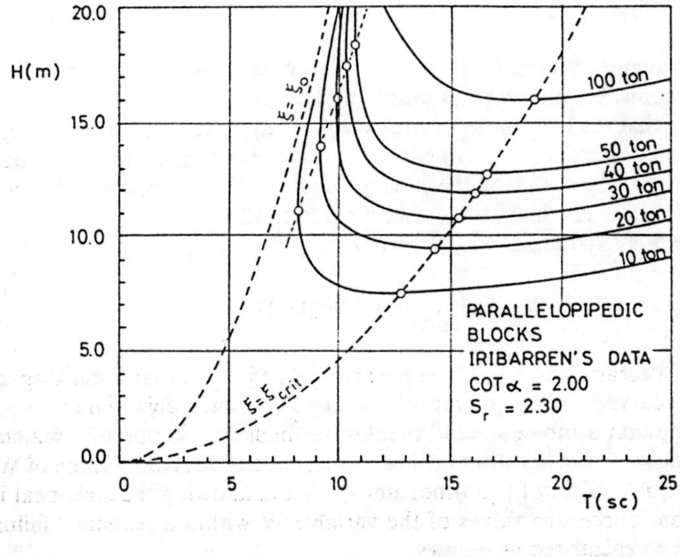

Figure 40. Variation of interaction curves with weight of armor units.

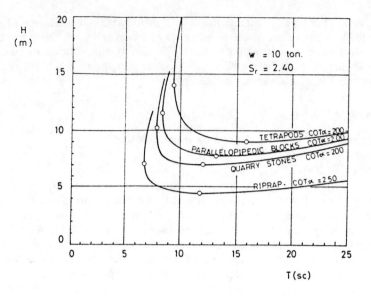

Figure 41. Interaction curves for different types of armor units.

It is evident that once slope characteristics (type of armor unit, α, γ_r, γ_w) are fixed, this weight depends exclusively on H and T or

$$W = f_0(H, T) \tag{54}$$

In case of irregular waves, the variable W may be considered a random variable depending upon the characterization of "each wave."

Assuming that the hypothesis of equivalence [73] is valid, it can be accepted that the distribution function of W within a sea state is obtained by assigning to each individual wave of a sea state, the same value of W that is produced by a periodic wave train of the same height and the same period.

Applying this hypothesis, one can write

$$F_w(W_0) = \text{Prob}(W \leq W_0) = \iint_D p^*(H, T) \, dH \, dT \tag{57}$$

where the integration domain, D, is the area defined by the wave breaking limit, and interaction curve $W = W_0$, where W_0 is a known armor unit weight.

Assuming that a rubble-mound breakwater under the action of a sea state *fails*, if at least one wave exists within the sea state, which produces a value of W greater than the actual weight of the armor units, W, and allowing the statistical independence among successive values of the variable W within a sea state, failure probability can be calculated as follows:

$$f = 1 - (F_w(W_0))^{3,600t/T_z} \tag{58}$$

where   t = duration of the sea state in hours
      T_z = mean zero upcrossing wave period in seconds
      f = failure probability

The following example analyzes failure probability of a rubble-mound breakwater having the following characteristics

Type of armor units: parallelepipedic blocks
  W_0 = 50.0 tons
cot α = 2.0
   γ_r = 2.3 t/m^3
   γ_w = 1.0 t/m^3
Depth at the toe of breakwater: d = 20.0 m
Horizontal bottom

Figure 42 presents the corresponding breaking limit and interaction curve. Figures 43 and 44 show results obtained for a variable sea state and durations of 1 and 6 hours, respectively.

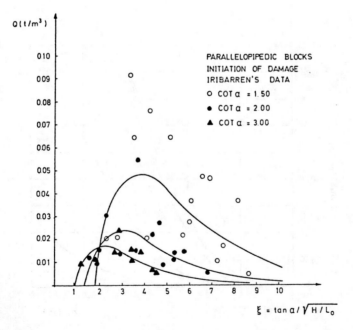

Figure 42a. Breaking limit and interaction curve for the example.

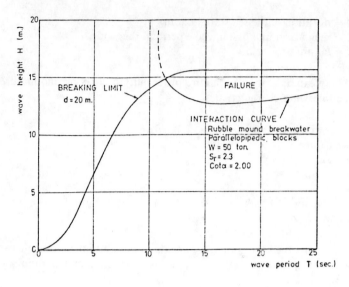

Figure 42b. (Continued)

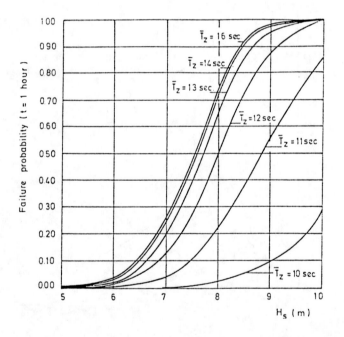

Figure 43. Failure probability for the example. Sea state duration 1 hour.

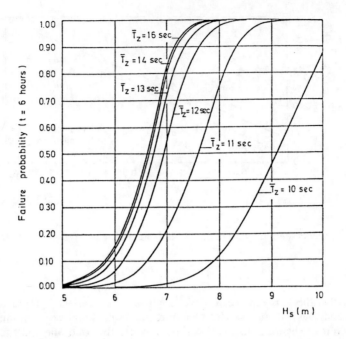

Figure 44. Failure probability for the example. Sea state duration 2 hours.

Influence of the Slope Geometry on the Slope Stability Under Irregular Waves. Sawaragi et al. [74] investigated whether the equilibrium, slope exists under irregular wave test conditions. To discuss the equilibrium slope quantitatively, the main dimensions are defined as shown. In Figure 45, special attention was given to the length of the plain part in the equilibrium slope.

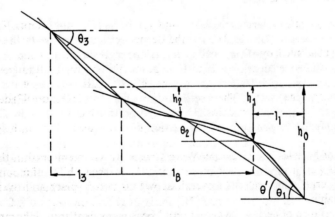

Figure 45. Definition sketch of a equilibrium slope.

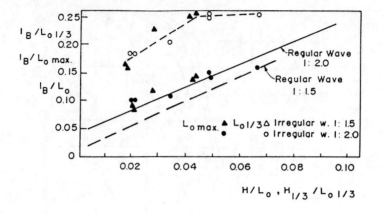

Figure 46. Length of the plain part of equilibrium slopes under irregular wave conditions [73a,b].

The relationship between the relative length of plain part $(1/L_0)$ and the wave steepness is shown in Figure 46. In the figure, the results obtained from the regular wave experiments by authors are also shown, where the solid line and the dashed line indicate the best fitted lines of regular wave conditions of the slope 1:2.0 and 1:1.5, respectively. Open symbols and black symbols indicate the relative length of plain part normalized by the significant wave length $(L_{0_{1/3}})$, and the maximum wavelength $(L_{0_{max}})$. In the figure, the relative length of plain part $l_B/L_{0_{1/3}}$ indicates very large values and $l_B/L_{0_{max}}$ shows nearly the same values as the results obtained in the regular wave experiment. As a result, Sawaragi et al. [74] concluded that the length of the plain part of equilibrium slope created by irregular waves is controlled by the maximum wavelength.

A practical case: San Ciprián (Spain). San Ciprián has 50-t dolos units. The slope angle equal to cot $\alpha = 1.33$ to 2.00. In the deeper sections breakwater head dolos have been substituted by 90-ton cubes on a slope angle equal to cot $\alpha = 2.5$. For other sections in water depth less than 10 m at low tide (spring tidal range is of the order 4.5 m) it was decided after three years of systematic survey of the dike to maintain the damaged sector. These sections show an S profile (Figure 47) developed by waves mostly with broken dolos. The evolved profile has an S-profile. This section resisted further deformation by the action of waves up to 12 m in height.

Stability of Mounds in Relation to Wave Groups. It was mentioned in the introduction that wave groups are very important as far as the stability of mound structures is concerned. This refers to overall as well as unit-in-place and overall unit structure stability.

The importance of certain "wave groups" became evident from laboratory and field experiences. Now it is possible to continue the "resonance and grouping con-

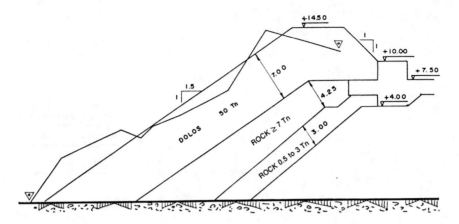

Figure 47. Typical section of San Ciprián breakwater.

cept" supporting the evidence of earlier observations by Bruun and Johannesson [12, 12a, 14], Günbak [27], Bruun and Günbak [10], Johnson et al. [44a], and Burcharth [15, 15a] and their statements on the importance of short groups, freak waves, and "jumps." An adequate evaluation of the effect of wave groups should be approached from a probabilistic point of view. In that case the approach should consider all the possibilities for failures as explained by Bruun [8, p. 431]. It is outside of the scope of this section to present this approach. The interested reader is referred to the original work. Also, in chapter 22 another probabilistic approach to the stability of mound breakwaters is described.

Three-Dimensional Hydrodynamic Effects

Stability of Mounds Under Oblique Wave Attack. At the International Navigation Congress in Rome (1953), Abecasis pointed out the lack of agreement between calculated formulas and the experience on stability of mounds for oblique wave attacks. Since then, only a few contributions have been made in this field, e.g. Iribarren [37], Van de Kreeke [84], and Whillock [87]. It is, however, generally accepted among engineers and researchers that the conventional formulas do not adequately cover oblique wave attacks.

The Technical Advisory Committee in the Netherlands [81], suggests that the run-up on an impermeable smooth slope under oblique wave attack is cos θ times the run-up under perpendicular wave attack, where θ is the angle of incidence. One explanation for this criterion may be given by observing that the slope of the breakwater in the direction of propagation is tan α cos θ. For smooth impermeable slopes and Ir < 2.3, up-rush according to Hunt [35] can be written as

$$Ru/H = Ir \tag{59}$$

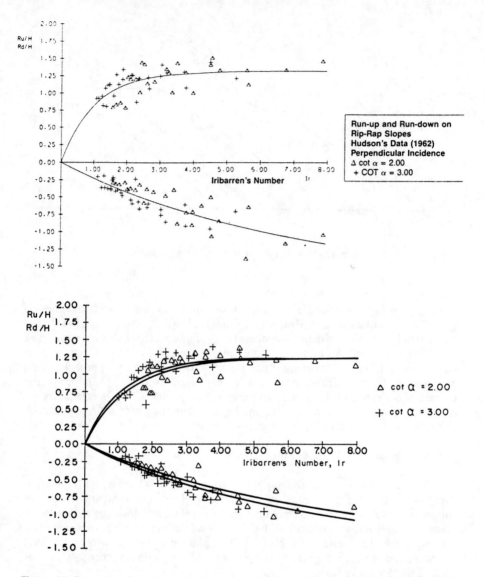

Figure 48. Run-up and run-down on rip-rap slope. Perpendicular incidence (a), $\theta = 30°$ (b), $\theta = 60°$ (c) [33].

For $\theta < 50°$, a comparison of this result with experimental data of Hosoi and Shuto [31a] indicates a reasonable degree of agreement, at least for breaking waves [3, 4].

In the following discussion, it is assumed that flow characteristics and stability change with respect to perpendicular wave incidence exclusively, as long as the slope varies. The mound slope in the direction of propagation is $\tan \alpha \cos \theta$, where

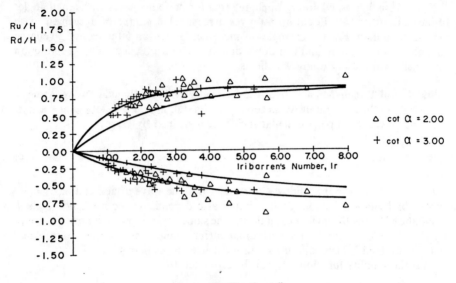

Figure 48. (Continued)

θ is the angle between the direction of propagation of waves and the perpendicular to the alignment of the breakwater.

Flow Characteristics on a Slope Under Oblique Wave Attack. Flow characteristics on a rough permeable slope under periodic waves with oblique wave incidence can be estimated by taking Iribarren's number in the direction of propagation as follows:

$$Z = A_z(1 - \exp(B_z Ir \cos \theta)) \tag{60}$$

A_z and B_z being the values for perpendicular incidence.

Figures 48a, b, and c show Hudson's data [32], taken from Günbak [26], for run-up and run-down on a rip-rap slope with angles of incidence of $\theta = 0°$, $30°$ and $60°$. Also shown are the curves corresponding to Equation 60.

The coefficients A_z, B_z, and the correlation coefficient, ρ_c, are given in Table 12.

Table 12
Coefficients of the Best Fit Curves for Hudson's Data

$\theta°$		A_z	B_z	ρ
0	Ru	1.3219	−0.9654	0.641
	Rd	1.7404	−0.1395	0.832
30	Ru	1.2433	−0.8682	0.680
	Rd	1.4863	−0.1620	0.905
60	Ru	0.9084	−0.8824	0.686
	Rd	0.7738	−0.3245	0.781

From these figures, it can be concluded that for periodic waves with small angles of incidence ($\theta < 45°$), Equation 60 gives a reasonable degree of agreement with experimental data. For larger angles of incidence, Equation 60 does not give large enough values of run-up and run-down due to a significant effect of wave refraction on the slope and other unknown effects.

Stability of Rubble-Mound Breakwaters Under Oblique Regular Wave Attacks. The weight of the armor unit, W, necessary for its stability on the slope under attack of regular waves with perpendicular incidence is defined by Equation 44:

$$W = \gamma_r H^3 R \Psi \tag{44}$$

The stability of a mound breakwater under oblique wave attack can also be expressed by Equation 44, considering that Ψ also depends on the incidence angle θ. Assuming effects by the incidence angle and the slope angle only and ignoring secondary effects such as refraction, longitudinal currents, and others, one may conclude that Equation 44 is also valid for small incidence angles ($\theta < 45°$).

Thus the stability function, Ψ_θ, can be estimated by

$$\Psi(\theta) = A_\theta(Ir_\theta - (Ir_0)) \exp(B_\theta(Ir_\theta - (Ir_0)_\theta), \qquad Ir_\theta \geq (Ir_0)_\theta \tag{45}$$

where A_θ and B_θ are the fit coefficients corresponding to the slope $\tan\alpha \cos\theta$ and perpendicular incidence, and

$$(Ir_0)_\theta = 2.654 \tan\alpha \cos\theta, \qquad Ir_\theta = \tan\alpha \cos\theta/\sqrt{H/L_0} \tag{46}$$

Evaluation of Oblique Wave Attack on the Stability of Mound Breakwaters. Stability conditions increase with decreasing slope, however this occurs only up to a certain slope angle. Once it is exceeded, the stability conditions worsen [37]. Table 13 provides the coefficients for the stability functions for tetrapods and dolos.

Table 13
Parameters of the Stability Function for Tetrapods and Dolos. Initiation of Damage. Perpendicular Incidence

Type of Amor Unit	cot α	A_w	B_w
Tetrapods	1.33	0.03380	−0.3141
(Iribarren's data)	1.50	0.02788	−0.3993
	2.00	0.02058	−0.5078
	2.50	0.04697	−0.4539
Dolos	1.50	0.04905	−0.4901
(Hydraulics Research	2.00	0.04201	−0.6548
Station's data)			

As mentioned before, the change of stability which is produced from a specific angle of the slope cannot be explained by a change in flow characteristics, but rather it is associated with the structural behavior of the granular system.

This idea seems to be confirmed by experimental results of Brebner [6] and Price [68]. Consequently, it is possible to recognize the maximum stability for a specific slope that depends largely on the type of armor unit. This optimum slope will be steeper and the maximum stability more pronounced, as the interlocking between armor units becomes more important [68] (see Table 10).

If the design slope is close to the slope for the optimum stability, and assuming that the breakwater is structurally isotropic, the stability of the breakwater decreases as the angle of incidence increases. If the design slope is much steeper than the optimum stability slope, the stability of the breakwater under oblique wave attack improves as the angle of incidence increases, at least up to $\theta = \cos^{-1}(1/\tan \alpha \cot \alpha_{\text{opt}})$.

Figure 49a–c shows the stability of the breakwater under oblique and perpendicular wave attack through their respective maxima of the stability function, $\psi_{\text{max}}(\theta)$ and $\psi_{\text{max}}(0)$, the variation of the ratio $\psi_{\text{max}}(\theta)/\psi_{\text{max}}(0)$ with the incidence angle, θ, for different kinds of armor units and design slopes. The stability functions for quarry stones under regular waves with perpendicular incidence have been taken from Losada and Giménez-Curto [53], and those for tetrapods and dolos are given in Table 13. In some cases the curves are schematic (dashed curves) due to the lack of experimental data.

The small amount of experimental data available on the oblique wave attacks roughly agrees with the above-mentioned results. Van de Kreeke [84] concluded, after experiments on rip-rap on a small scale, that for angles of incidence less than

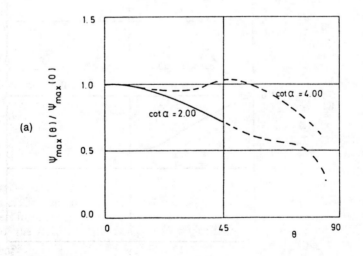

Figure 49. Effect of oblique wave attack on the stability of quarrystones (a), tetrapods (b) and dolos (c).

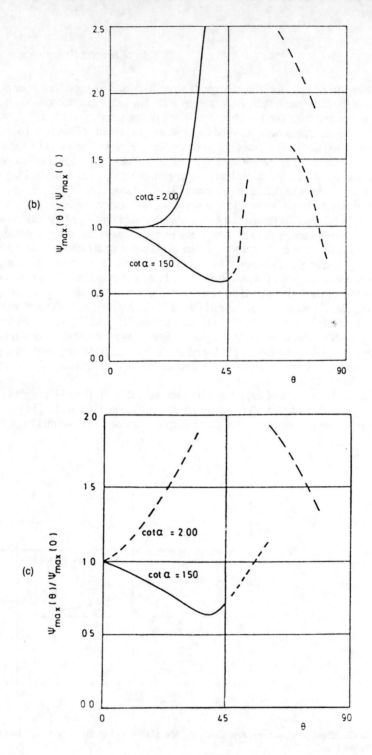

(b)

(c)

Figure 49. (Continued)

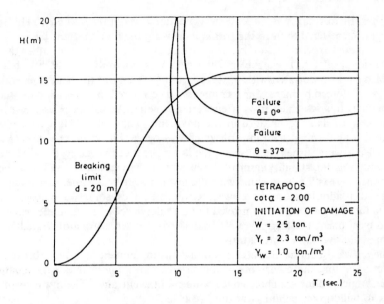

Figure 50. Effect of the wave incidence angle on the failure area for tetrapods.

45°, the stability of the breakwater is similar to that of perpendicular incidence. Whillock [87] presents results on the stability of dolos blocks under oblique wave attack. Despite the fact that the amount of data is small, it can be estimated that stability decreases as the angle of incidence increases, at least up to 60°.

Zwamborn and Beute [88] present data for dolos that show the same trends as in Whillock's study.

Stability of Rubble-Mound Breakwaters Under a Sea State with Oblique Wave Incidence. On the basis of stability functions for oblique wave incidence (Equation 45), stability interaction curves can be obtained [53]. The area between the interaction curve and breaking limit is the failure area. Generally, the failure probability of rubble-mound breakwaters under a sea state with oblique wave incidence can be calculated by considering the failure area and joint probability distribution of wave heights and periods [53]. Figure 50 shows the failure area for tetrapods for several angles of incidence.

Stability of Breakwater Heads. The head of the breakwater is usually just the extension of the mound, which is modified at the free end. The wave action on the head differs from the wave action on the trunk as the mound waves attack different sections of the head at various angles. In addition to the wave attack, currents generated by the wave breaking causes a "swash" across the slope. Such swash caused by breaking or surging waves may carry high velocities that affect stability, because the blocks are subjected to parallel flow [16].

It has, therefore, become a common practice to assign a lower K_D, Hudson coefficient to the head than to the trunk, increasing the block weight by 50 to 100%. Special model experiments on heads were often undertaken to account for the three-dimensional effects. The problem, however, was not only of stability, but other problems arise associated with the layout and geometry of the head. Generally, the head is reinforced by increasing its dimensions compared to the truck cross-sections. Sometimes this is achieved by a circular geometry. As such circles proved to be vulnerable to damage because in the navigation channel, heads were sometimes reinforced by turning them inward which was better, but more expensive. In some cases heads were turned out instead, the latter practice proved to be more efficient. Not only was the stability improved, but also the navigational conditions because the swash across the head slope with the inward-bent head generated waves inside the head in addition to a wave swash current. Besides, some wave energy was reflected into the entrance. This proved to be a safety problem for smaller vessels, and could even affect the larger vessels by its cross power, as demonstrated by navigational and hydraulic model tests.

The outward-bent head is also advantageous to sediment transport because of its deflection of longshore currents. A fourth advantage, applicable to the conditions in the Arctic, produces a changed ice pattern in the entrance. The inward-bent head tends to buildup ice behind it at the entrance.

Losada and Desiré [58] approached the problem of initiation of motion or block stability under horizontal (parallel) oscillatory flow from a sediment transport angle. The following expression for threshold value for movement was developed:

$$A/D = \alpha_s(\gamma'g/\omega^2 A) \tag{61}$$

where $\omega = 2\pi/T$

A = amplitude of water motion on the bed

D = grain (sphere) diameter

g = acceleration of gravity

$\gamma' = (\rho_s - \rho_w/\rho_w)$

α_s = coefficient that takes different values depending on the type of grain motion (damage). For initiation of motion Losada and Desiré [58] suggest $\alpha_s = 0.070$

Structural Unit Stability

Mound Breakwater as a Granular Medium. A rubble-mound breakwater may be considered as a granular medium completely occupied by granular material or a large number of solid particles (grains). These grains are loosely packed and cohesionless. They are defined by the following factors [87a]:

1. Density of grains
2. Absolute size of grains, grain size distributions
3. Geometry (shape of grains)

If the granular material is well mixed, then the granular medium may be considered homogeneous and isotropic, which implies that the statistical properties of the granular medium can be regarded to be independent of position and direction [87a].

More than 60 years ago, Terzaghi, wrote:

"The fundamental error was introduced by Coulomb, who purposely ignored the fact that sand consists of individual grains, and who dealt with the sand as if it were a homogeneous mass with certain mechanical properties. Coulomb's idea proved very useful as a working hypothesis for the solution of one special problem of the earth-pressure theory, but it developed an obstacle against further progress as soon as its hypothetical character came to be forgotten by Coulomb's successors."

Unfortunately, the same is true for the development of the analysis of the stability of rubble-mound breakwaters. The first approach and formula was established by Iribarren [37–39], who considered, in some way, the slope as a granular medium, introducing a friction parameter, μ, which had the function of describing the stress actions between armor units. This first effort was forgotten in later formulas, which included all factors, not directly, but evaluated by the formulas, in just one coefficient, K_D. That means without *any* attempt of understanding the phenomena involved, and that had *disastrous effects* on further developments.

An armor unit of the granular system is subject to external hydrodynamic forces and internal forces due to neighbor units (friction and interlocking forces). To displace an armor unit integrated in the main layer, the external forces must overcome the friction and interlocking existing among armor units. Friction affects the resistance to movement due to the "micro" roughness of armor units. Interlocking refers to resistance of a "macroscopic" type, depending upon the shape of the armor units.

If a threshold value of friction and/or interlocking has been exceeded, the only resistance that the armor unit offers against extraction by waves is its own weight.

The internal forces on each unit are transmitted through the contact points between the units. Each unit has a number of such contacts, which depend on its position on the slope and its shape and size. Without water, the granular medium transmits the weight of the units to the ground through the contacts by internal forces. The equilibrium condition of each unit is then due to the unit's weight and internal forces that in the more general case present a "hyperstatic equilibrium," as there are more unknown forces than equations. So, to evaluate contact forces in the granular medium, the number of contacts per unit must be known.

The University of Cantabria, Santander in Spain conducted four tests (slopes cot α = 1.5 and 2.0), with dolos units of 24-cm size in which the number of contact points per dolos were evaluated. Other workers, (e.g., Marsal [60]) also gave results of the number of contacts per particle for regular assemblies of uniform sizes of gravel with different packing densities. The conclusion of these tests is that the number of contact points may be considered a random variable (Figure 51). In the case of dolos, Table 14 gives the average number of contact per dolos and the standard deviation in each test.

Table 14
The Average Number of Contacts per Dolos and σ

Test No.	Average Number of Contact Points per Dolos	Standard Deviation
1	5.75	1.52
2	4.82	1.43
3	5.41	1.48
4	5.44	1.50

Figure 52 shows the distribution function of the number of contact points per dolos on Gaussian probability paper. It may be accepted that for a dolos mound the number of contacts has a Gaussian random distribution.

It is obvious that if the number of contact points change for each unit, the same occurs for the contact forces. This means that a granular medium develops a stress state in which some units receive and transmit more stress than others, developing main lines of stress transmission. Cundall and Stracks' computer program [18a] permitted an evaluation of stresses in a granular medium. Also, Rodriguez Ortiz

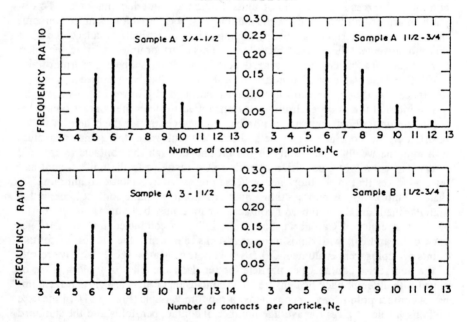

Figure 51. Statistical distribution of contacts per particle, dense uniform gravels [60].

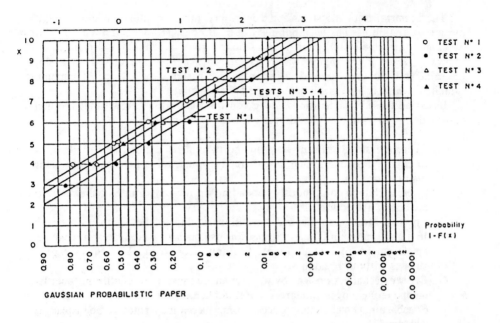

Figure 52. Distribution function of number of contact points of each dolos unit.

[71], conducted laboratory tests where the granular medium was built up with cylinders obtaining the stress distribution in the medium.

When the granular medium is subjected to a change in stress by external action, the stress transmission lines change. Under high interaction forces, structural transformations occur due to the units. The stress state of each unit, therefore, may change both in magnitude and in the direction of the contact forces.

A dispersion of the contact force intensities and a change in stresses induces rotations and displacements of units, which of necessity establishes a new state of equilibrium.

Applying this evaluation of the granular medium effects to a rubble-mound breakwater, it is necessary to consider average characteristics of friction, interlocking roughness, and permeability, which vary from one armor unit to another so that every unit has a different stability condition. The behavior of the main layer, as a granular medium, must be analyzed as a random distribution because the state of stress itself is random, so that the stability conditions of main layer armor units are highly variable from one armor unit to another initially and are changing with time under wave action.

These aspects have been confirmed by the static tests of movement of dolos units made by Price [68] and Losada and Giménez-Curto [56]. The forces needed to remove a unit were random and the statistical parameters of the distribution changed as the slope was affected by vibration or other disturbing forces.

The importance of the stress state developed in the granular medium to withstand external forces has been pointed out by Brebner [6], who showed how dolos obtained the same stability for flows as quarry rock in a horizontal plane. Dolos, however, resist much higher water velocities when they are placed on a slope. Losada and Giménez-Curto [55] showed the existence of a slope of maximum stability, which is a function of the type of armor unit.

Based on these considerations, some conclusions may be drawn that are useful in the design of a rubble-mound breakwater:

1. There are stress transmissions in the mound. It is possible to define lines of equal stress magnitude, but there is a remarkable heterogeneity in their distribution.
2. Stresses change continuously depending on the magnitude of change in the incident wave action.
3. The first stress state defined on a slope is due to the weight of the units. In some armor units, these stresses are sufficient to motivate rotations and displacements of contact points. The unit must be capable of resisting such stresses without breaking.
4. Every external action, e.g., by waves, change in water level, differential settlements, etc. changes the stress state and thereby the equilibrium condition of each unit. During this process, some pieces may rotate or be displaced/dislodged.
5. Until recently, the designer of special units, such as tetrapods, dolos, etc., has not considered the stress state and the continuous readjustment of stresses with time and wave action.
6. The stresses at the contact points may develop tension stresses on units where the contact is made by interlocking. So, the material (mass concrete in general) must be able to resist breaking. Mass concrete, however, does not resist tensile stresses.
7. Units provided with "legs" and "arms" develop a high level of interlocking. Increasing the size and weight of such units, increases the stress state on the slope. Also, increasing size increases tensile stresses on the units more quickly than the increase of resistance. It is easy to establish that an increase of the size of units, which develop high interlocking, increases the stress state. Consequently, external actions such as waves apply on an already stressed slope.
8. The problem of breakage of armor units must be considered statistically. The probability of failure is represented by the area below the intersection of two curves, one representing the resistance, the other the action (weight plus external action). If the resistance curve has low values or the unit weight develops high stresses, or they are developed by external actions, the probability of breakage may be high. As an example, small dolos of 5 t have a low probability of failure, but dolos of 50 t may easily be stressed by their own weight to an extent that the probability of failure becomes high.
9. An armor unit must resist all stresses developed before it is displaced from its location without breaking. Also, it is important that the units are capable

of withstanding the stresses developed during their movements along or away from the slope. First, the piece must resist the static stresses developed as well as those caused by rocking, and finally, stresses occurring during their "take-off" due to their bumping against other units. All of these items should be considered in design. If not, too many units may break even before they are subject to wave action.

10. In this respect, the breaking of a unit after its displacement should only be considered if the designer of the breakwater admits that displaced pieces may contribute to the development of a new shape of the slope, which is more stable than the original slope such as the S-slope case of San Ciprián Harbor in the northern part of Spain mentioned before.

Functional Evaluation of Armor Units. Before the designer decides which artificial unit should be used as armor, a thorough evaluation must be made of other types of units. Such an evaluation should cover functional, constructional, and economical aspects. In this section, only the functional aspects are considered. Only a few artificial concrete units such as akmons, dolos, and tetrapods are analyzed.

The function of the rubble mound is to protect a water area and to dissipate wave energy. The mound shall resist external and internal actions without damage or allow an admissible and preevaluated level of damage. The structure as a whole, as well as each of its components (units), must be able to resist all these actions.

After the casting, the units are placed in an armor layer on a structure of granular materials exposed to forces by neighboring blocks, transmitting these forces, plus the unit's own weight (in air or submerged, depending on its position), through sub- and core-layers to the foundation. Settlings of the structure induced by its own weight and by external forces, mainly wind waves, cause an adjustment of the position of all units inducing new internal stresses. Under wave attack, armor units are stressed and some units may rock and eventually become displaced or dislodged.

Initially, only blocks placed loosely in the granular medium will start rocking. During rocking, these blocks may impact other units or receive impacts from neighboring units. Displaced or dislodged units may hit other units. Heavy wave action may cause settling of the structure as a whole.

Roughly, the stresses induced on the units by external and internal actions depend upon their mass. The induced tensile stresses also depend upon the size of the units as do the resistance of the units. With increasing size of the units, forces cause the induced tensile stresses to increase more rapidly than the resistance of the sections of the unit.

Figure 53 shows schematically the probability density distributions of the induced stresses and the resistance of a unit. The intersection of both curves defines the probability of structure failure of the unit. Increasing the size of the unit causes both curves to move to the right, but the induced tensile curves move more quickly and consequently increase the intersection area (see Figure 53).

Heavy wave action displaces the unit from its position in the granular medium, with or without breaking, rotating and translating it along the slope, thereby impacting other units. Eventually, it stops due to the roughness of the slope, thereby

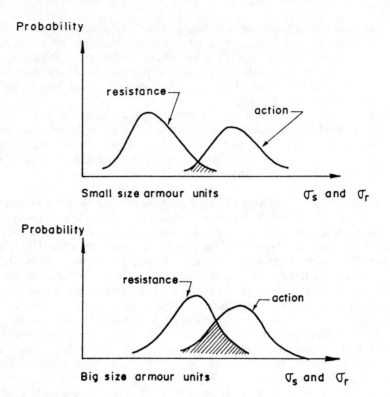

Figure 53. Schematic probability density distributions of induced stresses σ_s, and resistance, σ_r, of armor units.

reaching a new equilibrium position. During this process, it may break or break other armor units by bumping them.

The evaluation of armor units must cover the entire history of the units, from the time they were cast to the time they were displaced from their position. One should therefore distinguish between *structural* and *hydrodynamic stability*.

Structural stability includes the stability of the unit to resist stresses induced at its casting, placement, by the granular medium, and by its displacement and movement until it reaches final position. Construction includes stages when stresses develop during casting, curing, storing, and during transport and placement.

The granular sublayer induces stresses by roughness, interlocking and rocking, settling and adjustment of the main layer due to smaller waves or settling of the core and foundation. Finally, the unit must withstand stresses induced by displacements and movements on the slope.

Hydrodynamic stability only includes the stability of the armor units against displacement assuming that the units do not break.

Four geometrically different units have been considered—cubes or parallelo-pipedic, akmons, tetrapods and dolosse—presenting sequences in the development of "legs" and in consequences of interlocking. The development of legs came with the desire of weight reduction. Cubes have a height-width ratio of ~ 1, whereas dolos have a ratio of $\sim 0.30-0.40$. A simple analysis shows how the weights of units can be changed by the need for interlocking. Unfortunately, this philosophy proved to be problematic. New problems emerged that were ignored until very recently.

Units with legs develop high stresses induced by the construction itself, and by the block compound as a granular medium, inducing tensile stresses. To obtain high interlocking, it is necessary to use "legs," but this induces tensile and torsion stresses. Mass concrete does not withstand tensile stresses. To decrease stresses induced by the construction and by the granular medium, it is therefore necessary to be very careful in all construction processes to avoid that new additional stresses, e.g., thermal stresses.

These stresses increase with the mass and size of the unit. For example, dolosse weighing 50–150 t will fail by static action only due to load distributions.

The probability of having dolos locked almost by their own weight in a granular medium is very high and the probability of failure of a number of units in a mound is also high (see example by Mettam [60a]).

The probability of failure by construction and granular medium effects also increases with the increase of unit size. As an order of magnitude, the ratio of stresses of dolos weighing 2.7 t and 50 t is approximately 2.5.

Decreasing the length of the legs and increasing the trunk's cross-section lowers the probability of failure of the unit due to stresses by construction and granular medium effects. For cubes, this probability may be considered almost zero.

Tetrapods and akmons may be considered as "intermediates" between dolos and cubes. This in turn, means that only very large tetrapods (> 75 t) have a high probability of failure during construction and due to granular medium effects.

Different authors (see e.g. Burcharth [15]), have shown that for dolos the failure by impacts increases linearly with the size of the units, keeping the other characteristic factors constant. Generally, it may be said that for units with legs the probability of failure by impact increases with the size. This may also be true for blocks without legs, cubes, but the increase is much slower than for the "legged blocks," They are considered "brittle."

Slimmer dolos weighing more than 20 t have a relatively high probability of breaking before or during displacement. Through impacts, they may break other units on the slope and the probability for the increases with block size.

The probability of failure decreases for the same weight of the unit, moving from dolos, tetrapods, akmons to cubes. For cubes, the probability may be considered almost zero. Dolos of 40 t correspond to tetrapods of 70 t or 90 t. That means tetrapods of 40 t have a high probability of breaking (of the same order as dolos of 20 t. For akmons the same condition occurs in 70–90 t-weights.

Resistance to fatigue indicates the same trend. Legs are more vulnerable to fatigue forces than are units without legs. Increasing the size of the unit maintaining the same geometrical relationships decreases the resistance to fatigue.

Table 15
Stability Evaluations
(All units considered to have the same weight)

Armor Unit	Stability							
	Structural							Hydrodynamic
	Casting Construction	Granular Medium	Displacements					
		Interlocking			Rocking	Displacement	Impact	
	Roughness Micro, the Same for all Blocks	Macro	Settlement		St = stresses			
Dolos	Stresses increase with size	High level	High stresses Breaking of large sizes		High stresses with impacts and large sizes (> 20 ts) break.	Breaking of almost all sizes of units	Breaking	Optimum stability cot = 2.00
Tetrapod	Stresses increase with size	Medium level	Medium stresses		Medium stresses with impacts possibility of breaking large sizes (>40 ts)	Breaking of large sizes		Optimum stability cot = 2.50
Akmon	Lower stresses	Low level	Low level		Lower stresses	Some large sizes may break (> 70 ts)	Some break	Highest stability for lower slopes cot = 3.00
Cubes	Stresses very small by proper casting, curving and placement	No interlocking	Almost zero		Low stresses	No breaking	Some large sizes may break (>120 ts).	Highest stability for lower slopes cot > 3.00

Comparison of the stability of different units under wave action (assuming that they do not break) may be conducted by comparing the respective stability functions. Unfortunately, the limited data available and the use of many differing damage criteria make the comparison difficult, if not impossible.

Units that interlock have a maximum stability for a specific slope; the stability increases as the level of interlocking between blocks increases. Dolos have an optimum stability slope. For a slope of approximately 1:2, dolos need less weight to withstand the same waves as other types of blocks. The optimum slopes become milder as the legs or the capability to develop interlocking decreases and the response peak becomes less pronounced. This aspect is very important for oblique wave incidence as it always occurs at the breakwater head. Therefore, only for the specific optimum slope can one type of unit be better hydrodynamically another unit.

If the units have legs (interlocking), the superiority is not true for other slopes. That is one of the great dangers of the multilegged blocks, such as dolos, as stated by Brebner [6].

While multilegged blocks of relatively small size may be justified, the wisdom of using very large size interlocking blocks may be highly questioned. In all cases, a very careful control of manufacturing and construction procedures must be followed.

A summary of the views expressed in this section is given in Table 15. It may be useful for preevaluations before the type of armor unit is chosen. Some of the most popular shapes of units are shown in Figure 54.

Superstructure Stability

The superstructure in its simplest version is a crown covered with blocks, which are heavy enough to withstand the effects of overflowing water when waves overtop the structure. Often, such crowns are capped by heavy cast-in-place concrete slabs or blocks. The overflow water caused by uprush could damage the crown and the interior slope or perhaps crack the concrete slab if venting of trapped air is inadequate. The stability of the crown can best be evaluated by model experiments with random waves.

Often, superstructures include a wave screen. This could be very dangerous to the stability of the mound in front of the screen. Model experiments with realistic wave data can provide data on all forces on such a screen, also semitheoretical approaches are available.

Figure 55 show a cross section of a breakwater constructed on the Mediterranean coast of Turkey. Six hundred meters of this breakwater were damaged severely by a storm with a significant wave height of about 6.5 m and significant wave period of 10 sec. The damaged section of the breakwater after the storm is shown with dotted lines (Figure 55). The type of damage was first a sliding failure of the wave screen, followed by an erosion of backslope armor core and frontslope armor.

To predict the sliding stability of the wave screen defined in Figure 55 the following analytical model was developed. The model assumes wave run-up as a triangular wedge with an apex angle of 15° shown schematically in Figure 56. Figure 57 shows

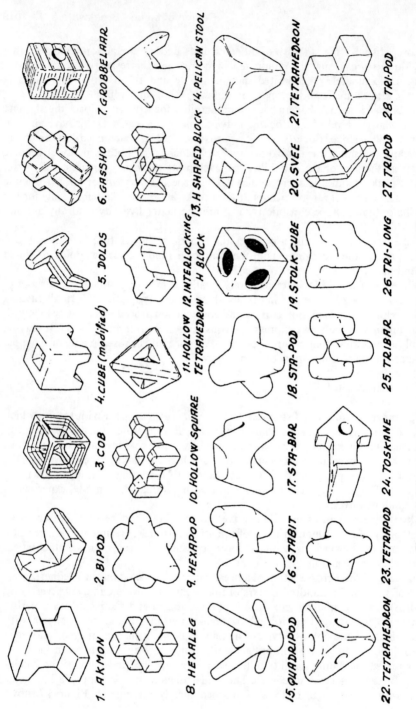

1. AKMON 2. BIPOD 3. COB 4. CUBE (modified) 5. DOLOS 6. GASSHO 7. GROBBELAAR

8. HEXALEG 9. HEXAPOD 10. HOLLOW SQUARE 11. HOLLOW TETRAHEDRON 12. INTERLOCKING H BLOCK 13. H SHAPED BLOCK 14. PELICAN STOOL

15. QUADRIPOD 16. STABIT 17. STA-BAR 18. STA-POD 19. STOLK CUBE 20. SVEE 21. TETRAHEDRON

22. TETRAHEDRON 23. TETRAPOD 24. TOSKANE 25. TRIBAR 26. TRI-LONG 27. TRIPOD 28. TRI-POD

Figure 54. Different kinds of concrete blocks (HRS, Wallingford Notes, 1978).

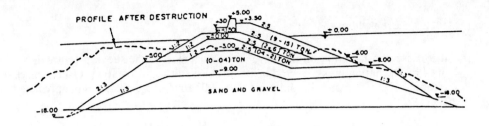

Figure 55. Antalyc main breakwater section before and after damage.

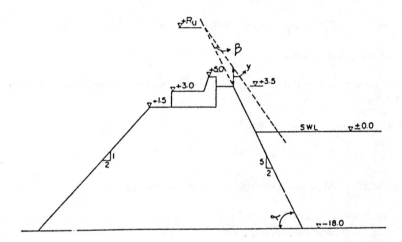

Figure 56. Schematic representation of hypothetical run-up.

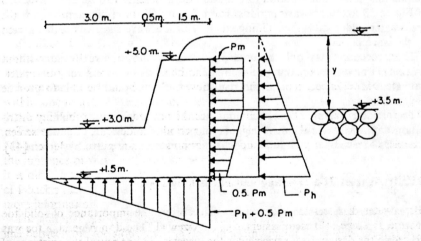

Figure 57. Pressure distribution on the wave screen.

the pressure distribution on the wave screen, where p_m is the shock pressure developed by stagnation pressures and p_h is the quasi-static hydrostatic pressure. In reference to Figures 56 and 57, and using $\gamma_w = 1.03$ t/m^3, these pressures are predicted as:

$$p_m = \gamma_w(\sqrt{gy})^2/2g = 0.51y \ (t/m^2) \tag{48}$$

$$P_h = \gamma_w \ (y + 2) = 1.03 \ (y + 2) \ (t/m^2) \tag{49}$$

$$y = (Ru - MWL/\sin \alpha)(\sin 15°/\cos(\alpha - 15°)) = 0.7(Ru - MWL) \tag{50}$$

MWL = Mean water level.

Using wave run-up data for a quarrystone breakwater the run-up is predicted as follows:

$$Ru = 0.4\xi H, \qquad \text{for } \xi \leq 2.5 \tag{51a}$$

$$Ru = H, \qquad \text{for } \xi > 2.5 \tag{51b}$$

The limit of sliding stability of the wall may be written as:

$$\frac{\text{Total vertical forces on the wall} \times \mu_f}{\text{Total horizontal forces on the wall}} = 1.0 \tag{52}$$

where μ_f is the friction coefficient of sliding between the bottom of the wall and its foundation stones. The solution of Equation 52, in reference to Figure 57 is plotted in Figure 58 for three wave periods. From Figure 58 it may be seen that, for the breakwater under study, the sliding stability of the wave screen is highly affected by the wave period.

This procedure may only be used for waves reaching the breakwater without breaking. For waves breaking in front of the breakwater, forces may be underestimated. Model experiments with realistic wave data should be able to provide design data.

The previous example clearly demonstrates the need for joint probability distribution data of individual wave heights and periods for design of a wave screen. Examples of results of hydraulic model studies on screen are given by Jensen [43].

Stability Against Toe Damage and Erosion at Toe

Breakwater disasters in recent years have proven the importance of solid toe structure. In some of these disasters, e.g., at Arzew el Djedid in Algeria, a toe was included in the design, but surveys after the disaster did not reveal the existence of any toe at all and hardly any toe-debris either. Apparently, this was because the toe was too small or it was poorly built. It was, however, supposed to have been

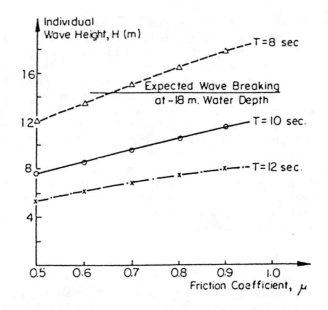

Figure 58. Wave conditions that start sliding of the wave screen.

built. The reasons for the toe failure could also be erosion in front of the toe causing undermining and sliding of the toe into the scour hole.

During down-rush, the toe is exposed not only to high velocities trying to push the toe armor out of place, but also to hydrostatic (fluidizing) pressures forces from inside the mound. For rubble-mound structures there are no simple empirical curves for minimum stone weight versus known design parameters.

Stability of the Bottom in Front of the Toe. The stability of the bottom in front of the toe in turn depends upon the soil condition, longshore current, velocities, wave action and on possible dredging work too close to the toe. While studies indicate that a scour hole in front of a rubble-mound structure may occur anywhere within one-fourth wavelength of the incident wave [31], the actual area to be protected is not generally that wide.

There is no general rule for the design of the toe including its mattress protection. Model experiments can provide some information on the stability of a toe under the influence of wave action in some cases combined with longshore currents, but it is difficult to quantify. Preliminary stone weight may be determined by the use of Isbach's theory (1935), CERC-*Shore Protection Manual* [79]. See Bruun [8] for more information.

Toe and mattress protection should extend as far out in front of the intersection line between the toe slope and the bottom as any major turbulence created by the toe, which may be seen in two-dimensional model experiments. If currents run along the structure, the toe must be expanded and the mattress protecting the toe against scour would have to be much wider, depending upon the strength of the current. The current pattern and velocities may then be determined by three-dimensional model experiments. A mattress of 10–30 m width may be necessary if currents are strong, such as at extreme ends of breakwaters or jetties when the bottom is fine sand, which is highly erodible. It is common to use core material for mattresses, but this may not be sufficient. Where currents are strong, a more substantial mattress, e.g., a graded filter, willow, mangle or fabric mattress with a cover of rock of adequate size to withstand a combined action of waves and currents, should be used. The gradation of the material used for the construction of the mattress and its cover layer should follow the Terzaghi filter ratios.

The safest way of preventing fine bottom materials, e.g., fine sand and silt, from penetrating into layers of coarse material is probably the use of a synthetic filter mat (geotextile) usually a fabric type with the fine mesh, which will not allow the material to pass through it in quantities. Geotextiles are commercially available, but they differ greatly in mesh size and tensile strength.

Scale Effects

Often it is necessary to check the design of the breakwater in a hydraulic model. Proper and correct scaling obviously is mandatory. The hydraulic model tests are based on and interpreted in agreement with the Froude similitude relationship.

The scale effects are caused by the lack of complete dynamic similarity. Special tests are necessary to determine the effects of linear scale and obtain scale-effect correction coefficients for predicting equations derived based on Froude's law.

Hudson and Keulegan [34], provided the following information:

"One such series of tests was conducted by Hudson and Jackson [34a] where a rubble-mound breakwater similar in cross section to that of an existing breakwater in San Pedro Bay, California, was modeled and tested by the Froude law using linear scales of 1:30, 1:45, and 1:60. The test results are compared one to the other, and with storm damage to the San Pedro breakwater. These results indicate that for the linear scales, prototype wave dimensions, and breakwater armor units used in these tests, the Froude law is sufficiently accurate for use in the design of such models."

Other tests, the results of which can be used to determine the scale effects and corrective coefficients, were conducted by Dai and Kamel [18b]. Their data, plotted to show the relation between $N_s = 1/\Psi$ and Re, Reynolds number, are given in Figure 59, the data points that are in the range of values of Re between 5.0×10^5 and 1.0×10^6 were obtained from tests conducted in the large wave flume at CERC. Data can be used as prototype values to obtain approximate corrective coefficients $(N_s)_p/(N_s)_m$ (p = prototype, m = model). However, more data points are considered necessary for Reynolds numbers from about 3.0×10^4 to 1.0×10^6 to ensure that accurate values of the ratio $(N_s)_p/(N_s)_m$ are obtained.

Sawaragi et al. [73b] verified the scale effects in model tests (rough quarry stone) by testing four different scales, where stability criteria at 0% and 15% damage were

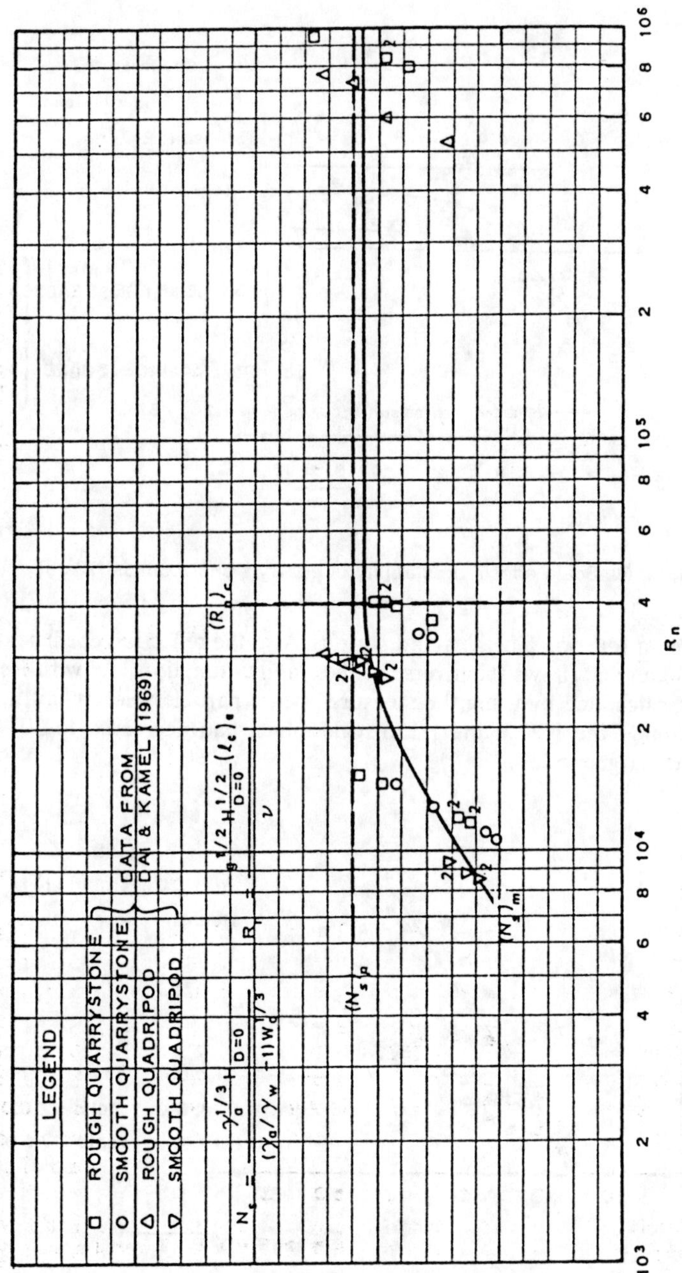

Figure 59. Scale effects of rubble mound stability models [18].

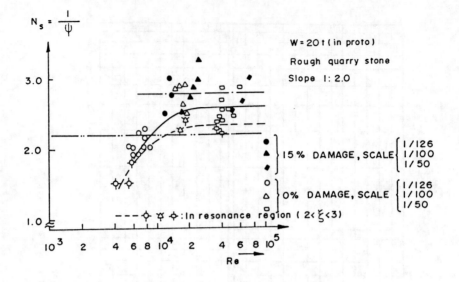

Figure 60. Scale effects on stability of quarry stone mounds [73a,b].

measured for various wave heights and periods. Also the reflection coefficients were calculated. Figure 60 shows the inverse of the stability function $1/\Psi$ with Reynolds number, Re, calculated by using the measured water particle velocity on the slope. At initial damage the $1/\Psi$ in the 1/126 scale model had decreased to 30–40% of those of other large models.

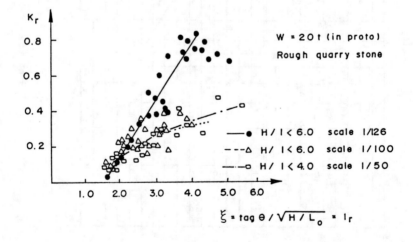

Figure 61. Scale effects on wave reflection [73a,b].

Figure 61 shows the reflection coefficient for individual models as a function of Ir. The scale effects on the reflection are presented clearly in the 1/126 scale model. It is noted that for Ir > 2.0 the differences in the K_R values are substantial.

It is generally accepted that scale effects are avoided if the model scale is larger than 1/60, but the scale may still be too small for practical experiments [8]. A comprehensive review of all aspects concerning modeling is given by Vasco Costa in Bruun et al. [8].

Hudson and Keulegan [34] give the following factors that influence the accuracy of model tests results (and must be considered in addition to those due to scale effects) in model design and operation:

1. Type of wave generator and the distance between the generator and the test structure.
2. Distance between the test structure and the wave absorber used in the shoreward end of the wave flume.
3. Reflection coefficient of the wave absorber.
4. Type, magnitude, and duration of attack of the test waves.
5. Stillwater level selected for testing.
6. Manner of determining the amount of damage to the test section when it is a rubble-mound structure.
7. Accuracy with which the wave dimensions are measured.
8. Other test conditions that must be selected by the laboratory engineer based on available prototype, data, and experience with similar model studies previously conducted.

Practical Data for Design

Wave Data. The wave data to be used for design shall be a true representation of nature in all details that influence structural function and stability. Consequently, all hydrodynamic aspects must be known and reproduced correctly.

While properly instrumented wave recording is able to describe all details of the actual wave motion, hindcasting can only provide certain characteristic values that are normally used in connection with the description of a sea state like H_s and T_s. For design, they are of limited value, but in connection with a wave spectrum of a selected "likely" type they may be used for developing details of wave conditions that are needed for a true hydrodynamic reproduction of such conditions, which are determining for stability. The JONSWAP-spectrum is now generally accepted as the most versatile spectrum adaptable to any location by quantification of certain parametric values. This may be done by a calibration based on actual records from the site in question.

Wave Conditions Determine Design. The wave conditions that determine stability also cause the most dangerous conditions for stability on short-term basis and are responsible for fatigue on short- and long-term basis. Such conditions can, with the present state of the art, be described by any formula or by any particular wave spectrum or by a "design wave." These principles are all outdated by experience.

Table 16
Design Criteria and Data on Waves

Waves	Character of Wave Data		
Short Term One or a few extreme storms possibilities for 3-dimensionality	**Wave Spectra** The absolute peak and local peaks	**Time Series** Groups Jumps Freaks	**Extremes** Hmax, Tmax, Hmax/T Values
Long-Term Repeated adverse conditions including all short term adverse conditions. For 3-dimensionality	Adverse wave conditions including extreme occurrences of low frequency (comparison with maintenance performed over several years).		

It is necessary to know the details of the actual wave action obtainable only by recordings at the site. Transfer of data from a neighboring location is risky unless all conditions are identical and they hardly ever are, particularly with respect to bathymetry. Table 16 summarizes design criteria and data on waves by Bruun [8].

Only minor damages may be acceptable for low-frequency short-term conditions. For long-term conditions of "fatigue nature" damages must not be allowed to develop beyond a certain point.

A particular concern is "fatigue." Fatigue has two meanings. One is fatigue by gradual displacement of units as previously mentioned. The other is fatigue of the materials used.

"Short-term" refers to severe wave conditions occurring during one or a few particular storms. "Storms" may be characterized:

1. *Descriptively* by the development of sea states through the generation, peak and attenuation phases.
2. *Hydrodynamically* by certain wave conditions or, explicitly, by sequences of waves that are particularly dangerous to stability including wave groups, "jumps" in wave action and "freak waves," which exert maximum forces of destructive nature on the mound. Such information can qualitatively be transferred from "earlier" or "similar" experiences to a particular site by proper calibrations to the site. Quantifications of actual levels of exposure may for extreme conditions be developed by extreme wave analyses, which will provide the extremes of wave heights and periods.

Short-term conditions also include the duration of storms of specific intensities.

"Long-term" refers to conditions that occur through many years of integrating the effects of short-term occurrences. This implies that the structure does not necessarily fail during severe short-term conditions, but that damages may develop through a number of such events by which the structure is gradually damaged, e.g., by departures of essential materials or by fatigue or other deterioration of the materials in the structure with particular reference to concrete blocks.

"Short-term" extreme conditions may be employed for design of certain structures of more "fragile" or "brittle" structural characteristics like some multilegged blocks, while "long-term" (repeated) conditions may determine the design of mound structures.

Three-Dimensional Data. Knowledge about the three-dimensionality of wave action is essential for design. If wave actions from different approach angles occur, it is essential for safe design to secure information about the three-dimensionality, which may be responsible for the generation of short-crested waves causing freak waves and dangerous wave groups.

Other Data. Other data needed for design includes

1. *Bathymetric data* which must be very detailed and include projections for the future development of a port facility and could include changes of the bottom topography.
2. *Geotechnical data* for foundation stability and for the stability of the bottom against erosion.
3. *Materials data*, including availability of materials, gradations of materials, soundness of materials, friction between layers of materials (geotechnical stability)
4. *Equipment data*, including data on transportation, handling, maintenance, communications.
5. *Labor availability*—skilled, unskilled labor, accomodations and facilities for labor.
6. *Environmental data*—the influence of the structure on the environment during construction (short-term and long-term effects), measures against possible adverse effects.
7. *Risk analysis and economic data*—aiming towards an optimum design considering all factors.

Construction

Construction of mound breakwaters has many variables, technical as well as commercial. Construction procedures depend upon materials and equipment available as well as upon the labor force which can be mobilized.

The first and most important principle of construction is that: *The breakwater shall be built as designed.*

Materials, Equipment, and Maintenance

Materials. Information on the availability of materials may be obtained from earlier mound structures, but in recent years breakwater construction called for the use of larger blocks, so it became necessary to investigate by blasting tests in quarries if such blocks could be produced economically. In some cases the quarries were located in the neighborhood of the site of the new port or port expansion, in other cases blocks had to be brought in by barges, rail, or trucks. Barge transport is usually the least expensive, but transportation costs may still be so high that concrete blocks may have to be considered. It occurred that difficulties arose on rock size and one had the choice between a gentle slope with a high consumption of materials or concrete blocks of heavier weight on a steeper slope. In developing countries the choice may then be the gentle slope.

It is an important requirement to the quarry that it yields a high percentage of heavy blocks. Quarries in granite, gabbro, and some basalts may yield 80% blocks, but the normal yield will be 30–40% larger blocks. Block size can be within limits determined by the blasting process. The normal quantity of explosives is 0.15–0.25 kg/m^3. Non-brisant explosives, like ammonium-nitrate, yield the highest percentage of larger blocks. Normal practice is for large blocks for armor on the seaside and smaller on the inside to be sorted out first, followed by filter blocks for sublayers. The remaining material is for core fill and "waste." Waste materials may be used for the lower part of core fill. In dumping the core fill, it should be realized that the largest pieces of rock always tend to come to rest in the lowest part of the slope. This can, to some extent, be remedied by building the lowest part of the core by floating equipment. If a mobile crane with a long jib is available, placement may be handled by a box with a shutter, long enough to hold one dump-truck load.

A core fill should never be too dense, as this will cause a buildup of hydrostatic pressure. A normal requirement is that core fill must only include 5% material of sand and pebble size.

Sublayers or filter layers should be built with a reasonable tolerance in thickness, e.g., $\pm 20\%$. The material must fulfil Terzaghi's filter ratios, $5d_{15} < D_{15} < 5d_{85}$. This can be handled by producing "ideal samples" in the quarry as well as on the construction site. A trained supervisor is then able to see if a load of sublayer material fulfills standard requirements. Placement of sublayers may be handled by land-based cranes with a long jib. The lower part of it may have to be placed from barges if the water is deep.

The armor block layer is most important for breakwater stability. It should be placed as soon as possible following the placement of sublayers to avoid damage to sublayer and core, which may be difficult to repair. It is practical to keep a sufficient number of blocks in stock at the site to enable rapid replacement in case of an unfavorable weather forecast. Blocks are brought out to the breakwater on trollies or trucks. The earlier practice of just dumping blocks directly from trucks or trollies caused losses of many blocks outside the desired profile.

Equipment. Crane capacity in tons and meters determine how far from the crane one is able to place blocks of adequate size. At large breakwaters it is, therefore, necessary to use floating equipment for placement of blocks in the lower slope, where exact placement is important to establish a solid foundation for the upper part of the slope.

A disadvantage of mound breakwaters of heavy armor blocks is the necessity of having a heavy crane. Such equipment is, however, usually not available in developing countries, where it may become necessary to use light equipment.

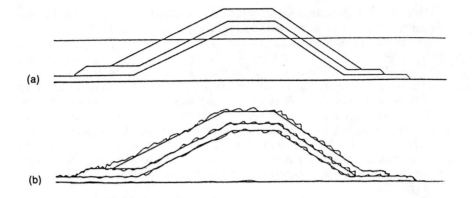

Figure 62. The drafting board breakwater (a); breakwater the way it was constructed (b).

The normal practice today is to place blocks directly by land-based cranes in this position. This is particularly practical at exposed sites. If weather conditions can be expected to stay stable at the site for a certain period of time, one may select a more rapid method of placement by simply dumping the armor blocks pell-mell, advancing the blocks just behind core and sublayers, and then moving in afterwards to adjust with a backhoe.

This has in many instances proven to be very practical, but it requires that additional blocks needed are available, and can be loaded and transported to the crane or backhoe for immediate placement, or after having been temporarily placed close to their final location in the breakwater. Such "double-handling" has proven to be technically as well as economically justified.

For the success of all construction work good supervision by experienced engineers and foremen is absolutely essential. So is a detailed professional planning of all phases of the works including coordination of all activities. This is mentioned in detail in the following section. And it should be remembered that practical aspects should be considered in the design (Figure 62A).

Maintenance. Finally, but *most important*: It is not enough to "complete the works" successfully. They shall also be maintained. The best maintenance, of course, is to avoid it. There are, however, many reasons for maintenance as described in the following sections. An obvious and often recorded reason is that the breakwater simply was not strong enough at certain sections. This, in turn, was often caused by shortcomings in knowledge about the actual wave action occurring along the breakwater. Or it could also be a result of changed wave action, e.g., by shoaling along the breakwater.

Maintenance includes many problems. The difficulty with maintenance operations often was that large equipment was no longer available for such operations. Attempts, therefore, were made to get by with smaller equipment handling smaller blocks. To stabilize such mounds mortaring was used. Cement, however, proved to be too rigid. Asphalt was much better, but required special mixing plants.

To evaluate maintenance steps properly it is necessary to understand the reason for damages. This may be obtained by model experiments, but field data are better. An example of such monitoring is given by Pope and Clark [67a] in a paper on "Monitoring of a Dolos Armor Cover, Cleveland." This program constituted aerial photography, wave measurements by pressure gauges, and armor unit surveys on a total of 32 units by which all movements (76 degrees of freedom) were recorded. It was found that movements had been fairly uniform throughout the trunk and slightly greater around the head section. Waterline blocks had generally moved more than crest units. Movements decreased with time. In addition, side-scan sonar imagery was used. It was found that although the individual dolos were too small to be identified within the structure slope, the structure toe was distinctive, changes in the structure slope were discernible, and general duplicity between side-scan runs was possible.

The merits of the survey were recordings of distinct movements, thereby providing a better understanding of the actual damages, or the initiation of damages.

Construction Practices: The Organization of the Work

Today "the contractor" is the man or the group that must not only execute the work, but plan and organize it in all details. To reach this objective the contractor must perform a sequence of actions, which may be summarized as follows:

1. Study the project in all its stages; analyze
2. Construction procedures
3. Alternatives
4. Time schedules
5. Construction systems
6. Facilities needed to do the work
7. Organizations of labor force
8. Supplies

The object of the preliminary study is to analyze the possibilities of solving the specific problems present in performing the work:

1. Access facilities
2. Installations of any kind that are needed
3. Wave and weather climates
4. Soils conditions
5. Communications
6. Supply market
7. Labor and personnel market

The final study must produce the construction procedures specifically including the following items:

• Planning of installations considering the following details:
  1. Access to the construction area and its yards
  2. Office buildings

3. Storage buildings and areas
4. Housing for employees and labor
5. Machine and repair shops
6. Mobilization of equipment
- Specific tasks as:
  1. Quarry preparation and organization
  2. Quarry opening
  3. Concrete manufacturing including casting yard and storage areas
  4. Harbor or pier for construction works
- Problems associated with:
  1. Start of the works
  2. Completion of works, closing down of operations.

Planning. Planning includes scheduling of the construction, which forecasting difficulties and deviations that may occur. The following index of planning may be considered:

1. Execution
2. Prefabrication
3. Transportation and handling

The "Gantt procedure" may be used as a planning model. It is necessary to consider (and to show diagrammatically) the dependencies and correlations of the different activities to be performed.

Breakwater work schedules depend much upon the sea state, and one of the most important functions of the contractor is to secure adequate equipment and manpower enabling him to fulfill all requirements to performance and time schedules. In this respect, it is necessary to accept that the mound is not considered "stable" until construction has been successfully completed in all phases.

Organization of the Construction. Before starting the construction it is necessary to study the need of staff, service, and production personnel (labor). It is also necessary to consider variances in the availability of labor and other personnel. Good organization also requires an adequate supply of materials, equipment and spare parts including:

1. Explosives
2. Drilling equipment
3. Cement and aggregates
4. Fuels and lubricants
5. Electric power
6. Equipment for casting, transportation, and handling

It is of primary importance to evaluate all the costs of supplies as they develop during the construction period.

The final item in the organization is to know the availability of all equipment needed to do the work, fixed as well as movable. And it cannot be stressed too

Table 17
Basic Costs in Breakwater Construction

Item	Definition	Subject
Labor	Cost/hour or unit	Wages, social charges, transports
Materials	Unit costs	Cost at source, transportation costs, cost of storage, cost of losses
Supplied	Unit costs of fuels and lubricants, power, explosives, et cetera	Cost at source, cost of transportation, cost of storage, cost of losses
Equipment	Unit costs all included of all services	Depreciation, maintenance including replacements
(Subcontracts)	Cost per unit or flat price	A number of specific tasks like quarrying

strongly that it is mandatory to include a certain safety factor when evaluating all heavy exposures that are vulnerable to damages and continuous heavy wear. The availability of standby and reserve capacity, therefore, is extremely important.

Cost Estimates. It is very important to monitor the actual costs of the construction and compare them to the predicted costs. Basic costs include the costs of labor (wages and salaries), materials, and supplies. They are listed in Table 17.
The economic planning may be organized as shown in Table 18.

Table 18
Economic Overall Planning

Direct Costs	All Materials
	Equipment for transport and handling (all costs including operation, maintenance, depreciation) Construction costs for all works Cost of supplies for construction works
Indirect Costs	**Construction and Maintenance Costs**
	Auxiliary installations including equipment Supplies for general auxilliary works General costs, salaries and other for auxiliary works: social, administrative, opening and closing or works Cost of insurance Cost of performance bonds

Installations Needed. One may distinguish between general and specific installations. The former are needed to do the work, but are not (cannot be) included as units of works. They are

1. Access facilities
2. Electric power, high and low voltage, lighting, etc., water supply, fire protection, supplies of compressed air
3. Repair shop
4. Offices and stores
5. Housing for labor and other personnel. Costs that are directly included in the construction are
   (a) Blasting of rock in quarry
   (b) Transportation and handling of rock, aggregates, and cement
   (c) Production of concrete in blocks and on site, curing, handling

Each specific item produces specific requirements related to the type of work and to the construction procedure.

Construction Plan. Table 19 gives an overall idea of such a plan.

In "production" of quantities one may distinguish between produced units counted in tons of rock and in tons or m^3 of concrete, and units placed in the structure counted in tons of rock placed by dump truck, crane or by barge; or in tons or m^3 of concrete blocks placed by crane or cast in situ in the structure.

In his planning of the works the contractor must attempt streamlining of all operations and assure that he, at any time, has the necessary reserve capacity available to advance works properly. These topics are dealt with in detail in Bruun, et al. [8].

Table 19
Construction Plan

Concrete Production	Quarry Production
Cement supply Aggregate supply Water supply Admixtures (if any) Storage	Explosives and equipment
Concrete plant Prefabrication Casting in situ	Drilling and blasting
Storage of blocks	Storage of rock for direct placement Storage of aggregates
Placement of blocks	Placement of rock

Examples

Mound Breakwaters in Spain (Bay of Biscay)

The purpose of this section is to review several mound breakwaters on the Spanish Coast of the Bay of Biscay (Cantabrian Sea), Figure 63. It also includes a summary of design criteria which offer a better understanding and evaluation of the breakwater's response.

It is outside the scope of these comments to criticize the failures. The intention is to illustrate the Spanish experience through old and new breakwaters. Four important rubble mounds, with artificial armor units are described: Bermeo, Bilbao, Gijón, and San Ciprián (Figure 63).

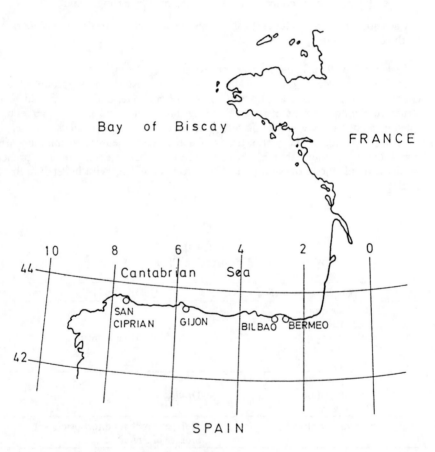

Figure 63. Cantabria Coast of the Bay of Biscay. General location of San Ciprián, Gijón, Bilbao and Bermeo harbors.

Wave Climate in the Cantabrian Sea. The waves reaching the Cantabrian Sea Coast are generated in the North Atlantic by the action of extratropical storms. The polar mass oscillations along the year define the path of the storms through the Bay of Biscay. Under such conditions, the winds are from west to northwest. Van Koten (1977) estimated the mode of the gradient wind speed, u_N (double exponential distribution) for the Cantabrian Sea Coast to be max $u_N = 40$ m/sec.

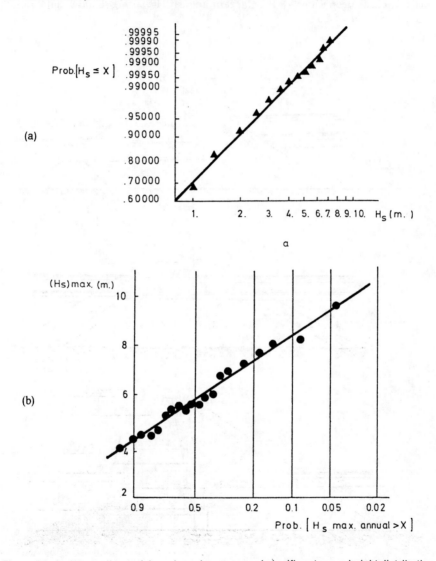

Figure 64a,b. Wave climate (a), and maximum annual significant wave height distribution (b), for Cantabrian Coast; Deep water.

Maximum frequency and intensities of waves occur from N 25 W to N 60 W. After visual data, Hogben and Lumb (1967) and instrumental data (Waverider buoy) recorded through five years at a depth of 35 m, the significant wave height distribution was obtained. The extremal significant wave height distribution was calculated by hindcasting from meteorological charts of 20 years using a spectral method, (Figure 64B). Both distributions are roughly representative of the wave conditions in deep water for the Cantabrian Sea. The spring semidiurnal tidal range is of the order of 4.5 m.

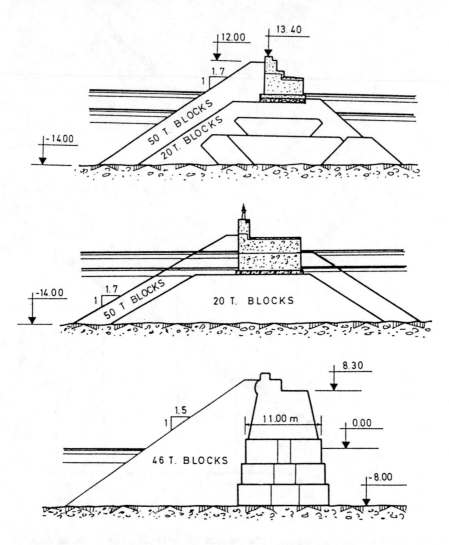

Figure 65. Bermeo breakwater, cross-sections.

Bermeo Harbor. The breakwater of Bermeo, Figure 65, protects a very important fishing harbor. The construction started in 1915 as a vertical wall. After several failures (breaking down the wall in many sections) it was decided (1951) to protect the wall with artificial armor units, parallelepipedic blocks of 46 t weight. The breakwater was extended to a 17-m depth in 1975.

The enlargement is characterized by a secondary layer of 20-t armor units while the head crown is constructed over a core of 20-t blocks. The blocks below mean water level have been placed from barges and those above mean water level by crane.

The response of the breakwater during its life was followed by aerial pictures. It can be concluded that since 1975 no block moved from its position above mean water level.

Bilbao Harbor. The Bilbao breakwater (Figure 66) is approximately 2,400 m long. It has been damaged twice since its completion in 1976. The first damage occurred in March 1976 and no reports were made. It was again severely damaged by waves of the storm of December 1976. Significant wave heights during the storm reached

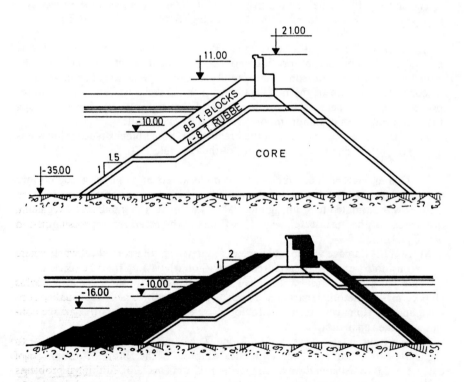

Figure 66. Bilbao breakwater, cross-sections.

Table 20

Breakwater	W (ton)	cot α	H_{min} (m)	$T_{H_{min}}$ (sc)	$H_{T_{min}}$ (m)	T_{min} (sc)
Bermeo (blocks)	50	1.7	10.8	15.0	15.4	9.7
Bilbao (blocks)	85	1.5	11.4	15.1	16.2	10.0
	150	2.0	17.7	19.7	25.6	12.6
Gijon (blocks)	120	1.6	13.7	16.6	19.5	10.9
San Ciprian (dolos)	50	2.0	12.2	16.0	17.5	10.4

Summary of minimum wave height and wave period that will start damage on related breakwaters.

7.90 m with a peak period 17.8 sec. During the storm the breakwater suffered several damage including breakdowns of the wave screen.

After model tests it was decided to rebuild the breakwater, increasing the weight of the parallelepipedic blocks up to 150 t and decreasing the slope to cot α = 2.

The head was constructed with floating caissons founded at the bottom and showed a marked instability.

There is no systematic survey of the breakwater.

The source of damage was the instability of the 85-t parallelepipedic blocks on a slope of cot α = 1.5 under action of waves higher than 12 m (Table 20).

Gijón Harbor. This breakwater (Figure 67), which now serves as a wharf is located at a depth of 23 m. Except for differential displacements of crown and head, constructed with floating caissons, there is no proof of slope failure. The main reason to construct the core of the breakwater with 90-t blocks was the lack of appropriate natural rock near the harbor. Apparently, the transmission of energy through the breakwater was of minor importance for harbor activities.

There is no systematic survey of the breakwater. Some blocks placed thirty years ago were broken due to a poor quality of the concrete.

San Ciprián Harbor. The rubble-mound breakwaters at San Ciprián Bay (Figure 68), were built in 1979. Important damage was discovered after the storm of March 1980. It was estimated that during the peak of the storm, the significant wave height, at the head of the breakwater, was H_s = 7 m, and the mean zero-upcrossing period was T_z = 14 sec.

Most of the damage was in a change of alignment in the north breakwater where numerous dolos units were fractured, but without departing from the section.

Some parts of the breakwater have been repaired with steel reinforced dolos (100 kg/m^3), while other parts have been replaced by blocks of high-quality concrete and the slope was decreased to cot α = 2.5. After two years the damage continues in the repaired area.

There are systematic surveys of the slope. The cause of failure is basically due to the lack of structural and hydrodynamical stability of the 50-t dolos on a slope of cot^{-1} α = 2.0 to withstand waves higher than 12 m (Table 20). Additional problems with poor-quality stones, concrete, and construction technique are unsolved.

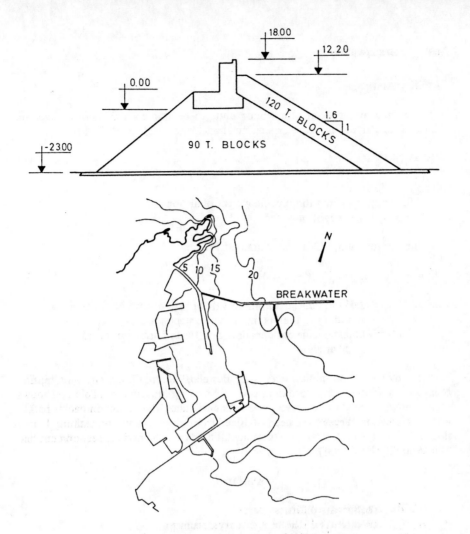

Figure 67. Gijón breakwater, cross-section, general plan.

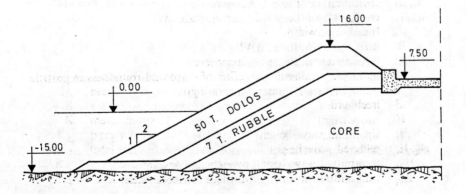

Figure 68. San Ciprián breakwater, cross-section.

Stability Analysis

The weight, W, necessary for armor units to be stable on the slope under the attack of regular waves with perpendicular incidence, is defined [55] by

$$W = \gamma_w R H^3 \Psi \tag{44}$$

where $R = S/(Sr - 1)^3$
   $S_r = \gamma_r/\gamma_w$, γ_r being the specific weight of armor units
   γ = specific weight of water

The stability function, Ψ, can be estimated [53] as:

$$\Psi = A_w(Ir - Ir_0) \exp(B_w(Ir - Ir_0)), \qquad Ir \geq Ir_0 \tag{47}$$

where $Ir_0 = 2.654 \tan \alpha$, the minimum value of Iribarren's Number, corresponding to the maximum wave steepness
   $A_w B_w$ = fitness coefficient depending on type of armor units and slope angle

Figure 69 shows interaction curves for Bermeo, Bilbao, Gijón, and San Ciprián breakwaters jointly with approximate wave breaking limit curves. Table 20 shows minimum wave height and wave period that will start the damage in each breakwater. Interaction curves have been obtained from the corresponding stability functions that give the best fit to the experimental data (refer to previous section entitled "The Stability Function").

Notation

A, B	coefficients of fitness curves
A_u, B_u	coefficients of the best fit curves, run-up
A_d, B_d	coefficients of the best fit curves, run-down
A_θ, B_θ	coefficients of the best fit curves, oblique incidence, stability
A_z, B_z	coefficients of the best fit curves
A_w, B_w	coefficients of the best fit curves, stability
B	breakwater width
B_s	breakwater width at MWL
B_c	breakwater width at the upper level
C_s	parameter evaluating the effect of shape and roundness in particle
D	grain diameter; domain (integrating)
F	freeboard
H	wave height
H_s	significant wave height
H_R, H_r	reflected wave height
H_{T_0}	transmitted wave height over the breakwater
H_{T_t}	transmitted wave height through the breakwater

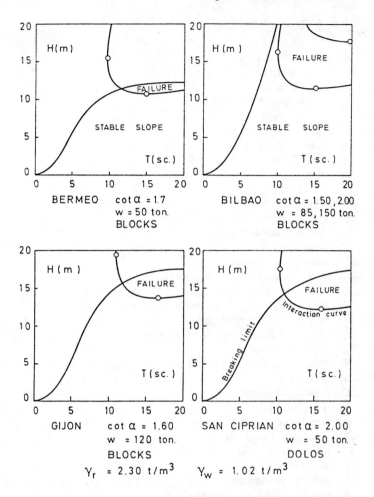

Figure 69. Interaction curves for Bermeo, Bilbao, Gijón and San Ciprián.

H_b breaking wave height

K   scattering wave coefficient

K   mean diameter of the secondary layer

K_{T_t} transmission coefficient through the breakwater

K_T total transmission coefficient (over and through the breakwater)

K_{T_0} transmission coefficient over the breakwater

K_R reflection coefficient

K_E dissipation coefficient
K_D Hudson coefficient
Ir   Iribarren number
Ir_0 limiting Iribarren number
L   wavelength
L_0 deep-water wavelength
$L_{0_{1/3}}$ significant wavelength
$L_{0_{wave}}$ maximum wavelength
Q   wave overtopping rate
R   function for specific density
R_u run-up
R_d run-down
R*   dimensionless freeboard
S_r relative armor density
N_s Hudson stability number
T   wave period
T_p peak wave period
$T_{0,1}$ zero-one moment wave period
T_z zero-upcrossing wave period
Z   flow characteristic variable
W   weight of the armor unit
W_i weight of the secondary layer units
Re   Reynolds number
N   number of overtopping waves
a   parameter
a_i width of berms
c   wave celerity
d   depth and height of berms
d*   dimensionless depth
e, e_i thickness of layer
h_i water depth
l   equivalent cube size
g   acceleration due to gravity
q   rate of overtopping averaged over the duration of the storm (Goda's diagram, Figures 22a-d) in m^3/m-s.
p   pressure
p_m shock pressure developed by stagnation pressures
p_h quasi-static hydrostatic pressure
t   time
u, u_{max} horizontal velocity and maximum velocity
u_N mode of the gradient wind speed (double exponential distribution)
v, v_{max}, v_{min} horizontal velocity wave and maximum and minimum velocity
u_c velocity of the wave front
z   dimensionless flow characteristic variable
l_B plane length in the S profile
r_i total number of occurences for a run of length
n   porosity

Greek Symbols

α dike slope angle

α_T coefficient in tansmission equation

α_R coefficient in reflection equation

β_K coefficient in transmission equation

β bottom slope angle

γ_r, γ_i specific weight of armor units and grains, respectively

γ_w water specific weight

δ water layer thickness

v kinematic viscosity

μ dynamic viscosity

λ breakwater width

ρ_s armor unit density

ρ_w water density

ρ_c correlation coefficient

γ $(\rho_s - \rho_w)\rho_w$

σ_s tensile strength

σ_r tensile resistance

ϵ wave spectrum parameter

v_0 parameter in the joint wave height-period distribution

ξ, ξ^* groupiness parameter

ϕ average angle of repose

ϕ stability function

ϕ_0 stability function in oblique incidence

μ_f friction coefficient wall-foundation stones

β_s parameter incorporating the effect of the scaling of the bed grains

σ phase difference

References

1. Allsop, N. W. H., 1983, "Low-Crest Breakwaters, Studies in Random Waves," Coastal Structures-83, ASCE.
2. Ahrens, J. P. and Mc Cartney, B. L., 1975, "Wave Period Effect on the Stability of Riprap," *Proc. Civ. Eng. Oceans*, III (1975), Vol. 2, pp. 1019–1034.
3. Battjes, J. A., 1974a, "Computation of Set-up, Longshore Currents, Run-up and Overtopping due to Wind Generated Waves," *Communications on Hydraulics*, Delft University of Technology, Rep. 74-2.
4. Battjes, J. A., 1974b, "Surf Similarity," *Proc. Conf. on Coastal Eng.*, 14th, Copenhagen, pp. 466–480.
5. Battjes, J. A. and Roos, A., 1975, "Characteristics of Flow in Run-up of Periodic Waves," *Communications on Hydraulics*, Delft University of Technology, Rep. 75-3.
6. Brebner, A., 1978, "Performance of Dolos Blocks in an Open Channel Situation," *Proc. Conf. Coastal Eng.*, 16th, Hamburg, pp. 2305–2307.
7. Bretschneider, C. L., 1959, "Wave Variability and Wave Spectra for Wind-Generated Gravity Waves," Beach Erosion Board, U.S. Army Corps. Eng., Tech. Memo. No. 118.
8. Bruun, P., (editor) 1985, "*Design and Construction of Mounds for Breakwaters for coastal protection.*" Elsevier.

9. Bruun, P., 1989. *Port Engineering*, 4th Edition, Volumes 1 (1400 pp.) and 2 (1200 pp.), The Gulf Publishing Co., Houston. See also "Stability and Fragility," *The Dock and Harbour Authority*, Vol. LXIII, No. 736, 1981.

9a. Bruun, P., 1979, "Common Reasons for Damage or Breakdown of Mound Breakwaters," *Coastal Engineering* 2, pp. 261–273.

10. Bruun, P. and Günbak, A. R., 1978, "Stability of Sloping Structures in Relation to $\xi = \tan \alpha / \sqrt{H/L_0}$ Risk Criteria in Design," *Coastal Eng.*, 1:287–322.

11. Bruun, P. and Günbak, A. R., 1977, "Risk Criteria in Design Stability of Sloping Structures in Relation to $\xi = \tan \alpha / \sqrt{H/L_0}$." Symp. Design Rubble-Mound Breakwaters, British Hovercraft Corporation, Isle of Whight, Paper No. 4.

12. Bruun, P. and Johannesson, P., 1977, "Parameters Affecting Stability of Rubble-Mounds," Closure. *ASCE J. Waterw.*, Port Coastal Ocean Div., 103 (WW4):533–566.

12a. Bruun, P. and Johannesson, P., 1976, "Parameters Affecting Stability of Rubble-Mounds," *Journal of Waterways, Harbor and Coastal Engineering Div.*, ASCE, Vol. 102, WW2, pp. 141–164.

13. Bruun, P. and Günbak, A. R., 1976, "New Design Principles for Rubble-Mound Structures," *Proc. 15th Conf. on Coastal Eng.*, Honolulu, Hawaii, pp. 2429–2473.

14. Bruun, P. and Johannesson, P., 1974, "A Critical Review of the Parameters Effecting the Design of Rubble-Mound Breakwaters," Rep. No. 3/74, Div. Post and Ocean Engineering, Norwegian Inst. of Tech., Trondheim.

15. Burcharth, H. F., 1981, "Full-Scale Dynamic Testing of Dolos to Destruction," *Coastal Engineering*, 4, pp. 229–251.

15a. Burcharth, H. F., 1979, "Effect of Wave Grouping on On-Shore Structures," *Coastal Engineering*, Vol. 2, No. 3, March, pp. 189–199.

16. Burcharth, H. F. and Thompson, A. C., 1983, "Stability of Armour units in Oscillatory Flow," *ASCE Coastal Structures*, 83:71–82.

17. Castro, E., 1933, Diques de escollera. Revista de Obras Públicas, Madrid, April 1933, pp. 183–185.

18. Cavanié, A., Arhan, M., and Ezraty, R., 1976, "A Statistical Relationship Between Individual Heights and Periods of Storm Waves." *Proc. BOSS'76*. Vol. II, Trondheim, pp. 354–360.

18a. Cundall, P. A., and Strack, O. D. L., 1979, "Discrete Numerical Model for Granular Assemblies," *Geotechnique*, Vol. 29, No. 1, March, p. 47–65.

18b. Dai, Y. B. and Kamel, A. M., 1969, "Scale-Effects Tests for Rubble-Mound Breakwaters: Hydraulic Model Investigation," Research Report H-69-2, U.S. Army Engineer Waterways Experiment Station, Vicksburg, MS, December.

19. Desire, J. M., 1985, "Comportamiento de sistemas granulares bajo la acción de flujos oscilatorios. Aplicación a diques rompeolas de bloques paralelepipédicos." Thesis for Dr. Eng. degree. E.T.S. Ingenieros de Caminos, Canales y Puertos. University of Santander. Spain (in Spanish).

19a. Eagleson, P. S. and Dean, R. G., 1961, "Wave-Induced Motion of Bottom Sediment Particles," *Trans. Am. Soc. Civil Engrs.* 126, pp. 1162–1189.

20. Galvin, C. J. Jr., 1968, "Breaker Type Classification on Three Laboratory Beaches," *J. Geophys. Res.*, 73:3651–3659.

21. Giménez-Curto, L. A., 1979, Comportamiento de los diques rompeolas bajo la acción del oleaje. (Behaviour of Mound Breakwaters under Wave Action). Ph.D. Thesis. University of Santander, Spain (in Spanish).

22. Goda, Y., 1985, *Random Seas and Design of Maritime Structures*, University of Tokyo Press.

23. Goda, Y., 1970, "A Synthesis of Breaker Indices," *Transactions of the Japanese Society of Civil Engineering*, Vol. 2, Part 2.

24. Goda, Y., 1969, "Reanalysis of Laboratory Data on Wave Transmission over Break-waters," Report of the Port and Harbour Research Institute, Vol. 18, No. 3.

25. Günbak, A. R., 1982, "Some Design and Modeling Problems of Rubble-Mound Break-waters," Proceedings of the Int. Coastal and Port Eng. in Developing Countries Conference, Colombo, Sri Lanka.

26. Günbak, A. R., 1979, "Rubble-Mound Breakwaters," Div. Port and Ocean Eng., The Norwegian Institute of Technology, Trondheim, Norway. Rep. 1-1979.

27. Günbak, A. R., 1978, "Test on a 1:2.5 Rubble Mound Breakwater Irregular Waves," *Div. Port Ocean Eng.* The Norwegian Institute of Technology. Trondheim, Norway. Rep. 2-1978.

28. Günbak, A. R., 1976, "The Stability of Rubble-Mound Breakwaters in Relation to Wave Breaking and Run-down Characteristics and to the $\xi \sim \tan \alpha \cdot T/\sqrt{H}$ number," *Div. Port and Ocean Eng.*, The Norwegian Institute of Technology, Trondheim, Norway, Rep. 1-1976.

29. Günbak, A. R. and Bruun, P. M., 1979, "Wave Mechanics Principles on the Design of Rubble Mound Breakwaters." *Proc. of the Int. Conf. on Port and Ocean Eng. Under Arctic Conditions.* Trondheim.

30. Hedar, P. A., 1960, "Stability of Rock-Fill Breakwaters." Akademiforlaget—Gumperts, Gøteborg.

31. Herbich, J. B., Murphy, H. D., and Van Weele, B., 1965, Scour Flat Sand Beaches Due to Wave Action in Front of Seawalls, *Proc. Coastal Engineering*, Santa Barbara Speciality Conf., ASCE.

31a. Hosoi, M. and Shuto, N., 1964, "Run-up Height on Single Slope Dike Due to Waves Coming Obliquely," *Proc. Coastal Eng. in Japan*, Vol. 7, pp. 95–99.

32. Hudson, R. Y., 1961, "Laboratory Investigation of Rubble Mound Breakwaters," *Trans. of the ASCE*, Vol. 126, Part IV, pp. 492–541.

33. Hudson, R. Y., 1959, "Laboratory Investigation of Rubble-Mound Breakwaters." *ASCE J. Waterw. Harbors Div.*, 85 (WW3):93–121.

34. Hudson, R. Y. and Keulegan, G. H., 1979, in *Coastal Hydraulic Models*, Special Report No. 5, Coastal Engineering Research Center.

34a. Hudson, R. Y. and Jackson, R. A., 1955, "Design of Tetrapod Cover Layer for a Rubble-Mound Breakwaters, Crescent City Harbor, Crescent City, California," Technical Memorandum No. 2-413, U.S. Army Engineer Waterways Experiment Station, Vicksburg, MS, June.

35. Hunt, T. A., 1959, "Design of Seawalls and Breakwaters," *ASCE, J. Waterw. Harb. Div.*, 85 (WW3):123–152.

36. Hydraulics Research Station, 1970, "High Island water scheme," Hong-Kong. Willingford, Rep. EX 532.

37. Iribarren, R., 1965, Formule pour le calcul des diques en enrochements naturels ou élements artificiels. XXI Int. Navigation Congr., Stockholm, Section II-1.

38. Iribarren, R., 1938, Una formula para el cálculo de los diques de escollera. July, 1938. Fluid Mechanics Laboratory, Univ. Calif., Berkeley, Tech. Rep. HE-116-295, 1948. Translated by D. Heinrich.

39. Iribarren, R. and Nogales, C., 1954, "Other Verifications of the Formula Calculating Breakwater Embankments," Permanent International Association of Navigation Congresses, PIANC, Bull. No. 39 (1954):119–139.

40. Iribarren, R. and Nogales, C., 1950, Generalización de la fórmula para el cálculo de los diques de escollera y comprobación de sus coeficientes. Revista de Obras Públicas, Madrid, May 1950, pp. 227–239.

41. Iribarren, R. and Nogales, C., 1949, Protection des ports. XVII International Navigation Congress, Lisbon, Section II-4.

42. Iversen, H. W., 1952, "Laboratory Study of Breakers," National Bureau of Standards, Washington, D.C., Circular 521.

42a. Jackson, R. A., 1968, "Design of Cover Layers for Rubble-Mound Breakwater Subjected to Non-breaking Waves," U.S. Army Engineer Waterways Experiment Station, Research Report. No. 2-11.

43. Jensen, O. J., 1984, *rubble-mound breakwater* (monograph) Danish Hydraulic Institute, Denmark.

44. Johannesson, P. and Bruun, P. M., "Hydraulic Performance of Rubble Mound Breakwaters, Reasons for Failure," Proceedings. The First Int. Conf. on Port and Ocean Eng. Under Arctic Conditions, Vol. 1, pp. 326–359, The Norwegian Inst. of Tech., Trondheim, Norway, 1971.

44a. Johnson, R. R., Mansard, E. P. D. and Ploeg. J., 1978, "Effect of Wave Grouping on Breakwater Stability," *Proc. 16th Coastal Eng. Conference*, Hamburg, Germany, Aug. 27–Sept. 3, ASCE, New York, 1979, Vol. 2, pp. 2228–2243.

45. Kamphuis, J. W. and Mohamed, N., 1978, "Run-up of Irregular Waves on Plane Smooth Slope," *ASCE J. Waterw. Port Coastal Ocean Div.*, 104(WW2):135–147.

46. Kemp, P. H. and Plinston, D. T., 1968, "Beaches Produced by Low Phase Difference." *Proc. of Am. Soc. of Civil Engineers. Journal of Hydraulics Division*, Vol. 94, HY 5.

47. Kristinsson, B. and Eliasson, J., 1978, "Stability Measurements on Rubble-Mound Breakwaters," *Coastal Eng.*, 2(1):85–91.

48. Kobayashi, N. A., OHa, A. K., Roy, I., 1987, "Wave Reflection and Run-up on Rough Slopes," *ASCE Waterway*; P.C. and O.E. Vol. 113, No. 3, pp. 282–300.

49. Kobayashi, N. and Jacobs, B. K., 1985, "Rip-rap Stability Under Wave Action," *ASCE Waterway, P.C. and O.E.* Vol. 111, No. 3, pp. 55–566.

49a. Kobayashi, Nobuhisa and Jacobs, Brian K., 1985, "Stability of Armor Units of Composite Slopes," *J. Waterways, Port, Coastal and Ocean Engineering*, Vol. VIII, No. 5, September, pp. 880–894.

50. Kobayashi, N. and Jacobs, B. K., 1985, "Stability of Armor Units on Composite Slopes," *ASCE Waterway, P.C. and O.I.*, Vol. 111, No. 5, pp. 880–894.

51. Lamarre, P., 1967, "Water-Wave Transmission by Overtopping of an Impermeable Breakwater," M.S. Thesis. M.I.T., Cambridge, Massachusetts.

52. Longuet-Higgins, M.S., 1975, "On the Joint Distribution of the Periods and Amplitudes of Sea Waters," *J. Geophys. Res.*, 80:2688–2694.

53. Losada, M. A. and Giménez-Curto, L. A., 1979a, "The Joint Effect of the Wave Height and period on the Stability of Rubble-Mound Breakwaters Using Iribarren's Number," *Coastal Eng.*, 3:77–96.

54. Losada, M. A. and Giménez-Curto, L. A., 1979b, "An Approximation to the Failure Probability of Maritime Structures Under a Sea State," *Proc. Int. Conf. on Port and Ocean Engineering under Artic Conditions*, (POAC), 5th., Trondheim, Norway, pp. 1269–1281.

55. Losada, M. A. and Giménez-Curto, L. A., 1980, "Mound Breakwaters Under Wave Attack," Int. Seminar on Criteria for Design and Construction of Breakwaters and Coastal Structures. Dep. of Oceanographical and Ports Engineering, University of Santander, Santander, Spain. Sect. II, pp. 127–238.

56. Losada, M. A. and Giménez-Curto, L. A., 1981, "Flow Characteristics on Rough, Permeable Slopes Under Wave Action," *Coastal Eng.*, 4:187–206.

56a. Losada, Miguel A. and Gimenez-Curto, Luis A., 1982, "Mound Breakwaters Under Oblique Wave Attack: A Working Hypothesis," *Coastal Engineering*, Vol. 6, No. 1, March, pp. 83–92.

57. Losada, M. A. and Desire, J. M., 1984, "Functional Comparison of Breakwater Armor Units." Internatl. Symp. on Marit. Struct. in the Mediterranean Sea. Athens.

58. Losada, M. A. and Desiré, J. M., 1985, "Incipient Motion on a Horizontal Granular Bed in Non-Breaking Water Waves," *Coastal Eng.*, 9:357–370.

59. Losada, M. A., Desiré, J. M. and Alejo, M., 1986, "Stability of Blocks as Breakwater Armor Units," *ASCE J. of Structural Engineering*, Vol. 112, No. 11, pp. 2392–2401.

59a. Magoon, O. T. and Baird, W. F., 1977, "Breakage of Breakwater Armor Units," *Proceedings of the Symposium on Design of Rubble-Mound Breakwaters*, British Hoovercraft Corporation, Isle of Wright.

60. Marsal, R. J., 1973, "Mechanical Properties of Rockfill." *Embankment Dam Eng.*, pp. 109–200, John Wiley and Sons (300 pp.).

60a. Mettam, J. D., 1976, "Design of Main Breakwater at Sines Harbor," *Proc. 15th Coastal Engineering Conference*, Hawaii, pp. 2499–2518.

61. Miche, R., 1944, Mouvements ondulatoires de la mer en profundeur constante ou décroissante. Ann. des Ponts et Chaussées, 114.

62. Michell, J. H., 1893, "On the Highest Waves in Water," *Philos. Mag.*, 36, No. 5.

62a. Miller, R. L. and Byrne, R. J., 1965, "The Angle of Repose of a Single Grain on a Fixed Bed," Tech. Rep. No. 4, Dept. Geophys. Sc., University of Chicago, May.

63. Moraes, C., 1970, "Experiments of Wave Reflexion on Impermeable Slopes," *Proc. Conf. on Coastal Eng.*, 12th., Washington, D.C., pp. 509–521.

64. Numata, A., 1976, "Laboratory Formulation for Transmission and Reflection at Permeable Breakwaters of Artificial Blocks." *Coastal Engineering in Japan*, Vol. XIX. pp. 47–58.

65. Ouellet, Y., 1972, "Considerations on Factors in Breakwater Model Tests," *Proc. Conf. Coastal Eng.*, 13th., Vancouver, pp. 1809–1825.

66. Patrick, D. A. and Wiegel, R. L., 1954, "Amphibian Tractors in the Surf," *Proc. Conf. on Ships and Waves*, 1st, p. 397.

67. Permanent International Association of Navigation Congresses, (PIANC), 1976. Final Report of the International Commission for the Study of Waves. Annexe Bull. No. 25 (Vol. III/1976).

67a. Pope, J. and Clark, D., 1983, "Monitoring of a Dolos Armor Cover, Cleveland, OH," *Proc. Coastal Structures Conference*, ASCE, Washington, D.C.

68. Price, W. A., 1979, "Static Stability of Rubble-Mound Breakwaters," *The Dock & Harbour Authority*, Vol. LX, No. 702, May 1979.

69. Reid, R. O. and Bretschneider, C. L., 1953, "Surface Waves and Offshore Structures," Texas A&M Research Foundation. Tech. Rep., October, 1953.

70. Ryu, C. R. and Sawaragi, T., 1986, "Wave Control Functions and Design Principles of Composite Slope Rubble-Mound Structures," *Coastal Engineering in Japan*, Vol. XXIX, pp. 227–240.

71. Rodriguez Ortiz, J. M., "Estudio del Comportamiento de Medio Granulares Heterogéneos mediante Modelos Discontinuous Analógicos y Matemáticos." Ph, D., Universidad Politécnica de Madrid. (in Spanish).

72. Saville, T., Jr., 1956, "Wave Run-up on Shore Structures," *ASCE J. Waterw. Harbours Div.*, 82(WW2), April, 1956.

73. Saville, T., Jr., 1962, "An Approximation of the Wave Run-up Frequency Distribution," *Proc. Conf. on Coastal Eng.*, 8th Mexico.

73a. Saville, T., Jr., 1963, "Wave Run-up on Composite Slopes," *Proc. 6th Conference on Coastal Engineering*, pp. 691–699.

73b. Sawaragi, T., Ryu, C. R. and Iwata, K., 1983, "Consideration of the Destruction Mechanism of Rubble-Mound Breakwater due to the Resonance Phenomena," *Proc. 8th Int. Harbor Cong.*, pp. 3.197–3.208.

73c. Sawaragi, T. and Iwata, K., 1973, "Some Consideration on Hydraulic Characteristics of Preforated Breakwater Quays," *Proc. of JSCE*, December, pp. 53–63.

73d. Sawaragi, T., Deguchi, I. and Hong, G. P., 1986, "Effect of Rubble-Mound Foundation of Composite Type Breakwater on Reduction of Reflection," *Proc. 5th APD-IAHR*, pp. 361–378.

74. Sawaragi, T., Ryu, C. R., and Kusumi, M., 1985, "Destruction Mechanism and Design of Rubble-Mound Structures by Irregular waves," *Coastal Engineering in Japan.* Vol. XXVIII, pp. 173–190.

75. Sawaragi, T., L. Iwata & Kobayashi, 1982, "Condition and Probability of Occurrence of Resonance on Steep Slopes of Coastal Structures," Coastal Eng. in Japan, 1982.

76. Seelig, W. N., 1980, "Two-dimensional Tests of Wave Transmission and Reflection Characteristics of Laboratory Breakwaters," C.E.R.C. Technical Report No. 80-1.

77. Sholtz, D. J. P. and Zwamborn, J. A., 1983, "Effect of the Waist Thickness on Stability of Dolos," Struc. Div., Coastal Eng. 1 Hydr., Natl. Res. Inst. for Oceanol., Council for Scient. 1 Ind. Res. (CSIR), Res. Rept. 556, Stellenbosch, South Africa.

78. Sollitt, C. K., and Cross, R. H., 1972, "Wave Transmission Through Permeable Breakwaters," *Proc. Conf. on Coastal Eng.*, 13th, Vancouver, pp. 1827–1846.

79. SPM, *Shore Protection Manual*, 1984, U.S. Army Corps of Engineering Research Center, Department of the Army Corps of Engineers.

80. Stoa, P. N., 1979, "Wave Run-up on Rough Slopes," U.S. Army Corps of Engineers, Coastal Engineering Research Center. Rep. CETA 79-1.

81. Technical Advisory Committee on Protection Against Inundation, 1974, *Wave Run-up and Overtopping*, Government Publishing Office, The Hague.

82. Tørum, A., Mathiesen, B. J., and Escutio, R., 1979, "Reliability of Breakwater Model Tests," Coastal Structures 79, ASCE, pp. 454–469.

83. U.S. Army Coastal Engineering Research Center, 1977, "Prediction of Irregular Wave Overtopping," CETA Report Nos. 77-2 and 77-7.

84. Van de Kreeke, J., 1969, "Damage Function of Rubble-Mound Breakwaters," *J. Waterw. Harbors Div.*, ASCE, 95 (WW3): 345–354.

85. Van der Meer, J. W. and K. W. Pilarczyk, 1984, "Stability of Rubble-Mound Slopes Under Random Wave Attack," Publication No. 332, Delft Hydraulic Laboratory, December 1984.

86. Van Oorschot, J. H. and d'Angremound, K., 1968, "The Effect of Wave Energy Spectra on Wave Run-up," *Proc. Conf. on Coastal Eng.*, 11th, London, pp. 888–900.

87. Whillock, A. F., 1977, "Stability of Dolos Blocks Under Oblique Wave Attack," Hydraulics Research Station, Wallingford, Rep. IT159.

87a. Yalin, M. S., 1977, *Mechanics of Sediment Transport*, 2nd Ed., Pergamon Press, Oxford, England.

88. Zwamborn, J. A. and Beute, J. A., 1972, "Stability of Dolos armor Units," ECOR Symp., S71, Stellenbosch, South Africa.

CHAPTER 22

PROBABILISTIC DESIGN OF BREAKWATERS

Jentsje W. van der Meer

Research Engineer
Harbours, Coasts and Offshore Technology Division
Delft Hydraulics, Emmeloord, The Netherlands

CONTENTS

Introduction

The purpose of the design of a revetment or breakwater is to obtain a structure that, during its construction and throughout its intended service life, has a sufficiently low probability of failure and of collapse. To achieve the best possible assessment of this, a risk analysis can be performed. The three main elements of the risk analysis are hazard, mechanisms, and consequence.

A risk analysis begins with the preparation of an inventory of the hazards and mechanisms. A mechanism is defined as the manner in which the structure responds to hazards. A combination of hazards and mechanisms leads, with a particular probability, to failure or collapse of the structure as a whole or of its components. Here only the mechanism of instability of the armor layer due to wave action is treated. A probabilistic calculation of the failure probability can be performed using the so-called reliability function, Z, with regard to the limit state considered. In its simplest form, Z = strength-load. Negative values of Z correspond to failure. The probability of failure can thus be represented symbolically as $P[Z < 0]$.

Application in Rubble-Mound Design

The various parameters in an armor layer design are given by two new stability formulas: For plunging waves:

$$H_s/\Delta D_{n50} * \sqrt{\xi_z} = aP^{0.18}(S/\sqrt{N})^{0.2} \tag{1}$$

For surging waves:

$$H_s/\Delta_{n50} = bP^{-0.13}(S/\sqrt{N})^{0.2}\sqrt{\cot \alpha}\xi_z{}^P \tag{2}$$

Description of the parameters was given in Chapter 18. The parameters in Equations 1 and 2 can be allocated to the strength and load parameters as follows:

Strength	Load
D_{n50}	H_s
Δ	T_z or H_s/L_z
$\cot \alpha$	N
P	

For armor layer design the damage level S is, in fact, equivalent to the failure criterion for the reliability function. This means that probabilities can be calculated for different damage levels. By rearranging Equations 1 and 2 the reliability function can be established. In this case the influence of the wave period is described by the fictitious wave steepness H_s/L_z, where $L_z = gT_z{}^2/2\pi$. The reliability function, Z, for plunging waves is described by:

$$Z = S^{0.2} * a6.2P^{0.18} \cot \alpha^{0.5} \Delta D_{n50} - (H_s + FH_s)(H_s/L_z)^{-0.25}N^{0.1} \tag{3}$$

For surging waves:

$$Z = S^{0.2} * bP^{-0.13} \cot \alpha^{0.5 - P} \Delta D_{n50} - (H_s + FH_s)(H_s/L_z)^{0.5P}N^{0.1} \tag{4}$$

where FH_s is a parameter to account for the uncertainty of the wave height (see Figure 1).

The long-term distribution of the wave height can be described by an exponential function:

$$P(H_s) \equiv P[H \le H_s] = 1 - \exp[-\{(H_s - C)/B\}^\gamma] \tag{5}$$

where C = the background noise level or lower-boundary
       B = scale parameter
       γ = shape parameter

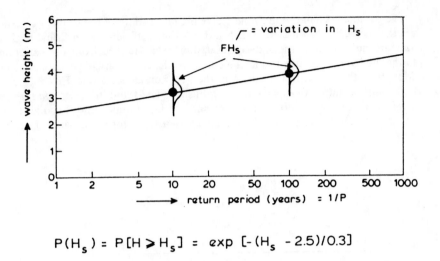

$$P(H_s) = P[H \geqslant H_s] = exp\,[-(H_s - 2.5)/0.3]$$

Figure 1. Long-term distribution of the wave height H_s with its variation FH_s.

The uncertainty of this long-term distribution is given by the FH_s parameter in Equations 3 and 4, which has an average value of zero and has a normal distribution. For the example given here, $C = 2.5$, $B = 0.3$, and $\gamma = 1.0$. This long-term distribution of the wave height is shown in Figure 1, together with the parameter FH_s. The 1/50 year wave height in this case, calculated using Equation 5 with $P = 1/50$, is 3.67 m. The values for the average and the standard deviation used for the computations are shown in Table 1.

Table 1
Parameters Used for Probabilistic Computations

Parameter	Distribution	Average	Standard Deviation
D_{n50}	normal	1.0 m	0.03 m
Δ	normal	1.6	0.05
cot α	normal	3.0	0.15
P	normal	0.5	0.05
N	normal	3,000	1,500
H_s	Weibull	B = 0.3	C = 2.5
FH_s	normal	0	0.25
H_s/L_z	normal	0.04	0.01
a (Equation 1)	normal	6.2	0.4
b (Equation 2)	normal	1.0	0.08

The parameters a and b in Table 1 give the uncertainty of the stability equations; a is the coefficient 6.2 in Equation 1 and b is the coefficient 1.0 in Equation 2. The standard deviations of the stability equations were derived from the variation of all the model test results around the curves of the equations. Figure 2 gives Equation 1 with the model test results and the 90% confidence levels. From this figure a standard deviation of $\sigma = 0.4$ was established. The standard deviation for Equation 2 was found to be 0.08. The uncertainty of Equations 1 and 2 is due to curve fitting, but also due to the random behavior of armor stones, which also occurs in nature.

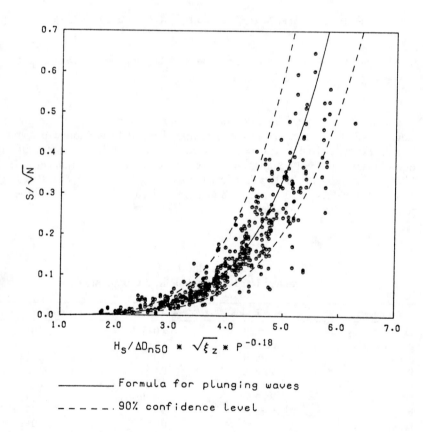

_____ Formula for plunging waves

_ _ _ _ _ .90% confidence level

Figure 2. Formula for plunging waves with test results.

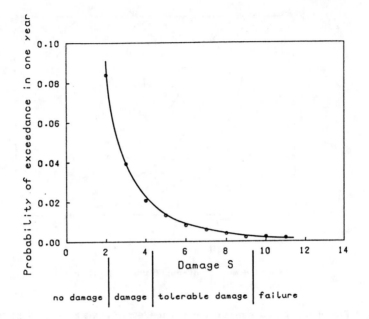

Figure 3. Probability of exceedance of the damage level S in one year.

Computations

The Level II First-Order Second-Moment (FOSM) with Approximate Full Distribution Approach (AFDA) method was used for the computations. General references on this aspect are Thoft-Christensen and Baker [1] and Hallam et al. [2]. These computations were performed for several damage levels, S. The results give the probability of occurrence of that damage level in one year. These probabilities per year are small and are shown in Figure 3. The horizontal axis shows the damage level S and the vertical axis shows the probability of exceedance of these damage levels in one year. The probability of exceedance in one year of the damage level S = 4, for instance, is equal to about 2%.

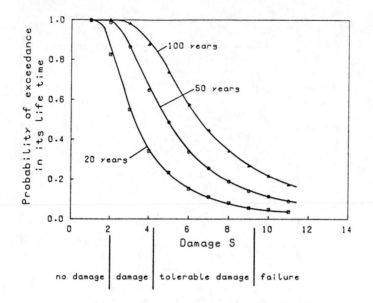

Figure 4. Probability of exceedance of the damage level S in the life time of the structure.

The probability of exceedance for an X year period can be obtained using

$$P[Z < 0; X \text{ years}] = 1 - [1 - P(Z < 0, 1 \text{ year})]^X \qquad (6)$$

Results, derived from Figure 3 using Equation 6, are shown in Figure 4. Curves are drawn for three lifetimes (X = 20, 50, and 100 years). From this figure it follows that the damage level S = 2, which means start of damage, will certainly occur in a lifetime (project life) of 50 years. Tolerable damage (S = 5 − 8) in the same lifetime will occur with a probability of 0.2 − 0.5. The probability that failure (filter layer visible) will occur in a lifetime of 50 years is less than 0.1.

Such probability curves can be used to make a cost optimization for the breakwater during its project life. This procedure is discussed in Nielsen and Burcharth [3] and Le Mehaute [4]. Probabilistic designs that consider other failure mechanisms for a breakwater are described in the CIAD report [5].

Conclusions

New stability equations have been derived from the results of extensive model investigations. The equations have been rewritten in the form of reliability functions. Level II computations were performed, which resulted in graphs showing the probability of exceedance of different damage levels during the project life of the structure.

The probabilistic design procedure has been used in an example. The same type of computations can be performed for other structures, using this example as a reference.

Notation

A	erosion area in a cross-section
a	coefficient 6.2 in Equation 1, used as a stochastic variable
AFDA	Approximate full distribution approach
B	scale parameter in exponential function
b	coefficient 1.0 in Equation 2, used as a stochastic variable
C	lower boundary in exponential function
D_{n50}	nominal diameter $(W_{50}/\rho_a)^{1/3}$
FH_s	uncertainty parameter of wave height H_s
g	acceleration due to gravity
H_s	significant wave height
L_z	deep-water wavelength $(gT_z^2/2\pi)$
N	number of waves (storm duration)
P	permeability coefficient
$P[Z < 0]$	probability of failure
S	damage level (A/D_{n50}^2)
T_z	average wave period
W_{50}	50% value of mass distribution curve
X	lifetime (project life) of the structure (years)
Z	reliability function

Greek Symbols

α	slope angle
γ	shape parameter in exponential function
Δ	relative mass density $(\rho_a/\rho - 1)$
ξ_z	surf similarity parameter $(\tan \alpha/\sqrt{H_s/L_z})$
ρ	mass density of water
ρ_a	mass density of stone
σ	standard deviation

References

1. Thoft-Christensen, P. and Baker, M. J., 1982, *Structural Reliability Theory and its Applications*, Springer Verlag, Berlin, West Germany.
2. Hallam, M. G., Heaf, N. I., and Wootos, I. R., 1977, *Rationalization of Safety and Serviceability factors in Structural Codes*, CIRIA report No. 63.
3. Nielsen, S. R. K. and Burcharth, H. F., 1983, "Stochastic design of rubble mound breakwaters," *Proceedings 11th IFIP Conf. on System Modelling and Optimization*, Copenhagen, Denmark, pp. 534–544.
4. Le Méhauté, B. and Wang, S., 1985, "Wave Statistical Uncertainties and Design of Breakwater," *J. WPC and OE*, ASCE, Vol. 111, No. 5.
5. CIAD Project Group, 1985, *Computer aided evaluation of the reliability of a breakwater design*, Zoetermeer, CIAD-III, the Netherlands.

CHAPTER 23

DESIGN OF SEAWALLS AND GROINS

Richard Silvester

Department of Civil Engineering
University of Western Australia
Nedlands, Australia

CONTENTS

Seawalls

Introduction

Seawalls, bulkheads or revetments are constructed parallel to the shoreline to protect an area of land or facilities against the sea. If the section of coast is not being eroded, such protection is not necessary, as a beach in equilibrium can well defend the hinterland. It may, therefore, be concluded that the original dearth of sediment supply will continue after the installation of the wall. Even if the wall is placed some distance back on the berm, the beach can continue to recede, because nothing has been done to obviate natural processes.

A beach berm, considered as that reasonably flat width of sand from the waterline to where vegetation commences, can be considered to have been removed out to sea and back again in the past two years. This is the reason for the lack of vegetation, because any seeds that had landed on this area would have been taken seaward by the storm waves [1]. When the swell returns the offshore bar, these seeds act like fine sediment and hence are sorted out to sea, never to return and germinate. Thus, a structure placed on the berm will leave insufficient material for the storm waves to construct a bar of adequate height to break incoming waves [2]. Hence, during a storm, waves will always be impacting on the wall. Even the subsequent swell will also be so reflected and create standing or short-crested waves that make it difficult for the berm to reform in front of the wall. These and other influences are discussed.

Various shapes of structure have been suggested, purportedly to better reflect waves and reduce run-up or overtopping. The effectiveness of this approach is outlined. The length and height of a seawall is dictated by the purpose(s) it is to serve, which may involve waves, storm surges, or tsunamis. The actual reach of water up a structure is determined by its shape, materials of construction, and slope of seabed fronting it. Where a crest height exceeds the crest of the wall, water will pour over it onto pavements or roadways adjacent to this protective device. The volume so involved needs to be calculated in order to design drains for its ready removal.

Influence of Reflection

The topic of scour around breakwaters is presented in Volume 2 and applies equally to seawalls and related structures. The obliquity of waves to the former is generally greater as they are angled about 45° to the shoreline. In deeper water wave direction is more angled to the coast than for a seawall, which is in shallower water and runs parallel to the coast. But, even so, some obliquity must be accepted, because if there was none, there would be no littoral drift and no erosion problem. This applies to both storm waves and swell.

Some thirty years ago, an eminent oceanographer told me, "There is no doubt about the efficiency of these seawalls, they reflect waves out to sea, never to be seen again. They are good disposers of energy." Little did he and many engineers realize that in so proceeding out to sea these reflected waves impose a second batch of erosive power to the seafloor. This is not just a doubling of the incident wave power, because the orbital motions of the water particles are completely different and conducive to sand suspension and transport parallel to the reflecting face [3].

The situation shown in Figure 1 of a wall constructed along portion of coast can be considered rather typical. It is seen that waves refracting shoreward are still angled to the face on arrival and hence will be reflected at an equal angle. The limiting orthogonals of these reflected waves are shown, which approach each other offshore as refraction seawards also occur. They may even cross, as illustrated, and so produce a wave caustic, implying an infinite concentration of energy. This results in wave breaking, not only for the reflected waves, but also for the incident waves in that area.

Consider now the zone in front of the wall where the intersection of incoming and outgoing crests doubles the wave height. These island crests propagate along the wall, providing a finite distance between crests normal to this face. This creates the term "short-crested," which phenomenon is discussed in Chapter 3 and also alluded to in Volume 2. The orbital motions are similar along alignments parallel

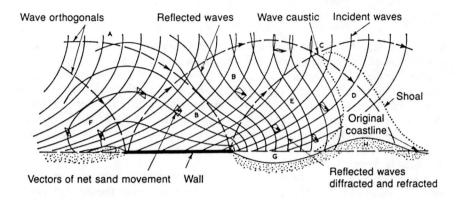

Wave orthogonals   Reflected waves   Wave caustic   Incident waves

Shoal

Original
coastline

Vectors of net sand movement   Wall

Reflected waves
diffracted and refracted

Figure 1. Influence of oblique wave reflection from a seawall.

to the wall, but vary across the crest distance normal to it. Besides excessive velocities, the water particles experience an enhanced mass transport, or net movement
each wave cycle, which is also along the wall, in the direction of island crest propagation. Overall, there is a strong capacity to scour the bed.

Thus, in the area of Figure 1 between the reflected wave orthogonals, material
is quickly removed downcoast beyond the limit of the seawall. But even there the
reflected waves are diffracting beyond the limiting orthogonal and also refracting
shoreward. This maintains the short-crested system into this area, continuing the
scouring process. This results in recession of the shoreline as shown. Such erosion
downcoast of seawalls is ubiquitous. On the upcoast end of the wall the diffraction
of reflected waves can create a net movement upcoast that could result in a slight
accretion, but this is of little consequence.

The excessive volume of sediment from in front of and just downcoast of the wall
is then influenced by the zone of little wave energy, in the lee of the wave caustic
previously mentioned. There the sediment is deposited due to the lack of power to
continue its longshore movement. It is only when a shoal has occurred that oribital
motions are sufficient to maintain transport in an equilibrium state. Such an accretion may result in the beach protruding out from the original shoreline.

The engineer thus observes a region of erosion from his wall to somewhere downcoast where conditions are excellent, with even some building out of the beach. His
first and probably his second reaction is to rectify the problem by extending the
wall to this stable section of coast. Needless to say, this will only exacerbate the
problem, or push it further downcoast, perhaps out of his jurisdiction. Such an
elongation provides a greater width of reflected waves and hence erosion of a larger
area of seabed. It is little wonder that it is so difficult to maintain a beach in front
of a seawall.

Types of Structure

Seawalls may be vertical, sloping, curved in either direction, and have various roughness elements on their faces. Such elements are small in character so that the wave treats them as a smooth surface. They therefore do not reduce run-up or concomitant overtopping to any significant degree. Where structures are placed well back from a beach, which may be considered as stable, they can serve to restrict flooding from the very infrequent storm surge with its high water levels. They also serve to contain inundation from tsunamis. It is first necessary to establish that the fronting beach is not likely to erode, or, if it is, to design some structures to retain sediment in place.

It is generally accepted [4] that seawalls, revetments, etc. cannot economically be built to a height that no overtopping will ever occur. Even though they may be designed for an existing offshore profile, it is difficult to predict what changes will occur over the life of the structure. As previously noted, continuous reflection of only swell waves can scour the bed for long distances from a wall face, making it easier for waves to apply their unbroken wave energy to the structure.

Wave Run-Up

The tests on this topic prior to 1966 have been brought together [4] in the form of multiple graphs of R/H_0' versus slope of structure for a range of H_0'/T^2, where R is the reach of waves above SWL, H_0' is the deep-water wave height for normal approach to the coast, and T is the wave period. It is preferable to use the dimensionless ratio H_0'/L_0 rather than the dimensional equivalent of H_0'/T^2, which is specific to the system of units used. This wave steepness will vary at the site dependent on the depth ratio d/L_0, and hence a different ratio of d/H_0' may be introduced, with curves grouping in increments of this parameter.

Such a presentation appears in Figure 2, for a horizontal bed meeting a straight smoothed face of slope 1:n with toe depth d. Two sets of curves are shown, for $d/H_0' = 1-3$ and > 3. Slopes range from 1:1.5 to 1:4, which is normal for most seawall type structures. For the case of slope 1:1.5 and $d/H_0' > 3$ the value of R/H_0' is constant at 2.4, but for all other cases the run-up ratio rises for decreasing wave steepness. This does not imply that the run-up itself increases because the wave heights are now less for a given wave period.

Where the bed adjacent to the seawall is not flat but sloped, the wave is more able to break on reaching the toe of the structure, which produces maximum run-up. Either side of these maxima a smaller wave steepness involves wave reflection, while for greater steepness the wave has broken before reaching the slope. These optimum curves can only be exhibited with d/L_0 curves and not with ranges of d/H_0'. For a bed slope of 1:10 adjacent to the wall values of R/H_0' are shown in Figure 3 versus H_0'/L_0 for a range of structural slopes and three groupings of d/H_0'. It is seen that the single curve for $d/H_0' = 0$, for all slopes, is below those for other d/H_0' values. The smaller this ratio the less is the runup, as to be expected. For the smallest deep-water wave steepness of 0.002 (equivalent to 0.5 m height of a

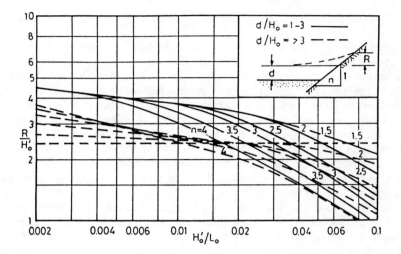

Figure 2. Run-up ratio versus deep-water steepness for a range of smooth impermeable slopes.

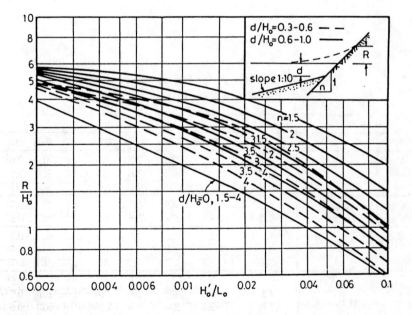

Figure 3. Run-up on smooth impermeable slopes with the seafloor sloped at 1:10.

12-sec wave) the run-up ratio varies from 4 to 5.8, which only involves run-up of 2 to 3 m.

Also included in the same reference [4] are graphs of run-up (R/H_0') versus H_0'/T^2 for various shapes of wall and specific d/H_0' values. A bed slope of 1:10 is also assumed. These are summarized in Table 1 for convenient comparison, but only to the first decimal place as any greater accuracy is not warranted for this phenomenon. These plotted to a logarithmic scale will result in either straight lines or smooth curves for ready determination from intermediate wave steepnesses. Otherwise, plain interpolation could suffice. The rip-rap values refer to stones placed up to two thicknesses on an impervious underlayer, they may be held in place with bitumastic mortar to prevent displacement.

Where a permeable rubble-mound slope exists, a certain amount of energy absorption occurs, thus reducing the run-up. This is exhibited in Table 2 for the case of zero bed slope and only for $d/H_0' > 3$. It is seen that these values rise to maxima for H_0'/L_0 around 0.12, which is approaching the incipient breaking wave in deep water. These run-up ratios are in the order of one third those for a smooth impermeable slope.

Tests have been conducted comparing monochromatic with spectral waves, but no significant difference was found on either plain or composite slopes [5]. Delft tests [6] indicated a higher run-up for wider spectra. A relationship based upon that of Hunt [7] for monochromatic waves was found satisfactory in the prediction

Table 1
Run-up Ratio (R/H_0') for Impermeable Seawalls
with Seabed Slope of 1:10 [33]

Wall Type	d/H_0'	H_0/L_0						
		0.002	0.004	0.006	0.01	0.02	0.04	0.08
Vertical	0	4.5	3.1	2.5	1.8	1.3	0.9	0.6
	1.5	3.4	3.1	3.0	2.8	2.5	2.3	2.1
	3.0	2.9	2.5	2.3	2.0	1.7	1.5	1.3
Curved to vertical	1.5	5.0	4.7	4.5	4.4	4.1	3.9	3.7
Curved to recurve	1.5	4.5	3.0	2.5	1.7	1.1	0.7	0.5
Stepped 1:1.5 slope	0	3.5	2.8	2.3	1.6	1.0	0.5	0.3
	1.5	3.7	3.2	3.0	2.8	2.2	1.9	1.7
	3.0	1.7	1.7	1.7	1.7	1.7	1.7	1.7
Rip-rap 1:1.5 slope	0	3.0	2.4	2.0	1.5	0.9	0.5	0.3
	1.5	4.1	3.2	2.8	2.0	1.5	1.0	0.7
	3.0	3.0	2.4	1.9	1.5	1.1	0.8	0.6

Table 2
Run-up Ratio (R/H_0') for Rubble-Mound Revetments for $d/H_0' > 3$ [33]

n	H_0/L_0						
	0.002	0.004	0.006	0.01	0.02	0.04	0.08
1.5	0.8	0.9	0.9	1.0	1.1	0.9	0.7
2.0	0.9	1.0	1.2	1.3	1.1	0.9	0.6
2.5	0.7	0.9	1.0	1.1	1.0	0.8	0.6
3.0	0.8	0.9	1.0	1.0	0.9	0.7	0.5
4.0	0.7	0.8	0.9	0.9	0.8	0.6	0.4
5.0	0.6	0.7	0.8	0.8	0.6	0.5	0.3

of run-up for 1:4 and 1:6 smooth impermeable slopes. It could be used with caution for other slopes:

$$R = CH_{1/3}(gT_{max}^2/2\pi H_{1/3})^{1/2}/n \tag{1}$$

where C is a factor varying with spectral width, which for a nearshore fully-arisen-sea gives $C = 0.7$. It is also dependent on frequency of exceedance and the value quoted is based upon 2% of the waves exceeding the run-up computed by Equation 1. For a narrow spectrum it should be reduced to 85%. The n value is the slope of the structure in terms of 1:n.

The term in the brackets of Equation 1 is virtually the reciprocal of a wave steepness, using local maximum spectral height $(H_{1/3})$ and deep-water length (L_0). The relationship of this breaking wave steepness in shoaling water can be shown to be [8].

$$(H_{1/3}/L_0)_{max} = 0.684d/L_0 \tag{2}$$

Inserting this into Equation 1 gives

$$R/H_{1/3} = 0.846(L_0/d)^{1/2}/n \tag{3}$$

which has been graphed in Figure 4 for a range of n. For a given depth at the toe of a seawall and known period at the peak of the spectrum of either a developing or fully developed sea the maximum wave height can be determined from Equation 2. With the depth ratio (d/L_0) so assessed the run-up can be found from Equation 3 or Figure 4, without wave hindcasting except for the derivation of the period at

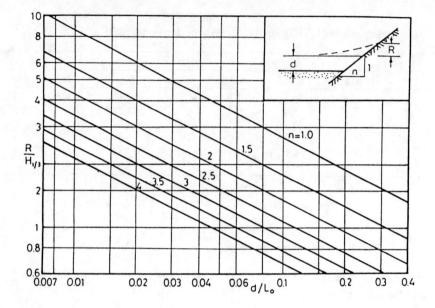

Figure 4. Run-up of storm waves on smooth impermeable slopes with fronting flat bed.

the spectral peak (T_{max}). This is given by the optimum wind speed U_{10} (knots) divided by 3 [8].

Overtopping

When the run-up of a wave exceeds the crest of a marine structure, overtopping will occur. This can produce serious results by way of flooding facilities landward of the revetment, or destruction of the top and leeward face of a breakwater where smaller armor units are generally used. It is necessary, therefore, to be able to assess the quantity of water passing over the top of the structure per wave period, or averaged over time. With respect to damage of breakwaters the velocity of such water is also significant.

The run-up computed previously is no longer applicable because the overtopping reduces the reflection and hence the extent of the standing wave. In Figure 5 the run-up (R) for various shapes of seawall is indicated. Many workers have carried out flume tests [9–12] while others have endeavored to derive a theory based upon a weir approach [13, 14]. The analysis of Kikkawa et al. [13] uses local wave dimensions and treats the overtopping as a flow over a broad-crested weir with changing upstream height. Their analysis appears to agree well with the test data available [13, 14], in spite of the assumption of a triangular shape for the wave crest rather

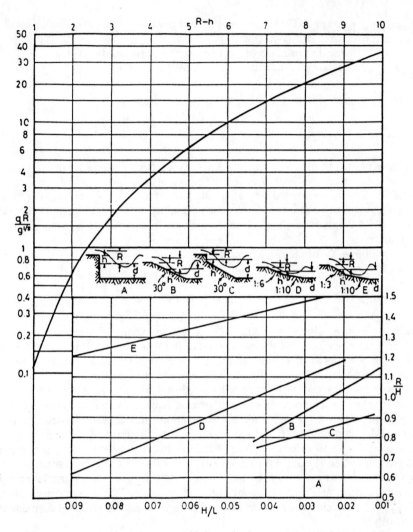

Figure 5. Run-up for the case of overtopping plus average discharge of water.

than a sinusoidal or cnoidal profile. By the time the wave reaches the crest of the dike it will either be a standing wave or be breaking. In either case the crest shape should be close to triangular. The equation so derived [14] can be put in the form

$$\frac{q_{ave}}{g^{1/2}H^{3/2}} = \sqrt{2}\,\frac{2}{15}\,m\left(\frac{R}{H}\right)^{3/2}\left(1 - \frac{h}{R_0}\right)^{5/2} \tag{4}$$

where q_{ave} = average discharge over the weir per unit length of dike
$\qquad\quad$ m = discharge coefficient
$\qquad\quad$ R = maximum reach of the overtopping wave above SWL
$\qquad\quad$ h = height of the structure above SWL

Using m = 0.6 [14] this Equation 4 can be converted to

$$q_{ave}R/g^{1/2} = 0.113(R - h)^{5/2} \qquad\qquad (5)$$

which is plotted in Figure 5. Any units may be used for q, R, and h with an appropriate value of g. It is seen that for the range of R − h of 1 to 10 the parameter $qR/g^{1/2}$ varies from around 0.1 to 35. Other shapes and proportions of seawall or revetment can be equated to the versions presented in Figure 5, or tests conducted to find R/H values for any given local wave steepness (H/L) with associated overtopping.

The volume V_T discharging over a length B of the dike in a wave period T is given by

$$V_T = q_{ave}TB \qquad\qquad (6)$$

with an average velocity v = $2q_{ave}/(R - h)$, assuming the discharge to occur as a rectangular block for half the wave period. Because the overtopping water body has been considered of triangular cross-section, this velocity should be doubled, but verification of such figures should be made in the laboratory.

Tsuruta and Goda [15] have used Equation 4 but modified it to obtain other dimensionless parameters, both for monochromatic waves and a spectrum. By using the fourth-order theory for standing waves and normal shoaling relationships, they derived the limiting ratio (H_0/d_c) at which no overtopping would occur for a given h/d value. This is sketched in Figure 6. They also showed that optimum overtopping occurs when $H_0/d \doteq 1.0$ to 1.3, or $H_{1/3}/d = 0.6$ to 0.8. This is when the wave is just breaking at the toe of the major slope. At this time the water at the crest is moving forward at about the speed of the wave or $\sqrt{gd}$. This is retarded to about 70% [5] of this velocity due to friction on the slope and the transfer of momentum vertically.

The effect of wind has been studied in wind-wave flumes [16], but the results are in terms of $U/\sqrt{gH_0}$ and are therefore difficult to apply. It appears that when d/L_0 is large, increased overtopping is produced by a following wind, probably due to the larger heights possible just before reaching the dike. With shallower conditions more breaking occurs offshore. Allowance should be made for doubling the discharge when a wind of 30 knots is blowing shoreward. The maximum H under such storm conditions is given by Equation 2 with a wave period of 10 sec.

Where waves are oblique to a structure, the bore from breaking is angled to the dike crest so that overtopping is reduced [9]. Also, the longshore component of this velocity interferes with the breaking of other waves, so that the discharge is

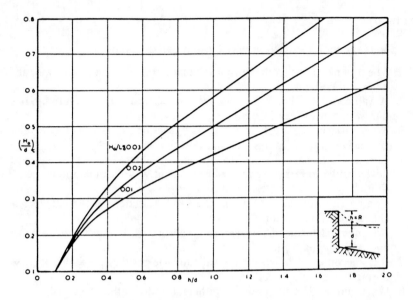

Figure 6. Limiting wave height for no overtopping.

lessened greatly overall. However, this does not preclude the spilling of large volumes where the wave crest meets the wall, but this discharge traverses the length of the dike. Where waves arrive at an angle θ to a seawall, the run-up is reduced by a factor K_θ as given in Table 3 [17]. These tests were for a slope of 1:2, but in the absence of further data they may be applied to other slopes. Such wave obliquity can result in severe scouring of the bed adjacent to a breakwater, as discussed in Volume 2, and hence depths at the toe can vary greatly. This can affect the size of waves impacting on the structure.

Table 3
Values of K_θ for Run-up of Waves Angled θ to Dike Slope of 1:2

H_0/L_0	0.01	0.015	0.02	0.025	0.03	0.04	0.05
$\theta° = 10$	0.97	0.97	0.97	0.97	0.97	0.97	0.97
20	0.94	0.94	0.94	0.94	0.94	0.94	0.94
30	0.90	0.91	0.91	0.90	0.90	0.89	0.88
40	0.88	0.88	0.89	0.87	0.86	0.85	0.84
50	0.80	0.79	0.78	0.75	0.73	0.70	0.65
60	0.77	0.72	0.62	0.54	0.48	0.41	0.34

Summary

The points raised in this section may be summarized as follows:

1. The original erosion will continue after the construction of a seawall and will be expedited by its presence.
2. A wall constructed on a berm leaves insufficient material to form an offshore bar, which can break incoming storm waves.
3. Waves arriving obliquely to a wall will generate short-crested waves that are conducive to scour in front of and downcoast of a wall.
4. Further downcoast of a wall the increased volume of material removed will be deposited to form a shoal before incident waves can continue the littoral drift.
5. Continuation of the wall along the eroded section to the silted area will enhance erosion offshore.
6. Roughness elements on impermeable walls have little effect on wave reflection and run-up on a wall.
7. It is uneconomical to construct walls to a height that precludes overtopping during the life of a structure.
8. Wave run-up depends upon wave height and length, slope of the wall, and depth at the toe.
9. Little difference occurs in wave run-up for monochromatic and spectral waves.
10. Wave overtopping reduces run-up values and depends upon wave characteristics and height of wall above SWL.
11. The run-up and volume of overtopping is increased by wind.

Groins

Introduction

Groins are structures that run normal to the coast and intercept the longshore transport of sediment within the surf zone. They have been used since the last century from the first sighting of the littoral current accompanying great suspension within breaking waves. They purport to interrupt this flow of material and hence retain it on an eroding section of shoreline. It becomes obvious that they are only effective when persistent waves are arriving obliquely to the coast, hence moving sand alongshore. Of course, if this were not the situation then there would not be an erosion problem. It is the fluctuations in supply of drift that cause beaches to recede and require some stabilization measure, of which groins are one of the oldest solutions.

An annotated bibliography has been prepared of papers dealing with groins up to the year 1971 [18]. It contains subject subheadings of beach dynamics, construction methods, groin dimensions, groin types, location, materials, patents, permeability, trade names, and types of investigation. Besides these the presentations consider such items as wave climate, groin orientation and spacing, downcoast erosion, scour at the toe, economics, and aesthetics. Most articles describe some new groin field, generally just after installation, with glowing reports of effectiveness, initially at least. Only a few report on long-term trends and deficiencies. However, it is through learning about the latter that improvements in design or alternative solutions are likely to arise. As Balsillie [19] observes about the bibliography, "It was determined that the majority of articles were introductory in nature, giving in many cases but a cursory glance at groin design and purpose."

The theories behind groin application are discussed, including spacing, length, height, orientation, and permeability. Model experiments involve topics such as groin cross-section, coarseness of sand, coastal profiles, types of wave, and effect of tides. Constructional problems include materials of construction, economics, aesthetics, and environmental issues. However, the effectiveness of groins is discussed first, showing where they serve their purpose and locations where they are likely to fail in their objectives. The reader can then judge as to whether he or she should pursue this revered but ancient mode of beach stabilization.

Governments, down to local authorities, have the task of designing structures to improve or maintain the coastal margin. In this they are helped or thwarted by the plethora of "experts" who have lived near it, or maybe only visited a few times in their lives, but know the simple answers to such complex questions. This is epitomized by Carey [20], who observed, "Small-town and district councils can seldom be induced to look ahead and provide the means of defense against the inevitable forces of attack. When they do so they are often denounced by the indignant ratepayer for the extravagance. I heard a case the other day of a local board which had spent money in building groynes (sic), and now said a sapient ratepayer, 'look at them, sir, they are covered with sand and shingle and completely buried, and our money is wasted.'"

Effectiveness of Groins

During that time of the year when swell waves are constantly arriving from some oblique direction, the littoral drift will accumulate upcoast of a structure placed across the surf zone. The shoreline will build out at an angle until it reaches the tip of the groin. Material will then by-pass this extremity and so feed the downcoast region that has suffered denudation while the upcoast has accreted. In the case of a field of groins it will build up against the second groin and so on along the field. This successive saturation of each compartment takes time, and a large volume of sand is unavailable to the zone downcoast of the last impediment. Hence, the larger the groin field the greater the erosion suffered in this area.

Longshore transport is not only effected in the surf zone, although this ribbon of water experiences the greatest movement of material. Offshore, beyond the breaker zone, shallow-water waves are shearing sediment into suspension and moving it, by mass-transport at the bed, in the direction of wave motion. The slope of the bed exerts its influence under gravity and hence sand particles move seaward, normal to the bed contours, during the trough cycle. In this manner sediment is oscillated in saw-tooth fashion along the coast, without moving laterally, toward or away from the beach. Now, if there is a dearth of material available from upcoast, to

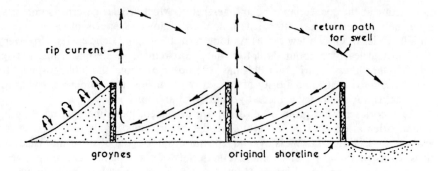

Figure 7. Formation of rip currents by storm waves.

replace that being removed by this longshore component of energy, it will exert its influence not only in the surf zone but also offshore.

Most groins are taken out to the breaker zone of the normal swell built profile, which is the closest it ever gets to the waterline. Outside this limit erosion can still occur, due to the decreased supply of sediment that existed prior to the groins, but nothing has been done by the construction to halt the offshore erosion. This has been observed on the Danish coast, where there are many kilometers of groins each 300 m apart, about which Lehnfelt and Svendsen [21] concluded, "The groins can, under favorable conditions, protect the bed of the sea from erosion as far as their extremities but not much further. Beyond the end of the groin erosion continues and it is evident that after a certain time this erosion will attack the groin and later the land itself."

But even the sediment accumulated between groins is in jeopardy when a cyclone passes along or across the coast, causing storm waves to arrive from a large fan of directions. These are not necessarily related to the swell arrival angle, being generally from the alternate quadrant [8]. Taking a resultant normal to the coast, these storm waves will be more angled to the triangular accumulations of sand than the original shoreline. They will therefore generate a strong littoral drift toward the downcoast side of the groins where a seaward rip-current forms. (See Figure 7). This carries the drift offshore where it is deposited further out to sea than if the original beach was forming an offshore bar. Some of this material will remain there to make up the scouring that has already occurred, as alluded to previously. That which is transported shoreward will form the beach berm much further downcoast than for a normal offshore bar. Thus a field of groins expedites the longshore removal of sediment from where it is required, with little returning to the compartments between groins. This requires them to be refilled in the manner previously discussed.

Suggestions have been made to angle the groin downcoast a little, or add an oblique leg to its toe, in order to protect the heel of the structure and reduce the

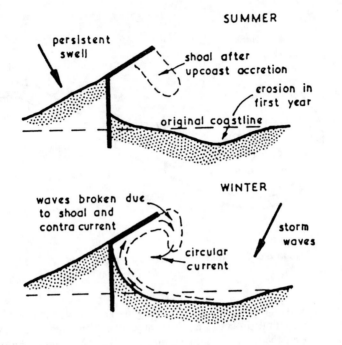

Figure 8. Influence of Y addition to normal groin.

full effect of rip currents [22, 23]. The use of the half Y shape, as illustrated in Figure 8, has the effect of twisting any current into a vortex, causing drift to be deposited closer offshore. The contra current to the incoming storm waves helps in their dissipation and this accretion process. Subsequent swell will sweep this sediment to shore and help maintain material on the leeward side of the groin, so protecting the heel. However, in an excessively erosive situation, even this design feature will not save the structure from being exposed and finally isolated from the shoreline.

Large fluctuations in littoral drift must be accepted as a fact of life. The greatest is of short-term duration, as storm sequences form an offshore bar from the berm, which is then returned to the beach by swell over a matter of days. During this short period, the bulk of littoral drift occurs [1, 2]. Storm wave attack and hence size of the bar is not uniform along the coast so that humps of material move along the coast at frequencies dictated by the number and spacing of storms in the region. Longer term variations in volumes of drift are caused by supply from flooding rivers, construction of marine structures such as breakwaters or groins, and dredging of channels across the continental shelf. All these can decrease the supply to any section of coast or provide a surfeit of sand over short time periods. Any measurements of shoreline fluctuation, by aerial photography or land surveys, will exhibit

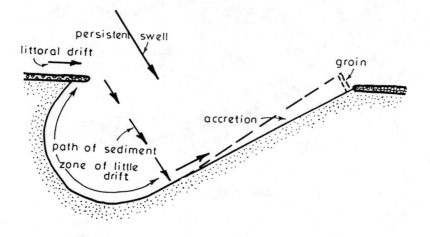

Figure 9. Locations of groins within natural shaped bays.

the excessively dynamic nature of this margin. The presence of groins has little effect on these natural processes as they may suffer complete saturation, with the shoreline beyond their tips, and two years later be left stranded in the sea [24].

As previously noted, groins are unlikely to retain sand where it is required for coastal defense without the presence of strong littoral drift. This is because the sporadic removal offshore of material so collected requires replacement by oblique swell waves. Even when concurrent reclamation is carried out with the installation of a groin field, the situation will become normal within a year, with the sequence as outlined previously. The excess of sand is carried downcoast as an extra large hump. Thus, it can be seen that groins achieve very little in stabilizing a coast in an erosive situation. Although Berg and Watts [25] stated the following over 20 years ago, the points are still relevant today: "Of the numerous types of structures developed for shore protection purposes, the groin is probably the most widely utilized although its functional behavior is perhaps the least understood. Examples may be found where a single groin or groin system achieved its intended purpose, while similar structures in different locations have provided little or no protection. In addition, there are a seemingly endless number of variations in groin designs, some of which have been purported to be the ultimate answer to shore erosion."

There are some locations where groins can be effective and others where they are not. The ubiquity of crenulate-shaped bays is presented in Volume 2 and it is in this context that groin installation should be considered. A bay, as depicted in Figure 9, could have littoral drift still arriving at its upcoast headland. This material does not then move around the complete periphery to arrive at the downcoast limit, but passes across the bay under the action of waves, which do not suffer diffraction. Thus, sediment reaches the bay at some point around the curve and is then transported towards the tangential section, as proven by tracer tests in the prototype [26]. The only longshore movement from the curved segment, including the area of greatest indentation, is that removed as the bay is eroded back to its static equilibrium shape. Any groins placed in this zone to prevent such denudation will fail miserably. However, groins placed on the tangential downcoast beach could accrete long segments of beach as the waves are only slightly angled to this shoreline. This difference in location could explain the conclusion reached by Balsillie and Berg [19]: "There are numerous examples where groins have fulfilled their purposes and as many others which have not, indeed some have actually intensified the problems they were intended to solve."

Theory of Groins

This section could well be commenced with a quotation from Wiegel [27]: "There is an extensive literature on the construction and operation of groin systems, much of which is controversial. Most prototype observations have been made of only the net result, with little or no observations of wave and current conditions associated with the movement of the beach sand. In fact there is little published information on prototype groin usefulness [28]."

Laboratory tests [29] found that groins should extend 40% to the predominant plunger line, presumably for the swell-built beach profile. Further extension resulted in scour downcoast. Other tests [30, 31] showed this distance could be up to 60% of the surf zone.

The spacing of groins has been examined [29, 30] and shown to be preferably 2 to 3 times the groin length. If it is desired to fill each compartment in a groin field to the maximum, the tips of successive groins could be considered control points of headland systems as in Volume 2. The line joining the tips then becomes the control line (see Figure 10). For stability the beach passing through the tip of the downcoast groin should be parallel to the wave crests on the orthogonal normal to them. The depth (d) at such a point should be used to determine d/L_0, where L_0 is the deep-water wavelength, for which the refraction angle is computed from some given deep-water approach direction of persistent swell. A straight wave crest line is then assumed through the tip of the upcoast groin, parallel to the crests in the downcoast region. This is angled β to the control line, as is the downcoast tangent of the beach line as depicted in the inset of Figure 10.

If the groin length (B) is taken to the point of the original shoreline, which is to be maintained, its angle (θ) to the wave crest line is $90° + \beta$. By using either Figure 9 or 10 of "Natural Shaping of Bays" (Volume 2), the ratio of groin length (B) to spacing (D) is equivalent to R/R_0 in the bay situation. These have been computed as reciprocals (or D/B) and graphed against wave obliquity at some reasonable depth beyond the groin tips. It is seen that ratios of 3 to 4 apply to waves angled 30° to 20° to the original shoreline, which is reasonable for depths beyond the breaker line. For example, waves of 9-secs period arriving from 45° to the coast in deep water will have crests angled at 20° in 5-m depth, which requires 4 times the groin length for full saturation to occur. Dunham [32] has suggested the use of

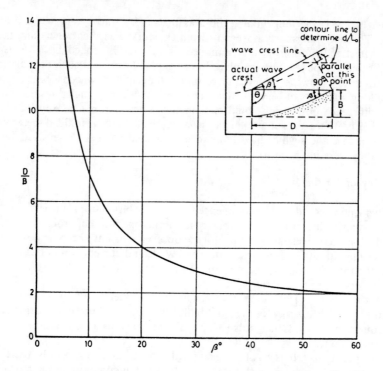

Figure 10. Ratios of groin spacing to groin length for sand saturation between.

very long groins, in order to achieve a segment of the bay in static equilibrium: "For this reason, they have sometimes been labeled 'barrier groins,' but regardless of designation, they are intended to serve as artificial headlands."

The heights of groins need not be much above the beach berm, which is the reach of the waves at high tide. If such structures are to be used for leisure activities, angling, etc. they should be elevated for safety reasons, perhaps with railings.

Orientation of groins can be summed up by the Coastal Engineering Research Center [33]: "Examples may be found of almost every conceivable groin alignment and advantages are claimed by proponents of each type." If angled slightly down-coast, they can provide a little curvature to the beach in the shadow zone and so reduce outflanking of the structure. They may also make it harder for rip currents to be deflected seaward. T or L shaped tips also achieve this but can suffer erosion during storms. If deviation from right angles to the original shoreline is contem-plated, the best orientation is normal to the expected waterline or parallel to ortho-gonals of the most persistent swell waves, as indicated in Figure 10.

Studies of inclination have been presented [34] and the conclusion reached that a downcoast inclination of 70° could be countenanced for wave obliquity of 20°.

From the inset of Figure 10 it is seen that θ is then 140° for $\beta = 30°$, which gives from Figure 9 (Volume 2, "Methods to Mitigate Scour"), D/B = 3.3 (B measured along the groin). If groins were normal to the coast, $\theta = 120°$ for which D/B = 2.95, thus increasing the volume of structures per unit length of shoreline by 12%. However, the inclined groins might need to be taken back to the original shoreline, even though the leeward beach will accrete along a portion of its length, in which case each structure is lengthened some 11%, thus almost balancing the apparent saving in the greater spacing ratio of 3.3.

Permeable groins can comprise piles driven about one diameter apart generally to LWM in an area of large tidal range. When driven over water they become expensive. The most recent discussion of this option by Bakker et al. [35], with five authors, should be considered most important, but a thorough analysis of their model tests and prototype observations is inconclusive. They cited ten locations on the Dutch coast where such pile screens had been installed with a small history of events. The conclusions reached for each are as follows:

Site 1. Artificial changes were too dominant to see the effect of screens.

Site 2. Leeside scour shifted to the end of the new screen system, from down-coast of a previous groin system. The authors believed this proved the efficiency of the screens, even though it was an accretionary situation as exhibited by the large dunes present.

Site 3. Currents were increased seaward and landward of the screens. "A diminution of the erosion in the last decade can be observed; however, long-term fluctuations may have played a role."

Site 4. "These screens and their effects were drastically affected by large-scale automonous morphological developments in this area."

Site 5. Accretion started 5 years before screens were inserted, and large accretion occurred due to closure of an adjacent channel.

Site 6. Long-term erosion was not stopped and the screens were outflanked, with rip currents encouraged by the screens.

Site 7. "Later on, this pile screen project was abandoned."

Site 8. Reeds were added and the beach was reshoveled, but even so landward and seaward erosion occurred.

Site 9. "Rather strong outflanking occurred near the dune foot, probably boosting the dune foot erosion rather than stopping it. For this reason the pile screens were removed in 1980."

Site 10. Erosion stopped between the screens but outflanking occurred.

From the details of each site it is strange that the authors could conclude, "Some of the pile screen projects, which have been implemented since 1965, have been a success, others failed." They admitted that statistical evidence was not forthcoming due to "the background noise." The fluctuations of sand supply, which is a fact of life on the coast, with offshore channels shifting, were not coped with by piles, many of which were washed out. To overcome outflanking they proposed installing piles well into the dunes and there was a need to remove mussels at the outer end. More flexibility was suggested in terms of adding or subtracting units, placing stones between double pile arrays, or beach renourishment. Such ad hoc manipulation does not appear good engineering practice.

Besides low cost, these structures supposedly reduced longshore currents, although laboratory tests indicated that with tidal currents and waves the velocities in the surf zone were enhanced. Only with waves normal to the beach, which is an unrealistic supposition, was this littoral current reduced. It was concluded also that there was "A more gradual velocity gradient and less turbulence near the seaward end (as compared to impermeable groins)." With the latter the shoreline is made more normal to the waves, which reduces the littoral current so that the previous observation is not correct. In fact higher velocities were found both seaward and shoreward of the screens in prototype situations.

Even though one of the expectations was reduction in rip currents, this was listed as a problem to be faced. In experiments longshore velocities seaward of the screens increased to 115% of those without screens, together with an offshore component that could carry sediment seaward. Perhaps the prior conclusion reached [19] is still applicable, namely, "On groin structures utilized today, there is a greater lack of adequate understanding of permeable structures than of any other type of groin design."

Thus from the initial critique of impermeable groins and subsequent discussion of papers presented, plus the presentation of the permeable alternative, some different approach to beach stabilization appears necessary. A conclusion reached by Balsillie and Berg [19] is relevant here: "By the very nature of beaches, that no two are the same, it is erroneous to assure that one specific groin design will provide the answer to all shore erosion problems."

It is not that sometimes a marine structure has not been as effective as desired by the designer, but that the deleterious influences on adjacent shorelines can end up with litigation. Lillevang [36] has discussed this type of responsibility with an introductory remark: "There are more individuals who are certain a groin will be beneficial than there are engineers whose experience tells them that one does not always achieve unmixed blessings when a groin is placed on a coastline."

References

1. Silvester, R., 1984, "Littoral Drift Caused by Storms," *Proceedings Symposium IUTAM on Seabed Mechanics*, pp. 217–222.
2. Silvester, R., 1984, "Fluctuations in Littoral Drift," *Proceedings 19th International Conference Coastal Engineering*, ASCE Vol. II, pp. 1291–1305.
3. Silvester, R., 1972, "Wave Reflection at Seawalls and Breakwaters," *Proceedings Institution of Civil Engineers*, Vol. 51, pp. 123–131.
4. *Shore Protection Planning and Design*, 1966, Technical Report No. 4., U.S. Army Coastal Research Centre, 3rd Edition.
5. Machemehl, J. L. and Herbich, J. B., 1970, *Effects of Slope Roughness on Wave Run-up on Composite Slopes*, Texas A&M University, COE Report No. 29.
6. Van Oorschot, J. N. and D'Angremond, K., 1968, "The Effects of Wave Energy Spectra on Wave Run-up," *Proceedings 11th International Conference Coastal Engineering*, ASCE Vol. II, pp. 888–900.

7. Hunt Jr., I. A., "Design of Seawalls and Breakwaters," *Proceedings Waterway and Harbor Division*, ASCE, Vol. 85 (WW3), pp. 123–152.
8. Silvester, R., 1974, *Coastal Engineering*. Vols. I and II, Elsevier, Amsterdam.
9. Ishihara, T. et al., 1960, "Wave Overtopping on Seawalls," *Proceedings Coastal Engineering in Japan*, Vol. 3, pp. 53–62.
10. Iwagaki, Y. et al., 1965, "Effects of Wave Height and Sea-Water Level on Wave Overtopping and Wave Run-up," *Proceedings Coastal Engineering in Japan*, Vol. 8, pp. 141–151.
11. Saville Jr., T., 1955, *Laboratory Data on Wave Run-up and Overtopping on Shore Structures*, Beach Erosion Board, Technical Memorandum No. 64.
12. Sibul, O. J. and Tickner, E. G., 1956, "*Model Study of Overtopping of Wind-Generated Waves on Levees with Slopes of 1:3 and 1:6*, Beach Erosion Board, Technical Memorandum, No. 80.
13. Kikkawa, H. et al., 1968, "Fundamental Study of Wave Overtopping on Levees," *Proceedings Coastal Engineering in Japan*, Vol. 11, pp. 107–115.
14. Shi-igai H. and Kono, T., 1970, "Analytical Approach on Wave Overtopping on Levees," *Proceedings 12th International Conference Coastal Engineering*, ASCE, Vol. I, pp. 536–574.
15. Tsuruta, S. and Goda, Y., 1968, "Expected Discharge of Irregular Wave Overtopping," *Proceedings 11th International Conference Coastal Engineering*, ASCE, Vol. II, pp. 833–852.
16. Iwagaki, Y. et al., 1966, "On the Effect of Wind on Waves Overtopping on Vertical Seawalls," *Bulletin of Disaster Prevention Research Institute, Kyoto University*, Vol. 16, pp. 11–30.
17. Hosoi, M. and Shuto, N., 1964, "Run-up Height on Single Slope Dike due to Waves Coming Obliquely," *Proceedings Coastal Engineering in Japan*, Vol. 7, pp. 95–99.
18. Balsillie, J. H. and Bruno, R. O., 1972, "*Groins: An Annotated Bibliography*, Coastal Engineering Research Center, U.S. Army Corps of Engineers, Misc. Paper No. 1–72.
19. Balsillie, J. H. and Berg, D. W., 1972, "State of Groin Design and Effectiveness," *Proceedings 13th International Conference Coastal Engineering*, ASCE, Vol. II, pp. 1367–1383.
20. Carey, A.E., 1907, "The Protection of Sea Shores from Erosion." *Journal Society of Arts*, pp. 650–663.
21. Lehnfelt, A. and Svendsen, S. V., 1958, "Thyboroen Channel—Difficult Protection Problem in Denmark," *Ingenioeren*, Vol. 2, pp. 66–74.
22. Berg, D. W. and Watts, G. M., 1967, "Variations in Groin Design," *Journal Waterways and Harbors Division*, ASCE, Vol. 93, No. WW2, pp. 79–100.
23. Petersen, M., "Review of German Experience on Coastal Protection by Groins." *Beach Erosion Board Bulletin*, No. 17, pp. 39–54 (translated by O. W. Kabelae).
24. Riedel, H. P. and Fidge, B. L., 1977, "Beach Changes at Swan Island," *Proceedings 3rd Australian Conference Coastal and Ocean Engineering*, pp. 163–169.
25. Berg, D. W. and Watts, G. M., 1965, "Variations in Groin Design," *Proceedings Coastal Engineering Santa Barbara Specialty Conference*, ASCE, pp. 763–797.
26. Hughs, E. P. C., 1957, "The Investigation and Design for Portland Harbour, Victoria," *Journal Institution of Engineers*, Australia, Vol. 29, pp. 55–68.
27. Wiegel, R. L., 1964, *Oceanographical Engineering*, Prentice Hall Incorporated.
28. Savage, R. P., 1959, *Laboratory Study of the Effect of Groins on the Rate of Littoral Drift*," U.S. Army, Corps of Engineers, Beach Erosion Board, Technical Memorandum, No. 114.
29. Nagai, S., 1956, "Arrangements of Groins on a Sandy Beach," *Journal Waterways and Harbors Division*, ASCE, Vol. 82, No. WW2, Paper No. 1063.
30. Horikawa, K. and Sonu, C., 1958, "An Experimental Study on the Effect of Coastal Groins," *Coastal Engineering in Japan*, Vol. 1, pp. 59–74.

31. Nagai, S. and Kubo, H., 1958, "Motion of Sand Particles between Groins," *Journal Waterways and Harbors Division*, ASCE, Vol. 84, No. WW5, Paper No. 1876.

32. Dunham, J. W., 1965, "Use of Long Groins as Artificial Headlands," *Proceedings Coastal Engineering Santa Barbara Specialty Conference*, ASCE, 1965, pp. 755–762.

33. *Shore Protection Manual*, 1984, Coastal Engineering Research Center, U.S. Corps of Engineers.

34. Barcelo, J. P., 1970, "Experimental Study of the Hydraulic Behaviour of Inclined Groyne Systems." *Proceedings 12th International Conference Coastal Engineering*, ASCE, Vol. II, pp. 1021–1040.

35. Bakker, W. T. et al., 1984, "Permeable Groynes: Experiments and Practice in the Netherlands." *Proceedings 19th International Conference Coastal Engineering*, ASCE, Vol. II, pp. 2026–2041.

36. Lillevang, O. J., 1965, "Groins and Effects—Minimizing Liabilities," *Proceedings Coastal Engineering Santa Barbara Specialty Conference*, ASCE, 1965, pp. 749–754.

CHAPTER 24

WAVE AND ICE FORCES ON ARTIFICIAL ISLANDS AND ARCTIC STRUCTURES

Jerry L. Machemehl

Associate Professor of Ocean and Civil Engineering
Texas A&M University
College Station, Texas, U.S.A.

CONTENTS

Introduction

The search for oil and gas in the Alaskan and Canadian Beaufort Sea has led to an increased interest in the powerful natural forces of the Arctic offshore. Arctic offshore structures are being designed for heavily ice-covered basins offshore Alaska and Canada. These structures are designed for loading generated by waves and perennial ice features. The global ice forces/loads govern the overall structural geometry and dimensions as well as the foundation design.

The Arctic offshore is almost completely ice covered for over nine months of the year, with varying degrees of ice movement and multi-year ice content. Multi-year ice may also invade during the open water period.

The Arctic engineer/design engineer must consider various ice events that may occur on the Arctic structure. Offshore Arctic ice features include first year sea ice, multi-year floes, pressure ridges, ice islands, and broken ice. These ice features occur in the landfast ice, shear zone, or pack ice. The severest impact event is created by a large multi-year floe. This event occurs in the pack ice at any time, and in the land-fast area during the open water season.

Forces on an Arctic structure are controlled by either the driving mechanism (i.e., wind and water currents) or the failure mechanism in the ice. Some ice failure mechanisms that have been considered are crushing, bending, buckling, splitting, and pressure ridge formation. The force level in an ice feature depends on the continuity, uniformity and strength of the ice as well as on the wind and current conditions.

Arctic Structures

Arctic structures can be classified as either narrow or wide as shown in Table 1. A narrow structure is defined in terms of the ice failure zone. Only one zone of ice failure will occur across the width of the narrow structure. Examples of narrow

Table 1
Application of Wave and Ice Loads for Structure Types in the
Artic Offshore Environment

Wave or Ice Features and Load Issues	Structure Types				
	Narrow			Wide	
	Slope-Sided or Conical	Vertical Sided	Multi-Legged	Slope-Sided	Vertical Sided
Local Wave Pressure					
Non-breaking	N.A.	A	A	N.A.	A
Breaking	A	A	A	AB	A
Ice Sheet or Floe					
Crushing	N.A.	A	A	AB	A
Vertical Bending	A	N.A.	N.A.	AB	N.A.
Buckling	A	A	A	AB	A
First-Year Ridges	A	A	A	A	A
Rubble	A	A	A	A	A
Multi-Year Floe	A	A	N.A.	A	A
Multi-Year Ridges	A	A	N.A.	A	A
Local Ice Pressure	A	A	A	A	A

Notes: A = The wave or ice load issue is applicable to the structure type. N.A. = The wave or ice load/ice feature is not applicable to the structure type. AB = Earth fill islands may behave as a sloping structure. Loads on islands may be calculated assuming vertical sides.

structures include:

1.
   width less than two/three times the thickness of the maximum expected ice feature (e.g., Cook Inlet structure/platform).
2. Vertical multi-leg structure (or nearly vertically-sided structure (with legs sufficiently spaced that independent zones of ice failure are experienced at each leg [34].
3. Sloping or conical structures designed to cause ice features to fail in bending (either upward or downward).

A wide structure is defined in terms of one or more failure zones. More than one zone of ice failure may occur across the width of the structure. Examples of wide structures include:

1. Slope-sided, large-diameter artificial island (e.g., BF-37 Island) as shown in Figure 1.
2. Vertically-sided, large-diameter caisson structure (e.g., Concrete Island Drilling System and Esso Steel Caisson Retained Island) as shown in Figures 2 and 3.

Figure 1. Arctic offshore exploratory drilling island.

Figure 2. Concrete island drilling system (CIDS) in the Alaskan Beaufort Sea.

Figure 3. Arctic offshore ice (Note: multi-year floe in center front.)

Environment

Open Water

The Alaskan and Canadian Beaufort Seas experience approximately 90 days of open water. Waves may be generated during late summer storms. Wave information for offshore Alaska areas for normal sea states can be found in the Climatic Atlas [4]. The sea states are limited by the presence of ice.

Ice-Covered Seas

Ice coverage offshore Canada and Alaska has been documented by Potocsky [58], Webster [92, 93], and La Belle, et al. [44].

Ice Zonation

The ice over the continental shelf of the southern Beaufort Sea can be divided into three zones: landfast ice zone, shear ice zone, and polar pack ice zone [38].

Landfast Ice Zone. The term fast ice refers to the ice nearshore that is relatively immobile for some unspecified time period during the winter. Fast ice generally consists mostly of seasonal ice grown in place, undergoes little deformation, and therefore is relatively smooth. The landfast ice may also contain pressure ridges, shear ridges, and hummock fields, which form mainly in early winter when new ice is thin. Tension and shearing also occur in the landfast zone, which results in cracks, leads, and dislocation of the various ice features. The outer boundary of the landfast ice zone is marked by a change from the relatively underformed smooth ice inshore to highly deformed ice offshore.

Shear Ice Zone. The term shear ice refers to the intensely deformed ice between the relatively immobile landfast ice zone and the mobile pack ice zone. The zone is dominated by shear ridges formed by the rubbing of the pack ice with the landfast ice. The shearing in the ice occurs at or near the offshore face of the features. Many of the large shear ridges are grounded, which helps to keep the landfast ice immobile. The inner 3.1 mi (5 km) of the shear zone contains the highest shear ridges.

Pack Ice Zone. The term pack ice refers to the permanent ice pack of the North Pole. The ice is mostly multi-year ice with comparatively low salinity. The pack ice has a westward movement pattern, which is a part of the general movement pattern called the Arctic Gyre. Movement of the pack ice is on the order of several miles per day near the edge of the pack.

Ice Movements

The Arctic ice pack is in constant motion. Large-scale ice movements are caused by major current systems (e.g., the Beaufort Gyre in the Arctic Ocean). Medium-scale movements are caused by storm winds, waves, and currents, while small-scale movements are associated with thermal changes in the pack. The winds and currents are, however, the dominant factors influencing motion in the ice field. Thorndike and Cheung [79], Thorndike and Colony [80], McNutt [46] and Thomas and Pritchard [78] have presented data on pack and landfast ice movement in the Beaufort, Chukchi and Bering Seas.

Winter Ice Movement. The winter ice movement in the nearshore area of the Beaufort Sea consists of a very slow and variable creep movement throughout the winter, superposed with several large and more sudden ice-movement "events," which are related to winter storms. Ice movements within the nearshore area depend on the site (i.e., the degree of exposure). The geography and environmental conditions generalized ice movements based on the degree of exposure or protection are shown in Tables 2 and 3 for the Beaufort Sea.

Table 2
Generalized Ice Movement for Beaufort Sea

Degree of Exposure	Ice Movement (Median) V_{med}		Ice Movement (Maximum) V_{max}		Maximum Excursion		Maximum Daily Movement Frequency For Jan.–May			
	(ft/hr)	(m/hr)	(ft/hr)	(m/hr)	(ft/mo)	(m/mo)	1.0 ft 0.3 m	≥5.0 ft ≥1.5 m	≥10.0 ft ≥3.0 m	≥100.0 ft ≥30.5 m
Very exposed	0.20	0.060	170.0	51.8	240.0	73.2	0.50	0.25	0.15	0.08
Exposed	0.10	0.030	50.0	15.2	100.0	30.5	0.30	0.15	0.08	0.04
Protected	0.02	0.006	1.5	1.5	10.0	3.1	0.40	0.05	0.00	0.00
Very protected	0.01	0.003	0.2	0.1	1.0	0.3	0.00	—	—	—

Table 3
Generalized Ice Movement Rates

Ice Movement Rates	Units	Beaufort Sea		Cook Inlet	Chukchi Sea		Navarin Basin	Norton Sound	St. George Basin
		Nearshore <60 ft <18 m	Offshore >60 ft >18 m		Northern	Southern			
Summer	kts per day	2–3	2–3	N/A	2–3	N/A	N/A	N/A	N/A
Freezeup/Breakup	kts per day	1–2	1–2	6–7	1–2	1–2	2–3	1–2	N/A
Midwinter	kts per day	0.01–0.02	0.2–0.6	6–7	0.8–1.0	0.8–1.0	2–3	1–2	2–3

Table 4
Ice Feature Statistics

Ice Movement Rates	Units	Beaufort Sea Nearshore <60 ft <18 m	Beaufort Sea Offshore >60 ft >18 m	Cook Inlet	Chukchi Sea Northern	Chukchi Sea Southern	Navarin Basin	Norton Sound	St. George Basin
Sheet Ice Thickness	ft	6–7	6–7	2–3	6–7	4–5	3–4	3–4	1–2
	m	1.8–2.1	1.8–2.1	0.6–0.9	1.8–2.1	1.2–1.5	0.9–1.2	0.9–1.2	–0.6
Rafted Ice Thickness	ft	15–20	20–25	4–5	15–20	15–20	10–20	12–20	8–15
	m	4.6–6.1	6.1–7.6	1.2–1.5	4.6–6.1	4.6–6.1	3.0–6.1	3.7–6.1	2.4–4.6
Multi-Year Floe Thickness	ft	25–30	25–30	N/A	25–30	15–20	N/A	N/A	N/A
	m	7.6–9.1	7.6–9.1	N/A	7.6–9.1	4.6–6.1	N/A	N/A	N/A
First-Year Ridge Thickness (Floating)	ft	30–75	100–140	10–12	100–140	80–120	80–100	30–50	70–90
	m	9.1–22.9	30.5–42.7	3.0–3.7	30.5–42.7	24.4–36.6	24.4–30.5	9.1–15.2	21.3–27.4
Multi-Year Ridge Thickness	ft	30–75	70–80	N/A	70–80	N/A	N/A	N/A	N/A
	m	9.1–22.9	21.3–24.4	N/A	21.3–24.4	N/A	N/A	N/A	N/A
Multi-Year Floe Diameter	mi	0.6	1–3	N/A	1–3	1–3	N/A	N/A	N/A
	km	1.0	1.6–4.8	N/A	1.6–4.8	1.6–4.8	N/A	N/A	N/A

Notes: "Ridge" thickness inclues the sail height and keel depth.

Summer Ice Movement. The summer ice movement in the nearshore area of the Beaufort Sea is very dynamic. Large ice movements are caused by storm winds and waves.

Ice Morphology

Sheet Ice. Ice occurs annually in the Alaskan Seas (i.e., Beaufort, Chukchi and Bering Seas). The thicknesses of the fast sheet ice (see Table 4) along the Alaskan coast have been documented by Bilello [7].

Rafted Ice. Rafting occurs when an ice sheet overrides and adjacent ice sheet. Rafted ice may be two or more ice sheets thick. The rafted sheets tend to bond together. Thicknesses and distribution of rafted ice (see Table 4) have been reported by Voelker, et al. [88].

First-Year Ridges. Ice sheets may fail by crushing, flexure, or buckling with resulting accumulations of ice blocks. The accumulated ice blocks form a first-year ridge with a sail of loosely consolidated blocks and a keel composed of both consolidated and unconsolidated blocks. Ridges normally form in early winter up to the middle of December. During the winter months, the ice has reached its maximum thickness and few ridges are formed (See Table 4). Activity increases again as summer breakup approaches. Martin and Bauer [47], Hibler [28], Tucker and Govoni [81] have compiled data on first-year ridges (i.e., cross section and frequencies) in the Beaufort and Bering Seas. Kreider and Thro [42] found the number of ridges in the Beaufort Sea varied from 7.7 to 13.9 ridges per mile. Ridge heights ranged from 4.6 to 4.9 ft (1.4 to 1.5 m). A 50-year frequency ridge was estimated to have a height of 12 ft (3.7 m). A ridge sail height-to-keel depth ratio of 1:4.5 has been reported by Hibler [28] for the Beaufort Sea. Consolidated ridge keels appear limited to 8–12 ft (2.4 to 3.7 m) below sea level in the Beaufort Sea. A sail height-to-unconsolidated keel depth of 1:3.13 have been reported by Voelker, et al. [88] for the Bering Sea.

Rubble Fields. These fields are areas of floating, deformed, usually first-year ice. Most rubble fields are created by compressional forces, which make the ice surface highly irregular. These rubble fields can form whenever sea ice is in motion. Rubble fields are frequently observed in the Beaufort Sea in the 30–60 ft (9.1–18.3 m) water depth range and along the shoal areas of the Chukchi and Bering Seas.

Multi-Year Ridges. These are pressure ridges that have survived two or more summer melt seasons (see Figure 4). They are commonly rounded and less steep than first-year ridges and are normally embedded in multi-year ice floes. Properties and cross sections of multi-year ridges have been investigated by Kovacs et al. [41], Hnatiuk, et al. [29] and Wright et al. [101]. Wright et al. [101] investigated fifteen multi-year ridges or ridge fragments in the Canadian Beaufort Sea. They found ridge thicknesses (see Table 4) ranging from 31.5 ft (9.6 m) to 15.7 ft (4.8 m). Kovacs [39, 40] and Wright et al. [101] found a fairly constant relationship between sail

Figure 4. Steel caisson-retained island (CRI) in the Canadian Beaufort Sea.

height and keel depth of multi-year ridges. They found the ridge sail-height to keel-depth ratio to be 1.0 to 3.3.

Kovacs [40] found the multi-year ridges in the Beaufort Sea were consolidated. The interblock voids were filled with fresh water from melted snow or ice from the summer melt season. Kovacs [40] found a mean brine free density of about 0.84 mg/m³. The apparent unconfined compressive strength was 1,016 to 1,161 psi (7 to 8 MPa) at −10°C.

Richter and Cox [63] conducted a series of uniaxial constant-strain-rate tests on sea ice samples obtained from Beaufort Sea ridges. The ice samples were loaded both parallel and perpendicular to the crystal axes. The strength ranged from 168 psi (1.16 MPa) to 1,090 psi (7.52 MPa) at a 10^{-5} sec^{-1} strain rate to 346 psi (2.39 MPa) to 1,580 psi (10.90 MPa) at a strain rate of 10^{-3} sec^{-1}. The ice strength decreased as the porosity increased. The salinity of the multi-year ridges averaged 2 ppt.

Ice Islands. These islands are tabular icebergs that have calved off the ice shelves of Ellesmere Island, Canada. Jeffries, et al. [31] has documented the frequency, size, and population of ice islands in the Beaufort Sea. Ice islands occasionally ground in 60–80 ft (18.3–24.4 m) water depths offshore Alaska.

Physical and Mechanical Properties

Physical Properties

Sea ice is a crystalline material. Its properties depend on the size and orientation of the crystals and its temperature, salinity, density, and impurities [94].

Crystal Structure. Sea ice grows as a sheet. The sheet is composed of columnar large-grained crystals. Impurities (e.g., sediments) can promote "seeding," which forms small granular ice crystals. A preferred crystal orientation occurs where ice is protected from movement. Crystal sizes generally increase as ice thickness increases.

Temperature. The temperature of sea ice is controlled primarily by air temperature, wind speed, and snow cover (i.e., snow cover has an insulating effect). The temperature gradient through first-year sheet ice and multi-year floes may be assumed to be linear ranging between the freezing point of seawater of 28.8°F (-1.8°C) at the lower surface and the average daily air temperature at the upper surface.

Salinity. Salt entrapped in sea ice is concentrated in small liquid brine pockets between ice crystals. First-year ice salinities normally range from 3 to 6 parts per thousand [13]. The salinity of multi-year ice is considerably lower, usually ranging from 1 to 2 parts per thousand [15]. Young sea ice may have salinity of 9 to 11 parts per thousand [47].

Brine Volume. The strength and elastic properties of sea ice are functions of its brine volume, μ_b which is related to the ice salinity and temperature.

First-Year Sea Ice. An empirical relationship of brine volume for first-year sea ice densities has been proposed by Frankenstein and Garner [23]:

$$\mu_b = S(0.532 - 49.185/T)$$
$$v_b = \mu_b \times 10^{-3} \tag{1}$$

where   S = salinity (ppt)
        T = ice temperature (°C)
        μ_b = brine volume (ppt)
        v_b = nondimensional brine volume

Multi-year sea ice: An empirical relationship of brine volume for multi-year sea ice or ice containing entrapped air or sand salts has been proposed by Cox and Weeks [14].

Impurities. As first-year sea ice melts, impurities, such as brine, are expelled through drainage channels creating voids that may weaken the ice. Impurities such as sediment, may strengthen the ice by initiating the growth of small, granular ice crystals.

Mechanical Properties

The mechanical properties of sea ice are dependent on many factors, including its crystalline structure, brine volume, temperature, and strain rate. Mechanical properties include ice strength (compressive, tensile, flexural, etc.).

Compressive Strength. The unconfined compressive (crushing) strength of sea ice is a complicated function of temperature, brine volume, crystal type, geometry and strain rate (i.e., compressive strength of sea ice is extremely sensitive to strain rate).

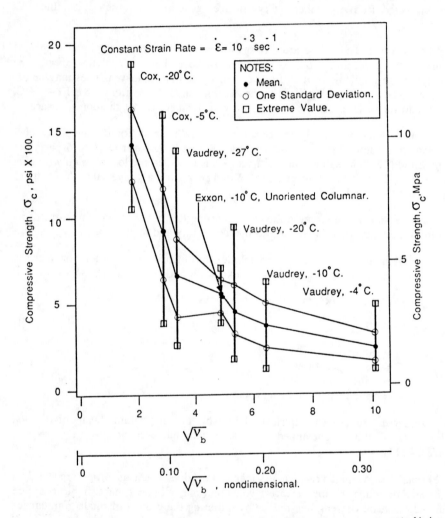

Figure 5. Sea ice horizontal unconfined compressive strength versus square root of brine volume [83].

Small Scale/Laboratory Tests. Numerous investigations [11, 15, 22, 56, 72, 84] have conducted small-scale laboratory tests. Unconfined compressive strength data are presented as a function of brine volume as shown in Figure 5 for a constant strain rate of 10^{-3} sec^{-1} and as a function of strain rate as shown in Figure 6, Wang [91], Bohon and Weingarten [8], and Sanderson [70] present different results on the effect of strain rate on compressive strength for rates above 10^{-3} sec^{-1}.

Large-Scale/Field Data. Such field tests have been conducted by Croasdale [16, 17], who was the first to measure the crushing strength of ice in the field. Croasdale measured ice pressures from 440 to 890 psi (3.0 to 6.1 MPa). (Note: The ice was essentially fresh i.e., salinity = 0.8 to 3.3 ppt; temp. = $-10°$F).

Tensile Strength. The uniaxial tensile strength of sea ice has been found to vary with salinity, temperature, sample orientation, and to a lesser extent, strain-rate. Generally, the tensile strength of a vertical sample along the grain is two or three

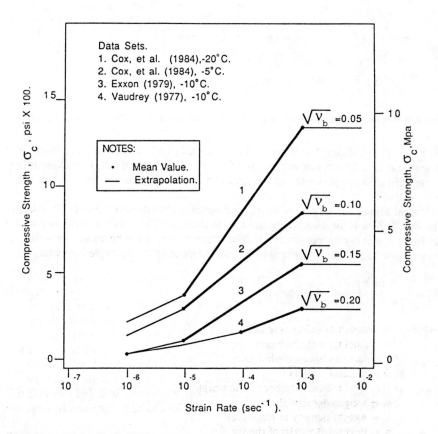

Figure 6. Sea ice horizontal unconfined compressive strength versus strain rate [83].

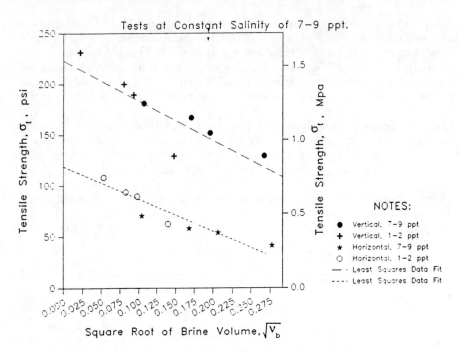

Figure 7. Sea ice tensile strength as a function of the square root of brine volume [19].

times that of a horizontal sample across the grain. The uniaxial tensile strength of a horizontal sample of columnar ice varies from 60 to 150 psi (0.4 to 1.0 MPa). Tensile strength data are presented as a function of brine volume as shown in Figure 7.

Flexural Strength. Flexural strength represents the tensile strength of the ice, as determined from beam bending tests with the elastic beam theory. Two types of flexural tests have been commonly used: simply supported beam and in-situ cantilever beam. The flexural strength can be determined from simple beam tests:

$$\sigma_f = \left[\frac{6}{Dh^2} \frac{P\ell}{4} \left(\frac{\rho_w - \rho_i}{8} \right) gbh\ell^2 \right] \tag{2}$$

where b = width of the simple beam
     h = thickness of the beam
     ℓ = length of the simple beam
     D = flexural rigidity
     P = load required to break the beam
     ρ_i = weight density of the ice
     ρ_w = weight density of the water
     σ_f = flexural strength of the ice

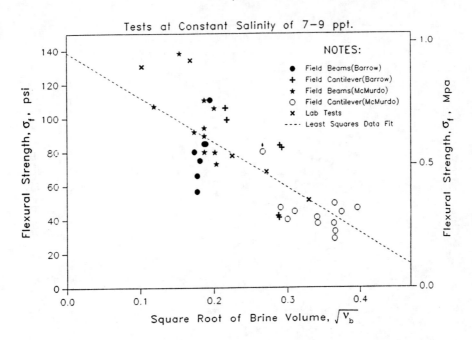

Figure 8. Ice flexural strength as a function of the square root of brine volume [84].

Dykins [19] and Vaudrey [84] determined flexural strength from large-scale field tests. They related flexural strength to brine volume as shown in Figure 8.

Shear Strength. The shear strength of sea ice has been found to vary with temperature and brine volume. Shear strength has been investigated by Butkovitch [10], Pounder and Little [59], Paige and Lee [55] and Dykins [19]:

• Butkovitch [10] conducted tests with a double shear device. The average shear strength was 233.0 psi (1.6 MPa) in the temperature range of −5 to −7°C and 334.0 psi (2.3 MPa) in the range of −10 to −13°C. The salinity of the ice was about 6%.
• Pounder and Little [59] carried out single direct shear tests on sea ice of various temperatures and grain structure. They obtained strengths in the range of 2.9 to 145.0 psi (0.02 to 1.0 MPa).
• Paige and Lee [55] carried out tests on specimens made from cores of natural sea ice. The shear strengths were in the range of 72.6 to 174.1 psi (0.5 to 1.2 MPa) with a significant dependence on brine volume.
• Dykins [19] used laboratory grown columnar-grained saline ice and obtained strengths in the range of 14.5 to 36.3 psi (0.1 to 0.25 MPa).

The shear strength of sea ice as a function of brine volume is shown in Figure 9.

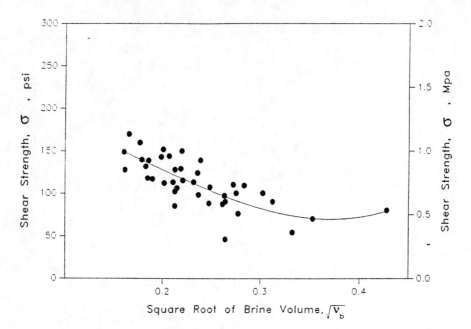

Figure 9. Sea ice shear strength as a function of the square root of brine volume [55].

Adfreeze Strength. The strength of the bond between ice and structure (i.e., ad-freeze strength) is important when predicting the magnitude of breakout loads on structures. Adfreeze strengths ranging from 30 to 120 psi (0.2 to 0.8 MPa) have been cited for uncoated steel and concrete structures [12, 54, 66, 67].

Apparent Elastic Modulus: The apparent elastic modulus of sea ice depends on the brine volume, temperature, and loading rate as well as direction of loading. Values for elastic modulus have been obtained from static measurements, but these are difficult to interpret because of the viscoelastic behavior of sea ice. Values of apparent elastic modulus as a function of brine volume are shown in Figure 10. Equation 3 has been used to determine the elastic modulus for a free floating ice sheet:

$$E = \frac{12\rho_w g(1 - v^2)\ell_c^{\,4}}{t^3} \tag{3}$$

where
t = ice thickness
ℓ_c = characteristic length
E = Young's/elastic modulus
$\rho_w g$ = weight density of sea water
v = Poisson's ratio

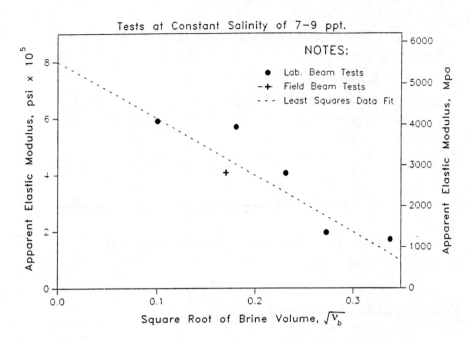

Figure 10. Apparent modulus of elasticity of sea ice as a function of the square root of brine volume [84].

Poisson's Ratio. For sea ice Poisson's ratio approaches 0.5 for small strain-rates. Poisson's ratio decreases to 0.35 for high strain-rates. For most engineering purposes, however, Poisson's ratio can probably be taken to be 0.3 to 0.4.

Wave Load Predictions

Wave Pressure Phenomena

The magnitude of the wave pressure against a wall depends on the wave conditions at the wall. The wave pressure varies from standing wave pressure to impulsive breaking wave pressure.

Wave Reflection

The wave conditions near a vertical wall are shown in Figure 11. The wave height existing at a vertical wall is the sum of the incident wave height, H_i and the reflected wave height, H_r:

$$H_w = (1 + C_r)H_i \tag{4}$$

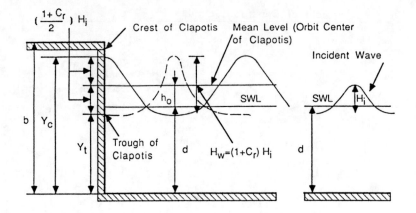

Figure 11. Definition sketch for nonbreaking waves [75].

where C_r = coefficient of wave reflection
H_i = incident wave height
H_r = reflected wave height
H_w = wave height at the vertical wall

The height of the standing wave for perfect reflection is given by Equations 5 and 6.

Standing wave crest on the wall:

$$y_c = d + h_0 + \left(\frac{1 + C_r}{2}\right)H_i \tag{5}$$

Standing wave trough on the wall:

$$y_t = d + h_0 - \left(\frac{1 + C_r}{2}\right)H_i \tag{6}$$

where C_r = coefficient of wave reflection
H_i = incident wave height
d = depth from still water level
h_0 = height of clapotis orbit center above the still water level
y_c = depth from standing wave crest
y_t = depth from standing wave trough

Pressure distributions of the crest and trough of a standing wave are shown in Figure 12.

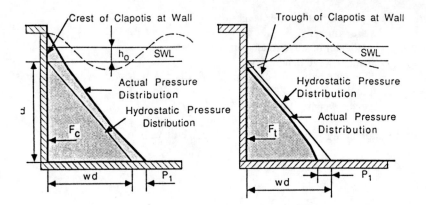

Figure 12. Pressure distributions for nonbreaking waves [75].

Nonbreaking Wave Forces on Vertical Walls

Static and dynamic pressures result from nonbreaking waves on a vertical wall. The static pressure is due to the water surface elevation, and the dynamic pressure is due to the collision between water particles and the vertical wall. Pressures on vertical walls due to nonbreaking waves have been studied by Sainflou [68], Rundgren [65], and Kamel [33]. Gourret [26], Miche [48], [68], Bièsel [6], Rundgren [65], Kishi [36], Tadjbakhsh and Keller [76] used second-order approximation. The wave pressure to the first order of approximation is

$$\frac{P}{\gamma} = h_0 + H_i \frac{\sinh(kh_0)}{\sinh(kd)\cosh(kd)} \sin \sigma t \sin kx_0 \tag{7}$$

where h_0 = height of standing wave orbit center above the still-water level
k = wave number
d = depth from still water level
x_0 = horizontal distance
t = time
H_i = incident wave height
P = wave pressure
γ = specific weight of fluid
σ = wave angular frequency

Pressure distributions of the crest and trough of a standing wave at a vertical wall are shown in Figure 12.

$$P_1 = \left(\frac{1 + C_r}{2}\right) \frac{\gamma H_i}{\cosh(kd)} \tag{8}$$

where   d = depth from still water level
     k = wave number
     C_r = coefficient of wave reflection
     H_i = incident wave height
     P_1 = difference between actual pressure distribution and hydrostatic pressure distribution
     γ = specific weight of fluid

The total nonbreaking wave force on a wall per unit wall length is

$$F_t = \frac{\gamma d^2}{2} + F_w \tag{9}$$

where   d = depth from still water level
     F_t = total wave force
     F_w = wave force
     γ = specific weight of fluid

Breaking Wave Forces on Vertical Walls

Waves breaking on structures are known to cause impact pressures of short duration, known as shock pressures, followed by secondary pressures of less intensity and longer duration. The phenomenon of shock pressure according to Bagnold [5] is caused by an adiabatic compression of air enclosed between the front face of a breaking wave and a vertical wall. The phenomenon of shock pressures has been studied in the laboratory by Bagnold [5], Denny [18], Ross [64], Carr [13], Leendertse [45], Nagai [52, 53], Kamel [33], Weggel [97], Weggel and Maxwell [95, 96], Rundgren [65], and Minikin [50, 51].

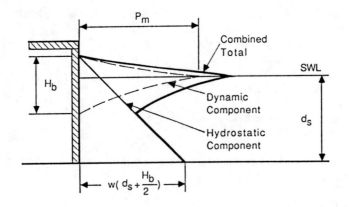

Figure 13. Minikin wave pressure diagram [51].

Minikin [50, 51] combined shock-pressure results with his own observations and developed an empirical equation for the maximum dynamic pressure:

$$\frac{P_m}{\gamma} = 101(d_s + D)\frac{d_w H_b}{DLD} \tag{10}$$

where
d_s = water depth at toe of wall
d_w = water depth one wavelength in front of the wall
H_b = breaker height
L_D = wave length in water depth D
P_m = maximum dynamic pressure
γ = specific weight of fluid

The distribution of dynamic pressure is shown in Figure 13. The pressure decreases parabolically from P_m at the SWL to zero at a distance of $H_b/2$ as shown in Figure 13. The force represented by the area under dynamic pressure distribution is given by

$$F_m = \frac{P_m H_b}{3} \tag{11}$$

where
F_m = force resulting from the dynamic component of pressure
H_b = breaker height
P_m = maximum dynamic pressure

The forces resulting from the hydrostatic pressure must be added to the dynamic force. The total breaking wave force on a wall per unit wall length is

$$F_t = F_m + \gamma \frac{\left(d_s + \dfrac{H_b}{2}\right)^2}{2} \tag{12}$$

where
d_s = water depth at toe of wall
F_m = force resulting from the dynamic component of pressure
F_t = total force
H_b = breaker height
γ = specific weight of fluid

Ice Load Predictions

Ice loads on structures consist of both global and local loads. The magnitude of the load depends on:

1. The geometry of the ice feature,
2. The physical and mechanical properties of the ice feature.
3. The velocity of the ice feature.

4. The environmental forces available to drive the feature.
5. The failure mode in the ice feature or in the surrounding ice sheet.
6. The non-simultaneous failure of the ice.
7. Simultaneous occurrence of more than one failure mode.
8. Friction between the structure and ice.
9. The inertial effects in both the ice and the structure.
10. The compliance of the structure.

Ice loads may be limited by ice strength, momentum, and driving force. Winkler and Reese [99] have proposed a method for evaluating structural loads considering both limitations in ice strength and in driving force.

Loads Limited by Ice Strength

Sheet or Floe Crushing

Empirical Method. The horizontal force exerted by sheet or floe crushing against a structure may be calculated as [37].

$$F = If_c\sigma_xDt \tag{13}$$

where f_c = contact factor
t = ice thickness
D = diameter or width of the structure (at the line of ice contact)
F = horizontal ice force
I = indentation factor
σ_x = unconfined compressive strength of the ice

in which $If_c\sigma_x$ is the average ice pressure and Dt is the exposed area of the structure.

Indentation Factor. The effect of the ice geometry on the failure mechanism is expressed through the indentation factor, I. The indentation factor is a function of the constitutive properties of the ice as well as its geometry. Indentation factors have been developed from plasticity analysis by assuming ductile behavior of the ice [61, 90]. Laboratory data analyzed in these studies have verified factors derived from plasticity analyses in which measured indentation pressure divided by calculated indentation factors agree with ice strength data over a range of strain rates. An indentation factor of 1.4 has been proposed for large aspect ratios (i.e., structure diameter to sheet ice thickness ratio) based on triaxial test data for granular freshwater ice. For granular sea ice, Exxon [22] proposed an indentation factor of 1.2 for a large aspect ratio. An example of indentation factors for laboratory grown columnar freshwater ice tend toward 3.0 for large aspect ratios. For a half space consisting of a Von Mises material, this factor will vary between 2.54 and 3.00.

Contact Factor. The contact factor is a reduction factor to allow for the fact that failure occurs in a brittle, nonsimultaneous mode over the loaded area of the ice. The contact factor can be expected to vary as a function of strain rate [49]. For the case of cylindrical indenters, Michel and Toussaint [49] suggested a value of 0.3 at the transition strain rate ($\dot{\epsilon} = 10^{-3} \sec^{-1}$).

Unconfined Compressive Strength of Sea Ice. The unconfined compressive strength of sea ice is extremely sensitive to strain rate, which is based on the instantaneous velocity of the ice cover. Strain rate data have been evaluated from field measurements at Tarsiut Island in 1982 [70], and Adams Island in 1982 and 1983 [24]. Exxon [22] has suggested using Equation 14 to calculate strain rate for large diameter structures (i.e., artificial islands):

$$\dot{\epsilon} = V/2D \tag{14}$$

where D = diameter
V = instantaneous velocity (velocity of the ice)
$\dot{\epsilon}$ = strain rate

Reference Stress Method. Pointer et al. [57] developed and applied the reference stress method to ice crushing. Ice loads calculated by the reference stress method are based on an analysis that combines theoretical results from linear elasticity or linear viscoelasticity and perfect plasticity to approximate power-law creep behavior. The steady state (secondary creep) load is then given by

$$P = \phi \, Dt \, F_\sigma \left[\frac{U/D}{\phi\psi} \right] \tag{15}$$

where   t = ice thickness
D = contact width (diameter)
$F_\sigma(X)$ = uniaxial stress corresponding to a uniaxial strain rate (X)
P = total ice load
U = ice velocity
ϕ, ψ = coefficients

Condition	ϕ	ψ
Plane strain (D/t 0)	$(\pi + 2)/\sqrt{3} = 2.986$	0.445
Intermediate D/t; free slip between ice and structure	$\text{Min} \begin{cases} 2.986 \\ (2/\sqrt{3})(1 + 1/4\sqrt{2}\,t/D) \end{cases}$	Between 0.445 and 0.385
Intermediate D/t; no slip between ice	$\text{Min} \begin{array}{l} 2.986 \\ (2/\sqrt{3})(1.5 + 1/4\sqrt{2}\,t/D) \\ (2/\sqrt{3})(1 + 1/2\sqrt{2}\left(\dfrac{t}{D}\right)^{1/2} + 1/4(t/D)) \end{array}$	
Plane stress (D/t → ∞)	$2/\sqrt{3} = 1.154$	0.385

$$\tag{16}$$

The coefficients are functions of the crystalline structure of the ice and the direction of the radial crack forming in the ice at the time of failure. A further discussion of the reference stress method can be found in Sanderson [70] and Walden et al. [89].

Cutoff Stress Method. This method was developed and applied to ice crushing by Walden et al. [89]. The method recognizes that a maximum value of ice strength exists and that it is associated with a change in failure mode from ductile to brittle. The cutoff stress method therefore determines the governing ice load rather than the movement-rate-dependent creep solutions specified by the reference stress method. The global ice load exerted on a structure by a sheet of columnar ice is given by

$$P = \sigma_{oc} \, Dt\left[1 - \sqrt{\frac{v}{v_0}}\right] \tag{17}$$

where t = ice thickness
  D = contact width (diameter)
  P = total ice load
  v = brine volume
  v_0 = reference brine volume
  σ_{oc} = critical normalized columnar ice stress

The critical normalized columnar ice stress represents the peak stress (normalized to zero brine volume) developed by a columnar ice sheet at the scale of an Arctic structure (i.e., contact area of 1,000 to 5,000 ft^2/100 to 500 m^2).

Sheet or Floe Bending

Ralston [62] used a limit analysis solution to evaluate the forces exerted by sheet ice upward bending failure against a conical structure.

Forces on a Conical Structure. The forces exerted by sheet ice or floe upward bending on a structure include:

1. The horizontal component of the force required to cause the ice to fail in bending:

$$[A_1\sigma_F t^2 + A_2\rho_w gtD^2]A_4 \tag{18}$$

2. The horizontal component of the force due to ice friction on the surface of the structure:

$$[A_3\rho_w gt_R(D^2 - D_T{}^2)]A_4 \tag{19}$$

3. The vertical component of the force required to cause the ice to fail in bending:

$$B_1 R_H \tag{20}$$

4. The vertical component of the force due to the weight of the ice on the structure:

$$B_2 \rho_w g t_R (D^2 - D_T^2) \tag{21}$$

The horizontal and vertical forces may be calculated from Equations 22 and 23, respectively:

$$R_H = [A_1 \sigma_F t^2 + A_2 \rho_w g t D^2 + A_3 \rho_w g t_R (D^2 - D_T^2)] A_4 \tag{22}$$

and

$$R_V = B_1 R_H + B_2 \rho_w g t_R (D^2 - D_T^2) \tag{23}$$

where
g = acceleration due to gravity
t = ice sheet thickness
t_R = ice ride-up thickness
A_1, A_2, A_3 and A_4 = ice force coefficients (see Figures 14 and 15)
B_1 and B_2 = ice force coefficients (see Figure 16)
D = waterline diameter of the cone
D_T = top diameter of the cone
R_H = horizontal force on the cone
R_V = vertical force on the cone
α = cone angle in radians with respect to the horizontal
ρ_w = unit mass of water
σ_f = sheet ice bending strength
μ = coefficient of friction between the cone and the ice.

Forces on an Inverted Conical Structure. The forces exerted by sheet ice or floe downward bending on a structure may be calculated from

$$R_H = [A_1 \sigma_F t^2 + (\tfrac{1}{9})A_2 \rho_w g t D^2 + (\tfrac{1}{9})A_3 \rho_w g t_R (D^2 - D_T^2)] A_4 \tag{24}$$

$$R_V = B_1 R_H + (\tfrac{1}{9})B_2 \rho_w g t_R (D^2 - D_T^2) \tag{25}$$

Ice force coefficients A_1 and A_2 for inverted conical structures are determined by entering Figure 14 with the ordinate $(\rho_w g D^2)/(9\sigma_F t)$.

Forces on Steep Cones or Very Wide Structures. Equations 22 through 25 are not appropriate for very wide structures or steep cone angles.

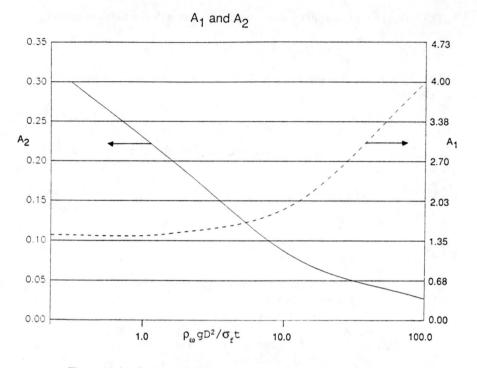

Figure 14. Ice force coefficients (A_1 and A_2) for plastic analysis [62].

Sheet or Floe Buckling

Sodhi [74] used the method of finite elements to investigate the buckling of a wedge shaped floating ice sheet. Results of the finite element solution for three different boundary conditions (i.e., fixed, hinged and frictionless) and two different wedge angles are shown in Figure 17. The buckling load obtained from Figure 17 is divided by the contact area to obtain the buckling pressure on the structure. If the calculated buckling pressure is greater than the pressure required to fail ice by crushing, then the ice is expected to fail by crushing rather than by buckling.

Loads Limited by Ice Feature Momentum

Large inertial ice forces occur when a moving ice feature encounters a structure. The momentum of the ice feature is gradually transformed into work done in failing and rotating the ice feature. The ice force varies with time depending on the strain rate and configuration of the contact zone. A conservative force may be obtained by multiplying the pressure from a pressure vs. area curve (see Figure 18) and the contact area. The analysis can be calibrated with field or model test results.

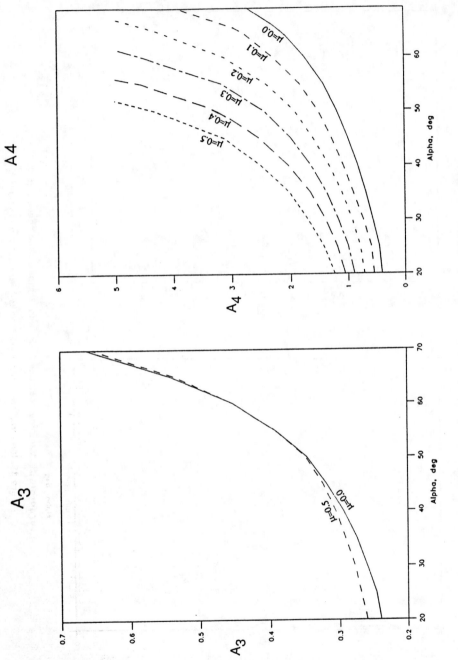

Figure 15. Ice force coefficients (A_3 and A_4) for plastic analysis [62].

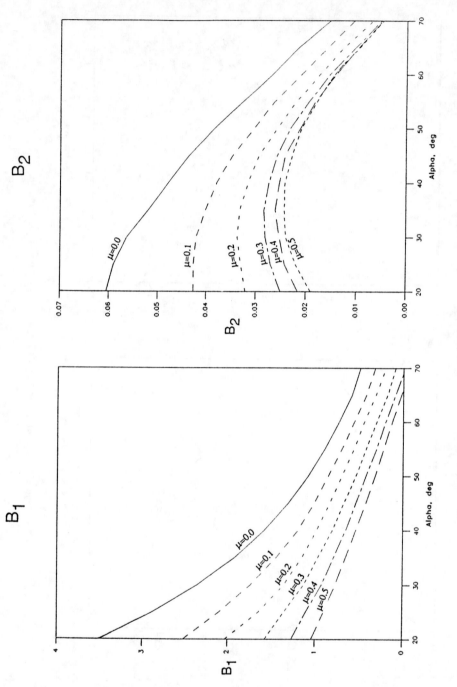

Figure 16. Ice force coefficients (B_1 and B_2) for plastic analysis [62].

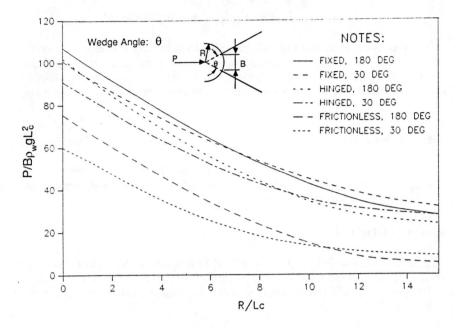

Figure 17. Ice wedge buckling [74].

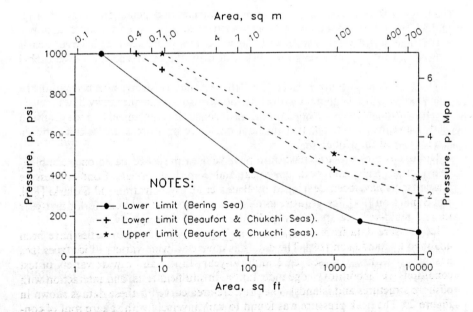

Figure 18. Design pressure, area curve, first year ice [82].

Forces Limited by Environmental Forces

The driving force for ice movement is provided by winds and currents. The forces are transmitted through the ice cover to grounded ice features (e.g., multi-year floes) and bottom-founded structures (e.g., caissons, caisson-retained islands, and islands). The force level in the ice cover depends on the continuity, uniformity and strength of the ice.

"Blocking" Ice Features

The ice cover may not provide sufficient force to fail "blocking" ice features. The "blocking" ice feature could become a mechanism for transmitting the load from the surrounding ice cover to a structure.

Limits to Driving Force

Vivatrat and Kreider [85] and Vivatrat [86] have discussed limits to the driving force. They presented estimates of the average ice force level due to environmental conditions and discussed the limitations due to the ice sheet failure and ridging in the ice cover.

Local Contact Pressure

The magnitude of local contact pressure on a structure depends on the environmental forces and the contact area. The contact pressure over a small area is primarily a function of ice strength, and the contact pressure over a large area is influenced not only by the ice strength but also by the magnitude of the global load.

The local contact pressure is larger than the uniaxial ice strength because of the confinement of the ice in contact with the structure. Confinement may be a function of structure geometry, decreasing with increasing side slope angle, and varying with loaded area. However, product of the average ice pressure and the contact area cannot exceed the global ice load.

Numerous pressure-area relationships have been proposed based on a combination of test results and both analytical and empirical models. Contact pressure relationships have been developed by Bruen et al. [9], Vivatrat and Slomski [87], and Sanderson [71]. Ice pressure as a function of contact area curves for first-year ice and multi-year ice are shown in Figures 18 and 19, respectively.

Ice pressure data from small, medium, large and meso-scale studies have been analyzed by Sanderson [69]. The data sets covered a wide variety of ice types (i.e., freshwater ice, first-year sea ice, and multi-year sea ice) and a wide variety of test conditions (i.e., laboratory edge indentation, in situ field tests, and interaction with offshore structures and islands). The pressure-area curve for these data is shown in Figure 20. The peak pressure was found to vary inversely with square root of contact area.

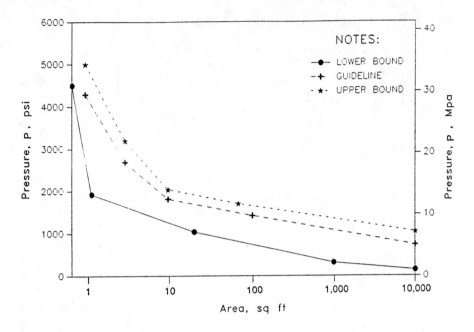

Figure 19. Design pressure, area curve, multi-year ice [82].

Ice Rubble Fields

Rubble fields are composed of ice blocks in a semi-organized arrangement. They are normally partially consolidated. The partial consolidation occurs at or near the sea surface and depends on the age and temperature of the rubble field.

Rubble fields fail against a structure by crushing. The crushing strength of ice rubble is assumed to be considerably lower than the crushing strength of individual ice pieces making up the rubble field. The upper bound force of a rubble field on a structure can be expressed as

$$F = \bar{\sigma} \, Dt \qquad (27)$$

where t = ice thickness (i.e., thickness of the ice field)
  D = diameter or width of the structure (at the line of ice contact)
  F = horizontal ice force
  $\bar{\sigma}$ = upper bound rubble field pressure

Prodanovic [60] has expressed the upper bound to rubble field pressure as

$$\bar{\sigma} = \sigma_{ps}\left[1 + \frac{at}{D}\left(1 + \frac{bt}{D}\right)\right] \qquad (28)$$

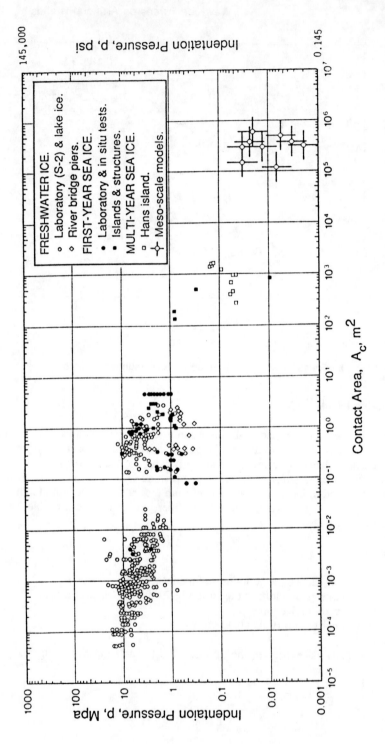

Figure 20. Plot of peak indentation pressure against contact area for two-dimensional indentation [71].

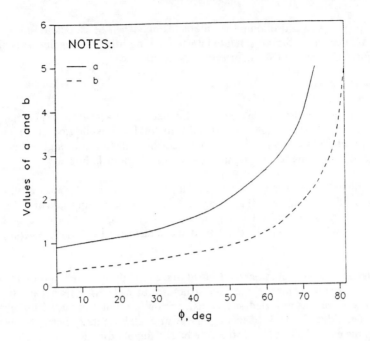

Figure 21. Values of parameters a and b [60].

where a, b = parameters, taken from Figure 21 (based on values of ϕ)
       t = ice thickness (i.e., thickness of the rubble field)
      D = diameter or width of the structure (at the line of ice contact)
    σ_{ps} = plane strain (confined) compressive strength of ice rubble
    $\bar{\sigma}$ = upper bound rubble to field pressure

and the plane strain compressive strength as

$$\sigma_{ps} = 2c \tan(\pi/4 + \phi/2) \tag{29}$$

where   c = cohesion of the ice rubble
    σ_{ps} = plain strain (confined) compressive strength of ice rubble,
    ϕ = effective angle of internal friction of the ice rubble

The cohesion according to Weiss et al. [98] is proportional to the thickness of the ice rubble, and the angle of internal friction is constant. The bound on cohesion has been expressed by Weiss et al. [98] as

$$0.35t \le c \le 1.0t \tag{30}$$

Loads from partially consolidated rubble fields may then be calculated as a combination of force due to the consolidated portion falling either in crushing or bending and the force necessary to shear or crush the ice rubble.

Multi-year Ridges

These ice ridges are also composed of individual ice blocks in a semi-organized arrangement. Multi-year ridges are partially to totally consolidated and may fail against a structure by crushing, bending, or shearing. Due to the strength of a multi-year ridge, it may come to rest against a structure without failing.

Conical/Slope Sided Structures. Conical/slope sided structures cause multi-year ice ridges to either fail in vertical bending or to ride-up the sloping side until limited by equilibrium considerations. Ice ridge forces may be computed by elastic methods [35], plastic limit analysis [90], discrete element methods [30], and experimental model tests.

Ice Ride-Up Analysis. Winkler and Nordgren [100] developed a model for calculating the force on a conical/slope sided structure during the ride-up of a multi-year iceridge. The ridge was modeled as an elastic beam in point contact with the rigid structure. The ridge was rotated through large angles about its centerline as it was pushed up the conical/slope sided structure by the surrounding ice. The forces com-

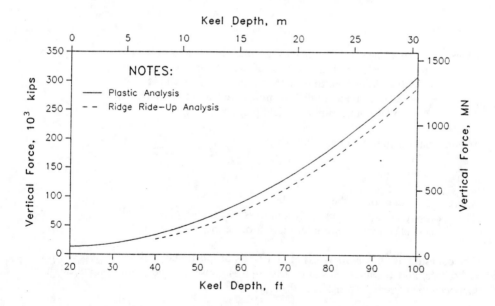

Figure 22. Vertical force from multi-year ridges for conical structures.

puted using the ice ridge ride-up analysis assume that the ridge is free-floating within a surrounding ice floe and that the ice-structure coefficient of friction is 0.15. The vertical forces are shown in Figure 22 for multi-year ridges.

Elastic Methods. Kim and Kotras [35] developed an analytical model to predict ridge bending failure loads. The method of Kim and Kotras [35] was based on Hetenyi's theory of an elastic beam on an elastic foundation. The ridge with attached ice sheet was simplified as an equivalent, infinitely long, floating, elastic beam. The ridge material was assumed to be elastic-brittle. Semeniuk [73] developed a computer program to calculate the force required to form a center crack to split the ridge into halves, and then, the force required to form a hinge crack to each half of the broken ridge. As soon as the flexural strength was reached, the ridge was assumed to break immediately without any residual strength left. The elastic method was found to underestimate the load resistance of the ridge. Abdelnour [2] employed a computer program to calculate vertical ridge loads for model tests of Edwards and Lewis [21] and Edwards and Abdelnour [20]. The analytical model of Kim and Kotras [35] was found to underestimate the ridge loads.

Plastic Limit Analysis. Wang [90] developed an analytical method to predict ridge bending failure loads. The method of Wang [90] was based on the upper bound limit analysis of the plastic theory. The ridge and the surrounding ice sheet were assumed to be elastic-perfectly plastic resting on an elastic-perfectly plastic foundation. The ridge forces computed from this method are upper bounds of the actual ridge forces encountered by a conical/slope sided structure. The horizontal force according to Wang [90] is

$$R_H V \geqq D_{br} + D_{bs} + D_{wr} + D_{ws} + D_f \tag{31}$$

where D_f = rate of energy dissipation due to friction between ridge and conical/slope sided structure
   D_{br} = rate of energy dissipation due to ridge bending
   D_{bs} = rate of energy dissipation due to ice sheet bending
   D_{wr} = rate of energy dissipation due to ridge weight (or buoyancy)
   D_{ws} = rate of energy dissipation due to ice sheet weight (or buoyancy)
   R_H = horizontal force that the ridge exerts on the conical/slope sided structure
   V = far field ice sheet velocity

Equation 31 is not a rigorous upper bound expression because the term due to friction is not a rigorous upper bound expression. The vertical force according to Wang [90] is

$$R_V = R_H(1 - \mu \tan \alpha)/(\mu + \tan \alpha) \tag{32}$$

where R_V = vertical force that the ridge exerts on the conical slope sided structure
   α = conical/slope sided angle
   μ = coefficient of friction

Numerical Methods. Both discrete element [30] and finite element models are available for computing ridge bending failure loads for conical/slope sided structures.

Non-Simultaneous Failure

Kry [43], Slomski and Vivatrat [87] and Ashby et al. [3] analyzed non-simultaneous failure of an ice feature on a wide structure. They hypothesized that large-scale failure occurs by successive fracture of independent zones. They analyzed the statistical sum of individual stress time series for a large number of zones. Kry [43] and Slomski and Vivatrat [87] concluded that the peak stresses over a large multi-zone area are lower than over the area of a single zone.

Other Load Factors and Considerations

Adfreeze Loads

When there is no significant or continuous ice movement, the sea ice freezes/bonds to the concrete and steel surfaces of arctic offshore structures. The adfreeze strength is dependent on temperature, salinity, and strain rate [32]. Adfreeze strengths between 3.0 psi (0.02 MPa) and 150 psi (1.03 MPa) have been reported by Oksanen [54] and Gershunov [25]. The force necessary to overcome the adhesion bond of ice pieces adfrozen to the surface of a conical structure is [1]

$$R_h = 2 \sum_{i=1}^{N} \frac{\cos(\theta_i - \gamma_i)}{\cos(\beta_i)} \left(\frac{w \sin \alpha + R_i \cos \psi_i}{\cos \gamma_i + R'} \right) \tag{33}$$

where
i = i-th ice piece
N = number of ice pieces on one quarter of the cone surface
R_h = horizontal force
R_i = force necessary to dislodge an individual ice piece
R' = adhesion bond force for the adfrozen unbroken sheet ice above the waterline
w = weight of an individual ice piece
$\alpha, \beta_i, \gamma_i, \psi_i$ = horizontal projection of tangent plane angles
γ_i = angle in a plane tangent to the cone surface

The sheet ice adfreeze bond is

$$R' = \tau_a A_s \tag{34}$$

where A_s = contact area of unbroken sheet ice frozen to the cone surface above the waterline
R' = adhesion bond force for the adfrozen, unbroken sheet ice above the waterline
τ_a = shear strength of bond ice-structure

The individual ice-piece adfreeze bond force is defined as

$$R_i = A_i C_a C_s \tau_a \tag{35}$$

where A_i = surface area of ice of the i-th piece
C_a = adfreeze area factor
C_s = a stress distribution factor
R_i = force necessary to dislodge an individual ice piece
τ_a = shear strength of bond ice-structure

Static and Dynamic Coefficients of Friction

An analysis of ice ride-up forces on a sloping surface requires an evaluation of the frictional characteristics of sea ice. Static and dynamic coefficients of friction for various ambient conditions of temperature, stress, and velocity have been reported by Saeki et al. [67]. Static coefficients of friction ranged from 0.2 to 0.3, and the dynamic coefficient of friction was 0.1. Dynamic coefficients of friction for rough and wet surfaces and for coated and uncoated steel have been reported by Tatinclaux and Murday [77]. Values of the dynamic coefficient of friction ranged from less than 0.05 to more than 0.20.

References

1. Acres, 1973, "Ice Adhesion Studies," APOA Project No. 57, Arctic Petroleum Operators Association.
2. Abdelnour, R., 1981, "Model Tests of Multi-year Pressure Ridges Moving Onto Conical Structures," Proceedings, Ice Symposium, IAHR, Quebec City, Canada, July 27–31, pp. 728–749.
3. Ashby, M., Palmer, A., Thouless, M., Goodman, D., Howard, M., Goodman, S. D., Howard, M., Hallam, S., Murrell, S., Jones, N., Sanderson, T., and Ponter, A., 1986, "Non Simultaneous Failure and Ice Loads on Arctic Structures," OTC Paper, Proceedings, Eighteenth Annual Offshore Technology Conference, Houston, Texas, May, pp. 399–404.
4. BLM, 1977, "Climatic Atlas of the Outer Continental Shelf Waters and Coastal Regions of Alaska," Atlas, U.S. Department of the Interior, AEIDC, Anchorage, Alaska.
5. Bagnold, R. A., 1939, "Interim Report on Wave Pressure Research," *Journal, Institution of Civil Engineers*, Vol. 12, No. 7, London, England, pp. 202–226.
6. Bièsel, F., 1952, "Equations Générales au Second Ordre de la Houille Irrégulière," *La Houille Blanche*, France, Vol. 5–6, pp. 372–376.
7. Bilello, M. A., 1980, "Maximum Thickness and Subsequent Decay of Lake, River and Fast Ice in Canada and Alaska," CRREL Report 80-06, U.S. Army Cold Regions Research and Engineering Laboratory, Hanover, New Hampshire, 160 pp.
8. Bohon, M. and Weingarten, J. S., 1985, "The Calculation of Ice Forces on Arctic Structures." Proceedings, Civil Engineering in the Arctic Offshore, San Francisco, California.
9. Bruen, F. J., Byrd, R. C., Vivatrat, V., and Watt, B. J., 1982," Selection of Local Design Ice Pressures for Arctic Systems," OTC Paper 4334, Proceedings, Fourteenth Annual Offshore Technology Conference, Houston, Texas, May, pp. 417–435.
10. Butkovitch, T. R., 1956, "Strength Studies of Sea Ice," Research Report RR-28, Snow, Ice and Permafrost Establishment, Willamette, Illinois.

11. Butkovitch, T. R., 1959, "On the Mechanical Properties of Sea Ice, Thule, Greenland," Research Report S4, SIPRE, U.S. Army.

12. Cammaert, 1986, "Adfreeze Forces on Offshore Platforms," Offshore Mechanics and Arctic Engineering Symposium, ASME, Tokyo, Japan.

13. Carr, J. H., 1954, "Breaking Wave Forces on Plane Barriers," Report No. E 11.3, Hydrodynamics Laboratory, California Institute of Technology, Pasadena, California.

14a. Cox, G. F. N. and Weeks, W. F., 1975, "Brine Drainage and Initial Salt Entrapment in Sodium Chloride Ice," CRREL Research Report 345, U.S. Army Cold Regions Research and Engineering Laboratory, Hanover, New Hampshire, Dec., 85 pp.

14b. Cox, G. F. N. and Weeks, W. F., 1982, "Equations for Determining the Gas and Brine Volumes in Sea Ice Samples," CRREL Report, U.S. Army Cold Regions Research and Engineering Laboratory, Hanover, New Hampshire, 11 pp.

15. Cox, G. F. N., Richter, J. A., Weeks, W. F., and Mellor, M., 1984, "A Summary of the Strength and Modulus of Ice Samples from Multi-Year Pressure Ridges," Proceedings, Third International Offshore Mechanics and Arctic Engineering Symposium, ASME, New Orleans, Louisiana, Feb. 12–17, pp. 126–132.

16. Croasdale, K. R., 1970, "The Nutcracker Ice Strength Tests, 1969–1970," 1PRT-9ME-70 Production Research and Technical Services Department, Imperial Oil Ltd., Calgary, Alberta, Canada, APOA Project No. 1, Arctic Petroleum Operators Association.

17. Croasdale, K. R., 1971, "The Nutcracker Ice Strength Tests, 1970–1971," 1PRT-3ME-71 Production Research and Technical Services Department, Imperial Oil Ltd., Calgary, Alberta, Canada, APOA Project No. 9, Arctic Petroleum Operators Association.

18. Denny, D. F., 1951, "Further Experiments on Wave Pressures," *Journal, Institution of Civil Engineers*, Vol. 35, London, England.

19. Dykins, J. E., 1971, "Ice Engineering-Material Properties of Saline Ice for a Limited Range of Conditions," Technical Report R720, Naval Civil Engineering Laboratory, Port Hueneme, California.

20. Edwards, R. Y. and Abdelnour, R., 1975, "Preliminary Modelling of the Process of Penetration of Pressure Ridges on Conical Structures," Report 62 C, ARCTEC, Canada, Ltd., May 24.

21. Edwards, B. Y., Jr. and Lewis, J. W., 1972, "Model Experiments to Determine the Forces Exerted on Structure by Moving Ice Fields," Report 00571-5, Arctec, Inc., Columbia, Maryland, March 6.

22. Exxon, 1979, Technical Seminar on Alaskan Beaufort Sea Gravel Island Design, Exxon Co., U.S.A., Houston, Texas, 18 Oct.

23. Frankenstein, G. and Garner, R., 1967, "Equations for Determining the Brine Volume of Sea Ice from -0.5 to -22.9 C, *Journal of Glaciology*, Vol. 6, No. 48.

24. Frederking, R., Wessels, E., Maxwell, J. B., Prinstenberg, S., and Sayed, M., "Ice Interaction with Adams Island, Winter 1983/1984," Proceedings, Seventh Symposium on Ice, International Association for Hydraulic Research, Hamburg, West Germany, Aug. 27–31.

25. Gershunov, E. M., 1984, "Shear Strength of Adfreeze Bond and Its Effect on Global Ice Load Applied to Mobile Offshore Drilling Units Under Arctic Conditions," OTC 4687, Proceedings, Sixteenth Offshore Technology Conference, Houston, Texas, pp. 357–362.

26. Gourret, M., 1935, "Sûr Mouvement Approché des Clapotis; Application en Digues Maritimes Verticales." *Annales des Ponts et Chausseés*, France Vol. 105, No. 16, pp. 337–451.

27. Hibler, W. D., et al., 1974, "Analysis of Shear Ice Deformation in the Beaufort Sea Using Satellite Imagery," in *The Coast and Shelf of the Beaufort Sea*, J. C. Reed and J. E. Sater, (eds.), Arctic Institute of North America, Arlington, Virginia, pp. 165–172.

28. Hibler, W. D., 1980, "Modeling a Variable Thickness Ice Cover," Monthly Weather Review, Vol. 168, No. 12, pp. 1943–1973.

29. Hnatiuk, J. and Johnson, G. H., 1973, "Environmental Conditions Influencing Arctic Decisions and Design Criteria," Proceedings, Fifth International Congress, Arctic Oil and Gas: Problems and Possibilities, French Foundation of Northern Studies, Le Havre, France.

30. Hocking, G., Mustoe, G. G. W., and Williams, J. R., 1985, "Influence of Artificial Island Side-Slopes on Ice Ride-up and Pile-up," Proceedings, Arctic '85, ASCE, San Francisco, California, March, pp. 185–192.

31. Jeffries, M. O., Sackinger, W. M., and Shoemaker, H. D., 1988, "Geometry and Physical Properties of Ice Islands," Proceedings, Port and Ocean Engineering Under Arctic Conditions," W. M. Sackinger and M. O. Jeffries (eds.), The Geophysical Institute, University of Alaska, Fairbanks, Alaska.

32. Jellinek, H. H., 1957, "Adhesive Properties of Ice," RR38, U.S. Army Cold Regions Research Engineer Laboratory, Hanover, New Hampshire, Sept.

33. Kamel, A. M., 1968, "Water Wave Pressures on Seawalls and Breakwaters," Research Report 2–10, U.S. Army Engineer Waterways Experiment Station, Vicksburg, Mississippi.

34. Kato, K. and Sodhi, D. S., 1983, "Ice Action on Pairs of Cylindrical and Conical Structures," CRREL Report 83-25, U.S. Army Cold Regions Research and Engineering Laboratory, Hanover, New Hampshire.

35. Kim, J. K. and Kotras, T. V., 1973, "Mathematical Model to Describe the Behavior of a Moving Ice Field Encountering a Conical Structure," Technical Report 0107, ARCTEC Canada, Ltd., Montreal, Canada, Dec. 28.

36. Kishi, 1957, "Clapotis in Shallow Water," *Journal Research*, Public Works Research Institute, Vol. 2, Paper No. 5, pp. 1–10.

37. Korzhavin, K. N., 1971, "Action of Ice on Engineering Structures," U.S. CRREL Translation TL260, Hanover, New Hampshire.

38. Kovacs, A. and Mellor, M., 1974, "Sea Ice Morphology and Ice as a Geological Agent in the Southern Beaufort Sea," in *The Coast and Shelf of the Beaufort Sea*. J.. C. Reed and J. E. Sater, (eds.) Arctic Institute of North America, Arlington, Virginia, pp. 113–116.

39. Kovacs, A., 1979, "Characteristics of Multi-Year Pressure Ridges," Proceedings, Seventh International Conference on Port and Ocean Engineering Under Arctic Conditions (POAC), Vol. 3, Technical Research Center of Finland, Helsinki, Finland.

40. Kovacs, A., 1983, "Characteristics of Multi-Year Pressure Ridges," Proceeding, Seventh International Conference on Port and Ocean Engineering Under Arctic Conditions (POAC 83), Vol. 3, Helsinki, Finland, pp. 173–182.

41. Kovacs, A., Weeks, W. F., Ackley, S., and Hibler, III, W. D., 1973, "Structure of a Multi-Year Pressure Ridge," *Arctic*, Vol. 26, No. 1, pp. 22–31.

42. Kreider, J. R. and Thro, M. E., 1981, "Statistical Techniques for the Analysis of Sea Ice Pressure Ridge Distributions," Proceedings, Conference on Port and Ocean Engineering Under Arctic Conditions (POAC 81), Vol. II, Quebec City, Quebec, pp. 789–798.

43. Kry, P. R., 1980, "Ice Forces on Wide Structures," *Canadian Geotechnical Journal*, Canada, Vol. 17, pp. 97–113.

44. LaBelle, J. C., et al., 1983, "Alaska Marine Ice Atlas," Report, Arctic Environmental Information and Data Center, University of Alaska, Fairbanks, Alaska, 302 pp.

45. Leendertse, J. J., 1961, "Forces Induced by Breaking Waves on a Vertical Wall." Technical Report 092, U.S. Naval Civil Engineering Laboratory, Port Hueneme, California.

46. McNutt, L., 1981, "Remote Sensing Analysis of Ice Growth and Distribution in the Eastern Bering Sea," *Bering Sea Shelf: Oceanography and Resources*, Vol. I, Hood and Calder (eds.), The University of Washington Press, Seattle, Washington, pp. 141–166.

47. Martin, S. and Bauer, J., 1979, "Bering Sea Ice—Edge Phenomena," from the Bering Sea Shelf: Oceanography and Resources, Vol. 1, Hood and Calder, (eds.), The University of Washington Press, Seattle, Washington, 1979, pp. 189–212.

48. Miche, R., 1944, "Mouvements Ondulatoires de la Mer en Profondeur Constante ou Décroissante," *Annales des Ponts et Chauseés*, Vol. 114, Paris, France.

49. Michel, B. and Toussaint, N., 1977, "Mechanics and Theory of Indentation of Ice Plates," *Journal of Glaciology*, Vol. 19. No. 81, p. 285–300.

50. Minikin, R. R., 1955, "Breaking Waves: A Comment on the Genoa Breakwater," *Dock and Harbour Authority*, London, England, pp. 164–165.

51. Minikin, R. R., 1963, *Winds, Waves and Maritime Structures Studies in Harbor Making and in the Protection of Coasts*, 2nd Rev. Ed., Griffin, London, England, 294 pp.

52. Nagai, S., 1960, "Shock Pressures Exerted by Breaking Waves on Breakwaters," *Journal, Waterways and Harbors Division, ASCE*, Vol. 86, WW 2, June.

53. Nagai, S., 1961, "Shock Pressures Exerted by Breaking Waves on Breakwaters," *Transactions, ASCE*, Vol. 126, Part IV, No. 3261.

54. Oksanen, P., 1981, "Friction and Adhesion of Ice," Proceedings, Ice Symposium, International Association Hydraulic Research (IAHR), Québec, Canada, pp. 628–640.

55. Paige, R. A. and Lee, C. W., 1967, "Preliminary Studies on Sea Ice in McMurdo Sound, Antarctica, During Deep Freeze 65," *Journal of Glaciology*, 6(46), pp. 515–528.

56. Peyton, H. R., 1966, "Sea Ice Strength," Report UAGR-182, Geophysical Institute, University of Alaska, Fairbanks, Alaska, 197 pp. 273.

57. Pointer, A. R. S., Palmer, A. C., Goodman, D. J., Ashby, M. F., Evans, A. G., and Hutchinson, J. W., 1983, "The Force Exerted by a Moving Ice Sheet on an Offshore Structure," *Cold Regions Science and Technology*, Vol. 8, Elsevier Science Publishers B.V., Amsterdam, The Netherlands, pp. 109–118.

58. Potocsky, G. J., 1975, "Alaskan Area 15- and 30-Day Ice Forcecasting Guide," N00 SP-263, Naval Oceanographic Office, U.S. Dept of the Navy, Washington, D.C., 190 pp.

59. Pounder, E. R. and Little, E. M., 1959, "Some Physical Properties of Sea Ice," *International Canadian Journal of Physics*, Canada, Vol. 37, pp. 443–473.

60. Prodanovic, A., 1979, "Model Tests of Ice Rubble Strength," Proceedings, Fifth International Conference on Port and Ocean Engineering Under Arctic Conditions (POAC 79), Trondheim, Norway, Vol. 1, pp. 89–105.

61. Ralston, T. D., 1978, "An Analysis of Ice Sheet Indentation," Proceedings, Ice Symposium, International Association Hydraulic Research (IAHR), Lulean, Sweden, pp. 13–31.

62. Ralston, T. D., 1979, "Plastic Limit Analysis of Sheet Ice Loads on Conical Structures," International Union of Theoretical and Applied Mechanics Symposium on Physics and Mechanics of Ice, Copenhagen, Denmark.

63. Richter, J. A. and Cox, G. F. N., 1984, "A Preliminary Examination of the Effect of Structure on the Compressive Strength of Ice Samples from Multi-Year Pressure Ridges," Proceedings, Third International Offshore Mechanics and Arctic Engineering Symposium, ASME, New Orleans, Louisiana, Feb. 12–17, pp. 140–144.

64. Ross, C. W., 1955, "Laboratory Study of Shock Pressures of Breaking Waves," TM-59, U.S. Army, COE, Beach Erosion Board, Washington, D.C., Feb.

65. Rundgren, L., 1958, "Water Wave Forces," Bulletin No. 54, Royal Institute of Technology, Division of Hydraulics, Stockholm, Sweden.

66. Sackinger, W. M., 1977, "Shear Strength of Adfreeze Bond of Sea Ice to Structures," Proceedings, Fourth International Conference on Port and Ocean Engineering Under Arctic Conditions (POAC 77), St. John's, Newfoundland.

67. Saeki, H., Ono, T., Karazawa, N., Sakai, M., and Tanaka, S., 1984, "The Coefficient of Friction Between Sea Ice and Various Materials Used in Offshore Structures," OTC Paper 4689, Proceedings, Annual Offshore Technology Conference, Houston, Texas.
68. Sainflou, G., 1928, "Essai sûr les Digues Maritimes Verticales," *Annales des Ponts et Chauseès*, Vol. 98, No. 4, Paris, France.
69. Sanderson, T. J. O., 1987, "A Pressure-Area Curve for Ice," in *Working Groups on Ice Forces*, CRREL Special Report 87-17, U.S. Army Cold Regions Research and Engineering Laboratory, Hanover, New Hampshire, pp. 75–98.
70. Sanderson, T. J. O., 1984, "Theoretical and Measured Ice Force on Wide Structures," Proceedings Seventh International Symposium on Ice, International Association of Hydraulic Research, Hamburg, West Germany, Aug. 27–31, pp. 151–207.
71. Sanderson, T. J. O., 1986, "A Pressure-Area Curve for Ice," Proceedings, International Association of Hydraulic Research, Ice Symposium, Iowa City, Iowa.
72. Schwartz, J. and Weeks, W. F., 1977, "Engineering Properties of Ice," *Journal of Glaciology*, Vol. 19, No. 8, pp. 499–530.
73. Semeniuk, A., 1975, "Computer Program to Evaluate the Forces Generated by a Moving Ice Field Encountering a Conical Structure," Report IPRT-21ME-75, Imperial Oil Ltd., Calgary, Canada, June.
74. Sodhi, D. S., 1979, "Buckling Analysis of Wedge-Shaped Floating Ice Sheets," Proceedings, Fifth International Conference on Port and Ocean Engineering Under Arctic Conditions, Trondheim, Norway, Vol. 1, pp. 797–310.
75. SPM, 1984, *Shore Protection Manual*, U.S. Army Coastal Engineering Research Center, Ft. Belvoir, Virginia.
76. Tadjbakhsh, I. and Keller, J. B., 1960, "Standing Surface Waves of Finite Amplitude." *Journal, Fluid Mechanics*, Vol. 8, Part 3, pp. 442–451.
77. Tatinclaux, J. C. and Murday, D., 1985, "Field Tests of the Kinetic Friction Coefficients of Sea Ice," CREEL Report 85-17, U.S. Army Cold Regions Research and Engineering Laboratory, Hanover, New Hampshire.
78. Thomas, D. and Pritchard, R., 1981, "Norton Sound and Bering Sea Ice Motion: 1981," Report No. 209, Flow Research Co., Kent, Washington.
79. Thorndike, A. and Cheung, J., 1977, "AIDJEX Measurements of Sea Ice Motion, April 1975–May 1976." Bulletin No. 35, Arctic Ice Dynamics Joint Experiment, University of Washington, Seattle, Washington.
80. Thorndike, A. and Colony, R., 1980, "Arctic Ocean Buoy Program Data Report, 1979," Polar Science Center, University of Washington, Seattle, Washington.
81. Tucker, W. B. III and Govoni, J. W., 1981, "Morphological Investigations of First-Year Sea Ice Pressure Ridge Sails," *Gold Regions Science and Technology*, Vol. 5, pp. 1–12.
82. Utt, M., 1985, personal communication.
83. Vaudrey, K. D., 1985, personal communication.
84. Vaudrey, K. D., 1977, "Ice Engineering—Study of Related Properties of Floating Sea Ice Sheets and Summary of Elastic and Viscoelastic Analyses," TR R860, U.S. Naval Civil Engineering Laboratory, 79 pp.
85. Vivatrat, V. and Kreider, J. R., 1981, "Ice Force Prediction Using a Limited Driving Force Approach," OTC Paper 4115, Thirteenth Annual Offshore Technology Conference, Houston, Texas, May, 4–7, pp. 471–479.
86. Vivatrat, V., 1982, "Strains and Strain Rates on Sea Ice Indentation," OTC Paper 4311, Proceedings, Fourteenth Annual Offshore Technology Conference, Houston, Texas, May, pp. 133–140.
87. Vivatrat, V. and Slomski, S., 1983, "A Probabilistic Basis for Selecting Design Ice Pressures and Ice Loads for Arctic Structures," OTC 4457, Proceedings, Offshore Technology Conference, Houston, Texas, May 2–5, pp.

88. Voelker, R., et al., 1981, "Assessment of Ice Conditions in the South Bering Sea Based on April 1980 USCGC Polar Class Trafficability Test Data," Report No. 500C-2, ARCTEC, Inc., Columbia, M.D.

89. Walden, J. T., Hallam, S. D., Baldwin, J. T. 1987, "An Explicit Technique for Calculating First Year Ice Loads on Structures," Proceedings, Sixth International Symposium. Offshore Mechanics and Arctic Engineering, ASME, Houston, Texas, Vol. 4, March 1–6, pp. 267–272.

90. Wang, Y. S., 1984, "Analysis and Model Tests of Pressure Ridges Failing Against Conical Structures," Proceedings, Seventh International Symposium on Ice, International Association for Hydraulic Research (IAHR), Hamburg, Germany, Aug. 27–31.

91. Wang, Y. S., 1979, "Crystallographic Studies and Strength Tests of Field Ice in the Alaskan Beaufort Sea," Proceedings, Fifth International Conference on Port and Ocean Engineering Under Arctic Conditions (POAC 79), Trondheim, Norway, pp. 651–655.

92. Webster, B. D., 1981, "A Climatology of the Ice Extent in the Bering Sea," Technical Memorandum NWS AR-33, National Weather Service, National Oceanic and Atmospheric Administration, Anchorage, Alaska, 38 pp.

93. Webster, B. D., 1982, "Empirical Probabilities of the Ice Limit and Fifty Percent Ice Concentration Boundary in the Chukchi and Beaufort Seas," Technical Memorandum NWS AR-34, National Weather Service, U.S. National Oceanic and Atmospheric Administration, Anchorage, Alaska, 9 pp.

94. Weeks, W. and Ackley, S., 1982, "Physical Properties of Sea Ice," CRREL Monograph 82-1, U.S. Army Cold Regions Research and Engineering Laboratory, Hanover, N.H.

95. Weggel, J. R. and Maxwell, W. H. C., 1970a, "Numerical Model for Wave Pressure Distributions," *Journal, Waterways, Harbors and Coastal Engineering*, ASCE, Vol. 96, No. WW3, pp. 623–642.

96. Weggel, J. R. and Maxwell, W. H. C., 1970b, "Experimental Study of Breaking Wave Pressures," Paper No. OTC 1244, Annual Offshore Technology Conference, Houston, Texas.

97. Weggel, J. R., 1968, "The Impact Pressures of Breaking Water Waves," Unpublished Dissertation, University of Illinois, Urbana, Illinois.

98. Weiss, K. T., Prodanovic, A., and Wood, K. N., 1981, "Determination of Ice Rubble Shear Property," Proceedings, Symposium on Ice, International Association for Hydraulic Research, Québec City, Québec, Canada.

99. Winkler, M. M. and Reese, A. M., 1986, "Probabilistic Model for Multiyear Ice Ridge Loads on Conical Structures," Proceedings, Eighth Ice Symposium, International Association for Hydraulic Research, Vol. 1, pp. 159–170.

100. Winkler, M. M. and Nordgren R. P., 1986, "Ice Ridge Ride-Up Forces on Conical Structures," Proceedings, Eighth Ice Symposium, International Association for Hydraulic Research, Iowa City, Iowa, Aug. 18–22, pp. 171–183.

101. Wright, B., Hnatiuk, J., and Kovacs, A., 1979, "Multi-Year Pressure Ridges in the Canadian Beaufort Sea," Proceedings, Fifth International Conference on Port and Ocean Engineering Under Arctic Conditions (POAC 79), Trondheim, Norway, pp. 107–267.

Bibliography

Agerton, D. J., 1981, "Large Winter Ice Movements in the Nearshore Alaskan Beaufort Sea," Proceedings, POAC 81, Vol. II, Quebec City, Quebec, 1981, pp. 599–608.

Blenkarn, K. A., 1970, "Measurement and Analysis of Ice Forces on Cook Inlet Structures," OTC 1261, Offshore Technology Conference, Houston, Texas, April 22–24, pp. 365–378.

Campbell, W. J., 1975, "Geophysical Studies of Floating Ice by Remote Sensing." *Journal of Glaciology*, Vol. 15, No. 73, 1975, pp. 305–328.

Croteau, P., Rojanski, M., and Gerwick, B. C., 1984, "Summer Ice Floe Impacts Against Caisson-Type Exploration and Production Platforms," *Journal of Energy Resources Technology*, OMAE, New Orleans.

Crowder, W. K., et al., 1973, "Meso-scale Deformation of Sea Ice from Satellite Imagery," in *Advance Concepts and Techniques in the Study of Snow and Ice Resources*, Comp. H. S. Santerford and J. L. Smith, National Academy of Sciences, Washington, D.C., pp. 563–573.

Danielewicz, B. W. and Metge, N., 1981, "Ice Forces on Hans Island," APOA Project No. 180, August.

de Rouville, A., Besson, P., and Petry, P., 1938, "État Actuel des Études Inernationales sur les Efforts Dus aux Lames," *Annales des Ponts et Chauseés*, Vol. 108, No. 2, Paris, France.

Dickins, D. and Wetzel, V., 1981, "Multi-Year Pressure Ridge Study-Queen Elizabeth Islands," Proceedings, Sixth International Conference on Port and Ocean Engineering (POAC), Quebec City, Quebec, Canada.

Engelbrektson, A., 1983, "Ice Force Design of Offshore Structures," Proceedings, International Conference on Offshore and Marine Technology, Gothenburg, Sweden, Mary 1–4.

Frederking, R. and Gold, L. W., 1975, "Experimental Study of Edge Loading of Ice Plates," *Canadian Geotechnical Journal*, Vol. 12, No. 4, pp. 456–463.

Hirayama, K Schwartz, J., and Wu, H. C., 1974, "An Investigation of Ice Forces on Vertical Structures," II HR Report No. 158, University of Iowa, Iowa City, Iowa.

Hirayama, K., Schwarz, J., and Wu, H. C., 1974, "An Investigation of Ice Forces on Vertical Structures," II HR Report No. 158, University of Iowa, Iowa City, Iowa.

Inoue, M. and Koma, N., 1985, "Field Indentation Tests on Cylindrical Structures," Proceedings, Eighth International Conference on Port and Ocean Engineering Under Arctic Conditions (POAC 85), Vol. 2, Ranssarssuaq, Greenland, Sept. 7–14, pp. 555–568.

Inoue, M. and Koma, N., 1985, "Field Indentation Tests on Cylindrical Structures," Proceedings, Eighth International Conference on Port and Ocean Engineering Under Arctic Conditions (POAC), Narssarssuaq, Vol. 2, Sept. 7–14, p. 555–568.

Iyer, S. H., 1983, "Size Effects in Ice and Their Influence on the Structural Design of Offshore Structures," Proceedings, Seventh International Conference on Port and Ocean Engineering Under Arctic Conditions (POAC 83), Vol. 3, Helsinki, Finland, April 5–9, pp. 414–432.

Kry, K. R., 1979b, "Stress Distribution During Continuous Crushing of Ice," APOA Project No. 148, Arctic Petroleum Operators Association.

Kry, P. R., 1979a, "High Aspect Ratio Crushing Test," APOA Project No. 93, Arctic Petroleum Operators Association.

Lecourt, E. J. and Benze, D. J., 1980, "Large-Scale Ice Strength Tests, 1979/1980," Report 535H, ARCTEC, Inc., Columbia, Maryland, Vol. 4, (Report of AOGA 107).

Lecourt, E. J. and Benze, D. J., 1981, "Large-Scale Ice Strength Tests, 1980/1981," Report 706F, ARCTEC, Inc., Columbia, Maryland, Vol. 3, (Report of AOGA 130).

Maattanen, M., 1981, "Experiences with Vibration Isolated Lighthouses," Proceedings, Sixth International Conference on Port and Ocean Engineering Under Arctic Conditions (POAC 81), Vol. 1, Quebec City, Canada, July 27–31, pp. 491–501.

Michel, B. and Blanchet, D., 1983, "Indentation of an S2 Floating Ice Sheet in the Brittle Range," *Annals of Glaciology*, Vol. 4, pp. 180–187.

Miller, T. W., McLatchie, A., Hedley, R. and Morris, G., 1974, "Ice Crushing Tests," APOA Project No. 66, Arctic Petroleum Operators Association.

Mohaghegh, M., 1973, "Determining the Strength of Sea Ice Sheets," AIDJEX Bulletin No. 18, University of Washington, Seattle, Washington.

Muraki, Y., 1966, "Field Observations of Wave Pressure, Wave Run-up and Oscillation of Breakwater," Proceedings, Tenth International Coastal Engineering Conference, ASCE, Vol. I, pp. 302–321.

Reimnitz, E. and Barnes, P. W., "Sea Ice as a Geologic Agent on the Beaufort Sea Shelf of Alaska," in *The Coast and Shelf of the Beaufort Sea*, J. C. Reed and J. E. Sater (eds.), Arctic Institute of North America, Arlington, Virginia, 1974, pp. 301–355.

Reimnitz, E., Toimil, L., and Barnes, P., "Arctic Continental Shelf Processes and Morphology Related to Sea Ice Zonation, Beaufort Sea, Alaska," AIDJEX Bulletin No. 36, University of Washington, Seattle, Washington, 1977.

Schulson, E. M. and Cannon, M. P., 1984, "The Effect of Grain Size on the Compressive Strength of Ice," Proceedings International Association for Hydraulic Research, Hamburg.

Schwartz, J., 1970, "The Pressure of Floating Ice-Fields on Piles," Proceedings, First Ice Symposium, International Association for Hydraulic Research, Reykjavik, Iceland.

Stringer, W. J., 1979, "Morphology and Hazard Related to Nearshore Ice in Coastal Waters," Proceedings, POAC 79, Norwegian Institute of Technology, Trondheim, Norway, pp. 1–22.

Stringer, W. J., "Sea Morphology of the Beaufort Shore Fast Ice," in *The Coast and Shelf of the Beaufort Sea*, J. C. Reed and J. E. Sater (eds.) Arctic Institute of North America, Arlington, Virginia, 1974, pp. 165–172.

Stringer, W. J., Barrett, S. A., and Schreurs, L. K., "Nearshore Ice Conditions and Hazards in the Beaufort, Chukchi, and Bering Seas," Report, UAGR No. 274, Geophysical Institute, University of Alaska, Fairbanks, Alaska, 1980, 161 pp.

Taylor, T. P., 1973, "Ice Crushing Tests 1973," APOA Project No. 52, Arctic Petroleum Operators Association.

Timco, G. W., 1986, "Indentation and Penetration of Edge-loaded Freshwater Ice Sheets in the Brittle Range," Proceedings, Fifth International Symposium on Offshore Mechanics and Arctic Engineering (OMAE), Tokyo, Japan, April.

Timco, G. W., 1986, "Indentation and Penetration of Edge-loaded Freshwater Ice Sheets," Proceedings, 4th International Symposium on Offshore Mechanics and Arctic Engineering (OMA), Tokyo, Japan, April.

Tucker, W., et al., 1979, "Sea Ice Ridging Over the Alaskan Continental Shelf," *Journal, Geophysical Research*, Vol. 84, No. 68, pp. 4885–4897.

Walsh, J. E., "A Data Set on Northern Hemisphere Sea Ice Extent, 1953–1976," in *Arctic Sea Ice*, M. Shartran (ed.), Pt. 1, Glaciology Data Report GD2, World Data Center for Glaciology (Snow and Ice), Instaar, University of Colorado, Bounder, Colorado, 1978, pp. 49–51.

Walsh, J. E., "Workshop on Snow Cover and Sea Ice Data 1979," Glaciological Data Report, GD-5, World Data Center for Glaciology, University of Colorado, Boulder, Colorado, 1979, 117 pp.

Weeks, W. F., 1984, "The Variation of Ice Strength Within and Between Multi-Year Pressure Ridges in the Beaufort Sea," Proceedings, Third International Offshore and Mechanics and Arctic Engineering Symposium, ASME, New Orleans, Louisiana, Feb. 12–17, pp. 134–138.

Weeks, W. F., Kovacs, A., and Hibler, W. D., III, 1971, Pressure Ridge Characteristics in the Arctic Coastal Environment," Proceedings, POAC 71, Vol. 1, Technological University of Norway, Trondheim, Norway, pp. 152–182.

Wright, B. D., Hnatiuk, J., and Kovacs, A., 1978, "Sea Ice Pressure Ridges in the Beaufort Sea," Proceedings, Ice Symposium, International Association Hydraulic Research, Lulea, Sweden, Aug. 17–19, pp. 249–271.

Zabilansky, L. V., Nevel, D. E. and Haynes, F. D., 1975, "Ice Forces on Model Structures," *Canadian Journal of Civil Engineering*, Vol. 2, pp. 400–417.

AUTHOR INDEX

Subject Index

A

Abbreviations, technical, 568, 585, 586

Accretion, 905, 1061, 1071

Additives, 932–934

ADI (alternating direction implicit), 567, 568, 569

Alameda beach data, 788

Algiers, 869

Amphidromic system, 540, 541

Analysis
  extremal, 468
  risk, 1051

Analytical approach, 101, 102, 106

Angle of approach, 104–106

Angular distribution function, 184

Angular frequency, 101, 102, 106

Annual maximum series, 388

Antifer, 868

Antipode position, 537

API (American Petroleum Institute), 516

Apra Harbor, 868

Arctic environment, 1085, 1086

Arctic gyre, 1086

Arctic structures
  artificial island, 1083, 1090
  caisson, 1083
  conical, 1083, 1114
  narrow, 1082
  vertical leg, 1083
  vertical multi-leg, 1083
  wide, 1083

Armor units, 862, 866, 870–876, 1052
  damage, 973, 985–987
  density, 984
  evaluation, 1015–1019
  friction, 973, 1011–1014
  interlocking, 973, 985, 1011–1014
  rocking, 1015

size, 946, 976
  sliding, 944
  stability, 944, 972ff, 1010ff

Artificial headlands, 1076

Artificial stone breakwater, 870–880. *See also* Breakwaters.

Ashdod, Israel, 869

Astronomical factors causing tides, 537–539, 559–560

Astronomically-induced ocean tide, 539–543

Atlantic Ocean tides
  K1 tide, 540–541
  K2 tide, 563–566

Atlantic Remote Sensing Land Ocean Experiment (ARSLOE), 486

Atmospheric pressure, 549, 553

B

Bar
  offshore, 1060, 1072–1073
  longshore, 50

Barnett formula, plotting position, 392

Baroclinic modes, 581

Barometric forcing, 549, 553

Barotropic mode, 581

Basin oscillations, 561–562, 570

Bathymetry, 862

Bays, 923

Bays, *See* Crenulate.

Beach, 1059, 1062
  accretion, 1061, 1070
  bar formation, 1060, 1072–1073
  berm, 1059–1060, 1072–1073, 1076
  breaker line, 1072, 1075
  erosion, 1061–1062, 1071–1072
  humps (of sand), 1074
  littoral current, 1070, 1078
  littoral drift, 1060, 1070–1074
  nourishment, 665–667
  offshore zone, 1072